Eighth Edition

Managerial Accounting

LANE K. ANDERSON
PhD, CPA, CMA
Ernst & Young Professor of Accounting
Texas Tech University

HAROLD M. SOLLENBERGER
DBA, CPA
Professor of Accounting
Michigan State University

COLLEGE DIVISION South-Western Publishing Co.

Cincinnati Ohio

AQ96HA   ISBN: 0-538-81326-1

1 2 3 4 5 6 7 8 9 D 0 9 8 7 6 5 4 3 2

Printed in the United States of America

Sponsoring Editor: Mark Hubble
Project Editor: Mary Draper
Production Editors: Leslie Kauffman and Mark Sears
Associate Editor: Rodd Whelpley
Marketing Manager: Jim Enders
Cover and Internal Design: Delgado Design
Cover Photo: Barbara Kasten, New York, NY

Material from the Uniform CPA Examination Questions and Unofficial
Answers, copyright © 1983, 1987 by the American Institute of Certified
Public Accountants, Inc., is reprinted or adapted with permission.
Material from the Certificate in Management Accounting Examination,
copyright © 1974, 1980, 1983, 1985 by the National Association of Accoun-
tants, is reprinted or adapted with permission.

Library of Congress Cataloging-in-Publication Data

Anderson, Lane K.
    Managerial accounting / Lane K. Anderson, Harold M. Sollenberger.
 -- 8th ed.
        p.   cm.
    Rev. ed. of: Managerial accounting / Carl L. Moore, Lane K.
Anderson, Robert K. Jaedicke. 7th ed. c1988.
    Includes index.
    ISBN 0-538-81326-1
    1. Managerial accounting. 2. Cost accounting.   I. Sollenberger,
Harold M. II. Moore, Carl L. Managerial accounting. III. Title.
HF5657.4.M66   1992
658.15'11--dc20
                                            91-46096
                                                CIP

Preface

The 1990s ushered in the era of international business that has resulted in significant changes to the business environment. Managers of U.S. companies can no longer restrict their thinking to country boundaries. Today, the world marketplace dominates almost every business decision. Accounting is changing to meet the ever-growing needs of fast-paced managers. Accounting information is becoming more accurate as managers seek ways to gain a competitive advantage.

In this, the eighth edition of MANAGERIAL ACCOUNTING, we have significantly revised materials to reflect the changes to accounting theories and practices already implemented, and those changes anticipated as the next century approaches. Even with change, this edition retains its central focus of explaining how accounting data can be used by managers for planning and decision making, control and performance evaluation, cost management, and product costing.

IMPORTANT NEW FEATURES IN THIS EDITION

The eighth edition of MANAGERIAL ACCOUNTING is not just another revision. This book has been significantly rewritten to (1) incorporate many of the useful suggestions received from our users and (2) to explore new developments in the changing business environment. The following materials are new to the eighth edition.

Activity-Based Costing (ABC)

Chapter 3 presents a conceptual foundation for activity-based costing (ABC), which is promoted as a means of improving the accuracy of tracing costs to products and services. ABC is on the cutting edge of new accounting concepts. Although Chapter 3 presents the conceptual basis, ABC concepts are incorporated into practical applications in those chapters covering planning and decision making, performance evaluation and control, and cost management. In Chapter 3 we also show how ABC ties into responsibility accounting.

Profit Analysis

The changing business environment suggests students need techniques to analyze every aspect of the income statement. While standard costs and variance analysis in a manufacturing setting is the traditional profit analysis covered by most managerial texts, Chapter 10 of this text presents gross profit analysis, contribution margin analysis, and operating expense analysis.

International Implications in a Changing Environment

In the new world economy, managers are faced with managerial accounting issues not previously dealt with. Chapter 16 covers the significant topics important to managers of companies having international operations or that are contemplating moving into the international arena. Although these issues are important to accountants as well, the emphasis is on how management can use the accounting information to better function in the global marketplace.

Financial Reporting of Cash Flows

The statement of cash flows is introduced as one of the required general-purpose financial statements. Chapter 18 provides thorough, understandable coverage of how the statements are prepared and what information they provide to managers. Both the direct and indirect methods of reporting operating cash flows are covered.

CHANGES FROM THE SEVENTH EDITION

In addition to those revisions discussed above are the following significant changes in the eighth edition:

- The text is reorganized into six parts: managerial accounting framework, product cost framework, planning and control framework, decision-making framework, special topics, and interfaces of financial and managerial accounting.
- Every chapter is revised to reflect current and emerging managerial accounting issues.
- Chapters on budgeting are streamlined and expanded to show both the budgeting process and the needed managerial coordination.
- Standard costs for material, labor, and overhead are combined in one chapter and simplified to highlight managerial uses of standard costs.
- Cost estimation is expanded to include time series considerations.
- Important materials that many instructors want the flexibility to cover or omit, or which add unnecessary complexity to chapter coverage, are moved to appendices. Topics covered in appendices include the following:
  —Service centers and support functions (appendix to Chapter 5)
  —Weighted average cost method (appendix to Chapter 6)
  —Three-variance analysis for standard overhead costs (appendix to Chapter 9)
  —Time value of money (Appendix B at the end of the book)
- The end-of-chapter exercises and problems have been expanded. Each chapter (except Chapter 1) offers between 25 and 35 exercises and problems. This volume and variety provides plenty of material for many different assignments over several semesters.
- Exercises and problems are structured from easy to complex so students are challenged at different levels of understanding.

ORGANIZATION OF MATERIAL

Learning Objectives.   Learning objectives identify the chapter contents and what the student should be able to do upon completing the end-of-chapter materials. They provide a guide to the study of each chapter.

Vignette.   Each chapter begins with a realistic business situation or problem that focuses on topics covered in the chapter. In many chapters, this vignette is the central illustration throughout the chapter. In other chapters, it becomes the problem for review at the end of the chapter. These vignettes provide a good introduction to the chapter and give the student a sense of the subject's importance.

Chapter Summary.   A brief synopsis of each chapter helps the student organize, review, and integrate key concepts. We have structured the summary around the learning objectives so the student can determine whether all learning objectives were covered.

Review Problem.   A review problem with solution enables the student to test the level of understanding of chapter material and obtain immediate feedback about appropriate answers.

Key Terms and Concepts.   Important terminology, definitions, and concepts appear in color throughout each chapter. These key terms and concepts are listed at the end of the chapter. A glossary of terms is provided at the end of the book.

Review and Discussion Questions.   Review questions provide a review of the chapter concepts in simple implementation situations. They are intended to stimulate thinking about issues related to the subject matter. These questions can be used to spark class discussion or provide themes for written reports.

Exercises.   Exercises usually cover one or two simple concepts with basic computations. They provide a good review of chapter materials without a lot of complexity.

Problems.   Problems include either more than one issue, challenging situations, complex computations or interpretative issues. Each problem is based on a realistic business situation.

Cases.   Cases have greater depth and complexity than problems. They are designed to help students integrate various concepts within the chapter and across several chapters. In some instances, the cases require creativity in arriving at solutions. This helps students develop their analytical skills.

End-of-Book Materials   Appendix A covers the accounting cycle and provides problems students can use to practice or review their skills. This appendix is for the student who needs a quick refresher of the accounting procedures for the accounting cycle.

Appendix B is a comprehensive treatment of the time value of money and the present value concept. It is review material for those who need a refresher. This material is essential for the chapters on capital investment decisions. The interest and annuity tables required for the present value issues in capital investment decisions are located at the back of the book.

WHERE AND HOW TO USE THE MATERIAL

MANAGERIAL ACCOUNTING is structured with a great deal of flexibility. You will find that the variety of chapters and the mix of materials within chapters allows you to structure a course and a plan for learning to your specific needs. You have a unique opportunity to design alternative courses for different levels of students. We have used this material with undergraduate students, MBA students, and participants in executive development programs. The text targets an introductory to intermediate level of exposure to the use of accounting information in management. We have consciously applied the accounting uses to all types of organizations whether manufacturing, service, merchandiser, or not-for-profit.

The book can be used at any of four levels: second semester principles, junior-level course between principles and cost accounting, junior-level non-accounting major managerial course, and graduate-level beginning managerial accounting.

The material within each chapter presents a broad mix of procedural, conceptual, interpretative and interrelated issues. The large number of exercises in each chapter provide opportunities for beginning students to explore simple issues at both the procedural and conceptual levels. The many problems present more practice with the subject matter, but the problems are provided for students who want to delve more deeply into the topic. Each chapter contains one or more cases that integrate many issues. These materials are excellent for graduate students or undergraduate students accustomed to dealing with cases.

For students who need a review of basic financial accounting, it may be helpful to start with Appendix A. This appendix deals concisely with the accounting cycle and provides problems which allow students to review the procedures related to the accounting cycle.

LEARNING AND TEACHING AIDS

Available to Instructors

Instructor's Resource Guide.   New for this edition, the instructor's resource guide is organized to provide a basis for developing class lectures, teaching transparencies to supplement classroom lecture, and a comprehensive guide to selecting exercises, problems, and cases. The instructor's resource guide should be particularly helpful to new instructors or graduate teaching assistants who wish to use the teaching notes and examples.

Solutions Manual.   The solutions manual contains answers to all review and discussion questions and detailed solutions for every exercise, problem, and case. Additional clarifying notes and suggestions are presented where appropriate.

Test Bank.   A test bank includes a variety of questions and short problems that are compatible and consistent with the text material. The questions provide multiple choice, true-false, and matching options. The questions within each option range from simple to complex to provide several alternative combinations to select from. Solutions to all questions and problems are included.

MicroSWAT III.   This is a microcomputer version of the test bank that permits individualizing each examination to your own circumstances. It is designed to save time in preparing and grading interim and final examinations.

Spreadsheet Applications.   These template diskettes are used with Lotus 1-2-3 for solving selected end-of-chapter problems that are identified in the textbook with the symbol in the margin. The templates allow instructors to pursue "what if" analysis so students can see immediately the impact of changes. These diskettes are provided free of charge from South-Western Publishing Co. to instructors at educational institutions that adopt this text.

Available to Students

Study Guide.   The study guide assists students in reviewing each chapter's content, in checking progress toward understanding concepts, and in preparing for examinations. The study guide includes chapter reviews and self-assessment questions, such as matching, true-false, multiple choice, and computational exercises. Solutions for all questions and exercises are included in the study guide. A glossary of key terms and concepts is also found in the study guide.

Check Figures.   Instructors may order check figures for students to use in verifying their solutions to end-of-chapter problems.

ACKNOWLEDGEMENTS

The eighth edition was completed with the input and assistance of many people. We owe a debt of gratitude and feel it important to recognize some special people, even with the risk that we may omit someone.

We thank the following faculty who reviewed the textbook for the previous edition and the manuscript for this new edition and who provided many helpful suggestions:

Charles D. Bailey
Florida State University

John W. Hardy
Brigham Young University

Robert J. Campbell
Miami University

Nancy Hill
DePaul University

James R. Davis
Clemson University

Will H. Owen
Mississippi State University

Maxwell P. Godwin
Southwest Texas State University

Stanley C. Salvary
Canisius College

Laverne E. Gebhard
University of Wisconsin—Milwaukee

Paul F. Williams
North Carolina State University

Quentin N. Gerber
St. Cloud State University

Richard E. Veazey
Grand Valley State University

Sanford C. Gunn
State University of New York at Buffalo

We also thank Alice B. Sineath, Forsyth Technical Community College, for reviewing the solutions to the exercises, problems, and cases; William Phipps, Vernon Regional Junior College, for reviewing the solutions in the test bank; and Pamela Anglin, Navarro College, for reviewing the solutions in the study guide.

We are grateful to a few special graduate students at Texas Tech University and Michigan State University who provided considerable assistance with various phases in completing this revision. They include G.R. Smith, Texas Tech University, and Bradley Saegesser and Michael Zweng at Michigan State University.

Permission has been received from the Institute of Certified Management Accountants to use questions and/or unofficial answers from past Certificate in Management Accounting (CMA) examinations. Also, our appreciation is extended to the American Institute of Certified Public Accountants for permission to use (or to adapt) selected problems from their examinations. These problems bear the notations CMA and AICPA respectively.

Lane K. Anderson
Harold M. Sollenberger

Authors

Professor Lane K. Anderson is the Ernst & Young Professor of Accounting at Texas Tech University. He received both an M.B.A. and a Ph.D. in Accounting at the University of Wisconsin—Madison, and a Bachelor of Science and a Master of Accountancy at Brigham Young University. Professor Anderson is a CPA and was awarded a Robert Beyer Gold Medal for his performance on the CMA examination. He is a member of and is active in academic and professional organizations such as the American Accounting Association, the Institute of Management Accounting (formerly the National Association of Accountants), the American Institute of Certified Public Accountants, and the National Contract Management Association.

Professor Anderson has served with Arthur Andersen & Company as a staff auditor, with Ernst & Young as a special consultant in government contract services practice, and on the staff of the Cost Accounting Standards Board. He is currently an active consultant with major aerospace and defense contractors on cost accounting matters related to government contracts.

Professor Anderson has over twenty years of experience teaching graduate and undergraduate courses in cost and managerial accounting and in accounting systems at Texas Tech University, the University of Maryland, and Brigham Young University. Several student organizations have honored him as an outstanding teacher.

Professor Harold M. Sollenberger is Professor of Accounting at Michigan State University. He received his M.B.A. and D.B.A. degrees from Indiana University and his Bachelor of Science from Shippensburg University. He is a CPA and was recognized nationally for his performance on that exam. He is a member of the Financial Executives Institute, the Institute of Management Accounting (formerly the National Association of Accountants), and the American Accounting Association.

At Michigan State University, Professor Sollenberger has served as Chairperson of the accounting and finance faculties. He currently serves as Faculty Coordinator of the Advanced Management Program and executive M.B.A. program. He has served as a consultant to C.P.A. firms, government units, professional associations, and industrial firms. He has taught at Indiana University and University of Southern California, and in the People's Republic of China. He has led numerous management study groups to Europe, Japan, Korea, and the PRC.

His teaching experience spans all levels of accounting instruction from introductory courses, to doctoral seminars, and to working managers in a wide variety of industries. Most recently, he has taught managerial accounting primarily to executive M.B.A. students and to undergraduates via a live instructional television system. Outside the university, Professor Sollenberger has taught in a wide variety of banking and credit union financial management schools. Known for his energetic, humorous, and participatory teaching style, he has received numerous awards for his teaching.

Contents

Part One

MANAGERIAL ACCOUNTING FRAMEWORK

Chapter One ❖ *Managerial Accounting and Management's*
Need for Information   2

Why Managers Need Accounting Information 3 • Planning and
Decision Making 4 • Performance Evaluation and Control 5 • Cost
Management 5 • Cost Determination 6 • Levels of Management 7 •
A Changing Business Environment 7 • Competitive Situation 7 •
Technical Evolution 8 • Management Complexity 9 • **The Objective of
Management** 9 • **The Accounting System as a Provider of Information**
10 • Financial Accounting 10 • Managerial Accounting 13 •
Differences between Managerial and Financial Accounting 13 •
Organization of the Firm 14 • **Role of the Management Accountant**
17 • Management Accountant 17 • Certified Management
Accountant 18 • Standards of Ethical Conduct 18

Chapter Two ❖ *Cost Concepts*   23

Nature of Cost 25 • Costs, Expenses, and Income Measurement 26 •
Cash Versus Accrual Accounting 26 • Comparing Service, Merchandising
and Manufacturing Organizations 26 • Traditional Grouping of Product
Costs—Manufacturing 31 • Manufacturing Flows of Costs 33 • **Cost
Behavior** 35 • Variable Costs 36 • Fixed Costs 36 • Nature of
Variable and Fixed Costs 38 • Relevant Range 39 • Semivariable and
Semifixed Costs 39 • **Cost Concepts for Planning, Acting, and
Controlling** 41 • Direct Costs Versus Indirect Costs 41 • Incremental
Costs Versus Average Costs 42 • Relevant Costs Versus Irrelevant
Costs 43 • Differential Cost, Indifference Points, and Opportunity
Cost 45 • Controllable Costs Versus Noncontrollable Costs 45 • Planned
Costs Versus Actual Costs 47

Chapter Three ❖ *Activity-Based Costing for Product Costing*
and Responsibility Accounting   74

Activity-Based Costing 77 • Issues Influencing Cost Management
Systems Design 78 • Definition of Activity-Based Costing 79 • Flow of
Costs Under Activity-Based Costing 81 • Influence of Product Mix
Complexity 86 • **A Comprehensive Activity-Based Costing Example** 87

x

Picturing the Cost Flows From Activities to Products 89 • Comparing ABC to Traditional Costing 93 • **Cost Management Issues 94** • Non-value-added Costs 95 • Performance Measurement 97 • Product Life-Cycle Costs 101 • **Responsibility Accounting 101** • Responsibility Centers 102 • Identifying Cost Centers 103 • Chart of Accounts Classifications 104 • Pyramid Reporting 107

Chapter Four ❖ *Cost-Volume-Profit Relationships*   134

Cost-Volume-Profit Analysis 136 • A Desired Profit Before Tax 137 • A Desired Profit After Tax 137 • Desired Profit as an Amount Per Unit or Percentage of Sales 138 • The Break-Even Chart 138 • Curvature of Revenue and Cost Lines 139 • **The Profit-Volume Graph 140** • Sales Volume 141 • Variable Costs 142 • Price Policy 144 • Fixed Costs 147 • Current Emphasis on Fixed Costs 148 • **Measures of Relationship Between Operating Levels and Break-Even Points 148** • Operating Leverage 149 • Margin of Safety 152 • Relationship Between Operating Leverage and Margin of Safety 154 • **The Sales Mix 154** • **Indifference Point 157** • **Other Contribution Margin Measurements 158** • Contribution Margin Per Unit of Scarce Resource 159 • Controllable and Segment Contribution Margins 159 • Illustration of All Contribution Margin Concepts 160

Part Two

PRODUCT COST FRAMEWORK

Chapter 5 ❖ *Introduction to Product Costing*   188

Product Cost Systems 189 • Production Environment for Job Cost 190 • Production Environment for Process Cost 191   **The Job Cost System 192** • Costing of Direct Materials 193 • Costing of Direct Labor 194 • Costing of Direct Materials and Labor and Cost Control 195 • **Simplified Approach to Costing Factory Overhead 196** • Computing the Overhead Rate 197 • Costing Variable Overhead 199 • Costing Fixed Overhead 200 • Disposition of the Overhead Variance 201 • **Multiple Overhead Rates 202** • **Departmental Versus Plant-Wide Overhead Rates 203** • Activity-Based Costing 204 • **The Concept of Capacity 205** • **Cost of Providing Services 207** • **A Job Cost Illustration 207** • **Appendix: Service Centers and Support Functions 214** • Select a Cost Driver 214 • Interdepartmental Support 215 • Other Issues 218

Chapter Six ❖ *Process Cost Accounting*   244

Overview of Process Costing of Output 246   Manufacturing
Environment 246 • Physical Flow of Products 246 • Focal Point for Cost
Accumulation 247 • **The Cost Elements 249** • Materials 249 •
Conversion Costs 249 • The Cost of Production Report 250 • **The
Equivalent Unit Concept 252** • Unit Costs 252 • Stage of
Completion 252 • Timing of Inputs 255 • Computational Steps 255 •
Cost of Production Report 259 • **Accountability in Subsequent
Departments 261** • Determine Physical Flow 262 • Calculate
Equivalent Units 263 • Compute Unit Costs 263 • Distribute Total Costs
to Units 263 • Determine Where Costs Are 264 • Cost of Production
Report 265 • **Management's Use of the Cost of Production Report 266** •
Modified and Hybrid Systems 267 • **Impact of Changing
Manufacturing Environment 268** • Simplification of JIT 268 • Activity-
Based Costing 268 • **Appendix: Weighted Average Cost Method 275** •
Computational Steps 275 • Accountability in Subsequent
Departments 279

Part Three

PLANNING AND CONTROL FRAMEWORK

Chapter Seven ❖ *Budgeting for Operations*   302

Budgeting: Implementing Planning and Control 304 • The
Relationship Between Planning and Budgeting 304 • A Planning and
Control System 305 • Purposes of Budgeting 307 • Budget
Preparation 311 • **Master Budget—An Overview 312** • Master Budget
for a Manufacturer 312 • Master Budget for a Nonmanufacturing
Company 317 • **The Starting Point 318** • Finding the Controlling
Constraint 319 • Sales Forecasting 319 • Formatting Budget
Schedules 321 • Independent and Dependent Variables 324 • **Other
Approaches to Budgeting 324** • Project Budgets 324 • Zero-Based
Budgeting 326 • Program Budgeting 327 • Probabilistic
Budgeting 327 • **Behavorial Side of Budgeting 329** • Top Management
Support 329 • Manager Expectations: Realism and Credibility 330 •
Budgetary Slack 330 • Institutionalizing Budgeting 331 • Human
Factors and Budget Stress 331 • Budgets Are Only One Aspect of
Planning and Control 331

Chapter Eight ❖ *Master Budgeting Example and Financial
                Modeling*   352

A Master Operating Budgeting Example 354 • Annual Goals and
Planning Assumptions 354 • Sales Forecast and Budget 357 •

Production Plan and Budgets 358 • Supporting Schedules 365 • Cost of
Products Manufactured and Sold Schedule 367 • Selling and
Administrative Expense Budgets 368 • Project Budgets 370 • Cash Flow
Forecast 370 • **The Example Completed: Forecast Financial Statements**
371 • Forecast Income Statement 372 • Forecast Balance Sheet 373 •
Forecast Statement of Cash Flows 374 • Master Budget Summary 375 •
Financial Planning Models 376 • Defining the Financial Planning
Model 376 • Elements of the Model 378 • Structuring the
Interrelationships 380 • "What If" Analysis 381

Chapter Nine ❖ *Profit Analysis Through Standard Costs*   418

Profit Analysis 419 • **The Use of Standards 421** • Definition of
Standard Costs 421 • Advantages of Standards 422 • The Quality of
Standards 423 • Revising the Standards 424 • **Standard Cost Sheet**
425 • **Standards for Materials 426** • Materials Price Variance 426 •
Materials Quantity Variance 429 • Interrelationships of Price and Quantity
Variances 431 • Control of Materials Acquisition 432 • **Standards for**
Labor 432 • Setting Rate Standards 433 • Time Standards 433 •
Accounting for the Rate and Efficiency Variances 434 • Causes of Labor
Variances 435 • Responsibility for Labor Variances 436 •
Interrelationships of Variances 436 • The Influence of Automation 437 •
Standards for Overhead 437 • Development of Overhead Rates 438 •
Flexible Overhead Budgets 439 • Framework for Two-Way Overhead
Variance Analysis 439 • **Plant Capacity and Control 443** • **Summary of**
Standard Cost Variances 444 • **Disposition of Variances 446** •
Standard Costs in a Process Cost System 446 • **Appendix 1: Some**
Quantitative Methods: Materials and Labor 450 • Materials 450 •
Labor—The Learning Curve 455 • **Appendix 2: Three-Variance Method**
for Overhead 456 • Framework for Three-Way Overhead Variance
Analysis 457

Chapter Ten ❖ *Profit Analysis—Gross Profit and Operating*
Expenses   487

Gross Profit Analysis 488 • Single Product Case 490 • Multiple
Product Case 491 • **Uses and Limitation of Gross Profit Analysis 496** •
Analysis of Operating Expenses 497 • **Contribution Margin Approach**
499 • Sales Price Variance 500 • Cost Variance 501 • Sales Quantity
Variance 502 • Summary of Contribution Margin Variances 502 • **Mix**
and Yield Variances 503 • Mix Variances 504 • Yield Variances 505 •
Interaction of Variances 506 • **Variable Costing 506** • Characteristics of
Variable Costing 506 • Comparing Variable Costing and Absorption
Costing 507 • Reconciliation of Variable and Absorption Costing 509 •
Arguments for Either Costing Method 510

Part Four

DECISION MAKING FRAMEWORK

Chapter Eleven ❖ *Managerial Decisions: Analysis of Relevant
                    Information*   546

The Decision-Making Process 548 • **Differential Analysis 550** • The
Basic Decision Rule 550 • Incremental Analysis and Total Analysis 551 •
An Example of Differential Analysis 552 • Policy Issues Affecting
Relevant Costing Decisions 554 • **Differential Analysis Decisions 555** •
Make or Buy Decisions 556 • Special Sales Pricing Decisions 562 • Use
of Scarce Resource Decisions 566 • Sell or Process Further
Decisions 570 • Add or Delete a Segment Decision 573 • Replace
Equipment Decision 576 • Capacity Expansion Decision 577 • **Costs and
The Pricing Decision   577** • Price Based on Full Cost 578 • Variable
Cost Pricing 579

Chapter Twelve ❖ *Capital Investment Decisions*   612

The Importance of Capital Investment Decisions 615 • **The Capital
Investment Decision 616** • Cash Flows 616 • Types of Projects 617 •
Time Perspective 618 • An Example—Equipment Replacement and
Capacity Expansion 618 • Relevant Investment, Revenue, and Cost
Data 619 • Formatting the Relevant Data 619 • **The Evaluation Methods
620** • Net Present Value Method 621 • Internal Rate of Return
Method 625 • The Payback Period Method 627 • Accounting Rate of
Return Method 628 • **Taxes and Depreciation 630** • Income Taxes and
Capital Investments 630 • Depreciation Expense and Taxes 631 • **Cost
of Capital 635**

Chapter Thirteen ❖ *Capital Investment Decisions: Additional
                     Issues*   658

Calculation Issues 659 • Uneven Project Lives 659 • Working
Capital 660 • Inflation and Future Cash 661 • Evaluation of Projects
With Different Initial Investments 662 • Gains and Losses on Asset
Disposals 664 • **Financing Versus Investment Decisions 665** • The
General Rules 665 • Lease Versus Purchase 666 • Two Examples 666 •
Accelerated Depreciation, MACRS, and The Tax Shield 667 • MACRS
Classes and Deduction Percentages 669 • Immediate Expensing of Assets
for Small Businesses 671 • An Example of MACRS 671 • **Post Audit of
Capital Investments 671** • **Problems of Uncertainty 673** • Risk
Percentage Factor 673 • Sensitivity Analysis 674 • Using Expected
Values 675 • **Capital Investments in Not-for-Profit Organizations 676** •
Social Costs of Capital Investment Decisions 676

Chapter Fourteen ❖ *Planning and Control in Decentralized Operations*   695

Review of Responsibility Centers   697 • **Advantages of Decentralization 698** • **Measurement of Financial Performance   699** • Return on Investment 700 • Residual Income 707 • **Performance Evaluation Systems in Service Organizations   708** • **Intracompany Transactions and the Transfer Pricing Problems   709** • Desired Qualities of Transfer Prices and Policies 711 • Transfer Prices 712 • Grading Transfer Pricing Methods According To the Criteria 719

Part Five

SPECIAL TOPICS

Chapter Fifteen ❖ *Cost Estimation*   750

Types of Cost Behavior   751 • Variable Cost 752 • Fixed Cost 752 • Semivariable and Semifixed Costs 752 • Other Cost Behavior 753 • **Significance of Cost Behavior to Decision Making and Control   753** • Trends in Fixed Costs 754 • Decision Making 754 • Planning and Control 755 • **Cost Estimation   755** • Account Analysis 756 • Engineering Approach 756 • Scattergraph and Visual Fit 757 • High-Low Method 759 • **Regression and Correlation Analyses   760** • Least Squares Method 761 • Quality of the Regression 763 • Output from Computer Analysis 768 • **Checking Some Inferences   768** • **Control Limits   769** • **Multiple and Nonlinear Regression   771** • Multiple Regression Model 771 • Quality of the Regression 772 • Concerns in Using Multiple Regression 772 • Nonlinear Regression 772 • Output From Computer Analysis 773 • **Time Series Approaches   773** • Trend Analysis 774 • Decomposition 775

Chapter Sixteen ❖ *International Implications in a Changing Environment*   800

International Environment   802 • Communications Differences 802 • Cultural Differences 803 • Environmental Differences 804 • **Setting Up Business in Other Countries   805** • Direct Investment 805 • Equity Investment in Other Companies 806 • Joint Ventures 806 • Franchising and Networking 807 • Barter Exchanges 808 • Countertrade 808 • **Differences in Accounting Rules and Financial Structure   809** • Accounting Rules 810 • Financial Structure 811 • International Accounting Standards 812 • **International Transfer Pricing   812** • Minimization of World-wide Income Taxes 813 • Minimization of World-wide Import Duties 813 • Avoidance of Financial Restrictions 813 • Management of Currency Exchange Fluctuations 814 • Gaining Host Country Approval 814 • **International Taxation   814** • Accounting for

Transactions in Foreign Currency 815 • Importing or Exporting Goods or Services 816 • Borrowing or Lending 819 • Hedging 820 • **Translation of Financial Statements of Foreign Affiliates 824** • **Performance Evaluation in the Multinational Company 825** • Financial Measures 825 • Nonfinancial Measures 826 • Budgets 826

Part Six

INTERFACES OF FINANCIAL AND MANAGERIAL ACCOUNTING

Chapter Seventeen ❖ *Financial Performance Analysis*   848

Uses and Users of Financial Performance Analysis 850 • **An Example Company—Amberg Lighting Equipment 852** • **Types of Financial Statement Analysis 854** • Comparative Statements 854 • Percentage Composition Statements 855 • Base-Year Comparisons 856 • Ratio Analysis 857 • **Financial Performance Analysis: Risks and Returns 858** • Liquidity 858 • Capital Adequacy 862 • Asset Quality 864 • Earnings 867 • Growth 871 • Market Performance 872 **Interrelationships of Risks and Returns 873** • Financial Leverage 873 • Earning Power Ratios 875 • Strategic Profit Model 876 • **Caveats in Using Financial Performance Analysis 876**

Chapter Eighteen ❖ *The Statement of Cash Flows*   905

Types of Cash Flows 909 • **Format of the Statement 910** • **Operations Cash Flows 912** • Indirect Method 912 • Direct Method 914 • **Preparing a Statement of Cash Flows 916** • **An Example 916** • Step 1: Formatting the Statement 918 • Step 2: Find the Change in Balance Sheet Accounts 918 • Step 3: Enter the "Answer" to the Statement of Cash Flows 918 • Steps 4, 5, and 6: Analyze Additional Data. Use T-Accounts to Analyze Certain Accounts. When an Account's Change is Explained, Check It Off and Move to the Next Data Item or Account Until All Accounts Are Checked. 918 • Step 7: Add Up the Operations, Investing, and Financing Sections and Balance to the Change in Cash, the "Answer" 926 • **If the Statement Does Not Balance 927** • **Operations Section Using the Direct Method 928** • **The Story the Statement Tells 929** • **Cash Flow Forecasting 931** • **Other Managerial Implications 931**

Appendix A
An Overview of the Accounting Process 967

Appendix B
The Time Value of Money 1008

Index   1033

Part One

Managerial Accounting Framework

Chapter One

Managerial Accounting and Management's Need For Information

 ❖ *Chapter Objectives*

After studying Chapter 1, you will be able to:
1. Describe the management activities of planning and decision making, performance evaluation and control, cost management, and cost determination.
2. Describe how to accomplish control through a budget.
3. Explain the changes taking place in the business environment and their influence on the use of accounting information.
4. Identify and describe the groups that have a primary interest in financial accounting information and those that have an interest in managerial accounting information.
5. Name and describe the basic differences between and similarities of financial accounting and managerial accounting.
6. List the functions of the controller.

Innovative Trailers, Inc. Needs Accounting Information

With growing numbers of manufacturers prodding their suppliers to commit to just-in-time (JIT) delivery, Innovative Trailers, Inc. figures it is time to market a novel concept for trucking. JIT is widely regarded as a major key to the efficiency of factories. Suppliers deliver their parts to the plant each day, sometimes even every hour, eliminating the costs of keeping large inventories on hand. But it means the suppliers need more trucks shuttling back and forth, and a factory's receiving docks can become jammed when supplies converge.

Innovative Trailers has developed a soft-sided trailer that dramatically speeds up loading and unloading—which means a supplier needs fewer trucks, because the few trucks they have spend more time on the road. The "soft" sides open like window drapes, thanks to a special, heavy-duty plastic. In rollover tests, the plastic proved strong enough to keep even heavy steel shipments from spilling.

The market not only looks good in the United States and Canada but also in Europe. Several European countries already have a form of curtain-side trailers. Some factories even permit their suppliers to send these trailers directly to the production floor for unloading.

As top management considers whether to move forward with production of the new styled trailers, a number of questions arise. How will the production start-up costs impact financial statements? How will reported profits change over the first five years of production? Will bankers want to extent any needed lines of credit? What does a trailer cost to make? How will it control the production costs? These, and many other questions, require information. Much of that information exists in or can be accumulated by the accounting system.

Many people view accountants as providers of information about the economic activity of an organization. The accounting system accumulates, classifies, and reports such information in a manner that meets your needs as a manager. This chapter introduces the different needs for which the various levels of management seek information, and the role accounting systems play in providing information. It will also introduce the people who typically deal with information about economic activity.

WHY MANAGERS NEED ACCOUNTING INFORMATION

Industry, together with federal, state and local governments, foundations and institutes, and other not-for-profit organizations, creates or causes events that we call economic activity. Taken together, all organizations represent a broad range of products and services. So you can get an idea of just how broad this range is, consider the sampling of industries within the American economy listed in Figure 1.1.

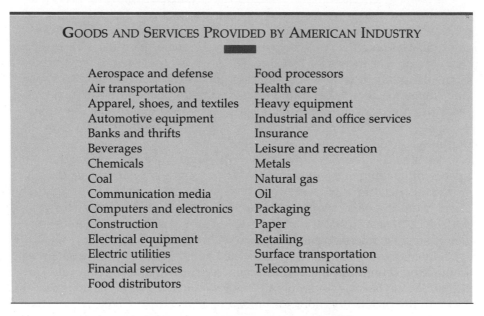

Figure 1.1   Goods and Services Provided by American Industry

If you were a manager in a company within any of the listed industries, you would spend huge chunks of time organizing personnel and arranging for materials and facilities so you could be productive. You would face numerous choices, priorities, organizational politics and culture, and the normal burdens of bureaucracy. In today's world, you would generally be data rich but information poor. The internal accounting system exists as a resource to accumulate relevant financial and nonmonetary data and convert them into meaningful information that meets managers' needs. The most common categories of needs are planning and decision making, performance evaluation and control, cost management, and cost determination for financial reporting.

Planning and Decision Making

Planning is formulating short-term and long-term goals and objectives, predicting potential results under alternative ways of achieving them, and deciding how to attain the desired results. A budget is the quantitative expression of planning. A **budget** is a plan showing how resources are to be acquired and used over a specified time interval. This definition emphasizes three critical elements: a plan, a set of resources, and a time interval.

Decisions during the planning process affect a number of areas. If you are a retailer, for example, should you increase or decrease selling prices? If you change, how will volume levels change? In operating a motel, will you include a restaurant or provide limousine service to the airport? In assembling a product, should you purchase a component part or make it within the company? As a manufacturer of kitchenware, should you change the methods for moving sheet metal through a stamping operation? If the product line is increased, when should you expand the work force? For improving the quality of final products, can you restructure production procedures to operate with zero defects? With demand increasing for certain product lines, at what point should you consider renting additional space or constructing new facilities?

Clearly, planning includes both short-term and long-term decisions. Short-term decisions relate primarily to current operations and the current period. Long-term decisions cover several years.

Performance Evaluation and Control

Planning, of course, is not enough. You must convert the plans into actions. As a manager, you will direct, coordinate, and control personnel and operations in order to realize your plans. Sometimes as operations progress you will find it necessary to revise the plans and to redirect activities along a course different from that originally plotted. That means establishing a monitoring system that compares the results of actions against plans. This process of comparing actions against plans is called **control**.

The budget serves as a basis for comparison and facilitates control while operations are underway. **Budgetary control** is the use of a budget for controlling operations. Figure 1.2 shows the interrelationship between budgeting and budgetary control.

Figure 1.2 shows that as action occurs we take a measurement and compare with the budget. If the comparison reveals that the plan is satisfactory but future plans can be refined, a feedback loop leads to input for future planning. If the comparison reveals unsatisfactory performance, we immediately take corrective actions to bring performance into line with the plan. If the measurement suggests changes for future control, a feedback loop leads to future control considerations.

Performance evaluation is comparing actual performance with plans and providing feedback for future planning and control. Since people act, performance evaluation affects how people behave. That means the methods and techniques you use to measure actions and the manner in which you communicate an evaluation influence how they are motivated. A positive environment increases productivity, while a negative environment promotes low morale and decreases incentive to meet plans.

Cost Management

Cost management is the process of managing the activities that cause the incurrence of costs. The emphasis, therefore, is on identifying, planning, and evaluating the activities that cause or drive costs. This implies managing both the activities and the amounts of costs tied to those activities. Cost management is related to a movement in the accounting world called activity-based costing. Traditionally, we traced costs to departments or some responsibility

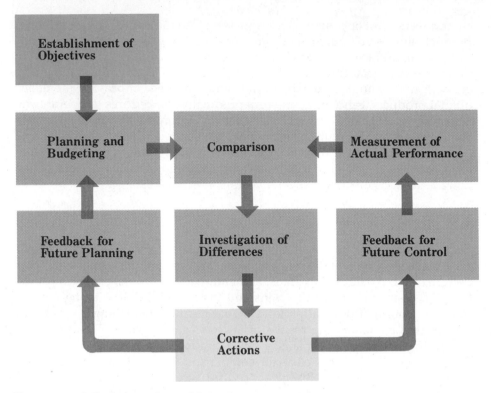

Figure 1.2   A Budgetary Control System

center. Employing cost management techniques, we now identify costs with activities, then trace that grouping of costs to processes, and subsequently associate those costs with products and services.

Cost management involves elements of both planning and control. We center planning around activities; we make measurements that are tied to activities; and we compare those actions with the plans. Control assumes holding the line on those planned costs. Cost management is broader because it addresses the issues of what causes costs and what changes are necessary to achieve specific goals. Thus, cost management techniques are important for providing relevant cost information that will satisfy the many information needs you, as a manager, will have.

Cost Determination

Cost determination, also known as product costing or inventory valuation and income determination, deals with measuring the total amount of resources used for something. The most common thing of concern is a product or service, but it also includes such items as contracts, a play, a building or piece of equipment, or a convention. In identifying costs with things, we follow the general concept of classifying costs as direct and indirect costs. (The concepts of direct and indirect costs will be covered in Chapter 2.) The primary focus is on the value added to goods or services by the productive effort of the organization. Cost determination will assist you in attaching costs to inventory, in arriving at cost-based selling prices, and in identifying costs incurred for services rendered to clients and other outsiders.

Levels of Management

Top, middle, and lower management each requires different types of information. A rough parallel exists between a manager's level in the organization and the type of accounting information needed.

Top management generally faces unstructured or semistructured problems that are resolved through strategic planning. These problems deal with product or service markets, the economy, competitors, availability of resources, and other outside factors that may affect the company. For this reason, some of the information used is from external sources. Top management's accounting information is usually highly summarized, encompasses a long time period, is future oriented, and deals with a variety of variables. It must be available on an irregular and infrequent basis.

Middle management deals with semistructured problems relating primarily to obtaining and using resources effectively and efficiently. Here, managers want information that will help formulate operating budgets; create capital spending plans; choose product improvements; plan staff levels; measure, evaluate, and improve performance of subordinates; and similar decisions.

Lower management faces semistructured or structured problems that deal with specific tasks. Each manager typically has authority to operate within a particular department or category of work. The types of decisions needed are usually known, and the required information and decision rules are usually identified explicitly, perhaps in the company's operating manual. Lower management needs information that is detailed, accurate, short term in nature, and provided frequently and routinely. Managers obtain such information mainly from sources within the organization.

A CHANGING BUSINESS ENVIRONMENT

The business environment is changing rapidly, both domestically and worldwide. These changes influence the way you and all managers conduct business. Consequently, they also affect the type of information you will use. For discussion purposes, we present the changes in three general areas: competitive situation, technical evolution, and management complexity.

Competitive Situation

Shifts in the competitive situation cause managers to find ways to reduce unit costs of products and services while providing improved product quality and customer service. In providing relevant information to meet new needs, accountants are rethinking how to accumulate and structure data into information. Too often information is flowing to managers that is not appropriate for the uses managers intend.

Perhaps the most obvious change is the globalization of business activity. **Globalization** can be defined as the act or state of becoming world wide in scope or application. Apart from this geographical application, globalization can also be defined as becoming universal. This second meaning implies both a harmonization of rules and a reduction of barriers that allow for the free flow of capital and permit all firms to compete in all markets. Business activity is spanning the globe to the point where capitalist philosophies now flourish in traditionally communistic countries. It is also breaking down country boundaries while recognizing cultural, competitive, legal, and political differences.

Another movement is called **world class manufacturing**. It emphasizes higher quality, lower investment in inventories, faster throughput, automation, and organizational flexibility to meet changing needs and advances in information technology. Many business people view companies with world class manufacturing as pioneers on the "cutting edge" of productivity in manufacturing, distribution, and management. A company on the cutting edge must surely have overcome quality issues and are eliminating waste and idle time through just-in-time systems.

Just-in-time (JIT) often applies to inventories and means holding inventories to a minimum. It is sometimes called a "zero-stock system" or "synchronous manufacturing." The objective of JIT is to obtain materials just in time for production, to move work in process from one work center to another just in time for the needs of the next work center, and to provide finished goods just in time for sale. All manufacturing facilities focus on a flow similar to a pipeline, with a uniform flow of parts, components, and subassemblies moving smoothly through the line. A natural by-product is the elimination or substantial reduction of inventory carrying costs. Advocates of JIT claim it results in (1) reduced material, work in process, and finished goods inventory; (2) increased equipment utilization; (3) reduced space needs; (4) increased employee productivity; (5) improved quality of the product, and (6) elimination of waste, defined as any unproductive effort. Successful implementation of a JIT system will also commit the company to use fewer suppliers and develop very close ties with those suppliers.

Technical Evolution

The technical evolution brings phrases like focused production, flexible manufacturing, computer-aided design, computer-aided manufacturing, and many others. Focused production is a movement to decrease the variety of products produced in each plant in order to manufacture the products and services that result in the highest contribution margins. Some companies even organize their plants into cells that focus the production of a group of machinery on a product line.

Flexible manufacturing is a movement to increase the variety of products that a given machine or group of machines can produce. The purpose is to reduce space, cost associated with machinery, set-up time and cost, and increase total throughput. By doubling the variety of products the same machinery can manufacture and halving the total variety of products, a company can cut the equipment required for production to about one-fourth.

Computer-aided design (CAD) is the use of high-quality graphics and software to design new products or change existing products. The software has the capacity to enlarge or reduce the product in size, show cross sections through the product at various lines, print out part specifications, and print out final blueprints for the entire product. CAD significantly reduces the engineering design time.

Computer-aided manufacturing (CAM) occurs when machines or entire production lines are run by computers. The time for setting the machine can be reduced from hours to seconds, and the settings are accurate. CAM allows one worker to oversee the activities and maintain three to ten production stations. Major systems such as "materials requirements planning" (MRP) and "manufacturing resource planning" (MRP II) are used to optimize the manufacturing process. The major advantage of CAM is an increase in output and quality.

In addition to these foregoing advances, the availability of PC computers and satellite transmission technology provides the capability of generating vast amounts of data and communicating them to any place in the world. PC computers permit managers and accountants to better manage their work and develop better data for important analyses. Satellite transmissions allow managers to transmit and receive needed information from far away countries in seconds.

Management Complexity

Management complexity is such a broad area that only a few points are mentioned here. Deregulation of services has changed the way companies view the future. Look at all the changes in the airline, telecommunications, and financial institutions. Automation now requires huge investments with high risks that require careful decision making in acquisition and efficient control to utilize properly the capacity created. Automation is also changing the way companies group and manage people. More data bases are now available, and management must carefully consider just what data it wants to use. The knowledge explosion is exponential, and data management will require skill from future managers. And a final comment relates to world politics and economics. No country is isolated. Political and economic events in one country have a ripple effect on the economies of other countries. Such unpredictable events require managers who are courageous, energetic, and innovative.

THE OBJECTIVE OF MANAGEMENT

If accounting information serves management, the accountant must consider the goals of management. That means that management must have goals. To many outsiders, management is striving only to increase business volume or to maximize profits. A commercial organization, of course, normally has an interest in profit because the owners will judge management on its ability to earn profit from the resources entrusted to its care. But many organizations do not even attempt to produce a profit. The success of a not-for-profit enterprise, for instance, is measured by the realization of an established common goal rather than in economic terms. A governmental agency is primarily concerned with providing a specific service to the public. Individuals may form an association for the purpose of promoting some common idea, with no revenue/cost intent beyond covering necessary expenses.

Regardless of the type of organization, economic realities are important. At a minimum, management must use its resources in a manner that attains desired goals in an efficient manner. A governmental unit, for example, may use the profit concept in measuring whether or not it uses resources effectively and efficiently.

Modern management recognizes that business enterprise is also responsible to many diverse groups, both inside and outside the organization. For example, the general public expects to receive dependable products at a fair cost, while the employees depend on the business for a means of livelihood. In addition, the community expects a business to be a good neighbor. Beyond these groups, there must be consideration given to the interests of owners and creditors. Most business people now acknowledge that the interests of each group are best served by the harmonious reconciliation of all interests. This is called goal congruence. Hence, the objective of maximizing the profits or the rates of return must be accomplished within socially and legally accepted bounds.

THE ACCOUNTING SYSTEM AS A PROVIDER OF INFORMATION

The accounting system generates much of the information that satisfies many of the foregoing needs. Two branches of accounting function within an organization, yet have very different purposes. One is called financial accounting, and the other is managerial accounting. Figure 1.3 depicts the primary purposes of each type of accounting and the interested parties.

Financial Accounting

Financial accounting is the branch of accounting that organizes accounting information for presentation to interested parties outside of the organization. The primary reports (known as financial statements) prepared under financial accounting are the balance sheet (sometimes called a statement of financial position), the income statement, and the statement of cash flow. The balance sheet is a summary of assets, liabilities, and owners' equity at a specified point

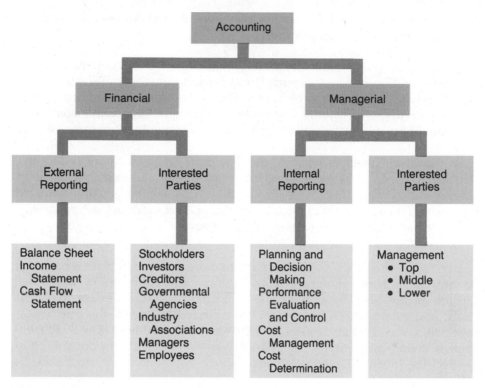

Figure 1.3   Scope of Financial and Managerial Accounting

in time. The income statement reports the change in owners' equity over a period of time resulting from the company's operations. The cash flow statement shows the changes in assets, liabilities, and owners' equity over a specific period of time as a consequence of operating, investing, and financing activities.

Without prescribed principles for accounting and reporting practices, those who rely on financial statements could easily be confused (or misled) by the variety of accounting presentations. Modern businesses are complex, and guidelines (known as generally accepted accounting principles) are provided for financial reporting. The Security and Exchange Commission and the Financial Accounting Standards Board are the overseers for providing appropriate principles. Other regulatory bodies, such as the Federal Power Commission, the Interstate Commerce Commission, state public utility commissions, and state insurance commissions, set forth more specific reporting requirements for organizations that fall within their jurisdictions. Internationally, each country has developed its own accounting principles. While similar in basic issues, different accounting guidelines influence business practices, managers' decisions, and financial results.

Groups outside an organization that use the organization's financial statements include owners, investors, creditors, taxing authorities, regulatory agencies, and industry associations. Even though financial accounting primarily serves outsiders, managers and employees within a company also have an interest in the information provided.

Owners, Investors, and Creditors   All organizations depend on some source of funding to begin, maintain, and expand operations. Private organizations rely heavily upon owners, investors (sometimes different from owners), and creditors (providers of short-term credit and long-term loans). Not-for-profit organizations rely on contributions and sometimes on governmental funding.

Owners and investors use accounting reports to assist them in deciding whether to continue as owners and investors. Financial statements also help lenders and contributors assess how well an organization is using available resources. Finally, potential owners, investors, and creditors use reports in selecting the most promising use of their money.

Taxing Authorities   The assessment of many types of taxes is based on accounting information submitted by the taxpayer. Examples of such taxes include income taxes, sales taxes, use taxes, franchise taxes, excise taxes, gift taxes, and estate taxes. These taxes are collected by school districts, cities, counties, states, port authorities, and the federal government. The most well-known taxing authority is the federal government with its tax collection agency, the Internal Revenue Service.

Regulatory Agencies   Local, state, and federal agencies regulate a substantial portion of the business activity in the United States. Although many facets of regulated activity are nonfinancial in nature, much of the regulation is implemented through or involves some accounting reporting. Regulated activities that require accounting reporting include prices charged by utilities, cost-based pricing for government contracts, minimum wages, and pension plan funding.

Industry Associations   Most industries have one or more associations that gather important statistics about the national and international industry, sponsor research studies, and lobby for favorable legislation at both the state and federal levels. Examples of industry associations include the Aerospace Industry Association, the Electronic Industry Association, and the American Hospital Association. Financial statements from companies within the industry allow associations to assess the health, stability, and direction of the industry.

Managers   The interest of a manager depends somewhat on the manager's position within the organization. At the higher levels of an organization, managers make policy decisions about the accounting system that affect the way accounting information is generated. These decisions ultimately affect how items appear in the financial statements. For example, decisions about depreciation methods, capital/expense criteria, and inventory methods will influence whether a cost item shows up as an asset on the balance sheet or an expense on the income statement.

All levels of managers make decisions that influence the magnitude of amounts in the financial statements. A decision to buy a new piece of equipment on credit, for example, increases the assets, liabilities, and depreciation expense. A decision to work overtime or hire more people increases labor costs and perhaps fringe benefits.

Employees   Based on financial statements and other information, employees make decisions about continued employment, union wage demands and contract negotiations, adequacy of pension plans, and viability of employee stock purchase or savings plans. Profit sharing programs involve employees in helping the company become financially successful and competitive.

Managerial Accounting

Managerial accounting, or management accounting, is the branch of accounting that deals with how accounting data and other financial information will meet the information needs of management. Because managerial accounting is designed to assist internal management, it is relatively free from the restrictions imposed by regulatory bodies and generally accepted accounting principles. It relies more upon concepts and applications that are useful for management's purposes. Specific applications depend on the needs and preferences of the manager rather than generally accepted guidelines. This means a manager has a wide range of accounting information from which to choose for a particular purpose.

The internal reporting activity typically focuses on the different areas of management information needs discussed earlier: planning and decision making, performance evaluation and control, cost management, and cost determination.

Differences between Managerial and Financial Accounting

Several important differences distinguish managerial accounting from financial accounting.

First, managerial accounting is not subject to the same rules, regulations, and principles as is financial accounting. No generally accepted accounting principles are promulgated for managerial accounting; no authoritative bodies exist that prescribe and audit for compliance, except for special circumstances that we will explore later in the text.

Another important difference between managerial and financial accounting is that financial accounting relies on accounting principles structured around the accounting equation: assets equal liabilities plus owners' equity. Financial statements reflect either a point in time or some change over time with respect to the accounting equation. Managerial reports, on the other hand, must have a structure which satisfies an individual manager's needs. These reports will often use estimates, are narrow in scope, and are seldom useful for anything other than the original purpose.

A third difference is the type of information presented in the reports prepared under financial and managerial accounting. Financial reports present monetary information while managerial accounting reports may also include nonmonetary information. Examples of nonmonetary information needed for decisions include quantities of raw materials in inventory, number of employees, units of product produced or sold, labor hours worked, average defective units, and so forth.

Another difference is that managerial accounting focuses on segments of the organization as well as on the whole organization. The primary interest of financial accounting is the company as a whole. In financial accounting, certain reporting requirements cause companies to subdivide assets, revenues, and profits according to main lines of business activity. In managerial accounting, however, the segment is of primary importance. Segments may be products, individual activities, divisions, plants, operations, tasks, or any other responsibility centers. The necessity for dividing the costs, revenues, assets, and liabilities among segments creates important allocation issues in managerial accounting that are not needed when the focus is the organization in total, as is the case for financial accounting.

Finally, managerial accounting, somewhat more than financial accounting, draws heavily on disciplines outside of accounting. Examples of frequently used business disciplines include finance, management, information systems, marketing, and production and operations management. The nonbusiness disciplines drawn on are computer science, economics, engineering, mathematics, operations research, psychology, sociology, and statistics.

Lest we leave the impression that managerial and financial accounting have nothing in common, two important similarities do exist. The accounting information system that accumulates and classifies information and generates financial statements is the same system used for many of the managerial accounting reports. Therefore, when the system accumulates and classifies information, it should do so in a format that accommodates both types of accounting.

The other similarity is the manner in which accountants measure the components of cost, assign costs to accounting periods, and allocate costs to segments. Many of the concepts developed for financial accounting for measuring and assigning costs are based on a rationale that is also appropriate for managerial accounting. When financial accounting develops a principle or concept that proves useful for managerial accounting, it is adopted for internal reporting.

ORGANIZATION OF THE FIRM

Responsibility for the design, implementation, and operation of the accounting system within a firm rests upon the chief financial officer and the operating staff. The abbreviated organization chart in Figure 1.4 shows how the

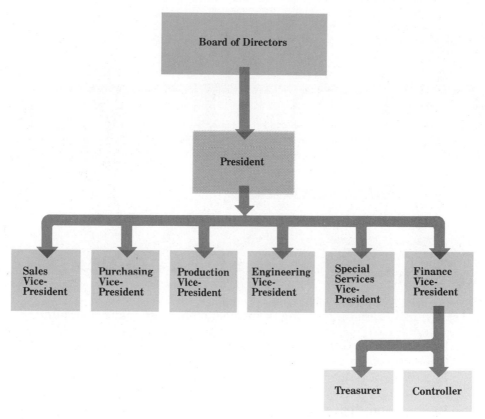

Figure 1.4   Organization Chart of a Manufacturing Company

finance vice-president, the treasurer, and the controller fit into the organization. Although the organization chart is for a manufacturing company, service organizations have similar positions or people with the same responsibilities.

The governing board that sets general policies for the entity is the board of directors, board of trustees, board of governors, or other designation according to the type of organization and custom. Responsibility for operating the entity on a day-to-day basis is vested in the president, who in turn delegates authority in various functional areas to vice-presidents.

The vice-president of finance is responsible for the accounting and monetary functions of the entity. The **treasurer**, operating under the vice-president of finance, is responsible for granting credit, collecting and depositing money, disbursing money, and obtaining credit. Essentially, the treasurer's function is a monetary function. The **controller**, on the other hand, has the general responsibilities listed as follows and outlined on the chart given in Figure 1.5:

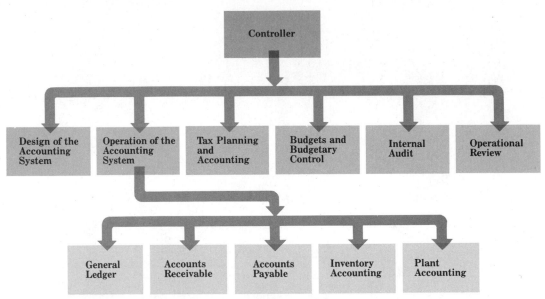

Figure 1.5 Responsibilities of the Controller

1. Design of the accounting system
2. Operation of the system:
   (a) General ledger
   (b) Accounts receivable
   (c) Accounts payable
   (d) Inventory accounting
   (e) Plant accounting
3. Tax planning and accounting
4. Budgets and budgetary control
5. Internal reviews for compliance with accounting policies and procedures
6. Operational review

The functions of the controller may be classified or handled in various ways, depending on company preference. Essentially the controller's function is an accounting function. The controller is responsible for the design and operation of the accounting system and the preparation of financial statements and reports that meet government or regulatory requirements. In addition, the controller is responsible for budgets, an internal review of operations for accuracy and conformity to policies, and a review of operations for the purpose of finding ways to improve profitability. In some organizations, the operational review is included as a part of the internal audit function.

In studying accounting, you first learn about the operation of an accounting system in a financial accounting course. Subsequent courses expand on financial accounting and deal with specialized topics such as information systems, tax accounting, and auditing. Managerial accounting concentrates on planning and operational review aspects and managerial concerns.

ROLE OF THE MANAGEMENT ACCOUNTANT

Although the top accounting-oriented people in an organization are the chief financial officer and the controller, the accounting and financial management functions contain a range of jobs. People seeking careers along this path are referred to as management accountants. This section describes the management accountant and some of the requirements that make management accounting a profession.

Management Accountant

A **management accountant** is an accountant who participates in all accounting work within the organization, including maintaining the accounting records, preparing financial statements, generating the many specialized managerial reports, and coordinating budgeting and reporting efforts. As Figure 1.6 shows, the management accountant combines the accounting data in various ways to carry out these functions.

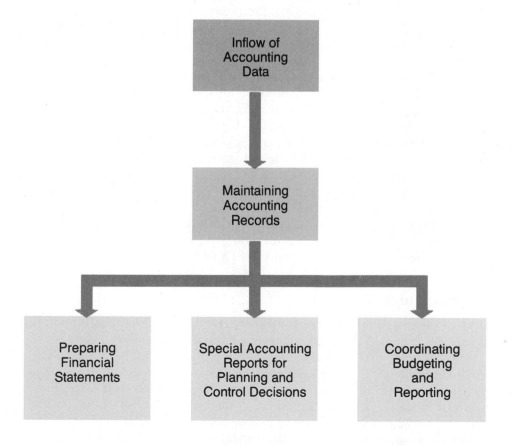

Figure 1.6   Responsibilities of the Management Accountant

The management accountant is not only a service arm to management but is also a part of management. The controller, for example, is responsible for the management of the entire accounting function, which includes selecting ways to process accounting data and present information in the various reports. The controller exercises managerial influence when answering questions like: What combination and quantity of reports should be prepared? How should they be prepared? What is the best method of collecting data? By the nature of accounting work, the management accountant applies management principles and often assists in the decisions made by management.

Certified Management Accountant

The Certified Management Accounting program recognizes an individual's achieving a specific level of knowledge and professional skill. Earning the certificate and becoming a Certified Management Accountant (CMA) is considered an important professional step for anyone desiring to become an active management accountant or financial manager. The CMA program was founded on the basic principle that a management accountant plays an influential role in the management process. The program highlights the contemporary role of the management accountant as a contributor to and a participant in management. Consequently, the person seeking the CMA designation must understand and work with all aspects of business.

To qualify for the CMA designation, candidates must pass a comprehensive four-part examination and must meet specific educational and professional standards. To maintain the designation, an individual must meet continuing educational requirements and adhere to the program's "Standards of Ethical Conduct for Management Accountants."

The four-part examination covers all of the areas important for the work of a management accountant. Part 1 is about economics, finance, and management. Part 2 covers financial accounting and reporting. Part 3 deals with management reporting, analysis, and behavioral issues. Part 4 is about decision analysis and information systems.

The Institute of Management Accountants (formerly called the National Association of Accountants) is the organization that promotes the CMA designation. The program receives its support from a wide range of companies.

Standards of Ethical Conduct

In the preceding pages, we discussed managers' needs for accounting information. We assumed also that whatever information the accounting system generates is presented fairly and timely for the purposes intended. An additional consideration is the accountant's professional conduct. Management accountants must maintain integrity and ethical behavior on their own behalf and must make top management aware of unethical behavior on the part of other people within the organization. This does not mean the management accountant is a policeman. Rather, the management accountant promotes and encourages ethical behavior in all aspects of business life.

The Institute of Management Accountants believes ethics is a cornerstone of its organization and recognized the importance of providing guidance in the area. In June 1983, it published "Standards for Ethical Conduct for Management Accountants." That statement is summarized in Figure 1.7.

The statement on ethical conduct requires management accountants to comply with the established policies of the organization. However, in the absence of such policies, the management accountant must exercise appropriate judgment when faced with ethical problems. More and more organizations are developing codes of ethical conduct and are instituting compliance programs. Because resolving ethical issues is complex, many accounting educational programs are incorporating studies on ethical behavior in their curricula.

SUMMARY

Managers in all types of organizations need accounting information to aid them in fulfilling their roles as efficiently and effectively as possible. The general areas for which they need accounting information are planning and decision making, performance evaluation and control, cost management, and cost determination. Short-term planning is usually reflected in budgets. The budget then becomes a base for comparing actual performance and implementing budgetary control. Cost management is also a planning and control mechanism but focuses on the activities which incur costs, not the responsibility centers to which costs can be traced.

Changes in the business environment affect the way companies do business and manner in which accounting information meets a manager's needs. Some of the recent changes represent competitive situations, technical evolution, and management complexity. The most notable changes are the globalization of business activity, institution of just-in-time systems, computer-aided design systems, and computer-aided manufacturing systems.

Accounting information is provided from a system that handles the requirements of two branches of accounting: financial accounting and managerial accounting. Financial accounting presents accounting information to parties outside the organization. The primary reports are the balance sheet, the income statement, and the cash flow statement. Outside parties interested in an organization's financial statements include (but are not limited to): owners, investors, taxing authorities, and industry associations. Financial reports must follow generally accepted accounting principles.

Managerial accounting organizes accounting information for use by internal management. It is relatively free from the restrictions of financial accounting. Internal reporting is generally directed to the four major areas mentioned above. The types of information needed vary with the level of management using the information.

ETHICAL CONDUCT

Competence

Management accountants have a responsibility to:
- Maintain an appropriate level of professional competence by ongoing development of their knowledge and skills.
- Perform their professional duties in accordance with laws, regulations, and technical standards.
- Prepare complete and clear reports and recommendations after appropriate analyses of relevant and reliable information.

Confidentiality

Management accountants have the responsibility to:
- Refrain from disclosing confidential information acquired in the course of their work except when authorized, unless legally obligated to do so.
- Inform subordinates as appropriate regarding the confidentiality of information acquired in the course of their work and monitor their activities to assure the maintenance of that confidentiality.
- Refrain from using or appearing to use confidential information acquired in the course of their work for unethical or illegal advantage either personally or through third parties.

Integrity

Management accountants have the responsibility to:
- Avoid actual or apparent conflicts of interest and advise all appropriate parties of any potential conflict.
- Refrain from engaging in any activity that would prejudice their ability to carry out their duties ethically.
- Refuse any gift, favor, or hospitality that would influence or would appear to influence their actions.
- Refrain from either actively or passively subverting the attainment of the organization's legitimate and ethical objectives.
- Recognize and communicate professional limitations or other constraints that would preclude responsible judgment or successful performance of an activity.
- Communicate unfavorable as well as favorable information and professional judgments or opinions.
- Refrain from engaging in or supporting any activity that would discredit the profession.

Objectivity

Management accountants have the responsibility to:
- Communicate information fairly and objectively.
- Disclose fully all relevant information that could reasonably be expected to influence an intended user's understanding of the reports, comments, and recommendations.

From: *Standards of Ethical Conduct for Management Accountants*, SMAIC, Montvale: Institute of Management Accountants (formerly National Association of Accountants), 1983.

Figure 1.7 Standards of Ethical Conduct

A management accountant is an accountant who participates in all of the accounting work within the organization. This position is not only a service arm for management but, because of the nature of the accounting work, it is also a part of management. The management accountant must apply management principles and often participates in management decisions.

TERMINOLOGY REVIEW

Budget (4)
Budgetary control (5)
Computer-aided design (CAD) (9)
Computer-aided manufacturing (CAM) (9)
Control (5)
Controller (15)
Cost determination (6)
Cost management (5)
Financial accounting (10)

Flexible manufacturing (8)
Globalization (8)
Just-in-time (JIT) (8)
Management accountant (17)
Managerial accounting (13)
Performance evaluation (5)
Planning (4)
Treasurer (15)
World class manufacturing (8)

QUESTIONS FOR REVIEW AND DISCUSSION

1. Explain how planning and decision making are related to performance evaluation and control.

2. List the sequence of steps in a budgetary control system.

3. Why does budgetary control have feedback loops for future planning and for future control?

4. Explain the significance of cost management and its emphasis on activities.

5. What is cost determination?

6. Which of the following four classes of management activities is most important? (If management did not do this, the company would be out of business.) Explain.
    (a) Planning and decision making
    (b) Performance evaluation and control
    (c) Cost management
    (d) Cost determination

7. What is meant by "world class manufacturing?"

8. Briefly explain what JIT is and what its benefits are.

9. What is the difference between focused production and flexible manufacturing?

10. Which groups (both inside and outside an organization) have an interest in financial statements issued by the organization? Give reasons for each group's interest.

11. Name the three financial statements prepared in financial accounting and released to outside parties. Briefly describe each one.

12. Compare and contrast the characteristics of accounting information needed by top management with accounting information used by lower management.

13. Briefly describe five ways in which financial accounting and managerial accounting are different. Name two ways in which they are the same or similar.

14. Why is financial accounting subject to more strict rules and regulations than managerial accounting?

15. Generally accepted accounting principles provide a distinction between and show a similarity of financial accounting and managerial accounting. Explain.

16. What objectives, other than profit, might be important to managers in an organization?

17. Why do service organizations, governmental units, and various not-for-profit organizations need managerial accounting?

18. A management accountant is both an information provider and a part of management. Explain.

19. Carlos Garcia, president of Garcia Food Processors, stated: "The controller in our organization frequently has more influence over the lower-level managers than our upper-level people have. This also seems to be the case with most of our clients." Why would he say this? Do you agree or disagree with the assessment of the president? Explain.

20. Briefly describe the management accountant's responsibility for ethical behavior with respect to competence, confidentiality, integrity, and objectivity.

21. What is the payoff for an organization to have a code of ethics that employees will follow?

Chapter Two

Cost Concepts

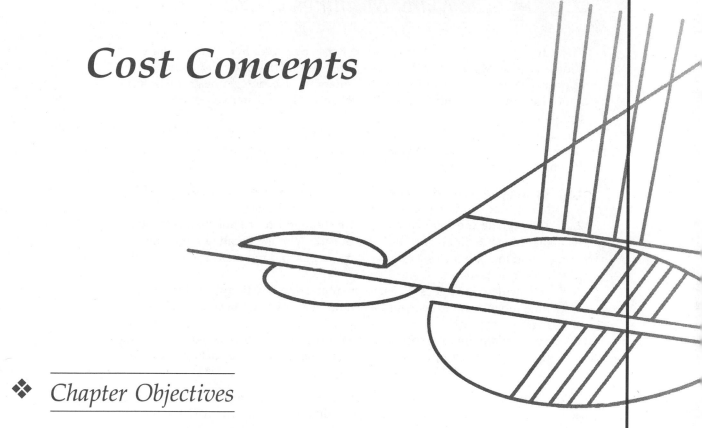

❖ *Chapter Objectives*

After studying Chapter 2, you will be able to:

1. Define and illustrate key concepts of cost.
2. Understand the differences in cost flows in service, merchandising, and manufacturing enterprises.
3. Define product cost elements.
4. Distinguish between variable and fixed cost behavior.
5. Distinguish various planning, decision, and cost concepts.

■ *The Many Meanings of Cost* ■

After the end of her Sophomore year, Kris's dad asks her, "What will your Junior year at Major State University cost us?" Kris gives the standard response: "Why?" She knows that the intended use determines which costs should be included and excluded from an analysis. That's common sense, right? Right!

Another answer to "what does it cost" could have been: "It depends." It depends on who the decision maker is and what the decision is. In this case, a few of the alternatives are:

1. To compare tuition costs among different schools. But Kris really likes Major State and would never think of changing schools.
2. To estimate the total basic cost of tuition and room and board to begin planning for financing the year ahead. A more detailed cost estimate would include the cost of trips home, social and recreation activities, and even this textbook.
3. To calculate the net cash cost after subtracting any financial aid and part-time job income to see what Kris and her dad must take from their savings or borrow.
4. To calculate the total cost of the year in college, given that Kris is passing up an attractive opportunity as a manager trainee at a local fast-food outlet for college life.

Matching cost patterns and alternatives is a large part of decision-making activities. In Kris's case, matching costs is difficult because many of these costs behave differently. Tuition may be a fixed amount per term at one school and paid on a per credit basis at another. A dorm cafeteria may have a 20 meal per week contract or a pay-as-you-eat plan. You could "eat out" or make it yourself in an apartment. Apartment rents can include or exclude utilities.

Understanding cost behavior and knowing which costs to consider and which to ignore are critical factors not only in everyday life situations, but also in business decisions. This chapter will explain much of the terminology needed to analyze these decisions and many other types of situations. Much of the analysis will be basic common sense. Assemble the relevant facts and make a rational decision. Even when we know the relevant quantitative facts, qualitative and strategic factors may cause us to select an alternative that is economically less attractive on the surface.

Managers measure and use costs in many different ways. Cost data are especially important in the following areas:

1. **Planning**. The estimation of future costs in budget preparation and planning activities.
2. **Decision Making**. The selection and formatting of costs relevant to a wide variety of decision-making processes.

3. **Cost Control**. The measurement of costs incurred and the comparison of these costs with budgets, goals, targets, or standards in directing an organization.
4. **Income Measurement**. The determination of the costs associated with the products and services sold to measure profitability of the firm, a segment of the business, a contract, a project, or a customer for a time period.

NATURE OF COST

A cost, broadly defined, is the amount of resource given up to obtain a given objective or object. Generally speaking, cost refers to the monetary measurement (exchange price) attached to the acquisition of goods and services consumed in an organization's activities. The monetary measurement is the cash outlay, but occasionally goods and services may also be acquired by giving up assets other than cash, such as securities, receivables, or property.

The cost objective or object is defined as any purpose for which costs are accumulated. A cost objective may be for making decisions, planning spending levels, or evaluating actual performance. It is the "why" of cost analysis.

Cost, in many respects, is an elusive term. It has meaning only in a specific set of circumstances and for a particular purpose. The cost to a buyer of an office desk, for example, is different from the cost to the manufacturer of that desk. An incremental cost carries a different meaning than a fixed cost. An opportunity cost has relevance to a decision while a sunk cost does not. Consequently, meaningful usage of the term "cost" requires a modifier that conveys the intended meaning for the circumstances involved. Each modifier implies certain attributes, and those attributes dictate the proper usage of costs.

Because many different kinds of costs exist, it is important to understand how one cost concept may be suitable for a given purpose while another concept would be entirely unsuitable. The problem of working with costs is simplified if one considers carefully how the costs are to be used. Costs are useful tools; just as a hammer is useful for driving nails but not for smoothing wood surfaces, so too are costs useful when used properly.

Business people undertake activities to achieve some output or result. Often these activities result in costs—purchasing materials, hiring people, renting space, and so on. Such activities are known as cost drivers. Finding the cause-and-effect linkage between costs and cost drivers is an important part of estimating, assigning, and controlling costs.

Managers, stockholders, employees, and other groups are interested in summarized cost data. However, frequently management requires more detailed information. For example, to manage an enterprise effectively, the costs of a given segment of the business such as a division or a product line must be known. Managers need to know the cost of producing and selling a given quantity of product. Detailed cost information is furnished by a cost accounting system and is used to control business activities, plan operations, and make decisions.

Costs, Expenses, and Income Measurement

If costs are the resources given up to obtain a given object, the object received may be consumed by the end of the period, or it may be part of an asset the firm still owns. In financial accounting, the consumed resource would be an expense, and the assets appear in the form of inventories or productive assets such as equipment. In many managerial analyses, the distinction between cost dollars and expense or asset dollars is clouded with the words cost and expense used interchangeably. Yet income measurement is important to management, and the fundamental financial accounting income measurement rules are applicable to managerial analysis.

Cash Versus Accrual Accounting

Clearly, cash flow has a heavy influence on managerial decisions. Yet, measurement of profit must include proper revenue recognition and expense matching rules. Accrual-based accounting methods, such as those used to measure receivables and payables, depreciation and amortization expenses, taxation expenses and payments, and historical asset costs are used to determine a company's financial profit. Often, however, this accrual-based accounting information is at odds with management's need for the type of cash-based accounting information useful for performing cash flow analyses. Knowing when to use cash and accrual numbers may have major impacts on specific decisions. In many cases, timing of cash flows is more critical to managers than precise accrual accounting numbers.

Comparing Service, Merchandising, and Manufacturing Organizations

Differences in measuring profitability for various types of organizations are largely a function of inventoried costs. Many similarities exist. Providing a service to a client in a law firm or repairing a washing machine in a fix-it shop is essentially the same as manufacturing pencils. In service industries, resources are brought together to produce the service, just as they are brought together to make the product in a factory environment.

Service organizations will maintain only supplies inventories. The merchandising firm buys and sells products and keeps inventories of merchandise. The manufacturing firm will buy materials or components and convert these inputs into a saleable product. The inventories here include both the purchased materials inputs and the in-process partially complete products, as well as completed and ready to sell inventories. Thus, the inventory and costing processes in a manufacturing firm have added complexity. Figure 2.1 compares income statements and selected balance sheet accounts for the three types of businesses.

INCOME STATEMENTS FOR THE YEAR 1995

	Service Firms	Merchandising Firms	Manufacturing Firms
	Adcom Communications	Karl's Supermarket	Premier Products
Sales..	$8,000,000	$8,000,000	$8,000,000
Cost of sales:			
Cost of goods manufactured:			
Beginning materials inventory......................			$ 465,000
+ Purchases of materials			2,323,000
Materials available for use.........................			$2,788,000
− Ending materials inventory......................			510,000
Materials used.....................................			$2,278,000
+ Direct labor			895,000
+ Manufacturing overhead			2,117,000
Manufacturing costs...............................			$5,290,000
+ Beginning work in process			427,000
Total manufacturing costs			$5,717,000
− Ending work in process..........................			408,000
Cost of goods manufactured			$5,309,000
Purchases		$6,892,000	
+ Beginning goods inventory		401,000	752,000
Goods available for sale...........................		$7,293,000	$6,061,000
− Ending goods inventory..........................		388,000	794,000
Cost of goods sold		$6,905,000	$5,267,000
Direct client expenses	5,788,000		
Gross margin	$2,212,000	$1,095,000	$2,733,000
Operating expenses:			
Selling expenses..................................	$ 511,000	$ 544,000	$ 985,000
Administrative expenses	1,267,000	263,000	1,019,000
Total operating expenses..........................	$1,778,000	$ 807,000	$2,004,000
Net operating income	$ 434,000	$ 288,000	$ 729,000

SELECTED BALANCE SHEET INFORMATION FOR THE YEAR 1995

Accounts receivable	$1,362,000	$ 81,000	$1,033,000
Materials inventory			510,000
Work in process inventory			408,000
Products inventory		388,000	794,000
Supplies inventory.................................	69,000	86,000	143,000
Accounts payable	229,000	112,000	459,000

Figure 2.1 Measuring Income in Service, Merchandising, and Manufacturing Firms

Service Organizations   A service business performs an activity for a fee. The costs of performing the service may include salaries of professionals and support personnel, supplies, purchased specialized services, and routine costs such as rent and utilities. As shown in Figure 2.1 the expenses of Adcom

Communications Company, a public relations firm, are reported as either direct client expenses or operating expenses. Some service organizations can identify direct costs of performing the services, as in the Adcom illustration, while others would group all expenses under the operating expenses section. The detail behind these numbers undoubtedly reflects specific revenues and expenses from individual contracts or projects that the firm handled during 1995.

Figure 2.2 shows the flows of costs in Adcom Communications. Those costs going to Direct Client Expense are the chargeable time of the firm's professional staff and any other costs that are traceable directly to specific client projects. All other costs are classified as either selling or administrative expenses. Essentially, all costs incurred by the firm are **period costs**, meaning that they become expenses of the time period when the cost is incurred. Only receivables and payables, supplies, depreciation, and perhaps costs that are not billed to clients would cause the reported expenses to differ from the cash costs.

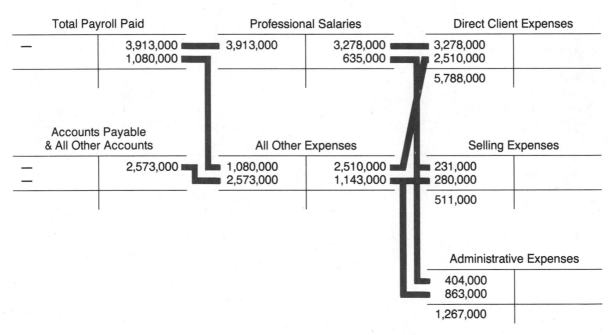

Figure 2.2 Service Organization Cost Flows

The problems of measuring performance, such as the profitability of a specific contract, and linking support costs in the firm to specific sources of revenue are surprisingly similar to manufacturing costing problems. These problems are discussed in later sections.

Merchandising Organizations   A merchandising business purchases products for resale. Generally, a merchandising firm is a link in the physical distribution chain, acting as a wholesaler or retailer. Figure 2.1 introduces

Cost of Goods Sold to the income statement of Karl's Supermarkets, operator of a retail store. Figure 2.3 shows the flow of costs through the relevant accounts. Again, behind the totals reported would be detailed revenues and costs of sales for various segments such as produce, hardware, meat, and grocery departments.

Any cost that is inventoriable is a **product cost**. In merchandising firms product cost includes the cost of merchandise plus in-bound freight and possibly certain internal merchandise handling costs. All other expenses in the supermarket operation are treated as period costs.

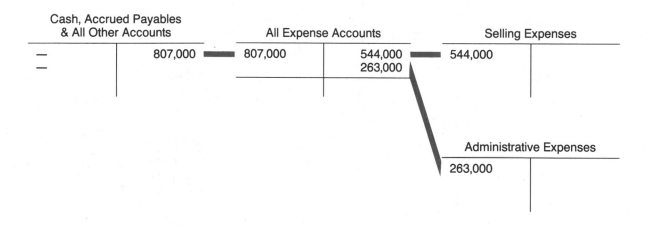

Figure 2.3   Merchandise Organization Cost Flows

Manufacturing Organizations   As Figure 2.1 illustrates, manufacturing firms have the most complex cost of goods sold activities. A new section, cost of goods manufactured, is introduced. The flows of costs, the variety of costs, the complexity of most manufacturing operations, and the cost and activity relationships that can develop create an environment that draws on all the skills and talents of production managers and managerial accountants.

Figure 2.4 illustrates a simplified version of Premier Products Company's factory where resources are brought together for producing automotive components. Premier is a producer of subassemblies for the auto industry. An assembly line in the factory is the focus of the "manufacturing" activities. Materials (primarily purchased parts and components) are purchased for use in production, and factory employees work to convert materials into finished products. Many support services are used, including materials handlers, equipment maintenance people, heat, power, employee benefits, factory accountants, and supervisors. Other expenses include depreciation on the building and equipment.

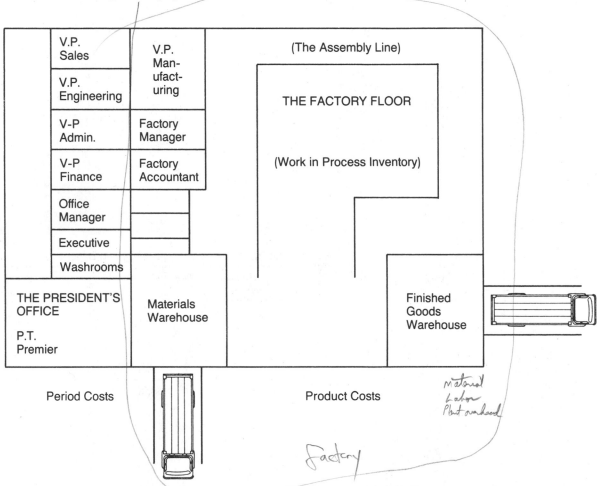

Figure 2.4 The Premier Products Company's Factory

In Figure 2.4, the firm is divided into the office area and the factory area. As a generalization, any expense incurred in the office area is an operating expense and, therefore, a period cost. Any cost incurred in the factory area is a manufacturing cost and, therefore, a product cost. Obviously, this is a simplified example and avoids some cost allocation problems, but the basic concept holds for nearly all costs. One accounting task for a manufacturer is to attach the resource costs to the finished units to measure product cost per unit.

Manufacturing requires three types of inventories—materials, work in process, and finished products. Materials purchases are received and inventoried in the materials warehouse, and the costs are recorded in **Materials Inventory**. When materials are needed and requisitioned for use on the factory floor, materials costs arc transferred to **Work in Process Inventory**. This term describes both the products that have been started but are not yet complete and the costs incurred for materials, workers, and other resources used in the production process. When products are completed, they are physically moved to the finished goods warehouse, and the product costs are also transferred to **Finished Goods Inventory**. These products are now ready for sale to customers. And when the sale takes place, the product costs are transferred to **Cost of Goods Sold**.

Traditional Grouping of Product Costs—Manufacturing

Figure 2.1 illustrates the income measurement for Premier Products. Often a product's cost is composed of three groups of manufacturing costs—materials, direct labor, and manufacturing overhead. While automated manufacturing and costing systems that link activities and costs can create more or fewer product cost groups, these three have historically been used in nearly all manufacturing cost systems.

Materials costs are the cost of physical components of the product. In some cases, natural resources such as oil, flour, or lumber are used. In other cases, partially processed components (another company's finished product) are the materials inputs. Often a complete list of all materials used in a product is prepared and is called a **bill of materials**. Assuming a perpetual inventory system, by adding materials purchases to beginning inventory and subtracting materials issued to the factory floor leaves ending materials inventory. Materials issued to the factory are **materials used**. Supplies and materials used in small quantities, such as glue and lubricants, are often called indirect materials and treated as manufacturing overhead costs.

Direct labor costs are the wages paid to workers who directly process the product. In Figure 2.4, assembly line workers would be direct labor. Direct labor cost could include fringe benefit costs, such as health insurance, pension costs, and various payroll taxes. For example, a $10 per hour wage rate might grow to nearly $20 per hour when all employer-paid benefit costs are added. Historically, wages of direct laborers were a major manufacturing cost. Today, as many factories become more and more automated, direct labor costs are shrinking as a percentage of total product cost. More indirect employees are needed for support activities—programming and repairing robotic equipment for example.

Manufacturing overhead costs include all manufacturing costs that are not materials or direct labor. Factory overhead[1] and indirect manufacturing costs are other names for these costs. Obviously, a wide variety of costs is included, such as maintenance employees' wages, salaries of factory managers, utilities

---

[1]The term "factory burden" is still common in practice, but "burden" is an archaic usage that we will not use in this text.

costs, factory and equipment depreciation, and repair costs. Potentially hundreds of different cost accounts could be grouped under manufacturing overhead. Often supplies like nails, glue, lubricants, and paints could be included in the materials group or in indirect materials which is an overhead cost. Likewise, certain workers' tasks could be called indirect labor in one company and direct labor in another. For example, materials handlers and quality control personnel could be accounted for as either direct or indirect labor. Generally, if the worker has direct contact with the product, the cost is direct labor. The cost of any support task is indirect labor.

If you can't trace directly or if allocated against the Indirect Cost

Materials and direct labor are often thought of as **direct product costs** since these costs are easily identified with specific products and units of product. Manufacturing overhead is thought of as **indirect product costs**. These manufacturing costs are not easily traced to specific products or units. For example, the plant manager's salary cannot be tied to specific units of a particular product in a multi-product factory, since the manager is responsible for all activities in the factory.

If in doubt of a direct cost, then classify as Indirect Cost,

A major problem in product costing is attaching manufacturing overhead to products. The simplest approach is to divide the number of units produced into total manufacturing costs. For example, a highly automated factory produces a variety of inexpensive calculators. The same production processes are used for all products with minimal "change over" costs. Three million calculators roll off the line every month. The basic integrated circuits distinguish the products. All other costs in the plant could be summed and divided by the number of calculators produced ($6,000,000 ÷ 3,000,000 = $2.00 per unit). Below are March production data by product line:

	Business	Scientific	General Purpose	Total
Materials costs	$3,600,000	$4,200,000	$1,500,000	$ 9,300,000
Indirect other costs				6,000,000
Total costs				$15,300,000
Units produced	1,200,000	1,200,000	600,000	3,000,000
Materials costs per unit	$3.00	$3.50	$2.50	$3.10
Indirect other costs per unit	2.00	2.00	2.00	2.00
Product cost per unit	$5.00	$5.50	$4.50	$5.10

Several approaches to product costing could be used. The easiest is to divide the total costs of $15,300,000 by 3,000,000 calculators. The $5.10 average cost hides the difference in cost of specific materials for each model. A second approach averages materials costs for each model and averages all other costs over all units. This produces a high cost of $5.50 for scientific models and a low cost of $4.50 for general purpose models. More complex costing would be needed if production processes for each model differed in some substantial way such as equipment used, time needed for assembly, or special testing. Even in this simple situation managers will want detailed information on the $6,000,000 of other costs. What are the individual expenses, who controls them, and what was the budgeted level of spending?

Materials and direct labor are often considered to be the **prime costs** of a product. These are the direct costs easily identifiable with a specific product.

Given the nature of manufacturing, direct labor and manufacturing overhead are known as **conversion costs**. In the factory, materials are "converted" into finished product using labor and all the factory's facilitating resources. Figure 2.5 diagrams these relationships.

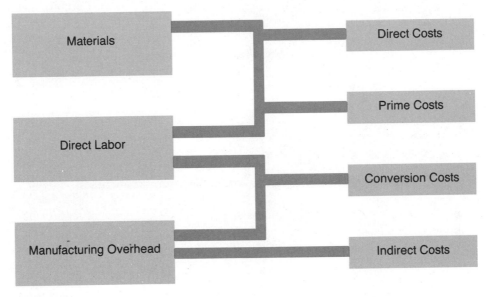

Figure 2.5   Product Costs and Product Cost Groups

Also, as the volume of production increases or decreases, certain costs increase or decrease with volume while others change little if any. Materials will move with production volume. Direct labor is often assumed to move with production. However, many union contracts guarantee workers minimum hours of employment even if production volume falls. Certain overhead costs will fluctuate with production volume such as supplies, support labor, and power costs. Others will remain largely constant, such as supervisory salaries, depreciation, insurance, and property taxes. Thus materials and direct labor are often assumed to be **variable product costs**, and manufacturing overhead will include both variable and **fixed product costs**. Behavior of these costs is discussed later.

Manufacturing Flows of Costs

Figure 2.6 ties the formal income statement in Figure 2.1 and the factory environment in Figure 2.4 together in a flow of costs through the manufacturing process. The Premier Products Company factory can be viewed as a bucket. Resource costs are dumped in, and costs of finished goods are poured out. The physical flow of production and accounting flow of costs are parallel views of the same activities. At the beginning of 1995, the bucket may already

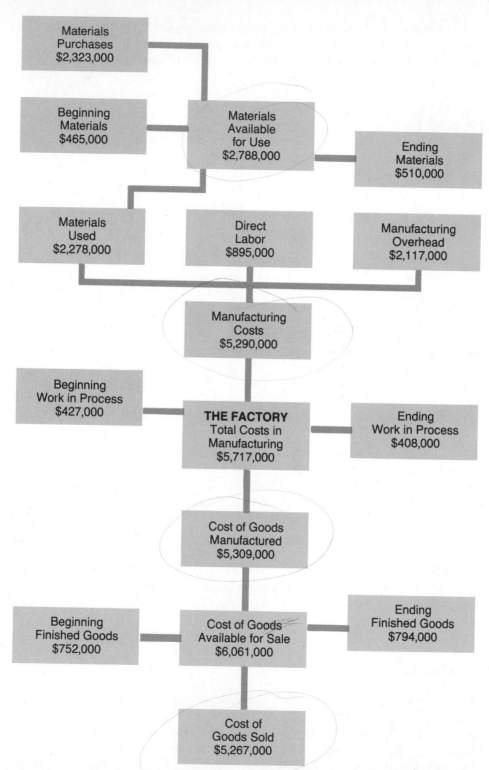

Figure 2.6 Flows of Products and Costs Through the Factory

contain costs from the prior time period. This is beginning work in process inventory. Materials is also a bucket where beginning inventory and purchases give the total materials available for use during this year. Materials used can be measured directly by adding the costs of materials transferred to the factory floor or by taking physical materials inventory counts and assuming that the rest was used. Most modern factories know where all materials are at all times. As direct laborers work and earn wages and as all other production costs are incurred, more costs are added to the work in process bucket.

The sum of materials, direct labor, and manufacturing overhead costs added to production is called **manufacturing costs** for that time period. When units are completed and transferred to finished goods inventory, costs attached to the completed units this period are poured out of the bucket. The cost of these products is called the **cost of goods manufactured**. At the end of the time period, the remaining costs in the bucket are ending work in process inventory.

At this point on Figure 2.1, the manufacturing and merchandising firms begin to look alike. Cost of goods manufactured in Premier is the same as purchases in Karl's Supermarket. Both firms will add beginning merchandise inventory or finished goods inventories to get **goods available for sale**. By subtracting ending finished goods inventory, we get **cost of goods sold**.

Understanding product costing is fundamental to many decision-making and income-measuring processes, but more critical to most management issues is how costs behave as circumstances change. The ramifications of cost behavior extend to all planning and controlling tasks.

COST BEHAVIOR

To say that a cost "behaves" in a certain way is somewhat misleading. A cost results from taking some action or from the mere passage of time. Something drives a cost—some activity, decision, or event. Selling one more hamburger involves a burger, a bun, a container, a napkin, and any condiments used. But selling one more hamburger has no impact on the cost of supervision, equipment rental, or advertising. The building lease costs will remain unchanged unless the lease calls for the rental payment to be a percentage of total sales dollars. Cost behavior, then, is the impact that a cost driver has on a cost.

Which costs can be expected to remain constant when the amount of work done increases or decreases? Also, which costs increase as more work is performed and decrease when less work is performed? If costs are to be estimated and controlled, we need to know whether or not the cost will change if conditions change and, if so, by what amount.

Cost behavior is often expressed in a dichotomous pattern—either variable or fixed. In the real world, many behavior patterns exist since most costs are not strictly variable or fixed. Thus the concepts of semivariable and semifixed costs add complexity to the study of cost behavior.

Variable Costs

A **variable cost** is a cost that varies in total amount in direct proportion to changes in activity or output. A decrease in activity brings a proportional decrease in the total variable cost; an increase in activity results in a proportional increase in the total variable cost. For example, direct materials cost is usually a variable cost with each unit manufactured requiring a certain quantity of material. Thus, the materials cost changes in direct proportion to the number of units manufactured.

A proportional relationship between an activity and an associated cost has this important characteristic: the variable cost expressed on a per unit basis remains constant throughout the relevant range of activity. The slope of the total variable cost curve represents the constant variable cost per unit. For example, if materials cost per unit were $4.00, the expression $4X$ would give the total variable cost at the X level of output. Figure 2.7 shows the behavior of variable costs in total and on a per unit basis.

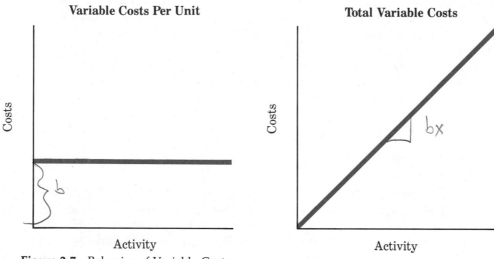

Figure 2.7   Behavior of Variable Costs

Fixed Costs

A **fixed cost** is constant in total amount when changes occur in activity level within some range of activity. Such costs as the plant manager's salary, depreciation, insurance, taxes, and rent usually remain the same regardless of whether the plant is above or below its normal level of operations. Fixed costs tend to be lumps of dollars instead of a rate like variable costs. A month's rent is quoted as an amount for the month, not as an amount per unit of output or even per hour of use. However, a fixed cost, like any cost, is subject to certain variations. Rent may increase or insurance costs may go up, but these changes are caused by factors independent of the firm's activity level.

By definition, the total fixed costs are constant, which means that the fixed cost per unit will vary. Figure 2.8 shows the behavior of fixed costs in total and on a per unit basis. When a company produces a greater number of units, the fixed cost per unit decreases. Conversely, when a smaller number of units are produced, the fixed cost per unit increases. This variability of fixed costs per unit creates problems in product costing. The cost per unit depends on the number of units produced or the level of activity achieved.

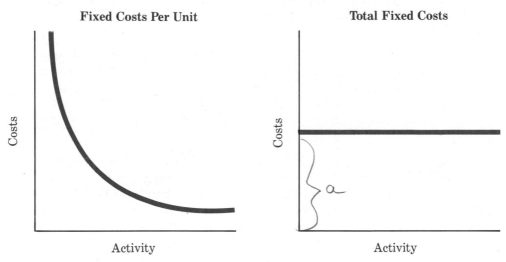

Figure 2.8   Behavior of Fixed Costs

Fixed costs by their nature do not change with volume. But certain fixed costs can be changed by management action. These are **discretionary fixed costs**. Discretionary fixed costs are expenditures that managers can elect to spend or not to spend. For example, a company might budget the cost of consultants for $20,000 per month for the coming year. But the contract says that the company can cancel the contract at any time. Management maintains discretion over the spending. On the other hand, if the contract guarantees the consultant a 12-month relationship and the contract has been signed, a **committed fixed cost** has been created. A committed fixed cost is one over which managers have lost control in the short run and must incur.

An interesting observation is needed here. Managers can, with time and intent, change the behavior of certain activities' costs in a firm. For example, variable direct labor costs can be converted to a fixed cost by guaranteeing employees "job security" for some period of time such as a three-year union contract. Or equipment could be leased on a short-term basis (day-to-day or even hourly) instead of purchasing—converting a fixed cost to a variable cost. Also, fixed cost automated equipment could be installed to replace high variable cost manual operations. Variable costs may be increased or decreased based on long-term competitive strategies and overt management decisions. Thus, analysts should recognize that managers have alternatives and can act to change cost behavior patterns.

Nature of Variable and Fixed Costs

The basic nature of variable and fixed costs is different. Variable costs are first expressed as a rate—cost per unit of activity. Variable costs can be converted to a total amount only by knowing the volume of activity achieved. Fixed costs are first expressed as an amount. Fixed costs can be converted to a rate only if a volume of activity or output is known. In the following example, the cost per unit of $7.00 and the total cost of $700,000 can be found only if the output of 100,000 units is known. If the units produced increased to 120,000, both the cost per unit and the total cost changes as shown below:

| | Costs of 100,000 Units | | Costs of 120,000 Units | |
	Cost Per Unit	Total Cost	Cost Per Unit	Total Cost
Variable costs	$4.00 ➡	$400,000	$4.00 ➡	$480,000
Fixed costs	3.00 ⬅	300,000	2.50 ⬅	300,000
Total costs	$7.00	$700,000	$6.50	$780,000

A decrease in the cost per unit from $7.00 to $6.50 is caused by spreading the $300,000 of fixed costs over more units—120,000 instead of 100,000. The increase in the total cost is caused by variable costs per unit for the additional 20,000 units. A decrease in volume would have a similar reverse impact—the cost per unit would increase and the total costs would decline.

In planning, decision making, or controlling, three factors must be known to perform analysis:

1.   The variable cost rate.
2.   The fixed cost amount.
3.   The level of activity or output.

These factors can be brought together in a **cost function**—an expression that mathematically links the costs, their behavior, and their cost driver. In our example, the expression would be total costs equal fixed cost plus variable cost per unit times the number of units produced or:

$$\text{Total cost} = \$300,000 + \$4X$$

Where X is the number of units produced.

One major danger in converting fixed cost lumps to costs per unit is that a user may misinterpret the unit cost number. It could be assumed that the variable cost is now the total cost per unit—forgetting that the fixed cost is sitting in the production cost budget as a fixed cost. At a different activity level, the per unit cost will be different. Even in working homework problems, students often use costs per unit in their analysis and are in danger of missing the impact of volume changes on total costs. An opposite problem exists if total costs for variable and fixed costs are used, since volume changes will have an impact on total variable costs and not fixed costs. The general warning: Beware of activity changes and their impacts on costs.

Relevant Range

In Figures 2.7 and 2.8 the cost lines are assumed to start at zero and go to a very large volume. Realistically, cost relationships only hold for a much narrower range of activity—a relevant range. A **relevant range** is the normal range of expected activity. Management does not expect activity to exceed a certain upper bound nor fall below a certain lower bound. Production activity is expected to be within this range, and costs are budgeted for these levels. In cost analysis, costs are planned and are expected to behave normally within the relevant range. Usually, past experience is the basis for estimating cost behavior, and the range of this experience establishes the relevant range.

In many cases, fixed costs are fixed, and variable costs are variable within the relevant range. Outside the upper range limit, additional fixed costs may be incurred—another supervisor if a second shift is needed. Also, the variable rate might change—economies of larger volume purchase contracts or higher overtime premiums if more work is added. Thus, assumptions are made in Figures 2.7 and 2.8 to extend the cost functions beyond the relevant range. In the above example, the change in volume was from 100,000 to 120,000 units. If we assume that these are the extreme points of the relevant range, the cost function of $300,000 plus $4 per unit is valid between 100,000 and 120,000 units as shown in Figure 2.9. If the relevant range was 110,000 to 115,000 units, our cost function may not be accurate or useful. Even within the relevant range we must be careful in making cost behavior assumptions.

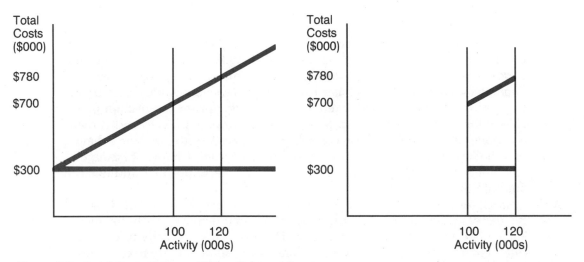

Figure 2.9   Total Costs Patterns With a Relevant Range

Semivariable and Semifixed Costs

Figure 2.10 illustrates a few cost functions that are neither strictly variable nor fixed. Many costs are **semivariable**, meaning they may change but not in direct proportion to the changes in output. Often, these costs have attributes of both variable and fixed costs. In Figure 2.10, Example A shows a cost that declines on a per unit basis as more is used. Perhaps lower purchase prices or greater efficiency in use of the materials could result in a lower per unit cost as volume increases. Example B shows a constant variable rate until a certain activity level is reached, then the variable cost per unit increases. Perhaps after employees work a 40-hour week, a 50 percent overtime premium must be paid.

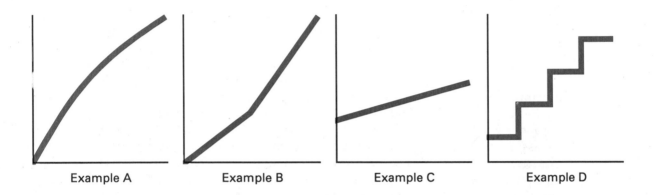

Example A   Example B   Example C   Example D

Figure 2.10   Examples of Semivariable and Semifixed Cost Patterns (X axis is activity level; Y axis is total costs)

Some semivariable costs, perhaps better called **mixed costs**, may be broken down into fixed and variable components, thus making it easier to budget and control costs and to apply cost data for decision-making purposes. Example C illustrates a cost pattern that has a fixed cost plus a variable rate. A telephone expense may include a basic fixed monthly charge for the connection plus a charge for each local call made. Many expenses have both fixed and variable components. Budgeting these costs requires special study of their behavior and the link between the cost driver and the cost itself. Chapter 15 examines techniques that can help separate the fixed and variable portions and that can quantify the cost function.

Semifixed costs are typified by step increases in costs with changes in activity. Increases are lumps of cost. This means that activity can be increased somewhat without an increase in cost. However, at some activity level, the total cost must be increased by a fixed amount to allow activity to continue to increase. Often, fixed and semifixed costs are capacity-providing costs such as rents and salaries. For example, a buyer in a purchasing department will be able to handle a certain volume of purchase orders. Beyond this buyer's maximum level, the company must hire another buyer if production continues to increase.

Example D illustrates a **step fixed cost**. Each step represents another lump of cost as another level of activity is reached. The width and height of each step depend on the specific cost involved. If many narrow steps exist within the relevant range, a step cost may approximate a variable cost pattern. On the other hand, very wide steps may encompass all or most of the relevant range and may approximate a fixed cost pattern. When neither the variable nor fixed approximation is reasonable, step costs must be explicitly recognized when they are used in planning and control decisions.

COST CONCEPTS FOR PLANNING AND CONTROLLING

Each managerial use of costs needs its own definition of cost. Often, terms can be explained using contrasts between terms and their definitions. In certain applications, great care must be exercised to distinguish different cost meanings, even subtle differences. In other situations, similar terms can easily be substituted for one another.

Direct Costs Versus Indirect Costs

Costs are sometimes defined as being direct or indirect with respect to some segment of the business—an activity, a department, or a product. If a cost can be specifically identified with or traced to the cost objective, it is a **direct cost** of that objective. A direct cost can also be called a traceable cost. To be a **traceable cost**, we must be able to track the cost to its cost objective with little doubt. The cost of a blue knob for Model X32 is a direct cost of Model X32 because it is traceable to that specific product. If no clear association between a cost and the cost objective is apparent, the cost is an **indirect cost**. For example, the cost to heat the factory is an indirect cost of the various products manufactured there. The distinction depends on whether or not the cost can be directly identified with the cost objective without forcing a link through assumptions or implications.

One aspect of direct versus indirect costs is determining whether a cost is direct or indirect at a given level of the organization. For example, the salary of the plant manager of Plant A is a direct cost of Plant A. But if multiple products are produced in Plant A, the manager's salary is indirect to the specific products. Thus, what is a direct cost for one purpose may be an indirect cost for another purpose.

An indirect cost can also be called a common cost or a joint cost. A **common cost** is incurred to benefit more than one business activity. In a university setting, the president's salary is a common cost to all colleges and departments within the university. Also, the college of business dean's salary is a direct cost to the college of business; however, the dean's salary is a common cost to all departments within the college of business. Since the cost is common to all departments, it cannot be a direct cost of any department.

A **joint cost** is applied to situations where multiple outputs are derived from the joint cost. For example, a barrel of crude oil can be processed into literally thousands of products. Even simple straight forward refining processes generate numerous final and intermediate products. The costs of the crude oil and the initial refining process are joint costs of the products produced. It is impossible to trace specific portions of the crude oil costs to specific products, and allocations of cost must be made to assign the joint costs.

An interesting side of this joint cost is the fact that the crude oil cost is a variable cost, but it is not traceable to a specific product. Yet in analyzing costs, variable costs are often, but not always, direct costs. Likewise, fixed costs are often thought of as indirect costs. Yet many fixed costs can be traced to a given cost objective. For example, if Ms. Hood owns three Burgers Plus fast-food outlets in a city and wants to measure each location's profitability, certain costs are direct and others indirect. Food and supplies costs are variable and direct. Location managers, rent, and depreciation expenses are probably fixed but also direct. The owner's salary, her home office expenses, and city-wide advertising costs are all indirect to each of the three locations. If she is interested in the profitability of specific product lines such as burgers, drinks, shakes, and fries, perhaps the only direct costs will be the food costs, while all others are indirect. Again, the "why do you want to know" question determines the definition of cost.

When costs cannot be traced to a particular cost objective such as products or departments, these indirect costs may need to be allocated. Using only direct costs may give an incomplete picture of an object's costs. Allocating indirect costs may help see a long-run cost pattern or may give a better idea of the total cost of providing a product or service. Indirect costs can be divided using some activity measure or common factor and allocated to cost objectives. The allocation process should attempt to link the cost and the cost objective. The main bases are cause and effect, use of the resource, and benefit received. Some indirect costs have more obvious links than others. For example, a repair department in a factory can look at how much time mechanics spend in each producing department. But the plant manager's salary is a true common cost of the entire factory. Some arbitrary proration must be done in this case.

Incremental Costs Versus Average Costs

A basic distinction in cost analysis is the difference between the cost of adding one more unit and the average cost of all units produced. **Incremental costs** are the costs incurred by adding more activity—more sales, another project, or a new department. Another term used to describe incremental cost is marginal cost. Often, **marginal cost** is thought of as the cost of adding one more unit of output or doing one more task. Incremental costs are often variable costs but can include any fixed costs that are also added as a result of the increased activity level. As one more unit is added, we eventually reach one of the steps where another lump of fixed costs must be added. These additional fixed costs would then be incremental fixed costs.

Incremental implies adding something. But the concept could also apply to deleting a segment. The term **decremental cost** could be used. But more commonly, costs that go away are called avoidable costs. An **avoidable cost** will be eliminated if a specific segment is eliminated. In a retail bakery chain, the utilities expense for the Pleasant Street store is a direct cost of that location. If that store is closed, the utilities can be turned off; and the costs will stop. The salary of the store manager might also be avoidable unless that person has an employment contract for a certain time period.

The **average cost** of a unit generally includes all costs for producing all units. An average product cost includes all materials, direct labor, and manufacturing overhead costs. The average cost will generally decline as volume of activity increases due to spreading the same fixed costs over more units. It averages variable and fixed product costs and direct and indirect product costs. The term full cost implies an all inclusive set of costs. But **full cost** also is commonly interpreted to be a full manufactured cost, excluding selling, administrative, and financing costs. The accountant's full cost definition is generally narrower than the economist's definition.

The incremental cost concept extends the cost behavior discussion. Which costs will change if a change in activity occurs? For example, if a supermarket manager is considering adding a pharmacy to its stores, what will change? The incremental costs will include facilities (equipment and remodeling), licenses, salaries of pharmacists and trained assistants, reporting and security costs, inventory holding costs, and the cost of sales. If we assume no space is added to the store, some other department will lose space and presumably sales. To make the decision, the expected changes in revenues and costs must be documented and planned. Competitive and strategic issues may be critical deciding factors, but knowing the incremental revenues and costs of the decision is fundamental to any analysis.

In many situations, the incremental or marginal cost per unit will be much more relevant to the decision than the average cost per unit. Incremental costs tend to focus on change, while averages tend to include fixed costs which will not change regardless of the decision. Care must be taken, however, not to ignore the long-run average cost of production. In the long run, all costs must be covered by revenue if the firm is to remain successful. Likewise, few decisions are truly short term in nature. Yet in assessing a decision to make a change, it is critical that the cost impact of the change be examined carefully through **incremental cost analysis**.

Relevant Costs Versus Irrelevant Costs

The key to incremental cost analysis is knowing which costs are relevant and which are irrelevant to the analysis. A **relevant cost** is a cost that changes its value as different alternatives are compared. If a cost increases, decreases, appears, or disappears as different courses of action are evaluated, it is relevant. The definition of irrelevant should be obvious. An **irrelevant cost** is one that does not change across alternatives. Being irrelevant does not mean that a cost is forgotten or that it need not be evaluated. It means that it is not one of the factors that will quantitatively affect the decision.

A relevant cost must also be a current or future value. This means that current market or cash values are used to evaluate all assets and liabilities. **Out-of-pocket costs** is the term used to describe relevant cash costs. In contrast to financial accounting, estimates of values must be used in many cases. Future values must be forecast in many cases. Heavy emphases are on cash flows and on knowing when the cash flows will occur. The credibility of forecasts of future values will influence the quality of the analysis. Many forecasts of costs are based on recent historical experiences. Experience has also given us opportunities to evaluate past decisions and to watch past cost relationships. But the decisions we make are about the present and future. We will invest time and money in analysis of these decisions. The more important the decision, the greater the investment in analysis must be. For example, the decision to invest in a new paint facility for an auto assembly plant is over $600 million dollars. Many years of analysis by a wide variety of individuals at nearly every level of the company will be incorporated into the project. Yet, the decision to change the oil in a company car will be made routinely using well established maintenance rules. The amount of dollars involved, the uniqueness of the task, and the strategic importance of the task are major factors in determining the amount of analysis needed.

If a cost does not change, it can be excluded from further analysis. A sunk cost is also a type of irrelevant cost. A **sunk cost** is a past or committed cost. It is an irreversible cost. Any cost incurred in the past is sunk, gone forever. Any asset obtained from the incurred cost can be used or sold, but its value is its present or future value—not the cost paid. Thus, any historical cost is a sunk cost. Also, payments required in any valid contractual commitment are sunk costs. These are **unavoidable costs**, costs that must be incurred.

To illustrate, assume that Summers Township purchased a water purification filter at a cost of $7,000. The township trustees are considering using the filter as part of a public swim facility improvement project. Or, if not used, it could be resold for $9,000. The cost has already been incurred and has no affect on any decision with respect to the use or disposal of the filter. The net benefit of each alternative is shown as follows:

	Including Past Filter Cost		Excluding Past Filter Cost	
	Use	Dispose	Use	Dispose
Increased revenue..................	$50,000		$50,000	
Other incremental costs	(38,000)		(38,000)	
Proceeds from filter		$ 9,000		$ 9,000
Cost of filter	(7,000)	(7,000)		
Net benefit	$ 5,000	$ 2,000	$12,000	$ 9,000

Note that the $7,000 cost of the filter is the same for each alternative, is a sunk cost, and can be ignored. The economic advantage of using the filter versus selling it is $3,000 whether the filter cost is included or excluded.

A major difference between financial and managerial accounting arises here. Historical costs, which are fundamental to most balance sheet asset values and income measurement, have little or no significance in managerial analysis. A past cost has no meaning in decisions to hold, use, or sell. Only current and future values have meaning. Even tax issues use historical costs only to determine current and future tax costs. The temptation to continue to use historical costs in decisions is great. But using any past cost will only distort the decision-making process.

Differential Cost, Indifference Points, and Opportunity Cost

Decision making requires comparing alternatives and selecting the best alternative. The focus is often on the differential costs. A **differential cost** is the difference in costs between one course of action and another. If the decision is to "do A" or "do B," the incremental revenues and costs of doing A are summed and compared to the incremental revenues and costs of doing B. Even "do A" or "not do A" comparisons are done the same way. In the Summers Township example above, the $3,000 is the differential cost.

In some situations, a mid-point or indifference point can be found. The **indifference point** is the activity level where a decision maker is indifferent between the two alternatives. For example, if Alternative A's operating costs are $1,000 plus $5 per unit and Alternative B's operating costs are $500 plus $10 per unit, the indifference point would be 100 units, shown as follows:

Alternative A		**Alternative B**
$1,000 + $5X	=	$500 + $10X
X	=	100 units

At X equals 100 the decision maker does not care which alternative is selected. If volume is under 100, Alternative B is preferred. If volume is over 100, Alternative A is preferred.

An opportunity cost is another version of differential cost. An **opportunity cost** is the income foregone by selecting another alternative. It is generally thought of as the value of the best alternative not taken. For example, we might have three job offers—one for $40,000 per year, another for $35,000, and a third for $28,000. By selecting the best offer of $40,000, our opportunity cost is $35,000, the next best alternative. We gave up $35,000 to get $40,000. The general decision rule would be that the opportunity cost should not exceed the value of the option selected.

Controllable Costs Versus Noncontrollable Costs

Another important aspect of cost is the distinction between costs that can be controlled and costs that cannot be controlled by a particular person. This cost classification, like the direct and indirect cost classification, depends on a point of reference. Costs are incurred with the authorization of some member of management. If a manager is responsible for a given cost, that cost is said to be a **controllable cost** with respect to that person. If the manager is not authorized to incur the cost, it is a **noncontrollable cost** with respect to that person. An entire cost control system rests on careful cost responsibility identification.

All costs are controllable at some level of management. Top management, including the board of directors, has broad authority over costs and directly or indirectly controls all costs in the firm. For example, top management can increase or decrease managerial salaries and can initiate or abandon major projects. Such costs are beyond the authority of intermediate or lower-level managers, however, and are noncontrollable at that level. A departmental supervisor, for example, may have control over the supplies used by the department but has no control over plant asset acquisitions (or resulting depreciation) allocated to the department. Costs should be budgeted by the manager who has responsibility for that cost. Also, a manager's cost report should emphasize the costs budgeted by that manager.

Direct costs and controllable costs are not necessarily the same. A cost may be a direct cost of a given department but may not be controlled by the departmental supervisor. For example, the salary of a departmental supervisor, which is a direct cost of the department, is controlled at a higher level of management rather than by the supervisor.

We should not assume that a cost is noncontrollable because it is a fixed cost. While a fixed cost, such as property insurance, may be noncontrollable at certain managerial levels, it is nevertheless subject to control by a manager who has the authority to obtain insurance coverage. Often there is a tendency to view a cost as either controllable or noncontrollable because it is either variable or fixed. It is as incorrect, however, to confuse cost behavior characteristics with controllability as it is to confuse cost behavior characteristics with the direct and indirect concept.

Time also plays a part in controllability. Assume that Keith Helsel manages the Myers Division of Turner Industries. Helsel controls all revenues and cost generating activities in his division. If Helsel tries to change plans, the time frame becomes an important limitation. If it is near noon, he has little power to change many costs before 5:00 p.m. today. If it is April and he wants to change the plans for the rest of the year, he has many more degrees of freedom. If it is late this year and he is building next year's plan, major changes could be made. The greater the time span, the more control a manager has.

Control may also be prescribed by company policy. Certain expenditure levels may be attached to each level of management. If an expense that is greater than a given manager's authority arises, approval must be sought from a higher level. Also, policies may explicitly place responsibility for certain decisions at specific levels or functions in the firm. Controllability is often specified by management level, by company policies, and by functional responsibilities.

It may seem that costs can be budgeted and reported quite easily on the basis of controllability, but such is not the case. Costs may be authorized by one individual and in that sense are controlled by that person; but other persons within the organization may influence the amount of the cost. Thus, control by one individual is not absolute.

For example, it may be more economical to have one service contract for repair and maintenance for the entire plant than to have several separate contracts negotiated by each of the departmental supervisors. One of the departmental supervisors may be given the authority to obtain the contract for all departments. This is similar to a personal situation in which one person plans a dinner party at a restaurant for several others. The person who has the authority to execute the plans has control in one sense but in another sense does not. Someone may order lobster, another a flaming desert, and so on. As a result, the budget may be exceeded; and the fault cannot be placed entirely with the person making the plans. Knowing the possible consequences of an over-budget situation will cause the manager to plan ahead and avoid the problem. Pre-selecting the menu at an agreed upon price per person would solve the problem.

A **cost control system**, where cost responsibility is identified and performance is compared to a plan, can be a subtle means of enforcing company policy. Decisions are made at the top management level which compel cost control at lower management levels. At all levels, supervisors are especially careful when costs are charged against them. Thus top management does not always have to spell out policy in a directive; lower levels of management will be guided according to how the costs are charged to their responsibility areas.

Costs that would normally be included in the reports of subordinates may be excluded if top management believes that the company will benefit from a more liberal policy. On the other hand, costs can be controlled more rigorously if they are authorized by and charged to a specific manager.

For example, a company may provide a copying service to expedite the duplication of forms and reports. The copying service may be given to all departments at no charge, thus encouraging the departmental supervisors to make full use of this service. However, if top management believes that the service is being drawn upon too freely, a charge may be made to the departments for this service. Managers, knowing that they will be charged for the service, may tend to use it more sparingly.

The successful operation of a cost control system depends to a large extent on the attitudes of company personnel. Some research has been done in the area of human behavior within organizations, but much still needs to be done. The central objective is to assign cost responsibility in such a way that individuals are motivated to act in the best interests of the company to achieve established goals. A policy that may work in one organization may not necessarily work in another because of the differences in the attitudes and behavior of the personnel.

Planned Costs Versus Actual Costs

Lists of managerial uses of accounting have planning and controlling at the top. A plan, also known as a **budget**, shows how resources are to be acquired and used over a specified time interval. The implication is that plans are made, actions are taken, and reports are prepared to show results. Comparing plan to actual is a fundamental managerial action.

Most managerial activity will deal with planning data. But follow-up and evaluation are critical steps in closing the plan, act, and control cycle. The very essence of control rests on the knowledge that actual results will be reviewed, compared to the plan, used to revise the ongoing plan, and used to reward managers. The absence of follow-up sends a message to managers that planning is not really important because deviations from plan are never reviewed.

Periodic control reports should monitor the plan versus actual status of operations. Generally, this month's actual results are compared to this month's budget, and the year-to-date results are also compared to budget.

Variances are shown as over or under budget, indicate possible operating problems, and are targeted for investigation.

An identification of trouble areas, however, is only the beginning of the control process. Questions must be asked. Is the difference between budgeted cost and actual cost significant enough to justify further investigation? What caused the variation? Is it likely that a variation from the budget will repeat in the future if action is not taken? It may be found that measures can be taken that reduce variations in the future. In some cases, the budgeted figure is found to be unrealistic and should be revised. Control reports are somewhat like switchboards that flash warning lights when trouble appears. They furnish the initial information that serves as a basis for making corrections.

Julie McGee is the plant manager of the Cleveland Plant of Alexander Fabrics, Inc. She is responsible for the costs that she authorizes for plant administration and for the costs authorized by the three departmental supervisors in the plant. Each month she will receive a report showing in summary form the costs incurred by her and by the departmental supervisors. Figure 2.11 is a report for the month of June.

ALEXANDER FABRICS, INC.
COST REPORT—DEPARTMENTAL COSTS
PLANT: CLEVELAND
MANAGER: JULIE MCGEE
PERIOD: MONTH OF JUNE 1995

	June			Year to Date		
	Budget	Actual	Variance Over (Under)	Budget	Actual	Variance Over (Under)
Plant administration:						
Salaries	$ 7,830	$ 8,460	$ 630	$ 47,550	$ 49,320	$ 1,770
Employee benefits	1,760	1,710	(50)	10,870	10,880	10
Insurance	250	250	0	1,500	1,500	0
Utilities	430	320	(110)	2,680	3,290	610
Supplies	170	180	10	3,140	2,610	(530)
Miscellaneous	1,510	1,700	190	7,020	8,190	1,170
Total administration	$ 11,950	$ 12,620	$ 670	$ 72,760	$ 75,790	$ 3,030
Department 1	68,210	68,970	760	386,420	385,280	(1,140)
Department 2	46,300	49,500	3,200	263,140	278,230	15,090
Department 3	23,970	23,920	(50)	143,810	143,670	(140)
Total	$150,430	$155,010	$4,580	$866,130	$882,970	$16,840

Figure 2.11   Management Control Report Comparing Actual to Plan

If McGee believes that costs incurred in a certain department are excessive, she can obtain a cost report for that department with the detailed costs broken down. For example, she may find the Department 2 costs to be excessive. After an investigation, the Department 2 supervisor and McGee may find that materials and supplies costs may be too high. At this point she and the supervisor can work together to find reasons why the actual costs exceeded budgeted costs.

Each supervisor receives a report similar to the one shown for McGee, showing costs that supervisor controls, including a summary of costs controlled by any subordinates. A network of reports showing a comparison of controllable costs with budgets extends all the way from the president's office to the lowest level of management.

In many other situations plans and decisions are made. Performance can only be measured against a benchmark. The budget or plan is the benchmark, and the actual results indicate success or lack of it. Each follow-up report must compare planned expenses and actual expenses and should show variances from budget. Managers can then follow up and make any changes needed.

SUMMARY

Different managerial needs require different costs. Some costs, such as fixed and variable costs, are useful in product costing and control of operations. Other costs, such as incremental costs and opportunity costs, are useful in decision making. Consequently, a manager's understanding of the cost concepts and terminology for planning, control, decision making, and income measurement is essential in order to select appropriate costs for the various situations. A starting point is realizing that the term "cost" has an elusive meaning without a modifying term attached to it.

In general, costs have many attributes, but the three most important ones for using cost concepts are cost behavior, traceability, and controllability. The question of what drives costs creates a linkage between cost causing activities in the firm, cost behavior, and cost control. Variable costs behave in a different manner than fixed costs; hence, they are planned for and controlled differently. Fixed costs, when converted to a per unit basis, can create difficulties in income measurement and decision making if managers are not aware of how to interpret the per unit numbers.

Traceability is the ability to identify a cost with an objective; objectives may be departments, products, projects, tasks, and so forth. Specific identification of a cost to an objective tags that cost as direct; nontraceability leads to indirect costs and possible cost allocations. Controllability refers to whether a specific manager has the authority to incur the cost and the responsibility for using the resource represented by the cost. This cost concept is important in evaluating a manager's performance, which is part of the control process.

Income measurement is important to any for-profit organization whether service, merchandising, or manufacturing. Manufacturing operations introduce more complex accounting flows of cost and add the need to calculate a product cost based on the resources used in the factory. Methods of treating cost flow are somewhat different for each of these organizations, so the methods of determining income also differ depending on the type of organization.

PROBLEM FOR REVIEW

The Vixon Corporation operates sales, administrative, and manufacturing activities from a facility in Philadelphia. It produces and sells a variety of products. Vixon's costs can be classified in several ways according to the cost terms introduced in this chapter. The following selected costs relate to the corporation's activities and particularly to the factory's Department 4, one of its production departments.

(1) Materials used on products in Department 4
(2) Wages, production personnel in Department 4
(3) Factory taxes and insurance
(4) Lubrication oils for equipment in Department 4
(5) Wages, factory equipment maintenance mechanics
(6) Factory heat and power
(7) Salary, factory manager
(8) Equipment depreciation in Department 4
(9) Salary, supervisor of Department 4
(10) Building depreciation
(11) Sales commissions paid on product sales
(12) Salary, sales manager
(13) Advertising agency costs
(14) Travel and entertainment
(15) Computer operating costs

Required:

Based on reasonable assumptions about a manufacturing firm, classify each cost as:

(a) Variable or fixed cost.
(b) Controllable or noncontrollable by the manager of the department.
(c) Product or period costs.
(d) Direct or indirect to the cost objective (the product or department depending on the answer to part c).

Solution:

Cost Item	Variable Cost	Fixed Cost	Controllable by Dept. 4 Manager Yes	No	Product Cost	Period Cost	Direct Cost	Indirect Cost	Comments
(1) Materials	X		X		X		X		Direct if used in Department 4.
(2) Wages, production, Department 4	X		X		X		X		Word "wages" implies hourly pay. Assumes employees are paid hourly and hours vary with output.

Cost Item	Variable Cost	Fixed Cost	Controllable by Dept. 4 Manager		Product Cost	Period Cost	Direct Cost	Indirect Cost	Comments
			Yes	No					
(3) Factory taxes and insurance		X		X	X			X	
(4) Lubrication oils Department 4	X		X		X			X	Probably semivariable.
(5) Wages, factory equipment maintenance		X		X	X			X	Probably fixed within relevant range, influenced by Department 4 manager.
(6) Factory heat and power		X		X	X			X	Probably semifixed within relevant range.
(7) Salary, factory *manager* supervision		X		X	X			X	
(8) Equipment depreciation Department 4		X		X	X		X		Direct cost of Department 4, but not controllable since manager can not buy and sell equipment.
(9) Salary, supervisor of Department 4 . . .		X		X	X			X	Direct cost of Department 4, but manager does not control his/her own salary.
(10) Building depreciation		X		X	?	?		X	If building is factory, then cost is product; if office, then cost is period; and if both, then cost must be allocated between factory and office activities.
(11) Sales commissions	X			X		X	X		Considered direct as to specific products since commissions are paid on specific products.
(12) Salary, sales manager		X		X		X		X	Assume fixed salary and no commissions.

Cost Item	Variable Cost	Fixed Cost	Controllable by Dept. 4 Manager		Product Cost	Period Cost	Direct Cost	Indirect Cost	Comments
			Yes	No					
(13) Advertising agency costs.............		X		X		X		X	Probably fixed because of contract.
(14) Travel and entertainment	X			X		X		X	Cost could be semivariable. Assumed to be sales related.
(15) Computer operating costs.............		X		X		X		X	Computer center probably serves all areas of firm. Department 4 manager might influence a small portion of cost.

TERMINOLOGY REVIEW

Average cost (43)
Avoidable cost (42)
Bill of materials (31)
Budget (47)
Committed fixed cost (37)
Common cost (41)
Controllable cost (45)
Conversion costs (33)
Cost (25)
Cost control (25)
Cost control system (47)
Cost drivers (25)
Cost objective or object (25)
Cost of goods manufactured (35)
Cost of goods sold (31)
Decision making (24)
Decremental cost (42)
Differential cost (45)
Direct cost (41)
Direct labor costs (31)
Direct product costs (32)
Discretionary fixed costs (37)
Finished goods inventory (31)
Fixed cost (36)
Fixed product costs (33)
Full cost (43)

Income measurement (25)
Incremental costs (42)
Incremental cost analysis (43)
Indifference point (45)
Indirect cost (41)
Indirect product costs (32)
Irrelevant costs (43)
Joint cost (41)
Manufacturing costs (35)
Manufacturing overhead costs (31)
Marginal cost (42)
Materials inventory (31)
Materials used (31)
Mixed costs (40)
Noncontrollable cost (45)
Opportunity cost (45)
Out-of-pocket costs (43)
Period costs (28)
Planning (24)
Prime costs (32)
Product cost (29)
Relevant cost (43)
Relevant range (39)
Semifixed costs (40)
Semivariable cost (39)
Step fixed cost (40)

Sunk cost (44)   Variable cost (36)
Traceable cost (41) *(direct cost)*   Variable product costs (33)
Unavoidable costs (44)   Work in process inventory (31)

QUESTIONS FOR REVIEW AND DISCUSSION

1. Why must the term "cost" have an adjective attached to it to have meaning to a manager?

2. Describe the basic cost behavior of variable, fixed, and semivariable costs, both in total amount and on a per unit basis.

3. Identify at least two ways in which fixed costs pose difficulties for cost accountants and managers.

4. What does the mathematical expression $\$100,000 + \$12X$ mean in terms of measuring product cost?

5. (a) A controller in a recent speech said, "I rarely see a real variable cost or a truly fixed cost." What did she mean?

    (b) Further in her speech she said, "Some of my friends define semivariable costs, semifixed costs, step costs, and mixed costs differently; some of my other friends often use these terms interchangeably. And I like all my friends." Was she just trying to be funny or is there truth in her quip?

6. Distinguish among the following terms: Cost of goods manufactured, cost of goods sold, and manufacturing costs.

7. Use the letters for each of the following cost groups to create a formula for each of the terms listed.

    A. Fixed manufacturing overhead   F. Direct materials purchases
    B. Variable manufacturing overhead   G. Direct materials used
    C. Total manufacturing overhead   H. Direct labor
    D. Beginning work in process   I. Ending work in process
    E. Beginning finished goods inventory   J. Ending finished goods inventory

    Terms: Prime costs, conversion costs, direct costs, indirect costs, total factory costs to be accounted for, costs transferred to finished goods inventory, and goods available for sale.

8. Using T-accounts and a factory diagram similar to Figure 2.2, show the parallel flows of costs and products through a manufacturing process.

9. A fixed product cost is a lump of dollars incurred during a time period. A variable product cost is a rate per unit of production activity. To find total product costs or the cost per unit, what other data do we need to know?

10. Comment on the validity of the following statements:
    (a) All sunk costs are irrelevant.
    (b) All irrelevant costs are past costs.
    (c) All relevant costs are present or future amounts.
    (d) All future costs are relevant costs.
    (e) A cost can be relevant for one decision and irrelevant for another decision.

11. Define an opportunity cost and explain its relevance to decision making. When would a decision maker look at the opportunity cost of a decision?

12. How can an individual cost be both a direct and an indirect cost? A controllable and a noncontrollable cost? Give examples.

13. Assume that you are the chairperson of the department of accounting at your school. You are evaluating the costs of offering the Managerial Accounting course versus other accounting, business, and school-wide courses. Give an example of a direct cost, a common cost, an indirect cost, a controllable cost, a variable cost, a fixed cost, an opportunity cost, an avoidable cost, and an out-of-pocket cost.

14. Assume that you are a student in a managerial accounting course. You are analyzing your costs of taking this course. Give an example of a direct cost, a common cost, an indirect cost, a controllable cost, a variable cost, a fixed cost, an opportunity cost, an avoidable cost, and an out-of-pocket cost.

15. Will an allocated cost normally be reduced by the elimination of a department? Explain. Give one example of a case in which the allocated cost would be reduced and one case in which it would not be reduced.

16. Explain how time has an effect upon the controllability of cost.

17. Willard Rose supervises the fabricating department at Specialty Sheet Metal, Inc. The factory accountant includes Willard's salary among the direct costs in the departmental cost report. Willard claims his salary is noncontrollable and should not be in the cost report for the department he supervises. Is Willard correct? Explain.

18. Period costs differ from product costs. How do they differ, and why is the distinction important?

19. Name the three traditional cost elements in a manufactured product. How can these elements be attached to the product? Explain.

EXERCISES

1. **Classifying Cost Behavior.** Classify each of the following costs as variable, fixed, semivariable, or step costs:
   (a)   Raw materials used in production.
   (b)   Salary of the supervisor in the fabricating department.
   (c)   Salaries of buyers in the purchasing department.
   (d)   Straight-line depreciation on equipment.
   (e)   Computer services costs, based on usage.
   (f)   Computer services costs, based on predetermined percentage of the EDP budget.
   (g)   Salaries of the security guards at gates to a plant.
   (h)   Insurance premiums covering a plant and its equipment.
   (i)   Equipment maintenance costs.
   (j)   Sales commissions.
   (k)   Salaries of receiving department inspectors.
   (l)   Electric power in a factory where a minimum charge is made for kilowatt usage up to a certain usage plus an additional charge per kilowatt hour thereafter.

2. **Relevant Inventory Costs.** Wellington Stitch manufactures designer jeans. At the end of the current year, the inventory for one line of jeans had become obsolete. The cost of producing this inventory was $50,000. Geri Wilder, a product line manager, estimated that a little rework on the obsolete line, at a cost of $8,000, would yield a product suitable

for a nearby discount clothing store. The discount store would pay $15,000. Or, Geri figured, the jeans could be sold "as is" to a company in northern Mexico for $6,000, although Wellington would have to pay the $750 freight charges. She could also sell the jeans as material waste to a recycling firm for $1,200 today.

Required:
1. What is the sunk cost in this situation?
2. Which is the best alternative of those presented? Why?
3. Geri could store the jeans for a cost of $150 per month. She says "I think this style will return in, oh, maybe 8 or 10 years." She guesses that the jeans might be sold for "up to $30,000 then," considering storage damage and no inflation. Does this information affect your analysis?

3. **Product Line Decision.** Any one of three different product lines can be produced by Meyers Parts Company with the present equipment in one of the divisions. The annual depreciation of the equipment is $16,200; and the annual cost to operate the equipment, regardless of product line manufactured, is $3,600.

   Product A is expected to yield sales revenue of $88,000 a year with increased costs of production amounting to $39,000. Product B should yield sales revenue of $65,000 a year with increased costs of $19,000. Product C should yield sales revenue of $157,000 with increased costs of $115,000.

Required:
1. Which of the three product lines offers the best profit potential based on the information given? Show computations.
2. Identify the irrelevant costs.
3. What is the opportunity cost of selecting the most profitable product line?

4. **Cost Classification.** Selected costs associated with several manufacturing operations are shown below:

   (a) Plant manager's salary.
   (b) Lubricating oils for machines.
   (c) Brass rods used in making plumbing products.
   (d) Starter motors to be installed in new automobiles.
   (e) Depreciation on the building that includes both the factory and the home office.
   (f) Labor in the repairs and maintenance section.
   (g) Salary of the supervisor in the grinding department.
   (h) Crude oil used in a refining process.
   (i) Janitorial supplies for a sales branch office.
   (j) Wages of artists preparing ads for a grocery chain.
   (k) Wages of executive secretaries in an advertising agency.
   (l) Depreciation on administrative office furniture.
   (m) Property taxes on the plant.
   (n) Depreciation on equipment used in an egg sorting process.
   (o) Salary of the corporate controller.
   (p) Sales commissions of the marketing staff.

Required:
   Set up columns to classify each cost by cost behavior (variable, semivariable, or fixed) with respect to activity; by product or period cost; and then as direct or indirect as to specific products.

5. **Opportunity Cost and Relevant Costs.** Cynthia Good is considering the possibility of obtaining an advanced degree from Clearwater University. She already has credits toward the degree and estimates that she can obtain the degree in one year. To do this, however, she must give up her job that pays a salary of $25,000 per year. Living costs, whether she goes on for the degree or not, are estimated at $16,000 for the year. In addition, the cost of tuition and books at the university will amount to $6,200.

Required:
1. What is the opportunity cost if Good decides to return to school?
2. What is the sunk cost in this decision? What is the differential cost in the decision?

6. **Cost Classifications.** Marie Cobb is the manager of Department 7 and has the authority to buy supplies, hire labor, maintain equipment, and incur telephone and postage charges for the department. Various costs for the month of April 1993 are as follows:

Plant superintendent's salary	$ 8,000
Factory heat and light	3,200
Telephone and postage—Department 7	1,100
Plant maintenance and repairs	1,700
Equipment maintenance charges—Department 7	2,600
Supplies used—Department 7	1,400
Salary—Marie Cobb	2,500
Labor cost—Department 7	14,600
Plant depreciation	3,000
Equipment depreciation—Department 7	2,300
Total	$40,400

Required:
1. List the costs that can be controlled by Marie Cobb.
2. List the costs that can be directly identified with Department 7.
3. List the costs that will be allocated to Department 7.

7. **Cost Term Definitions.** Indicate what cost term is being defined in each of the following sentences:
   (a) Cost per unit that decreases as more units are produced in a given time period.
   (b) Activity levels within which the firm is expected to operate and can predict costs.
   (c) Costs that are expensed within a given time period and not inventoried.
   (d) Cost that management has obligated itself to incur in the future.
   (e) A cost that will go away if an activity is eliminated.
   (f) Profit that is given up by accepting a different option.
   (g) A cost that is managed by a specific manager.
   (h) A cost incurred to produce more than one product that cannot be easily traced to each product.
   (i) Total product cost divided by total units produced.
   (j) The cost of adding one more unit of output.
   (k) A cost that is traceable to a particular cost objective but cannot be controlled by the manager responsible for that cost objective.
   (l) Product cost that is not materials or direct labor.

8. **Unit Product Cost.** Chemicals costing an average of $6 for each medical test in a local lab are needed to complete a specific testing procedure. Four tests can be completed in an hour by a skilled technician with a labor cost of $18 per hour, including most payroll fringe benefits. The lab's total fixed overhead cost amounts to $120,000 per year. Other

variable costs are $16 per technician hour. It is estimated that no less than 20,000 tests are to be performed next year. In a relatively poor year, 24,000 tests would be done. If the company were to operate at an average or normal level, it would do 28,000 tests. With very good business conditions, it would be possible to make 32,000 tests.

Required:

1.   What would be the relevant range of activity for the lab?
2.   Determine the variable cost per test and the fixed cost per test under each of the four activity levels stated.
3.   On a graph, plot the total variable costs and the fixed costs patterns.
4.   If part-time lab technicians cannot be found and the lab must hire a full-time technician for each 2,000 hours of test work needed, graph the labor cost pattern for performing the tests over the relevant range. (Assume that a full-time technician costs $36,000 per year.)

9.   **Income Measurement in Manufacturing.** Yong Lee Manufacturing Company of Hong Kong used materials costing $180,000 in the production of 10,000 units of product. No materials were on hand at the beginning or at the end of the year. Labor costing $50,000 was used in producing the units. Other costs of manufacturing, such as factory supervision, heat and light, taxes, and insurance, are all fixed costs and amounted to $100,000 for the year. No finished goods inventory existed at the beginning of the year, and 8,000 units of product were sold during the year.

Required:

1.   Compute the unit cost of manufacturing the product. Show the unit cost broken down by cost element: direct materials, direct labor, and factory overhead.
2.   Show where the total costs put into production this year are at the end of the year.

10.   **Income Measurement in a Service Organization.** PC Programming develops microcomputer business software to meet specific needs of its clients. Accounting records show the following transactions and amounts for the current month:

Amounts billed to clients	$50,000
Direct labor payroll (1,000 hours)	15,000
Direct overhead costs applicable to client jobs	12,000
Marketing expenses	3,000
Office expenses	7,500
Other administrative expenses	2,200

Required:

Prepare an income statement including a gross margin for client jobs.

11.   **Cost Flows in Manufacturing.** Analyze the following cases:

A.   The work in process of Page Corporation increased $11,500 from the beginning to the end of November. Costs incurred during November were $12,000 for materials used, $63,000 for direct labor, and $21,000 for overhead. Find the cost of goods manufactured for November.

B.   In the Essells Company, costs incurred during November were $15,000 for materials purchased, $40,000 for direct labor, and $50,000 for overhead. Materials inventory decreased by $4,000. If the cost of goods manufactured in November is $99,000 and the beginning work in process inventory was $28,000, find the ending work in process inventory.

C.   In the Myers Company the cost of goods sold for November was $156,000, finished goods inventory decreased by $13,000, and the work in process inventory increased by $9,000. Find the total manufacturing costs for November.

12.   **More Cost Flows in Manufacturing.** Gluk Company provided the inventory balances and manufacturing cost data shown below for the month of January:

	January 1	January 31
Inventories:		
Direct materials	$?	$20,000
Work in process	20,000	25,000
Finished goods	30,000	28,000

	Month of January
Manufacturing overhead	$100,000
Cost of goods manufactured	235,000
Direct materials used	90,000
Direct materials purchased	100,000
Direct labor	?

Required:

1.   What was the total amount of direct labor during January and what was the beginning (January 1) direct materials inventory?
2.   T-account the flows of costs through the appropriate accounts for January.

13.   **Searching for Unknowns in Manufacturing Costs Flows.** Doe Company, Rae Company, and Me Company produce musical products. Operating results for the past year include these amounts:

	Doe Company	Rae Company	Me Company
Sales	$?	$ 80,000	$?
Direct materials	20,000	?	22,000
Direct labor	30,000	20,000	15,000
Manufacturing overhead	40,000	25,000	?
Manufacturing costs	?	?	?
Beginning work in process	4,000	9,000	9,000
Ending work in process	12,000	4,000	6,000
Cost of goods manufactured	?	69,000	61,000
Beginning finished goods	6,000	?	8,000
Ending finished goods	21,000	22,000	?
Cost of goods sold	?	?	65,000
Gross margin	?	18,000	24,000
Operating expenses	25,000	?	13,000
Net income	6,000	(1,000)	?

Required:

Find the missing values. Helpful hint: Set up a manufacturing cost of sales format and plug in the known values.

14.   **Components of Product Cost.** Using the following lettered items, create a formula for finding the values listed at the top of the next page:

A. Materials purchased
B. Materials used
C. Direct labor
D. Manufacturing overhead
E. Beginning materials inventory

F. Ending materials inventory
G. Beginning work in process inventory
H. Ending work in process inventory
I. Beginning finished goods inventory
J. Ending finished goods inventory

Required:

Create a formula for:

0. Example: Conversion costs = C + D
1. Cost of goods manufactured =
2. Manufacturing costs =
3. Prime costs =
4. Beginning materials inventory (E) =
5. Goods available for sale =
6. Cost of goods sold =

15. **Product Cost in a Service Business.** The Dunn Partners developed a plan for 1993 and has reported the following results for the first quarter for their Sun City Pharmacy:

	Budget	Actual	Difference
Number of prescriptions filled	20,000	22,000	2,000
Pharmacists' salaries	$60,000	$66,000	$ 6,000
Variable overhead costs	20,000	21,500	1,500
Fixed overhead costs	60,000	59,000	(1,000)

Pharmacists' salaries are considered fixed, because, when they work overtime hours, it is for no extra pay.

Required:

1. What was the budgeted cost and the actual average cost of filling a prescription during the first quarter of 1993?
2. Given the budgeted expense and activity levels and the actual volume of prescriptions filled, what amount should have been budgeted for costs of filling prescriptions? Prepare a revised budget and compare it to actual to find a new difference between budgeted and actual expenses.

16. **Income Statement Formatting.** A partial trial balance of the Brown Corporation as of December 31, 1993 follows:

Purchases of raw materials	$160,000
Direct labor	225,000
Indirect labor	40,000
Factory rent	84,000
Office rent	48,000
Depreciation—machinery	35,000
Depreciation—office equipment	8,000
Insurance factory	18,000
Salespersons' salaries	72,000
Repairs and maintenance—machinery	12,000
Administrative salaries	50,000
Miscellaneous factory	26,000
Miscellaneous office	40,000
Sales	850,000

January 1 inventories are:		December 31 inventories are:	
Raw materials	$ 45,000	Raw materials	$ 40,000
Work in process	30,000	Work in process	35,000
Finished goods	125,000	Finished goods	110,000

Required:

Using a good format, prepare an income statement with a cost of goods manufactured section.

PROBLEMS

2-1. **Identifying Cost Patterns.** Match the following graphs with the descriptions given at the top of the next page:

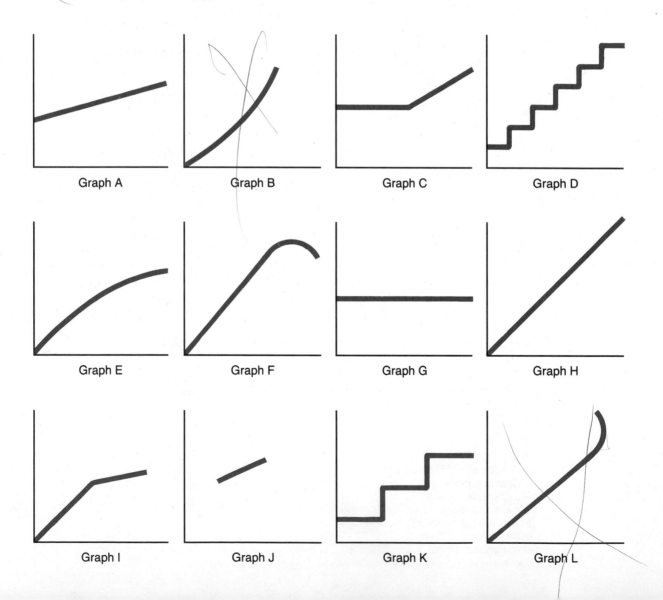

Graph A   Graph B   Graph C   Graph D

Graph E   Graph F   Graph G   Graph H

Graph I   Graph J   Graph K   Graph L

_G_ **1.** Straight-line depreciation (a classic fixed cost).

_K_ **2.** Shift supervision salaries (shifts added as demand increases).

_B_ **3.** Cost of vegetables for a cannery which are purchased from nearby farmers. As the quantities purchased increase, higher transportation costs are incurred to truck the vegetables to the cannery from further distances.

_H_ **4.** Commissions paid to salespersons on sales.

_L_ **5.** Labor costs including overtime and weekend premiums when production volume exceeds regular hours production capacity.

_J_ **6.** Mixed cost within a relevant range.

_A_ **7.** a + bx where "a" and "b" are not equal to zero.

_C_ **8.** Water and waste water minimum fixed cost plus a rate per gallon beyond a base quantity.

_F_ **9.** Certain annual payroll taxes that are based on the first $20,000 of wages earned by each employee each year. Most employees earn more than this annually.

_I_ **10.** Cost of hourly messenger service for a regional bank with a reduced rate after 2,000 hours of chargeable time.

_D_ **11.** Computer equipment costs to add additional telephone operators for a telemarketing firm.

_E_ **12.** Materials costs when discounts are received when we purchase larger quantities.

2-2. **Determining Unknowns.** Find the missing values in the following manufacturing income statement:

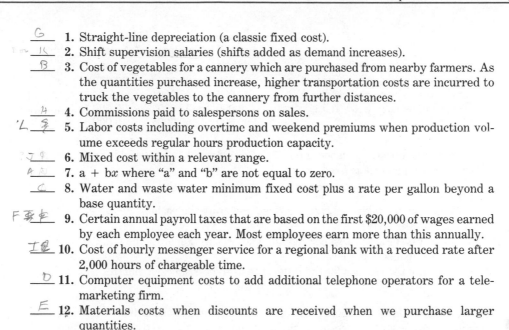

	1992	1993	1994
Sales	$?	$113,700	$ 130,000
Cost of goods sold:			
Materials inventory 1/1	$ 8,000	$ 6,000	$?
+ Materials purchases	?	20,000	30,000
Materials available	$?	$ 26,000	$?
− Materials inventory 12/31	?	9,000	12,300
Materials used	$ 7,200	$ 17,000	$?
Direct labor	20,000	23,500	?
Manufacturing overhead	16,000	21,300	24,000
Total manufacturing costs	$53,000	$ 61,800	$ 90,900
+ Work in process inventory 1/1	12,000	18,000	16,300
− Work in process inventory 12/31	?	16,300	22,300
Cost of goods manufactured	$?	$ 63,500	$ 84,900
+ Finished goods inventory 1/1	?	21,000	18,300
Goods available for sale	$62,000	$ 84,500	$103,200
− Finished goods inventory 12/31	21,000	?	20,000
Cost of goods sold	$ 41,000	$?	$ 83,200
Gross profit	$49,000	?	$ 46,800

2-3. **Changing Unit Costs.** Keller Company is a manufacturer of rivets made from special alloys. Its manufacturing costs for the first three months of 1994 were as follows:

	Monthly Budget	Actual Costs		
		January	February	March
Direct materials and direct labor	$ 80,000	$ 73,000	$ 80,900	$ 77,000
Depreciation of machinery and building	30,000	30,000	30,000	30,000
Supervision salaries and benefits	40,000	40,000	41,000	41,000
Utilities for the factory	36,000	37,000	35,500	36,000
Rivet output (units)	200,000	180,000	210,000	190,000

Direct materials and labor and utilities are thought to be variable costs, and the other costs are planned as fixed costs.

Required:
1.   What was the budgeted cost per rivet? Separate the variable and fixed cost components per rivet.
2.   What was the actual cost per rivet for each month? Separate the variable and fixed cost components per rivet.
3.   What are the reasons for the difference in rivet costs each month?

2-4.   **Unit Cost and Volume.** Hackert Service Company refurbishes utility meters in older neighborhoods. Estimated costs for the next three months of activity are as follows:

	Meters Serviced	
	500	1,000
Labor costs...	$15,000	$30,000
Replacement parts	10,000	20,000
Other variable operating expenses	6,000	12,000
Fixed operating expenses	18,000	18,000
General and administrative expenses	12,500	15,000

Required:
1.   What are the total operating costs at each level?
2.   What are the total operating costs per meter serviced at each level? Separate the variable and fixed cost components.
3.   What kind of cost is the general and administrative expenses? How can it be broken down?
4.   What are the total costs per meter at each level?
5.   Create a cost formula for Hackert to estimate the firm's total costs for any other volume.

2-5.   **Cost Flows Through T-Accounts.** Use T-accounts to show the flow of costs and revenues through the accounting system of Halpin Corporation during July of 1994. Accounts to be used:

Cash	Direct Labor Cost
Accounts Receivable	Manufacturing Overhead Expenses
Materials Inventory	Accumulated Depreciation
Supplies Inventory	Cost of Goods Sold
Work in Processing Inventory	Sales
Finished Goods Inventory	Accounts Payable

Transactions:

$A + E = L + OE + R$

1.   Beginning balances:

Materials Inventory	$128,000	Cash	$ 36,000
Supplies Inventory	65,000	Accounts Receivable	122,000
Work in Process Inventory ..	82,000	Accounts Payable	49,000
Finished Goods Inventory ...	172,000	Accumulated Depreciation ...	56,000

2.   Purchases of materials on account: $360,000
3.   Purchases of supplies on account: $86,000
4.   Materials requisitioned for production: $385,000
5.   Supplies used in production: $93,000
6.   Direct labor wages paid: $98,000
7.   Depreciation expense on factory building and equipment: $22,000
8.   Indirect labor wages and supervisory salaries paid: $186,000
9.   Utilities expenses paid: $26,000
10.   Other factory expenses paid: $83,000
11.   Completed production for July: $845,000
12.   Sales on account recorded for July: $1,262,000
13.   Collection of receivables: $1,195,000
14.   Cost of goods sold in July: $870,000
15.   Cash payments to vendors: $468,000

2-6.   **Cost Identification of Product Costs.** A small regional bakery, Aunt Bert's Bakery Goodies, normally produces 200,000 pies per year in its pie department. Fixed costs are added to the pies assuming a normal production level. The cost report for the recently completed year is as follows:

Direct materials	$ 93,000
Direct labor	116,000
Supervision...	135,000
Supplies used	15,000
Maintenance in pie department	22,000
Depreciation on pie department equipment	32,000
Telephone expenses...	8,000
All utilities	36,000
Insurance and taxes	16,000
Rent...	48,000
Total costs	$521,000

Direct materials, supplies used, and direct labor are the only costs that vary with production. The costs of plant occupancy (utilities, insurance and taxes, and rent) are allocated to the pie department on the basis of the space occupied by pie making.

Required:
1.   Determine the per pie variable and fixed costs and total costs of producing pies.
2.   Determine the total direct pie costs and the per pie direct cost.
3.   If a pie is sold for $2.90 per pie:
     (a) Will variable costs be covered?
     (b) Will all direct costs be covered?
     (c) Will all product costs be covered?
4.   Assume that next year only 150,000 pies will be manufactured, what price is needed if a profit of $60,000 is desired after total costs are covered?

2-7. **Product Costs and Control.** Heavy metal barrels, used as containers for roofing, asphalt, aluminum paint, and various industrial materials, are manufactured by MVM Containers Company. The cost of the materials for each of these containers is $7.25; the labor cost per container is $2.00. Various supplies used in production cost $1.50 per container.

The other costs to operate the department in which these containers are made are fixed costs and have been estimated for the year as follows:

Supervision.	$85,000
Equipment and operating costs	6,000
Repairs and maintenance of equipment.	3,500
Depreciation of equipment	1,500
Total	$96,000

The supervisor of this department controls all of these costs with the exceptions of depreciation of equipment and the supervisor's own salary of $48,000, which is included in the total cost of supervision.

Factory overhead for the entire plant is allocated to the departments on the basis of a factor that combines space occupied with the number of employees. The department in which these containers are produced is expected to be allocated 30 percent of the total plant cost of $240,000. This department produces only this type of container.

Required:
1. What is the variable cost per container? What are the prime costs per container?
2. What are the conversion costs per container if 120,000 containers are produced?
3. Identify the costs controlled by the department supervisor.
4. What is the total cost per container, if MVM produces 120,000 containers per year? If MVM produces 150,000 containers per year?

2-8. **Controllable and Noncontrollable Costs.** The manager of Department 3 of Tulsa Tool Company is responsible for the acquisition and use of materials and supplies in the department, maintenance and repair of equipment, training, and miscellaneous expenses. The manager also hires personnel and sets wage rates. The superintendent of the division, however, acquires equipment used in the departments and is responsible for building occupancy costs such as depreciation of the building, utilities, taxes, and insurance. Building occupancy costs have been allocated to the departments.

A budget report for Department 3 for the month of March 1994 follows:

	Budget	Actual	Variance Over (Under) Budget
Materials and supplies	$ 7,300	$ 7,420	$120
Salary of department manager	3,000	3,000	—
Wages.	19,500	19,300	(200)
Maintenance and repairs of equipment	1,700	1,740	40
Building maintenance	2,600	2,950	350
Depreciation—equipment.	1,200	1,200	—
Depreciation—building	2,300	2,300	—
Taxes and insurance—building	850	850	—
Utilities	1,400	1,870	470
Training.	830	780	(50)
Miscellaneous department expenses	220	210	(10)
Total	$40,900	$41,620	$720

Required:

1. List the direct costs of Department 3.
2. Prepare a cost report that shows only the costs controlled by the department manager.

2-9. Income Statement Preparation. The Giffin Corporation produces heavy duty riding garden tractors and has the following balances in its operating accounts (in millions of dollars) for 1995:

Sales	$700
Selling and Administrative Expenses	100
Factory Supplies Used	10
Factory Utilities	30
Indirect Labor	60
Purchases of Direct Materials	125
Direct Labor	100
Depreciation—Factory Building and Equipment	80
Factory Supervisory Salaries	40
Miscellaneous Factory Overhead	35
Direct Materials, December 31, 1994	15
Work in Process, December 31, 1994	10
Finished Goods, December 31, 1994	70
Direct Materials, December 31, 1995	20
Work in Process, December 31, 1995	5
Finished Goods, December 31, 1995	?

Records show that 120,000 units were transferred to finished goods inventory in 1995; and, of those units, 110,000 were sold. Giffin uses a FIFO inventory system for all inventories.

Required:

Complete an income statement including the cost of goods manufactured and sold for the year ended December 31, 1995.

2-10. Cost Control and Emergencies. Stan Chang says that he does not have control over some of the costs charged to him. For example, his supervisor may at times accept orders that must be completed in a very short time, making it necessary for Chang to hire temporary labor at a cost of $12 per hour. Also, materials and supplies may have to be obtained under emergency conditions at unfavorable terms. The budgeting process is very difficult, he states, because of the many uncertainties.

Last year, Chang estimated the cost of materials and supplies at $116,000. Repairs and maintenance are his responsibility, as well as telephone, office supplies, and postage expense. The estimate for telephone expense last year was $4,600; for office supplies, $17,300; and for postage, $14,400. Maintenance costs were budgeted at $21,600. Included in the budget was Chang's salary of $30,000. Regular labor cost was budgeted at $83,000. Temporary labor was budgeted at 800 hours for a cost of $9,600. General factory overhead allocated to the department was budgeted at $72,000. Machinery and equipment are the responsibility of plant management. Depreciation is not charged to the departments.

Actual costs charged to Chang's department for the year are:

Materials and supplies	$127,000
Salary (Chang)	30,000
Wages, regular	83,000
Wages, temporary labor	26,400
Telephone	5,300
Office supplies	17,200
Postage	14,600
Maintenance	23,700
Allocated factory overhead	78,000
Total	$405,200

Required:

1. Comment on the merits of Chang's argument with respect to cost control.
2. Compare actual and budgeted costs for the year, showing variances. Which variances appear to be caused by the short-timeframe orders Chang mentioned?

2-11. **Cost Behavior and Planning.** McConnell Inc. manufactures and sells a single product with a price of $50 per unit. The following estimated annual cost data have been prepared for the upper and lower levels of the firm's relevant range of activity:

	Lower Level	Upper Level	F, V, SV
Production (units)	5,000	7,500	
Manufacturing costs:			
Direct materials	$ 50,000	$ 75,000	_____
Direct labor	40,000	60,000	_____
Overhead:			
Indirect labor	$ 21,000	$ 28,500	_____
Supplies	20,000	30,000	_____
Depreciation	12,000	12,000	_____
Distribution expenses:			
Salespersons	$ 45,000	$ 62,500	_____
Travel	8,000	8,000	_____
Advertising	5,000	5,000	_____
Other	29,000	41,500	_____
General and administrative expenses	30,000	37,500	_____
Total	$260,000	$360,000	

Required:

1. Classify each individual element of cost according to its behavior pattern (fixed, variable, or semivariable).
2. Prepare a diagram for each of the following: revenue, total variable costs, total fixed costs, and total semivariable costs. (Four diagrams)
3. Prepare one diagram that includes all three cost groups. Indicate the relevant range and the total costs at zero activity and at the lower and upper levels of the relevant range.
4. Express the total cost line shown in Part 3 in equation format.

2-12. **Finding Unknown Amounts.** For each of the cases, find the unknowns designated by letters. Each case is independent.

	Firm 1	Firm 2	Firm 3	Firm 4
Direct materials inventory, 1/1	$ 6,400	$ F	$ 6,900	$ 1,500
Direct materials inventory, 12/31	5,400	4,600	5,500	P
Direct labor	13,000	8,000	K	6,000
Factory overhead.....................	29,000	7,600	13,000	Q
Purchases of direct materials	9,000	7,000	L	8,000
Direct materials used	A	G	9,400	5,600
Sales	B	33,800	55,000	40,000
Cost of goods sold	C	22,000	M	17,000
Cost of goods manufactured	50,000	H	N	18,100
Manufacturing costs	D	21,500	O	18,100
Finished goods inventory, 1/1	8,000	4,000	7,800	6,000
Finished goods inventory, 12/31	5,300	5,300	6,200	R
Gross profit.........................	11,300	I	12,000	S
Work in process, 1/1	E	4,800	1,300	T
Work in process, 12/31	2,000	J	300	2,500

2-13 **Planning Costs.** Kevin Fletcher has just been appointed supervisor of the maintenance department of Helton Insurance Companies. This department services equipment in all departments of the headquarters building. To a large extent, costs are influenced by the demands from other departments.

In preparing the budget, Fletcher reviews the budget requests from those departments that have requested hours of service from his department as follows:

Requesting Department	Hours Requested
8	3,000
11	2,500
14	1,000
19	3,500

Fletcher has discussed the service requests with his division head, Laurie Owens. She advises him that the supervisor of Department 8 tends to overestimate requirements and that the budget will be more realistic if reduced by 20 percent of the hours requested. Conversely, the supervisor of Department 11 is likely to underestimate and to come in with last minute requests that will probably add as much as 500 hours to the budget.

All workers in Fletcher's department are to receive a wage rate of $15 per hour, and each will be expected to work 2,000 hours per year which leaves about 1,500 hours of usable time after training and non-chargeable work. Fletcher has the authority to hire an assistant at a salary of $24,000 per year, and his own salary has been established by Owens at $37,000.

Parts required for the year are estimated to cost $123,000. Other costs related to departmental operation have been budgeted as follows:

Supplies	$39,000
Utilities	11,500
Plant occupancy cost allocated	14,000
Total	$64,500

Owens states that top management does not like to see much overtime but recognizes that some of the requested work may need to be done on overtime. She advises that 500 hours of overtime premium be budgeted. Overtime premium is 50 percent of the regular wage rate.

Required:

From the information given, prepare a cost budget for Fletcher's department including the estimated number of employees needed to cover the requested maintenance hours.

2-14. **Cost Decision.** Alpine Sheet Metal Works uses one area of its plant for record storage. The plant superintendent complains that this is a waste of valuable space that could be put to productive use or at least rented to some other company. The records could be microfilmed at a one-time cost of $20,000, and an annual maintenance and updating cost would be $8,000. The space released can be rented to Ruther Truck Lines at an annual rental of $29,000.

A second option is manufacturing a new line of product in this space. Marketing studies and cost estimates show that the new product can be expected to produce the following results each year:

Net sales..		$268,000
Materials.......................................	$83,000	
Labor..	31,200	
Other additional costs.........................	17,800	
Allocated costs of the plant (based on space occupied):		
Heat and light.................................	14,500	
Repairs and maintenance	14,000	
Taxes and insurance...........................	19,000	
Supervision....................................	52,000	
Depreciation	28,000	
Total costs of new product line		259,500
Income before income tax		$ 8,500

The superintendent is disappointed to learn that the new product will contribute relatively little to the total operation and is inclined to rent the space to Ruther Truck Lines.

Required:
1. Identify the relevant costs for each alternative.
2. What would each alternative contribute to profits of Alpine?
3. Identify the opportunity cost in this decision.

2-15. **Cost Analysis Without Measurable Outputs.** Four Oaks Public Library has four areas, classified by type of books and other reading materials. The four areas are Technical, Historical, General, and Children. The library board of trustees is reviewing budget data and actual spending. Budget and actual direct costs of operating each area for the first quarter of 1994 are as follows:

	Technical	Historical	General	Children
Budget...........................	$105,000	$50,000	$52,000	$30,000
Actual:				
Salaries......................	$ 58,000	$31,000	$34,000	$23,000
Books	39,400	8,900	12,600	7,200
Periodicals	8,300	3,100	3,700	2,300
Supplies	2,900	3,200	2,800	2,600

The costs of operating the library as a total entity follow:

Building occupancy and utilities.	$40,000
Library administration	75,000
Order department	50,000

Other data with respect to library areas are:

			Recent Monthly Activity			
	Percentage of Space Occupied	Number of Employees	Order Requests Processed	Number of Customers Serviced	Books Checked Out	Fees & Revenue Generated
Technical	20%	8	150	800	300	$1,600
Historical	30	6	10	200	1,200	388
General.	20	5	50	600	2,000	487
Children	15	3	40	900	1,500	106
Administration	15	6	50			
Total	100%	28	300	2,500	5,000	$2,581

Required:
1. Prepare a report showing the direct costs, allocated costs (if appropriate), and budget comparisons for each library area.
2. Why would a detailed analysis of costs be important to the library management?
3. Discuss alternative ways of analyzing the costs of operating the areas and in measuring performance. Advantages, disadvantages, problems, possible criteria, measures of customer service, activity indicators, cost drivers, and social benefits. What additional data might be collected to help the analysis?

2-16. **Differential Revenues and Opportunity Costs.** Sundown Refining is a small refining operation in Kansas. Its primary products are gasoline and No. 6 fuel oil. All crude oil goes first into the atmospheric tower for distillation. The output is gasoline, No. 6 fuel oil, and a residual fuel oil. Both of the fuel oils can be further processed in a catalytic cracker (known as the cat cracker). The decision to process the fuel oils further depends on market conditions and the current cat cracker utilization.

The refinery currently has on hand an additional 30,000 gallons of No. 6 fuel oil. This fuel oil can either be sold to a distribution network at $0.50 per gallon or processed through the cat cracker to generate gasoline, which sells at $0.90 per gallon. Delia Garcia, the production manager, must make a decision on the routing of the additional fuel oil.

The cat cracker has the following yield for processing fuel oil: gasoline, 75 percent; residual fuel oil, 20 percent; and loss, 5 percent. The operating costs are largely fixed costs and are budgeted at $10,000 per month plus $0.10 per gallon of input fuel. Residual fuel is a by-product with an insignificant sales value. The cat cracker is currently operating at 80 percent capacity. Full capacity is 100,000 gallons of input fuel.

Required:
1. Should the fuel oil be processed through the cat cracker to obtain gasoline? Why?
2. What is the opportunity cost of this decision?

2-17. **Costing Services for a Consulting Firm.** Tom Toliver has his own consulting practice and specializes in training programs on motivation and employee relationships. He maintains an office at a suburban location, but his training programs are almost always at the client's office. Toliver's policy is to charge clients with all costs directly related to the job (such as travel, special materials development, and copying of materials) plus a billing rate per hour for his time. The billing rate is set to cover his estimated operating expenses and provide him with $3,500 per month for living expenses. In the past, Toliver has averaged 120 billable hours a month, but economic conditions are causing a decline in demand for his services.

The estimated operating expenses for the upcoming month are:

Secretarial support	$1,000
Office rent (includes utilities)	500
Telephone	250
Office supplies	170
Depreciation on office equipment	80
Miscellaneous expenses	260
	$2,260

Toliver's current commitments involve an estimated 80 hours of billable time for the month, and he is looking for more work. Grace Brian, owner of Brian's Apparel, would like him to run a two-day workshop (8 hours each day) for her employees. She is willing to pay $1,000 plus any direct expenses. Toliver estimates the workshop will entail 4 hours of billable time outside of the actual workshop.

Required:
1. What is Toliver's required billing rate assuming his normal 120 billable hours per month work load? With only 80 billable hours per month?
2. Assume that Toliver's current clients (80-hour commitment per month) have agreed to pay the 80-hour billing rate from Part 1 above. Should Toliver accept Grace Brian's offer?
3. Assume that the competitive environment suggests a billing rate no higher than the 120-hour rate calculated in Part 1 above and that Toliver can find additional work at this rate. Should Toliver accept Grace Brian's offer?

2-18. **Cost Flow—Merchandise and Manufacturing.** Winston Steel Company manufactures tubular steel furniture. The tubing that is used to produce the furniture is purchased from Martinelli Distributors. Martinelli Distributors is not a manufacturer. Martinelli buys the tubes of steel and resells to customers without doing any work to convert the tubes to other forms.

Martinelli had no inventory on hand at the beginning of the year. During the year, the distributor purchased tubing at a cost of $380,000. The costs per unit remained the same throughout the year. Tubing with a cost of $310,000 was sold during the year. Operating costs of sales and office salaries, advertising, taxes and insurance, rent, heat and light, and telephone in aggregate amounted to $65,000 and were period costs for the year. Sales revenue was $435,000.

Winston Steel Company had no inventory of materials at the beginning of the year. Tubing having a cost of $175,000 was purchased from Martinelli Distributors. Other materials costing $275,000 were also purchased. At the end of the year, Winston Steel Company counted materials inventory and assigned a cost of $50,000 to this inventory.

During the year, Winston Steel operated at a normal capacity of 80,000 product units. Labor cost of manufacturing was $240,000. Various other costs of manufacturing, such as plant supervision, factory taxes and insurance, factory heat and light, and factory telephone, amounted to $120,000.

Winston Steel Company also incurred selling and administrative expenses for the period, such as sales and office salaries, advertising, rent, taxes and insurance, and telephone. These operating expenses for the year amounted to $130,000. During the year, 75,000 units of furniture were sold for $900,000. No inventory of partially completed or completed furniture was on hand at the beginning of the year.

Required:
1.   Prepare a summary income statement for the year for Martinelli Distributors showing revenue, cost of goods sold, and operating expenses.
2.   Compute the cost for Winston Steel Company to produce a unit of furniture. Show the unit cost by each cost element: direct materials, direct labor, and manufacturing overhead.
3.   Prepare a summary income statement for the year for Winston Steel Company showing revenue, cost of goods sold, and operating expenses.

CASE 2A—THE GINGERBREAD LADY

The Gingerbread Lady has a part-time business of producing and selling gingerbread houses for Christmas. Production starts in late October and runs four consecutive weeks. To meet health codes, she rents a kitchen at a nearby preschool and bakes and decorates the houses there. She can use the kitchen only on Friday evenings and all day Saturdays and can produce, at most, 300 houses in one weekend. The rent per weekend is $60. Consequently, the Gingerbread Lady can produce, at most, 1,200 houses for the season. Materials and labor costs amount to $2.50 per house. The houses are sold at various bazaars throughout the community. The Gingerbread Lady thinks that she can charge whatever the market will bear at each bazaar.

Four bazaars have been announced this year. For some reason, all of the bazaars this year are being held at the same time, thus forcing the Gingerbread Lady to choose which bazaar she will attend. Each bazaar, expressed as an alternative, is shown as follows with the anticipated selling price and its specific costs:

Alternative A: A private athletic club with an elite membership sponsors this two-day bazaar. It charges a flat fee of $25 per day for each seller. The Gingerbread Lady feels a selling price of $6.75 per house is appropriate. From past experience, she knows she can sell 200 houses with follow-up orders for 150 houses.

Alternative B: A two-day neighborhood bazaar is held in the lower-middle income part of the city. She will charge $5.95 per house and must pay a flat fee of $15 per day. She can sell, at most, 400 houses.

Alternative C: This two-day bazaar is held in a community center in another lower-middle income section of the city. Here the price is a bit lower at $5.45. The center charges $12 per day for each seller participating in the bazaar. Based on last year's records, the Gingerbread Lady can sell 500 houses in the two days.

Alternative D: The local university sponsors a three-day bazaar and charges each seller 10 percent of the gross revenue from sales as a fee. Because of the student population, the Gingerbread Lady will charge $5.00 per house. But she thinks she can sell 600 houses during the three days.

She has already determined it is not worthwhile to her to be in business if she cannot make a minimum of $1.25 per house.

Required:

1. Prepare an analysis showing which bazaar the Gingerbread Lady should pick for this year.
2. If the Gingerbread Lady could hire someone to handle the next most attractive (profitable) bazaar for her, what is the maximum amount she could pay and at least break even?
3. If the Gingerbread Lady could hire other people to handle additional bazaars and pay them 50 percent of any profits over $1.25 per house as their wage, for which bazaars should she produce?

Chapter Three

Activity-Based Costing for Product Costing and Responsibility Accounting

 Chapter Objectives

After studying Chapter 3, you will be able to:
1. Explain the interrelationship between cost drivers, activities, and products in an activity-based costing system.
2. Describe the key components and cost flows in an activity-based costing system.
3. List and explain the key objectives of a cost management system.
4. Identify and understand the need to eliminate non-value-added activities.
5. Define the major components of a responsibility accounting system.
6. Describe how control can be accomplished through responsibility accounting.

Why Profitable Products Aren't Necessarily as Profitable as they Look

Alexus Plumbing Fixtures is a $100 million manufacturer of plumbing fixtures. It has a vertically integrated 720,000 square foot factory encompassing everything from die casting, screw machines, pipe threading, chrome plating, stamping, polishing, and assembly. It also sells an enormous number of product variations extending into the hundreds of thousands, including available functions, styles, finishes, and substitutions. These factors contribute to a large overhead structure that amounts to almost 60 percent of the cost of goods sold. The cost accounting system identifies materials, labor, and overhead costs with each department, and the departmental costs are allocated to products on the basis of direct labor identified with that department. Alexus is losing money. Management wants to reduce costs and improve profitability.

Members of the management team recently attended a management seminar and heard a speaker mention the benefits of activity-based costing. The speaker said that companies similar to Alexus, who permit many options in their products, are losing money because the company pushes products that look profitable based on a faulty cost accounting system. Alexus executives believe they should study their business to see if activity-based costing would alleviate some of their cost problems and help them control costs better.

Stan Stanslovsky, plant controller and something of a computer jock, came back from the meeting and began to think about alternative costing approaches. He figured that a major change in the product costing system would take months, maybe years, and would cost hundreds of thousands of dollars. He remembered his younger days as a budget analyst in the sales division of a food products company. They always had test markets going to try new ideas. Why couldn't he "test" a different product costing approach, he wondered.

Stan selected a small product line of water filters. Two departments were nearly exclusively devoted to the filter products. Most products were simple assembly tasks; a few were complex; and some required either manual or automated steps. He studied past costs and activity levels. He talked to the plant's production planners and engineers and workers and managers in both departments. After about a month of work, he recreated the unit costs of the filters for the first quarter of the year. He emphasized links between costs incurred and activities.

He found that frequent setups to change from producing one filter to another took time and stopped production. Some filters had low demand, others were high volume sellers. He linked some costs to machine usage, others to direct labor hours expended. Instead of having materials, direct labor, and overhead cost groups, Stan had grouped costs by materials, materials handling, all labor wages and benefits, machine usage costs, setup costs, supervision, and general factory overhead.

He found that some products were under-costed, some over-costed, while about half didn't change much. The new costs of certain key products were over 50 percent off. Were the old costs or his new costs right? Well, he knew his new numbers were only estimates, but they were so different that Alexus' pricing formulas, cost analyses, and decision-making data could all be substantially off base.

He began to show his results to others who had gone to the seminar— production, sales, and financial people. A few scoffed, but Stan got a lot of responses like: "I thought that might be the case," and "I always wondered about those cost numbers."

But Stan knew the big test would be to get budget money to make changes in the cost accounting system itself. Would people be willing to pay for better information?

Two major forces have come together to put great pressure on managerial accountants to provide improved cost information about their firms' products and services. These are global competition and automation in the work place.

1. **Global competitiveness**. Most companies in nearly every industry face increased competition from direct competitors whether from across the street or halfway around the world. Whether the technology is old (making iron and steel) or new (making high definition televisions), the needs for accurate and relevant product cost data have grown dramatically. Competitiveness also means knowing the costs of product quality, reliable delivery, and waste—unproductive effort. Cost control takes on new meaning if a competitor can sell an item at a price that is 10 percent lower than another company's production cost and still make money on the sale. More complex cost analysis brings a realization that traditional cost systems are not using the "right" variables or collecting cost data in enough detail.

2. **Automation of the work place**. Dramatic changes in production have also taken place. Another "industrial revolution" is what some people have called it. Computer power has introduced concepts like computer-aided design (CAD) and computer-aided manufacturing (CAM), flexible manufacturing systems (FMS), and robotics. Computer power has allowed precise tasks to be programmed and machines to be designed to do those tasks. Likewise, computer power has enabled production managers to coordinate thousands of events, transactions, and possible courses of action. One outcome is a shift from heavy dependence on labor to technology. Direct labor costs were often a major product cost, and labor activity often reflected general activity in the plant. Now, in many factories, direct labor is a minor piece of a product's total cost. Other production costs have grown tremendously because of equipment

costs and support personnel needed to coordinate production. New activity measures are needed to link resources used with production activities.

The very computer power that has changed production must also be applied to cost accounting. First, costs of using resources are among the thousands of events and transactions mentioned above that production managers are analyzing. The days of separate cost accounting systems for financial reporting and data systems for production management are past. Second, what had been cost prohibitive in terms of cost systems is now reasonable. Memory capacities, computation speed, communication networks, and equipment availability are building blocks that make data collecting, analysis, and reporting relatively inexpensive when compared to the value created.

Competition and automation have focused attention on getting more accurate, timely, and relevant product costs. The same concern can be expressed for all uses of cost information, applicable to all cost objectives. The concepts are very simple and have always been at the heart of cost accounting—link the cost of resources used to the activity using the resource and link the activity to the product being produced. This has become known as activity-based costing.

This chapter presents the conceptual foundation for activity-based costing as a means of improving the accuracy of assigning costs to cost objectives—primarily to products and services. And to create the structure necessary to classify, plan and control, and report costs, a responsibility accounting system is defined and discussed in conjunction with activity-based costing.

ACTIVITY-BASED COSTING

Activity-based costing focuses on finding the cost of producing a product or service. Many of the managerial accounting functions presented in the following chapters of this book depend on quality cost data. These functions and the chapters impacted include:

1. **Planning and controlling production costs.** Product costing systems are discussed in Chapters 5 and 6. Budgeting itself, explained in Chapters 7 and 8, depends on understanding cost behavior and the links between planned activities and planned costs.

2. **Pricing products and bidding on new work.** Relationships between volumes, product costs, and profits are discussed in Chapter 4.

3. **Making incremental decisions and competitive analyses.** Relevant product costs are key elements of the type of incremental decisions presented in Chapter 11. Even intracompany sales and divisional evaluations, discussed in Chapter 14, depend on accurate product cost information.

4. **Evaluating capital investments which would expand production or introduce new products.** Chapters 12 and 13 focus on capital investment

decisions which depend on accurate forecasts of new product costs or expected cost reductions.

5.   **Designing and engineering products and production processes.** Standard costing, discussed in Chapters 9 and 10, uses product specifications to develop product costs. More accurate product cost data can highlight high cost or problem activities that can be redesigned.

In Chapter 2, we introduced cost of goods manufactured and the three traditional groups of costs—materials, direct labor, and manufacturing overhead. Once materials and direct labor were linked with products because of their obvious direct relationships, all other costs were traditionally lumped together as overhead. One activity measure, often direct labor, was used to attach all overhead to products. Many different overhead costs were combined and included:

1.   Plant supervision salaries
2.   Materials handling costs
3.   Plant engineering costs
4.   Set-up or change-over costs
5.   Supplies and indirect materials
6.   Depreciation, taxes, and insurance on equipment
7.   Energy and other utility costs
8.   Repair and maintenance costs

Each of these costs behaves differently, since each cost is created by different activities. Often, each product uses different amounts of each resource. In most situations more groupings of costs are necessary to show clear links between the costs of resources used and outputs. Ideally, every cost could be traced directly to specific products. This is just not possible. If we produce a million units of different types and sizes of batteries in a factory, can the manager's $100,000 salary be traced to each battery? No. Can we link this cost and certain factory activities, then link the activity costs and the different production groups, and then link product group costs and product units? Yes, with careful study.

Issues Influencing Cost Management Systems Design

The underlying theme of product costing systems is that product costs are so critical to managerial decisions that greater precision and accuracy are needed today than were demanded in the past. Thus, a major effort is underway in many companies to upgrade their product costing systems.

The level of detail that a product cost system needs must be based on the following considerations:

1.   The competitive environment, which will impact the degree of accuracy needed and the toleration of product costing errors.
2.   The homogeneity or heterogeneity of the products produced.
3.   The complexity of the production process.

4. The volumes of each product produced.
5. The cost of measuring and collecting activity and cost data.
6. The impacts more accurate and relevant data will have on managerial behavior.

Such systems are expensive to design and to operate. Yet the value of better product cost information can also be extremely high.

Definition of Activity-Based Costing

Activity-based costing (ABC) is a system of accounting that focuses on activities performed to produce products. Activities become the fundamental cost accumulation points. Costs are traced to activities, and activities are traced to products based on each product's use of the activities. These relationships for allocating costs to products are expressed pictorially in Figure 3.1.

Figure 3.1   An Overall View of ABC Cost Linkage

Under activity-based costing, an effort is made to identify and account for as many costs as possible as direct costs of production. Any cost that can possibly be traced to a particular product or product line is treated as a direct cost. For example, under the traditional costing system, the cost of set-up time (the factory down time from converting from producing one product to another) is included in manufacturing overhead and applied to products on the basis of direct labor hours. Under ABC, set-up time is measured for each product line, and set-up costs are directly assigned to each part or product.

An ABC system identifies the major activities in a production process, aggregates those activities into activity centers, accumulates costs in activity centers, selects cost drivers that link activities to products, and traces the costs of activities to products. An **activity center** is a segment of the organization for which management wants to report separately the cost of the activities performed. Consequently, we use a mechanism for assigning a given activity's pool of costs called a cost driver. A **cost driver** is an event, action, or activity that results in incurring costs. It is any factor that causes costs to change. The basic concept is that cost drivers, such as set-up time, measure the amount of resources a specific product uses of a particular set of resources—the group of activities. As activities occur, we identify performance measures that can be used for various purposes. This basic concept is depicted in Figure 3.2.

Although not always obvious, several different cost drivers could link an activity's costs and the cost objective. A cost function is created from the

Activity center [handwritten margin note]

activity's costs and the planned cost driver activity level. In the materials handling case in Figure 3.2, assume that the cost driver selected is the pounds of materials moved. The planned material handling costs are divided by the planned pounds to be moved. A cost per pound is the cost function. Then, the actual pounds handled in the production of a product times the cost per pound is the amount of materials handling costs assigned to that product. Again, the overall process is to identify the best cost driver that links costs and activities; then use that cost driver to link activities with products (or other cost objectives).

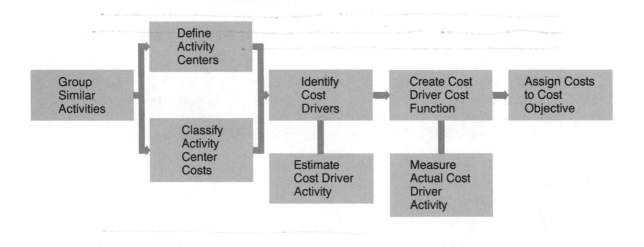

Example: Moving and handling materials in the factory:

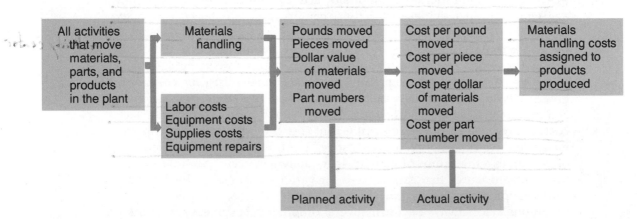

Figure 3.2   An Overall View of the ABC Process

Flow of Costs Under Activity-Based Costing

In applying the definition of ABC to a specific organization, we follow five basic steps:

1. Assemble similar actions into activity groups.
2. Classify costs by activity group and by kind of expense.
3. Select cost drivers.
4. Calculate a cost function to link costs and cost drivers with resource use.
5. Assign cost to the cost objective.

These steps are consistent with Figure 3.2.

Group Similar Actions   The number of actions performed in any organization can be quite numerous. Although the ideal is to relate the cost of every action to a cost driver and then to the product, the costs of accomplishing this can far exceed the benefits. Therefore, actions are combined into activity groups. Treating collections of actions as activities eliminates the need to measure and track the performance of individual actions and costs.

One meaningful way of grouping actions is to classify them with different levels of activities. A common outline is unit-level activities, batch-level activities, product-level activities, and facilities-level activities. Figure 3.3 illustrates the four types. **Unit-level activities** are performed each time a unit is produced. These are repetitive activities. Direct labor or machine hours are examples. Costs of these activities vary with the number of units produced. **Batch-level activities** are those performed each time a batch of goods is produced. Machine setups, order processing, and material handling are related to batches rather than individual units. The costs of these activities vary according to the number of batches but are common or fixed costs for all units in the batch. **Product-level activities** are those performed as needed to support the production of each different type of product. Maintaining bills of materials and routing information, processing engineering changes, testing routines, and handling materials are examples of activities in this category. **Facility-level activities** are those which simply sustain a facility's general manufacturing process. These costs are common to a variety of products and are the most difficult to link to product specific activities.

Traditionally, we classify factory overhead costs as variable and fixed. Relative to volume of outputs, costs of unit-level activities are predominately variable costs while costs of the other three levels are predominately fixed costs. However, separately identifying batch-, product-, and facility-level activity centers helps in selecting cost drivers. Often, the cost perspective changes: many costs that are fixed relative to units of output are now variable costs relative to the cost driver. This is particularly true for batch- and product-level activities. Costs of facility-level activities remain in the primarily fixed category and are often apportioned or allocated to products in some arbitrary manner.

Classify Costs By Activity Group And By Kind Of Expense   Once the actions are grouped into activities, the next step is identifying the costs with the activities. As will be discussed later under responsibility accounting,

Unit-Level Activities

Activities:
   Assembly activities
   Stamping activities
   Machining activities

Resources used:
   Labor wages and benefits
   Materials used
   Supplies used
   Energy consumed

Cost drivers:
   Labor hours used
   Machine hours used
   Direct costs of production
   Number of units produced

Batch-Level Activities

Activities:
   Batch change-overs (setups)
   Materials preparation
   Order processing

Resources used:
   Labor costs of setups
   Labor costs to prepare jobs
   Labor costs to process orders
   Batch handling office costs

Cost drivers:
   Number of batches
   Number of setups
   Number of orders processed

Facility-Level Activities

Activities:
   Plant supervision
   Occupancy
   Personnel administration

Resources used:
   Plant depreciation, taxes, & insurance
   Salaries of plant management
   General training

Cost drivers:
   Number of employees in production
      activity centers
   Allocation percentages
   Direct costs of production
   Volume of units produced

Product-Level Activities

Activities:
   Production scheduling
   Product design
   Parts and product testing
   Special handling and storage

Resources used:
   Specialized equipment
   Labor costs of design
   Files and records maintenance

Cost drivers:
   Number of products
   Number of parts

Figure 3.3   Levels of ABC Activity Groups

the coding and classifying of cost data at this early point determine the level of detail and the break-downs of cost data available to managers for all cost analysis purposes later. A chart of accounts or a data base classification scheme will identify the type of cost by natural classification: salary, postage, telephone, repair, supplies, etc. A second code will identify the activity center. In responsibility accounting, this is called a cost center. An activity center and a cost center are both commonly defined as the smallest part of an organization around which we will want to accumulate costs. In fact in most carefully defined cost systems, the terms activity center and cost center can be used interchangeably.

Select Cost Drivers   Direct costs can be traced immediately to a product without the need for a cost driver, using the costs themselves as the cost driver. All other manufacturing costs need links between cost, activity, and product. Cost drivers are the links. A cost driver can link a pool of costs in an activity center to the product. Or a cost driver can link costs in one activity center to activities in another activity center. Multiple layers of activities can exist. One activity relates to another activity, which may relate to still another activity before relationships to products are identified. Figure 3.4 gives an example of the variety of these relationships.

The first box at the top is the total costs of manufacturing during a production period. The costs are classified by activity center code and by natural expense type. As will be discussed later, a manager is responsible for each activity center and the costs incurred in that center.

A **preliminary stage cost driver** links costs of resources consumed (inputs) in an individual activity to other activity centers. Cost drivers moving costs from one activity center to another are preliminary stage cost drivers. **A primary stage cost driver** links costs in an activity center directly with products. Some costs, such as batch-level activity centers cost in Figure 3.4, are initially assigned to a primary stage activity center and only need a single stage assignment process. These primary stage centers may collect reassigned costs from numerous preliminary stage activity centers—based on cost drivers that reflect activity and resources used.

The activity centers are typically one of four types as described above. Direct costs of unit-level activity centers are assumed in Figure 3.4 to be always traceable to specific products. Batch-level activity centers should also be traceable to specific products but often use a cost driver. Product-level activity centers may be related to a specific product or may be grouped by activities before being assigned to products at the primary stage. Facility-level activity centers may go through multiple preliminary stages before arriving at a direct link with products.

ABC systems differ from traditional cost accounting systems in the number and variety of cost drivers used to trace costs. Traditional cost accounting systems use very few drivers—often only direct labor hours or dollars. ABC systems, on the other hand, may use a multitude of cost drivers that relate costs more closely to the resources consumed and the activities occurring.

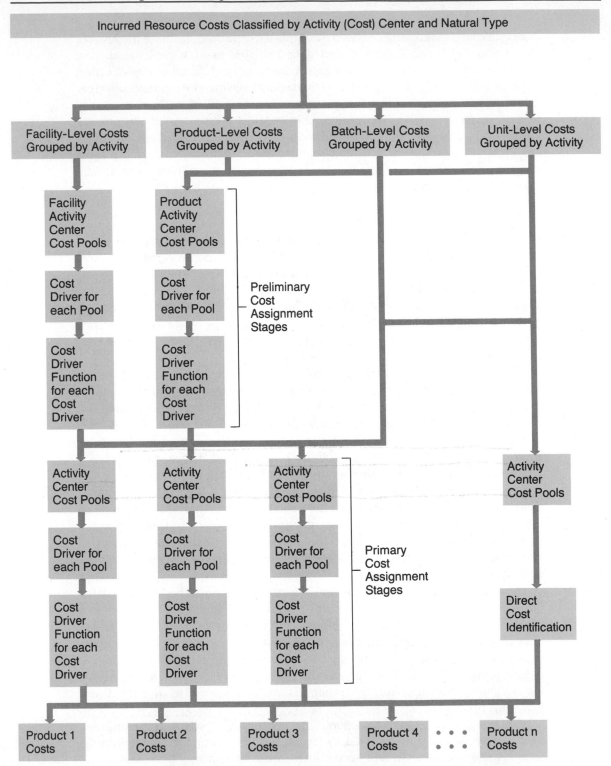

Figure 3.4 Relationships of Activity Cost Centers, Cost Drivers, Cost Functions, and Product Costs

Although not comprehensive, Figure 3.5 gives examples of cost drivers one might find in an ABC system.

COST DRIVERS

Number of products or units	Number of purchasing and ordering hours
Number of labor minutes per piece	
Amount of labor cost incurred	Number of customer options per product
Value of materials in a product	
Number of material moves	Number of accessories
Number of materials handling hours	Number of times ordered
Number of times handled	Number of units scrapped
Number of parts received per month	Number of engineering product change orders
Number of part numbers maintained	
Number of part numbers in a product	Number of die impressions
Amount of hazardous materials	Number of units reworked
Number of new parts introduced	Volume of scrap—by weight or units
Number of setup hours	Number of customer orders processed
Number of setups	
Number of machine hours used on a product	Square feet used by an activity
	Number of employees
Number of vendors	

Figure 3.5   Cost Drivers Used in Actual ABC Systems

Calculate a Cost Function   In Figure 3.4, a cost function is used to convert the pool of costs and cost driver data into a rate per cost driver unit, a percentage of other cost amounts, or an allocation percentage. This cost function could be based on either planned or actual activity levels. In Chapter 5, we discuss the creation of predetermined overhead rates using planned activity levels. Using actual activity levels and costs for example, if the set-up activity center cost pool totaled $25,000 and if set-up hours were the cost driver and were 500 hours, the cost function would be $50 per set-up hour. Costs are then distributed to products using set-up hours incurred.

Assign Costs to Cost Objectives   The final step is distributing costs to the users of the resources. The cost pool, the cost driver, and the cost function now combine to determine how much cost is charged to each resource user. If this is at a preliminary stage, the users are predominately other activity centers. Thus, a group of costs are now reassigned to other cost pools based on use. If the activity center is at the primary stage, the users are the products themselves. In the set-up example, if 60 hours of set-up time were used for Product A's production, $3,000 would be charged to Product A. All costs entering the manufacturing process during a given time period are eventually assigned to products.

Influence of Product Mix Complexity

The primary goal of ABC for product costing is to generate accurate product costs. In general, this means the cost accounting system must handle the complexity of production while minimizing possible distortions caused by cost assignment processes. The complexity of product mix plays a significant role in determining whether the costs of two or more activities can be combined and traced to a product by means of a single cost driver and still be assigned accurately. If a company wants more accurate product costs, it must increase the number of activity centers, cost pools, and cost drivers. Since the introduction of a new cost driver in the system has a cost/benefit value, most companies will face a trade-off between more cost drivers, greater detail, and more expensive data processing versus more data aggregation and less expensive data processing. Several important issues relate to selecting cost drivers and they include:

1.   Product diversity (homogeneity or heterogeneity).
2.   Batch-size diversity.
3.   Relative costs of activities aggregated.

Product diversity refers to the degree to which products differ in the number of activities (that is, resources or inputs) required by each product. The greater the difference in how two different products use resources or inputs, the greater the distortion a single cost driver will make in tracing costs to the products. For example, producing an ornate bathroom faucet fixture may consume labor-intensive production resources while a kitchen sink faucet may consume machine-intensive resources.

Some products are simply larger than other products. A console model versus a portable model is an example. The size influences how the product is produced and which resources are required. The complexity of a product is determined by the differences in how a product is manufactured and the number of options a manufacturer has for its products. Deluxe models and products with many customer options, for example, increase the manufacturing difficulty. Each option adds an extension to the production process. However, supervision and other departmental costs are not necessarily influenced by these options. Material inputs may differ by product. Some materials may require more handling from the receiving dock through the storeroom to the production floor. In other cases, certain materials may require longer machining time or more time in trimming processes. Some products may have a high degree of vertical integration—from raw materials to finished products. Others are assembled from purchased parts.

Batch-size diversity occurs when products are manufactured in different sized batches. Batches refer not only to production orders but to order quantities of raw materials and to shipping batch sizes. In an automotive stamping plant, a weekly run of hood stampings for a popular model may be 3,000 units, while a very similar but higher priced model may have a biweekly run of 500. Although we normally think of differing batch sizes when we produce different products, batch-size diversity can also occur with the same product over time. For instance, this week the production order consists of 500 units. Due to an increase in demand, the production schedule for next week calls for an order of 800 units. Frequency of batch runs may also require that more attention be given to minimizing set-up time and cost. In traditional cost systems, set-up costs were added to other overhead costs, losing the separate identity and cost detail of set-up activities. Set-up hours may be more appropriate than number of setups. Just-in-time production encourages producing only what is needed immediately—often smaller batches and more frequently.

Relative differences in activity costs, depending on the level of aggregation, influence whether more cost drivers are necessary to trace costs of activities to products. The rule of thumb is that activities can be grouped until the costs traced to a product using a grouped cost driver differ materially from the tracing that would take place if the individual activities used their own unique cost driver. What is material will depend on the issues introduced earlier in the chapter.

If computer resources were free and if managers had unlimited amounts of analysis time, more and more detail could be captured and evaluated. Since this is not the case, very practical decisions must be made. In large ABC applications, the number of cost drivers (both preliminary and primary) used across an entire plant may be as low as 20 to a high of several hundred. Often, a high percentage of costs are assigned using a small number of drivers. The cost system's design should allow judgments to be made about the number of cost pools and cost drivers and should allow for cost pools and cost drivers to be changed easily when the need arises.

A COMPREHENSIVE ACTIVITY-BASED COST EXAMPLE

The controller and the production manager of Freeman Metal Products have just completed the installation of an activity-based costing system in their factory. The firm's products are primarily replacement parts sold to the construction and farm equipment industry. The actual plant is a complex of nearly 20 producing and 15 support departments and several hundred basic products are routinely produced plus many custom variations. Many orders are for small quantities, while others are standing orders for thousands of units per month. To simplify the example, only 4 facility-level activity centers, 3 support activity centers, and 4 producing activity centers are illustrated. Also, only 5 products are shown. Production volume for October, 1995 is as follows:

	Product A	Product B	Product C	Product D	Product E
Units Produced	22,000	15,000	40,000	6,000	3,000

The activity centers, direct costs for October, 1995, and cost drivers are as follows:

ACTIVITY CENTER INFORMATION

Activity Center Code	Activity Center	Direct Costs	Direct Product Costs		Other Costs	Cost Driver Selected
			Materials	Labor		
110	Plant Administration	$ 50,000			$ 50,000	Allocation %
120	Occupancy	60,000			60,000	Square feet used
130	Data Processing	30,000			30,000	Transactions processed
140	Personnel Benefits	60,000			60,000	Percent of payroll cost
210	Setup Operations	30,000			30,000	Setups
220	Materials Handling	50,000			50,000	Percent of materials dollars used
230	Shipping	40,000	$ 5,000		35,000	Shipments
310	Fabricating	160,000	90,000	$ 30,000	40,000	Machine steps
410	Heat Treating	50,000	20,000	10,000	20,000	Treatment hours
420	Machining	50,000	15,000	20,000	15,000	Machine hours
430	Assembly	110,000	40,000	40,000	30,000	Labor hours
	Total	$690,000	$170,000	$100,000	$420,000	

Activities were grouped and activity centers were determined as a result of special studies. Cost drivers were selected after analysis of past cost behavior and activity levels within each activity center. The cost driver data for the preliminary stage cost assignments are as follows:

COST DRIVER DATA

Activity Center Code	Activity Center	Cost Driver Activity	Activity Centers Using Resources and Receiving Costs						
			210	220	230	310	410	420	430
110	Plant Administration: Allocation % . . . . . . (1 % equals $500)	100%	6%	8%	6%	20%	20%	20%	20%
120	Occupancy: Square feet used . . ($.50 per square foot)	120,000	4,000	16,000	4,000	28,000	20,000	24,000	24,000
130	Data Processing: Transactions . . . . . . ($.10 per transaction)	300,000	5,000	160,000	5,000	40,000	20,000	30,000	40,000
140	Personnel Benefits: % of payroll . . . . (1/3 of payroll)	$180,000	$13,500	$21,000	$21,000	$42,000	$12,000	$22,500	$48,000
220	Materials Handling: per materials $ . . . . ($.50 per dollar)	$170,000			$5,000	$90,000	$20,000	$15,000	$40,000

Each activity center has one cost driver. The cost driver activity becomes the base for determining which other activity centers used a given activity center's resources. For example, occupancy activities include general plant maintenance, property taxes, common utilities, and similar common costs. The cost driver selected was square feet of plant used by each activity. Direct occupancy costs were $60,000 which allow the controller to develop a cost function of $.50 per square foot occupied. Notice that Materials Handling serves all production activity centers and the shipping support activity center but not Setup Operations or itself. The full development of the Materials Handling cost function of $.50 per dollar of materials handled must await further cost assignments shown in Figure 3.6.

With preliminary cost assignments made using cost drivers and cost functions given above, the remaining activity centers contain either direct product costs or costs to be assigned to products using primary cost drivers. The direct costs and cost driver functions are as follows for each product:

Activity Center Code	Activity Center	Cost Driver Activity	Cost Driver Activity Linked to Each Product				
			Product A	Product B	Product C	Product D	Product E
210	Setup Operations:						
	Number of setups	200	5	50	20	80	45
	($200 per setup)						
230	Shipping:						
	Shipments....................	100	5	10	20	35	30
	($500 per shipment)						
310	Fabricating:						
	Machine steps	25,400	2,600	4,400	6,400	8,000	4,000
	($5 per step)						
410	Heat Treating:						
	Treatment hours	1,000	200	300	0	300	200
	($56 per hour)						
420	Machining:						
	Machine hours	500	100	150	80	120	50
	($110 per hour)						
430	Assembly:						
	Labor hours	2,500	500	400	600	300	700
	($36.80 per hour)						

As can be seen, different products use different amounts of the resources in each activity center. From the production volume data given earlier, we can see that total volume, batch size, complexity, conversion efforts, and shipping tasks vary dramatically among the 5 products.

Picturing the Cost Flows From Activities to Products

Cost assignments to products for each batch, product, and unit activity centers are shown in the previous examples but depend on the cost assignments from other activity centers. To track all cost assignments, Figure 3.6 presents a work sheet of the cost flows from activity centers to products. Figure 3.7 diagrams the activity centers and the flows into and out of each center and finally to each product. For example, total costs accumulated in the Materials Handling Activity Center 220 is $85,000 which includes $50,000 of direct costs and $35,000 of assigned costs from Activity Centers 110, 120, 130, and 140 as shown in Figure 3.6. The cost driver is dollars of materials handled which totalled $170,000. Thus, the cost function is $.50 per dollar of material moved. Materials handling costs are assigned to Activity Centers 230, 310, 410, 420, and 430.

Activity Center Code		Direct and Assigned Product Costs					
		Product A	Product B	Product C	Product D	Product E	110
	Materials Costs	.....	.....	.....	.....	.....	.....
	Labor Costs	.....	.....	.....	.....	.....	.....
	Direct Other Costs	.....	.....	.....	.....	.....	$50,000
110	Plant Administration:						
	Driver: allocation %	.....	.....	.....	.....	.....	(50,000)
120	Occupancy:						
	Driver: square feet used	.....	.....	.....	.....	.....	.....
130	Data Process:						
	Driver: transactions	.....	.....	.....	.....	.....	.....
140	Personnel Benefits:						
	Driver: % of payroll $	.....	.....	.....	.....	.....	.....
210	Setup Operations:						
	Driver: Setups	$ 1,000	$ 10,000	$ 4,000	$ 16,000	$ 9,000	.....
220	Materials Handling:						
	Driver: % of material. $	.....	.....	.....	.....	.....	
230	Shipping:						
	Direct: Materials	1,000	500	2,000	600	900	.....
	Driver: Shipments	2,500	5,000	10,000	17,500	15,000	.....
310	Fabricating:						
	Direct: Materials	10,000	5,000	40,000	25,000	10,000	.....
	Direct: Labor	12,000	3,000	3,000	8,000	4,000	.....
	Driver: Machine steps	13,000	22,000	32,000	40,000	20,000	.....
410	Heat Treating:						
	Direct: Materials	3,000	6,000	0	6,000	5,000	.....
	Direct: Labor	2,000	2,000	0	3,000	3,000	.....
	Driver: Treatment. hrs.	11,200	16,800	0	16,800	11,200	.....
420	Machining:						
	Direct: Materials	5,000	2,000	6,000	1,000	1,000	.....
	Direct: Labor	2,000	8,000	4,000	4,000	2,000	.....
	Driver: Machine hrs.	11,000	16,500	8,800	13,200	5,500	.....
430	Assembly:						
	Direct: Materials	12,000	2,000	20,000	4,000	2,000	.....
	Direct: Labor	8,000	6,000	10,000	5,000	11,000	.....
	Driver: Labor hrs.	18,400	14,720	22,080	11,040	25,760	.....
	Product Costs	$112,100	$119,520	$161,880	$171,140	$125,360	
	Units Produced	22,000	15,000	40,000	6,000	3,000	
	Cost Per Unit	$ 5.0955	$ 7.9680	$ 4.0470	$28.5233	$41.7867	
	Total Costs	$690,000					

Figure 3.6 Calculation of Product Cost Using Activity-Based Costing for Cost Assignment

In Figure 3.6, preliminary cost assignments are made to other activity centers. In turn the primary cost assignments go to products. For example, the Machining Activity Center 420 incurred $15,000 of materials costs, $20,000 of labor costs, and $15,000 of other traceable costs. Additional costs were assigned to Machining: $10,000 from Plant Administration, $12,000 from Occupancy, and so on. A total of $40,000 of additional costs were charged to

Activity Centers

120	130	140	210	220	230	310	410	420	430
.....	.....	.....	.....	.....	$ 5,000	$ 90,000	$ 20,000	$ 15,000	$ 40,000
.....	.....	.....	.....	.....	.....	30,000	10,000	20,000	40,000
$ 60,000	$ 30,000	$ 60,000	$ 30,000	50,000	35,000	40,000	20,000	15,000	30,000
.....	.....	.....	3,000	4,000	3,000	10,000	10,000	10,000	10,000
(60,000)	.....	.....	2,000	8,000	2,000	14,000	10,000	12,000	12,000
.....	(30,000)	.....	500	16,000	500	4,000	2,000	3,000	4,000
.....	.....	(60,000)	4,500	7,000	7,000	14,000	4,000	7,500	16,000
.....	.....	.....	(40,000)	.....	.....	.....	.....	.....	.....
.....	.....	.....	.....	(85,000)	2,500	45,000	10,000	7,500	20,000
.....	.....	.....	.....	.....	(5,000)	.....	.....	.....	.....
.....	.....	.....	.....	.....	(50,000)	.....	.....	.....	.....
.....	.....	.....	.....	.....	.....	(90,000)	.....	.....	.....
.....	.....	.....	.....	.....	.....	(30,000)	.....	.....	.....
.....	.....	.....	.....	.....	.....	(127,000)	.....	.....	.....
.....	.....	.....	.....	.....	.....	.....	(20,000)	.....	.....
.....	.....	.....	.....	.....	.....	.....	(10,000)	.....	.....
.....	.....	.....	.....	.....	.....	.....	(56,000)	.....	.....
.....	.....	.....	.....	.....	.....	.....	.....	(15,000)	.....
.....	.....	.....	.....	.....	.....	.....	.....	(20,000)	.....
.....	.....	.....	.....	.....	.....	.....	.....	(55,000)	.....
.....	.....	.....	.....	.....	.....	.....	.....	.....	(40,000)
.....	.....	.....	.....	.....	.....	.....	.....	.....	(40,000)
.....	.....	.....	.....	.....	.....	.....	.....	.....	(92,000)

Figure 3.6 (Cont.)   Calculation of Product Cost Using Activity-Based Costing for Cost Assignment

Activity Center 420. Now a total of $90,000 of costs have passed through the Machining Activity Center in October. These costs were all assigned to products: materials costs using the physical materials, labor costs using the employees' time, and other costs using machining hours as its cost driver.

Total product costs can be accumulated from all activity centers that can trace costs directly to products. The list of costs for Product A totals $112,100.

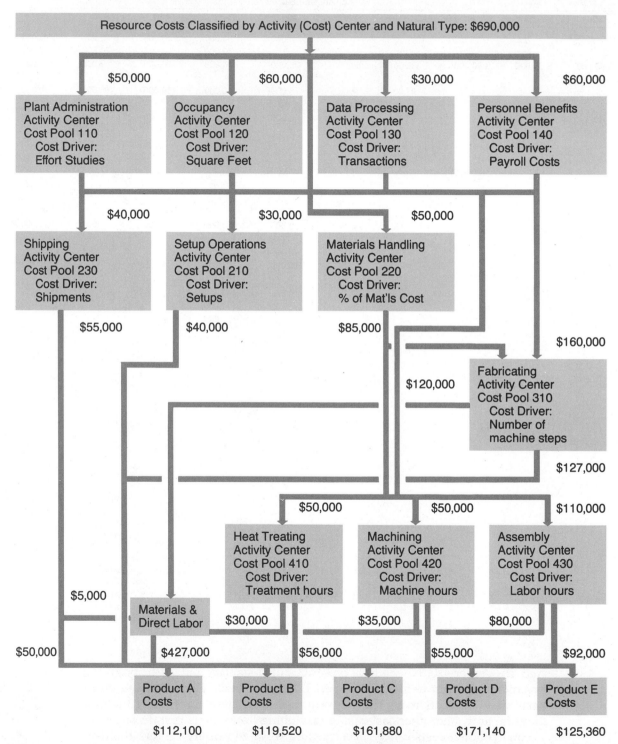

Figure 3.7 Diagram of Activity Centers, Cost Flows, and Product Costs

During October, 22,000 units were produced giving a cost per unit of $5.0955. Product A production report for October would appear as follows:

Product: Product A	**Units produced:** 22,000 units	
Period: October 1995		

	Costs Incurred	Cost Per Unit
Materials costs:		
Fabricating	$ 10,000	$ .4545
Heat treating.............................	3,000	.1364
Machining	5,000	.2273
Assembly	12,000	.5455
Shipping	1,000	.0455
Total	$ 31,000	$1.4092
Labor costs:		
Fabricating	$ 12,000	$ .5455
Heat treating............................	2,000	.0909
Machining	2,000	.0909
Assembly	8,000	.3636
Total	$ 24,000	$1.0909
Other costs:		
Setup costs.............................	$ 1,000	$ .0455
Fabricating overhead costs	13,000	.5909
Heat treating overhead costs	11,200	.5091
Machining overhead costs	11,000	.5000
Assembly overhead costs................	18,400	.8364
Shipping costs	2,500	.1136
Total	$ 57,100	$2.5955
Total product costs	$112,100	$5.0956*

* Difference due to rounding the individual cost per unit costs.

Comparing ABC to Traditional Costing

As discussed, traditional costing systems often paid less attention to the cause and effect relationships between resources used and production activities. Assume that the prior costing system in use by Freeman Metal Products assigned overhead costs to products using direct labor dollars. Let us also assume that the preliminary cost assignment steps would be the same under either approach. This is a simplifying assumption since traditional cost systems would probably have used more arbitrary bases for facility-level costs than the ABC system. Using direct labor dollars as the only cost driver is a common approach to assigning overhead. Since $420,000 of total overhead costs were incurred and total direct labor was $100,000, an overhead rate of $4.20 for each $1 of direct labor would be added to each product. If costs were grouped by materials, direct labor, and overhead, the product costs would be as follows:

	Total	Product A	Product B	Product C	Product D	Product E
Direct materials	$170,000	$ 31,000	$ 15,500	$ 68,000	$ 36,600	$ 18,900
Direct labor.	100,000	24,000	19,000	17,000	20,000	20,000
Overhead costs						
(420 % of labor).	420,000	100,800	79,800	71,400	84,000	84,000
Total product costs	$690,000	$155,800	$114,300	$156,400	$140,600	$122,900
Units produced		22,000	15,000	40,000	6,000	3,000
Traditional cost per unit		$7.0818	$7.6200	$3.9100	$23.4333	$40.9667
ABC cost per unit from above		$5.0955	$7.9680	$4.0470	$28.5233	$41.7867
Difference:						
Traditional minus ABC costs		$1.9863	$(.3480)	$(.1370)	$(5.0900)	$(.8200)
Percentage of ABC cost.		39.0 %	(4.4 %)	(3.4 %)	(17.8%)	(2.0 %)

A dramatic picture appears. Using a costing system very common in many companies today, two of five products have large cost differences—Products A and D. Freeman had been using a cost overstated by 39 percent when selling Product A. This is a far more profitable product than Freeman management had thought. Freeman may be losing Product A business because of its higher than necessary price.

Notice that four of the five products have higher costs under ABC. These products are less profitable than previously thought—particularly Product D. Product D is low volume with many setups and high shipping costs. Under traditional costing, set-up costs and shipping costs were rolled into the total overhead and not traced to specific products. Products B, C, D, and E prices might need to be raised to cover their actual use of production resources.

Whether ABC costs are "correct" or not, they would appear to be more accurate than the traditional costs. ABC makes a greater effort to match resource use, costs, activities, and products.

COST MANAGEMENT ISSUES

In Chapter 1 we defined cost management as the process of managing the activities that cause the incurrence of costs. This implies managing both the activities and the amounts of costs tied to those activities. When management implements a cost management system in an organization, it needs a foundation on which to build. The appropriate foundation assumes that cost management has the following four objectives:

1.   To measure the cost of the resources consumed in performing the organization's significant activities.
2.   To identify and eliminate non-value-added costs. We often focus on production time to find non-value-added effort. Activities and their costs that can be eliminated without deterioration of product quality and value increase profitability and can reduce total production time.

3. To determine efficiency and effectiveness performance measures for all cost generating activities.

4. To identify and evaluate activities that can improve performance at any stage of the product life cycle.

The first objective was the subject of our discussion on activity-based costing. Issues regarding the remaining objectives are presented in the following sections.

Non-Value-Added Costs

An emphasis of cost management on activities can help management to identify non-value-added costs and eliminate the activities that cause them. This is often called waste—any resource-using activity that does not add value. A key goal of production managers is to eliminate waste and, thereby, have an efficient and productive operation.

Time is perhaps the most valuable manufacturing resource. Study of non-value-added time in manufacturing operations takes the following six forms: process time, inspection time, move time, wait time, storage time, and product flow time.

Process time is the time during which a product is undergoing conversion activities which transform raw materials into finished products. Although most people view process time as the sum of many value-added activities, the presence of inefficiency or other nonproductive time represents non-value-added activities. Managers must continually review processes to catch inefficiencies that can creep in over time and to change processes to improve throughput.

Just-in-time production concepts are fundamental building blocks for reducing process time. Many companies have physically reorganized their factories to encourage faster throughput. Figure 3-8 illustrates a restructuring of a plant to reduce process time. The traditional plant has large inventories, much material movement within the plant, and a mixing of fabricating and assembly tasks. The just-in-time plant produces only when parts and products are needed, carries narrow safety stock inventories, has a north-to-south flow of production, and organizes production around product families (similar production requirements). Effort is made to integrate manufacturing with product design, production engineering and planning, and cost analysis.

The implication is that greater output can be achieved with the same equipment, people, and space—waste is reduced.

Inspection time is the amount of time spent assuring that the product is of high quality. Typically, materials and components are inspected upon arrival. Then inspection occurs at various points during and at the conclusion of the production process. It is difficult to say whether inspection procedures result in non-value-added costs without detailed knowledge of the production technology and inspection procedures. However, many companies are striving to reduce the costs of maintaining product quality and are working virtually to eliminate the costs of reworking defective products. Consequently, we see zero defects and total quality control programs to sensitize employees to the need for eliminating spoiled and defective units. The argument is that quality is built into and not inspected into the product.

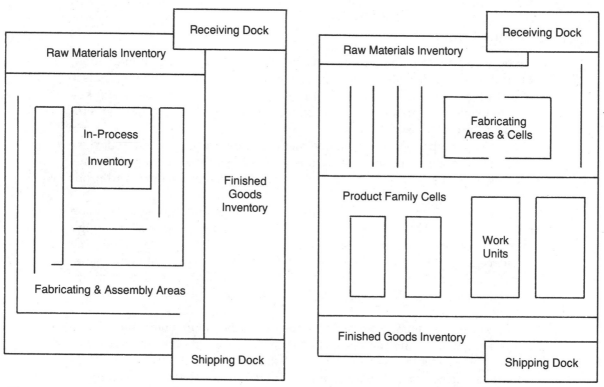

Traditional Factory Layout With Large Materials, In-Process, and Finished Goods Inventories

Just-In-Time Factory Layout With a Pull-Through Flow, Few Inventories, and Integrated Manufacturing

Figure 3.8   Traditional Factory Versus Just-In-Time Factory Layouts

Move time is the time spent moving raw materials, work in process, or finished products between operations within the plant. This includes the activities associated with receiving materials, moving them into storage, moving materials and components to the first production operation, moving partially completed products from one work center to the next or from one department to another, and moving the completed product to the finished goods storage area to await shipping. Many companies refer to these activities as material-handling operations. Move time is a non-value-added activity. A certain amount of move time is necessary in any production process but proper sequencing of operations and tasks and implementing automation technologies can significantly reduce move time. Figure 3.8 illustrates the importance of an efficient flow through the factory to minimize materials movement.

Wait time is the amount of time that materials or work in process spend waiting for the next operation. This includes the time that materials, components, and partially completed product spend in queues immediately preceding an operation and in holding areas located near or next to each department waiting for the next production operation. Wait time potentially represents a significant non-value-added cost. A company's working capital is tied up in work in process, and space is unnecessarily wasted on numerous production queues and holding areas. Even in the simple diagrams in Figure 3.8, we can see that space released from having inventory sitting around waiting for the next production step can be used to expand production. The ultimate goal of just-in-time inventory and production philosophy is to eliminate wait time completely. Japanese companies using Kanban and JIT systems have proven that remarkable reductions in in-process inventories can be made. For example, a car assembly plant producing seventy cars per hour may have less than one hour's supply of engines in the plant at any time. In Detroit, a car begins its two hour trip along an assembly line while in a supplier's seating plant an electronic message is received to trigger assembly of that car's seats. The seats are built and delivered to the car assembly line before the car arrives at the seat installation point.

Storage time is the time during which finished products are held in stock before shipment to customers. It includes the time products spend in storage and the time spent in packaging activities in preparing final products for shipment. Traditionally, companies have stored large inventories of finished products to avoid stock outs. Similar to waiting time, storage time ties up a company's working capital in inventories and requires large amounts of space devoted to storage activities. While not applicable to all manufacturing operations, produce-to-order is a goal—produce products only after a sales order is received. Improvements in order entry systems and shortened lead times in production scheduling can give the appearance of a produce-to-order operation.

Product flow time is the clock time for an average unit to go from the beginning of the production process to completion and shipment. This time is equal to productive time plus wasted time, such as moving, waiting, or setting up. More specifically, it is the processing time plus inspection time plus waiting time plus move time.

Performance Measurement

As changes occur in the operating environment, the traditional measures of performance are being re-examined. New measures are being adopted to better fit the concepts of activity-based costing and cost management. In addition, accountants are measuring performance in new areas of operations, areas that have normally been outside of the accountants' domain or are new because of needs that innovative and automated environments create. This section gives a glimpse of some of the critical changes taking place.

Nonfinancial Measures   Accountants have traditionally focused on financial measures of performance, such as variations from budgeted or standard costs. Such measures are still important, but a broader evaluation including nonfinancial measures are necessary. For example, physical measures (such as cycle time, value-added direct labor, or defective product rates) are playing greater roles in helping managers achieve high quality and competitive operations. To illustrate, let's look at measures for cycle time, value-added direct labor, and labor content.

Manufacturing cycle efficiency (MCE) is a measure of the amount of product flow time which consists of process time. It is the following ratio:

$$\text{Manufacturing cycle efficiency} = \frac{\text{Process time}}{\text{Product flow time}}$$

Remember that product flow time is the sum of process time, inspection time, wait time, and move time. The goal is to keep MCE as high as possible. Although 100 percent is the theoretic ideal, the operations of many manufacturing companies range from the 60 to 90 percent levels and the percentage cannot improve without major restructuring.

The total labor expended for the benefit of the product or service is segregated into direct and indirect labor. **Direct labor** is all labor that can be specifically identified with a product or service in an economically feasible manner. **Value-added direct labor** is that portion of direct labor that changes raw materials into a finished product or service that is delivered to a customer. For example, value-added direct labor fabricates, assembles, and finishes products. Non-value-added labor moves, inspects, stores, examines, or otherwise handles the products without adding customer value. **Indirect labor** is labor that is not readily traced to a product or service. Indirect workers supervise, repair, manage, purchase, inspect, record, advise, or otherwise support the direct workers. Traditionally, indirect workers are non-value-added. In labor-intensive activities, one measure of performance for labor is the **value-added labor ratio** or ratio of value-added time to total time:

$$\text{Value-added labor ratio} = \frac{\text{Value-added direct labor}}{\text{Total direct and indirect labor}}$$

The ratio also may be computed in terms of number of employees or payroll. One goal is to reduce the number of supervisors, managers, clerical staff, accountants, engineers, inspectors, and all others that are non-value-added workers.

In many operations, direct labor is being replaced by automated equipment, and indirect labor now includes technicians needed to program, set up, and maintain the equipment. Often, the distinction between direct and indirect is blurred or eliminated. Team approaches to production (work units or product family cells as shown in Figure 3.8), guaranteed wage labor contracts, and broader job classifications have further eroded the importance of direct labor as a cost group. In fact, another labor performance measure is the percentage of total labor cost in the total product cost or the **labor content percentage:**

$$\text{Labor content percentage} = \frac{\text{Total direct and indirect labor}}{\text{Total product cost}}$$

The goal would be to reduce this percentage and increase the productivity of all labor dollars.

Many more nonfinancial measures are necessary. Some measures currently exist while others are developed as managers perceive the need. We have presented only a few ideas of nonfinancial measures to show some of the changes that are currently taking place in identifying better performance measures.

Product Quality   Customers are demanding quality products. Although quality can be improved by implementing a just-in-time philosophy throughout purchasing and production activities, certain measures of performance for quality are necessary. One common financial measure is a period report covering the costs budgeted and incurred for quality assurance activities. A number of nonfinancial measures are also helpful in assessing and maintaining quality. Customer acceptance measures, for instance, focus on the extent to which a company's customers perceive its product to be of high quality. These include such measures as counts of customer complaints, warranty claims, products returned, and repeat sales. In-process quality measures look at product quality during production. Rework, defects, and scrap measures are used to keep these items to a minimum. Products are also selected at random or statistically sampled during the various stages of production for testing. Defect rates are measured, and corrective actions specified.

A third area of quality relates to purchased materials and parts. The pressure is on purchasing agents to acquire high quality inputs to meet materials requirements at low costs. One measure is the rating of suppliers on the basis of the quality of their materials, delivery performance, and customer service. Also, waste, scrap, and defects occurring during production that are traceable to materials are identified with specific suppliers.

Productivity   Increasing pressure from global competition has caused many companies to focus on better measures of productivity. The most common measure of productivity is the relationship of inputs to outputs. Traditionally, accountants have associated productivity with variances calculated for quantity, efficiency, mix, yield, and capacity. In other words, the goal was cost minimization. In other cases, measures were developed that were nothing more than quantities of output divided by quantities of inputs. Today, we are looking for more detailed, meaningful measures. Activity-based costing can pinpoint high cost activities. Engineers can design for greater production efficiency and defect elimination. For example, a machine manufacturer might look for the number of machines produced per day per employee. A car assembly operation might look for the square footage required per day per car. An electrical generating plant might keep track of the tons of coal required to generate a thousand kilowatt hours of electricity. The measures are oriented toward specific activities and evaluate management control over these activities.

Computer-integrated manufacturing (CIM) is an attempt to optimize the entire plant's production by planning which departments will produce which parts and products in what order and when. Formerly, each department's efficiency was measured and keeping all departments running at full speed was the goal. Now in CIM, certain departments may be idled until their resources are needed. This is "pull through" production and part of the JIT philosophy. Produce only what is needed immediately. Performance measures must therefore evaluate a unit based on its production assignment, not necessarily its capacity. Responsibility for productivity is now moved to higher management levels and away from the individual activity center or cost center manager.

Inventory Reduction   Huge investments in inventories, ordering costs, and carrying costs can include significant amounts of non-value-added costs. To remain price competitive, every effort is needed to reduce or eliminate inventories. The just-in-time philosophy focuses on keeping inventories at low or zero levels for materials and parts at every stage of production. Therefore, inventory control measures are used to minimize non-value-added costs. Such measures may include average inventory values, average time that various categories of materials are held or inventories are standing in a production operations, and inventory turnovers. Measures like the manufacturing cycle efficiency also relate to inventory reduction because nonprocessing time—inspection, move, and wait times—is much of the reason why inventories exist.

Machine Maintenance   If our efforts to reduce inventories are successful, we shift our focus to the company's capability of producing goods quickly. We must keep production equipment and machinery operating. Therefore, performance measures will look at machine down time, machine availability, and maintenance schedules. Some companies even make a distinction between bottleneck and non-bottleneck machinery. A bottleneck operation is one that limits the production capacity of the entire facility. It is vital that the machinery in bottleneck operations be available 100 percent of the time, excluding time for routine required maintenance.

Delivery Performance   As a final point, assume that we have done a super job of reducing many non-value-added activities and eliminating others. Still, we are not successful until quality product is delivered on time and at the right place to the customer. Some companies have a goal of filling 100 percent of their orders on time. Common measures of delivery performance include the percentage of orders filled, the percentage of on-time deliveries, and the average time between the receipt of a customer order and delivery of the goods. Monitoring customer back orders also tells us how many orders were not filled from stock or on time and how long a customer had to wait for an order. A desirable piece of information often impossible to measure is business lost because of delivery failure. Many managers believe that the "competitive ball game" is won or lost with product quality and delivery performance.

Product Life-Cycle Costs

A new area of cost management is product life-cycle costing, which is the accumulation of costs for activities that occur over the entire life cycle of a product. A product's life cycle begins with its inception, and continues through five stages: product planning, preliminary design, detailed design, production, and product logistics support. In our traditional cost accounting systems, we have accumulated only those costs related to production, only one of the five stages. As product life cycles become shorter, due to rapid technological change, the costs of the other stages are gaining in significance. And, the major portion of these costs is committed early in the product's life cycle. We are now at the point where the costs of each stage should be accumulated and identified with the product.

RESPONSIBILITY ACCOUNTING

Responsibility accounting has no universal definition, but it does mean that the accounting system is focused on managerial concerns. "Responsibility" implies that a manager's actions are controlled by comparing actual performance to a plan. Plans are created by managers for their respective areas of responsibility and are compared to their actual results for those areas. Authority and control are linked through responsibility for planning, executing, reporting, and analyzing.

A responsibility accounting system brings discipline to planning and control tasks. These same basic elements remain very visible from accounting systems in small firms to the most sophisticated planning systems in large, complex organizations.

The basic elements of responsibility accounting are:

1. Responsibility center identification (often defined as activity centers as in activity-based costing or more generally as cost, profit, or investment centers)—to segment the organization into small sets of similar activities.
2. Chart of accounts classification—to classify accounting data by their natural characteristics.
3. Budgeting system—to create a quantitative plan of action that sets approved revenue, expense, and other financial performance levels.
4. Control-based reports—to report actual versus plan for expenses, revenues, and other financial and activity measures such as cost drivers.
5. A roll-up reporting capability—to summarize lower level units at higher management levels along responsibility channels.

The budgeting system is discussed at length in Chapters 7 and 8. But it must be recognized here that management planning and control depend heavily on a well-developed budgeting process. A basic budget system also includes:

1. A planning schedule—to establish responsibility for planning tasks, a timetable, and required reviews and approvals.

2.   Involvement of all managers—to allow people who know situations best to create the budget and to build their commitments to the plan.

3.   Follow-up and plan updating steps—to review budget variances and to revise and extend the plan.

Strictly speaking, cost control is not so much a control of costs as it is a control over the people who incur the costs. No one likes to be controlled; however, any effort, if it is to be successful, depends on the willingness of people to accept certain objectives. For purposes of cost control, the relevant costs are the costs that can be identified with the individual who controls, authorizes, or causes the incurrence of costs.

In Chapter 2, we defined the terms controllable and noncontrollable. The definitions are now linked to organizational structure and to performance assessment.

Responsibility Centers

From an organizational viewpoint, responsibility accounting focuses attention on a responsibility center. A **responsibility center:**

1.   Is any organizational unit where management control exists over incurring cost or generating revenue. Organizational units may be departments, plants, divisions, subsidiaries, groups, or an entire organization.

2.   Is any organization that has a specific manager responsible for its activities.

Other terms are used to identify various types of responsibility centers. They are activity center (a term defined earlier in the chapter), cost center, profit center, and investment center. Figure 3.9 illustrates the three types of responsibility centers plus activity centers.

A **cost center** is a responsibility center where control exists over incurring costs. All costs must be assigned to a cost center. A cost center is the smallest unit of an organization around which costs are accumulated. Often, the unit is defined by an organization chart. Yet, when needed, even organizational units can be further subdivided into more cost centers if costs can better be grouped for planning, control, or costing purposes. The discussion on defining activity centers in activity-based costing is directly tied to responsibility accounting here. If a cost center is determined to have several cost drivers, it should be divided into more cost centers or activity centers so that homogeneous activities and costs can be grouped together.

A **profit center** is a responsibility center where control exists over generating revenue. A profit center manager has both cost and revenue responsibilities. Often, sales organizations are profit centers, or at least exert some contribution margin responsibility. Managers with product line responsibility might include both manufacturing and marketing. Managers of branches or regions have both sales and expense control and are profit centers.

An **investment center** is a responsibility center where control exists over costs, revenues, and the investment in assets used or managed. Typically, divisions of large organizations may be viewed by top management as essentially a separate business entity. Managers are given responsibility for revenues and expenses plus the authority to acquire or dispose of assets.

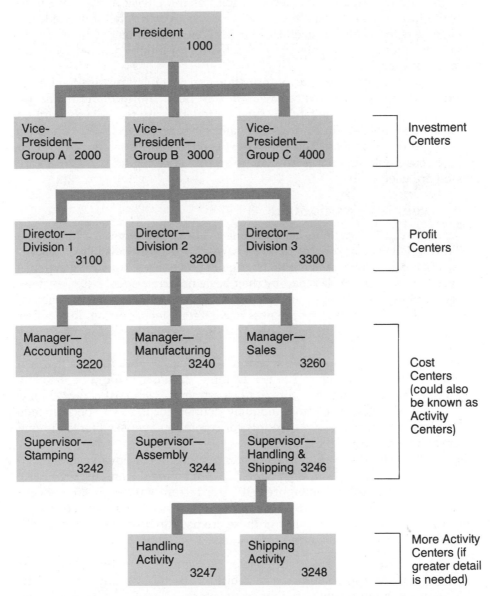

Figure 3.9   Responsibility Centers: Investment Centers, Profit Centers and Cost Centers Including Activity Centers

Identifying Cost Centers

In many cases cost centers parallel the boxes on the organization chart. Figure 3.9 also illustrates the linkage between a firm's organization chart and its cost center coding. The organization chart structure and grouping of operating activities should be studied before cost centers are defined. A logic is often applied to the numbering system—different parts of the organization, levels of management, superior/subordinate links, etc. For example, the first digit indicates the Group structure; the second indicates the Division; the third indicates the functional area; and the last digit gives greater detail if needed. If a manager is responsible for several activities in one cost center, a further breakdown can be made to separate different activities for linking a cost driver with the costs of each activity.

Too many cost centers cut key information and cost relationships too finely. Yet, data aggregation and summarization start here. If important details are lost initially, they are gone forever. Cost centers that are too broadly defined will lose detail needed for control and many other purposes in later analyses including product costing. The same cost-benefit comparisons done in activity-based costing to determine how many activity centers and cost drivers are needed are used here.

Chart of Accounts Classifications

Designing a chart of accounts is hardly one of life's exciting tasks. However, a carefully detailed chart of accounts is the second half of responsibility accounting's classification system. But equal budgeting focus is on operating expense accounts. Expenses are classified by their basic nature: wages, supplies, telephone, repairs, depreciation, etc. Again too much detail smothers analysis, and too few accounts loses the fineness needed for later reporting. Remember that the chart of accounts is tied to the cost center structure giving a two-way expense classification.

Figure 3.10 presents a sample structure of a chart of accounts for the firm organized as shown in Figure 3.9. For example, 3248-6320 would be the code for equipment repairs in the Shipping Department. Each cost center should have its set of expense accounts uniquely defined for its own special needs while using identical expense accounts for common expenses like telephone expense in every cost center.

Figure 3.11, shown on page 106, is a cost center report from an actual metal forming factory. This is from Cost Center 3242 in Figure 3.9 and uses the basic chart of accounts outlined in Figure 3.10. This factory has nearly 80 cost centers. Approximately four hundred different expense accounts are used in various cost centers. Twenty to thirty of these are used in a typical cost center.

Several observations about the control report in Figure 3.11:

1. The breakdown among controllable, semicontrollable, and allocated is an excellent approach to signal which costs and variances should be analyzed more carefully in that cost center.
2. The monthly and year-to-date comparisons of actual to budget give a look at the current situation, the annual trend, and the size of the variances from budget.
3. Cost drivers that relate overhead costs to products or to other activities in the plant are given at the bottom of the report. Budget and actual activity levels help interpret the results.

PARTIAL CHART OF ACCOUNTS

1000	Assets	5000	Selling & Administrative Expenses
1100	Cash	5100	Salary Expenses
1110	Checking Accounts	5110	Manager Salary Expense
•	•	5120	Staff Salary Expense
1200	Accounts Receivable	•	•
•	•	5400	Advertising Expense
•	•	•	•
1300	Inventories	6000	Manufacturing Expense
•	•	6100	Direct Manufacturing Expenses
2000	Liabilities	6110	Direct Labor Wages
•	•	6160	Direct Materials
•	•	6200	Manufacturing Overhead
3000	Equities	6210	Machine Expenses
•	•	6211	Machine Setup
•	•	•	•
4000	Revenues	6320	Repairs Expenses—Equipment
4100	Product Line A	•	•
4110	Product A-1	6520	Depreciation Expenses—Equipment
•	•	•	•
4900	Miscellaneous Revenue	7000	Gain and Loss Items

Figure 3.10   Sample Chart of Accounts Structure

Other minor but interesting items appear:

1. Probably a classification error was made in September for a repair of equipment. It was charged to 330 Repairs—Dies & Fixtures and created an over budget variance while 320 Repairs—Equipment shows an under budget variance of about the same amount.

2. The overall performance of manager Kannisoni in the controllable and semicontrollable categories was very close to the budget for September. But because of an extraordinarily large charge in 6780 General Reallocations, the cost center's total expenses appear to be about $6,000 over budget. Manager Kannisoni should not be penalized for this noncontrollable expense overrun.

While the inclusion of the allocated expenses section may be useful for accounting completeness or for product costing purposes, it has little useful managerial impact. Including allocated costs in the manager's responsibility report violates the basic principle of responsibility accounting—account for what you control. It would be better behaviorally if these expenses never appeared on the cost center report.

Management has other options in presenting reports for responsibility centers. One possibility is to segregate variable and fixed costs for each line item so that potentially two cost lines would appear for each cost category.

Cost Center: Stamping
Cost Center #: 3242

Period: September 94
Manager: I. Kannisoni

	Monthly Actual	Budget	(Over) or Under	Year-to-Date Actual	Budget	(Over) or Under
Workers	12.0	12.0	0	11.3	11.5	.2
Direct labor hours	1920	2016	96	16450	17460	1010
6110 Direct Labor Cost	23465	24192	727	206211	209520	3309
6160 Direct Materials Used	0	0	0	0	0	0
Overhead expenses:						
Controllable expenses:						
6211 Machine Setup	3703	3424	(279)	29920	30608	688
6212 Down Time	1076	1680	604	13357	13286	(71)
6215 Maintenance Labor	430	639	209	4205	3016	(1189)
6245 Hourly Overtime Premium	761		(761)	3094		(3094)
6271 Hourly Fringe Benefits	11222	12000	778	106112	103506	(2606)
6330 Repairs—Dies & Fixtures	10671	7319	(3352)	78971	77446	(1525)
6351 Abrasives & Lubricants	8	20	12	708	236	(472)
6369 Miscellaneous Expense	110	140	30	1193	1198	5
6441 Rework	68	22	(46)	479	206	(273)
6443 Scrap	1247	1242	(5)	8730	13827	5097
Total controllable expenses	29296	26486	(2810)	246769	243329	(3440)
Semicontrollable expenses:						
6220 Other Indirect Labor	1807	1658	149	14740	14219	(521)
6243 Hourly Union Time	691	731	40	6371	6513	142
6260 Salaries	2507	2045	(462)	16914	18105	1191
6272 Salaried Benefits	424	518	94	4138	4812	674
6320 Repairs—Equipment	7066	10069	3003	82987	80253	(2734)
6420 Factory Utilities	337	139	(198)	2564	3888	1324
Total semicontrol. expenses	12832	15160	2328	127714	127790	76
Allocated expenses:						
6510 Depreciation—Building	271	117	(154)	1588	962	(626)
6520 Depreciation—Equipment	4070	4070	0	36630	36630	0
6540 Property Taxes	1342	1342	0	12078	12078	0
6770 Warranty			0			0
6780 General Reallocations	33945	27653	(6292)	260230	244201	(16029)
Total allocated expenses	39628	33182	(6446)	310526	293871	(16655)
Cost center overhead	81756	74828	(6928)	685009	664990	(20019)
Total cost center expenditures	105221	99020	(6201)	891220	874510	(16710)
Activity measures:						
Number of stampings (000)	179.7	175.0	4.7	1563	1575	(12)
Tons of materials processed	145.1	150.0	(4.9)	1320	1350	(30)
Operating machine hours	1145.0	1209.6	(64.6)	10419	10476	(57)

Figure 3.11   Example of a Cost Center Control Report

Pyramid Reporting

A pyramid reporting structure is used to report on each individual's area of responsibility. Individuals at the bottom of the organization chart receive reports on individual activities within their area of control. Individuals in middle and upper levels of management receive reports containing summary information on the results of individual activities over which they have control.

The report in Figure 3.11 is reviewed by manager Kannisoni's superior. The results of this cost center would be summarized at the next higher level, in the control report for Cost Center 3240 Manager of Manufacturing in Figure 3.9. All cost centers for Division 2 are summarized in the control report for profit center 3200 along with other Division 2 responsibility centers. Division 2 is summarized in the Group B Vice-President's investment center report along with all divisions reporting to the group vice-president. All responsibility centers eventually report to the President in the firm-wide control reports. In all reports, actual is compared to budget on monthly and year-to-date bases.

SUMMARY

Activity-based costing is a system of accounting that focuses on activities performed to produce products. This makes activities the primary building block in cost accumulation. Cost drivers are used to identify costs with activities and to identify activities with products. Preliminary-stage cost drivers assign support activity costs to other activity centers. Primary-stage cost drivers relate costs of activities to products.

In designing an activity-based costing system, five basic steps are followed. First, assemble similar actions into activity groups. This process involves categorizing activities as unit level, batch level, product level, and facility level. Second, classify costs by activity group and by kind of expense. Third, select the appropriate preliminary stage and primary stage cost drivers. The purpose of this process is to eliminate distortions in the cost allocations to product that result from product mix complexity. Activity-based costing considers the possible inaccuracies caused by product diversity and batch-size diversity. Fourth, calculate a cost function to link costs and the cost driver activity. Finally, fifth, assign the costs to the cost objective—often the product cost.

Cost management is the process of managing the activities that cause the incurrence of costs. This implies managing both the activities and the amounts of costs tied to those activities. In performing cost management, four key objectives are essential: (1) measure the cost of resources consumed in significant activities; (2) identify and eliminate non-value-added costs; (3) determine the efficiency and effectiveness performance measures for all cost generating activities; and (4) identify and evaluate activities that can improve performance at any product life-cycle stage.

The emphasis on value-added costs means reviewing activities and eliminating those that do not add value to the product. The product flow time is composed of process time, inspection time, move time, waiting time, and storage time. The most common place to look for non-value-added activities is in inspection, move, waiting, and storage time.

As changes occur in the operating environment of organizations, other areas are being examined for improvements. Managements are currently focusing on performance measurement, product life-cycle costs, and justifying capital expenditures.

Responsibility accounting is an approach to accountability that identifies costs with the responsible person. First, responsibility centers are identified. Second, costs are classified by controllability and by type. Third, a budget sets targets and limits. Fourth, control reports are prepared to show budget versus actual and variances. Thus, planned and actual performance is tied to a specific person.

PROBLEMS FOR REVIEW

Review Problem A

Wacker Company has identified the following activity centers and preliminary stage cost drivers:

Activity Center	Cost Driver
Purchasing	Number of purchase orders
Material handling	Number of parts
Setups	Number of setups
Cutting	Number of parts
Assembly	Direct labor hours
Painting	Number of units painted

Two customer orders came in for the month. The cost drivers appearing on each order are as follows:

	Order 1	Order 2
Number of purchase orders	1	2
Number of parts	10	5
Number of setups	3	1
Direct labor hours	25	15
Number of units painted	12	24

Required:

Assuming the company traditionally allocated all of these costs using direct labor hours, how would activity-based costing, with the above cost drivers, improve the allocation of costs to products on the two customer orders?

Solution:

Only one activity center, Assembly, uses direct labor hours to link costs with orders. Direct labor hours do not represent any of the other activity centers. Order 1 would receive 62.5 percent of the combined costs because it uses that portion of total direct labor hours. Consequently, the costs charged to both orders will be distorted.

By identifying each activity center separately with its own cost driver, the company has a better measure of resources consumed for each customer order. Order 2 will receive twice the purchasing cost; Order 1, twice the material handling and cutting costs; Order 1, three times the setup cost; and Order 2 twice the painting cost. A better matching of resources consumed on each order is achieved by using activity-based costing.

Review Problem B

Mike Schwartz is responsible for the Finishing Activity Center at Alexus Plumbing Fixtures. A budget for the center for July, 1995 is as follows:

Materials and supplies	$ 9,640
Labor	7,320
Supervision	3,000
Fuel	1,680
Telephone	430
Postage	260
Taxes and insurance	1,750
Heat and light	1,540
Repairs and maintenance	1,870
Depreciation—equipment	900
Other allocated plant costs	3,400
Total	$31,790

The actual cost of materials and supplies for the month was $9,570; labor, $7,480; and fuel, $1,710. Telephone amounted to $480. Repairs and maintenance cost was $1,850. Heat and light cost was $1,600, and the other allocated plant costs were $5,700. All other costs were in agreement with the budget.

The cost of supervision, taxes and insurance, heat and light, depreciation of equipment, and other allocated plant costs are not controllable by Schwartz.

Required:
Prepare a responsibility report showing a comparison of the actual and budgeted costs for July. Separate the controllable costs from the uncontrollable costs in the report.

Solution:

Report: Cost Center Performance Report   **Date:** July, 1995
Cost Center: Finishing Activity Center   **Manager:** Mike Schwartz

	Actual	Budget	Over/ (Under) Variance
Controllable costs:			
Materials and supplies	$ 9,570	$ 9,640	$ (70)
Labor	7,480	7,320	160
Fuel	1,710	1,680	30
Telephone	480	430	50
Postage	260	260	0
Repairs and maintenance	1,850	1,870	(20)
Total controllable costs	$21,350	$21,200	$ 150

	Actual	Budget	Over/ (Under) Variance
Noncontrollable costs:			
Supervision................................	$ 3,000	$ 3,000	$ 0
Taxes and insurance.......................	1,750	1,750	0
Heat and light............................	1,600	1,540	60
Depreciation—equipment...................	900	900	0
Other allocated plant costs.................	5,700	3,400	2,300
Total noncontrollable costs.................	$12,950	$10,590	$2,360
Total cost center costs	$34,300	$31,790	$2,510

TERMINOLOGY REVIEW

Activity-based costing (ABC) (79)
Activity center (79)
Batch-level activities (81)
Batch-size diversity (86)
Cost center (102)
Cost driver (79)
Direct labor (98)
Facility-level activities (81)
Indirect labor (98)
Inspection time (95)
Investment center (102)
Labor content percentage (98)
Manufacturing cycle efficiency (MCE) (98)

Move time (96)
Preliminary stage cost driver (83)
Primary stage cost driver (83)
Process time (95)
Product diversity (86)
Product flow time (97)
Product-level activities (81)
Profit center (102)
Responsibility center (102)
Storage time (97)
Unit-level activities (81)
Value-added direct labor (98)
Value-added labor ratio (98)
Wait time (97)

QUESTIONS FOR REVIEW AND DISCUSSION

1. Describe the relationship between resources, activities, and products.

2. What is a cost driver? What is its role in tracing costs to products?

3. Identify the five basic steps in applying the definition of activity-based costing.

4. Why are actions grouped into activities instead of being treated individually?

5. Define an activity center. How many activity centers can be in one production department?

6. What is the purpose for grouping actions into specific categories of unit-level activities, batch-level activities, product-level activities, and facility-level activities?

7. Describe the difference between unit-level activities, batch-level activities, and product-level activities.

8. How might the definitions of variable and fixed costs be changed in an activity-based costing system?

9.   Explain the difference between a preliminary stage cost driver and a primary stage cost driver.

10. Explain the purpose of a cost function that will use cost driver data.

11. What is meant by product diversity?

12. How can batch-size diversity influence the costs assigned to products?

13. List the four objectives of a cost management system.

14. What is meant by the term "non-value-added costs"? Give three examples.

15. List and define the six ways that time is spent in a manufacturing process. Which of these types of activities are likely candidates for non-value-added activities? Explain.

16. Define the term "manufacturing cycle efficiency."

17. Explain the value-added labor ratio.

18. What is product quality? Why is it an important consideration to an on-going, profitable company?

19. Why should product life cycles be a consideration in cost management?

20. Identify and describe the basic elements of responsibility accounting.

21. What is a responsibility center?

22. What are the similarities and differences between an activity center, a cost center, and profit center?

23. Why is a well-understood organization chart an important element in responsibility accounting?

24. What is meant by pyramid reporting in responsibility accounting?

EXERCISES

1.   **Grouping of Similar Activities.** Seguin Electronics, Inc. makes an avionics circuit board for private aircraft manufacturers. The production process takes place in three departments. The following costs were budgeted for February:

Computer programming—production	$ 18,000
Custodial wages—plant	4,500
Depreciation—machinery	120,000
Depreciation—plant	60,000
Electricity—machinery	11,600
Electricity—plant	7,400
Engineering design	45,000
Equipment maintenance—wages	14,100
Equipment maintenance—parts and supplies	2,900
Heating—plant	3,200
Inspection—production	3,800
Insurance—plant	10,000
Property taxes	9,300
Raw materials, components, subassemblies	330,000
Set-up wages	14,000

Required:

1. Identify each of the costs listed on page 111 as one of the following:

   (a) A unit-level activity.   (b) A batch-level activity.
   (c) A product-level activity.   (d) A facility-level activity.

2. Specify an appropriate cost driver for tracing to the products the costs as they are associated with the various levels of activities identified above.

2. **Classifying Cost Drivers.** Kerrville Curios Manufacturing has identified the following cost drivers in its operations:

Allocation percentages	Number of orders processed
Labor hours used	Number of parts
Machine hours used	Number of products
Number of batches	Number of setups
Number of employees in each production activity center	Number of units of product

   Required:

   Classify each of the above cost drivers as unit-level, batch-level, product-level or facility-level. If a cost driver would fit more than one category, explain why that would be.

3. **Activity Groupings and Cost Drivers.** Wind-Driven Products, Inc. uses JIT manufacturing and has the production process organized into manufacturing cells where each cell produces either a single product or a major subassembly. Cell workers are responsible for a quality completed product, setting up machinery, and maintaining all machinery in the cell. The following are the costs incurred either within each cell or for the benefit of each cell:

(a) Raw materials	(j) Oil for lubricating machinery
(b) Direct labor	(k) Cell equipment maintenance
(c) Salary of a cell supervisor	(l) Parts for machinery
(d) Salary of the plant manager	(m) Power
(e) Salaries of janitors	(n) Costs to set up machinery
(f) Salary of an industrial engineer	(o) Taxes on plant and equipment
(g) Overtime wages for cell workers	(p) Insurance on plant and equipment
(h) Plant depreciation	(q) Pencils and paper for cell supervisor
(i) Depreciation on machinery	

   Required:

   1. Identify which of the above costs can be identified directly with products without the use of cost drivers.
   2. Group the remaining costs by similar activities.
   3. Identify an appropriate cost driver for assigning the costs of grouped activities to the product. (It is possible for some groupings to have a cost driver to trace the costs to another grouping of activities before assigning costs to products.)

4.   **Cost Driver Identification.** A list of activity groups is shown below:

(a)	Machinery maintenance	(f)	Janitorial
(b)	Storeroom	(g)	Personnel
(c)	Cafeteria	(h)	Purchasing
(d)	Medical clinic	(i)	Inspection
(e)	Day Care	(j)	Computer Services

Required:
For each activity grouping listed, select one or two cost drivers that are logical for tracing costs from the activity grouping to cost objectives and products.

5.   **Preliminary Stage Cost Drivers.** Potter Manufacturing has the following groupings of activities and primary stage cost drivers:

Activity (Cost Center) Grouping	Primary Stage Cost Driver
Purchasing	Number of parts
Production—labor-paced assembly	Direct labor hours
Production—machine-paced assembly	Machine hours
Production—quality testing	Testing hours
Marketing and distribution	Number of finished units sold

The costs that have been identified with "Production—labor-paced assembly" either directly or indirectly are shown below:

(a)   Production manager's salary and office expenses. An analysis of his time shows that he spends 70% on labor-paced assembly, 20% on machine-paced assembly, and 10% on quality testing.
(b)   Supervisor's salary.
(c)   Supplies and other indirect materials costs.
(d)   Repair and maintenance costs. This work is performed by a separate support function called "Maintenance."
(e)   Fringe benefit costs of all workers in the labor-paced assembly activity.
(f)   Heat, light, and power costs.
(g)   Depreciation on equipment.
(h)   Janitorial costs. This work is performed by a separate janitorial support function.
(i)   Plant security costs.
(j)   Plant insurance costs.

Required:
Explain how preliminary cost drivers are used to trace each of the costs to the Production—labor-paced assembly activity grouping. Include in your discussion a suggested cost driver for each cost.

6.   **Impact of Grouping Activities.** Perrington Water Treatment Services has one division that manufactures two models of residential water treatment systems. The controller is considering implementing an activity-based costing system for overhead costs. In looking at the operations for the past year, the following overhead costs were reported:

Materials handling	$120,000
Receiving	40,000
Engineering	90,000
Depreciation on machinery	60,000
Power	30,000
Setups	84,000
Maintenance	80,000
Packing for shipment	35,000
Total	$539,000

The controller is looking at two alternative approaches. The first is to find a cost driver for each cost. The second is to group some of the costs and select a cost driver for the grouping. Tentative groupings and their cost drivers are:

(a) Materials-related costs (Cost driver = Materials dollars):
   Materials handling.
   Receiving.
(b) Engineering (Cost driver = Engineering labor hours).
(c) Manufacturing overhead (Cost driver = Machine hours):
   Depreciation on machinery.
   Power.
   Setups.
   Maintenance.
(d) Packing for shipment (Cost driver = Number of orders shipped).

The following activity information is available for the past year for the two models.

	Standard	Deluxe
Units produced	10,000	20,000
Direct labor hours	10,000	20,000
Machine hours	20,000	40,000
Number of moves for materials handling	2,000	4,000
Engineering labor hours	5,000	3,000
Number of orders received	600	400
Number of setups	70	30
Maintenance hours used	1,500	2,500
Kilowatt hours	15,000	30,000
Number of orders shipped	2,000	3,000
Materials	$80,000	$240,000

Required:
1. Using the costs and activity information, determine how much of the overhead costs would be charged to each model if costs were traced to products under the controller's first alternative.
2. Using the costs and activity information, determine how much of the overhead costs would be charged to each model if costs were traced to products under the controller's second alternative.
3. Explain how grouping of costs influences the costs traced to the products.

7. **Non-Value-Added Costs.** El Paso Denim Jeans, Inc. manufactures denim jeans in a process that passes through three departments. The output of each department is immediately transferred to the next department to await further work in the new department. Output from the last department in the process represents the completed

product, which goes to finished goods inventory to await shipping. Specifically, dyed denim cloth bales are released from the storeroom (materials inventory) and moved to the Cutting Department where the fabric is cut to patterns. The cut pieces are sorted into sets of jeans. Any miscut pieces are scrapped. The sets move to the Stitch and Form Department. There the pieces are sewn together. Thread, zippers, and snaps are added during this process to make the completed jeans. The jeans are sent to the Inspection and Finishing Department. Inspection makes certain jeans meet quality standards; spoiled and defective jeans are removed from the process. Spoiled jeans go to the scrap pile. Inspectors must determine the extent of defect in those jeans considered defective. If the defect can easily be corrected, the jeans go back into the process where the work will be done. If the defect cannot be corrected, the jeans are treated as seconds and are sold in factory outlets and discount stores, unlabeled, as seconds. Those jeans successfully passing inspection move to the labeling tables where brand labels are stitched on each pair of jeans. The completed jeans move to the warehouse where they become part of the finished goods inventory.

Required:
1. Identify the activities in the denim jeans production process that fall into process time, inspection time, move time, wait time, and storage time.
2. List the activities in the denim jeans production process that are candidates for non-value-added activities.

8. **Non-Value-Added Costs in a Doctor's Office.** Dr. Wally Johnson has his own medical practice. He specializes in the treatment of diabetics. His staff consists of a receptionist, two nurses, a lab technician, and a dietitian. As patients enter the outer office, they check in with the receptionist. The patient then waits until called by a nurse. When called, the patient moves from the waiting room to the inner offices. The patient must weigh in and is then assigned a room for the rest of the work and conferences. The nurse assigning the patient to a room gathers all the personal data for updating the medical records, such as insulin dosage, medication, illnesses since last visit, and so forth. The nurse also takes an initial blood sample for blood sugar test and performs a blood pressure test. The patient then waits until the doctor comes in. After the doctor's conference, the nurse returns to take more blood samples, depending on what is ordered by the doctor. The patient then waits until the dietitian comes to review eating habits and talk about how to improve eating and weight control. The patient returns to the receptionist to pay for the office visit and to schedule the next visit.

Required:
1. Identify the activities in the doctor's office that fall into process time, inspection time, move time, wait time, and storage time.
2. List the activities in the doctor's office that are candidates for non-value-added activities. Explain why you classify them as non-value-added activities.

9. **Value-Added Labor.** Joshi, Inc. produces air pumps in a small factory in Green Bay, Wisconsin. The company employs eleven people with nine direct and two indirect laborers. Compensation costs for the nine direct workers are treated as follows:

(a) Three fabricators who cut and grind metal parts from raw steel, aluminum, and brass.
(b) One parts inspector who examines and approves parts produced.
(c) One warehouse stocker who keeps parts in inventory and stocks bins used by assembly workers.

(**d**)   One molder who molds vinyl seals and plastic fittings by using an injection molder.

(**e**)   Two assemblers who assemble parts into product.

(**f**)   One product inspector who inspects the final product.

Required:

1.   Categorize each of the nine workers as value-added or non-value-added workers.

2.   Compute the value-added labor ratio.

10.   **Value-Added Labor.** KATT Country is an FM radio station with the current country hits. The station has the following employees and wages paid for September, 1995:

	Number of Employees	Wages & Salaries	Totals
Lead disc jockeys	8	$2,000	$16,000
Support disc jockeys	9	1,500	13,500
News and weather staff	3	1,700	5,100
Engineering staff	5	2,100	10,500
Supervisors/managers	5	2,300	11,500
Account executives	6	1,200	7,200
Clerical/office staff	4	1,100	4,400
Totals	40		$68,200

Required:

1.   Compute the ratio of value-added employees to total employees in terms of number of employees.

2.   Compute the ratio of value-added employees to total employees in terms of total compensation paid.

11.   **Production Efficiency—Nonfinancial Data.** Adrian Sargent's Advanced Plastics (ASAP) manufactures a wide range of plastic-based products for automobiles, airplanes and boats. The company has the reputation for delivering high-quality products on time. Each month the CFO issues a production efficiency report. The data compiled on these reports for the third quarter of 1995 are as follows:

	July	August	September
Manufacturing cycle efficiency	94%	96%	92%
Total set-up time (in hours)	62	60	58
Overtime hours	70	73	76
Power consumption in kilowatt-hours (000s omitted)	802	832	838
Machine downtime (hours)	15	10	20
Number of unscheduled machine maintenance calls	0	0	1
Inventory value/sales revenue	4%	4%	5%
Number of defective units received in raw materials orders	2	1	0
Number of defective units—in process	35	40	55
Number of defective units—finished goods	18	12	24
Percentage of customer orders filled	100%	100%	100%
Percentage of on-time orders delivered	99%	98%	94%
Number of products returned by customers	0	0	1

Required:

Categorize each of the above nonfinancial performance measures as one of the following:

1. Production processing and productivity.
2. Product quality and customer acceptance.
3. Delivery performance.
4. Inventory control.
5. Machine maintenance.

12. **Evaluation of a Responsibility Report.** Carolina Widget Works prepared the following responsibility report for its milling shop cost center:

CAROLINA WIDGET WORKS
MILLING SHOP COST CENTER
RESPONSIBILITY REPORT
FOR THE WEEK ENDED APRIL 9, 1994

Supervisors responsible: Kelli Tunnell
Brent Droll
Cheryl Broadway

	Budget	Actual	Variance
Direct labor	$ 21,000	$ 21,057	$ 57 U
Materials:			
Metal G1-P20	80,000	79,250	750 F
Metal K8-x10	40,000	41,010	1,010 U
Manufacturing overhead (variable and fixed) . .	29,000	31,000	2,000 U
Allocated administrative costs from the central office	5,100	6,050	950 U
Total costs	$175,100	$178,367	$3,267 U

Required:
Given the concepts of responsibility accounting, evaluate the appropriateness of this report.

13. **Type of Responsibility Centers.** The list below describes a variety of business situations:
    (a) A convenience store that is one of several owned by a chain. The goods to be sold and the selling prices are all determined by the corporate office.
    (b) The assembly department of a private airplane manufacturer.
    (c) The janitorial department of an office furniture manufacturer.
    (d) The women's department in a large retail store. The buyer for the department decides which items are purchased. The supervisor of the women's department decides the selling prices.
    (e) The marketing department of a local TV station.
    (f) The purchasing department for a large electronics company.
    (g) The parts department of an automobile dealership.
    (h) The PC product line produced by a major computer manufacturer that is organized by product lines.
    (i) The technical support department for a large computer software company. Customers can call an 800 number and ask questions about problems they are experiencing with software purchased from the company.
    (j) The car pool operation for a city government. City officials needing cars check out the car for the days of travel.

Required:

For each of the business segments, indicate if it is more likely organized as a cost center, a profit center, or an investment center. State any additional assumptions you feel are necessary in order to classify a situation.

14. **Controllable Versus Noncontrollable in a Responsibility Report.** The costs listed below relate to the Potash Processing Plant, a cost center of Ashco, Inc.

(a) The plant's share of costs incurred by the corporate vice president of manufacturing. The share is an allocation to the plant based on equal shares to all plants under the VP's direction.

(b) Electricity used in the plant.

(c) Depreciation on plant equipment.

(d) Direct labor used in the plant.

(e) Insurance for the plant. The amount of insurance is negotiated by the corporation's Insurance Department. The amount determined in negotiation is paid by the corporate headquarters and charged to the plant.

(f) The revenue received from selling items manufactured by the plant. The corporate Marketing Department finds customers and negotiates selling prices.

(g) Indirect material and supplies used in the plant.

(h) The corporate office maintains a Legal Department. A share of legal costs is allocated to the plant on the basis of the plant's revenue.

(i) Salaries of production foremen. The number of foremen is determined by the number of shifts and the number of direct workers assigned to each shift. The plant manager has final approval of the production schedule.

(j) Cost of space provided for internal auditors. Corporate internal auditors visit the plant each quarter. The plant manager is required to provide ample working space and equipment for the auditors.

Required:

Top management has decided that only those items controllable by a manager will be included in the responsibility report for that manager. Which of the items would be included on the responsibility report for a manager of Potash Processing Plant? Consider each situation independently.

15. **Performance Report with a Budget Formula.** Desert Rat Rentals has one department totally dedicated to dune buggies. The company rents them by the day and mileage. The company's cost analyst developed the following annual budget formula for each cost related to the dune buggies:

Cost Item	Formula
Fuel	$0.25 per mile
Oil	0.10 per mile
Chassis and other lubricants	0.05 per mile plus $ 1,000
Repairs	0.06 per mile plus 1,200
Property taxes	1,300
Depreciation	2,500
Parking fees	2,000
State registration and licenses....................	600
Comprehensive and liability insurance	1,600
Total budget formula	$0.46 per mile plus $10,200

During the year just ended, the records of Desert Rat Rentals show the dune buggies were driven 24,000 miles and the following expenses were incurred:

Fuel	$6,220
Oil	2,515
Chassis and other lubricants	2,190
Repairs	2,705
Property taxes	1,410
Depreciation	2,500
Parking fees	2,400
State registration and licenses	730
Comprehensive and liability insurance	1,600

Required:

Prepare a responsibility performance report for the Dune Buggy Department for the year. Show budget, actual results, and variances.

16. **Responsibility Reporting.** The chart of accounts for Hubert Company shows expense classifications as follows:

5000 Selling Expenses
6000 Manufacturing Expenses
6100   Direct Materials
6200   Direct Labor
6300   Manufacturing Overhead
7000 Administrative Expenses

The following accounts and amounts (with 000s omitted) were taken from the accounting and budgeting records for June:

Acct. No.	Account Name	June Actual	June Budget	Year-to-Date Actual	Year-to-Date Budget
5110	Advertising	$ 125	$ 135	$ 833	$ 810
5120	Bad Debt Expense	37	36	218	216
6310	Depreciation—Factory Machinery	45	45	275	280
7110	Depreciation—Office Equipment	17	16	102	96
6200	Direct Labor	749	751	4,599	4,506
6320	Factory Rent	244	244	1,464	1,464
6330	Factory Utilities	34	33	237	218
6340	Indirect Labor	176	174	1,056	1,044
6100	Direct Materials	1,319	1,388	8,178	8,328
6350	Property Taxes—Factory Machinery	19	21	114	126
7120	Property Taxes—Office Equipment	7	8	42	48
6360	Repairs and Maintenance—Factory	47	50	351	320
7130	Salaries of Administrative Personnel	1,687	1,601	9,122	9,606
5130	Sales Commissions	109	111	754	670

Required:

Prepare a responsibility performance report for manufacturing overhead. Show budget, actual results, and variances for the month and year-to-date.

PROBLEMS

3-1. **Classifying Cost Drivers.** The Sage Company has identified the following cost drivers in its operations:

Direct labor hours   Number of purchase orders sent
Machine hours   Number of purchase orders received
Direct materials dollars   Number of shipments made
Number of products ordered   Number of shipments of materials re-
Number of special components   ceived
Number of set-up hours   Hours of inspections
Number of setups   Number of employees
Sales in dollars and units   Number of heat treatment hours
Number of parts   Number of solder joints
Number of customer orders processed   Dollars of value added

Required:

Classify each of the above cost drivers as unit level, batch-level, product-level, or facility-level. If a cost driver would fit more than one category, explain why.

3-2. **Activity Identification and Cost Driver Selection.** Stemmons Company has the following costs in its chart of accounts:

(a) Salaries of Purchasing Agents
(b) Secretarial and Clerical Costs in the Purchasing Department
(c) Personnel and Supplies in the Receiving Department
(d) Personnel and Supplies in Production Scheduling and Control
(e) Personnel and Supplies in Inventory Storerooms
(f) Direct Material
(g) Direct Labor
(h) Indirect Material
(i) Indirect Labor
(j) Factory Supervision
(k) Factory and Equipment Maintenance
(l) Personnel Training Programs
(m) Hiring Costs
(n) Personnel and Supplies in Industrial Engineering
(o) Personnel and Supplies in Packing and Shipping
(p) Personnel and Supplies in the Accounting Department
(q) Personnel and Supplies in the Advertising Department
(r) Personnel and Supplies in Market Research
(s) Personnel and Supplies in Product Design Engineering
(t) Cost of Product Advertising
(u) Cost of Institutional Advertising
(v) Research and Development
(w) Charitable Donations
(x) Dues to the Trade Association

The controller has identified a number of cost drivers and they follow:

1. Number of purchase orders placed.
2. Pounds, gallons, and so forth, of items purchased.

3. Number of production shop orders active.
4. Number of machine hours.
5. Number of direct labor hours.
6. Number of units manufactured.
7. Number of persons employed.
8. Number of customer orders shipped.
9. Dollar volume of sales.

Required:
(1) Identify each of the above costs with one of the following:
   (a) Unit-level activities.   (b) Batch-level activities.
   (c) Product-level activities.   (d) Facility-level activities.
(2) Specify an appropriate cost driver from the list given that can be used for tracing the costs as they are associated with the various levels of activities to the next cost objective or products, whichever is appropriate. If an appropriate cost driver is not on the list, state so.

3-3. **Grouping Similar Activities.** HealthCare Products is organized functionally into three divisions: Operations, Sales, and Administrative. Purchasing, receiving, materials and production control, manufacturing, factory personnel, inventory stores, and shipping activities are all under the control of the vice-president for operations. Advertising, market research, and sales are all the responsibility of the vice-president in sales. And accounting, budgeting, the firm's computer center, and general office management are all delegated to the controller (Administrative). The following costs are found in the company as a whole:

(a) Depreciation on factory equipment.
(b) Depreciation on office equipment.
(c) Depreciation on factory building.
(d) Advertising manager's salary.
(e) Assembly foreman's salary.
(f) Salespersons' salaries.
(g) Salespersons' travel expenses.
(h) Supplies used in the factory Machining Department.
(i) Advertising supplies used.
(j) Electricity consumed in the Assembly Department.
(k) Lost material (scrap) in a Machining Department.
(l) Direct labor in the Assembly Department.
(m) Supplies used in the Sales Office.
(n) Sales commissions.
(o) Packing supplies.
(p) Cost of hiring new employees.
(q) Payroll fringe benefits for workers in the Shipping Department.
(r) Supplies used by Production Scheduling.
(s) Cost of repairing parts improperly manufactured in the Machining Department.
(t) Paint used in the Assembly Department.
(u) Heat, light and power for the factory.
(v) Leasing of computer equipment used in the Accounting Department.

Required:
1. Identify each of the above costs with the appropriate division: Operations, Sales, Administrative.

2. Identify each of the costs with one of the following:
    (a) Unit-level activities.   (b) Batch-level activities.
    (c) Product-level activities.   (d) Facility-level activities.
    Organize these classifications by division: Operations, Sales, Administrative.
3. Specify an appropriate cost driver for tracing the costs as they are associated with the various levels of activities to the next cost objective or products, whichever is appropriate.

3-4. **Preliminary Stage and Primary Stage Cost Drivers.** Refer to the data in Problem 3-3 above. HealthCare Products is interested in using activity-based costing to identify as many costs as possible to the products. These costs will be used for planning and control decisions rather than for inventory valuation. The controller decided that all operation costs will be related to products but only those sales and administrative costs that are classified as unit-level, batch-level, or product-level costs should be related to products.

Required:
1. Using preliminary stage cost drivers, explain how individual items of costs will be traced to activity groupings.
2. Using primary stage cost drivers, show how the costs should be related to products.
3. Explain why it is necessary to use preliminary stage and primary stage cost drivers.

3-5. **Activity-Based Costing.** Heidkamp Manufacturing has grouped activities into five categories: Building, Repair, Computer, Machine, and Finishing. Building charges its costs to all of the other groupings based on square footage. Repair charges its costs only to Machine and Finishing. Computer has both outside and inside business. It uses computer hours as the cost driver for charging costs to work performed. Currently, 30% of the computer service is provided to outside customers while 70% goes to inside users. Machine uses set-up hours as the cost driver for 40% of its costs. The other 60% uses machine hours as cost driver. All costs of Machine are charged to products. Finishing uses transactions as the cost driver for 70% of its costs, and the other 30% has product flow time as the cost driver. All costs of Finishing go to products.

The current month's costs for each grouping, prior to charging costs from one grouping to another, are as follows:

Building	$864,800
Repair	500,000
Computer	300,000
Machine	400,000
Finishing	200,000

The operating statistics for the month for each category follow:

	Building	Repair	Computer	Machine	Finish.
Floor space (in sq. ft.) . . .		9,000	19,000	14,400	57,600
Repair hours	8,000			22,400	9,600
Computer hours*				16,800	4,200
Set-up hours				5,000	
Machine hours				100,000	
Transactions					400,000
Product flow time (in hrs.)					20,000

* The total computer hours is 30,000 but 30% of those relate to outside work. Therefore, 30% of the computer costs should be designated for outside work.

During the month, a number of jobs were worked on. The following two jobs were started and completed during the month. Following are the operating statistics for each job:

	#TK451	#RG566
Set-up hours	200	50
Machine hours	100	300
Transactions	200	100
Product flow time	80	900

Required:
1. Using the indicated preliminary stage cost drivers, determine the total dollars that will be charged into Machine and Finishing.
2. Using the indicated primary stage cost drivers, determine the total amount of costs charged to each of the two jobs.

3-6. **Activities and Cost Drivers for an Employment Agency.** Midwest Relocation Services is an employment agency working specifically with mid-level executives looking for new career opportunities or seeking employment after a layoff. The company views its product as placements. These are identified in four categories: employer-paid fee, applicant-paid fee, out-placement contract, and executive-search contract.

   The agency incurs a number of costs in performing its services. However, those costs classified as operating expenses are as follows:

Acct #	Account Title
402	Salaries and Wages
403	Payroll Taxes
404	Employee Benefits
408	Office Supplies (postage, stationery, etc.)
409	Dues and Publications
410	Utilities
412	Rent
413	Repairs and Maintenance (contracted from outside)
420	Business Promotion
421	Auto Expenses
422	Travel Expenses
430	Professional Fees
432	Collection Expenses
435	License
441	Property Taxes
444	Insurance Costs
445	State Franchise Tax
447	Bad Debt Expense
448	Depreciation and Amortization
449	Miscellaneous

Required:
1. Classify each cost as related to unit-level, batch-level, product-level, or facility-level activities. Indicate an appropriate cost driver for each cost.
2. With the information from (1) above, group costs into logical activity groups and specify a cost driver for each activity group.
3. Explain what differences exist between applying activity-based costing to a manufacturing firm and to an employment agency.

3-7.   Non-Value-Added Costs. Donut Depot manufactures donuts that are available fresh every day at several stores throughout Dallas. Donuts left over at the end of the day are packaged and sold at a reduced price as day-old donuts. Donuts not sold by the end of the second day are contributed to the local food bank (a food supply to help welfare families in the metroplex). The production process consists of the following steps:

(a)   Ingredients such as flour, sugar, and cooking oil, are received, inspected, and placed in the storeroom until requisitioned by production.

(b)   Upon requisition, the ingredients are transported from the storeroom to the production area and staged at the mixing department.

(c)   Ingredients are blended into a dough mixture in 40-pound batches in six heavy-duty mixers.

(d)   The dough is rolled out on large boards and left to rise in a holding area.

(e)   When the cutting machines are ready, the boards are moved to the machines and the donuts cut. Cut donuts and donut holes move to the deep fry area. Leftovers from each cutting are accumulated, re-rolled on another board, and processed through the cutting machine. At the end of the production day, leftovers and unprocessed dough on boards are thrown in the trash.

(f)   The cut donuts and donut holes are placed on wire trays and taken to the cooking area, where the trays are stacked until ready for cooking.

(g)   The cooks empty the trays into large vats of hot cooking oil where the donuts and donut holes are, in effect, fried in a sea of oil.

(h)   The cooked products are removed from the vats and placed on drying pads which absorb the excess oil from the donuts. While the product is drying, it is inspected. Misshaped donuts are removed from the good batch and set aside for disposal. What the crew doesn't eat is thrown out at the end of the production shift.

(i)   After drying, the products are placed on large square boards and moved to the finishing area where they will be coated with glaze, icing, powdered sugar, coconut, candy chips, etc.

(j)   After allowing the coating to settle or dry, whichever is the case, the donuts are placed in boxes of 4 dozen each. Donut holes are placed in boxes with 100 donut holes per box. The boxes are moved to the shipping area to await the trucks that will deliver them to the various retail outlets.

(k)   Each morning the delivery trucks return the unsold donuts delivered the previous day. (For some reason donut holes are always sold out.) The day-old donuts are repackaged in plastic bags. Each bag contains one dozen donuts and is marked "day-old." The packages are then returned to the retail outlets. On the second day, any unsold packages are returned to the shipping area. At the end of the day, these packages are delivered to the food bank.

Required:

1.   Identify the activities in the donut production process that fall into process time, inspection time, move time, wait time, and storage time.

2.   List the activities in the donut production process that are candidates for non-value-added activities.

3-8.   Non-Value-Added Costs. HomeTech Manufacturing, Inc. specializes in making products that represent the latest materials and technologies available. The company has a reputation for excellent quality and for entering the market with the best products at reasonable prices.

   The Cookware Division has two product lines: Chef's Delight, a 9-piece set, and Gourmet Ease, a 20-piece set. Chef's Delight is top quality featuring anodized solid-spun aluminum for fast, even heat conductivity and satin finish for easy cleaning. It has bright stainless steel lids and nickel-plated cast iron handles. Stamping operations are needed for the pots, frying pans, and lids. Handles attached to all pots and pans require a molding operation. The handles for each lid are made from stainless steel rods that are bent to shape and flattened where attached to lids. In finishing and assembly, holes are drilled into each pot, pan, and lid so handles can be attached with screws. The pieces are polished and assembled and placed in the finished goods warehouse. The production costs for the set of Chef's Delight are as follows:

	Total 9 Pieces	Average Per Piece
Material	$ 92.70	$10.30
Stamping and molding:		
Direct labor	10.80	1.20
Overhead	32.40	3.60
Finishing and assembly:		
Direct labor	18.00	2.00
Overhead	27.00	3.00
Total	$180.90	$20.10

Inspection takes place at the end of each major operation. The outlines and trimmings resulting from the stamping, molding, and drilling are scrap, which is sold for the value of the materials. Work from the drilling operation through final assembly that does not meet quality standards is either spoilage or defective work, depending on the inspector's decision. Spoilage goes with the scrap. Defective units are reworked and returned to good products.

Required:
1. List the probable activities in the Chef's Delight production process that are candidates for non-value-added activities.
2. It is often said, "There is no free lunch." Where in the costs of the product will the costs of scrap, spoilage, and rework appear?
3. List some of the things the company might do to eliminate non-value-added activities.

3-9. **Cost of Breakage and Defective Customer Service.** Carolina Trucking Co. hauls goods in the Carolinas, Georgia, and Florida. The company guarantees arrival at the designated place within an agreed two-hour period. Penalty for late arrival is 10 percent off the shipping rate. The penalty for being a day late is 20 percent of shipping rates. Each additional day costs an additional 20 percent. The following portion of shipments will arrive late:

More than 2 hours but less than 1 day late	3%
1 day late	2%
2 days late	1%

Breakage of shipped goods results in additional costs related to replacing the goods, reshipping them to their destination, and the disruption of the customer's business. The company follows the policy of paying replacement costs on all broken goods, refunding shipping charges on damaged shipments, and paying a 30 percent surcharge on the replacement cost for business interruption. Approximately 1 percent of goods shipped (in dollar value) will be damaged in shipment.

During July 1995, Carolina Trucking expects to make 642 shipments with total revenues (before breakage and defective service) of $6,420,000. The average shipment is expected to have a $8,000 replacement cost. The variable costs are 70 percent of the billed shipping rate. Fixed costs are $900,000 per month.

Required:

1. Prepare an estimate of the penalties, or revenue lost, from late shipments during July 1995.
2. Prepare an estimate of the cost of shipments with breakage.
3. Assume the company can make systems changes and implement training programs that will reduce the late shipments to:

More than 2 hours late but less than 1 day	2%
1 day late	1%
More than one day	0%

The percentage of goods shipped that would be damaged could be cut in half. How much could the company afford to pay for such changes and programs?

3-10. **Value-Added Labor Concept.** Below is a listing of different business enterprises.

(a) Airline
(b) A CPA firm
(c) Radio station
(d) Clinic specializing in sports injuries
(e) Rehabilitation and therapy center for accident and surgery patients
(f) Member of a nationwide budget motel chain
(g) Travel agency
(h) Retail department store
(i) Automobile garage for repairs and servicing
(j) Funeral home

Required:

For each of the organizations, identify the value-added direct workers.

3-11. **Responsibility Accounting and Pyramid Reporting.** Pampa Packaging Materials Corporation has two plants, one in Illinois and one in Tennessee. Each plant has a Forming and Packing Department.

Production for the forming department of the Illinois Plant is estimated at 1,500 tons for June. The budgeted costs per ton are as follows:

Direct materials	$ 8
Direct labor	15
Factory overhead	9
Total per ton	$32

Total budgeted production costs for the packing department are $33,000 for June. Budgeted costs for the plant manager's office are $57,000.

Budgeted costs for the Tennessee Plant total $67,000. The vice-president of production is responsible for both plants and her office has expenses budgeted at $74,000. Budgeted expenses for the company's vice-president of marketing and his office are $112,600. The company's president is budgeting $140,000 for his office.

Actual expenses for June for the 1,500 tons produced are as follows:

President's office	$142,300
Vice-president of marketing	109,800
Vice-president of production—office	75,500
Total cost of Tennessee Plant	70,100

Illinois Plant:	
Plant manager's office	$ 58,300
Packing department	34,900
Forming department:	
Direct materials	10,600
Direct labor	23,400
Factory overhead	13,200

Required:
Prepare a responsibility report showing the details of the budgeted, actual, and variance amounts for the following:
(a)   Forming Department in Illinois Plant
(b)   Plant Manager for the Illinois Plant
(c)   Vice-President of Production
(d)   President of the company

3-12. **Relationship of Actual, Budget, Variance.** The following partial performance report is available for the Fabrication Cost Center of Womble Metal-Benders, Inc.

	Actual	Budget	Variance
Units produced	40,000	40,000	—
Direct materials	$ 60,000	$?	$(2,000)*
Direct labor	?	?	3,000
Total prime costs	$260,000	$?	$ 1,000
Variable factory overhead:			
Supplies	$ 20,000	$21,000	$?
Maintenance wages	?	5,000	(800)
Power	?	2,500	?
Total variable overhead	$?	$28,500	$(1,300)
Fixed factory overhead:			
Indirect labor salaries	$ 18,000	$17,500	$?
Depreciation	?	8,000	600
Insurance	?	?	?
Other	7,200	?	200
Total fixed overhead	$ 40,300	$?	$?
Total costs of cost center	$?	$?	$(1,000)

* Note: Parentheses indicate a favorable variance—actual is less than budget.

Required:
Find the missing amounts in the cost center performance report.

3-13. **Evaluation of a Responsibility Report.** The Argon County Hospital is located in the county seat. Argon County is a well-known summer resort area. The county population doubles during the vacation months. The hospital is organized into several departments. Although it is a relatively small hospital, its pleasant surroundings have attracted a well-trained and competent medical staff.

An administrator was hired a year ago to improve the business activities of the hospital. Among the new ideas he has introduced is responsibility accounting. This program was announced along with quarterly cost reports supplied to department heads. Previously cost data were presented to department heads infrequently. Excerpts from the announcement and the report received by the laundry supervisor are presented as follows:

"The hospital has adopted a 'responsibility accounting system.' From now on you will receive quarterly reports comparing the costs of operating your department with budgeted costs. The reports will highlight the differences (variations) so you can zero in on the departure from the budgeted costs (this is called 'management by exception'). Responsibility accounting means you are accountable for keeping the costs in your department within the budget. The variations from the budget will help you identify what costs are out of line, and the size of the variation will indicate which ones are the most important. Your first such report accompanies this announcement."

The annual budget for the year was constructed by the new administrator. Quarterly budgets were computed as one-fourth of the annual budget.

ARGON COUNTY HOSPITAL
PERFORMANCE REPORT—LAUNDRY DEPARTMENT
JULY–SEPTEMBER

	Budget	Actual	(Over) Under Budget	Percent (Over) Under Budget
Patient days	9,500	11,900	(2,400)	(25)
Pounds processed—Laundry	125,000	156,000	(31,000)	(25)
Costs:				
Laundry labor	$ 9,000	$ 12,500	$ (3,500)	(39)
Supplies	1,100	1,875	(775)	(70)
Water, water heating and softening	1,700	2,500	(800)	(47)
Maintenance....................	1,400	2,200	(800)	(57)
Supervisor's salary	3,150	3,750	(600)	(19)
Allocated administration costs	4,000	5,000	(1,000)	(25)
Equipment depreciation	1,200	1,250	(50)	(4)
	$ 21,550	$ 29,075	$ (7,525)	(35)

Administrator's Comments: Costs are significantly above budget for the quarter. Particular attention needs to be paid to labor, supplies, and maintenance.

The administration compiled the budget from an analysis of the prior three years' actual costs. For that three-year period costs were increasing from one year to the next with more rapid increases occurring between the second and third year. The administrator considered establishing the budget at an average of the prior three years' costs, hoping that the installation of the system would reduce costs to this level. However, in view of the rapidly increasing prices, he finally chose last year's costs less 3% for the current budget. The activity level measured by patient days and pounds was set at last year's volume, which was approximately equal to the volume of each of the past three years.

Required:
1. Comment on the method used to construct the budget.
2. What information should be communicated by variations from budgets? (Hint: Consider those factors over which the manager of the laundry department has control.)
3. Explain strengths and weaknesses of this report.

(ICMA adapted)

3-14. **Performance Report for Advertising Agency.** Mooney Advertising, Inc. is noted locally for its artwork, copywriting services, and media selection. The accounting classifications for its overhead, selling, and administrative expenses are:

6000	Overhead Costs
7000	Selling Expenses
8000	Administrative Expenses

An account listing with amounts (with 000s omitted) for April and the year-to-date is as follows:

Acct. No.	Account Name	April Actual	April Budget	Year-to-Date Actual	Year-to-Date Budget
7010	Account Executive Salaries......	$10	$12	$ 44	$ 48
7040	Advertising....................	2	2	10	8
7020	Clerical Salaries	4	3	11	12
7030	Commissions...................	8	9	31	35
6280	Depreciation	10	10	40	40
7280	Depreciation	2	3	9	12
8280	Depreciation	5	5	20	22
6250	Equipment Rental..............	1	1	2	5
7250	Equipment Rental..............	0	1	3	6
8250	Equipment Rental..............	2	1	6	5
6210	Indirect Labor	20	22	90	100
6230	Insurance.....................	3	3	10	12
7230	Insurance.....................	4	5	16	15
8230	Insurance.....................	4	3	10	16
6290	Miscellaneous	1	1	3	5
7290	Miscellaneous	0	1	2	4
8290	Miscellaneous	2	3	6	9
8020	Office Salaries.................	21	18	86	72
8030	Office Supplies	3	2	16	18
8010	Officers' Salaries	50	50	200	200
8070	Officers' Life Insurance	1	1	4	4
6270	Payroll Taxes	2	3	9	12
7270	Payroll Taxes	1	1	4	4
8270	Payroll Taxes	2	2	8	7
8040	Postage	2	3	9	11
8060	Professional Fees..............	6	7	28	25
6240	Telephone	1	1	3	4
7240	Telephone	4	3	18	19
8240	Telephone	5	6	20	25
7050	Travel and Entertainment	5	7	18	28
8050	Travel and Entertainment	7	6	25	24
6220	Utilities	9	10	44	40
8220	Utilities	1	1	5	6
7220	Utilities	7	6	30	32

Required:

Prepare a performance report for each of the following areas. Show actual, budget, and (over) under budget for the current month and for the year-to-date.
(a)   Overhead.
(b)   Selling.
(c)   Administrative.

3-15. **Performance Report for a Grocery Store.** McInnes Groceries of Heber Valley maintains tight control on its operating expenses through the use of budgets. The monthly and year-to-date budgets are based on formulas the chief accountant developed. The following information is the accounts and monthly budget formulas (annual budget formulas are found by multiplying the fixed costs by the number of months):

Account	Formula
Payroll	$50,000 + 6% of revenues
Store Supplies	1% of revenues
Advertising	$4,000 + 1% of revenues
Equipment Rental	$8,000
Payroll Taxes	10% of payroll
Taxes and Licenses	$4,500
Accounting and Legal Fees	$1,500 + 0.5% of revenues
Travel and Entertainment	$2,000 + 1.5% of revenues
Charitable Contributions	$100 + 0.5% of revenues
Telephone	$400 + 0.5% of revenues
Utilities	$2,300
Leasing	$9,000
Insurance	$2,600
Depreciation on Equipment	$4,700
Gas and Oil for Vehicles	2% of revenues
Repairs for Vehicles	$900 + 2% of gas and oil

The accounting records for May show the following actual dollar amounts:

	Current Month	Year-to-Date
Revenues	$300,000	$1,700,000
Payroll	$ 69,000	$ 362,000
Store Supplies	3,600	15,000
Advertising	6,010	38,150
Equipment Rental	8,100	37,220
Payroll Taxes	6,240	31,860
Taxes and Licenses	4,500	22,500
Accounting and Legal Fees	2,760	14,800
Travel and Entertainment	8,000	41,740
Charitable Contributions	1,600	8,000
Telephone	3,100	9,500
Utilities	2,900	12,400
Leasing	9,000	45,000
Insurance	2,800	14,200
Depreciation on Equipment	5,000	25,000
Gas and Oil for Vehicles	7,330	36,720
Repairs for Vehicles	1,047	5,235

Required:

Prepare a responsibility performance report for the above operating expenses. Show the current month and year-to-date information for actual, budget, and (over) under budget. Separate the report into three sections for costs: variable costs, semi-variable costs, and strictly fixed costs.

3-16.   **Responsibility Accounting and Pyramid Reporting.** The Jacksonville Slugger Division of Georgia Pine Products, Inc. produces baseball bats in its South Georgia Plant. The factory consists of two production departments: Cutting and Finishing. Each department has a supervisor who is responsible for the cost of materials issued to the department and costs of labor and overhead used in the department. The vice-president of production is over the two production departments. He reports to the divisional president along with the vice-presidents of sales, finance, personnel, and computer services.

During April 1995, the Cutting Department completed and transferred 70,000 units. No beginning or ending inventories existed in the Cutting Department during April. All materials issued to the department during the month were used. The budget for April was based on 75,000 units. The budgeted costs for the month are based on the following formula:

Materials (35 oz. of wood at $.02 per oz.)	$.70 per unit
Direct labor (.03 hrs. at $5 per hour)	$.15 per unit
Variable overhead (.03 hrs. at $4 per hour).................	$.12 per unit
Fixed overhead	$45,000 per month

The Finishing Department had no beginning or ending inventories for April. All 70,000 units received from the Cutting Department during the month were completed and transferred to the finished inventory warehouse. The budget called for 75,000 units to be produced in the Finishing Department during April. The budgeted costs for the month are based on the following formula:

Varnish (.10 gals. at $3.40 per gal.)	$.34 per unit
Direct labor (.05 hrs. at $5 per hour)	$.25 per unit
Variable overhead (.05 hrs. at $7 per hour).................	$.35 per unit
Fixed overhead	$22,500 per month

Relevant cost data for the month are summarized as follows:

Cutting Department:
Materials purchased	190,000 lbs. of wood for $59,850
Materials issued.........................	168,600 lbs.
Direct labor	2,200 hours for $10,780
Actual overhead	$57,500

Finishing Department:
Varnish purchased.......................	8,280 gals. for $27,324
Varnish issued	6,820 gals.
Direct labor	3,510 hours for $17,550
Actual overhead.........................	$43,390

Other departmental cost data:

	Budgeted	Actual
Personnel Department	$47,200	$51,100
Computer Services	23,500	22,900
Sales Department	63,600	65,800
Finance Department	29,100	34,000
Office of the V.P. of Production	16,100	14,700
Office of the Divisional President	25,900	27,200

Required:
Prepare cost performance reports for:
(a)   The Cutting Department supervisor.
(b)   The Finishing Department supervisor.
(c)   The Vice-President of Production.
(d)   The Divisional President.

CASE 3A–LEDA LEARNING SYSTEMS

LEDA Learning Systems has many divisions, each specializing in some aspect of education and training. One responsibility center in the Professional Seminar Division is Government Contract Accounting Seminars. Since this responsibility center is profit oriented, it is treated as a profit center for performance evaluation purposes.

Because the Department of Defense is tightening up its spending habits, many companies are cutting back on sending their people to on-site presentations of training seminars and hiring seminars. Actual results and variances for the last fiscal year for Government Contract Accounting Seminars are as follows:

	Actual	Variance*
Seminar participants	7,020	1,380 U
Number of seminars given	175	25 U
Revenues	$1,404,000	$396,000 U
Costs which vary with number of participants:		
Food	$ 70,200	$ 10,800 F
Workbooks and handouts	274,890	85,110 F
Costs which vary with number of seminars:		
Instructors' fees	$ 280,000	40,000 F
Rental of sites	21,600	2,630 U
Equipment rental (overhead projectors, etc.)	8,110	510 U
Fixed costs of Government Contract Accounting Seminars:		
Salaries of managers and assistants	$ 124,000	4,000 U
Office expenses	13,000	640 U
Promotion of seminars	89,000	7,500 F
Divisional overhead allocated to this profit center	$ 389,000	9,000 F
Total expenses	$1,269,800	$144,630 F
Profits	$ 134,200	$251,370 U

* U = Unfavorable
  F = Favorable

Seminars are one, two, and three days. The average number of seminars last year was two days. Course schedules permit eight hours of instruction each so that those desiring continuing education credits for CPA certificates, licenses, or other requirements can have a full eight hours of credit per course. The manager's salary, included above, is $60,000, and it had been budgeted at that level.

Required:

1.   Since this responsibility center is a profit center, the presumption is the manager of Government Contract Accounting Seminars controls the revenues. The factors influencing revenues are the number of seminar participants and the number of seminars. Does the manager really control these two factors? Explain.

2.   In general, are the variances in this report controllable by the manager of the profit center? (Hint: What level of activity is the budget based on?)

3.   Which of the costs and related variances are not controllable by the manager?

4.   What suggestions can you give for improving the usefulness of the above report?

5.   Prepare a performance report which you believe describes the performance of the manager better than the above report. A budget column is not necessary but may be helpful.

Chapter Four

Cost-Volume-Profit Relationships

❖ *Chapter Objectives*

After studying Chapter 4, you will be able to:

1. Identify the interacting factors and assumptions that make cost-volume-profit analysis possible.
2. Calculate the effect on profits of changes in selling prices or changes in variable costs.
3. Show how changes in fixed costs affect break-even points and profits.
4. Explain operating leverage, and describe how it can be an advantage when sales volume is increasing but a disadvantage when sales volume is declining.
5. Describe the margin of safety concept, and calculate a margin of safety for any given situation.
6. Find the break-even point and any desired level of profit when multiple products are sold in combination.
7. Calculate the indifference point for two products that will compete for the same resources.
8. Identify the different measures of contribution margin, and explain what the elements of each are.

"Can You Lose a Little on Each One, But Make it Up on Volume?"

Skip Johnson, owner of C&J Clothiers, started his business over twenty-five years ago. During that time, he enjoyed a number of upswings and weathered several downturns in the economy. He has such a reputation for stocking the finest men's clothing in the state and for providing customer service at such a high quality that people mail or call in orders from hundreds of miles away. The business has realized many profitable years and provided a high standard of living for Skip and his family.

But times are changing. Personnel costs continue to rise, particularly fringe benefits like medical insurance premiums. Crude oil prices are increasing which influences the prices of thousands of products based on oil derivatives. Additionally, the increased costs greatly influence the costs of operations for hundreds of manufacturing and service organizations. At the same time, the take-home pay of most people is increasing slower than the rise in the cost of the goods and services they buy. Consequently, Skip faces a declining customer base. Skip has slashed operating costs, but he still faces shrinking profit margins.

Because of high profitability in the past, Skip never analyzed the relationships among revenues, costs, and volume to see how they relate to profit levels. Now, Skip is wondering how far sales can drop before he sees the red ink of losses. With that information, he hopes to identify what changes will keep operations profitable. Skip sees many other businesses closing their doors and is fearful he will have to follow suit someday. He just doesn't know what factors will influence his future profits.

A management, similar to Skip Johnson of C&J Clothiers, desirous of estimating profits at specific operating levels, preparing budgets, or controlling costs effectively and efficiently needs an understanding of how revenues, costs, and volume interact to provide profits. With this understanding, management performs any number of analyses that fit in a broad category we call **cost-volume-profit analysis**. At a minimum, management must identify its activities and cost drivers and the variable and fixed costs incurred as a result of these activities and cost drivers. The accuracy of cost behavior estimation depends heavily on the condition of the data available within a company and the methods used to separate variable and fixed components.

Cost-volume-profit analysis, as its name implies, looks at the interaction of factors that influence the level of profits. Although the name cost-volume-profit leaves us with the impression that only cost and volume determine profits, a number of important factors exist that determine whether we have profits or losses and whether profits increase or decrease over time. The key factors are:

1. Selling prices.
2. Volume of sales.
3. Unit variable cost.
4. Total fixed cost.
5. Sales mix (combinations in which various product lines are sold).

Although many important relationships exist among these factors, three are basic for the remainder of this chapter. One relationship is between variable costs and sales. The excess of sales revenue over variable cost is called the **contribution margin**. The contribution margin also equals the sum of fixed costs and profits. A second relationship is between contribution margin and profit. The contribution margin per unit multiplied by the change in volume of sales equals the change in profits. Therefore, the financial impact of decisions involving volume changes can be assessed using contribution margin. A third relationship is between fixed costs and the contribution margin. When the two equal, the company has a break-even point; profit is zero.

Skip Johnson will have a better idea of how to manage his business if he understands its activities and cost drivers (as discussed in Chapter 3) and if he knows which of the foregoing factors he controls. Even though cost-volume-profit analysis does not guarantee profitable operations, it certainly paints the picture of where operations are and what needs changing to move in a specific direction.

COST-VOLUME-PROFIT ANALYSIS

Cost-volume-profit analysis, also called **break-even analysis,** is an analysis of the factors that interact to influence the amounts of profit. One significant volume level is the **break-even point**, where total revenue equals total costs. It indicates how many units of product must be sold or how much revenue is needed to at least cover all costs.

Each unit of product sold is expected to yield revenue in excess of its variable cost and thus contribute to the recovery of fixed costs and provide a profit. The point at which profit is zero means that the contribution margin is equal to the fixed costs. Sales volume must increase beyond the break-even point for a company to realize a profit.

Let's take a look at a simple example of the relationships. Assume that a company manufactures and sells a single product line as follows:

	Dollars	Percentage of Selling Price
Unit selling price	$25	100%
Unit variable cost	15	60
Unit contribution margin	$10	40%
Total fixed cost	$100,000	

Each unit of product sold contributes $10 to the recovery of fixed costs and to provide a profit. Hence, the company must sell 10,000 units in order to break even. The 10,000 units sold will result in a total contribution margin of $100,000, and that equals the total fixed cost. A break-even point in units is calculated by dividing the contribution margin per unit into the total fixed costs to be recovered.

$$\frac{\$100,000 \text{ (total fixed cost)}}{\$10 \text{ (unit contribution margin)}} = 10,000 \text{ units}$$

A break-even point measured in dollars of revenue can be computed directly by dividing the contribution margin percentage, in this case 40 percent, into the total fixed cost. When 40 percent of the revenue, that is the contribution margin, is equal to the fixed cost of $100,000, the company will break even.

$$\frac{\$100,000 \text{ (total fixed cost)}}{40\% \text{ (contribution margin percentage)}} = \$250,000 \text{ revenue}$$

We could have arrived at the same number by using the 10,000 units at the break-even point times the selling price: $10,000 \times \$25 = \$250,000$.

A Desired Profit Before Tax

In business, a break-even operation is not satisfactory but serves as a base for profit planning. Continuing with the illustration, assume that management has set a profit objective of $200,000 before income taxes and that the income tax rate is 40 percent. The profit before tax is treated as if it were an additional fixed cost in the computation of units to be sold or revenue required to attain the objective. The general formula is below:

$$\frac{\text{Fixed cost} + \text{Profit before tax}}{\text{Contribution margin (per unit or percentage)}} = \text{units or revenues}$$

We can just insert the appropriate amounts to calculate the units or revenue dollars where profits will equal $200,000.

$$\frac{\$100,000 + \$200,000}{\$10 \text{ (unit contribution margin)}} = 30,000 \text{ units}$$

$$\frac{\$100,000 + \$200,000}{40\% \text{ (contribution margin percentage)}} = \$750,000 \text{ revenue}$$

A Desired Profit After Tax

The profit objective may be stated as a profit after income taxes. If such is the case, the profit before tax is determined by the following formula:

$$\text{Profit before tax} = \frac{\text{Profit after tax}}{(1 - \text{tax rate})}$$

In the example given at the bottom of page 137, assume that a profit after income taxes has been budgeted at $120,000 and that the income tax rate is 40 percent. The profit before tax is then calculated as follows:

$$\text{Profit before tax} = \frac{\$120,000}{(1 - .40)} = \frac{\$120,000}{.60} = \$200,000$$

We now use the previous formulas for finding specific points and compute the same results of 30,000 units and $750,000 revenue.

Desired Profit as an Amount Per Unit or a Percentage of Sales

Management may also state the profit objective as either an average profit per unit or as a percentage of sales (rate of return or profit margin). Assume the profit objective is stated at $2 profit per unit. The formula for calculating the number of units which attains the profit objective is below:

$$\frac{\$100,000 \text{ (fixed cost)}}{\$10 \text{ (unit contribution margin)} - \$2 \text{ (profit per unit)}} = 12,500 \text{ units}$$

If instead of a per unit profit, management stated the profit objective as a 20 percent profit margin before taxes, the appropriate formula is below:

$$\frac{\$100,000 \text{ (fixed cost)}}{40\% \text{ (contribution margin percentage)} - 20\% \text{ (profit margin)}} = \$500,000 \text{ revenue}$$

The Break-Even Chart

Total revenue and total cost at different sales volumes can be estimated and plotted on a **break-even chart.** The information shown on the break-even chart can also be given in conventional reports, but it is often easier to grasp the fundamental facts when they are presented in graphic or pictorial form. Dollars are shown on the vertical scale of the chart, and the units of product to be sold are shown on the horizontal scale. The total costs are plotted for the various quantities to be sold and are connected by a line. Total revenues are similarly entered on the chart.

The break-even point lies at the intersection of the total revenue and the total cost lines. Losses are measured to the left of the break-even point, the amount of the loss at any point being equal to the dollar difference between the total cost line and the total revenue line. Profit is measured to the right of the break-even point, and at any point is equal to the dollar difference between the total revenue line and the total cost line. This dollar difference is the contribution margin per unit multiplied by the volume in excess of the break-even point.

In Figure 4.1, a break-even chart has been prepared using the following data. The selling price is $25 and the unit variable cost is $15 over the range of units sold. (For multiple product situations, the sales mix, or product combination problem, is discussed in a later section.)

	Units of Product Sold					
	5,000	**10,000**	**15,000**	**20,000**	**25,000**	**30,000**
Total revenue.	$125,000	$250,000	$375,000	$500,000	$625,000	$750,000
Total cost:						
Variable	$ 75,000	$150,000	$225,000	$300,000	$375,000	$450,000
Fixed	100,000	100,000	100,000	100,000	100,000	100,000
Total cost	$175,000	$250,000	$325,000	$400,000	$475,000	$550,000
Profit (loss).	($50,000)	0	$ 50,000	$100,000	$150,000	$200,000

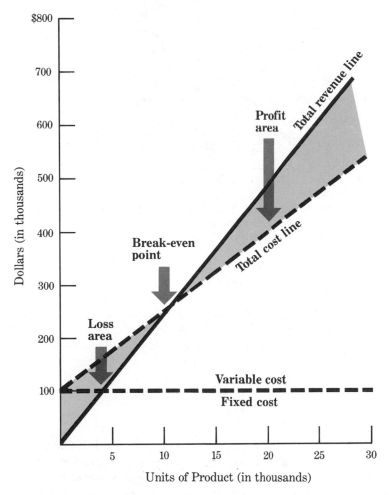

Figure 4.1   Break-Even Chart

Curvature of Revenue and Cost Lines

In some cases, revenue and cost cannot be represented by straight lines. If more units are to be sold, management may have to reduce selling prices. Under these conditions, the revenue function is a curve instead of a straight line. Cost may also be nonlinear depending on what changes take place as volume increases. The cost curve may rise slowly at the start but rise more steeply as volume is expanded. This will occur if the variable cost per unit becomes higher as more units are manufactured. Also, fixed costs might change as volume increases. For example, volume increases might cause a jump in supervision, equipment, and space costs. Therefore, it may be possible to have two break-even points as shown in Figure 4.2.

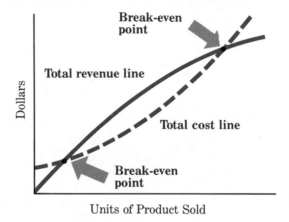

Figure 4.2   Break-Even Chart with Two Break-Even Points

In many cases, however, revenue and cost can be represented by straight lines. Any given company probably operates within certain volume ranges where revenue and cost can be plotted without any noticeable curvature. This is called the **relevant range**. If the revenue and the cost curves begin to converge, the company is not maximizing its profit. Total cost is increasing faster than total revenue; that is, each unit sold is adding more to cost than to revenue.

THE PROFIT-VOLUME GRAPH

A **profit-volume graph**, or **P/V graph**, is sometimes used in place of or along with a break-even chart. Profits and losses are given on the vertical scale; and units of product, sales revenue, and/or percentages of capacity are given on the horizontal scale. A horizontal line is drawn on the graph to separate profits from losses. The profit or loss at each of various sales levels is plotted. These points are then connected to form a profit line. The slope of the profit line is the contribution margin per unit if the horizontal line is stated as units of product and the contribution margin percentage is stated as sales revenue.

The break-even point is the point where the profit line intersects the horizontal line. Dollars of profit are measured on a vertical scale above the line, and dollars of loss are measured below the line. The P/V graph may be preferred to the break-even chart because profit and loss at any point can be read directly from the vertical scale; but the P/V graph does not clearly show how cost varies with activity. Break-even charts and P/V graphs are often used together, thus obtaining the advantages of both.

Data used in the earlier illustration of a break-even chart in Figure 4.1 have also been used in preparing the P/V graph in Figure 4.3.

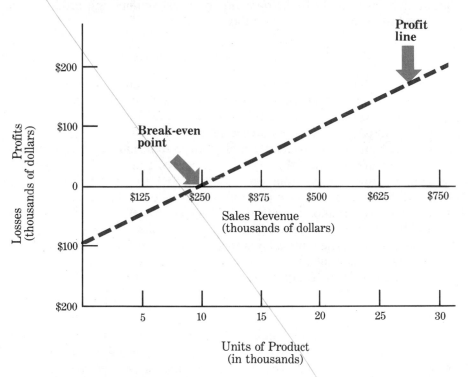

Figure 4.3   Profit-Volume Graph

The profit-volume graph is a convenient device to show how profit is affected by changes in the factors that affect profit. For example, if unit selling price, unit variable cost, and total fixed cost remain constant, how many more units must be sold to realize a greater profit? Or, if the unit variable cost can be reduced, what additional profit can be expected at any given volume of sales? The effect of changes in sales volume, unit variable cost, unit selling price, total fixed cost, and sales mix is discussed in the following paragraphs.

Sales Volume

For some companies, substantial profits depend on high sales volume. For example, if each unit of product is sold at a relatively low contribution margin, high profits are a function of selling in large quantities. This is more significant when the fixed cost is high. For an illustration, consider a company that handles a product with a selling price of $1 per unit. Assume a variable cost of $.70

per unit and a fixed cost of $180,000 per year. The contribution margin must be $.30 per unit, calculated as follows:

Selling price	$1.00
Variable cost	.70
Contribution margin	$ .30

Before any profit is realized, the company must sell enough units for the total contribution margin to recover the fixed cost.

Fixed cost ÷ Contribution margin = Break-even point
$180,000 ÷ $.30 = 600,000 units

Therefore, 600,000 units must be sold just to break even. For every unit sold in excess of 600,000, a $.30 profit before tax is earned. In such a situation, the company must be certain that it can sell substantially more than 600,000 units to earn a reasonable profit on its investment.

When products sell for relatively high contribution margins per unit, the fixed cost is recaptured with the sale of fewer units, and a profit can be made on a relatively low sales volume. Suppose that each unit of product sells for $1,000 and that the variable cost per unit is $900. The fixed cost for the year is $180,000. The contribution margin percentage is only 10 percent, but this is equal to $100 from each unit sold. The break-even point will be reached when 1,800 units are sold. The physical quantity handled is much lower than it was in the preceding example, but the same principle applies. More than 1,800 units must be sold if the company is to produce a profit.

Variable Costs

The relationship between the selling price of a product and its variable cost is important in any line of business. Even small savings in the variable cost can add significantly to profits. A reduction of a fraction of a dollar in the unit cost becomes a contribution to fixed cost and profit. If 50,000 units are sold in a year, a $.10 decrease in the unit cost becomes a $5,000 increase in profit. Conversely, a $.10 increase in unit cost decreases profit by $5,000.

Management is continually searching for opportunities to make even small cost savings. What appears trivial may turn out to be the difference between profit or loss for the year. In manufacturing, it may be possible to save on materials cost by using a cheaper material that is just as satisfactory. Using materials more effectively can also result in savings. Improving methods of production may decrease labor and overhead costs per unit.

A small savings in unit cost can give a company a competitive advantage. If prices must be reduced, the low-cost producer will usually suffer less. At any given price and fixed cost structure, the low-cost producer will become profitable faster as sales volume increases.

The following operating results of three companies show how profit is influenced by changes in the variable cost pattern. Each of the three companies sells 100,000 units of one product line at a price of $5 per unit. Each has an annual fixed cost of $150,000. Company A can manufacture and sell each unit at a variable cost of $2.50. Company B has found ways to save costs and can produce each unit for a variable cost of $2, while Company C has allowed its unit variable cost to rise to $3.

A difference of $.50 in unit variable cost between Company A and Company B or between Company A and Company C adds up to a $50,000 difference in profit when 100,000 units are sold. The low-cost producer has a $1 per unit profit advantage over the high-cost producer. If sales volume should fall to 60,000 units per company, Company B would have a profit of $30,000, Company A would break even, and Company C would suffer a loss of $30,000.

	Company A	Company B	Company C
Number of units sold	100,000	100,000	100,000
Unit selling price	$5.00	$5.00	$5.00
Unit variable cost	2.50	2.00	3.00
Unit contribution margin	2.50	3.00	2.00
Contribution margin percentage	50%	60%	40%
Total sales revenue	$500,000	$500,000	$500,000
Total variable cost	250,000	200,000	300,000
Total contribution margin	$250,000	$300,000	$200,000
Fixed cost	150,000	150,000	150,000
Income before income tax	$100,000	$150,000	$ 50,000

The same results are shown in the P/V graph in Figure 4.4:

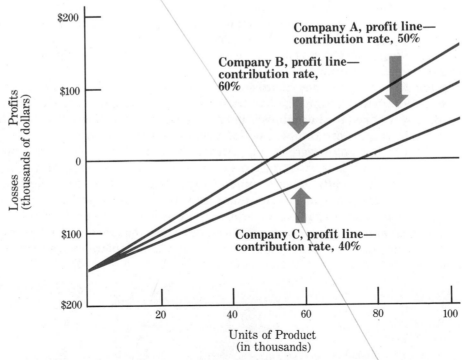

Figure 4.4   Comparing P/V When Variable Costs Differ

The profit line for each company starts at a loss of $150,000, the amount of the fixed cost. When 40,000 units are sold, a difference of $20,000 occurs between each profit line. The lines diverge as greater quantities are sold; at the 100,000-unit level, the difference is $50,000 between each profit line. Company B can make a profit by selling any quantity in excess of 50,000 units, but Company C must sell 75,000 units to break even. With its present cost structure, Company C will have to sell in greater volume if it is to earn a profit equal to profits earned by Company A or Company B. Company C is the inefficient producer in the group and, as such, operates at a disadvantage. When there is enough business for everyone, Company C will earn a profit but will most likely earn less than the others. When business conditions are poor, Company C will be more vulnerable to losses.

Price Policy

One of the ways to improve profit is to get more sales volume; and to stimulate sales volume, management may decide to reduce prices. But results may not be as anticipated. It does not necessarily follow that sales volume will be increased by reducing prices. If the demand for the product is perfectly inelastic, volume will not respond to a change in price. The price reduction will result only in lower profit.

Suppose, however, that greater quantities can be sold at a lower price. The advantage, if there is one, is soon eliminated if competitors retaliate by lowering their prices also. The market will eventually be shared as it was before, and possibly with lower profits for all. Even assuming that competitors will not react to price reductions, still no guarantee exists that profit can be increased by increasing sales. In fact, profit may decline in the face of increased sales, if the new price is set too low. It may turn out that more effort is being put forth to get a smaller return.

While sales volume may increase with reductions in price, it may not increase enough to overcome the handicap of selling at a lower price. This point is often overlooked by the optimistic business person who believes that a small increase in volume can compensate for a slight decrease in price.

Price cuts, like an increase in the variable unit cost, decrease the contribution margin. On a unit basis, price decreases may appear to be insignificant; but when the unit differential is multiplied by thousands of units, the total effect may be tremendous. Perhaps many more units must be sold to make up for the difference. Company A, for example, hopes to increase profit by selling more units; and to sell more, it plans to reduce the unit price by 10 percent. The present price and cost structure and the one contemplated are shown as follows:

	Present Price and Cost	Contemplated Price and Cost
Selling price	$5.00	$4.50
Variable cost	2.50	2.50
Contribution margin	$2.50	$2.00
Contribution margin percentage	50%	44.4%

At present, one-half of each dollar in revenue can be applied to fixed cost and profit. When sales are twice the fixed cost, Company A will break even. This means that 60,000 units yielding a revenue of $300,000 must be sold if fixed cost is $150,000. But when the price is reduced, less than half of each dollar can be applied to fixed cost and profit. To recover $150,000 in fixed cost, unit sales must be 75,000 ($150,000/$2 per unit contribution margin). The revenue must be $337,500 (75,000 units × $4.50 per unit). Not only must total revenue be higher but, with a lower price per unit, more units must be sold to obtain that revenue.

To overcome the effect of a 10 percent cut in price, sales volume in physical units must be increased by 25 percent.

75,000	units to be sold at lower price to break even
60,000	units to be sold at present price to break even
15,000	increase in number of units

$$\frac{15,000}{60,000} = \text{¼ or 25\% increase}$$

Sales revenue must be increased by 12 1/2 percent, as calculated below:

$337,500	sales revenue needed at new break-even point
300,000	sales revenue needed at present break-even point
$ 37,500	increase in sales revenue

$$\frac{\$ 37,500}{\$300,000} = \text{⅛ or or 12 1/2\% increase}$$

The present income before income tax of $100,000 can still be earned if 125,000 units are sold for a total revenue of $562,500, as shown below:

	Present Operation	Comtemplated Operation
Number of units sold	100,000	125,000
Sales	$500,000	$562,500
Cost of goods sold	250,000	312,500
Contribution margin	$250,000	$250,000
Fixed cost	150,000	150,000
Income before income tax	$100,000	$100,000

After selling 125,000 units, the company can improve its profit, but at a slower rate than when it operated with a price of $5. For every $4,500 increase in revenue, profit increases by $2,000. At present, a $4,500 increase in revenue beyond the break-even point yields $2,250 in profit. A P/V graph showing these changes appears in Figure 4.5.

The increase in sales volume required to overcome the effect of a price reduction is proportionately greater when the contribution margin percentage is relatively low at the start. If each unit of product makes only a modest contribution, then a reduction in price makes it all the more difficult to recover the fixed cost and to earn a profit.

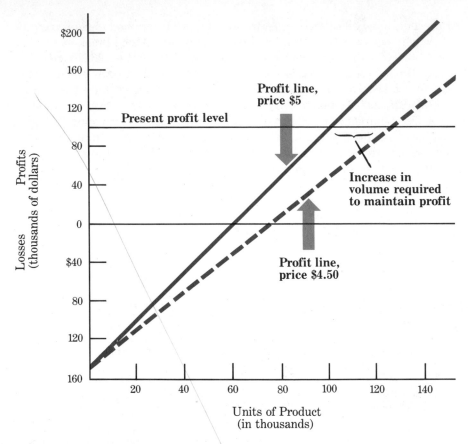

Figure 4.5   Effect of a Price Reduction on Profit

It may seem, at first, that the price should not be reduced. The handicap imposed by the decrease in price appears to be overwhelming; yet, in many circumstances, profit can be increased by lowering prices. A savings in variable cost, for example, can be passed along to the customer. The contribution margin remains the same; and if more units can be sold, an increase in profit will follow. Even with no change in variable cost, increased profit may be realized by lowering prices, provided that sales volume can be increased by more than enough to make up for the effect of the decrease in price.

The policy with respect to price will depend on the long-range and short-range objectives of management. In any event, it is important for management to know the consequences of adopting a certain course of action. That way, management can cut prices with a full knowledge that an immediate reduction in profits will occur. Management accepts this disadvantage in the hope that the company can establish itself as a volume producer in the market. Another company, whose management is not informed with respect to cost-volume relationships, may cut prices in an attempt to gain immediate profit; then when the profit does not materialize, the management will be unpleasantly surprised. Chapter 11 will discuss additional aspects of price policy.

Fixed Costs

A change in fixed cost has no effect on the contribution margin. Increases in fixed cost are recovered when the contribution margin from additional units sold is equal to the increase in fixed cost. Because fixed cost is not part of the contribution margin computation, the slope of the profit line on a P/V graph is unaffected by changes in fixed cost. The new profit line is drawn parallel to the original line, and the vertical distance between the two lines, at any point, is equal to the increase or the decrease in fixed cost.

The P/V graph in Figure 4.6 shows the results of an increase in fixed cost from $600,000 to $700,000. The product sells for $5 per unit, variable cost is $3 per unit, and the contribution margin per unit is $2. Under the new fixed cost structure, the profit line shifts downward and at any point the new line is $100,000 lower than it was originally. To maintain the same profit as before, 50,000 more units must be sold.

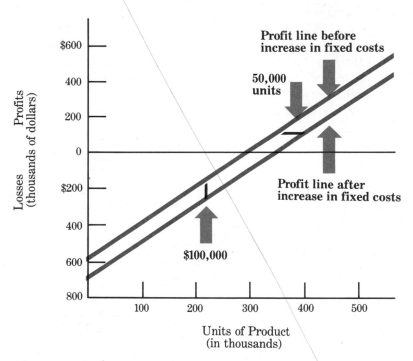

Figure 4.6   Increase in Fixed Cost

Decreases in fixed cost will cause the profit line to shift upward. The total contribution to fixed cost and profit can be reduced by the amount of the decrease in cost without affecting profit. The lower sales volume now needed to maintain the same profit can be calculated by dividing the unit contribution into the decrease in fixed cost. The new profit line is parallel to the original line at a vertical distance equal to the decrease in fixed cost.

Current Emphasis on Fixed Costs

Two important developments are currently causing management to take a closer look at fixed costs:

1. The trend toward automation and the resulting increases in fixed costs.
2. The reduction in sales volume in some heavy industries making it necessary for management to cut fixed costs if the company is to earn profits.

A company with increasing fixed costs must obtain more sales volume, or increase the contribution margin rate, or both if a certain profit level is to be maintained. The company that is forced to accept a lower volume of sales will have to reduce fixed costs if it is to operate at a given profit level.

For example, suppose that Stellar Company operated for several years with sales revenue of approximately $10,000,000, with a contribution margin of 30 percent, and with fixed costs of $2,000,000. In those years, the income before income taxes each year was $1,000,000. Then, foreign imports cut into its share of the market, and sales were further reduced as customers began to use substitute products. Sales are now down to $5,000,000 a year with no prospect for improvement in upcoming years. The company is currently operating at a loss of $500,000 a year, but management has found a way to reduce fixed costs by 50% so that the company can survive at a lower level of operations. Income statements for the previous good years, the current lean years, and the expected good years are given as follows:

	Previous Good Years	Current Lean Years	Expected Good Years
Sales	$10,000,000	$5,000,000	$5,000,000
Variable costs	7,000,000	3,500,000	3,500,000
Contribution margin	$ 3,000,000	$1,500,000	$1,500,000
Fixed costs	2,000,000	2,000,000	1,000,000
Profit (loss)	$ 1,000,000	$ (500,000)	$ 500,000

MEASURES OF RELATIONSHIP BETWEEN OPERATING LEVELS AND BREAK-EVEN POINTS

Companies want to know where they are with respect to the break-even point. If they are operating around the break-even point, management may be more conservative in its approach to implementing changes and mapping out new strategies. On the other hand, if they are operating well away from the break-even point, management will be more liberal because the downside risk is not as great. Two measures that relate to this distance between a break-even point and the current or planned operating volume are operating leverage and margin of safety. These measures are the subject of the following sections.

Operating Leverage

Operating leverage is a measure of the effect a percentage change in sales revenue has on profit before taxes. It is a principle by which management in a high fixed cost industry with a relatively high contribution margin percentage (low variable costs relative to sales revenue) can increase profits substantially with a small increase in sales volume. The measure is a ratio of the contribution margin divided by profit.

$$\frac{\text{Contribution margin}}{\text{Profit before taxes}} = \text{Operating leverage factor}$$

We typically call this ratio the operating leverage factor or the degree of operating leverage. It is related to the distance between the break-even point and a current or expected sales volume because the difference between the contribution margin and the profit before taxes is the fixed cost. As profit moves closer to zero, the closer the fixed costs are to the contribution margin, and the closer the company is to the break-even point. The ratio is designed to yield a high number when close to the break-even point and a progressively lower number as sales volume increases.

With a relatively small increase in sales volume, profits will increase by the percentage increase in sales volume multiplied by the operating leverage factor. Simply stated, a company with high fixed costs will have to sell in large volume to recover the fixed costs. However, if the company also has a high contribution margin ratio, it will move into higher profits very quickly after the break-even volume is attained. Hence, a fairly small percentage increase in sales volume (computed on a base that is already fairly large) will increase profits rapidly.

For example, suppose that Gamma Company has been selling 8,750 units of a product each year as follows:

Unit selling price	$20
Unit variable cost	12
Unit contribution margin	$ 8
Contribution margin percentage ($8 ÷ $20)	40%
Fixed cost for the year	$60,000
Units sold	8,750
Sales revenue	$175,000
Variable costs	105,000
Contribution margin	$ 70,000
Fixed costs	60,000
Profit	$ 10,000

The operating leverage factor for this situation is 7 and is computed as follows:

$$\frac{\$70{,}000 \text{ (Contribution margin)}}{\$10{,}000 \text{ (Profit)}} = 7 \text{ (Operating leverage factor)}$$

At a sales volume of 8,750, if sales volume can be increased by an additional 10 percent, profit can be increased by 70 percent:

Percentage increase in sales volume		Operating leverage factor		Percentage increase in profit
10%	×	7	=	70%

A 10 percent increase in sales volume will increase sales from 8,750 units to 9,625 units, (8,750 × 1. 1). Operating leverage suggests then that the profit should be $17,000 ($10,000 × 1.7). The following income statement shows that a 10 percent increase in sales volume results in a 70 percent increase in profits.

Units sold	9,625	(10% increase)
Sales revenue	$192,500	(10% increase)
Variable cost	115,500	
Contribution margin............................	$ 77,000	
Fixed cost.......................................	60,000	
Profit	$ 17,000	(70% increase)

As sales volume increases away from the break-even point, contribution margin and profit move closer together; thus, the operating leverage factor decreases. In the example given, yet another 10 percent increase in sales will produce only a 45 percent increase in profit. The new operating leverage factor, with a contribution margin of $77,000 and a profit of $17,000, is 4.53.

$$\frac{\$77{,}000 \text{ (Contribution margin)}}{\$17{,}000 \text{ (Profit)}} = 4.53 \text{ (Operating leverage factor)}$$

Units sold	10,588	(10% increase)
Sales revenue	$211,760	(10% increase)
Variable cost	127,056	
Contribution margin............................	$ 84,704	
Fixed cost.......................................	60,000	
Profit	$ 24,704	(45.3% increase)*

*Increase is not exactly 45.3 percent due to initial rounding of the units sold to the nearest whole number.

Operating Leverage with High Fixed Cost   The magnitude of the operating leverage factor is directly related to the level of fixed cost. In order to see the impact of fixed cost, let's look at two companies: Alpha and Beta. Both companies sell the same product at the same price and have identical sales volume. The only difference between the two companies is the level of fixed cost. An income statement for each company follows:

	Alpha Company	Beta Company
Units sold	16,250	16,250
Sales revenue	$325,000	$325,000
Variable cost	195,000	195,000
Contribution margin................................	$130,000	$130,000
Fixed cost	120,000	60,000
Profit	$ 10,000	$ 70,000
Operating Factor:		
(contribution margin/profit)	13.0	1.857

Beta Company has a small advantage from operating leverage, but Alpha Company—operating with twice as much fixed cost—has a much larger operating leverage factor. Therefore, Alpha will benefit more from leveraging than will Beta. To see what this means for the companies, consider a 10 percent increase in sales volume. The operating leverage factors indicate that Alpha should realize a 130 percent increase in profit while Beta will increase only 18.57 percent.

	Percentage increase in sales volume		Operating leverage factor		Percentage increase in profit
Alpha	10%	×	13.0	=	130%
Beta	10%	×	1.857	=	18.57%

	Alpha Company	Beta Company
Units sold (10% increase)	17,875	17,875
Sales revenue (10% increase)......................	$357,500	$357,500
Variable cost (10% increase)	214,500	214,500
Contribution margin................................	$143,000	$143,000
Fixed cost	120,000	60,000
Profit	$ 23,000	$ 83,000
Percentage increase in profit:		
(change in profit/old profit)	130%	18.57%

To understand why the company with a higher level of fixed costs receives the benefits of leveraging, we must understand how fixed costs fit in the formula for computing the operating factor. Below is the original formula with a restated formula:

$$\frac{\text{Contribution margin}}{\text{Profit}} = \frac{\text{Contribution margin}}{\text{Contribution margin} - \text{Fixed cost}}$$

As fixed costs increase, the numerator of the formula gets smaller which means the answer is larger. The higher the fixed costs, the closer the company is to break even and the greater the percentage change in profits is from a change in sales. Alpha company has a higher percentage change in profit because its fixed costs are higher.

Operating Leverage in a Declining Market   A company like Alpha Company, with relatively high fixed costs, will increase profits remarkably with only modest increases in sales volume; but when sales volume declines—even by a small amount—profits will also decrease more rapidly. Returning to the original sales volume for both companies, assume that sales volume for both decreases 10 percent. Alpha Company's profit will decrease 130 percent while Beta Company's will decrease only 18.57 percent. This means that Beta Company will still earn a profit but Alpha Company will sustain a loss.

	Alpha Company	Beta Company
Units sold (10% decrease)	14,625	14,625
Sales revenue (10% decrease)	$292,500	$292,500
Variable cost (10% decrease)	175,500	175,500
Contribution margin	$117,000	$117,000
Fixed cost	120,000	60,000
Profit (loss)	$ (3,000)	$ 57,000
Percentage decrease in profit: (change in profit/old profit)	130%	18.57%

The basic message for the company with a high operating leverage factor is to be conservative on sales volume issues and to look closely at those cost elements that will reduce break-even points. The most significant reduction in break-even points will come from reducing the level of fixed cost. Decreases in variable cost per unit will increase the contribution, which decreases break-even points.

Margin of Safety

The **margin of safety** is the excess of actual sales over sales at the break-even point. The excess may also be computed as a percentage of actual sales. The margin of safety, expressed either in dollars or as a percentage, shows how much sales volume can be reduced without sustaining losses. The formulas for calculating margin of safety are below:

$$\text{Margin of safety in dollars} = \text{Actual or expected sales} - \text{Break-even sales}$$

$$\text{Margin of safety in percentage form} = \frac{\text{Margin of safety in dollars}}{\text{Actual or expected sales}}$$

For our purposes, margin of safety is the percentage form. Therefore, unless otherwise specified, a reference to margin of safety will mean a percentage.

The margin of safety is computed on page 153 from income statements given for XyFont Company and Zebra Company. XyFont Company is in a better position to absorb a reduction in sales and will not reach the break-even point until sales decline by 50%. The contribution margin percentage is relatively low, and for every dollar decrease in sales, the contribution margin will decrease by only $.20. Also, fixed costs are at a lower level. In contrast, Zebra

Company will find that the contribution margin will decline rapidly with a decrease in sales. For every dollar decrease in sales, the contribution margin will decrease by $.40. In addition, the fixed costs are higher. If Zebra Company is to improve its margin of safety, it must lower the break-even point or increase sales volume.

When FC=↑ then C M will ∆ faster

	XyFont Company		Zebra Company	
	Dollars	**Percentage of Sales Revenue**	**Dollars**	**Percentage of Sales Revenue**
Sales revenue	$1,000,000	100%	$1,000,000	100%
Variable cost	800,000	80	600,000	60
Contribution margin ...	$ 200,000	20%	$ 400,000	40%
Fixed cost	100,000		300,000	
Profit	$ 100,000		$ 100,000	

Break-even sales:

$$\frac{\$100,000 \text{ (Fixed cost)}}{20\% \text{ (Contribution margin rate)}} = \$ 500,000$$

$$\frac{\$300,000 \text{ (Fixed cost)}}{40\% \text{ (Contribution margin rate)}} = \qquad\qquad \$ 750,000$$

Margin of safety in dollars:

$$\begin{array}{l}\$1,000,000 - \$500,000 \\ \text{(Actual sales less} \qquad = \quad \$ 500,000 \\ \text{break-even sales)}\end{array}$$

$$\begin{array}{l}\$1,000,000 - \$750,000 \\ \text{(Actual sales less} \qquad = \qquad\qquad \$ 250,000 \\ \text{break-even sales)}\end{array}$$

Margin of safety as a percentage:

$$\frac{\$500,000}{\$1,000,000} = \qquad 50\%$$

$$\frac{\$250,000}{\$1,000,000} = \qquad\qquad\qquad 25\%$$

The margin of safety gets larger as sales volumes increase away from the break-even point. Therefore, it is a measure of the distance sales volume is from the break-even sales volume. Consequently, a margin of safety becomes a concern to a company when it has a sales volume above the break-even volume and the market is declining. When the market is increasing, the margin of safety is nice to know but it does not usually play a significant factor in management's plans.

Relationship Between Operating Leverage and Margin of Safety

A relationship exists between operating leverage and margin of safety that suggests when each method of analysis might be most useful. The relationship is an inverse one, expressed in the following formula:

$$\text{Operating leverage factor} = \frac{1}{\text{Margin of safety}}$$

or

$$\text{Margin of safety} = \frac{1}{\text{Operating leverage factor}}$$

Using the data from XyFont Company above, the operating leverage factor using the straight-forward approach is calculated as follows:

$$\frac{\$200,000 \text{ (Contribution margin)}}{\$100,000 \text{ (Profit)}} = 2$$

Using the inverse relationship, we already know the margin of safety is 50% and that yields the operating leverage factor computed as below.

$$\frac{1}{50\% \text{ (Margin of safety)}} = 2$$

We have already seen in the foregoing discussions that operating leverage factors are higher near break-even points and decrease as sales volume increases. Margins of safety are quite the opposite. They are low near break-even points and get larger with increases in sales volume. But, that is exactly what the inverse relationship tells us.

THE SALES MIX

When selling more than one product line, the relative proportion of each product line to the total sales is called the **sales mix.** With each product line having a different contribution margin, management will try to maximize the sales of the product lines with the higher contribution margins. However, a sales mix results because there are limits to the quantities of any given product line that can be produced, and there may also be certain market limitations on how much can be sold.

When products have their own individual production facilities and fixed costs are specifically identified with the product line, cost-volume-profit analysis is performed for each product line. However, in many cases, product lines share facilities and the fixed costs related to many products. For such a situation, cost-volume-profit analysis requires averaging of data by using the sales mix as weights. Consequently, a break-even point can be computed for any assumed mix of sales, and a break-even chart or P/V graph can be constructed for any sales mix. But any one graph will have a constant sales mix for the entire range of volumes covered by the cost and revenue lines. If the sales mix changes, a new set of cost and revenue lines is needed.

Let's consider an example of cost-volume-profit analysis with a sales mix. Assume that the following budget is prepared for the sale of three product lines in combination. Fixed costs are budgeted at $500,000 for the year:

Product Lines	Unit Sales Volume (Units)	Unit Selling Price	Unit Variable Cost	Contribution Margin Dollars	Contribution Margin Percentage
JP-1	20,000	$50	$20	$30	60
KQ-9	10,000	50	30	20	40
TS-3	10,000	50	40	10	20
	40,000				

The break-even point in units is computed using a weighted average contribution margin as follows:

Product Lines	Sales Mix Proportions		Unit Contribution Margin	Weighted Contribution Margin
JP-1	50%	×	$30	$15.00
KQ-9	25%	×	20	5.00
TS-3	25%	×	10	2.50
Weighted contribution margin				$22.50

$$\frac{\$500{,}000 \text{ (Fixed cost)}}{\$22.50 \text{ (Weighted contribution margin)}} = 22{,}222 \text{ total units}$$

The detailed composition of sales and contribution margins at this level is as follows:

Product Lines	Sales Mix Proportions		Total Units		Units of Product		Unit Contribution Margin		Contribution Margin
JP-1	50%	×	22,222	=	11,111	×	$30	=	$333,330
KQ-9	25%	×	22,222	=	5,555	×	20	=	111,100
TS-3	25%	×	22,222	=	5,555	×	10	=	55,550
Break-even contribution margin*									$499,980

* Approximately equal to fixed cost of $500,000. Difference is due to rounding.

If you want the sales revenue at the break-even point directly, it is calculated as we did earlier in the chapter. Simply divide the weighted contribution margin percentage into the fixed costs. Individual product line revenues will be the total revenues multiplied by individual sales mix proportions. For example, let's look at more information about the illustration we started with.

| | Product Lines | | | |
	JP-1	KQ-9	TS-3	Total
Units to be sold	20,000	10,000	10,000	40,000
Sales	$1,000,000	$500,000	$500,000	$2,000,000
Variable cost	400,000	300,000	400,000	1,100,000
Contribution margin	$ 600,000	$200,000	$100,000	$ 900,000
Less fixed cost				500,000
Budgeted profit before income taxes				$ 400,000

As shown in the following calculations, the weighted contribution margin percentage is 45 percent, and revenue at the break-even point is $1,111,111.

$$\frac{\$900,000 \text{ (Total contribution margin)}}{\$2,000,000 \text{ (Total sales revenue)}} = 45\%$$

$$\frac{\$500,000 \text{ (Fixed cost)}}{45\% \text{ (Weighted contribution margin percentage)}} = \$1,111,111$$

If the actual sales mix changes from the budgeted sales mix, the break-even point and other factors of cost-volume-profit analysis may change. During the next year, for instance, assume the company operated at the capacity budgeted with fixed cost of $500,000. The unit selling prices and variable costs were in agreement with the budget. Yet, with the same revenue of $2,000,000, the profit before income taxes was considerably lower than anticipated. The difference was due to a changed sales mix. Assume actual results were as shown below. Instead of earning $400,000 before income taxes, the company earned only $200,000. Sales of Products KQ-9 and TS-3, the less profitable lines, were much better than expected. At the same time, sales of the best product line, Product JP-1, were less than expected. As a result, the total contribution margin was less than budgeted, so income before income tax was also less than budgeted.

Product Line	Quantity Sold	Unit Contribution Margin	Total Contribution Margin	Sales Revenue
JP-1	5,000	$30	$150,000	$ 250,000
KQ-9	20,000	20	400,000	1,000,000
TS-3	15,000	10	150,000	750,000
Total contribution margin			$700,000	$2,000,000
Less fixed cost			500,000	
Actual profit before income taxes			$200,000	

One way to encourage the sales force to sell more of the high contribution margin lines is to compute sales commissions on the contribution margin and not on sales revenue. If sales commissions are based on sales revenue, a sales force may have a high volume of sales of less profitable product lines and still earn a satisfactory commission. But if sales commissions are related to contribution margin, the sales force is encouraged to strive for greater sales of more profitable products, and, in doing so, will help to improve total company profits.

INDIFFERENCE POINT

Management will often face a situation where it must decide which of two products to produce or services to offer when available capacity permits only one. Too many managers will make the decision on the basis of break-even points and contribution margins. They ignore the range of potential volume in which production and sales will likely operate.

Suppose Carrollton Plastics has two products: Plastimax, with a contribution margin of $50 and identifiable fixed costs of $30,000; and Pyrexl, with a contribution margin of $40 and identifiable fixed costs of $22,000. The company has capacity to produce either product but not both. Assume that fixed costs are entirely avoidable. Which product should the company produce? The decision depends on where the anticipated sales volume will be.

Our analysis requires a profit function for each product which is expressed as follows:

$$(\text{Contribution margin per unit} \times \text{Volume}) - \text{Fixed cost} = \text{Profit}$$

Applying this formula to each product, we have two profit functions, as shown below:

$$\text{Profit (Plastimax)} = \$50x - \$30,000$$
$$\text{Profit (Pyrexl)} = \$40x - \$22,000$$

The next step is to calculate the break-even points in units. These points give the minimum quantities a company is willing to produce.

$$\text{Plastimax: } \$30,000 \div \$50 = 600 \text{ units}$$
$$\text{Pyrexl: } \$22,000 \div \$40 = 550 \text{ units}$$

Given a choice, we will not produce less than 600 units of Plastimax nor 550 units of Pyrexl.

Next, we calculate the point at which the profit functions intersect. This is the point at which the total profit from each product is identical. Therefore, set the profit functions equal to each other and solve for the number of units:

$$\$50x - \$30,000 = \$40x - \$22,000$$
$$10x = 8,000$$
$$x = 800 \text{ units}$$

The point of intersection is known as an **indifference point** because the profit of each product is the same. At 800 units, management can select either product with identical results. If expected sales volume is less than 800 units, management will prefer one product to the other. At points above 800 units, management will prefer the other product.

Knowing the contribution margins for each product, the break-even points, and the indifference point, we can construct the following decision table:

Anticipated Range of Volume	Preferred Product
0 – 549	Neither product
550 – 799	Pyrexl
800	Indifferent
801 and above	Plastimax

Initially, some managers will question selecting Pyrexl in the range of 601 – 799 units because Plastimax has the higher contribution margin per unit and sales are above its break-even point. Pyrexl will earn a profit at any point above 551 units. Although Plastimax is profitable with 601 units and above, its profit does not catch up to Pyrexl until the indifference point.

The point of this discussion is to show that management cannot make a decision without knowing the anticipated volume at which the product selected will be sold. Then, if the products or services under examination have intersecting profit functions, the indifference point should enter into the analysis. You should recognize that not all profit functions will intersect, in which case, an indifference point does not exist.

We have used the indifference point concept above to help select between products. The same analysis is appropriate when a company wants to select one production process over another. For example, management may have one option to install a labor-intensive process and another option for a capital-intensive process. Which process should it select? Management must determine the contribution margin for the product related to the new process and the fixed costs of the process. With this information, we repeat the steps from above that lead to a decision table. Management then gets estimates of sales volume and compares those to the points in the decision table.

OTHER CONTRIBUTION MARGIN MEASUREMENTS

We have defined the contribution margin with respect to individual products or services. The basic definition we have used for the contribution margin is sales minus variable cost. Although we have not used the term thus far, a more appropriate term is variable contribution margin because all variable items (revenue and costs) are included in the calculation. The variable costs include both product and period variable costs. This is the contribution that pays for fixed costs and then provides a profit. There are other ways of formulating and expressing a contribution margin. In this section, we look at other expressions of the contribution margin concept. The first one measures a contribution for a unit of resource. The second one ties contribution margin to organizational units and their managers.

Contribution Margin Per Unit of Scarce Resource

Management is expected to earn an adequate return on invested resources. Selecting a product mix on the basis of contribution margins per unit or expanding production to utilize limited capacity can lead to an inefficient use of resources. With existing facilities and productive resources, management should seek the best **contribution margin per unit of the limiting or scarce factor**. The scarce factor, in some cases, may be hours of labor time; or it may be space used for production. For example, assume that three product lines can be produced and sold as follows:

Product Line	Unit Contribution Margin (1)	Production Hours Per Unit of Product (2)	Contribution Margin Per Hour(1) ÷ (2)
Turk	$10	5	$2
Russ	6	2	3
Gee	4	1	4

How should the company use its resources? In order to see how this information helps in selecting a sales mix, assume production capacity of 10,000 hours. The contribution margin per unit tells us that the company should produce all of Gee it can; then move to Russ, and finally to Turk. But, the market place plus other commitments can also be limiting concerns. Assume, therefore, that the market will not absorb more than 1,000 units of Gee and that a current commitment requires that the company produce 1,500 units of Turk. The mix is computed below:

Production hours available		10,000
Gee (1,000 × 1 hour)	1,000	
Turk (1,500 × 5 hours)	7,500	8,500
Hours available for Russ		1,500

Units of Russ (1,500 ÷ 2) = 750

Therefore, the current mix that best utilizes capacity is 1,500 units of Turk; 750 units of Russ; and 1,000 units of Gee. As market conditions and other commitments change, the company should increase Gee and decrease Turk.

Chapter 11 discusses in more detail the applications of contribution margin per unit of scarce resource.

Controllable and Segment Contribution Margins

The next contribution margin concept looks at managerial control and is applicable where a manager has revenue and cost responsibility. Costs controllable by the manager are subtracted from sales to provide a **controllable contribution margin** or controllable margin. It represents the amount available to pay for the noncontrollable expenses and to provide a profit for the company as a whole. Notice that this contribution margin indicates by what amount revenue exceeds the costs controlled by the manager. Therefore, it is a measure used to evaluate a manager's performance. However, it is important to note that the controllable contribution margin is not a manager's contribution to the company's profits, since many noncontrollable costs may exist and must be paid before any profit is generated for the organization as a whole.

The costs that are controllable by a manager could include the variable product costs, any period variable costs such as commissions paid to sales persons, and any fixed costs that the manager controls such as salespersons' salaries. The exact content of controllable costs depends on the situation at each company.

The next contribution margin is the **direct or segment contribution margin** or segment margin. The direct contribution margin is sales minus all direct costs of the segment. (The definitions for direct and indirect were discussed in Chapter 2.) For example, the direct contribution margin for a branch office is sales less all product costs, less branch operating costs, less any other cost that can be traced to the branch. This amount is the branch's contribution to pay for home office costs and any other indirect costs of the organization and to generate company profit.

Illustration of All Contribution Margin Concepts

It is possible to illustrate nearly all of the variations in contribution margin in one example. Let us revisit the Burgers Plus illustration from Chapter 2. The owner is Ms. Hood and there are three outlets around town. Figure 4.7 presents a summary income statement, expanded for the Grand Avenue location.

The only contribution margin measure not illustrated is contribution margin per unit. Since a small cola and a large double cheeseburger cannot be equated, the unit measure is not relevant. However with more information, the contribution margin for fries, shakes, burgers, etc. can be analyzed. Pricing, product offerings, and production costs are all part of the profit analysis. In a business like this every product must contribute to paying for indirect costs and generating profit. For example, the Grand Avenue location had $185,000 in sales in September. The breakdown of sales and variable food costs was:

	Burgers	Fries	Shakes	Drinks	Others	Total
Sales	$ 81,000	$ 36,000	$ 14,000	$ 39,000	$ 15,000	$185,000
Variable food costs	38,880	14,400	7,700	14,820	9,300	85,100
Food contribution margin	$ 42,120	$ 21,600	$ 6,300	$ 24,180	$ 5,700	$ 99,900
Food contribution margin percentage	52%	60%	45%	62%	38%	54%

More detail could be developed for each product in each product line. Notice that the Other Variable Costs (probably supplies and condiments) could not be traced accurately to each product line. The variable contribution margin can be expressed as a dollar amount or a percentage. The food contribution margin and the variable contribution margin will be watched carefully from month to month for trends and any significant changes.

BURGERS PLUS
CONTRIBUTION ANALYSIS BY STORE
FOR THE MONTH OF SEPTEMBER

	River Road	Pine Street	Grand Avenue		Totals
Sales	$120,000	$ 96,000	$185,000	100%	$401,000
Variable food costs . . .	$ 55,500	$ 46,000	$ 85,100	46%	$186,600
Other variable costs . .	6,000	4,500	11,100	6%	21,600
Total variable costs . . .	$ 61,500	$ 50,500	$ 96,200	52%	$208,200
Variable contribution margin	$ 58,500	$ 45,500	$ 88,800	48%	$192,800
Direct controllable fixed costs	12,600	13,900	20,400		46,900
Controllable contribution margin	$ 45,900	$ 31,600	$ 68,400		$145,900
Direct noncontrollable fixed costs	24,400	21,300	38,900		84,600
Direct contribution margin	$ 21,500	$ 10,300	$ 29,500		$ 61,300
Common corporate costs					36,900
Net profit					$ 24,400

Figure 4.7   Contribution Margin Analysis By Store

The direct controllable fixed costs will include any fixed cost that the individual store managers can control, including perhaps shift managers' salaries if the stores are open 24 hours a day. Also, certain costs like local advertising or promotions costs, cleaning costs, and maintenance costs might be called controllable costs. The controllable contribution margin is the profit basis on which the Grand Avenue manager will be evaluated and rewarded (a bonus for strong profit improvement or performance).

The direct noncontrollable fixed costs include two major expenses—the store manager's salary and occupancy costs (rent or depreciation). Both expenses can be easily traced to specific locations and are not controllable by the store manager. Certain other costs could fall into this category by being direct but not variable and not controllable. It is this direct or store contribution margin that is used to measure the profit performance of the store itself.

At this point, measuring segment or store profitability stops. Direct contribution margin is the finest tuned profit measure that is free of broader cost allocations. All other costs not already deducted are considered common or indirect costs. These could be allocated on some basis; but the concept of contribution margin analysis ends prior to allocation of common costs. Part of the aura is the visual nature of contribution margin. It is easily understood, seen, and measured. Allocations may distort all three.

Ms. Hood now has numerous versions of profitability for each location. She will use each to answer specific questions about her products, managers, and stores. More detail may be needed, but the profit measuring framework has been put in place. Many managerial decisions will use contribution margin analysis. When the nonspecific term contribution margin is used, it generally means variable contribution margin. But as in most cases in life, play it safe—define which contribution margin you are talking about.

SUMMARY

In planning profit, management considers sales volume, selling prices, variable costs, fixed costs, and the sales mix. When the contribution margin is equal to fixed costs, the company breaks even. A desired profit level can be attained when the contribution margin is equal to the fixed costs plus the desired profit before income taxes. Break-even charts or profit/volume graphs are visual representations of profits or losses that can be expected at different volume levels.

In making plans, management can review various alternatives to see how they will affect profit. For example, what will likely happen if the selling price is increased or if the variable cost is decreased? Often a relatively small change in variable cost per unit will have a relatively large effect on profit. Prices may be cut to increase sales volume, but this will not necessarily increase profit. Profit may or may not increase in the short run, or lower profit may be accepted in the short run if increased profit can be anticipated in the long run.

Recent developments such as increased automation tend to increase the importance of fixed costs in the total cost structure. With a relatively high contribution margin rate and relatively high fixed costs, a small percentage increase in sales volume can be translated into a substantial increase in profits. This principle, known as operating leverage, can also work against a company when sales volume is decreasing. When a company is operating at volume levels higher than the break-even point, the margin of safety becomes an important part of a cost-volume-profit analysis.

When more than one product line is sold, the relative proportion of total sales for each product line is known as the sales mix. In order to maximize profit, management will try to maximize the sales of product lines with higher contribution margin rates. A break-even point and break-even units for each product line can be computed for any given sales mix. Other measures of contribution margin are explained and their uses discussed, including: contribution margin per unit of scarce resource, controllable contribution margin, and segment contribution margin.

PROBLEM FOR REVIEW

Foxx Company manufactures a water sealant at the Orange County Plant. This sealant is used to stop leaks in basements or in concrete retainer walls. In 1994, the company sold 1,600,000 gallons of the sealant at a price of $3.00 per gallon with a variable production cost per gallon of $1.50. The fixed manufacturing costs were $1,550,000.

In 1995, new automated equipment will be used in production. This will increase the fixed manufacturing costs for the year to $1,785,000. The variable production cost per gallon has been estimated at $1.30 per gallon.

The sales division estimates that sales volume can be increased by 12.5 percent in 1995. The board of directors asks you to determine what effect these changes will have on the manufacturing profit after considering income taxes at 40 percent of income before taxes.

Required:

1. Prepare an income statement for manufacturing operations for both 1994 and 1995 (include all of the expected changes).
2. For 1994, compute the break-even point in gallons and revenues.
3. For 1995, compute the break-even point in gallon and revenues.
4. Using the cost and revenue data for 1994, consider each of the following situations independently:
    (a) What is the effect on the break-even point in gallons for the decrease in variable cost from $1.50 per gallon to $1.30 gallon.
    (b) What is the effect on the break-even point in gallons for the increase in fixed cost of $235,000.
5. For 1994, calculate the operating leverage factor and the margin of safety.
6. For 1995, calculate the operating leverage factor and the margin of safety, after making all estimated changes.
7. Using 1,800,000 gallons as a base, assume that sales volume in 1995 can be increased further to 1,890,000 gallons. Determine the percentage increase in sales and in profit before taxes under this assumption. What is the operating leverage factor?

Solution:

1.

FOXX COMPANY
ORANGE COUNTY PLANT
INCOME STATEMENT—MANUFACTURING

	1994	1995
Sales:		
(1,600,000 × $3.00)	$4,800,000	
(1,800,000* × $3.00)		$5,400,000
Variable production cost:		
(1,600,000 × $1.50)	2,400,000	
(1,800,000 × $1.30)		2,340,000
Contribution margin	$2,400,000	$3,060,000
Fixed production cost	1,550,000	1,785,000
Income before income taxes	$ 850,000	$1,275,000
Income taxes, 40%	340,000	510,000
Net profit	$ 510,000	$ 765,000
*Sales in gallons, 1994	1,600,000	
12.5% increase	200,000	
Estimated sales in gallons, 1995	1,800,000	

2.   For 1994, break-even point in gallons and revenues:

$$\frac{\$1,550,000 \text{ (Fixed cost)}}{\$1.50 \text{ (Unit contribution margin)}} = 1,033,333 \text{ gallons}$$

$$\frac{\$1,550,000 \text{ (Fixed cost)}}{50\% \text{ (Contribution margin percentage)}} = \$3,100,000$$

3.   For 1995, estimated break-even point in gallons and revenues:

$$\frac{\$1,785,000 \text{ (Fixed cost)}}{\$1.70 \text{ (Unit contribution margin)}} = 1,050,000 \text{ gallons}$$

$$\frac{\$1,785,000 \text{ (Fixed cost)}}{56.667\% \text{ (Contribution margin percentage)}} = \$3,150,000$$

4.   (a) Change in variable cost:
New break-even point:

$$\frac{\$1,550,000 \text{ (Fixed cost)}}{\$1.70 \text{ (Unit contribution margin)}} = 911,765 \text{ gallons}$$

Old break-even point . . . .   1,033,333 gallons
Decrease in break-even point . . . .   121,568 gallons

(b) Change in fixed cost:
New break-even point:

$$\frac{\$1,785,000 \text{ (Fixed cost)}}{\$1.50 \text{ (Unit contribution margin)}} = 1,190,000 \text{ gallons}$$

Old break-even point . . . .   1,033,333 gallons
Increase in break-even point . . . .   156,667 gallons

5.   Operating leverage and margin of safety for 1994:
Operating leverage:

$$\frac{\$2,400,000 \text{ (Contribution margin)}}{\$850,000 \text{ (Profit before tax)}} = 2.82$$

Margin of safety:

$$\frac{\$4,800,000 \text{ (Current revenues)} - \$3,100,000 \text{ (Break-even revenues)}}{\$4,800,000 \text{ (Current revenues)}} = 35.4 \text{ percent}$$

6.   Operating leverage and margin of safety for 1995:
Operating leverage:

$$\frac{\$3,060,000 \text{ (Contribution margin)}}{\$1,275,000 \text{ (Profit before tax)}} = 2.40$$

Margin of safety:

$$\frac{\$5,400,000 \text{ (Current revenues)} - \$3,150,000 \text{ (Break-even revenues)}}{\$5,400,000 \text{ (Current revenues)}} = 41.7 \text{ percent}$$

7.   Percentage increase in sales volume:

$$\frac{90,000 \text{ (additional gallons)}}{1,800,000 \text{ (original estimate of gallons to be sold)}} = 5\% \text{ sales volume increase}$$

Estimated profit with sales of 1,890,000 gallons:

Contribution margin (1,890,000 × $1.70)	$3,213,000
Fixed cost	1,785,000
Estimated income before income taxes	$1,428,000

Percentage increase in profit before taxes:

Revised additional estimate	$1,428,000
Original estimate	1,275,000
Increase in profit	$ 153,000

$$\frac{\$153,000 \text{ (Increase in profit)}}{\$1,275,000 \text{ (Original estimate)}} = 12\% \text{ increase in profit}$$

$$\frac{\$3,060,000 \text{ (Contribution margin, original estimate)}}{\$1,275,000 \text{ (Income before taxes, original estimate)}} = 2.4 \text{ operating leverage factor}$$

Percentage Increase in Sales Volume		Operating Leverage Factor		Percentage Increase in Profit
5%	×	2.4	=	12%

TERMINOLOGY REVIEW

Break-even chart (138)
Break-even point (136)
Contribution margin (136)
Contribution margin per unit of limiting
or scarce factor (159)
Controllable contribution margin (159)
Cost-volume-profit analysis or break-
even analysis (136)
Direct or segment contribution margin
(160)

Indifference point (157)
Margin of safety (152)
Operating leverage (149)
Profit-volume (P/V) graph (140)
Relevant range (140)
Sales mix (154)
Variable contribution margin (158)

QUESTIONS FOR REVIEW AND DISCUSSION

1. Identify the interrelated factors that are important to profit planning.

2. When the total contribution margin is equal to the total fixed cost, is the company operating at a profit or at a loss? Explain.

3. If the total fixed cost and the contribution margin per unit of product are given, explain how to compute the number of units that must be sold in order to break even.

4. Describe the components of a break-even chart.

5. If the total fixed cost and the percentage of the contribution margin to sales revenue are given, explain how to compute the sales revenue at the break-even point.

6. If the total fixed cost and the percentage of the variable cost to sales revenue are given, is it possible to compute the sales revenue at the break-even point? Explain.

7. Can there be two break-even points? If so, describe how the revenue and cost lines would be drawn on the break-even chart?

8. In conventional practice, there is only one break-even point. Why?

9. Is it possible to compute the number of units that must be sold to earn a certain amount of profit after income tax? Explain.

10. How does a P/V graph differ from a break-even chart? Which form of presentation is superior?

11. When the contribution margin is high in relation to sales revenue, is the slope of the profit line on the P/V graph relatively steep or flat?

12. If there is an increase in the variable cost per unit of product, is there any effect on the profit line on the P/V graph? Explain the effect.

13. If there is a decrease in the selling price per unit of product, is there any effect on the profit line on the P/V graph? Explain the effect.

14. A 10% decrease in the selling price of a product has the same effect on profits as a 10% increase in the unit variable cost of the product. Is this true? Explain.

15. What does the slope of the P/V graph represent?

16. Does the slope of the profit line on the P/V graph change when the total fixed cost is increased or decreased? How is the profit line affected by changes in the total fixed cost?

17. Explain how an advantage can be obtained by accepting an increase in fixed costs in exchange for a reduction in the unit variable cost. (Consult the Problem For Review.)

18. What is operating leverage? How can it work against a company?

19. Define margin of safety. How is a margin of safety related to operating leverage?

20. What is the meaning of a break-even point where multiple products are present? Explain the meaning in terms of the individual products.

21. Given an instance in which a company has the ability to produce two products but the capacity to produce only one, explain the significance of the break-even points and an indifference point.

22. Identify and define at least four versions of contribution margin. If you managed a local outlet of Hot'n'Juicy Burgers, how might each be used?

EXERCISES

1. **Break-Even Point.** Prairie View Wineries, Inc., conducts tours through its wine processing facility. The tours are free and are included as part of the sales promotion program. Estimates show that the cost per tourist is $4.50 plus an additional fixed cost for the year of $60,000. An average of 30,000 tourists can be expected each year. The average contribution margin per case of wine sold is $15.

    Required:
    Calculate how many cases of wine must be sold in order to cover the total average cost of the tours.

2. **Break-Even Point.** Craig Lejewski operates a health club in Cleveland. Annual memberships are sold, and nonmembers may pay for individual sessions. Lejewski states that the average revenue amounts to $20 per patron visit. He has estimated the variable cost at $2.50 per patron visit and the fixed cost per year at $35,000. Next year, the fixed cost is expected to increase to $43,750.

    Required:
    1. How many patron visits were required last year for Lejewski to break even?
    2. Under the new fixed cost structure for next year, how many patron visits are needed to break even?
    3. How many patron visits above the break-even point are required next year to earn a profit of $17,500.

3. **Break-Even Point.** The president of Weyland Supply Company is concerned about increased costs to purchase a hardware item that is sold by the company through one of its retail outlets. Last year the variable cost per unit of product was $18. Next year the variable cost is expected to increase to $22 per unit. The selling price per unit, however, cannot be increased and will remain at $25 per unit. The fixed costs amount to $63,000.

    Required:
    1. What was the break-even point in units of product last year?
    2. What was the break-even point in sales dollars for last year?
    3. How many units of product must be sold next year in order to break even?
    4. How many sales dollars will generate break-even volume for next year?

4. **Planned Profit Before Income Taxes.** Huseman Appliances, Inc., is planning operations for the next year. The total contribution margin has been estimated at 40 percent of sales revenue. The 40 percent contribution margin rate is considered to be more probable, but there is a possibility that the contribution margin rate will only be 35 percent. The owner has budgeted fixed costs at $840,000 for the year and has set a profit before income taxes goal of $560,000.

    Required:
    1. How much revenue will be needed to reach the profit goal if the contribution margin rate is 40 percent?
    2. How much revenue will be needed to reach the profit goal if the contribution margin rate is 35 percent?
    3. Calculate the margin of safety at each contribution rate.

5. **Planned Profit After Income Taxes.** Jessica VanBakel notes that if her company is to keep up with the competition, she must obtain the latest type of equipment. If new

equipment is obtained, fixed costs are expected to increase from $640,000 a year to
$1,000,000. On the other hand, the contribution margin rate is expected to increase from
30 percent to 40 percent.

VanBakel has set a profit objective of $300,000 after income taxes at a tax rate of
40 percent.

Required:
1.   Compute the sales revenue needed to meet the profit objective with a 30 percent
     contribution margin rate and lower fixed costs.
2.   Compute the sales revenue needed to meet the profit objective with a 40 percent
     contribution margin rate and higher fixed costs.
3.   Determine the operating leverage for (1) and (2) above.

6.   **Planned Profit After income Taxes.** WestOak Catering Service has budgeted a 12
     percent of sales after tax profit. Management has agreed that this level of profit is
     needed in order to yield a reasonable return on the owners' investment. Fixed costs
     have been budgeted at $456,000 for the year, and the contribution margin rate has been
     estimated at 30 percent. The income tax rate is 40 percent.

Required:
1.   How much revenue will be needed to realize the profit objective?
2.   By how much does this revenue exceed the break-even revenue?
3.   Calculate the margin of safety for the profit objective.

7.   **Break-Even Point and Profits.** Kerri Mayo has observed that there is a demand for
     small tables for personal computers and printers. Retail office furniture outlets are
     charging from $300 to $500 for a table. Kerri believes that she can manufacture and sell
     an attractive small table that will serve the purpose for $180. The cost of materials,
     labor, and variable overhead per table is estimated at $100. The fixed costs consisting of
     rent, insurance, taxes, and depreciation are estimated at $18,000 for the year. She
     already has orders for 180 tables and has established contacts that should result in the
     sale of 150 more tables.

Required:
1.   How many tables must Kerri make and sell in order to break even?
2.   How much profit can be made from the expected production and sale of 330 tables?
3.   What is the margin of safety for 330 tables sold?
4.   How many tables are needed for a profit objective of $8,000?

8.   **Effect of a Price Reduction.** Vacation Motel is presently charging $45 a night for a
     room. The variable cost per room per night has been estimated at $20. Fixed costs for
     the year have been estimated at $236,250. The motel has the capacity to operate at
     15,000 room days a year. Room days are equal to the number of rooms multiplied by
     number of days. With the present price structure, the motel has been operating at only
     9,500 room days a year.

The manager believes that the motel cannot compete on a service basis with chain
motels and that occupancy can be increased by reducing the room rate to $30 a night.
The owner states that with a rate of $30 a night, the motel cannot earn a profit even with
100 percent occupancy.

Required:
1.   How much profit is earned per year now with an occupancy of 9,500 room days?
2.   Calculate the degree of operating leverage at 9,500 room days.

3.   With the new price structure, how many room days will be needed to earn the same profit that is being earned now?

4.   Is the owner correct in stating that a profit cannot be earned with a rate of $30 a night? Explain.

9.   **Effect of a Variable Cost Increase.** Jason Fabricators produces a component that is sold for $80 per unit. Last year the variable cost to produce and sell each unit was $60. Next year, materials and labor costs are expected to increase, so the variable cost per unit will be increased to $65. The selling price cannot be increased. The fixed costs last year were $285,000 and are expected to be the same next year.

The president of the company is concerned about how much additional sales volume will be required next year in order to earn the profit before taxes that was earned last year. Last year the profit before income taxes averaged $12 per unit.

Required:
1.   How many units were sold last year?
2.   How many more units must be sold next year in order to earn the same average profit per unit that was earned last year?
3.   Compare the margin of safety for each of the two points.

10.   **Effect of a Fixed Cost Increase.** The president of Erik Manufacturing Company is concerned about the increasing fixed manufacturing costs. Last year, the fixed manufacturing costs were $267,000. This year, the fixed manufacturing costs increased to $345,000. The fixed selling and administrative costs of $180,000 were the same for both years. The company operated in both years with an average contribution margin rate of 30 percent. It earned a profit before income taxes of $345,000 last year.

Required:
1.   What was the sales revenue last year?
2.   How much would sales revenue have had to increase this year in order for the company to have earned the same profit this year as it did last year?
3.   Calculate the margin of safety for each year. Which year was better?

11.   **Indifference Point.** Celebration, Inc. has two products it would like to offer for sale but has capacity enough for only one of the products. The contribution margin for Markit-right is $10 and would require $18,000 of fixed costs. Note-Taker would generate a $15 contribution margin, but have fixed costs of $30,000. Rozalyn Johnson, President, is trying to decide which product to bring to market.

Required:
1.   Calculate the break-even point for each product.
2.   Calculate the indifference point for the two products.
3.   Specify the range of volumes over which each product would be preferred.

12.   **Multiple Product Analysis.** A division of Roswell Products, Inc. manufactures and sells two grades of canvas. The contribution margin per roll of Lite-Weight canvas is $25, and the contribution margin per roll of Heavy-Duty canvas is $75. Last year this division manufactured and sold as many rolls of one type of canvas as the other. The fixed costs were $675,000, and the profit before income taxes was $540,000.

During the current year, 14,000 rolls of Lite-Weight canvas were sold; and 6,000 rolls of Heavy-Duty canvas were sold. The contribution margin per roll for each line remained the same, and the fixed cost remained the same.

Required:
1.   How many rolls of each grade of canvas were sold last year?
2.   How much profit was earned during the current year?
3.   Assuming the same sales mix experienced in the current year, compute the number of units of each grade of canvas that should have been sold during the current year in order to earn the $540,000 profit that was earned last year.

13.   **Segment Performance.** The following data in thousands are from the Long Segment of the Horn Company:

Allocated corporate expenses	$ 45
Direct noncontrollable expenses	60
Variable cost of products sold	350
Variable selling expenses	20
Revenue	600
Direct controllable expenses	40
Unallocated corporate expenses	105
(Three profit centers of equal size exist in the company.)	

Required:
Measure the profitability of the Long Segment and the Long Segment manager.

14.   **Direct and Indirect Cost.** Ajay Brown Manufacturing operates with three divisions: A, B, and C. Division A produces revenue of $1,400,000 for the year; Division B produces revenue of $700,000; and Division C produces $700,000. The total costs for the year for each division are given below:

	Divisions			
	A	B	C	Total
Materials, labor, and other variable costs	$ 520,000	$335,000	$381,000	$1,236,000
Direct controllable fixed costs	311,000	153,000	264,000	728,000
Direct noncontrollable fixed costs	60,000	83,000	70,000	213,000
Allocated company costs	150,000	150,000	150,000	450,000
Total costs	$1,041,000	$721,000	$865,000	$2,627,000

Required:
1.   What are the relevant costs and revenues to evaluate each division manager?
2.   What are the relevant costs and revenues to evaluate each division?
3.   Which division(s) earn enough to cover their controllable costs of operations?
4.   Which division(s) cover their direct costs of operations?

15.   **Contribution Margin Definitions.** In the following income statement format are several classifications of costs, each of which are labeled a, b, c, or d. Identify with an a, b, c, or d how each of the specific costs listed would be classified from the perspective of a manager for a local fast food branch owned by a company that has 12 similar branches in the same metropolitan area.

**Cost
Classification**

		Sales
a	–	Variable Costs
		Variable Contribution Margin
b	–	Controllable Direct Fixed Costs
		Controllable Contribution Margin
c	–	Noncontrollable Direct Fixed Costs
		Direct Contribution Margin
d	–	Allocated Common Costs
		Net Income

Costs:

_a_   **1.** The burger wrapper and biodegradable box costs.

_c_   **2.** Monthly rent on the building where the branch is located. (Lease is long term, is a constant amount each month, and was negotiated by the home office. Alternative thought: what if rent were based on a percentage of sales?)

_d_   **3.** The president's salary.

_b_   **4.** The utilities costs. (These have been roughly the same for several years except for inflation.)

_c_   **5.** The branch manager's salary.

_b_   **6.** The assistant manager's salaries.

_a_   **7.** Food costs.

_b_   **8.** Advertising costs, the local branch's cost of distributing coupons in local newspapers.

_d_   **9.** Advertising costs, television ads placed by the home office not mentioning each location.

_a_   **10.** Wages of part-time "associates" who staff the counters and the kitchen.

16.   **Margin of Safety.** Julie Rowley, chairman of the board of Kaufman Products Company, noted that profits decreased from 1994 to 1995. Increases in sales volume have not added enough contribution margin to compensate for the increase in fixed costs. Summary income statements for each of the two years are given as follows:

	1994	**1995**
Sales	$32,000,000	$36,000,000
Variable costs	24,000,000	27,000,000
Contribution margin	$ 8,000,000	$ 9,000,000
Fixed costs	5,000,000	6,500,000
Income before income taxes	$ 3,000,000	$ 2,500,000

Rowley exclaims, "At the rate we are going with large increases in fixed costs, we will be at our break-even point even with increases in sales."

Required:

1. Compute the margin of safety in both dollars and as a percentage for both 1994 and 1995.

2. Does Rowley have reason for concern? Explain.

17. **C-V-P Analysis with Various Changes.** Herkloz Company sold 20,000 units of its single product during the past year at a selling price of $20.00. The contribution margin percentage was 40 percent and fixed costs for the year were $80,000.

Required:
1. Determine the margin of safety for the company's last year's results.
2. Assuming the company could maintain the same selling price and cost structure as last year, what would the profit be under each of the following independent situations for next year:
    (a) The selling price decreases $2 per unit and sales volume increases by 15 percent?
    (b) The selling price increases $1.50 per unit, sales volume decreases 10 percent, and fixed costs increase $10,000.
    (c) The selling price remains the same, but variable costs increase $1 per unit and fixed costs decrease $15,000.

PROBLEMS

4-1. **Cost, Volume, and Profit Relationships.** Data with respect to a basic product line sold by Carroll Stores are given as follows:

Selling price per unit	$50
Cost per unit.	30
Contribution margin per unit.	$20

The fixed costs for the year are $360,000. The income tax rate is 40 percent.

Required:
1. Determine the number of units that must be sold in order to break even.
2. If a profit before income taxes of $270,000 is to be earned, how many units of product must be sold?
3. If a profit after income taxes of $180,000 is to be earned, how many units of product must be sold?
4. If the selling price per unit is reduced by 10 percent, how many units must be sold to earn a profit of $8 per unit before income taxes?
5. Assume that the selling price remains at $50. How many units must be sold in order to earn a profit of $8 per unit before income taxes if the variable cost per unit increases by 10 percent?
6. Why does a 10 percent decrease in the selling price have more effect on the contribution margin than a 10 percent increase in the variable unit cost?

4-2. **Margin of Safety and Operating Leverage.** The Waterford Division of Maxus Products manufactures a component used in the production of garden tractors. Marty Story, the president of the division, states that the division has the capacity to produce 5,000 units of this component each month. The fixed costs of production are $10,000 each month.

Story admits that it will take some time before the plant has enough orders to operate at capacity, but sales should range between 3,000 and 4,000 units a month. She is interested in looking at what happens to the margin of safety and the operating leverage over a range of activity. To help with this analysis, the accountant tells you that each unit is sold for $20, and the variable unit cost is $15.

Required:
1. Calculate the margin of safety for 3,000 and 4,000 units.
2. Calculate the degree of operating leverage for 3,000 and 4,000 units.
3. Determine the expected manufacturing profit or loss at 3,000 units and at 4,000 units.
4. What do the margin of safety and degrees of operating leverage tell you about what will happen to profit as sales move from 3,000 to 4,000 units?

4-3. **C-V-P and Ratios.** The vice-president of sales, Michael Demski, estimates that the variable cost per product unit will increase from $80 to $85. The selling price is expected to remain at $100. The fixed costs for the year amount to $400,000. Last year the company sold 30,000 units of product and expects to sell the same quantity this year.

Demski is concerned about the loss in profitability because of increased costs. He asks you to prepare an evaluation of what changes are taking place.

Required:
1. What is the contribution margin percentage (ratio) for this and last year?
2. What is the break-even point in sales dollars for this and last year?
3. Calculate the margin of safety for last year and this year.
4. Calculate the degree of operating leverage for last year and this year.
5. Explain what would happen to profit this year if the sales volume could be increased by 15 percent.

4-4. **Sales Promotion and Profits.** Kleen Kar Wash charges $5.95 for a car wash. The variable costs of supplies, labor, etc., are estimated at $3.25 per car. The fixed overhead is $2,000 per month. During an average month, the company will wash 1,400 cars.

Jerry Cummings, the manager, has made arrangements with a fast food outlet nearby to distribute coupons valued at $1 toward food purchases. Kleen Kar Wash will pay 50 cents for each coupon and will distribute one coupon with each car wash. The cost to promote this premium will be $150 each month. With the coupons, Cummings believes that volume will increase to 1,800 cars per month.

Required:
1. What is the average profit each month without the premium?
2. What will the profit be with the premium if Cummings' estimates are correct?
3. Suppose that Cummings is incorrect and that only 1,200 cars are washed each month, even with the promotion. Compute the expected profit.

4-5. **Costs and Profit Planning.** Meng Tan recently retired from the Coast Guard and plans to use his boat for fishing excursions. He has estimated costs as follows.

Pole rental per person	$ .75
Bait bucket per person	.75
Fuel cost per season	800.00
Dock rental per season	400.00
Boat maintenance per season	1,200.00
Depreciation of boat per season	3,000.00
Taxes and permits per season	400.00
His own salary per season	3,000.00

A part-time worker is to be hired to dress the fish for the customers. This worker will receive a salary of $1,000 for the season plus a piece rate wage for each customer.

Tan would like to earn a profit of $5,000 each season after his own salary and estimates that the revenue from 4,000 customers will be $46,000.

Required:
In order to meet his profit objective, what is the maximum piece rate per customer that Tan can pay to a part-time worker?

4-6. **Estimating a Selling Price.** Kaylene Bays and her brother, Francis, would like to make extra money when they have time away from their studies at Wisconsin State University. They are skilled in carpentry and plan to build and sell rustic lawn chairs.
    Estimates of the cost to make and sell each chair are as follows:

Lumber and other materials	$30
Labor (wages to student helpers)	15
Commission to stores selling the chairs	8% of selling price

Radio and direct mail advertising is estimated at a total cost of $5,000. A pickup truck to transport the chairs can be rented at a cost of $1,000. Kaylene and Francis each plan to earn a profit of $4,500 for their efforts. This amount was arrived at by considering what they could earn if they used their time in another way.
    Kaylene believes that 800 units can be made and sold. Francis is more optimistic and believes that 900 units can be made and sold. Both agree that the price must be less than the commercial price of $98 per chair.

Required:
1. Compute a selling price to obtain the desired profit if 800 chairs are sold.
2. Compute a selling price to obtain the desired profit if 900 chairs are sold.
3. Assume that the selling price is based upon the sale of 800 chairs but that 900 chairs are actually sold. How much additional profit will each of them make?
4. Assume that the selling price is based upon the sale of 800 chairs but that only 700 chairs are actually sold. How much profit will each of them make?

4-7. **Step Costs and Ratios.** The Styro Company produces a small electronic dictionary that it sells wholesale for $20 per unit. The variable manufacturing costs are $8 up through 5,000 units and $6 beyond that point. The variable selling and marketing costs are $2 per unit. Total fixed costs are $30,000 for volume through 5,000 units and $36,000 beyond that point.

Required:
1. Compute the break-even point in units and in sales dollars.
2. Starting with 1,000 units above the break-even point and running to 10,000 units, compute each of the following:
    (a) Total contribution margin
    (b) Profit before taxes
    (c) Margin of safety
    (d) Operating leverage
3. Explain how changes in contribution margin relate to changes in profit before taxes before and after 5,000 units.

4-8. **Effect of Variable and Fixed Cost Changes.** Paco Manufacturing Company is considering the acquisition of new equipment. If purchased, the equipment will increase the contribution margin rate from 40 percent to 50 percent. The fixed costs will also increase from $1,000,000 to $1,200,000 per year.

Last year the company earned an income before income taxes of $200,000 on sales of $3,000,000. The board of directors would like to improve the profitability during the current year.

Required:
1. Prepare a table for last year showing the sales dollars and profit before taxes over a range extending from sales of $2,000,000 to $4,000,000, inclusive, with intervals of $500,000.
2. Repeat (1) above for this year.
3. Does it appear that the new equipment can improve profitability at all levels of operation? Explain.

4-9. **Operating Leverage and Margin of Safety.** The vice-president of sales, Walter Speed, observed that the company has operated with a 40 percent contribution margin percentage but that the fixed costs are relatively large at $2,000,000 per year. The income before income taxes this year was only $400,000 on net sales of $6,000,000. He sees an opportunity to increase sales to $6,300,000 next year but is concerned that such a small increase in sales will have relatively little impact on profit inasmuch as the fixed costs are so high.

Required:
1. Compute the degree of operating leverage for both this year and next year. Assume sales revenue for next year can be increased to $6,300,000.
2. Explain why the profit can be increased by a relatively large amount with only a modest increase in revenue.
3. Calculate the margin of safety for both this year and next year, assuming sales revenue can be increased to $6,300,000 for next year.
4. Does the margin of safety give any additional information not available through the operating leverage? Explain.

4-10. **Change in Operating Leverage.** Operating results for three years are given as follows for Loeb Consultants:

	1992	1993	1994
Net revenues	$19,000,000	$20,000,000	$21,000,000
Variable costs	9,000,000	9,500,000	10,000,000
Contribution margin	$10,000,000	$10,500,000	$11,000,000
Fixed costs	8,500,000	8,500,000	8,500,000
Income before income taxes	$ 1,500,000	$ 2,000,000	$ 2,500,000

The president of the company, Eric Regen, wonders why the profit increased by a third with just over a 5 percent increase in revenues from 1992 to 1993, and yet increased by only 25 percent from 1993 to 1994 with the same dollar increase in revenues.

Required:
1. Compute the operating leverage for 1992 and 1993. Explain how the operating leverage is related to the profit increases.
2. Compute the break-even point in dollars for each of the three years.
3. Calculate the margin of safety for each of the three years. Explain how the margin of safety relates to the profit increases.

4-11. Change in Sales Mix. Payless Office Furniture sells desks, chairs, and tables. Budgeted sales and profits for this year are estimated as follows:

	Desks	Chairs	Tables	Total
Sales	$400,000	$900,000	$700,000	$2,000,000
Variable costs	300,000	450,000	510,000	1,260,000
Contribution margin	$100,000	$450,000	$190,000	$ 740,000
Fixed costs				350,000
Income before taxes				$ 390,000

In reviewing actual results for the year, the manager wonders why the actual profit for the year was less than the budgeted profit, considering that selling prices and costs conformed to the budget and that sales revenue agreed with the budget. Actual sales by product line are given as follows:

Desks	$ 700,000
Chairs	400,000
Tables	900,000
Total revenue	$2,000,000

Required:
1. Compute the sales revenue of each product that would be sold at the break-even point under the budgeted data.
2. Compute the sales revenue of each product that would be sold at the break-even point under the actual sales mix.
3. Calculate the profit before income taxes for the actual sales mix, assuming variable costs maintained the budgeted relationship and actual fixed costs equaled budgeted fixed costs.
4. Explain to the manager why the actual profit decreased from the budgeted profit.
5. Compute the margin of safety on both a budgeted and actual basis. Explain what changes took place in the margin of safety and why.

4-12. Segment Profitability. Illinois Transportation runs passenger and freight services between Chicago airports and down-state cities. The owner, Walter Gruber, is an operations-wise manager. He has recently heard about a "segment contribution margin" approach at a university continuing education program. The following data are available for the first half of 1994:

Total revenue was $5.0 million, of which $3.5 million was freight traffic and $1.5 million was passenger traffic. Of the passenger revenue, 60 percent was generated by Route 1, 30 percent by Route 2, and 10 percent by Route 3.

Total direct controllable fixed costs were $600,000, of which $500,000 was spent on freight traffic. Of the remainder, $40,000 could not be traced to specific routes, although it was clearly applicable to passenger traffic in general, and Routes 1, 2, and 3 incurred costs of $30,000, $18,000, and $12,000, respectively.

Total direct noncontrollable costs, which were not regarded as being controllable by segment managers, were $500,000, of which 80 percent was traceable to freight traffic. Of the 20 percent traceable to passenger traffic, Routes 1, 2, and 3 should be charged $40,000, $20,000, and $15,000, respectively; the balance was not traceable to a specific route.

Total variable costs were $3.2 million, of which $2.0 million was freight traffic. Of the $1.2 million traceable to passenger traffic, $670,000, $400,000, and $130,000 was incurred by Routes 1, 2, and 3, respectively.

The common fixed costs not clearly traceable to any part of the company amounted to $500,000. Walter has always allocated these on a percentage of sales.

Required:
1. Walter asks you to prepare an earnings statement that shows the performance of each segment of the firm by various types of contribution margin.
2. Briefly describe what the results tell Walter.

4-13. Indifference Point, Operating Leverage, and Margin of Safety. Candice Company has decided to introduce a new product. The new product can be manufactured by either a capital intensive method (more fixed assets) or a labor intensive method. The manufacturing method will not affect the quality of the product. The estimated manufacturing costs by the two methods are as follows:

	Capital Intensive	Labor Intensive
Raw materials per unit	$5.00	$5.60
Direct labor per unit:		
1/2 hr. at $12	6.00	
48 min. at $9		7.20
Variable overhead per unit:		
1/2 hr. at $6	3.00	
48 min. at $6		4.80
Directly traceable fixed overhead	$2,440,000	$1,320,000

Candice's market research department has recommended an introductory unit sales price of $30. The selling expenses are estimated to be $500,000 annually plus $2 for each unit sold regardless of manufacturing method.

Required:
1. Calculate the estimated break-even point in annual unit sales of the new product if Candice Company uses the:
   (a) Capital-intensive manufacturing method.
   (b) Labor-intensive manufacturing method.
2. Determine the annual unit sales volume at which Candice Company would be indifferent between the two manufacturing methods. Prepare a decision table showing at which quantities the company would prefer one manufacturing method over the other.
3. Calculate the operating leverage and margin of safety at the indifference point for each manufacturing method.
   (a) Which manufacturing method has the better margin of safety if sales volume were to decrease below the indifference point? Explain.
   (b) Which manufacturing method will increase profits the most as sales volume moves beyond the indifference point? Explain.
4. Identify the business factors other than operating leverage and margin of safety that Candice must consider before selecting the capital-intensive or labor-intensive manufacturing method.

(ICMA Adapted)

4-14. **Break-Even Points with Step Costs.** Brauer Company produces a hand-held electronic dictionary/thesaurus that it markets through office suppliers and discount stores. Production costs for a normal monthly volume of 10,000 units are as follows:

Direct materials	$60,000
Direct labor	73,000
Variable factory overhead	38,000
Fixed factory overhead	60,000

At 12,000 units or more, the fixed factory overhead increases to $70,000 per month. Brauer incurs selling and administrative expenses at a variable rate of $.10 per unit sold and $7,500 per month. The current price at which Brauer Company sells its dictionary/thesaurus is $25.20.

Required:
1. Compute the contribution margin per unit and the contribution margin percentage. (Round the percentage to three decimal places, if necessary.)
2. Compute the break-even point in units and in dollars of revenues.
3. What is the expected monthly profit for 10,000 units?
4. If the company wants a 10 percent return on sales, how many units must it sell?
5. If the company wants an average profit per unit of $4, how many units must it sell?
6. How many units must the company sell to achieve a profit of $30,000.

4-15. **Step Costs, Operating Leverage, and Margin of Safety.** Pyle Electronics produces DataStore, a hand-held computer the size of a typical calculator, which is used to store addresses and telephone numbers and keep current lists, such as to-do lists and shopping lists. Pyle's wholesale price is $21 per unit. The variable manufacturing costs are $9 per unit for 5,000 units or less. If more than 5,000 units are sold, the variable manufacturing costs decrease by $2 per unit. Variable selling and administrative expenses are $2 per unit sold. The total fixed costs for the company are $32,000 for 5,000 units or less. They increase $6,000 when production and sales exceed 5,000 units.

Required:
1. Compute the break-even point in units and in dollars of revenue.
2. Starting with 1,000 units and moving in increments of 1,000 units up to a total of 10,000 units, compute the following:
   (a) Total contribution margin.
   (b) Operating leverage factor.
   (c) Margin of safety.
   (d) Profit before income taxes.
3. Prepare a cost-volume-profit graph for Pyle Electronics, covering the range of 0 units to 10,000 units.

4-16. **Break-Even Analysis.** The owners of Evening Star Motel want to know potential maximum profits and the break-even occupancy for the operation. Evening Star Motel is a budget operation to attract business people and families traveling on low budgets. A study of costs shows a difference between summer and winter operations. Swimming pool maintenance adds to summer costs while utilities (heat and light) add to winter costs. Variable costs have been determined on the basis of cost per room occupied per day and are set forth as follows:

	Cost Per Room
Laundry	$1.90
Heat and light (summer)	1.10
Heat and light (winter)	2.20
Repairs	.75
Supplies	1.60
Taxes and insurance	3.60
Maintenance	1.50
Pool maintenance (summer only)	.60

Fixed costs per month of operation have been estimated as follows:

Housekeeping	$14,000
Management	17,000
Desk service	2,700
Repairs and maintenance	1,600
Taxes	1,430
Insurance	1,120
Heat and light	1,000
Depreciation—motel	26,000
Depreciation—furnishings	12,500
Pool maintenance and personnel (summer only)	1,800

Evening Star has 300 rooms and charges $40 per room per night. Summer is relatively short and is defined as June, July, and August. All other months are designated as winter months. A month consists of 30 days for making calculations. Maximum capacity for a month would be 9,000 room days (300 rooms × 30 days).

Required:
1. Compute the maximum operating income that can be expected for a summer month, and the maximum income for a winter month.
2. What is the break-even point in terms of room days for summer? For winter? Also state the break-even point as a percentage of total capacity for both summer and winter.
3. Based on advance reservations and normal expectations, Evening Star Motel plans for 5,000 room days in August. Determine the estimated operating income for August. Also determine the percentage of capacity expected for August.

4-17. **Profitability of New Equipment.** Don Keefer, the production superintendent, has recommended that Jovanovich Equipment Company purchase automated machines to replace the old machines presently in service. The president of the company, Lee Hopkins, is skeptical.

"You know," the president states, "that our contribution margin rate is low to start with, and we need more fixed cost like a drowning man needs a drink of water. From what you have told me, this new equipment will add $800,000 a year to our fixed manufacturing cost."

An income statement for the past year is given as follows:

Net sales	$16,000,000
Cost of goods sold	13,500,000
Gross profit	$ 2,500,000
Operating expenses	1,300,000
Income before income taxes	$ 1,200,000
Income taxes (40 percent)	480,000
Net income	$ 720,000

Fixed production costs of $1,500,000 are included in cost of goods sold, and fixed costs of $500,000 are included in operating expenses.

"The savings in variable costs will more than make up for the increased fixed production costs," Keefer replies. "Materials now cost $4,000,000, but their use can be cut by 10 percent by more efficient handling that will reduce breakage. But the real savings is labor. Labor cost can be reduced from $6,000,000 to $5,000,000 when operating at last year's volume level. Furthermore, variable overhead can be reduced from $2,000,000 to $1,000,000. What you lose by increased fixed cost will be made up and more by reduced variable costs that result in a better contribution margin rate."

"You're wrong about one thing," Hopkins answers. "The increased prices for materials will cancel out any saving in materials use."

"Even so, the new equipment is a good deal," the superintendent replies.

Required:
1. Does it appear that the new equipment will improve profits? Base your calculations on the same sales revenue as the past year and all statements made.
2. What was the total contribution margin rate in the past year?
3. Under the new plan, what is the expected total contribution margin rate?

4-18. **Effect of Changes on Profits.** The management of Allison Plastics, Inc. is in the process of preparing a budget for the next year. The company manufactures car mats, dishware, and figures that can be used as decorations or as toys for children. Some changes in prices and costs are expected along with changes in sales volume. Data from operations for the past year are as follows:

	Figures	Mats	Dishware
Units sold	550,000	1,200,000	350,000
Unit selling price	$12.00	$8.00	$40.00
Variable costs per unit:			
Materials	$3.00	$3.00	$12.00
Indirect materials and supplies	.40	.40	1.00
Labor	1.50	1.50	6.00
Packing and shipping	.60	.60	1.50
Utilities	.50	.50	.50

Fixed costs:	
Supervision	$ 230,000
Employee benefits	765,000
Postage and telephone	73,000
Property taxes and insurance	126,000
Heat and light	192,000
Repairs and maintenance	94,000
Depreciation	86,000
Advertising	549,000
Travel and entertainment	162,000
Sales office, other sales expense	236,000
Office and administration	372,000
	$2,885,000

Sales volume of figures for next year is expected to be 80% of the volume for the past year. The sales volume of mats is expected to remain constant. The volume of dishware sales should increase by 10 percent if the advertising budget is increased by

$170,000. The selling price of figures is to be reduced to $10 per unit, and the selling price of mats is to be increased to $9 per unit.

Materials prices next year per unit of product have been estimated as follows:

Figures	$ 3.50
Mats	3.50
Dishware	14.00

Labor cost for next year is estimated at $2 per unit for both figures and mats. For dishware, labor is estimated at $7 per unit. The utility costs are estimated at $1 next year for each unit of each product line. Fixed costs, with the exception of the advertising previously referred to, will probably increase by 10 percent. Income taxes are at 40 percent of income before income tax.

Required:
1. Compute the contribution margin and percentage of contribution margin per unit of each product for the past year.
2. Compute the contribution margin and percentage of contribution margin per unit of each product according to the estimates for the next year.
3. Determine the net income for the past year. (Show contribution margin by product line.)
4. Determine the expected net income next year. (Show contribution margin by product line.)
5. Will the expected volume increase in dishware sales more than compensate for the expected cost increases in dishware? Show computations.
6. Compute the break-even point for the given sales mix of each year. Explain the break-even point change between years.

4-19. Indifference Point, Operating Leverage, and Margin of Safety. DeFeis Printing Company specializes in high quality printed advertising materials. The company's operations are highly automated, resulting in less waste and in low unit costs. A unit of printing product consists of 1,000 pages. The company's accountant has developed the following cost structure for a typical month:

Variable costs:	
Direct materials	$ 17 per unit
Direct labor	12 per unit
Variable overhead	8 per unit
Fixed costs:	
Fixed printing overhead	23,000 per month
Other fixed costs	12,000 per month

DeFries Printing's managers expect the industry to go slowly into recession and the number of orders eventually to decrease from the current level of 9,000 units per month to 7,000 units. A severe recession, which DeFries' management gives a 20 percent chance of occurring, could reduce orders to 6,000 units per month. In an effort to reduce costs, the managers are considering replacing their automated processes with older, more labor-intensive models. The switch would increase labor costs per unit to $14, but would reduce fixed printing overhead by $8,000 because of greatly reduced leasing costs. Revenue and materials costs would remain unchanged. The average selling price per unit is $44.

Required:

1. Assuming the normal month of 9,000 units, compute the following for both the newer equipment and the older equipment:
   - (a) The monthly profit.
   - (b) The operating leverage factor.
   - (c) The margin of safety.
2. Using the operating leverage factor in (1b) above, estimate the profits at 7,000 and 6,000 units for both the newer equipment and the older equipment.
3. At what sales volume is the profit earned with newer equipment equal to the profit earned with older equipment?
4. In the face of decreasing demand, which alternative should management take? Explain.

4-20. **C-V-P Analysis for a Hospital.** Bedford Hospital operates a general hospital but rents space and beds to separately owned entities providing specialized services such as pediatrics and psychiatrics. Bedford charges each entity for common services, such as patients' meals and laundry, and for administrative services, such as billings and collections. Space and bed rentals are fixed amounts per year, based on the number of beds.

Bedford charged the pediatrics service with the following costs for the year ended June 30, 1995:

	Patient Days Variable	Bed Capacity (Fixed)
Dietary...	$ 600,000	—
Janitorial	—	$ 70,000
Laundry.......................................	300,000	—
Laboratory	450,000	—
Pharmacy	350,000	—
Repairs and maintenance	—	30,000
General and maintenance	—	1,300,000
Rent..	—	1,500,000
Billings and collections	300,000	—
Total	$2,000,000	$2,900,000

During the year ended June 30, 1995, pediatrics charged patients an average of $300 per day, had a capacity of 60 beds, and had total revenue of $6,000,000. Pediatrics also employed the following personnel:

	Annual Salaries (each)
Supervising nurses	$25,000
Nurses	20,000
Aides.....................................	9,000

Bedford requires that separately owned departments employ the following minimum numbers of personnel, based on patient days:

Annual Patient Days	Aides	Nurses	Supervising Nurses
Up to 21,900	20	10	4
21,901 - 26,000	26	13	4
26,001 - 29,200	30	15	4

Pediatrics always employs the minimum requirements in each category. These salaries are therefore fixed within ranges of annual patient days.

Pediatrics operated at 100 percent of capacity on 90 days in 1995. It is estimated that during those 90 days, the demand for beds exceeded the capacity by about 20. Bedford could make an additional 20 beds available for pediatrics during the year ending June 30, 1996. The additional beds would increase pediatrics' fixed charges.

Required:
1. Determine the break-even point for pediatrics, expressed as the number of patient days, for the year ended June 30, 1996, if it does not rent the additional 20 beds. Assume that the revenue, cost per patient day, cost per bed, and salary rates will remain the same as they were in the previous year.
2. Assume that all of the data related to 1995 will hold for 1996, except that pediatrics will rent the additional 20 beds and therefore increase its per bed charges. Demand for beds will be the same in 1996 as it was in 1995. Determine the increase or decrease in profit for pediatrics that would accompany renting the additional beds.

(AICPA adapted)

CASE 4A–TWINKLE TOY COMPANY

Thomas Anthony and his wife Susan as a hobby designed and produced toys which they gave to family and friends at Christmas, on birthdays, and for other occasions. These toys were well received, and a number of people asked to buy additional ones that they could give as gifts. The couple was encouraged to open their own production facilities by the local manager of a chain store. Finally, on January 1991, they formed Twinkle Toy Company. The "Twinkle" coming from the obvious gleam in all children's eyes after receiving one of the toys. Sales during the first year were well over half a million dollars. Financial data in thousands for the first five years and estimated data for 1996 are as follows:

	1991	1992	1993	1994	1995	1996
Sales	$630.0	$787.5	$945.0	$1,500.0	$1,950.0	$2,100.0
Variable costs	516.6	605.0	725.0	825.0	950.0	1,350.0
Contribution margin	$113.4	$182.5	$220.0	$ 675.0	$1,000.0	$ 750.0
Fixed costs	42.2	45.0	57.0	110.0	145.0	187.0
Operating profit . . .	$ 71.2	$137.5	$163.0	$ 565.0	$ 855.0	$ 563.0
Interest expense . .	5.0	8.0	16.0	24.0	21.0	21.0
Profit before tax . . .	$ 66.2	$129.5	$147.0	$ 541.0	$ 834.0	$ 542.0
Income taxes	26.5	51.8	58.8	216.4	333.6	216.8
Profit after tax.	$ 39.7	$ 77.7	$ 88.2	$ 324.6	$ 500.4	$ 325.2

Total industry sales are quite stable, but because of fads and fashions, individual companies often experience considerably more instability than the industry has. Twinkle Toys, for example, missed the market in 1993, when its new designs were not especially well received. Therefore, sales did not increase as rapidly as the Anthonys thought they should have.

Sales instability, along with the seasonal nature of industry, presents a financial planning dilemma for most toy companies. About 80% of all sales occur during the months of September and October, when stores are stocking up for the holiday season. Collections are not generally received until January and February, after stores have their Christmas receipts for cash sales and credit card collections. Twinkle Toys follows the same sales and cash collection pattern as the industry, but its production is seasonal as well. About 70 percent of the output is produced during the April through September period. Then 30 percent of the output is produced during the remaining five months of the year.

Production costs have increased dramatically during the last couple of years. A main plant was built in 1994, with additional capacity acquired through leasing space within the neighboring industrial park. Inefficiencies associated with the lack of centrally located production facilities and the need to train new employees during peak production periods have contributed to the deteriorating cost situation. Estimates for 1996 in the foregoing chart assume the company will continue to operate without changes discussed below.

Susan Anthony believes that the company should buy the land adjacent to the present plant, construct an integrated production facility, and produce at a more uniform rate throughout the year. She believes the new plant should be large enough to accommodate projected sales demand for upcoming years. Expenditures for this proposal amount to $1.1 million, all to be financed by a ten-year loan. If this proposal is accepted, variable costs will approximate 75 percent of sales, and fixed costs will be about $380,000.

Increasing fixed costs within a company that experiences fluctuating sales has always troubled Tom. He believes the company should follow a conservative path which would slow down the rate of expansion and hold the present position. Tom's proposal would result in variable costs at approximately 85% of sales, with fixed costs amounting to $300,000. Although Tom feels his wife's aggressive approach has helped attain the growth rate the company has enjoyed, he is concerned that continuing such an approach now could jeopardize the company's existence.

Required:
1. Using the techniques and tools discussed in the chapter, analyze the situation facing Twinkle Toy Company and develop the basis for what you would recommend the Anthonys should do.
2. What additional information would you like to have available to clarify issues or provide data that would make your recommended decisions easier to make?

CASE 4B—RADEN PAPER COMPANY

Raden Paper Company produces four basic paper product lines at one of its plants: computer paper, paper napkins, place mats, and poster board. Materials and operations vary according to the line of product. The market has been relatively good. The demand for napkins and place mats has increased with more people eating out, and the demand for the other lines has been growing steadily.

The plant superintendent, Marcella Owens, while pleased with the prospects for increased sales, is concerned about costs:

"We hear talk about a paperless office, but I haven't seen it yet. The computers, if anything, have increased the market for paper. Our big problem now is the high fixed cost of production. As we have automated our operation, we have experienced increases in fixed overhead and even variable overhead. And, we will have to add more equipment since it appears that we need even more plant capacity. We are operating over our normal capacity as it is.

"The place mat market concerns me. We may have to give up printing the mats. Our specialty printing is driving up the variable overhead to the point where we may not find it profitable to continue with that line at all."

Cost and price data for the next fiscal quarter are given as follows:

	Computer Paper	Napkins	Place Mats	Poster Board
Estimated sales volume in units	30,000	120,000	45,000	80,000
Selling prices	$14.00	$7.00	$12.00	$8.50
Materials costs	6.00	4.50	3.60	2.50

Variable overhead includes the cost of hourly labor and the variable cost of equipment operation. The fixed plant overhead is estimated at $420,000 for the quarter. Direct labor, to a large extent, is salaried; and the cost is included as a part of fixed plant overhead. The fixed overhead is charged to products on the basis of 42,000 machine hours per quarter. The superintendent's concern about the eventual need for more capacity is based on increases in production that may reach and exceed the practical capacity of 60,000 machine hours.

In addition to the fixed plant overhead, the plant incurs fixed selling and administrative expenses per quarter of $118,000.

"I share your concern about increasing fixed costs," the supervisor of plant operations replies. "We are still operating with about the same number of people we had when we didn't have this sophisticated equipment. In going over our needs and costs, it appears to me that we could cut fixed plant overhead to $378,000 a quarter without doing any violence to our operation. This would be a big help."

"You may be right," Owens responds. "We forget that we have more productive power than we once had, and we may as well take advantage of it. Suppose we get some hard figures that show where the cost reductions will be made."

Data with respect to production per machine hour and the variable cost per hour of producing each of the products are given as follows:

	Computer Paper	Napkins	Place Mats	Poster Board
Units per hour	6	10	5	4
Variable overhead per hour	$9.00	$6.00	$12.00	$8.00

"I hate to spoil things," the vice-president of purchasing announces. "But the cost of our material for computer stock is now up to $7.00. Just got a call about that this morning. Also, place mat material will be up to $4.00 a unit."

"On the bright side," the vice-president of sales reports, "we have firm orders for 35,000 cartons of computer paper, not 30,000 as we originally figured."

Required:

1.   From all original estimates given, prepare an estimated income statement by product line for the next fiscal quarter. Also, show the contribution margins per unit and the total unit costs.

2.   Prepare an income statement as in part 1 above with all revisions included.

3.   For the original estimates, compute each of the following:

   (a)   Break-even point for the given sales mix.

   (b)   Operating leverage factor for the estimated sales volume.

   (c)   Margin of safety for the estimated sales volume.

4.   For the revised estimates, compute each of the following:

   (a)   Break-even point for the given sales mix.

   (b)   Operating leverage factor for the estimated sales volume.

   (c)   Margin of safety for the estimated sales volume.

5.   Comment on Owens's concern about the variable cost of the place mats.

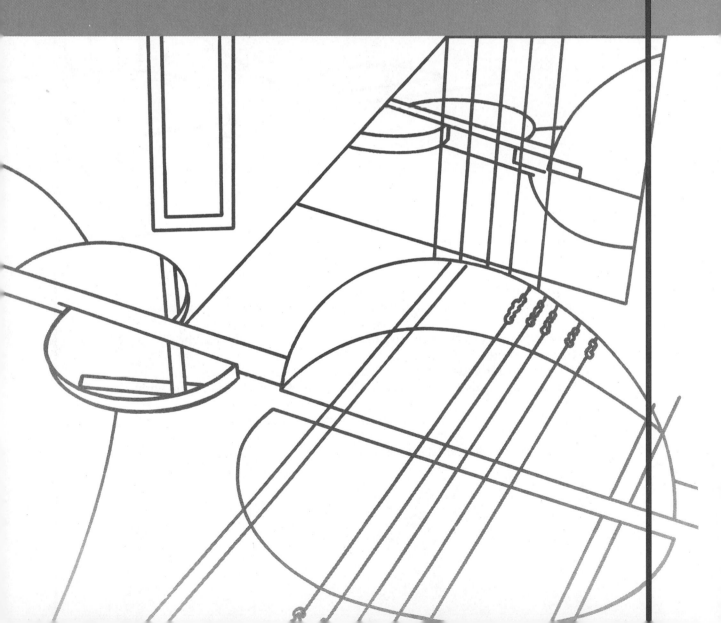

Part Two

Product Cost Framework

Chapter Five

Introduction To Product Costing

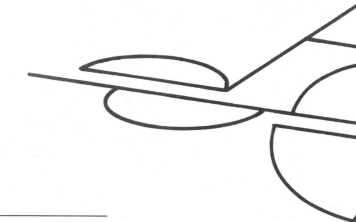

❖ Chapter Objectives

After studying Chapter 5, you will be able to:

1. Identify the circumstances in which a job cost system and a process cost system are appropriate.
2. Describe how direct materials, direct labor, and factory overhead are costed to products when a job cost system is used.
3. Calculate plant-wide and departmental factory overhead rates.
4. Explain how activity-based costing improves the costs identified with products.
5. Identify the main differences between various concepts of plant capacity.
6. Explain why services or products should be costed by using an overhead rate computed at normal operating capacity.

◾ *What is the Cost of a Backpack?* ◾

As a government man working out of Denver, Dell Freeman satisfied his love for the outdoors by working as a part-time wilderness guide and cross-country ski instructor. He also found himself either redesigning or making the equipment he needed, such as pull-along sleds and backpacks. When people started buying his sleds, he used his savings as seed money for a new business. Now his most notable product is a unique collapsible teepee-shaped tent.

Freeman started his enterprise with a firm hope of making a profit and he has realized profits in the past. However, times are changing. Revenues for this year have reached $1.8 million and are expected to increase in the future. Costs are, on the other hand, increasing faster than revenues. Freeman does not know what his profit margins are for sleds, backpacks, and tents because he has no idea what it costs him to make a product. Most of his accounting has been a "shoebox approach" where receipts, deposit slips, and invoices go into a box. Periodically, a local CPA firm sends a staff accountant to sort out the box's contents and prepare financial statements.

Right now, Freeman needs cost information about production and his accounting system does not provide it. For example, What does it cost to produce one unit of each of his products? Are production costs higher this month than last month? With profits going down, which products are losing profit margin. And, behind all of these questions is: Which costs are production costs? Freeman needs an accounting system that will provide cost information for the many needs he has now and in the future.

This chapter discusses the accounting for production costs and presents ways to identify costs with products. Accounting for direct materials and direct labor comes first. Then, accounting for factory overhead covers the simple to more complex situations. The chapter describes the type of manufacturing environment appropriate for job cost and process cost systems. However, the chapter then concentrates on the job cost system. The process cost system will be covered in Chapter 6.

PRODUCT COST SYSTEMS

The production of goods and services involves costs. As mentioned in Chapter 2, these costs are typically classified as materials, labor, and factory overhead. The flow of these costs through the accounts and into an income statement is summarized in Figure 2.1. Managers are interested in identifying unit costs for purposes of establishing inventory values for the balance sheet and cost of goods sold for the income statement. Managers also want to know the costs of individual customer orders or the costs to perform certain services so they can evaluate the profitability of their goods and services. Unit costs are used by many managers to accomplish an assortment of needs.

The method of accumulating costs and tracing them to products and services is closely associated with the type of operations a company has and the purposes for which unit costs are needed. The primary reasons organizations want a cost accounting system are to: (a) identify costs with work performed; and (b) provide cost information that will aid in planning and decision making, performance evaluation and control, and cost management.

The principles underlying cost accounting are applicable to manufacturing companies, wholesalers, retailers, and service organizations. Many nonmanufacturing companies may not incorporate a procedure in the cost accounting system for identifying the costs to specific customer orders. Instead, a separate analysis of those costs may be prepared for information purposes. For example, a hospital will make an analysis showing the cost to render a given type of medical treatment or the cost of outpatient care. A contractor, on the other hand, will accumulate costs by project. If a contractor is constructing a new bridge for the state, for instance, the contractor will identify and trace the costs to the bridge project.

Identifying and tracking costs in a not-for-profit organization take on a different viewpoint. A university may be more interested in the estimation, measurement, and control of a program to train mathematics teachers. Or, a museum may want to determine the cost of having a particular exhibit for a season.

Regardless of the type of organization, costs are identified as direct costs when they can be readily connected to an objective. Indirect costs, which can not as easily be connected to an objective, must be allocated using some reasonable basis for allocation. Because the principles used in tracing costs are more clearly identified in a manufacturing setting, accounting for the manufacturing costs can often be adapted for a wide variety of applications. Manufacturing costs are accumulated and assigned to products through the use of one of two basic cost accounting systems:

1.   The job cost system.
2.   The process cost system.

The production environment, which translates into the nature of the product or service and the type and number of operations, is the primary consideration in selecting a cost accounting system. Therefore, we consider the different production environments and whether job cost or process cost is appropriate.

Production Environment for Job Cost

The environment appropriate for a job cost system is typified by one-of-a-kind, customized, or special-order products and services. This means the products or services have two dominant characteristics:

1.   Products or services are unique and are produced or rendered individually, in lots, in batches, or in some other group.

2.   Products or services receive varying degrees of the inputs, such as materials, labor, and overhead.

Examples of products that fit these characteristics are office buildings, residential housing, NASA spacecraft, custom equipment, and office furniture. Examples of services include health care, accounting, legal, family counseling, insurance agencies, auto repairs, plays and concerts, and fund-raising campaigns.

The uniqueness of a product or service determines what work will be performed and the type and sequence of operations. This, in turn, determines the degree of material, labor, and overhead related to the work. Since the degree of input will be different, unit costs can easily vary among similar products. As a result, prices for these products or services are cost-based; i.e., accumulating costs by customer or source of an order. For example, a company that builds military equipment to support soldiers in a desert setting will generally have cost-based prices, and the company will use a job cost system.

Production Environment for Process Cost

Process costing is appropriate when operations represent mass production or continuous processing. In this situation, each unit of product or service within the same category is identical. Examples include processed foods, candy, oil refining, rubber, and automobile assembly. Products or services produced in this environment have two dominant characteristics:

1.   Products or services are identical or similar and are produced or rendered on a continuous basis.
2.   Products or services receive substantially identical amounts of materials, labor, and overhead.

The main difference between mass-produced services and mass-produced products is that labor and overhead are the significant cost elements for service. Although materials may be present, their costs are generally insignificant. Examples include most banking services, baggage handling at bus depots or airports, insurance claims processing, and credit checking.

The production environment here is typically categorized as one which yields commingled products, fabricated products, or assembled products. **Commingled products** exist when one unit of the product cannot be distinguished from any other unit. One pound of sugar is indistinguishable from another pound unless contained in some way. Products that fit in this category include flour, oil, electricity, textiles, processed foods, and paper. **Fabricated products** involve reshaping materials through a cutting, stamping, or molding operation. Examples include tires, nuts and bolts, automobile body panels, ash trays, and silverware. **Assembled products** are those that bring parts and subassemblies together for an assembly operation. Each product passes through the same assembly operations. Examples include kitchen appliances, calculators, computers, telephones, and commercial airplanes.

THE JOB COST SYSTEM

The **job cost system** accumulates separately the costs of materials, labor, and overhead for the job, whether a job of one unit or a job of many units. The computer assigns each job a number for purposes of tracking the work tied to the job and accumulating the costs of that job. Daily, weekly, or monthly cost summaries for each job are generated by the computer system. These summaries are referred to as **job, work, or production orders**. The file of production orders in process constitutes a subsidiary ledger in support of the work in process account in the general ledger. An example of a completed production order for Job 216 is shown in Figure 5.1.

PRODUCTION ORDER

Customer ___Roth Supply Co.___   Job Order ___216___

Description ___Welded Parts Code #735___   Date Started ___1/19/95___

Quantity ___1,000___   Date Completed ___1/27/95___

Materials			Labor			Overhead	
Date	Code	Amount	Date	Hours	Amount		
Jan. 19	52	$3,130	Jan. 19 to 23	140	$1,120	Director Labor Hours	200
						Overhead Rate	$6.00
						Applied Overhead	$1,200
23	68	350	Jan. 26 to 27	60	480		
						Summary	
						Direct Materials	$3,480
						Direct Labor	1,600
						Factory Overhead	1,200
						Total Cost	$6,280
						Unit Cost	$6.28
	Total	$3,480	Total	200	$1,600		

Figure 5.1   A Completed Production Order.

Now, let's turn to the accounting for the cost elements that make up a job. First, we look at the costing of direct materials.

Costing of Direct Materials

Materials are the raw materials, purchased parts, and purchased or subcontracted assemblies and subassemblies. **Direct materials** are the quantities of materials that are identified with the production of a specific product, that are easily and economically traced to the product, and whose cost represents a significant part of the total product cost. All other materials and supplies that become part of a product or are consumed in production are called **indirect materials**.

The costs associated with acquiring materials and having them ready for production typically fall into five categories:

1. The acquisition cost (purchase price or production cost) of the materials.
2. In-transit charges such as freight, insurance, storage, customs and duty charges.
3. Credits for trade discounts, cash discounts, and other discounts and allowances.
4. The costs of purchasing, receiving, inspection, and storage activities.
5. Miscellaneous items, including income from the sale of scrap and spoiled units, obsolescence, and other inventory losses.

Categories 1 through 3 are the costs typically included as the cost of a quantity of materials, whether direct or indirect materials. Categories 4 and 5 are treated as factory overhead. We allocate those costs to products in one of the several approaches that will be discussed later in the chapter.

The determinant of which materials to buy is the **bill of materials** generated by the engineers. This document lists all materials needed to produce one unit of each product. It will also give the sequence in which the material will enter production. Once a decision is made about the quantity of products to produce, the bill of material is used to determine how much materials should be acquired.

When materials are purchased on account for $75,000, an entry is made to debit Materials (the control accounting for materials inventory) and to credit Accounts Payable as follows:

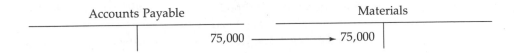

Production managers requisition from the storeroom the quantities of each type of material required for a specific job. Thus, each requisition becomes the basis for charging materials used to a specific job. Assume that the requisitions for a week show that direct materials costing $60,000 have been transferred from the materials inventory to production. The total of $60,000 is recorded as a credit to Materials. The work in process account is a focal account for the entry of the costs of production. (The costs of the three cost elements—direct materials, direct labor, and factory overhead—are funneled through this account, as will be shown later.) It is therefore the control account for all in-process activity. The entry to cost materials used in production for the week is given as follows:

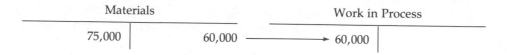

Materials			Work in Process
75,000	60,000	→ 60,000	

The costs that make up the $60,000 are also charged to each job or production order. These summaries form the subsidiary ledger that back up the work in process account.

Costing of Direct Labor

Factory labor is the total labor expended for the benefit of production. **Direct labor** is all labor that can be specifically identified with a product in an economically feasible manner. **Indirect labor** is labor that is not readily traced to a product. Because of the changes in the production environment in many companies and the emphasis on a just-in-time philosophy, a new term related to labor is value-added direct labor. We defined value-added labor and presented an efficiency measure in Chapter 3. For our purposes here, we will not make a distinction in our accounting between value-added and non-value-added labor. Remember though that value-added direct labor changes materials into a finished product. For example, value-added direct labor fabricates parts, assembles products, and finishes products. Non-value-added direct labor moves, inspects, stores, examines, or otherwise handles the product without adding value to the customer.

Labor costs include the wages and salaries of the employees plus any additional expenditure made by an employer on behalf of an employee. These typically include bonuses, overtime premiums, shift differentials, employer's payroll taxes, and fringe benefits. Wages and salaries are the typical costs tied to labor differentiated as direct and indirect labor. The additional costs are usually treated as part of the factory overhead costs.

Factory payroll is recorded by a debit to Payroll with offsetting credits to Employees Income Tax Payable, other liability accounts for payroll deductions, and Wages Payable as follows:

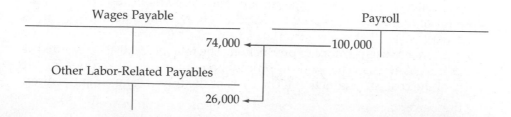

Wages Payable		Payroll	
	74,000 ←	—100,000	
Other Labor-Related Payables			
	26,000 ←		

In this example, for the sake of simplicity, we have assumed that all labor is direct labor. In practice, some idle time and set-up time for production workers exists. Hence, a portion of the payroll, even a payroll for only production workers, will consist of pay for some hours that cannot be charged to any production order. This cost will be a part of factory overhead, along with the cost of hospitalization, sick pay, or other benefits that cannot be identified with orders of production.

Labor time tickets or labor time reports will show how much of the labor time and cost is to be charged to each job in Work in Process. In this example, the payroll cost represents 10,000 direct labor hours at $10 each. The work in process control account will be debited for a total of 10,000 direct labor hours at $10 each, or for $100,000, as shown:

Payroll		Work in Process	
	100,000	100,000 → 100,000	

Costing of Direct Materials and Labor and Cost Control

Production supervisors, in planning their operations, may estimate the direct materials and direct labor cost for each job for which they are responsible. They subsequently measure the actual cost and compare it with the estimates, taking into account the stage of completion for each job. For example, a report on production may be prepared as follows:

DIRECT MATERIALS

Job Number	Estimate	Actual	Dollar Variance Over (Under)	Percentage of Completion
1017	$22,000	$21,000	$(1,000)	100%
1018	19,500	20,000	500	100
1019	10,000*	14,000	4,000	50
1020	5,000*	5,000	0	25
Total	$56,500	$60,000	$ 3,500	

* Estimates adjusted to percentage of completion basis.

The variance column shows the differences between estimated and actual amounts. The total estimates for each job have been adjusted by the percentage completed so that a valid comparison can be made with the actual amounts. The total direct materials cost of Job 1019 was estimated to be $20,000. The job is 50 percent complete as to direct materials and that equates to an estimated cost of $10,000 (50 percent of $20,000).

A report that compares actual direct labor hours with the estimated hours can reveal whether or not more hours are being used on a job than expected. Again, the estimates are made comparable with the actual results by determining the percentage of work completed and applying that percentage to the total estimate. For example, Job 1020 is only 10 percent complete with respect to direct labor. The total estimate on that job for direct labor hours must have been 4,500 hours if 450 hours is 10 percent of the total estimate, as shown:

DIRECT LABOR HOURS

Job Number	Estimate	Actual	Direct Labor Hour Variance Over (Under)	Percentage of Completion
1017	4,450*	4,000	(450)	80%
1018	1,800*	2,000	200	50
1019	3,300*	3,500	200	50
1020	450*	500	50	10
Total	10,000	10,000	0	

* Estimates adjusted to percentage of completion basis.

The report on direct labor hours can be converted to a direct labor cost report by multiplying the direct labor hours by the direct labor hour rate (in this case, $10), as shown in the following report:

DIRECT LABOR COST

Job Number	Estimate	Actual	Direct Labor Dollar Variance Over (Under)	Percentage of Completion
1017	$ 44,500*	$ 40,000	$(4,500)	80%
1018	18,000*	20,000	2,000	50
1019	33,000*	35,000	2,000	50
1020	4,500*	5,000	500	10
Total	$100,000	$100,000	$ 0	

* Estimates adjusted to percentage of completion basis.

Supervisors are able to use such cost information as they follow each job from its inception to completion. As a **cost overrun** (unfavorable variation from estimate) develops, they can take corrective measures. The preceding example shows that Job 1019 is 50 percent completed with respect to both direct materials and direct labor and that more materials and more hours were used than anticipated. Knowing what caused the overrun may enable the supervisor to find ways to reduce cost. Or, it may be found that the estimate was unrealistically low; in this case, budgets are revised.

SIMPLIFIED APPROACH TO COSTING FACTORY OVERHEAD

Factory overhead, unlike direct materials and direct labor, cannot be requisitioned or measured directly as a cost of any particular job, production order, or service. Factory overhead consists of a variety of costs such as indirect materials, indirect labor, insurance, depreciation, utilities, repair and mainte-nance, and taxes, all of which are indirectly related to the products. The indi-rect nature of overhead costs with respect to the products or services creates a difficulty in identifying production costs with each unit. For our purposes, we take an overall, simplified approach to costing of factory overhead to prod-ucts. This is to convey the concepts involved. Later in the chapter, we expand to treatments of overhead costs, such as departmental rates and activity-based costing.

For the discussion that follows, factory overhead is attached to products or services by means of a cost driver that is identifiable to the products. This cost driver serves as a bridge between factory overhead and the products. Often the cost driver chosen for overhead allocation is direct labor hours, machine hours, or direct labor cost. Factory overhead is budgeted for the year, and the activity behind the cost driver is also budgeted. The budgeted activity is divid-ed into the budgeted overhead to obtain an **overhead rate.** Products then are assigned overhead cost by multiplying the actual quantities of the activity by the rate calculated.

The cost driver chosen as a basis for overhead allocation should be related logically to both the overhead and the product. If machinery plays an impor-tant role in the manufacturing operation, the overhead cost likely consists of power cost, lubrication, maintenance, repairs, depreciation, and other costs closely related to machine operation. The benefits received by the products can probably be best measured against the cost of the machine hours used in their production. Therefore, these overhead costs should be allocated to the products on a machine-hour basis. For other departments in the plant that are more labor intensive than capital intensive, direct labor cost or direct labor hours may be more appropriate for overhead allocation.

Computing the Overhead Rate

The calculation of an overhead rate is illustrated by assuming that several factory overhead budgets are prepared for various levels of operating activity. A series of budgets for various levels of operating activity is called a **flexible overhead budget.** This is a budget based on a formula that expresses the budgeted overhead at any point within the relevant range. The formula recog-nizes that some costs are variable and some are fixed. An example of such a budget is shown at the top of page 198.

In this example, the 10,000 budgeted direct labor hours level is selected as the level for obtaining a product costing rate. Note that the variable cost is $3 per hour at any level of operation, whereas the fixed rate depends on the number of direct labor hours used in the computation. The total rate per 10,000 direct labor hours is computed as $8 per hour.

$$\frac{\text{Budgeted factory overhead}}{\text{Budgeted direct labor hours}} = \frac{\$80,000}{10,000} = \$8 \text{ per direct labor hour}$$

	Budgeted Direct Labor Hours			
	6,000	8,000	10,000*	12,000
Budgeted factory overhead:				
Variable:				
Indirect materials	$ 7,500	$10,000	$12,500	$15,000
Repairs and maintenance.........	5,700	7,600	9,500	11,400
Power and light	4,800	6,400	8,000	9,600
Total......................	$18,000	$24,000	$30,000	$36,000
Fixed:				
Indirect labor and supervision	$18,000	$18,000	$18,000	$18,000
Repairs and maintenance.........	6,500	6,500	6,500	6,500
Power and light	5,500	5,500	5,500	5,500
Factory rent	8,000	8,000	8,000	8,000
Depreciation of equipment	12,000	12,000	12,000	12,000
Total......................	$50,000	$50,000	$50,000	$50,000
Total budgeted overhead	$68,000	$74,000	$80,000	$86,000
Rate per direct labor hour:				
Variable......................	$ 3.000	$ 3.000	$ 3.000	$ 3.000
Fixed	8.333	6.250	5.000	4.167
Total.......................	$11.333	$ 9.250	$ 8.000	$ 7.167

* Level selected to determine the overhead rate for applying overhead costs to products.

During the year, the products passing through the plant are charged on the basis of this predetermined rate. Assume that 10,000 hours of direct labor are used during the year. While the manufacturing operation was going on, various entries were made to cost the products. If done in aggregate, one summary entry would show the following:

Applied Factory Overhead	Work in Process
80,000 ⟶	80,000

As each job goes through production, an overhead charge at the predetermined rate of $8 for each direct labor hour worked is made to the job. The cost shown for Job 1018 may now be summarized at this stage of its production as follows:

Direct materials	$20,000
Direct labor (2,000 hours at $10 per direct labor hour)	20,000
Factory overhead (2,000 hours at $8 per direct labor hour)	16,000
Total cost	$56,000

Costs for direct materials, direct labor, and factory overhead are accumulated for jobs throughout the production process. At its completion, the cost of a job is transferred out of work in process and into finished goods.

Why does the accountant go to so much trouble in assigning factory overhead cost to the products using a predetermined rate? Why not wait until the end of the year when actual data are available for factory overhead costs and direct labor hours? A predetermined overhead rate is preferred for two major reasons. The first is the timing of factory overhead cost incurrence. For example, air conditioning costs in the summer for many companies in the sunbelt tend to be higher than heating costs are in the winter. Should we allocate the higher air conditioning costs to products just because the products were manufactured during the summer? The facilities and workers must be maintained no matter what the weather outside. Because the facilities and workers benefit production throughout the year, a predetermined overhead rate is used to average the costs over all units of output for the year.

The second reason for using a predetermined overhead rate is the potential fluctuation in the activity represented by the cost driver. Most companies do not have a constant level of activity every month. For example, employees take vacations during the summer months; operations are scaled back to accommodate major repairs and maintenance; production ceases while a change over in tooling occurs; or the doors are closed for the week between Christmas and New Year's Day. A predetermined overhead rate averages costs over the units of work regardless of when work is performed. This way a product is not penalized because it was produced during a period of low volume.

One additional advantage is the availability of costs during production for use in pricing and bidding. Companies are always trying to bring in orders for various products. The use of a predetermined overhead rate permits preparation of bids on major orders or pricing individual customer requests.

Costing Variable Overhead

In the following example, the total cost is estimated at $29,000 for a production order. Direct labor cost amounts to $10 per direct labor hour, and variable overhead cost is at the rate of $3 per direct labor hour. Fixed overhead is ignored in this example. Estimated direct labor hours total 1,000 hours for the job. Because of revisions in the production process, the job can now be completed in 950 direct labor hours.

Original Estimate
(1,000 direct labor hours)

Direct materials	$16,000
Direct labor (1,000 × $10)	10,000
Variable overhead (1,000 × $3)	3,000
Total	$29,000

Revised Estimate
(950 direct labor hours)

Direct materials	$16,000
Direct labor (950 × $10)	9,500
Variable overhead (950 × $3)	2,850
Total	$28,350

By saving 50 hours of direct labor, the company can reduce the cost of this job by $650 (the difference between the original estimate and the revised estimate). The savings is a decrease in direct labor of $500 and a decrease in variable overhead of $150. Management recognizes that substantial savings in cost are possible by finding ways to reduce labor time or other factors related to variable overhead. One very important function of management is to review operations closely with the objective of reducing production time and cost. Small savings in time can be translated into substantial cost savings when volume of production is considered.

Costing Fixed Overhead

Assume now that the full cost of the job is to be computed with an apportioned share of the fixed overhead included. The fixed overhead cannot be controlled by job or project. It is allocated to the work by the use of an hourly costing rate. The budget for fixed overhead in this example is $50,000, and the company is generally expected to operate at 10,000 direct labor hours a year. The fixed overhead rate is $5 per direct labor hour, calculated as follows:

$$\frac{\$50,000 \text{ fixed overhead}}{10,000 \text{ direct labor hours}} = \$5 \text{ per direct labor hour}$$

The full cost estimate of the production order is given as:

Original Estimate
(1,000 direct labor hours)

Direct materials	$16,000
Direct labor (1,000 × $10)	10,000
Variable overhead (1,000 × $3)	3,000
Fixed overhead (1,000 × $5)	5,000
Total	$34,000

Revised Estimate
(950 direct labor hours)

Direct materials	$16,000
Direct labor (950 × $10)	9,500
Variable overhead (950 × $3)	2,850
Fixed overhead (950 × $5)	4,750
Total	$33,100

Now there is an additional savings of $250 due to charging less fixed overhead to the job. The total fixed costs are not influenced by the job and the company still incurs the costs. For variable costs, when the activity does not occur, the variable costs are saved. But the only way to save fixed costs is to eliminate facilities or salaried people.

In the above situation, if the company actually operated at 10,000 direct hours during the year, all of the fixed overhead of $50,000 would be absorbed by the jobs. If, however, only 8,000 direct labor hours are worked, only $40,000 of the fixed overhead would be costed to the products by using the fixed overhead rate of $5 per direct labor hour that was established for 10,000 direct labor hours:

$$8,000 \text{ actual hours} \times \$5 \text{ fixed overhead} = \$40,000 \text{ fixed overhead}$$
$$\text{rate per hour} \qquad\qquad \text{costed to products}$$

The difference between the budgeted fixed overhead and the fixed overhead costed to products by the use of the predetermined fixed overhead rate is designated as a **capacity variance,** or **volume variance.** In this case there is a $10,000 capacity variance as shown:

Budgeted fixed overhead	$50,000
Fixed overhead costed to products	40,000
Capacity variance	$10,000

The selection of a capacity concept is discussed later in this chapter; the reasons for a capacity variance are considered further in Chapter 9.

Disposition of the Overhead Variance

While the products are costed using a predetermined overhead rate, actual overhead costs are incurred and recorded as debits to Factory Overhead. At the end of the year, after all adjusting entries have been made, the factory overhead accounts might have balances as follows:

Factory Overhead		Applied Factory Overhead	
81,500			80,000

Not all of the actual factory overhead was charged to products. The difference, or variance, of $1,500 can be closed to Cost of Goods Sold at the end of the year or, if desired, can be allocated to Cost of Goods Sold, Finished Goods, and Work in Process on the basis of relative cost. If too little overhead has been costed to the products, the variance is called **underapplied or underabsorbed overhead.** On the other hand, if too much overhead has been costed to the products, the variance is called an **overapplied or overabsorbed overhead.** The entry to close out the actual overhead, the applied overhead, and the variance is given as follows:

Factory Overhead				Applied Factory Overhead		
81,500	Closing	81,500		Closing	80,000	80,000

Cost of Goods Sold	
Closing	1,500

Applied:

Variable overhead applied:	
10,000 hours × $3 per hour	$30,000
Fixed overhead applied:	
10,000 hours × $5 per hour	50,000
Total overhead applied	$80,000
Actual overhead	81,500
Underapplied overhead	$ 1,500

The underapplied factory overhead means nothing more than the actual costs were not absorbed by the products manufactured. Underapplied overhead occurs in these situations:

1. We produced less than expected, or
2. We spent more than expected.

Overapplied amounts can also occur. When that happens, the variance is credited to Cost of Goods Sold. Overapplied overhead occurs in these situations:

1. We produced more than expected, or
2. We spent less than expected.

More detailed reasons for the difference is the subject of Chapter 9.

MULTIPLE OVERHEAD RATES

Some reasonable, casual, or beneficial relationship should exist between the costs accumulated in factory overhead accounts, the cost driver selected, and the products or services to which the costs will be allocated. Simply stated: The activity (as represented by the cost driver) related to the products or services is the reason factory overhead costs are incurred. That means a relationship exists between the activity, the cost driver, and the factory overhead costs. For example, if a company uses direct labor hours as a cost driver for the labor activity, we expect factory overhead costs to consist primarily or exclusively of costs that support direct workers. Such costs may include supervision and facilities for work places, as well as travel, training, and fringe benefits of workers.

In all of the examples to this point in the chapter, we have assumed that only one cost driver is appropriate for the total factory overhead. We discussed in Chapter 3 that the diversity of products and services and the diversity of operations or tasks in the production process will distort cost allocations for many companies. Therefore, this section looks at other approaches to refining the allocation process. We look first at departmental (or activity center) rates and then at a more detailed approach through activity-based costing.

DEPARTMENTAL VERSUS PLANT-WIDE OVERHEAD RATES

The greater the differences in products, the more the diversity that exists in the operations. Departmental overhead rates will assign costs more accurately to products than will one plant-wide overhead rate. A plant-wide factory overhead rate can only be justified for a company making one or two products.

For an example, consider The Paint Farm. It finishes furniture for local manufacturers. The furniture passes through two major activity centers that form the two departments in the process: sanding and painting. A summary of direct labor and factory overhead costs for each department during the last month is below:

	Sanding	Painting	Total
Direct labor	$ 37,000	$ 26,500	$ 63,500
Factory overhead.........................	74,000	79,500	153,500

Factory overhead is allocated to products on the basis of direct labor dollars. Dividing the factory overhead costs by direct labor dollars gives the following departmental and plant-wide overhead rates:

Sanding ($74,000/$37,000)   = 200%
Painting ($79,500/$26,500)   = 300%
Plant-wide ($153,500/$63,500) = 241.7%

Let's see the difference the rates have in allocating factory overhead costs to a job that has $86 of Sanding direct labor and $32 of Painting direct labor. That is a total labor cost of $118.

Plant-wide overhead rate ($118 × 241.7%) $285.21

Departmental overhead rates:
  Sanding ($86 × 200%) $172
  Painting ($32 × 300%)...................................   96 $268.00

The departmental rates allocate costs considering the characteristics of the product or job involved. The plant-wide rate averages all products and jobs.

In the above example, the same cost driver was selected for each department. A more common situation is where departments have different cost drivers. For example, a Fabrication Department may use direct labor hours; a Machining Department, machine time; a Production Engineering Department, direct labor cost. As a company looks for ways to trace more accurately costs to products, it will look more closely at the production and support activities. This leads us to activity-based costing.

Activity-Based Costing

We discussed the concepts of activity-based costing in Chapter 3. That discussion included the relationship of activities, cost drivers, and products, and presented many examples of cost drivers. In this section, we apply those concepts to the allocation of factory overhead costs to jobs.

The basic idea behind activity-based costing is to define the discrete activities for which costs are incurred. Preliminary-stage cost drivers identify costs with groupings of activities, called cost pools, and primary-stage cost drivers trace cost pools to products. In the following example, costs are already identified with a grouping of activities. Our task is to provide predetermined overhead rates for each grouping.

The following summary shows the costs for each overhead cost pool, cost drivers, budgeted amounts, and predetermined rates for Northwest Metal Fabricators:

Overhead Cost Pool	Overhead Cost	Cost Dirver	Budgeted Level for Cost Driver	Predetermined Overhead Rate
Purchasing and material-related	$ 250,000	Materials costs	$2,000,000	12.5% of materials cost
Product engineering	110,000	Engineering hours	5,500 hours	$20 per hour
Factory occupancy	300,000	Machine hours	100,000 hours	$3 per hour
Fringe benefits	80,000	Direct labor cost	$1,000,000	8% of direct labor cost
Machine depreciation	450,000	Machine hours	100,000 hours	$4.50 per hour
Machine set-up costs	75,000	Number of setups	1,000 setups	$75 per setup
General manufacturing costs	200,000	Machine hours	100,000 hours	$2 per hour
	$1,465,000			

The company has just completed a customer order with following cost driver information related to the order:

Materials cost	$40,000
Direct labor cost	$10,000
Engineering hours	45
Number of setups	3
Machine hours	28

The factory overhead cost charged to this job using the predetermined overhead rates is calculated as follows:

Purchasing and material-related costs (12.5% × $40,000)	$5,000
Product engineering ($20 × 45)	900
Factory occupancy ($3 × 28)	84
Fringe benefits (8% × $10,000)	800
Machine depreciation ($4.50 × 28)	126
Machine setups ($75 × 3)	225
General manufacturing costs ($2 × 28)	56
Total overhead costs charged to job	$7,191

Let's compare this result to the outcome from using a plant-wide rate based on machine hours. The plant-wide predetermined overhead rate would be:

$$\$1,465,000 \div 100,000 = \$14.65 \text{ per machine hour}$$

The cost charged to the above job would only be $410.20 ($14.65 × 28 machine hours). A plant-wide rate leads to a major distortion in cost allocation. This means that other jobs would have to subsidize the above job if a plant-wide rate were used. Activity-based costing is better because it more accurately traces costs to the job that causes the costs.

THE CONCEPT OF CAPACITY

We often use several definitions of **capacity**—the activity that is transformed into the amount of product or service a company can render within a given interval of time. A restaurant manager, for example, may define capacity as the number of patrons that can be served over the dinner hour, or the manager of a motel may look upon capacity as the number of rooms available to rent on a given night. Often, the following definitions of capacity are found to be useful:

1. Ideal capacity.
2. Practical capacity.
3. Expected capacity.
4. Normal capacity.

Ideal capacity, as the term would imply, is the maximum amount of product that can be manufactured or maximum service that can be rendered with available facilities. This is often too perfect a goal to be realized and is generally recognized to be the absolute limit. Certain interruptions and inefficiencies in production are to be expected.

Practical capacity is full utilization of facilities with allowance made for interruptions and inefficiencies. For example, production will be slowed down or stopped at times because of breakdowns, shortages of labor and materials, or retooling. These possibilities are taken into account in arriving at practical plant capacity.

Expected capacity is the level of operation budgeted or estimated for the current period. This may be at or below practical plant capacity. It is the level at which management expects to operate during the next month or year.

Normal capacity is generally a balance between practical plant capacity and sales demand in the long run. Over a period of years, the peaks and valleys of customer demand are leveled out by averaging, and the point of average plant utilization is considered to be normal capacity.

The overhead rate for costing products or services is computed using the normal level of operations. If a portion of the fixed overhead is not costed to products with a rate determined at normal capacity, management is informed by the capacity (or volume) variance that the company is operating below the average or normal level. Perhaps this can be corrected by a greater sales effort or by better coordination between production and sales.

It may seem, at first, that factory overhead per unit should be calculated at the expected level of operation for the next year. After all, why should a normal overhead rate per unit be used when you already know that the company may be operating at below that level? A rate computed at the expected level of operation will come closer to costing all of the overhead to the products, and product cost will be more in line with actual cost. If the company plans to operate below normal capacity, an overhead rate computed at the expected level of operations will result in more of the fixed overhead being assigned to each unit of product.

For example, assume that the normal level of operation is 200,000 machine hours and that 100,000 units of product can be manufactured in that time. The fixed overhead for the year is budgeted at $500,000. The normal fixed overhead per unit of product is then $5 as computed as follows:

$$\frac{\text{Budgeted fixed overhead}}{\text{Units produced at normal capacity}} = \frac{\$500,000}{100,000} = \$5 \text{ Fixed overhead per unit}$$

But management expects to operate at only 100,000 machine hours next year and produce 50,000 units of product. An overhead rate at expected capacity would be $10 per unit of product:

$$\frac{\text{Budgeted fixed overhead}}{\text{Units produced at expected capacity}} = \frac{\$500,000}{50,000} = \$10 \text{ Fixed overhead per unit}$$

The problem with using an overhead rate based on expected, rather than normal capacity, occurs when determining the selling price of the product. If selling prices are set by adding a markup to total cost, the price will be higher when fewer units are produced. With a higher price under competitive conditions, customers may be lost, thereby aggravating a condition that is already below normal.

For this reason, the objective is not necessarily to assign all overhead costs to the products. The products should bear the normal overhead costs, and the unabsorbed or overabsorbed fixed overhead should be recognized as a variance. This approaches the ideal of obtaining a standard product cost and not a cost that includes all of the fixed overhead. Explicit recognition of the variance provides management with information to control the operation or to make decisions. (The capacity variance is a measurement of the underutilization or overutilization of the plant and should not be buried in a higher product cost.)

COST OF PROVIDING SERVICES

An entity that provides services instead of tangible products may not operate with a formal cost accounting system but will nevertheless measure performance by class of service and by customer groups. A hotel, for example, may provide an exercise room for use by its guests. The cost of supplies used exclusively for the exercise room, such as rubbing lotions and bandages, along with the salaries and wages of the room's employees, such as the manager and exercise class instructors, are identified with the exercise function. Also, a portion of the cost of special equipment used (depreciation) and other overhead costs increased by operating this service will be included. These costs can be used as a basis for deciding how much must be added to a guest's bill to cover costs and allow for profit. Also, as the service is provided, does the amount of customer patronage justify continuance of the service? Can other features be provided at a certain cost to attract more customer attention? Properly assigning costs to the exercise room will give the manager the accounting information needed to answer these questions.

Accounting and legal services are examples where the organization may want costs accumulated by client number or case. In this situation, each client number or case becomes a job with costs traced to the individual jobs as we do with individual products. No formal inventory account for work in process exists, but an account is used that serves as the equivalent, such as "Costs of Unbilled Work."

A JOB COST ILLUSTRATION

Summarized cost data for the year ended April 30, 1995, are presented below for Clark Machine Company to illustrate job cost procedures using historical cost.

Historical cost is the actual cost that has been incurred, and in this chapter it was assumed that the actual or historical cost was to be assigned to the products to the extent that this was possible. In Chapter 9, a standard cost accounting system will be discussed.

Note that the entries given are in composite form. In practice many repetitious entries are made to record individual transactions that take place during the fiscal year. The sequential order of the cost transactions should also be considered. For example, the budget of factory overhead and the overhead rate calculation are made before the beginning of the fiscal year. The predetermined overhead rate must be calculated from a budget of factory overhead so that products will be assigned the proper overhead cost. Only at the end of the year will the company know that 220,000 direct labor hours are used, and that the actual factory overhead cost is $1,336,200. Throughout the year, the company purchases materials and incurs labor and factory overhead costs as products are continually worked on, completed, and sold. At the same time, costs are traced to the products and released as expenses when the products are sold.

Clark Machine Company
Transactional Data
For the Year Ended April 30, 1995

1. Materials purchased during the fiscal year totaled $840,000.
2. Direct materials requisitioned for production cost $631,400. Included in this amount is the materials cost for Job 216 of $3,480. Indirect materials costing $47,200 were also requisitioned.
3. Factory payrolls in total amounted to $1,874,000. The income taxes withheld from the employees' wages totaled $393,400, and the deduction for FICA taxes withheld amounted to $106,600.
4. A distribution of the factory labor cost of $1,874,000 shows that $1,760,000 was direct labor while the remaining $114,000 was indirect labor. The portion of the direct labor cost that pertained to Job 216 was $1,600.
5. Factory overhead at the normal operating level of 250,000 direct labor hours results in an overhead rate of $6 per direct labor hour. During the year, direct labor workers recorded 220,000 labor hours.
6. The factory overhead, in addition to the indirect materials and the indirect labor, amounted to $1,175,000. Included in this amount is depreciation of $120,000 and the employer's share of FICA taxes of $106,600. The balance of the overhead was acquired through accounts payable. Job 216 was completed with 200 direct labor hours. The production order for Job 216 was shown in Figure 5-1.
7. Jobs completed and transferred to stock during the year had costs of $2,945,200.
8. The cost of orders sold during the year was $2,320,000.
9. Applied Factory Overhead and Factory Overhead are closed at the end of the fiscal year with the variance written off to Cost of Goods Sold.

The transactions are entered in the accounts as follows:

1. Purchase of materials. (The cost of each type of material is also entered on the individual materials inventory cards.)

Accounts Payable		Materials	
	840,000 ⟶	840,000	

2. Materials issued to production. (Requisitions are the basis for entries reducing materials inventory, and for posting direct materials costs to each job and posting indirect materials costs to the factory overhead accounts.)

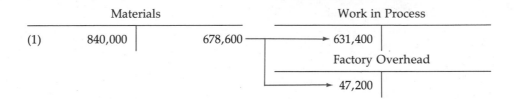

	Materials			Work in Process	
(1)	840,000		678,600 ⟶	631,400	

Factory Overhead

47,200

3.   Aggregate factory payrolls:

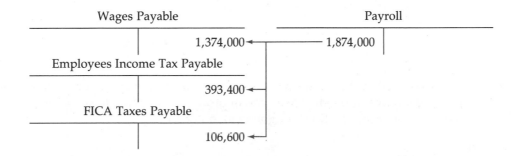

Wages Payable		Payroll	
	1,374,000 ⟵	1,874,000	

Employees Income Tax Payable

393,400 ⟵

FICA Taxes Payable

106,600 ⟵

4.   Payroll distribution for the year. (A classification of labor time by jobs is shown on labor time tickets. These tickets are the basis for distribution of direct labor cost to individual jobs and for posting indirect labor cost to the factory overhead subsidiary ledger.)

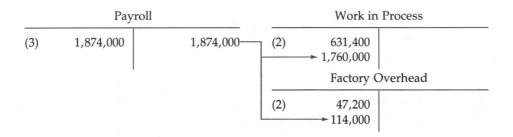

	Payroll			Work in Process	
(3)	1,874,000	1,874,000 ⟶	(2)	631,400	
				1,760,000	

Factory Overhead

| (2) | 47,200 |
| | 114,000 |

5.   Factory overhead applied. (Factory overhead applied to products on direct labor hour basis: 220,000 hours × $6 rate = $1,320,000.)

Applied Factory Overhead		Work in Process	
	1,320,000 ⟶	(2)	631,400
		(4)	1,760,000
			1,320,000

6.   Actual factory overhead (in addition to indirect materials, indirect labor, and employer's share of FICA taxes).

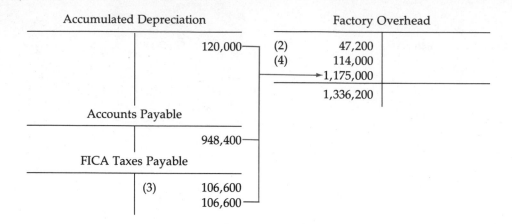

Accumulated Depreciation		Factory Overhead	
	120,000	(2) 47,200	
		(4) 114,000	
		→1,175,000	
		1,336,200	

Accounts Payable	
	948,400

FICA Taxes Payable	
(3) 106,600	
106,600	

7.   Work completed during the year and transferred to stock. (Completed jobs are removed from the file of jobs in process and moved to subsidiary ledger supporting the finished goods inventory.)

Work in Process		Finished Goods	
(2) 631,400	2,945,200 ————→	2,945,200	
(4) 1,760,000			
(5) 1,320,000			
3,711,400			

8.   The cost of goods sold. (Deductions are recorded in the finished goods inventory ledger. Entries are also made in records supporting billings to customers for the sales.)

Finished Goods		Cost of Goods Sold	
(7) 2,945,200	2,320,000 ————→	2,320,000	

9.   Closing of Applied Factory Overhead and Factory Overhead accounts. (Actual overhead is not absorbed as a part of the product cost. The excess is closed to Cost of Goods Sold.)

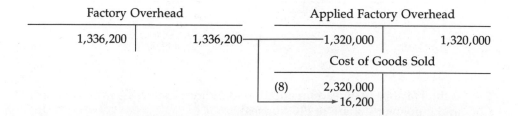

Factory Overhead		Applied Factory Overhead	
1,336,200	1,336,200 —	—1,320,000	1,320,000

Cost of Goods Sold	
(8) 2,320,000	
→ 16,200	

SUMMARY

One of the objectives in cost accounting is to determine the cost to render a given service, to manufacture a given quantity of product, or to complete some project. The two most common cost accounting systems for achieving this objective are the job cost system and the process cost system. A job cost system is appropriate when the product or service is one-of-a-kind, customized, or special ordered by a customer. A process cost system is appropriate when the operations represent mass production or continuous processing. This production environment is typically characterized by commingled products, fabricated products, or assembled products.

A job cost system accumulates separately the costs of materials, labor, and overhead for the job, whether the job is one unit or many units. Materials are identified as direct or indirect. If direct, the materials are charged directly to the specific job. If indirect, the materials are referred to as indirect materials or supplies and their costs are included in factory overhead. Labor follows the same type of distinctions.

Factory overhead is budgeted at the normal operating level and divided by a budgeted cost driver that relates overhead cost to the products. The cost driver selected may be direct labor hours if the overhead consists largely of labor-related costs and labor support costs, such as supervision and fringe benefit costs. The cost driver "direct labor hours" serves as a bridge between the product and the overhead costs. On the other hand, machine hours may be more appropriate if a large part of the overhead is lubrication, maintenance, and other costs generally related to machine operation. Both the overhead cost and the cost driver are budgeted at a normal level of operations, and the rate calculated is used to allocate overhead to services or products. Factory overhead rates can be plant-wide rates, departmental rates, or activity rates, depending on the diversity of the products and the diversity of the operations. Activity-based costing is the preferred approach when considerable product or operation diversity exists.

Actual costs are accumulated, and comparisons of actual and estimated costs for each service or job help management to control costs. Actual overhead incurred can be compared with the overhead applied to the services or products. If any factory overhead is unabsorbed through allocation (or if overhead is overabsorbed), management can use this information to control the operation. A favorable or unfavorable capacity variance is a measure of how well the plant is being utilized.

PROBLEM FOR REVIEW

Johnson Schuman owns and operates a plumbing and heating company. Two overhead rates are used in applying overhead costs to the jobs. One rate is based on direct labor hours, and the other is based on machine hours. The machine is a backhoe used in digging service lines. Overhead costs of operating the backhoe are kept separately, so that only the jobs requiring the use of the backhoe are charged an overhead rate per machine hour. Overhead for the year is budgeted for a normal operating capacity of 6,000 direct labor hours and 1,800 machine hours (hours of backhoe operation). The overhead budgets are given as follows:

	Budget at 6,000 direct labor hours	Budget at 1,800 machine hours
Budgeted factory overhead:		
Supplies	$ 3,800	
Indirect labor	24,000	
Supervision..............................	50,000	
Payroll taxes.............................	18,200	
Telephone................................	2,600	
Heat and light...........................	3,200	
Rent—building	15,000	
Insurance and taxes	4,000	$ 1,400
Fuel	1,800	4,800
Depreciation—equipment.................	2,200	8,600
Miscellaneous	1,200	
Lubrication		1,600
Maintenance.............................		3,700
Repairs		1,500
Total overhead budget	$126,000	$21,600

On February 1, the cost of work in process is $440 and consists of only one job, the job for W. Hartenstine. Details with respect to the cost of the Hartenstine job are as follows:

Direct materials	$112
Direct labor..	160
Overhead	168
Cost at February 1	$440

Costs and other data pertaining to jobs worked on during February are as follows:

	Direct Materials	Direct Labor	Labor Hours	Machine Hours
W. Hartenstine	$ 135	$ 320	16	—
C. Lasher	246	560	28	—
P. Romero	230	240	12	—
(machine hours)....................	—	125	—	5
M. Tellerico........................	84	60	3	—
All other jobs	842	14,000	500	160
Totals	$1,537	$15,305	559	165

The direct labor cost is $20 per hour of ordinary labor and $25 per hour of backhoe operation.

All orders were finished during February with the exception of the Tellerico order which is still in process.

Required:

1. Compute an overhead rate per direct labor hour and an overhead rate per machine hour.
2. Prepare a summary of costs incurred for work done in February.
3. Prepare a summary of work in process that shows the costs in process during the period and the cost of goods completed.
4. Give the costs of each job listed, identifying costs by the cost elements: direct materials, direct labor, overhead-labor, and overhead-machine.

Solution:

1.

$$\frac{\text{Budget of overhead for direct labor hours}}{\text{Budget of direct labor hours}} = \frac{\$126,000}{6,000} = \$21 \text{ per direct labor hour}$$

$$\frac{\text{Budget of overhead for machine hours}}{\text{Budget of machine hours}} = \frac{\$21,600}{1,800} = \$12 \text{ per machine hour}$$

2. Costs of work performed during the period:

Materials	$ 1,537
Payroll	15,305
Applied overhead—labor (559 hours × $21)	11,739
Applied overhead—machine (165 hours × $12)	1,980
Cost of work performed during the period	$30,561

3. Summary of work in process and calculation of costs of goods completed:

Work in process at February 1	$ 440
Add February costs	30,561
	$31,001
Less cost of incomplete Tellerico job	207*
Cost of work completed in February	$30,794

* Work in process at February 28 for Tellerico job:

Direct materials	$ 84
Direct labor	60
Overhead labor (3 hrs. × $21)	63
Total cost	$ 207

4. Detailed costs of each job:

	Direct Materials	Direct Labor	Overhead —Labor	Overhead —Machine	Total Cost
W. Hartenstine	$ 247	$ 480	$ 504	$ 0	$ 1,231
C. Lasher	246	560	588	0	1,394
P. Romero	230	365	252	60	907
M. Tellerico	84	60	63	0	207
All other jobs	842	14,000	10,500	1,920	27,262
Total costs	$1,649	$15,465	$11,907	$1,980	$31,001

Combine the cost of February 1 Work in Process for Hartenstine with the current cost of the job to get the total cost of the Hartenstine job.

For each job, multiply the direct labor hours given by the $21 overhead rate per direct labor hour.

For each job, where appropriate, multiply the machine hours by the $12 overhead rate per machine hour.

❖ *APPENDIX*

SERVICE CENTERS AND SUPPORT FUNCTIONS

Most companies have several departments or functions involved directly or indirectly in producing goods or rendering services. The manner in which departmental overhead rates are developed depends on the interrelationships among the several types of departments.

Producing departments are organizational units most closely tied to the productive effort that results in products or services to customers. On the other hand, **service centers and support functions** provide supporting services that facilitate the activities of the manufacturing process. For our purposes, we will refer to these support services as service centers. They include, for example, maintenance, quality control, cafeterias, internal auditing, personnel, accounting, production planning and control, or medical facilities. Although they do not have a direct relationship to output, service and support function costs support production and become part of the cost of a finished product or service. In some limited cases, a service center provides support services for producing departments and customer service for outside customers. Examples of these services include engineering consulting, research and development, computer systems design, copying services, and laboratory services.

In the chapter, we did not address the specifics of allocating the costs of service centers with reciprocal relationships. Here we look at the procedures for allocating such costs. A reciprocal relationship exists when service centers provide service to each other.

SELECT A COST DRIVER

Service center costs are allocated to producing departments by means of a cost driver. Any number of cost drivers for calculating a rate may be appropriate depending on the nature of the support activity. Examples of cost drivers that could be used are given in Figure 5.2

POSSIBLE COST DRIVERS FOR SELECTED SERVICE CENTERS	
Service Center	**Cost Drivers**
Purchasing	Number of orders, cost of materials, line items ordered
Receiving and inspection	Cost of materials, number of units, number of orders, labor hours
Storerooms	Cost of materials, number of requisitions, number of units handled, square or cubic footage occupied
Personnel	Number of employees, labor hours, turnover of labor
Laundry	Pounds of laundry, number of items processed
Cafeteria	Number of employees
Custodial services	Square footage occupied
Repair and maintenance	Machine hours, labor hours
Medical facilities	Number of employees, hours worked
Factory administration	Total labor hours, number of employees, labor cost
Power	Kilowatt hours, capacity of machines

Figure 5.2   Cost Drivers Used for Service Centers

INTERDEPARTMENTAL SUPPORT

Once a cost driver is selected, an allocation rate is computed in the same manner we did for factory overhead costs. Two common approaches are available for allocating the costs of service centers when interdepartmental support (reciprocal relationships) exist: direct method, and step (sequential) method. In describing the two approaches, only support departments with reciprocal services will be illustrated.

To illustrate the two methods of allocating service center costs, we will use the operating data from Telico Manufacturing. The company makes several products in a single factory. It has three service centers and two producing departments. Budgeted data for the coming year appear below:

	Square Feet	Employees	Overhead Costs
Service centers:			
Building services	100	30	$165,000
Personnel	200	20	90,000
Administration	800	20	330,000
Producing departments:			
Fabrication	1,000	30	265,000
Assembly	2,000	90	420,000

Building Services costs are allocated on square footage; Personnel and Administration on employees. Fabrication will have an overhead rate based on machine hours, and Assembly will use direct labor hours. Budgeted machine hours in Fabrication are 50,000; direct labor hours in Assembly are 120,000.

Direct Method

The **direct method** allocations are made from each service center to producing departments in proportion to activity performed for the producing departments. Thus, the direct method does not assign costs to other service centers for work performed for other service centers. Allocation of service center costs uses only that operating data pertaining to producing departments. Once the support and service centers have their costs allocated, producing departmental overhead rates are calculated per unit of activity.

Square footage for Fabrication is 1,000 and for Assembly is 2,000. This forms the allocation base of 3,000 square feet. Building Services is then prorated over Fabrication and Assembly as follows:

Fabrication	1,000 sq. ft.	⅓ × $165,000 =	$ 55,000
Assembly	2,000 sq. ft.	⅔ × $165,000 =	110,000
Total	3,000 sq. ft.		$165,000

The same approach follows for Personnel and Administration. These are summarized below:

Fabrication	30 employees	25% × $ 90,000 =	$ 22,500
Assembly	90 employees	75% × $ 90,000 =	67,500
Total	120 employees		$ 90,000
Fabrication	30 employees	25% × $330,000 =	$ 82,500
Assembly	90 employees	75% × $330,000 =	247,500
Total	120 employees		$330,000

The other way to perform these allocations is to divide the service center cost by the cost driver and apply the resulting rate to the producing department. For example, the Building Services would have a rate of $55 ($165,000 ÷ 3,000) per square foot.

The results of service center allocations and the subsequent calculation of overhead rates for the producing departments are summarized below:

	Building Services	Personnel	Adminis- tration	Fabri- cation	Assembly
Costs	$165,000	$90,000	$330,000	$265,000	$420,000
Building services ..	(165,000)			55,000	110,000
Personnel		(90,000)		22,500	67,500
Administration			(330,000)	82,500	247,500
	$ 0	$ 0	$ 0	$425,000	$845,000
Machine hours				50,000	
Overhead rate per machine hour				$ 8.50	
Direct labor hours					120,000
Overhead rate per direct labor hour					$ 7.04

Step (Sequential) Method

The **step (sequential) method** is an attempt to consider reciprocal services. However, recognition of those services is a one-way process. The service centers are arranged in a sequence, and their costs are allocated one after the other. The first service center's costs are allocated to all subsequent service centers and producing departments. The second service center's cost is then allocated to all subsequent service centers and producing departments, but not back to the first service center. This process continues until all service centers' costs have been allocated to producing departments.

The square footage for Personnel is 200; Administration is 800; Fabrication is 1,000; and Assembly is 2,000. This forms the allocation base of 4,000 square feet. Building Services is then prorated over remaining service centers and producing departments as follows:

Personnel	200 sq. ft.	5% × $165,000 =	$ 8,250
Administration	800 sq. ft.	20% × $165,000 =	33,000
Fabrication	1,000 sq. ft.	25% × $165,000 =	41,250
Assembly	2,000 sq. ft.	50% × $165,000 =	82,500
Total	4,000 sq. ft.		$165,000

Personnel receives an allocation of Building Services costs. These must be added to the costs already in Personnel to determine the allocation of Personnel costs. The new Personnel costs total $98,250 ($90,000 + $8,250). The allocation occurs as follows:

Administration	20 employees	$2/14$ × $98,250 =	$ 14,035*
Fabrication	30 employees	$3/14$ × $98,250 =	21,054
Assembly	90 employees	$9/14$ × $98,250 =	63,161
Total	140 employees		$ 98,250

* This figure has been rounded down.

After allocating Building Services and Personnel, the Administration costs for the next step of the allocation are $377,035 ($330,000 + $33,000 + $14,035). These costs are allocated below:

Fabrication	30 employees	25% × $377,035 =	$ 94,259
Assembly	90 employees	75% × $377,035 =	282,776
Total	120 employees		$377,035

The results of service center allocations and the subsequent calculation of overhead rates for the producing departments are summarized below and at the top of the following page:

	Building Services	Personnel	Administration	Fabrication	Assembly
Costs	$165,000	$90,000	$330,000	$265,000	$420,000
Building services ..	(165,000)	8,250	33,000	41,250	82,500
	$ 0	$98,250			
Personnel		(98,250)	14,035	21,054	63,161
		$ 0	$377,035		
Administration			(377,035)	94,259	282,776
			$ 0	$421,563	$848,437

Machine hours	50,000	
Overhead rate per machine hour	$ 8.431	
Direct labor hours		120,000
Overhead rate per direct labor hour		$7.07

How do you arrange the order of service centers? The order is determined from a survey of the services rendered by each service center. In some instances, the survey will show interdepartmental services for some service centers are so insignificant they can be ignored. The general rule is to sequence service centers in the order of amount of services provided to other service centers—going from greatest to least. What constitutes "greatest amount of service"? One interpretation is the rendering of service to the greatest number of other service centers. Another is the amount of cost in the service center; the service center with the highest amount of costs goes first. It is not clear which interpretation should be applied. The real issue is to set up a sequence that will provide reasonable and logical allocations.

OTHER ISSUES

Two other issues influence the way we allocate service center costs: treatment of revenues and allocating costs by behavior. These issues are presented here.

Treatment of Revenues

Most service centers are simply cost centers and thus generate no revenues. A few, such as the cafeteria, may charge employees or other outside parties for the services they perform. Any revenues generated should be offset against the service center costs. That means for both the direct method and the step method, we allocate the costs less the offset. In this manner, other service centers and producing departments will not be required to bear costs for which the service center has already been reimbursed.

Allocating Costs by Behavior

Whenever possible, service center costs should be separated into variable and fixed classifications and allocated separately. This approach is appropriate to avoid possible inequities in allocation, as well as to provide data for planning and decision making, performance evaluation and control, and cost management.

As a general rule, variable costs should be charged to other service centers and producing departments on the basis of the activity that controls the incurrence of the cost involved. This way, the service centers and departments directly responsible for the incurrence of servicing costs are required to bear the cost in proportion to their actual usage of the service involved.

The fixed costs of service centers represent the cost of providing capacity. As such, these costs are most equitably allocated to consuming service centers and producing departments on the basis of predetermined amounts. In this way, the amount of cost to be allocated is determined in advance of the period in which service will be rendered. Once determined, the amount does not change from period to period. Typically, the amount charged is based either on the service centers' and producing departments' peak-period or long-run average servicing needs.

TERMINOLOGY REVIEW

Assembled products (191)
Bill of materials (193)
Capacity (205)
Capacity or volume variance (201)
Commingled products (191)
Cost overrun (196)
Direct labor (194)
Direct materials (193)
Direct method (216)
Expected capacity (205)
Fabricated products (191)
Flexible overhead budget (197)
Ideal capacity (205)
Indirect labor (194)

Indirect materials (193)
Job cost system (192)
Job, work, or production order (192)
Normal capacity (205)
Overapplied or overabsorbed overhead (201)
Overhead rate (197)
Practical capacity (205)
Producing departments (214)
Service centers and support functions (214)
Step (sequential) method (217)
Underapplied or underabsorbed overhead (201)

QUESTIONS FOR REVIEW AND DISCUSSION

1. Under what conditions would a job cost system be appropriate? A process cost system?

2. What is the distinguishing characteristic of a commingled product?

3. What is the difference between a fabricated product and an assembled product?

4. What is the purpose of a job, work, or production order?

5. Describe briefly how costs flow through the accounts in job costing for a manufacturer. How would this change for a service organization?

6. What is a bill of materials? Why is it important to the acquisition of materials?

7. What are the cost elements associated with the materials acquisition process? Which ones are likely to be included in the cost of materials charged as direct or indirect materials?

8. What are the three criteria for determining whether materials are direct or indirect?

9. What form is used to identify materials with a production order?

10. What are the cost elements associated with labor? Which ones are likely to be included in the cost of direct or indirect labor? Where are the other cost elements accumulated for charging to products?

11. What form is used to identify direct labor with a production order?

12. Explain why a budget is used in costing factory overhead rather than waiting to assign actual overhead cost after the end of the year.

13. What is the basis for selecting a cost driver to be used in costing factory overhead?

14. What is the total cost savings if 80 direct labor hours can be saved when direct labor cost per hour is $7, and variable overhead per direct labor hour is $5?

15. What account is credited when factory overhead cost is assigned to work in process?

16. How is the difference between the actual factory overhead and the overhead assigned to the products handled at the end of the year?

17. Explain under what circumstances departmental rates are preferred to a plant-wide factory overhead rate.

18. Describe how overhead rates determined using activity-based costing differ from departmental overhead rates.

19. What is the difference between practical and normal capacity?

20. If the company does not expect to operate at normal capacity during the next year, why should the products be costed by using an overhead rate determined at normal capacity?

21. (Appendix) What is the difference between a service center and a producing department?

22. (Appendix) How do service center costs enter into the final cost of products and services?

23. (Appendix) How are service center costs allocated to other service centers and producing departments under the direct method? Under the step method?

24. (Appendix) If a service center generates revenues of some type, how do these revenues enter into the allocation of service costs to other service centers and producing departments?

EXERCISES

1. **Cost of Orders.** Costello Repair Services specializes in the routine maintenance and repair of power lawn mowers and other small machines. Three orders (#721, #722, and #723) were started and completed in March. Materials costing $41 were used on order #721, materials costing $17 were used on order #722, and materials costing $8 were used on order #723. Labor is paid at a uniform rate of $8.50 per hour, and overhead is applied at 80 percent of labor cost. During the month, 3 labor hours were used for order #721, 2 hours for order #722, and 4 hours for order #723.

   Required:
   Compute the cost of each order, showing separately the cost of materials, labor, and overhead.

2. **Tracing the Cost Flow.** Carterville Tool & Die Company used $816,250 in direct materials in April for the production of various orders. Direct labor cost for the month was $275,400. Factory overhead is costed to production at 150 percent of direct labor cost.

No orders were in process at the beginning and end of the month. All work was delivered to customers.

Required:
Prepare T-accounts to record the costs entered in production, the transfer of costs to finished goods, and the transfer of costs to cost of goods sold.

3.   **Tracing the Cost Flow.** During the fiscal year, Weiskoff Instruments, Inc. purchased direct materials costing $415,200 and used direct materials costing $297,300 in production. Indirect materials costing $28,100 were used and recorded as factory overhead. Factory payrolls amounted to $242,000 in direct labor and $54,000 in indirect labor. Factory overhead, in addition to indirect materials and indirect labor, amounted to $42,000 (record as a credit to Accounts Payable). Factory overhead is applied to the production orders at 50 percent of direct labor cost. The cost of production orders completed during the fiscal year was $428,000. The cost of goods sold was $342,000, and sales revenue was $487,000. No inventories were on hand at the beginning of the fiscal year.

Required:
1.   Enter the transactions directly into T-accounts. Refer to the job order cost illustration in this chapter as an example. Close the factory overhead variance directly into Cost of Goods Sold. The T-accounts you will need are the following:

Materials	Cost of Goods Sold
Payroll	Factory Overhead
Work in Process	Applied Factory Overhead
Finished Goods	Accounts Payable
Wages Payable	Sales
Accounts Receivable	

2.   Prepare a summary statement showing sales revenue, cost of goods sold, and gross margin for the fiscal year.

4.   **Factory Overhead Rates.** Jensen Supply Company normally operates at 450,000 direct labor hours a year. At this level of operation, variable overhead has been budgeted at $337,500, and fixed overhead has been budgeted at $1,012,500.

Required:
1.   Compute the total factory overhead rate per direct labor hour at normal capacity.
2.   Determine the variable portion of the overhead rate at normal capacity. What would the variable overhead rate be if normal capacity were 400,000 direct labor hours instead of 450,000 hours? Assume that variable cost varies in direct proportion with hours of operation.
3.   Determine the fixed portion of the overhead rate at normal capacity. What would the fixed overhead rate be if 400,000 direct labor hours were considered normal capacity? Explain why the rate differs depending upon the level set as normal capacity.

5.   **Overhead Rates for a Service Enterprise.** Mountain Horn Hostel was purchased by a naturalist who hopes to show people the value of wildlife and also provide them with a pleasant vacation retreat. Costs are budgeted for the year and will be allocated over the 120 days of the tourist season. The hostel has a normal capacity of 100 persons per day. Using the cost information, the owner hopes to develop a billing rate per person per day that will yield an acceptable profit.
      Costs for the year were estimated as follows:

Kitchen and dining room costs	$172,000
Housekeeping costs	68,000
Taxes and insurance	18,000
Repairs and maintenance	21,000
Utilities	37,000
Grounds and pool maintenance	11,000
Salaries of drivers and guides	54,000
Operating cost—buses and vans	9,000
Depreciation—buses and vans	18,000
Depreciation—buildings	12,000
Total estimated cost	$420,000

A friend of the naturalist offers advice: "Your idea of normal capacity is full capacity. What about rainy days and cancellations? You'll be lucky to have 80 people a day. And if snow comes early, count on a 100-day season. That's my idea of normal."

Required:
1. Compute a cost per person per day using the naturalist's concept of normal.
2. Compute a cost per person per day using the friend's figures.
3. Explain the difference in the results of the two computations.

6. **Factory Overhead Rates.** Mendez Specialities Company prepared a flexible budget of factory overhead for the year. The budget is summarized as follows:

Budgeted machine hours	150,000	200,000	250,000
Variable overhead	$300,000	$ 400,000	$ 500,000
Fixed overhead	600,000	600,000	600,000
Total overhead	$900,000	$1,000,000	$1,100,000

Required:
1. If 200,000 machine hours are considered to be a normal level of operation, determine the factory overhead rate. Give the variable and fixed portions of the rate.
2. Assume that the company operated at an actual level of 150,000 machine hours. How much variable overhead would be apportioned to the products by using the rate determined at 200,000 machine hours? Would all of the variable overhead budgeted for 150,000 machine hours be absorbed? Explain.
3. Assuming again that the company operated at 150,000 machine hours, how much of the fixed overhead would be apportioned to the products by using the rate determined at 200,000 machine hours?
4. Explain why all of the budgeted fixed overhead would not be absorbed at 150,000 machine hours. What name is given to the difference between the budgeted fixed overhead and the fixed overhead absorbed by the products?

7. **Factory Overhead Costing.** Abrahms Manufacturing Company estimated variable factory overhead costs at $6 per machine hour. Fixed factory overhead was budgeted at $600,000 for the year. Normal capacity is 120,000 machine hours for the year.

The company actually operated at 125,000 machine hours for the year. Variable overhead for the year was $750,000, which is exactly the amount that would be budgeted for 125,000 machine hours. Actual fixed overhead was $600,000 as budgeted.

Required:
1. Compute the factory overhead rate, breaking it into a variable and a fixed rate.

2. Determine the balance of actual overhead in Factory Overhead (the factory overhead control account) before closing.
3. Determine the balance of Applied Factory Overhead before closing.
4. Was there a capacity variance for the year? If so, explain why and determine the amount of the variance.

8. **Departmental Factory Overhead Rates.** Chin Chow Products, Inc. operates with two manufacturing departments. Shaping and Forming uses more machinery and equipment, and the overhead rate is based on machine hours. Assembly is more labor intensive, and the overhead rate is based on direct labor hours. Budgeted hours and budgeted overhead at normal capacity are given below for each department:

	Departments	
	Shaping and Forming	Assembly
Budgeted machine hours	150,000	
Budgeted direct labor hours......................		50,000
Budgeted overhead............................	$450,000	$250,000

Order #878 required 50 hours of machine time in Shaping and Forming and 30 direct labor hours in Assembly.

Required:
1. Compute the overhead rates for each of the two departments.
2. Determine the factory overhead applied to Order #878 in each of the two departments.

9. **Flow of Cost.** At the beginning of 1995 Danzi Company had the following inventory balances:

Materials Inventory	$27,000
Work in Process Inventory	48,000
Finished Goods Inventory	34,000

During the year materials costing $152,600 were purchased. Materials requisitioned for jobs cost $98,000, and indirect materials costing $42,000 were charged to Factory Overhead. Factory payrolls were $212,000 with income taxes withheld of $43,000 and FICA taxes withheld of $17,000. Indirect labor included in the payrolls at $71,000 was charged to Factory Overhead. All other labor was direct labor charged to the jobs. Factory overhead was applied to the jobs at the rate of $8 per machine hour. During the year, the company operated at 45,000 machine hours and incurred factory overhead costs of $259,000 (in addition to the indirect materials and indirect labor as stated above). Depreciation of $47,000 was included in the $259,000 of factory overhead costs.

Products costing $465,000 were completed during the year, and the cost of goods sold was $480,000.

Required:
1. Set up T-accounts as follows and enter beginning balances where appropriate:

Materials Inventory
Work in Process Inventory
Finished Goods Inventory
Payroll
Factory Overhead
Applied Factory Overhead

Accumulated Depreciation
Income Taxes Withheld
FICA Taxes Withheld
Wages Payable
Accounts Payable
Cost of Goods Sold

2.   Enter transactions directly into the T-accounts. Close Factory Overhead and Applied Factory Overhead with the variance closed to Cost of Goods Sold.

10.   **Analysis of Job Orders.** Data from three production orders completed by Araceli Products Company are given as follows:

	Production Orders		
	163	164	165
Direct materials	$ 5,600	$3,800	$2,600
Direct labor	4,500	2,700	3,000
Applied factory overhead	2,400	900	1,200
Total cost	$12,500	$7,400	$6,800
Direct labor hours	600	300	400
Number of units produced	1,000	500	200

Required:
1.   What was the direct labor rate per hour on each of the orders?
2.   What was the overhead rate per hour on each of the orders, assuming this rate was based on direct labor hours?
3.   Compute the total cost per unit of product on each order.

11.   **Departmental and Plant-wide Overhead Rates.** Yellowhouse Toy Company manufactures small battery-powered cars that children under eight years of age can drive around a house or yard. Currently, the company has two models: Speed Demon and Cadillac Classic. Both cars sell well. The company processes the cars in three departments: Fabrication, Assembly, and Painting. The departmental budgets for the current year are below:

	Overhead Costs	Machine Hours
Fabrication	$ 730,000	25,000
Assembly	260,000	13,000
Painting	10,000	12,000
	$1,000,000	50,000

The estimated machine hours for a batch of 50 of each of the cars are:

	Speed Demon	Cadillac Classic
Fabrication	50	90
Assembly	75	40
Painting	35	20
	160	150

Required:

1. Compute overhead rates for each department and for the plant in total.
2. Compute the estimated overhead cost per batch of each car using:
    (a) A plant-wide rate.
    (b) Departmental rates.
3. Explain why a different cost exists for the cars depending on the use of a plant-wide rate or departmental rates.

12. **Divisional and Facility-wide Overhead Rates.** Goshen Research Laboratories performs contract research for government and commercial applications. It is located in the Salt Lake Valley where it has access to a labor market with advanced scientific and engineering degrees. Utah has several major universities graduating people who want to pursue careers while remaining in Utah. The company is divided into six divisions with appropriate support and ancillary facilities. Each division is housed in its own building within the industrial complex.

The company bills its customers based on the cost of research work. Costs included are for direct equipment, direct man hours, and overhead. The current overhead rate used for billing purposes is the facility-wide rate which is $31.25 per hour for this year. The overhead costs and labor hours by division are as follows:

	Overhead (Thousands)	Labor Hours (Thousands)
Thermal	$ 3,760	160
Solar	13,120	800
Aquatic	2,975	170
Laser	113,400	2,250
Gases	16,471	910
Mechanical	37,290	1,695
Totals	$187,016	5,985

Several customers, particularly government agencies, question the overhead rate because it is too high for their projects.

Required:

1. Calculate overhead rates for the overall facility and for each of the six divisions.
2. Show how much overhead would be charged to each of the following projects with a facility-wide overhead rate and then with divisional rates:
    (a) Project #95106: Soil Conservation of Semi-Arid Lands. Funded by the Department of Interior. During 1995, this project had 31,400 hours of work recorded on it. Sixty percent of those hours are from the Thermal Division, and 40 percent are from the Solar Division.
    (b) Project #95111: Coal Gasification Project. Funded 30 percent by the State of Utah, 50 percent by the Department of Energy, and 20% by a private utilities company. This project absorbed 47,500 hours, of which 23,200 were in the Laser Division with the remaining hours coming from the Mechanical Division.

13. **Activity-Based Costing and Cost Drivers.** Jilliard Company manufactures two types of medical syringes: low-unit and med-unit. The overhead activities, costs, and related data are as follows:

	Low-Unit	Med-Unit	Activity Center Costs
Receiving orders	100	150	$ 7,500
Machine hours	12,000	13,000	125,000
Setups.....................................	45	20	9,750
Shipping orders	200	400	30,000

Required:

1.   Identify the appropriate cost driver for each activity center and compute a rate for each center.
2.   Allocate the overhead costs to the two products using the rates from (1) above.
3.   Assume the total costs of all activity centers are allocated on the basis of machine hours. Calculate the overall rate and allocate overhead costs to the two products using that rate.
4.   Explain why the costs allocated to the two products differ in (2) and (3) above.

14.   **Product Cost Buildup.** Delerico Manufacturing Company makes a variety of backpacks. The activity centers and budgeted information for the year are:

Activity Center	Overhead Costs	Cost Driver	Activity Center Rate
Material handling ..	$ 300,000	Weight of materials	$0.30 per lb. of material
Cutting............	1,800,000	Number of shapes	3.00 per shape
Assembly	4,600,000	Direct labor hours	12.00 per labor hour
Sewing	1,200,000	Machine hours	8.00 per machine hour

Two styles of backpacks were produced in December, the EasyRider and the Overnighter. The quantities and other operating data for the month are:

	EasyRider	Overnighter
Direct material pounds	50,000	15,000
Assembly direct labor hours.......................	7,500	1,200
Sewing machine hours	12,500	1,800
Units produced....................................	5,000	1,000
Number of shapes	35,000	15,000

Required:

1.   Using the activity center rates, find the total overhead costs charged to each product during the month.
2.   Calculate a per unit cost for each backpack.
3.   With the information given, compute the budgeted level for each cost driver upon which the activity center rates were based.

15.   **Allocating Service Center (Appendix).** The Lemler Company manufactures 3½″ computer disks with two service centers and three producing departments. The budgeted data for June 1995 are:

	Overhead Cost	Labor Hours	Machine Hours	Employees
Service centers:				
Plant Administration	$ 50,000	10,000		20
Personnel	35,000	20,000		25
Producing departments:				
Cutting.....................	225,000	25,000	200,000	150
Assembly	375,000	35,000	150,000	225
Finishing	400,000	30,000	20,000	175

Plant administrative costs are allocated on the basis of labor hours, and personnel is allocated on the basis of the number of employees. The overhead rates in cutting and assembly are based on machine hours. The overhead rate in Finishing is based on labor hours.

Required:
1. Using the direct method, allocate the service center costs to the producing departments and calculate overhead rates for each producing department.
2. Using the step method, allocate the service center costs to the producing departments and calculate overhead rates for each producing department. If necessary, round all dollar allocations to producing departments to the nearest dollar. (Allocate service centers in the order of plant administration and personnel.)

16. **Allocating Service Center Costs.** (Appendix) Jacksboro Manufacturing, Inc. shows the following estimated operating statistics for this year:

	Personnel Transactions Processed	Number of Employees	Space Occupied (Square Feet)
Service centers:			
Utilities......................	10	80	1,000
Cafeteria	20	25	8,000
Personnel	15	50	2,000
Producing departments:			
Cutting......................	80	900	70,000
Finishing	20	600	30,000

Budgeted overhead costs for the year and the cost driver for each department are as follows:

	Overhead	Cost Driver
Utilities	$30,000	Square footage
Cafeteria	20,000	Number of employees
Personnel	10,000	Number of personnel transactions
Cutting.......................	80,000	Machine hours
Finishing	60,000	Direct labor hours

Cutting budgeted 20,000 machine hours for the year while Finishing budgeted 15,000 direct labor hours.

Required:

1. Using the direct method, allocate the service center costs to the producing depart-ments and calculate overhead rates for each producing department.
2. Using the step method, allocate the service center costs to the producing depart-ments and calculate overhead rates for each producing department. If necessary, round all dollar allocations to producing departments to the nearest dollar. (Allo-cate service centers in the order of utilities, cafeteria, and personnel.)

17. **Direct and Step Method for Developing Overhead Rates.** (Appendix) Dabling Cre-ations is in the process of developing overhead rates for the coming year. The budgeted information for its three support functions (Repair, Factory Office, and Personnel) and two operating departments (Fabrication and Finishing) is as follows:

	Repair	Factory Office	Person-nel	Fabri-cation	Fin-ishing	Total
Overhead	$22,500	$29,000	$21,000	$44,250	$46,750	$163,500
Service hours	200	800	1,200	9,000	7,000	18,200
Square footage ...	2,000	1,000	500	6,500	8,000	18,000
Number of employees	30	20	80	240	620	1,000

The Repair Department is responsible for providing maintenance to all departments. Its costs are allocated using service hours as the cost driver. Factory Office includes factory scheduling, storage, and all accounting functions. Its costs are allocated using square foot-age. Personnel handles the hiring, training, and terminating of all employees for the compa-ny. Its costs are allocated using number of employees as the cost driver. Fabrication is machine-intensive so the cost driver is machine hours. The budgeted machine hours are 10,000 hours. Finishing is labor intensive and uses direct labor hours as the cost driver. The budget calls for 20,000 direct labor hours during the period.

Required:

1. Calculate the overhead rates for Fabrication and Finishing assuming the support functions are allocated with the direct method.
2. Calculate the overhead rates for Fabrication and Finishing assuming the support functions are allocated with the step method. Use the sequence of Repair, Factory Office, and Personnel.

PROBLEMS

5-1. **Factory Overhead Rates.** Irish Products Company manufactures a product line that has a direct materials cost of $21 per unit and a direct labor cost of $14 per unit. Factory overhead is applied to production on the basis of machine hours with five units of prod-ucts produced each machine hour. Under normal conditions, the company operates at 150,000 machine hours each year and produces 750,000 units of product.

The following is a summarized flexible budget for the year.

Machine hours	100,000	150,000	200,000
Variable overhead	$ 600,000	$ 900,000	$1,200,000
Fixed overhead	600,000	600,000	600,000
Total overhead......................	$1,200,000	$1,500,000	$1,800,000

Required:

1. Compute the overhead rate per machine hour at normal operating capacity.
2. Determine the total unit cost of the product at the normal operating capacity of 150,000 machine hours.
3. If normal operating capacity were 200,000 machine hours, what would be the total overhead rate per machine hour?
4. If the company operated at 200,000 machine hours and made 1,000,000 units of product during the year, what would the capacity variance be? Would the fixed overhead be overapplied or underapplied? (Use 150,000 machine hours as normal.)

5-2. **Fixed Overhead and Hours of Operation.** Jack Bickham has prepared a budget of overhead cost for Sutherland Industries, Inc. at the normal level of operations and at the expected level of operations for the next year, shown as follows:

	Normal Level	Expected Level
Direct labor hours	150,000	120,000
Variable overhead	$ 750,000	$ 600,000
Fixed overhead	1,200,000	1,200,000
Total overhead	$1,950,000	$1,800,000

Bickham states, "We cost our products by using an overhead rate computed at normal capacity; but it seems to me that if we used a rate computed at expected capacity, we wouldn't have such a large overhead variance at the end of the year. What makes it worse is that we have so much fixed overhead."

During the next year the company operated at 120,000 direct labor hours and incurred overhead cost as follows.

Variable overhead	$ 605,000
Fixed overhead	1,200,000
Total overhead	$1,805,000

Required:

1. Compute an overhead rate per direct labor hour at normal operating capacity.
2. Compute an overhead rate per direct labor hour at the expected level of operating capacity.
3. Determine the under- or overapplied amount when the rate is figured at normal capacity and when the rate is figured at expected capacity.
4. Point out the fallacy in Bickham's argument.
5. Is Bickham correct in stating that the variance is worse because of the relatively large fixed overhead? Explain.

5-3. **Cost of Service.** Calico Library, located in a small western city, depends upon donations and membership dues for support. The membership dues are applied to the annual cost of operation, and donations are used to make additions to the library.

In 1995, the library plans to add bookmobile service for subscribers living in outlying areas. Each person would pay an annual subscription fee, with the fee to be based on miles driven and number of persons served in each district. Miles driven and number of persons to be served by the bookmobile have been estimated for 1995 as follows:

District	Miles per Year	Number of Subscribers
Dry Canyon	6,000	600
Sand Valley	1,000	200
Castle District.......................................	2,000	400
Little Stream	5,000	800
Totals	14,000	2,000

Costs of van operation each year, including depreciation, have been estimated at $10,500 plus the salary of a driver at $31,500. These costs are to be apportioned first on the basis of mileage driven per district and then by the number of subscribers per district.

The library board believes that the subscribers in outlying areas should also bear their share of general library overhead estimated at $210,000 for 1995. A total of 50,000 subscribers (including those in outlying areas) are to share this cost.

Required:

Based on the information given, determine the fee for a subscriber in each district served by the bookmobile.

5-4. **Costs of Individual Orders.** During August, Altamont Machine Company started production orders 116, 117, and 118. Order 115 was in process at the beginning of the month with direct materials costs of $35,000, direct labor costs of $21,000, and applied factory overhead of $25,200. During the month, direct materials were requisitioned, and direct labor was identified with the orders as follows:

Order No.	Direct Materials	Direct Labor
115	—	$26,000
116	$39,000	45,000
117	53,000	47,000
118	47,000	16,000

Factory overhead is applied to the orders at 120 percent of direct labor cost.

Orders 115, 116, and 117 were completed and sold in August. Order 118 was incomplete on August 31.

Required:

1. Determine the cost of each order by cost element.
2. What was the total cost of direct materials requisitioned in August and charged to Work in Process?
3. Determine the cost of goods sold in August.
4. What was the Work in Process balance on August 31?

5-5. **Cost of Contracts.** Pfeffer Contracting Company repaves highways and does excavation work. On January 1, 1994, the Eastern Highway Project was in process with costs as follows:

Materials	$810,000
Labor...	420,000
Contract overhead..	210,000

During 1994, the company incurred costs for various projects as follows:

	Eastern Highway	State University	Clover Estates	Route 691	Market Street	Totals
Materials.........	$215,000	$1,780,000	$ 170,000	$3,720,000	$350,000	$ 6,235,000
Labor............	170,000	1,420,000	590,000	1,480,000	260,000	3,920,000
Overhead	85,000	710,000	295,000	740,000	130,000	1,960,000
Totals	$470,000	$3,910,000	$1,055,000	$5,940,000	$740,000	$12,115,000

Contract overhead is costed to the projects at 50 percent of labor cost. Actual overhead cost for 1994 was $2,090,000. Included in the actual overhead cost is $290,000 for indirect materials, $950,000 for indirect labor, and $510,000 for depreciation. All other overhead cost is credited to Accounts Payable.

Pfeffer Contracting Company uses Contracts in Process instead of a work in process account. Projects completed do not pass through a finished goods account but are charged directly to Cost of Completed Projects.

All projects, with the exceptions of the State University Project and the Market Street Project, were completed during the year.

Required:
1. Using T-accounts, show the costs charged to Contracts in Process.
2. Prepare a summary of the actual overhead costs charged to Contract Overhead. This should give the total balance on the debit side of the Contract Overhead account.
3. Using T-accounts, show the costs transferred to Cost of Completed Projects.
4. Using T-accounts, close the actual and applied overhead costs with the under- or overapplied amount closed directly to Cost of Completed Projects.
5. Determine the total cost of the Eastern Highway Project and the cost of Contracts in Process at the end of the year. (Show detail by project and cost element.)

5-6. Job Order Cost Transactions. A summary of manufacturing cost transactions for Modern Motors, Inc. for 1995 is as follows:

(a) Materials costing $1,157,000 were purchased from suppliers on account.
(b) Materials were requisitioned during the year as follows:

Direct materials....................................	$791,000
Indirect materials (factory overhead)	147,000

Included were direct materials requisitions of $21,000 for order 115.

(c) The factory payroll for the year amounted to $488,000. FICA taxes withheld amounted to $33,000, income taxes withheld amounted to $87,000, and the amount paid to the employees was $368,000.
(d) The factory labor was utilized as follows:

Direct labor	$338,000
Indirect labor (factory overhead)	150,000

Included in the direct labor cost was $22,500 identified by labor time tickets with order 115.

(e) Factory overhead was applied to production at 150 percent of the direct labor cost.
(f) Factory overhead cost during the year, in addition to the cost of indirect materials and indirect labor previously referred to, amounted to $173,000. Included in this

amount was depreciation of $52,000. Credit the balance of this cost to Accounts Payable.

(g)   Orders costing $1,218,000 were completed during the year. Order 115 is included among the completed orders.

(h)   Goods costing $1,075,000 were sold to customers on credit terms for $1,830,000.

Required:

1.   Using T-accounts, record transactions (a)-(h) and close the factory overhead variance to Cost of Goods Sold.

2.   Compute the total cost and cost per unit of order 115 assuming that 10,000 units were produced on that order.

5-7.   **Incomplete Data.** The Paddle Shop, Inc. keeps accounting and cost records on a personal computer. During the month of January, data were lost as a result of errors made by a new operator. Fortunately, some data were retrieved and are set forth below:

(a)   The debit balance in the payroll account was $150,000. This balance included $30,000 in indirect labor that was charged to the Factory Overhead account.

(b)   The debit balance in the factory overhead account totaled $175,000. This balance included the indirect labor from above.

(c)   The company uses an Applied Factory Overhead account, but information on its balance was lost. Factory overhead is applied to the products at 150% of direct labor cost.

(d)   The work in process inventory account showed a January 1 balance of $62,000. Materials requisitioned and charged to Work in Process during the period amounted to $117,000. The balance in Work in Process on January 31 was $77,000.

(e)   The Finished Goods Inventory balance at January 1 was $31,000.

(d)   Cost of Goods Sold had a debit balance of $346,000. This amount did not include an under- or overapplied factory overhead.

Required:

1.   From the information given, determine the direct labor and the factory overhead applied to production in January.

2.   What was the cost of work completed and transferred to the finished goods inventory for the month?

3.   How much should the finished goods inventory cost on January 31?

4.   Has overhead been overapplied or underapplied? Determine the under- or overapplied factory overhead in January.

5-8.   **Incomplete Data.** You find that the cost records at Sabath Tool & Die Company have been poorly maintained. Some information has been entered, but other information is missing. Fortunately, the information given is correct.

The costs for jobs 686, 687, and 688 are to be determined. The direct materials cost is $528 for job 686 and $715 for job 687. The cost of direct materials requisitioned during the month for all other jobs, except job 688, cost $4,820. No jobs were in process at the beginning of the month. The total cost of direct materials requisitioned during the month was $6,913.

Labor is paid at a uniform rate of $10 an hour. Job 686 required 82 direct labor hours, and job 688 required 43 direct labor hours. A total of 760 direct labor hours were worked during the month. The direct labor cost of all other jobs, with the exception of the three jobs being considered, was $5,850.

Two machine hours are used for each direct labor hour. Overhead is applied at a rate of $4 per machine hour. The actual overhead cost for the month was $6,320. Jobs 686, 687, and 688 were completed during the month.

Required:
1. Compute the costs for jobs 686, 687, and 688. Show costs by cost element.
2. Determine the amount of factory overhead applied to all orders during the month.
3. What was the amount of the under- or overapplied factory overhead?
4. You have received a telephone call from the plant manager requesting the total cost per unit on job 686. There were 50 units of product on this order. What is the total cost per unit?

5-9. **Effect of Overhead Cost on Product Cost.** Fixed factory overhead is a large part of total product cost for High Plains Technology, Inc. A flexible overhead budget for the year is given as follows in summary form:

Machine hours	200,000	250,000	300,000	350,000
Variable overhead	$ 800,000	$1,000,000	$1,200,000	$1,400,000
Fixed overhead	1,800,000	1,800,000	1,800,000	1,800,000
Total overhead	$2,600,000	$2,800,000	$3,000,000	$3,200,000

Under normal conditions, the company operates at 300,000 machine hours a year. Management believes that the normal level of operation should be increased to 350,000 machine hours, inasmuch as the company has been operating at approximately this level for the past few years.

The company has followed the practice of billing customers at 150 percent of total materials, labor, and factory overhead cost.

An opportunity to reduce variable overhead cost to $3.50 per machine hour has been found. The factory superintendent would like to see the effect on product cost and selling price if the savings in variable overhead and the revised concept of normal hours of operation are put into use. One standard order is to be used as a model. The direct materials and direct labor costs of this order are as follows:

Direct materials	$1,350
Direct labor	240

This order requires 50 machine hours, and consists of 200 units.

Required:
1. At the present time, what is the variable overhead cost per machine hour? Is this true at all machine-hour levels?
2. What is the fixed overhead cost per machine hour at 300,000 machine hours?
3. What is the fixed overhead cost per machine hour at 350,000 machine hours?
4. Use the order given as a model. Compute the total cost, unit cost, and unit selling price for each of the alternatives listed as follows:
    (a) Variable overhead cost is $4 per hour and 300,000 machine hours is the normal level of operation.
    (b) Variable overhead cost is $4 per hour and 350,000 machine hours is the normal level of operation.
    (c) Variable overhead cost is $3.50 per hour and 300,000 machine hours is the normal level of operation.
    (d) Variable overhead cost is $3.50 per hour and 350,000 machine hours is the normal level of operation.

5-10. **Factory Overhead Cost Control.** Kathryn Lemmon is the supervisor of Department 5 in the Tulia plant of Oklahoma Instrument Company. She is responsible for the cost of direct materials, direct labor, and variable overhead costs incurred in this department. The fixed overhead cost is not under her jurisdiction.

During May, actual factory overhead costs for Department 5 were as follows:

Actual Variable Overhead

Indirect materials	$ 19,400
Supplies	14,200
Telephone	700
Heat and light	1,600
Power	7,000
Repairs and maintenance	3,200
Total variable overhead	$ 46,100

Actual Fixed Overhead

Indirect labor	$ 61,000
Supervision	42,000
Heat and light	7,000
Repairs and maintenance	9,000
Depreciation	21,000
Total fixed overhead	$140,000
Total actual overhead	$186,100

The department operated at 45,000 direct labor hours during May. A budget of factory overhead for 45,000 direct labor hours is below:

Budgeted Variable Overhead

Indirect materials	$ 16,500
Supplies	12,400
Telephone	700
Heat and light	1,550
Power	7,000
Repairs and maintenance	2,350
Total variable overhead	$ 40,500

Budgeted Fixed Overhead

Indirect labor	$ 61,000
Supervision	42,000
Heat and light	7,000
Repairs and maintenance	9,000
Depreciation	21,000
Total fixed overhead	$140,000
Total budgeted overhead	$180,500

Variable overhead is costed to the products at the rate of $.90 per direct labor hour, and fixed overhead is costed to the products at the rate of $2.80 per direct labor hour.

Required:

1.   How much overhead was costed to the products in May?
2.   Compute the under- or overapplied factory overhead for May.
3.   How much of the under- or overapplied factory overhead can be attributed to operating below the normal capacity?

4. Prepare a responsibility cost report for Lemmon showing all actual variable overhead costs, all budgeted variable overhead costs, and variances for each cost listed.
5. Identify any items of overhead that are over the budgeted amount by more than 10 percent.

5-11. Automation and Cost. In 1994, Pioneer Motors, Inc. automated its production lines. As a result, virtually all of the labor that directly related to creating the products was eliminated. A smaller labor force is required, and the remaining workers are primarily monitoring machine operation and product quality. What was once classified as direct labor is now reclassified as indirect labor.

Total budgeted manufacturing costs for 1994 as a labor-intensive operation are compared with the budgeted costs for 1995 with a machine-intensive operation, as shown in the following table. In both years, the budgets are for a normal level of operation. When the company operated with more labor, overhead was assigned to the products on the basis of 400,000 direct labor hours. Under the automated operation, the rate is based on 500,000 machine hours.

	Budgets	
	Labor Intensive Operation	Machine Intensive Operations
Direct materials	$4,870,000	$4,630,000
Direct labor	3,260,000	0
Supervision.....................................	730,000	550,000
Indirect labor	880,000	2,720,000
Payroll taxes and fringe benefits	421,000	344,000
Supplies and indirect materials	310,000	325,000
Lubrication	76,000	217,000
Power	142,000	319,000
Maintenance—equipment	115,000	436,000
Repairs—equipment..............................	132,000	117,000
Depreciation—equipment..........................	48,000	382,000
Taxes and insurance.............................	126,000	133,000
Heat and light..................................	38,000	46,000
Other utilities	17,000	19,000
Depreciation—plant	80,000	80,000

One of the production managers states that the total overhead costs of manufacturing are higher than they were before and that the company didn't save anything by automating the production lines. The vice-president of production disagrees: "While total overhead costs may be higher," he agrees, "the increased productivity makes it possible for us to serve a growing market with lower costs per unit of product."

The following table shows the cost data for a large order assuming it were produced under each production process:

	Labor-Intensive Operation	Machine-Intensive Operation
Direct materials	$640,000	$615,000
Direct labor	680,000	0
Direct labor hours	60,000	0
Machine hours	0	30,000
Number of product units	100,000	100,000

Required:
1. Compute an overhead rate for both the labor-intensive operation and the machine-intensive operation.
2. Determine the total and unit cost of the large order under both types of operation.
3. Comment on the positions taken by the production manager and the vice-president of production.

5-12. **Departmental and Plant-wide Rates.** Purinton Printing Products has one division that makes rollers for printing presses. The rollers vary in size from ¼ inches to 8 inches in diameter. Fabrication and Finishing are the two departments within this division. The company uses machine hours as the base for allocating factory overhead costs to products. The budgeted data for the two departments for the coming year are below:

	Fabrication	Finishing	Totals
Machine hours	90,000	30,000	120,000
Overhead costs	$2,232,000	$252,600	$2,484,600

The machine hours for a batch of 100 units for two different products are given as:

	Fabrication	Finishing	Totals
½" roller..................................	4	8	12
6½" roller	9	6	15

The prime costs per batch for these two products are:

	½" roller	6½" roller
Direct materials:		
Fabrication	$ 18.90	$ 33.40
Finishing	9.70	11.50
Direct labor:		
Fabrication	48.10	187.30
Finishing	37.80	32.20
Total prime costs	$114.50	$264.40

Required:
1. Compute the departmental overhead rates for Fabrication and Finishing using machine hours as the cost driver.
2. Compute a plant-wide overhead rate using machine hours as the cost driver.
3. Compute the overhead cost per batch of product assuming:
   (a) The plant-wide rate.
   (b) The departmental rates.
4. Compute the total cost per unit of each product assuming:
   (a) The plant-wide rate.
   (b) The departmental rates.

5-13. **Departmental Rates versus Company-wide Rates.** Kool-Air Galore, Inc. manufactures air conditioners for automobiles. The company designs its products with flexibility to accommodate many makes and models of automobiles. The main products are MaxiFlow and Alaska. MaxiFlow uses a few complex fabricated parts, but these have been found easy to assemble and test. On the other hand, Alaska uses many standard parts but has a complex assembly and test process. The following planning information is available for 1996 on each department:

	Overhead Costs	Machine Hours
Radiator parts fabrication	$ 80,000	10,000
Radiator assembly, weld & test	100,000	20,000
Compressor parts fabrication	120,000	5,000
Compressor assembly and test	180,000	45,000
	$480,000	80,000

A production batch of 20 units uses each of the following hours in these departments:

	MaxiFlow	Alaska
Radiator parts fabrication	28	16
Radiator assembly, weld & test	30	74
Compressor parts fabrication	32	8
Compressor assembly and test	26	66
	116	164

Required:
1. Compute the departmental overhead rates using machine hours as the cost driver.
2. Compute a company-wide overhead rate using machine hours as the cost driver.
3. Compute the overhead cost per batch of MaxiFlow and Alaska assuming:
   (a) The company-wide rate.
   (b) The departmental rates.
4. Compute the total cost per unit of MaxiFlow and Alaska assuming:
   (a) The company-wide rate.
   (b) The departmental rates.

5-14. **Overhead Cost Drivers (Activity-Based Costing).** The controller of Stark Chemical Supply has established the following activity centers with overhead costs and related cost drivers:

Activity Centers	Budgeted Overhead Costs	Cost Driver	Budgeted Level for Cost Driver
Materials handling	$120,000	Weight of raw materials	60,000 pounds
Machine setups	240,000	Number of setups	120 setups
Hazardous waste control . . .	60,000	Weight of Hazardous materials	12,000 pounds
Quality control	85,000	Number of inspections	1,000 inspections
Other	205,000	Machine hours	102,500 hours

An order for 1,000 boxes of a powdered chemical has the following production requirements:

Raw materials ....   10,500 pounds
Machine setups ....   5 setups
Hazardous materials ....   1,850 pounds
Inspections ....   13 inspections
Machine hours ....   490 machine hours

Required:

1.   Compute the overhead rates for each activity center.
2.   Using the rates for (1) above, charge overhead costs to the order for 1,000 boxes of powdered chemical.
3.   Calculate the cost per box of powdered chemical.
4.   Assume the company allocates overhead costs on a plant-wide basis using machine hours.
      (a)   Compute the plant-wide overhead rate.
      (b)   Charge overhead costs to the order for 1,000 boxes of powered chemical.
      (c)   Calculate the cost per box of powdered chemical.
5.   Explain why the cost per box differs under the two methods.

5-15. Overhead Rates and Unit Costs (Activity-Based Costing). Hertzlott Machine Shop makes replacement parts for automotive transmissions. It produces three basic products: gears, shafts, and casings. The company is budgeting activity for 1996. The activity centers, costs, and cost drivers are as follows:

Activity Center	Budgeted Costs	Cost Driver
Materials handling	$ 312,400	Direct materials cost
Production scheduling.....................	116,000	Number of production orders
Setups..................................	144,600	Number of setups
Manual machinery	986,000	Direct labor hours
Automated machinery	3,212,000	Machine hours
Finishing	1,798,000	Direct labor hours
Packaging and shipping	234,000	Number of orders shipped

The following data are predicted for 1996:

	Gears	Shafts	Casings
Units produced..................................	10,000	2,000	700
Direct materials cost per unit	$60	$80	$100
Number of production orders	40	20	10
Number of setups	20	10	14
Direct labor hours	20,000	10,000	8,400
Machine hours	30,000	15,000	2,800
Number of orders shipped	1,000	1,500	70

Required:

1.   Compute an overhead rate for each activity center. Round calculations to four decimal places.
2.   Compute an overall rate for the combined activities based on direct labor hours. Round calculations to four decimal places.

3. Show how much overhead is budgeted for gears, shafts, and casings using the activity center rates and the overall rate.
4. Calculate an overall rate for the combined activities based on the total number of units.
5. Show how much overhead is budgeted for gears, shafts and casings using the rate in (4) above.
6. Explain why the overhead costs differ in (3) and (4) above.

5-16. **Support Function Allocation.** (Appendix) El Paso Women's Clothing specializes in designer skirts which it manufactures to customer order. The budgeted data for its main plant for 1996 are:

| | Support Functions | | Producing Departments | |
	Adminis-tration	Mainten-ance	Cutting	Sewing
Overhead costs	$80,000	$30,000	$500,000	$600,000
Labor hours		10,000	50,000	80,000
Machine hours			100,000	150,000
Square feet...................	4,500	7,000	50,000	25,000

During the year, Skibells Co. placed an order that was started and completed by year's end. Data for this job include the following information:

	Cutting	Sewing
Direct materials	$95,000	$21,000
Direct labor hours	7,000	15,000
Direct labor costs....................................	$56,000	$120,000
Machine hours	16,000	30,000

Required:
Treat each of the following requirements independently:

1. The company follows a policy of applying overhead for the entire plant on the basis of machine hours.
   (a) Calculate a plant-wide overhead rate based on machine hours.
   (b) Apply overhead to the Skibells job.
2. The company follows a policy of allocating support functions to the producing departments using the direct method. Plant Administration costs are allocated on direct labor hours; Maintenance on square feet; Cutting on machine hours; and Sewing on direct labor hours.
   (a) Allocate support function costs to producing departments.
   (b) Calculate overhead rates for producing departments.
   (c) Apply overhead to the Skibells job.
3. The company follows a policy of allocating support functions to the producing departments using the step method. Plant Administration is allocated first in the step method. Plant Administration costs are allocated on direct labor hours; Maintenance on square feet; Cutting on machine hours; and Sewing on direct labor hours.
   (a) Allocate support function costs to producing departments.
   (b) Calculate overhead rates for producing departments.
   (c) Apply overhead to the Skibells job.

4.   Prepare a summary of the results of allocating overhead to the Skibells job in each of the three alternatives. Explain why the differences in overhead costs occur.

5-17. **Service Center Cost Drivers—Direct and Step Methods.** (Appendix) Kruk Creative Productions, Inc. shows the following estimates for its support functions for 1995:

	Number of Employees	Square Meters of Floor Space	Hours of Repairs and Maintenance Used	Kilowatt Hours of Power Used
Support functions:				
Administration	45	12,000	20	6,000
Personnel	5	1,000	5	500
Cafeteria	20	5,000	10	4,000
Building and Grounds ...	10	1,000	40	2,000
Repairs and Maintenance	10	1,000	80	500
Power	25	5,000	100	1,000
Producing depts.:				
Cutting................	45	20,000	380	80,000
Grinding	100	30,000	460	66,000
Assembly	90	40,000	240	30,000
Finishing	50	10,000	170	50,000

Administration, Personnel, and Cafeteria are allocated using the number of employees. Building and Grounds uses square meters of floor space. Repairs and Maintenance uses repair hours. Power is based on kilowatt hours used.

Required:
1.   Prepare a summary that shows the percentage of each support function allocated to the producing departments, assuming the direct method of allocating support functions is used. (Round calculations to four decimal places.)
2.   Prepare a summary that shows the percentage of each support function allocated to the remaining functions and producing departments, assuming the step method of allocating support functions is used. (Round calculations to four decimal places.) For purposes of this allocation, assume a sequence in the same order listed in the problem above.
3.   Prepare a summary that shows the percentage of each support function allocated to the remaining functions and producing departments, assuming the step method of allocating support functions is used. (Round calculations to four decimal places.) For purposes of this allocation, assume the following sequence: Administration, Power, Personnel, Cafeteria, Repairs and Maintenance, Building and Grounds.
4.   Explain why the sequencing of support functions is important for step method allocations.

CASE 5A—UPTON, INC.

Upton, Inc. manufactures a line of home furniture. The company's single manufacturing plant consists of the Cutting, Assembly, and Finishing Departments. Upton uses departmental rates for applying manufacturing overhead to production and maintains separate manufacturing overhead control and manufacturing overhead applied accounts for each of the three production departments.

The following predetermined departmental manufacturing overhead rates were calculated for Upton's fiscal year ending May 31, 1995:

Department	Rates
Cutting..	$2.40 per machine hour
Assembly	$5.00 per direct labor hour
Finishing	$1.60 per direct labor dollar

Information regarding actual operations for Upton's plant for the six months ended November 30, 1994, is presented below:

	Department		
	Cutting	**Assembly**	**Finishing**
Manufacturing overhead costs...............	$22,600	$56,800	$98,500
Machine hours	10,800	2,100	4,400
Direct labor hours	6,800	12,400	16,500
Direct labor dollars	$40,800	$62,000	$66,000

Based upon this experience and updated projections for the last six months of the fiscal year, Upton revised its operating budget. Projected data regarding manufacturing overhead and operating activity for each department for the six months ending May 31, 1995, are presented as follows:

	Department		
	Cutting	**Assembly**	**Finishing**
Manufacturing overhead costs...............	$23,400	$57,500	$96,500
Machine hours	9,200	2,000	4,200
Direct labor hours	6,000	13,000	16,000
Direct labor dollars	$36,000	$65,000	$64,000

Diane Potter, Upton's controller, plans to develop revised departmental manufacturing overhead rates that will be more representative of efficient operations for the current fiscal year ending May 31, 1995. She has decided to combine the actual results for the first six months of the fiscal year with the projections for the next six months to develop revised departmental overhead rates. She then plans to adjust the manufacturing overhead applied accounts for each department through November 1994, to recognize the revised overhead rates. The analysis is presented below as prepared by Potter from general ledger account balances as of November 30, 1994.

Account	Direct Materials	Direct Labor	Manufacturing Overhead	Account Balance
Work in Process Inventory	$ 53,000	$ 95,000	$ 12,000	$ 160,000
Finished Goods	96,000	176,000	48,000	320,000
Cost of Goods Sold	336,000	604,000	180,000	1,120,000
	$485,000	$875,000	$240,000	$1,600,000

Required:

1.   Determine the balance of the manufacturing overhead applied accounts as of November 30, 1994, before any revision for the:
   (a)   Cutting Department.
   (b)   Assembly Department.
   (c)   Finishing Department.
2.   Calculate the revised departmental manufacturing overhead rates that Upton, Inc., should use for the remainder of the fiscal year ending May 31, 1995.
3.   Prepare an analysis that shows how the manufacturing overhead applied accounts should be adjusted as of November 30, 1994, and use T-accounts to record adjustments to all general ledger accounts that are affected.

(ICMA adapted)

CASE 5B—WADSWORTH & CAPELL LEGAL SERVICES (Appendix)

Wadsworth & Capell Legal Services is a large law office in St. Louis. It is organized into three operating departments: Criminal, Civil, and Personal & Family Services. Support functions include a secretarial pool and a research center. An administrative function is responsible for managing the entire company. Wadsworth & Capell follows the practice of allocating support functions to the three operating departments in order to establish a cost-based charge for pricing the various legal services to clients. Administrative costs are not allocated (they are treated as period costs in the income statement), but they are recovered through the profit margin developed as a percentage of all other costs.

Budgeting for the upcoming fiscal year has resulted in the following costs charged directly to all functions and departments:

	Secretarial	Research	Criminal	Civil	Personal & Family
Salaries and wages ...	$80,000	$120,000	$300,000	$400,000	$100,000
Fringe benefits	5,600	11,200	30,000	40,000	10,000
Depreciation on equipment, fixtures, and furniture	8,000	16,000	24,000	32,000	8,000
Supplies	16,000	3,200	4,500	6,000	1,500

The indirect costs that are prorated to administration, support functions, and operating departments are of four varieties: insurance, leasing, utilities, and janitorial services. The following means are used to prorate indirect costs:

(a)   Insurance costs ($160,000) are for malpractice coverage and for equipment, fixtures, and furniture. The premium ($36,000) representing coverage on equipment, fixtures, and furniture is prorated on the basis of book value. The remainder of the $160,000 is for malpractice. Since malpractice relates to people, the proration is based on the number of people in each department.
(b)   Leasing costs ($96,000) are incurred for the office space occupied by the firm. Therefore, these costs are prorated based on square footage occupied.
(c)   Utilities costs ($60,000) are for heat, light, and water. They are prorated on the basis of square footage occupied.

(d)   Janitorial services ($36,000) to keep the offices clean are contracted out. These costs are prorated on square footage.

In allocating the support functions to the operating departments, the secretarial pool is allocated on the basis of secretarial time. The Research Center is allocated on the basis of salaries and wages. Overhead rates for the operating departments are determined by using salaries and wages in the Criminal and Civil Departments, and staff time in Personal and Family Services. The following budgeted data are available for the allocation bases:

	Adminis-tration	Secre-tarial	Research	Criminal	Civil	Personal & Family
Number of people	2	4	6	4	6	2
Book values	$10,000	$70,000	$80,000	$120,000	$160,000	$40,000
Square footage	1,000	2,000	2,000	1,500	2,500	1,000
Staff time (hours)	4,000	8,500	12,500	9,000	12,500	5,000
Secretarial time (hours)	500	200	2,000	2,000	3,000	1,000

Required:
1.   Complete the proration of indirect costs to all support functions and operating departments. Show the sum of direct and indirect costs in each function and department.
2.   Explain why the proration of indirect costs is necessary.
3.   Using the direct method, allocate the service functions to the operating departments and develop the overhead rates for each of the operating departments. (Round dollar allocations to the nearest dollar and overhead rates to four decimal places.)
4.   Using the step method, allocate the service functions to the operating departments and develop the overhead rates for each of the operating departments. The Secretarial Pool is allocated first. (Round dollar allocations to the nearest dollar and overhead rates to four decimal places.)
5.   Compare the answers in (3) and (4) and explain why the differences occurred. Is the direct method used in (3) or the step methods used in (4) preferred? Why?

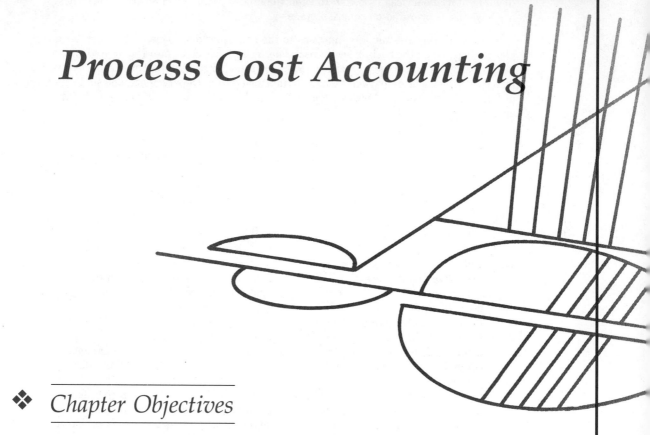

Chapter Six

Process Cost Accounting

❖ *Chapter Objectives*

After studying Chapter 6, you will be able to:
1. Describe the cost flow through the accounts for a process cost system.
2. Compute the equivalent units of production and unit costs using FIFO.
3. Use the results of unit cost computations in tracing the flow of costs through the accounts.
4. Prepare a cost of production report.
5. Explain the impact of a previous department's activities on the cost accountability of the current department.
6. List several ways in which management can use departmental unit costs as a tool in evaluating departmental performance.
7. Explain the impact that changes in the manufacturing environment have on process cost accounting.

Finding Unit Costs in a Process Cost Environment

VITA-LIFE, Inc. specializes in multi-vitamin and mineral food supplements made from concentrated extracts of nutrient-rich plants, such as alfalfa, watercress, parsley and acerola cherries. Probably the ultimate food supplement VITA-LIFE produces is its maxi-max vitamin/mineral tablets. Production of maxi-max consists of nine processes:

1. Harvesting. Leafy, nutrient-rich plants are cut in the fields.
2. Dehydration. Moisture is removed in seconds so nutrients are left intact.
3. Milling. Plant materials are ground to a fine flour.
4. Extraction. Alfalfa flour is combined with parsley and watercress and fed into extractors.
5. Concentration. Extracted material goes to special evaporators which quickly concentrate the material in a high vacuum.
6. Blending. Concentrated material is blended with specially cultured yeast, rich in B vitamins.
7. Compounding. Remaining natural ingredients (such as tricalcium phosphate, cod liver oil, mixed tocopherols from vegetable oils, kelp, bone meal, magnesium oxide, cobalamin concentrate, and iron) are added.
8. Tableting. Material, which is now granular in consistency, is compressed into tablets. Tableting machines can produce in excess of 10 million tablets per shift.
9. Coating. Tablets are sealed, packaged, and enclosed in cellophane to assure freshness. Each package contains 100 tablets, which is basically a one month supply at one tablet each meal, three meals a day.

Some of these processes are combined in departments, cost centers, or other activity centers. Milling and extraction are in the Milling Department; blending and compounding in the Blending Department; and tableting and coating in the Tableting Department. The other processes are in their own individual departments.

How does VITA-LIFE, Inc. determine the cost of packages produced and sold?

This chapter discusses the factors a company considers in identifying the cost of processes with the products it sells and then in reporting those costs to appropriate managers. Although the following discussion focuses on a manufacturing environment, the concepts presented are appropriate in service and merchandising organizations.

OVERVIEW OF PROCESS COSTING OF OUTPUT

A **process cost system** identifies manufacturing costs with individual departments for an interval of time. Costs are not charged to specific units or orders as work is performed but unit costs are based on costs incurred during a interval of time and on the volume of output during the same interval. The unit cost of a final product will be the sum of all manufacturing costs allocated to the product by each department the product passed through during manufacturing. The concepts and procedures for calculating unit costs are discussed later in the chapter.

The characteristics of a process cost setting are the environment, physical flow of products, and the focal point for cost accumulation. Each of these is presented below.

Manufacturing Environment

The manufacturing environment for which process cost accounting is most appropriate is one in which products are mass produced or result from continuous processing. In this situation, each unit that goes through the same process is identical to the other units. Examples include candy, soft drinks, clothing, chemicals, and most processed foods. In addition, individual operations can be suitable for process cost accounting if every product passing through the operation has the same work performed on it. For instance, cars and airplanes on an assembly line have the same assembly operations performed during the assembly process.

Physical Flow of Products

In a process system, a product may flow through several operations on its way to completion. For example, materials may start in a blending operation. Both the physical units and costs will be identified for the blending operation over a period of time, such as a month. When the units are completed in the blending operation, the units with their costs are transferred to the next operation, in this case, the grinding operation. Additional costs will be incurred and accounted for in the grinding operation. At the completion of the grinding operation, the units and accumulated costs of preceding operations will be transferred to the last operation in this example, the finishing operation. The flow of units and costs for this example are shown in Figure 6.1.

In some types of operations, a subassembly may be produced on a separate production line for addition to the product at a later stage. For example, assume that the main production line extends from Department A to Department C. A subassembly line, consisting of Departments W and X, produces a component that is brought into the main line in Department C. A diagram showing the flow of units and costs in this case is given in Figure 6.2.

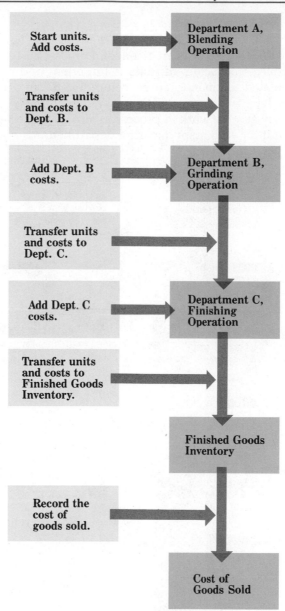

Figure 6.1 Flow of Units and Costs in a Process Manufacturing System

Focal Point for Cost Accumulation

The materials, labor, and factory overhead are traditionally identified with specific departments or operating centers. This differs from job cost systems which identify costs with specific batches or customer orders. In this chapter, the term department will be used as a generic term and will cover the traditional concepts of department, operating or work center, operation, task, activity center, and responsibility center. As a result of charging costs to departments, few detailed records are needed in process costing. Recording the flow and end-of-period status of units is important and can be estimated, manually calculated, or monitored by computer. Because costs need to be identified with departments, a process cost system normally includes accounting transfers between the work in process inventory control accounts with at least one account for each manufacturing department.

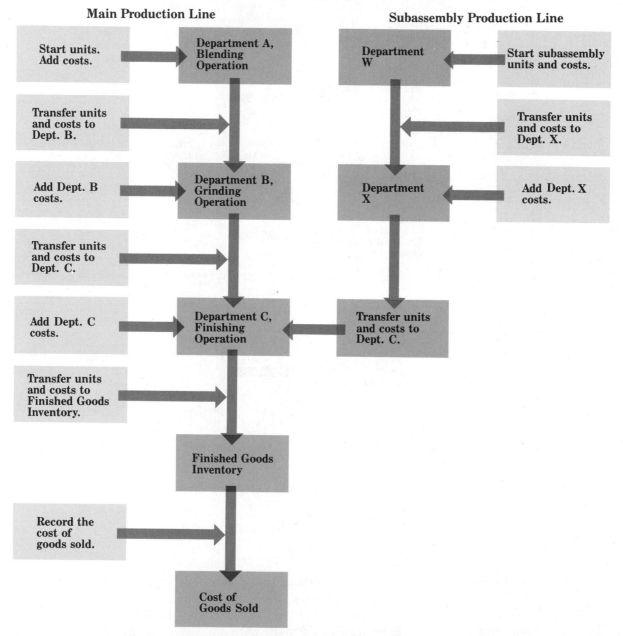

Figure 6.2   Flow of Units and Costs for Subassembly Components

THE COST ELEMENTS

The cost elements in a process cost environment depend on whether the organization is a manufacturing, merchandising, or service organization. Since a manufacturer probably has more detailed costs, we discuss here the two major elements of materials and conversion costs.

Materials

Materials are requisitioned for use in a specific department and the materials costs are accumulated by the department for a specific time interval. Although materials can be added in any department, they are often issued from the storeroom to the first operating department in the process. The concept of accounting for materials costs does not depend on whether materials are added in the first department or in subsequent departments.

Two major differences in accumulating materials costs between the job cost system and the process cost system should be noted. Materials costs are identified with departments and then with individual units in a process cost system. Materials costs bypass departments and are charged to specific jobs in a job cost system. Also, because materials costs are accumulated for a period of time and averaged over all units receiving material content during the period, the emphasis on distinguishing between direct materials and indirect materials is not considered critical to accurate unit costs. In other words, the averaging of costs is broader in a process cost system than in a job cost system.

Conversion Costs

The labor and overhead costs are called **conversion costs**. Materials are introduced in a processing system, and labor and overhead are used to convert raw materials to a finished product. Because these costs are so often entering the process at the same time, we combine them for illustrations throughout the chapter. This assumes that overhead is applied to production using direct labor hours or dollars. Where another cost driver is used, we separate the two cost elements.

The labor is measured monthly, by department, and without specific order. Labor time tickets may be used for payroll accounting but are not used to measure time taken to complete a single order. Like materials, little emphasis is placed on distinguishing precisely between direct labor and indirect labor.

Factory overhead costs are accumulated by department. Typically, we record them in a departmental overhead control ledger by type of expense or by natural expense accounts. Overhead costs are charged to departments through predetermined overhead rates for each department. In most of our illustrations, the manufacturing overhead appears to be actual overhead. However, the costs represent charges based on predetermined overhead rates. Since we discussed in Chapter 5 how an organization would accumulate actual factory overhead costs and apply factory overhead costs, we will not repeat the coverage here. We assume that factory overhead is accumulated and applied using a departmental basis.

The Cost of Production Report

A departmental **cost of production report** is a cost report that is divided into three major sections: one related to quantities and two related to costs. These sections are as follows:

1. Physical quantities:
   (a) Quantities charged to the department.
   (b) Quantities accounted for.
2. Costs charged to the department.
3. Costs accounted for.

As an example of a simplified cost of production report the Machining Department for Beyer Manufacturing Company is given in Figure 6.3. It is for the month of September 1996. At the beginning of the month, 15,000 partially completed units were in work in process. During the September, 100,000 units were placed in production. The beginning inventory of work in process

BEYER MANUFACTURING COMPANY
MACHINING DEPARTMENT
COST OF PRODUCTION REPORT
FOR THE MONTH OF SEPTEMBER 1996

1. Quantities:

Units charged to department:

In process, beginning	15,000
Started in September	100,000
Total units charged to department	115,000

Units accounted for:
Completed and transferred to Assembly:

From beginning inventory	15,000
Started and completed in September	80,000
Total units transferred out	95,000
In process, ending inventory	20,000
Total units accounted for	115,000

2. Costs charged to department:

In process, beginning	$ 30,000
September costs	182,000
Total costs charged	$212,000

3. Costs accounted for:

Completed and transferred out:
In process, beginning (15,000 units):

Cost at September 1	$ 30,000
Cost to complete work in process, beginning	12,000
	$ 42,000
Started and completed in September (80,000 units)	160,000
Total cost of work transferred out (95,000 units)	$202,000
In process, ending (20,000 units)	10,000
Total costs accounted for	$212,000

Figure 6.3 Example of Cost of Production Report

(15,000 units) was finished in Machining and transferred to the Assembly Department together with 80,000 units that were started and completed. At the end of September, 20,000 partially completed units are in inventory. We have not addressed the stage of completion of the partially completed units. That subject is discussed in the next section of this chapter.

The Machining Department is one segment of the total cost flow through the accounting system. Figure 6.4 presents a diagram of cost flow from the work in process—machining account to the work in process—assembly account to the finished goods account to the cost of goods sold account. Notice that the data for the Machining Department appear on the cost of production report on page 250.

COST ELEMENTS   **ACCOUNTS**

WORK IN PROCESS—MACHINING

Balance, beginning of month	30,000	(2) 202,000
Materials	(1) 92,000	
Labor	(1) 45,000	
Factory overhead	(1) 45,000	

WORK IN PROCESS—ASSEMBLY

Balance, beginning of month	23,000	(4) 278,820
Cost transferred in from Machining	(2) 202,000	
Labor	(3) 66,000	
Factory overhead	(3) 33,000	

FINISHED GOODS

Balance, beginning of month	70,000	(5) 231,910
Cost transferred in from Assembly	(4) 278,820	

COST OF GOODS SOLD

Cost of goods sold in August	(5) 231,910	

(1) Record materials, labor, and overhead to the Machining Department.
(2) Transfer costs of completed units from Machining to Assembly.
(3) Record labor and overhead to the Assembly Department.
(4) Transfer costs of completed units from Assembly to finished goods inventory.
(5) Record the cost of units sold.

Figure 6.4   Flow of Costs from Work in Process through Cost of Goods Sold

The balances of the inventory accounts on September 30 are given as follows:

Work in Process—Machining $10,000
Work in Process—Assembly   45,180
Finished Goods Inventory 116,910

THE EQUIVALENT UNIT CONCEPT

The primary goal of any cost accounting system is to identify costs with products for purposes of determining ending inventories for work in process and finished goods and of establishing the cost of goods sold amount. In determining work in process inventories, process cost accounting attaches costs to units completed in one department and transferred to the next department in the sequence. Costs are attached to units in inventories whether or not the units are wholly or partially completed. The mechanism for tracing costs to units is a unit cost.

Unit Costs

When calculating unit costs, we typically think of a fraction similar to the following:

$$\text{Unit cost} = \frac{\text{Departmental costs}}{\text{Units produced or work done}}$$

Applying this fraction to the typical process cost situation is complicated by two major factors: (1) the stage of completion of units in beginning inventory, units started and completed, and units in the ending inventory; and (2) the different points in time that materials and conversion costs enter a departmental process. This means that units produced is not a good measure for determining an appropriate unit cost. Consequently, an equivalent unit must be identified. An **equivalent unit** represents the theoretical number of units that could have been produced had the resources been applied to starting and completing units. We will discuss the two major issues above in the following sections and then move to the computational steps.

Stage of Completion

The physical flow of completed products from a work in process inventory is usually viewed as follows:

Units in beginning work in process inventory
+   Units of product started during the period
-   Units in ending work in process inventory
Units completed and transferred out

In a process cost system, the units in the beginning and ending inventories are usually at a different stage of completion, and the completed units contain units that may have required different work to complete them during this period. The **stage of completion** is the average percentage of work completed on a unit of product at any point in time. For a department, three distinct groupings of products are identified:

1. Partially completed units in the beginning inventory completed during the current period. The work to complete these units is represented by 100 percent less the stage of completion when the period started.
2. Units started and completed during the period. The work completed is represented by 100 percent.
3. Partially completed units at the end of the period. The work completed is represented by stage of completion at the end of the period.

If all three of these groups are summed, the result is equivalent units for this time period—the work done by the workers in this department. This is the number of units that could have been produced if all production were started and completed during the period, assuming no beginning or ending work in process inventories.

For example, the Seminole Metal Works has a machining department. On March 1, 15,000 units were in process and were 60 percent completed. During the month, 200,000 units were added to the department's operations. On March 31, 20,000 units were in process and were 30 percent completed. Following our formula from above, the number of units complete is calculated as follows:

Units in beginning inventory	15,000
+ Units started during period	200,000
− Units in ending inventory	20,000
Units completed and transferred	195,000

In order to calculate the equivalent units for the month, we need to compute the units started and completed during the month. Assuming the physical flow through the department is first-in, first-out (FIFO), the units in the beginning inventory are the first units completed and the ending inventory consists of units started but not completed. Therefore, we have two ways of computing the units started and completed, as follows:

Units completed and transferred	195,000
− Units in beginning inventory	15,000
Units started and completed	180,000

or

Units started during the period	200,000
− Units in ending inventory	20,000
Units started and completed	180,000

Figure 6.5 displays this same information graphically:

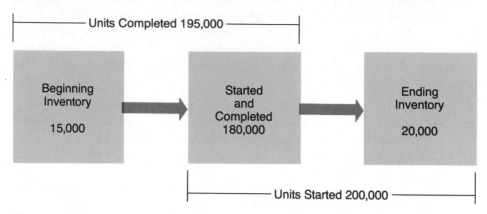

Figure 6.5 Physical Flow of Units

We now have the three groups of units and their stage of completion which are necessary to find the number of equivalent units. One way to calculate the equivalent units is as follows:

To complete, beginning inventory [15,000 × (100% − 60%)]	6,000
Started and completed (180,000 units × 100%)	180,000
Ending inventory (20,000 units × 30%)	6,000
Equivalent units	192,000

Two other methods are available for calculating equivalent units. One is called the "units completed method" which will be illustrated later in this chapter. The other method is the "units started method." They give the same equivalent units results, as follows:

Units completed method:

Units completed (195,000 units × 100%)	195,000
+ Ending inventory (20,000 units × 30%)	6,000
− Beginning inventory (15,000 units × 60%)	9,000
Equivalent units	192,000

Units started method:

Units started (200,000 units × 100%)	200,000
+ To complete, beginning inventory [15,000 × (100% − 60%)]	6,000
− To complete, ending inventory [20,000 × (100% − 30%)]	14,000
Equivalent units	192,000

Either of these two methods may be used if a manager is working only with equivalent units and unit costs. However, if a cost of production report is prepared, these methods do not have the information readily available for supporting the figures in that report.

Timing of Inputs

Materials, labor, and factory overhead are the inputs to the production process. These inputs may enter at different points during the process. The most common situation is for materials to enter at the beginning of a departmental process and for labor and factory overhead to be added continuously throughout the process. Consequently, it is possible for some units in process to have all of their material content but only part of the labor and factory overhead. In other processes, the materials may be added continuously or at the end of the process. For our purposes, unless otherwise mentioned, materials will be added at the beginning of the process, and labor and factory overhead will enter the process together and be added continuously or evenly throughout a process.

In order to calculate unit costs when inputs have different timing for entering a process, it is necessary to calculate the equivalent units for each cost input. Therefore, one equivalent unit computation is for materials and another computation is for conversion costs. Rather than illustrate this procedure now, the illustration in the computational steps below will show how these separate equivalent units are used to establish unit costs.

Computational Steps

Charging physical units to a department and accounting for those units are generally clerical functions. Likewise, the identification of the costs charged to a department is a relatively simple function. However, distributing the costs to work completed and ending inventories requires a computation of unit costs, an easy task, but one that requires an understanding of several steps. These steps are set forth as follows:

1.   Determine physical flow of units.
2.   Calculate equivalent units.
3.   Compute unit costs.
4.   Distribute total costs to units.
5.   Determine where costs are.

The last step provides a check figure for determining if the four previous steps were completed accurately. This step verifies that the total costs distributed to the units equal the total costs charged to the department.

Each of these steps is presented below as part of developing a cost of production report.

We assume a **first-in, first-out (FIFO) cost method** in progressing through the five computational steps. Under FIFO, the older costs are transferred out first and the more current costs are transferred out next. Only the most recent costs are held as ending inventory. With the FIFO cost method, the equivalent units are literally the units that could have been completed if all efforts during the period were devoted to starting and completing units, allowing no partially completed units. Usually, however, some units will be in a stage of partial completion at both the beginning and the end of the month. The beginning work in process units are completed during the month, and a start has been made on the units in ending work in process.

To illustrate the computational steps, consider the following data from Deming Container Corporation. Deming Container produces large trash containers for residential use. Garbage trucks, using lift systems, empty the containers into the trucks. The containers are produced in three departments: Fabrication, Welding, and Finishing. All metal enters production at the beginning of the Fabrication Department operations. The metal is cut and molded there. Costs incurred are both materials and conversion costs. The Welding Department welds all cuts and the external parts needed for lifting. Conversion costs are the only costs incurred in welding. The Finishing Department incurs costs for sanding rough edges, installing lids, and painting. The materials cost is for the paint that is added at the end of the process. Conversion costs are added throughout the finishing operations. We illustrate the Fabrication Department here. Its activity for May 1994 is summarized below:

Work in process, May 1, 1994:	
Units	4,000
Stage of completion:	
Materials	100%
Conversion costs	40%
Costs:	
Materials	$400,000
Conversion costs	80,000
Beginning inventory total cost	$480,000
Units started	12,000
Units completed and transferred	14,000
Current period costs:	
Materials	$1,200,000
Conversion costs	650,000
Total costs added	$1,850,000
Work in process, May 31, 1994:	
Units	2,000
Stage of completion:	
Materials	100%
Conversion costs	30%

Determine Physical Flow of Units   Determining the physical flow of units for a department involves identifying the units in the beginning inventory, the units started during the period, the units completed and transferred out during the period, and the units in the ending inventory. These are whole units, stage of completion is not an issue here. The flow of units represents the quantities portion of the cost of production report and appears as follows:

Quantities:

Units charged to Fabrication Department:

In process, beginning	4,000
Started in production	12,000
Total units charged	16,000

Units accounted for by Fabrication Department:

Completed and transferred out:

From beginning inventory	4,000
Started and completed:	
(12,000 − 2,000 or 14,000 − 4,000)	10,000
Total units transferred out	14,000
In process, ending	2,000
Total units accounted for	16,000

Calculate Equivalent Units   Equivalent units are computed by multiplying physical units by the percentage of work completed on them. For our example we would have the following calculation:

	Materials	Fabrication Conversion
To complete beginning inventory:		
4,000 × (100% − 100%)	0	
4,000 × (100% − 40%)		2,400
Units started and completed:		
10,000 × 100%	10,000	10,000
Ending inventory completed:		
2,000 × 100%	2,000	
2,000 × 30%		600
Equivalent units (work done)	12,000	13,000

An alternate calculation (units completed method) can be used to find equivalent units. It is, however, not as helpful when preparing a cost of production report. This method is presented below:

	Materials	Fabrication Conversion
Units completed (14,000 × 100%)	14,000	14,000
Ending inventory:		
2,000 × 100%	2,000	
2,000 × 30%		600
Works to be done	16,000	14,600
Beginning inventory:		
4,000 × 100%	(4,000)	
4,000 × 40%		(1,600)
Equivalent units (work done)	12,000	13,000

Compute Unit Costs   The unit costs for materials and conversion costs are calculated from the current month's costs and the equivalent units. The costs for which the Fabrication Department will be held accountable are:

	Materials	Conversion	Total
Beginning inventory...........	$ 400,000	$ 80,000	$ 480,000
Current month	1,200,000	650,000	1,850,000
Total costs	$1,600,000	$730,000	$2,330,000

With the current month's costs and the equivalent units from above, the cost for the current month is divided by the equivalent units for the month to obtain a unit cost:

	Materials	Conversion
Current month	$1,200,000	$650,000
Equivalent units	12,000	13,000
Unit costs	$100	$50

A piece of information that can be used by managers is given in the beginning work in process inventory. These dollars represent costs from the prior period, in this case, the previous month. Thus, we have unit cost information about the units in the beginning inventory as follows:

$$\frac{\text{Materials costs}}{\text{Equivalent units for materials}} = \frac{\$400,000}{4,000} = \$100 \text{ per unit}$$

$$\frac{\text{Conversion costs}}{\text{Equivalent units for conversion}} = \frac{\$80,000}{1,600} = \$50 \text{ per unit}$$

These unit costs are identical to those for the current period, although such a case will not always occur.

Distribute Total Costs to Units   The distribution of costs to units using the foregoing unit costs and equivalent units is shown on page 259.

Note the sequence of computations. First, the old costs in the beginning work in process are transferred out. Then, the cost to complete the beginning work in process is computed. The costs associated with units started and completed come next. Sum all of these costs, and we have the cost of goods completed and transferred out. Finally, the costs of the work done on the units still in process on May 31 is determined.

Often the unit cost calculations result in the need to round to some decimal place. The more decimal places used, the less the rounding error in total dollars assigned to units completed and units in ending inventory. If rounding errors occur, it is customary to adjust the costs assigned to units completed to compensate for the rounding error.

Costs accounted for:

	Materials	Conversion Costs	Total
Completed and transferred to Welding Department:			
Work in process, May 1:			
Cost at May 1	$ 400,000	$ 80,000	$ 480,000
Cost to complete beginning inventory:			
(2,400 equivalent units × $50)	0	120,000	120,000
	$ 400,000	$200,000	$ 600,000
Started and completed:			
Materials:			
(10,000 equivalent units × $100)	1,000,000		
Conversion:			
(10,000 equivalent units × $50)		500,000	1,500,000
Total costs of completed units	$1,400,000	$700,000	$2,100,000
Work in process, May 31:			
Materials:			
(2,000 equivalent units × $100) . . .	200,000		
Conversion:			
(600 equivalent units × $50)		30,000	230,000
Total costs accounted for	$1,600,000	$730,000	$2,330,000

Determine Where Costs Are   This final step in the computational process is really a check to see that all costs charged to the department are charged to units completed and units in the ending inventory. For instance, the total costs charged to the Fabrication Department are $2,330,000. When we finish distributing the costs to the units completed and units in the ending inventory, the sum should also equal $2,330,000. For the full detail, consider the following summary:

Costs charged to department:

	Materials	Conversion Costs	Total
Work in process, May 1	$ 400,000	$ 80,000	$ 480,000
Costs added during month	1,200,000	650,000	1,850,000
Total costs charged	$1,600,000	$730,000	$2,330,000
Total costs accounted for (taken from previous step)	$1,600,000	$730,000	$2,330,000

This check shows that materials and conversion costs charged to the department have indeed been distributed to all units.

Cost of Production Report

The five computational steps provide all of the calculations needed to prepare a cost of production report for May. This report is summarized in Figure 6.6.

DEMING CONTAINER CORPORATION
FABRICATION DEPARTMENT
COST OF PRODUCTION REPORT
FOR THE MONTH OF MAY 1994

Quantities:
Units charged to department:

In process, beginning	4,000
Started in production	12,000
Total units charged to department	16,000

Units accounted for:
Completed and transferred out:

From beginning inventory	4,000
Started and completed	10,000
Total units transferred out	14,000
In process, ending	2,000
Total units accounted for	16,000

Costs charged to department:

	Materials	Conversion Costs	Total
Work in process, May 1	$ 400,000	$ 80,000	$ 480,000
Costs added during month	1,200,000	650,000	1,850,000
Total costs charged	$1,600,000	$730,000	$2,330,000

Costs accounted for:

	Materials	Conversion Costs	Total
Completed and transferred to Welding Department:			
Work in process, May 1:			
Cost at May 1	$ 400,000	$ 80,000	$ 480,000
Cost to complete beginning inventory:			
(2,400 equivalent units × $50)	0	120,000	120,000
	$ 400,000	$200,000	$ 600,000
Started and completed:			
Materials:			
(10,000 equivalent units × $100)	1,000,000		
Conversion:			
(10,000 equivalent units × $50)		500,000	1,500,000
Total costs of completed units	$1,400,000	$700,000	$2,100,000
Work in process, May 31:			
Materials:			
(2,000 equivalent units × $100)	200,000		
Conversion:			
(600 equivalent units × $50)		30,000	230,000
Total costs accounted for	$1,600,000	$730,000	$2,330,000

Additional calculations:

	Materials	Conversion
Current month's costs	$1,200,000	$650,000
Computation of equivalent units:		
To complete beginning inventory:		
4,000 × (100% − 100%)	0	
4,000 × (100% − 40%)		2,400
Units started and completed:		
10,000 × 100%	10,000	10,000
Ending inventory completed:		
2,000 × 100%	2,000	
2,000 × 30%		600
Equivalent units (work done)	12,000	13,000
Equivalent unit costs....................	$100	$50

Figure 6.6 Cost of Production Report for Fabrication Department

In T-account form, the transactions reflected in the cost of production report would be summarized in the following general cost flow:

Work in Process—Fabrication		Work in Process—Welding	
Beg. Inventory 480,000	Completed	Transferred in	
Materials 1,200,000	2,100,000 ——————→ 2,100,000		
Conversion 650,000			
End. Inventory 230,000			

ACCOUNTABILITY IN SUBSEQUENT DEPARTMENTS

The procedures are the same for subsequent departments in the processing operation. In departments after the first, however, unit costs must be computed for the accumulated work done in earlier departments as well as for the work done in the present department. For example, if operations cover 10 departments, Department 10 would compute a unit cost for the work done in the preceding 9 departments and a unit cost for its own work.

The equivalent units for work done in preceding departments are the actual physical units. There is no need to compute what fraction of the work has been done since all the work that can be done in earlier departments has been done;

otherwise, the units would not be in the present department. We refer to this cost element as **transferred-in costs.**

Continuing with the Deming Container Corporation illustration, consider the results in the Welding Department—the second department in the sequence. No new materials enter here, so the cost elements are transferred-in costs and conversion costs. The departmental activity for May 1994 is summarized below:

Work in process, May 1, 1994:	
Units	1,000
Stage of completion:	
Transferred in from Fabrication	100%
Conversion costs	20%
Costs:	
Transferred in from Fabrication	$ 150,000
Conversion costs (from April)	5,000
Beginning inventory total cost	$ 155,000
Units started (transferred in from Fabrication)	14,000
Units completed and transferred to Finishing	13,000
Current period costs:	
Transferred in from Fabrication	$2,100,000
Conversion costs	353,600
Total costs added	$2,453,600
Work in process, May 31, 1994:	
Units	2,000
Stage of completion:	
Transferred in from Fabrication	100%
Conversion costs	40%

Determine Physical Flow

The physical flow of units is identified as the units in the beginning inventory, the units started during the period, the units completed and transferred out during the period, and the units in the ending inventory. For the Welding Department, this flow appears as follows:

Quantities:	
Units charged to Welding Department:	
In process, beginning	1,000
Started in production	14,000
Total units charged	15,000
Units accounted for by Welding Department:	
Completed and transferred out:	
From beginning inventory	1,000
Started and completed:	
(14,000 − 2,000 or 13,000 − 1,000)	12,000
Total units transferred out	13,000
In process, ending	2,000
Total units accounted for	15,000

Calculate Equivalent Units

Equivalent units are computed by multiplying physical units by the percentage of work completed on them. For our example we would have the following calculation:

	Trans-ferred In	Welding Conversion
To complete beginning inventory:		
1,000 × (100% − 100%)	0	
1,000 × (100% − 20%)		800
Units started and completed:		
12,000 × 100%	12,000	12,000
Ending inventory completed:		
2,000 × 100%	2,000	
2,000 × 40%		800
Equivalent units	14,000	13,600

Compute Unit Costs

The unit costs for transferred-in units and conversion costs are calculated from the current month's costs and the equivalent units. The costs for which the Welding Department will be held accountable are:

	Trans-ferred In	Welding Conversion	Total
Beginning inventory	$ 150,000	$ 5,000	$ 155,000
Current month	2,100,000	353,600	2,453,600
Total costs	$2,250,000	$358,600	$2,608,600

With the current month's costs and the equivalent units from above, the cost for the current month is divided by the equivalent units for the month to obtain a unit cost:

	Trans-ferred In	Welding Conversion
Current month	$2,100,000	$353,600
Equivalent units	14,000	13,600
Unit costs	$150	$26

Distribute Total Costs to Units

The distribution of costs using the foregoing unit costs is as follows:

Costs accounted for:

	Trans-ferred In	Welding Conversion	Total
Completed and transferred to Finishing Department:			
Work in process, May 1:			
Cost at May 1	$ 150,000	$ 5,000	$155,000
Cost to complete beg. inventory:			
(800 equivalent units × $26)	0	20,800	20,800
	$ 150,000	$ 25,800	$175,800
Started and completed:			
Transferred in:			
(12,000 equivalent units × $150) . .	1,800,000		
Conversion:			
(12,000 equivalent units × $26) . . .		312,000	2,112,000
Total costs of completed units	$1,950,000	$337,800	$2,287,800
Work in process, May 31:			
Transferred in:			
(2,000 equivalent units × $150)	300,000		
Conversion:			
(800 equivalent units × $26)		20,800	320,800
Total costs accounted for	$2,250,000	$358,600	$2,608,600

As can be seen, the treatment of transferred-in costs is exactly like materials added at the beginning of the departmental operations. If materials were also added in the Welding Department, we would, in effect, have two materials amounts for which equivalent units are needed.

Determine Where Costs Are

The total costs charged to the Welding Department are $2,608,600. Costs distributed to the units completed and units in the ending inventory should sum to $2,608,600. Let's check by performing the following calculation:

Costs charged to department:

	Trans-ferred In	Welding Conversion	Total
Work in process, May 1	$ 150,000	$ 5,000	$ 155,000
Costs added during month	2,100,000	353,600	2,453,600
Total costs charged	$2,250,000	$358,600	$2,608,600
Total costs accounted for (taken from previous step)	$2,250,000	$358,600	$2,608,600

This schedule shows that all costs charged to the Welding Department have been distributed to all units.

Cost of Production Report

The five computational steps provide all of the calculations needed to prepare a cost of production report for May. This report is summarized in Figure 6.7.

DEMING CONTAINER CORPORATION
WELDING DEPARTMENT
COST OF PRODUCTION REPORT
FOR THE MONTH OF MAY 1994

Quantities:
Units charged to department:

In process, beginning	1,000
Started in production	14,000
Total units charged to department	15,000

Units accounted for:
Completed and transferred out:

From beginning inventory	1,000
Started and completed:	
(14,000 − 2,000 or 13,000 − 1,000)	12,000
Total units transferred out	13,000
In process, ending	2,000
Total units accounted for	15,000

Costs charged to department:

	Trans- ferred In	Welding Conversion	Total
Work in process, May 1	$ 150,000	$ 5,000	$ 155,000
Costs added during month	2,100,000	353,600	2,453,600
Total costs charged	$2,250,000	$358,600	$2,608,600

Costs accounted for:

	Trans- ferred In	Welding Conversion	Total
Completed and transferred to Finishing Department:			
Work in process, May 1:			
Cost at May 1	$ 150,000	$ 5,000	$ 155,000
Cost to complete beginning inventory:			
(800 equivalent units × $26)	0	20,800	20,800
	$ 150,000	$ 25,800	$ 175,800
Started and completed:			
Transferred in:			
(12,000 equivalent units × $150)	1,800,000		
Conversion:			
(12,000 equivalent units × $26)		312,000	2,112,000
Total costs of completed units	$1,950,000	$337,800	$2,287,800
Work in process, May 31:			
Transferred in:			
(2,000 equivalent units × $150)	300,000		
Conversion:			
(800 equivalent units × $26)		20,800	320,800
Total costs accounted for	$2,250,000	$358,600	$2,608,600

Additional calculations:	Trans- ferred In	Welding Conversion
Current month's costs	$2,100,000	$353,600
Computation of equivalent units:		
To complete beg. inventory:		
1,000 × (100% − 100%)	0	
1,000 × (100% − 20%)		800
Units started and completed:		
12,000 × 100%	12,000	12,000
Ending inventory:		
2,000 × 100%	2,000	
2,000 × 40%		800
Equivalent units (work done)	14,000	13,600
Equivalent unit costs	$150	$26

Figure 6.7   Cost of Production Report for Welding Department

In T-account form, the transactions reflected in the cost of production report would be summarized in the following general cost flow:

Work in Process—Welding		
Beg. Inventory 155,000	Completed	
Transferred in 2,100,000		2,287,800
Conversion 353,600		
End. Inventory 320,800		

Work in Process—Finishing	
Transferred in	
2,287,800	

MANAGEMENT'S USE OF COST OF PRODUCTION REPORTS

Internal accounting reports often serve only to attach dollar magnitudes to the events about which managers already know. For example, managers know about volumes, inefficiencies, and scrap, but they do not know the costs related to them. However, the information provided by a cost of production report can be used by managers in several different ways.

When unit costs for materials and conversion costs change from one period to the next, a manager should ask why. Why is a materials price higher or lower? What causes conversion costs to change? The manager has to find the answers in order to ensure that the numbers reported represent reality and are accurate. Sometimes managers intuitively know the numbers are either correct or incorrect because of their experiences.

Cost of production reports for several periods in succession can show trends. Here certain questions arise. Are inventories bouncing around, or are they stable? Why? Why are unit costs steadily moving up, or why are they erratic? Are we changing the mix of workers as reflected in labor cost changes? These and many other questions help managers understand their working environment and the company's focus much better.

If unit costs are identified as variable and fixed costs, a manager can perform different cost-volume-profit analyses. Naturally, a sequence of departments that depends on one another must cooperate in some of these analyses in order for the company to have the greatest benefit.

Many other uses are available. The above are cited only to show that the cost of production reports are more than mere printing on paper.

MODIFIED AND HYBRID SYSTEMS

A wide variety of products, processes, and industries presents complex situations where classification of an accounting system as a job cost or process cost system is not easy. Modifications and adaptations are made to the accounting system to meet the needs of specific situations. This leads us to other systems that we categorize as modified cost systems and hybrid cost systems.

A **modified cost system** is one in which one or more elements of cost use job costing while the other cost elements use process costing. For example, a manufacturer of men's shirts will make different sizes and styles and use different fabrics. However, the operations of cutting the fabric and the sewing on of collars, sleeves, buttons, and labels are essentially the same for each shirt. Consequently, the manufacturer can group the shirts by sizes, styles, and fabric and treat the costing of materials using job costing. Then, the labor and factory overhead costs for the operations can use a process cost system.

A **hybrid cost system** is one in which one type of costing system (job costing or process costing) is used for one phase of the production process, and another system is used for a subsequent production process. For example, in manufacturing cars the various parts, subassemblies, engines, transmissions, and so forth may be produced where a job costing system is used. In assembly, every car, regardless of model, has the same assembly operations performed. Therefore, the labor and factory overhead costs of the assembly operations may be accounted for using a process cost system. Hybrid cost systems can follow a number of sequences depending on the particular production process.

Except in the simplest of cases, pure job costing or process costing does not exist. There is usually some modification. Managers and those aspiring to become managers need to understand their own organization's system in order to evaluate the cost information generated by that system.

IMPACT OF CHANGING MANUFACTURING ENVIRONMENT

As discussed in Chapters 1 and 3, many changes have occurred and are occurring in the manufacturing environment. Some of these changes can have a dramatic impact on the way costs are accumulated and the way unit costs are calculated. The two most significant changes in the environment relate to just-in-time systems and activity-based costing.

Simplifications of JIT

For companies adopting a **just-in-time (JIT) philosophy**, the expectation is to reduce or eliminate inventories. If a company implements JIT throughout its operations, the final departments in the process output the products just in time to be shipped; parts, components, and subassemblies are manufactured just in time to meet the final department's needs and so on back through the process. Even in the beginning, materials are received just in time to enter the appropriate department.

JIT can significantly simplify accounting for a process cost system. Partially completed units within each department will be kept as low as possible, meaning that most of the costs incurred during the period are tied to goods completed. This encourages more accurate estimations of stage of completion and unit costs. In addition, little need exists to transfer costs from one department to the next. The costs of the period can be recorded directly to the cost of goods sold account. Process costs per unit can still be computed but more on a daily or weekly basis. The unit costs will be calculated using units produced rather than equivalent units.

Many managers believe that a system truly operating under JIT will have no inventories and, therefore, no need for a process cost system. Because the process flow time is not zero, some items are always in production in a partially completed stage. Process costing becomes greatly simplified in such a setting, but it is not eliminated.

Activity-Based Costing

Activity-based costing (ABC), as discussed in Chapter 3, traces costs to the activities that cause costs. Consequently, we pay greater attention to the activities than to either departments or the cost elements—materials, labor, and overhead. Now, we are interested in identifying the important activities affecting the production process and relate those activities to the products. We may apply the concept of equivalent units to such activities as purchasing, materials handling, setup, quality control, or production scheduling. That leads to a potentially large number of activities for which equivalent units will be calculated. If the goal is providing greater accuracy in product costs, identifying costs to activities and using cost drivers to trace the costs to equivalent units will, in many cases, prove effective. The extent to which ABC will influence how we use a process cost system will depend on a company's product mix complexity for any period.

For some companies, the nature of the activities and cost drivers will be very different from what we considered in Chapter 3. For example, consider a paperboard machine at the Timberline Paperboard plant. It runs 24 hours per day, 7 days per week. The machine processes 23 different grades of paperboard. The production schedule requires producing all 23 grades within an approximate two-week time interval. The stock flow (pulp) is mixed in the head box and applied to a porous wire mesh. In the press section, the pulp mixture is forced against the wire with pressure and suction to eliminate water within the mixture and form the desired paperboard attributes. The material moves on to the drying section along a fabric carrier where it passes over numerous cylindrical dryers which are heated with steam.

After the drying process, the paperboard advances to the size press where various coatings are applied. The calendar stack section presses the material to reduce variation across the width and length of the sheet thereby improving the surface quality of the paperboard. The coater section applies a clay-based opaque material to the sheet, if required by engineering specifications. Finally, long sections of paperboard in a continuous sheet, termed reels, are rolled up directly from the paper machine to await shipment. Any subquality paperboard within reels is separated from the acceptable quality during a rewinding operation.

Since all of the good output can be sold, the company is vitally concerned about minimizing poor quality output. The activities that will greatly influence the amount of high- versus low-quality output will include factors centered around such activities as the composition of each crew working the machine, the specific shift during the day, the grade produced, breaks taken by the crew, change in grades during the process, shift changes, and downtime. In the typical process cost system, we do not normally attribute cost incurrence to these things. However, in an ABC system, we identify the set of activities that causes costs and uses those activities to relate the costs to the final products. In the past, the activities mentioned have been identified as influencing the quantity of good output, but their costs were hidden in the materials, labor and factory overhead costs.

SUMMARY

In many operations, products are continuously manufactured through a series of departments. Physical units and costs are identified with the departments. Unit costs are used in tracing the costs through the various departments and to the finished goods inventory account.

Unit costs in a process cost system are computed by dividing the appropriate current costs by the related equivalent units. The inventory costing method used is the first-in, first-out method. This assumes the beginning inventory is completed before new units started are completed. Costs incurred are assumed to flow in the same manner.

In subsequent departments, transferred-in units and costs become a separate cost element in the calculation of unit costs. Equivalent units for transferred-in costs are treated as though they were materials added at the beginning of the process.

Because manufacturing situations will vary from one company to another, modifications and adaptations to the cost accounting system must be made. Modified and hybrid cost systems are common. A modified cost system will have some elements of cost using job costs and other elements of cost using process costs. A hybrid cost system will have one department on a job cost basis and another department on a process cost basis.

Changes taking place in the manufacturing environment have an impact on a process cost system. Some changes, such as JIT, can simplify the calculation of unit costs. Other changes, such as activity-based costing, can increase the number of cost elements that must be considered when determining the unit costs.

PROBLEM FOR REVIEW

We have used the Deming Container Corporation for an illustration of performing the computational steps and preparing a cost of production report. In the chapter, two departments were used: Fabrication and Welding. Building on that information, the problem for review will use the last department in the sequence—the Finishing Department.

The Finishing Department receives product from the Welding Department, performs several operations to complete the product, and paints it. Therefore, the cost elements for this department are transferred in, materials, and conversion costs. Painting occurs at the end of the process; therefore, material is added at the end rather than the beginning. Having material added at the end means that no material is in the ending inventory.

A summary of the data for May 1994 in the Finishing Department follows:

Work in process, May 1, 1994:	
Units	3,000
Stage of completion:	
Transferred in from Welding	100%
Materials	0%
Conversion costs	10%
Costs:	
Transferred in from Welding	$ 525,000
Conversion costs	6,000
Beginning inventory total cost	$ 531,000
Units started (transferred in) from Welding	13,000
Units completed and transferred to finished goods	15,000
Current period costs:	
Transferred in from Welding	$2,287,800
Materials	225,000
Conversion costs	260,100
Total costs added	$2,772,900

Work in process, May 31, 1994:
Units   1,000
Stage of completion:
  Transferred in from Welding 100%
  Materials 0%
  Conversion costs 60%

Required:

1. Perform the computational steps on the Finishing Department data.
2. Prepare a cost of production report for May 1994.

Solution:

1. Computational Steps
Step 1: Determine physical flow

Quantities:
Units charged to Finishing Department:
In process, beginning inventory   3,000
Started in production   13,000
Total units charged to department   16,000

Units accounted for by Finishing Department:
Completed and transferred out:
  From beginning inventory   3,000
  Started and completed:
  (13,000 − 1,000 or 15,000 − 3,000)   12,000
Total units transferred out   15,000
In process, ending inventory   1,000
Total units accounted for   16,000

Step 2: Calculate equivalent units

	Trans- ferred In	Materials	Finishing Conversion
To complete beginning inventory:			
3,000 × (100% − 100%)	0		
3,000 × (100% − 0%)		3,000	
3,000 × (100% − 10%)			2,700
Units started and completed:			
12,000 × 100%	12,000	12,000	12,000
Ending inventory completed:			
1,000 × 100%	1,000		
1,000 × 0%		0	
1,000 × 60%			600
Equivalent units	13,000	15,000	15,300

Step 3: Compute unit costs

	Trans-ferred In	Materials	Finishing Conversion	Total
Current month	$2,287,800	$225,000	$260,100	$2,772,900
Equivalent units	13,000	15,000	15,300	
Unit costs	$175.985	$15.00	$17.00	

Step 4: Distribute total costs to units

Costs accounted for:

	Trans-ferred in	Materials	Finishing Conversion	Total
Completed and transferred out:				
Work in process, May 1:				
Cost at May 1	$ 525,000	$ 0	$ 6,000	$ 531,000
Cost to complete beginning inventory:				
Materials:				
(3,000 eq. units × $15)	0	45,000		
Conversion:				
(2,700 eq. units × $17)			45,900	90,900
	$ 525,000	$ 45,000	$ 51,900	$ 621,900
Started and completed:				
Transferred in:				
(12,000 eq. units × $175.985)	2,111,820			
Materials:				
(12,000 eq. units × $15)		180,000		
Conversion:				
(12,000 eq. units × $17)			204,000	2,495,820
Total costs of completed units................	$2,636,820	$225,000	$255,900	$3,117,720
Work in process, May 31:				
Transferred in:				
(1,000 eq. units × $175.985)	175,985			
Materials:				
(0 eq. units × $15)		0		
Conversion:				
(600 eq.units × $17)			10,200	186,185
Total costs accounted for.....................	$2,812,805	$225,000	$266,100	$3,303,905

The rounding difference of $5 would normally be included with the total costs of completed units. In the cost of production report shown on pages 273 and 274, we will show the costs of units started and completed as $2,495,815 instead of $2,495,820.

Step 5: Determine where costs are

	Trans- ferred In	Materials	Finishing Conversion	Total
Work in process, May 1 ...	$ 525,000	$ 0	$ 6,000	$ 531,000
Costs added during month	2,287,800	225,000	260,100	2,772,900
Total costs charged	$2,812,800	$225,000	$266,100	$3,303,900
Total costs accounted for (Taken from previous step)	$2,812,800*	$225,000	$266,100	$3,303,900

* $5 rounding difference omitted here.

2.   Cost of Production Report

The four computational steps provide all of the calculations needed to prepare a cost of production report for May. This report is summarized below and on the following page:

DEMING CONTAINER CORPORATION
FINISHING DEPARTMENT
COST OF PRODUCTION REPORT
FOR THE MONTH OF MAY 1994

Quantities:
Units charged to department:

In process, beginning	3,000
Started in production	13,000
Total units charged to department	16,000

Units accounted for:
Completed and transferred out:

From beginning inventory	3,000
Started and completed: (13,000 − 1,000 or 15,000 − 3,000)	12,000
Total units transferred out	15,000
In process, ending	1,000
Total units accounted for	16,000

Costs charged to department:

	Trans- ferred In	Materials	Finishing Conversion	Total
Work in process, May 1	$ 525,000	$ 0	$ 6,000	$ 531,000
Costs added during month	2,287,800	225,000	260,100	2,772,900
Total costs charged	$2,812,800	$225,000	$266,100	$3,303,900

Costs accounted for:

	Trans-ferred In	Materials	Finishing Conversion	Total
Completed and transferred out:				
Work in process, May 1:				
Cost at May 1	$ 525,000	$ 0	$ 6,000	$ 531,000
Cost to complete beginning inventory:				
Materials:				
(3,000 eq. units × $15)	0	45,000		
Conversion:				
(2,700 eq. units × $17)			45,900	90,900
	$ 525,000	$ 45,000	$ 51,900	$ 621,900
Started and completed:				
Transferred in:				
(12,000 eq. units × $175.985) . . .	2,111,815*			
Materials:				
(12,000 eq. units × $15)		180,000		
Conversion:				
(12,000 eq. units × $17)			204,000	2,495,815
Total costs of completed units	$2,636,815	$225,000	$255,900	$3,117,715
Work in process, May 31:				
Transferred in:				
(1,000 eq. units × $175.985) . .	175,985			
Materials:				
(0 eq. units × $15)		0		
Conversion:				
(600 eq.units × $17)			10,200	186,185
Total costs accounted for	$2,812,800	$225,000	$266,100	$3,303,900

Additional calculations:

	Trans-ferred In	Materials	Finishing Conversion
Current month's costs	$2,287,800	$225,000	$260,100
Computation of equivalent units:			
To complete beginning inventory:			
3,000 × (100% − 100%)	0		
3,000 × (100% − 0%)		3,000	
3,000 × (100% − 10%)			2,700
Units started and completed:			
12,000 × 100%	12,000	12,000	12,000
Ending inventory:			
1,000 × 100%	1,000		
1,000 × 0%		0	
1,000 × 60%			600
Equivalent units	13,000	15,000	15,300
Equivalent unit costs	$175.985	$15.00	$17.00

* Stated as 2,111,815 rather than 2,111,820 to compensate for $5 rounding difference.

In T-account form, the transactions reflected in the cost of production report would be summarized as follows:

Work in Process—Finishing			Finished Goods Inventory	
Beg. Inventory	531,000	Completed	Transferred in	
Transferred in	2,287,800	3,117,715 ———————→	3,117,715	
Materials	225,000			
Conversion	260,100			
End. Inventory	186,185			

❖ *APPENDIX*

WEIGHTED AVERAGE COST METHOD

An alternative to the first-in, first-out cost method for calculating equivalent units is the weighted average cost method. This method averages the costs of the beginning work in process inventory and the current production. Thus, the method assumes that the started and completed units for the period are the units completed (regardless of when the units were started). Equivalent units are calculated as the sum of the units completed during the period and the ending work in process inventory multiplied by its stage of completion.

The weighted average cost method is easier and simpler than FIFO because it does not require tracking the costs in the beginning inventory separately from those costs added during the current period. It is justified on the basis of convenience and simplicity. One can argue that a process which produces identical or similar units should generate the same unit costs from one month to the next. In addition, if beginning and ending inventories do not differ significantly from period to period the costs per unit are relatively stable. However, the weighted average method commingles costs and production efforts of two time periods. The resulting product costs do not match production management's measures of inputs and outputs.

COMPUTATIONAL STEPS

The same computational steps apply to the weighted average cost method as are appropriate to the FIFO cost method. A slight difference occurs in the cost accountability section of the cost of production report. In this section, costs are distributed to units completed and units in the ending inventory. The weighted average cost method will usually have different unit costs.

We continue the example of the Deming Container Corporation in the chapter. For the Fabrication Department, we prepared the cost of production report using the FIFO cost method. Below, we apply the weighted average cost method to the Fabrication Department data.

Determine Physical Flow

Determining the physical flow for a department involves identifying the units in the beginning inventory, the units started during the period, the units completed and transferred out during the period, and the units in the ending inventory. These are whole units; stage of completion is not at issue. The flow of units represents the quantities portion of the cost of production report and appears as follows:

Quantities:
Units charged to Fabrication Department:

In process, beginning	4,000
Started in production	12,000
Total units charged	16,000

Units accounted for by Fabrication Department:

Completed and transferred out	14,000
In process, ending	2,000
Total units accounted for	16,000

Calculate Equivalent Units

Since equivalent units ignore the partially completed beginning inventory, only units completed and units in ending inventory are considered. For our example, we would have the following calculation:

	Materials	Conversion
Units completed: 14,000 × 100%	14,000	14,000
Ending inventory:		
2,000 × 100%	2,000	
2,000 × 30%		600
Equivalent units	16,000	14,600

Compute Unit Costs

The unit costs for material and conversion costs are calculated from the total costs and the equivalent units. The costs for which the Fabrication Department will be held accountable are:

	Materials	Conversion	Total
Beginning inventory...............	$ 400,000	$ 80,000	$ 480,000
Current month	1,200,000	650,000	1,850,000
Total costs	$1,600,000	$730,000	$2,330,000

Unit costs are calculated by using the equivalent units from above and dividing them into the total costs:

	Materials	Conversion
Total costs	$1,600,000	$730,000
Equivalent units	16,000	14,600
Unit costs	$100	$50

These unit costs are identical to those calculated using the FIFO cost method. Usually, some difference will occur in the numbers, but generally not a significant one.

Distribute Total Costs to Units

The distribution of costs using the foregoing unit costs is as follows:

Costs accounted for:	Materials	Conversion	Total
Completed and transferred to Welding Department:			
Materials:			
(14,000 eq. units × $100)	$1,400,000		
Conversion:			
(14,000 eq. units × $50)		$700,000	$2,100,000
Total cost of completed units	$1,400,000	$700,000	$2,100,000
Work in process, May 31:			
Materials:			
(2,000 eq. units × $100)	200,000		
Conversion:			
(600 eq. units × $50)		30,000	230,000
Total costs accounted for	$1,600,000	$730,000	$2,330,000

Determine Where Costs Are

The total costs charged to the Fabrication Department are $2,330,000. After distributing the costs to the units completed and units in the ending inventory, the sum of that distribution should equal $2,330,000. The following schedule checks this equality:

	Materials	Conversion	Total
Beginning inventory.................	$ 400,000	$ 80,000	$ 480,000
Current month	1,200,000	650,000	1,850,000
Total costs	$1,600,000	$730,000	$2,330,000
Total costs accounted for (from previous step)	$1,600,000	$730,000	$2,330,000

Cost of Production Report

The five computational steps provide all of the calculations needed to prepare a cost of production report for May. The report prepared under the weighted average cost method appears below:

DEMING CONTAINER CORPORATION
FABRICATION DEPARTMENT
COST OF PRODUCTION REPORT
FOR THE MONTH OF MAY 1994

Quantities:
Units charged to department:
In process, beginning	4,000
Started in production..	12,000
Total units charged to department	16,000

Units accounted for:
Completed and transferred out	14,000
In process, ending	2,000
Total units accounted for	16,000

Costs charged to department:

	Materials	Conversion Costs	Total
Beginning Inventory	$ 400,000	$ 80,000	$ 480,000
Costs added during month	1,200,000	650,000	1,850,000
Total costs charged..............	$1,600,000	$730,000	$2,330,000

Costs accounted for:

	Materials	Conversion Costs	Total
Completed and transferred to Welding Department:			
Materials:			
(14,000 eq. units × $100)	$1,400,000		
Conversion:			
(14,000 eq. units × $50)		$700,000	$2,100,000
Total costs of completed units	$1,400,000	$700,000	$2,100,000
Work in process, May 31:			
Materials:			
(2,000 equivalent units × $100)	200,000		
Conversion:			
(600 equivalent units × $50) ..		30,000	230,000
Total costs accounted for	$1,600,000	$730,000	$2,330,000

Additional calculations:

	Materials	Conversion
Total costs	$1,600,000	$730,000
Units completed: 14,000 × 100	14,000	14,000
Ending inventory:		
2,000 × 100%	2,000	
2,000 × 30%		600
Equivalent units	16,000	14,600
Equivalent unit costs	$100	$50

ACCOUNTABILITY IN SUBSEQUENT DEPARTMENTS

The procedures are the same for subsequent departments in the processing operation. In departments after the first, however, unit costs must be computed for the accumulated work done in earlier departments as well as for the work done in the present department.

The equivalent units for work done in preceding departments are the actual physical units. There is no need to compute what fraction of the work has been done since all the work that can be done in earlier departments has been done, or the units would not be in the present department.

Following through with the Deming Container Corporation illustration, consider the results in the Welding Department—the second department in the sequence. There is no material entered here, so the cost elements are transferred-in costs and conversion costs.

Determine Physical Flow

The physical flow of units is identified as the units in the beginning inventory, the units started during the period, the units completed and transferred out during the period, and the units in the ending inventory. For the Welding Department, this flow is identical to the FIFO method and appears as follows:

Units charged to Welding Department:
In process, beginning	1,000
Started in production	14,000
Total units charged	15,000

Units accounted for by Welding Department:
Completed and transferred out	13,000
In process, ending	2,000
Total units accounted for	15,000

Calculate Equivalent Units

Equivalent units are computed by multiplying physical units by the percentage of work completed on them. For our example we would have the following calculation:

	Trans- ferred In	Conversion
Units completed:		
13,000 × 100%	13,000	13,000
Ending inventory:		
2,000 × 100%	2,000	
2,000 × 40%		800
Equivalent units	15,000	13,800

Compute Unit Costs

The unit costs for transferred-in units and conversion costs are calculated from the total costs and the equivalent units. The costs for which the Welding Department will be held accountable are:

	Trans- ferred In	Conversion	Total
Beginning inventory..................	$ 150,000	$ 5,000	$ 155,000
Current month	2,100,000	353,600	2,453,600
Total costs	$2,250,000	$358,600	$2,608,600

With the total costs and the equivalent units from above, the total cost for the month is divided by the equivalent units for the month to obtain a unit cost:

	Trans- ferred In	Conversion
Total costs	$2,250,000	$358,600
Equivalent units	15,000	13,800
Unit costs	$150	$25.986

Distribute Total Costs to Units

The distribution of costs using the foregoing unit costs is as follows:

Costs accounted for:

	Trans- ferred In	Conversion	Total
Completed and transferred to Finishing Department:			
Transferred in:			
(13,000 eq. units × $150)	$1,950,000		
Conversion:			
(13,000 eq. units × $25.986)		$337,818	$2,287,818
Total cost of completed units	$1,950,000	$337,818	$2,287,818
Work in process, May 31:			
Transferred in:			
(2,000 eq. units × $150)	300,000		
Conversion:			
(800 eq. units × $25.986)		20,789	320,789
Total costs accounted for	$2,250,000	$358,607	$2,608,607

As can be seen, the treatment of transferred-in costs is exactly like materials added at the beginning of the departmental operations. If materials were also added in this department, we would have one equivalent unit calculation for transferred-in units and one for the new materials.

Determine Where Costs Are

The total costs charged to the Welding Department are $2,608,600. After completing the distribution of costs, the costs transferred out and the costs in the ending inventory should sum to $2,608,600. We check this equality as follows:

	Trans-ferred In	Conversion	Total
Beginning inventory	$ 150,000	$ 5,000	$ 155,000
Costs added during month	2,100,000	353,600	2,453,600
Total costs charged	$2,250,000	$358,600	$2,608,600
Total costs accounted for (from previous step)	$2,250,000	$358,607	$2,608,607

We have a rounding difference in the conversion costs. When we prepare the costs of production report, we will adjust the cost of units completed to compensate for rounding.

Cost of Production Report

The five computational steps provide all of the calculations needed to prepare a cost of production report for May. This report is summarized below and on the following page:

DEMING CONTAINER CORPORATION
WELDING DEPARTMENT
COST OF PRODUCTION REPORT
FOR THE MONTH OF MAY 1994

Quantities:
Units charged to department:

In process, beginning	1,000
Started in production	14,000
Total units charged to department	15,000

Units accounted for:

Completed and transferred out	13,000
In process, ending	2,000
Total units accounted for	15,000

Costs charged to department:

	Trans-ferred In	Welding Conversion	Total
Beginning inventory	$ 150,000	$ 5,000	$ 155,000
Costs added during month	2,100,000	353,600	2,453,600
Total costs charged	$2,250,000	$ 358,600	$2,608,600

Costs accounted for:

	Trans-ferred In	Welding Conversion	Total
Completed and transferred to Finishing Department:			
Transferred in:			
(13,000 eq. units × $150)	$1,950,000		
Conversion:			
(13,000 eq. units × $25.986) ..		$ 337,811 *	$2,287,811
Total costs of completed units	$1,950,000	$ 337,811	$2,287,811
Work in process, May 31:			
Transferred in:			
(2,000 equivalent units × $150)	300,000		
Conversion:			
(800 equivalent units × $25.986)		20,789	320,789
Total costs accounted for	$2,250,000	$ 358,600	$2,608,600

Additional calculations:

	Trans-ferred In	Welding Conversion
Total costs	$2,250,000	$358,600
Units completed: 13,000 × 100%...	13,000	13,000
Ending inventory:		
2,000 × 100%	2,000	
2,000 × 40%		800
Equivalent units (work done)	15,000	13,800
Equivalent unit costs	$150	$25.986

* The $7 rounding difference has been compensated for here.

TERMINOLOGY REVIEW

Conversion costs (249)
Cost of production report (250)
Equivalent unit (252)
First-in, first-out (FIFO) cost method (255)

Hybrid cost system (267)
Modified cost system (267)
Process cost system (246)
Stage of completion (253)
Transferred-in costs (262)

QUESTIONS FOR REVIEW AND DISCUSSION

1. What is the focal point for cost accumulation in a process cost system?

2. What accounting report is the major document for a process cost system?

3. List the five computational steps necessary to account for costs in a process cost system.

4. Explain how equivalent units are computed under the FIFO method of inventory accounting.

5. How are the unit costs computed under the FIFO method of inventory accounting?

6. Why are equivalent units for materials usually different from equivalent units for conversion costs?

7. Explain why the equivalent units of work done in preceding departments are equal to the actual number of units charged to the subsequent department.

8. At what stage of completion are transferred-in units from the ending work in process inventory of a subsequent department?

9. Why should we distinguish between transferred-in costs and those related to materials added in a subsequent department.

10. What purpose does the quantity section of a cost of production report serve?

11. How can management use a cost of production report?

12. Distinguish between a modified cost system and a hybrid cost system.

13. Explain how a just-in-time environment can simplify a process cost system.

14. (Appendix) What is the distinction between equivalent units under the FIFO method and equivalent units under the weighted average method?

15. (Appendix) Under what circumstances will both FIFO and weighted average yield the same equivalent units?

16. (Appendix) On a cost of production report, the costs of units completed and transferred out are treated one way under the FIFO method and a different way under the weighted average method. Explain this difference.

EXERCISES

1. **Physical Flow.** The work in process inventory in Operation 1 on July 1, was 2,500 units. During July, 60,000 units were completed in Operation 1 and transferred to Operation 2. The ending work in process inventory in Operation 1 was 3,500 units.

   Required:
   1. Compute the number of units started into production.
   2. Compute the number of units started and completed.

2. **Equivalent Units.** Carroll Fisheries raises cutthroat trout for local restaurants. The process involves three ponds: raising, growing, and fattening. Fingerlings are grown after hatching in the raising pond. At a specified point, the fingerlings are moved to the growing pond, where they mature. After maturing, the fish are transferred to the fattening pond. The growing pond had 5,000 fingerlings on April 1, that were 10 percent complete for the growing pond. The fish represent materials. During the month, an additional 30,000 fingerlings were put into the pond. By the end of April, 28,000 fish had been moved to the fattening pond. The fingerlings remaining in the growing pond were 30 percent complete.

   Required:
   1. Determine the equivalent units for fingerlings.
   2. Determine the equivalent units for conversion costs.

3.   **Unit Cost Computation.** On November 1, 15,000 units were in process in Department 1 that were 100 percent complete for materials (materials are added at the beginning of the process) and 60 percent complete for conversion costs. The cost of the beginning work in process inventory was $15,000 for materials and $4,500 for conversion costs. In November, 200,000 units were started in process. Material costs for the month were $205,000. Conversion costs amounted to $370,000. On November 30, 30,000 units were in process that were 30 percent complete for conversion costs.

Required:
1.   Compute the equivalent units and unit cost for materials.
2.   Compute the equivalent units and unit cost for conversion costs.

4.   **Distribution of Total Cost.** There were 5,000 units in process in the Cutting Department of Rosella Company at the beginning of February. These units had materials and conversion costs of $48,000 and were 60 percent complete for conversion costs. Material is added at the beginning of the process. During February, 60,000 units were started. The ending inventory for the month totalled 8,000 units, 25 percent complete for conversion costs. The unit cost calculation shows $4 for materials and $8 for conversion costs in February.

Required:
1.   Compute the cost of units completed and transferred to the next department.
2.   Compute the cost of units in the ending inventory for the month.

5.   **Cost of Production Report.** Schulteis Chicken Farms raises chicks to the egg-laying stage and then moves the hens to the laying sheds. Information about the Chick Raising Operation for March 1994 is:
  (a)   Beginning inventory of chicks is 12,000, 100 percent for chicks and 20 percent for raising costs.
  (b)   Beginning inventory costs are $12,960 for chicks and $1,153 for raising costs.
  (c)   Chicks added during March totalled 20,000.
  (d)   Costs incurred during the month are $20,000 for chicks and $12,180 for raising costs.
  (e)   Ending inventory at March 31, consisted of 2,000 chicks, 100 percent complete for chicks and 70 percent for raising costs.

Required:
    Prepare a cost of production report for the Chick Raising Operation for March 1994.

6.   **Unit Costs—Subsequent Departments.** Wilson Ceramics Company produces a figurine in five operations. On June 1, there were 4,000 figurines in process in Operation 5 that were 25 percent complete in Operation 5. The cost of work in process in Operation 5 consisted of $1,000 in cost from the four earlier operations and a $200 cost of Operation 5. During June, 10,000 figurines were received from Operation 4 at a cost of $3,000. In Operation 5, the beginning work in process was completed, and 7,000 units were started and completed. The processing costs in June in Operation 5 amounted to $2,200. On June 30, there were 3,000 units in process, 1/3 complete as to work in Operation 5.

Required:
1.   Calculate equivalent units and unit cost of work done in the preceding operations and transferred into Operation 5 in June.
2.   Determine the equivalent units and unit cost of work done in Operation 5 for June.

7. **Units Costs—Subsequent Departments.** Cochrane Candy Company manufactures candy bars in unit lots consisting of 24 bars to a unit. The January 1 inventory consisted of 6,000 units in process in Department 4 that were 2/3 complete in that operation. The work in process on January 1 included costs of $30,000 incurred in earlier departments and $4,000 in Department 4. During the month of January, Department 4 received 50,000 units from Department 3 at a cost of $272,400.

Processing costs in the month of January in Department 4 amounted to $55,400. Department 4, the last processing department, completed and transferred 53,000 units to the finished goods inventory. On January 31, there were 3,000 units in process in Department 4 that were 1/3 completed in that department.

Required:
1. Compute the equivalent units and unit cost of work done in the preceding departments transferred into Department 4 during January.
2. Compute the equivalent units and unit cost of work done in the Department 4 for January.

8. **Cost Accountability—Subsequent Departments.** Axiom Products, Inc. manufactures a vitamin product in five operations. On July 1, Department 5 had 8,000 units in process that were 25 percent complete for conversion costs in Department 5. Material (a coating) is added at the end of the process in Department 5. The cost of the beginning work in process incurred in earlier operations was $48,000, and the cost in Department 5 was $1,000. During July, Department 5 received 70,000 units from Department 4 at a cost of $420,000. July conversion costs for Department 5 were $36,000. The material costs added in the department were $17,000. Department 5 started and completed 60,000 units in July. The work in process inventory on July 31 of 10,000 units was 60 percent complete in Department 5.

Required:
1. What was the total cost of work transferred to the finished goods inventory in July?
2. Determine the cost of work in process inventory in Department 5 on July 31.

9. **Unit Cost—Weighted Average Cost Method.** (Appendix) On December 1, Department K had 10,000 units in process that were 40 percent completed for conversion costs. The cost of the beginning work in process inventory was $20,000. In December, 150,000 units were started in process. Conversion costs in December amounted to $720,000. On December 31, the department had 20,000 units in process that were 40 percent complete for conversion costs.

Required:
1. Compute the equivalent units.
2. Determine the unit cost.

10. **Cost Accounting—Weighted Average Cost Method.** (Appendix) The beginning work in process in Department A1 on September 1 consisted of 40,000 units of product. During the month of September, 150,000 units were completed and transferred to Department A2. The September 30 work in process inventory in Department A1 consisted of 60,000 units that were 20 percent completed in that department. The unit cost, as computed by the weighted average cost method, was $6.

Required:
1. Compute the total cost of work transferred to Department A2.
2. Compute the total cost of work in process at September 30.

11. **Units Costs—Subsequent Departments.** (Appendix) Work Exercise 7 using the weighted-average cost method.

12. **Cost Accountability—Subsequent Departments.** (Appendix). Work Exercise 8 using the weighted-average cost method.

13. **Equivalent Units.** Calculate the equivalent units for each of the following independent situations.
     (a) Department MK had 5,000 units in process on April 1 which were 60 percent complete for conversion costs. Materials are added at the beginning of the departmental process and conversion costs are added uniformly throughout the process. During April, a total of 80,000 units were completed and transferred to Department PQ. On April 30, the in-process inventory consisted of 8,000 units that had 25 percent of the work completed.
     (b) During July, Department XY started to process 180,000 units. At the beginning of the month, 12,000 units were in process, 90 percent complete for materials and 70 percent complete for conversion costs. On July 31, the in-process inventory was 10,000 units, which were 50 percent complete for materials and 40 percent complete for conversion costs.
     (c) The beginning inventory in process in the Sewing Department on August 1 consisted of 15,000 units that were 100 percent complete for transferred-in costs, 60 percent complete for materials and 50 percent complete for conversion costs. The Cutting Department transferred in 250,000 units during August. At the end of the month, the in-process inventory of 20,000 was 20 percent complete for materials and conversion costs.
     (d) On May 1, Activity Center 123 had 30,000 units in process that were 30 percent complete regarding conversion costs. Materials are added at the end of the process in this activity center. During May, Activity Center 816 transferred 320,000 units to Activity Center 123. A total of 340,000 units were completed during May and transferred to Activity Center 963. The work in process inventory on May 31 was 60 percent complete regarding conversion costs.

14. **Equivalent Units.** (Appendix) Work Exercise 13 using the weighted-average cost method.

15. **Processing Costs.** Hubert Products Company produces an oven cleaner. The chemical mixture is transferred to the Final Mix Department where an inert material is added to the mixture. Because evaporation equals the amount of inert materials added, quantities do not increase. Subsequent to the Final Mix Department, the product is packaged and shipped. The equivalent units (in gallons) and costs for the Final Mix Department were computed as follows:

	Transferred In	Materials	Conversion
Beginning work in process	0	6,000	1,200
Started and completed	40,000	40,000	40,000
Ending work in process	3 000	3,000	1,800
Equivalent units	43,000	49,000	43,000
Equivalent unit costs	$2.10	$0.10	$0.20

Required:
1. Compute the current period costs for:
    (a) Transferred-in costs.
    (b) Materials.
    (c) Conversion costs.
2. If the beginning work in process inventory was valued at $12,600, what would be the cost of goods completed?

16. **T-Account Flow with Process Costs.** Southwest Paper Company manufactures paper from pine logs in a continuous process. Its operations are divided into three activity centers: Stripping, Mixing, and Pressing. The Stripping Center strips the bark off the logs and chips the log into small pieces. The Mixing Center mixes the chips with chemicals in a vat. The Pressing Center presses the chemically dissolved pulp into paper.

The process does not change, and the company's operations move at a constant speed so that beginning and ending inventories are always in the same amount and at the same stage of completion. For this reason, the inventories of work in process are not considered in determining production for each period.

The company completed the following transactions during one week in August:
(a) Purchased on credit three car load lots of logs for $2,700 and one tank car of chemicals for $1,000.
(b) Placed two car loads of logs and half the chemicals into process.
(c) Labor for the week was as follows:

Stripping Center	$1,500
Mixing Center	700
Pressing Center	900
Factory indirect labor	800

(d) Manufacturing overhead (other than indirect labor) was as follows:

Depreciation	$400
Machinery repairs	100
Power	100
Supplies	50
Taxes	100

(e) The company applies manufacturing overhead to departments on the basis of 50 percent of direct labor costs.

Required:
Show the flow of costs for each of the above transactions using T-accounts. Separate work in process accounts exist for each activity center.

PROBLEMS

6-1. **Flow of Process Cost.** LeMay Cookie Company manufactures a line of chocolate cookies in three processing operations. The product is perishable, and no work in process inventories are on hand in any of the operations at the end of the month. During the month of June, 500,000 units were processed completely in all three operations, transferred to finished goods inventory, and sold. Processing costs for the month were as follows:

Department A:
Materials	$165,000	
Labor	25,000	
Overhead	20,000	$210,000

Department B:
Labor	$ 80,000	
Overhead	40,000	120,000

Department C:
Labor	$ 60,000	
Overhead	45,000	105,000

Required:
1. Using T-accounts for the work in process inventories of each operation, trace the flow of costs through the three operations and into cost of goods sold.
2. Determine the total unit manufactured cost.
3. Determine the addition to unit cost by each of the three operations.

6-2. **Flow of Process Cost.** A vitamin product is manufactured in three operations by Bocian Health Products, Inc. No work in process existed on August 1 in any of the three operations, but 10,000 units were in process in each operation at the end of August. The percentage of the work in process that was completed in each operation at August 31 is given as follows:

Department 1	40%
Department 2	60%
Department 3	20%

Costs in the three departments for August were as follows:

	Departments		
	1	2	3
Materials	$ 94,000	0	0
Labor	47,000	$30,000	$14,400
Overhead	47,000	21,600	7,200
Totals	$188,000	$51,600	$21,600

During August, 100,000 units were started in process in Department 1.

Required:
1. For each department, compute the unit cost of work done in that department and the cumulative unit cost of work done including preceding departments costs.
2. Using T-accounts for each department, trace the flow of costs through the three departments and into finished goods inventory.
3. Assume that 50,000 units were sold during the month. What amount will appear in the cost of goods sold account?

6-3. **Cost of Production Report.** Pfeffer Specialty Foods, Inc. prepares and cans tasty Italian foods in three processing operations. All materials are added at the beginning of the first operation. Data for the month of May in Operation A are given as follows:

	Units
Work in process, May 1	5,000
Units started in process	120,000

	Costs
Work in process, May 1:	
Materials	$ 15,000
Labor and overhead	2,000
May costs:	
Materials	$360,000
Labor and overhead	232,000

The beginning overhead was 20 percent complete for labor and overhead. During the month, 115,000 units were completed and transferred to Operation B; and 10,000 units that were 20 percent complete as to labor and overhead were in process in Operation A at May 31.

Required:
1. Prepare a cost of production report for Operation A for the month of May.
2. Explain how management might use this cost of production report.

6-4. **Cost of Production Report.** Bigalow Robotics, Inc. manufactures a small robot that can be moved around a room by remote control. It can be used as a novelty to serve food and drinks to guests, and, with a special attachment, it can vacuum the carpet.

The materials are all added at the beginning of the Assembly Operation (the first operation). Labor and overhead are added during the month. Data for the month of July in the Assembly Operation are given as follows:

Units:	
Work in process, July 1	20,000
Units started in process	250,000
Total units charged	270,000

Costs:	
Work in process, July 1:	
Materials	$ 240,000
Labor and overhead	80,000
	$ 320,000
July costs:	
Materials	$3,500,000
Labor and overhead	1,457,280
	$4,957,280

The inventory of work in process on July 1 was complete as to materials but only 1/4 complete as to labor and overhead. On July 31, the inventory consisted of 20,000 units that were 40 percent complete with respect to labor and overhead.

Required:
1. Prepare a cost of production report for the Assembly Operation for the month of July.
2. Explain how management could use this report.

6-5. Explanation of Approach to a Cost of Production Report—Dept. 1. A production report for the month of May is given as follows for Department 1 of Enid Chemical Company:

Quantities:

Units charged to department:

Work in process, May 1 (40% complete)	500
Started in May	2,000
Total units charged	2,500

Units accounted for:

Transferred to Dept. 2	2,200
Work in process, May 31 (1/2 complete)	300
Total units accounted for	2,500

Costs charged to department:

Work in process, May 1	$ 800.00
Processing cost, May	9,020.00
Total cost charged	$9,820.00

Costs accounted for:

Transferred to Dept. 2:

Work in process, May 1	$ 800.00
Cost to complete work in process, May 1	1,258.60
Started and completed	7,132.09
	$9,190.69
Work in process, May 31	629.30
Total cost accounted for	$9,819.99*

* Difference caused by rounding.

Required:

1. Explain what the above cost of production report tells you about the quantity flow and the cost flow.
2. Explain why equivalent units are preferred to total units produced in determining costs of units completed and units in ending inventory.
3. What additional information can this report give a manager?
4. Calculate how many units were started and completed during the month of May.

6-6. Cost Accountability—Two Months. Conrad George, Inc. manufactures a single product that goes through a mixing operation followed by a drying operation. The data for the Mixing Department for October and November are:

	October	November
Beginning inventory	0	600
Units started during month	12,400	13,100
Units completed and transferred	11,800	13,300
Costs put into production:		
Materials	$258,640	$271,760
Labor and factory overhead	526,860	569,770
Ending inventory	600	400
Stage of completion for ending inventory:		
Materials	90%	50%
Labor and factory overhead	60%	30%

Required:
1. Prepare a cost of production report for October. Round unit costs to five decimal places and total dollars to the nearest dollar.
2. Prepare a cost of production report for November. Round unit costs to five decimal places and total dollars to the nearest dollar.

6-7. **A Comparison of Actual and Estimated Unit Cost.** Sylvia Whitman, controller of Schoewe Company, has estimated unit costs at various operating stages in the production of a new potato snack. The unit cost of work done in Operation 1, according to budget estimates, should be $2.50, consisting of a unit cost of $1.60 for materials and a unit cost of $.90 for labor and overhead. All materials are added at the beginning of the operation, and labor and overhead are added as the work progresses. Cost and production data for Operation 1 are given as follows for the month of October:

Quantities:

Units charged to operation:

Work in process, October 1 (40% complete as to labor and overhead)	10,000
Started in production	150,000
Total units charged	160,000

Units accounted for:

Transferred to Operation 2............................	155,000
Work in process, October 31 (20% complete as to labor and overhead)	5,000
Total units accounted for	160,000

Costs charged to operation:

Work in process, October 1:		
Materials	$ 16,000	
Labor and overhead	5,400	$ 21,400
October costs:		
Materials	$240,000	
Labor and overhead	182,400	422,400
Total costs charged....................................		$443,800

Required:
1. Prepare the cost accountability section of a production report for Operation 1 for the month of October.
2. Compare the actual unit cost with the estimated unit cost. Identify separately any variance of materials cost and any variance of labor and overhead cost.

6-8. **Cost Accountability—Two Months.** (Appendix) Work Problem 6-6 using the weighted-average cost method.

6-9. **A Comparison of Actual and Estimated Unit Cost.** (Appendix) Work Problem 6-7 using the weighted-average cost method.

6-10. **Unit Cost and Cost Accountability.** Hunsicker Mills, Inc. processes a grain product in three operations. Operation 3 had 9,000 units in process on November 1 that were 60 percent complete with respect to work done in Operation 3. The cost of this work in process was as follows:

Cost of work in preceding operations $18,000
Cost of work in Operation 3 2,700

Units were transferred from Operation 2 to Operation 3 during November. The cost of the 80,000 units transferred in from earlier operations was $167,800.

In Operation 3, 85,000 units were completed and transferred to Finished Goods. Costs in November in Operation 3 were $31,700.

The work in process inventory on November 30 was 25 percent complete in Operation 3.

Required:

1.   Compute the unit costs for work done in preceding operations and in Operation 3. (Round computations to three decimal places.)

2.   Prepare a cost accountability section of a production report for Operation 3 for November.

3.   Explain what information the beginning inventory gives you about the cost of work performed during October in Operation 3.

6-11. **Cost of Production Report.** Swiss-Works, Inc. is a manufacturer of a digital watch. Materials are added to production at the beginning of the manufacturing process, and factory overhead is applied to each product at the rate of 60 percent of direct labor costs. Its operations for June show ending inventories of work in process and finished goods as reflected in the general ledger:

	Units	Costs
Work in process (50% complete for labor and overhead)	300,000	$870,000
Finished goods	200,000	$900,000

No finished goods inventory existed on June 1. The operating data for the month are:

		Costs	
	Units	Materials	Labor
Work in process, June 1 (80% complete for labor and overhead costs)...............................	200,000	$ 200,000	$ 315,000
Units started during June	1,000,000		
Materials costs		1,300,000	
Labor costs			1,780,000
Units completed	900,000		

Required:

1.   Calculate the unit costs for June for:
     (a)   Materials
     (b)   Labor
     (c)   Overhead

2.   Prepare a cost of production report for June.

3.   Using T-accounts prepare a summary of cost flow from work in process inventory through finished goods to cost of goods sold.

6-12. Subsequent Departments. Desert Fragrance Products, Inc. manufactures a full line of cosmetics and fragrances. A perfume for teenagers requires processing in three sequential operations: Blending, Cooking, and Packaging. Materials are added on a continuous basis in Blending and at the end of Packaging. No materials are added during Cooking. Conversion costs are added uniformly throughout all departments. A summary of operating data for April appears as:

	Operations		
	Blending	**Cooking**	**Packaging**
Quantities (units in gallons):			
Beginning inventory..................	32,000	19,200	27,200
Started or transferred in	104,000	?	?
Completed or transferred out	112,000	?	?
Ending inventory	24,000	14,400	12,800
Stage of completion:			
Beginning inventory:			
Transferred in......................	-	100%	100%
Materials	20%	-	0%
Conversion costs	20%	40%	20%
Ending inventory:			
Transferred in......................	-	100%	100%
Materials	30%	-	0%
Conversion costs	30%	25%	60%
Costs:			
Beginning inventory:			
Transferred in......................	-	$ 79,680	$146,880
Materials	$ 15,360	-	-
Conversion costs	11,200	9,600	4,352
Current period costs:			
Materials	$251,520	-	$ 65,280
Conversion costs	183,400	$ 130,900	99,328

Required:

1. Prepare a cost of production report for each of the three operations. Round unit cost computations to four decimal places and dollar amounts to nearest dollar.

2. Using T-accounts, show the flow of dollars into and out of the three work in process accounts for the operations and into finished goods.

6-13. Subsequent Departments. (Appendix) Work Problem 6-12 assuming the Blending and Cooking Operations use the weighted-average cost method and the Packaging Operation uses the FIFO cost method.

6-14. Several Months. Mountain Valley Winery started operations three years ago and is gaining a reputation for quality. The accounting system is evolving and has not been fully formalized. A chief accountant has been hired to bring order to the paper shuffling. In the process, the chief accountant has gathered data to prepare cost of production reports for Activity Center A for the first three months of the current fiscal year (April, May, and June). This information is as follows:

	April	May	June
Gallons:			
Beginning inventory.....................	10,000	?	?
Started in production	80,000	65,000	70,000
Completed	70,000	60,000	?
Ending inventory	?	?	20,000
Stage of completion:			
Beginning inventory.....................	60%	30%	70%
Ending inventory	30%	70%	40%
Cost data:			
Beginning inventory:			
Materials	$ 10,000	?	?
Conversion costs	20,000	?	?
Current period:			
Materials	$ 80,000	$ 66,000	$ 70,000
Conversion costs	170,000	142,000	156,000

Materials are added at the beginning of Activity Center A. Conversion costs flow uniformly throughout the process.

Required:
1. Compute the physical flow of product for each of the three months.
2. Prepare a cost of production report for each of the three months.
3. Analyze the cost of production reports for each month and comment on:
    (a)   Unit costs for materials and conversion costs.
    (b)   Stage of completion for inventories.

6-15. **Costs Flow Through T-Accounts.** Lupe Manufacturing Company produces a single product. Its operations are a continuous process through two activity centers: Machining and Finishing. Materials are added at the start of production in each department. For November, the following transactions took place:
(a)   Purchased materials on credit costing $435,400.
(b)   Started 80,000 units in production in the Machining Center. The direct materials cost $240,000 and indirect materials cost $8,100. The Machining Center had no beginning work in process inventory.
(c)   Salaries and wages paid for the month show the following labor costs:

	Machining	Finishing
Direct labor	$140,000	$141,500
Factory indirect labor	30,000	6,700

(d)   Factory overhead is applied at 100% of direct labor cost in Machining and at 20% of direct labor cost in Finishing.
(e)   Actual factory overhead costs for Machining, other than indirect materials and indirect labor, totaled $100,000.
(f)   Machining completed 60,000 units and transferred them to Finishing. The units remaining in Machining were 100% complete for materials and 50% complete for conversion costs.
(g)   No beginning inventory was in Finishing on November 1. Direct materials costs added in Finishing were $88,500; indirect materials were $2,400.
(h)   Actual factory overhead costs for Finishing, other than indirect materials and indirect labor, were $16,600.

(i)   50,000 units were completed in Finishing and transferred to finished goods. Units remaining in Finishing were 100% completed for materials and 70% completed for conversion costs.

(j)   After sales, 10,000 units remained in finished goods inventory.

Required:

1.   Using T-accounts, trace the costs reflected in the transactions through the appropriate accounts.

2.   Close any under- or overapplied factory overhead for Machining and Finishing to Cost of Goods Sold.

6-16. Analysis of a Work in Process Account. Broadway Pharmaceutical Company manufacturers a tablet for allergy sufferers. Ingredients are all added at the beginning of the Blending Operation. Conversion costs flow uniformly throughout the process. Tableting and Coating are operations downstream from Blending. Information on the Blending Operation for October is as follows:

Work in Process—Blending Operation

October 1, balance (100,000 units 40% complete for conversion costs) $151,760	Completed and transferred to Tableting: Units - ? Costs - ?
Direct materials added (1,000,000 units) 1,310,000	
Direct labor costs ?	
Factory overhead (applied at 180% of direct labor cost) 396,000	
October 31, balance (200,000 units 70% complete for conversion costs ?	

The October 1 balance consists of the following cost elements:

Direct materials	$128,000
Direct labor	8,800
Factory overhead	14,960
Total	$151,760

Required:

1.   Compute the amount of direct labor cost for the period.

2.   Calculate the unit costs for direct materials, direct labor, and factory overhead for the current month (October). Direct labor and factory overhead should be separate; do not combine them into one figure.

3.   Prepare a cost of production report for the Blending Operation.

4.   Calculate the unit costs for direct material, direct labor, and factory overhead in the inventory at the beginning of October.

5.   Compare the unit costs computed in (2) and (4) above. Explain what information this comparison gives a manager.

6-17. Analysis of a Work in Process Account. (Appendix) Work Problem 6-16 using the weighted average cost method.

6-18. Two Departments for Two Months. Southwest Collections, Inc. publishes books about the southwestern United States. The company operates with two basic production departments: Printing and Binding. After binding, the books go to the warehouse for shipping to bookstores. Materials are added at the beginning of each department and conversion costs occur evenly throughout the whole process.

The following operating information for the two departments is available for September and October:

	September	October
Printing:		
Beginning inventory:		
Units (number of books)	10,000	?
Stage of completion for conversion	20%	?
Costs:		
Materials	$ 1,000	?
Conversion	2,500	?
Units started during month	90,000	60,000
Units completed during month	80,000	?
Costs added during month:		
Materials	$ 9,000	$ 7,500
Conversion	83,700	57,750
Ending inventory:		
Units (number of books)	?	20,000
Stage of completion for conversion	75%	70%
Binding:		
Beginning inventory:		
Units (number of books)	2,000	4,000
Stage of completion for conversion	20%	50%
Costs:		
Transferred in	$ 2,000	?
Materials	100	?
Conversion	200	?
Units transferred in during month	80,000	?
Units completed during month	?	45,000
Costs added during month:		
Materials	$ 4,000	$ 7,500
Conversion	39,800	25,300
Ending inventory:		
Units (number of books)	4,000	?
Stage of completion for conversion	50%	30%

Required:
1. Prepare cost of production reports for the Printing Department for each month.
2. Prepare cost of production reports for the Binding Department for each month.
3. Compare the unit costs for materials and conversion costs between the two months for each department. Comment.

6-19. Two Departments for Two Months. (Appendix) Work Problem 6-18 using the weighted average cost method.

6-20. Change in Units Between Departments. Artistic Beauty, Inc. has a fragrance division that manufactures men's after-shave. Each after-shave is processed through three departments: Blending, Cooking, and Bottling. The Blending Department mixes dry chemicals and spices according to a recipe. The resulting dry powder moves to the Cooking Department where liquid is added to the powder and the mixture is cooked. The hot liquid moves to the Bottling Department for cooling and bottling. The FIFO cost method is used in both departments. Operating data for December in Blending and Cooking are:

	Blending	Cooking
Work in process, December 1:		
Units	8,000 lbs.	5,000 gal.
Costs:		
Transferred in	-	$10,250
Materials	$ 3,600	800
Conversion costs	12,800	2,375
Units started or transferred in	82,000 lbs.	31,000 gal.
Units completed and transferred out	78,000 lbs.	32,500 gal.
Current period costs for the month:		
Materials	$ 38,700	$ 4,992
Conversion costs	124,160	29,906

The beginning inventory in the Blending Department was 20 percent complete. The ending inventory was 80 percent complete. Materials and conversion costs are added to Blending uniformly throughout the process.

Materials in the Cooking Department consist of distilled liquid and the powder from Blending. These are added at the start of the process. Overhead occurs evenly in the process. The beginning inventory was 50 percent complete and the ending inventory was 40 percent complete.

Required:
1. Prepare a cost of production report for the Blending Department.
2. Prepare a cost of production report for the Cooking Department.

CASE 6A–BOZEMAN HI-TECH PRODUCTS

Bozeman Hi-Tech Products manufactures a product that is accounted for under a process cost system in the assembly and finishing departments. Recently, the production superintendent was reviewing the cost of production reports for the two departments. His intuition suggested something was wrong with the reports. He asked the departmental managers if they had reviewed the reports to which they both said yes. However, both managers acknowledged that the reports must be in error because they didn't agree with the operating facts. One manager suggested the Accounting Department had screwed up again.

You have been asked to review the departmental cost of production reports and determine what adjustments should be made. You have the following information available to you:

	Assembly	Finishing
Units:		
Beginning inventory	10,000	12,000
Units started	20,000	?
Units completed and transferred	26,000	?
Ending inventory	4,000	10,000
Costs:		
Materials costs added	$22,000	$14,000
Labor costs	8,000	12,000

In the Assembly Department, materials are added at the beginning of the process and conversion costs enter evenly throughout the operation. Beginning work in process was 50 percent complete for conversion costs. Beginning inventories include $6,000 for material and $2,000 for conversion costs. Overhead is applied at the rate of 50 percent of labor dollars. Ending inventory was 40 percent completed. The FIFO method is used.

In the Finishing Department, materials are added at the end of the process. Conversion costs occur uniformly throughout operations. Beginning work in process in the Finishing Department was 75 percent complete for conversion costs. Beginning inventories include $10,000 for transferred-in costs and $10,000 for conversion costs. Overhead is applied at the rate of 100 percent of labor dollars. Ending inventory was estimated to be 25% complete. The FIFO method is used.

Excerpts from the cost of production reports are as follows:

Assembly Department:

Cost of goods completed (26,000 × $1.2667)		$32,934
Ending inventory:		
Materials (4,000 × $.9333)	$ 3,733	
Conversion costs (4,000 × $.3334)	1,333	5,066
Total costs accounted for		$38,000

Additional computations:

	Materials	Conversion Cost
Costs in process, beginning	$ 6,000	$ 2,000
Current period costs	22,000	12,000
	$28,000	$14,000
Computation of equivalent units:		
Units completed	26,000	26,000
Ending inventory	4,000	4,000
Equivalent units	30,000	30,000
Equivalent unit cost	$ .9333	$ .3333

Finishing Department:

Cost of goods completed		$59,790
Ending inventory:		
Transferred in (10,000 × $1.2667)	$12,667	
Material (10,000 × $.5385)	5,385	
Conversion costs (2,500 × $.4364)	1,091	19,143
Total costs accounted for		$78,933

Required:

1. Prepare a corrected cost of production report for the Assembly Department. Identify the errors, if any, in the original cost of production report.
2. Prepare a corrected cost of production report for the Finishing Department. Identify the errors, if any, in the original cost of production report.
3. Using T-accounts, make the necessary entries to correct the costs that are transferred from the Assembly Department to the Finishing department and from the Finishing Department to the finished goods inventory.

CASE 6B—GULF COAST PIPELINES

Gulf Coast Pipelines, Inc. is a liquid petroleum pipeline transportation company. The line running from Corpus Christi to Kansas City is a 30 inch, high pressure line which moves product at an average of 8 miles per hour. A filled line contains 28 million barrels of product which travel an average 192 miles per day. The line speed can be increased safely to about 280 miles per day or slowed to almost a stop. The line can be filled to capacity or be partially empty. Over certain segments the line moves faster than elsewhere as more product is placed in and taken out. The line carries various products including crude oil of varying weights, home heating oil, and numerous other petroleum products. As a transportation company, Gulf Coast Pipelines does not own the products transported. Instead, it is paid a fee for its services based on moving 10,000 barrels (420,000 gallons) of product 1 mile. The variable cost of running the line is for the 30 pumping stations along the line: the higher the traffic, the higher the fuel cost for pumping. The other cost of running the line is overhead cost, which relates to line maintenance. One unit is considered to be moving 10,000 barrels one mile.

On April 1, 1995, the Corpus Christi to Kansas City line had 1.44 million units in process (18 million barrels that were to be transported an average of 800 miles), which were 60% complete. During the month the line completed 12 million units of delivered product and had ending units in process of 2 million units (20 million barrels to be transported 1,000 miles) that were 40% complete. The beginning units in transit had accumulated costs of $8,800,000 of which $2,400,000 were variable costs. During the month, the Corpus Christi to Kansas City line had $33,420,800 in variable costs and $81,168,800 in fixed costs. The completed deliveries were billed at $134,400,000 for services.

Required:

1. What is the nature of the costs incurred as to direct materials, direct labor, variable or fixed overhead?
2. Why should this application be considered for a modified process cost system?
3. Compute the equivalent units of production for the Corpus Christi to Kansas City line. (Round to 4 places, if needed.)
4. Compute a cost per unit of output for variable and fixed costs.
5. What were the profits before administrative expenses and taxes during April 1995?
6. What were the costs of the units in transit on April 30, 1995?

Part Three

Planning and Control Framework

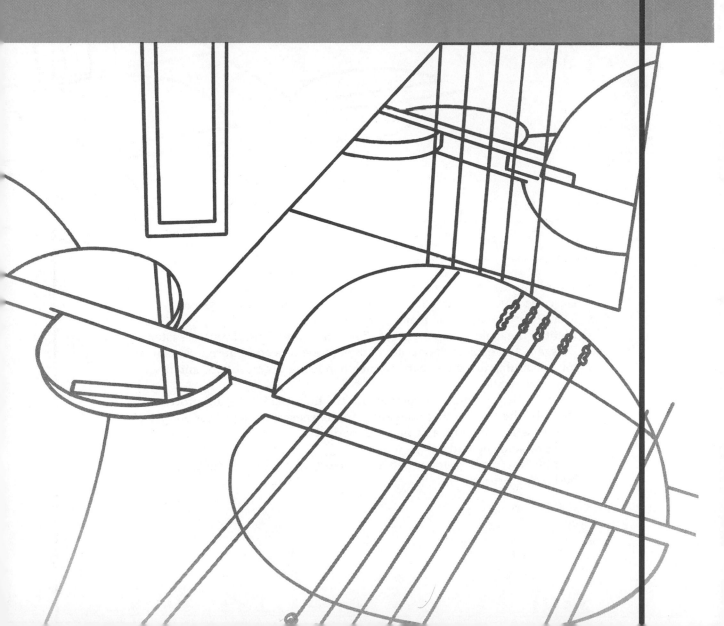

Chapter Seven

Budgeting For Operations

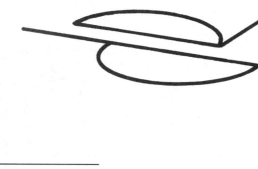

❖ *Chapter Objectives*

After studying Chapter 7, you will be able to:
1. Describe how budgeting fits into the planning and control system.
2. Identify and explain the major purposes of budgeting.
3. Identify the major components of a financial planning and control system.
4. Diagram and explain the master budget sequences and interrelationships for a manufacturing company, a merchandising organization, and a service organization.
5. Describe the operating budgeting and the financial budgeting processes.
6. Describe the use of other budgeting approaches such as project budgets, zero-based budgeting, and program budgets.
7. Use probabilistic budgeting.
8. Identify the major human behavior factors that affect budgets and the budgeting process.

To Budget or Not to Budget . . . The Answer is Clear!

Mention the words "planning" or "budgeting" to Marty Hartsock, president of Macon Industries, and you get a reaction ranging from disdain to outright hostility. She has been heard to say:

1. "How can I plan? Things always change so fast!"
2. "My business isn't suited to anything so formal. My managers and I need to be flexible, fast on our feet, and ready to change direction overnight, if need be."
3. "The budget always says we can't do it. I just say, 'Do it!' "
4. "The budget reports always tell me where I've been, never where I'm going."
5. "That's the accountant's budget; it doesn't tell me what my problems are and what to do about them!"
6. "We can't wait for approvals and variance reports. Budgets hold us back!"

Hartsock even has a coffee cup that has "Budgets Are For Wimps!" printed on it. She believes intuition and drive, not meaningless reports, are what got the company where it is today: "The easiest way to lose our edge is to start acting like paper shufflers!" she continues. Each of her comments could have some truth in it, but more likely the comments together reflect a serious deficiency in the firm's management process—little or no planning and little ability to measure performance.

A close friend says plans and budgets strike terror in Hartsock because her "style" is threatened. She likes to operate quickly and decisively, while keeping others in the dark. If she uses a budget, her underlying assumptions can be examined and questioned. Hartsock is afraid she might have to admit that she has no idea where the company is going and that her success has had nothing to do with brains or a superior product.

Recently, a situation arose where Hartsock thought employees were making too many "bad calls" on key decisions. She was surprised by the responses she got when she asked several department managers what was wrong. Each complained about indecisiveness at the top; how management kept changing its mind, and how even the simplest decisions were held up indefinitely. In the confusion, employees found it hard to have any sense of direction or get anything done.

Plans and budgets involve anticipating events, setting a plan of action, and taking action to ensure they impact the organization in the most favorable way. A simple but often misunderstood concept is the key to budgeting: planning is not deciding what to do in the future; it is deciding what to do now to assure a future. This chapter discusses the concepts, tools, and processes needed to develop a master budget.

BUDGETING: IMPLEMENTING PLANNING AND CONTROL

Planning and control consists of an overall process with budgeting being an important part. **Planning** can be viewed as a framework within which managers anticipate future events, develop a plan of action, and estimate future revenues and costs. **Control** is the process of using feedback on actual operations to report results versus plan, to evaluate performance, and to measure achievement of plans and goals and deviations from policies. We define a **budget** as a plan showing how resources are to be acquired and used over a specified time period.

A fundamental ingredient needed to get budgeting off to a successful start is management's interest in setting goals and objectives. **Goals and objectives** are statements about the desired position of the organization in the future or about the direction important variables should take in determining the long-term destiny of the organization. They not only describe specific performance targets but also give calendar dates by which desired performance should be attained. A profit goal might be, for example, to earn an annual 15 percent after-tax return on stockholders' equity or to generate an annual 10 percent growth in sales.

Once the goals (direction and motivations) and objectives (quantified performance targets) are set, desired outputs have largely been identified. Now, the budgeting process determines the inputs of various activities needed to achieve the projected overall outputs.

The Relationship Between Planning and Budgeting

Planning identifies a desired output while budgeting identifies inputs needed to achieve that output. Thus, management uses the planning process to establish programs, make basic policies, and set goals and objectives for the overall organization. Budgeting, as a part of the planning process, coordinates the details of the many activities needed to implement the programs that meet the company's goals and objectives.

Figure 7.1 shows two bands linked together. The inner band is the basic management process of planning, acting, evaluating and controlling, and giving feedback. The outer band shows the budgeting cycle of building the master budget, recording and classifying data about actual results, preparing and using performance reports, and updating the budgeting process. At each inner circle step, managers must use the outer circle tools to plan and control. The outer boxes must be designed to meet the needs of the managers at each stage.

Another observation is that the bands are complete circles and continuous over time. In a normal system, the plan will determine actions; actions generate performance results, and results are evaluated and create the basis for revising the budget in the next cycle.

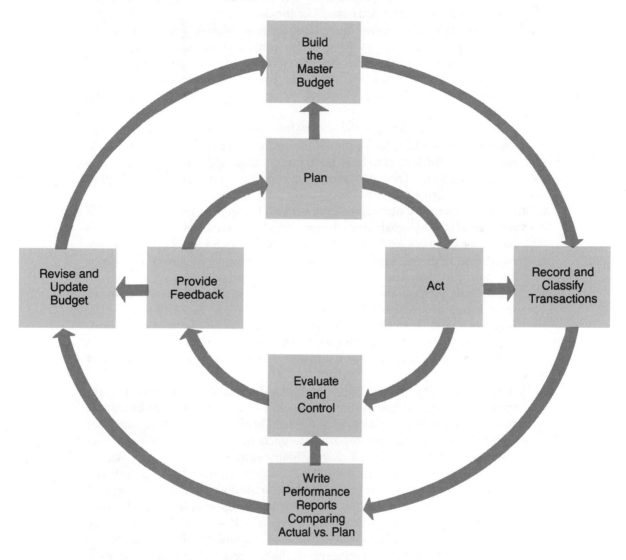

Figure 7.1   Interaction of the Managerial Process and the Budgeting System Process

A Planning and Control System

Describing planning and control can be a nebulous task. A common set of techniques includes most, if not all, of the following tools and processes:

1. **A strategic planning process**. This formal long-range planning effort must define the firm's **mission** (why the firm exists), the **long-range goals** (what level of achievement it hopes to enjoy), and a **strategic plan** (what markets, products, price policies, resource needs, and production capabilities the firm will have). Strategic and long run are not synonymous, but most strategic plans lay out goals, directions, and resource needs for a 3-to-5 year time frame or longer.

2. **A set of goals, objectives, and planning assumptions for annual planning.** The strategic plan is divided into annual segments. The most current year in the strategic plan is the basis for the master budget. Specific annual goals and objectives that move the firm toward the longer run strategic goals form the planning targets for the annual budgeting process.

3. **A business plan**. Creating the annual business plan is the task of evaluating the firm's goals, its strengths, its business opportunities, its weaknesses, and the tactics to be used to build a firm-wide set of priorities for the coming year. This plan should be consistent with the strategic plan developed above.

4. **A management by objectives system (MBO)**. An MBO system personalizes the firm-wide goals to each manager. Each manager develops a personal set of goals and plan of achievements to be fulfilled which are consistent with the firm-wide plans. Each manager is committed to his or her own program and to the firm's overall plans and goals.

5. **A planning process and timetable**. A time schedule for budgeting would include dates for starting the process, for submitting first and succeeding budgets drafts, for reviews and approvals at various levels of the firm, and for final review and approval by the president or board of directors of the firm. Basically, the formal process establishes who does what and when.

6. **A responsibility accounting system**. As discussed in Chapter 3, a responsibility accounting system is needed to establish responsibility and control for revenues, costs, and assets. Through this system, data are collected, classified, and reported to each manager and for each segment. The system includes responsibility centers as cost, profit, or investment centers; a detailed chart of accounts or data bases to capture relevant data elements in every transaction; and a reporting system that links revenues and costs to the controlling manager and compares budget to actual dollars on a periodic and year-to-date basis. The reporting system should have a roll-up capability that summarizes for each higher level of management the lower-level managers' performances.

7. **A performance evaluation feedback and follow-up process that uses periodic control reports and budget data to compare actual and budgeted items by area of responsibility**. Explanation of variances from budget is required along with recommended management actions needed to correct problem areas.

8. **A process for updating the budget**. No budget can be approved and forgotten. Actual events differ from the plan. For example, in banking, interest rates are forecast but often move in a different direction. In manufacturing, materials costs may increase dramatically. In sales, a major customer may expand or contract. All of these create a need to update or revise the budget. Many firms have a formal updating cycle, either semi-annually, quarterly, or even monthly. An update is often called a **rolling update (or continuous budget)**. As another month of actual results arrives (say March of 1994), a new month of forecast is added (March of 1995). A twelve-month planning horizon is always maintained.

9. **A reward or bonus system**. Rewards can provide incentives for managers who achieve their unit's budget goals and/or their personal planning goals or MBO targets. Tying performance to compensation appears to be an increasingly common practice.

10. **Financial modeling**. Capabilities for computer generated "what if" scenarios are now nearly a requirement of any financial planning system. The ability to test a financial plan by changing key variables allows managers to find a feasible plan that meets the firm's goals and objectives without laborious trial and error methods of the past. Computer power and software capabilities now make simulating nearly every aspect of the plan fast and economical.

11. **Participatory budgeting**. It is assumed that every manager in the firm is involved in the planning and control system. Once the goals, objectives, and **planning assumptions** are handed down from the executive level, plans and budgets are constructed from the bottom up. This is sometimes called "grass roots" budgeting. Interactive cycles of plan, review, and change may flow up and down the organization to arrive at an acceptable budget that all levels can approve. Participation applies to planning, execution of the plan, and evaluation of the results.

The length of the budget period may be a week, a month, a quarter, a year, or even more than a year. The duration depends on how the budget is to be used. Normally, a budget is made for a year and is divided into months or quarters of a year. A budget for the acquisition of capital investments may be made for 5 or more years into the future. The plans for later years will probably be somewhat indefinite, because they are based on long-term prospects. With the passage of time, the plans should be revised to reflect current conditions.

Purposes of Budgeting

Some form of budgeting is important to all organizations. The advantages of budgeting almost always clearly outweigh the costs and efforts required by the process. Although many reasons for budgeting can be cited, the key purposes are:

1. To formalize the planning process.
2. To create a basis for performance evaluation.

3.   To coordinate and integrate management's efforts by focusing on goals and objectives.
4.   To create a plan of action.
5.   To identify constraints and realities.
6.   To aid in resource allocation.
7.   To create an "aura of control."
8.   To help motivate managers and employees positively.

Formalize the Planning Process   Perhaps the foremost advantage of budgeting is that it forces managers to think ahead. A look into the future invariably compels top management to set goals and objectives. Middle and lower managers are then led to consider current problems, as well as problems which may develop in the future, and to formulate approaches for coping with them.

Budgeting tends to move an organization from a reactionary mode, in which management simply reacts to problems, to an anticipation mode, in which problems are foreseen and positive action is taken. Too often, without budgeting, managers operate as fire fighters —solving one emergency after another. They simply have no time for planning beyond today and tomorrow, nor for looking for positive measures and preventative actions.

Create a Basis for Performance Evaluation   Any actual result is meaningless unless it is compared to a target, a plan, or a budgeted number. A budget is a benchmark against which we can measure actual results and evaluate managers' performances. Significant variances between actual and planned results may require explanations and, often, corrective action by the manager responsible for the activities.

One major benefit of a benchmark is that managers will know what is expected of them. To the extent that managers actively participate in the decisions built into a budget, they carve out their own tasks and establish benchmarks against which they will be measured. As a basis for judging performance, budgeted activity is regarded as far more relevant than historical data. The major drawback of using historical data is that inefficiencies in past performance may be concealed and allowed to continue. Also, changes in economic conditions, technology, competition, and personnel make comparisons of present with past performance invalid. Carefully budgeted data are more realistic for performance evaluation because the budget sets the level of desired performance. The manager can work toward these levels.

The planning activity also provides a basis for reporting actuals. If sales are planned along product lines, the actual results should be reported by product lines. If budgets are prepared in each cost center, reports should be designed around the cost center structure.

Evaluation of performance must occur at several levels. First, performance evaluation at the managerial level occurs where controllable revenue and expenses are measured. This segment is also evaluated using direct revenue and expenses. The firm as a whole is also evaluated. Generally, budgeting follows controllability; but often traceability is also included in budget preparation and evaluation.

Coordinate and Integrate Management's Efforts   Coordination and integration involve the meshing and balancing of an organization's resources so that overall goals and objectives are attained. The budget is the plan of action for the entire organization and must reflect the coordinated efforts of all segments of the organization. The budgeting process demands that managers open up lines of communication within the organization: (1) up and down organizational lines from subordinates to supervisors and (2) across organizational lines between managers of various functions.

In upward communication, the budgeting process provides the mechanism for a manager to communicate needs to higher management levels. In downward communication, top management spells out the goals and objectives of the firm and its expectations of individual managers.

Coordination across organizational lines is necessary due to the interdependence of activities. For example, purchasing managers integrate their plans with production requirements; production managers use the sales budget to help them anticipate and plan for materials, employees, and productive facilities; and personnel must know the needs of all departments before it can plan for employee recruitment and training.

Create a Plan of Action   The planning process brings together ideas, forecasts, resource availabilities, and financial realities to create a plan that meets the firm's goals and objectives. Now what? Use it! Make decisions that implement the plan. Follow the budgeted marketing plan, schedule production according to the sales and production plans, and buy materials according to the materials needs budget. The master budget is not an accountant's toy. It should be the operating bible for all managers in the firm. Sure, conditions change. The budget will need updating regularly, but it must be a plan that is "bought into" by all managers—top, middle, and lower levels. Building a budget and then putting it on a shelf waste the resources put into the budget creation effort, and budgeting is not cheap. It also means that managers retreat to a "seat of the pants" management style that loses the benefits of a coordinated and goal-directed benchmark for performance evaluation.

Identify Constraints and Realities   Every organization has some aspect of its activities that is a bottleneck to completing goals and objectives successfully. One machine may operate slower than the preceding machines feeding into it; a service department may suffer high absenteeism; or a hotel cannot remake rooms fast enough. Whatever the constraint, budgeting helps identify it and provides management with an opportunity to plan how to resolve it. If not treated in advance, these constraints become likely spots for unanticipated emergencies and "fire fighting."

Also, a change in one area can easily create tremendous conflicts or operating inefficiencies in other parts of the firm. Now is the time to test loads, links between activities, staffing priorities, the reasonableness of assumptions, and goal attainment. Dollarizing plans forces reality onto planners. Managers must make difficult choices when resources are scarce. Compromises, trade-offs, and actual rejection of attractive alternatives may be needed to build a plan that is achievable, is consistent with the long-range goals, and meets the current year's goals.

Aid in Resource Allocation   "We'll do this if we get budget approval." "If I get the budget 'green light' to hire another person, we can tackle your project." "If I can convince my boss to budget more funds for marketing, we can expand our market penetration." These are very typical managerial comments about getting or losing resources. Budget time is when many resources are allocated or reallocated. Once an allocation is in a budget or not in a budget, the dollars are hard to move or to change. While seemingly a mere accounting task, the budget process, if handled properly, can be a powerful managerial tool for rewarding past achievements and selecting the most promising future uses of funds.

Generally, resources (people, money, time, equipment, etc.) are in short supply and must be rationed to the highest bidders. The bids are often promises of profits. For example, if $1 spent in Department A could earn $3 but that same $1 could be spent in Department B to earn $4, we would select Department B's project. Many other factors come into play. Many times the budget approval process is the main hurdle to get new funds or to keep existing levels of funding.

Create an "Aura of Control"   The expression "in control" can mean many things; but, in a management sense, it implies that an organization has an effective set of controls in place to ensure that its managers understand their authority and limits. They understand their responsibilities and execute them. A budget system can serve as a disciplinarian or "cop" for fiscal issues in the firm. An "aura of control" means that employees feel that management has control over business activities and that policies are in place and followed. Budget approval to spend, budget control reports on spending, and budget change approvals are all part of the psychology of budgets.

As in other areas, too much of a good thing can kill an organization. Too much dependence on budget authority can stifle creativity, can block necessary managerial actions, and can cause a manager to "choke on a gnat" while an "elephant" of a problem is ignored.

Help Motivate Managers and Employees Positively   A budget system can often have a negative image: it's hard work to create the budget; nobody cares about the budget; and only bad things happen when budget reports appear. Ah, but now the good news:

1.   People who help to prepare budgets for their area will have a commitment to the budget and take pride in achieving "their" plan.

2. Through the budget, managers can see how their part of the puzzle fits with all the other pieces to form the whole—the firm-wide plan.

3. A fair and active budget review, approval, and follow-up process tell managers that a "work hard, keep your head up, keep your nose clean, and good things will happen" attitude works.

4. Promotions and raises should be based on job performance, and achieving budget goals and objectives is a major part of that job evaluation.

5. Many firms have incentive systems in place that reward managers for strong performance, including achieving budgeted goals and targets.

Managers must work at making the budgeting process meaningful as a guide to action and as a performance benchmark. Rewards for achieving or exceeding goals should be equally as important as chastisement for falling below the target. Managerial attitudes play a tremendous role in determining how the budgeting system is viewed by each manager and employee. The goal should be to have the system pay dividends to itself by using the planning and control system to promote improved teamwork, more involvement in improving processes, and achieving greater goal congruency throughout the organization.

Budget Preparation

In budgeting, all functions and activities of the business are carefully interlocked. Plans for the manufacturing division must be tied to plans for the sales division. If large shipments are to be made to customers during particular months, the manufacturing division should have the products ready at that time. At a still earlier date, the materials to be used in production have to be ordered, allowing enough time for their receipt from suppliers and their use in manufacturing. This concept of timing and coordinating activities applies in all areas of budgeting.

A budget is prepared by combining the efforts of many individuals. Those who are in charge of a particular function or activity make up the budget estimates. Estimates for individual departments or divisions are adjusted and consolidated into one budget for the entire function. For instance, sales estimates may be made by regional sales managers, with the approved estimates being combined into one sales estimate for the company. At the same time, several functions, such as sales, production, product engineering, purchasing, and so forth, are coordinated so that all of the budgets fit together properly using a common set of key activity variables.

Ordinarily, individuals prepare budgets for their own departments or responsibility centers. This self-created budget has certain distinct advantages, as follows:

1. The person closest to an activity should be able to make reliable estimates.

2. The person who makes the estimate tends to feel like a member of the team.

3.   The person who feels like a team member will make every effort to fulfill a self-created budget.

4.   The person is forced to assume the responsibility for performance—a built-in control mechanism of the self-created budget.

The self-created budget, however, is not necessarily approved as originally presented. If too much freedom is allowed, the budget may offer no challenge. It can also offer an opportunity for undeserved credit for favorable budget comparisons. Before budgets are accepted, they are reviewed by higher levels of management. If changes are to be made, they can be discussed, and compromises can be reached that are acceptable to all concerned.

The person in immediate contact with an activity is in a good position to make budget estimates. However, an individual whose energy is devoted to one thing may have a narrow viewpoint or exaggerate the activity's importance, forgetting that it is only a part of a larger activity. For instance, a regional salesperson may wonder why a product line that has sold successfully has been discontinued. The top executive group, however, may have discovered that the sales and profits in total were not sufficient to justify continued production.

Top management and the lower levels of management work together to produce the budget. As a general rule, those who are in higher positions are not familiar with the details of an activity and depend on their subordinates for underlying information. On the other hand, the top executives of the firm know more about the business as a whole, are better informed with respect to the general business outlook, and take a broader point of view.

MASTER BUDGET—AN OVERVIEW

The annual budgeting effort is commonly called the **master budget** or, in some firms, the **profit plan** or **comprehensive budget.** Although a master budget usually covers a one-year period in detail, it may be prepared on a month-by-month basis for the year and may extend in summary form several years into the future. For whatever period of time, the master budget begins with a sales budget and concludes with pro forma financial statements.

This section reviews the ingredients that make up a master budget for manufacturing and for nonmanufacturing companies.

Master Budget for a Manufacturer

Master budget terminology and classifications may differ among manufacturing organizations, but we will use the terms and classifications to describe the master budget and its supporting schedules as shown in Figure 7.2. In Chapter 8, a comprehensive example is developed which illustrates each schedule and its format. Figure 7.2 references the appropriate Chapter 8 illustration.

THE STRUCTURE OF A MASTER BUDGET FOR A MANUFACTURER

I. Annual Goals and Planning Assumptions
  A. Operating and financial goals
  B. Planning assumptions
    1. Product cost and price data (Schedule 1)
    2. Operating activity assumptions (Schedule 2)
    3. Financial activity assumptions (Schedule 3)
    4. Beginning balance sheet data (Schedule 3)

II. Operating Budget
  A. Sales forecast and budget (Schedule 4)
  B. Production plan for the plant and schedules for cost centers (Schedule 5)
  C. Manufacturing cost budgets by cost center
    1. Direct materials requirements and purchases budgets (Schedules 6 & 7)
    2. Direct labor budget (Schedule 8)
    3. Manufacturing overhead budgets
      (a) Flexible manufacturing overhead budget (Schedule 9)
      (b) Operating manufacturing overhead budget (Schedule 10)
  D. Supporting Schedules
    1. Accounts receivable—credit and collections (Schedule 11)
    2. Inventories—levels and valuation (Schedule 12)
    3. Accounts payable—purchases and payments (Schedule 13)
  E. Cost of goods manufactured and sold schedule (Schedule 14)
  F. Operating expenses budgets
    1. Selling expenses budget (Schedule 15)
    2. Administrative expenses budget (Schedule 16)
  G. Cash flow forecast—receipts, disbursements, and cash balance (Schedule 18)

III. Project Budgets (Schedule 17)
  A. Capital expenditures budget
  B. Research and development budget
  C. Other special budgets

IV. Forecast Financial Statements
  A. Forecast statement of income and expense
  B. Forecast balance sheet
  C. Forecast statement of cash flows

Figure 7.2   The Master Budget Structure

The interrelationships among master budget components are shown on the flowchart in Figure 7.3.

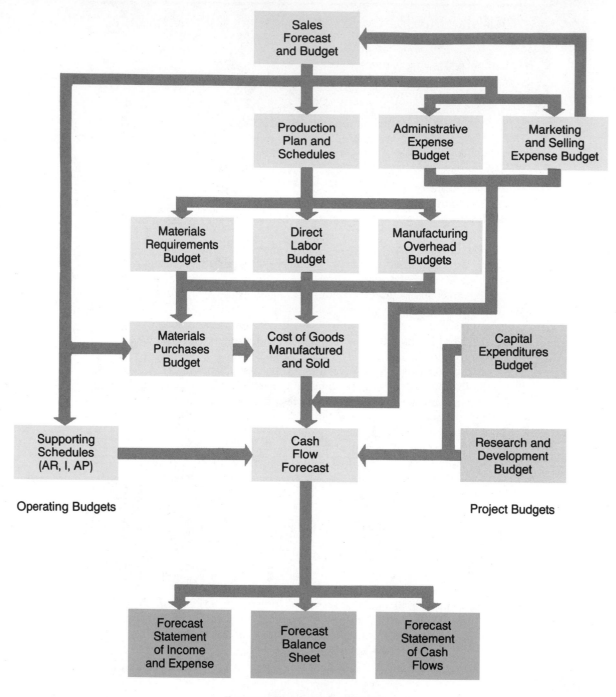

Figure 7.3 Components of the Master Budget

Operating Budgets   The **operating budget** is a formal document that summarizes the expected results of an organization's revenue and expense transactions for a future period, usually one year. The cash flow forecast brings together all the events that generate and use cash. The summary of the operating budget is the forecast financial statements for the year. All of the budgets within the operating budget are, in effect, supporting schedules to the forecast statement of cash flow and the income statement.

The day-to-day activities of any business are the operating activities—those activities performed in conducting the daily affairs of the business. These activities are interdependent parts of the operating cycle. The operating cycle is illustrated by following a circular sequence of events from the purchase of materials on account to paying those bills with cash collected from sales to customers. The cycle, as shown in Figure 7.4, can be thought of as "cash to cash."

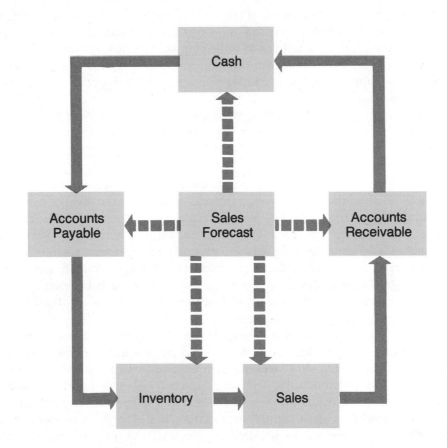

Figure 7.4   The Operating Cycle

A manufacturing or merchandising company must have inventory to sell. In merchandising, purchases of inventory are generally financed through payables, although direct cash purchases occasionally occur. In manufacturing, materials and manufacturing overhead are often financed through payables. Cash is used to pay for labor and to liquidate the payables.

Sales relieve finished goods inventory and create receivables. The company ships the goods, invoices customers, and at some point collects cash. Once receivables are collected, cash is available to renew the cycle. In the process of converting inventories into cash through sales, the company hopes to generate a sufficient gross margin to cover selling and administrative expenses and to provide for profit.

The sales forecast is at the center of the operating cycle because it influences the targets set for managing the cycle. For example, the sales forecast determines the need for minimum cash and inventory levels; it impacts decisions on when to make purchases and to incur payables; and it helps determine the credit terms needed to generate sales and control receivables.

Detailed budgets for various cost centers and accounts support the summarized budgets. For example, a cash flow budget for March can be broken down into weekly cash flow schedules to anticipate payroll dates, loan payments, and other critical short-term cash flow dates. Detailed weekly or even daily production plans by specific machine or person are developed from the basic monthly plan.

All of the activities within the operating cycle form the crux of the income statement. Consequently, the operating budget is the heart of the master budget.

Cash Flow Forecast   Cash forecasting is an integral part of cash management. **Cash management** is planning and controlling the level of cash balances over a specified time interval. Cash planning has many time frames. Often, three can be identified: long-term cash flow planning, annual cash forecasting, and short-term daily or weekly cash management. Cash balances in most organizations consist of transaction cash, accommodation cash, and excess cash. These distinctions are not often used in cash budgeting or in financial reporting, but they are important to the treasurer of an organization who is responsible for cash management.

Transaction cash is the cash balance required to carry on operations. The organization usually looks to collections on receivables and cash sales as major sources of operating cash. Operating cash expenditures are mostly payables and payroll. **Accommodation cash** refers to cash balances kept in financial institutions to pay for financial services received. The level of accommodation cash is influenced by many factors, such as the types of banking services used, the volumes of transactions handled by the financial institutions, and the specific fees paid for services. Cash balances in excess of operating cash and accommodation cash are referred to as **excess cash**. Obviously, the opposite situation also exists and could be called a cash deficit, which must be covered by reduced spending, increased collections, or borrowings.

Idle cash is a nonearning asset. The objective of an organization is to maintain cash balances as low as possible yet meet operating needs. Firms want to speed up collections and defer cash payments. Methods of lowering cash balances include centralizing cash management, using bank lock boxes for collections, shortening the time between shipment and invoicing, and rescheduling payment dates.

The treasurer will generally invest excess cash in highly liquid and secure temporary investments with income potential. A business may have excess cash at some time during the year because of seasonal sales patterns and anticipation of major cash outflows, such as capital expenditures, taxes, and dividend or interest payments.

Any organization providing products or services to customers must have cash flow to survive. For example, a public relations firm provides a variety of services to its clients; but it must pay for salaries, travel, support services, rent, and other costs. Clients are billed but wait another 30 days to pay. Thus, it is possible that a firm collects cash 30, 60, or 90 days after paying many of its expenses. A means of financing these timing differences must be arranged. Lines of credit and other borrowing arrangements are prearranged to make cash available when needed.

A cash flow forecast in its simplest form is nothing more than a list of cash inflows and outflows by time period. The level of detail is determined by the time period, the supporting schedules available, and the need for the information.

Project Budgets   While the time frame of most budgeting activities is 12 months, a variety of activities use a **project budget**. The task being budgeted might take three months, two years, or five years to complete. Examples of these activities are capital expenditures such as new construction or equipment replacement, research and development programs, and information systems development projects. Many run three, five, or even ten years into the future. The project budgets can have major impacts on planned cash flows and on the forecast income statement and balance sheet. Capital expenditures budgets are discussed in Chapters 12 and 13.

Forecast Financial Statements   The **forecast financial statements** focus on the financial results of the operating budget and project budgets. These are the forecast statement of income and expense, the balance sheet, and the statement of cash flows. Details of financial statement forecasting are discussed in the next chapter. The statement of cash flows is discussed in additional detail in Chapter 18.

Master Budget for a Nonmanufacturing Company

How does a master budget differ for a merchandising or service organization? The budgeting concepts used by a manufacturer are essentially the same. However, nonmanufacturing company differences do exist, and the major ones are summarized on the next page.

Merchandising Organization   A merchandising operation is a distribution point without the worries and complexities of producing a product. Consequently, the merchandiser has no need for a production budget or a manufacturing cost budget with their supporting budgets for direct materials, direct labor, and factory overhead. Instead, a purchasing budget—which incorporates consideration of merchandise inventories—is a major focus in budgeting. Although a cost of goods manufactured budget is no longer needed, most merchandising companies will concentrate on a gross margin (gross profit) budget, which combines the sales and cost of goods sold budgets. Operating expenses may be different in nature in the merchandising organization, but the functional classifications of selling and administrative expenses remain. The basic difference between a master budget for a manufacturer and a merchandiser is in the activities budgeted between the sales budget and the cost of goods sold budget.

Service Organization   A service organization is similar to a merchandiser and goes through much the same budgeting process. But without a physical product to sell, the typical concerns about the purchasing budget or about inventories are not present. A cost of services budget may be prepared, but a common approach is to budget labor and overhead as a part of operating expenses.

Budgets for many service firms such as engineering and design firms, advertising agencies, accounting and legal firms, and even a wide array of retail companies will budget revenues by project, by client or customer, or by service line. Project-oriented firms may well budget very much like manufacturing companies except that materials will likely become a supply or overhead item. The service is much like a product. Labor or professional salaries will be the dominant cost budgeted. Also, overhead budgets for client support personnel and other "product" expenses will be budgeted like manufacturing overhead with overhead charged directly to a project or applied like manufacturing overhead on an activity basis. The cost of services budget could well look like the cost of goods manufactured budget in a factory setting.

THE STARTING POINT

Successful budgeting rests on strong and visible support of planning by top management. If executives emphasize planning, updating and revising budgets, and evaluating performances using budget comparisons, other managers will see that financial planning and control are major parts of the "corporate culture." Planning will become part of a manager's instinctive acts.

In reality, the starting point in preparing the master budget is the planning necessary to begin. Thus, the controller's office personnel sets the wheels in motion by preparing forms, schedules, and supporting forecast data. The executive officers often meet to set goals, targets, and assumptions. This is planning to plan. But the starting point of the actual planning cycle must be determined. What is planned first?

Finding the Controlling Constraint

Regardless of the organization, the starting point of the budget effort should be the most constraining variable. Generally, this is sales. Most firms are working to generate more sales. But other variables might be more limiting in specific cases, such as:

1. Machine capacity in a specialized production area (plastic extruding equipment in a plastic bottle plant).
2. Skilled personnel in a labor-intensive or high technology area (tax accountants in an accounting firm or skilled die makers in a tool and die shop).
3. Floor space in a retail outlet in a key high-traffic location (the first floor in a major downtown department store).
4. Salespersons' time used to make calls on customers (traveling sales reps who must decide which customers to call on and how frequently to demonstrate new products).
5. Tables in a restaurant (where demand for reservations cannot be met).
6. Seats in a theater (where the seating capacity is generally reached for most shows offered).

Most of the nonsales constraints are temporary or self-imposed. Often, seasonal sales peaks exceed normal capacity. Also, equipment or personnel limits can be eliminated by buying or hiring more resources. When a variable other than sales constrains a firm's operation, it becomes the starting point for planning. Maximizing the profitability of floor space in a retail store means eliminating items that may sell well but generate low margins. Contribution margin per square foot will be the starting point in retail forecasting.

However, the sales variable continues to be the primary limiting factor over years and across most firms.

Sales Forecasting

A realistic sales budget serves as a keystone for the master budget, as can be seen from the master budget flowchart in Figure 7.3 and the operating cycle diagram in Figure 7.4. The activities and the budgets for all phases of the business operation are influenced by sales. Plant production is geared to the expected demands of customers as set forth in a sales budget, and the cost of selling the product and administering the business is also planned in relation to sales activity. Selling expenses such as advertising, travel, and entertainment are not only dependent upon sales activity but also help to create it. Thus, a certain degree of interdependence exists. Capital expenditures, on the other hand, are only indirectly related to the sales of any one year. Ordinarily, long-range plans for asset acquisitions are not curtailed because of estimates of reduced sales in any given year. The plans, however, may be postponed or revised if little prospect exists for sales recovery over the long run.

The **sales forecast** is based on a variety of interlocking factors, such as pricing policy, the general economic outlook, conditions within the industry, governmental policies, historical patterns, and the position of the company in the economy. In relatively large companies, an economic forecasting department or a division of the controller's department devotes its full time to economic forecasting, with forecasts prepared not only for the immediate future, but for five to ten years ahead.

A sales forecast can be built using data from many sources. The major sources are presented here:

1.   **Analysis of historical sales to create trends and a momentum forecast.** If past sales were 10,000 units, future sales should be 10,000 plus a growth percentage. Knowing sales trends over time can form the basis for setting sales targets for future periods. Recognizing product life cycles, seasonal patterns, customer growth patterns, and past product sales results allows marketing managers to bring their knowledge and experience of the market place to bear on the forecasting task.

2.   **Grass roots forecasts by customers and by products prepared by salespersons.** Building a sales forecast by estimating sales by customer for all products that a customer buys or by products for all buyers of that product is a common approach for companies that have sales staffs. This empirically created estimate of sales is truly linking specific customer demand to the forecast. Salespersons may even ask customers for input—what each one expects to purchase over the coming year. Specific sales budgets can be set by product and by customer. Sales from past years can be detailed to provide one basis for estimating possible future sales. The regional sales managers and salespeople can prepare sales estimates for the coming year in light of past sales and their expectations of the future.

3.   **Statistical analysis of sales and economic data.** Time series and correlation analysis can be used to look at variables over time and in relation to other variables. Sales forecasts are sometimes made on this more scientific basis by fitting the business activity of the company to published indexes and reports on the economy at large. A given company may find that its activity tends to follow the Federal Reserve Board's Index, statistics on bank deposits, national disposable income, consumer spending indices, population trends, and so forth. Computer models are used to analyze diverse information in many combinations and test the findings for validity. Various factors that have a bearing on sales can be brought together in weighted formulas. Experimentation and computer testing reveal whether or not the statistical weights used in any of the formulas are valid. If a reasonable degree of correlation is found in any formula tested, that formula may be used in estimating the sales potential.

4. **Market research analysis of promotion and sales efforts, market structure, and market share.** Market research examines the potential market and strategies to reach the market and obtain specific market share objectives. Promotional and advertising resources are budgeted to obtain the maximum sales or maximum contribution margin given the expenditures. The objective is to reach the point where the marginal cost of promotion is equal to the marginal revenue generated.

Many factors operate to complicate sales forecasting. A company may appear at first to fit into a particular industry grouping, yet upon closer examination it may be found that the company handles many different lines of products and has the attributes of several industries. In addition, products may be sold through various channels in different countries. Some products, such as food and clothing, are sold to the consumer; while other products are indirectly related to consumer demand. For example, basic products such as glass, steel, and aluminum are not sold to the consumer directly but are used in the manufacture of other products. The demand for basic products that are used in making other products is said to be a **derived demand** Sales forecasts for these products depend on forecasts and data prepared for other industries. If products are sold to automobile manufacturers, then the demand is derived from forecasts of new car sales.

These approaches are not independent. More than likely, all are brought to bear on the forecasting problem. Each different method tests the assumptions and the data of the others. When put together by sales and marketing management, the marketing plan and the sales forecast are interdependent. Figure 7.3 shows the cross linkage. Sales forecasting is part science and part art. But responsibility for the forecast must be set, since many plans, decisions, and actions result from the agreed upon sales budget.

Formatting Budget Schedules

Structure and format simplify the preparation of budget schedules. Aligning time periods in columns and flowing information sequentially keep the tremendous amount of data organized and understandable. Once an item is budgeted for one time period, a pattern is established for the remaining time periods. Often, data from one time period (or column) are needed in a prior or following time period (column). For example, assume that:

1. Sales for the first four months of 1995 are forecast to be $50,000, $60,000, $70,000, and $80,000 respectively.
2. Cost of sales is 60 percent.
3. Beginning inventory is $20,000.
4. Ending inventory is to be budgeted at 40 percent of next month's cost of sales.

The format and data for forecasting purchases for the first quarter are:

	January	February	March	April
Sales	$50,000	$60,000	$70,000	$80,000
Cost of sales (60 percent)	30,000	36,000	42,000	48,000
Product needs:				
Cost of sales	$30,000	$36,000	$42,000	
Ending inventory (40 % of next				
month's cost of sales)	14,400	16,800	19,200	
Total needs....................	$44,400	$52,800	$61,200	
Product supply:				
Less beginning inventory	20,000	14,400	16,800	
Required purchases	$24,400	$38,400	$44,400	

Now let us assume that the sales will be collected as follows: 60 percent in the month of sale, 20 percent in the month after the sale, and 18 percent in the second month after the sale. Uncollectables are estimated to be 2 percent of sales. The beginning accounts receivable balance is $40,000, made up of 25 percent November sales and 75 percent December sales.

The format and data for cash receipts forecasting for the same three months of 1995 are as follows:

	January	February	March
Cash collections of receivables:			
November sales:			
[($40,000 × .25) ÷ .20] × .18	$ 9,000		
December sales:			
[($40,000 × .75) ÷ .40] × .20 and × .18	15,000	$ 13,500	
January sales:			
$50,000 × .60 and × .20 and × .18....	30,000	10,000	$ 9,000
February sales:			
$60,000 × .60 and × .20		36,000	12,000
March sales:			
$70,000 × .60			42,000
Total cash collected from sales	$ 54,000	$ 59,500	$63,000

The key to formatting budget schedules is to organize data by columns and rows. The January column contains all data needed to find cash collections for January. The January sales row is converted into cash collections for each month that cash is to be received and is shown in the January, February, and March columns. This columnar format can be carried through all master budget schedules.

Often, budget schedules are measured in physical units and not dollars. For example, unit sales are forecast to be 10,000, 12,000, 13,000, 15,000, and 14,000 for the first five months of 1996. Production could also be set in units. First, let us assume that inventory of finished units should be 40 percent of next month's sales. Sales and ending inventory create the required needs. Purchases and beginning inventory meet the needs. The beginning inventory on January 1, 1996 is 4,000 units. For the first four months, the format would be:

PRODUCTION PLAN
(IN UNITS)

	January	February	March	April	May
Production needed:					
Sales	10,000	12,000	13,000	15,000	14,000
Ending inventory	4,800	5,200	6,000	5,600	
Total needed	14,800	17,200	19,000	20,600	
Less beginning inventory	4,000	4,000	5,200	6,000	
Required production	10,800	13,200	13,800	14,600	

Other approaches to production planning could be formatted. Assume that production managers decided to produce at an even rate over the first four months and let inventory fluctuate from month to month, but not let the quarterly beginning and ending inventory figure change. The production and inventory plan in units would appear as follows:

PRODUCTION AND INVENTORY PLAN
(IN UNITS)

	January	February	March	April	Total
Production (50,000 ÷ 4) . . .	12,500	12,500	12,500	12,500	50,000
Sales	10,000	12,000	13,000	15,000	50,000
Change in inventory	2,500	500	(500)	(2,500)	0
Add beginning inventory	4,000	6,500	7,000	6,500	4,000
Ending inventory	6,500	7,000	6,500	4,000	4,000

Notice that the production plan format changes to meet the planning needs but the columnar structure continues. Also, a logic of working down through the planning problem keeps the data organized and ready for other schedules and later columns. For example, the production in units found above will be needed in the materials requirements and purchases schedules, direct labor schedule, and manufacturing overhead schedules.

Links among schedules require an order and sequential set of calculations. A typical pattern is sales determine production, production determines materials needs, materials needs determine materials purchases, purchases determine cash disbursements for payables, cash disbursements help determine the need for borrowings, and borrowings finally determine interest expense and interest payments.

Occasionally, circular reasoning, where A depends on the value of B and B depends on the value of A, arises. For example, the amount of cash we need to borrow may well depend on the interest we need to pay on the money we borrow. Planning assumptions may be needed to eliminate these problems. Often, when working on spreadsheet software, you are warned that the formulas have circular reason which should be corrected to avoid errors in the forecast numbers.

The example presented in Chapter 8 uses these formatting guides and calculation sequences and can be used for illustrations of particular schedules.

Independent and Dependent Variables

The planning assumptions and sales forecasts are called **independent variables**, meaning they can be changed by the planner or budget analyst. These could also be called external values, since they must be defined before the budget is assembled and often very early in the planning process. All remaining values in the budget are formula driven, using the independent variables or other already determined values. These calculated values are called **dependent variables**, meaning that this value is determined by other variables. In many cases, the dependent variables are found by using independent variables such as sales and a formula such as percentage of sales collected in the month of sale.

In the typical master budget situation, the independent variables would be all the planning assumptions, product cost and price data, and the sales forecast. All other values in the schedules and statements are dependent variables. In spreadsheet software logic, independent variables are constants or formulas. The dependent variables are found by creating a cell formula.

OTHER APPROACHES TO BUDGETING

So far we have discussed budgeting in terms of a master budget and its components. The concept of budgeting can have different connotations depending on the organization involved and the organization's purpose. This section highlights other approaches to budgeting that may be appropriate.

Project Budgets

Some budgets are oriented to particular events and serve as guidelines to the probable results of such events. Project budgets allow these events to be planned and controlled using time schedules, financial budgets, and responsibility assignments. Project budgeting areas include:

1. Construction projects.
2. Information systems projects.
3. Research and development projects.
4. Model-year projects (launching new models).
5. Engineering product design projects.
6. Training programs.
7. Advertising or public relations programs.
8. Government contracts.
9. Audits.
10. Renovation of buildings and equipment.

Project management has been a source of many problems, in particular time schedule and spending overruns. Many projects are one-time efforts, like constructing a headquarters building or designing a order-entry system for our marketing department. Research and development management often presents the classic management dilemma: an unknown final result, difficulty in defining intermediate evaluation points, and working in technologically underdeveloped areas.

Budgets must be developed around stages and units of work. Timetables, deadlines, decision points, and spending authorizations must be linked. Also, a reporting system that requires reviews of spending and progress to date is vital to management control. Once a project budget is established, actual costs can be compared with the budget to monitor the performance of the project. However, an overall picture may not be adequate as a means of overall and direct control. Various people may be responsible for individual costs within the project. Performance reports must, therefore, be geared to the level of accountability of people who control the costs.

Two management concerns exist: How did we do? And, what should we do now? These use different views of the same data. One looks back at resources used, and the other looks forward to resource needs and benefits.

As an example, assume that a systems development project is budgeted at $100,000 and should take 6 months to complete. It is to save the firm $150,000 in costs. It is now 3 months into the project, and $40,000 has been spent. The manager in charge estimates that it is one-third done and will take another 6 months and $90,000 to complete. Current estimates show the savings to be only $120,000. How should the current status be evaluated? If the project is one-third done, the manager is behind in time and money as follows:

SYSTEMS PROJECT

	Original Project	Revised Budget	Incremental Dollars From This Point	Budgeted Progress To Date (1/3)	Actual Results	(Over)/Under Budget
Savings.....	$150,000	$120,000	$120,000			
Costs.......	$100,000	$130,000	$ 90,000	$ 33,333	$ 40,000	($ 6,667)
Time	6 months	9 months	6 months	2 months	3 months	(1 month)

Using the original budget, the project is a month behind schedule and over spent by $6,667. If the budget is revised and if new time and cost estimates are used, the project appears to be on time and under budget.

	Revised Budget	Budgeted Progress To Date (1/3)	Actual Results	(Over)/Under Budget
Costs.......	$130,000	$43,333	$ 40,000	$ 3,333
Time	9 months	3 months	3 months	On Time

The following conclusions can be made:

1. The original budget is valuable as the original base for planning resource needs. It is also the control base for evaluating actual performance to budget. Even when the budget is revised, reference to the original budget is often useful managerial information.
2. The revised budget serves as a base for resource planning from this point on. It is not a valid base for comparison with actual results for the total project since the over or under budget variances to date are rolled into the revised budget.

Also, after the costs and benefits are revised, the original project would appear unprofitable and should be rejected. If we were to make the original decision all over again, knowing what we know now, we would have rejected the project. However, using incremental analysis the additional costs are $90,000 with $120,000 of future benefits to be gained. This may still be an attractive project and worthy of continuation.

Careful monitoring of project status (costs and accomplishment) is critical to avoiding serious out-of-control situations. It also assumes that managers have ethical standards which prevent complicity to hide project problems and deliberate efforts to circumvent project controls.

Zero-Based Budgeting

Zero-based budgeting was introduced into certain business and government organizations because managers were dissatisfied with existing budgeting processes. Under the **zero-based budgeting** concept, all spending is planned as if the task were new. A zero expenditure level is assumed until a manager can justify a higher level of spending. This is different from most budgeting processes, which often start with current levels of expenditures and evaluate increases only.

Two basic steps in zero-based budgeting stand out:

1. Developing decision packages—analyzing and describing each significant activity in one or more decision packages.
2. Ranking decision packages—evaluating and ranking these decision packages in order of importance through cost-benefit analysis, subjective priority setting and evaluation, or some other set of criteria.

The purpose of developing and ranking decision packages is to aid management in allocating all available resources. The most important activities in the ranking will get the resources first. The lower ranking decision packages receive resources only if the resources are available.

Zero-based budgeting has limitations. The process often generates a large volume of paperwork; hence, many managers have found that decision packages are unmanageable with the volume of paperwork usually increasing geometrically with organization size. Many observers have concluded that zero-based budgeting may be more useful to the managers who formulate the budget than to top managers who decide on the decision packages. Also, experience shows that managers quickly learn how to "play games" with the decision packages. In other words, this approach to budgeting may not result in any significant reallocation of resources.

The basic idea of seriously examining each expense regardless of its pedigree or purpose is vital to all budgeting efforts. Segmenting larger tasks into smaller units to be evaluated is also a key to all planning and control tasks. It can be argued that, with effective traditional budget logic and execution, zero-based budgeting is not needed and would not have received attention.

Program Budgeting

Program budgeting also called **planning, programming, and budgeting system (PPBS)**, is more commonly associated with not-for-profit organizations. Program budgets focus on the outputs of programs rather than specific inputs. A program is a specific activity or a set of activities established to achieve an objective. For example, a city might set an objective to minimize loss of life and property from fire. This could include fire prevention activities, fire fighting training, public education on fire prevention, and fire regulations and inspections. A vigorous fire prevention project might be budgeted instead of a new fire truck. PPBS is a formal planning system that uses a program budget and emphasizes cost-benefit analysis. It has three major characteristics:

1. It develops a program structure with a statement of goals and objectives for each program—a fundamental evaluation of mission and purpose.
2. It identifies evaluation criteria and desired outputs—forces priority setting.
3. It assumes a zero base as a starting point—similar to zero-based budgeting.

The key to successful PPBS is forcing managers to back away from their own operations and evaluate the overall objectives. But this is also the disadvantage of PPBS: managers must link all activities to the organization's mission and objectives; and the process is time-consuming and complex. Measuring benefits and cost effectiveness is a difficult and, at times, impossible task.

Probabilistic Budgeting

Probabilities reflect the likelihood that certain business conditions will occur. When risk exists that a particular variable might move within a range of values, using probabilities to express those possible outcomes helps the budgeting process to be more realistic. The effects of a particular change in any factor can be determined. In other words, the sensitivity of profits to changes in factors such as sales volume and prices can be tested; this provides management with data to help identify areas needing close attention.

A simple illustration is given to show how probabilities can be applied in determining the **expected value** (the average or mean value) of sales, costs, and profits. Assume, for example, that a company plans to sell one product line next year at a price of $20 a unit. Probability estimates have been made for sales volume and variable costs per unit. (The variable costs per unit vary with prices of inputs but not with changes in the expected sales volume.)

Sales Volume (number of units)	Probabilities	Variable Unit Costs	Probabilities
150,000	.20	$15	.80
200,000	.70	10	.20
250,000	.10		1.00
	1.00		

In this illustration, the relationship of individual probabilities to their respective sales volume and variable unit costs is the basis for understanding the total expected value of the contribution margin and the expected value of profits. The total expected values of sales, variable costs, and the contribution margin are as follows:

Sales Volume	Probabilities	Expected Value (units)
150,000	.20	30,000
200,000	.70	140,000
250,000	.10	25,000
Expected sales volume (units)		195,000
Expected sales (195,000 units x $20)		$3,900,000

Variable Unit Costs	Probabilities	Expected Value
$15	.80	$12
10	.20	2
Expected cost per unit		$14
Expected variable costs (195,000 units × $14)		2,730,000
Expected contribution margin		$1,170,000

If the two sets of probabilities are combined the following expected contribution margin is found:

	Sales Revenue −	Variable Cost =	Contribution Margin	Probabilities Sales ×	Cost =	Joint	Expected Value
Possible outcomes: Sales of 150,000 units (20 %) Unit variable cost:							
$15	$3,000,000	$2,250,000	$ 750,000	.20 ×	.80 =	.16	$ 120,000
10	3,000,000	1,500,000	1,500,000	.20 ×	.20 =	.04	60,000
Sales of 200,000 units (70 %) Unit variable cost:							
$15	$4,000,000	$3,000,000	$1,000,000	.70 ×	.80 =	.56	$ 560,000
10	4,000,000	2,000,000	2,000,000	.70 ×	.20 =	.14	280,000
Sales of 250,000 units (10 %) Unit variable cost:							
$15	$5,000,000	$3,750,000	$1,250,000	.10 ×	.80 =	.08	$ 100,000
10	5,000,000	2,500,000	2,500,000	.10 ×	.20 =	.02	50,000
Total expected value of contribution margin							$1,170,000

The probabilistic approach to budgeting can provide possible outcomes for a combination of different factors under conditions of uncertainty. Past experience coupled with a careful analysis of the future can serve as a basis for establishing probability estimates. For each particular circumstance, the probable profit will vary according to the combination of conditions. Admittedly, probability estimates will not be precise, but they can be more accurate than rough approximations or intuitive judgments.

Models may be built that incorporate probability analysis with respect to economic conditions, sales volumes, prices, and costs. Using a computer, the models may be tested in simulation studies to determine expected profit levels if certain probabilistic estimates are made.

BEHAVORIAL SIDE OF BUDGETING

All organizations are made up of people who will perform a multitude of activities in pursuit of the organization's goals and objectives. Top management must know what effects its planning and control tools and techniques will have on the people within the organization. Likewise, management must also appreciate how the behavior can affect the results of applying specific approaches. Budgets have the potential to motivate workers to reach for higher levels of activity and increased efficiency and productivity. Therefore, this section explores the common behavioral implications of the budgeting process.

Top Management Support

Heavy involvement of top management in the planning and control process has been implied earlier. Budgeting success at middle and lower management levels is highly correlated with executive-level participation in the formation and use of budgets. Nothing will destroy the effectiveness of the budgeting process quicker than lower-level managers' perceptions that top managers do not support the process. All top management actions must cement the impression that a commitment exists for budgeting and performance reporting.

A demonstration of support involves at least four important ingredients. First, top management must establish clearly delineated lines of authority and responsibility. Second, appropriate goals and objectives that other management levels can easily translate into activities must be developed. Third, top management must actively review and approve budgets and follow-up on budget variances. This conveys the importance they attach to budgeting. And fourth, top management must exhibit a positive attitude toward involving lower management levels in the process.

Managerial Expectations: Realism and Credibility

Managers who participate in preparing budgets and who feel that budgets represent "fair" standards receive personal satisfaction from accomplishing the goals and objectives set forth in the budget. Consequently, budgets become a positive motivator and bring out the best in people. But because of unrealistic management expectations, budgeting too often fosters feelings of animosity toward the budgeting process and threatens the security and self-esteem of the people involved.

Management can create negative budgeting attitudes in several ways. One of these is using budgets, or giving the impression they are being used, to squeeze every ounce of productivity out of employees, or solely to identify poor performers, or as a means of restricting an employee's ability to perform. If budget variances are always viewed as "bad news," subordinates will quickly adjust their behavior to avoid negative evaluations. Necessary managerial actions may not be taken because of the fear of penalties. Unless top management is willing to recognize the need for flexibility, reality, and positive change, lower management support quickly dissipates.

Budgetary Slack

Budgetary slack, also called "padding the budget," occurs when managers intentionally request more funds than needed to support the budgeted level of activities or underestimate revenues that may be generated by those activities. Padding indicates either poor relations between top management and the lower management levels or poor administration of the budgeting process.

A common instance of padding occurs when lower-level managers know from past experience that their budget requests will be cut by upper-level managers without careful review. Their response is to pad certain expenses or "low-ball" revenue estimates. In turn, upper-level managers, knowing that lower-level managers pad their budgets, automatically raise the level of anticipated revenues and cut budgeted expenses. Now the organization has a vicious circle of counter-productive activity.

Some organizations experience a different phenomenon. As the budget period progresses, it becomes apparent that the organization's short-term objectives are not going to be met, and top management institutes strenuous cost-cutting measures. Upper-level management issues an edict that all segments must cut costs by some percentage, say 10 percent of budget. Since this can be demoralizing to those managers who did not build "fat" into their budgets, managers resort to padding for self-preservation. While upper-level management may perceive their cost-cutting approach as "fair," in reality it suffers three weaknesses: organizational differences are ignored, resource allocations consistent with the firm's long-run goals are obliterated, and executive management is viewed as being arbitrary, capricious, and ignorant of the needs of specific programs under its control.

The most effective weapon against "slack" is a careful and rigorous review of budgets by line managers. To be effective, the reviewers must know the inner workings of the units reporting to them. It means that nonaccounting managers must be able to read and interpret budget data and control reports. It also implies close working relationships between the controller's office and the responsible line managers.

Institutionalizing Budgeting

In many organizations with extensive experience in budgeting, the budgeting process itself can become almost mechanical with little creative thought applied. Often forms must be prepared, detailed instructions followed, and routine approvals given without clear relevance to the business plan or operating problems of the organization. The budget becomes "the accountants' budget," not the plan of action. Managerial creativity might not be encouraged—so much in this column and not more than that in that column. And once the budget is approved and in place a manager might say: "Wow! The budget's done for this year. Now I don't have to worry about it until next year!" It is clear that this manager does not expect to use the budget as the plan of action or to be evaluated meaningfully as actual results roll in.

The danger is that budget preparation takes on an identity of its own— either as an accounting requirement, as a perfunctory task, or a set of forms to be completed. Linking budget dollars to the firm's plans, goals, and objectives gives the budget process relevance, both for the firm as a whole and for specific managers.

Human Factors and Budget Stress

Budgets are a basis for directing and controlling activities and establishing a discipline within an organization. The tightness of budgets necessarily depends on a number of factors including the degree of stability and ability to predict future results with a given function, the operating experience of managers, and the closeness of supervision. Of particular note is the reaction each manager has to budgets and budget stress. Some people need close guidelines and a "fear of God" approach, while others operate best with broad degrees of freedom. Supervisors and upper-level managers must make careful judgments about how tight the budget numbers should be for each manager. Remember, the goal is to generate the greatest good from each manager's area of responsibility and to maximize goal achievement for the whole organization.

Budgets Are Only One Aspect of Planning and Control

While responsibility accounting, budgeting systems, and budget reports are certainly key parts of an organization's planning and control activities, other planning and control tools can be used as a support or as a substitute for budgeting. Training, policies and procedures, supervision, automation, quality of personnel, staff support, standards, development of other planning tools, and the degree of centralization or decentralization all help determine the level of importance attached to the budgeting process. And this level of dependence changes over time as organizations become more mature, change managerial philosophies, or encounter operating or financial problems.

SUMMARY

Perhaps the major functions of management are to plan and control the activities of an organization. Planning and controlling include a system of tools and techniques that starts with a strategic plan, uses a responsibility accounting system, and concludes with feedback on actual results compared to the plan. The glue that often holds the planning activities together is the budget. Eight different purposes of budgeting were outlined. These establish budgeting as a versatile tool and a framework for carrying out management's responsibilities.

The master budget is the summary of the operating, project, and financial budgets. The operating budget begins with a sales budget, carries on to production and all manufacturing cost budgets, includes the operating expense budgets, and ends with a cash flow forecast. The keystone to the operating budget is the sales budget, which is based on a sales forecast.

Other budgeting approaches were presented. Project budgets are prepared for plans that span the normal annual time frame or are non-routine in nature. Zero-based budgeting and program budgeting are innovative approaches to prioritizing resources. Probabilistic budgeting gives managers an opportunity to bring various estimates of key variables into the budgeting process.

A concluding consideration is management's concern for the influence the budgeting process has on people and how people affect the budgeting process. Areas of particular importance are top management's support of the budget, managerial expectations, budgetary slack, and budget stress.

PROBLEMS FOR REVIEW

Review Problem A

The production manager of the Morris Company wishes to maintain an inventory of materials equal to production needs for the next two months because of potential delays in obtaining shipments from his Korean supplier. Each unit takes 4 pounds of material which costs $3 per pound. Finished goods inventory is usually maintained at 60 percent of the following month's sales. The sales budget for the first 8 months of 1996 in units is as follows:

Month	Budgeted Sales
January	12,000
February	16,000
March	15,000
April	16,000
May	20,000
June...	15,000
July	18,000
August..	22,000

As of December 31, 1995, 100,000 pounds of materials and 8,000 units of finished goods were on hand.

Required:

Prepare a budget for production in units and a materials requirements budget in pounds showing purchases in pounds and dollars for as many months as possible.

Solution:

Production Plan in Units:

	January	February	March	April	May	June	July	August
Sales.........................	12,000	16,000	15,000	16,000	20,000	15,000	18,000	22,000
Ending inventory (60% of next month)	9,600	9,000	9,600	12,000	9,000	10,800	13,200	?
Total units needed	21,600	25,000	24,600	28,000	29,000	25,800	31,200	
Beginning inventory available	8,000	9,600	9,000	9,600	12,000	9,000	10,800	
Production required	13,600	15,400	15,600	18,400	17,000	16,800	20,400	

Material Requirements and Purchases Budget:

	January	February	March	April	May	June	July
Production required	13,600	15,400	15,600	18,400	17,000	16,800	20,400
Pounds per unit........................	4	4	4	4	4	4	4
Pounds required	54,400	61,600	62,400	73,600	68,000	67,200	81,600
Ending inventory (next 2 months of production requirements)	124,000	136,000	141,600	135,200	148,800	?	?
Total pounds needed	178,400	197,600	204,000	208,800	216,800		
Beginning inventory available	100,000	124,000	136,000	141,600	135,200		
Materials purchases	78,400	73,600	68,000	67,200	81,600		
Cost per pound	$ 3	$ 3	$ 3	$ 3	$ 3		
Materials purchases in dollars............	$235,300	$220,800	$204,000	$202,200	$244,800		

Review Problem B

The supervisor of the economic forecasting department has estimated that a 70 percent probability exists that sales volume for next year will be 400,000 units of product if the selling price is established at $6 per unit. A 30 percent probability exists that sales will be 300,000 if the selling price is established at

$8 per unit. Variable cost per unit is estimated at $4 per unit with a probability of 60 percent and at $5 per unit with a probability of 40 percent. Fixed costs for the next year have been estimated at $250,000.

Required:

Compute the expected value of net operating income for next year.

Solution:

	Sales Revenue	Variable Cost	Contribution Margin	Probabilities			Expected Value
				Sales ×	Variable Cost =	Joint	
Possible outcomes: Sales of 400,000 units at $6 per unit (70 %): Variable costs per unit:							
$4 (60 %)	$2,400,000	$1,600,000	$ 800,000	.70 ×	.60 =	.42	$332,000
5 (40 %)	2,400,000	2,000,000	400,000	.70 ×	.40 =	.28	112,000
Sales at 300,000 units at $8 per unit (30 %): Variable costs per unit:							
$4 (60 %)	$2,400,000	$1,200,000	$1,200,000	.30 ×	.60 =	.18	$216,000
5 (40 %)	2,400,000	1,500,000	900,000	.30 ×	.40 =	.12	108,000
Total expected contribution margin							$768,000
Less estimated fixed costs..							250,000
Expected net operating profit							$518,000

TERMINOLOGY REVIEW

Accommodation cash (316)
Budget (304)
Budgetary slack (330)
Cash management (316)
Comprehensive budget (312)
Control (304)
Dependent variables (324)
Derived demand (321)
Excess cash (316)
Expected value (327)
Goals and objectives (304)
Forecast financial statements (317)
Independent variables (324)
Long-range goals (306)
Master budget (312)

Mission (306)
Operating budget (315)
Planning (304)
Planning assumptions (307)
Profit plan (312)
Program budgeting or planning, programming, and budgeting system (PPBS) (327)
Project budget (317)
Rolling update (or continuous budget) (307)
Sales forecast (320)
Strategic plan (306)
Transaction cash (316)
Zero-based budgeting (326)

QUESTIONS FOR REVIEW AND DISCUSSION

1.   What is the relationship between planning and control?

2.   What is a budget? How is budgeting related to performance evaluation?

3.   Differentiate between long-range goals and objectives and the master budget's goals and objectives.

4.   List the major components of a planning and control system.

5.   Identify and explain five purposes of budgeting.

6.   Reread the vignette about Marty Hartsock at the beginning of the chapter. Comment on each of her comments about budgeting. Why do you think she thinks that way? What retort might you give to each comment?

7.   Which is a better basis for judging actual results, budgeted performance or past performance? Explain.

8.   How do the elements of a responsibility accounting system help link planning and control?

9.   In most cases, what is the limiting factor in the preparation of a budget for a manufacturing firm? For a merchandising firm? For a service firm?

10.   Suggest several approaches to generating a sales forecast.

11.   Name and explain the use of the major budget schedules that create the data needed for the cost of goods manufactured budget. See Figures 7.2 and 7.3.

12.   Why is formatting important in preparing budget schedules? What is the basic structure of the format?

13.   What similarities exist between labor planning and materials purchases planning?

14.   How do zero-based budgeting and program budgeting differ from the more traditional approach to budgeting?

15.   What is the difference between an independent variable and a dependent variable in the budgeting process? Give three examples of each.

16.   Which of the costs normally included in a factory overhead budget would require no cash disbursement?

17.   What limits are placed upon the sales division by the manufacturing division?

18.   Explain how a cash budget differs from a budgeted income statement.

19.   . Differentiate among transaction cash, accommodation cash, and excess cash.

20.   How is a cash budget used in planning short-term bank loans and short-term investments?

21.   What are the advantages and disadvantages in holding large cash reserves?

22.   What important factors must be considered in planning cash receipts? What must be considered in planning cash payments to vendors?

23.   General and administrative expenses are usually considered to be fixed in amount and influenced very little by changes in sales activity. Explain.

24.   For what kind of business activities is a project budget useful?

25.   When probabilities are estimated for various possible contribution margins, what is meant by the term "expected value of the contribution margin?"

26.   Why are the human behavior concerns in budgeting important? Identify several concerns and explain.

27.   What is "budgetary slack?" Is it good or bad? Why "yes" <u>and</u> "no?"

EXERCISES

1.   **Needed Purchases.** Stew Crumbaugh, controller of Ink Supply, Inc., estimated sales for the third and fourth quarters at $750,000 and $800,000 respectively. The estimated gross profit rate is 40 percent. The June 30 inventory at cost is $120,000. The targeted inventory at the end of the third quarter is to be 20 percent of fourth quarter sales volume.

Required:
What quantity of inventory should be purchased in the third quarter?

2.   **Budget Comments.** Comment briefly on the following quotes about budgeting by another textbook author:

(a)   "One major criticism of budgeting is that it is used as a 'cost reduction' tool rather than a 'cost control' tool. . . . The objective of the budget is to control costs at an efficient level of operation."

(b)   "There are generally three benefits of allowing employees to participate in developing the budget: (1) employees tend to accept the budget as their own plan of action, (2) participation tends to increase morale among employees and toward management, and (3) employee cohesiveness is increased and productivity will also increase if dictated by the group norm."

(c)   "Even though budgets are quantitative tools, considerable emotion is connected with both the controller and the controlled. The individual in control often uses the budget as a medium of personality expression. The people being controlled often have feelings of fear and anxiety because their success and promotion are tied directly to the budget."

3.   **Materials Requirements.** Stewart Co. produces plastic buckets. The following budget data are available:

(a)   Ending Finished Goods Inventory: 20% of next quarter's sales

(b)   Ending Materials Inventory: 30% of next quarter's production

(c)   Forecast sales for each quarter of 1995 are 1,000, 1,100, 1,200, and 1,300 buckets, respectively.

(d)   Two pounds of plastic are needed for each bucket. January 1, 1995 inventories are the correct levels as to percentage of sales and production.

Required:
How many pounds of plastic must be purchased for the first two quarters of 1995 to meet the buckets sales forecast?

4.   **Expected Value of Profit.** The sales manager of the Zweng Corporation Economic Forecasting Department has estimated that a 40 percent probability exists that sales volume for next year will be 600,000 units of product if the selling price is established at $7 per unit. A 60 percent probability exists that sales will be 500,000 units if the selling price is established at $8 per unit. Variable cost per unit is estimated at $6 (with a probability of 20 percent) or $5 (with a probability of 80 percent). Fixed costs for the next year have been estimated at $800,000.

Required:
Compute the expected value of net income before income tax for next year.

5. **Flexible Budgeting.** The Cuney Company operates a mobile pizza business. Estimates of monthly costs at two levels of sales are as follows:

	20,000 Pizzas	30,000 Pizzas
Pizza ingredients	$20,000	$30,000
Truck rental and salaries	25,000	25,000
Gas, part-time help, etc.	20,000	26,000

Required:
Cuney has estimated sales for the month to be 28,000 pizzas. Help prepare an expense budget for next month.

6. **Purchase Requirements.** Verbat Company has asked you to help prepare a materials purchases schedule. Verbat produces two products called DSDD and SSSD. A special compound called "A1" is used in differing amounts in each product. "A1" is forecast to cost $10 per pound. Production levels by month and pounds per unit of product are as follows:

	DSDD Units	SSSD Units	Pounds of "A1" Per Unit
January	300	100	DSDD unit: 2 lb. of A1
February	400	120	SSSD unit: 3 lb. of A1
March	600	150	
April	500	200	

Inventory of "A1" begins at 200 on January 1 and is to increase by 20 pounds per month.

Required:
Find the amount of "A1" that must be purchased each month and the dollar value of those purchases.

7. **Sales and Purchases.** Dawe Company sells course note packets for courses with high enrollments at Prestige University. Each one sells for $10, and the purchase cost is $6 per packet. Dawe keeps an inventory of 40 percent of next month's forecast sales. Each month Dawe pays suppliers 70 percent of the current month's purchases and the rest is paid the following month. The Spring semester's sales budget is:

	January	February	March	April	May
Sales	$ 6,000	$ 4,000	$ 3,000	$ 6,000	$1,000

Required:
1. Give Dawe's budgeted purchases per month through April.
2. Show Dawe's cash payments to suppliers per month from February through April.

8. **Forecast Cash Receipts.** The Hackstock Co. sells saw blades for industrial use. The company sales are 80 percent on account and 20 percent for cash. Sales on account are collected as follows: 30 percent in the month of sale, 50 percent the next month, and the remainder in the second month after the sale.

The accounts receivable balance on January 1 was $ 40,000 ($5,000 from November sales and $35,000 from December). The sales forecast for the first half of next year is:

January	$100,000	April	$140,000
February	90,000	May....................	150,000
March	120,000	June	160,000

Required:

Find the forecast cash receipts for each month of the first quarter.

9. **Forecast Cash Payments.** Hal's Soft Shoe Shop is preparing its cash budget for the month of November. The following information is available about its operation:

November beginning inventory	$18,000
Estimated November cost of goods sold	90,000
Estimated November ending inventory............................	16,000
Estimated November payments for purchases made prior to November	21,000
Estimated November payments for purchases made in November	80 percent

Required:

What are the estimated cash payments in November for Hal?

10. **Sales Budget.** Peale Manufacturing Company produces two product lines. The Sales Department estimates that 150,000 units of Product 1 will be sold next year, and that 240,000 units of Product 2 will be sold. Product 1 will be sold at $8 per unit, and Product 2 will be sold at $10 per unit. Product 1 is expected to sell more heavily during the first half of the year, with 40 percent of total sales in the first quarter, and another 40 percent in the second quarter. Of the remaining units, 20,000 will be sold in the third quarter, and the rest will be sold in the fourth quarter. Sales for Product 2 will be evenly distributed over the four quarters.

Required:

Prepare a budget of sales, both in units and in dollars, by product line for each quarter.

11. **Cash Budgeting.** Caveney Corporation is preparing a cash budget for 1996 using the following data:

(a) Each month, 60 percent of sales are on credit. Credit sales are collected 70 percent in the month of sales and 30 percent the next month.

(b) Cost of goods sold is 70 percent of sales. Of purchases, 60 percent are paid when purchased with the rest being paid the next month.

(c) Planned inventory should be 40 percent of the next month's sales. Budgeted purchases in February were $60,000.

(d) All other expenses are $10,000 per month including $2,000 of depreciation expense. These are paid when incurred.

(e) Forecast cash balance as of March 1 is $20,000.

Budgeted sales for a portion of 1996 were:

February	$ 90,000
March	120,000
April	110,000
May	100,000

Required:

Create a cash forecast for March.

12. **Project Budgeting.** We have approved a 6-month $200,000 systems project to improve office communications. Intangible benefits of $150,000 per year have been promised. We are now 4 months into the project. People and equipment expenses have been $160,000, and we think it will take another 3 months and $80,000 to finish the project.

Required:
1. From a control perspective, how are we doing?
2. From a planning perspective, how do we see the future?

13. **Production Plan.** Betz Company's sales budget shows the following projections for the year ending December 31:

Quarter	Number of Units
First	60,000
Second	80,000
Third	45,000
Fourth	55,000
Total	240,000

Inventory at December 31 of last year was budgeted at 18,000 units. The quantity of finished goods inventory at the end of each quarter should equal 30 percent of the next quarter's budgeted sales of units.

Required:
According to the production budget, how many units should be produced during the first quarter?

14. **Net Sales Budget.** Klems Machine Company has prepared a sales budget for next year for its major product line. The estimated units to be sold are as follows:

Quarter	Number of Units
1	15,000
2	20,000
3	30,000
4	20,000

The selling price for the first half of the year has been estimated at $500 per unit and will be increased to $540 a unit for the second half of the year.

Judging from past experience, 1 percent of gross sales will be deducted for sales returns and allowances. Also, it is likely that an additional 2 percent of gross sales will prove to be uncollectible.

Required:
Prepare a budget of gross and net sales revenue by quarters for the budgeted income statement and for the cash budget.

15. **Net Sales Budget.** Western Trails, Inc. has estimated sales volume for the next year as follows:

	Products		
	1	**2**	**3**
First quarter	30,000	60,000	70,000
Second quarter	25,000	50,000	90,000
Third quarter................................	15,000	40,000	120,000
Fourth quarter	10,000	30,000	140,000
Annual totals	80,000	180,000	420,000

Product 1 is expected to sell at $2 per unit, Product 2 at $4 per unit, and Product 3 at $6 per unit. Sales returns and allowances are estimated at 3 percent of gross sales revenue, and uncollectible accounts are estimated at 2 percent of gross sales revenue.

Required:

Prepare a budget of gross and net sales revenue by quarter and by product line for the budgeted income statement and for the cash budget.

16.   **Production and Inventories.** Handorf Company has irregular sales volume during the year, and management is planning to produce at a uniform rate with inventories increasing or decreasing throughout the year. A sales budget in product units is forecast for the first six months of 1996 as follows:

Months	**Units**
January	40,000
February	25,000
March	45,000
April	20,000
May	40,000
June...	30,000

The production cycle is short and work in process inventories are insignificant. An inventory of 10,000 units was on hand at January 1, and 20,000 units of inventory are planned for June 30.

Required:

Prepare a production schedule that will have level production each month while showing the expected inventories at the end of each month.

17.   **Production and Inventories.** The production manager of Gomez Company plans to have an inventory on hand at the end of each month that will be equal to 30 percent of the sales of the next month. The actual inventory is at the needed level for the end of June. A sales budget for the next seven months is as follows:

Months	**Units**
July	40,000
August..	50,000
September	60,000
October...	70,000
November..	60,000
December..	50,000
January...	60,000

Required:

Prepare a production budget for the last six months of the year.

18. **Budget Limits.** Rollin Parts, Inc. has the capacity to manufacture 400,000 units of a certain product line each year. Each unit of product requires 2 pounds of a metal that is difficult to obtain. The sales department estimates that 300,000 units of product can be sold next year. The purchasing department states that 30,000 pounds of the metal are on hand at the beginning of the year and that only 290,000 pounds can be purchased on the market next year. The purchasing department has found a company that is willing to produce 100,000 units of product on a contract basis. That company has enough of the required metal on hand to make the 100,000 units.

Required:
1. What is the limiting factor in budgeting next year?
2. How many units of the product can be produced internally and sold next year?
3. What is the maximum forecast sales possible for next year?

19. **Labor Cost Budget.** Budget plans of Baxter Supply Company are being revised for the last two quarters of 1995. Two product lines are manufactured. Under the revised plan, production in units of product is estimated as follows:

	Product Lines	
	1	2
Third quarter.	12,000	15,000
Fourth quarter	16,000	18,000

The labor rate per hour is to be $10 during the third quarter. On October 1, a $.50 per hour raise contained in the Baxter labor contract with its union will go into effect. Production plans indicate that 15 minutes are required to produce each unit of Product 1 and that 20 minutes are required to produce each unit of Product 2.

In preparation of the budget, provision is to be made for the fringe benefit costs such as pensions and medical health insurance. The total fringe benefit cost is to be estimated at 55 percent of the hourly labor cost for the third quarter. Other union agreement changes will increase the fringe cost to 60 percent of the hourly labor cost for the fourth quarter.

Required:
1. Prepare a budget showing the direct labor cost for each product line and in total for each quarter.
2. Add a section to the direct labor cost schedule showing the estimated fringe benefit cost and total labor cost for each quarter.

PROBLEMS

7-1. **Purchases Budget.** In the production of a line of product, Kim Li Company uses 4 units of Material R and 2 units of Material S. All materials are purchased in the month before the units are scheduled for completion. The production cycle takes about a week, and all units of product are sold in the month following completion.

The cost per unit of materials is estimated to be $4 for Material R and $7 for Material S. A production schedule for June, 1996 through January, 1997 inclusive follows:

	Units of Product To Be Completed
June, 1996	42,000
July	46,000
August	48,000
September	47,000
October	51,000
November	54,000
December	60,000
January, 1997	65,000

Required:

1. Prepare a budget schedule for each of the last six months of 1996 showing how much of each material must be purchased.
2. Convert the budget of purchases in units to a total purchases dollar budget.
3. Compute the cost of materials in cost of goods sold for October, November, and December.

7-2. **Purchases Budget.** The Resnick Processing Company has prepared production estimates for the two product lines that it manufactures as shown in the following table:

	Units of Product	
	Product A	Product B
June, 1995	2,000	3,500
July	2,600	3,200
August	4,200	2,400
September	5,800	2,200
October	6,000	2,000
November	3,200	3,500
December	2,500	4,600
January, 1996	2,000	5,000

The production planner wants an inventory stock on hand of about one week's production at all times (about 25 percent of the following month's production). One part, Panel 435781, is used in both products. Requirements per unit of product and prices are as follows:

	Panels Per Unit		Per Unit Part Price
	Product A	Product B	
Panel 435781	2	5	$6

The purchasing department has located a new supplier of Panel 435781 who can furnish the material in the desired quality and quantity at a cost of $5.40 per unit. The present contract for delivery expires on September 30, 1995, and a contract with the new supplier will be made for deliveries after that date.

Required:

1. Prepare a purchases budget in units of materials and in dollars for each month from July to December, inclusive.
2. For the fourth quarter, compute the total cost savings in the cost of materials purchased that can be expected by dealing with the new supplier.

7-3.   **Supplies and Labor Cost.** The Greenberg Health Clinic serves as an outpatient clinic for the citizens in the Brant City area. Medicines, drugs, and various medical supplies must be obtained, and cost estimates must be made for each month. In addition to physicians who are available on a contract basis at a cost of $50,000 a month, nurses salary costs are $40,000 a month. Other employees are engaged on a part-time basis at a cost of $11.00 per hour. Past experience shows that one part-time person is required for every 50 patients served in a month. The typical part-time employee works 100 hours in a month.

The costs of medicines and various supplies varies at the rate of $5 per patient served plus a fixed cost of $15,000 for medicines and supplies each month.

An estimate was made of patients to be served in the last quarter of the year:

	Number of Patients
October	900
November	1,100
December	1,200

Required:

1.   Prepare a schedule showing the cost of the medicines and other supplies for each month.
2.   According to the estimates, how many part-time people will be needed each month, and at what cost?
3.   Prepare a budget schedule showing the costs of contract services, salaries, medicines and other supplies, and part-time labor cost for each month.

7-4.   **Project Management.** In the Osann Corp. an advertising project is forecast to cost $100,000, generate $200,000 in additional variable contribution margin, and take 6 months to complete.

It is now 4 months into the project and $60,000 has been spent. Ossan estimates that it is one-third done and that it will take another 8 months and $100,000 to complete the project. Current estimates now show that the forecast additional variable contribution margin will be $160,000. Osann is at a "go" or "no go" point on this project.

Required:

1.   How does Osann report the project relative to the budget?
2.   How does Osann report this project in its "plan of action," if approved for continuation?
3.   Should the project be "canned" or continued at this "go" or "no go" point?

7-5.   **Labor Cost Budget.** Cutter Cartons Inc. manufactures two basic lines of product— Sturdee and Rain-Proof. Past experience has shown that 10 units of Sturdee can be produced each labor hour and that 8 units of Rain-Proof can be produced each labor hour. Direct labor is paid at the rate of $12 per hour, and each employee works approximately 400 hours of productive time each quarter. Production has been estimated for 1996 as follows:

	Units	
	Sturdee	Rain-Proof
First quarter	12,600	12,000
Second quarter	16,200	9,000
Third quarter	14,400	15,000
Fourth quarter	14,400	18,000

Required:

1. Prepare a schedule showing the total direct labor hours needed each quarter to meet the production requirements.
2. Add to the schedule prepared in part 1 to show the direct labor cost budget each quarter.
3. How many employees will be needed each quarter?

7-6. **Direct Labor Cost Budget.** Barbara Gonzalez, Inc. manufactures three gardening tools: a grass trimmer, a hedge trimmer, and a brush cutter. Qualified employees number 15 at the present time, and new employees will be engaged as production increases. Each employee works approximately 160 hours a month and is paid at the rate of $9.60 per hour. Production budgets in units of product are given as follows:

	Product Lines		
	Grass Trimmer	**Hedge Trimmer**	**Brush Cutter**
March	6,000	3,000	1,000
April	9,000	3,000	1,000
May	12,000	6,000	2,000
June....................	15,000	7,500	2,000
July	12,000	6,000	3,000
August..................	9,000	3,000	1,000

The direct labor time required for one person to assemble and test each unit of product has been estimated as follows:

Grass trimmer	10 minutes
Hedge trimmer	15 minutes
Brush cutter	30 minutes

Required:

1. Prepare a budget of direct labor hours for each month and convert it into a budget of direct labor cost.
2. How many employees will be needed for production each month?

7-7. **Budgeted Income Statement.** Benaglio Plastic Products had inventories of 75,000 pounds of raw materials and 25,000 units of finished product at the start of the year. Sales forecasts for the first seven months are as follows:

January	40,000 units
February	55,000 units
March	50,000 units
April	70,000 units
May	60,000 units
June...	70,000 units
July	60,000 units

Benaglio maintains a finished goods inventory equal to 40 percent of the forecast sales of the next month, and a raw materials inventory equal to 30 percent of the next month's production requirements. Each unit of product requires 3 pounds of raw materials at $5 per pound.

The budgeted direct labor cost is $8 per hour, and each finished unit requires 30 minutes. Variable factory overhead is $5 per direct labor hour. Fixed factory overhead, including depreciation of $30,000, totals $45,000 per month. Normal capacity is 60,000 units per month.

Selling and administrative expenses are $2 per unit sold plus $20,000 per month, of which $15,000 is depreciation. The income tax rate is 40 percent. The selling price is $32 per unit.

Required:

1. Prepare a budgeted cost per unit for goods manufactured. Include supporting schedules needed to calculate product cost components.
2. Prepare budgeted income statements for the first four months of the year. (Assume the inventories are on a FIFO basis. The beginning inventory of raw materials is valued at $5 per pound; finished goods at $16 per unit.)

7-8. **Sales Budget from Incomplete Data.** You have been working on the budget for 1996 for WWWW Company. The president, Will Nelson, is holding a key meeting in a Seoul, Korea parts supplier plant at 9:00 a.m. on Thursday. Mr. Nelson wants the sales and production budgets in units for the Detroit plant for next year. It's now 2:00 p.m. on Wednesday in Detroit, twelve hours behind Seoul. The information can be sent by fax to the WWWW Seoul office.

You have certain data on your desk but nothing about units to be sold. Available information reveals that 4 pounds of materials are required for each unit of product manufactured. An inventory of 160,000 pounds of materials is to be on hand at the beginning of the year and throughout the year.

Materials can be used in production during the quarter acquired. Purchases for the year have been planned as follows:

	Pounds of Materials
First quarter	1,200,000
Second quarter	1,500,000
Third quarter	2,000,000
Fourth quarter	2,500,000

Each pound of material purchased costs $2.40. The inventory of finished goods is 12,000 units at the beginning of the year. This inventory is to be increased by 1,000 units each quarter until year end, when it will have increased to 16,000 units.

Required:

1. Prepare schedules to support your calculation of the sales budget by quarters in units of product.
2. Prepare a budget of sales in dollars assuming a selling price per unit of product of $60.
3. You have finished the sales schedule by 4:00 p.m. Now convert the materials purchases budget into dollars and determine the cost of materials in cost of goods sold.

7-9. **Probabilistic Budgeting.** Jacobs Manufacturing Company is in the process of preparing its operating budget for next year. Bill McCarthy, the controller, wants to include in the budget documents a budgeted income statement based on probabilities. In visiting with selling, production, and administrative personnel, McCarthy has obtained estimates and probabilities for each area.

The sales estimates, with associated selling prices and probabilities, are as follows:

Units	Selling Price	Probability
800,000	$25	.20
700,000	28	.30
600,000	32	.40
500,000	36	.10

Variable manufacturing costs will either be $8 per unit, with a probability of 80 percent, or $10 per unit, with a probability of 20 percent. Fixed manufacturing costs have a 90 percent chance of being $100,000 and a 10 percent chance of being $120,000. Variable selling and administrative expenses are estimated at $2, $3, or $4, with probabilities of 20 percent, 70 percent, and 10 percent respectively. Fixed selling and administrative expenses have a 60 percent chance of amounting to $50,000 and a 40 percent chance of being $60,000.

Required:
Prepare a budgeted income statement based on expected values.

7-10. **Cash Budget.** The Builders Wholesale Store makes about 20 percent of its sales for cash. Credit sales are collected 20, 50, and 25 percent in the month of sale, month after, and second month after sale, respectively. The remaining 5 percent become bad debts. The store tries to purchase enough goods each month to maintain its inventory at two and one-half times the following month's budgeted sales. All of its purchases are subject to a 2 percent discount if paid within 10 days and the store takes all discounts. Accounts payable is then equal to one-third of that month's net purchases. Cost of goods sold, without considering the 2 percent discount, is 60 percent of selling prices. The firm records inventory at gross, taking the cash discounts to the income statement. The store pays all of its other expenses in the month incurred.

The store manager has asked you to prepare a cash budget for April and you have gathered the following data:

Sales:

January	$240,000
February	220,000
March	280,000
April	300,000
May	350,000
Cash at April 1	$35,000
Selling and administrative expenses budgeted for April	86,000*

* Includes $20,000 of depreciation expense.

Required:
Prepare a cash budget for April.

7-11. **Comprehensive Production Budget.** VanLeer Manufacturing Company produces and sells a specialty industrial liquid cleaning fluid. The product is sold in units of one barrel equal to 42 gallons. The selling price per barrel is $125. Finished goods inventory at September 1 was 14,800 barrels at a cost of $1,243,200. The finished goods inventory at September 30 is expected to increase by 1,700 barrels. The company expects to sell 90,000 barrels during the month. In costing all inventories, the company uses the FIFO method.

Raw materials consist of three different chemicals referred to as W8, X2, and Z4. Each barrel of final product requires 21 gallons of W8, 14 gallons of X2, and 7 gallons of Z4. Materials inventory information is as follows:

Materials	Inventory at September 1		Inventory at September 30	
	Gallons	Unit Cost	Gallons	Unit Cost
W8	60,000	$ .75	57,000	$ .80
X2	40,000	.85	38,500	.90
Z4	20,000	1.20	19,500	1.20

Unit costs in the ending inventory represent the anticipated costs for materials purchased during the month.

Two hours of direct labor are needed to produce one barrel of final product. Direct labor workers are paid $13 per hour. Factory overhead is segregated into fixed and variable costs. Variable factory overhead is expected to be $3.40 per direct labor hour, while fixed factory overhead should be $1,834,000 for the month. Fixed factory overhead is applied to work in process on the basis of barrels processed.

Required:
Prepare each of the following budgets for September:
1. Production budget.
2. Direct materials purchases budget.
3. Direct labor budget.
4. Cost of goods sold budget.

7-12. **Budgeting Cash.** The following data are part of the information being used to prepare the master budget for the Soft Surf Water Bed Shoppe:

Planned cash balance, May 1, 1996...............................	$ 60,000
Sales for May (50% collected in the month of sale, 40% the next month, and 10% the third month).......................................	800,000
Customer receivables as of May 1:	
From March sales...	70,000
From April sales..	450,000
Merchandise purchases for May (40% paid in month of purchase, 60% paid the next month).......................................	500,000
Inventory increase for May......................................	20,000
Payroll earned in May...	95,000
Payroll paid in May..	88,000
Three-year insurance policy renewal due on May 1 (to be paid in cash)	3,600
Other expenses for May (payable in May)...........................	41,000
Depreciation for month of May	2,000
Accrued taxes for May (payable in December).......................	6,000
60-day bank note due May 15....................................	175,000
Interest payable on bank note due May 15	10,000
Accounts Payable on May 1 (from merchandise purchases)	240,000

Required:
Using the information above, prepare a cash budget showing expected cash receipts and disbursements and a pro forma income statement for the month of May 1996.

7-13. **Cash Forecasting.** John Iannotti is preparing his budgets for 1996. He has written the following on a pad of legal paper:

Forecast Sales		Actual 12/31/95 Balance Sheet Data	
January	$70,000	Cash	$ 8,000
February	90,000	Accounts Receivable	20,000
March	80,000	Inventory	60,000
April	60,000	Accounts Payable	45,000

Other data are as follows:

(a) Sales are on credit with 40 percent collected in the month of sales and 60 percent next month.

(b) Cost of sales is 60 percent of sales.

(c) Other variable costs are 10 percent of sales, paid in the month incurred.

(d) Inventories are to be 150 percent of next month's budgeted sales requirements.

(e) Purchases are paid in the month after purchase.

(f) Fixed expenses are $3,000 per month; all require cash.

Required:

Prepare a cash budget for February.

7-14. **Budgeted Income Statement for a Service Organization.** The Rest-Rite Motel is a low-priced motel in a small New Mexico community along Interstate 40. It has 50 rooms, each with two double beds. Roll-away beds are available for $2 per night. The rates are $18 for one person, $10 for the next person, and $3 for each additional person beyond two.

During April, the motel manager expects an 80 percent occupancy rate. Past experience suggests the average number of people per room during a spring month is three. The manager estimates that 60 nights of roll-away beds can be expected during April.

Laundry costs average $0.50 per person per night. Cleaning workers earn $5.50 per hour, and it takes 30 minutes to clean each room. Other variable operating costs (utilities, for example) are $5 per occupied room per night. Maintenance and grounds personnel cost about $1,500 per month. Two clerks each have a salary of $1,000 per month. Depreciation is $2,000 per month. Other cash fixed expenses are $900 per month.

Required:

Prepare a budgeted income statement for April.

7-15. **Comprehensive Operating Budget.** Shell Environmental Systems, Inc. manufactures and distributes a portable air purification system and a drinking water treatment system. Reg Kittle, chief accountant, is in the process of budgeting operations by quarter for the upcoming year, 1995.

The air purifier sells for $500 and volume is expected to grow at the rate of 5 percent quarterly over the next two years. A water treatment unit sells for $200 and volume will grow at 3 percent quarterly for the next 18 months. Selling expenses are budgeted as a percentage of total sales dollars: salaries are 5 percent, commissions are 10 percent, advertising is 5 percent, and other expenses are $40,000 per quarter. General and administrative expenses are approximately 3 percent of sales plus $50,000 per quarter. The income tax rate is 40 percent.

Direct labor is $12 per hour, and the factory overhead rate is 110 percent of direct labor cost. Materials are purchased such that 40 percent of materials needed for a quarter are available at the beginning of the quarter; the other 60 percent is purchased during the quarter needed. No work in process inventories are needed, but finished goods inventory is budgeted for one half of the sales forecast for the upcoming quarter. Other manufacturing statistics are as follows:

Product	Material Cost Per Unit	Labor Time Per Unit
Air purifier	$150	5 hours
Water treatment	80	2 hours

The company produced and sold, during the fourth quarter of 1994, 1,060 air purifiers and 1,970 water treatment units. The ending finished goods inventory was at 50 percent of the anticipated sales for the first quarter of 1995. The ending materials inventory for the fourth quarter of 1994 was 40 percent of the anticipated production requirements for the first quarter of 1995. The costs of the fourth quarter of 1994 are the same as those anticipated for 1995.

Required:

Prepare the following budgets for each quarter and for the year in total for 1995:

1. Combined sales budget and selling expense budget. Show the sales budget in units and in dollars.
2. Production budget showing units in finished goods inventories, unit production, and the costs of goods manufactured.
3. Budgeted income statement.

7-16. Interpreting Overhead Budget Data. The following data come from a manufacturing overhead section of a master budget for Rose Products:

MANUFACTURING OVERHEAD FLEXIBLE BUDGET—1995

	Expected Annual Production of Units			
	24,000	26,000	28,000	30,000
Variable overhead:				
All variable expense	$36,000	$39,000	$42,000	$45,000
Fixed overhead:				
All cash fixed expense	$36,000	$36,000	$36,000	$36,000
Depreciation	6,000	6,000	6,000	6,000
Total fixed expense	$42,000	$42,000	$42,000	$42,000
Total flexible overhead budget	$78,000	$81,000	$84,000	$87,000
Variable overhead rate per unit			$ 1.50	
Fixed overhead rate per unit			1.50	
Manufacturing overhead rate per unit			$ 3.00	

MANUFACTURING OVERHEAD BUDGET—1995

	Q - 1	Q - 2	Q - 3	Q - 4	Total
Budgeted volume (units)	6,800	6,500	6,900	7,400	27,600
Variable overhead budget	$ 10,200	$ 9,750	$ 10,350	$ 11,100	$ 41,400
Fixed overhead budget	10,500	10,500	10,500	10,500	42,000
Total overhead budget	$ 20,700	$ 20,250	$ 20,850	$ 21,600	$ 83,400
Variable overhead applied	$ 10,200	$ 9,750	$ 10,350	$ 11,100	$ 41,400
Fixed overhead applied	10,200	9,750	10,350	11,100	41,400
Total overhead applied	$ 20,400	$ 19,500	$ 20,700	$ 22,200	$ 82,800
Over or (under) applied	$ (300)	$ (750)	$ (150)	$ 600	$ (600)

Required:

1. Which data in the manufacturing overhead flexible budget above are probably independent variables? Which are dependent variables?
2. What was the apparent normal capacity? Explain how you know this.

3.   Explain the over or (under) applied overhead variance for each quarter and in total. Why is it under applied for the year?

4.   Based on the data shown and your knowledge of flexible budgeting, how much overhead is Rose Products expecting to spend in 1995?

7-17. **Behavioral Effects of Budgeting.** Rouge Corporation is a medium-size company in the steel industry with six divisions located in different geographical sectors of the United States. Considerable autonomy in operational management is permitted in the divisions, partly due to the products produced and markets served. Corporate management establishes divisional budgets using prior year data adjusted for industry and economic changes expected for the coming year. Budgets are prepared by year and by quarter, with top management attempting to recognize problems unique to each division. Once the year's divisional budgets are set by corporate management, they cannot be modified by division management.

The budget for calendar year 1995 projects total corporate net income before taxes of $3,750,000 for the year, including $937,500 for the first quarter. Results of first quarter operations presented to corporate management in early April showed corporate net income of $865,000, which was $72,500 below the projected net income for the quarter. The St. Louis Division operated at 4.5 percent above its projected divisional net income, while the other five divisions showed net incomes with variances ranging from 1.5 to 22 percent below budgeted net income.

Corporate management is concerned with the first quarter results because they believed strongly that differences between divisions had been recognized. An entire day in late November of last year had been spent presenting and explaining the corporate and divisional budgets to the division managers and their division controllers. A mid-April meeting of corporate and division management has generated unusual candor. All five division managers with results below plan cited reasons why first quarter results in their respective divisions represented effective management and were the best that could be expected. Corporate management has remained unconvinced and informs division managers, "Results will be brought into line with the budget by the end of the second quarter."

Required:

1.   Identify and explain the major disadvantages in the procedures employed by Rouge Corporation's corporate management in preparing and implementing divisional budgets.

2.   Discuss the behavioral problems that may arise by requiring Rouge Corporation's division managers to meet the quarterly budgeted net income figures, as well as the annual budgeted net income. (ICMA Adapted)

CASE 7A—Remley Fixtures Company

Remley Fixtures Company is planning to expand beyond the industrial market that it now serves with materials handling units to produce and sell snowmobiles and trail bikes for the consumer market. The president of the company, Orville Stokes, estimates that the company must invest $1,800,000 in new equipment at the initial stage. He wants to know how much cash flow can be provided by operations next year to apply toward acquiring the equipment, and how much of the cost will have to be financed.

The sales division estimates sales revenue next year at $8,500,000. However, if economic conditions deteriorate, sales revenue may be only $6,500,000.

Cost of goods sold has been estimated at 70 percent of revenue. A possibility exists that the company will have to absorb cost increases that cannot be passed along to customers. In this case, the cost of goods sold will be 80 percent of revenue. With sales down to $6,500,000, the cost of goods sold will definitely be 80 percent of revenue. Revenues, operating expenses, and probabilities of occurrence have been estimated for each of the three alternatives as follows:

Alternative	Revenues and Cost of Goods Sold	Operating Expenses	Probabilities
1.........	Sales at $8,500,000 with 70 percent cost of goods sold	$1,050,000	30 %
2.........	Sales at $8,500,000 with 80 percent cost of goods sold	1,200,000	50 %
3.........	Sales at $6,500,000 with 80 percent cost of goods sold	1,100,000	20 %

Depreciation of $280,000 is included in operating expenses under each alternative, and depreciation of $350,000 is included in cost of goods sold for each alternative. Income taxes are estimated at 40 percent of income before income taxes.

In making the transition, equipment will be sold for $680,000, net of income taxes. A payment of $350,000 is to be made on long-term notes. Dividends of $300,000 are to be paid under each alternative.

Required:

1.   Prepare a statement to show the forecast cash flow provided by operations under each assumption and the expected cash flow in total.

2.   Continue the forecast statement to show how much additional cash will be needed to finance the new project after considering all of the information given. Show the impact of all three assumptions and the expected cash flow in total.

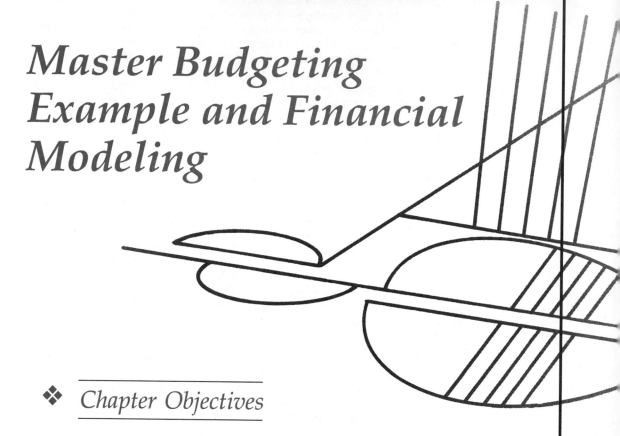

Chapter Eight

Master Budgeting Example and Financial Modeling

❖ *Chapter Objectives*

After studying Chapter 8, you will be able to:
1. Prepare schedules for all elements of the operating budget.
2. Complete the master budget with preparation of a forecast income statement, balance sheet, and statement of cash flows.
3. Show the use of flexible budgeting in a master budget.
4. Identify the primary components of financial planning models.
5. Understand the basic format and calculation sequences for preparing budgets and supporting schedules.
6. Understand the need for simulation capabilities in budget preparation and "what if" analyses.

Ben's Budget Inquisition and Renee's Response

Ben Hall, president of Hall Associates, Inc., has just reviewed a first draft of the 1995 budget for his labor relations consulting firm. The firm has 25 employees, operates in a three state area of the northeastern United States, provides services to small businesses and school systems, and participates in mediation and arbitration activities in the public sector. Increases in his own labor costs, uncertainty about future demand for the firm's services, and questions about how his employees react to budgets and budget pressures have him concerned about what he calls "the ethics and realities" of budgeting and financial planning. He shares much of the budget information with his key managers. They have provided their best thoughts on revenue potential for 1995. People costs and their benefit programs have been rising at a rate of 15 percent for 3 years. Business revenues have grown only 12 percent over that same time period.

Recently, Renee Foresman, controller of Hall Associates, purchased a budgeting software package from a firm specializing in financial planning assistance for consulting-type firms. After some work with the software firm, Renee has installed the master budgeting module on her desk-top computer. Her first effort was to transfer the 1994 budget numbers from each department to the computer. Then she prepared Ben's first budget draft. This morning, she met with Ben about the budget numbers. He asked a long list of questions about the budget assumptions, the numbers, and meeting the firm's budget goals. Most of the questions will take hours, if not days, to get solid answers. Another module of the software package is a planning model that will take the master budget data and allow Renee to change a wide variety of variables and quickly recalculate a "new" budget.

This seems like a godsend to Ben. He sends Renee off to "play with her new toy" and to come back tomorrow with outputs to answer his questions. Renee finds that the financial model will answer many of the questions, but the answers give Ben a chance to ask more and more informed questions. A number of the questions Ben raised really need inputs from his operating managers. How he, Renee, and the other managers act and react to the simulation results will impact budget revisions for Hall Associates' operations.

Chapter 8 will illustrate a comprehensive master budget which was introduced and discussed in Chapter 7. Financial modeling will be introduced as a powerful tool to test the master budget's numbers, assumptions, and achievement of its goals. Modeling leads to "what if" analysis of any or all of the budget's assumptions, interrelationships, and managerial assertions about the coming year's activities. Based on the budgeting discussion in Chapter 7, a master budget will be developed for a hypothetical firm. Then, financial modeling is explained and discussed, and several "what ifs" will be presented as illustrations of financial simulation.

A MASTER OPERATING BUDGETING EXAMPLE

To illustrate the master budget sequence of preparing budget components and the format of the budget schedules, a comprehensive example is presented and explained.[1] The company is Marshall Products Company. It is a small manufacturer of wood products. In recent years, its primary products are ceremonial podiums which are sold to chapters of the Podium Speakers Society of America (PSSA). Graduates of the Society's speaker training program are given a wooden podium as a symbol of public speaking prowess. Marshall Products has an exclusive arrangement with the PSSA that requires the local chapters to purchase the podiums from Marshall Products at previously agreed upon prices. Two styles of podiums are produced—the JR EXEC and the EXEC. Chapters of the PSSA give the EXEC model to honors graduates and the JR EXEC to all others.

Marshall Products has a factory with two production departments: Department 1 where the wood is cut, rough finished, and assembled; and Department 2 where the trim is attached, a PSSA supplied emblem is applied, a polyurethane finish is applied, and packing and shipping are done. A small sales office and administrative staff complete the organization.

Each year, Marshall Products prepares a master budget on a quarterly basis and generally follows the structure shown in Chapter 7, Figure 7.2. As in most budgeting situations, Marshall Products' dollar amounts are rounded to eliminate cents, and physical measures are often rounded to whole units. The budget modeling program used to prepare the budget will keep track of all decimal places in its memory. This will, throughout this master budgeting example, cause certain columns or rows to appear to add incorrectly, but overall accuracy is maintained.

Annual Goals and Planning Assumptions

Marshall Products begins the planning process with a planning meeting at a local resort each August. Key managers discuss their area of responsibility and present strengths, opportunities, problems, and last year's results.

Operating and Financial Goals   At the planning session, a set of goals and targets for the coming calendar year is agreed upon and are as follows for the coming year:

---

[1]The Marshall Products Company case has an accompanying software spreadsheet template on an instructor's diskette for classroom use.

		1995 **Forecast Value**
Growth:	10% growth in sales (1994 sales were $680,000)	17.47%
Profitability:	10% return on equity	11.01%
Capital:	Total debt to equity less than 25%	26.27%
Liquidity:	Current ratio of better than 3:1	5.95:1
Other Goals:	Reduce inventory by 10% from beginning levels	13.14%
	Cost of podiums below 65% of sales price—JR EXEC	58.95%
	Cost of podiums below 65% of sales price— EXEC	63.26%

These are measured using beginning and ending balance sheet and annual income statement numbers. Based on the forecast developed by Marshall for 1995 (shown in later schedules), all goals except the capital goal are met. Other operating goals and targets related to efficiency and operating management were also set but are not presented here because they do not relate directly to the budget process.

Planning Assumptions   Certain data and relationships are needed to begin the planning process. These include beginning balances, operating activity assumptions, and finance assumptions.

Product Cost and Pricing Data   The first planning data, presented on page 356, are the costs of both JR EXEC and EXEC models. Material, labor, and overhead are listed for both podiums by price and quantity of each resource used. The list of materials is often called a **bill of materials**. The labor shows costs and hours in each department. A more detailed set of labor processes is used to plan labor schedules in each department. Manufacturing overhead uses a fixed and variable breakdown. In Department 1, overhead is applied to podiums using machine hours, because of the heavy use of machinery in cutting and sanding. In Department 2, direct labor hours are used as the cost driver because of the labor-intensive finishing process. Shipping costs per unit are considered to be selling expenses and are not product costs. Podium prices are negotiated between the PSSA and Marshall Products each fall as an early part of the planning process.

Operating Assumptions   A variety of planning details is needed to prepare the budgets. Most of these come from past experience, from estimates of beginning balances, and from forecasts of 1995. Schedule 2, shown on page 356, presents these initial assumptions.

The operating assumptions include percentages, specific budgeted amounts for certain accounts to prepare overhead rates, and any other constant that will be needed in calculations. In real life, expected inflation rates, salary increase percentages, growth rates in certain activities, and staffing levels are commonly included.

SCHEDULE 1
BILL OF MATERIALS, QUANTITIES, COSTS, AND PRICE SHEET

		JR EXEC		EXEC	
	Cost	Quantity	Per Unit	Quantity	Per Unit
Materials:					
Plywood (square feet)........................	$ 0.2750	12.00	$ 3.300	16.00	$ 4.400
Wood screws (unit)	0.0215	18.00	0.387	24.00	0.516
Trim (feet)................................	0.0850	15.00	1.275	18.00	1.530
Total materials			$ 4.962		$ 6.446
Direct labor:					
Department 1 (direct labor hours).............	$10.00	0.20	$ 2.000	0.25	$ 2.500
Department 2 (direct labor hours).............	12.00	0.50	6.000	0.75	9.000
Total direct labor			$ 8.000		$11.500
Variable manufacturing overhead:					
Department 1 (machine hours)	$ 7.20	0.20	$ 1.440	0.25	$ 1.800
Department 2 (direct labor hours).............	4.00	0.50	2.000	0.75	3.000
Total variable overhead			$ 3.440		$ 4.800
Fixed manufacturing overhead:					
Department 1 (machine hours)	$15.00	0.20	$ 3.000	0.25	$ 3.750
Department 2 (direct labor hours).............	6.00	0.50	3.000	0.75	4.500
Total fixed overhead			$ 6.000		$ 8.250
Total manufacturing overhead................			$ 9.440		$13.050
Total manufactured podium cost..............			$22.402		$30.996
Sales price			$38.00		$49.00

SCHEDULE 2
OPERATING ASSUMPTIONS

Inventory data:	Plywood (sq feet)	Wood Screws (boxes)	Trim (feet)	JR EXEC	EXEC
Beginning inventory	10,000	22	9,000	1,300	200
Ending Inventory as a percentage of next quarter's requirements	20.00%	20.00%	10.00%	25.00%	25.00%
Accounts Receivable:					
Sales percentage collected this quarter					75.00%
Uncollectible accounts percentage					2.00
Sales return percentage expected					1.00
Discount percentage on this quarter's sales collected this quarter					2.00
Accounts Payable:					
Purchases percentage paid this quarter					60.00%
Discount percentage on this quarter's purchases paid this quarter					2.00
Manufacturing activity base:					
Department 1—budgeted machine hours rounded to nearest 200 hours					4,200
Department 2—budgeted labor hours rounded nearest to 500 hours					11,000
Manufacturing overhead expense data:					
See Schedule 9 for budgeted variable rates and fixed amounts.					

Selling expense data:	JR EXEC	EXEC
Sales commissions	4.00%	6.00%
Shipping expenses	$1.35	$1.65

See Schedule 15 for budgeted specific account amounts.
Administrative expense data:
See Schedule 16 for budgeted specific account amounts.

Financial Planning Assumptions   Borrowing and investing, cash levels, and balance sheet starting points are the independent variables needed to complete the cash flow forecast and pro forma (or forecast) financial statements.

SCHEDULE 3
FINANCING ASSUMPTIONS

Cash, taxes, and capital balances:

Cash balance—minimum balance	$ 15,000
Cash balance—maximum balance...	$ 25,000
Borrowing and investment incremental amount	$ 5,000
Income tax rate (federal, state, and local)	40.00%
Interest rate on bank borrowings and investments (annual)	12.00%
Quarterly principal payment on notes payable	$ 1,000
Capital stock—outstanding stock (24,000 shares).............................	$ 240,000
Dividend rate—per share per quarter	$ 0.10

Other balance sheet accounts and balances as of December 31, 1994:

Cash	$ 15,000
Accounts Receivable	58,000
Building and Equipment	350,000
Accumulated Depreciation	(100,000)
Other Assets	10,000
Accounts Payable	10,300
Taxes Payable..	2,000
Long-Term Notes Payable	64,000

Capital expenditures:

	First Quarter	Second Quarter	Third Quarter	Fourth Quarter
Capital expenditures by quarter	$8,000	$0	$10,000	$15,000

With these details given, the only remaining independent variable needed is the sales forecast.

Sales Forecast and Budget

The sales forecast is based on past sales, the PSSA's enrollment forecast, and contacts with most major chapters around the country. It is prepared using a rolling five quarter time frame. A fifth quarter of sales data is needed to complete a number of fourth quarter schedules.

The physical quantities are independent variables. The dollar amounts are found by using the physical units and the prices from Schedule 1. A small sales returns allowance of 1 percent of sales is forecast. Also, the format of the four quarters, an annual total, and an as needed fifth quarter are established.

SCHEDULE 4
SALES FORECAST BY PRODUCT BY QUARTER

	First Quarter	Second Quarter	Third Quarter	Fourth Quarter	Total	Fifth Quarter
Unit sales						
JR EXEC	3,200	3,200	3,600	3,800	13,800	3,500
EXEC	1,200	1,400	1,500	1,500	5,600	1,300
Sales dollars						
JR EXEC	$121,600	$121,600	$136,800	$144,400	$524,400	$133,000
EXEC	58,800	68,600	73,500	73,500	274,400	63,700
Total gross sales	$180,400	$190,200	$210,300	$217,900	$798,800	$196,700
Less returns	(1,804)	(1,902)	(2,103)	(2,179)	(7,988)	(1,967)
Net sales dollars	$178,596	$188,298	$208,197	$215,721	$790,812	$194,733

Production Plan and Budgets

A production plan is prepared by product using beginning finished podium inventory, the sales forecast, and desired ending inventory levels for each product and for each production department or cost center. In this example, work in process inventory is assumed to be so small and unchanging that it is immaterial to both the planning and the product costing tasks. If work in process were substantial, the beginning level would be known, a desired ending level would be set, and production would be determined.

Key relationships in this production plan are the percentages of sales that should be on hand at the end of each quarter. Note the format of the schedule as discussed earlier. Production is planned in greater detail than by quarter as shown here. Each product's production schedules would be built by day, week, or month and by specific operation within each producing department.

From Schedule 5 through the end of the master budget, all numbers are calculated using data from Schedules 1 through 4. All values from this point on are dependent variables using the independent variables from Schedules 1 through 4.

A company may choose to operate at a fairly uniform level through the year; or, conversely, it may prefer to manufacture products as needed. With sales fluctuating through the year, inventories will increase or decrease if production is held at a constant level. When production moves with sales, the inventories will not vary to any extent; but production will go up or down with sales. Either approach to the production problem has its cost advantages and disadvantages, and the less costly method will generally be selected.

When production is stabilized at a certain level, the manufacturing costs tend to be more uniformly distributed throughout the year. Plant and labor resources will not be overloaded in some months only to remain idle during others. However, other problems arise when production is stabilized. Inventories of finished product will build up when sales volume is low and will fall during high demand seasons. The variations in inventory will create carrying costs. Funds may be invested in inventories when they could be used elsewhere to better advantage. Carrying costs often run at least 25 percent of the inventory value. Often some compromise is made, while a tendency toward JIT production exists.

SCHEDULE 5
PRODUCTION PLAN BY PRODUCT BY QUARTER

	First Quarter	Second Quarter	Third Quarter	Fourth Quarter	Total	Fifth Quarter
JR EXEC:						
Unit sales	3,200	3,200	3,600	3,800	13,800	3,500
Ending finished goods	800	900	950	875	875	800
Total needs	4,000	4,100	4,550	4,675	14,675	4,300
Beginning finished goods...................	(1,300)	(800)	(900)	(950)	(1,300)	(875)
Production	2,700	3,300	3,650	3,725	13,375	3,425
EXEC:						
Unit sales	1,200	1,400	1,500	1,500	5,600	1,300
Ending finished goods	350	375	375	325	325	350
Total needs	1,550	1,775	1,875	1,825	5,925	1,650
Beginning finished goods...................	(200)	(350)	(375)	(375)	(200)	(325)
Production	1,350	1,425	1,500	1,450	5,725	1,325

Materials Requirements Budget   The materials list was given in Schedule 1. Deciding which materials to schedule (such as wood screws) and which to consider supply items (such as polyurethane) is a product manager's or controller's decision. The quantities of materials used in each unit are specified in Schedule 1. These are based on experience or engineering studies and form the basis for standard costs which are discussed in Chapter 9. The units of materials needed to meet the production requirement were determined by multiplying the product units to be made by the units of materials required for each unit of product.

SCHEDULE 6
MATERIALS REQUIREMENTS

	First Quarter	Second Quarter	Third Quarter	Fourth Quarter	Total	Fifth Quarter
Plywood—in square feet						
JR EXEC	32,400	39,600	43,800	44,700	160,500	41,100
EXEC	21,600	22,800	24,000	23,200	91,600	21,200
Total plywood (sq ft)	54,000	62,400	67,800	67,900	252,100	62,300
Wood Screws—in 000s						
JR EXEC	48.60	59.40	65.70	67.05	240.75	61.65
EXEC	32.40	34.20	36.00	34.80	137.40	31.80
Total screws (000)	81.00	93.60	101.70	101.85	378.15	93.45
Trim—in feet						
JR EXEC	40,500	49,500	54,750	55,875	200,625	51,375
EXEC	24,300	25,650	27,000	26,100	103,050	23,850
Total trim (feet)	64,800	75,150	81,750	81,975	303,675	75,225

The 32,400 square feet of plywood needed for JR EXEC in the first quarter is found by multiplying 12 square feet per unit (Schedule 1) times the 2,700 units to be produced (Schedule 5). In more complex production situations, the accumulation of parts and materials needs is called a **bill of materials explosion**. All uses of the same part in different products are added together to find the total usage across the entire product line for the time period. Computer software for production planning such as Materials Requirements Planning (MRP) is used to plan needs and to issue purchase orders for the needed amounts when inventory levels reach a certain point. Schedules 6 and 7 are combined automatically.

Materials Purchases Budget   Purchases, like production, are planned in relation to desired inventory levels which are given in Schedule 2. Inventories

SCHEDULE 7
MATERIALS PURCHASES BUDGET

	First Quarter	Second Quarter	Third Quarter	Fourth Quarter	Total
Plywood requirements:					
Production requirements	54,000	62,400	67,800	67,900	252,100
Ending inventory	12,480	13,560	13,580	12,460	12,460
Total needs	66,480	75,960	81,380	80,360	264,560
Beginning inventory	(10,000)	(12,480)	(13,560)	(13,580)	(10,000)
Purchases (sq. feet)	56,480	63,480	67,820	66,780	254,560
Purchases ($)	$15,532	$17,457	$18,651*	$18,365	$ 70,004
Wood screw requirements:					
Production requirements	81.00	93.60	101.70	101.85	378.15
Ending inventory	18.72	20.34	20.37	18.69	18.69
Total needs	99.72	113.94	122.07	120.54	396.84
Beginning inventory	(22.00)	(18.72)	(20.34)	(20.37)	(22.00)
Purchases (000)	77.72	95.22	101.73	100.17	374.84
Purchases ($)	$ 1,671	$ 2,047	$ 2,187	$ 2,154	$ 8,059
Trim requirements (rounded to the nearest foot):					
Production requirements	64,800	75,150	81,750	81,975	303,675
Ending inventory	7,515	8,175	8,198	7,523	7,523
Total needs	72,315	83,325	89,948	89,498	311,198
Beginning inventory	(9,000)	(7,515)	(8,175)	(8,198)	(9,000)
Purchases (feet)	63,315	75,810	81,773	81,300	302,198
Purchases ($)	$ 5,382	$ 6,444	$ 6,951	$ 6,911	$ 25,687
Total purchases	$22,585	$25,948	$27,788	$27,429	$103,750

* This calculation generates a purchase cost of $18,650.50. This number is rounded to the nearest dollar. This is the first of many rounded amounts in this comprehensive illustration. The spreadsheet software keeps track of all significant digits in calculations and then rounds to the specified level. Therefore, certain columns and rows which include rounded numbers may not add as shown. For example, the purchase cost in the total column for plywood shows $70,004, while the four quarters' numbers add up to $70,005 resulting from rounding up in quarters three and four. Budgeting rarely needs detail beyond whole dollars. Financial modeling software often will maintain the high level of accuracy that computers can automatically give. Therefore, the minor inconvenience of having a column of rounded numbers not add up exactly is a benefit in the overall model's accuracy level.

should be planned so that they vary only within maximum and minimum limits. These limits are set for each material by estimating delivery time, rate of usage, and frequency of ordering. Carrying a supply that is greatly in excess of current need is expensive. Conversely, inventory balances can be trimmed to a point where a real risk exists that shortages will interrupt production if shipments are not received in time.

The 56,480 square feet of plywood purchases in the first quarter is the result of the production requirements from Schedule 6 plus the desired ending inventory based on second quarter production minus the assumed beginning inventory. Costing of purchases uses Schedule 1 prices for material items.

The purchasing department is in the best position to furnish data with respect to estimated costs. It maintains contact with suppliers and knows what prices are offered by competing firms. Even so, the task of estimating future prices is difficult. In addition to the cost of the materials themselves, other costs should be included as a part of the materials cost. Freight on incoming materials and the cost of purchasing, receiving, handling, and storing materials are a part of materials cost. Usually it is difficult to relate these costs to any specific item of material purchased; as a matter of expediency, they are often budgeted as a part of factory overhead.

Direct Labor Budget   The direct labor budget is estimated first by the number of labor hours required—per unit hours (Schedule 1) times the units to be made (Schedule 5). Hours per podium are set again by past experience or by industrial engineering studies. In either event, adjustments most likely will be made. New production methods may bring about savings in labor time, thus making past records of performance obsolete. Allowances also are made for idle time, set-up time, training, and other variations from the expected level of work. Using 2,000 hours per year as a per employee estimate, Department 1 needs between 2 and 3 direct laborers. Department 2 needs between 5 and 6. This assumes fully productive persons and no overtime. Actual employment is the responsibility of the plant management.

The hourly labor cost per hour can be the "straight wage" rate with all payroll taxes and fringes included in manufacturing overhead. Or the rate could be the "loaded wage rate," which includes all or most fringes, expected overtime premiums, and even unproductive time. The differences can be dramatic. For example, the current United Automobile Workers contract with the major U. S. auto companies provides an average straight wage of about $15 per hour, while the loaded rate (even excluding unproductive time) is nearly $30 per hour.

In Schedule 8 on page 362, the 540 hours in Department 1 for JR EXEC in the first quarter is found by multiplying .2 hour per unit (Schedule 1) times 2,700 units (Schedule 5) to be produced. Hours are summed and multiplied by the appropriate wage rates (Schedule 1).

SCHEDULE 8
DIRECT LABOR REQUIREMENTS

	First Quarter	Second Quarter	Third Quarter	Fourth Quarter	Total
Department 1					
JR EXEC	540.00	660.00	730.00	745.00	2,675.00
EXEC	337.50	356.25	375.00	362.50	1,431.25
Total labor hours	877.50	1,016.25	1,105.00	1,107.50	4,106.25
Total direct labor costs—Department 1	$ 8,775	$ 10,163	$ 11,050	$ 11,075	$ 41,063
Department 2					
JR EXEC	1,350.00	1,650.00	1,825.00	1,862.50	6,687.50
EXEC	1,012.50	1,068.75	1,125.00	1,087.50	4,293.75
Total labor hours	2,362.50	2,718.75	2,950.00	2,950.00	10,981.25
Total direct labor costs—Department 2	$ 28,350	$ 32,625	$ 35,400	$ 35,400	$ 131,775
Total labor budget	$ 37,125	$ 42,788	$ 46,450	$ 46,475	$ 172,838

The definition of what is direct and indirect varies considerably and, therefore, affects both labor costs and manufacturing overhead. Even within the same company, a union contract in one plant may specify job classifications that are combined in another contract for a second plant. Labor hours are also broken down by seniority, with estimated rates applied in the calculation of a labor cost budget. Estimates are more difficult to make if a contract change is anticipated during the year or if cost-of-living increases and other indefinite factors play a part in the determination of wage rates.

With an increasing trend towards automation, many employees who once were hourly workers will now be paid salaries. Their work will be as monitors of the operations as opposed to the direct labor effort of converting materials into finished products. Thus, many blue-collar workers will become white-collar workers, whose salaries may be classified under fixed factory overhead.

Manufacturing Overhead Budgets   Budgeting manufacturing overhead takes two forms—creating the expected overhead spending patterns using a flexible budget and budgeted spending and applied overhead levels.

Flexible Budget for Manufacturing Overhead   Normal or expected activity levels, planning variable and fixed overhead items, selecting an activity base for applying overhead, and setting the overhead rates are all done as part of the annual budgeting process. Schedule 9 is the output of this process. The expected activity base selected for Department 1 was machine hours because most of the overhead costs were machine related and much of the work in Department 1 used saws, sanders, and other woodworking equipment. Department 2 work is predominately to finish sanding, trimming, and applying the urethane finish—heavily labor dependent. Expected machine and labor hours were summed and rounded to an expected level of activity (4,200 machine hours and 11,000 labor hours). Using the budgeted expenses and the expected activity level given in Schedule 2, variable and fixed overhead rates were determined. These are calculated on Schedule 9 and appear on Schedule 1.

SCHEDULE 9
MANUFACTURING OVERHEAD FLEXIBLE BUDGET

Department 1 (Cost Center # 1)

Activity Base: Machine Hours

		Machine Hour Activity			
		3,800	4,000	4,200	4,400
Variable expenses:	Rate/Hr			Expected	
Supplies	$ 0.40	$ 1,520	$ 1,600	$ 1,680	$ 1,760
Indirect labor	1.50	5,700	6,000	6,300	6,600
Fringes	4.45	16,910	17,800	18,690	19,580
Power—variable	0.25	950	1,000	1,050	1,100
Maintenance	0.60	2,280	2,400	2,520	2,640
Total variable expenses	$ 7.20	$ 27,360	$ 28,800	$ 30,240	$ 31,680
Fixed expenses:	Amount				
Depreciation	$20,000	$ 20,000	$ 20,000	$ 20,000	$ 20,000
Property taxes	4,000	4,000	4,000	4,000	4,000
Supervision	25,000	25,000	25,000	25,000	25,000
Power—fixed	1,000	1,000	1,000	1,000	1,000
Allocations and other	13,000	13,000	13,000	13,000	13,000
Total fixed expenses	$63,000	$ 63,000	$ 63,000	$ 63,000	$ 63,000
Total Department 1 overhead		$ 90,360	$ 91,800	$ 93,240	$ 94,680
Overhead rates:				Expected	
Department 1—variable rate		$ 7.20	$ 7.20	$ 7.20	$ 7.20
Department 1—fixed rate		16.58	15.75	15.00	14.32
Department 1—overhead rate		$ 23.78	$ 22.95	$ 22.20	$ 21.52

Department 2 (Cost Center # 2)

Activity Base: Labor Hours

		Budgeted Direct Labor Hours			
		10,000	10,500	11,000	11,500
Variable expenses:	Rate/Hr			Expected	
Supplies	$ 0.20	$ 2,000	$ 2,100	$ 2,200	$ 2,300
Indirect labor	0.40	4,000	4,200	4,400	4,600
Fringes	3.05	30,500	32,025	33,550	35,075
Power—variable	0.15	1,500	1,575	1,650	1,725
Maintenance	0.20	2,000	2,100	2,200	2,300
Total variable expenses	$ 4.00	$ 40,000	$ 42,000	$ 44,000	$ 46,000
Fixed expenses	Amount				
Depreciation	$10,000	$ 10,000	$ 10,000	$ 10,000	$ 10,000
Property taxes	3,000	3,000	3,000	3,000	3,000
Supervision	31,000	31,000	31,000	31,000	31,000
Power—fixed	2,000	2,000	2,000	2,000	2,000
Allocations and other	20,000	20,000	20,000	20,000	20,000
Total fixed expenses	$66,000	$ 66,000	$ 66,000	$ 66,000	$ 66,000
Total Department 2 overhead		$106,000	$108,000	$110,000	$112,000
Overhead rates:				Expected	
Department 2—variable rate		$ 4.00	$ 4.00	$ 4.00	$ 4.00
Department 2—fixed rate		6.60	6.29	6.00	5.74
Department 2—overhead rate		$ 10.60	$ 10.29	$ 10.00	$ 9.74

For many companies, the best opportunity for cost savings lies in the factory overhead area. Direct materials costs and direct labor costs are often determined by factors that are beyond the control of management. A small waste in the use of some lubricant, for example, is unimportant if only one machine is considered, but when this waste is multiplied by all machines in the plant, the loss may be substantial.

Spending and Applied Manufacturing Overhead Budgets   With the overhead rates and the budgeted activity levels by department, the budgeted manufacturing overhead budget and the budgeted applied overhead budget can be prepared. The machine hour activity levels come from the times per unit in Schedule 1 and the production plan. The budgeted amounts for each expense for each quarter are the amounts the production supervision is expected to spend given that activity. Notice that fixed costs remain fixed.

At the bottom of each department's budget is the planned applied overhead. This will differ from the budgeted spending level because the quarterly activity level is not exactly equal to one quarter of the annual expected activity level. For example, Department 1's first quarter's activity is budgeted at 877.50 machine hours. Using the overhead rates developed in Schedule 9, the applied overhead is $19,480.50. That is $22.20 per machine hour ($7.20 variable and $15.00 fixed) times 877.5 hours. Fixed overhead is budgeted evenly through the year and is $15,750 per quarter ($63,000 total fixed expenses from Schedule 9 divided by four). The overhead is under-applied by $2,587.50, which is the budgeted $15,750 minus the applied fixed overhead of $13,162.50 ($15.00 per hour x 877.5 hours).

It may seem strange to budget over- or underapplied overhead, but unless the expected or normal activity is exactly equal to the budgeted production activity an overhead variance must exist and must be budgeted. In this case, the entire year's budget produces an underapplied manufacturing variance of $1,519, which will be taken to the income statement. Even on a quarterly basis, the first and second quarters are budgeted to operate below the expected activity level and have underapplied overhead. And the third and fourth quarters should operate above the expected activity level and have overapplied overhead.

SCHEDULE 10
MANUFACTURING OVERHEAD BUDGET BY COST CENTER

Department 1 Budget	First Quarter	Second Quarter	Third Quarter	Fourth Quarter	Total
Machine hour activity	877.50	1,016.25	1,105.00	1,107.50	4,106.25
Variable overhead:					
Supplies	$ 351	$ 407	$ 442	$ 443	$ 1,643
Indirect labor	1,316	1,524	1,658	1,661	6,159
Fringes	3,905	4,522	4,917	4,928	18,273
Power—variable	219	254	276	277	1,027
Maintenance	527	610	663	665	2,464
Total variable expenses	$ 6,318	$ 7,317	$ 7,956	$ 7,974	$ 29,565

Department 1 Budget	First Quarter	Second Quarter	Third Quarter	Fourth Quarter	Total
Fixed overhead:					
Depreciation....................................	$ 5,000	$ 5,000	$ 5,000	$ 5,000	$ 20,000
Property taxes	1,000	1,000	1,000	1,000	4,000
Supervision	6,250	6,250	6,250	6,250	25,000
Power—fixed..................................	250	250	250	250	1,000
Allocations and other	3,250	3,250	3,250	3,250	13,000
Total fixed expenses..........................	$15,750	$15,750	$15,750	$15,750	$ 63,000
Total overhead—Dept. 1	$22,068	$23,067	$23,706	$23,724	$ 92,565
Applied overhead	$19,481	$22,561	$24,531	$24,587	$ 91,159
Over- (Under-) applied	$ (2,588)	$ (506)	$ 825	$ 863	$ (1,406)
Over- (Under-) applied YTD.......................	$ (2,588)	$ (3,094)	$ (2,269)	$ (1,406)	$ (1,406)

Department 2 Budget	First Quarter	Second Quarter	Third Quarter	Fourth Quarter	Total
Direct labor activity	2,362.50	2,718.75	2,950.00	2,950.00	10,981.25
Variable overhead:					
Supplies	$ 473	$ 544	$ 590	$ 590	$ 2,196
Indirect labor	945	1,088	1,180	1,180	4,393
Fringes	7,206	8,292	8,998	8,998	33,493
Power—variable	354	408	443	443	1,647
Maintenance	473	544	590	590	2,196
Total variable expenses	$ 9,450	$10,875	$11,800	$11,800	$ 43,925
Fixed overhead:					
Depreciation...................................	$ 2,500	$ 2,500	$ 2,500	$ 2,500	$ 10,000
Property taxes	750	750	750	750	3,000
Supervision	7,750	7,750	7,750	7,750	31,000
Power—fixed..................................	500	500	500	500	2,000
Other allocation	5,000	5,000	5,000	5,000	20,000
Total fixed expenses...........................	$16,500	$16,500	$16,500	$16,500	$ 66,000
Total overhead—Dept. 2	$25,950	$27,375	$28,300	$28,300	$109,925
Applied overhead	23,625	27,188	29,500	29,500	109,813
Over- (Under-) applied	$ (2,325)	$ (188)	$ 1,200	$ 1,200	$ (113)
Over- (Under-) applied YTD.......................	$ (2,325)	$ (2,513)	$ (1,313)	$ (113)	$ (113)
Total manufacturing overhead.......................	$48,018	$50,442	$52,006	$52,024	$202,490
Total applied	$43,106	$49,748	$54,031	$54,087	$200,971
Total over- (under-) applied.........................	$ (4,913)	$ (694)	$ 2,025	$ 2,063	$ (1,519)
Total over- (under-) YTD	$ (4,913)	$ (5,606)	$ (3,581)	$ (1,519)	$ (1,519)
Cash outflow (Total overhead minus depreciation expense)	$40,518	$42,942	$44,506	$44,524	$172,490

Supporting Schedules

To complete the budget, several supporting schedules are needed. These are prepared by the accounting staff, but are important to cash flow forecasting and the calculation of cost of podiums manufactured and sold. Our assumptions about collections, payments, and ending balances were given in Schedule 2, Operating Assumptions. We can now develop forecasts for accounts receivable, inventories, and accounts payable.

SCHEDULE 11
ACCOUNTS RECEIVABLE

	First Quarter	Second Quarter	Third Quarter	Fourth Quarter
Beginning balance	$ 58,000	$ 44,649	$ 47,074	$ 52,049
Net sales	178,596	188,298	208,197	215,721
Total receivables	$236,596	$232,947	$255,272	$267,770
Decreases in receivables:				
Collections—prior quarter	$ 53,360	$ 41,077	$ 43,309	$ 47,885
Collections—this quarter (after discounts)	131,268	138,400	153,025	158,555
Total cash collections	$184,628	$179,477	$196,333	$206,440
Cash discounts	2,679	2,824	3,123	3,236
Uncollectables—prior quarter	4,640	3,572	3,766	4,164
Total credits	$191,947	$185,873	$203,222	$213,840
Ending balance	$ 44,649	$ 47,074	$ 52,049	$ 53,930

Using Schedule 2 data, the percentage of net sales collected in the current quarter is 75 percent, uncollectible accounts is 2 percent of net sales and written off in the next quarter, and cash discounts are 2 percent of collections of the current quarter's net sales.

SCHEDULE 12
INVENTORY—COST BASIS

	Beg. Inv.	First Quarter	Second Quarter	Third Quarter	Fourth Quarter
Materials Inventory:					
Plywood—square feet	$ 2,750	$ 3,432	$ 3,729	$ 3,735	$ 3,427
Wood screws—000 units	473	402	437	438	402
Trim—feet	765	639	695	697	639
Total materials	$ 3,988	$ 4,473	$ 4,861	$ 4,869	$ 4,468
Finished goods inventory:					
JR EXEC	$29,123	$17,922	$20,162	$21,282	$19,602
EXEC	6,199	10,849	11,624	11,624	10,074
Total finished goods	$35,322	$28,770	$31,785	$32,905	$29,675
Total inventory	$39,310	$33,243	$36,646	$37,775	$34,143

Inventory values use quantities from Schedules 5 and 7 and costs from Schedule 1.

SCHEDULE 13
ACCOUNTS PAYABLE

	First Quarter	Second Quarter	Third Quarter	Fourth Quarter
Beginning balance	$10,300	$ 9,034	$10,379	$11,115
Purchases on account	22,585	25,948	27,788	27,429
Total payables	$32,885	$34,982	$38,168	$38,544
Decrease in payables:				
Cash payments—prior quarter	$10,300	$ 9,034	$10,379	$11,115
Cash payments—this quarter	13,280	15,257	16,340	16,128
Total cash payments	$23,580	$24,291	$26,719	$27,243
Cash discounts	271	311	333	329
Total debits	$23,851	$24,602	$27,052	$27,572
Ending balance	$ 9,034	$10,379	$11,115	$10,971

Schedule 2 indicates 60 percent of purchases are paid in the current quarter less a 2 percent discount. The remainder is paid in the next quarter.

Cost of Products Manufactured and Sold Schedule

Now all the elements are in place to prepare a schedule of the cost of goods manufactured and sold. While every entry on the schedule is not specifically shown in another schedule, all are easily calculated from the data now assembled. The breakdown of costs by JR EXEC and EXEC is needed to analyze the profitability of each product. These data will be entered in summary form on the income statement.

SCHEDULE 14
COST OF PODIUMS MANUFACTURED AND SOLD SCHEDULE

	First Quarter	Second Quarter	Third Quarter	Fourth Quarter	Total
JR EXEC:					
Manufacturing costs:					
Materials costs:					
Plywood used	$ 8,910	$ 10,890	$ 12,045	$ 12,293	$ 44,138
Wood screws used	1,045	1,277	1,413	1,442	5,176
Trim used	3,443	4,208	4,654	4,749	17,053
Total materials used	$ 13,397	$ 16,375	$ 18,111	$ 18,483	$ 66,367
Direct labor..............................	21,600	26,400	29,200	29,800	107,000
Manufacturing overhead applied	25,488	31,152	34,456	35,164	126,260
Cost of JR EXECs made	$ 60,485	$ 73,927	$ 81,767	$ 83,447	$299,627
Plus: beginning JR EXEC inventory	29,123	17,922	20,162	21,282	29,123
Less: ending JR EXEC inventory	(17,922)	(20,162)	(21,282)	(19,602)	(19,602)
Cost of JR EXECs sold	$ 71,686	$ 71,686	$ 80,647	$ 85,128	$309,148

	First Quarter	Second Quarter	Third Quarter	Fourth Quarter	Total
EXEC:					
Manufacturing costs:					
Materials costs:					
Plywood used	$ 5,940	$ 6,270	$ 6,600	$ 6,380	$ 25,190
Wood screws used	697	735	774	748	2,954
Trim used	2,066	2,180	2,295	2,219	8,759
Total materials used	$ 8,702	$ 9,186	$ 9,669	$ 9,347	$ 36,903
Direct labor.............................	15,525	16,388	17,250	16,675	65,838
Manufacturing overhead applied	17,618	18,596	19,575	18,923	74,711
Cost of EXEC made	$ 41,845	$ 44,169	$ 46,494	$ 44,944	$177,452
Plus: beginning EXEC inventory	6,199	10,849	11,624	11,624	6,199
Less: ending EXEC inventory	(10,849)	(11,624)	(11,624)	(10,074)	(10,074)
Cost of EXECs sold	$ 37,195	$ 43,394	$ 46,494	$ 46,494	$173,578
Total cost of podiums sold....................	$108,882	$115,081	$127,141	$131,622	$482,725
Over- (Under-) applied overhead	(4,913)	(694)	2,025	2,063	(1,519)
Adjusted total cost of podiums sold	$113,794	$115,775	$125,116	$129,559	$484,244

Schedule 14 brings together all production costs from Schedules 5 through 11. An interesting proof can be made. Using product costs from Schedule 1 and sales from Schedule 4, cost of JR EXEC and EXEC sold can be calculated quickly. These numbers can be checked against the sums of materials, labor, and applied overhead and the changes in inventories. For each product and each quarter these two numbers should match. They do in this case. Notice that the over-or under-applied overhead adjusts the total cost of podiums sold.

Selling and Administrative Expense Budgets

The cost of promoting, selling, and distributing the products is budgeted by combining the costs into a **selling or marketing expense budget**. Although the selling cost is not included as a part of product cost, it is frequently broken down by product lines, sales regions, customers, salespersons, or by some other significant unit basis. Cost analysis can be applied in planning sales activity, revealing what it probably costs to sell different quantities and combinations of products. The goal is to match sales spending with sales potential. Thus, selling expenses can also be budgeted by area of responsibility and can be used as a basis for control.

Many selling expenses bear no direct relationship to sales and may be arbitrarily determined by managerial policy. Promotional expenses and shipping expenses, for example, are dependent upon sales; but they are also influenced by other factors. Frequently, these expenses not only are governed by sales but also help to determine sales. Distribution expenses vary according to the destination of the products and agreements reached with customers.

SCHEDULE 15
SELLING EXPENSES BUDGET

	First Quarter	Second Quarter	Third Quarter	Fourth Quarter	Total
Commissions—JR EXEC	$ 4,864	$ 4,864	$ 5,472	$ 5,776	$ 20,976
Commissions—EXEC	3,528	4,116	4,410	4,410	16,464
Advertising	2,000	2,000	1,000	1,000	6,000
Sales salaries	7,500	7,500	7,500	7,500	30,000
Bad debt expense	3,572	3,766	4,164	4,314	15,816
Other sales expenses	3,000	2,000	4,000	1,000	10,000
Shipping expenses—JR EXEC.	4,320	4,320	4,860	5,130	18,630
Shipping expenses—EXEC	1,980	2,310	2,475	2,475	9,240
Total selling expenses	$30,764	$30,876	$33,881	$31,605	$127,126
Total cash selling expenses	$27,192	$27,110	$29,717	$27,291	$111,310

The cost of administration and the cost of maintaining a corporate form of business are frequently combined into an **administrative expense budget**. Administrative cost, like manufacturing and selling costs, is broken down for control purposes. Budgets of costs chargeable to individual administrative supervisors provide a basis for comparison to actual costs. In this illustration, specific amounts budgeted for each expense are then divided equally into the four quarters. As in other fixed expense accounts, this need not be the case. Often staff changes could cause certain quarters to have greater or lesser expenses.

SCHEDULE 16
ADMINISTRATIVE EXPENSES BUDGET

	First Quarter	Second Quarter	Third Quarter	Fourth Quarter	Total
Clerical expenses	$ 8,750	$ 8,750	$ 8,750	$ 8,750	$ 35,000
Supplies	1,250	1,250	1,250	1,250	5,000
Executive salaries	15,000	15,000	15,000	15,000	60,000
Other administrative expenses	2,000	2,000	2,000	2,000	8,000
Total administrative expenses	$27,000	$27,000	$27,000	$27,000	$108,000

Few administrative expenses are directly volume related. With major swings in volume or growth over time, these expenses will shift and increase. Often, staff salaries seem to contain an inherent growth variable. All organizations must guard against seemingly necessary growth in these nonproducing areas. Governments, universities, and major corporations alike have an ability to grow layers of "white collar" staff which represent overhead that must be supported by the revenue generating activities of the organization.

Project Budgets

The need for project budgets in this example is limited. Marshall Products has a small capital investment budget which was listed in Schedule 3. These expenditures are brought together in Schedule 17.

SCHEDULE 17
CAPITAL INVESTMENT PROJECT BUDGET

	First Quarter	Second Quarter	Third Quarter	Fourth Quarter	Total
Projects:					
Equipment purchases........................	$ 8,000	$ 0	$10,000	$15,000	$33,000
Research and development...............					0
Other project budgets......................					0
Total project expenditures...............	$ 8,000	$ 0	$10,000	$15,000	$33,000

Much detailed work and approvals are needed to support these brief project budget numbers.

Cash Flow Forecast

Now that all the operating budget elements have been put into place, the time for summarizing the separate but linked plans has arrived. The first summary is the preparation of the cash flow forecast. Nearly every schedule contains cash flow information. The basic structure is to list receipts and disbursements and summarize the cash balance, its changes, and any needed investing and borrowing activities.

This cash flow forecast is different in structure from the statement of cash flow discussed in Chapters 7 and 18. But the basics are similar. No major distinction is drawn between operations, investing, and financing; but the items could easily be regrouped. Generally, all inflows are listed, and then all outflows are listed. In Schedule 18, each cash flow item is given a reference for its source. The interest and tax calculations reflect calculations done for income statement and balance sheet purposes. Also, project cash flows such as capital expenditures are included.

A key part of cash flow forecasting is to plan for cash deficits or surpluses. If the cash balance falls below the minimum desired level (given in Schedule 3), bank borrowings or sales of investments are needed. If the cash balance goes above the maximum level, the excess cash should be invested to ensure maximum earnings on the firm's assets. These calculations at the bottom of the Schedule 18 show that the firm is forecast to generate extra cash. Using $5,000 increments for borrowing or investing cash given in Schedule 3, the budgeted total excess cash in 1995 is $25,000. Based on these results, the long-term notes payable might be reduced, higher dividends could be paid, or the plant and equipment could be modernized or expanded faster.

The cash flow forecast is partly operations budgeting and partly financial budgeting. It does bring together all the cash flows from wherever they are generated in the firm.

SCHEDULE 18
CASH FLOW FORECAST

	Source	First Quarter	Second Quarter	Third Quarter	Fourth Quarter	Total
Cash receipts:						
Collections of accounts	Schedule 11	$184,628	$179,476	$196,333	$206,440	$766,878
Interest received	Balance sheet	0	150	450	600	1,200
Other receipts	Various				0	0
Total cash received...........		$184,628	$179,626	$196,783	$207,040	$768,078
Cash disbursements:						
Materials purchases	Schedule 13	$ 23,580	$ 24,291	$ 26,719	$ 27,243	$101,833
Direct labor payroll	Schedule 8	37,125	42,788	46,450	46,475	172,838
Manufacturing overhead	Schedule 10	40,518	42,942	44,506	44,524	172,490
Selling expenses	Schedule 15	27,192	27,110	29,717	27,291	111,310
Administrative expenses	Schedule 16	27,000	27,000	27,000	27,000	108,000
Interest payments	Balance sheet	1,920	1,920	1,890	1,860	7,590
Tax payments	Balance sheet	2,000	1,144	4,278	7,260	14,682
Dividend payments	Schedule 3	2,400	2,400	2,400	2,400	9,600
Project expenditures	Schedule 17	8,000	0	10,000	15,000	33,000
Note payable repayment	Schedule 3	1,000	1,000	1,000	1,000	4,000
Other payments..............	Various					0
Total cash payments		$170,735	$170,595	$193,960	$200,054	$735,343
Cash receipts minus disbursements		$ 13,893	$ 9,031	$ 2,824	$ 6,987	$ 32,735
Plus: beginning cash	Schedule 3	15,000	23,893	22,924	20,748	15,000
Cash available................		$ 28,893	$ 32,924	$ 25,748	$ 27,735	$ 47,735
Less: excess cash on hand		(5,000)	(10,000)	(5,000)	(5,000)	(25,000)
Plus: new borrowing needed		0	0	0	0	0
Ending cash balance		$ 23,893	$ 22,924	$ 20,748	$ 22,735	$ 22,735
Cumulative borrowings..........		$ 0	$ 0	$ 0	$ 0	$ 0
Cumulative investments		$ 5,000	$ 15,000	$ 20,000	$ 25,000	$ 25,000

THE EXAMPLE COMPLETED: FORECAST FINANCIAL STATEMENTS

The operating budgets build the base for the coming year's activities. But the operating data also determine the financial results for the year.

Consolidation of the operating numbers into the forecast financial statements is frequently the responsibility of the controller of the firm. These statements are reviewed carefully by the firm's executives. The results are compared to the annual financial goals set earlier. In this example, the schedules used as sources of the account balances are listed to help explain the income statement and balance sheet numbers.

Forecast Income Statement

A forecast income statement is prepared from the budget data for the year. The forecast or pro forma income statement is a summary of the expected revenue and expense budgets and shows whether the annual profit goals can be realized. The forecast makes it easier to evaluate the overall operation. Management can compare its actual income statements with the estimated statements as the year progresses. If budgeted profits are to be realized, adjustments may have to be made as operations progress. Perhaps the budget itself requires revision. At the end of the year, a comparison of actual results with the budget may indicate areas of operation that deserve more attention in the future. Or, comparisons may reveal ways to prepare more realistic budgets.

MARSHALL PRODUCTS COMPANY
FORECAST STATEMENT OF INCOME AND EXPENSE
FOR THE FORECAST YEAR ENDED DECEMBER 31, 1995

	First Quarter	Second Quarter	Third Quarter	Fourth Quarter	Total	Source
Sales:						
Sales of JR EXEC..................	$121,600	$121,600	$136,800	$144,400	$524,400	Sch. 4
Sales of EXEC....................	58,800	68,600	73,500	73,500	274,400	Sch. 4
Total gross sales.................	$180,400	$190,200	$210,300	$217,900	$798,800	
Less: sales returns	(1,804)	(1,902)	(2,103)	(2,179)	(7,988)	Sch. 4
Net sales	$178,596	$188,298	$208,197	$215,721	$790,812	
Cost of goods sold:						
Cost of JR EXECs sold	$ 71,686	$ 71,686	$ 80,647	$ 85,128	$309,148	Sch. 14
Cost of EXECs sold	37,195	43,394	46,494	46,494	173,578	Sch. 14
Total cost of podiums sold	$108,882	$115,081	$127,141	$131,622	$482,725	
Manufacturing variances	4,913	694	(2,025)	(2,063)	1,519	Sch. 10
Total cost of podiums sold	$113,794	$115,775	$125,116	$129,559	$484,244	
Gross margin on sales	$ 64,802	$ 72,523	$ 83,081	$ 86,162	$306,568	
Selling and administrative expense	57,764	57,876	60,881	58,605	235,126	Sch. 15,16
Operating income	$ 7,038	$ 14,647	$ 22,200	$ 27,556	$ 71,442	
Other income:						
Interest income	$ 150	$ 450	$ 600	$ 750	$ 1,950	Calculated
Purchase cash discounts	271	311	333	329	1,245	Sch. 13
Interest expense	(1,920)	(1,890)	(1,860)	(1,830)	(7,500)	Calculated
Sales cash discounts	(2,679)	(2,824)	(3,123)	(3,236)	(11,862)	Sch. 11
Net income before taxes	$ 2,860	$ 10,694	$ 18,150	$ 23,570	$ 55,275	
Income tax expenses	1,144	4,278	7,260	9,428	22,110	Calculated
Net income........................	$ 1,716	$ 6,417	$ 10,890	$ 14,142	$ 33,165	

As can be seen, the sales revenue, cost of goods sold, and selling and administrative expenses information are summarized from earlier schedules. The over- or underapplied overhead is brought from Schedule 10. The other income and expense items and income taxes expense are calculated from data given as financial assumptions or in an earlier schedule.

In practice, a forecast income statement is broken down by months or weeks. In addition, it is subdivided according to product lines, sales regions, and customer groupings. From an analysis of these subdivisions, management can determine which products, regions, or customer groups are most profitable. The actual information is compared to the sales forecast data to update the sales forecast data base.

Forecast Balance Sheet

The forecast or pro forma balance sheet indicates the firm's financial position for some later date. Like the income statement, it is a summary statement that

	December 31, 1994	March 31, 1995	June 30, 1995	September 30, 1995	December 31, 1995	Source
MARSHALL PRODUCTS COMPANY						
FORECAST BALANCE SHEETS						
END OF FORECAST PERIOD						
Assets:						
Cash	$ 15,000	$ 23,893	$ 22,924	$ 20,748	$ 22,735	Sch. 18
Short-Term Investments ..	0	5,000	15,000	20,000	25,000	Sch. 18
Accounts Receivable	58,000	44,649	47,074	52,049	53,930	Sch. 11
Less: Allowance for Bad Debts	(4,640)	(3,572)	(3,766)	(4,164)	(4,314)	Sch. 11,15
Inventory...............	39,310	33,243	36,646	37,775	34,143	Sch 12
Interest Receivable	0	150	450	600	750	Inc. Stat
Current Assets	$107,670	$103,364	$118,329	$127,008	$132,244	
Building and Equipment ..	$350,000	$358,000	$358,000	$368,000	$383,000	Sch. 3,18
Less: Accumulated Depreciation	(100,000)	(107,500)	(115,000)	(122,500)	(130,000)	Sch. 3,10
Other Assets	10,000	10,000	10,000	10,000	10,000	Sch. 3
Total Assets	$367,670	$363,864	$371,329	$382,508	$395,244	
Liabilities and Equity:						
Accounts Payable	$ 10,300	$ 9,034	$ 10,379	$ 11,115	$ 10,971	Sch. 13
Taxes Payable	2,000	1,144	4,278	7,260	9,428	Sch. 3, Inc. Stat
Bank Borrowings	0	0	0	0	0	Sch. 18
Interest Payable	1,920	1,920	1,890	1,860	1,830	Inc. Stat
Total Current Liabilities...	$ 14,220	$ 12,098	$ 16,547	$ 20,235	$ 22,229	
Long-Term Notes Payable	64,000	63,000	62,000	61,000	60,000	Sch. 3,18
Total Liabilities	$ 78,220	$ 75,098	$ 78,547	$ 81,235	$ 82,229	
Capital Stock	$240,000	$240,000	$240,000	$240,000	$240,000	Sch. 3
Retained Earnings	49,450	48,766	52,782	61,273	73,015	Sch. 18, Inc. Stat
Total Equity	$289,450	$288,766	$292,782	$301,273	$313,015	
Total Liabilities and Equity ..	$367,670	$363,864	$371,329	$382,508	$395,244	

depends on the various individual budgets which have been prepared. Rarely will an account be budgeted directly on the balance sheet. Thus, it is the sum of other budgeting efforts. It can be compared with historical statements to show how the accounts will be affected by operations during the budget year. The same type of historical financial statement performance analysis discussed in Chapter 17 should be applied to the forecast statements.

The forecast balance sheet also serves as a point of reference during the year. Interim statements prepared at various dates can be compared with corresponding budget statements. It may be possible to detect unfavorable variations that should be corrected during the year, or the budget itself may require revision.

Forecast Statement of Cash Flows

The statement of cash flows is explained in detail in Chapter 18. A forecast statement of cash flows is a summary of operating, financing, and investing activities over the fiscal year, expressed in cash terms. Financing activities include obtaining resources from owners and creditors, providing owners with dividends, and repaying creditors. Investing activities include buying

MARSHALL PRODUCTS COMPANY
FORECAST CASH FLOW STATEMENTS
FOR THE FORECAST YEAR ENDED DECEMBER 31, 1995

	First Quarter	Second Quarter	Third Quarter	Fourth Quarter	Total
Cash flow from operating activities:					
Net income...............................	$ 1,716	$ 6,417	$ 10,890	$ 14,142	$ 33,165
Add:					
Depreciation expense.........................	7,500	7,500	7,500	7,500	30,000
Change in net accounts receivable..............	12,283	(2,231)	(4,577)	(1,731)	3,744
Change in inventories.........................	6,067	(3,403)	(1,129)	3,632	5,167
Change in interest receivable	(150)	(300)	(150)	(150)	(750)
Change in accounts payable	(1,266)	1,345	736	(144)	671
Change in taxes payable	(856)	3,134	2,982	2,168	7,428
Change in interest payable	0	(30)	(30)	(30)	(90)
Cash flow from operations	$ 25,294	$ 12,432	$ 16,222	$ 25,407	$ 79,335
Cash flow from investing activities:					
Equipment purchases...........................	$ (8,000)	$ 0	$(10,000)	$(15,000)	$(33,000)
Short-term investments purchases	(5,000)	(10,000)	(5,000)	(5,000)	(25,000)
Cash flow from investing	$(13,000)	$(10,000)	$(15,000)	$(20,000)	$(58,000)
Cash flow from financing activities:					
Dividends paid................................	$ (2,400)	$ (2,400)	$ (2,400)	$ (2,400)	$ (9,600)
Notes payable repaid	(1,000)	(1,000)	(1,000)	(1,000)	(4,000)
Cash flow from financing	$ (3,400)	$ (3,400)	$ (3,400)	$ (3,400)	$(13,600)
Change in cash balance	$ 8,893*	$ (969)*	$ (2,176)*	$ 1,987	$ 7,735

* Difference due to rounding to whole dollars.

and selling productive assets and financial investments. Operating activities include the normal business transactions that the firm conducts on a day-to-day basis. But, to complete the master budget for the Marshall Products Company, it is necessary to give a forecast statement of cash flows.

From this report, operations generated nearly $80,000 which was used to purchase equipment and acquire short-term investments. These numbers can be taken from the balance sheet, cash flow forecast, and initial assumptions.

Master Budget Summary

Several observations should be made about the master budget discussion and example:

1. The budget should be self balancing. As a test of completeness, the balance sheet should balance at the end of the budget period. This means that all accounting issues in the plan have been included in the statements. Mechanically, the budget balances.
2. The budget should be tested for reasonableness in all areas and departments. The tests should include:
    (a) Reviewing the reasonableness of the critical independent variable (most often the sales forecast) as a key evaluation step.
    (b) Sensitivity analysis to determine whether small changes in key values will cause major changes in profitability or cash flow.
    (c) "What if" analysis to determine whether a better combination of budgeted efforts would produce a stronger plan.
    (d) Rechecking and approval by all levels of management involved in the planning effort.
3. The final budgeted results should be analyzed for achievement of the original planning goals and objectives.

Many iterations may be needed to arrive at a budget that managers can "buy into," satisfies top management's goals, and pushes the firm toward its long-range goals.

This budgeting process assumes active participation of managers in each department and subunit of the firm. Costs are budgeted in each cost center. Cost drivers are used to measure expected activity and to forecast costs at those levels. The quality of these estimates determines the value of the budget as a plan of action. The effectiveness of the budgeting process also affects our ability to control costs, to cost products accurately, and to make decisions using the budget data.

In this example, the assumptions used in Schedules 1, 2, and 3 merely appeared. Developing these inputs is a difficult and critical step. As can now be seen, changes in prices, balances, percentages, and needs can have major impacts on cash flows, profits, account balances, and financing needs.

FINANCIAL PLANNING MODELS

We are living in a rapidly changing environment. The problem is how to cope with the changes. One tool now widely available for managing change is a financial planning model. **Modeling** is a meaningful abstraction of reality where key variables and relationships are mathematically represented. In the past 10 years, computer capabilities have brought financial modeling and simulation to even the smallest firms. **Simulation** is using a model to test policies, decisions, and alternative forecast scenarios. This section defines a financial planning model and types of models and looks at the uses of financial simulation. The major application, testing plans using "what if" analysis, is illustrated.

Defining the Financial Planning Model

In its most basic sense, a model is a meaningful abstraction of something real. A **financial planning model** converts an organization's accounting and other processes into a series of equations. These equations represent the interrelationships existing within an organization. The object is to simulate, using the computer, all significant definable processes that may affect the organization and to arrive at a realistic representation of actual results. The successful operation of any model depends on defining relationships, identifying key variables, and inputting accurate, complete, and timely data.

Successful models are developed for specific purposes and users. The objective of a model should be defined clearly before it is developed. The level of sophistication depends on the scope and complexity of the problem to be modeled, modeling and computer experience of the user, ease of use, availability of data, and the degree of accuracy needed. In its simplest form a model might take a column of a spreadsheet and multiply it by a growth percentage to create a forecast in another column. On the other hand, a large model might require a mainframe computer and consider thousands of variables and make millions of calculations.

The master budget is an excellent example of defining the interrelationships that describe an organization's operating and financial functions, its inputs, and its outputs. The system supporting the master budget contains the firm's goals, product prices and costs, production and inventory decision rules, relationships of indirect costs to cost objectives, and other operating and financial data and assumptions. If the model is adequately specified, an old balance sheet is combined with the relationship equations and independent variable data to generate a new balance sheet. All other operating and financial schedules and statements are also produced. The time frame could be multi-year, annual, monthly, or even weekly.

Financial planning models:

1.   Help develop and test planning goals and operating and financial policies.

2. Perform "what if" analysis to:
    (a) Evaluate results of complex decisions.
    (b) Measure impacts of policy changes.
    (c) Measure impacts of price and cost changes.
    (d) Measure the potential for achieving financial goals and targets.
3. Help assess long-range impacts of specific strategies.
4. Demonstrate results of planning without incurring the costs of making the decisions in the real world by:
    (a) Indicating the direction and magnitude of change.
    (b) Identifying early warning signals that may require managerial attention.
    (c) Fine tuning actions in combination decisions to find optimal points.
    (d) Allowing advocates of competing strategies to "strut their stuff."
5. If tied directly to the master budget, help speed up budget consolidation, give fast feedback for budget revisions, and provide increased time for budget analysis.
6. Provide an educational tool that can help illustrate the financial planning process, the integration of the budget steps, and the ties among complementary and conflicting goals.

Output from a financial planning model is typically in the form of income statements, balance sheets, cash flow statements, capital expenditure projections, and schedules for analysis of plans. Financial models come in all sizes, modes, and complexity. Usually, the model will be used repeatedly over time. Rarely is a model developed for one-time use. The range of model types includes:

1. **Manual calculations** which follow a series of steps, involve a limited amount of data and interrelationships, and rarely require a large number of iterations.
2. **Spreadsheet software** (generally personal computer based) that can be:
    (a) Developed by a user for a specific application.
    (b) Purchased from a software vendor and modified for a user's unique characteristics.
    (c) Purchased software on a use-as-received basis.
3. **Stand alone programmed software** developed for personal computers, minicomputers, and mainframes that are similar to spreadsheet software. These models exist separately from a firm's accounting transaction and reporting systems. Needed data can be downloaded and uploaded to and from the model. This type includes the broadest array of products from simple to complex. Models are offered by vendors for under $100. At the other end of the spectrum, companies have invested hundreds of thousands of dollars in developing their own models. If industry and firm uniqueness and specific purpose can be built into the software, buying a product from a vendor is often less costly than a self-developed model.

4. **Modeling capabilities integrated into the accounting systems** of the firm. The model is nearly indistinguishable as a separate accounting unit. All aspects of the accounting and finance function are modeled as a general management activity and not as separate accounting and finance applications. This will be the eventual situation for all companies. Few firms are presently at this stage of modeling. But as new accounting and operating information systems are designed and implemented, more modeling will be integrated.

The variety of products is large and growing. Need and cost are moving in opposite directions.

Elements of the Model

A financial planning model consists of three significant elements: inputs, the model itself, and outputs. These are combined to create a mathematical representation of the organization it models. In Figure 8.1 on page 379, the basic modeling elements are illustrated and linked.

Inputs   Inputs are historical data bases, economic and other forecast information, operating and financial factors, management policies, planning assumptions, and model queries. The historical data bases include the detailed financial statement account balances, transaction summaries, statistical relationships, economic data, nonfinancial quantitative data, and other data bases needed in specific industries such as banking. The forecast information may be internally generated, developed from external sources, or even purchased from vendors of forecast data.

Operating factors represent capacity constraints, physical relationships of equipment and production processes, customer demand and credit terms, product bills of materials and processes, inventory and warehousing links, shipping and delivery time schedules, and staffing levels. Financial factors include cash collection and payment patterns, borrowing and investing policies, capitalization issues, taxes, and accounting policies and practices.

Management policies involve goals setting, pricing, promotional efforts, debt/equity relationships, dividends, salary and benefits practices, and all other decision rules that affect the financial affairs of the firm directly and indirectly. Often management guidelines or constraints are needed to serve as **parameters** or boundaries for model variable values and to keep the model "in control." Planning assumptions include the items already illustrated in the master budget example plus anticipated inflation rates, salary and benefits costs, growth in markets, and other forecasting guides.

Model queries are the changes in the independent variables that are made to run the model and to do "what ifs." If prices or costs are to be changed, someone must enter the new values. This is defining the modeling problem, posing the "what if" question, and entering any new assumptions or data. Also, **management overrides** may be allowed to provide managers with a mechanism to supersede statistical projections or other modeled values that are unrealistic.

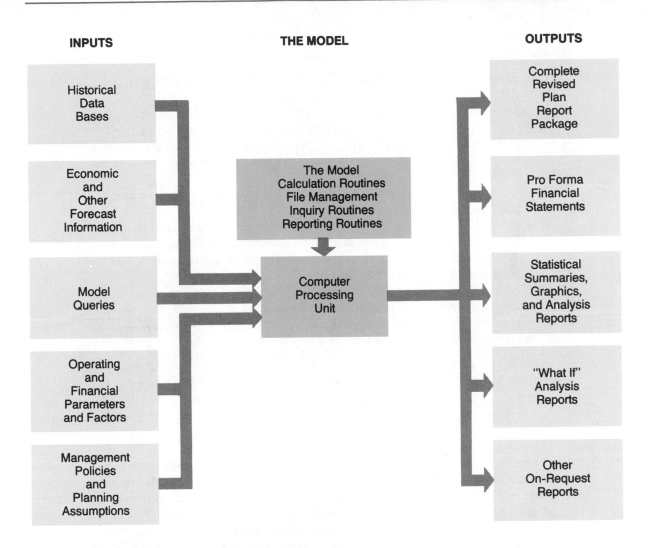

Figure 8.1 Elements of the Financial Planning Model

In master budgeting terminology, the inputs are the independent variables. Also, a new term, **constants**, plays an important role. Clearly, any data from external sources are independent variables. Historical data are hardly variables since they are fixed and cannot change. These data are constants. Operating and financial factors, management policies, and planning assumptions are independent variables in most models since the data items and relationships are defined by management or can change if management decides to change the linkages.

The Model   The second element is the model itself—a core of subroutines, interrelationships, and computer power that makes the model work. Calculation routines, file management processes, reporting routines, and user inquiry routines are the major components. While the essential resource is often computer power, modeling calculations may also require:

1. Statistical routines for projecting, curve fitting, seasonality factors, confidence interval setting, and even probability measurement.
2. Formulas for measuring capacity, yields from resources, input/ output relationships, production and distribution linkages, and other fixed or given interrelationships. (Whether a particular relationship is a given or a managerial input depends on managerial intent and the specific situation.)
3. Optimization routines in situations that call for maximization or minimization of some goal or objective.
4. Interactive capability to allow users to perform "on-line what ifs."
5. File management capabilities for automatic updating and easy downloading of data from other accounting systems for new actual results and other changes in data files.
6. Accrual accounting rules, account summarization, accounting balancing routines, and report preparation routines.
7. Ideally, flexibility and expandability to allow the model to grow as users gain experience and make more demands on the model.

While not all these tools are necessary, they do represent typical needs of computer-based models. Most of these tools will not be visible to the user. For example, a bank financial planning model needs to know that February 1996 has 29 days and not 28. But few users will consciously think about this minute detail.

Outputs   The third element is the model's output: revised plans, pro forma financial statements, statistical summaries, "what if" analyses, and other reports requested by managers. These reports can be hard copy output, screen displays, or graphs and other displays. Outputs are often **"what if" analyses** where different values are inserted for independent variables. "What ifs" can be compared to the base budget, prior period actuals, or other "what if" scenarios. A key to multiple runs is to identify the "what if" changes made that created the new output. In the heat of budget analysis, prior versions may need to be referenced and labelled to avoid confusion with other "what ifs." To use the model's output, a well-defined report package that allows managers to create relevant report formats and comparisons should be available. To the extent possible, the report formats should parallel the regular management reports. Often a set of reports is prepared as a package. Managers come to expect this set and know where to look for key ratios, earnings or cash flow impacts, and specific items within their areas of responsibility.

Structuring the Interrelationships

In structuring the interrelationships used by the model, the primary purpose is to transfer the computational burden from the user to the computer. The user is the beginning point. The new model user needs tutorials, learning aids, menus, and often explanations of basic model relationships. An experienced, but nontechnical, user will quickly see more interrelationships that will make the model more representative of the real world. An experienced and computer-savvy user will want an ability to add, adapt, and change interrelationships and linkages. The "walk before you run" adage has validity when learning to use financial planning models.

Which relationships should be modeled and which should be ignored? The criteria should include:

1. Materiality: Is it big enough to count?
2. Controllability: Can management do something about it?
3. Sensitivity: If it changes, will the change have major impact on key variables?
4. Explainability: Can the relationship be logically described?
5. Historical support: Do past data support the linkage?
6. Computational necessity and completeness: Are the calculations needed to create accuracy or accounting validity?
7. Managerial believability: Must the links be included because key managers will look for the linkage to decide on the model's trustworthiness?

Care must be taken when building the model to keep the model simple enough to manage and operate and yet capture the essential elements of the decision or environment being modeled.

"What If" Analysis

To demonstrate "what if" analysis in a modeling environment, several examples will be taken from the master budget illustration begun in Chapter 7 and completed earlier in this chapter. Let us assume that the controller of Marshall Products now has the budget as prepared. But several specific nagging questions are bothering the president. Four of these are:

1. Product cost changes.
2. Sales forecast changes.
3. Inventory policy changes.
4. Collections and payables assumptions changes.

Each will be examined and compared to original forecast data.

Example 1—Product Cost Changes   Wood prices may increase substantially over the next year. The increases may be as much as 10 percent on plywood and 8 percent on trim. The president wonders what the impact will be on earnings after tax and on the earnings goals of Marshall Products.

Product costs from Schedule 1:

| | | Original Forecast | | | | "What If" Change | | |
| | | JR EXEC | | EXEC | | | JR EXEC | EXEC |
	Price	Quantity	Total	Quantity	Total	New Price	Total	Total
Materials:								
Plywood (sq ft)...........	$0.2750	12.00	$3.30	16.00	$4.40	$0.3025	$3.63	$4.84
Wood screws (unit).......	0.0215	18.00	0.39	24.00	0.52	0.0215	0.39	0.52
Trim (feet)..............	0.0850	15.00	1.28	18.00	1.53	0.0918	1.38	1.65
Material total			$4.96		$6.45		$5.39	$7.01

The impacts of the changes on net income and on certain goals are:

	Original Forecast	"What If" Change	Percent Change
Net income...	$33,165	$27,583	(16.83%)
Goals:			
Profitability goal: 10% return on equity.................................	11.01%	9.21%	(16.34%)
Product cost below 65% of sales price—JR EXEC	58.95%	60.09%	1.93%
Product cost below 65% of sales price—EXEC	63.26%	64.40%	1.80%

The 10 and 8 percent changes in wood materials costs translate into over a 16 percent decrease in net income. The drop in net income causes the return on equity percentage to drop below the 10 percent goal. If the wood cost increases occur, management will have to raise prices, reduce other costs, act now to sign long-term purchase contracts at current lower prices, or take some other earnings improving action. The increased total product cost of EXEC also approaches the 65 percent of sales price level. This goal may well be used by management to signal potential profit problems. This "what if" scenario will also apply to labor cost negotiations, overhead cost changes, and marketing and distribution cost changes.

Example 2—Sales Forecast Changes   To sell 13,800 units of JR EXEC and 5,600 units of EXEC, the Podium Speakers Society of American will need to increase enrollments about 10 percent. If economic conditions cause growth to be only 5 or 6 percent, sales could be 100 units less each quarter of each product. The president asks what the impact will be on net income after taxes and on the sales and earnings goals of Marshall Products.

	Original Forecast	"What If" Change	Percent Change
Units of sales (1994 units sold were 17,650)	19,400	18,600	(4.12%)
Net income...	$33,165	$23,965	(27.74%)
Goals:			
Growth goal: 10% growth in sales dollars (1994 sales dollars were $680,000)	17.47%	12.35%	(29.31%)
Profitability goal: 10% return on equity....................................	11.01%	8.07%	(26.70%)
Product cost below 65% of sales price—JR EXEC	58.95%	59.72%	1.31%
Product cost below 65% of sales price—EXEC	63.26%	64.08%	1.30%

The slower growth (5 percent instead of 10 percent) has a dramatic impact on profits. Prices were increased from 1994 levels, since units sales are to increase by only 10 percent while sales dollars are to jump by 17 percent. Net income under the "what if" change drops by over 25 percent. The sales dollar growth still reaches the 10 percent target, but return on equity drops to 8 percent. An interesting aside that would not be obvious is an increase in unit costs. With lower volumes, the activity bases for overhead application in the factory would drop causing manufacturing overhead rates to increase. Again, as in Example 1, the unit cost of EXEC comes close to the 65 percent target. This "what if" shows that a 4 percent change in sales has a 27 percent impact on profits.

Example 3—Inventory Policy Changes

To respond to the erratic patterns of certain PSSA chapters, the president is thinking about keeping more finished podiums on hand at the end of each quarter. The current policy is to have 25 percent of next quarter's sales in ending inventory. The president wonders what impact a 50 percent policy will have on cash flow and inventory goals.

	First Quarter	Second Quarter	Third Quarter	Fourth Quarter	Total
Original Forecast from Schedule 18:					
Cash receipts minus disbursements	$ 13,893	$ 9,031	$ 2,824	$ 6,987	$ 32,735
"What If" Change:					
Cash receipts minus disbursements	$ (4,692)	$ 1,419	$ 1,312	$ 8,425	$ 6,464
Difference	$(18,585)	$ (7,612)	$ (1,512)	$ 1,438	$(26,271)

	Original Forecast	"What If" Change	Percent Change
Net income	$33,165	$36,359	9.63%
Goals:			
Profitability goal: 10% return on equity	11.01%	12.02%	9.17%
Reduce inventory by 10% from beginning levels	13.14%	(62.20%)	(573.36%)
Product cost below 65% of sales price—JR EXEC	58.95%	58.25%	1.19%
Product cost below 65% of sales price—EXEC	63.26%	62.51%	1.19%

The finished podiums inventory change would have a dramatic impact on cash flow. Over 1995, forecast net cash inflows would drop by over $26,000. In fact, Marshall Products would have to borrow funds in the first quarter when the new policy would have the greatest impact on production and cash outflows. The goal of inventory reduction is thrown out the window—inventories grow by over 60 percent.

An interesting sidelight is the improved profitability and lower product cost percentages. This is a result of higher production levels and higher activity levels for overhead application—the reverse of Example 2. This is a very short-lived earnings shot, since the major earnings gain comes in the first quarter. In later quarters, the cost of carrying the extra inventory overcomes the lower product costs as can be seen from the net income numbers from the original and "what if" forecasts:

	First Quarter	Second Quarter	Third Quarter	Fourth Quarter	Total
Original forecast net income	$ 1,716	$ 6,417	$10,890	$14,142	$33,165
"What If" Example 3 net income........................	$ 6,036	$ 6,502	$10,605	$13,216	$36,359

On into 1996, the cost of carrying the extra inventory will probably by about $3,000 to $4,000 per year.

Example 4—Collections and Payables Assumptions Changes   Recent national economic problems may make credit tighter. The president thinks chapters will be paying Marshall Products much slower, changing the receivables collected in the month of sale from 75 percent to 50 percent. To offset this, Marshall Products could delay paying some of its payables in the month incurred, dropping the payment percentage from 60 percent to 50 percent, without hurting its credit rating. The president wonders what this would do to Marshall Product's cash flow pattern.

	First Quarter	Second Quarter	Third Quarter	Fourth Quarter	Total
Original Forecast from Schedule 18:					
Cash receipts minus disbursements................	$ 13,893	$ 9,031	$ 2,824	$ 6,987	$ 32,735
"What If" Change:					
Cash receipts minus disbursements................	$(25,329)	$ 6,863	$ (2,057)	$ 4,889	$(15,635)
Difference..	$(39,222)	$ (2,168)	$ (4,881)	$ (1,098)	$(48,370)

	Original Forecast	"What If" Change	Percent Change
Goals:			
Liquidity goal: Current ratio of better than 3:1	5.95:1	3.21:1	(46.05%)

The drain on cash is very large, approaching $50,000 for the year. By year end, no short-term investments will exist and bank borrowings will increase by $25,000. Receivables and payables will grow, but the biggest impact is moving from an excess cash position to a serious cash deficit. If a credit crunch occurs, interest rates probably will also increase causing interest expenses to grow. The president will want to study this forecast with great care.

"What if" analysis can be applied to any independent variable in the model. Combinations of changes can be handled quickly and easily. Often obvious impacts will show up, but surprising results also appear. The "what if" analysis can be used to make decisions and to anticipate changed conditions that will force changes in strategy and in the plan of action.

Financial modeling and business simulation have become an industry itself within a very short time period. Many firms are in the business of supplying software, consulting on planning systems, and providing planning data. All this has occurred within the past ten years.

SUMMARY

A master budget example was developed to show the integrative nature of the various budget schedules. These schedules were brought together as a complete set, as new forecast financial statements were built and balanced.

A major development over the past 10 years is the computer power brought to bear on simulation and applied to financial modeling. In developing a financial planning model, the master budget is probably the best source for understanding the interrelationships that describe the operating and financial functions and the organization's objectives, inputs, and outputs. The ability to model the master budget and to test every controllable decision and assumption has tremendously increased the analysis of the plan of action. Even testing goals and objectives for realism has increased budgeting believability for management. This chapter, defined modeling, described its benefits, and explained its elements. Using the example master budget, several "what ifs" were run to test alternative scenarios.

PROBLEM FOR REVIEW

The Gizmo Company manufactures two varieties of gizmos: regular and deluxe. The company is now in the process of preparing its master budget by quarter for 1995. Mike Binder, Budget Director, has gathered the information from all departments and is ready to compile the operating budget part of the master budget. The following data represent expectations for 1995.

Product cost build up based on past and desired performance levels is as follows:

	Regular	Deluxe
Materials:		
AX-89 metal costing $1.80 per sheet	$ 3.60	$ 5.40
M172P component part costing $3.40 per unit	10.20	13.60
Total materials cost per unit	$ 13.80	$ 19.00
Direct labor costing $9.00 per hour	13.50	18.00
Manufacturing overhead costing $13.50 per direct labor hour	20.25	27.00
Total cost per unit	$ 47.55	$ 64.00
Selling price	$100.00	$135.00

For the upcoming year, the company is planning to have quarterly ending inventories at 20 percent of sales units anticipated for the next quarter. The year will begin with 1,000 units of regular, at a cost of $47,550, and 250 units of deluxe, at a cost of $16,000. Sales for each quarter are expected to be:

GIZMO SALES FORECAST

	First Quarter	Second Quarter	Third Quarter	Fourth Quarter	Total
1995:					
Regular	5,000	6,000	5,500	7,000	23,500
Deluxe	1,200	1,500	1,500	2,000	6,200
1996:					
Regular	5,700	6,800			
Deluxe	1,600	2,100			

Experience has shown that 3 percent of gross sales revenues will be returns and allowances during the quarter of sale. Uncollectible accounts represent 2 percent of gross sales revenues.

Beginning and ending inventories for work in process will be negligible. That is, all production for a quarter should be started and completed during that quarter. Normal capacity for operations is 12,000 direct labor hours per quarter.

Materials inventories are expected to be 40 percent of the next quarter's anticipated production requirements. Beginning inventories consist of 2,500 AX-89 sheets at a cost of $4,500 and 3,000 M172P component parts at a cost of $10,200.

At normal capacity, the following formulas are used to budget the various factory overhead costs for each quarter:

Depreciation	$21,000 per quarter		
Fringe benefits			$1.80 per direct labor hour (DLH)
Indirect labor			4.40 per DLH
Repair and maintenance	4,500 per quarter	plus	1.30 per DLH
Supervision	18,000 per quarter		
Supplies			1.20 per DLH
Taxes and insurance	3,500 per quarter		
Utilities	1,000 per quarter	plus	0.80 per DLH
Total	$48,000 per quarter	plus	$9.50 per DLH

Selling expenses are either fixed or vary with the number of units sold. They are:

Shipping and delivery	$1.00 per unit
Supplies	0.10 per unit
Telephone	0.50 per unit
Advertising	$6,000 per quarter
Depreciation	1,500 per quarter
Rent	12,000 per quarter
Salaries	20,000 per quarter
Travel and entertainment	4,500 per quarter
Utilities	700 per quarter

General and administrative expenses are budgeted at $75,000 for each quarter of 1995. Of that amount, $15,000 is depreciation expense. The research & development expense budget for the year are shown on page 387.

The company has investment income and interest expense which is recognized as other income and expense in the income statement. Investment income is received at the end of each quarter, as shown below.

	First Quarter	Second Quarter	Third Quarter	Fourth Quarter	Total
Research & development........................	$ 25,000	$ 31,000	$ 29,000	$ 37,000	$122,000
Investment income	2,800	2,800	5,600	6,440	17,640
Interest expenses		900			900

Income taxes are at a 40 percent rate.

Required:
Prepare each of the following budgets by quarter for 1995:

1. Sales revenue budget.
2. Production budget.
3. Purchases budget.
4. Direct labor budget.
5. Manufacturing overhead budget.
6. Selling expense budget.
7. Forecast cash flow statement.
8. Forecast income statement.
9. Forecast balance sheet as of December 31, 1995.

Solution:
1. **Sales revenue budget.** The unit sales forecast and prices generate the estimate of future revenues:

GIZMO SALES REVENUE BUDGET

	First Quarter	Second Quarter	Third Quarter	Fourth Quarter	Total
Gross sales:					
Regular......................................	$500,000	$600,000	$550,000	$700,000	$2,350,000
Deluxe	162,000	202,500	202,500	270,000	837,000
Total	$662,000	$802,500	$752,500	$970,000	$3,187,000
Less:					
Returns and allowances......................	19,860	24,075	22,575	29,100	95,610
Net sales	$642,140	$778,425	$729,925	$940,900	$3,091,390
Less:					
Uncollectible accounts	13,240	16,050	15,050	19,400	63,740
Net collectible sales	$628,900	$762,375	$714,875	$921,500	$3,027,650

2. **Production budget.** The extra columns that reflect data for the first and second quarters of 1996 are added only because these data are necessary for calculating budgeting information for quarters in 1995.

GIZMO PRODUCTION BUDGET

| | 1995 | | | | | 1996 | |
	First Quarter	Second Quarter	Third Quarter	Fourth Quarter	Total	First Quarter	Second Quarter
Regular Gizmos:							
Units to be sold	5,000	6,000	5,500	7,000	23,500	5,700	6,800
Add: Ending inventory	1,200	1,100	1,400	1,140	1,140	1,360	
Total needed	6,200	7,100	6,900	8,140	24,640	7,060	
Less: Beginning inventory	1,000	1,200	1,100	1,400	1,000	1,140	
Units to be produced	5,200	5,900	5,800	6,740	23,640	5,920	
Deluxe Gizmos:							
Units to be sold	1,200	1,500	1,500	2,000	6,200	1,600	2,100
Add: Ending inventory	300	300	400	320	320	420	
Total needed	1,500	1,800	1,900	2,320	6,520	2,020	
Less: Beginning inventory	250	300	300	400	250	320	
Units to be produced	1,250	1,500	1,600	1,920	6,270	1,700	

3. **Purchases budget.** Units and dollars can be combined in one budget. Remember the materials amounts must be computed by multiplying units to be produced by the material requirements of each unit.

GIZMO PURCHASES BUDGET

| | 1995 | | | | | 1996 |
	First Quarter	Second Quarter	Third Quarter	Fourth Quarter	Total	First Quarter
AX-89 production requirement:						
Regular	10,400	11,800	11,600	13,480	47,280	11,840
Deluxe	3,750	4,500	4,800	5,760	18,810	5,100
Total product needs	14,150	16,300	16,400	19,240	66,090	16,940
Add: Desired ending inventory	6,520	6,560	7,696	6,776	6,776	
Total production needs....................	20,670	22,860	24,096	26,016	72,866	
Less: Beginning inventory	2,500	6,520	6,560	7,696	2,500	
Units to be purchased	18,170	16,340	17,536	18,320	70,366	
Budgeted purchases cost	$32,706	$29,412	$31,565	$32,976	$126,659	
M172P production requirement:						
Regular	15,600	17,700	17,400	20,220	70,920	17,760
Deluxe	5,000	6,000	6,400	7,680	25,080	6,800
Total product needs	20,600	23,700	23,800	27,900	96,000	24,560
Add: Desired ending inventory	9,480	9,520	11,160	9,824	9,824	
Total production needs....................	30,080	33,220	34,960	37,724	105,824	
Less: Beginning inventory	3,000	9,480	9,520	11,160	3,000	
Units to be purchased	27,080	23,740	25,440	26,564	102,824	
Budgeted purchases cost	$92,072	$80,716	$86,496	$90,318	$349,602	

4. **Direct labor budget.** This budget is based on multiplying the units to be produced by the number of direct labor hours required for each unit.

GIZMO DIRECT LABOR BUDGET

	First Quarter	Second Quarter	Third Quarter	Fourth Quarter	Total
Hours worked:					
Regular	7,800	8,850	8,700	10,110	35,460
Deluxe	2,500	3,000	3,200	3,840	12,540
Total hours worked	10,300	11,850	11,900	13,950	48,000
Labor rate per hour	$ 9	$ 9	$ 9	$ 9	$ 9
Budgeted labor cost	$92,700	$106,650	$107,100	$125,550	$432,000

5. **Manufacturing overhead budget.** The variable overhead costs are calculated by multiplying the variable rate by the direct labor hours in the direct labor budget in (4) above.

GIZMO MANUFACTURING OVERHEAD BUDGET

	First Quarter	Second Quarter	Third Quarter	Fourth Quarter	Total
Variable overhead:					
Fringe benefits	$ 18,540	$ 21,330	$ 21,420	$ 25,110	$ 86,400
Indirect labor	45,320	52,140	52,360	61,380	211,200
Repairs and maintenance	13,390	15,405	15,470	18,135	62,400
Supplies	12,360	14,220	14,280	16,740	57,600
Utilities	8,240	9,480	9,520	11,160	38,400
Total variable overhead	$ 97,850	$112,575	$113,050	$132,525	$456,000
Fixed overhead:					
Depreciation	$ 21,000	$ 21,000	$ 21,000	$ 21,000	$ 84,000
Repairs and maintenance	4,500	4,500	4,500	4,500	18,000
Supervision	18,000	18,000	18,000	18,000	72,000
Taxes and insurance	3,500	3,500	3,500	3,500	14,000
Utilities	1,000	1,000	1,000	1,000	4,000
Total fixed overhead	$ 48,000	$ 48,000	$ 48,000	$ 48,000	$192,000
Total factory overhead	$145,850	$160,575	$161,050	$180,525	$648,000

6. **Selling expense budget.** The variable selling expense is based on the units sold. Units are an independent variable, not calculated in a preceding budget.

GIZMO SELLING EXPENSE BUDGET

	First Quarter	Second Quarter	Third Quarter	Fourth Quarter	Total
Variable selling expenses:					
Shipping and delivery	$ 6,200	$ 7,500	$ 7,000	$ 9,000	$ 29,700
Supplies	620	750	700	900	2,970
Telephone	3,100	3,750	3,500	4,500	14,850
Total variable expenses	$ 9,920	$12,000	$11,200	$14,400	$ 47,520

	First Quarter	Second Quarter	Third Quarter	Fourth Quarter	Total
Fixed selling expenses:					
Advertising	$ 6,000	$ 6,000	$ 6,000	$ 6,000	$ 24,000
Depreciation	1,500	1,500	1,500	1,500	6,000
Rent	12,000	12,000	12,000	12,000	48,000
Salaries	20,000	20,000	20,000	20,000	80,000
Travel and entertainment	4,500	4,500	4,500	4,500	18,000
Utilities	700	700	700	700	2,800
Total fixed expense	$44,700	$44,700	$44,700	$44,700	$178,800
Total selling expense	$54,620	$56,700	$55,900	$59,100	$226,320

7. **Cash flow forecast.** The cash flows from all the above schedules are brought together in total receipts and disbursements.

GIZMO CASH FLOW FORECAST
FOR THE YEAR ENDED DECEMBER 31, 1995:

	First Quarter	Second Quarter	Third Quarter	Fourth Quarter	Total
Cash balance, beginning	$ 15,000	$ 10,560	$ 50,482	$ 50,520	$ 15,000
Budgeted receipts:					
Collections on receivables:					
Previous quarter's sales	$120,000	$188,670	$228,713	$214,463	$ 751,845
Current quarter's sales	440,230	533,663	500,413	645,050	2,119,355
Total collections	$560,230	$722,333	$729,125	$859,513	$2,871,200
Redemption of securities	0	0	0	0	0
Interest received	2,800	2,800	5,600	6,440	17,640
Total cash receipts	$563,030	$725,133	$734,725	$865,953	$2,888,840
Cash available	$578,030	$735,692	$785,207	$916,472	$2,903,840
Budgeted disbursements:					
Materials purchases:					
Previous quarter's payments	$ 7,000	$ 12,478	$ 11,013	$ 11,806	$ 42,297
Current quarter's payments	112,300	99,115	106,255	110,965	428,635
Total materials payments	$119,300	$111,593	$117,268	$122,771	$ 470,932
Direct labor	92,700	106,650	107,100	125,550	432,000
Manufacturing overhead	124,850	139,575	140,050	159,525	564,000
Selling expense	53,120	55,200	54,400	57,600	220,320
General and administrative expense	60,000	60,000	60,000	60,000	240,000
Research and development expense	25,000	31,000	29,000	37,000	122,000
Income tax payments	104,500	62,292	87,870	81,060	335,722
Plant expansion	0	0	100,000	200,000	300,000
Interest expense paid	0	900	0	0	900
Dividends paid	18,000	18,000	18,000	18,000	72,000
Total cash payments	$597,470	$585,210	$713,688	$861,506	$2,757,874
Excess (Deficiency) of cash	$ (19,440)	$150,482	$ 71,520	$ 54,966	$ 145,966
Investment of excess cash	0	(70,000)	(21,000)	(4,000)	(95,000)
Borrowings	30,000	0	0	0	30,000
Repayment of loans	0	(30,000)	0	0	(30,000)
Cash balance, ending	$ 10,560	$ 50,482	$ 50,520	$ 50,966	$ 50,966

8.   **Forecast income statement.** The quarterly statement of earnings is critical to assessing the success of the budget in achieving the profit goals of the firm.

GIZMO FORECAST INCOME STATEMENT
FOR THE YEAR ENDED DECEMBER 31, 1995

	First Quarter	Second Quarter	Third Quarter	Fourth Quarter	Total
Net sales	$642,140	$778,425	$729,925	$940,900	$3,091,390
Cost of goods sold:					
Beginning inventory	$ 63,550	$ 76,260	$ 71,505	$ 92,170	$ 63,550
Current production	327,260	376,545	378,190	443,367	1,525,362
Total	$390,810	$452,805	$449,695	$535,537	$1,588,912
Less: Ending inventory	76,260	71,505	92,170	74,687	74,687
Cost of goods sold	$314,550	$381,300	$357,525	$460,850	$1,514,225
Over- (under-) applied overhead....	(6,800)	(600)	(400)	7,800	0
Adjusted cost of goods sold......	$321,350	$381,900	$357,925	$453,050	$1,514,225
Gross margin	$320,790	$396,525	$372,000	$487,850	$1,577,165
Operating expenses:					
Selling expense	$ 54,620	$ 56,700	$ 55,900	$ 59,100	$ 226,320
Uncollectible accounts	13,240	16,050	15,050	19,400	63,740
General and administration expense	75,000	75,000	75,000	75,000	300,000
Research and development expense	25,000	31,000	29,000	37,000	122,000
Total operating expenses.........	$167,860	$178,750	$174,950	$190,500	$ 712,060
Operating income	$152,930	$217,775	$197,050	$297,350	$ 865,105
Other income and expenses:					
Investment income	$ 2,800	$ 2,800	$ 5,600	$ 6,440	$ 17,640
Interest expense	0	(900)	0	0	(900)
Net other income and expenses	$ 2,800	$ 1,900	$ 5,600	$ 6,440	$ 16,740
Income before income taxes	$155,730	$219,675	$202,650	$303,790	$ 881,845
Income tax (40 percent)	62,292	87,870	81,060	121,516	352,738
Net income.......................	$ 93,438	$131,805	$121,590	$182,274	$ 529,107

9.   **Forecast balance sheet as of December 31, 1995.** The year-end balance sheet shown on page 392 gives the financial end point of the budget year.

TERMINOLOGY REVIEW

Administrative expense budget (369)
Bill of materials (355)
Bill of materials explosion (360)
Constants (379)
Financial planning model (376)
Management overrides (378)
Model queries (378)
Modeling (376)

Parameters (378)
Pro forma (or forecast) financial statements (357)
Selling or marketing expense budget (368)
Simulation (376)
"What If" analyses (380)

GIZMO FORECAST BALANCE SHEET
AS OF DECEMBER 31, 1995

Assets:
  Current assets:
    Cash .... $ 50,966
    Marketable securities   165,000
    Accounts receivable, net   276,450
    Inventories:
      Finished goods $74,687
      Materials 45,599   120,286
    Total current assets .... $ 612,702
    Plant and equipment, net of accumulated depreciation   678,750
  Total assets $1,291,452

Liabilities:
  Current liabilities:
    Accounts payable .... $ 12,329
    Estimated income tax payable ....   121,516 $ 133,845
  Stockholders' equity:
    Capital stock $600,000
    Retained earnings   557,607
  Total equities   1,157,607
  Total liabilities and equity... $1,291,452

QUESTIONS FOR REVIEW AND DISCUSSION

1. How is a production budget translated into a materials purchases budget?

2. Why do the formats suggested in Chapter 7 make the preparation of the schedules in the example in Chapter 8 easier to complete?

3. What is the difference between the flexible manufacturing overhead budget and the spending and applied overhead budget?

4. From the master budget example, identify the independent variables. Which schedules contain only dependent variables?

5. Why is it important that the balance sheet balance in budgeting?

6. Explain why cash receipts from customers may not fall in the same fiscal period as sales revenues.

7. What budgets are combined in planning a cash disbursements budget?

8. Considering the master budgeting example, what steps could be taken to even out the effect of differences in the flow of cash over the year?

9. Describe the primary components of the three basic elements of a financial planning model.

10. What does "what if" analysis mean?

11. Is a computer necessary to do financial modeling in today's business environment?

12. How can simulation be used in helping to create a budget?

13. A model in its most basic sense is a meaningful abstraction of reality. Explain how this concept applies to financial planning models.

14. A financial planning model should help management perform its functions better. Give an example of how a financial planning model could be helpful to a bank. To a travel agency. To an automotive parts manufacturer.

15. From a "what if" perspective, how does the pattern of collecting accounts receivable affect planned cash disbursements for direct material purchases?

16. Considering the "what if" examples presented in the chapter, what other "what ifs" could you suggest and why would they be important?

17. John Gaetz, controller of a local hospital, said the following about financial modeling at a recent meeting of the Tri-City Accountants Society: "The first financial model was A = L + OE." Comment.

EXERCISES

1. **Purchases and Cash Payments.** A production budget by fiscal quarter for Knowlton Company is given as follows:

	Units
First quarter	24,000
Second quarter	30,000
Third quarter	32,000
Fourth quarter	42,000

Four units of materials are used in producing each unit of product. Each unit of materials costs $.60. The materials inventory is to be equal to 25 percent of production requirements for the next quarter. This requirement was met at the beginning of the year. Production for the first quarter following the budget year is estimated at 28,000 units.

Accounts payable for materials purchased is estimated at $38,400 at the beginning of the current budget year. It is estimated that accounts payable at the end of the quarter for materials purchased will be equal to 40 percent of the purchases during the quarter.

Required:
1. Determine the number of units of materials to be purchased each quarter.
2. Determine the cost of materials to be purchased by quarters.
3. Estimate the payments to be made each quarter for materials.

2. **Sales and Collections.** Henderson Neat Shirts Co. sells shirts and is budgeting for 1996. The beginning actual Accounts Receivable, Inventory (at cost) and Accounts Payable balances and partial 1996 sales data are given at the top of the following page:

Beginning Balances (1/1/96):
Accounts Receivable.. $200,000
Inventory (at cost) 150,000
Accounts Payable 100,000

1996 Data:	First Quarter	Second Quarter
Sales	$600,000	$800,000
Cost of sales	360,000	480,000

Required:
1. Quarterly ending inventory should be 60 percent of the next quarter's expected sales volume. Find the budgeted purchases of shirts during the first quarter.
2. Sales are all on credit, and 80 percent is collected in the quarter of sale. The remainder is collected in the next quarter. Find the budgeted cash collections for the second quarter.

3. **Revised Production Budget.** By the middle of September, the sales manager of Powell Supplies Inc. realized that the original forecast for the fourth quarter would have to be revised. The original forecast showed that 160,000 units would be sold in October, 220,000 units would be sold in November, 270,000 units would be sold in December, and 300,000 units would be sold in January. It now appears that sales will be as follows:

Months	Units
October	150,000
November	200,000
December	230,000
January	240,000

Normally, 200 units of this product can be produced in one hour of machine time. An inventory equal to 20 percent of the estimated sales for the next month is to be on hand at the end of each month, and the company plans to have 32,000 units in the inventory on September 30.

Required:
1. Prepare production and machine-hour budgets for the three months of the fourth quarter using the original forecast.
2. Prepare revised production and machine-hour budgets for the three months of the fourth quarter using the revised sales forecast. (Assume that the inventory is to be 32,000 units on September 30 in either case.)
3. How many hours of production machine time can be released each month for other work in this department by the expected reduction in sales?

4. **Forecast Cash Payments.** Stock & Stem Company's January 1 actual inventory was $5,000 and payables were $3,000. Cost of goods sold for January, February, and March were $30,000, $35,000, and $40,000 respectively. The purchases policy says that ending inventory should be 20 percent of next month's cost of sales. Of purchases, 40 percent is paid in the current month and the rest in the next month.

Required:
Find the forecast cash payments for February.

5. **Direct Materials Purchases and Cash Payments.** The Schubert Company prepared a production budget for the first months of 1996 as follows:

	Units
January	18,000
February	16,000
March	20,000
April	24,000

Two units of Material 03 are required for each unit of product at a cost per unit of $1.50. One unit of Material 08 is required for each unit of product at a cost per unit of $5.

Forty percent of both materials needed in a month must be purchased in the preceding month. Thirty percent of the materials cost is paid during the month of purchase, and the other 70 percent is paid in the following month. Accounts payable at the beginning of January for material purchases is estimated at $44,000.

Required:
1. Determine the number of units to be purchased each month.
2. Determine the cost of purchases by month.
3. Prepare a budget of cash payments for materials by month.

6. **Production Schedules.** Olympia Candies is preparing a budget for the second quarter of the current calendar year. The March ending inventory of merchandise was $106,000, which was higher than expected. The company prefers to carry ending inventory amounting to the expected sales volume of the next two months. Purchases of merchandise are paid half in the month of purchase and half in the month following purchase, and the balance due on accounts payable at the end of March was $24,000.

Budgeted sales are as follows:

April	$40,000	July	$72,000
May	48,000	August	56,000
June	60,000	September	60,000

Required:
1. Assuming a 25 percent gross profit margin is budgeted, prepare a budget showing the following amounts for the months of April, May, and June:
   (a) Cost of goods sold.
   (b) Purchases required.
   (c) Cash payments for merchandise.
2. Assuming the balance on accounts receivable at the beginning of April was $35,000 and all customers pay three fourths in the month of sale and one fourth in the month following the sale, prepare a budget showing the cash receipts from accounts receivable for April, May, and June.

7. **Cash Collections and Receivables.** Past experience has demonstrated that 70 percent of the net sales billed in a month by Meyer Company is collected during the month, 20 percent is collected in the following month, and 10 percent is collected in the second following month.

A record of estimated net sales by month is given as follows:

1995	November	$450,000
	December	460,000
1996	January	480,000
	February	420,000
	March	500,000
	April	550,000
	May	600,000
	June	700,000

On January 1, 1996, the net accounts receivable balance is planned at $183,000.

Required:

Prepare a schedule of expected collections on accounts receivable for each of the first six months of 1996, and show the estimated balance of net accounts receivable at the end of each month.

8. **Cash Receipts from Sales.** Ponytail Productions has actual and anticipated revenues as follows:

Actual:		
July		$67,000
August		69,000
Budgeted:		
September		72,000
October		75,000
November		80,000
December		90,000

The controller has maintained a record of collections and has established the following pattern:

Month of sale	60%
First month after sale	30%
Second month after sale	5%
Third month after sale	3%
Uncollected	2%

Required:

Calculate the amount of cash the company is budgeting for collection by month in the fourth quarter of the year.

9. **Budget Schedules.** The following data apply to the Borden Hardware Store and its 1997 budget:

Forecast Sales

January	$60,000
February	50,000
March	80,000
April	90,000

Balance Sheet Data
December 31, 1996

Cash	$ 8,000
Accounts receivable:	
November sales	16,000
December sales	50,000
Inventory	54,000
Accounts payable (merchandise)	27,000

Other data are as follows:
(a) Sales are on credit with 60 percent of sales collected in the month after sale, 40 percent in the second month after sale.
(b) Cost of sales is 60 percent of sales.
(c) Other variable costs are 10 percent of sales, paid in the month incurred.
(d) Inventories are to be 150% of next month's budgeted sales requirements.
(e) Purchases are paid for in the month after purchase.
(f) Fixed expenses are $3,000 per month; all require cash.

Required:
1. Prepare budgets of purchases for each of the first three months of 1997.
2. Prepare separate budgets of cash receipts and disbursements and a cash budget for each of the first three months of 1997.
3. Prepare a budgeted income statement for the first quarter of 1997.

10. **Production Cost Budget.** A budget of the number of product units to be manufactured next year was prepared by Saunders Metals Company and is given as follows:

First quarter	48,000
Second quarter	56,000
Third quarter	64,000
Fourth quarter	60,000

A year's cost estimates are based on the previous year's actual costs. The direct materials cost per unit is estimated at $6. Direct labor cost is budgeted at $4 per unit, and factory overhead is to be applied at 200 percent of direct labor cost; 80 percent of the production for the quarter is to be sold in the quarter, and 20 percent of the production is to be sold in the following quarter. An inventory of 12,000 units on hand at the beginning of the budget year is to be sold in the first quarter.

Required:
1. Prepare a schedule showing the production costs for each quarter and for the year.
2. Compute estimated cost of goods sold for each quarter and for the year.

11. **Cash Payments for Operations.** Sargetis Paper Products, Inc. averages a gross profit of 30 percent. Sales for August were $500,000. The beginning inventory balance for August was $15,000 higher than the ending inventory balance. The accounts payable account had a balance of $45,000 at the beginning of August, and a balance of $52,000 at the end. The selling and administrative expenses are paid in the month incurred. Such expenses follow the formula of 5 percent of sales plus $25,000 per month, including depreciation expense of $10,000.

Required:
Compute the amount of cash payments made for operations during August.

12. **Estimated Income Statement.** Garrett Appliances Inc. prepared a budget for 1997 by quarters. Data from the budget appear as follows:

	Materials Purchased	Beginning Materials Inventory
First quarter	$280,000	$60,000
Second quarter	360,000	75,000
Third quarter	400,000	50,000
Fourth quarter	300,000	40,000
First quarter, 1998		40,000

Direct labor is budgeted at $140,000 each quarter with factory overhead estimated at 200 percent of direct labor cost. Selling and administrative expenses are budgeted at $115,000 each quarter. Net sales are budgeted by quarters as follows:

First quarter	$860,000
Second quarter	940,000
Third quarter	990,000
Fourth quarter	960,000

The amount of finished goods is estimated to be $120,000 at the beginning of the year. It is expected to increase to $150,000 by the end of the first quarter and will remain at that level until the end of the year when it will be reduced to $120,000.

Required:
Prepare an estimated income statement for each quarter and for the year. Income tax is estimated at 40 percent of income before income tax.

13. **Cash Budget.** Jennifer Witte is preparing a budget of cash receipts and disbursements for Gourmet Food Services, Inc. Some sales are for cash, and the rest of the sales is on a contract basis and is billed. Sales and collection data for April to August are as follows:

	Cash Sales	Billed Sales	Total
April	$65,000	$40,000	$105,000
May	72,000	46,000	118,000
June	84,000	68,000	152,000
July	88,000	72,000	160,000
August	86,000	70,000	156,000

Of the billed sales, 65 percent is collected during the month of sale, and the other 35% is collected in the following month.

Food costs amounting to 75 percent of sales must be paid during the month. Operating costs of $24,000 must be paid each month. Food costs will increase to 80 percent of sales in June. The cash balance at May 1 amounted to $7,000. If the cash balance is over $20,000 on August 31, Witte and the other stockholders will receive the excess as dividends.

Required:
1. Prepare a budget of cash receipts and disbursements for each month, May to August, inclusive.
2. Compute the amount, if any, that can be paid in dividends at the end of August.

14. **Budgeted Balance Sheet.** You have been asked to prepare a budgeted balance sheet on December 31, 1996, for Griffen Stores, Inc. A balance sheet at December 31, 1995, was as follows:

Assets:

Cash	$ 82,000
Accounts Receivable	112,000
Inventory	136,000
Building and Fixtures, net	358,000
Total Assets	$688,000

Liabilities and Equities:

Accounts Payable	$ 62,000
Capital Stock	300,000
Retained Earnings	326,000
Total Liabilities and Equities	$688,000

Cash receipts for the year are collections on accounts receivable amounting to $846,000. Cash payments are budgeted at $838,000. Included in those payments are payments of $126,000 for various expenses that do not flow through accounts payable. Credits to accounts payable for the year, estimated at $715,000, all result from merchandise purchased. Cash payments are all for expenses or purchases. Depreciation expense is estimated at $75,000. Net sales are estimated at $930,000. The inventory of merchandise is expected to increase to $147,000 by the end of the year.

Required:
From the information given, prepare a budgeted balance sheet at December 31, 1996. Prove the retained earnings balance by computing the net income. 1996 income tax is estimated at 40 percent of income before income tax and will be paid after December 31, 1996.

PROBLEMS

8-1. **Materials Cost.** Cahill Products Inc. plans to produce the following number of units of product in each of the months given:

October	15,000
November	25,000
December	30,000
January	35,000

Materials are to be purchased in the month before they are needed in production. This requirement was met for October production. Three gallons of Material A costing $3 per gallon is required for a unit of product. Two pounds of Material B costing $5 per pound is required for a unit of product.

Of the amounts owed to materials vendors, 60 percent are paid in the current month and the remainder in the next month.

Required:

1. Prepare materials requirements and purchases schedules in physical units for October, November, and December.
2. Prepare a schedule showing purchases costs for October, November, and December.
3. Prepare a schedule of cash payments needed to cover materials costs for October, November, and December.

8-2. **Payments for Materials.** Emery Mills Inc. is hard pressed for cash to meet scheduled payments for materials and other costs. A month is required for production, and materials are purchased as production progresses. All production is sold during the following month.

In the production operation, there is a natural loss of materials so that the final output is equal to only 80 percent of the input. Sales by month have been budgeted as follows:

	Units
June	200,000
July	240,000
August	320,000
September	280,000
October	300,000

Each unit is sold for $6.50. Half of the amount billed is collected during the month sold, with the other half being collected during the next month.

The materials used in production cost $.65 a unit, and 4 units of materials are in each completed unit of product. Costs of operation, other than materials cost, amount to $500,000 each month and must be paid during the month. Purchases are paid for in the month following purchases.

Required:

1. Determine the cost of purchases for July, August, and September.
2. Compute the expected cash inflow from customers, and subtract estimated disbursements, for July, August, and September.
3. Can the company meet the demands for cash each month?

8-3. **Factory Overhead Budget.** An overhead cost budget for the next year is being prepared by Riley Supply Company. Past studies indicate that costs have followed behavior patterns as shown as follows:

	Variable Cost Per Machine Hour
Indirect materials and supplies	$ .77
Heat, light, and power	1.50
Repairs and maintenance	5.00
Lubrication	.65

In addition, management estimates fixed factory overhead costs as follows:

Supervision.	$86,000
Indirect labor	72,000
Heat, light, and power.	21,000
Repairs and maintenance	23,000
Taxes and insurance.	17,000
Depreciation	29,000
Total	$248,000

A fixed overhead rate of $3.00 per machine hour has been established for costing the fixed overhead to the products. During the next year, the company plans to manufacture 425,000 units of product. Products are manufactured at the rate of 5 units per hour.

Required:
1.   Prepare a factory overhead budget showing variable and fixed costs separately.
2.   For each unit of product, compute budgeted applied variable and fixed overhead.
3.   Determine the budgeted over- or underapplied manufacturing overhead, if any.

8-4.   **Expenses and Cash Disbursements.** Kate Hollander, the treasurer of McCoy Ancient Studies Association, is planning an expense budget for 1996. Rent for the office is expected to amount to $6,000 for the year and will be paid in a lump sum during December of 1996.

Insurance costing $840 for the year is to be prepaid in January for the entire year. Salaries for the employees have been budgeted at $72,000 for the year and will be paid at about the time that the services are rendered. Salaries are evenly distributed throughout the year.

An outside service has been engaged to obtain speakers and to schedule visits to archaeological digs during the year. The entire cost for the year, estimated at $36,000, must be paid during September. It is estimated that the services will be distributed throughout the year as follows:

First quarter	$ 3,000
Second quarter	12,000
Third quarter.	15,000
Fourth quarter	6,000

Telephone and postage have been budgeted at $600 each quarter with payment being made during the quarter. Travel expenses of $6,000 for the year will be paid during the second quarter with the cost being equally divided between the second and third quarters of the year.

Depreciation on office furniture and various implements has been estimated at $600 for the year. Supplies costing $300 are to be used each quarter with payment for the entire year being budgeted for February.

Required:
1.   Prepare an accrual expense budget for Kate Hollander for 1996 by quarters.
2.   Convert the expense budget into a cash payments budget for 1996 by quarters.

8-5.   **Cash Forecasting.** Mr. Kelkar has started a used computer store. He needs to look carefully at his cash flows. He has provided the following budget data for 1997:

	Actual and Budgeted Account Balances	
	Balance At 12/31/96	Balance At 12/31/97
Cash	$ 4,000	$ 7,000
Accounts Receivable............................	12,000	20,000
Inventory.....................................	40,000	30,000
Prepaid Expenses	5,000	7,000
Accounts Payable	$19,000	$26,000
Wages Payable	4,000	6,000
Income Taxes Payable	10,000	6,000
Interest Payable................................	2,000	1,000

1997 Income Statement

Sales	$100,000
Cost of goods sold	75,000
Gross profit..	$ 25,000
Operating expenses (Including depreciation expense of $3,000)........	11,000
Operating income	$ 14,000
Interest expense	3,000
Income before taxes	$ 11,000
Taxes expense	5,000
Net income	$ 6,000

Required:

Prepare a cash forecast for 1997 for Kelkar's budgeted operations.

8-6. **Cash Flows and "What If."** C. J. Kraner, a member of the board of directors of Jordan Markets Inc., is concerned about the ability of the company to repay a loan in the amount of $250,000 that matures on June 30, 1996. In addition to the principal of the loan, the company must pay interest of $50,000.

The cash balance at January 1, 1996 is $82,000. Sales for December, 1995 through June 1996 have been budgeted as follows:

	Net Sales
December, 1995	$236,000
January, 1996	137,000
February	142,000
March	182,000
April...	170,000
May	156,000
June...	148,000

Cash sales each month are equal to approximately 30 percent of net sales. Collections on accounts receivable are expected as follows:

60 percent collected during the month of sale
40 percent collected in the following month

Total cash disbursements are estimated at $115,000 each month.

Required:

1. Prepare a cash budget for each month and for the first six months of 1996 in total.
2. Will the company be able to pay the loan with interest as of June 30 and still maintain a cash balance of no less than $60,000 on June 30?
3. If actual sales are 10 percent lower than the forecast each month while cash expenses drop by only $5,000 per month, what will happen to Jordan's ability to pay off the loan and keep the cash balance at the desired level?
4. If the sales and expenses fall as in Part 3 and collections patterns change to 40 percent collected in the current month and 60 percent in the following month, what will happen to the Jordan's cash situation?

8-7. **Cash Budget.** The Isett Company has planned a cash budget for the first six months of 1995. Estimates show that $60,000 should be collected in March and June for dividends received on investments in the stock of other companies. Each month, fixed operating expenses for wages, rent, heat and light, etc., must be paid in the amount of $220,000.
Collections on accounts receivable are estimated as follows:

60	percent collected in month of sale
25	percent collected in month following the sale
15	percent collected in second month following the sale

Payments for merchandise purchased are scheduled so that 70 percent of the payments are made in the month of purchase with the balance paid in the following month. The cash balance is estimated at $175,000 for January 1, 1995.
Estimated net sales and purchases by month are as follows:

	Net Sales	Purchases
November, 1994	$560,000	$320,000
December	550,000	380,000
January, 1995	640,000	420,000
February	700,000	400,000
March	650,000	350,000
April	580,000	280,000
May	460,000	260,000
June	520,000	260,000

An income tax payment of $100,000 is to be made in February, and a payment of $150,000 is to be made in June. A loan repayment of $80,000 will be made in February with interest added at $12,000. Assume interest expense is 1 percent of the loans outstanding each month and paid each month.

Required:
Prepare a budget of cash receipts and cash payments for each month. If a minimum cash balance of $150,000 must be available at the end of each month, identify the months, if any, when short-term loans will be required and the amounts of the loans. Also, indicate months, if any, when short-term loans can be repaid.

8-8. **Cash Budget and Revisions.** Sharon Williams, as a consultant to Gold and Gilmore, Inc., has advised management that collections on accounts receivable will likely be slower than in the past. If at all possible the company should try to reduce operating costs.

A budget of revenue for each month from November, 1996 to June, 1997 is as follows:

	Revenue
November, 1996	$450,000
December	430,000
January, 1997	420,000
February	400,000
March	350,000
April	330,000
May	280,000
June	250,000

Collections are expected be different for the first and second quarter's sales as follows:

First Quarter Sales	Second Quarter Sales	
70 percent	50 percent	Collected in the month of billing
20 percent	30 percent	Collected in the following month
5 percent	15 percent	Collected in the second following month

The remaining percentage owed may not be collectible.

Various costs of operation that must be paid are estimated at $300,000 per month. In addition, the company has had a tradition of paying dividends of $80,000 in March and $80,000 in June. The cash balance on January 1, 1997, is expected to be $93,000.

Required:

1. Prepare a cash budget for each month from January to June, inclusive.
2. Do you believe that Williams' concern is justified? Explain.

8-9. **Cash and Short-Term Loans.** Every year Bear River, Inc. has operated at about the same level, but sales vary substantially by season. As a result, the company needs short-term credit that is to be paid when the cash position improves.

Sales revenue for December 1995 and for each of the first six months of 1996 has been budgeted as follows:

	Revenue
December, 1995	$540,000
January, 1996	620,000
February	580,000
March	360,000
April	270,000
May	130,000
June	120,000

Sixty percent of the revenue is to be collected in the month billed with 40 percent collected in the following month. Cash payments have been budgeted at a steady rate of $400,000 per month.

The cash balance at January 1, 1996 is $100,000 but is to be maintained at approximately $120,000 throughout the year. Cash in excess of that amount is to be invested in U.S. treasury bills, and loans are to be made as necessary.

Required:
Prepare a cash budget for the first six months of 1996, indicating how much excess cash can be invested and how much cash must be borrowed. For purposes of the problem, ignore interest earned and interest expense.

8-10. Product Cost Budget. The Litewait Metals Company plans to manufacture 600,000 standard components for use in all its product lines next year. Powdered metals that cost $8 per unit of product will be used.

Direct labor cost for part of the year will be at a rate of $12 an hour, and 5 units are to be produced each hour. The cost per hour will likely increase to $14 an hour after 300,000 units of product are made with no change expected in productivity per hour.

The factory overhead is fixed and is budgeted at $1,500,000 for the year. The company plans to operate at a normal capacity of 120,000 direct labor hours next year.

Required:
1.   Compute the estimated cost of production next year by cost element.
2.   Determine the average estimated cost per unit of product next year.

8-11. Product Cost Budget. The management of Ingram Glass Products is aware of increased competition in the industry and has taken steps to better control costs. Product costs for last year are given as follows on a per unit basis:

	Product Lines		
	1	**2**	**3**
Direct materials	$ 6.00	$ 3.00	$ 5.00
Direct labor	3.00	2.00	3.00
Applied factory overhead	3.00	2.00	3.00
Total unit cost	$12.00	$ 7.00	$11.00

The direct materials are manufactured by another division of the company and has agreed to lower direct materials costs by 10 percent for the next year.

Direct labor cost will increase from $12 to $15 an hour, but increases in productivity are planned. Fixed overhead cost will be increased by $30,000 a year. The revision of the production process will make it possible to manufacture 6 units of Product 1 in one hour, 8 units of Product 2 in one hour, and 10 units of Product 3 in one hour.

Last year the company operated at a normal capacity of 200,000 direct labor hours with budgeted and actual factory overhead cost of $2,400,000. Next year, normal capacity is to be redefined at 180,000 direct labor hours with factory overhead (including the fixed overhead increase of $30,000) amounting to $1,860,000.

Last year the company manufactured the following quantities of products.

Product Lines	Number of Units
1	300,000
2	240,000
3	340,000

The same quantities are to be manufactured this coming year.

Required:

1.   Determine the cost of production this coming year in total and on a unit-of-product basis.
2.   Compute the expected cost saving in total compared with last year.

8-12.   **Estimated Financial Statements.** Norris Fasteners, Inc. has budgeted operations for each quarter of 1995. Budget data are given as follows:

	Net Sales	Production Cost	Operating Expenses
First quarter	$750,000	$480,000	$145,000
Second quarter	800,000	500,000	160,000
Third quarter...........	850,000	520,000	170,000
Fourth quarter	900,000	500,000	175,000
First quarter, 1996	800,000	520,000	170,000

Finished goods inventory has been planned as follows:

January 1, 1995...	$120,000
April 1, 1995..	135,000
July 1, 1995	130,000
October 1, 1995..	140,000
December 31, 1995......................................	125,000

Included in production cost each quarter is $120,000 in depreciation, and depreciation of $30,000 is included in each quarter in operating expenses. All production cost and operating expenses with the exception of depreciation are to be paid during the quarter.

Collections on sales are planned at 60 percent during the quarter of the sale and 40 percent during the quarter following the sale. The balance of collections on net sales for the fourth quarter of 1994 has been estimated at $280,000 and is to be included in total receipts for the first quarter of 1995.

Materials are purchased as needed in production and are not held in inventory. Income tax is estimated at 40 percent of income before income tax, and is paid during the subsequent quarter. Dividends of $100,000 are to be paid in June and again in December if covered by sufficient profits. No dividends will be paid if the profits for the year are less than $300,000.

A summary balance sheet at December 31, 1994 is given as follows:

NORRIS FASTENERS, INC.
BALANCE SHEET FOR DECEMBER 31, 1994

Assets:	
Cash	$ 115,000
Accounts Receivable.......................................	280,000
Inventory	120,000
Plant and Equipment, net of accumulated depreciation	1,450,000
Total Assets	$1,965,000
Liabilities and Equities:	
Estimated Income Taxes Payable.............................	$ 55,000
Capital Stock	1,500,000
Retained Earnings	410,000
Total Liabilities and Equities..................................	$1,965,000

Required:

1.   Prepare an estimated income statement for each quarter and for the year.
2.   Prepare a balance sheet at the end of each quarter of 1995.

8-13. Financial Planning Model. Canerdy Merchandiser would like to implement a financial planning model to aid in its monthly and annual budgeting process. Rochelle Canerdy, accountant, has identified the following relationships among the key planning variables.

1.   Sales volume (in units) is increasing at the rate of 4 percent per month. The selling price is $25 per unit.
2.   All sales are on credit. Collections are received 40 percent in the month of sale, 50 percent in the month after the sale, and 10 percent two months after the sale.
3.   Inventory is maintained at 120 percent of the following month's forecast sales.
4.   Purchases are paid 50 percent in the month of purchase and 50 percent in the month after purchase. Each unit costs $13.
5.   The operating expenses are both variable and fixed. The variable costs average 20 percent of each month's revenue. Fixed costs, including depreciation of $30,000, total $65,000 per month. All costs are paid in the month incurred.

Required:
Prepare a series of equations that may be used to represent the following relationships:

1.   Sales volume for the current month.
2.   Revenue for the current month.
3.   Purchases for the current month (units).
4.   Purchases for the current month (dollars).
5.   Cost of goods sold for the current month.
6.   Operating expenses for the current month.
7.   Net income for the current month.
8.   Cash receipts for the current month.
9.   Cash disbursements for the current month.
      For simplicity, use the following notations:

S_t	=	Current month's volume (units)
R_t	=	Revenue for the current month (dollars)
P_t	=	Current period purchases in units
$\$P_t$	=	Current period purchases in dollars
CGS_t	=	Cost of goods sold for the current month
OE_t	=	Operating expenses for the current month
NI_t	=	Net income for the current month
CR_t	=	Cash receipts for the current month
CD_t	=	Cash disbursements for the current month
I_t	=	Inventory at the end of the current month
$t-1$	=	Last month
$t-2$	=	Two months ago
$t+1$	=	Next month

8-14. Budgeted Savings—Materials and Labor. Paul Homan is concerned about losses of materials in production, especially since the prices of materials may increase. Data with respect to materials for one of the major product lines are given as follows:

	Quantity Per Unit In Final Product	Materials Price Per Pound
Material A	24 pounds	$.12
Material B	12 pounds	.08
Material C	12 pounds	.08

The product weight yield is 75 percent of the input for all three materials.

The labor rate is $14.40 an hour, and 12 finished units are made each hour. Overhead varies at $2.00 per unit of product. The fixed overhead is budgeted at $2,700,000 for the next quarter. The company costs only the variable costs to the product.

Homan believes that the yield from materials should be increased to 80 percent of input for all materials. Also, with some changes in production methods, 15 finished units should be made each hour.

During the next quarter, the company plans to produce and sell 1,800,000 finished units at a price of $14 per unit.

Required:

1.   Prepare a budgeted income statement for the manufacturing operation under present conditions without savings in materials or labor time.
2.   "What if" Homan:
     (a)   Achieves the planned savings in materials yield.
     (b)   Implements the planned labor saving changes.
     (c)   Achieves the planned savings in materials yield and the planned labor saving changes.

     How much will each alternative contribute to manufacturing profits?

8-15.   **Forecasting Income and Cash.** Green Company recently (late December, 1994) negotiated a $100,000 bank loan from the 3rd National Bank of Cleveland. As part of the loan agreement the bank requires a cash flow forecast for the current year. This will help determine whether the company can repay the loan. The following December 31, 1994, data are available:

Assets:	
Cash	$ 15,000
Account Receivable	110,000
Inventory	100,000
Equipment	600,000
Accumulated Depreciation	(250,000)
Total Assets	$575,000
Liabilities and Equities:	
Account Payable	$ 56,000
Wages Payable	15,000
Bank Loan	100,000
Capital Stock	250,000
Retained earnings	154,000
Total Equities	$575,000

Other data relating to 1995 include:

(a)   Sales are expected to be $1,000,000. Accounts receivable at year end is expected to be $140,000.

(b) Cost of goods sold is expected to be $400,000, and year end inventory is expected to be $150,000.

(c) Accounts payable is expected to be $15,000 higher.

(d) Wages payable is expected to be $22,000 at year end, and the wages expense is expected to be $230,000.

(e) Depreciation expense will be $50,000.

(f) Other expenses, all paid in cash, are expected to be $95,000, including interest on the loan.

(g) Cash expenditures for plant and equipment are expected to be $160,000.

(h) Green expects to pay a dividend of $40,000.

Required:

1. Calculate the net income for 1995.
2. What is the cash provided by operations in 1995?

8-16. Financial Planning Model. For a number of years now, Quinn Rappard Corporation has had difficulty in budgeting its monthly income statement and forecasting the monthly cash flows. As an outside consultant, you have been hired by the controller to develop a rudimentary financial planning model that will lead to a budgeted monthly income statement and budgeted monthly cash receipts and cash disbursements.

Upon investigation, you have found that the following relationships exist:

(a) Sales revenue is growing at one half of one percent a month.

(b) Sixty percent of each month's sales are for cash; the remaining 40 percent are credit sales.

(c) Credit sales are collected at 50 percent in the month of sale, 45 percent in the month after the sale, and 5 percent in the second month after the sale.

(d) Cost of goods sold has averaged 75 percent of sales.

(e) Purchases in units each month equal the forecast sales units for the next month.

(f) Purchases are paid 70 percent in the month of purchase, with half of these qualifying for a 2 percent cash discount. The remaining 30 percent is paid in the following month.

(g) The monthly operating expenses are 1 percent of monthly sales revenue plus fixed costs of $20,000, of which $2,000 is depreciation. These expenses are paid in the month incurred.

(h) Income taxes are ignored on a monthly basis.

Required:

Prepare a series of equations, based on the foregoing relationships, that will allow the company to budget net income and cash flow.

8-17. Quarter Cash Budget. McCubbin & Michaels, a prominent distribution company, has asked your assistance in preparing cash budget information for the last three months of 1997. The interim balance sheet for the third quarter (dated September 30, 1997) shows the following balances:

Cash	$142,100
Marketable Securities	200,000
Accounts Receivable.	807,750
Inventories	752,388
Accounts Payable	354,155
R & D Payables	9,450
Selling and Administrative Payables.	43,750

The chief financial officer provides you with the following information based on experience and management policy. All sales are credit sales and are billed the last day of the month of sale. Customers paying within 10 days of the billing date may take a 2 percent cash discount. Sixty percent of the sales is paid within the discount period in the month following billing. An additional 25 percent also pays in the month following billing, but these payments are not subject to the cash discount. The remaining 10 percent is collected in the second month following billing. Additional cash of $24,000 is expected in October as a result of renting unnecessary warehouse space.

Sixty percent of all purchases, selling and administrative expenses, and research and development expenses are paid in the month incurred. The remainder is paid in the following month. Ending inventories are set at 130 percent of the next month's budgeted cost of goods sold. The company's gross profit averages 30 percent of sales for the month. Selling and administrative expenses follow the formula of 5 percent of the current month's sales plus $75,000, which includes depreciation of $5,000. Research and development expenses are budgeted at 3 percent of sales.

Actual and budgeted sales information is as follows:

Actual:
August	$750,000
September	787,500

Budgeted:
October	$826,800
November	868,200
December	911,600
January	930,000

The company acquired equipment costing $250,000 cash in November. Dividends of $45,000 will be paid in December.

The company would like to maintain a minimum cash balance at the end of each month of $120,000. Any excess amounts go first to repayment of short-term borrowings and then to investment in marketable securities. When cash is needed to reach the minimum balance, the company policy is to sell marketable securities before borrowing the cash.

Required:
1. Compute the accounts receivable balance at the end of December, 1997. (Round all calculations to the nearest dollar for each part of this problem.)
2. Compute the accounts payable balance at the end of December, 1997.
3. Prepare a cash budget for each month in the last quarter of 1997 and for the quarter in total.

8-18. **Estimated Cash Flow.** The controller of Colfax Services, Inc. observes that accounts receivable are expected to decrease by $47,000 from March 31, 1996 to June 30, 1996. In preparation for increased activity in the summer months, however, the inventory of materials and supplies will also increase by $62,000. Also, accounts payable will likely increase by $38,000.

Early in July, short-term loans of $150,000 must be paid along with the regular quarterly dividend of 40 cents on each of the 60,000 outstanding shares of capital stock. Plans have been made to acquire new office equipment at a cost of $38,000, with payment being made by mid-July. The cash balance on March 31, 1996 was $142,000. Without considering the results of operations in early July, can the company meet its obligations for cash payments without reducing the cash balance below $120,000?

An estimated income statement for the latest quarter is:

COLFAX SERVICES, INC.
ESTIMATED INCOME STATEMENT
FOR THE QUARTER ENDED JUNE 30, 1996

Service revenue	$528,000
Cost of materials and supplies used	$136,000
Operating expenses (including depreciation of $81,000)	177,000
Interest expense	23,000
Total deductions from revenue	$336,000
Income before income taxes	$192,000
Income taxes	78,000
Net income	$114,000

Required:
1. Does it appear that operations in the quarter ended June 30, 1996 can supply sufficient cash to meet payment obligations in early July, while maintaining a cash balance of at least $120,000?
2. Prepare a forecast cash flow schedule to support your position.

CASE 8A—Adelberg Electronics, Inc.

Adelberg Electronics, Inc. designs and manufactures measurement and computation products and systems used in a variety of organizations. Its principal products are integrated instruments and computer systems, with associated software; test and measurement instruments; medical electronic equipment and systems; and instrumentation and systems for chemical analysis.

As a member of the budgeting team, your assignment is to prepare the budgeted balance sheet, based on information provided by other members of the team. The actual balance sheet for the end of 1998 follows:

ADELBERG ELECTRONICS, INC.
BALANCE SHEET
DECEMBER 31, 1998
(IN MILLIONS OF DOLLARS)

Current Assets:		
Cash	$ 479	
Accounts Receivable—Net	590	
Inventories	511	
Prepaid Expenses	30	$1,610
Property, Plant, and Equipment.	$1,397	
Less: Accumulated Depreciation	462	935
Total Assets		$2,545

Current Liabilities:
Accounts Payable	$ 249	
Accrued Income Taxes	132	
Other Accrued Liabilities	280	$ 661
Long-Term Debt		143
Total Liabilities		$ 804

Stockholders' Equity:
Common Stock	$ 356	
Retained Earnings	1,385	1,741
Total Liabilities and Equity		$2,545

Joe Silk, another member of the team, has furnished you with the following budgeted income statement for the current year:

BUDGETED INCOME STATEMENT
FOR THE YEAR ENDED DECEMBER 31, 1999
(IN MILLIONS OF DOLLARS)

Sales revenue		$3,253
Cost of goods sold		1,583
Gross profit		$1,670
Operating expenses:		
Marketing	$590	
General and administrative	358	
Research and development	343	1,291
Net income before taxes		$ 379
Provision for income taxes		134
Net income after taxes		$ 245

The controller has also furnished you with a number of assumptions, policies, and other information as follows:

1. The company has made arrangements to acquire property, plant, and equipment during the year for $339 million. Long-term debt will finance $18 million and cash will be used for the remainder.
2. All sales are on credit. Collections on credit sales for the year are budgeted for $3,218 million.
3. Several account balances are planned for changes.
    (a) Inventories will decrease by $15 million.
    (b) Other accrued liabilities will increase $70 million.
    (c) Prepaid expenses will increase $10 million.
4. Depreciation expense in the income statement totals $105 million.
5. Payments will be made on accounts payable, $2,682 million; and on accrued income taxes, $179 million.
6. Common stock was sold to employees in a special stock purchase plan for $34 million.
7. Dividends of $29 million will be declared and paid during the year.

Required:

Prepare a budgeted balance sheet, based on the results of the budget work sheet. Prepare any schedules needed to summarize the above information.

Case 8B—Buzby Invisible Dog Products[1]

The Buzby Invisible Dog Products (BIDP) markets products it purchases from various suppliers from its small corporate offices. The current products are novelty items—two forms of dog leashes for "invisible dogs." The items are called Lil Feefee and Big Bowser. Buzby has obtained an agreement with several beach resort shops and a few tourist traps to provide leashes to their various locations.

These stores are good customers, and the present demand for both forms of leashes is expected to hold for several years. It is somewhat seasonal with tourist locations having particularly strong sales during the summer months. Each year, Buzby negotiates volumes and prices with the representatives of these stores and estimates his operating costs. Based on these negotiations and other factors, Buzby begins to plan for the next year. BIDP prepares a profit plan for each year on a quarterly basis. The profit planning process uses the following basic input factors:

1. Assumptions, operating guidelines, product cost and price data, and beginning levels (Schedule 1).
2. Sales forecast by quarter by product in units (Schedule 2).

These factors are independent variables. All other values are dependent variables and are calculated from the independent variables. From these factors, an entire profit plan can be prepared. BIDP uses a microcomputer and spreadsheet software to assist the profit plan preparation. Using this system BIDP is able to construct a comprehensive profit plan and is able to test or change key factors quickly. These changes are often called "what if" questions since BIDP management is interested in knowing the impact on profits or cash flow if a change is made.

SCHEDULE 1
PROFIT PLANNING ASSUMPTIONS

Maximum cash balance	$10,000
Minimum cash balance	6,000
Minimum incremental borrowing amount	1,000
Annual interest rates on borrowings and investments	12%
Income tax rate (taxes paid on positive net income only)	40%

Product information:	Lil Feefee	Big Bowser
Unit sales price	$11.00	$14.00
Unit purchase cost	5.50	6.00

Percent of sales collected in next quarter	40%
Percent of purchases paid in next quarter	30%
Ending inventory level:	
Percent of next quarter's sales	30.00%
12/31/94 Lil Feefee inventory—units	5,000 units
12/31/94 Big Bowser inventory—units	3,000 units
Semiannual dividends paid in 1st and 3rd quarters	$1,000
Quarterly note payable principal payment	2,000

---

[1]The case has an accompanying spreadsheet template on an instructor's diskette.

Selling and administrative expenses: (annual)

Shipping out costs	$0.50 per unit
Shipping in costs	$0.10 per unit
Sales commissions	4%
Wages and salaries.....................................	$86,000
Rent expense	34,000
Depreciation expense	12,000
Other cash expenses	24,000
Lil Feefee fixed expenses...............................	12,000
Big Bowser fixed expenses	15,000

Beginning Balance Sheet (12/31/94):

Cash	$ 6,000	Bank Borrowings.........	$	0
Short-Term Investments	2,000	Accounts Payable........		20,000
Accounts Receivable....	25,000	Taxes Payable		2,000
Equipment (Net)........	100,000	Dividends Payable		2,000
		Notes Payable...........		40,000
		Capital Stock		40,000

Other assumptions:

1. If short-term bank borrowings are needed, cash is borrowed for the entire quarter.
2. If short-term investments are made, the investment is made for the entire quarter.
3. Short-term borrowings and investments should not exist in the same quarter.
4. Taxes and interest are assumed to be accrued in one quarter and paid in the next quarter.

SCHEDULE 2
SALES FORECAST—1995

	1995 Total	Q - 1	Q - 2	Q - 3	Q - 4	Q - 5
Units:						
Lil Feefee units ..	48,000	10,000	14,000	12,000	12,000	11,000
Big Bowser units	11,700	2,500	3,500	3,000	2,700	3,000
Total units	59,700	12,500	17,500	15,000	14,700	14,000

Required:

1. Using spreadsheet software, prepare the following 1995 budget schedules and statements by quarter:
   (a) Purchasing plan schedule in units and dollars.
   (b) Selling and administrative expenses budget.
   (c) Supporting schedules for:
      (1) Accounts receivable.
      (2) Inventories.
      (3) Accounts payable.
   (d) Cash flow forecast
   (e) Forecast statement of income
   (f) Forecast balance sheet
   To facilitate "what ifs," you will want to avoid the use of actual independent variable values in the cell formulas.

2.   Using the spreadsheet developed in Part 1, show the impact on net income and on cash short-term borrowings and investments for the following "what ifs:"
    (a)   A change in the sales forecast:

REVISED SCHEDULE 2
SALES FORECAST—1995

	1995 Total	Q - 1	Q - 2	Q - 3	Q - 4	Q - 5
Units:						
Lil Feefee units ..	40,000	9,000	12,000	10,000	9,000	10,000
Big Bowser units	11,000	2,400	3,300	2,800	2,500	2,800
Total units	51,000	11,400	15,300	12,800	11,500	12,800

    (b)   A change in costs and prices of Lil Feefee and Big Bowser:

	Lil Feefee	Big Bowser
Product Information:		
Unit sales price	$12.00	$16.00
Unit purchase cost.	6.00	7.00

    (c)   A change in percentages for:

First:	Percent of sales collected in next quarter	60.00%
Second:	Percent of purchases paid in next quarter	20.00%
Third:	Ending inventory level percent of next quarter's sales	50.00%
Fourth:	All three changes above occurring together.	

    (d)   Comment on the impacts each "what if" has on cash flows and net income.

CASE 8C–Stoner Rock Soup'n Sales Company[2]

    Don Stoner, low man on the accounting totem pole in the Plain and Ordinary Company, was sitting in his office recently day dreaming about a more exciting life. He saw himself as owner of the Stoner Rock Soup'n Sales Company. In his dream, he had created the newest taste sensation—rock soup. He combined a secret formula, water from an isolated mountain spring, and skilled elves to produce two products—Hard Rock and Soft Rock soup. He dreamed that his planning and control systems were working well. It was late in 1996, and he was at his personal computer building the profit plan for 1997. He had his budget spreadsheet humming. Numbers were flying, assumptions were made, and formats were in place.

---

[2]The case has an accompanying software spreadsheet template on an instructor's diskette with data and formats for schedules 1, 2, and 3 presented in the case and formats for Schedules 7, 8, and 13 plus the Cash Flow Forecast and the Forecast Statements of Income and Expense and Financial Position.

Amazingly, he found a partial spreadsheet file for the Stoner Rock Soup'n Sales Company, which included the following formatted schedules:

1. Schedule 1—Profit Planning Assumptions (presented below with data included on the instructor's template accompanying the case).
2. Schedule 2—Product Cost Sheet (presented below with data included on the instructor's template accompanying the case).
3. Schedule 3—Sales Forecast—1997 (presented below with data included on the instructor's template accompanying the case).
4. Schedule 7—Manufacturing Overhead Flexible Budget (in cases) (formatted on the instructor's template accompanying the case).
5. Schedule 8—Manufacturing Overhead Budget—1997 (formatted on the instructor's template accompanying the case).
6. Schedule 13—Cash Flow Forecast (formatted on the instructor's template accompanying the case).
7. Forecast Statement of Income and Expense (formatted on the instructor's template accompanying the case).
8. Forecast Statement of Financial Position—12/31/96, 3/31/97, 6/30/97, 9/30/97, and 12/31/97 (formatted on the instructor's template accompanying the case).

Required:

You are the only one in the office in whom Don feels he can confide. He feels he needs a little break but wonders if you would look at the plan on the spreadsheet and see if you can complete the schedules. Don wants to know if he can really make money from rock soup and if the balance sheet balances at the end of 1997. Being a good friend of Don's, and knowing he needs all the help he can get, you review the data and get to work. You glance at the schedules and see the attached data and formats. You see the following schedules are missing entirely:

1. Schedule 4—Production Plan—1997.
2. Schedule 5—Materials Requirements.
3. Schedule 6—Direct Labor Requirements.
4. Schedule 9—Selling and Administrative Expenses Budget.
5. Schedule 10—Accounts Receivable.
6. Schedule 11—Ending Inventories.
7. Schedule 12—Accounts Payable.

You hope to have the profit plan finished by the time Don returns:

SCHEDULE 1
PROFIT PLANNING ASSUMPTIONS

Percent of sales collected this quarter	70.00%
Percent of purchases paid for in current quarter	75.00%
Inventory Levels:	
Materials—percent of next quarter's requirements	30.00%
Finished goods—percent of next quarter's sales	30.00%
12/31/96 Materials:	
Rocks	35,000 pounds
Cans	3,000 cans
12/31/96 Finished Goods: Hard Rock	1,000 cases
Soft Rock	600 cases

Cash and other planning information:

Dividends paid (7/31/97)	$ 15,000
Notes payable repaid (7/1/97)	$ 10,000
Equipment purchased (1/1/97)	$ 20,000
Normal production capacity	30,000 cases
Variable manufacturing overhead per case	$ 1.00 per case
Cash fixed manufacturing overhead (annual)	$ 52,000
Manufacturing depreciation expense per year	$ 8,000
Selling expenses (annual)	$100,000
Sales commissions	5.00%
Administrative expenses (annual)	$100,000
Minimum cash balance	$ 12,000
Maximum cash balance	$ 18,000
Incremental investments and borrowings amount	$ 1,000
All interest rates	12.00%
Income tax rate	34.00%

Beginning financial position:

Cash	$15,000	Accounts Payable	$8,000
Short-term investments ..	0	Taxes Payable	1,000
Accounts receivable	25,000	Bank Borrowings	0
Equipment (net)	80,000	Notes Payable	40,000
		Capital Stock	50,000

SCHEDULE 2
PRODUCT COST SHEET

	Price	Quantity	(Case = 24) Hard Rock	Quantity	(Case = 24) Soft Rock
Materials (per case):					
Rocks (pounds)	$0.1265	36.00	$ 4.55	33.00	$ 4.17
Can (lids and label)	$0.1200	24.00	2.88	24.00	2.88
Water (gallons)	$0.0345	7.00	0.24	9.00	0.31
Total materials			$ 7.68		$ 7.37
Direct labor:					
Cooking and drying	$10.00	0.2875	$ 2.88	0.3255	$ 3.26
Canning and packing	9.00	0.1005	0.90	0.1650	1.49
Total direct labor			$ 3.78		$ 4.74
Manufacturing overhead:					
Variable (per case)	$1.00	1	$ 1.00	1	$ 1.00
Fixed (per case)	2.00	1	2.00	1	2.00
Total overhead			$ 3.00		$ 3.00
Total product cost (per case of 24 cans)			$14.46		$15.11
Sales price (per case of 24 cans)			$22.00		$32.00

SCHEDULE 3
SALES FORECAST—1997

	Q - 1	Q - 2	Q - 3	Q - 4	Q - 5
Hard Rock (cases)	3,900	6,200	6,000	4,100	4,100
Soft Rock (cases)	2,000	2,500	3,100	1,900	2,200

Chapter Nine

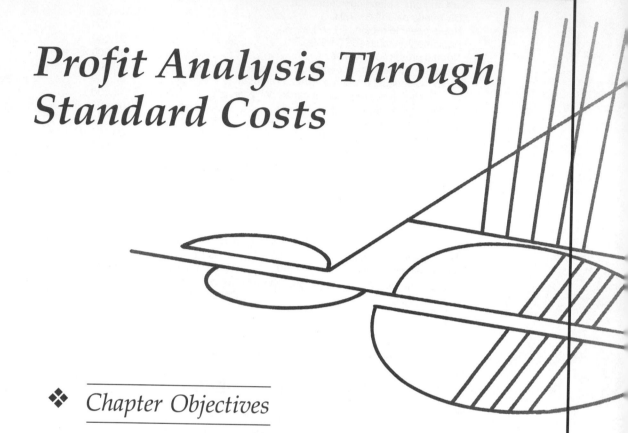

Profit Analysis Through Standard Costs

❖ *Chapter Objectives*

After studying Chapter 9, you will be able to:
1. Explain the significance of profit analysis for an organization.
2. Describe the major characteristics and conditions of a standard cost system.
3. Compute materials price and quantity variances, and identify potential causes of such variances.
4. Compute labor rate and efficiency variances, and identify potential causes of such variances.
5. Describe the interrelationships that exist among material and labor variances.
6. Explain the major considerations that are the basis of standard costs for overhead.
7. Distinguish between a budget variance and a capacity variance for overhead.
8. Explain why the capacity variance is related only to fixed overhead costs.
9. Explain how standard costs can be used in a process cost system.

■ *Where Do I Start With Standard Costs?* ■

Von Matheson, President of Colexus, Inc., just returned from a reunion of his graduating MBA class. During the day of activities, he talked with several of his classmates who have become extremely successful in various businesses. One of those classmates suggested to Von that adoption of a standard cost system eliminated most of her firm's unacceptable scrap and spoilage, caused an examination of nonvalue-added activities, and substantially reduced several inefficient operations.

Von did not know whether his single product operation would really benefit from a standard cost system. If he did make the change, which manufacturing costs should be put on standards? How do you set up standards? When do variances mean something? Isn't a standard cost system costly to use? Isn't it a pain in the neck? Wouldn't a tight budget do the same thing?

This was more than Von could deal with. He decided to bounce the idea of standard costs off his controller.

In measuring success in any undertaking, a comparison is usually made between actual performance and expected performance. Any difference is a variance. An appropriate manager is then left with the responsibility to explain the what, why, and how of the variance. In doing so, the manager must understand the influence of key variables on the actual results, focus on areas that deserve more detailed investigation, and determine changes that must be made in future planning and control. This chapter introduces the concept of profit analysis and then concentrates on the variances associated with a standard cost system for direct materials, direct labor, and factory overhead. Chapter 10 extends these concepts to analyzing revenues and operating expenses.

PROFIT ANALYSIS

Profit is an overall measure of how well an organization is doing. A profit variance then is the difference between the actual net income and the planned net income for the same period. The causes of such a variance are related to the various elements that make up net income: revenues, cost of goods sold, and operating expenses. The level of detail needed for identifying the causes depends on individual situations, but each new layer of detail is tied to some common components. Figure 9.1 shows a disaggregation of the profit variance into more detailed elements.

In order to have a variance, a baseline is necessary with which to compare actual results. Common baselines are a prior month or year, a budget, a flexible budget, or a standard. The analysis of a profit variance will necessarily look at each significant area in the income statement, and each one will have a

	Actual	Budget	Variance	
Revenues	$385,000	$365,000	$ 20,000	
Cost of goods sold	282,500	227,250	55,250	U
Gross profit or margin	$102,500	$137,750	$ 35,250	U
Operating expenses	81,250	90,000	8,750	U
Net income	$ 21,250	$ 47,750	$ 26,500	U

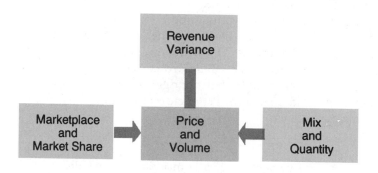

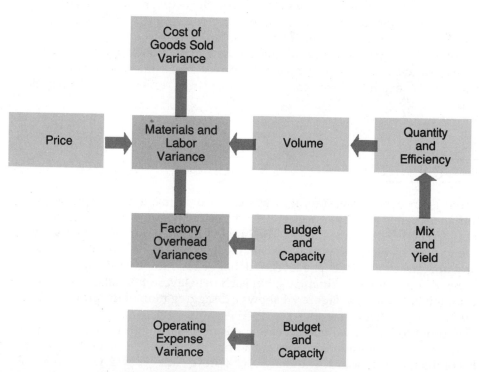

Figure 9.1   Detailed Levels of Variances

baseline that management feels is appropriate for the circumstances. The analysis then looks at causes of variation from the baseline.

For purposes of discussing an approach to profit analysis, we begin with cost of goods sold and the issues related to product costs. Revenues and operating expenses are taken up in the next chapter.

The cost of goods sold, comprised of the cost of materials, labor, and factory overhead, is generally the most significant cost in the income statement. Consequently, companies expend a great deal of effort to manage and control the underlying cost of goods manufactured. Managers can easily cite examples of how small savings on a unit basis or on a single operation or task performed add many dollars to profit. One common management control technique is a standard cost system. The following discussion will show how standard product costs aid profit analysis.

THE USE OF STANDARDS

Although a standard may be used as a basis for management and control by service industries, retailers, manufacturers, or governmental and not-for-profit entities, the procedures discussed here are focused on a manufacturing setting. However, the concepts discussed here have wide application to other organizations and to other types of costs. For example, the driver of a delivery truck is expected to handle a certain number of deliveries in a normal day. The number of expected or normal deliveries serves as a standard for the measurement of performance.

Standard costs are appropriate where an organization has standard products, services, or repetitive operations; and where management controls the factors comprising a standard cost. Some examples of where these conditions can exist are listed below:

1. Filling prescriptions in a pharmacy.
2. Picking orders in a warehouse.
3. Preparing food in a restaurant.
4. Answering telephones in travel agencies, airlines, customer service departments, and computer technical hotlines.
5. Processing orders in a mail-order house.
6. Calling on customers (by phone or door-to-door).
7. Processing computer center transactions from a modem.

Definition of Standard Costs

A **standard cost** for a product consists of a **price standard** (a generic term that means price for material, rate for labor, and rate for factory overhead) and a **quantity standard** (a generic term that means quantity for material, time for labor, and activity or volume for factory overhead). Setting standards for price and quantity will involve management judgments, industrial engineering studies, work measurement studies, vendor analyses, union bargaining, as well as a number of other techniques. The combination of price and quantity yields what is planned or expected for a specific interval of time and a set of conditions.

The standard cost is generally stated on a per unit basis: per unit of quantity, per unit of time, per unit of activity, or per unit of product. Once set, these standards remain unchanged as long as there is no change in the methods of operation or factors that influence quantities or in the unit prices of materials, labor, and factory overhead.

Advantages of Standards

A standard cost system presents many advantages to an organization. Although the primary purpose has always been cost control, properly set standards will have many other advantages. This section covers five major advantages of standard costs.

Cost Control   Cost control is comparing actual performance with the standard performance, analyzing variances to identify controllable causes, and taking action to correct or adjust future planning and control. As we shall see in later sections of this chapter, costs can change for at least four reasons: (1) changes in levels of prices or rates, (2) changes in efficiency, (3) changes in activity or volume, and (4) changes in the mix or yield. Variance analysis must identify these changes as well as the managers responsible for these changes so that adjustments can be made to the standards or good performance can be rewarded.

Standard cost accounting follows the principle of **management by exception.** Actual results that correspond with the standards require little attention. The exceptions, however, are emphasized. Management by exception can be desirable because it highlights only those weak areas that require management's attention. A behavioral effect occurs when management by exception is applied to people. If a worker is ignored when operating according to the standard and is noticed only when something is wrong, the worker may become resentful and perform less satisfactorily. While it may be argued by some that the worker is being paid to operate at standard, the human factor cannot be ignored. Without recognition, the worker becomes discontented; and this discontent may spread throughout the organization with a loss of both morale and productivity.

Cost Management   Cost management is related to cost control, but here the emphasis is on establishing the level of costs that becomes the benchmark for measuring performance. It can be as simple as decreasing the costs of operations through improved methods and procedures, better selection of resources (human, materials, and facilities), or eliminating unnecessary (nonvalue-added) activities. As standards are set and periodically reviewed, operations can be analyzed to identify waste and inefficiency and to eliminate their sources. These reviews can also be times to acknowledge better than expected performance; appreciation will motivate employees to continue looking for better ways to operate. A standard cost system creates an environment in which people become cost conscious, always looking for improvements in the process.

Decision Making   If standards are set at currently attainable levels (a concept discussed below in quality of standards), the standard costs are useful in making many types of decisions. For example, some common decisions are regular, special order, or transfer pricing; sell or process further; make or buy; and cash planning. When an analysis is used as the basis for setting the standard costs, managers need not perform new analyses for each decision.

Recordkeeping Costs   A standard cost system saves recordkeeping costs, not in initially starting the system, but in the long-run operations of the system. When using actual costs, each item of material issued from a storeroom has its cost that came from a specific purchase order. The cost transferred to work in process inventory is calculated using an inventory cost method: specific identification, FIFO, LIFO, moving average, or weighted average. For companies with thousands of different material categories in stock, identifying costs to move to work in process inventory can be an enormous task. When standard costs are in place, each item in the same material classification has the same standard cost. Therefore, costs transferred to work in process inventory are the product of a standard cost per unit and the number of units issued. This same process applies to work in process inventory transfers to finished goods. All inventories have their standard costs, and balances are always stated at standard.

Inventory Valuation   A standard cost system records the same costs for physically identical units of materials and products; an actual cost system can record different costs for physically identical units. Differences between the two costs tend to be waste, inefficiency, and nonvalue-added activities. Such items, if incurred at all, are period costs and excluded from inventory amounts. They should not be capitalized and deferred in inventory values. Therefore, standards provide for a more rational cost in valuing inventories.

Occasionally, efficiencies will also be one of the differences between actual and standard costs. That means that performance has been better than expected. If this situation will continue in the future, the standards are revised. Otherwise, the current standards still provide a more rational basis for putting costs on products.

The Quality of Standards

The term "standard" has no meaning unless we know on what the standard is based. A standard may be very strict at one extreme or very loose at the other extreme. We broadly classify standards as strict or tight standards, attainable standards, and loose or lax standards.

No easy solution exists to how standards should be set. The objective, of course, is to obtain the best possible results at the lowest possible cost. Often human behavior becomes the dominate concern in setting standards. A very high standard may motivate some employees to produce exceptional results. On the other hand, a standard that is too high and cannot be reached may discourage employees and will produce only modest results. In setting a level of standards, management must consider the employees, their abilities, their aspirations, and their degree of control over the results of operations.

Strict Standards

Strict standards are set at a maximum level of efficiency, representing conditions that can seldom, if ever, be attained. They ignore normal materials spoilage and idle labor time due to such factors as machine breakdowns. This standard appears to represent perfection, something few employees will achieve. Although a standard should challenge people, a standard that is virtually unattainable will not motivate most employees to do their best. An employee is more likely to put forth increased effort when feeling successful. In other words, a person increases aspirations with success while the aspiration level is lowered with failure.

In addition, variances from strict standards have little significance for control purposes. There will never be a favorable variance, only zero or unfavorable variances. In fact, most variances will be large and unfavorable. The question is "What does such a variance measure?"

Attainable Standards

Attainable standards can be achieved with reasonable effort. Perhaps the standards should be somewhat lower than what can be achieved by earnest effort. With success the employees gain confidence and tend to be more productive. For a more experienced group of workers, an exacting standard may serve as a challenge that motivates an employee to higher levels of performance. With less experienced workers, standards may have to be set at a lower level at first. As learning takes place, the standards may be raised. Increases in standards should be made with caution and should be accepted by the employees as being fair.

Managers should expect to see favorable and unfavorable variances with an attainable standard. Some employees will meet and exceed the standard with reasonable effort, while others will not meet the standard because of poor performance.

Loose Standards

Loose standards tend to be based on past performance and represent an average of prior costs. They include all of the inefficiency and waste in past operations. Such standards are not likely to motivate employees to high performance. The very nature of loose standards means less than efficient performance. As a result, variances from loose standards are almost always favorable and provide little useful information for the control of operations.

Revising the Standards

Standard costs should be reviewed periodically to see if revisions are necessary to keep them at the selected level of quality. Although many factors may combine that determine the best time to review standard costs, they should be reviewed at least once a year. Otherwise, they may not be current. This does not mean waiting until the end of the year. Companies with thousands of items on standards will have a department that spends full time reviewing standards throughout the year.

A key as to when to review standards is to identify changes taking place that outdate the existing standards. Let's look at a few of the changes that typically call for a revision to one or more standard costs:

1. Increases or decreases in the price levels of specific materials and supplies.
2. Changes in the payment plan or wage schedule.
3. Modifications of material type or specifications.
4. Acquisitions of new equipment or disposition of old equipment.
5. Modifications of operations or procedures.
6. Additions or deletions of product lines.
7. Expansions or contractions of facilities.
8. Changes in management policies that affect the amount of costs and the way costs are accumulated and identified with activities, operations, and products.

Management policies can have a significant impact on standard costs. Examples of the most common policy areas are the definition of capacity, the classification of fringe benefits, depreciation methods, and capitalization and expense policies. Capacity definitions influence the level of waste and inefficiency that management will tolerate and the amount of fixed costs applied to individual units of an operation, task, or product. A redefinition of capacity can be due to changes in the number of shifts, in the hours of operation with given shift schedules, or in demand for the product or service. Fringe benefits can appear in several ways, any of which can influence a product cost significantly. Management can classify any element of fringe benefit cost as a direct cost of the product, an indirect cost through a labor-related cost pool, a direct cost through a factory overhead cost pool, or a period cost through a general and administrative cost pool. Management determines which depreciation methods are in use. One common policy is to change from a declining balance method for existing equipment to a straight-line method at about the mid-life point of the asset life. Occasionally, management will change the method applied to new equipment purchased. The criteria for capitalization and expenses determine which costs are capitalized as assets to be charged to operations through depreciation and amortization and which costs are charged immediately upon incurrence. Any change in the criteria alters the treatment of those costs affected.

Throughout the chapter, we assume the standards are entered into the formal accounting system. Many companies do not follow this practice. Instead, they use standards as a part of statistical supplements in arriving at information for control purposes. Revision of standards is much more critical if the standards are the basis for product costing.

STANDARD COST SHEET

Once standards have been set for each component of cost, the costs are summarized in a **standard cost sheet** Here we reflect the cost of each category of direct material used, the cost of each direct labor operation employed, and the cost of all overhead tasks, operations, processes, and support functions applied to a unit of final product. Standard cost sheets can be extremely lengthy or very simple depending on the product and manufacturing process.

Colexus, Inc., uses a standard cost system in accounting for its only product, Colex. The standards currently are as follows:

Component	Cost of Component	Total Unit Cost
Materials	3 lbs. at $4.00 per pound	$12.00
Direct labor	1/2 hour at $7.00 per hour	3.50
Variable overhead	1/2 hour at $6.00 per hour	3.00
Fixed overhead	1/2 hour at $9.00 per hour	4.50
Total cost per unit		$23.00

This standard cost sheet gives the total unit cost of each product produced. It says that for each completed unit, three pounds of direct materials at a total cost of $12 is taken from materials inventory and charged to work in process inventory. Also $3.50 is charged for direct labor; and a total of $7.50 in overhead costs are applied. Nothing is noted here about the actual costs incurred because all production is carried only at standard cost. Thus, when a completed unit of product is transferred from work in process inventory to finished goods inventory and later to cost of goods sold, the cost is $23. The standard cost sheet becomes the basis for all accounting entries related to the product.

As we move to standards for materials, direct labor, and factory overhead, we need to know the volume of output and the material quantities allowed for that volume in order to calculate certain variances. We look to the standard cost sheet to find the allowed amounts. The volume of output will be expressed as units of product or equivalent units, depending on the circumstances in production.

STANDARDS FOR MATERIALS

Standards are established for the cost of obtaining materials and for the quantities to be used in production. Managers then compare actual costs against these standards to ascertain variances. Basically, two types of variances exist: price and quantity. Different variances may be developed for specialized purposes, but they can always be classified as variations in the price of materials or in the quantities used, or as a combination of price and quantity. If the actual cost is greater than the standard cost, the variance is an **unfavorable variance;** if actual cost is less than the standard cost, the variance is a **favorable variance.**

Materials Price Variance

A **materials price variance** measures the difference between the prices at which materials are acquired and the prices established in the standards.

What is in the standard, how a variance is calculated, and potential causes of variances are now explained.

Setting the Price Standard   A standard price is set for each category of material the company expects to use. The cost elements that make up the standard are a matter of management policy. Although the purchase price is the dominant element, other costs may also be included. For example, additional costs may include the cost of insurance for materials in transit, the cost of transporting materials, various cash and trade discounts, and costs of receiving and inspecting materials at the receiving dock. Once management decides on the elements, the next step is assessing prices. We do not discuss the estimation techniques here, but common approaches to determining amounts include:

1. Statistical forecasting.
2. Knowledge and experience in the particular type of business.
3. Weighted average of prices in most recent purchases.
4. Prices agreed upon in long-term contracts or purchase commitments.

Why should we be concerned about the cost elements in the materials price variance? When variances occur, we look for changes in the cost elements to give us explanations for the causes.

Accounting for a Price Variance   A materials price variance is isolated at the time we purchase materials. We record the actual quantity of materials purchased in the materials inventory at standard prices. We record the liability to the supplier at actual quantities and actual prices. Any difference between the two amounts is recorded as a price variance.

To illustrate, assume that the purchasing department for Colexus, Inc., bought 40,000 pounds of materials for $159,200, which is $3.98 per pound. To make the example easier to follow, we will use the following symbols:

$$AQP = \text{actual quantity purchased}$$
$$AP = \text{actual price}$$
$$SP = \text{standard price}$$
$$MPV = \text{materials price variance}$$

The cost flow of actual and standard costs through the accounts would appear in T-account form as shown at the top of the following page:

To calculate the variance without thinking in terms of accounts, the information from the T-accounts can be summarized into convenient formulas as follows:

$$AP \times AQP = \$3.98 \times 40,000 = \$159,200$$
$$SP \times AQP = \$4.00 \times 40,000 = \$160,000$$
$$MPV = (AP - SP) \times AQP = \$.02 \times 40,000 = \$800 \text{ Favorable}$$

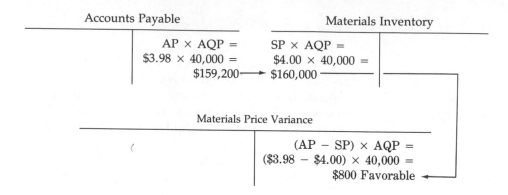

Note that the actual quantity is used in all calculations. Only the prices differ. A materials price variance can be either favorable or unfavorable when actual costs are compared with standard costs. In this illustration, the materials price variance is favorable because the materials were purchased at a cost below the standard.

Causes of the Price Variance   A variance occurs for any number of reasons. If the variance is significant, we must identify causes. If performance is deemed good, the responsible people should be praised and, where appropriate, rewarded. If the investigation finds out-of-control situations, corrections can be made so variations are eliminated in the future. Identifying the cause of variances leads us to examine the things that are changing with the cost elements that make up the standard. In some cases, we are just simply using outdated standards, and we need to adjust them.

Although many causes for variances pertain to any given situation, a list of the common sources appears below:

1. Random fluctuations in market prices.
2. Material substitutions.
3. Market shortages or excesses.
4. Purchasing from vendors other than those offering the terms used in the standard.
5. Purchasing higher or lower quality materials.
6. Purchasing in nonstandard or uneconomical quantities.
7. Changes in the mode of transportation.
8. Changes in the production schedule that result in rush orders or additional materials.
9. Unexpected price increases.
10. Fortunate buys.
11. Failure to take cash discounts.

Responsibility for the Price Variance   The purchasing department is usually charged with the responsibility for price variances. If the purchasing function is carried out properly, the standard price should be attainable. When lower prices are paid, a favorable materials price variance is recorded, indicating that the purchasing department was under the standard; higher prices are reflected in an unfavorable materials price variance. Sometimes the cause of price variances really should be charged to a production department instead of to the purchasing department. For example, two specific cases exist: (1) if a rush order is caused by production activity, and (2) if production people request a specific brand name for a material rather than allowing the purchasing department to buy by specifications.

Periodic reports show how actual prices compare with standard prices for the various types of materials purchased. Reports on price variances may be made as frequently as daily but will generally be weekly and monthly. They reveal which materials, if any, are responsible for a large part of any total price variation and can help the purchasing department in its search for more economical vendors.

Materials Quantity Variance

Materials are withdrawn and used in production, but the actual quantity used may be more or less than specified by the standards. The variation in the use of materials is called a **materials quantity variance.** Other names for the variance are materials usage variance, materials use variance, and materials efficiency variance. This section discusses the factors that influence the variance and its causes.

Setting the Quantity Variance   The quantity factor in a material standard cost is based on engineering specifications, blueprints and designs, bills of materials, and routings. Taken together, these items specify the quality, size, thickness, weight, and any other factor necessary for a good unit of final product. We also include in the quantity factor any desired allowances for normal acceptable waste, scrap, shrinkage, and spoilage that may occur during the manufacturing process. Like the price variance, we will look to these elements of the quantity factor when variances occur.

Accounting for a Quantity Variance   As materials are used, the work in process account is increased by the standard quantity used multiplied by the standard price. The materials account is decreased by the actual quantity used multiplied by the standard price. Returning to Colexus, Inc., assume that 31,000 pounds of material are withdrawn from Materials Inventory for use in the production of 10,000 units of final product. Because the standard cost sheet indicates only three pounds should be used for each final product, the standard quantity of material that should have been used is 30,000 pounds (3 lbs. x 30,000 units of final product).

For our example, we will use the following symbols in equation form:

$$SP = \text{Standard price}$$
$$AQU = \text{Actual quantity used}$$
$$SQ = \text{Standard quantity allowed}$$
$$MQV = \text{Materials quantity variance}$$

The cost flow of actual and standard costs through the accounts would appear in T-account form as follows:

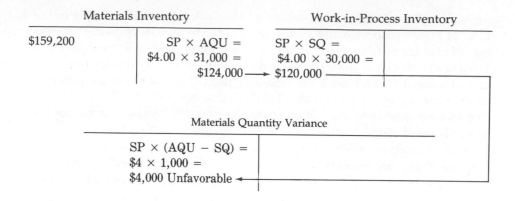

To calculate the variance without thinking in terms of accounts, the above information can be summarized into convenient formulas as follows:

$$SP \times AQU = \$4.00 \times 31,000 = \$124,000$$
$$SP \times SQ = \$4.00 \times 30,000 = \$120,000$$
$$MQV = SP \times (AQU - SQ) = \$4.00 \times 1,000 = \$4,000 \text{ Unfavorable}$$

In the first two equations, we use the standard unit price but the quantities differ. In one case, we use the actual quantities issued from the storeroom. In the other, we use the standard materials quantity allowed for each good unit of final product. Because only quantities can differ in the equations, we call any variation a quantity variance. The variance for Colexus, Inc., is unfavorable because the amount of materials used is greater than the amount called for by the standard.

The foregoing explanations apply to direct materials. Indirect materials are those that are used for something other than the direct manufacture of a product. When indirect materials are used by the maintenance department, the actual quantities are removed from materials inventory at standard price times actual quantities used and recorded in the maintenance department overhead account at the same amount. No variances are measured.

Causes of the Quantity Variance   What causes a materials quantity variance? To answer this question, we look to the elements that make up the quantity standard and the specific situation. Examples of common causes include:

1. Changes in product specifications.
2. Material substitutions.
3. Breakage during the handling of materials in movement and processing.
4. Workers improperly using the materials.
5. Machine settings operating at nonstandard levels.
6. Waste.
7. Pilferage.

Responsibility for the Quantity Variance   Ordinarily, materials quantity variances are chargeable to production departments. They often arise as a result of wasteful practices in working with materials, or they arise because of products that must be scrapped through faulty production.

Reports on the quantities of materials used are made to the responsible production department supervisor. A production supervisor, for example, may receive daily or weekly summaries showing how the quantities used in the department compare with the standards. At the operating level, managers can control directly the use of materials. Often reports on variations from standard are for physical quantities only. Managers do not need immediate feedback from a cost report. Daily or weekly cost reports simply tell managers the financial magnitude of variations and serve as a reminder that corrections should be made before losses become too great.

Summary reports of actual and standard materials consumption given in dollars, with variances and percentages of variances, also go to the plant superintendent at least monthly. If the variances in any department are too large, the superintendent can localize the differences and take steps to reduce them. During the month, of course, the operating managers will watch materials use; and if they have been doing their jobs properly, the accumulated variances for the month should be relatively small.

Interrelationships of Price and Quantity Variances

We have treated the materials price and quantity variances as though they are independent and unrelated. In many cases, the event that causes one variance also causes the other. For example, assume the purchasing department buys a lower-grade material at a substantially reduced price. This generates a favorable price variance for purchasing. When those materials reach production, they result in a higher than normal waste. This gives the operating supervisors unfavorable quantity variances. Keeping the two variances in isolation makes the purchasing agent look good while the operating supervisors turn in poor performances. In reality, both variances are the responsibility of the purchasing department. If the variances net out favorable, the purchasing decision has benefited the company. On the other hand, a net unfavorable variance is a loss to the company.

The operating people can also influence the price variance. If improperly adjusted machines, for instance, generate a higher than usual waste, more materials may be needed from the storeroom. When a production supervisor requisitions the materials and the storeroom manager realizes sufficient quantities are not available, a request is made to the purchasing department to order more. To keep the production schedule current, a rush order is issued. The higher prices paid for a rush order will result in an unfavorable price variance.

The warning of these situations is simple: Investigation of variances must not be done in isolation.

Control of Materials Acquisition

Control over materials begins with procurement. The purchasing department will seek a reliable supplier whose materials meet the quality standard in the desired quantity at the lowest price. After receiving purchase requisitions from individual departments, the purchasing department places the order for the materials. As materials arrive at the receiving dock, they are counted, inspected, and turned over to the storekeeper.

Invoices received by the accounting department for materials purchased are compared against purchase orders and receiving reports to determine whether or not the company was properly billed for materials ordered and received. Computations on the invoices are checked, and the verified invoices are filed by the dates when payments must be made.

The storekeeper is the only person with access to the physical materials, which are stored in an enclosed area to prevent theft or loss. A store ledger clerk maintains an accounting record of the quantities of materials received and withdrawn. Incoming items are entered from receiving reports on inventory cards or a computer terminal to reflect the inventory subsidiary ledger. The requisition forms for materials to be withdrawn for production support the entries for inventory withdrawals. The physical inventory kept by the storekeeper should be in substantial agreement with the book record revealed by independent counts. The separation of the duties acts as a check on both the storekeeper, who realizes that a book record of the inventory is being maintained, and the stores ledger clerk, who has no access to the physical inventory and thus no reason to falsify the record. This separation of physical custodianship of property and the responsibility for accountability follows a general principle of internal control: One person should control the physical asset while another person maintains the accounting record. This is true not only in inventory accounting but also in accounting for cash, securities, and other business assets.

STANDARDS FOR LABOR

We can set standards for direct labor and measure variances from the standards in much the same way as we did for materials. The price factor is called rate; the quantity factor is time. When we refer to variations in time, we will use the term efficiency. The **labor rate variance** measures the difference between the actual wage rate paid and actual hours worked (actual wages earned) and the actual hours multiplied by the standard labor rates. The **labor efficiency variance** is the difference between the actual hours worked and standard hours required for production multiplied by the standard labor rate. We will discuss in this section the important aspects of setting labor standards, accounting for variances, and identifying causes of variances.

When discussing standards for labor, we assume direct labor only. Indirect labor, in the form of people working in the manufacturing departments who are not working directly on products or the time people work that is classified as idle time, is part of the payroll system. These costs are distributed from payroll to the factory overhead and become part of overhead standards. Therefore, indirect labor is not discussed here.

Setting Rate Standards

Standard cost systems rely on individual labor rates by skill level classification for better control and accuracy. However, in some cases, standard rates can be set for cost centers or departments. Regardless of how it is structured, the underlying wage or salary rate established as the standard rate will be either established through contract negotiations or by the prevailing rates in the location where the work is performed. The details for selecting skill level classifications cover training, education, experience, special physical abilities, and set of task specifications.

When setting the standard rates, management must decide whether to use a basic labor rate or a "loaded" labor rate as the standard. A "loaded" labor rate includes labor-related costs such as overtime premiums, shift premiums, bonuses and incentives, payroll taxes, and fringe benefits. Those factors not included in the labor rate standard will be included in overhead. Therefore, management will look at the advantages of treating these cost factors as direct costs or as indirect costs. For example, if the company is performing contracts for the federal government, the company would typically recover more of its costs through the "loaded" standard labor rate.

Setting Time Standards

Time standards are more difficult to establish than material quantity standards. Peoples' productivity is the basis for setting time standards; and, as you know, people tend to differ in behavior from one time to the next. Setting time standards involves answering two questions: (1) What operations are performed? and (2) How much time should we spend in each operation for the product or service? The answer to the first question is determined by reviewing operations and procedures, process charts, and routing lists. The answer to the second question will be determined from one or more of the following:

1. Operation and body movement analysis. (This involves dividing each operation into the elementary body movements such as reaching, pushing, turning over, etc. Published tables of standard times are available for each movement. These standard times are applied to the individual movements and added together for the total standard time per operation.)
2. Time and motion studies conducted by industrial engineers.
3. Averages of past performance, adjusted for anticipated changes.
4. Test runs through the production process for which standards are to be set.

Accounting for the Rate and Efficiency Variances

Unlike materials, we cannot purchase labor and store it until needed. We purchase and use labor at the same time. Therefore, we discuss the accounting for both variances at the same time.

Colexus, Inc., shows a payroll for its direct workers of $35,616 and 4,800 hours. That gives an actual rate of $7.42 per hour. We have already seen the company produced 10,000 good units. The standard cost sheet tells us that each completed unit requires 1/2 hour of direct labor time. Hence, we were allowed 5,000 hours (1/2 × 10,000 units of product).

For our example, we will use the following symbols in equation form:

$$
\begin{aligned}
AR &= \text{Actual rate} \\
SR &= \text{Standard rate} \\
AH &= \text{Actual hours} \\
SH &= \text{Standard hours allowed} \\
LRV &= \text{Labor rate variance} \\
LEV &= \text{Labor efficiency variance}
\end{aligned}
$$

The cost flow of actual and standard costs through the accounts would appear in T-account form as follows:

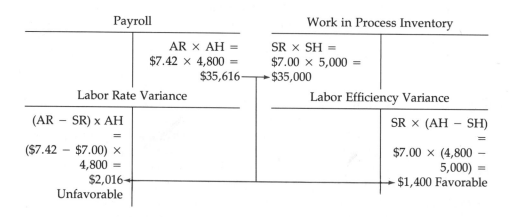

A labor rate variance results whenever the actual rate paid a worker differs from the standard rate. Calculating a labor rate variance requires holding the actual hours constant while comparing the difference in rates, as summarized below:

$$
\begin{aligned}
AR \times AH &= \$7.42 \times 4,800 = \$35,616 \\
SR \times AH &= \$7.00 \times 4,800 = \$33,600 \\
LRV = (AR - SR) \times SH &= \$\ .42 \times 4,800 = \$\ 2,016 \text{ Unfavorable}
\end{aligned}
$$

The variance is unfavorable because the actual rate exceeds the standard rate.

The labor efficiency variance (also called quantity, time, or usage variance) is the result when workers use times that differ from the standard. We calculate the variance by holding the rate constant while comparing the difference in times. The following summarizes this procedure:

$$SR \times AH = \$7.00 \times 4,800 = \$33,600$$
$$SR \times SH = \$7.00 \times 5,000 = \$35,000$$
$$LEV = SR \times (AH - SH) = \$7.00 \times (200) = \$1,400 \text{ Favorable}$$

The variance is favorable because the actual hours worked are less than the standard hours allowed for the 10,000 units of final product produced.

Because the hours are purchased and used at the same time, we can use an alternate approach to calculating the variances:

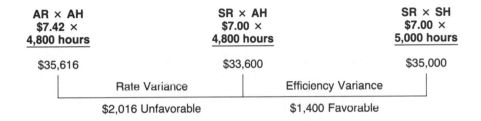

AR × AH	SR × AH	SR × SH
$7.42 ×	**$7.00 ×**	**$7.00 ×**
4,800 hours	**4,800 hours**	**5,000 hours**
$35,616	$33,600	$35,000
	Rate Variance	Efficiency Variance
	$2,016 Unfavorable	$1,400 Favorable

Causes of Labor Variances

Labor rates are usually set by contract, negotiations, or federal laws or regulations. So, why would a labor rate variance occur? Two basic reasons exist. First, labor rates often represent an average for a task, operation, or work center. If a departmental manager shifts workers around because of sudden changes in personnel requirements or a shortage of personnel, the average rate can easily change depending on how the shift relates to higher-paid or lower-paid workers. A second reason is that standard labor rates may include cost elements beyond the basic labor rate. Any changes in overtime worked, shift differentials, payroll taxes, or fringe benefits will show up in a labor variance if these elements are part of the standard rate.

Labor efficiency relates to how many units are completed per actual hour for each task, operation, or process. Any number of reasons exist for why productivity varies from the level assumed in the standard time. Some of the common causes of a labor efficiency variance include the following:

1. Use of lower-skilled or higher-skilled workers.
2. Effects of the learning curve.
3. Lower-quality or higher-quality materials to work on.
4. Changes in production methods.
5. Changes in production scheduling.
6. Installation of new equipment.
7. Poorly maintained equipment or machine malfunction.
8. Delays in routing work, materials, tools, or instructions.
9. Insufficient training, incorrect instructions, or worker dissatisfaction.

Responsibility for Labor Variances

Labor rate and efficiency variances are charged to the department managers who have control over the use of workers. Although a labor rate variance is important to understand and control, managers tend to concentrate more on the labor efficiency variance because it has a greater impact on capacity utilization and the department's ability to meet production schedules. Labor efficiency is compared by department and by job with established standards. Daily or weekly reports to department managers and the plant superintendent help to locate and solve difficulties on a particular job or in a department. Differences between jobs and departments may show that a job cannot be handled at the standard labor cost or that a department is not managed properly.

Interrelationships of Variances

As we saw with materials, variances should not be analyzed in isolation from one another. The event that causes one variance can easily be the same cause for one or more other variances. Because we can improve future planning and cost control when we identify and understand the interrelationship, we now look at interrelationships among labor variances and between materials and labor.

Labor Rate and Efficiency Variances   People perform the productive effort; thus, the rate of pay and the time required are related. Because so many relationships can exist between the two, we cite only a few examples here to aid in identifying what to look for in a specific operation.

Assume a number of workers are in various military reserve units that have been called up to active duty. As a temporary measure, a manager has two options: (1) employ temporary workers or (2) shift other workers internally and add overtime. Using temporary workers may be cheaper (they may also be more expensive depending on the situation); but they are not as experienced with the equipment, procedures, and processes. They will take more time than the standard allows. Therefore, the hiring of temporary workers will result in both rate and efficiency variances. The second option is to move workers around and use overtime. The move will put differently skilled workers on new jobs. The move can create either a favorable or unfavorable rate variance depending on the mix of workers. Their experience levels may be higher or lower than the specific job required and can result in an efficiency variance. Adding overtime will affect a rate variance depending on how the company treats the overtime premium. Efficiency should not be an issue of overtime unless the workers become less productive through fatigue.

In another case, suppose a worker is having difficulties working on a particular machine. The worker is taking more time than standard to complete good units. The manager, trying to keep production on schedule and not lose capacity to inefficiency, shifts a more skilled, higher paid worker into the job. The higher paid worker will yield an unfavorable rate variance but can reduce the unfavorable efficiency variance or create a favorable one.

Materials and Labor Variances   Materials and labor variances can also be related to the same source. For our purpose, we give two examples. Assume, for instance, that a purchasing agent has a fortunate buy on a lower-quality grade of material. The "good buy" yields a favorable materials price variance for purchasing. However, when the materials are used in production, they crumble and create more waste than anticipated. That means more materials are needed and an unfavorable materials quantity variance arises. A department manager, desiring to minimize the lost time, moves higher-skilled people to the operation where the higher waste occurs. This action leads to a labor rate variance and may influence the magnitude or the direction of a labor efficiency variance.

In another case, a worker starts the shift fatigued and stressed. His lack of concentration results in higher waste which takes more time. That results in unfavorable materials quantity and labor efficiency variances. Because more materials are need, the manager requisitions materials from the storeroom. The storekeeper finds fewer materials available than now required. Purchasing is asked to place a rush order so that production can proceed with minimum delay. The rush order will increase the purchasing costs and that means an unfavorable materials price variance.

The Influence of Automation

We are seeing a trend where many companies are automating various aspects or even all aspects of their production. The purpose of this movement is to increase productivity and quality while keeping unit costs low. With automatic equipment, the need for high levels of direct labor is substantially reduced. Direct labor in such an environment becomes such an insignificant element of cost that variances have little meaning.

In some industries, automation may not go beyond a certain point; in which case, direct labor will remain a smaller but significant cost element. However, with a great deal of automation, direct labor time becomes more dependent upon the speed of a machine operation than upon the speed of individual workers. Hence, labor efficiency is more related to machine efficiency than to the efficiency of the worker. This means a labor efficiency variance will still carry little meaningful information.

STANDARDS FOR OVERHEAD

The factory overhead costs consist of all manufacturing costs that are not classified as direct materials and direct labor. Examples of factory overhead costs include indirect materials and supplies, indirect labor, maintenance and repairs, lubrication, power, factory property taxes and insurance, and depreciation. Service organizations will have similar overhead costs related to providing services. In a standard cost, we apply the standard overhead costs to products and services. We accumulate the actual overhead costs and compare them to the applied amounts to determine whether the standards were met.

Variances from the standard help to direct management's attention to situations where costs should be controlled more closely, where the standards should be revised, or where managers should be praised and rewarded for good performance.

Development of Overhead Rates

Standard costs for manufacturing overhead have price and quantity factors, just like direct materials and direct labor. Price is reflected in one or more overhead rates; quantity is the measure of activity. Price and quantity in this case are closely linked. In developing standard overhead rates, five major considerations must be evaluated.

First, which cost elements are included in manufacturing overhead? We need to identify the costs such as indirect materials, indirect labor, fringe benefits, payroll taxes, utilities, property taxes, insurance, depreciation and security. When certain variances occur, these items will be examined for specific changes.

The second consideration is the measure of activity for relating overhead costs to products. A **measure of activity** for this purpose represents the factor that best expresses how costs change as volume increases or decreases. As noted in earlier chapters, we refer to the measure of activity as an allocation base or cost driver. Although many factors can influence costs, we select the dominant cost driver. The common ones are direct labor hours or costs, machine hours, and units of products. In Chapters 3 and 5, we examined activity-based costing and the identification of cost drivers that cause costs. Our use of the measure of activity above is the same as a primary-stage cost driver in those discussions. For standard costs, the appropriate measure must be selected if variances are to provide any meaningful information.

Third, closely related to the measure of activity is the concept of capacity and its anticipated level for the current period. We discussed several concepts in Chapter 5. The capacity concept selected and the determination of its level for the current period significantly influence overhead rates as a result of the presence of fixed costs.

A fourth consideration is cost behavior. The behavior of each cost within factory overhead is important because management plans for and controls variable costs differently than it plans for and controls fixed costs. Consequently, distinguishing variable from fixed overhead costs aides in analyzing variances for cause and responsibility. Standard cost systems typically split overhead rates and identify appropriate ones for variable overhead costs and for fixed overhead costs. In separating the variable and fixed cost rates, different measures of activity may be used for each cost behavior.

The fifth consideration is at which level the overhead rates should be set: by task, by machine or labor operation, by activity center, by department, by plant or overall. For a single product operation, plant-wide rates for variable and fixed costs are sufficient. The greater the product and operation diversity, the more likely it is that rates are calculated for smaller groupings of costs. For our illustration with Colexus, Inc., we assume an overall level merely to illustrate the concepts. The same considerations will apply should a company compute rates by task, activity center, and so forth.

Flexible Overhead Budgets

As we have seen in previous chapters, a **flexible overhead budget** is based on a formula that expresses the budgeted overhead at any point within the relevant range. The formula recognizes that some costs are variable and some are fixed. The following schedule shows the flexible overhead budget formula for Colexus, Inc. We are assuming here that the measure of activity is direct labor hours.

Cost Item	Fixed Cost	Variable Cost per Direct Labor Hour
Indirect materials	—	$ 1.90 per hour
Hourly indirect labor	—	1.27 per hour
Supervision.................................	$21,000	—
Repair and maintenance	3,600	1.11 per hour
Utilities and occupancy.....................	10,580	1.00 per hour
Depreciation................................	13,800	—
Miscellaneous costs	520	.72 per hour
	$49,500	$ 6.00 per hour

The flexible budget formula is: $49,500 + ($6.00 × hours). Since we know that the hours are related to units of product in terms of two units per hour, we can restate the formula as: $49,500 + ($3.00 × units of product). Typically, we would have multiple products using different amounts of direct labor which would require the use of the basic formula. As a sidelight, the overhead rates are also available from these numbers, if we assume a capacity level of 5,500 direct labor hours or 11,000 units of product. For variable costs, the rate is $6.00 per hour or $3.00 per unit (1/2 hour × $6.00). The fixed costs are $9.00 per hour ($49,500/5,500 hours) or $4.50 per unit (1/2 hour × $9.00).

The significance of the flexible overhead budget becomes apparent in the next section where we identify variances for overhead costs.

Framework for Two-Way Overhead Variance Analysis

Because different factors give rise to under- or overapplied overhead, we need a framework to identify the areas of potential causes of variations. In our framework, we compare actual overhead costs with a flexible budget and with the applied overhead to arrive at two possible variances: budget variance and capacity variance.

To begin, we need to know the actual overhead costs and the applied overhead costs. We have already seen for Colexus, Inc., that the company produced 10,000 units during the month. Actual overhead costs for the month are $31,500 variable and $50,000 fixed. Our factory overhead accounts would then show the following information:

Actual costs:		
Variable...	$31,500	
Fixed	50,000	$81,500
Applied costs:		
Variable ($3.00 × 10,000 units)	$30,000	
Fixed ($4.50 × 10,000 units).........................	45,000	75,000
Underapplied		$ 6,500

Remember, the cost per unit for variable and fixed overhead is calculated in advance and appears on the standard cost sheet for individual products. Therefore, the rates used above are applied directly to actual units or equivalent units of product.

The next step is to compare the actual costs and applied costs with the flexible budget for 10,000 units produced. The following table summarizes this information:

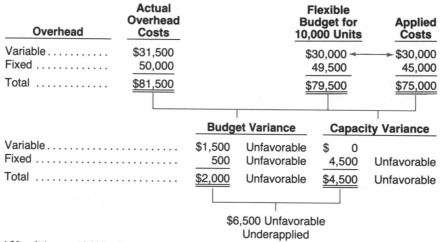

Overhead	Actual Overhead Costs		Flexible Budget for 10,000 Units	Applied Costs
Variable...........	$31,500		$30,000 ⟶	$30,000
Fixed	50,000		49,500	45,000
Total	$81,500		$79,500	$75,000

	Budget Variance		Capacity Variance	
Variable......................	$1,500	Unfavorable	$ 0	
Fixed	500	Unfavorable	4,500	Unfavorable
Total	$2,000	Unfavorable	$4,500	Unfavorable

$6,500 Unfavorable
Underapplied

* $6 × ½ hour × 10,000 units

Budget Variance   A budget variance is the difference between actual overhead costs and the flexible budget for actual units produced. It is also called a **controllable variance**. This variance is deemed controllable by the appropriate operating departments. In the foregoing example, the variance is unfavorable, which means more dollars were spent than were budgeted for 10,000 units. A more detailed examination of the variance is needed to identify areas where managers need to take some action. One approach for providing greater detail is to show the budget variance by individual cost item with the use of the flexible overhead formula, as shown in the table on the following page:

A number of causes may exist for either a favorable or an unfavorable budget variance. The common causes will fall into one of four categories:

1.   Price changes in the individual cost components making up overhead costs.
2.   Quantity changes in individual items within overhead cost components, probably in the variable overhead area.

Cost Item	Actual Overhead	Flexible Budget for 10,000 units	Budget Variance
Indirect materials	$10,250	$ 9,500	$ 750 U
Hourly indirect labor	6,250	6,350	100 F
Supervision	21,400	21,000	400 U
Repair and maintenance	9,050	9,150	100 F
Utilities and occupancy	15,930	15,580	350 U
Depreciation	13,800	13,800	0
Miscellaneous costs	4,820	4,120	700 U
	$81,500	$79,500	$2,000 U

3.   Estimation errors in segregating variable and fixed costs.
4.   Any overhead costs that are incurred or saved because of inefficient or efficient use of the underlying activity measure (machine hours or labor hours, for example).

The estimating errors come in two varieties: (1) the inaccuracies in predicting what will occur in the future, and (2) the reliability of approximations made in separating overhead costs into variable and fixed categories. The inefficient or efficient use of activity relates to the fact that in an activity (labor worked, for example) overhead costs are incurred to support that activity. If the activity is inefficient, overhead costs support inefficiency. On the other hand, if the activity does not occur, overhead costs are not incurred to support it. Therefore, efficient use saves overhead costs.

Capacity Variance   The capacity variance (also called a volume variance) is the difference between the flexible budget for the actual units produced and the amounts applied to work in process inventory. Because the variable overhead costs are the same in each column, the capacity variance is the difference between the budgeted fixed overhead and the applied fixed overhead. Therefore, the capacity variance is the amount of budgeted fixed overhead not applied (unfavorable) or the amount applied in excess of the budgeted fixed costs (favorable). A capacity variance, then, occurs when actual production differs from the capacity level used to calculate the standard fixed overhead rate.

Continuing with the previous example, we know that fixed overhead for the month was budgeted at $49,500 and that 5,500 direct labor hours or 11,000 units of product constitute a normal level of operation. We see that the standard overhead rate for costing products is computed at the normal capacity level, so in this case it is $4.50 per unit of product.

$$\frac{\$49,500 \text{ (Budgeted fixed overhead)}}{5,500 \text{ (Hours of direct labor)}} = \$9.00 \text{ per hour}$$

We convert the hourly rate to a rate per unit of product with the following computation:

1/2 hour per unit of product × $9.00 = $4.50 per unit

During the month Colexus, Inc., manufactured 10,000 units of product. Fixed overhead is costed to the products by multiplying the standard rate of $4.50 per unit by the 10,000 units of output.

$$\$4.50 \times 10{,}000 \text{ units of product} = \$45{,}000 \text{ applied}$$

Fixed overhead budget..	$49,500
Fixed overhead applied	45,000
Capacity variance (unfavorable)	$ 4,500

Figure 9.2 illustrates a graphical approach to the capacity variance concept.

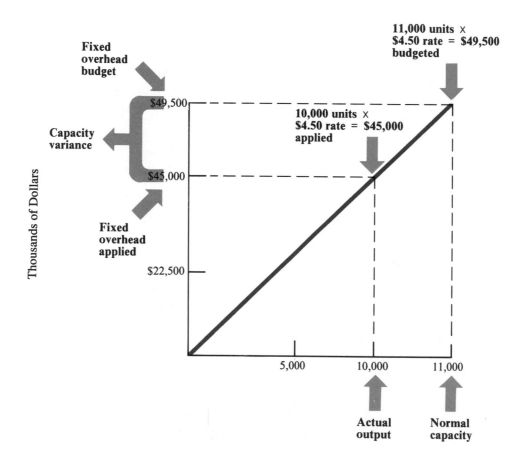

Units of Product

Figure 9.2   Analysis of Capacity Variance

The diagonal line on the graph represents the amount of fixed overhead applied for various units of product manufactured. It rises at the rate of $4.50 per unit of product and reaches the $49,500 budgeted fixed overhead level at 11,000 normal capacity. However, the company only produced 10,000 units of product. With the rate of $4.50 per unit, only $45,000 of the budgeted fixed overhead was applied. The difference between the budgeted fixed overhead and the fixed overhead applied is the capacity variance, as designated on the vertical scale.

Earlier in the chapter we presented the budget variance for individual categories of overhead costs. We could extend the idea to the capacity variance but we do not gain additional information from further detail. The capacity variance is an overall issue and has little to do with individual costs.

PLANT CAPACITY AND CONTROL

In general, we consider the capacity variance as an item the production departments do not control. The plant produces what marketing identifies as the sales requirements. Therefore, the production departments cannot be held responsible if the sales demand does not absorb production at a normal level of plant operation. Other factors, however, may contribute to producing below capacity. Some of these factors are controllable (or somewhat controllable) by production departments. Excessive machine downtime (due to poor maintenance, for example) or inefficient production scheduling could be problems traceable to production managers. Lack of rapidity in completing tasks due to unskilled workers is a factor we would expect to some degree, but an excess of this condition may also be traceable to one or more production managers.

Let's look at an example of some of the factors. In the preceding example, normal capacity was defined at 5,500 direct labor hours or 11,000 units of product. Normal capacity, as defined in Chapter 5, represents the average level of actual plant operation over the years. Practical plant capacity, on the other hand, is the level at which the plant can operate if all facilities are used to full extent. Some allowance is made under this definition for expected delays because of changes in machine setups, necessary maintenance time, and other interruptions. Hence, practical capacity is less than theoretical maximum capacity that could be obtained only under ideal conditions.

A comparison of the actual output with the output for practical plant capacity broadly measures the failure of the plant to operate at the level for which the plant was designed. Assume, for example, that Colexus, Inc., has a plant that can reasonably be expected to produce 15,000 units a month. Yet only 10,000 units were produced. The **idle capacity** is defined as the difference between the practical capacity and the actual production for a given month.

Practical capacity.	15,000 units
Actual production.	10,000 units
Total idle capacity	<u>5,000 units</u>

The idle capacity can be analyzed further to determine why the plant was not used as intended. Assume that the sales budget shows that 12,000 units were to be sold during the month but that orders for only 11,500 units were received. The differences between practical capacity, sales budget, sales orders received, and actual production are illustrated as follows:

Practical capacity	15,000	
		3,000 (1)
Sales budget	12,000	
		500 (2)
Sales orders received	11,500	
		1,500 (3)
Actual production	10,000	

1. **Practical capacity minus sales budget.** The difference between the practical plant capacity and the sales budget for the month requires further investigation. Perhaps the company was overly optimistic and provided too much plant capacity. Or the sales department may not be obtaining potential available sales. Additional analysis may reveal the nature of the problem and provide a foundation for improvements.

2. **Sales budget minus sales orders received.** The difference between the sales budget for the month and the sales orders received is a measurement of the inability of the sales department to meet the budget quota. Perhaps the sales quota was too high, or the sales department was not sufficiently aggressive.

3. **Sales orders received minus actual production.** The difference between the sales orders received and actual production reflects a mixture of idle time and inefficiency. We saw earlier that Colexus, Inc., used 4,800 hours to produce 10,000 products and 5,000 hours were allowed. The 200 hours of efficiency, in this case, freed enough hours for an additional production of 400 units (1/2 hour per unit $\times$ 200 hours). The difference between the sales orders received and the expected production for the time used (11,500 − 9,600 = 1,900 units) is a measurement of idle time. The idle time may be chargeable to poor production scheduling or to some other lapse in production management that caused production to fall below scheduled customer deliveries.

In order to simplify our example, we gave no allowance for inventories at either the beginning or the end of the period. In practice, adjustments must be made for units carried over as inventory or for units remaining on hand at the end of the month.

The significance of the variances may be emphasized by considering the dollar effect. If the sales department fails to meet the sales quota, the company loses profit on lost sales. Arguments can be made that the additional units could only be sold by reducing prices or that the cost estimates are not entirely accurate. Nevertheless, this approach to the problem can be helpful in that it points out how dollars of profit may be sacrificed by not using the facilities as intended.

SUMMARY OF STANDARD COST VARIANCES

We have completed a number of variance computations for the cost elements of production. Figure 9.3 contains a summary of all variances and the means for calculating them. The Figure also emphasizes that the costs charged to units produced are the standard costs. Therefore, work in process inventory and all subsequent accounts containing product costs will be stated at standard.

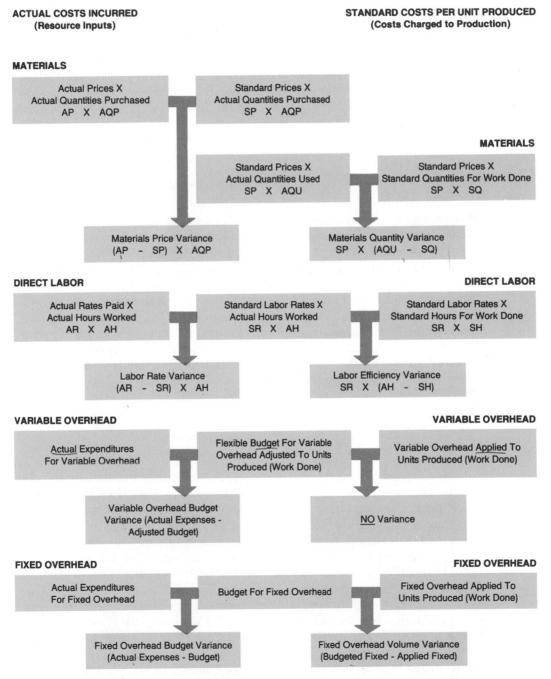

Figure 9.3 Summary of Standard Cost Variances

DISPOSITION OF VARIANCES

In our discussion of materials and labor variances, we set up separate variance accounts. Factory overhead variances, although identified separately in worksheet analysis, are left combined in the under- or overapplied amounts. Now, at the end of each period, variances accounts must be closed. Where do these variances go? As a practical matter, all standard cost variances will go to cost of goods sold. The most common practice is to close the variance accounts directly to cost of goods sold; thus, treating them as period costs. Occasionally, if the variances are significant in amount, they will be prorated to the appropriate materials, work in process, and finished goods inventories and cost of goods sold. We assume here that variances will be closed to the cost of goods sold account.

STANDARD COSTS IN A PROCESS COST SYSTEM

Throughout this chapter, we have alluded to units as actual units of production or equivalent units. Standard costs are appropriate for job cost systems or process cost systems. Where we have a process cost system, the equivalent units are calculated using the FIFO method discussed in Chapter 6. Remember that equivalent units can be different for materials, labor, and overhead.

One convenience realized in a standard cost system is the availability of unit costs without the computation we did in Chapter 6. Since standard costs are predetermined, we simply multiply the equivalent units by the appropriate standard costs to determine costs of goods completed and costs of the ending inventory. Except for the use of equivalent units, variance analysis in a process cost system does not differ from the analysis used in a job cost system.

SUMMARY

Profit becomes part of most performance measures used to evaluate managers or some segment of the organization. Any time actual performance varies from expectations, explanations for the differences are sought. Once reasons for or causes of variations are identified, changes can be made in the future through the planning process or control mechanisms. Common categories of variances are usually isolated as a first step in looking for explanations.

One aid to the analysis is the use of a standard cost system for costs that ultimately flow into cost of goods sold. Standard cost systems operate effectively in situations where standardized products or standardized operations exist. Although the primary advantage of such a system is cost control, several other advantages can also be achieved: cost management, decision making, savings in recordkeeping costs, and more rational inventory valuation.

A standard cost for a product or service consists of a price factor and a quantity factor. These become the basis for computing and analyzing variances. The quality of a standard is expressed as strict, attainable, or loose or lax. The preferred standard for all purposes is one that is current and attainable.

A standard cost sheet is a basic element of the standard cost system. Here the standard quantities and prices are stated for direct materials, direct labor, and all factory overhead. The standard cost sheet gives the total unit cost that is attached to a completed unit of a given product. It, therefore, facilitates the accounting for costs as they flow from work in process to finished goods to cost of goods sold.

Materials variances are set after considering the purchase price and other dollar amounts to be included and after determining the quantities needed for the intended operations. A materials price variance occurs anytime the actual price differs from the standard price. The variance is calculated as the actual price less the standard price times actual quantity purchased. A materials quantity variance is caused by using more or less materials than set by the standard. This variance is calculated as the standard price times the actual quantity used less the standard quantity allowed. Price variances are the responsibility of the purchasing department while quantity variances are the responsibility of production department managers.

In establishing labor standards, management looks at what operations are performed, how much time should be spent in each operation, what labor skills are needed to perform the operations, and what rate should be paid. The standard labor rate is the base rate of pay plus any other costs associated with labor that management chooses to include. A labor rate variance occurs any time the actual rate differs from the standard rate. The variance is the difference between the actual rate and the standard rate times the actual hours worked. A labor efficiency variance is caused by using more or less time than the standard specifies. This variance is calculated as standard rate times the difference between actual hours worked and the standard hours allowed. Both variances generally are the responsibility of production department managers.

Standards for factory overhead are set after considering five important factors: the cost elements to include in the standards, the measure of activity that best relates the costs to the work done, the capacity concept for the selected measure of activity, the cost behavior of each element of overhead cost, and the rate structure, whether by task, operation, process, department, or overall.

During any period, the actual overhead cost can differ from the overhead applied to products or services using the standards. In order to understand the significance of the under-or overapplied amounts, we calculate a budget variance and a capacity variance. A budget variance is the difference between actual overhead costs incurred and the flexible budget for the actual number of units of product produced. It represents those overhead cost elements over which department managers have control. The capacity variance is the difference between the flexible budget for the actual units produced and the amounts applied to work in process. This variance consists only of fixed overhead costs and represents the amount by which actual production differed from planned capacity.

PROBLEM FOR REVIEW

The Houston plant of Enrico Instruments, Inc. manufactures an electrical surge protector. The standard cost per unit of this product is as follows:

Direct materials: 5 units of material x $2 standard price	$10
Direct labor: 1/2 hours x $6 standard labor rate	3
Overhead: 3 machine hours x $8 standard overhead rate	24
Standard production cost per unit	$37

The total factory overhead at normal operating capacity has been budgeted at $480,000; and 60,000 machine hours or 20,000 units of product have been budgeted at normal capacity. The overhead rate per machine hour is $8.

Summary transactions and cost data pertaining to the year are as follows:

1. Materials purchases were 100,000 units at a unit cost of $2.04.
2. Direct materials issued to production were 93,000 units. Actual units of product manufactured during the year totalled 18,000 units.
3. Factory payroll totalled $159,500, of which indirect labor was $110,000.
4. Actual direct labor hours and rates:

    7,500 hours at $6
    500 hours at $9

5. Factory overhead other than indirect labor:

Indirect materials	$129,000
Reduction of prepaid insurance	2,000
Accrued expenses	109,500
Depreciation	86,000

    Variable factory overhead costs totaled $146,500. Fixed costs were $290,000. These amounts include indirect labor and the above listed costs.

6. Actual machine hours totaled 54,500 hours.
7. No units were in process at either the beginning or the end of the year. During the year, 18,000 units of product were manufactured, and 17,000 units were sold.
8. A portion of the flexible overhead budget is given in summary form as follows:

	Percentage of Normal Operating Capacity			
	70%	80%	90%	100%
Standard production in units of product	14,000	16,000	18,000	20,000
Budgeted machine hours	42,000	48,000	54,000	60,000
Variable overhead	$126,000	$144,000	$162,000	$180,000
Fixed overhead	300,000	300,000	300,000	300,000
Total overhead.................	$426,000	$444,000	$462,000	$480,000

Required:

Compute the following standard cost variances:

1. Materials price variance and materials quantity variance.
2. Labor rate variance and labor efficiency variance.
3. Overhead variances: Budget variance and capacity variance. Show what portion of the variances is variable and fixed.

Solution:

1. Materials price variance and materials quantity variance:
    a) Materials price variance:

$$
\begin{aligned}
\text{AP} \times \text{AQP} &= \$2.04 \times 100{,}000 = \$204{,}000 \\
\text{SP} \times \text{AQP} &= \$2.00 \times 100{,}000 = \$200{,}000 \\
\text{MPV} = (\text{AP} - \text{SP}) \times \text{AQP} &= \$.04 \times 100{,}000 \quad = \$4{,}000 \text{ Unfav.}
\end{aligned}
$$

    b) Materials quantity variance:

$$
\begin{aligned}
\text{SP} \times \text{AQU} &= \$2.00 \times 93{,}000 = \$186{,}000 \\
\text{SP} \times \text{SQ} &= \$2.00 \times 90{,}000 = \$180{,}000 \\
\text{MQV} = \text{SP} \times (\text{AQU} - \text{SQ}) &= \$2.00 \times 3{,}000 \quad = \$6{,}000 \text{ Unfav.}
\end{aligned}
$$

2. Labor rate variance and labor efficiency variances:
    a) Labor rate variance:

$$
\begin{aligned}
\text{AR} \times \text{AH} &= && \$49{,}500^* \\
\text{SR} \times \text{AH} &= \$6.00 \times 8{,}000 = && \$48{,}000 \\
\text{LRV} = (\text{AR} - \text{SR}) \times \text{SH} &= && \$\ 1{,}500 \text{ Unfav.}
\end{aligned}
$$

    * 7,500 hours at $6.00 + 500 hours at 9.00

    (The actual labor rate is not necessary to calculate the labor rate variance. However, the actual rate is required if the formula LRV = (AR − SR) × SH is used. The actual rate is found by dividing actual cost of $49,500 by 8,000 actual hours. The rate is $6.1875.)
    b) Labor efficiency variance:

$$
\begin{aligned}
\text{SR} \times \text{AH} &= \$6.00 \times 8{,}000 \quad = \$48{,}000 \\
\text{SR} \times \text{SH} &= \$6.00 \times 9{,}000 \quad = \$54{,}000 \\
\text{LEV} = \text{SR} \times (\text{AH} - \text{SH}) &= \$6.00 \times (1{,}000) = \$6{,}000 \text{ Favor.}
\end{aligned}
$$

3. Overhead variances:
    a) Under- overapplied overhead:

Actual costs:		
Indirect labor	$110,000	
Indirect materials	129,000	
Reduction of prepaid insurance	2,000	
Accrued expenses	109,500	
Depreciation	86,000	$436,500
Applied costs:		
$24.00 × 18,000 units		432,000
Underapplied		$ 4,500

b) Budget variance:

Actual overhead costs		$436,500
Budgeted overhead costs at 18,000 units:		
Variable	$162,000	
Fixed	300,000	462,000
Budget variance—favorable		$ 25,500

c) Capacity variance:

Budgeted overhead costs at 18,000 units:		
Variable	$162,000	
Fixed	300,000	$462,000
Applied overhead		432,000
Capacity variance—Unfavorable		$ 30,000

d) Summary of overhead variances:

Overhead	Actual Overhead Costs	Flexible Budget for 18,000 Units	Applied Costs
Variable	$146,500	$162,000	$162,000
Fixed	290,000	300,000	270,000
Total	$436,500	$462,000	$432,000

Variable	$15,500 Favorable	$ 0
Fixed	10,000 Favorable	$ 30,000 Unfavorable
	$25,500 Favorable	$ 30,000 Unfavorable
	Budget Variance	Capacity Variance

$4,500 Unfavorable
Underapplied

❖ APPENDIX 1

SOME QUANTITATIVE METHODS: MATERIALS AND LABOR

MATERIALS

Many different quantitative methods have been developed for use in planning inventory levels, timing the cycle for reorders, and estimating optimum order sizes. Computer programs have been designed to account for and handle the flow of inventory information.

Balancing Order and Storage Costs

One frequently used quantitative application deals with obtaining the lowest possible cost of ordering and storing materials. When materials are stored, the company has to use space that has a rental value, to carry additional insurance, and to invest funds in inventories that reduce the availability of funds for other purposes. In some industries, the cost to order may be trivial; hence, the problem of balancing order and storage costs does not exist.

However, in industries that deal with bulky materials, the costs of receiving and handling a shipment may be substantial. For example, it may be necessary to authorize overtime pay for someone to be available when a shipment arrives. Also, by placing frequent orders, the company may be losing quantity discounts that could be obtained by purchasing in bulk. Perhaps the savings to be obtained from placing large orders more than compensate for the increased storage costs.

Management must consider various factors, and these factors should be quantified, if possible. Normally the cost of ordering increases as orders are placed more frequently, but the cost of storage decreases. The total cost may be at a minimum when the two costs are approximately equal.

Calculating Order and Storage Costs

The order and storage costs can be tabulated under different assumptions as to the number of orders placed and the inventory investment. Assume that a company predicts that 3,000 units of a certain material are needed next year. Each unit costs $6. Past experience indicates that the storage costs are approximately equal to 10 percent of the inventory investment. The cost to place an order amounts to $9. If only one order were placed for the year, it would be for 3,000 units, and the average number of units held in the inventory during the year would be 1,500 (3,000 divided by 2) assuming a uniform rate of withdrawal. With two orders, 1,500 units would be purchased on each order, and the average inventory would be only 750 units. The cost to order and store the inventory is computed and set forth in the table below. Computations are made for a varying number of orders placed and a varying investment in inventory. The company should place ten orders each for 300 units. The storage cost of $90 is equal to the total ordering cost at this point, and the combined costs are at a minimum.

Number of Orders	Number of Units per Order	Average Inventory	Cost of Average Inventory	10% Storage Cost	Order Cost ($9 Each Order)
1	3,000	1,500	$9,000	$900	$ 9
2	1,500	750	4,500	450	18
3	1,000	500	3,000	300	27
4	750	375	2,250	225	36
5	600	300	1,800	180	45

Number of Orders	Number of Units per Order	Average Inventory	Cost of Average Inventory	10% Storage Cost	Order Cost ($9 Each Order)
6	500	250	$1,500	$150	$ 54
7	429	215	1,290	129	63
8	375	188	1,128	113	72
9	333	167	1,002	100	81
10	300	150	900	90	90
11	273	137	822	82	99
12	250	125	750	75	108

This same result can be computed by use of the **economic order quantity** formula:

$$Q = \sqrt{\frac{2\,DO}{S}}$$

Where Q = optimum quantity per order (unknown)
D = annual demand for materials expressed in units of material—3,000 units
O = cost per order placed—$9.00
S = storage cost per unit—$0.60 (10% of material cost,$6.00)

This formula was derived as follows:

$$\text{Cost to order} = \frac{\dfrac{\text{Annual demand}}{\text{Optimum quantity}}}{\text{per order}} \times \frac{\text{Cost per}}{\text{order}} \quad \text{or} \quad \frac{DO}{Q}$$

$$\text{Cost to store} = \frac{\dfrac{\text{Optimum quantity}}{\text{per order}}}{2^*} \times \frac{\text{Storage}}{\text{cost}} \quad \text{or} \quad \frac{QS}{2^*}$$

* Divide by 2 to get an average.

$$\frac{DO}{Q} = \frac{QS}{2}$$

$$DO = \frac{Q^1S}{2}$$

$$Q^2S = 2\,DO$$

$$Q^2 = \frac{2\,DO}{S}$$

$$Q = \sqrt{\frac{2\,DO}{S}}$$

The optimum order quantity can be computed directly from the formula, using inventory data as shown previously:

$$Q = \sqrt{\frac{2 \times 3,000 \times \$9.00}{\$0.60}}$$

$$Q = \sqrt{\frac{54,000}{.6}}$$

$$Q = \sqrt{90,000}$$

$$Q = 300 \text{ units}$$

The annual requirement of 3,000 units purchased on the basis of 300 units per order would require the placing of ten orders (3,000 units divided by 300 units per order).

Time to Order

Forecasting the most probable quantity used during a period of time is an important element in the decision about the most economical quantity to order. As a control measure, some flexibility must be allowed in case a quantity larger than was forecast is used. An excessive investment in inventory is certainly not desirable, but some buffer stock should be held to guard against not having inventory available when actual use exceeds the estimated use.

When placing an order, recognition should be given to the time that will elapse between the placement of the order and the actual receipt of the quantity ordered. This is called **lead time.** Sufficient quantities of inventory must be on hand to provide for operations during this lead time.

Some companies will physically segregate the inventory estimated for the lead time; it may be marked and placed in a separate box, for example. When the supply reaches the point where this portion of the inventory is to be used, an order must be placed. If estimates are made correctly, the materials will be received before the special stock is exhausted. Or a computer program may trigger orders when the supply on hand is down to an order point. Figure 9.4 illustrates the concept of timing the orders.

In the example displayed graphically in Figure 9.4, the quantity to be ordered, based on the optimum or economic order quantity, is 750 units. When the expected use reaches the 250 units of minimum stock for the lead time, an order should be placed for 750 units. The units should be received when the lead time expires, thus bringing the inventory to its expected maximum level of 750 units.

The dotted line shows that the actual use was more than expected. When this situation occurs, an order placed when the inventory is estimated to reach 250 units will result in a period of shortage. The actual inventory is being depleted more rapidly than expected, and the order is placed too late. The inventory situation should be monitored, and an order should be placed at 350 units (as shown by the dotted lines) to allow time for delivery with more rapid consumption. Furthermore, if it is perceived that the actual use will continue to be more than expected, the minimum inventory level and the economic order quantity will have to be recomputed.

Storage Cost and Changing Production Runs

The economic order quantity (EOQ) model is only one application used to minimize costs when one cost is increasing while another cost is decreasing. In planning the size of a production run, for example, we incur the equivalent of order costs. We call them set-up costs. These costs include the costs to change machine settings and the costs of idle labor time while the machines are reset to produce another product line. Because set-up costs tend to be high, management may be inclined to operate by producing large batches of a product

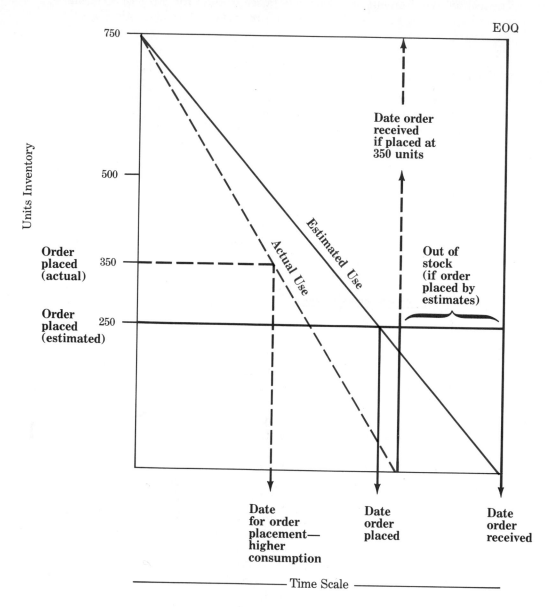

Figure 9.4   Timing Placement of Orders

and storing relatively large quantities as inventory. But, costs are also associated with inventory storage and financing charges and the risk of breakage and
spoilage. With short production runs, the costs to store inventory decrease.
With long production runs, the costs to store larger inventories increase. The
objective is to minimize the combined cost. As with order and storage costs,
the total cost is often at a minimum when the two costs are approximately
equal.

As an example, assume that the setup is $20 and that the cost to store inventory is 20% of inventory cost. Inventory cost is $30 per unit; hence, storage cost is $6 per unit. Annual demand for this product is 24,000 units. How many units should be manufactured in each batch to minimize combined costs of set-up changes and storage cost? The answer can be calculated using the following formula:

Q = optimum size of production run (unknown)
D = demand—24,000 units
C = set-up costs, similar to order cost in EOQ—$20
S = storage cost per unit—20% of $30, or $6

$$Q = \sqrt{\frac{2\ DC}{S}}$$

$$Q = \sqrt{\frac{2 \times 24{,}000 \times \$20}{\$6}}$$

$$Q = \sqrt{160{,}000}$$

Q = Optimum production run = 400 units

$$\frac{24{,}000 \text{ units demanded}}{400 \text{ units per production run}} = 60 \text{ production runs}$$

The minimum combined cost is $2,400 at 60 production runs for the year as shown in the following table:

Number of Runs	Number of Units per Run	Average Inventory	Cost of Average Inventory	20% Storage Cost	Setup Cost	Combined Cost
50	480	240	$7,200	$ 1,440	$1,000	$2,440
60	400	200	6,000	1,200	1,200	2,400
70	343	172	5,160	1,030	1,400	2,430

Other factors can also be considered. If the plant is operating at close to capacity, management may prefer to accept some additional storage cost (in order to save the time taken to change the machine settings) and not risk a failure to meet production quotas. However, with some automated equipment, a change in machine setting may require only a simple change in the program. Hence, the problem is relevant only if set-up costs are significant.

LABOR—THE LEARNING CURVE

In many industries, labor is a substantial part of the cost of production. Management applies quantitative methods in attempting to calculate how much labor time should be used in carrying out certain functions. Time and motion studies, that take into account human limitations, can help to determine how much labor time is required for an operation.

Management can obtain additional profit from increased productivity. With more units manufactured in a given time period, a greater manufacturing margin occurs even after sharing the benefits of increased productivity with the employees. Management is constantly trying to upgrade the skills of employees and to increase their efficiency through education and motivation.

We call the rate of learning a new task a **learning curve**. The curve shows that the average time to manufacture a unit will decrease as workers gain experience with a task. The initial or start-up phase is called the **learning phase**. Assume, for example, that the first batch of 100 units to be manufactured is produced in 500 labor hours. After this experience, the workers can produce the next 100-unit batch in less time. Perhaps the second 100-unit batch can be produced in 300 hours. An additional batch of 200 units may be produced with an additional 480 hours. When an optimum point is reached, no further increases in productivity can be expected and productivity is said to be at the **static phase**.

The foregoing example illustrates an 80 percent learning curve. This rate of learning means that when production doubles, the cumulative average time per unit decreases to 80 percent of the previous cumulative average time.

Units Per Batch	Cumulative Number of Units	Hours Per Batch	Cumulative Hours	Cumulative Average Hours Per Unit*
100	100	500	500	5.0
100	200	300	800	4.0 *
200	400	480	1,280	3.2 *

* Cumulative average is 80 percent of previous cumulative average.

The learning rate may be such that when the production is doubled, the cumulative average time per unit is 70 percent, 60 percent, or any other percentage of the previous cumulative average time per unit. At some point, the learning stage is completed and further increases in productivity cannot be expected. Experience with the learning rates for certain types of functions may be used in predicting expected results. Figure 9.5 shows the foregoing data for the 80 percent learning curve plotted on a graph.

❖ *APPENDIX 2*

THREE-VARIANCE METHOD FOR OVERHEAD

In many business situations, management needs more information about factory overhead costs in order to investigate variances and make appropriate

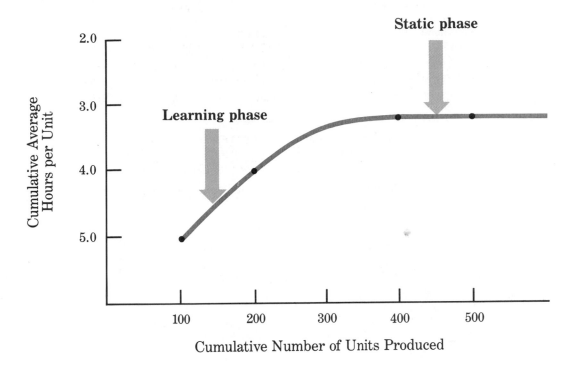

Figure 9.5   An 80 Percent Learning Curve

adjustments. For example, measuring efficiency through comparing input activity bases with output activity bases provides a particularly helpful expansion to the variance analysis. Consequently, we move from the two-variance approach discussed in the chapter to a three-variance method. The information is available also to expand to four variances.

FRAMEWORK FOR THREE-WAY OVERHEAD VARIANCE ANALYSIS

The difference between the two-way and the three-way variance analysis is the treatment of the budget or controllable variance. The budget variance is divided into a spending variance and an efficiency variance. The capacity variance is the same in both approaches.

To show how the variances fit together, we need to remember that overhead costs for Colexus, Inc., are related to direct labor hours. The actual direct labor hours worked were 4,800. Since Colexus produced 10,000 units of product, they were allowed 5,000 (1/2 hour × 10,000 units) direct labor hours. Based on the variable and fixed costs we have shown in the chapter, and remembering that the underapplied overhead was $6,500, we have the following framework:

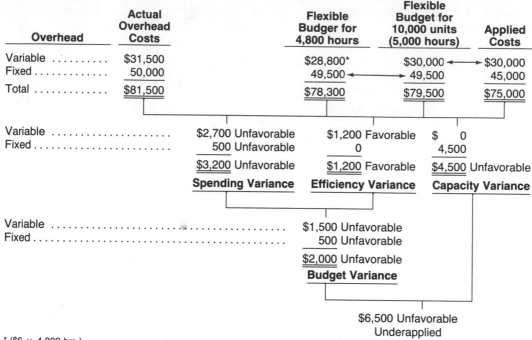

Overhead	Actual Overhead Costs		Flexible Budget for 4,800 hours	Flexible Budget for 10,000 units (5,000 hours)	Applied Costs
Variable	$31,500		$28,800*	$30,000 ◄────►	$30,000
Fixed	50,000		49,500 ◄──────	49,500	45,000
Total	$81,500		$78,300	$79,500	$75,000

Variable		$2,700 Unfavorable	$1,200 Favorable	$ 0	
Fixed		500 Unfavorable	0	4,500	
		$3,200 Unfavorable	$1,200 Favorable	$4,500 Unfavorable	
		Spending Variance	**Efficiency Variance**	**Capacity Variance**	

Variable	$1,500 Unfavorable	
Fixed	500 Unfavorable	
	$2,000 Unfavorable	
	Budget Variance	

$6,500 Unfavorable
Underapplied

* ($6 × 4,800 hrs.)

Spending Variance

A **spending variance** is the difference between the actual overhead cost and the flexible overhead budget for the actual activity base (hours of operation in our example). The variance assumes that the best measure of the amount spent on overhead is based on the actual activity base. In other words, the actual overhead for the above data is what was spent to work 4,800 direct labor hours, and this amount is compared with the budget for those hours.

A spending variance is similar to the combination of the price (or rate) variances and the quantity (or efficiency) variances in direct materials and direct labor. It shows that either one or both of the prices paid for overhead goods or services and the quantity used were not in agreement with the budget. A separate price or quantity variance is calculated.

The causes of variations include three of those categories presented for the budget variance:

1. Price changes in the individual cost components making up overhead costs.
2. Quantity changes in individual items within overhead cost components.
3. Estimation errors in segregating variable and fixed costs.

Efficiency Variance

The **efficiency variance** is the difference between the flexible budget for actual activity base and the flexible budget for standard activity base allowed for actual units of product produced. Because fixed overhead costs are identical in both budgets, the efficiency variance consists only of differences in variable overhead costs. Therefore, we have an alternate means of calculating the variance. The formula is similar to that used for materials quantity and labor efficiency variances: standard variable overhead rate per hour times the difference between actual activity base and the standard activity base allowed. For Colexus, Inc., the efficiency variance is favorable because the workers needed less than the standard hours allowed to complete the 10,000 units of product.

The term "efficiency" is in some sense a misnomer because it does not measure the efficient or inefficient use of individual overhead items. These are included in the spending variance. The efficiency variance measures the additional overhead costs incurred or saved as a result of inefficient or efficient use of the activity upon which overhead is based. That is, overhead must be incurred to support activity. If the activity is inefficient, overhead costs are incurred to support inefficiency. If management is efficient in using the activity, overhead costs are saved.

When direct labor hours are the measure of activity, a relationship exists between the labor efficiency variance and the overhead efficiency variance they move in the same direction. If labor hours are inefficiently used, the labor efficiency variance measures the labor costs incurred for that inefficiency and the overhead efficiency variance is the additional overhead cost incurred to support the inefficient labor. A favorable labor efficiency variance means the overhead efficiency variance must be favorable also. Consequently, to find the causes of an overhead efficiency variance for a direct labor activity base, we just need to look for the causes of inefficient or efficient labor.

Four-Way Analysis

Some managers prefer an additional level of detail. We already know that an efficiency variance is variable cost only and a capacity variance is fixed cost only. Since overhead costs are segregated into variable and fixed, if we split the spending variance into variable and fixed components, we have four variances: variable overhead spending, variable overhead efficiency, fixed overhead spending, and fixed overhead capacity.

TERMINOLOGY REVIEW

Attainable standards (424)
Budget variance (440)
Capacity variance (441)
Controllable variance (440)
Cost control (422)
Economic order quantity (452)
Efficiency variance (458)
Favorable variance (426)
Flexible overhead budget (439)

Idle capacity (443)
Labor efficiency variance (432)
Labor rate variance (432)
Lead time (453)
Learning curve (456)
Learning phase (456)
Loose standards (424)
Management by exception (422)
Materials price variance (426)

Materials quantity variance (429)
Measure of activity (438)
Price standard (421)
Quantity standard (421)
Spending variance (458)

Standard cost (421)
Standard cost sheet (425)
Static phase (456)
Strict standards (424)
Unfavorable variance (426)

QUESTIONS FOR REVIEW AND DISCUSSION

1. Explain the significance of profit analysis for an organization.

2. Under what conditions will a standard cost system work best?

3. Define a standard cost. Explain what constitutes the components of a standard cost.

4. What are the five major categories of advantages for a standard cost system? Why are they important?

5. Point out advantages and disadvantages of following the principle of management by exception.

6. What are some of the aspects of human behavior that must be considered in setting standards? Relate these to the quality of standards.

7. Which level of standard (tight, attainable, loose) will give the lowest standard cost per unit? Explain.

8. Standards should be reviewed from time to time and examined for possible revision. What are the events that call for a review of standards?

9. A standard cost sheet is a key component of a standard cost system. Describe a standard cost sheet and explain why it is significant.

10. Define a materials price variance. What determines whether it is favorable or unfavorable?

11. In purchasing materials, what amounts are recorded in Accounts Payable and what amounts in Materials Inventory?

12. Describe five potential causes of a materials price variance.

13. Define a materials quantity variance.

14. As materials are issued from the storeroom, what amounts are credited to the Materials Inventory and what amounts are charged to Work in Process?

15. List and explain five potential causes of materials quantity variances.

16. Who is responsible for a materials price variance? For a materials quantity variance?

17. Explain how the purchase of materials at less than the standard price may have an adverse effect upon the use of materials in production.

18. How are labor rate variances and labor efficiency variances computed?

19. The departmental supervisor assigned 3 people with a labor rate per person of $6 an hour to a project with a standard labor rate of $5 an hour. Each person spent 70 hours on this project. What effect will this have on the labor rate variance?

20. List five causes of a labor rate variance.

21. List five causes of a labor efficiency variance.

22. Give an example of how a labor rate variance and a labor efficiency variance are related.

23. Give an example of how labor variances and materials variances are related.

24. Discuss the major considerations in the development of factory overhead rates.

25. Explain briefly how under- or overapplied factory overhead can be analyzed into a budget variance and a capacity variance.

26. Define a budget variance and list the major categories of causes of variances.

27. Define a capacity variance and explain why it consists solely of fixed factory overhead costs.

28. Can a capacity variance be controlled? Explain.

29. What is the primary difference between using standard costs in a job cost system and a process cost system?

EXERCISES

1. **Standard Cost Sheet.** Murry Company manufactures special electronic equipment and parts. It has adopted a standard cost system with separate standards for each part. A special electronic "black box" has standards set with the following components. Materials include both iron and copper. Each "black box" requires 5 sheets of iron which cost $3 per sheet and 4 spools of copper at $3.50 per spool. Four hours of direct labor are needed for producing each box and the standard rate per hour is $6. Overhead costs are charged to products on the basis of direct labor time. The overhead rates are: variable $3 per hour, and fixed $2 per hour.

    Required:
    Prepare a standard cost sheet that shows the standard cost per unit for each "black box."

2. **Standard Cost Sheet.** The Crenshaw Company installed a standard cost system in order to achieve better cost control and to facilitate the task of charging costs to its product. The company produces a single product which has standards set for direct materials, direct labor, and manufacturing overhead. The product requires six kilograms of direct materials that cost $4.50 per kilogram. The standard calls for eight hours of direct labor time with a rate of $6.50 per hour. Manufacturing overhead is applied on the basis of machine hours at the rate of $4 per machine hour. The product uses 1.5 machine hours. Three-fourths of the manufacturing overhead rate is for fixed costs.

    Required:
    Prepare a standard cost sheet that shows the standard cost per unit for each product.

3. **Materials Variances.** A printed circuit used in the production of fuel-injected engines has a standard cost of $3 per unit. The standard calls for one printed circuit per engine. Last month, Capetini Automotive purchased 150,000 printed circuits at a cost of $2.91 per unit and 30,000 circuits at a cost of $3.15 per unit. The production department required 180,000 printed circuits to produce 178,500 engines.

Required:
1. Determine the materials price variance.
2. Determine the materials quantity variance.
3. Using T-accounts, show the accounts and amounts involved in the purchasing of the printed circuits and the issuing of the printed circuits to work in process.

4. **Materials Price Variance.** Three types of materials, designated as Basic, Filler, and Lining, are used by VanErik Construction Suppliers in the production of insulating blocks. Data with respect to April purchases are as follows:

Materials	Number of Units Purchased	Standard Unit Cost	Actual Unit Cost
Basic	15,000	$ .60	$ .65
Filler..........................	7,000	1.00	1.15
Lining........................	9,000	2.00	1.80

Required:
1. Determine the total materials price variance for the month of April.
2. Determine the individual materials price variance for the month of April.
3. Which calculation gives more information about price variances: the total price variance or the individual price variances? Explain.

5. **Materials Variances (Missing information).** In May, Muleshoe Equipment Corporation purchased 50,000 parts of a material at a total cost of $125,000. During the month, 46,000 parts having a standard unit cost of $2.20 were used in production. The materials quantity variance for the month was unfavorable by $6,600. According to the standards, 5 parts should be used for each unit of product.

Required:
1. Calculate the materials price variance.
2. How many units of product were made?
3. How many units of material should have been used in production?
4. How many dollars should be charged to Work in Process for materials requisitioned?

6. **Materials Variances.** A tricycle is manufactured by Cycle Specialties, Inc. Standard quantities and costs of the parts are as follows:

Description	Parts per Tricycle	Cost per Unit of Part
Wheels	3	$3.00
Frame	1	2.50
Handle bars	2	.80
Fenders..	3	.60
Steering assembly	1	1.00

This year, the company assembled 60,000 tricycles. No materials were on hand either at the beginning or at the end of the year. The quantities purchased and used in production are given at actual costs as follows:

Description	Number of Parts Used	Actual Cost
Wheels	182,000	$582,400
Frames	60,800	145,920
Handle bars	121,000	84,700
Fenders..	183,000	109,800
Steering assemblies	60,000	72,000

Required:

1. Compute the materials price variance and the materials quantity variance for each component.
2. Determine the total materials price variance and the total materials quantity variance.
3. Identify components with relatively large price variances and components with relatively large quantity variances.

7. **Materials Variances.** The Kala Company has the following data for the month of November 1995:

Materials purchased, 2,600 kilograms	$8,580
Materials used in production	1,320 kilograms
Units of product manufactured	17,000
Materials quantity variance	$384 Unfavorable
Standard price per kilogram..............................	$3.20

Required:

1. Find the standard quantity of materials allowed for the units of product manufactured.
2. Determine the materials price variance.
3. Trace the materials costs and variances through T-accounts with Work in Process Inventory as the final account.

8. **Selection of Labor Standards.** Four employees each work 38 hours a week in an assembly operation. Standard production for the week was established at 2,280 assemblies, or at a rate of production of 15 assemblies per labor hour. A person from time study has observed that it is possible to make 20 assemblies an hour, and this rate has been set as the new standard.

Production data for one week under the new standard are set forth as follows:

Employee	Hours Worked	Units Assembled
1	38	660
2	38	590
3	38	630
4	38	620

The standard labor rate per hour is $12. During this week, a materials quantity variance due solely to above normal scrap and waste was $2,500. Also, 500 units that had been fully assembled were rejected by an inspector.

Required:

1. What was the standard labor cost per assembly under the old standard of 15 assemblies per hour?

2.   What was the anticipated labor cost per assembly under the new standard of 20 assemblies per hour?

3.   What was the actual labor cost per assembly during the week (after deducting the rejected units)?

4.   Comment on the new labor standard and possible reasons for the losses.

9.   **Labor Variances.** Karlsruhe Mueslix Werke manufactures a popular German breakfast cereal. The company adopted a standard cost system that has the following labor standards for 10,000 cartons of Mueslix:

	Rate	Hours	Standard Cost
Crushing	20 DM	100	2,000 DM
Baking	12	40	480
Mixing	16	20	320
Packaging....................................	12	40	480
		200	3,280 DM
Labor cost per carton			0.328 DM

During September 1995, the company produced 830,000 cartons and had the following actual costs and hours:

	Cost	Hours Worked
Crushing	159,358 DM	8,400
Baking	52,752	3,820
Mixing	29,172	1,410
Packaging.......................................	29,368	2,653
	270,650 DM	16,283

Required:

1.   Calculate the labor rate variance for each of the four departments.

2.   Calculate the labor efficiency variance for each of the four departments.

3.   Using T-accounts, show the amounts of labor costs in payroll, variances, and work in process.

10.   **Labor Efficiency Variance.** Wallmouth Instruments, Inc. operates with an automated production line that, to a large extent, serves as a pacesetter in determining the speed of production per hour. However, the line has to be slowed up whenever the workers fall behind. (Mondays are always slow days.) Standards indicate that 10 units of product should be manufactured each hour with a standard labor rate of $10 per hour. Last month, 22,500 units of product were manufactured in 2,500 direct labor hours.

Required:

1.   What was the labor efficiency variance last month?

2.   Determine the amount of direct labor cost charged to work in process last month.

11.   **Labor Variances.** The payroll for Medical Claims Processors for the year was $516,000. Income taxes of $105,000 and FICA taxes of $42,000 were withheld, and employee voluntary withholdings totaled $4,000. The net amount paid to employees was $365,000. Included in the total payroll was indirect labor of $141,000 (not on an hourly basis).

The standard labor rate of $5.00 per hour was paid for 60,000 hours, and $7.50 per hour was paid for 10,000 hours. The company processed 550,000 claims during the year. Standards show that eight claims should be processed each hour.

Required:
1. Calculate the labor rate variance.
2. Calculate the labor efficiency variance.
3. Using T-accounts, show how much direct labor cost was charged to work in process and the various payroll accounts.

12. **Materials and Labor Variances with Incomplete Data.** Carl Blaine asks for your help in organizing information about direct materials and direct labor in the Operations Department of Blaine Parts Company for the month of May. He has developed the following information himself.

Standard price per sheet of material...................	$6
Standard number of sheets of material per unit of product	5
Actual sheets of material used at standard unit price......	$636,000
Increase in materials inventory	6,000 sheets
Materials price variance	$15,000 (unfavorable)
Materials quantity variance	$36,000 (unfavorable)
Standard units of product to be produced each direct labor hour	2
Standard labor cost per hour	$10
Labor rate variance	$3,000 (unfavorable)
Labor efficiency variance	$2,000 (favorable)
Actual direct labor payroll	$41,000

Required:
1. What was the actual cost of materials purchased?
2. How many units of product were made?
3. Determine the standard direct materials cost of production for the month.
4. Determine the standard direct labor cost of production for the month.
5. How many actual direct labor hours were used in production for the month?

13. **Materials and Labor Variances with Incomplete Data.** The cost accountant for Billings Plastics, Inc. has provided you with actual and standard cost data for one of the basic product lines for the month of February:

	Direct Materials	Direct Labor
Purchased and used at actual cost, 38,000 units ...	$104,500	
Actual direct labor payroll.......................		$63,000
Standard material units per product unit	2	
Standard labor time per product unit		20 minutes
Standard price per unit of materials	$ 2.50	
Standard direct labor rate per hour...............		$10
Labor rate variance (unfavorable)		$6,000

During February, 18,000 units of product were manufactured.

Required:
1. Determine the materials price variance.
2. What was the standard cost of the standard units of direct materials used in production?

3. Compute the materials quantity variance.
4. How many direct labor hours were used in February?
5. Compute the labor efficiency variance.
6. What was the standard cost of direct labor charged to work in process?

14. **Overhead Variances.** Carrollton Delivery Service delivers packages in Dallas and hires drivers to make deliveries. An average standard time has been established to make a delivery. According to the standards, it should be possible to make one delivery per hour. The office is centrally located, and it takes about as much time to deliver to one location as it does to another. Fixed costs have been budgeted at $240,000 for the year. Under normal conditions, the company expects to make 60,000 deliveries a year. The variable cost has been budgeted at $12 per hour. Last year, the company made 63,000 deliveries in 59,000 hours and incurred a total cost of $988,000, including the fixed cost.

Required:
1. Compute the standard cost of making a delivery.
2. How much overhead costs were charged to deliveries in total during the year?
3. Determine the budget variance.
4. Determine the capacity variance.

15. **Overhead Variance Analysis.** A flexible budget for Jimbo Casting Company is given in summary form as follows:

Machine hours	60,000	70,000	80,000	90,000
Variable overhead	$240,000	$280,000	$320,000	$360,000
Fixed overhead	480,000	480,000	480,000	480,000
Total overhead	$720,000	$760,000	$800,000	$840,000

The standard rate of production is 6 units per machine hour, and normal capacity has been defined at 80,000 machine hours. In 1995, the company manufactured 420,000 units of product in 70,000 machine hours. Actual variable overhead was $287,000, and the fixed overhead was $475,000.

Required:
1. Compute the amount of under- or overapplied overhead.
2. Compute the budget variance.
3. Explain the major causes of a budget variance.
4. Compute the capacity variance.
5. Cite three possible reasons for the existence of this capacity variance.

16. **Budget Variance for Individual Costs.** Suzi Stephens, manager of the Machining Department at Mayfield Industries, Inc., has estimated overhead costs for August at an expected operating level of 6,000 machine hours. Past experience indicates a rate of cost variability per hour as follows:

Lubrication	$.75
Supplies	.30
Power	.25
Repairs	.50
Maintenance	.80

Costs that are fixed for the month are budgeted as follows:

Supervision..	$ 4,500
Indirect labor	11,500
Heat and light...	3,200
Taxes and insurance.....................................	1,600
Depreciation	1,800

During the month of August, the department produced the quantity of product that should have been produced in 5,000 hours in a total of 5,500 hours and incurred the following overhead costs:

Lubrication	$ 3,900
Supplies	1,700
Power	1,500
Repairs	2,800
Maintenance...	4,300
Supervision...	4,000
Indirect labor	12,000
Heat and light...	3,200
Taxes and insurance.....................................	1,400
Depreciation	1,600
Total	$36,400

Required:
1. Prepare a budget of overhead costs for 5,000 machine hours.
2. Compare the actual overhead costs with the budget for 5,000 machine hours. Show budget variances for each item.
3. Explain what factors could cause the budget variance to arise.

17. **Fixed Overhead Relationships.** University Medical Center has a radiology department that operated at 50,000 standard hours last year. The standard calls for 5 patients per hour and the department actually handled 9,000 patients. Fixed overhead data are given as follows:

Fixed overhead charged to patients	$630,000
Unfavorable capacity variance.....................................	350,000

Required:
1. What was the fixed overhead budget last year?
2. What was the fixed overhead rate per patient?
3. How many patients were considered to be normal?
4. Would the capacity variance have been smaller or larger if the radiology department had processed 12,000 patients?

18. **Economic Order Quantity.** (Appendix 1) A chemical used in the production of plate glass is purchased in bulk. Over the course of a year, 10,000 tons of this chemical are required. It costs $25 to process and receive each order. Storage costs are equal to 20 percent of the $10 cost per ton.

Required:

1. How many orders should be placed in a year, and how many tons should be received on each order to minimize the combined costs of ordering and storing the chemical?
2. Prove that this cost is minimal by showing the combined cost of the optimum number of orders, the combined cost for one order more than optimal, and the combined cost for one order less than optimal.

19. **Economic Order Quantity.** (Appendix 1) Storey Magic Robots, Inc. has reached its capacity to produce a component part for one of its most popular robots. Purchasing has found a supplier for the part that will meet the anticipated delivery schedule. The contract calls for a total of 2,000 parts over the next year. Order costs will be $18 per order, and the carrying costs are $5 per unit per year. The purchase price is $25 per part. The lead time is 30 days. No stockouts are allowed.

Required:

1. Find the economic order quantity that minimizes total cost.
2. Calculate the reorder point.
3. The cost accountant has just informed you that an error was made in calculating the ordering cost per order. The cost should be $32 instead of $18. Explain the effect of this error on the cost of maintaining inventory. Show supporting calculations.

20. **Learning Curve.** (Appendix 1) Skyway Technic, Inc. is planning to submit a bid on equipment to be used in space exploration. Experience on similar contracts indicates that a 70 percent learning curve may be appropriate in estimating labor hours and costs. The first 500 units of this equipment will require an estimated 10,000 labor hours. The next 500 units should be completed in 4,000 hours. Another 1,000 units should follow the 70 percent learning curve, after which the learning process will be completed. The labor rate per hour is $20.

Required:

1. What will be the cumulative average hours per unit after production of the third batch (1,000-unit batch)? (Assume a 70 percent learning curve.)
2. Estimate the labor cost per unit after the completion of the learning process.

21. **Learning Curve.** (Appendix 1) A potential customer approaches Elliot, Inc. with a proposal to buy seven complex agricultural pumps for a total of $2,000. The pump was a new product and only one unit has been produced and that at the request of another customer. The following cost data are available on the first pump:

Direct materials (15 pounds at $2 per pound)	$ 30
Direct labor (50 hours at $10 per hour)	500
Variable overhead ($2 per direct labor hour)	100
Fixed overhead ($1 per direct labor hour)	50
Total cost	$680

The engineering department believes an 80 percent learning curve exists for this situation. Also, if the bid is accepted, the company will be eligible for a 3 percent quantity discount on direct materials.

Required:
Estimate the profit or loss Elliot, Inc. would realize if it accepted the proposal for the seven pumps.

22. **Overhead Variance Analysis.** (Appendix 2) Refer to the following Exercises and perform the indicated analysis.
    1. Exercise 14: Calculate spending and efficiency variances.
    2. Exercise 15: Calculate spending and efficiency variances and explain why the efficiency variance yields the results it does.
    3. Exercise 16: Calculate spending and efficiency variances for each item and calculate a total capacity variance.

23. **Three-way Overhead Analysis.** (Appendix 2) The manufacturing overhead costs of Jacobi Industries, Inc., are on a standard cost system. The flexible overhead budget formula is:

    Fixed costs: $100,000 per period
    Variable costs: $10 per unit

    Each unit of product requires 2 hours of machine time. Normal production is 25,000 units per month.
    During the most recent period, 42,000 hours were worked in producing 20,000 units of product. The actual manufacturing overhead costs totaled $350,000, of which $120,000 was fixed cost.

    Required:
    1. Calculate the under- or overapplied manufacturing overhead.
    2. How much of the total overhead variance is fixed cost and how much is variable cost?
    3. Compute the spending and efficiency variances.
    4. Compute the capacity variance.
    5. Prove that the spending, efficiency, and capacity variances account for the total overhead variance.

24. **Labor and Four-way Overhead Analysis.** (Appendix 2) Direct labor and overhead standards per finished unit for Hereford Metals Company are as follows:

    Direct labor: 10 hours at $5.00 per hour
    Variable overhead: 10 hours at $2.00 per hour
    Fixed overhead: 10 hours at $3.00 per hour

    Budgeted fixed overhead costs per month are $150,000. During March, 5,000 finished units were produced. Direct labor costs were $234,000 (52,000 hours). Actual variable overhead costs were $103,000 and actual fixed overhead costs were $147,000.

    Required:
    1. Determine the rate and efficiency variances for direct labor for March.
    2. Compute the under- or overapplied manufacturing overhead for the month.
    3. Calculate the spending, efficiency, and capacity variances for the month.
    4. Explain how the labor efficiency and overhead efficiency variances are related.
    5. Split the spending variance into its variable and fixed components.

PROBLEMS

9-1. **Standard Cost Sheet—Materials and Labor.** An industrial solvent with the brand name Vanex is produced by Lemann Chemical Company and sold in 25-liter drums. Data with respect to materials and labor are given as follows:

1. A batch of 1,500 liters of Vanex is made from an input of 1,500 liters each of Disix and Pryl. In the boiling operation, 50 percent of the volume of both Disix and Pryl is lost through evaporation.
2. At the end of the boiling operation, 2 kilograms of Bondit are added to each 1,500-liter batch. (This has no measurable effect on volume.)
3. A worker can process one 25-liter drum in 20 minutes.
4. At the final inspection, two 25-liter drums are rejected out of every ten drums received from the production line.
5. Standard materials prices and the labor rate are as follows.

Disix...	$ 2.00 per liter
Pryl	1.50 per liter
Bondit	6.00 per kilogram
Labor rate	12.00 per hour

Required:

Prepare a standard cost sheet that shows the standard materials and labor cost for each 25-liter drum of completed product.

9-2. **Standard Cost Sheet—All Cost Elements.** Wellington Office Furniture is a well-known supplier of quality office furniture. It is currently setting up a standard cost system to cover all of its products. One of the products is the Home Office Workstation for those who operate a business out of their home. The production process for this workstation involves four departments: Cutting, Assembly, Staining, and Finishing. Materials, labor and overhead costs are accumulated by department.

Raw materials include lumber, stain, drawer handles and fixtures, screws, dowels, and glue. Each workstation requires 64 feet of lumber at $1.60 per foot. Drawer handles and other drawer fixtures are $16.80 per workstation. Stain is .80 gallons at $16.70 per gallon. Screws, dowels, and glue are included in the overhead costs of the assembly department. Lumber enters the process in the Cutting Department; drawer handles and other drawer fixtures in the Assembly Department; and stain in the Staining Department.

Direct labor occurs in cutting, assembly, and finishing. Cutting requires 30 minutes per workstation with labor at $9.50 per hour. Assembly requires two hours per workstation with a labor cost of $11.60 per hour. Finishing requires 20 minutes with a labor cost of $7.80 per hour. Staining is an automated department and has no direct labor.

Factory overhead is applied to workstations by department on the basis of direct labor hours in the three departments with direct labor. Cutting is $10 per hour; Assembly is $9.50 per hour; and Finishing is $9.00 per hour. The Staining Department overhead is applied on the basis of machine time and the rate is $18 per machine hour. Each workstation requires one-fourth of an hour of machine time.

Required:

Prepare a standard cost sheet that shows all of the elements of cost for a completed workstation. For convenience, identify the cost elements by department.

9-3.   Comparison of Materials Cost, Two Plants. Redwood Coatings Company manufactures a roof coating and sealant product in 5-gallon pails in both the Holton plant and the McHugh plant. Materials cost is a large part of the total cost and varies from month to month. Standard quantities of materials used to manufacture each 5-gallon pail and the standard prices are as follows:

	Standard Quantities	Standard Prices
Oil	5 gallons	$3.00 per gallon
Metal	2 pounds	2.50 per pound
Sealer	10 ounces	.10 per ounce

Production and cost data for the two plants for both June and July are given as follows:

	Holton Plant	McHugh Plant
Product units manufactured:		
June...	80,000	50,000
July	85,000	60,000
Quantity of materials used:		
June:		
Oil	416,000 gals.	252,000 gals.
Metal	163,000 lbs.	102,000 lbs.
Sealer	800,000 oz.	502,000 oz.
July:		
Oil	427,000 gals.	320,000 gals.
Metal	170,000 lbs.	126,000 lbs.
Sealer	855,000 oz.	604,000 oz.

The actual prices for the materials purchased and used were the same for both plants. All materials purchased were used in production:

	Actual Unit Prices	
	June	July
Oil	$3.40	$3.45
Metal	2.30	2.40
Sealer	.12	.13

Required:
1. Compute the total materials price variance by ingredient for both June and July.
2. Compute the materials quantity variance by ingredient for each plant for each month.
3. Which plant had the larger quantity variance in June? Which had the larger quantity variance in July?

9-4.   Substituting Factors of Production. Denise Warren, vice-president of production at Vanity Fabrics, Inc., believes that a net savings in production cost can be realized by using stronger and more expensive yarn in production. In her opinion, far too much labor time is wasted in working with poor grade yarn that breaks or gets jammed in the knitting machines.

At the present time, 20,000 product units are made with a total of 200,000 yards of yarn costing $.12 cents a yard. With a better grade of yarn costing $.25 cents a yard, the same number of units could be made with 160,000 yards of yarn.

The standard labor rate is $8.50 per hour, and the standard time to make 20,000 units with the cheaper yarn is 20,000 hours. Warren estimates that with the better yarn, only 16,000 hours will be needed for 20,000 product units.

Required:

1. Calculate the standard costs of yarn and labor when using the cheaper yarn.
2. Calculate the standard costs of yarn and labor when using the more expensive yarn.
3. Does a net cost savings exist with the better yarn?
4. If there is not a net cost saving, what is the total variance in labor efficiency that the company can incur before the more expensive material becomes the better alternative?

9-5. **Reconstructing Actual Costs from Outputs.** NuMade Company manufactures a number of different products. Its most profitable product comes from a division in northern Mexico, which has the following standard cost sheet:

Materials (2 kilograms at 8,500 pesos per kilogram)	17,000 pesos
Labor (0.5 hours at 12,000 pesos per hour)	6,000
Overhead (18,000 pesos per labor hour)	9,000
Total product cost	32,000 pesos

Income statements are prepared for each product line on a monthly basis. At the end of a recent month, the following income statement information was available for the above product:

		(000 omitted)
Sales (45,000 pesos × 92,000 units)		4,140,000
Cost of goods sold at standard (32,000 pesos × 92,000 units)		2,944,000
Gross profit at standard		1,196,000
Manufacturing cost variances:		
Materials price	7,500 F	
Materials quantity	8,500 U	
Labor rate	5,900 U	
Labor efficiency	12,000 F	5,100
Adjusted gross profit		1,201,100

Materials purchases for the month were 300,000 kilograms. The division produced 120,000 units, with no work in process inventories at the beginning and ending of the month. All variances are closed to the Cost of Goods Sold Account at the end of each month.

Required:

1. Calculate the actual materials price per kilogram.
2. Calculate the number of kilograms of materials actually used in production.
3. Calculate the actual number of labor hours worked.

9-6. Interrelationship of Materials and Labor Variances. Vicki Jaedicke, purchasing agent for Rainelle Products, Inc., was pleased to report that she bought 50,000 units of a plastic part for $15,000, lower than the standard cost of $22,500. The part also was a lower grade than called for by the standard. According to standards, 5 of these parts should be used in the production of each unit of product.

When these parts were used in production, breakage was higher than normal. To keep the abnormal breakage to a minimum, the operating manager shifted more skilled workers into the operations where breakage occurred. The standard labor rate for this operation was $7 per hour. One half hour is the standard time for the operation for each final product.

Last month, the company used 42,000 plastic parts and 3,300 hours in the production of 6,000 units of product. The labor cost was $31,750.

Required:

1. Compute materials price and materials quantity variances.
2. Compute labor rate and labor efficiency variances.
3. Combine the four variances to obtain the net effect. Did the purchasing agent save the company money in buying the non-standard plastic parts?
4. Show which variance amounts would be assigned to the purchasing agent and which would be assigned to the operating manager.

9-7. Evaluation of Four Plants. Bethel Automotive, Inc. produces a unit of product at four plants: Hill, Valley, Ridge, and River. Standard materials and labor costs per unit of product are the same at all plants and are given as follows:

Direct materials per product unit:

Metal sheets—5 units @ $2	$10
Purchased part—3 units @ $1	3
Standard materials cost	$13

Direct labor per product unit:

1/2 hour @ $10	5
Standard materials and labor cost	$18

Actual production data for each of the four plants for June, July, and August are given as follows:

	Plants			
	Hill	Valley	Ridge	River
June:				
Units produced	80,000	50,000	60,000	100,000
Units of materials used:				
Metal sheets	402,000	252,000	335,000	510,000
Purchased part	241,000	151,000	215,000	305,000
Labor hours	42,000	27,000	40,000	49,000
July:				
Units produced	95,000	40,000	70,000	110,000
Units of materials used:				
Metal sheets	480,000	212,000	375,000	550,000
Purchased part	275,000	122,000	225,000	335,000
Labor hours	48,000	21,000	42,000	53,000

August:

Units produced.....................	100,000	45,000	65,000	120,000
Units of materials used:				
Metal sheets.....................	505,000	230,000	330,000	608,000
Purchased part...................	310,000	140,000	200,000	362,000
Labor hours	50,000	23,000	38,000	58,000

Required:

1. Compute the materials quantity variance for each month for each plant.
2. Compute the labor efficiency variance for each month for each plant.
3. If the market weakens, which plant is most likely to be closed down? Explain.

9-8. **Materials and Labor—Missing Information.** You have been asked to provide your supervisor with cost information about the operations in the Racine plant. Unfortunately, you are furnished with only partial information; you must calculate much of what is needed. The information you have to work with is as follows:

1. The company purchased 350,000 units of direct materials for the Racine plant last month. The standard cost per unit is $3.10.
2. Raw materials at the beginning of the month at the standard price cost $52,700.
3. Raw materials at the end of the month at the standard price cost $108,500.
4. The materials price variance was unfavorable by $175,000.
5. The materials quantity variance was unfavorable by $21,700.
6. Actual direct labor cost was $320,000, but the labor rate variance was unfavorable by $10,000.
7. Actual direct labor hours were 32,000.
8. The plant manufactured 65,000 units of product.
9. The labor efficiency variance was favorable by $15,000.

Required:
 Using the data above, furnish the following information:
a) Actual quantity of raw materials withdrawn from inventory for use in production at the standard price.
b) Actual cost of materials purchased.
c) Number of units of raw material needed for each unit of product according to the standard.
d) Standard direct materials cost of production.
e) Standard direct labor cost of production.
f) The standard labor rate per hour.
g) Standard labor hours per product unit.

9-9. **Overhead in an Automated Operation.** Sachi Kato observes, "The nature of costs has changed since Kato Windings Company installed more automated equipment. At one time, direct labor was an important factor. With automation, direct labor is essentially a fixed cost with workers monitoring the operation on television screens. Variable overhead cost is lower, and is related to hours of machine operation. On the other hand, fixed cost is much higher than it was in a labor-oriented operation. However, the production line can only move so fast," she states. "If it is stepped up, too many pieces are broken."

 Yoko Kato, the production manager, says, "We may not obtain much more savings from increases in productivity. Additional savings will have to come by holding fixed costs down and receiving a large volume of orders."

 Data from last year are given as follows:

Variable cost per machine hour..	$4
Number of standard units of product per machine hour.............	100
Fixed overhead budget...	$6,000,000
Normal number of product units produced in a year	60,000,000
Actual hours of operation	500,000
Actual product units produced	58,000,000
Actual overhead cost:	
Variable overhead	$1,935,000
Fixed overhead	6,030,000

Required:

1. What was the standard variable overhead cost per product unit and the standard fixed overhead cost per product unit?
2. How much overhead was applied to production for the year?
3. Determine the following variances:
   a) Overhead budget variance
   b) Overhead capacity variance
4. Prepare a graph that shows how a capacity variance arises in this case.

9-10. Complete Variance Analysis and Cost Flow. Sudan Machine Company operates with a standard cost accounting system and uses cost variances as a means of detecting costs that may require more control. A standard cost sheet for a component that is manufactured exclusively in one plant is given as follows:

Direct materials (6 units @ $4)	$24.00
Direct labor (1/2 hr. @ $8)	4.00
Variable overhead (3/4 machine hour @ $4).........................	3.00
Fixed overhead (3/4 machine hour @ $16)	12.00
Standard unit cost	$43.00

Data from the past year are given as follows:

1. Purchased 2,000,000 units of materials at a cost of $7,540,000.
2. Manufactured 300,000 units of product.
3. The fixed overhead budget for the year was $6,400,000.
4. Used 1,812,000 units of material in production.
5. Used 200,000 direct labor hours.
6. Actual labor cost was $1,610,000.
7. Worked 190,000 actual machine hours.
8. The actual variable overhead was $880,000.
9. The actual fixed overhead was $6,321,000.
10. Fixed overhead was applied to the products by using a rate computed for a normal production of 400,000 product units.
11. Of the 300,000 complete units, 250,000 units were sold.

Required:

1. Determine the following variances:
   a) Materials price variance.
   b) Materials quantity variance.
   c) Labor rate variance.
   d) Labor efficiency variance.
   e) Overhead budget variance.
   f) Overhead capacity variance.
2. Which is the largest unfavorable variance that may be controllable by production management?
3. If the capacity variance is unfavorable by a large amount, what steps may be taken in the future to correct it?

4. Using T-accounts, trace all of the costs through the accounts and close all variances to Cost of Goods Sold. Show the ending balances in the following accounts:
    a) Materials Inventory.
    b) Work in Process Inventory.
    c) Finished Goods Inventory.
    d) Cost of Goods Sold.

9-11. Budget and Capacity Variances. Revchek Manufacturing bases its factory overhead on the flexible budget equation expressed as:

$$\$33,000 + (\$2.40 \times \text{direct labor hours})$$

Normal production is based on 12,000 direct labor hours. Standards call for two direct labor hours per unit of completed product. For the current period, the operating results were as follows:

Actual direct labor hours worked	11,400
Units produced	5,800
Actual variable overhead costs	$28,460
Actual fixed overhead costs	$31,950

Required:
1. Calculate the overhead rates for variable and fixed overhead that would be used to apply overhead to products.
2. Calculate the under- or overapplied overhead for the period.
3. Determine the following variances:
    a) Overhead budget variance.
    b) Overhead capacity variance.
4. How much of the budget variance is due to variable costs and how much is due to fixed costs?

9-12. Overhead Variances for a Department. The following flexible budget information has been prepared for the Fabrication Department of Abbott Industries:

Machine hours at normal capacity	5,000
Variable overhead:	
Indirect labor	$3,500
Supplies	2,500
Repairs and maintenance	1,000
Electricity, other than lighting	5,000
Total variable overhead	$12,000
Fixed overhead:	
Supervision	$3,000
Supplies	1,700
Repairs and maintenance	3,000
Depreciation on machinery	6,500
Insurance	1,800
Property taxes	1,000
Heating	600
Lighting	400
Total fixed overhead	$18,000
Total factory overhead	$30,000

Factory overhead is allocated on the basis of machine hours. The standard calls for ten units of product per machine hour.

At the end of May, 4,650 machine hours were actually worked and 48,530 units of product were produced. The following actual overhead costs were incurred:

Variable overhead:	
Indirect labor	$3,400
Supplies	2,200
Repairs and maintenance	960
Electricity, other than lighting	4,740
Total variable overhead	$11,300

Fixed overhead:	
Supervision	$3,100
Supplies	1,650
Repairs and maintenance	3,200
Depreciation on machinery	6,500
Insurance	1,900
Property taxes	1,100
Heating	845
Lighting	405
Total fixed overhead	$18,700
Total factory overhead	$30,000

Required:

1. Prepare a report that shows each category of overhead cost with individual budget variances.
2. What are the major potential causes of the budget variances?
3. Calculate an overall capacity variance for the department.

9-13. Optimum Lot Size for Production. (Appendix 1) Carol McGee, a plant supervisor at Dayton Suppliers, believes the company is making a mistake by producing in large lot sizes. She recognizes that there is a cost of $60 (in idle time and other costs) associated with changing a machine setting when a new batch is to be run. But, in her opinion, the cost to store large amounts of product in the warehouse exceeds the cost of changing a production run.

"For example," she stated, "We just completed a run of 1,500 units on a product where annual sales are only 75,000 units. This product has a cost of $500 per unit, and the cost of storage is 20 percent, or $100 a unit."

Required:

1. How many units should be made on a production run to minimize the combined costs of resetting equipment and storage? What is the minimum combined cost?
2. What is the combined cost of resetting equipment and storage when 1,500 units are made on a run?

9-14. Economic Order Quantities. (Appendix 1) Filtration Systems Shoppe has a line of kitchen water filtration and treatment systems that the company retails for $240. The purchase price from its supplier is $165 per unit. Annual demand runs about 800 units. Insurance during shipment adds $2 per unit and freight averages $8 per unit. The clerical processing costs of placing an order are $25 per order. The company's cost of capital for its various sources of funds is 16 percent. It takes five days from the time an order is released until the units are delivered. The retail store is open every day except for a few special holidays (assume 360 days). The store currently orders 50 units each time an order is placed.

Required:

1. Compute the carrying cost per unit. (Hint: determine the cost invested per unit and multiply that amount by 16 percent.)
2. How many units should be ordered under economic order quantities? How many orders per year does that result in?
3. What is the reorder point?
4. Compared to current ordering policies, how much can the company save in carrying and ordering costs if it uses economic ordering quantities?

9-15. **Learning Curves.** (Appendix 1) Western Space Systems, Inc. is developing a new but complex part for a sophisticated Star Wars missile. In making the first unit, the company used 500 direct labor hours at a cost of $8,000. The Engineering Department is estimating a learning curve but hasn't decided whether it is 80 percent or 90 percent.

Required:

1. Determine the cumulate average work-hours per unit under an 80 percent and a 90 percent learning curve for a total of:
   a)   2 units.
   b)   4 units.
   c)   8 units.
   d)   16 units.
2. After completing the first unit, a prime contractor has ordered 15 additional units. What is the estimated direct labor cost for this order:
   a)   For an 80 percent learning curve?
   b)   For a 90 percent learning curve?
3. Suppose the actual learning curve realized in producing the additional 15 units was 85 percent, what is the additional cost or savings on the order as compared to an 80 percent and a 90 percent learning curve?

9-16. **Learning Curves and CVP Analysis.** (Appendix 1) CalMain Industries, Inc. is considering introducing a new product to its product lines which will sell at $1,700 per unit. The Engineering Department has studied the product design and the production process and arrived at the following estimates:

1. Labor will follow an 80 percent learning curve.
2. The first unit of product will require 100 direct labor hours.
3. The labor rate is $10 per hour.
4. Variable factory overhead is $4 per direct labor hour.
5. Fixed factory overhead will increase $5,000 per year as a result of this product.
6. Materials will cost $100 per completed unit of product.

Required:

1. Assuming there is no constraint on the available labor time during the year, how many units of the new product would have to be produced and sold in order to break even?
2. Assuming that maximum labor time available is 300 hours during the year, how many units of new product can be produced? Will the company break even within that constraint?
3. Returning to (1) above, if the company could improve its learning rate to 75 percent, how many more units could it produce at the break-even point for an 80 percent learning curve?

9-17. **Comprehensive Variance Analysis.** Alexander Company uses a standard cost system and isolates the following six variances for the appropriate departments:

Materials price variance	Labor efficiency variance
Materials quantity variance	Overhead budget variance
Labor rate variance	Overhead capacity variance

The company uses direct labor as the measure of activity for each of the producing departments.

Required:

For each of the following independent events indicate which variances would be affected. Briefly explain why they would be affected, and indicate whether the effect is favorable or unfavorable. If more than one variance is affected in a given situation, limit your discussion to the two or three most important variances for that situation.

a)   Demand exceeded expectation and the number of units produced during the year was much greater than the number planned.

b)   Because of an improperly adjusted machine, more materials were wasted than anticipated. When the department supervisor requisitioned more material from the storeroom, no material was there. A rush order for more materials was placed and the materials arrived by special delivery by the end of the day.

c)   A purchasing agent bought substandard material at a large savings. Because of the lower quality of material, more scrap was produced and an additional employee was hired to assist in the cutting operation.

d)   Several customer rush orders were accepted and placed into production. The orders were completed within the standard time allotted; however, overtime was required in order to meet the customers' delivery schedule.

e)   A new union contract at the beginning of the year required an increase in labor rates. Adjustments to the standard wage rates were made as required at the beginning of the year. During the year, the rate of inflation in the economy was lower than what was predicted for the contract wage rates.

f)   Due to food poisoning in the plant cafeteria, several highly skilled workers from one department were sick for two days. The department supervisor hired temporary, unskilled production-line workers to substitute for the skilled workers. The wages for the temporary help was less than standard and their output was also less than standard.

g)   Because of more than usual machine breakdowns, repair and maintenance personnel used more supplies than the overhead budgets called for.

h)   A brown out caused by the overload of extra power usage in the city resulted in machines not able to run at full power for four hours during a second shift.

i)   A forklift driver inadvertently ran into a large machine, dumping his load, and stopping the machine. Several direct labor workers and the machine operator helped clean up the mess and got the machine going again.

j)   A new quality control inspector was less strict than policy called for and units that should have been reworked were passed over, released to the finished goods warehouse, and sold to customers.

9-18. **Comprehensive Variance Analysis.** (Appendix 2) Refer to Problem 9-17. Work the problem using overhead spending variance and overhead efficiency variance instead of the overhead budget variance.

9-19. **Effect of Saving Labor Time.** (Appendix 2) Clyde Pritchard believes that the cost of production can be reduced by saving labor time and recommends that the workers be encouraged to increase productivity by paying a labor bonus equal to 80 percent of the labor cost for time saved.

"That doesn't leave very much advantage for the company, only 20 percent of the cost for time saved," George McHale replies. "That's only part of it," Pritchard answers. "How about the saving in variable factory overhead, which varies at the rate of $10 per direct labor hour?"

The standard direct labor rate per hour is $12, and the standard rate of production is set at 6 units per hour. Last month, 42,000 units of product were manufactured in 6,800 hours. Pritchard believes that 42,000 units could be made in 6,000 hours with the proposed labor bonus as an incentive.

Required:
1. Compute the labor cost at standard for the 6,800 hours and the labor cost at standard for 6,000 hours. Include the 80 percent bonus for saving 800 hours in the costs of the 6,000 hours.
2. How much variable overhead would be saved if the hours were reduced from 6,800 to 6,000 hours?
3. Do the benefits of the incentive program exceed the costs? (Hint: Compute the net savings to the company after the labor bonus, including the savings of variable factory overhead.

9-20. Efficiency or Capacity Variance. (Appendix 2) Lopez Metals Company produces a magnetic instrument at the San Jose plant. A standard cost accounting system is used. When operating at a normal capacity of 300,000 machine hours, the plant should produce 1,200,000 units of this instrument. In the past few years, the company has been able to sell only 800,000 units of this product line each year. Management is aware of the relatively high fixed overhead costs budgeted at $4,800,000 for the year and of the need to operate as closely to normal capacity as possible.

The company has two categories of variable overhead: one varies at the rate of $3 per unit of product, the other, which is based on machine hours, varies at $2.00 per unit of product. This means a total of $5.00 is charged to each product for variable overhead.

Last year the plant operated at 250,000 machine hours and produced 800,000 units of this product line. The standard variable overhead cost is $8 per machine hour and the company incurred $2,050,000 of actual variable overhead. It incurred $4,800,000 in fixed overhead.

One of the production supervisors, Ernesto Valdez, has stated that some improvement has been made in operating more closely to normal capacity. "By operating at 250,000 machine hours, the plant is up to 5/6 of normal capacity. If the plant had operated at only 200,000 hours, as it did the year before last, we would have absorbed only 2/3 of the fixed overhead. This year the unfavorable capacity variance is only $800,000. The year before that, the unfavorable capacity variance was $1,600,000."

The supervisor of another department, Julio Diaz, disagreed and replied, "You can't eliminate a capacity variance by using more hours. Ernesto, you are confusing the concept of a capacity variance with an efficiency variance."

Valdez answered by saying, "An efficiency variance involves only the variable overhead and has nothing to do with what we are discussing, the absorption of fixed overhead."

Required:
1. Calculate both the overhead efficiency variance and the capacity variance for both years.
2. Explain what the efficiency variance measures as compared to what the capacity variance measures.
3. Which of the two supervisors is correct? Explain.

9-21. Multiple Products and Overhead Analysis. (Appendix 2) Ohio Electrical Instruments manufactures three product lines used by the military services: electronic support devices (SD), electronic counter measure devices (CMD), and electronic counter counter measure devices (CCD). The company has one large production facility in Columbus. Most of the components are manufactured by various divisions, although a few components are purchased from outside vendors. The Assembly Department is responsible for the final assembly of all three products.

Assembly operations are labor intensive and operate under a standard cost system. Because overhead costs are driven by direct labor hours, overhead is applied to each product on that basis. The standard overhead costs for Assembly on each of the three products are as follows:

	Hours	Variable	Fixed	Total	Per Unit
SD	3.0	$10.00	$7.50	$17.50	$52.50
CMD	4.0	10.00	7.50	17.50	70.00
CCD	5.0	10.00	7.50	17.50	87.50

Normal capacity for Assembly is 36,000 direct labor hours per month.

During January, the Assembly Department had the following production performance:

	Units	Hours Worked
SD	3,800	10,900
CMD	2,700	10,400
CCD	2,200	11,500

Actual variable overhead amounted to $326,540 for the month. Actual fixed overhead totaled $271,000. No in-process inventories existed at the beginning and end of the month.

Required:

1. How many standard direct labor hours were allowed for actual production in Assembly during the month?
2. Calculate the under- or overapplied overhead for the month.
3. Calculate the following overhead variances:
   a) Variable spending variance.
   b) Variable efficiency variance.
   c) Fixed spending variance.
   d) Fixed capacity variance.
4. Explain how the variable efficiency variance is related to direct labor.
5. Explain how the variable efficiency variance and the fixed capacity variance are related.

9-22. Standard Cost and Variances. (Appendix B) Arcela Containers, Inc., has four operating divisions. The controller wants monthly reports on the operations of each of the divisions and for the total company. One of the reports is to give the manufacturing overhead spending variance, the manufacturing overhead efficiency variance, and the capacity variance.

Data for each of the divisions are given as follows. (All figures are in thousands.)

	Divisions			
	1	**2**	**3**	**4**
Budgeted variable overhead at normal capacity	$40	$60	$100	$400
Budgeted fixed overhead	$60	$90	$150	$100
Normal capacity, labor hours	20	10	20	50

Operating data for the months of August, September, and October are given as follows. (All figures are in thousands.)

	Divisions			
	1	**2**	**3**	**4**
August:				
Actual manufacturing overhead	$92	$155	$240	$487
Actual labor hours	14	10	19	48
Standard labor hours for work done	15	8	20	45
September:				
Actual manufacturing overhead	$83	$188	$226	$498
Actual labor hours	12	15	16	50
Standard labor hours for work done	14	12	12	50
October:				
Actual manufacturing overhead	$76	$197	$233	$475
Actual labor hours	9	16	18	47
Standard labor hours for work done	10	15	16	50

Required:

1. Prepare monthly reports for each division for August, September, and October and for the company as a whole. Show the following variances:
    a) Manufacturing overhead spending variance.
    b) Manufacturing overhead efficiency variance.
    c) Manufacturing overhead capacity variance.

2. Identify the division(s) with the worst spending variance, the worst efficiency variance, the worst capacity variance for each of the three months.

3. If the economy turned down, which division is most likely to run into problems first? Explain.

9-23. **Process Costs and Standard Cost Variances.** Webb & Company is engaged in the preparation of income tax returns for individuals. Webb uses the FIFO method and actual costs for financial reporting purposes. However, for internal reporting, Webb uses a standard cost system. The standards, based on equivalent performance, have been established as follows:

Labor per return..	5 hrs at $20 per hour
Overhead per return	5 hrs at $10 per hour

For March 1994 performance, budgeted overhead is $49,000 for the standard labor hours allowed. The following additional information pertains to the month of March:

Inventory data:

Returns in process, March 1 (25% complete)	200
Returns started in March	825
Returns in process, March 31 (80% complete)	125

Actual cost data:

Returns in process, March 1:	
Labor	$6,000
Overhead	2,500
Labor, March 1 to 31, 4,000 hours	89,000
Overhead, March 1 to 31	45,000

Required:

1. Using the FIFO method, compute the following for each cost element:
    a) Equivalent units of performance.
    b) Actual cost per equivalent unit.
2. Compute the actual cost of returns in process at March 31.
3. Compute the standard cost per return.
4. Prepare a schedule for internal reporting analyzing March performance, using the following variances, and indicating whether these variances are favorable or unfavorable:
    a) Total labor.
    b) Labor rate.
    c) Labor efficiency.
    d) Total overhead.
    e) Overhead capacity.
    f) Overhead budget.

(AICPA Adapted)

CASE 9A–WINN'S BICYCLES, INC.

Winn's Bicycles, Inc., is a large manufacturer located in Denver. Its usual production of bicycles is 10,000 units per year. The company has been a leader in the 21-speed bike industry for several years. However, with increasing competition and a higher public emphasis on quality, Winn has been searching for ways to maintain quality and cut costs. John Jackson, production planner, suggested that starting at the beginning of 1994 the company invest in higher quality materials and hire more experienced workers at a slightly higher pay rate.

The company has used a standard cost system for the past five years. The current standard costs for one bicycle, based on production of 10,000 units, are as follows:

Materials	$ 60
Direct labor (4 hours at $10)	40
Variable overhead (based on labor)	20
Fixed overhead (based on labor)	8
Standard cost per bicycle	$128

Jeffrey Winn, President, is skeptical about decreasing costs by increasing materials and labor costs. However, after much debate, he agrees to try the changes for one year beginning with January 1994.

Because the exact costs of changes were not known at the beginning of 1994, the existing standard costs were retained. That means, the changes will be in the variances from standard costs. For 1994, the company only produced 9,500 bicycles because the market place showed a decreasing demand. The following data shows the actual results for the year with 9,500 bicycles:

1. $617,500 of materials were purchased and used. No quantity variance existed, so any differences were due solely to price changes.
2. Direct labor was $249,375 for 23,750 direct labor hours.
3. Actual variable overhead totaled $163,000.
4. Actual fixed overhead totaled $80,000.

Mr. Winn was pleased with the results. Even though production was down 500 bicycles, the difference in costs was significant. He would like to know why.

Required:

1. Compute all appropriate variances for the following categories:
   a) Materials.
   b) Labor.
   c) Overhead.
2. Explain how any of the variances interrelate (have the same basic cause).
3. Explain which of the variances are controllable.
4. Assuming that the actual cost results for 1994 represent the new standard performance, calculate the new standard cost per bicycle, showing separately the materials, labor, and overhead components. (Normal production is still based on 10,000 bicycles.)

CASE 9B—AUTOMOBILE SUPPORT COMPANY[1]

The following transcript was prepared from a recording of a recent meeting of executives of the Automobile Support Company.

Location:	Seventh Floor Conference Room
Time:	10:00 Monday Morning
Meeting:	Special Executive Meeting
Present:	Bob Sharp—President
	Gloria Finan—Controller
	Charlie Smith—Assistant Controller
	Bill Plankton—Plant Manager
	Henry Wills—Sales Manager
	Julie Sheehan—Purchasing Manager

Bob Sharp: Good morning. As you recall, Thursday's operations review meeting was chaotic. Many of the variances from standard costs that showed up in the interim financial statements did not seem to be controllable, and some of you questioned the entire accounting system. I asked Gloria to look into our standard costing methods and report back to us today. Gloria, have you come up with anything?

Gloria Finan: I think so, Bob. As you know, for many years we have used a standard costing system in which standards are only adjusted annually. At year end, we determine the actual cost to produce the products then in inventory. These costs become the standards for the next year. This has worked well for the interim financial reports that we must provide to shareholders and others. We are able to create these reports without the need of expensive, and disruptive, interim costing of inventories. But the system has been less than satisfactory for internal purposes such as controlling costs through variance calculation and analysis. I asked my new assistant, Charlie Smith, to work out a system that would satisfy both stockholders and management. Charlie recently received an MBA from State University and has strong opinions about proper feedback and control. I brought Charlie with me today so that he could give us his recommendations in person. Charlie?

Charlie Smith: Thanks, Gloria. I think I have a solution that will satisfy everybody. The basic complaint about the present system is that the standards are out of date every time costs change. My proposal is simple—let's use two sets of standards. One set will be changed only once a year as is our current practice and will be used for our interim financial statements. This will satisfy that need. The other set will be changed continually to keep material, labor, and overhead costs (and standard quantities) current. This will result in variances that reflect true efficiencies and inefficiencies, and should satisfy our internal needs. I've worked out current standards and could implement them this week if you wish.

Bill Plankton: This looks very interesting, Charlie, but I wonder if I might ask a couple of questions?

Charlie Smith: Of course.

Gloria (aside to Charlie):   Look out!

Bill Plankton: Under your proposed system two sets of books for inventories are needed. There will be two sets of variances, which may differ in amount considerably, and two sets of inventory values for Raw Materials, Work in Process and Finished Goods. Would this not be both confusing internally and a concern externally to tax officials, regulatory agencies, and even stockholders if word leaked out in the press about our having dual sets of books? I say we go with one system, and since we all understand the old one I see nothing wrong with sticking with it, imperfect though it may be.

While I'm at it, I may as well get something else off my chest. Our internal reports always show production inefficiencies as variances which are blamed on the plant, while the sales department gets none of the blame and all of the glory. Can't we have a system that shows variances from budget for (1) sales prices, (2) sales volume, and (3) changes in sales mix? Aren't these more important to the company's long-term success than cost variances, regardless of whether you look at them from a current or an old standard?

Charlie Smith: Well . . .

Henry Wills: Now Bill, let's not get worked up over things we can't control. Don't blame Sales when the market is soft. Let's concentrate on controlling costs.

Bill Plankton: How can we control costs when we keep getting rush orders that we have to fill? Our guys have to interrupt production runs and work overtime two to three times a week just to help your salesmen keep their customers happy. And guess who gets blamed for those cost overruns?

Julie Sheehan: Well, I like Charlie's idea of using current standards, but I think in the future we should take his plan one step further. Why not develop "prospective" standards. By this I mean, when we set our standards at the beginning of the year, we should anticipate the cost increases which will occur during the year and build these into the standards. In the purchasing department this would reward timely purchasing decisions with favorable price variances. Right now the only time we get favorable price variances is when we get quantity discounts for purchasing in bulk.

Henry Wills: That might help with price variances but it would not help with efficiency variances. It would also mean we would still need two sets of standards—current standards for use in providing sales with current product costs, and the prospective standards for the cost system.

Charlie Smith: We could set price standards prospectively and efficiency standards currently. The latter would require that we devise a procedure to keep our book inventory from going out of whack. I agree we would need two sets of standards.

Gloria Finan: Since you brought it up, Julie, I must tell you that a number of purchasing's bulk orders have cost us more in inventory carrying costs than we have saved in price discounts. So even the favorable variances you mention were erroneous indicators of good performance. I don't think Charlie's plan addresses that issue, and it probably should.

Bob Sharp: Sorry Charlie, but I think that there are a number of additional ideas mentioned today that deserve attention. The use of two sets of standards; the use of prospective standards; changing standards as costs change and repricing inventories so inventory variances are not created. Gloria, could you and Charlie report back to us on Friday after considering the strengths and weaknesses of the issues brought up today? Thank you. This meeting stands adjourned.

Charlie (to Gloria as they head back to their offices): I thought you were on my side, Gloria.

Required:

1. What are the objectives for a standard cost system? How are these objectives being met and not met with the current system?
2. Prepare a set of recommendations for changes in the system. What implementation issues will be raised by your recommendations?

Chapter Ten

Profit Analysis - Gross Profit and Operating Expenses

 ## ❖ Chapter Objectives

1. Identify the components of gross profit analysis for single product and multiple product situations.
2. Calculate the following variances for the appropriate situations: sales price, cost, sales volume, sales mix, and sales quantity.
3. Identify and calculate the operating expenses variances.
4. Explain the difference in gross profit variances if a contribution margin approach is used.
5. Calculate mix and yield variances for both materials and labor.
6. Prepare a variable costing income statement.
7. Reconcile the differences between absorption costing net income and variable costing net income.
8. Explain and compare the major arguments supporting both variable costing and absorption costing.

What is Happening to Profits at Creative Weddings?

Creative Weddings, Inc., will do anything for a wedding but conduct the marriage ceremony. It is noted for decorating reception facilities, providing formal wear for the wedding party, baking the wedding cake, and providing and serving all refreshments. It designs photography packages for the couple and families.

One division of the company specializes in producing wedding invitations, napkins, and albums. A summary of budgeted and actual results for the just completed year follows:

	Actual	Budget	Variance
Sales	$385,000	$365,000	$ 20,000
Cost of sales	282,500	227,250	55,250
Gross profit	$102,500	$137,750	$ (35,250)
Operating expenses	81,250	90,000	(8,750)
Net profit	$ 21,250	$ 47,750	$ (26,500)

David Taylor, division manager, is concerned about the changes taking place in his profits and the factors causing those changes. He knows that prices and volume interact but is concerned that other factors influence profitability. He is planning for future operations and needs to make decisions about what changes to make and which direction the business should take. He asks for your help.

GROSS PROFIT ANALYSIS

One useful technique that will explain changes in revenue and cost of goods sold is called **gross profit analysis**. **Gross profit (or gross margin)** is sales revenue minus the cost of those sales. Analysis of gross profit uses an approach similar to standard cost variance analysis, although standards are not essential for the analysis. In fact, we will not use standard costs until after we explain the general approach to gross profit analysis. Then we modify the analysis for situations where standard costs are used. The factors we will emphasize in the analysis are changes that result from one or a combination of several of the following:

1.   Changes in selling prices (sales price variance).
2.   Changes in volume sold as reflected in the number of units sold (sales quantity variance).
3.   Changes in volume sold as reflected in the sales mix (sales mix variance).
4.   Changes in the cost elements in cost of goods sold (cost variance).

The framework we will use to identify these changes is depicted in Figure 10.1.

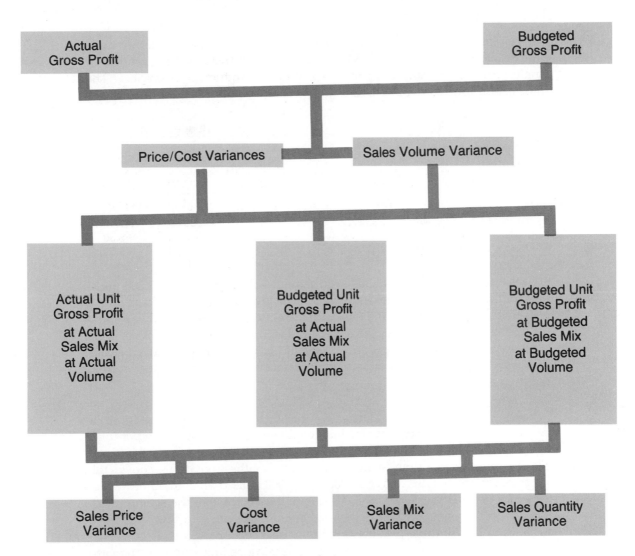

Figure 10.1   General Framework for Gross Profit Analysis

This framework shows only the relationships in a general sense. The actual formulas for calculating the variances are presented in the appropriate sections that follow. Also, we are comparing actual against budgeted data. For companies that want to compare this period against last period, the last period results are treated as budgeted data in the framework.

Later in the chapter we will present an analysis approach for the operating expenses. After that, we will show how to identify variances for an income statement formatted in a contribution margin approach. Variable costing is a product costing concept that fits well into the contribution margin approach and is widely used for internal reporting purposes. Therefore, the subject will be covered as a part of our profit analysis.

Single Product Case

The easiest illustration of the approach to a gross profit analysis is the single product case. For Creative Weddings, Inc., we will treat the invitations as a single product and ignore for the present other products and services. The information for the invitations is as follows:

	Actual	Budget	Variance
Volume in packages	15,000	10,000	5,000
Sales	$225,000	$200,000	$25,000
Cost of sales	187,500	120,000	67,500
Gross profit..............................	$ 37,500	$ 80,000	$ (42,500)
Selling price per package	$15.00	$20.00	$(5.00)
Cost per package	$12.50	$12.00	$.50
Gross profit per package	$2.50	$8.00	$(5.50)

Gross profit decreased $42,500 even though volume increased 5,000 packages and sales revenue increased $25,000. The gross profit per package took a nose dive. We can separate the total variances into components that will show the effects of changes in sales price, cost, and volume. There is no mix variance because we have only one product. We could split the volume between sales and cost of sales, but the source of the variance is a change in sales volume, not production volume.

Sales Price Variance   The **sales price variance** is the change in gross profit due to a difference between budgeted and actual selling price per unit. Its computation is the difference between actual unit selling price and budgeted unit selling price times actual units sold. For the invitations above, the variance is ($15.00 − $20.00) × 15,000 = $75,000 unfavorable. In other words, the gross profit decreased by $75,000 due to the decrease in the selling price. For possible reasons why such a variance might occur, see the sales price variance in the multiple product case in the next section.

Some managers follow a strategy of decreasing selling prices to increase volume and assume that the volume will make up the revenue shortfall from price changes. If this strategy works, the manager is viewed as a genius. We need not mention how people view managers who guess wrong. We already know that the gross profit decreased for the period.

Cost Variance   The **cost variance** is the change in gross profit due to an increase or decrease in unit cost. The computation is similar to the sales price variance; we substitute unit costs for unit selling prices. The formula is the difference between actual cost per unit and budgeted cost per unit times actual units sold. Creative Weddings, Inc. has a cost variance of ($12.50 − $12.00) × 15,000 = $7,500 unfavorable. Either in the production of invitations or in the buying of materials, an increase in costs occurred and that naturally has a negative impact on gross profit.

Sales Volume Variance   The **sales volume variance** is the increase or decrease in gross profit resulting from the difference between the planned and actual number of units sold. The variance is computed by the formula: (actual units sold − budgeted units sold) × budgeted gross profit per unit. For the above data, the sales volume variance is (15,000 − 10,000) × $8.00 = $40,000 favorable. It is favorable because the actual volume is higher and that should increase gross profit.

Comparing this with the sales price variance, we see that a lower price decreased gross profit more than the volume increase improved gross profit. Therefore, if management was following a strategy of lowering prices to increase volume, and thus to increase total gross profit, the strategy was not successful.

Summary of Gross Profit Variances   Since we are analyzing the difference between actual and budgeted amounts, the total of all variances should equal this difference. We know that the gross profit difference is $42,500 unfavorable. The following is a summary of the three variances:

Sales price variance	$75,000 U
Cost variance	7,500 U
Sales volume variance	40,000 F
Change in gross profit	$42,500 U

Multiple Product Case

Few companies make or sell only one product. Most will have many products, with the selling prices, cost of goods sold, and gross profit varying widely among the products. Therefore, we approach the analysis knowing a mix of products exists. To begin with, let's summarize the data for Creative Weddings, Inc. for three products that will be used in the analysis.

	Actual	Budget	Variance
Invitations:			
Volume in packages	15,000	10,000	5,000
Sales	$225,000	$200,000	$ 25,000
Cost of sales	187,500	120,000	67,500
Gross profit	$ 37,500	$ 80,000	$(42,500)
Selling price per package	$ 15.00	$ 20.00	$ (5.00)
Cost per package	12.50	12.00	.50
Gross profit per package	$ 2.50	$ 8.00	$ (5.50)
Napkins:			
Volume in packages	8,000	7,500	500
Sales	$ 72,000	$ 75,000	$ (3,000)
Cost of sales	40,000	41,250	(1,250)
Gross profit	$ 32,000	$ 33,750	$ (1,750)

	Actual	Budget	Variance
Selling price per package	$ 9.00	$ 10.00	$ (1.00)
Cost per package	5.00	5.50	(.50)
Gross profit per package	$ 4.00	$ 4.50	$ (.50)
Albums:			
Volume in units	5,500	6,000	(500)
Sales	$ 88,000	$ 90,000	$ (2,000)
Cost of sales	55,000	66,000	(11,000)
Gross profit	$ 33,000	$ 24,000	$ 9,000
Selling price per unit	$ 16.00	$ 15.00	$ 1.00
Cost per package	10.00	11.00	(1.00)
Gross profit per package	$ 6.00	$ 4.00	$ 2.00
Total gross profit	$102,500	$137,750	$(35,250)
Average gross profit	$ 3.596	$ 5.862	$ (2.266)

With this data, we will analyze gross profit by identifying four variances: sales price, cost, sales mix, and sales quantity.

Sales price variance   When selling prices per unit change, total sales revenue will change and that means a change in gross profit. The sales price variance is calculated for each product individually using this formula: actual sales units times the difference between the actual selling price and budgeted selling price. This is done as follows:

	Actual Sales units	Difference in Prices	Variance
Invitations	15,000	$(5.00)	$75,000 U
Napkins	8,000	$(1.00)	8,000 U
Albums	5,500	$ 1.00	5,500 F
			$77,500 U

With the exception of the albums, prices decreased; and the increase in the album prices was not sufficient to offset the other price decreases. Therefore, an unfavorable sales price variance exists.

A sales price variance may be caused by many factors, some of which are the following:

1.   Changes in the economy.
2.   Reactions to competitive changes.
3.   Changes in pricing policies.
4.   Changes in marketing strategy.
5.   Unplanned price discounts or changes in authority to offer discounts.
6.   Changes in customers' perception of quality and service.
7.   Opening of a new marketing territory.
8.   Altering of the marketing channels used.

Isolating variances gives a basis for understanding potential causes of variations. Once causes are identified and investigated, management can take corrective action or make adjustments to policies and procedures; whatever is necessary. Without investigating variances, management ignores the possibility that the variances are controllable and will reoccur in the future. The only reason for not investigating a variance is the cost/benefit of investigating variances. Therefore, management by exception is applied to variance investigation.

Cost variance   The formula for a cost variance uses the same factors as the sales price variance, except the cost per unit replaces the selling price. This variance can and should be further analyzed into materials, labor and overhead variances. (See Chapter 9.) Creative Weddings, Inc. would have the following calculation:

	Actual Sales Units	Difference in Prices	Variance
Invitations	15,000	$ .50	$7,500 U
Napkins............................	8,000	$ (.50)	4,000 F
Albums	5,500	$(1.00)	5,500 F
			$2,000 F

Costs per unit were down on two of the three products. Only one product showed a cost increase. The net effect was in favor of the downward movement in costs. Therefore, gross profit increased by $2,000 as a result of the cost changes.

The causes for the cost variance depend on whether the company is a manufacturer or merchandiser. In a manufacturing operation, the variance measures the production managers' failure to maintain control over direct materials, direct labor, and factory overhead, or their ability to invoke efficiencies that had not been planned. In a merchandising operation, the cost variance relates to the purchasing agents or buyers and measures their ability to control purchases. Service organizations usually do not record a cost of services rendered, so they would not have a cost variance.

Sales Volume Variance   As in the single product case, the sales volume variance measures the increase or decrease in gross profit resulting from changes between the planned units and the actual units sold. We calculate the variance as the difference in units times the budgeted gross profit per unit. The reason we use the budgeted gross profit is that the effects of differences between actual sales prices and budgeted sales prices and actual costs and budgeted costs are removed in calculating the sales price variance and cost variance. That leaves budgeted prices and costs, the difference of which is budgeted gross profit. The calculation of the volume variance for our example is:

	Actual Sales Units minus Budgeted Sales Units	Budgeted Gross Profit	Variance
Invitations	15,000 − 10,000 = 5,000	$8.00	$40,000 F
Napkins...............	8,000 − 7,500 = 500	4.50	2,250 F
Albums	5,500 − 6,000 = (500)	4.00	2,000 U
			$40,250 F

In the multiple product situation, the volume variance is difficult to interpret because it combines the interaction of changes in the sales mix and changes in the quantities. Therefore, it is customary to analyze the sales volume variance in terms of sales mix and sales quantity.

Sales Mix Variance   A **sales mix variance** measures the impact on gross profit of shifts in the units sold toward the more profitable or less profitable products. A favorable variance occurs when a company either sells fewer units of less profitable products or sells more units of more profitable products. On the other hand, an unfavorable variance occurs when a company sells more units of less profitable products or sells fewer units of more profitable products. The definition of which products are more or less profitable is based on a comparison of each product's budgeted gross profit with the average budgeted gross profit for all products in the mix. If the individual gross profit is less than the average, the product is less profitable.

The sales mix variance is the difference between the actual units at actual mix and the actual units restated at the budgeted mix, with that difference multiplied by the difference between the individual budgeted gross profit and the average budgeted gross profit. The budgeted mix is calculated below:

	Budgeted Units	Budgeted Mix Proportions
Invitations	10,000	10,000 ÷ 23,500
Napkins..................................	7,500	7,500 ÷ 23,500
Albums	6,000	6,000 ÷ 23,500
	23,500	

Now, we restate the total actual units of 28,500 to the budgeted mix, as follows:

	Total Actual Quantity × Mix Proportion
Invitations	28,500 × (10,000 ÷ 23,500) = 12,128
Napkins.............................	28,500 × (7,500 ÷ 23,500) = 9,096
Albums	28,500 × (6,000 ÷ 23,500) = 7,276*
	28,500

* This figure has been rounded down to facilitate the illustration.

The next step is to multiply the difference between the actual units and restated units by the difference between the budgeted gross profit and the average budgeted gross profit:

	Actual Units	Actual Units Restated	Unit Difference	Difference in Gross Profit	Variance
Invitations .	15,000 −	12,128	=	2,872	× ($8.00 − $5.862) =	$6,140 F
Napkins ...	8,000 −	9,096	=	(1,096)	× ($4.50 − $5.862) =	1,493 F
Albums ...	5,500 −	7,276	=	(1,776)	× ($4.00 − $5.862) =	3,307 F
	28,500	28,500				$10,940 F

The sales mix variance is important because some products contribute more to profit than others. This variance gives a manager the magnitude of the impact a change in sales mix has on gross profit. In the above situation, the shift in sales mix was favorable—a shift to the most profitable product and away from the less profitable products.

We have variances isolated by individual product. However, since the change in mix means a shift from one product to another, interpreting individual variances will only have meaning when related to the other products. Management is more interested in identifying the cause of the shift in mix, and the total sales mix variance gives us the information needed. However, sales mix variances for individual products do not provide additional information content.

Common causes of a sales mix variance, which is normally the responsibility of the marketing function, are:

1. Upturns or downturns in the economy that cause people to alter buying habits.
2. Changes in customer tastes and attitudes.
3. Changes in advertising and promotional expenditures.
4. Changes in marketing strategies.
5. Changes in pricing policies.
6. Changes in customers' perception of quality and service.
7. Opening a new marketing territory.
8. Altering the marketing channels used.

Notice that several of these causes are similar to the causes of the sales price variance. The reason is simply that customers will react by altering buying habits as the relationship of prices among the products changes.

Sales Quantity Variance   **The sales quantity variance** occurs when total actual units sold differs from the total budgeted units. The calculation is the difference between total actual units and total budgeted units times the average budgeted gross profit. For our case, the calculation yields: $(28,500 - 23,500) \times \$5.862 = \$29,310$ favorable. The sales quantity variance is favorable because the total units sold were greater than the total units budgeted.

The sales quantity variance is usually considered only in total. A variance for individual products does not provide additional information about the potential reasons for the existence of a quantity variance.

The sales quantity variance can be caused by many factors, such as unanticipated changes in general economic conditions, differences in the effectiveness of salespeople or the advertising program, or the changes in the credit policy. It can be influenced by the same causes we identified for the sales price variance and sales mix variance.

In larger companies, the variance is isolated separately for each distribution channel, for each geographic region, and possibly for each product line. Reporting by distribution channel indicates whether the variance occurred in wholesale or retail divisions. A geographic identification helps to show where the activities need investigation. A separation according to product line directs the investigation to the product lines that were causing the sales quantity variance. Separation also permits performance reporting along the lines of responsibility.

Summary of Gross Profit Variances   As we saw earlier, the total gross profit varied from the budget by $35,250. The sum of all variances should equal the total variance. The four variances are as follows:

Sales price variance		$77,500 U
Cost variance		2,000 F
Sales volume variance:		
Sales mix variance	$10,940 F	
Sales quantity variance........................	29,310 F	40,250 F
Decrease in gross profit		$35,250 U

Even though some variances are favorable, the net effect of all variances is an unfavorable variance in gross profit. The variances are significant, and management must investigate them to find which causes are controllable and can be corrected. This investigation will help management decide courses of action for future operations.

Modifications for Standard Costs   We assumed a budgeted cost figure for our gross profit analysis. The cost variance indicated any change in unit costs. When a standard cost system is used by a company, both the cost of sales at actual and budget are stated at the same standard unit costs. This is reasonable since units are transferred from work in process to finished goods to cost of sales at standard cost. Any difference between actual costs and standard costs has already been isolated during production. (See Chapter 9 for this process.) What does this mean for our gross profit analysis? It only means that we will not have a cost variance; it is zero. Therefore, the variances will be for sales price, mix, and quantity.

USES AND LIMITATIONS OF GROSS PROFIT ANALYSIS

The gross profit analysis identifies weak spots in performance for the period covered by the gross profit calculation. Since gross profit is the joint responsibility of the marketing and production functions, the gross profit analysis brings together these two major functional areas. The marketing function must explain the changes in sales prices, the shift in the sales mix, and the change in total units sold. The production function must explain any changes in costs. To the extent that changes in the sales mix or total units result from the production function's inability to meet planned production according to sales needs, production managers must explain why those changes occurred.

Responsibility for gross profit changes rests with different managers within the organization. Increases or decreases in selling prices (other than discounts) generally are in the domain of top management. Sales managers are typically responsible for the increases or decreases in sales volume and the shifts in sales mix. One or more production managers are responsible for cost changes due to efficient and inefficient production operations, for spending levels, and for adherence to planned production schedules.

Even though responsibility for one or more variances can be charged to specific people, not all gross profit variances have the same level of significance. For example, top managers may view volume changes as more important than sales price changes. Certainly, decreases in unit fixed costs traceable solely to increases in the volume of production activity mean less than lower unit fixed costs achieved through more efficient use of direct materials and direct labor or through a savings in some area of factory overhead.

As useful as we find gross profit analysis, the approach suffers several limitations. We present only the three most critical ones here. First, although we have defined variances with specific formulas, the boundary between one variance and another is "fuzzy" at best. The tool is important for direction and magnitude of the variances but not for precise measurement. Every variance has some intersecting or overlapping point with another variance which raises questions about whether we are giving the proper interpretation to the variance in a specific situation. Second, the budget plan for the period and the actual results do not necessarily represent what the manager should have accomplished during the period. For example, as conditions changed, did the manager respond to those changes in an optimal way? This is not measured in the variance analysis. And third, the analysis does not indicate why certain things occurred or how variances are interrelated. For instance, why were sales price changes large or small; why did volume fail to meet projections; or why did the mix shift from the most profitable product to the least profitable product? On a related issue, volume may be down because sales prices went up or volume may be up because the least profitable product was underpriced.

Variance analysis is nothing more than a series of computations that identify differences and label them as favorable or unfavorable. Identifying the underlying causes of these variances is left to the initiative of individual managers. Our variance computations merely focus the areas so managers can direct their investigation of causes in the most fruitful directions.

ANALYSIS OF OPERATING EXPENSES

Operating expenses (sometimes called nonmanufacturing expenses) are the selling, marketing, and distribution expenses plus general and administrative expenses. In this section, we will use the terms marketing expenses and administrative expenses when we detail operating expenses.

Administrative expenses are often the most difficult to manage because the relationship between inputs and outputs is not well defined. They are typically discretionary expenses that fall into the category of normal and necessary business expenses. The discretionary aspect of the expenses is that management sets a ceiling on costs for a particular set of tasks. For example, how much should the Accounting Department spend during the next month?

Management authorizes a certain amount, but it is only loosely related to the overall activity of the business for the month. Consequently, we must exercise caution in interpreting any variances calculated.

The framework for variance analysis compares the difference between actual and budgeted operating expenses and isolates two variances: spending and volume. These variances are presented schematically in Figure 10.2.

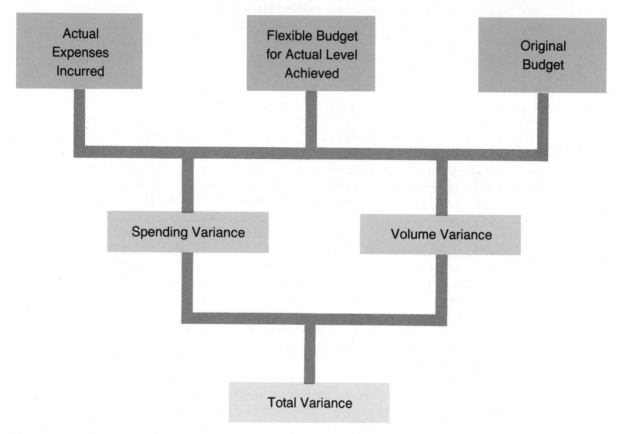

Figure 10.2   Framework for Operating Expense Variance Analysis

At the end of the period, we calculate a flexible budget for the actual level of operations achieved. The **spending variance** (some accountants call it a budget variance) is the difference between what we actually spent and what we should have spent at that same level of activity. A **volume variance** is the difference between the flexible budget and the original (master or static) budget. The difference represents the fact we planned to operate at one level and operated at a different level.

For Creative Weddings, Inc., the operating expenses are as follows:

Actual operating expenses	$81,250
Budgeted operating expenses	90,000
Favorable variance in operating expenses	$ 8,750

The budgeted amount is based on 15 percent of budgeted sales ($365,000 × 15% = $54,750) plus $35,250 of fixed costs. Since the actual sales are $385,000, we can establish a flexible budget based on the formula of 15 percent of sales plus $35,250. For our analysis, we do not need a segregation of the actual variable and fixed costs, but we need that segregation for a flexible budget. This information is as follows:

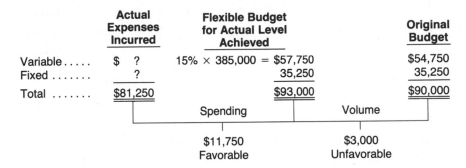

	Actual Expenses Incurred	Flexible Budget for Actual Level Achieved	Original Budget
Variable.....	$?	15% × 385,000 = $57,750	$54,750
Fixed	?	35,250	35,250
Total	$81,250	$93,000	$90,000

Spending — $11,750 Favorable

Volume — $3,000 Unfavorable

These variances relate in part to the variable and fixed nature of the operating costs. A spending variance consists of both variable and fixed costs, and the volume variance consists only of variable costs. (The nature of the volume variance here is different from and unrelated to the capacity variance in factory overhead costs. The capacity variance is only fixed costs.) The spending variance is controllable by managers of the appropriate activities and functions; the volume variance is caused by changes in its activity base. For example, where sales revenue is the measure of activity in our illustration, the volume variance is related to those factors causing the change in sales revenue.

The spending variance is the result of the responsible manager's efforts to keep spending in line with the amount expected at that level of activity. Besides estimating errors in specifying fixed and variable cost elements, this variance includes price and quantity differences identified with individual expense categories within the marketing expenses and administrative expenses.

The volume variance is the difference between two budget calculations made at two different levels—the actual level and the planned level. The reasons for operating at other than the planned level could be the result of random economic events, but, more than likely, one or more identifiable factors are related to the marketplace and overall business environment.

CONTRIBUTION MARGIN APPROACH

A contribution approach is popular in many organizations for internal profitability and performance reporting. The basic format of a contribution approach is revenues less variable costs (to arrive at a contribution margin) less fixed costs (to get the operating profit). Gross profit is not a component of this approach.

We have previously defined **contribution margin** as the excess of sales revenue minus variable costs. The analysis of this margin still yields sales price, cost, sales mix, and sales quantity variances. However, the dollar components of the variances differ from those we saw in the gross profit analysis because fixed costs are segregated.

For an illustration, we will consider the Matheson Cleaner Fluids Company. It produces and sells premium, standard, and economy cleaners for commercial use. Its budget for September is as follows:

	Premium	Standard	Economy	Total
Sales in gallons	20,000	20,000	40,000	80,000
Sales revenues	$320,000	$180,000	$224,000	$724,000
Variable costs	220,000	160,000	100,000	480,000
Contribution margin	$100,000	$ 20,000	$124,000	$244,000*
Fixed costs				150,000
Net profit				$ 94,000

* Average budgeted contribution margin: $244,000 ÷ 80,000 = $3.05

Actual results for the month were reported as follows:

	Premium	Standard	Economy	Total
Sales in gallons	25,000	15,000	50,000	90,000
Sales revenues	$406,250	$135,000	$275,000	$816,250
Variable costs	287,500	112,500	120,000	520,000
Contribution margin	$118,750	$ 22,500	$155,000	$296,250
Fixed costs				155,000
Net profit				$141,250

What are the causes of the $47,250 favorable variance in net profit? Answering that question begins with an analysis of the contribution margin in terms of sales price, cost (variable cost in this case), sales mix, and sales quantity. Using the techniques we covered in the gross profit analysis, we will now calculate the variances for the contribution margin. The variance on fixed costs is the same analysis we did for operating expenses; therefore, we will not repeat that one here.

Sales Price Variance

The sales price variance occurs when the actual sales price differs from the budgeted sales price. The formula for each product is actual sales units times the difference between actual sales price and budgeted sales price. For Matheson Cleaner Fluids Company, the variance is:

	Actual Sales units	Difference in Prices	Variance
Premium	25,000	($16.00 − $16.25)	$6,250 F
Standard	15,000	($ 9.00 − $ 9.00)	0
Economy	50,000	($ 5.60 − $ 5.50)	5,000 U
			$1,250 F

One product increased its price while one product decreased. The net effect is an increase to the contribution margin by $1,250.

Cost Variance

The variable costs in this illustration consist of manufacturing, marketing, and administrative variable costs that are identified with each product. The formula for calculating a cost variance is the same as that used for the sales price variance.

	Actual Sales units	Difference in Costs	Variance
Premium	25,000	($11.00 − $11.50)	$12,500 U
Standard	15,000	($ 8.00 − $ 7.50)	7,500 F
Economy	50,000	($ 2.50 − $ 2.40)	5,000 F
			$ 0

The costs varied unfavorably on one product and varied favorably on two products. The net effect is interesting because the increases and decreases canceled each other to yield a zero total cost variance by coincidence. Therefore, in this case variable cost changes do not influence the changes in contribution margin. Even though the total variance is zero, the individual variances may still need investigation to identify underlying causes and make adjustments where appropriate.

Sales Mix Variance

The sales mix variance measures the change in the contribution margin due to a shift in the mix of products sold. The budgeted mix is:

	Gallons	Budgeted Mix Proportion
Premium	20,000	25%
Standard	20,000	25%
Economy	40,000	50%
	80,000	

Restating the 90,000 gallons actually sold into terms of the budgeted mix gives the following:

	Total Gallons × Mix Proportion
Premium	90,000 × 25% = 22,500
Standard	90,000 × 25% = 22,500
Economy	90,000 × 50% = 45,000

Finding the difference between the actual gallons and the restated mix and multiplying by the difference between the budgeted contribution margin and average budgeted contribution margin result in a sales mix variance:

	Actual Units	Actual Units Restated		Unit Difference	Difference in Contribution Margin	Variance
Premium	25,000 −	22,500	=	2,500	× ($5.00 − $3.05) =	$ 4,875 F
Standard	15,000 −	22,500	=	(7,500)	× ($1.00 − $3.05) =	15,375 F
Economy	50,000 −	45,000	=	5,000	× ($3.10 − $3.05) =	250 F
	90,000	90,000				$20,500 F

The shift in mix was away from the least profitable product toward the two more profitable products. The result is an increase in contribution margin of $20,500.

Sales Quantity Variance

The change in the contribution margin due to quantity changes is related to the difference between the total actual gallons sold and the total gallons budgeted. We already know that the total actual gallons exceeded the budgeted gallons and that means a favorable variance. The dollar amount of that variance is the difference in total gallons times the average budgeted contribution margin. The calculation is: $(90,000 − 80,000) \times \$3.05 = \$30,500$ favorable. As we mentioned earlier, a separate calculation for individual products does not give meaningful information. (The proper calculation for individual products is beyond our work here.)

Summary of Contribution Margin Variances

The change in contribution margin should be explained by the variances we have calculated. The change we attempt to explain is:

Actual contribution margin	$296,250
Budgeted contribution margin	244,000
Favorable variance in contribution margin	$ 52,250

The four variances that identify major areas that will help explain the increase in contribution margin are summarized as follows:

Sales price variance	$ 1,250 F
Cost variance	0
Sales mix variance	20,500 F
Sales quantity variance.	30,500 F
Variance in contribution margin	$52,250 F

MIX AND YIELD VARIANCES

In many operations a recipe or formula is used to indicate the specifications for each category of material or class of labor. An individual fruit pie, for instance, has a recipe for the materials that go into the dough and into the filling. A CPA firm may have a mix of partners, senior managers, managers, seniors, and staff for specific types of audits. If the multiple materials (or labor) are to some extent interchangeable or if the mix can be altered to improve a yield, a new set of variances will help us identify the influence of mix and yield. In effect, we replace the materials quantity variance and labor efficiency variance with mix and yield variances.

The variances we previously calculated for materials and labor were based on changes in a price factor and a quantity factor. Addition of mix and yield variances bring a third element: the recipe or formula mix.

Because mix and yield variances are calculated in exactly the same way for both materials and labor, the illustration in this section will cover materials only.

The Cameron Plant has a standard cost system for its many products. One of its products is a soil treatment compound for cotton farmers in the southwest. This compound has the following materials mix for a 150 kilogram package:

		Standard Cost	
Materials	**Kilograms**	**Per Kilogram**	**Per Package**
Melmor	60	$1.50	$ 90.00
Nacmor	30	1.00	30.00
Oramor	70	.80	56.00
Total	160		$176.00

Notice that each package weighing 150 kilograms requires 160 kilograms of materials. This is an 93.75 percent yield from our input of materials. Alternatively, this difference is a 6.67 percent shrinkage based on output.

During a recent production run, the company produced 3,000 packages (each weighing 150 kilograms). The actual quantities of materials used are given below:

Materials	**Kilograms**
Melmor	186,000
Nacmor	90,000
Oramor	214,000
Total	490,000

Because materials price variances have already been eliminated in recording materials in inventory, we need only be concerned about the standard price (SP), actual quantities (AQ), actual mix (AM), standard quantities (SQ), and standard mix (SM) for compound materials mix and yield variances. The basic framework is as follows:

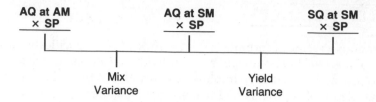

Mix Variances

A **mix variance** shows the cost change that results from combining quantities of material or labor in a ratio that differs from standard specifications. Materials mix variances come from changing the recipe or formula. They are common in industries such as chemicals, food processing, textiles, and pharmaceuticals. Labor mix variances occur when operations are performed by teams consisting of workers earning different rates and the composition of the team or the relationship in hours worked among team members changes.

The materials mix variance is caused by a difference between the actual mix of materials used in production and the standard materials that should have been used. We already have the actual quantities and the actual mix. The next step is to calculate the standard mix for the total actual quantities:

Melmor:	60 ÷ 160 × 490,000 = 183,750 Kilograms
Nacmor:	30 ÷ 160 × 490,000 = 91,875
Oramor:	70 ÷ 160 × 490,000 = 214,375
	490,000 Kilograms

The materials mix variance computation is:

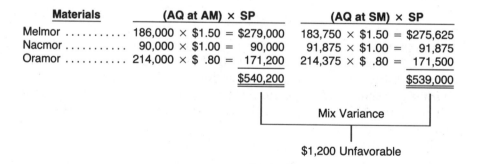

Materials	(AQ at AM) × SP	(AQ at SM) × SP
Melmor	186,000 × $1.50 = $279,000	183,750 × $1.50 = $275,625
Nacmor	90,000 × $1.00 = 90,000	91,875 × $1.00 = 91,875
Oramor	214,000 × $ .80 = 171,200	214,375 × $ .80 = 171,500
	$540,200	$539,000

Mix Variance

$1,200 Unfavorable

In this example, there was a shift in the proportions that resulted in a higher cost to the company. The company used less of the cheapest materials and increased the amount of the most expensive material. The net effect of the shift was $1,200 higher spending than expected.

Notice that we have used the individual materials to calculate a total variance. It seems plausible to have a mix variance associated with each material. Using the above computation to find the individual variances gives results that are meaningless. A different calculation is possible, which does not change the total variance but gives sense to the individual mix variances. It is similar to the manner in which we calculate a sales mix variance.

Yield Variances

A **yield variance** shows the cost change that results from an actual yield of finished product that is different from the standard quantity of product established for a given input of materials or labor. Yield variances are typical when losses are inherent in the production process and can produce actual yields that differ from standard yields for the inputs of materials and labor. Companies using yield variances often express performance as a percentage, such as 98 percent yield.

Yield variances cause changes in the average costs for both materials and labor. A substandard yield means that fewer units of finished products are available for the materials or labor input to production. This means the costs of materials or labor to produce one unit of good output increase.

For our current situation, a materials yield variance occurs when the output from production, given a specific amount of materials input, differs from the output established as the standard yield. The computation of the variance is the difference between the total actual quantities of materials used in production using the standard mix and the standard quantities allowed for the completed product. For the Cameron Plant illustration, the total actual quantities are 490,000 kilograms, and the actual output was 3,000 packages of 150 kilograms each. The total actual quantities as stated at the standard mix were calculated as part of the mix variance and appear as:

$$
\begin{array}{lll}
\text{Melmor:} & 60 \div 160 \times 490,000 = & 183,750 \\
\text{Nacmor:} & 30 \div 160 \times 490,000 = & 91,875 \\
\text{Oramor:} & 70 \div 160 \times 490,000 = & \underline{214,375} \\
& & \underline{490,000}
\end{array}
$$

The standard quantities for the 3,000 packages are calculated as:

$$
\begin{array}{lll}
\text{Melmor:} & 60 \times 3,000 = & 180,000 \\
\text{Nacmor:} & 30 \times 3,000 = & 90,000 \\
\text{Oramor:} & 70 \times 3,000 = & \underline{210,000} \\
& & \underline{480,000}
\end{array}
$$

We have two approaches to calculating the yield variance. The first one is below:

Materials	(AQ at SM) × SP	(SQ at SM) × SP
Melmor	183,750 × $1.50 = $275,625	180,000 × $1.50 = $270,000
Nacmor	91,875 × $1.00 = 91,875	90,000 × $1.00 = 90,000
Oramor	214,375 × $ .80 = 171,500	210,000 × $ .80 = 168,000
	$539,000	$528,000

Yield Variance

$11,000 Unfavorable

Similar to the mix variance, yield variances for individual materials require a special calculation to give meaningful results. The above amount is a straight-forward approach to the total variance.

The second approach to calculating the yield variance is to compare what the actual input should have yielded with the actual yield:

Standard yield of actual input:	
490,000 kilograms ÷ 160 kilograms....................	3,062.5 packages
Actual yield.......................................	3,000 packages
Difference in yield	62.5 packages
Times standard materials cost per package	$ 176
Unfavorable yield variance...........................	$11,000

Interaction of Variances

In the above situation, both the mix and yield variances are unfavorable. Situations exist where a shift in mix can cause variances such that one is favorable and the other is unfavorable. Managers will look at the net effect to determine whether the change in mix saved or lost money for the company.

VARIABLE COSTING

Variable costing is an approach to product costing that allocates only variable manufacturing costs (direct materials, direct labor, and variable factory over-head) to items produced. Thus, inventoriable costs are limited to the variable manufacturing costs; and period costs include all fixed costs and variable non-manufacturing costs. Absorption costing the method we typically use for external income statement reporting, allocates all manufacturing costs (vari-able and fixed) to products. This section compares these two costing methods.

Characteristics of Variable Costing

The primary characteristic differences in the costing methods are in the cost elements for product costs, the difference in inventory values, and the difference in profits. The following summary should highlight that the sole differ-ence between the two costing approaches is the treatment of the fixed manufacturing costs. Absorption costing includes these costs in product costs while variable costing considers them in period costs to be included with the operating expenses.

Cost Category	Variable Costing	Absorption Costing
Direct materials	Product	Product
Direct labor.................................	Product	Product
Variable factory overhead	Product	Product
Fixed factory overhead	**Period** ←———————→	**Product**
Marketing expenses	Period	Period
Administrative expenses......................	Period	Period

Variable costing uses a contribution approach as a reporting format. That means the variable marketing and administrative costs are in the computation of the contribution margin. However, variable marketing and administrative costs are not product costs.

Selecting variable costing or absorption costing has an impact on inventory values and profits because the treatment of fixed factory overhead is different. Although the profit can differ under the two costing methods, profit under variable costing is not always higher or lower than absorption costing. The difference between profits under the two methods is determined by the relationship of production to sales. We have three possibilities, as follows:

		Net Income	
Production units equal sales units..........................	AC	=	VC
Production units greater than sales units (building inventory)....	AC	>	VC
Production units less than sales units (liquidating inventory)	AC	<	VC

AC = absorption costing
VC = variable costing

The magnitude of any difference in profits is a function of the fixed manufacturing costs per unit and the change in inventory levels.

Another observation about the difference between the two methods is the profit patterns over time with respect to production and sales strategies. Let's take the case of a constant production schedule over time while sales are allowed to fluctuate each period. The absorption costing net income will fluctuate up and down with sales but the constant production will have a leveling effect on the swings. In other words, the peaks will not be as high nor as low as the corresponding sales. Variable costing net income, on the other hand, will have swings the match those of sales, in both direction and relative height and depth. For the situation where production fluctuates while sales remain rather constant, a different story is told. Absorption costing net income will fluctuate with production, in both direction and relative height and depth. Variable costing net income will remain constant to correspond with sales.

Comparing Variable Costing and Absorption Costing

Let's assume that Kim Chang Company produces a single product, a vibrating sofa chair. In its first year, 1994, the company planned to make 120,000 chairs, actually produced 100,000 chairs, and sold 75,000 chairs at $135 wholesale. The costs for the year are below:

Manufacturing costs:
    Materials .... $19.00 per unit
    Labor .... 18.00 per unit
    Variable overhead .... 15.00 per unit
    Budgeted fixed overhead ($1,200,000 ÷ 120,000 units).... 10.00 per unit
    Actual fixed overhead ($1,200,000 ÷ 100,000 units) ...... 12.00 per unit

Marketing and administrative costs:
    Variable .... $13.00 per unit sold
    Fixed $800,000

The absorption costing income statement that reflects these results is as follows:

KIM CHANG COMPANY
INCOME STATEMENT (ABSORPTION COSTING)
FOR THE YEAR ENDED DECEMBER 31, 1994

Sales revenue ($135 × 75,000)		$10,125,000
Cost of sales: _(19+18+15)_		
Variable ($52 × 75,000)	$3,900,000	
Fixed ($10 × 75,000)	750,000	
Capacity variance ... _(2× 100,000)_	200,000	4,850,000
Gross profit		$ 5,275,000
Marketing and administrative expenses:		
Variable ($13 × 75,000)	$ 975,000	
Fixed	800,000	1,775,000
Net profit		$ 3,500,000

The variable costing income statement would not have a capacity variance because the fixed manufacturing costs are period costs and are, therefore, not charged to inventories. A variable costing income statement would be as follows:

KIM CHANG COMPANY
INCOME STATEMENT (VARIABLE COSTING)
FOR THE YEAR ENDED DECEMBER 31, 1994

Sales revenue ($135 × 75,000)		$10,125,000
Variable costs:		
Manufacturing ($52 × 75,000)	$3,900,000	
Marketing and administrative ($13 × 75,000)....	975,000	4,875,000
Contribution margin		$ 5,250,000
Fixed costs:		
Manufacturing	$1,200,000	
Marketing and administrative	800,000	2,000,000
Net profit		$ 3,250,000

Notice that the variable costing profit is lower than the profit from absorption costing. Why does this happen? The next section answers this question.

Reconciliation of Variable and Absorption Costing

The difference in net profit figures is due solely to the treatment of fixed manufacturing costs. Absorption costing includes those costs in the inventory costs; variable costing treats them as expenses to be charged to the period incurred. During any given time period, the amount of fixed costs in inventory will increase or decrease as production differs from sales. If production is greater than sales (as is the case above), fixed costs will be deferred to future periods in the inventory under absorption costing. These costs would be expensed under variable costing. Therefore, absorption costing will have a higher net profit. Conversely, if sales are greater than production, fixed costs in the beginning inventory are released in the current period and added to the fixed costs incurred during the current period. That means higher fixed costs in the income statement under absorption costing than under variable costing and the result is a lower net profit for absorption costing.

In the simplified case in which fixed overhead costs per unit are the same in beginning and ending inventories, the difference in net profits is exactly equal to the change in inventory units times the fixed overhead rate per unit. For Kim Chang Company, the change in inventory is:

Units produced	100,000
Units sold	75,000
Increase in inventory	25,000

Using a predetermined fixed overhead rate of $10 per unit, the difference in net profits is: $10 × 25,000 units = $250,000. Let's check the results as follows:

Absorption costing net profit	$3,500,000
Variable costing net profit	3,250,000
Difference	$ 250,000

When the fixed overhead costs are different in the beginning and ending inventories (typical when a company uses actual costs instead of predetermined overhead), the reconciliation of net profit figures involves more than just the change in inventories. To illustrate this, let's use the predetermined overhead rate information and perform the following calculation:

Net profit before taxes—absorption costing	$3,500,000
Add: Fixed costs brought into period through beginning inventory ($10 × 0 units)	0
	$3,500,000
Less: Fixed costs deferred in ending inventory ($10 × 25,000 units)	250,000
Net profit before taxes—variable costing	$3,250,000

In our case, no beginning inventory existed. Had we started the period with a beginning inventory, the units would have been multiplied by the fixed costs per unit in that inventory.

The reconciliation of net profits between the two costing methods is independent of inventory cost flow assumptions. That means a company can use FIFO, LIFO, or some average cost method, and the reconciliation of net profits follows the same procedures.

Arguments for Either Costing Method

Any manager can make a valid case for either variable or absorption costing. However, the primary arguments for and against are summarized in the discussion below:

1. **Short term versus long term**. Those who favor variable costing (we will call them the variable costers) believe it focuses on the short-term consequences of accounting and is more realistic of the way managers make decisions. Those who favor absorption costing (we will call them the absorption costers) assume that the long-run performance is more important and that absorption costing more appropriately reflects long-term consequences.

2. **Behavior of managers**. Variable costers assume that managers can easily adapt to a new accounting method with little cost. They further argue that managers will be rewarded for playing games with absorption reports. They specifically refer to a manager's ability to manipulate net profit by increasing or decreasing inventory levels that are valued under absorption costing. The absorption costers admit that occasional short-term decisions (i.e., amount of ending inventory to hold) will be made incorrectly. However, over the long term, the mistakes will be more obvious, and the "games" will be found out by competent superiors. Absorption costers might assert that incompetent managers cannot be suddenly rehabilitated by a change in accounting methods.

3. **Variable versus fixed costs**. Variable costers believe that costs can be easily and meaningfully divided into variable and fixed categories and that using a contribution margin is much more useful for planning and decision making and for control and performance evaluation. Since absorption costing is primarily for external reporting purposes, absorption costers do not see this distinction as meaningful for reports. They will also argue that managers can still make the cost behavior distinctions for internal purposes. They also point out that the variable/fixed split is not easily made in practice.

4. **External versus internal reports**. Variable costers argue that allowing external reporting requirements dominate how useful and meaningful information should be reported is not a valid philosophy for competent management. Since information should be geared to the needs of management, external requirements should not drive the internal accounting system. Absorption costers argue that to have one set of requirements for external reporting and another set for internal reporting gives managers conflicting and inconsistent information. It also forges an image that the company is hiding something in the two approaches.

Neither variable costing nor absorption costing is correct or incorrect. Their usefulness correlates with management's attitudes and with philosophies of organizational behavior. This means that some companies will find variable costing extremely useful while other companies will find it less meaningful.

Since the major difference between the two methods is the treatment of fixed costs as product or period costs, the difference in net profits disappears where little or no inventory of work in process or finished goods exists. For companies implementing JIT production procedures, inventories will be eliminated or substantially reduced. Hence, the difference in costing method loses significance in this environment. Also, this controversy is irrelevant to service organizations.

We do not want to create the impression that the contribution approach to reporting is irrelevant in any situation or for any organization. The contribution approach has many advantages for all types of reporting. The issues above relate only to the treatment of fixed costs as product or period costs.

SUMMARY

Gross profit analysis is one approach to evaluating changes that result in favorable or unfavorable variances in gross profit. A sales price variance indicates the differences caused by changes in sales prices. A cost variance isolates the dollar amount associated with changes in costs of goods sold. A sales mix variance, for a company with multiple products, measures the change in gross profit due to shifts in the sales mix of the products. A sales volume variance (sales quantity variance for companies with multiple products) measures changes due to higher or lower total units sold than expected.

Operating expenses can also be analyzed by using variances. Spending and volume variances are the two most commonly calculated. A spending variance shows the difference between actual expenses and a flexible budget for the level of activity achieved. It consists of variable and fixed costs. The volume variance is the difference between the flexible budget and the budget for the original level planned. It consists only of variable costs.

Gross profit analysis and variances for operating expenses can also be applied when the income statement is prepared under a contribution approach. The variances for a contribution margin are sales price, cost (variable only), sales mix, and sales quantity. For the fixed costs, the only variance is a spending variance.

When a production process is based on a recipe or formula for inputs of various categories of materials and classes of labor and the materials and labor are somewhat interchangeable, a new set of variances occur. Mix and yield variances replace the materials quantity variance and labor efficiency variance. Mix variances show the cost changes due to combining quantities of materials or labor in a ratio that differs from standard specifications. Yield variances show the cost changes that result from an actual yield of finished product that is different from the standard yield for given inputs of materials or labor.

Variable costing includes only variable manufacturing costs as an element of product cost. The traditional method of income statement preparation is called absorption costing. It includes fixed manufacturing costs as an element of product cost. As a result of this difference, net profit under the two methods will not necessarily be the same. Anytime production exceeds sales, absorption costing yields a higher net profit; when sales exceed production, variable costing yields a higher net profit. The arguments for and against using either costing method apply to individual situations and management philosophy. Neither method is inherently correct or incorrect.

PROBLEMS FOR REVIEW

Review Problem A

Moats Designer Interiors produces three products that are somewhat interchangeable in the marketplace. Budgeted and operating results for the month were as follows:

	Sales Units	Sales Revenue	Cost of Sales	Gross Profit
Budget:				
AB-3	25,000	$ 500,000	$ 300,000	$200,000
AC-4	10,000	600,000	400,000	200,000
AD-5	15,000	1,050,000	975,000	75,000
	50,000	$2,150,000	$1,675,000	$475,000*
Actual:				
AB-3	27,000	$ 540,000	$ 270,000	$270,000
AC-4	8,000	520,000	320,000	200,000
AD-5	19,000	1,501,000	1,368,000	133,000
	54,000	$2,561,000	$1,958,000	$603,000
Variance in gross profit				$128,000

* Average budget gross profit: $475,000 ÷ 50,000 = $9.50

The marketing expenses are based on a budget formula of $20,000 plus 5 percent of sales revenue. Actual marketing expenses for the month are $132,400. Administrative expenses follow a budget formula of $50,000 plus 2 percent of sales revenue. Actual administrative expenses for the month totaled $89,200.

Required:

1.   Calculate the following variances and show that they equal the change in gross profit:

    a)   Sales price variance.
    b)   Cost variance.
    c)   Sales mix variance.
    d)   Sales quantity variance.

2.   Calculate individual spending and volume variances for:
    a)   Marketing expenses.
    b)   Administrative expenses.

Solution:

1.   a) Sales price variance:

	Actual Sales Units	Actual Price − Budgeted Price	Variance
AB-3	27,000	($20.00 − $20.00)	$ 0
AC-4	8,000	($65.00 − $60.00)	40,000 F
AD-5	19,000	($79.00 − $70.00)	171,000 F
			$211,000 F

b) Cost variance:

	Actual Sales Units	Actual Cost − Budgeted Cost	Variance
AB-3	27,000	($10.00 − $12.00)	$54,000 F
AC-4	8,000	($40.00 − $40.00)	0
AD-5	19,000	($72.00 − $65.00)	133,000 U
			$79,000 U

c) Sales mix variance:

	Budgeted Units	Budgeted Mix Proportions
AB-3	25,000	50%
AC-4	10,000	20%
AD-5	15,000	30%
	50,000	

Restate the total actual units of 54,000 to the budgeted mix, as follows:

	Total Actual Quantity × Mix Proportion
AB-3	54,000 × 50% = 27,000
AC-4	54,000 × 20% = 10,800
AD-5	54,000 × 30% = 16,200
	54,000

	Actual Units	Actual Units Restated	Difference	Difference in Gross Profit	Variance
AB-3	27,000	27,000	0	$ 8.00 − $9.50	$ 0
AC-4	8,000	10,800	(2,800)	$20.00 − $9.50	29,400 U
AD-5	19,000	16,200	2,800	$ 5.00 − $9.50	12,600 U
	54,000	54,000			$42,000 U

d) Sales quantity variance:

(Actual units − budgeted units) × average budgeted gross profit
(54,000 − 50,000) × $9.50 = $38,000 F

Summary of variances:

Sales price variance .... $211,000 F
Cost variance ....   79,000 U
Sales mix variance ....   42,000 U
Sales quantity variance......................................   38,000 F

Increase in gross profit .... $128,000 F

2.   a) Marketing expenses:

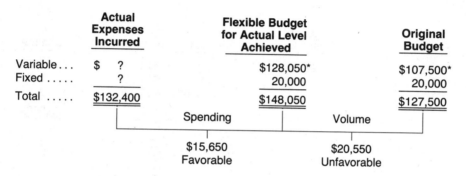

	Actual Expenses Incurred		Flexible Budget for Actual Level Achieved		Original Budget
Variable...	$?		$128,050*		$107,500*
Fixed	?		20,000		20,000
Total	$132,400		$148,050		$127,500

	Spending		Volume
	$15,650 Favorable		$20,550 Unfavorable

* 5% × $2,561,000 and 5% × $2,150,000

b) Administrative expenses:

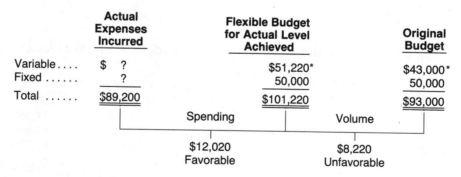

	Actual Expenses Incurred		Flexible Budget for Actual Level Achieved		Original Budget
Variable....	$?		$51,220*		$43,000*
Fixed	?		50,000		50,000
Total	$89,200		$101,220		$93,000

	Spending		Volume
	$12,020 Favorable		$8,220 Unfavorable

* 2% × $2,561,000 and 2% × $2,150,000

Review Problem B

The sales manager of Remagen Machine Company, Inc., objects to the accounting procedure in costing the manufactured products. She states that sales were lost from a failure to grant price concessions to customers. By including fixed overhead as a part of product cost, the costs are, of course, higher than they would be under variable costing. As a result, the president is reluctant to authorize sales below the full cost. But at any price above the unit variable cost, the sales manager states that the company can earn additional profits. Furthermore, she believes that the income statements give a false picture by shifting fixed costs from one year to another as a part of inventory cost.

The chief financial officer defends the accounting policy. The objective, he says, is to maintain prices and gain a reputation for quality products at an established price. Too many companies, he continues, have been shortsighted and have spoiled their markets at an established price by granting price concessions merely to get volume. Profits are not earned until after all costs are covered, and each unit of product should bear a share of the fixed overhead.

Cost and sales data are given for the past 3 years:

Year	Units Produced	Units Sold
1992	20,000	16,000
1993	25,000	22,000
1994	25,000	30,000

No inventories were on hand at the beginning of 1992. The company increased inventories over the three years in anticipation of growth in sales volume. Manufacturing cost per unit was constant throughout the three years and appears as:

Materials	$140
Labor	80
Variable overhead	40
	$260

The fixed factory overhead of $8,750,000 each year has been applied to the product units on the basis of normal production of 25,000 units per year and amounts to $350 per unit. The marketing and administrative expenses have averaged $40 per unit sold for variable costs and a total of $750,000 per year. The selling price remained the same throughout the three years at $720 per unit.

Required:

1. Prepare an income statement using absorption costing for each of the three years.
2. Prepare an income statement using variable costing for each of the three years.
3. Reconcile the difference in profits between the two statements for each of the three years.

Solution:

1. Three-year comparative income statement with absorption costing:

REMAGEN MACHINE COMPANY, INC.
INCOME STATEMENT (ABSORPTION COSTING)
FOR THE YEARS 1992, 1993, AND 1994

	1992	1993	1994
Units sold	16,000	22,000	30,000
Units produced	20,000	25,000	25,000
Sales	$ 11,520,000	$15,840,000	$21,600,000
Cost of goods sold:			
Inventory, beginning	$ 0	$ 2,440,000	$ 4,270,000
Current production at $610 per unit	12,200,000	15,250,000	15,250,000
	$ 12,200,000	$17,690,000	$19,520,000
Inventory, ending	2,440,000	4,270,000	1,220,000
Cost of goods sold	$ 9,760,000	$13,420,000	$18,300,000
Capacity variance	1,750,000	0	0
Adjusted cost of goods sold	$ 11,510,000	$13,420,000	$18,300,000
Gross profit	$ 10,000	$ 2,420,000	$ 3,300,000
Marketing and administrative expenses:			
Variable	$ 640,000	$ 880,000	$ 1,200,000
Fixed	750,000	750,000	750,000
	$ 1,390,000	$ 1,630,000	$ 1,950,000
Net profit (loss)	$ (1,380,000)	$ 790,000	$ 1,350,000

2. Three-year comparative income statement with variable costing.

REMAGEN MACHINE COMPANY, INC.
INCOME STATEMENT (VARIABLE COSTING)
FOR THE YEARS 1992, 1993, AND 1994

	1992	1993	1994
Units sold	16,000	22,000	30,000
Units produced	20,000	25,000	25,000
Sales	$ 11,520,000	$15,840,000	$21,600,000
Variable cost of goods sold:			
Inventory, beginning	$ 0	$ 1,040,000	$ 1,820,000
Current production at $260 per unit	5,200,000	6,500,000	6,500,000
	$ 5,200,000	$ 7,540,000	$ 8,320,000
Inventory, ending	1,040,000	1,820,000	520,000
	$ 4,160,000	$ 5,720,000	$ 7,800,000
Marketing and administrative expenses:			
Variable	640,000	880,000	1,200,000
Total variable costs	$ 4,800,000	$ 6,600,000	$ 9,000,000
Contribution margin	$ 6,720,000	$ 9,240,000	$12,600,000
Fixed costs:			
Manufacturing	$ 8,750,000	$ 8,750,000	$ 8,750,000
Marketing and administrative	750,000	750,000	750,000
	$ 9,500,000	$ 9,500,000	$ 9,500,000
Net profit (loss)	$ (2,780,000)	$ (260,000)	$ 3,100,000

3. Reconciliation of net profits between the two costing methods:
   Change in units approach:

	1992	1993	1994
Change in inventory	4,000	3,000	(5,000)
Fixed overhead	× $350	× $350	× $350
	$ 1,400,000	$1,050,000	$(1,750,000)

Step approach:

	1992	1993	1994
Net profit—absorption costing	$(1,380,000)	$ 790,000	$ 1,350,000
Add: Fixed costs in beginning inventory:			
$350 × 0	0		
$350 × 4,000		1,400,000	
$350 × 7,000			2,450,000
	$(1,380,000)	$2,190,000	$ 3,800,000
Less: Fixed costs in ending inventory			
$350 × 4,000	1,400,000		
$350 × 7,000		2,450,000	
$350 × 2,000			700,000
Net profit—variable costing	$(2,780,000)	$ (260,000)	$ 3,100,000

TERMINOLOGY REVIEW

Absorption costing (506)
Contribution margin (499)
Cost variance (490)
Gross profit analysis (488)
Gross profit (or gross margin) (488)
Mix variance (504)
Operating expenses (497)
Sales mix variance (494)

Sales price variance (490)
Sales quantity variance (495)
Sales volume variance (491)
Spending variance (498)
Variable costing (506)
Volume variance (498)
Yield variance (505)

QUESTIONS FOR REVIEW AND DISCUSSION

1. What is the difference between gross profit and contribution margin?

2. What are the principal factors influencing gross profit for single products? For multiple products?

3. Why should gross profit and contribution margin variances be based on different activity measures than manufacturing cost variances?

4. Explain why a single product firm will not have a sales mix variance in a gross profit analysis.

5. From where does a cost variance come?

6. When is it appropriate to compute sales mix and sales quantity variances rather than a single sales volume variance?

7. Cite several causes for each of the following variances:
   a) Sales price variance.
   b) Cost variance.
   c) Sales mix variance.
   d) Sales quantity variance.

8. How do changes in the sales mix influence profits?

9. Explain why an increased sales volume in units sold is not always a way to earn higher profits.

10. A company sells a variety of products with different gross profit margins. Explain how it is possible for total gross profit to move in the opposite direct from sales revenue even though selling prices and unit costs remain the same.

11. Explain how a sales mix variance differs from a sales quantity variance.

12. What effect do standard costs in manufacturing have on a gross profit analysis?

13. We normally assume that the production function does not influence sales price, mix, or quantity variances. The responsibility for these variances usually rests with the marketing function. How could the production function have a direct impact on sales mix or sales quantity variances?

14. Any production variances isolated in a standard cost system must be disposed of by the end of the period. Significant variances are prorated to appropriate inventory accounts and Cost of Goods Sold. Insignificant variances are closed to Cost of Goods Sold. Explain how the disposition of variances influences the analysis of gross profit. How would the summary of variances for reporting purposes change?

15. Identify three limitations of gross profit analysis.

16. What are the components of a spending variance for operating expenses? How does a volume variance differ from a spending variance?

17. Why is an understanding of cost behavior important to interpreting operating expense variances?

18. When performing a contribution margin analysis, how will variable marketing or administrative costs be included in calculating sales mix and sales quantity variances?

19. Why will fixed operating expenses be subject only to a spending variance calculation when a contribution margin analysis is used?

20. Differentiate between variable costing and absorption costing.

21. Why is it impossible for a company to incur an overhead capacity variance when variable costing is used?

22. Explain whether variable costing or absorption costing will have the higher net profit under each of the following conditions:
   a)   Production equals sales.
   b)   Production exceeds sales.
   c)   Production is less than sales.

23. How is it possible to increase net profit using absorption costing when sales are not increasing?

24. Identify the four major categories of arguments for variable costing or absorption costing.

25. A company had a highly labor-intensive manufacturing process. Recently it implemented robotics and a number of other technological changes that made the process capital intensive. What impact would this change make on the inventory valuations for variable costing and for absorption costing?

26. How is it possible to show zero profit at a break-even point using variable costing, but show a profit using absorption costing?

27. Under what conditions should a materials quantity variance be divided into materials mix and yield variances?

28. Should labor mix and yield variances be calculated and reported when the production manager has no control over the number of workers of each category? Explain why or why not.

EXERCISES

1. **Gross Profit Analysis with a Single Product.** The following information pertains to the single product of Colby Company:

	Budget	Actual
Sales units	2,500	3,000
Sales	$20,000	$22,500
Cost of sales	15,000	19,500
Gross profit	$ 5,000	$ 3,000

Required:

Compute the following gross profit variances:
a) Sales price variance.
b) Cost variance.
c) Sales volume variance.

2. **Gross Profit and Operating Expense Analysis with a Single Product.** Greensboro Designer Lamps prepared the following budgetary information for June 1995 for its Teen Lamp line:

Sales revenue (24,000 lamps)	$528,000
Cost of goods sold	312,000
Gross profit	$216,000
Operating expenses:	
($1 per lamp sold + $46,000)	70,000
Net profit	$146,000

Actual operations resulted in the production and sale of 25,000 units at an average selling price of $20 per unit. The cost of goods sold per unit equaled the budgeted unit cost. The operating expenses totaled $65,000.

Required:
1. Prepare an income statement that compares actual and budgeted amounts and shows the variance.
2. Determine the following gross profit variances:
   a) Sales price variance.
   b) Cost variance.
   c) Sales volume variance.
3. Determine the variances for the operating expenses:
   a) Spending variance.
   b) Volume variance.

3. **Contribution Margin Analysis for a Single Product.** Auto-Alarm, Inc. manufactures an auto alarm that attaches to the steering wheel. Each alarm has a budgeted wholesale price of $110. For April, the budget called for 2,000 alarms produced and sold with variable costs totalling $120,000. Fixed costs appeared in the budget at $50,000 for the month. During the month, the company actually produced and sold 1,900 alarms at an average wholesale price of $112. The variable costs were $55 per unit and fixed costs were $52,000.

Required:
1. Compute the contribution margin under budgeted and actual results.
2. Determine the following contribution margin variances:
   a) Sales price variance.
   b) Cost variance.
   c) Sales volume variance.

4. **Profit Analysis in Single Product Case.** The Suitland Company manufactures a single product. In the first quarter of 1994, it realized the following results:

	Actual	Budget	Variance
Sales revenue	$420,000	$400,000	$20,000
Variable costs	280,500	240,000	40,500
Contribution margin	$139,500	$160,000	$(20,500)
Fixed costs	132,500	120,000	12,500
Net profit	$ 7,000	$ 40,000	$(33,000)

Rita Suitland, President, expresses concern over the company's inability to achieve the budgeted profit level. She notes that the sales price increased $2 per unit in an attempt to cover higher materials and labor costs. The increased price apparently influenced volume because only 35,000 units were sold. That is 5,000 units less than budgeted. The variable and fixed costs include all variable costs of manufacturing, marketing, and administration.

Required:
1. Calculate the following contribution margin variances:
   a) Sales price variance.
   b) Cost variance.
   c) Sales volume variance.
2. Show that the above variances equal the change in contribution margin.
3. Calculate the following fixed cost variances:
   a) Spending variance.
   b) Volume variance.

5. **Variances for Individual Operating Expenses.** Anemia Manufacturing Company uses a budget formula for estimating its marketing and administrative expenses. The fixed and variable components of this formula for individual costs are:

Cost Category	Fixed Cost Per Month	Variable Cost Per Unit Sold
Salary and wages	$1,750	$0.90
Rent of space..................................	1,000	0.60
Freight out	0	0.15
Miscellaneous	250	0.05
	$3,000	$1.70

The company budgeted 10,000 units of sales for the month. It actually sold 9,200 units and incurred the following marketing and administrative expenses:

Salary and wages	$10,230
Rent of space...	6,710
Freight out	1,280
Miscellaneous	680
	$18,900

Required:
For each of the individual cost categories, compute the spending and volume variances, and indicate whether they are favorable or unfavorable.

6. **Analysis of Operating Expenses.** Sonora Company has marketing and administrative expenses that follow a fixed and variable cost behavior as follows:

Fixed cost per month	$15,000
Variable cost, based on sales	6%

Sales were budgeted at $150,000 for the month. Actual sales were $160,000 and marketing and administrative expenses were $24,000.

Required:
1. Compute the following marketing and administrative expense variances, and indicate whether they are favorable or unfavorable.
    a)   Spending variance.
    b)   Volume variance.
2. Explain whether the costs in each of the two foregoing variances are fixed or variable.

7. **Gross Profit Analysis for Multiple Products.** Waverly Brothers Company has two major products that it has been distributing through a network marketing organization in the southeastern United States. The data from 1993 showed the following results:

	Suede	Hi-gloss
Units sold	200,000	300,000
Sales price per unit	$5.00	$6.00
Cost of sales per unit	3.00	3.20

Comparable data for 1994 appear as follows:

	Suede	Hi-gloss
Units sold	120,000	380,000
Sales price per unit	$5.50	$5.90
Cost of sales per unit	3.10	3.00

Required:

1. Determine the change in gross profit between the two years.
2. Compute the following gross profit variances:
   a)   Sales price variance.
   b)   Cost variance.
   c)   Sales mix variance.
   d)   Sales quantity variance.
3. Cite four potential causes for the mix variances in (2) above.

8.   **Gross Profit and Operating Expense Analysis.** Chavez Walkie-Talkie makes two models of its favorite product. Budgeted and actual results for 1994 appear in the following income statement:

CHAVEZ WALKIE-TALKIE
INCOME STATEMENT
FOR THE YEAR ENDED DECEMBER 31, 1994

	Budget	Actual
Units:		
Distance	3,000	3,200
Around Town	6,000	6,300
Sales revenue	$1,080,000	$1,120,850
Cost of sales	756,000	829,445
Gross profit	$ 324,000	$ 291,405
Operating expenses	174,000	198,000
Net profit	$ 150,000	$ 93,405
Selling prices per unit:		
Distance	$ 166.00	$ 162.25
Around Town	97.00	95.50
Cost of sales per unit:		
Distance	$ 116.20	$ 120.07
Around Town	67.90	70.67

Operating expenses follow a budget formula of $10 per unit sold plus $84,000.

Required:

1. Determine the change in gross profit between budget and actual.
2. Calculate all appropriate gross profit variances for this situation.
3. Compute spending and volume variances for the operating expenses.
4. Explain how the sales quantity variance and the volume variance for operating expenses are related.

9. **Analysis of Contribution Margin.** Fairpoint-Ross Distributing has developed the following monthly budget for its two versions of a product:

	Regular	Deluxe	Total
Sales units	240,000	120,000	360,000
Revenues	$2,400,000	$2,160,000	$4,560,000
Variable costs	1,200,000	930,000	2,130,000
Contribution margin..................	$1,200,000	$1,230,000	$2,430,000

Actual results for the month were:

	Regular	Deluxe	Total
Sales units	250,000	100,000	350,000
Revenues	$2,750,000	$1,800,000	$4,550,000
Variable costs	1,375,000	750,000	2,125,000
Contribution margin..................	$1,375,000	$1,050,000	$2,425,000

Required:
1. Prepare an analysis of changes in the contribution margin that shows the following variances:
    a) Sales price variance.
    b) Cost variance.
    c) Sales mix variance.
    d) Sales quantity variance.
2. Comment on the possible interrelationships among the four variances in (1) above.

10. **Analysis of Contribution Margin.** The Frenchglen Company shows the following budgeted and actual data for sales and variable costs of each of its three products for December 1995:

	Units	Unit Sales Price	Variable Cost Per Unit
Budget:			
ChemTech	20,000	$10.00	$6.00
AgriGro	18,000	12.00	7.00
WeedOut..........................	12,000	6.00	2.50
Actual:			
ChemTech	19,000	$11.50	$6.00
AgriGro	18,000	10.50	7.25
WeedOut..........................	13,000	6.30	2.30

Required:
1. Compute the contribution margin at both the budget and actual levels, showing sales revenue, variable costs, and contribution margin.
2. Determine the following variances for the contribution margin:
    a) Sales price variance.
    b) Cost variance.
    c) Sales volume variance.
    d) Sales mix variance.
    e) Sales quantity variance.

3.   Show that the sales mix and sales quantity variances equal the sales volume
      variance.
4.   Show that the variances in (2) above explain the change in contribution margin.

11. **Variable and Absorption Costing Income Statements.** Casselton Agricultural Prod-
     ucts, Inc. started producing and selling a new product in 1994. Selected operating re-
     sults for this new product line for its first year of operations are as follows:

Units	
Produced	16,000
Sold	14,500
Sales price per unit	$ 12
Variable costs:	
Direct materials	$44,000
Direct labor	36,000
Factory overhead	16,000
Marketing and administration	12,000
Fixed costs:	
Factory overhead	$40,000
Marketing and administration	20,000

Required:
1.   Prepare an income statement for the year using the variable costing method.
2.   Prepare an income statement for the year using the absorption costing method.
3.   Prepare a reconciliation of net profits resulting from the two methods.

12. **Variable Costing.** Last year Rhao & Sons Co. operated at 250,000 units when it had a
     normal capacity of 300,000. The income statement for the year, prepared on an absorp-
     tion costing basis, is given below:

Units made and sold	250,000
Sales revenue	$2,000,000
Cost of goods sold (includes a capacity variance)	1,500,000
Gross profit	$ 500,000
Marketing and administrative expenses (includes variable costs of	
$125,000)	225,000
Profit before income taxes	$ 275,000
Income taxes	110,000
Profit after income taxes	$ 165,000

     The fixed manufacturing cost per unit of product is $3.00.

Required:
     Revise the income statement to place it on a variable costing basis.

13. **Variable Costing and Inventory Increase.** In 1994, Criswell Manufacturing Company
     plans to operate at normal capacity and manufacture 400,000 units of product. Sales for
     the year have been estimated at 350,000 units with total revenue at $17,500,000. The
     cost of the 20,000 units in the finished goods inventory on January 1, 1993, was $600,000.

Included in this amount was $400,000 in fixed manufacturing overhead. No changes in fixed manufacturing costs are expected in 1994, and the variable cost per unit of product will also remain unchanged.

Required:

1. Prepare an estimated income statement for 1994 under absorption costing.
2. Prepare an estimated income statement for 1994 under variable costing.
3. Explain why the income from manufacturing is higher under absorption costing than under variable costing. Your explanation should also include a flow of fixed costs under absorption costing in which you identify the fixed cost coming in with the beginning inventory, new fixed costs, and fixed costs deferred in the ending inventory.

14. **Unequal Sales and Production and Variable Costing.** Treadwell Memory Chips reduced its finished goods inventory in 1995 from 80,000 units at the beginning of the year to 50,000 units. Fixed manufacturing overhead of $1,360,000 was applied to the 170,000 units produced during the year. The manufacturing overhead capacity variance for the year was $240,000 unfavorable. Variable manufacturing cost per unit was $9. Each unit of product was sold for $20.

Required:

1. Prepare an income statement for the manufacturing operation in 1995 using absorption costing.
2. Prepare an income statement for the manufacturing operation in 1995 using variable costing.
3. Provide a reconciliation for the difference in profit between the two methods.

15. **Mix and Yield Variance Analysis.** Moab Automotive Products, Inc. blends chemicals and petroleum products such as antifreeze, windshield washer fluid, oil additives, and gasoline additives. One of the gasoline additives is a blend of methane, ethane, and alcohol. The following standard product cost specification has been developed for each 100-barrel batch of the product.

	Standard Input Quantity	Standard Price per Barrel
Methane	60 barrels	$ 5.00
Alcohol	50 barrels	$10.00
Ethane.	10 barrels	$ 8.00
	120 barrels	

Due to evaporation and spillage, the standard yield is expected to be 20 barrels less than the total raw materials input.

During September 1995, the company produced 50,000 barrels of additive. The following production results were reported:

Inputs Consumed	Quantity	Costs
Methane	32,000 barrels	$146,250
Alcohol	28,000 barrels	266,000
Ethane.	45,000 barrels	361,250
	105,000 barrels	$773,500

Required:
1. Calculate the materials price and quantity variances.
2. Calculate the materials mix variance.
3. Calculate the materials yield variance.
4. Show that the sum of the materials mix and yield variances is equal to the materials quantity variance.

16. **Labor Mix and Yield Variances.** Wyocena Specialty Products, Inc., has developed standard labor cost specifications for the labor input of its current major product:

> Class A Skill: 3 hours at $15
> Class B Skill: 5 hours at $10

During January, the company produced 10,000 units of this product and incurred the following labor costs:

> Class A Skill: 28,000 hours for $ 448,000
> Class B Skill: 64,000 hours for   704,000
> $1,152,000

Required:
1. Compute the labor rate variance.
2. Compute a total labor efficiency variance.
3. Compute the labor mix variance.
4. Compute the labor yield variance.
5. Show that the sum of the mix and yield variances equals the total labor efficiency variance.

17. **Materials and Labor Mix and Yield Variances.** Winnett Fixtures makes Execu-Tech, a product that requires two types of materials and two classes of labor. The following specifications for materials and labor appear on the standard cost sheet:

Materials:
LM-24 (20 units at $4 per unit) .... $ 80
Walnut (10 units at $5 per unit) 50 $130

Labor:
Class 1 (12 hours at $10 per hour) $120
Class 2 (4 hours at $13 per hour) 52 $172

For March, the company produced 1,500 units of Execu-Tech. Materials and labor results were:

Materials:
LM-24 (31,500 units) $133,875
Walnut (14,950 units) 76,245 $210,120

Labor:
Class 1 (17,450 hours) $177,990
Class 2 (5,950 hours) 77,350 $255,340

Required:
1. Calculate the following variances for materials:
   a) Materials price variance.
   b) Materials mix variance.
   c) Materials yield variance.
2. Calculate the following variances for labor:
   a) Labor rate variance.
   b) Labor mix variance.
   c) Labor yield variance.

PROBLEMS

10-1. Gross Profit and Contribution Margin Analysis with Single Product. Dorchester Company developed the following budget for the first quarter of 1995:

Sales (10,000 units)			$200,000
Cost of goods sold:			
Inventory, January 1 (2,000 units at $12).....		$ 24,000	
Cost of goods manufactured:			
Variable costs.........................	$88,000		
Fixed costs	44,000	132,000	
		$156,000	
Inventory, March 31 (3,000 units at $12)		36,000	120,000
Gross profit			$ 80,000
Operating expenses:			
Variable (per unit sold)		$ 30,000	
Fixed		20,000	50,000
Net Income			$ 30,000

During the quarter, actual sales were 11,000 units and total revenue was $231,000. Production totaled 12,000 units with fixed costs of $45,000 and variable costs of $102,000. Beginning inventory costs were $8 variable and $4 fixed. Marketing and administrative expenses were $34,000 for variable costs and $21,000 for fixed costs.

Required:
1. Prepare an income statement for the actual results of the first quarter. Use the same format as the budgeted income statement above.
2. Perform a gross profit and operating expense analysis and determine the following variances:
   a) Gross profit variances:
       i)   Sales price variance.
       ii)   Cost variance.
       iii) Sales volume variance.
   b) Operating expenses:
       i)   Spending variance.
       ii)   Volume variance.
3. Prepare an income statement that shows the budgeted and actual information in a contribution margin format.
4. Perform a contribution margin and operating expense analysis and determine the following variances:

    a)   Contribution margin variances:
         i)   Sales price variance.
         ii)   Cost variance.
         iii) Sales volume variance.
    b)   Operating expenses:
         i)   Spending variance.
         ii)   Volume variance.

10-2. Gross Profit Analysis for Single and Multiple Products. Kruk Company produces and sells two versions of its electronic Bible: standard and student. The budgeted sales and cost of sales for 1994 are as follows:

	Standard	Student
Sales units	10,000	5,000
Sales revenue	$2,750,000	$1,000,000
Cost of sales	1,650,000	650,000
Gross profit.....................................	$1,100,000	$ 350,000

The actual figures for 1994 show the following sales and operating results:

	Standard	Student
Sales units	12,000	9,000
Sales revenue	$3,072,000	$1,845,000
Cost of sales	2,040,000	1,199,250
Gross profit.....................................	$1,032,000	$ 645,750

Required:
1. Treating each version of the electronic Bible as a single product, calculate the following gross profit variances:
    a)   Sales price variance.
    b)   Cost variance.
    c)   Sales volume variance.
2. Treating the two products as a mix, calculate the following gross profit variances:
    a)   Sales price variance.
    b)   Cost variance.
    c)   Sales mix variance.
    d)   Sales quantity variance.
3. Give possible reasons why the variances in (2) occurred. Include any interrelationships of variances you think are pertinent.
4. Explain how the sales volume variance in (1a) is related to the sales mix and sales quantity variances in (2).

10-3. Contribution Margin Analysis for Multiple Products. Permian DuneBuggy Company is the distributor of dune buggies that are popular in southwest Texas. Three models are available and they have the following budgeted information for the year:

	Dust Eater	Track Maker	Sand Blaster
Sales units	300	200	100
Selling price	$2,500	$3,500	$4,500
Distributor cost	1,500	2,100	2,800
Handling expenses	150	200	250
Contribution margin	850	1,200	1,450

Actual results for the year varied from the plan for several reasons. Due to major weather conditions in Japan, certain parts for the Track Maker were delivered late to the manufacturer and all distributors were cut back on the number of Track Makers available to them. Consequently, Permian DuneBuggy had only 150 units which it sold. The Sand Blaster had a safety issue raised by a consumer group which caused the manufacturer to discontinue the model. Distributors were instructed to sell their stocks at substantially reduced prices. The distributor cost remained at $2,800 but the selling price for Permian DuneBuggy was $3,000. They had only 50 units in stock and sold all of them. Because of the high demand for dune buggies, the customers gobbled up the Dust Eater. The company was able to purchase and sell 600 at an average selling price of $2,650. The handling costs averaged 10% of the distributors' costs. The distributors' cost for the Dust Eater turned out to be $1,450 per unit and the Track Maker was $2,150 per unit.

Required:

1. Prepare a contribution margin income statement that shows the budgeted results for each of the dune buggies and in total.
2. Prepare a contribution margin income statement that shows the actual results for each of the dune buggies and in total.
3. Calculate the following contribution margin variances:
    a) Sales price variance.
    b) Cost variance.
    c) Sales mix variance.
    d) Sales quantity variance.
4. Explain why the variances occurred. (What is the source of the variances?)

10-4. **Contribution Margin Analysis for Services Lines.** Duncan Tour Service arranges and conducts travel tours for vacationists in the eastern states. Three basic tours are conducted: New York City, Cape Cod, and Williamsburg. Prices and variable costs per person have been estimated for each tour in 1995 as follows.

	Price	Variable cost
New York City	$400	$250
Cape Cod	350	175
Williamsburg	540	360

The fixed costs, such as the salaries of the managers and tour guides and office rent, have been estimated at $800,000 for the year.

An estimated income statement in summary form is given as follows:

	Total	New York	Cape Cod	Williamsburg
Number of customers	10,000	6,000	1,500	2,500
Revenue	$4,275,000	$2,400,000	$525,000	$1,350,000
Total cost*	3,462,500	1,980,000	382,500	1,100,000
Estimated income	$ 812,500	$ 420,000	$142,500	$ 250,000

*The fixed costs have been allocated to each tour on the basis of the estimated number of customers to be served.

Actual results for 1995 yield the following numbers:

	Customers	Price	Variable Cost
New York City	7,000	$390	$255
Cape Cod	1,000	330	175
Williamsburg	4,000	500	350
Fixed costs totaled $810,000.			

Required:

1. Restructure the estimated income statement into a contribution margin approach income statement.
2. Determine the actual contribution margin and actual profit.
3. For the contribution margin approach, calculate the following variances:
    a)   Sales price variance.
    b)   Cost variance.
    c)   Sales mix variance.
    d)   Sales quantity variance.
4. Calculate spending and volume variances for the fixed costs.
5. Present a rationale for why the change in profits went in the direction it did.

10-5. **Comprehensive Operating Expense Variance Analysis.** The Pomeroy Manufacturing Company budgeted 180,000 sales units for November. The product has a budgeted selling price of $21 and a manufacturing cost of $11.50 per unit. The company's flexible expense budget shows the following budget formulas for the operating expenses:

Administrative salaries and wages:	$50,000 + $.04 per unit sold
Sales salaries and wages:	$20,000 + $.06 per unit sold
Utilities:	$11,500 + $.15 per unit sold
Supplies:	$0.10 per unit sold
Travel and entertainment:	$.95 per unit sold
Depreciation:	$61,000
Property taxes:	$2,000

At the end of November, the accounting records showed the company had sold 195,000 units for a total of $4,000,000 and a cost of goods sold of $2,240,000. Actual costs for the operating expenses were:

Administrative salaries and wages	$56,800
Sales salaries and wages	33,600
Utilities	38,500
Supplies	19,560
Travel and entertainment	183,250
Depreciation	61,000
Property taxes	1,850
Total	$394,560

Required:

1. Prepare an income statement showing columns for both actual and budgeted results.
2. Calculate a spending variance for each of the individual operating expenses.
3. Calculate a volume variance for each of the individual operating expenses.
4. What type of cost behavior appears in the spending variance? What type appears in the volume variance?

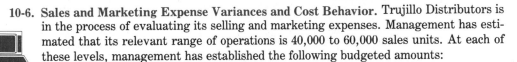

10-6. Sales and Marketing Expense Variances and Cost Behavior. Trujillo Distributors is in the process of evaluating its selling and marketing expenses. Management has estimated that its relevant range of operations is 40,000 to 60,000 sales units. At each of these levels, management has established the following budgeted amounts:

Sales units	40,000	60,000
Sales and marketing expenses:		
Transportation	$110,000	$150,000
Credit and collections	57,000	65,000
Direct selling......................................	19,800	26,200
Advertising and promotion	11,000	14,000

The company planned to operate at 48,000 units during 1995. It actually achieved 50,000 units during the year. Although the president is not comfortable that his managers are good cost estimators and feels they are not controlling costs, the accounting system is able to differentiate between variable and fixed costs. Actual costs incurred for sales and marketing activities are as follows:

	Variable	Fixed
Transportation	$109,000	$31,000
Credit and collections	23,505	42,185
Direct selling......................................	18,730	7,485
Advertising and promotion	7,248	4,690

Required:

1. Identify the budget formula for each individual sales and marketing expense.
2. Prepare an analysis for each expense that shows the spending and volume variances.
3. Do the variances suggest that the managers are good estimators of costs or that they may have difficulty controlling costs? Explain.

10-7. Variable Costing and Two Product Lines. Shupe Garden Implements manufactures lawn rakes and shovels at the Ames plant. Data with respect to sales and production have been estimated for next year as follows:

	Rakes	Shovels
Estimated units to be sold	240,000	160,000
Unit selling price	$3.50	$6.00
Unit variable cost of manufacturing....................	1.75	2.75
Production time per unit of product....................	10 min.	30 min.

The fixed overhead of the Ames plant is apportioned to the products at the rate of $3.00 each production hour. Total corporate fixed overhead of $300,000 has been apportioned to the Ames plant, but this is not apportioned to the products. Next year the company is expected to operate at normal capacity.

Required:
1. Assuming a variable costing approach, prepare an income statement that will show for each product line and in total:
    a) The contribution margin.
    b) The apportioned fixed overhead.
    c) The profit for each product.
    d) The final profit after recognizing apportionment of the corporate fixed overhead. (This assumes a variable costing approach.)
2. What is the expected total unit cost of each product line without apportioning the corporate fixed overhead?
3. Apportion corporate fixed overhead to each product on the basis of production time. Now, what is the expected total unit cost of each product line?
4. Which unit cost number would be best to use in establishing a cost-based selling price?

10-8. **Variable and Absorption Costing and Profit at the Break-Even Point.** The president of Schaucer Supply Company, Lola Schaucer, is surprised to learn that the company earned a profit in 1994 even though sales were at the break-even point.

"When we were going over the budget for 1994," she said, "I was told that we would have a poor year and could expect to break even with sales of only 206,000 units. Now, I find that we earned a small profit with sales of 206,000 units, although selling prices and costs were as budgeted. I am not complaining about a profit, mind you, but I can't understand how a profit can be made when operating at the break-even point."

Data pertaining to 1994 are given as follows:

$$\frac{\$3{,}090{,}000 \text{ (fixed production cost)}}{\$15 \text{ (unit contribution margin)}} = 206{,}000 \text{ units break even}$$

Unit selling price	$35
Unit variable cost	20
Unit contribution margin	$15

Fixed production costs are applied to products at $5 per unit, with 600,000 units being defined as normal production for a year. The inventory of finished goods was 30,000 units on January 1, 1994, and 80,000 units on December 31, 1994. The marketing and administrative expenses were fixed costs in the amount of $90,000. The income tax rate was 40 percent of profit before income taxes.

Required:
1. Prepare an income statement for 1994 using absorption costing.
2. Prepare an income statement for 1994 using variable costing.
3. Explain to the president how a small profit was made when using absorption costing and sales were at the break-even point
4. Explain whether the absorption costing income statement or the variable costing income statement gives the more realistic results.

10-9. Conversion of Absorption Costing to Variable Costing. Vanguard Electrical Supply Company manufactures electric switches and timing devices in three operating divisions: Utility, Household, and Commercial. An income statement, showing the results for each division, is given for 1994. The company operated at normal capacity in 1994 with total fixed manufacturing overhead of $8,900,000. Inventories were increased during the year in anticipation of more sales volume in 1995.

VANGUARD ELECTRICAL SUPPLY COMPANY
INCOME STATEMENT
FOR THE YEAR 1994
(IN THOUSANDS)

	Utility	Household	Commercial	Total
Net sales.....................	$6,200	$5,150	$6,300	$17,650
Cost of goods sold:				
Inventory, beginning	$ 540	$ 240	$ 150	$ 930
Production cost	5,400	4,000	4,200	13,600
Cost of merchandise available for sale	$5,940	$4,240	$4,350	$14,530
Less inventory, ending	900	640	900	2,440
Cost of goods sold	$5,040	$3,600	$3,450	$12,090
Manufacturing profit	$1,160	$1,550	$2,850	$ 5,560

The plant controller, Margaret Hubert, believes that profits may be higher than they would be otherwise because of fixed costs being carried over to the next year as a part of inventory. She would like to have the statement revised to a variable costing basis, and would like to know the manufacturing contribution margin for each division.

Additional analysis shows the units and unit variable costs as follows. There are no partially completed units.

	Utility	Household	Commercial
Units in beginning inventory	30,000	15,000	10,000
Units produced.......................	300,000	250,000	280,000
Units in ending inventory	50,000	40,000	60,000
Unit variable manufacturing cost	$6	$6	$5

Required:
1. Prepare an income statement on a variable costing basis that shows a contribution margin and direct profits by division and in total.
2. Prepare a reconciliation between the variable costing and absorption costing income statements. This reconciliation should show results by division and in total.
3. How much of the fixed cost was carried over to 1995 as a part of ending inventory cost for each division?

10-10. Creating Profits through Accounting Methods. The vice-president of sales, Dorey Rosen, gives the bad news to J. R. Wagoner, the vice-president of production: "Our sales volume will be 20 percent less than the 400,000 units we produced and sold last year. So, we may as well forget about year-end bonuses."

Wagoner smiles and replies, "We'll just pump the inventories up by producing 500,000 units. There is plenty of storage area in the warehouse."

"We'll never get away with it. The president will see what we are doing," Rosen answers.

"No, he knows nothing about accounting. Let me handle it, and we'll still get our bonuses."

Last year the company operated at normal capacity and made and sold 400,000 units of product. A summary manufacturing income statement is given as follows:

Units sold	400,000
Net sales...	$18,000,000
Cost of goods sold:	
Inventory, Jan. 1	$ 175,000
Production cost	14,000,000
Cost of merchandise available for sale........................	$14,175,000
Less inventory, Dec. 31	175,000
Cost of goods sold...	$14,000,000
Income from manufacturing	$ 4,000,000

Product cost includes fixed manufacturing overhead of $20 per product unit.

Required:

1.   How is Wagoner planning to build up the profits?
2.   Prepare an estimated income statement for the next year assuming that Rosen's estimate of sales is correct and that 500,000 units of product are manufactured. Use absorption costing.
3.   Recast the last year's manufacturing income statement and the estimated statement for this year on a variable costing basis.
4.   Discuss whether J.R. Wagoner is behaving in an ethical manner.

10-11. **Comparison of Absorption and Variable Costing.** Randolph Frame Factory has just completed three years of operation. Amy Randolph, president, has reviewed the audited financial statements for those three years and compared them to the statements her chief accountant prepared for internal use. She questions why the two sets of financial statements have different net income numbers. When asked about this, the chief accountant responded that the audited statements were prepared using absorption costing and the internal statements used variable costing. Amy still didn't understand why differences in net income would appear. She wants an analysis of the two results.

The selling price and cost data are identical for each of the three years and appear as follows:

Selling price per unit	$15.00
Manufacturing costs:	
Direct materials cost per unit	$2.80
Direct labor cost per unit....................................	4.70
Variable factory overhead per unit	.50
Fixed factory overhead in total................................	$120,000
Marketing and administrative expenses:	
Variable...	25% of sales
Fixed	$35,000

Units:

Year	Production	Sales
1992	60,000	50,000
1993	60,000	55,000
1994	50,000	60,000

The company uses a predetermined overhead rate for fixed costs based on normal capacity of 60,000 units per year.

Required:
1. Prepare a three-year comparative income statement using absorption costing.
2. Prepare a three-year comparative income statement using variable costing.
3. Reconcile the net income figures of absorption costing and variable costing for each of the three years.
4. Using a graph with sales units on the horizontal axis and dollars on the vertical axis, plot and connect the following points:
   a) Net income and sales units assuming absorption costing.
   b) Net income and sales units assuming the variable costing.
   c) The difference in net income between the two costing methods and their related sales units.
5. What conclusions can you derive from the graph in (4) about the advantages of the variable costing approach?

10-12. **Marketing and Administrative Expenses Analysis.** Hasluck Nwamadi, president of Nigerian Enterprises, a wholly-owned subsidiary of Worldwide Books, Inc., is concerned that marketing and administrative expenses are out of control. He is asking for your help to understand the costs and to identify possible ways of keeping the costs under control. He shows you the following report of actual costs for the month. You notice that someone entered the budget formula to the side of each cost.

Marketing expenses:

Sales salaries......................	$35,500	(4% of sales, $10,000 fixed)
Advertising	7,120	(1% of sales)
Sales expenses	15,240	(2% of sales, $2,000 fixed)
Misc. expenses	3,500	(1/2% of sales)
Depreciation	10,130	($10,000 fixed)
Total...........................	$71,490	

Administrative expenses:

Executive salaries	$20,000	($20,000 fixed)
General expenses	24,660	(3% of sales, $5,000 fixed)
Depreciation	4,950	($5,000 fixed)
Insurance	3,770	($3,000 fixed)
Property taxes	2,080	($2,000 fixed)
Total...........................	$55,460	

The company had budgeted $800,000 in sales for the month but actual sales showed a decrease and amounted to $700,000.

Required:

1.   Prepare a report that shows for each individual cost:
   a)   The actual costs.
   b)   Flexible budget at $700,000 sales.
   c)   Original budget at $800,000 sales.
   d)   Spending variance.
   e)   Volume variance.

2.   Explain whether this report indicates that the marketing and administrative costs are out of control.

10-13. **Gross Profit Analysis.** Artistic Beauty, Inc. is a high quality cosmetic company that sells its extensive product lines through high-end department stores. One product line consists of five products in hair care mousses: styling mousse, normal to oily mousse shampoo, normal to oily mousse rinse, normal to dry mousse shampoo, normal to dry mousse rinse. Units are defined in terms of cases. The sales representatives have considerable flexibility in negotiating wholesale prices with customer department stores.
   Actual production and sales data for May are as follows:

	Styling Mousse	N/O Shampoo	N/O Rinse	N/D Shampoo	N/D Rinse
Number of cases	8,000	3,000	4,000	7,000	5,000
Average selling price per case..................	$49.74	$48.93	$48.93	$52.29	$52.29
Average variable production cost	14.92	14.68	14.73	15.69	15.41
Average fixed production cost	5.00	5.00	5.00	5.00	5.00

   June operations are now complete and the actual production and sales data are available as follows:

	Styling Mousse	N/O Shampoo	N/O Rinse	N/D Shampoo	N/D Rinse
Number of cases	6,000	3,000	3,000	6,000	4,000
Average selling price per case..................	$51.23	$47.82	$48.99	$50.25	$50.78
Average variable production cost	14.92	15.01	14.88	14.13	14.21
Average fixed production cost	5.60	5.60	5.60	5.60	5.60

   The product line manager is concerned over the drop in volume from May to June. The sales representatives indicated that decrease in volume was costing them commissions and they were trying to negotiate higher prices to maintain their own income level. The primary change in variable production costs related to a change in quantities of ingredients purchased. The fixed production costs were higher basically because of a volume decrease.

Required:

1.   Prepare the gross profit section of an income statement for both May and June, and show the total variances for sales revenue, variable costs, fixed costs, and gross profit.

2. Analyze the gross profit to find the following information:
   a) Sales price variance.
   b) Cost variance.
   c) Sales mix variance.
   d) Sales quantity variance.
3. Summarize the variances and ascertain that the variances explain the change in gross profit.
4. Do the results suggest that the sales representatives were increasing prices as volume dropped? Explain.
5. Without calculating the variances, explain how the variances in a contribution margin analysis would differ from the variances you have calculated above.

10-14. **Labor Mix and Yield Variances.** Carter, Powell, Axelton & Co. is a regional CPA firm headquartered in Atlanta with offices throughout the southeastern United States. The firm has adopted a standard mix of personnel and time worked for each 100 billed hours of audit work:

	Cost	Hours	Standard Cost
Partners	$90	5	$ 450
Managers	40	20	800
Seniors	25	40	1,000
Staffs	18	60	1,080
Totals		125*	$3,330
Cost per Hour Billed			$33.30
Cost per Input Hour			$26.64

* Note that the firm expects that on average 80% of audit input hours will be billable to specific clients.

During February, the firm had the following results for the Atlanta audit practice:

	Cost	Time Sheet Hours
Partner	$ 63,056	901
Manager	141,700	4,109
Senior	216,621	9,208
Staff	248,096	12,412
Total	$669,473	26,630

Audit hours billed to clients: 20,500 Hours

Required:
1. Compute the audit labor rate variance for each level and the total.
2. Compute a audit labor efficiency variance for each level.
3. Compute the audit labor mix and yield variances. Explain how the mix and yield variances are related to the total audit labor efficiency variance.
4. Prepare a report by audit level of the costs and variances for the audit partner in charge.

10-15. **Contribution Margin Analysis with Materials Mix and Yield Variances.** Rio Grande Canners purchases fruit from the many growers in the Rio Grande Valley of south Texas. The company processes the fruit for canning. During processing, the fruit is graded into three classes: (1) Grade A, canned and sold under its own label; (2) Grade B, canned and sold to discount food chains; and (3) Grade C, which consists of pieces, canned and sold in Mexico.

Each ton of raw fruit (2,000 pounds) should yield 1,800 pounds of salable product. The standard specifications for the mix of grades per ton of fruit is 900 pounds of Grade A, 600 pounds of Grade B, and 300 pounds of Grade C. The processing costs are fixed and run about $20,000 per month. In a normal month, the company will process forty tons of fruit. Raw fruit has a standard cost of $0.75 per pound. The budgeted selling prices, although fruit is sold in cans, average per pound at: Grade A, $2.00; Grade B, $1.50; and Grade C, $0.80.

During May, forty tons of raw fruit were purchased at $0.65 per pound. The fixed processing costs equaled the budgeted amount of $20,000. Processing resulted in the following output and actual selling prices:

	Output	Selling Price
Grade A	34,000 pounds	$2.25
Grade B	28,000 pounds	1.60
Grade C	10,000 pounds	.90
	72,000 pounds	

Required:
1. Prepare an income statement using a contribution margin approach that shows the budgeted amounts (assuming forty tons of raw fruit input) and actual amounts.
2. Perform a contribution margin analysis that shows the following variances:
    a) Sales price variance.
    b) Cost variance (should be zero because of standard costs).
    c) Sales mix variance.
    d) Sales quantity variance.
3. Calculate materials mix and yield variances. Explain how they relate to the contribution margin analysis.

10-16. Materials and Labor Mix and Yield Variances. Fertilizer Innovators, Inc. was founded at a time when farmers planted higher acreage levels to offset several years of bad harvests. The company has been extremely successful helping farmers get greater yields from their crops. Terry Mathis, President, purchased a failing company that produced high phosphorous fertilizer for wheat and corn crops. He renovated the plant and added specialty fertilizers for all types of fruits and vegetables. With the standardized procedures for each product line, the company implemented a standard cost system.

In the fall of this year, the company introduced a fertilizer that focuses on next spring's home gardening market. The company says this fertilizer should be spread in February in southern states and in March or early April in northern states. Packages were produced in 25 pound units. Standard direct material and direct labor costs for one 25 pound package are as follows:

Material:
Ingredient MP100—6 lbs. @ $3.00	$18.00	
Ingredient RS044—12 lbs. @ $1.80	21.60	
Ingredient WT857—7 lbs. @ $0.80	5.60	$45.20

Direct Labor:
Unskilled—2 hours @ $4.35	$8.70	
Skilled—1/2 hour @ $8.20	4.10	$12.80

November turned out to be an off month. The supplier for Ingredient RS044 had a strike, making it difficult to procure sufficient quantities of the ingredient. The company altered the recipe so more of the other ingredients were used in the mix. A Hepatitis exposure put several skilled workers off the job for several days, and some temporary workers were hired to pick up the slack that the full-time unskilled workers could not handle. Material and labor costs recorded in completing 10,000, 25-pound bags of fertilizer were as follows:

Material:
Ingredient MP100—91,000 lbs. @ $2.90	$263,900
Ingredient RS044—60,000 lbs. @ $2.10	126,000
Ingredient WT857—109,000 lbs. @ $0.90	98,100

Direct labor:
Unskilled—31,000 hours @ $4.75	$147,250
Skilled—2,500 hours @ $8.20	20,500

Required:
1. Compute the following variances for material:
    a) Materials price.
    b) Materials mix.
    c) Materials yield.
2. Compute the following variances for direct labor:
    a) Labor rate.
    b) Labor mix.
    c) Labor yield.
3. Present an explanation of how the variances may be interrelated for the set of circumstances that occurred during the year.

CASE 10A—KRQ INDUSTRIES, INC.

The management of the Brownville Plastics Division of KRQ Industries, Inc. is considering ways to improve profitability by expanding the sales volume of the more profitable lines. In trying to rank the five product lines by profitability, there is a question of how the fixed manufacturing costs should be allocated.

The Brownville division makes five plastic product lines as follows.

1. Clear plastic handles for small tools, such as screwdrivers.
2. Plastic cases for flashlights, cameras, projectors, etc.
3. Kitchenware (plates, cups, and saucers).
4. Ornamental light globes.
5. Novelties and toys.

The materials vary according to the product line. In some cases, a clear plastic is processed; and in other cases, colors are added. Also, the processing operation depends upon the type of product made.

Sales and production cost data for the year are given as follows.

	Handles	Cases	Kitchenware	Light Globes	Novelties
Units sold*	150,000	80,000	120,000	90,000	60,000
Selling price	$9.00	$15.00	$16.00	$14.00	$5.00
Materials cost	1.80	3.50	4.80	4.20	1.60
Labor time per unit	20 min.	30 min.	40 min.	20 min.	10 min.

*Units are batches or lots as defined for each product line.

The sales volume as given is considered to be typical. The labor rate per hour is $9.00, and variable overhead varies at the rate of $6.00 per labor hour. The fixed manufacturing overhead for the year has been budgeted at $550,000. Selling and administrative costs follow a budget formula of 4 percent of total revenue plus fixed costs of $325,000.

The president of the company, Holly Mercer, asks, "How should we allocate the fixed costs of production in solving for the profitability of each product line? I have heard suggestions that the costs should be allocated on the basis of the relative market values. Joe Henderson, our production superintendent, has suggested that the fixed costs should be allocated on the basis of the revenues minus the direct costs of production. Any other thoughts?"

"Does it really matter how the fixed costs are allocated if we are trying to find out which lines are more profitable?" inquires Dave Lopez, the sales manager. "As I understand it, we are operating at normal capacity now. We can handle more business, but we should be concentrating on the promotion of the more profitable lines."

Henderson breaks in, "But, Dave, there can be no profit until all costs are recovered. If a product line can't cover its share of fixed costs, we shouldn't be making it."

"Can you determine exactly how much fixed cost should be identified with any one product line?" Lopez asks.

"Why don't we work it out both ways?" the president answers. "Let's get an income statement showing fixed production costs allocated on the basis of revenue, another income statement with the fixed costs allocated on the basis of revenue minus the variable costs, and still another income statement showing the contribution of each line over its variable costs. On that last statement, we should have the contribution margin per unit of product. While we are at it, let's determine contribution margin per product line per hour. Then, we can see how our time can be used to the best advantage. That will give Dave a better idea about which lines are more important to us."

Required:

1. Prepare income statements as requested by the president.
2. Comment on the positions taken by Joe Henderson and Dave Lopez.
3. Which income statement approach gives the most meaningful information for the managers involved? Explain.

CASE 10B—CAROWAY & COLLINS TOOLS, INC.

Caroway & Collins Tools, Inc., is a worldwide company that manufactures quality tools for the home and work. Its products fall roughly into five groups: power tools; accessories and fastenings for power tools; outdoor products; service parts, repair and maintenance; and household products. Information taken from the 1993 and 1994 consolidated income statement is as follows (000 omitted):

	Years Ended September 30,	
	1994	**1993**
Net sales	$1,791,194	$1,732,278
Costs and expenses:		
Cost of products sold	$1,160,379	$1,107,228
Marketing and administrative	575,490	531,763
Interest expenses	59,074	58,265
Other income	(38,492)	(20,253)
Restructuring costs	—	215,100
	$1,756,451	$1,892,103
Net profit (loss) before income taxes	$ 34,743	$ (159,825)
Income taxes (benefits)	7,200	(1,400)
Loss on early extinguishment of debt	21,239	—
Net profit (loss)	$ 6,304	$ (158,425)

A discussion of the consolidated operations gives selected details of happenings over the two years. They are summarized below.

Net Sales: Retail activity in the United States continued at a slow pace, and inventory levels in retail and wholesale distribution channels remained above last year's levels. As a result, sales by the company into these channels during fiscal 1994 were below last year's levels. Sales of power tools were comparable to last year; however, sales of household products were below last year's level. Sales of outdoor products and service increased over the previous year by 15 percent and 16 percent, respectively. Competition remains keen across many product lines and has limited the opportunities for pricing action.

As in the United States, retail sales in Europe remained weak, and competitive pressures stayed intense. European sales, however, were favorably affected by the strengthening of most currencies relative to the dollar. Excluding this positive effect and minimal price increases, sales volume decreased in Europe for the second consecutive year. Sales in other areas including Canada, Latin American, and Australia showed some growth which was primarily attributable to an increased emphasis on housewares and a strong market in Brazil. The following is the breakdown of sales:

	1994	1993
Consolidated sales	$1,791	$1,732
United States	$1,001	$1,047
Europe	514	435
Other	276	250

Although consolidated sales increased slightly, sales volume actually decreased about 4 percent between years.

Cost of Products Sold: Manufacturing costs as a percentage of sales have steadily increased. This increase was the result of the continuing high overhead costs as a consequence of reduced production, increased automation, and changes in production mix, all of which have aggravated the existing plant underutilization problem. These higher costs have been partially offset by reduced labor rates and materials costs. Additional charges for inventory obsolescence and other write-offs associated with the company's decision to discontinue certain unprofitable or low margin products were also included in cost of products sold during fiscal 1994.

Marketing and Administrative Expenses: Marketing and administrative expenses as a percentage of sales were 32.1 percent in 1994 as compared to 30.7 percent in 1993. The increase was primarily the result of higher product distribution costs as the company expanded its distribution network in the United States to service customer needs more efficiently. Implementation costs were also incurred to reorganize the corporate and group organizational structures and to achieve company-wide cost reductions. Advertising and promotional expenses, although lower than in fiscal 1993 as a percentage of sales, remained at a level necessary to support the company's continued introduction of new products and to promote existing products in an effort to stimulate sales in a weak retail environment.

Interest Expense: Interest expense was about the same level as last year as higher average borrowing levels and the impact of currency translation on foreign denominated debt were offset by reduced interest rates and the positive effect of the January 1994 equity offering.

Other Income: Other income for 1994 of $38.5 million included an $18.2 million gain on the sale of foreign currency exchange agreements. Excluding this transaction, other income was at about the same level as in prior years and was primarily interest earned on short-term investments.

Restructuring Costs: The primary objective of the major manufacturing restructuring program is to improve the plant utilization rate through a combination of plant closings, facilities consolidations, and rationalization and selective product sourcing.

Required:
1.   An outsider does not have all of the data available to perform a gross profit analysis that an insider does. Describe how you would approach a gross profit analysis and an expanded profit analysis for Caroway & Collins Tools, Inc.
2.   Using your approach, perform an analysis generating appropriate variances. Explain your variances in terms of the information contained in the discussion of the consolidated operations.

CASE 10C—MARKLEY DIVISION

The Markley Division of Rosette Industries manufactures and sells patio chairs. The chairs are produced in two versions—a metal model and a plastic model of lesser quality. The company uses its own sales force to sell the chairs to retail stores and to catalog outlets. Generally, customers purchase both the metal and plastic versions.

The chairs are produced on two different assembly lines located in adjoining buildings. The division management and sales department occupy the third building on the property. The division management includes a division controller responsible for the division's financial activities and the preparation of reports explaining the differences between actual and budgeted performance. The controller structures these reports such that the sales activities are distinguished from cost factors so that each can be analyzed separately.

The operating results for the first quarter of the fiscal year as compared to the budget are presented below:

MARKLEY DIVISION
OPERATING RESULTS FOR THE FIRST QUARTER

	Actual	Budget	Favorable (Unfavorable) Relative To The Budget
Sales in units:			
Plastic model	60,000	50,000	10,000
Metal model	20,000	25,000	(5,000)
Sales revenue:			
Plastic model	$630,000	$500,000	$130,000
Metal model	300,000	375,000	(75,000)
Total sales revenue	$930,000	$875,000	$ 55,000
Less variable costs:			
Manufacturing (at standard):			
Plastic model	480,000	400,000	(80,000)
Metal model	200,000	250,000	50,000
Selling:			
Plastic model	37,800	30,000	(7,800)
Metal model	18,000	22,500	4,500
Contribution margin (at standard):			
Plastic model	$112,000	$ 70,000	$ 42,200
Metal model	82,000	102,500	(20,500)
Less other costs:			
Variable production cost variances from standards	$ 49,600	—	$ (49,600)
Fixed manufacturing costs	49,200	48,000	(1,200)
Fixed selling and administrative costs	38,500	36,000	(2,500)
Corporate offices allocation	18,500	17,500	(1,000)
Total other costs	$155,800	$101,500	$ (54,300)
Divisional operating income	$ 38,400	$ 71,000	$ (32,600)

The budget for the current year was based on the assumption that Markley Division would maintain its present market share of the estimated total patio chair market (plastic and metal combined). A status report had been sent to corporate management toward the end of the second month indicating that the division operating income for the first quarter would probably be about 45% below budget: the estimate was just about on target. The division's operating income was below budget even though industry volume for patio chairs increased by 10% more than was expected at the time the budget was developed.

The manufacturing activities for the first quarter resulted in the production of 55,000 plastic chairs and 22,500 metal chairs. The costs incurred by each production unit in the first quarter are presented next:

	Plastic Model	Metal Model
Direct materials purchased:		
Plastic (60,000 @ $5.65)	$339,000	
Metal (30,000 @ $6.00)		$180,000

	Plastic Model	Metal Model
Direct materials used:		
Plastic (56,000 @ $5.00)	$280,000	
Metal (23,000 @ $6.00)		$138,000
Direct labor:		
9,300 hours @ $6.00 per hour	55,800	
5,600 hours @ $8.00 per hour		44,800
Manufacturing overhead:		
Variable:		
Supplies	43,000	18,000
Power	50,000	15,000
Employee benefits	19,000	12,000
Fixed:		
Supervision	14,000	11,000
Depreciation	12,000	9,000
Property taxes and other items	1,900	1,300

The standard variable manufacturing costs per unit and the budgeted monthly fixed manufacturing costs established for the current year are presented next:

	Plastic Model	Metal Model
Direct materials	$5.00	$6.00
Direct labor:		
1/6 hour @ $6.00 per hour	1.00	
1/4 hour @ $8.00 per hour		2.00
Variable manufacturing overhead:		
1/6 hour @ $12.00 per hour	2.00	
1/4 hour @ $8.00 per hour		2.00
Standard variable manufacturing cost per unit	$8.00	$10.00
Budgeted fixed costs per month:		
Supervision	$4,500	$3,500
Depreciation	4,000	3,000
Property taxes and other items	600	400
Total budgeted fixed cost per month	$9,100	$6,900

Required:

1. Explain the variance in Markley Division's contribution margin attributable to sales activities by calculating:
   a) Total sales price variance.
   b) Total sales mix variance.
   c) Total sales volume variance.

2. What portion of the sales volume variance, if any, can be attributed to a change in Markley Division's market share?

3. Analyze the variance in Markley Division's variable manufacturing costs ($49,600) in as much detail as the data permit.

4. Based on your analysis prepared for requirements (1), (2), and (3) above:
   a) Identify the major cause of Markley Division's unfavorable profit performance.
   b) Decide if Markley's management attempted to correct this problem. Explain.
   c) Discuss other steps, if any, that Markley's management could have taken to improve the division's operating income.

(ICMA Adapted)

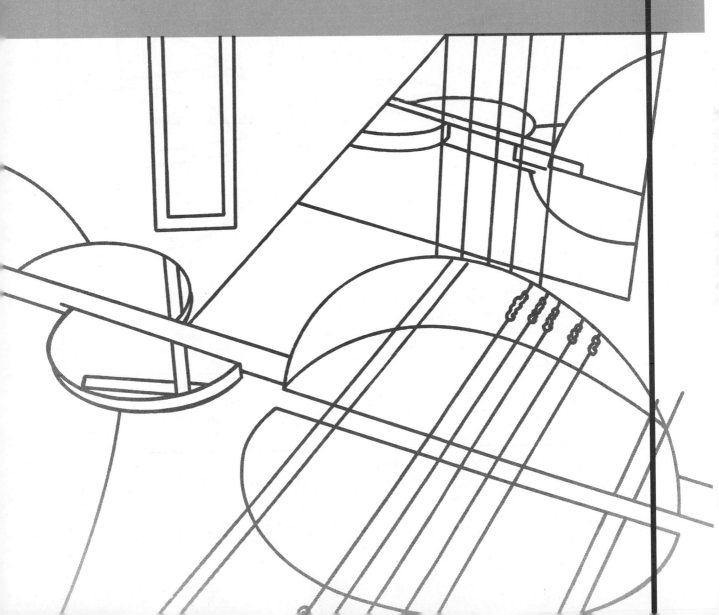

Part Four

Decision Making Framework

Chapter Eleven

Managerial Decisions: Analysis of Relevant Information

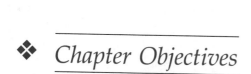

❖ *Chapter Objectives*

After studying Chapter 11, you will be able to:

1. Describe the decision-making process.
2. Understand the use of differential analysis in making basic decisions.
3. Understand how to identify and use relevant costs and revenues in decision making.
4. Identify the decision type; know the basic decision rule and guidelines; consider major constraints, assumptions, and underlying concerns; format the problem data for analysis; and apply the decision logic to similar real-life problems.
5. Evaluate make or buy, special sales pricing, scarce resource, process further, and add or delete a segment decisions.
6. Explain the role of cost information in product pricing decisions.

■ *Decisions, Decisions, Decisions* ■

Jim Rich operates a series of take-out ribs and sandwich shops, called Rich Ribs, in the suburbs of Midwest City. Before leaving on vacation, Jim asked his controller Jill Murad to prepare cost analyses of several decisions he has been considering. He met with Jill and outlined each issue.

Issue # 1:   A major local firm has called Jim and asked whether a deal could be arranged to serve Rich Ribs in their cafeteria at a special event and maybe more regularly later, depending on the employees' reaction. Jim's company name may or may not be identified. The company's price is roughly 60 percent of the Rich Ribs a la carte menu price.

Issue # 2:   The Riverwood shop has been showing a monthly net operating loss for the last six months. The shop's lease expires at the end of the year. Also, a new mini shopping mall is opening in a part of the city not presently served by Jim's shops. Jim could close the Riverwood shop and shift the manager to a new mall shop.

Issue # 3:   A local bakery with an excellent reputation in the area has offered to sell Jim bread sticks. Jim includes a serving of bread sticks with every take-out dinner order. Jim bakes his own bread sticks in his kitchen every day and is proud of their quality, but the bakery price offer seems very low.

Issue # 4:   Jim is thinking of adding pizza to his menu, but the kitchen facility's capacity would be stretched severely if he keeps all other menu items. He wants to use his kitchen capacity in the most profitable way.

Jim has a "common sense feel" about the answers to these decisions, but he needs economic proof. He looks to Jill to assemble, analyze, and present the relevant information for each issue. He must then weigh all the quantitative and qualitative factors and make the decision.

Yes, "decisions, decisions, decisions" is a common lament. But decision making is action taking. It is the exciting part of management. Experiences and skills of managers are brought to bear on specific problems. The decision may be very significant, such as when and where to build a new $4 billion manufacturing facility. Or it may be mundane, such as should we photocopy a report for a key meeting or send it to a copy center down the street. In either case, consciously or subconsciously, managers follow a process: define the problem, consider alternatives, collect and analyze data, and make a decision. The decision must be implemented and should be evaluated after the fact.

This chapter looks at a set of decisions that requires an organized decision making process and focuses on the use of cost data in making the decisions.

These decisions are grouped by common types that occur in all business activities and even in our personal lives.

The decisions, the methodologies, the data analyzed, and the decision time frames presented here are necessarily simplified. The real world offers much more complexity. Decisions are about the future. Much uncertainty exists. In our textbook problems, we consider only a few of the variables that impact the results of decisions. Black and white print also implies a certainty about the future that real decision makers strangely do not have available. Also, in reality, literally hundreds of variables are moving in different directions at the same time. Helping managers to use an order and a process, select relevant variables, and add format to the analysis are the goals of this chapter.

The steps in the decision-making process and how each step impacts the management accounting task will be developed on a general basis and then extended to each decision type studied.

The major decision types analyzed in this chapter are:

1. Make or buy.
2. Special sales pricing.
3. Use of scarce resources.
4. Sell or process further.
5. Add or delete a segment.

The replace equipment and expand capacity decisions are introduced and developed further in Chapters 12 and 13.

For each decision type, we define the problem, develop the decision rules, design a format for analysis, and apply differential analysis to help select an alternative. In addition to the quantitative analysis, major qualitative issues that influence the decision will be examined.

THE DECISION-MAKING PROCESS

All managerial decision making should be made with the mission and the strategic goals of the firm in mind. A key to effective decision making is an organized approach to a problem. Organization implies structure and methodology, not arbitrariness or rigidity in using mechanical or traditional rules. Also, certain issues with short-term or long-term impacts must be considered. The care put into each decision often determines the level of outcome. Still, the best process and even the best decision does not guarantee a successful outcome. The future determines its own fate, but the best prepared decision is more likely to produce the desired result than any other selection.

Over the years many lists of decision-making elements have been developed. As a reference point the following set of decision steps will be used:

1. **Define the decision issue.** A careful definition of the problem's scope is a key to much higher quality analysis of alternatives in later steps. Seeing the strategic, competitive, and organizational factors helps focus on real decision issues and not merely on obvious or surface problems.

2. **Specify the decision objective and decision rule.** Often the decision objective is already known, such as profit maximization. Other situations may call for the greatest efficiency, sales maximization, most persons served, or lowest cost. Knowing the overall goal sets the decision objective. In applying a decision objective to any situation, we normally refer to a **decision rule.** One or more decision rules guide a decision maker in selecting relevant data and in choosing an alternative.

3. **Identify the alternatives. Alternatives** are the options available to the decision maker. It requires creativity to see the broadest array of options and experienced judgment to select alternatives that are realistic. Even with simplifying assumptions and by limiting the number of alternatives considered, a manager may still be left with a complex problem. Further analysis may eliminate or introduce other alternatives.

4. **Collect relevant data on the alternatives.** Simplifying assumptions must be made in order to proceed in a practical way, given time and investigation cost limits. Data collection is a cost and benefit problem. Will benefits from an improved decision be greater than the additional time and cost spent collecting more data? Theoretically, we would stop collecting data when the marginal cost of collection equals the marginal benefit of a better decision. Practically, we are often constrained by time and available data. Most data will be estimates of the future, but historical data are often the bases of forecasts. Understanding past costs and providing ready access to cost detail are major tasks of managerial accountants.

5. **Format and analyze information about each alternative.** Organizing the decision data often simplifies the decision task. A decision maker should link the type of decision with a specific format for analyzing the information. A specific format can identify missing data, help compare alternatives, and focus the decision maker's attention on the decision's relevant revenues and costs. The managerial accountant's responsibility is to organize the relevant quantitative data for analysis. To the extent possible, the non-financial advantages and disadvantages should also be part of the evaluation package presented to the decision maker.

6. **Make the decision.** Given the decision rule, select the alternative that gives the greatest benefit. Having said that, we must recognize that the basic quantitative analysis is one part of the decision. Strategic issues, long-run impacts, qualitative factors, and even emotional and personal biases may influence the decision maker. But the relevant data form the foundation for the analysis.

7. **Implement the decision.** Now the obvious should take place. A decision has been selected; implement it. Implementation may take minutes or years. Some decisions require much analysis and nearly instant execution, such as the purchase of an investment security. Others require little analysis; but need long lead times and careful follow through, such as complying with new clean air regulations.

8. **Evaluate the results of the decision.** Some decisions are routine. Feedback on actual results automatically adds to the analysis of similar future decisions. For others, we are interested in closing the control cycle. Hav-

ing a follow-up process tells managers that their performance will be evaluated. History shows that these after-the-fact reviews have mixed effectiveness, but they are necessary control links.

Each step helps move the decision maker closer to achieving the best outcome for the firm. Cost and revenue data often play vital roles in evaluating alternatives and in selecting the best economic result. Performing all eight steps of the decision-making process completes the plan and control cycle.

DIFFERENTIAL ANALYSIS

Differential analysis is the use of relevant revenues and costs to make decisions. Basic rules guide the use of differential analysis in general and within each decision type.

The Basic Decision Rule

The basic differential analysis decision rule is:

> Select the alternative that gives the greatest incremental profit.

Incremental profit is the difference between the relevant revenues and the relevant costs of each alternative. Relevant revenues and relevant costs are defined as the current and future values that differ among the alternatives considered. In most cases the term "incremental" is used as a substitute for "relevant." In choosing among alternatives, all past and committed costs and costs that remain the same across all alternatives should be ignored.

Discussion here generally assumes that the decision objective is profit maximization unless another objective is specifically set. The time frame is generally short term, but the time frame is related to policy issues discussed in the next section.

A decision is frequently either:

1. Do it, or don't do it.
2. Do A, or do B, or do C, or etc.

In the first case, the status quo is the base; and the "do it" alternative will have incremental revenues and costs attached to it. In the second, incremental revenues and costs for each alternative are measured. In either case, the selection will be based on which alternative generates the highest incremental profit. Incremental profit is measured using contribution margin analysis. The definition of **contribution margin analysis** is incremental revenues minus incremental costs. In cost reduction cases, the lowest cost would be the most attractive. The lowest cost alternative would generate the highest profit for the firm assuming all other factors are constant.

Also relevant revenues are often assumed to be cash inflows, and relevant costs are cash outflows. The term <u>out-of-pocket costs</u> refers to costs that are paid out in cash. If cash flow and accrual income numbers differ, the managerial focus will be on cash flow. For short-term decisions, cash flow timing is probably not critical. But when the time frame is extended beyond the current year, the timing of cash flows is relevant to the evaluation of decision alternatives. These longer term cash flows are discussed in Chapters 12 and 13.

In many cases, the availability of capacity will impact decisions. Capacity costs are frequently fixed costs and are irrelevant to most short-term decisions. A relevant factor is the **opportunity cost** of the capacity. If excess capacity exists and no alternative uses are apparent, the opportunity cost is zero—no relevant costs and no lost contribution margin. If capacity is scarce, costs of acquiring additional capacity and the alternative uses of capacity must be considered.

Incremental Analysis and Total Analysis

Differential analysis compares alternatives by comparing incremental contribution margins. One important task of the managerial accountant is data formatting so that relevant data are displayed in a logical format and are easily understood. The format should focus on key issues surrounding the decision rule. The same problem can be formatted in many ways. The order of calculation is a matter of personal logic in many cases. In our discussion of each decision type, a preferred format will be presented. Often, the data requirements, availability of data, or the complexity of a specific decision may dictate a particular format and approach.

Two commonly used approaches are applicable to all decision types—the incremental analysis approach and the total analysis approach. The **incremental analysis approach** will include only the incremental revenues and costs of each alternative, excluding any irrelevant data. The **total analysis approach** will show the results for the total firm with the alternative included and then without the alternative. If adding a new product is being considered, the format is:

Incremental Analysis Approach	**Total Analysis Approach**
Incremental revenue from new product - Incremental costs from new product	Total firm revenue with new product - Total firm costs with new product
Incremental contribution margin from new product	Net income with new product
	Total firm revenue without new product - Total firm costs without new product
	Net income without new product
	Net income with new product - Net income without new product
	Incremental contribution margin from new product

Clearly, the two approaches yield the same incremental contribution margin. The total analysis approach has the advantage of showing the impacts of a decision on all aspects of firm. If adding the new product is independent of all other products, the incremental approach appears to be simpler and easier to evaluate. But, if the new product has complementary or substitution effects on other products, the total analysis approach may be the easier approach. In either case, only relevant revenues and costs will change; and the incremental contribution margin will still be the same.

An Example of Differential Analysis

Steinhour Fabrics is located in Atlanta. Mr. Steinhour recently purchased a small manufacturer of inexpensive backpacks for college students. He produces several styles and colors, but all products are essentially the same. He has just finished the profit plan for 1994, and a simplified income statement appears as follows:

STEINHOUR FABRICS
INCOME STATEMENT
FOR THE YEAR ENDED DECEMBER 31, 1994

Sales (100,000 units × $10)		$1,000,000
Cost of sales:		
Variable production costs ($3 per unit)	$300,000	
Other factory costs	300,000	600,000
Gross profit		$ 400,000
Selling costs (15 % × sales)	$150,000	
Administrative overhead	150,000	300,000
Net income before income tax		$ 100,000

Mr. Steinhour has concluded that he is using 80 percent of capacity. He is currently considering several alternatives to increase capacity utilization and profits. His analysis shows the best scenarios to be:

1. Maintain the status quo.
2. Expand sales of backpacks to 125,000 by lowering the selling price from $10 to $9 per unit.
3. Expand the product line to include a hip pack for bikers and walkers. He estimates the sales price to be $6 per unit with commissions remaining at 15 percent. These units would have a variable production cost of $2.25 per unit. If he sells 25,000 units, the remaining capacity will be used.

The three alternatives compare as shown in Figure 11.1 for contribution margin per unit and total contribution margin income:

	Alternative 1	Alternative 2	Alternative 3 Backpacks	Alternative 3 Hip Packs	Total
Units of sales	100,000	125,000	100,000	25,000	
Sales price	$ 10.00	$ 9.00	$ 10.00	$ 6.00	
Variable costs:					
Production costs	$ 3.00	$ 3.00	$ 3.00	$ 2.25	
Selling costs	1.50	1.35	1.50	.90	
Total variable costs	$ 4.50	$ 4.35	$ 4.50	$ 3.15	
Contribution margin per unit	$ 5.50	$ 4.65	$ 5.50	$ 2.85	
Sales	$1,000,000	$1,125,000	$1,000,000	$150,000	$1,150,000
Variable costs:					
Production costs	$ 300,000	$ 375,000	$ 300,000	$ 56,250	$ 356,250
Selling costs	150,000	168,750	150,000	22,500	172,500
Total variable costs	$ 450,000	$ 543,750	$ 450,000	$ 78,750	$ 528,750
Variable contribution margin	$ 550,000	$ 581,250	$ 550,000	$ 71,250	$ 621,250
Fixed costs:					
Other factory costs	$ 300,000	$ 300,000			$ 300,000
Administrative costs	150,000	150,000			150,000
Total fixed costs	$ 450,000	$ 450,000			$ 450,000
Net income before taxes	$ 100,000	$ 131,250			$ 171,250

Figure 11.1   Total Analysis Approach to Differential Analysis

Notice that this presentation is a total analysis approach. The total firm's results are shown. Alternative 2 increases net income to $131,250, a differential increase of $31,250. Alternative 3, with the new hip pack, increases net income by $71,250. In Alternative 3, the fixed costs are not allocated between the two products since no basis is presented nor does a need exist. Fixed costs are assumed not to change under any alternative and are ignored. In fact, the differences in net income exactly match the changes in variable contribution margin. Also, if taxes are considered, additional taxes would be a relevant cost.

The basic sales of at least 100,000 units holds for all alternatives. However, in Alternative 2, the price drops and the sales increase by 25,000 units. Thus, the sales revenue from the common 100,000 backpacks could be relevant for all alternatives. Or the price reduction of $1 per unit in Alternative 2 could be considered a negative revenue item only for Alternative 2, and the $1,000,000 in sales ignored. An incremental analysis approach would appear as shown in Figure 11.2 on page 554.

The incremental contribution margin of each alternative matches the increase in net income before taxes. No mention is made of the original sales of 100,000 units or the fixed costs which did not change. All comparisons are made to Alternative 1, the status quo. Therefore, no change is shown for Alternative 1.

	Alternative 1	Alternative 2	Alternative 3 Backpacks	Hip Packs	Total
Incremental sales ($9 × 25,000)	$ 0	$ 225,000	$ 0	$ 0	$ 0
Lost revenue from price reduction [($9-$10) × 100,000]		(100,000]			
Sales of hip packs ($6 × 25,000)				150,000	150,000
Incremental production costs of backpacks ($3 × 25,000)		(75,000)			
Incremental production costs of hip packs ($2.25 × 25,000)				(56,250)	(56,250)
Incremental sales commissions (15 % × increased revenue)		(18,750)		(22,500)	(22,500)
Incremental contribution margin	$ 0	$ 31,250			$ 71,250

Figure 11.2   Incremental Analysis Approach to Differential Analysis

Based on the quantitative data presented, Steinhour would select Alternative 3. Before the decision is made, long-term considerations should be thought through. Is the hip pack consistent with the firm's product plans? Will entering this market attract other competitors? Is pricing designed to fill capacity or to fit the overall firm pricing policy? Will additional equipment be needed to support the new product or to meet future growth in regular backpacks? Although supposedly a short-term incremental decision, these questions lead to concern about policy issues.

Policy Issues Affecting Relevant Costing Decisions

Knowing the relevant costing decision criteria and how to apply differential analysis gives the decision maker a powerful bag of tools to work out a wide variety of problem areas. But as with all real-world issues, the decision-making path has more complexity than the basic rules imply. The differential analysis model is so simple and appealing that we can easily be lulled into a false sense of confidence.

It is important, then, to remember two interrelated areas of concern that keep appearing: first, the time frame of the differential analysis decision, and, second, the strategic considerations that must be evaluated when decisions are made. These policy concerns hover over the analysis of all decision types.

The Time Frame   We make certain assumptions in differential analysis. A short-term horizon is assumed, variable costs are relevant, most fixed costs are irrelevant, and alternatives are evaluated that can be implemented quickly. However, managers must recognize that all important decisions have both short- and long-term impacts. In many cases, investments must be made that last longer than the immediate time frame. Decisions made today often cannot easily be reversed tomorrow. Also, profitable decisions made on a one-time basis or made for an immediate gain may change the options available to managers in the long run. Customers, competitors, employees, and suppliers react to our actions. They learn to interpret our actions over time. Short-term thinking for near-term profit may damage an overall business strategy.

We must quickly add that over dependence on long-term costing, where average costs and revenues dominate, can create even worse problems. Relevant costing is still applicable to longer time frames. In the long run, sunk costs are still irrelevant.

The incremental cost and revenue analysis discussed and illustrated in the following pages assumes the use of relevant costing and a bias toward short-term thinking. But the long-term impacts must be considered as we evaluate alternatives.

Strategic Planning Issues   A firm's strategic plan looks at product offerings, pricing strategies, competitive positions, and financial performance goals. Often, these are "long haul" policies that are implemented on a short-term basis by tactics and decision guidelines.

By adopting relevant costing principles as the primary decision philosophy, managers can let the "tail wag the dog." Incremental decisions are just that, additions to the margin—often small increments. The major pricing, production, and marketing decisions must follow the long-term strategies that have been carefully thought through.

Often decisions are masked as short term, when they are really policy-making, long-term decisions. For example:

1.   The one-time special sale becomes repeat business and a growing segment of total sales.
2.   Regular customers seek price breaks to compete with buyers of off-brand look-alikes.
3.   A cheaper lower quality source for parts eventually hurts a firm's image as a producer of quality products. This same out-sourcing undermines the harmony the company has worked hard to develop with its labor union.
4.   By temporarily stopping production of a seasonally unprofitable product a company loses market share for an entire product line.

These and more examples of "wise" short-term decisions having a negative impact on long-term results should cause us to be leery of adopting differential analysis as our sole approach to decision making. Relevant costing is still a fundamental analytical approach. The main caveat is that no decision can be made in isolation. Decision makers must be sensitive to these important time frame and strategic implications.

DIFFERENTIAL ANALYSIS DECISIONS

Decision types are analyzed to create a framework for managerial decision making. These types are simplified to illustrate the basic decision analyses and are make or buy, special sales pricing, use of scarce resources, sell or process further, add or delete a product, replace equipment, and expand capacity. Again, the real world is more complex in that many decisions are combinations of several types. But the basic questions appear again and again in different forms in all kinds of organizations. While the decision rules may differ, the same decision types are relevant to profit and non-profit organizations and to service, merchandising, and manufacturing organizations.

For each decision type, we define the basic question, cite applications, specify key decision criteria and basic guidelines, present a data analysis format, highlight major qualitative factors, and develop an example.

Make or Buy Decisions

The basic make or buy decision asks the question: should we make the item or perform the service ourselves, or should we purchase the item or service from a vendor?

A wide variety of situations falls within this decision type. In fact, nearly all products and services offered on the market today result from basic make or buy decisions. A sample of these decisions includes:

The "Make" Alternative	The "Buy" Alternative
Make a component part in our factory.	Buy it from a nearby vendor, a non-union factory in another state, a foreign manufacturer, or another division of our own company.
Service our own company cars.	Contract maintenance from a local garage.
Operate our own shipping fleet of trucks.	Hire various freight companies.
Clean our own offices.	Hire a cleaning service.
Run our own printing shop.	Contract with local printers.
Manage our own data processing operation.	Hire a facilities management company.
Make our own potato salad for our restaurant.	Buy potato salad from a local delicatessen.

As can be seen, this sample includes decisions that may need investments in long-term assets, cause major shifts in operations, and examine qualitative issues.

A firm may make this decision for various reasons, including to:

1. Reduce costs.
2. Use or to free up capacity.

3. Improve delivery performance.
4. Improve the quality of the product or service.
5. Encourage greater competitiveness of internal operations by comparing performance and cost to outsiders.
6. Gain access to new technology.
7. Avoid or to free up investment of scarce funds or to obtain high returns on new investments.
8. Integrate operating activities.

The answer could be to "make" or "buy." Our task is to assemble the relevant costs for the decision.

The Key Decision Rule and Guidelines   The key decision rule is: If the out-of-pocket costs of buying the product or service are less than the out-of-pocket costs of making the product or service, buy it. If not, make it.

Out-of-pocket costs are the relevant costs in this decision. The decision rule is still to earn the highest profit. But since the make or buy decision generally deals only with costs, the decision rule is to minimize cost.

The decision could be either to buy a part we currently produce or to make a part we currently purchase. The cost analysis is the same either way. If we are **out-sourcing,** or buying from a vendor, the relevant cost concept is avoidable costs. If we are going to consider **in-house sourcing,** or making the part ourselves, the relevant cost concept is incremental costs.

The relevant costs of the make decision are the direct costs incurred in making the product. These include variable costs of materials, direct labor, and any variable manufacturing overhead. Fixed costs could include any costs that could be added if the part is made. Also, any special costs that can be traced to the part such as unique tooling costs or any supplies that would otherwise not be needed are relevant to the decision. Costs of handling materials, production support, insurance, and other services that would be added are viewed as direct costs. General factory overhead is rarely impacted by the make or buy decision unless it is so major that the entire plant is closed or other substantial changes are made.

The relevant costs of the buy decision are the purchase cost of the product, shipping and handling costs, and any cost incurred to get the purchased part into usable position. Inspection and testing costs are examples. Another relevant cost issue is the alternative use of the space vacated if the part is now purchased. The space could be rented at some market rate, used by another department, or used by us to produce other parts.

Data Analysis Format   The make or buy data analysis format merely lists the relevant costs to make and the relevant costs to buy. One approach is to organize the data in T-account form as follows:

Make Costs		Buy Costs	
Materials	$	Purchase cost plus	
Direct labor and other		transportation and any	
variable factory costs	$	direct handling costs	$
Direct fixed costs	$		
Any other avoidable or			
incremental costs	$		
Cost of additional space	or	Less incremental revenue or	
needed to make	$	benefit from use of released	
		space	($)
Total make cost	**$**	**Total buy cost**	**$**

The objective is to show the net relevant cost of making and the net relevant cost of buying. Notice any costs that do not change are not shown on either side, since they are irrelevant. The obvious costs of making (all direct product costs) and of buying (the purchase cost) are easily listed on the appropriate side. Several other items can be either an additional cost on one side or a negative cost on the other side. For example, if purchasing a part is being evaluated, the factory space no longer needed can be rented or used to produce other parts. If rented for $10,000 a year, the $10,000 can be seen as a reduction in the buy cost, since by buying we earn the revenue. Or it can be seen as an additional make cost, since by making we forego a $10,000 opportunity cost. Either way works. But either omitting the $10,000 or counting it double is incorrect.

Because both fixed and variable costs may be part of the analysis, the expected volume must be used to arrive at a total cost. Whether total dollars or cost per part is used, the number of parts is relevant. At times quoting costs on a per unit basis can imply that all costs are variable. Knowing the total cost and its composition becomes critical.

The bottom line is the comparison of the total make cost and the total buy cost. Pick the lower cost.

An Example   Epper Company has asked for bids from several suppliers for a control subassembly, a unit needed in the production of several models of their Superior Line of lighting fixtures. Epper has made these units for the past several years along with control units for other products. Epper thinks the 1995 production requirements will be 30,000 units. The Universal Wiring Company responded with the most attractive bid and offered to sell the subassembly for $3 per unit delivered. Inspection and quality control checks would cost Epper about $3,000.

Epper's 1994 product cost sheet shows the following production costs per part, based on actual production of 25,000 units:

	Per Unit	Total Cost
Materials	$1.25	$31,250
Direct labor	.60	15,000
Variable manufacturing overhead	.50	12,500
Fixed manufacturing overhead	1.00	25,000
Total	$3.35	$83,750

All costs are direct costs, except fixed manufacturing overhead. The only direct cost in fixed manufacturing overhead is $6,000, which is the cost of renting specialized equipment required for the subassembly.

The company has been operating at 85 percent of the factory's normal capacity. General factory overhead is $190,000 per year at whatever level of output is attained. The specialized equipment which the subassembly uses has been fully utilized. If the subassembly is purchased, Epper could use the equipment to complete another control device. That work must now be subcontracted to a local electrical shop for a net additional cost of $12,000 per year. If Epper did not use the special equipment, it could be returned; the rent avoided; and the space used for storage. Rental of equivalent space would cost $4,000 next year.

To arrive at a decision, the decision rule of least cost is set; and the alternatives must be identified. The alternatives are:

1. Make the control subassembly.
2. Buy the control subassembly, and:
    (a) Use the specialized equipment to complete the other control device; or
    (b) Eliminate the specialized equipment using the space as storage.

The analysis is complicated by the optional use of the equipment. Before we examine the make or buy choice, let us examine the 2a and 2b options. The relevant costs of these two are not really a make or buy problem, but rather determining the opportunity cost of the specialized equipment. The relevant costs are:

	Use Equipment	Eliminate Equipment
Savings from eliminating equipment		$ 6,000
Savings from eliminating space rental		4,000
Savings from eliminating subcontracting	$12,000	
Total savings	$12,000	$10,000
Net advantage of using the equipment	$ 2,000	

At this point, we can narrow the alternatives to (1) make or (2a) buy the subassembly and use the equipment to eliminate the subcontracting work.

Make Costs		Buy Costs	
Materials	$37,500	Purchase cost	$ 90,000
Direct labor	18,000	Inspection and quality	
Variable overhead	15,000	control	3,000
		Subcontracting savings . .	(12,000)
Total make costs	$70,500	Total buy costs	$ 81,000
Net make advantage	$10,500		

We can make several observations about these data:

1. The variable costs on both the make and the buy sides are relevant.
2. The total unit-cost comparison of $3.35 to $3.00 hides the cost behavior patterns that exist. Likewise, using only variable costs could also lead to mistaken conclusions.
3. The volume to be used is 30,000 units (the expected volume) and not the 25,000 units (the current volume).
4. The $190,000 of general factory overhead is irrelevant and is ignored. The $1 per unit of fixed manufacturing overhead can be converted into $25,000 of fixed costs applied to these units. Of that, $6,000 was a direct fixed cost meaning that $19,000 was applied overhead. This indicates that this operation had 10 percent of the general factory overhead applied to it. If we buy, this $19,000 will not go away and will have to be applied to the other 90 percent of factory activity (or to the subcontracting brought in-house).
5. The opportunity cost of the equipment is $12,000 and could be an additional cost of the make option or (as shown) a savings under the buy option.
6. Notice that once the $12,000 opportunity cost for use of the equipment was established, the $6,000 cost of renting the equipment was irrelevant because the equipment was used in both the make and the buy alternatives.
7. The net advantage can be stated as: continue to make and save $10,500.

Another way to analyze all three options at the same time would be as follows:

	Make (Alternative 1)	Buy, Use Equip. (Alternative 2a)	Buy, Rent Space (Alternative 2b)
Variable production costs .	$70,500		
Equipment rental costs . .	6,000	$ 6,000	
Purchase costs		90,000	$90,000
Inspection and QC costs .		3,000	3,000
Subcontracting savings . .		(12,000)	
Storage rental savings . .			(4,000)
Net total costs	$76,500	$87,000	$89,000

Notice that the relevant amounts differ because of the inclusion of the third alternative. Also, the totals differ from the earlier format, but the differential advantage of make over the better buy option is still $10,500. The differential between 2a and 2b is still $2,000.

Qualitative Factors   The make or buy decision has been shown to be a basic least cost choice. But many subtleties surround the decision. In the above example, only quantitative monetary facts were considered. Every fact has qualifiers attached to it. Quality, delivery, labor force, and investment implications are among the key issues.

Often, product and service quality is the highest ranking factor and could support either the make or buy side. By making the product, we can control the environment, train workers, and ensure quality of all aspects of production. On the other hand, the particular part may require highly technical production. We may not have much experience. Whereas an outside supplier may specialize in this work, may be faster, and produce a higher quality product. Quality in many areas can be so important that cost differentials will be ignored to get higher quality.

Delivery capability in just-in-time production systems becomes critically important. Again, perhaps in-house production has an advantage since the comprehensive production planning system can build timely schedules to produce on an "as needed" basis. Or the outside supplier may use delivery capability as a key competitive issue and may well be able to meet complex and short time frame requirements better. Delivery requirements can also counter cost advantages.

Labor stability is another major make or buy consideration. For the United Auto Workers Union and the major American auto producers, out-sourcing has become one of the major areas of contention in labor negotiations. The auto companies have historically been rather vertically integrated, some more than others. The companies, in trying to become more competitive with foreign imports, have attempted to shift production to lower cost suppliers. These suppliers may be non-union and operate in lower cost geographic areas. Many of these suppliers are "leaner and meaner" competitors than the captive divisions of the auto makers themselves. The UAW is concerned about job losses of its members. Labor contract provisions guarantee levels of in-house production. Labor implications affect how management analyzes make or buy policies and specific decisions. Labor harmony may easily outweigh product cost considerations.

Another labor issue is more local. If we have a skilled workforce and we decide to buy the part, these workers undoubtedly will move to other jobs. Thus, losing this base of workers, we may not be able to resume making the part in the future. This is particularly true in service areas. Services often call for special skills and training that may be difficult to replace. Also, a functioning unit often blends skills and long experience, which may be impossible to recreate.

Global business transactions mean that we not only decide to make or buy, but, if we make, where do we make it? If we buy, where do we buy? Brazil, Mexico, Korea, Japan, and eastern or western Europe are some of the possible source countries. Also, many multinational firms have facilities in a wide variety of countries and can shift production around the world depending on production costs, quality, materials proximity, and product demand.

Investment in equipment, inventories, and space is often a major commitment in make or buy decisions that we ignore in short-run analysis. In fact in the example above, the specialized equipment was assumed to be rented to avoid the long-term investment issues. Generally, equipment is purchased and used over multiple years. Alternative uses of equipment, buying or disposition of productive assets, building or liquidating inventories, and leasing assets all add capital-budgeting ramifications. These are discussed in Chapters 12 and 13.

Often, business dealings operate through contracts and other long-term arrangements. In current business environments, companies are attempting to develop stronger customer-supplier links and are moving more to systems approaches to solving problems. This means integration of data systems, product design, production, delivery, and product subsystems. Labor contracts, personnel policies, and quality of work life programs have changed the way personnel expansions and reductions are managed.

One last issue is the future of general factory overhead in situations where buy decisions are being considered. In the Epper example, general factory overhead was $190,000. Through a cost allocation process, $19,000 ($25,000 − 6,000) was applied to the 25,000 subassembly units. The $190,000 is assumed to continue even though factory activity will perhaps decline. As more and more parts are out-sourced, fewer and fewer products remain to absorb the overhead. The $190,000 are real expenses and eventually must be reduced or other work added to take up the production slack. Serious management decisions at higher levels must be made. This does not lessen the need to look at make or buy decisions at all levels, but it does open the task to broader analysis than the basic decision implies.

Special Sales Pricing Decisions

The basic special sales pricing decision asks the question: Should we seek sales of non-regular products or to non-regular customers at prices that are generally lower than regular sales to regular customers?

This decision type evaluates additional sales opportunities using contribution margin analysis. It is the sales side of the make or buy problem. Often, one company's make or buy problem is another company's special sales pricing problem. Examples of special sales applications are to:

1. Use excess production capacity by generating discount priced sales.
2. Generate sales that only cover out-of-pocket costs to keep a workforce employed during a recession.
3. Make a one-time sale to get rid of stale merchandise.
4. Respond to a request for a special feature or an economy model from a regular customer.
5. Price for entry into a new competitive market.
6. React to predatory pricing strategies of a competitor.

In certain situations, even regular business can be priced using contribution margin analysis. Clearly, knowledge of cost behavior, volumes, and capacities is a major influence in pricing and marketing activities.

The Key Decision Rule and Guidelines   The key decision rule is: Subject to the following specific guidelines, if we earn a positive contribution margin on the special sale, make the sale.

The guidelines necessary to allow the basic rule to work are:

1.   Excess capacity should exist, with no alternative use of the capacity. This allows the opportunity cost of using the capacity to be zero or at least very low.
2.   The special sale should not interfere with regular business, and the special sale should be in a market segment different than our other business. The sale will then be incremental revenue.
3.   The expectation is that this is a one-time deal, will not become regular business, and will not share the general overhead burden of regular sales.

In true special sales situations, all these guidelines should be met. Otherwise, the analysis of the special sale will have additional relevant revenues and costs to consider.

Relevant revenues are the incremental revenues from the special sale. If any regular sales are lost, the negative changes in revenues are relevant. The relevant costs are any cost incurred to produce the special sales units. Generally, these will be the product's variable costs adjusted for the special sale's requirements. Additional costs could include special parts, incremental supervision, overtime premiums, sales costs, and shipping costs.

Expressed another way, the minimum price will be the out-of-pocket costs plus any opportunity cost of making the sale (profits from regular sales lost, production foregone, etc.). The economic rule is to produce and sell until the marginal revenue equals marginal cost. If capacity exists, we will continue to produce and sell as long as incremental revenue exceeds incremental cost.

Data Analysis Format   Formatting data for special sales decisions focuses on the new sales and added costs as follows:

Incremental revenue	$
Additional variable production costs	($)
Other additional direct production costs	($)
Additional variable sales and distribution costs	($)
Other additional direct sales and distribution costs	($)
Incremental contribution margin	$

Only relevant revenues and costs are shown. The variable production costs must be adjusted from the regular-business variable costs for any changed features of the special units such as a different cabinet finish or the use of heavy-duty shock absorbers. For labor costs, changed processes need to be considered as well as any overtime premiums. Use of any additional resources, supervision, inspection, licenses, or packaging materials will be included.

Selling costs need attention. Usual commissions may or may not be applied. Shipping costs may be higher or lower. Generally, variable costs will vary, and fixed costs will be fixed unless otherwise indicated.

An Example   Assume that Plante Company's capacity is 90,000 units, including 15,000 units made on overtime. Plante is currently producing and selling only 80,000 units of a men's winter hats each year in its northeastern U.S. market at a price of $8 per unit. Variable production cost is $3 per unit, and annual fixed factory overhead cost is $200,000. Variable sales and shipping costs are $.50 per unit; all operating fixed costs are $120,000. The profit calculation is as follows:

Sales (80,000 units × $8)		$640,000
Factory costs:		
Variable (80,000 units × $3)	$240,000	
Fixed overhead	200,000	440,000
Gross profit		$200,000
Operating expenses:		
Variable sales and shipping expenses	$ 40,000	
Fixed expenses	120,000	160,000
Net income		$ 40,000

A European catalog company approaches Plante with an order for 10,000 units at $6 each. Sales in Europe should not affect Plante's regular market. The special sales units would require inserting a new label and would be made during overtime hours, adding $.80 per unit to the factory variable cost. The overtime supervisor would be paid a $500 bonus for the extra work. The entire lot would be packed and shipped to Europe for $2,000. The analysis shows:

Incremental sales	$60,000
Incremental variable factory costs (10,000 × $3)	(30,000)
Additional variable factory costs (10,000 × $.80)	(8,000)
Additional fixed supervision costs	(500)
Additional shipping costs	(2,000)
Incremental contribution margin	$19,500

Incremental profit of $19,500 is added to the $40,000 from regular business to produce an estimated net income of $59,500 after the special sale to Europe. Plante adds to total profit by accepting the special order even though the special price of $6 is $1.50 below the average cost of $7.50 (total product and operating expenses divided by 80,000 units). At a price of $6, the order will contribute $2.20 per unit ($6 − $3 − $.80) toward any additional fixed costs, original fixed costs, and profit.

Factory and operating fixed costs are unchanged and can be ignored, except for additional specific supervision and shipping costs. Notice that the variable sales and shipping costs are also irrelevant, because data indicated they would not be applicable to the special sale.

Market Not Segmented   This example illustrates why some firms make price concessions in periods of excess capacity. However, accepting sales at special prices is generally a good policy only when the special market can be kept separate from the regular market. And this is a marketing, not a cost, problem. For example, in the preceding illustration, assume that the foreign market begins to affect the domestic market to the extent that the domestic price drops from $8 per unit to $7.60 per unit (a 5 percent drop). In this case, the firm's profit calculation for the next period would appear as follows:

Original net income from sales of 80,000 units	$40,000
Add incremental contribution margin from European sales	19,500
Less lost revenue from price reduction of $.40 per unit on regular sales	
(80,000 units × $.40)	(32,000)
Net income after special sale and regular sales reduction	$27,500

As can be seen, if the special market price influences the domestic market, the profit decreases from $40,000 to $27,500 rather than increasing to $59,500. If the line of demarcation between the European and the domestic market cannot be maintained, then a lower price is bound to dominate, maybe even below $7.60. The special sales pricing policy would be a poor policy for the firm to follow. Of course, any pricing policy can lead to poor results if the decision maker fails to properly assess market conditions. The problem lies not in the fact that variable costs instead of full costs were used, but that the market conditions were not properly assessed.

No Excess Capacity   Let us examine one more variation of this example. Assume that Plante's capacity was only 85,000 units instead of 90,000 units and that the European order is an all or nothing situation. By accepting the order, 5,000 units of regular business must be given up.

Incremental contribution margin from European sale		$19,500
Revenue from lost regular sales (5,000 × $8)	$(40,000)	
Variable factory cost of lost sales (5,000 × $3)	15,000	
Variable sales and shipping costs (5,000 × $.50)	2,500	
Contribution margin from lost sales		(22,500)
Impact on contribution margin after considering lost sales		$ (3,000)

Losing 5,000 units of regular sales to accommodate the 10,000 unit European sale will cost Plante profits. Based on this analysis Plante will probably reject the European sale.

Qualitative Factors   The major qualitative issue is a strategic concern. Product pricing is a key market positioning tool. Capacity use is a key resource of management concern. The special sales price decision can allow short-term decisions to preempt strategic plans. The first question a special order opportunity should trigger is: How does the sale fit the long-term market positioning goals of our products? Tied to this question is a second: Is using capacity for this sale consistent with the plans for using the firm's production capabilities? The decision guidelines presented above (excess capacity, segmented market, and one-time deal) are tactical rules to help prevent obvious short-term thinking from damaging long-run strategies. Each firm must answer the markets issue for itself. Should we build a premium product and price image? Discount deals may destroy that image. Do we have dealers depending on our pricing and product image stability? Will customers not really see similarities between our regular products and our special products? In many cases, short-term gains come at the expense of long-term market position.

The guideline on one-time deals is easily violated. Accepting one more one-time deal becomes an easy path to follow. When we repeat one-time deals, we begin to allocate a portion of our capacity to low profit business on a regular basis. Then, if the market segmentation guideline does not hold, regular business begins to shrink and special sales business will expand. Certain customers will be paying prices that cover all costs, while others will pay only a portion of the firm's operating costs.

All the caveats about contribution margin analysis and pricing are intended to point to the possible dangers in using a powerful tool that measures relevant costs and revenues. Relevant costing and pricing can be linked within any time frame—short or long. The keys are understanding the cost behavior patterns and separating relevant and irrelevant revenues and costs. Tying the contribution margin analysis to a company's pricing strategies is management's responsibility.

Use of Scarce Resource Decisions

The basic scarce resource decision asks the question: When a productive resource is limited, how do we allocate the use of scarce resources?

The scarce or limited resource decision is an extension of the special sales pricing decision except that no excess capacity exists. In fact, the problem is a common situation. Often several constraints exist for any decision. Examples are diverse, as shown in the table on page 567.

In all these situations, contribution margin analysis can be used. But instead of a direct contribution margin as in the special sales pricing decision, a contribution margin per unit of scarce resource is the relevant profit measurement. **Contribution margin per unit of scarce resource** is the contribution margin per unit divided by the amount of scarce resource used by each unit. For example, assume that Product 28 has a $10 per unit contribution margin and uses 30 minutes of a polishing machine that is a major bottleneck in the factory. Then, $10 divided by .5 hour tells us that the contribution margin per hour of polishing machine time is $20 per hour for Product 28.

It should be obvious that another approach to the same issue is: What price should be charged for various products or services that use given amounts of the scarce resource?

A complicating issue arises when we face more than one resource constraint. In the Product 28 example, molding capacity might also be a constraint in addition to the polishing machine problem. These multiple constraint problems use the same contribution margin data plus analytical tools like linear programing to find an optimal solution.

Scarce Resource	Issue
Specialized machine time.	What are the most profitable products per machine hour to produce?
Skilled employees time.	What is the most profitable work they can do per hour?
Space in a department store.	What is the most profitable use of the usable square footage?
Salesperson time during a sales call.	Which products should they attempt to sell during the limited time allowed them?
An accountant doing tax returns.	Which kinds of tax returns (simple to complex) should the accountant do?
A seat in a restaurant.	Which menu items generate the most profit per seat per dinner hour?
Spending a fixed advertising budget.	Which media spending will generate the most profit?
Student study time.	How much time should be spent on which courses to earn the highest grade average?

The Key Decision Rule and Guidelines   The scarce resource decision rule is: Select the products or services with the highest contribution margin per unit of scarce resource, which will give the combination of products that yields the highest total profit for the firm.

The rule means that the scarce resource controls the sales mix. Maximum profit per unit of scarce resource, the input, is the objective. The scarce resource constraint is generally a temporary situation. Often, we can hire or train more skilled workers, buy more equipment, rent additional space, etc. Thus, the problem is more like a short-term decision than the prior decisions.

The guidelines needed to apply the rule include:

1. The product with the highest contribution margin per unit of scarce resource is picked, then the second highest, and so on until the resource is fully utilized.

2. The amount of resource needed for each product or service must be known. Also, the contribution margin per unit of product or service must be known.

3. Minimum sales levels may be needed to meet sales demand and contract requirements. Sales potential may create a maximum sales level. The limits may indicate possible product pricing problems.

4. The contribution margin definition generally used is the variable contribution margin which is divided by the amount of resource used. If substantial direct fixed costs exist, they must be included in the analysis.

5. Any allocated indirect fixed costs are irrelevant to the product choice decision and should not be part of the analysis.

If a product's demand is unlimited, we generally find that it is the only product produced if it yields the most profit per unit of scarce resource. Maximum and minimum sales levels can be set to override the decision model's recommendation. From our earlier example, if Product 28 is the most profitable, the recommendation would be to produce all 28s. If our marketing people tell us that we can only sell 10,000 units of 28, we produce only 10,000 units. This may free machine time for the next most profitable product.

Also, a Product 32 may have been excluded because it has a low contribution margin per machine hour. But, if we have a contract requiring us to deliver 5,000 units of 32 at the current price, we must produce 5,000 units of 32. Required production further constrains machine time available for the most profitable products.

If we have normal sales levels for each product, we may be able to incorporate direct fixed costs into the analysis. This must be done carefully, understanding that fixed costs are being converted into a rate which makes them appear to be variable costs. The incorporation of these fixed costs is much like the activity-based costing analysis discussed in Chapter 3. There, formerly indirect costs assigned to products are converted to direct costs or at least are assigned using appropriate cost drivers.

Data Analysis Format and an Example   Formatting data for analyzing the scarce resource decision focuses on finding the contribution margin per unit and the scarce resource per unit used by each product. In either case, the objective is to work toward a profitability ranking of all products.

As an example of the format and the analysis, the Museum Repos Company (MRC) produces a series of reproductions of well-known sculptures. Finish work is done by four highly skilled artists. Only these persons can do the intricate carving and polishing needed to finish the pieces. MRC cannot produce enough units to meet the sales demand. Data from 1993 show four of the pieces MRC makes.

	Piece A	Piece B	Piece C	Piece D
Sales price per unit	$250	$350	$600	$1,000
Variable cost per unit	150	150	240	550
Assigned fixed cost per unit	50	110	120	200
Level of sales (units)	1,000 units	200 units	500 units	500 units
Hours of detail work per unit	2 hours	5 hours	6 hours	10 hours

The data format uses contribution margin analysis as follows:

	Piece A	Piece B	Piece C	Piece D
Sales price per unit	$250	$350	$600	$1,000
Variable cost per unit	150	150	240	550
Piece contribution margin per unit	$100	$200	$360	$ 450
Hours of detail work per unit	2 hours	5 hours	6 hours	10 hours
Contribution margin per hour of detail work (contribution margin per unit divided by hours per unit)	$50	$40	$60	$45
Priority: Highest piece profitability	2nd	4th	1st	3rd

Assuming that the four artists will have available about 2,000 hours of work time per year, we should use the 8,000 total hours as follows:

Produce	Piece	Hours Per Unit	Units	Hours Required	Remaining Available Hours	Contribution Margin Per Hour	Contribution Margin
					8,000		
1st	Piece C	6	500	3,000	5,000	$60	$180,000
2nd	Piece A	2	1,000	2,000	3,000	$50	100,000
3rd	Piece D	10	300	3,000	0	$45	135,000
Total hours used				8,000			$415,000

Not Produced:

Piece D	200 units
Piece B	200 units

The result is that all units of Pieces C and A and only 300 units of Piece D are made. The detail artists capacity is entirely used. The remaining 200 units of Piece D and all 500 units of Piece B will not be produced. This product mix will generate the highest total contribution margin given the limited artist capacity.

Note that the assigned fixed costs are not included in the analysis. The fixed costs are assumed to be indirect costs and will be incurred regardless of which products are made. The method of applying overhead to units uses activity bases and may cause different amounts of overhead to be applied to each product. But the amount of fixed costs incurred will not change.

Qualitative Factors   The fundamental qualitative issues in the scarce resource analysis are the basic questions of price and product offerings. Is only our firm's capacity limited or is the market place demand driven? Prices should be set based on competition and customer demand. The scarce resource analysis will highlight possible poor pricing positions of specific products. In the MRC example, prices of Pieces B and D might be raised to improve the contribution margin per hour of artist time and to match or exceed Piece C's level. Also, the question of whether certain products should be made at all can be raised. Often, low volume products may have unusually high set-up costs and other one-time costs. This might explain why Piece B has the highest ratio of fixed costs applied to product cost. More data are needed, but the analysis points to a problem with Piece B.

Also of concern is the use of the scarce resource itself. Can steps be taken to conserve capacity, to substitute less critical resources, and to buy additional capacity? After this analysis has been done, we can get an estimate of the value of additional capacity. In the MRC example, another employee working 2,000 hours per year would produce the following additional contribution margin:

	Hours Per Unit	Units	Hours Required	Contribution Margin Per Unit	Additional Contribution Margin
Piece D	10	200	2,000	$45	$90,000

The added contribution margin is $90,000. At that price, can we hire, recruit, or train another detail artist? Probably, yes.

The basic analysis ignores the complementary aspect of various products in a product line. To be in a market may require a complete offering, a full menu, or a complete set of departments. To offer less may cause us to lose customer interest and even access to customers.

The pricing question raised earlier also affects the expected volume of sales for each product. The inverse relationship between price and demand points to the need for a strategic pricing and capacity use policy, as discussed under the special sales pricing decision.

In the long term, more capacity, better utilization, or pricing changes will shift the decision away from a scarce resource problem. Yet, when business is too strong, the common sense rule of taking only the most profitable business should guide our decisions.

Sell or Process Further Decisions

The basic question in the sell or process further decision is: Should the product be sold as is or should it be processed further? A sell-or-process decision is characterized by a situation where a partially processed product can be produced and sold at a certain point in production, or it can be processed further and sold as a finished product. In other cases, additional features could be added to an existing product. Or, a sequence of services sold separately could be "bundled" into one service and sold as an integrated service.

A case common to process further decisions is where multiple products result from a process further step. These are called **joint products**, and the process step is called a **split-off point**.

Key Decision Rule and Guidelines   The key decision rule is: If the revenue after processing further minus the incremental costs of the processing is greater than the revenue if sold as is, process further. Or, expressed in the classic incremental form, is the incremental revenue from processing further greater than the incremental costs? If yes, do it.

The basic guidelines needed are:

1. All additional processing costs are assumed to be incremental.
2. Only costs incurred during the additional processing are relevant to the decision. Costs incurred prior to the split-off point are common to both sell and process further alternatives, cannot change, and are, therefore, irrelevant.
3. The decision is independent of the product costing task. In product costing, prior costs can be attached to units by arbitrarily splitting costs among the joint products. Here again, the only relevant revenues and costs are current and future values.
4. The basic decision also assumes that products are *either* sold as is *or* processed further. In many cases, we could do *both*—sell as is *and* sell after processing further. This alternative depends on available capacity and specific product profitability.

The decision task is to remember to always look forward and never backward. We are standing here today with something of value and looking to the future. We can sell it now. Or, we can do additional work on it, spend more money, and sell it in the future. Any past cost cannot be changed and is common to both alternatives. The decision assumes we are now at the intermediate step, not starting from the beginning.

Data Analysis Format and Examples   We can analyze data using either the incremental or total analysis versions. The incremental analysis format is:

Revenue from sale after processing	$
Less revenue from sale before processing	−$
Incremental revenue from processing	$
Less additional processing costs	−$
Contribution margin from processing further	$

Assume, for example, that a line of unpainted hardwood desks for home office use sells for $180 with a manufacturing cost of $100. The company can stain the desks at an additional cost of $30 each, yielding a desk that sells for $225. Due to market demand, the company could only sell 500 stained desks. The analysis follows:

Revenue from sale of stained desks (500 units @ $225)	$112,500
Less: Revenue from sale of unstained desks (500 units @ $180)	90,000
Incremental revenue	$ 22,500
Less: Cost of staining (500 units @ $30)	15,000
Incremental contribution margin from processing further	$ 7,500

The decision is obvious: stain and sell 500 desks.

Finding the additional profit of $7,500 from further processing the desks made three important assumptions. First, it is assumed that the cost of manufacturing the desk is irrelevant, because that cost is the same for each alternative—unstained or stained. Second, we assume that the company has capacity to process desks further without taking something away from the production and sales of other desks. And third, we assume that the only costs of further processing are variable costs. The company does not need to incur additional fixed costs for further processing. If these assumptions are not valid for a situation, the costs of further processing must be adjusted to reflect those facts.

Joint Products—Produce All or None   Another common situation is the joint product decision. Often, natural resource decisions result in many different intermediate stages and many different end products. Assume that we produce an industrial wax base with a sales value of $4 per gallon. The manufactured cost is $3.25 per gallon. We can process 60,000 gallons of the industrial wax through a process that gives us equal amounts of three high quality auto waxes: Super Gloss, Shiner, and Deep Glow. Performing the process represents the split-off point, that is to say the point at which we can sell the wax base as is or go ahead and make the three high quality waxes. The cost of further processing is $40,000. The market values of the three waxes are $6, $5, and $4.80 per gallon, respectively. Should we process further?

Revenue from processing further:

	Quantity	Price	Revenue
Super Gloss	20,000	$6.00	$120,000
Shiner	20,000	$5.00	100,000
Deep Glow	20,000	$4.80	96,000
Total			$316,000
Less cost of processing further			40,000
Net revenue from processing further			$276,000
Less revenue lost from industrial wax ($4 × 60,000 gallons)			240,000
Incremental contribution margin from processing			$ 36,000

The decision is to process further. Notice that the industrial wax production cost is not included since it is a common cost.

Joint Products—Process Which Products Further
If the process costs were variable costs and if any one or all of the auto waxes could be produced without any relation to the others, what should be done? Assume that the variable costs per gallon were $1, $1.25 and $.40 respectively. The analysis on a per gallon basis would be:

	Process Further Price		Industrial Wax Price		Incremental Revenue		Additional Processing Costs		Incremental Contribution Margin	Process Further?
Super Gloss	$6.00	−	$4.00	=	$2.00	−	$1.00	=	$1.00	Yes
Shiner	$5.00	−	$4.00	=	$1.00	−	$1.25	=	$ (.25)	No
Deep Glow	$4.80	−	$4.00	=	$ .80	−	$ .40	=	$ .40	Yes

Super Gloss and Deep Glow would be processed further, but Shiner has a negative incremental contribution margin relative to industrial wax and would not be produced. This assumes that we can sell all the industrial wax we can produce. If we must make a choice because of a limited supply of industrial wax, we would make Super Gloss first and then Deep Glow.

Joint Products—Setting Priorities
If we could produce as much as we can sell of all products, our priorities would be Super Gloss, Deep Glow, industrial wax, and finally Shiner. Shiner is the least attractive product, but it still generates a profit ($5.00 − $4.50) after the industrial wax product cost of $3.25 and the $1.25 of additional processing costs. The $3.25 is relevant only if we cannot sell all the industrial wax we can produce.

Qualitative Factors   The guidelines listed above highlight the qualitative issues. The short-term version of this decision assumes further processing stages can be shut down or started up with little cost impacts. In many processing operations, significant capacity costs exist. In real life, metals commodity prices often determine whether copper, zinc, and gold mines operate or temporarily suspend production. Prices of retail, wholesale, and "on the hoof" products and process costs at each stage in beef cattle, pork, and poultry operations are constantly monitored in order to make proper sell or process further decisions. In many cases, basic operating costs are significant and do not disappear if processing stops. If these costs continue, they are still irrelevant, but must be paid.

Again, the basic analysis and decision rules do work, but the long-run ramifications must always be included.

Add or Delete a Segment Decision

The basic decision question is: Is the firm more profitable with or without the segment?

Examples of this decision include:

1. Opening or closing a branch of a retail store.
2. Adding or eliminating a product in a product line or adding or eliminating an entire product line.
3. Adding or eliminating a specialized service in a hospital.
4. Opening or closing a claims office of an auto insurance firm.

In each of these examples, the question of whether the firm is better off with or without the particular segment hinges on the segment's contribution to the profits of the firm as a whole. A **segment** is a subset of the total business.

The decision analysis must look at the strategic value of the segment to be added or deleted. Then the analysis must look at the contribution the segment makes to profits and must resist the temptation to focus on net income of the segment.

Key Decision Rule and Guidelines   The key decision rule is: If the firm's profits are higher after adding the segment or deleting the segment, take the action that will enhance overall profitability.

This rule assumes that the following guidelines are in place:

1. Segment evaluations use direct contribution margin.
2. The basic analysis ignores complementary and substitution effects on other segments but includes them to form a complete picture.
3. Segment eliminations focus on lost revenue and avoidable costs.
4. Segment additions focus on incremental revenues and costs.

To make this judgment, direct contribution margin for the segment must be known. This means including revenues, cost of sales, and any other costs that are avoidable or incremental.

Figure 11.3 shows two income statements for the Brooks Store and a breakdown for its three departments. One is a net income format with indirect costs arbitrarily divided among the three departments. The other is in contribution margin format and stops measuring departmental profitability at the direct contribution margin level.

BROOKS STORE
COMPARATIVE INCOME STATEMENTS
(EXPRESSED IN THOUSANDS)

	Net Income Approach				Contribution Margin Approach			
	Dept A	Dept B	Dept C	Totals	Dept A	Dept B	Dept C	Totals
Sales.........................	$400	$500	$100	$1,000	$400	$500	$100	$1,000
Cost of sales	200	320	60	580	$200	$320	$ 60	$ 580
Variable sales commissions					40	50	10	100
Total variable costs.............					$240	$370	$ 70	$ 680
Gross margin	$200	$180	$ 40	$ 420				
Variable contribution margin					$160	$130	$ 30	$ 320
Operating expenses:								
Direct selling & administrative expenses:								
Variable & fixed	$ 80	$ 90	$ 20	$ 190				
Fixed					40	40	10	90
Direct contribution margin					$120	$ 90	$ 20	$ 230
Indirect operating expenses								150
Allocated equally	50	50	50	150				
Total operating expenses........	$130	$140	$ 70	$ 340				
Net income....................	$ 70	$ 40	$ (30)	$ 80				$ 80

Figure 11.3   Comparative Departmental Profit Measurements for the Brooks Store, a Merchandising Firm

The net income approach shows Department C to be losing money. The temptation to evaluate a segment's performance by allocating all costs to the segments is appealing from a completeness perspective. But segment net income sends misleading signals. Now, by reorganizing the data into a contribution margin format, it can be seen that the firm would be worse off by $20,000 (the lost contribution margin of Department C), if Department C were eliminated. None of the indirect costs currently allocated to Department C would disappear. This assumes that all Department C revenues, variable costs, and direct fixed costs are avoidable.

Data Analysis Format and an Example   Either the incremental approach or total analysis approach could be used. In a basic analysis, the incremental analysis approach highlights the revenue and expense changes and is easier to construct. However, where complementary and substitution effects are considered, the total analysis approach may show more clearly the effects of all changes in other departments.

Let's assume that Brooks sees the negative net income from Department C and considers eliminating it. Also, assume that deleting C has no impact on A and B or on indirect expenses. The incremental analysis shows:

Department C revenue lost	$(100)
Department C cost of sales avoided	60
Department C variable selling expenses avoided	10
Department C direct fixed expenses avoided	10
Department C lost direct contribution margin	$ (20)

The lost contribution margin is negative meaning that Brooks would lose $20,000 in profits. In this example, we would keep Department C. If this number were positive, we would delete the department because the relevant costs exceed relevant revenues.

Now, let us add some complexity to the example. Assume that if C is deleted, Department A will expand into C's space, add 10 percent to its sales and its variable costs, and add $8,000 to direct fixed costs. Also, assume that customers of C also made purchases in Department B. By dropping C, B's sales decline by 20 percent. To show all these changes a total analysis approach will be used in Figure 11.4.

BROOKS STORE
TOTAL ANALYSIS OF DELETING DEPARTMENT C
(EXPRESSED IN THOUSANDS)

	With Department C-- Contribution Margin Approach				Without Department C-- Contribution Margin Approach		
	Dept A	Dept B	Dept C	Totals	Dept A	Dept B	Totals
Sales	$400	$500	$100	$1,000	$440	$400	$840
Variable costs:							
Cost of sales	$200	$320	$ 60	$ 580	$220	$256	$476
Variable sales commissions	40	50	10	100	44	40	84
Total variable costs	$240	$370	$ 70	$ 680	$264	$296	$560
Variable contribution margin	$160	$130	$ 30	$ 320	$176	$104	$280
Fixed direct expenses:							
Selling & administrative expenses	40	40	10	90	48	40	88
Direct contribution margin	$120	$ 90	$ 20	$ 230	$128	$ 64	$192
Indirect operating expenses				150			150
Net income				$ 80			$ 42

Figure 11.4   Total Analysis of Deleting Department C

The analysis shows a $38,000 decline in profits. The growth in Department A gains $8,000. But the loss of sales in Department B loses $26,000, and the elimination of Department C loses $20,000. Expansion of A does not cover the lost contribution margin from C. The lost sales in B compound the negative impact of dropping C. Reject the change.

Qualitative Factors   Again, the short-term emphasis may hide the long-term costs of expansion or contraction. Adding a product may require sizable investments in inventories or production facilities. Dropping a product may release funds and free equipment and space. Thus, even after considering strategic issues, the quantitative analysis in many cases requires long-term financial factors.

The add or delete decision is tied to the scarce resource decision. The decision to drop or add is rarely an isolated decision. What will replace the dropped segment? What does the new segment replace? The opportunity cost is generally not zero, must be quantified, and is compared to the incremental change in contribution margin.

Also, while the complementary and substitution effects have been shown already, the subtle impacts on other products and departments are often difficult to measure before the fact. While direct contribution margin is used, certain direct costs may be neither entirely avoidable nor controllable by the decision maker. History also shows that cost contraction is much more difficult to manage than cost expansion.

Replace Equipment Decision

This decision asks the question: Is greater benefit (lower cost or higher profit) received from obtaining new equipment or keeping the old equipment?

To decide this question, the cost of operating or the profit earned from using the old equipment must be known. The new equipment brings two costs: first, the incremental cost of the new equipment; and second, the reduced operating costs or increased contribution margin earned from the new equipment.

To avoid multi-year investment considerations (which will be discussed in Chapter 12), we have assumed that the old and new equipment are rented. The analysis then becomes a combined add and delete decision. We delete the old equipment with its relevant revenues and costs and add new equipment with its relevant revenues and costs.

For example, a computer center has reached an activity level that requires two Model 310 mainframe units. These machines have a total annual rental cost of $500,000. Operating costs add another $200,000. In the next year, capacity will be exhausted requiring a third Model 310: $200,000 in added rent and $40,000 in added operating costs. A larger and faster Model 420 would have more capacity than the three Model 310s combined: rent for $720,000 per year and an operating cost of $150,000 per year. With this simplified data, the analysis is:

Rent of three Model 310s avoided	$700,000
Operating costs of three Model 310s avoided	240,000
Rent of Model 420 incurred	(720,000)
Operating costs of Model 420 incurred	(150,000)
Savings from renting Model 420	$ 70,000

The decision would be to replace the three Model 310s with a Model 420. Notice that the comparison is between three Model 310s and one Model 420. The future need for a third 310 is a given.

While renting or leasing equipment is common, purchasing equipment is the basic method of acquiring new assets. The investment is made today, and benefit is earned over the life of the asset. The basic data in the example beg the questions of what are the one-time conversion costs, what is the value of the old equipment, and how long will the old and new equipment last. These costs and time frames must be known to evaluate all aspects of the decision. This is a Chapter 12 task.

Capacity Expansion Decision

The expand capacity decision is in reality an add a segment decision and generally requires an investment to buy more equipment, space, or inventory. Expansions without any major investment can be analyzed in the same manner as in adding a segment. Where new investment is needed, capital investment analysis must be used. Again, Chapter 12 discusses these issues.

COSTS AND THE PRICING DECISION

One of most difficult and critical decisions faced by the manager is the pricing. A firm's pricing policy is a major part of its overall strategic marketing position. Costs often play a major role in pricing decisions in firms that have large capital investments, operate in mature markets, or operate in rate-regulated industries. In other firms, prices are functions of demand-oriented market places. Even here costs still play an important role, since relative product profitability is a major performance indicator. Also, global competitiveness has introduced market price as a starting point in product design and costing—a competitive market price minus a desired markup equals an allowable product cost.

In some situations, no pricing decision is needed. Market conditions may be such that widespread competition sets a universal price. For example, the major decision with agricultural products is determining what quantity to produce. However, in situations where the decision maker does have some control over price, information about both product supply and demand is needed. The cost side of the pricing decision is emphasized in this discussion; demand is considered, but is the responsibility of product planning or marketing managers.

Price Based on Full Cost

Markup pricing methods are widely used. To arrive at the price, a cost per unit is computed; and then a **markup**, stated as a percentage of cost, is added. The purpose of the markup is to provide for a profit. The term "cost" as used in this method is ambiguous until carefully defined. Two definitions are possible: variable cost or full cost.

The most widely used markup pricing form is based on full cost. **Full cost** is often assumed to be full manufactured cost, including fixed and variable product costs. Full cost is then used to set a price, usually by adding a percentage of full cost, to cover operating expenses and to generate an adequate profit.

The Fixed Cost Problem   The proper treatment of fixed cost presents a problem in full cost pricing. As volume increases, the fixed cost and full cost per unit decrease. If price follows cost, price goes down and further spurs demand. Unfortunately, the opposite is more distressing. As volume decreases, full cost increases. As price goes up, demand falls and volume declines again—a downward spiral. Hence, any attempt to consider the demand situation in establishing the full cost of the product involves circular reasoning.

Full cost pricing does have the following potential problems:

1. Full product cost per unit is accurate at only one level of volume.
2. Rarely does a full cost reflect incremental cost changes when volume changes.
3. To get to a product cost, numerous arbitrary allocations of costs have to be made.
4. A full cost-based price will almost guarantee that a "wrong" price will be selected.
5. Changes in full cost per unit do not reflect cost behavior as volume changes.

It does, however, offer some counter benefits:

1. Using full costs allows all products to bear a "fair share" of all costs that must be covered.
2. Rarely do decisions have only short-term impacts, and long-term costs patterns may behave like average or full unit costs.
3. Full product cost is more conservative and may generate a "wrong price," but the margin of error is often smaller than possible under a variable costing approach.

In any particular situation, however, it may be that no other pricing method gives any better result than full cost pricing. It is usually easier to criticize a pricing method than to recommend a better one.

The Allocation Problem   When two or more products are produced, the problem of how to allocate joint costs is encountered in full cost pricing. Although the allocation problem has been discussed in previous chapters, it is reviewed here. The earlier discussions were primarily concerned with cost allocation problems in cost accounting systems, where data are used primarily for inventory valuation and income determination. The problem is much the same in pricing. For this reason, full cost data developed in cost accounting are often used in full cost pricing. At the very least, cost accounting data provide a starting point for pricing purposes. In addition to the problem of how to allocate joint costs, note that the allocation process itself can involve high clerical costs when cost and product structures are complicated.

In choosing the basis of allocation for inventory costing and income determination, the rules of "use," "causality," and "benefit received" by the product can be used. In general, accountants try to allocate these common costs according to the resources consumed or the benefit received by the cost object (in this case the products). The argument is frequently made that machine-related overhead costs should be assigned to products on the basis of machine time but that labor-related overhead should be assigned on the basis of labor hours. This uses the activity base and the cost driver concepts. A link between resources used, their costs, and production activities is established. A product using more labor hours bears a greater portion of the labor-related costs, while a product using more machine time bears a greater portion of the machine-related costs.

A question arises, however, as to whether or not the cost drivers provide a good allocation base for setting prices. This is not an easy question to answer. It is sometimes argued that full cost pricing should give a "fair price" that assures social approval of the price. If this argument is valid, perhaps the allocation of common costs according to resource consumption is an acceptable basis for determining full cost and thus price. The manager could publicly defend such a price, if required. However, in seeking a price that provides the greatest positive difference between revenue and cost, it is difficult to see how the dual problems of cost allocation and choosing the volume over which to spread the fixed cost can be satisfactorily resolved.

Variable Cost Pricing

Another approach to cost-plus-a-markup pricing is to use variable cost rather than full cost as the cost base. One major advantage of this approach is that some of the difficulties of allocating indirect cost and spreading fixed costs can be avoided. To exploit the advantages of the variable cost approach, however, it is necessary to have reasonably accurate estimates of product demand. If such estimates are available and if variable costs are used, it may be possible to arrive at a price that approaches a maximum profit position. At the very least, such a procedure may consider more of the pertinent factors of a price decision than does the full cost approach. Even in long-term strategic planning, where all costs are assumed to be variable, pricing to maximize long-term profits is a key financial guideline.

In special sales pricing discussions above, caution was expressed about the realism of assumptions needed to make variable cost pricing fit the firm's long-run strategy. Yet, it is possible to build a pricing procedure for regular products using variable cost as a base. The use of variable cost pricing is frequently associated with a problem such as overcapacity. But beyond these cases, a careful study of variable cost pricing gives additional insights into pricing issues. The variable cost method is not a cure-all; but, although not widely accepted in business circles, it has many features that should be considered in setting prices.

If variable cost is used, the markup that is added must be large enough to cover all fixed costs and to provide a profit. A danger always exists that variable cost may, in time, come to be looked upon as the full cost; and in such instances the results would be disastrous. Prices that cover only a portion of total costs will, in the long run, lead to serious earnings problems. Also, the potential harm that a wrong markup percentage can do is greater under variable costing than under full costing.

Another reason why variable cost pricing is not widely accepted has to do with the inability of many conventional accounting systems to measure variable costs properly. Most systems are not geared to separate variable and fixed costs, and a careful review of job and process costing provides convincing evidence of this. The historical reason for this situation is the overwhelming influence that inventory costing and income determination have had on cost systems. Full cost has been considered the most acceptable base for income determination due to the accounting principles that require product costs to include all costs of production. The benefit principle also reinforces the valuation of inventory at full cost. In past decades, it was clerically not possible in many firms to measure both full cost and variable cost. However, computer systems now make it possible to measure almost any incremental quantity that is of use to management; thus, variable cost pricing is now more operational.

An important advantage of a detailed investigation of variable cost pricing is seeing a stronger relationship between the markup percentage and the market-demand function. In pricing policy, even if cost can be determined, it is still necessary to add the markup in order to establish a price. If the markup is too high, the price is too high; and the firm may price itself out of the market. If the markup is too low, the firm's price is too low; and it loses profits. Hence, the proper markup is related to the market situation.

SUMMARY

Managers in any organization must make decisions, some affecting operations in the short run, while others have long-run implications. This chapter established a framework for decision making and identified the steps necessary to make and implement decisions involving costs and revenues.

Differential analysis can be applied to a wide variety of decisions. The basic rule is to select the alternative that gives the greatest incremental profit. Incremental profit is the difference between the relevant revenues and the relevant costs of each alternative. Relevant revenues and costs are defined as the current and future values that differ among the alternatives considered. In most cases the term "incremental" is used as a substitute for "relevant." All past and committed costs and costs that remain the same across all alternatives should be ignored.

The decision types examined in detail were: make or buy, special sales order, scarce resource, sell or process further, and drop or add a segment. For each decision type, the key decision rule and guidelines were stated, and a format for analyzing relevant data was developed. In every decision, the short-term and long-term implications must be examined. While the basic decision assumes a short-term time frame, the real-world applications often include long-term elements.

Qualitative issues affect every decision examined with strategic and policy concerns looming in the background. These were discussed for each decision type.

Finally, the role of costs in the pricing decision was briefly discussed using full cost pricing and variable-cost pricing approaches. While pricing issues appeared in most of the decision discussions, the use of costs for pricing must be handled carefully. Managers responsible for market positioning and product planning use many tools, including cost data, to develop pricing strategies and policies.

PROBLEMS FOR REVIEW

Review Problem A

The Roed Corporation incurs the following estimated annual costs in making a part for one of its products:

	Total Costs for 20,000 Units
Direct Labor	$200,000
Direct Materials	600,000
Factory Overhead:	
Variable	300,000
Fixed	380,000

The Stauffer Company offers to sell the same parts for $60 per unit. If the parts are purchased from Stauffer, plant space currently used by Roed for making the parts can be rented out for $60,000 a year. Also, $120,000 of the fixed factory overhead could be avoided if the part is purchased.

Required:
What should Roed do?

Solution:
Create a T-account format and insert the relevant data:

Make			Buy	
Direct labor	$200,000		Purchase cost	
Direct materials	600,000		($60 × 20,000 units) ...	$1,200,000
Variable factory				
overhead	300,000			
Avoidable fixed factory			Rent from released	
overhead	120,000		space	(60,000)
Total "make" cost	$1,220,000		Total "buy" cost	$1,140,000

The decision, based on the quantitative facts, would be to buy the part and save $80,000.

Review Problem B   ~~Special pricing~~

Chiddick, Inc. sells a product called Teris at a price of $21 per unit. Chiddick is currently producing 200,000 units and is operating at <u>full capacity</u>. The costs per unit of Teris are as follows:

Direct materials	$ 4	
Direct labor	5	
Overhead	9	(60 percent of which is fixed) FC = 5.4 VC = 3.6
	$18	

A special order to buy 20,000 units was received from Lintol & Saegesser, an import/export firm in Beijing, PRC. Additional shipping costs incurred on this special order would be $2 per unit.

Required:

What is the minimum price per unit that Chiddick should set for the Beijing order?

Solution:

In sorting out the facts of the special pricing problem, Chiddick must determine whether:

1. Excess capacity exists—no, Chaddick is operating at full capacity.
2. Order will not interfere with regular business—probably okay since the order is from Beijing.
3. Has a positive contribution margin—this will depend on the price selected.

Since no excess capacity exists, Chiddick must take sales away from regular customers to sell to Lintol & Saegesser. It must earn at least the same contribution margin from the Beijing sale as from his regular sales. Since the Beijing sale will cost $2 per unit more in shipping costs, Chiddick must set the selling price at $23 per unit. This is the $21 regular price plus the $2 of additional shipping costs.

Please note that if Chiddick had excess capacity the price would need to cover only the incremental costs of producing the additional units. This would be: $4 for materials, $5 for labor, $3.60 for variable overhead, and $2 for shipping costs or a total of $14.60.

Review Problem C *Process further*

The Eckel Corporation produces products A, B, and C from a joint process. Joint production costs to produce A, B, and C were $60,000 and are allocated to A, B, and C according to number of units. Each product may be sold at its split-off point or processed further.

Product	Units Produced	Sales Price Per Unit at Split-Off	Sales Price Per Unit if Processed Further
A	20,000	$3	$6
B	20,000	4	8
C	20,000	7	9

Additional processing costs are $1 per unit for each unit processed further.

Required:

If Eckel only has $40,000 available for further processing, what would be the highest additional contribution margin it could earn from processing further?

Solution:

Find the incremental profit per unit for each product:

Product	Sales Price at Split-Off	Sales Price if Processed Further	Incremental Revenue	Incremental Cost	Incremental Contribution Margin	Rank
A	$3	$6	$3	$1	$2	2
B	4	8	4	1	3	1
C	7	9	2	1	1	3

Since each unit costs $1 to process further, Eckel can process 40,000 units. It will process Product B first, then A, and finally C if any funds are left. To process all of Product B will cost $20,000. This leaves $20,000 to process Product A. Processing all of Product A will cost another $20,000 and take all the remaining processing funds. No funds remain to process Product C, even though Eckel could earn a positive contribution margin from processing Product C further.

Eckel would earn an additional contribution of $100,000 as follows:

Product A:	($3 × 20,000 units)	−	($1 × 20,000 units)	=	$ 40,000
Product B:	($4 × 20,000 units)	−	($1 × 20,000 units)	=	60,000
Incremental contribution margin:					$100,000

Review Problem D *Add a Drop*

The Oetting Corporation has three product lines. Last year's costs for each product are as follows:

	Alpha	Beta	Gamma	Total
Sales	$ 230	$ 270	$ 360	$ 860
Variable costs	(120)	(150)	(170)	(440)
Unavoidable fixed costs	(60)	(60)	(60)	(180)
Avoidable fixed costs	(80)	(50)	(80)	(210)
Net Income	$ (30)	$ 10	$ 50	$ 30

Assume Ms. Oetting, the company president, is not impressed with the performance of product line Alpha and is deciding whether to eliminate it.

Required:

Is this a good decision and what is the impact of eliminating Alpha on the net income of the company?

Solution:

Two approaches can be taken: the incremental approach and the total approach. The incremental approach will show the lost revenues and the avoidable costs of Alpha:

Sales lost	$(230)
Variable costs avoided	120
Fixed costs avoided	80
Contribution margin lost	$ (30)

If Alpha is dropped, Ms. Oetting's profits will decline by $30.

The total approach will show the same thing. Total revenues and costs will show the following:

Sales	$630	($860 − $230)
Variable costs	(320)	($440 − $120)
Unavoidable fixed costs	(180)	No change
Avoidable fixed costs	(130)	($210 − $80)
Net income	$ 0	

After Alpha is dropped, Ms. Oetting is just breaking even instead of earning $30 in profits. She should keep Alpha, unless a more profitable alternative is found to replace Alpha.

Review Problem E

Rann Manufacturing has expanded into a new facility where it has excess capacity of 2,000 machine hours per month. The marketing manager has found three products the company could produce to take advantage of the extra capacity. Fixed overhead costs are applied to the units at $5 per unit. Data on these three products are:

	Products		
	A	B	C
Selling price per unit	$20	$25	$30
Variable cost per unit	8	15	17
Contribution margin per unit	$12	$10	$13
Less fixed costs per unit	5	5	5
Net profit per unit	$ 7	$ 5	$ 8
Units per machine hour	6	7	5

Required:

If the company has an objective to maximize total profitability, what order of preference would the company select for production?

Solution:

	Products		
	A	B	C
Selling price per unit	$20	$25	$30
Variable cost per unit	8	15	17
Contribution margin per unit	$12	$10	$13
Times units per machine hour	6	7	5
Contribution margin per machine hour	$72	$70	$65
Order of preference for production	1st	2nd	3rd

Notice that the fixed costs are irrelevant to the decision.

TERMINOLOGY REVIEW

Alternatives (549)
Contribution margin analysis (550)
Contribution margin per unit of scarce resource (566)
Decision objective (549)
Decision rule (549)
Differential analysis (550)
Full cost (578)
In-house sourcing (557)
Incremental analysis approach (551)
Incremental profit (550)

Joint products (570)
Markup (578)
Markup pricing method (578)
Opportunity cost (551)
Out-sourcing (557)
Out-of-pocket costs (550)
Relevant cost (550)
Relevant revenue (550)
Segment (573)
Split-off point (570)
Total analysis approach (551)

QUESTIONS FOR REVIEW AND DISCUSSION

1. Distinguish among the terms decision objective, decision rule, and decision guideline as used in the chapter. Show how the terms apply to one of the decision types discussed.

2.   Describe the steps in the decision-making process. In which steps does the managerial accountant play major roles?

3.   Why is identifying a decision's alternatives one of the most important steps in the decision-making process?

4.   Stan Hayhow, owner of several small local businesses, said recently: "The general rule I follow in making short-run decisions is that variable costs are almost always relevant and fixed cost are almost always irrelevant." Do you agree? Why or why not?

5.   Distinguish between:
     (a) Incremental cost and full cost.
     (b) Irrelevant cost and sunk cost.
     (c) Opportunity cost and differential cost.

6.   Joe Abbott of Quick Supply says he prefers the incremental analysis method because it eliminates all unnecessary data. Jan Gilbert of Office Managers, Inc. prefers the total analysis approach. Explain the difference between incremental analysis and total analysis as alternate means for providing data for decision making.

7.   Often, relevant costing decisions are described as short-term decisions. Is this valid? Is it a safe statement?

8.   "A rational person should be able to look at the relevant dollars and cents and make a sound decision." Agree or disagree? Why?

9.   Identify the guidelines that should be met for a special sales pricing decision using variable and direct fixed costs as a pricing base.

10. The president of Bethany Company said, "Accounting data are useful for predicting the results of various alternatives, but, in my company, the final selection of an alternative often depends on other factors." Explain the meaning of this statement.

11. How can opportunity costs be used in deciding whether a product should be sold in a partially completed state (intermediate product) or finished and sold as a completed product?

12. Artkraft Company produces two products in Department R. Product R-3 has a contribution margin of $60. Product R-7 has a contribution margin of $40. Explain under what conditions the company would be more profitable producing Product R-7, assuming it could sell all it produces of either product.

13. Why might a company produce a subassembly at a higher cost, rather than buy the same subassembly from an outside supplier?

14. In deciding to add or to delete a line of business, what version of profitability should be used? Explain.

15. Explain how a special sales decision in one firm might be a make or buy decision in another firm.

16. If a restaurant owner considers adding a new main course and deleting another for profitability purposes, what decision rule should be applied? This is what type of decision?

17. Although a special order would have contributed $75,000 to profits and the company had excess capacity, management rejected the order. What are the possible reasons for management's action?

18. In markup pricing, what elements must be covered by the markup when full costs are used? What elements must be covered when variable costs are used?

19. Explain how the treatment of fixed costs presents a problem in full cost pricing.

20. The marketing vice-president of Janelle Fabrics says that product prices should always be set by supply and demand in the market place to ensure high sales levels. The controller says that product prices should always be based on cost to ensure profitability. Is either correct? Does a middle ground exist?

EXERCISES

1. **Special Sales.** A. L. Anthony Company sells product A at a price of $30 per unit. Anthony's manufactured cost per unit based on the full capacity of 200,000 units is as follows:

Direct materials	$10
Direct labor	5
Overhead	12
	$27

The manufacturing overhead is one-third variable and two-thirds fixed.

A Japanese firm has offered to buy 20,000 units. Additional shipping costs of this order would be $2 per unit. Anthony has sufficient existing capacity to manufacture the additional units. The Anthony sales manager wants to earn $40,000 from this sale.

Required:
What is the minimum price per unit Anthony should charge?

2. **Make or Buy.** Sumners Corporation manufactures a subassembly HQ-101 for use in its major product. The costs per unit for 40,000 units of HQ-101 are as follows:

Direct materials	$14
Direct labor	4
Variable overhead applied	8
Fixed overhead applied	11
Total unit cost..	$37

Fryman Suppliers has offered to manufacture 40,000 units of HQ-101 for Sumners Corporation at a unit cost of $30. If Sumners accepts the offer, it could eliminate $6 per unit of the fixed overhead cost. In addition, Sumners could use the space in the production of another subassembly and save $70,000 in costs for that subassembly's operation.

Required:
1. Format the relevant data and recommend a decision to Sumners.
2. What factors other than the quantitative analysis does Sumners need to consider?

3. **Relevant Costs and Revenues and Opportunity Cost.** Zybura Company has 3,000 obsolete aluminum parts that are carried in inventory at $45,000, which was the original

production cost. The parts can be reworked at a cost of $5,000 and sold for $20,000. Otherwise, the company can sell the parts as scrap for $9,000, less disposal costs of $500. Zybura could also continue to hold the inventory at a cost of $4,000 per year.

Required:
1. What are the relevant costs and revenues for each alternative?
2. What is the best course of action?

4. **Incremental vs. Total Analysis Approaches.** Taylor Company currently produces 6,000 units per month of its major product. Financial data for a recent month are as follows:

Sales	$240,000
Variable costs	144,000
Fixed costs	60,000

The company would like to expand its operations to 7,000 units per month. Fixed costs would increase $10,000 because of the expansion.

Required:
1. Use the total analysis approach to evaluate the decision.
2. Use the incremental analysis approach to evaluate the decision.

5. **Scarce Resource Decision..** The Soma Company can produce three different products— Able, Baker, and Charlie. Because of unusual demand, all orders cannot be filled for the products. All variable dollar amounts are direct, but fixed costs are allocated on a per-unit basis. Soma has 2,000 hours of production time.

	Able	Baker	Charlie
Sales price	$50	$40	$30
Variable costs	30	25	20
Fixed costs	10	10	10
Production time per unit	1 hour	.5 hour	.2 hour

Required:
1. Assume that Soma can sell all of any product produced, what should Soma produce?
2. Assume that Soma can sell only 3,000 units of each product. What priorities should be set for the production manager of Soma to maximize profits?

6. **Process Further Decision.** Silver Bullet Refining produces naphtha, kerosene, and other distillates from a joint process costing $120,000 for a certain volume of crude oil. From this process, 1,000 barrels of naphtha have been produced and have been allocated $35,000 of the joint costs. They can be sold at the split-off point for $60 per barrel, or they can be further processed into other products and sold at $85 per barrel. The processing cost for further refining 1,000 barrels of naphtha is $20,000.

The other distillates can be sold now for $80,000 or processed further at a cost of $40,000 and sold for $110,000. Kerosene can be sold for $60,000 at the split-off point. Kerosene is also allocated $35,000 of the joint process costs.

Required:

1. Determine whether the 1,000 barrels of naphtha should be sold now or after additional processing.
2. What is the most Silver Bullet can pay for crude oil and not lose money on refining?

7. **Eliminating a Department.** ABCDE Department Store has 5 departments—A, B, C, D, and E. Department E is being evaluated using the data below for the store:

	All Others	Department E	Total
Sales	$4,500,000	$ 500,000	$5,000,000
Cost of sales	2,200,000	300,000	2,500,000
Gross margin	$2,300,000	$ 200,000	$2,500,000
Rent and services	$ 800,000	$ 200,000	$1,000,000
Direct salaries	450,000	50,000	500,000
Advertising allocation	450,000	50,000	500,000
Total expenses..................	$1,700,000	$ 300,000	$2,000,000
Net profit (loss)	$ 600,000	$ (100,000)	$ 500,000

Rent and Services is a corporate committed fixed expense and is allocated evenly to the 5 departments. Advertising will not change regardless of the decision, and is allocated using sales dollars. ABCDE is evaluating Department E's future.

Required:

Comment on the following statements about Department E:

(a) It is earning $100,000 in variable contribution margin for ABCDE.
(b) It is earning $150,000 in direct contribution margin for ABCDE.
(c) It is a $100,000 drain on the profitability of ABCDE.
(d) The company's overall profitability without Department E would be $600,000.

8. **Make or Buy Indifference Point.** Dave Simmet has found a manufacturer that will charge $40 per unit plus $200,000 for special equipment and dies for a lens and lens holder assembly for an overhead projector. But he thinks he can make it himself for the following costs:

Prime costs...	$21
Other variable costs	3
Total variable costs	$24

Simmet knows that incremental salaries, equipment rentals, and other fixed costs to make the assembly will run $360,000 per year. Common costs of manufacturing are applied to products at 60 percent of prime costs. Simmet plans to sell these projectors for $150 per unit.

Required:

Find the volume of sales units needed to cause Simmet to be indifferent between making the lens and lens holder assembly or buying it.

9. **Product Combination Decision.** Data concerning four product lines are as follows:

	Product Line			
	A	**B**	**C**	**D**
Selling price per unit	$300	$250	$130	$ 70
Variable cost per unit	250	80	50	40
Hours required for each unit	5	10	4	2
Maximum market potential (units)	No Limit	6,000	8,000	4,000
Total fixed cost.....................	$100,000			
Total hours available	96,000 hours			

Required:

1. Based on these data, choose the best product combination.
2. How would the answer change if the company were required to deliver 2,000 units of each product to a major distributor? The maximum market potential includes the major distributor's units.

10. **Process or Sell Decision.** The Smokie Meat Company produces a meat product which can be sold after slaughtering without additional processing, or it can be processed (smoked) and then sold. For the next month the company has scheduled production of 30,000 units of the product which, if sold unprocessed, would bring a selling price of $12 per unit. Variable costs associated with producing the unprocessed product are $7 per unit, and the fixed cost of the facilities used for producing the unprocessed product is $55,000 for the month. If 30,000 units of the unprocessed product are produced, the entire capacity of that part of the plant will be used. However, unused capacity in the part of the plant used for the smoking process will exist. If the 30,000 units are smoked, this capacity, which would otherwise be idle, will be entirely used.

The additional variable cost, mainly for heat and smoking ingredients, is estimated to be $5 per unit, and the selling price of the processed product is $17.50 per unit. The monthly fixed cost of depreciation on the portion of the facility used for smoking the meat amounts to $18,000. This cost is fixed regardless of whether or not the product is processed further.

Required:

Prepare an analysis to help the manager decide whether the 30,000 units should be sold processed or unprocessed.

11. **Equipment Replacement.** Consider the following two situations:

Situation A: Halo Enterprises is considering plans to rent a new power generator system for its agricultural business. It currently uses a system that rents for $20,000 per year and has annual operating costs of $24,000. The new system will rent for $30,000 per year and have annual operating costs of $10,000. Both systems will perform the same function.

Required:

Should Halo change to the new system?

Situation B: Last week Palo Enterprises purchased a new irrigation system called Spray costing $60,000. Its annual cash operating costs are estimated to be $35,000. It has a 4-year useful life and no residual value. Today, a salesman has offered Palo a new system called Sprinkle that will cost $60,000, and will also have a 4-year useful life with no residual value. The Spray equipment can be traded-in for a $10,000 allowance. The annual cash operating costs of Sprinkle are estimated to be $20,000.

Sales of $400,000 and other operating expenses of $180,000 per year will be the same under either alternative.

Required:

Ignoring the time value of money, should Palo purchase the Sprinkle system?

12. **Elimination of a Product Line.** The Haverick's Old General Store is currently divided into three departments. Over the past several months, sales and profit have declined, although the situation is now considered stable. Department 2 has begun to show a loss, and the owner, Joan Haverick, is thinking of discontinuing it. The space could be rented to a chain shoe store which would pay a flat fee of $12,000 a month to Haverick.

The following is an income statement for last month, considered to be typical. Costs of goods sold are variable costs. Sales salaries are fixed but directly identifiable with each department and could be avoided if the department were eliminated. The fixed administrative costs (allocated equally to all departments) would not change in total if the department were eliminated.

| | Department | | | |
	1	2	3	Total
Sales	$185,000	$80,000	$135,000	$400,000
Costs:				
Cost of goods sold............	$ 96,000	$44,000	$ 70,000	$210,000
Sales salaries	28,000	8,000	24,000	60,000
Fixed administrative cost	30,000	30,000	30,000	90,000
Total cost	$154,000	$82,000	$124,000	$360,000
Income before income tax	$ 31,000	$ (2,000)	$ 11,000	$ 40,000

Required:

Prepare an analysis and advise Haverick whether the department should be discontinued and the space rented.

13. **Special Sales Pricing.** The Chung Company is selling 80,000 units of a product at $10 per unit. The variable cost is $6 per unit, and the annual fixed cost is $120,000. A discount house has offered to buy 10,000 additional units of the product which would be slightly modified, but the modifications would not affect production cost. The discount house will pay $7 per unit.

Required:

1. If the two markets can be distinguished, should the order be accepted (assuming capacity exists and has no other use)?
2. The manager feels that the two markets might not be distinguished and that the lower price would cause regular sales to fall by 5,000 units. Should Chung accept the discount house offer?
3. If the discount house offer is raised to $9 per unit and competition resulting from the special sale causes the regular price to drop to $9.50 to maintain the same regular sales volume, should Chung accept the discount house offer?

14. **Explaining Profit Differences.** The Sneed Company sells for $26 per unit a product which has a variable cost of $17 per unit. The planned sales for the coming year are 100,000 units. With annual fixed cost of $540,000, the controller estimates the following profit per unit:

Selling price per unit		$26.00
Variable cost per unit	$17.00	
Fixed cost per unit	5.40	22.40
Profit per unit		$ 3.60

During the year, the company actually produced and sold 90,000 units; and the president, based on the controller's calculations, estimated the profit to be $324,000. When the statements were prepared, the profit was $270,000, even though actual costs behaved as estimated.

Required:
Prepare an analysis to show why the profit was $90,000 lower than had been estimated and $54,000 below the president's calculations.

15.   **Special Sales Pricing.** Muir Company manufactures study lamps. The budget for next year calls for sales of 500,000 lamps at $17 each. Variable costs are $9 per lamp, and fixed costs are budgeted at $3,000,000 or $6 per lamp. Recently, a purchasing agent from Nationwide Discount Superstores offered to buy 100,000 lamps at a price of $13.50 each. By working overtime and extra shifts, Muir would have sufficient capacity. Additional overtime premiums would be $75,000. Additional supervision costs are $20,000. Total selling and administrative expenses will not change if the order is accepted.

Muir's finance manager argues that "With the extra volume the full cost of regular sales would be reduced from $15 per unit to $14. At this level Muir would make an extra $1 per unit on all regular sales, but still lose money on the special sales because of overtime costs and the lower price."

He thinks that the "economics of the deal" are too risky and that the deal violates the firm's strategic pricing policies that have helped Muir create a reputation for quality.

Required:
1.   Is the finance manager's quantitative analysis sound?
2.   What does the finance manager mean by "too risky?" And why might this be a violation of the firm's pricing policies?

16.   **Make or Buy.** Roto Inc. makes steel blades for lawn mowers that it assembles and sells. The cost accounting system gives the following data:

Units produced	100,000 units
Materials	$ 60,000
Direct labor	20,000
Variable manufacturing overhead	60,000
Fixed manufacturing overhead	90,000

Roto has an opportunity to purchase its 100,000 blades from an outside supplier at a cost of $2.20 per blade. Inspection of the purchased blades will cost an additional $5,000 in the quality assurance department. Certain leased equipment costing $30,000 and included in fixed overhead can be avoided if the blades are purchased. The released space could be used to make another part that is now purchased, which would save Roto $46,000.

Required:
On quantitative terms, should Roto buy the blades from the outside supplier?

17. **Segment Profit Performance Analysis.** Blaufuss Sausages has a central processing plant and three stores. Recently, profits have been declining. The projected 1994 income statement for the three stores appears below:

	Main Street	King Street	Queen Street	Total
Sales	$ 200	$ 175	$ 190	$565
Product cost of sausages . . .	(120)	(100)	(110)	(330)
Gross margin	$ 80	$ 75	$ 80	$235
Direct store expenses	(60)	(85)	(35)	(180)
Allocated administrative overhead expenses	(25)	(15)	(20)	(60)
Net income	$ (5)	$ (25)	$ 25	$ (5)

Required:
   If all revenues and expenses are as presented above and each store is independent of all others, what will each of the following actions do to Blaufuss Sausages' profits?
(a) Eliminate Main Street store.
(b) Eliminate King Street store.
(c) Eliminate Main and King Street stores.
(d) Close all stores.
(e) Open a fourth store so that the allocated administrative overhead expenses can be allocated over four stores. (Assume that the new store will have a zero net income.)

18. **Full Cost Pricing.** The Dual Track Company produces two products, A and B. Data on cost and production are as follows:

	Product A	Product B
Materials cost per unit.	$35	$16
Labor hours required per unit	3	2
Hourly labor rate	$15	$12
Planned production	20,000 units	40,000 units

Annual fixed overhead costs amount to $840,000.

Required:
   Assuming the manager wants to set a price with a 10 percent markup based on full cost, prepare an analysis showing what the selling prices for each product would be if the fixed overhead costs were allocated using:
(a) The total number of planned production units.
(b) Total planned direct labor hours.

19. **Markup Pricing.** Assume that the following cost analysis has been performed for a specific customer order for Lila Products, Inc. The president, Lila Ganong, is experimenting with different pricing strategies. She thinks 100,000 units can be sold. Fixed costs have been allocated using various activity bases.

	Per Unit	Total
Manufacturing costs—variable	$4.25	$425,000
Manufacturing costs—direct fixed	1.50	150,000
Manufacturing costs—indirect fixed	3.75	375,000
Manufacturing costs—total	$9.50	$950,000
Selling expenses—variable	$1.80	$180,000
Selling expenses—indirect fixed	1.45	145,000
Selling expenses—total	$3.25	$325,000

Required:

What markup percentage is needed to earn $120,000 if the price is set:

(a)   Assuming that the order is a one-time sale?

(b)   Assuming that the order will become part of Lila's regular product line?

20.   **Cost Analysis and Pricing.** Sales in the Jackson office of Fast Print Company for 1994 were $475,000. The costs were:

Materials and variable supplies costs	$200,000
Direct labor costs	100,000
Occupancy and other fixed operating costs	100,000
Total	$400,000

For most printing jobs, a cost-plus pricing policy is used. To find a job's cost, estimated labor costs are doubled to cover labor and overhead and added to estimated materials costs. The total job cost is then multiplied by 120 percent to calculate customer price.

A local supermarket advertising manager has come to see the office manager with an offer. She will bring a weekly advertising piece to be printed which will be mailed to local residents. The printing job would require $200 of materials and supplies and $100 of direct labor time. She is willing to pay $450 per week and would like a one-year contract. The Jackson office manager rejects the offer since it violates his pricing strategy.

Required:

1.   Is the supermarket business profitable for Fast Print:

(a)   On a one-time basis?

(b)   As a regular (annual) basis?

2.   What qualitative issues might impact your answer?

PROBLEMS

11-1   **Make or Buy Decision.** Ling Automotive Systems is introducing a new electronic wiring system for the original-equipment auto market. The system requires an electronic-controlled motor that the firm does not currently produce. Production engineering has talked to several suppliers. The best bid is from Fiero Electronics at $23 per unit for any volume within the firm's relevant range. Delivery must be guaranteed on a JIT basis.

Ling's production manager believes that he can make the motor although additional space and machinery would be required. The firm now leases, for $80,000 per year, space that could be used to make the new motors. However, the space is now used to assemble another sub-system. Ling would have to lease additional space in an adjacent building for the assembly process. That space rents for $175,000 per year. It is suitable for assembly work but not for motors production. Additional equipment needed to produce the motors could be rented for $200,000 per year.

The controller has developed the following unit costs based on the expected demand of 100,000 units per year:

Materials	$10.00
Direct labor	4.00
Rent for space	.80
Machinery rental	2.00
Other costs	10.00
Total cost	$26.80

The "other costs" figure includes $6 per unit of allocated fixed overhead and $4 of variable overhead costs.

Required:

Determine whether Ling should make or buy the motors.

11-2   **Relevant Costs.** Celeste Granger is a sales representative in southwest Texas for Precise Images Equipment. The company has asked her to expand her territory to cover El Paso in west Texas. This expansion will increase Granger's mileage by 12,000 miles per year. To see whether this proposal is worthwhile to the company, Granger's supervisor has asked her to estimate the additional costs expected per year.

Granger drives an average of 40,000 miles per year without the proposed expansion. She keeps good records of her travel expenses, and her records show the following automobile expenses for 40,000 miles:

Estimated variable costs:	
Gasoline	$ 4,000
Routine maintenance (oil, tires, minor repairs, etc.)	1,600
Estimated annual costs:	
Insurance	960
Licenses and taxes	200
Depreciation (based upon a 2-year ownership policy and straight-line depreciation)	6,000
Total expenses	$12,760

Revenues in El Paso using an independent service company have been about $80,000 with a variable contribution margin of 35 percent after paying a 10 percent sales commission to the service company. Granger's personal calls could increase sales by 50 percent. She is paid a 5 percent commission in addition to her salary. By shifting her territory, possible sales growth in her existing territory might not be fully realized, costing the firm $10,000 in contribution margin next year.

Required:

Prepare an analysis of differential costs and revenues between the status quo alternative and the alternative to expand the territory.

11-3   **Determining the Least-Cost Alternative.** McNulty Construction, Inc. plans to erect a new building. It will use part of the space for its own offices and lease the balance of the space to tenants. The company has two alternatives: (1) do its own construction work or (2) use an independent contractor.

If the company does its own construction work, it will not be able to handle outside construction contracts that would contribute $600,000 to net income. The costs attributable to these outside contracts are excluded from both sets of the estimated costs of operation shown below. These estimates have been prepared to show the expected results for the coming year when the office building will be built.

	McNulty's Estimated Yearly Operating Costs (Building Constructed by Independent Contractor)	McNulty's Estimated Yearly Operating Costs (Building Constructed by McNulty Construction)
Materials.............................	$6,000,000	$7,000,000
Construction labor.....................	3,000,000	4,800,000
Indirect materials and supplies	315,000	400,000
Supervision	650,000	780,000
Taxes and insurance	50,000	70,000
Maintenance and repairs	106,000	106,000
Truck and equipment operation	91,000	91,000
Depreciation..........................	60,000	60,000
Travel	40,000	43,000
Telephone and utilities	107,000	107,000
Miscellaneous	10,000	10,000

The independent company has bid $3,500,000 for the job.

Required:
1. Which of the two alternatives should be selected to obtain the lowest construction cost? (Ignore income taxes.)
2. Given the goal of maximizing the company's financial returns, which alternative should be selected?

11-4. **Evaluating a Segment.** Mr. Yablanka has recently inherited a chain of about 90 bakery shops in Chicago from his mother-in-law. Several new outlets are opened and old ones are closed annually. He is in the process of evaluating the performance of each location and of all his store managers. He is currently evaluating Store 54, managed by a relatively experienced manager. Business statistics for the company and Store 54 data are as follows (dollars are in 000s):

	Company Data	Store #54
Sales	100%	$ 400
Costs:		
Cost of baked goodies	35%	$ 150
Store salaries and wages	20	110
Store occupancy costs	30	120
Home office expenses	10	50
Total expenses...............................	95%	$ 430
Net income	5%	$ (30)

The store's lease is a 5-year commitment for $40,000 per year. If Store 54 is closed, another nearby store would pick up $50,000 of Store 54's lost gross margin. Store 54's manager has a 5-year personal services contract for $30,000 per year and will be transferred to a new store being opened. All other salaries and occupancy costs can be eliminated. Home office expenses are allocated evenly among the 90 stores.

Required:
1. Should Store 54 be closed now? Why or why not?
2. If a 6-month reprieve is given the manager of Store 54, in what areas should the manager focus attention?

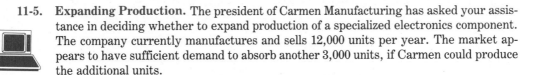

11-5. Expanding Production. The president of Carmen Manufacturing has asked your assistance in deciding whether to expand production of a specialized electronics component. The company currently manufactures and sells 12,000 units per year. The market appears to have sufficient demand to absorb another 3,000 units, if Carmen could produce the additional units.

Each component currently sells for $70. The total costs during this past year when 12,000 components were produced were:

Direct materials	$144,000
Direct labor	96,000
Other variable factory expenses	120,000
Fixed factory expenses	240,000
Variable selling expenses	24,000
Fixed selling and general expenses	150,000

The company maintains no inventory, since it can sell the products as fast as they come off the production line.

The president notes that costs will increase in some areas. Direct materials will increase 5 percent; the other variable factory expenses will increase 10 percent; and fixed factory expenses and fixed selling and general expenses will each increase by $5,000.

Production can be expanded by 3,000 units (for a total of 15,000 units) without incurring any new fixed factory expenses. However, producing in excess of 15,000 units will require new equipment that will add $60,000 to the fixed factory expenses. This equipment would allow the company to expand to a total of 18,000 units.

Required:
1. Prepare an income statement showing the net income before taxes with sales of 12,000 units, 15,000 units, and 18,000 units.
2. What would you advise the president to do in this case?

11-6. Evaluating a New Sales Segment. Bambery Steering Inc. is presently operating at 75 percent of practical capacity, producing about 200,000 units annually of a patented power steering system component. Bambery recently received an offer from a Korean truck manufacturer to purchase 40,000 components at $8 per unit. Bambery has not previously sold systems internationally.

Budgeted production costs for 200,000 and 250,000 units are as follows:

Units	200,000	250,000
Costs:		
Direct material	$ 600,000	$ 750,000
Direct labor	240,000	300,000
Factory overhead	800,000	900,000
Total costs	$1,640,000	$1,950,000
Cost per unit	$8.20	$7.80

John Capers, VP Sales, thinks accepting the order will get the company's "foot in the door" of the expanding international market, even if the company loses a little on this order.

Marge Horne, VP Engineering, feels that any new market should first show its profitability and that this offer is below last year's cost per unit of $8.20. "This guarantees a loss on the order," she says.

Gino Minutelli, the treasurer, has made a quick computation indicating that accepting the order will actually increase dollars of gross margin.

Required:
1. Estimate Bambery's variable cost per unit.
2. Show how Marge and Gino are analyzing the situation. Using the facts as given, what does the incremental analysis of the additional 40,000 units show?
3. What major non-quantitative factors might affect the decision to accept or reject the special order.

11-7. **Alternative Uses of Capacity.** Harris Equipment Manufacturing built a new facility five years ago but has only been able to use 60 percent of its capacity to build a major machine products line. Management would like to use the excess capacity and has three possibilities. Only one of the three may be selected.
   (a) Harris could produce an additional 600 units per year of its most popular machine and focus new marketing efforts on the European metal parts producers. Management estimates that additional freight costs would amount to $550 per machine and fixed factory overhead would increase by $150,000. To cover the additional cost, the selling price per machine on European sales would be increased by $1,100 per machine. Incremental international selling costs would be about $200,000 per year. Harris has earned a contribution margin of $1,800 on each unit in the past.
   (b) Harris could produce and market a smaller model of an existing laser lathe. The capacity could be used to produce 200 units per year that would sell for $15,500 each. Management has estimated the following unit variable costs.

Direct materials	$3,000
Direct labor	1,500
Variable overhead	2,000
Variable selling	500
Total costs	$7,000

The new lathe would require additional fixed costs of $700,000 in fixed overhead and $250,000 in fixed selling expenses.
   (c) Olson Testing Company has offered to lease the facilities at $45,000 per month plus 10 percent of the net revenues generated from the facilities by Olson. Net revenues are estimated at $2,200,000 per year.

Required:
1. Which of the three alternatives should management select?
2. What is the opportunity cost of this decision?

11-8. **Dropping a Product.** The Leverenz Corp. runs a speciality food and novelty products firm. He buys rattlesnakes from "snake hunters" in west Texas, paying an average of $10 per snake. Each snake comes complete. He produces canned meat, cured hides, and rattles. At the end of a recent season, Mr. Leverenz is evaluating his financial results:

	Meat	Hides	Rattles	Total
Sales	$ 30,000	$ 8,000	$ 2,000	$ 40,000
Cost of snakes	(18,000)	(4,800)	(1,200)	(24,000)
Gross profit	$ 12,000	$ 3,200	$ 800	$ 16,000
Processing costs	$ (6,000)	$ (900)	$ (600)	$ (7,500)
Common costs	(4,000)	(600)	(400)	(5,000)
Operating expenses	$ (10,000)	$ (1,500)	$ (1,000)	$ (12,500)
Income (loss)	$ 2,000	$ 1,700	$ (200)	$ 3,500

The cost of snakes assigned to each product is based on ratio of cost to revenue (60 percent). Processing costs are direct costs. Common costs are allocated on the basis of direct processing costs and are unavoidable.

Mr. Leverenz has a philosophy of "every tub on its own bottom" and is determined to cut his losses on rattles.

Required:
1. Is he really "losing" money on rattles? Explain.
2. An old miner has offered to buy every rattle "as is" without processing for $.50 per rattle. Will this eliminate the "loss" problem and improve his profitability?

11-9. Value of Additional Information. Three of your friends (Doug, Dan, and Dave) are playing a "who done it" game at a party. Another friend, Doris, paid $15 to get key pieces of evidence about the "crime." Doris could sell her information to Doug, Dan, and Dave for $10 each. Instead of selling the information now, Doris could buy more information and collect different revenues from each. The amount of the revenue depends on what each person thinks it will be worth. Doris's cost of collecting more information and her new revenue estimates are:

	Cost of More Info	Doris' Revenue After Buying More Info
Doug	$15	$20
Dan	$ 5	$18
Dave	$ 8	$15

Required:
When should Doris try to collect from each of your friends—now or after buying more information?

11-10. Expansion and Elimination of a Division. AGRI Corporation is a corporate farmer with operations in the Pacific Northwest, Iowa, and Texas. Due to weather conditions and a downturn in the market, the Texas operations have produced marginal results for several years. Management is considering discontinuing its operations in Texas. However, the company must still meet current contractual commitments to provide certain commodities to processors. If closed, all direct Texas costs can be avoided.

Management has provided the following projection of operations for the upcoming year ($000 omitted).

	Total	Northwest	Iowa	Texas
Sales	$6,600	$3,200	$2,000	$1,400
Variable cost	$1,188	$ 527	$ 380	$ 281
Direct fixed costs:				
Operations	2,170	985	635	550
Administrative...................	1,650	840	420	390
Home office—allocated	792	396	252	144
Total costs	$5,800	$2,748	$1,687	$1,365
Net income	$ 800	$ 452	$ 313	$ 35

Management believes it has two alternatives to evaluate:

(a) Close the Texas operations and lease the assets, realizing an annual net return of $125,000, and enter into an agreement with a competitor to fill the contractual commitments. Under this agreement, AGRI Corporation would receive 15 percent of the net sales from these commitments, and net sales are estimated at $600,000.

(b) Expand in Iowa by using presently idle space to service the customers of the discontinued Texas operation. The move would result in several changes in Iowa as follows:

	Increase over Current Operations
Total sales	40%
Total variable cost	50%
Fixed operations cost	20%
Fixed administrative cost	10%
New transportation cost	$88,000

Under both alternatives, the home office expenses will remain the same in total. If the Texas operations are eliminated, the home office expenses will be allocated only to the Northwest and Iowa operations.

Required:
1. Should AGRI Corporation discontinue its Texas operations?
2. If the Texas operations are closed, how should AGRI satisfy its contractual commitments?

11-11. **Incremental Versus Total Analysis Approaches.** McGee Manufacturing operates a plant in Oregon for the production of a special wooden molding used on desktops. The company operates one shift and produces 150,000 packages annually that sell for $15 each to specialty producers. The product has a derived demand sufficient to warrant considering the doubling of production. Information on current production is as follows:

Direct material cost	$6.25 per unit
Direct labor cost at 50,000 hours	$12.00 per hour
Other variable production and selling costs...................	$105,000
Fixed production and selling costs	$387,000

To increase sales to 300,000 units per year, the company will need a second shift. Direct materials cost would remain the same per unit. Because labor efficiency is expected to be higher than on existing production, it is estimated that only 42,000 direct labor hours will be needed on the second shift. The labor rate, including shift premium, would average $15.00 per hour. Other variable production and selling costs will jump to $1.00 per package. Additional fixed cost of $180,000 per year will be incurred.

Required:
1. Evaluate the second shift using the incremental analysis approach.
2. Evaluate the firm as a whole if the second shift is implemented using the total analysis approach.

11-12. Extension of Manufacturing Process. Little Folks Fun Things Inc. manufactures the components used in the production of swing sets, play pens, and other children's yard toys. These components are not painted or processed further. Instead, they are sold to other manufacturers for completion or are sold to distributors for sale as unfinished items requiring further work.

The play pen components, for example, are sold to other manufacturers or to stores for $33 per set. Approximately 45,000 of these sets are sold each year. The president of the company, Connie Zimmerman, believes that the company can do the finishing work and sell the completed play pens at a price of $49 per unit.

The controller of the company has provided the following cost data for use in analysis:

Cost to manufacture unfinished play pens (45,000 units):	
Direct materials	$ 360,000
Direct labor	540,000
Manufacturing overhead applied at the rate of $5 per machine hour	225,000
Total production cost..	$1,125,000
Estimated cost to finish 45,000 units:	
Additional direct materials	$ 67,500
Additional direct labor cost	292,500
Additional variable overhead	90,000
Annual salary of supervisor hired for finishing operation	32,000
Other additional fixed costs	60,000
Total additional cost	$ 542,000

Required:
1. Using the data given, compute the economic advantage or disadvantage of the finishing operation.
2. Identify the costs that are irrelevant costs with respect to this decision?
3. Identify the opportunity cost in the decision to finish.
4. If the market declines so that only 20,000 finished units can be sold each year, compute the advantage or disadvantage in the finishing operation.

11-13. Use of Capacity. Duncan Specialty Compounds manufactures chemical compounds for industrial use. Department 23 produces related products—Pre and Post. Pre can be sold for $3.00 per pound or processed further and sold as Post. Pre can also be bought from other suppliers at a market price of $3 per pound plus $.25 per pound for transportation. One pound of Pre is used to produce one pound of Post. Post has been selling for $7.20 for several years, but the price has recently fallen to $6.80. Production could be Pre only, Pre and Post, or Post only.

Department 23's available capacity is 300,000 hours. It takes one hour to make 10 pounds of Pre and two hours of additional processing to make 10 pounds of Post.

Sue Martin, the vice-president of marketing, has analyzed the markets and costs. She thinks that Post production should be halted when Post's price falls below $6.55 per pound. At that point, the profit from a pound of Post would be less than two times the profit from a pound of Pre. She says this is important since Post uses twice as much production time as Pre. She cites the following data:

Department 23 Analysis of Pre:

Selling price, net of any selling costs		$3.00
Direct materials and labor	$1.95	
Manufacturing overhead	.60	
Cost per pound		2.55
Operating profit per pound		$ .45

Department 23 Analysis of Post:

Selling price, net of any selling costs		$6.80
Cost of 1 pound of Pre (from above)	$2.55	
Additional direct materials and labor	1.90	
Manufacturing overhead	1.20	
Cost per pound		5.65
Operating profit per pound		$1.15

Direct materials and labor costs are variable. Manufacturing overhead is fixed and is allocated to products by budgeting the total overhead for the coming year and dividing by the total hours of capacity available.

Required:

Is Sue Martin correct about her production recommendation? Recommend a production plan.

11-14. Product Combination Decision. The Merkle Company sells three products which can be sold in any combination so long as no more than 210,000 machine hours are used. All costs are variable (labor and materials) except for the rental cost of the production facility, which is $480,000 per year. The economic data for each product are as follows.

	Product L	**Product M**	**Product N**
Selling price per unit	$20	$15	$10
Variable cost per unit	11	9	6
Machine hours per unit	3 hours	4 hours	1 hour

Required:

1. In the absence of any market constraints, what is the most profitable combination of products, and what is the profit?
2. If the market for Product N is limited to 90,000 units, with no market limitation on the other products, how does this change the best product combination and the profit?
3. What is the best product combination (and the profit) if a shortage of materials for Product L limits the production of that product to 30,000 units, and there is still a market limit of 90,000 units of Product N?

11-15. Make or Buy Decision. The Prada Company produces a part used in the final assembly of its main product. Two manufacturing operations are required to produce the part. Typical annual production of the part is 160,000 units. The estimated current costs are as follows:

Operation 1:

Materials	$144,000
Direct labor	52,000
Variable overhead	140,000
General overhead	95,000
Total cost, Operation 1	$431,000

Operation 2:

Direct labor	$ 90,000
Variable overhead	50,000
General overhead	60,000
Total cost, Operation 2	$200,000

The general overhead is fixed. The other costs are variable. Operation 1 can be eliminated if these parts are purchased from an outside vendor. The vendor will supply 160,000 units a year at $2.00 per unit. These parts would still have to be processed through Operation 2. The Prada Company would have to pay freight of $12,000 per year on the purchased parts. If Operation 1 is eliminated, the space can be rented for $14,400 per year.

Required:

Prepare an analysis to help the company decide whether to purchase the parts or to continue to manufacture them in Operation 1.

11-16. Make or Buy Decision. Perkins Company produces a line of iron and steel building products. The product lines include numerous subassemblies and parts. Many of these parts can be either produced in Department 8 by Perkins or out-sourced from parts suppliers. Several of these parts are listed below with their related cost and production data, including their normal batch sizes and the estimated cost of each set up:

	Iron Frames #10	Steel Frames #11	Steel Housing #12	Assembly Unit #13
Materials cost per unit.............	$5.00	$6.00	$18.00	$8.00
Variable labor cost per unit	1.50	1.00	5.00	3.00
Overhead cost per unit excluding set-up costs).....................	4.50	3.00	15.00	9.00
Units required....................	80,000	40,000	15,000	100,000
Hours required per unit............	1 hour	4 hours	5 hours	2 hours
Batch size (in units)...............	10,000	10,000	3,000	5,000
Estimated set-up cost per batch	$4,000	$3,000	$3,000	$2,000
Outside prices per unit	$10.00	$11.00	$32.00	$18.00

These four parts can be produced or purchased. Department 8's facilities are flexible in that these parts can be produced in any combination. The materials and labor are considered to be variable costs. Batch sizes and set-up costs have been estimated based on past experience. Overhead costs are fixed, except for setup costs. Total overhead is assigned to products at the rate of 300 percent of direct labor cost. This rate is a predetermined rate established from the factory overhead budget.

The capacity of the producing department is 300,000 machine hours. Consider the contribution margin to be the difference between the outside purchase price and the appropriate costs of manufacturing.

Required:

Using contribution margin analysis, show the manager how much of each product to manufacture and how much of each to purchase. What is the dollar contribution associated with your solution?

11-17. **Direct Contribution Margins.** The Ashwell Company makes three products. Revenue and cost data for a typical month are as follows ($000 omitted):

| | Products | | | |
	J	K	L	Total
Sales	$300	$500	$800	$1,600
Variable costs	90	200	400	690
Contribution margin	$210	$300	$400	$ 910
Fixed costs:				
Separable and avoidable	$ 90	$100	$120	$ 310
Joint, allocated on sales dollar basis	60	100	160	320
Total Fixed costs:	$150	$200	$280	$ 630
Profit	$ 60	$100	$120	$ 280

Required:

Answer each of the following questions independently.

(a) The firm is considering the introduction of a new Product M to take the place of J. Product M would sell for $12 per unit, have variable costs of $5 per unit, and incremental fixed costs of $104,000. How many units of Product M would have to be sold to maintain the existing income of $280,000?

(b) K could increase sales by 20 percent by reducing variable contribution margin to 45 percent and increasing separable and avoidable fixed costs by $40,000. Should Ashwell do this?

(c) Rank each product by total sales, variable contribution margin percentage, direct contribution margin percentage, and net profit percentage. How might each measure be used?

11-18. **"Lose a little on each one, and make it up on volume."** The James Company currently sells three products whose quantities, selling prices, and variable costs are as follows:

Product	Quantity	Selling Price	Variable Cost
110	10,000	$22	$14
111	15,000	12	7
112	25,000	27	16

The fixed cost for the operation is $350,000, and it is allocated on the basis of the total units produced. The plant is currently at capacity, and each unit requires the same production time. The following cost report for Product 111 shows that this product is not profitable:

Selling price per unit		$12
Variable cost per unit	$7	
Fixed cost per unit	7	14
Net profit (loss) per unit		$ (2)

Part A: The above report causes the sales manager to argue that Product 111 should be dropped from the product line, stating that it is difficult to make up on volume what is lost on the individual unit.

Required:
1. If no alternative exists for the use of capacity, should Product 111 be dropped?
2. If Product 111 is dropped, what happens to the net profit per unit of Product 110?
3. If Product 111 is dropped, how many more units of Product 112 need to be sold to maintain current profit levels?

Part B: Assume the same situation as in Part A. However, if Product 111 is dropped, no additional units of Product 110 or Product 112 can be sold. The sales manager finds another product, 113, which can be sold for $8 and has a variable cost of $6.00. In addition, it takes only one half the time to produce Product 113 as it takes to produce Product 111. Sufficient sales can be generated to use the capacity freed by dropping Product 111.

The sales manager argues that Product 113 should be added and Product 111 should be dropped, saying, "It is true that the contribution margin of Product 113 is only $2.00 per unit; but since more units of Product 113 can be produced, the fixed cost per unit will also go down. We'll make more money on our other products. As a matter of fact, the fixed cost per unit on all units will drop by $1.62—from $7 to $5.38 ($350,000 divided by 65,000)—if we switch to Product 113."

Required:
Is the sales manager right? How much would the price on Product 113 have to be increased before it would be as profitable as Product 111? Explain the error in the sales manager's reasoning.

11-19. **Scarce Resources with Other Constraints.** Data concerning four product lines are given below:

	Product Lines			
	A	**B**	**C**	**D**
Selling price per unit	$13	$20	$5	$25
Variable cost per unit	$ 6	$ 5	$2	$16
Allocated common costs per unit	$ 4	$ 8	$1	$ 3
Units produced per hour	4 units	2 units	8 units	3 units
Maximum sales limit	5,000 units	5,000 units	10,000 units	No limit
Minimum production requirements	1,000 units	None	2,000 units	1,200 units

There are 6,000 total hours available. Minimum production requirements are needed to meet existing sales contracts. Marketing has provided a "best estimate" of the maximum sales we can expect for each product, including the minimums.

Required:
Based on the above data, choose the best product combination.

11-20. Pricing Decision. The Baker Company is currently producing and selling two products, X and Y. The data on costs, selling prices, and volume are given as follows:

	Product X	Product Y
Selling price per unit	$16	$25
Variable cost per unit—labor and materials	11	15
Fixed overhead cost per unit allocated to products	5	5
Units sold	10,000	40,000

The total fixed overhead is $250,000 per year and is allocated equally since each product requires equal production time. Product Y requires a higher-priced material, which explains why the variable cost of this product is higher than for Product X.

A major company in the industry is looked on as a price leader. Most of the smaller companies follow its actions on price setting. Recently, this company reduced the price on Product X to $14. The sales manager and the president of Baker Company are attempting to determine what to do in response to this action. The sales manager estimates that if the price on Product X is held at $16, sales will probably decline to 8,000 units. If the company follows the price decrease and reduces the price of Product X to $14, it is estimated that volume can be maintained at 10,000 units. However, the sales manager notes that Product X is already incurring zero profit at the selling price of $16 and suggests to the president that the product be dropped entirely. Such an action would provide unused capacity, since no more units of Y can be sold and no substitute product is immediately available. Whatever is done, argues the sales manager, the price on Product X should not be reduced to $14, since the action will result in a loss per unit of $2.

Required:

Advise the president on the proper course to follow. Include consideration of short-run and long-run issues. Use the data above to support your advice.

11-21. Special Sales Pricing. The Dell Company produces a limited line of plastic containers that are used to store and ship certain chemical compounds. The capacity of the plant is 100,000 factory processing hours—a measure used internally to indicate factory activity. It can produce two containers per factory processing hour. For the last few years, the company has been producing about 180,000 containers per year; but the prospects for the coming year look very bright. Several new industrial plants have recently located in the area, and the company management believes that the excess capacity can now be used. The average price of the standard container is $220 per unit with the following cost structure:

	Cost per Unit
Materials	$130
Labor	20
Overhead	42
Total	$192

The materials and labor are considered to be variable costs. The total overhead is fixed and is allocated to the products on the basis of hours. The rate calculation is as follows:

$$\frac{\text{Estimated overhead}}{\text{Hours of capacity}} = \frac{\$8,400,000}{100,000} = \$84 \text{ per hour}$$

The price of $220 per standard container is now fairly well established within the industry. The company set this price by adding a profit of $28 per unit to the full cost.

The company has been approached by a contracting officer for the government to build 10,000 special containers. The materials cost has been estimated to be $25 less per unit than on standard containers. Factory usage and labor time will be about the same. The sales manager has calculated the price for the contracting officer as follows:

	Cost per Unit
Materials	$105
Labor	20
Overhead	42
Total	$167
Markup	28
Price	$195

The contracting officer, in reviewing the calculation, notices that the markup based on cost for the special container ($28 ÷ $167 = 16.8% approximately) is higher than for the standard container ($28 ÷ $192 = 14.6% approximately). The officer argues that the price on the special container should be reduced so as to make the special container no more profitable than the standard container.

Required:

Assuming that the company wants to set the special container price to make it no more profitable than the standard container, is the $195 price "fair?" Evaluate the contracting officer's reasoning with respect to the markup percentage. What price should Dell charge?

11-22. Allocation of Production Between Manufacturing Plants. The Eagle Company has two plants producing an equivalent grade of inexpensive alloy from a material which is a waste product in the manufacture of steel. One plant is located in Indiana and the other in Pennsylvania. The Indiana plant has been operating at 70 percent of capacity producing 2,800 tons of alloy per period, and the Pennsylvania plant has been operating at 60 percent of capacity producing 3,600 tons per period. Each ton of alloy requires a ton of materials—the waste metal. The price of the materials is $30 per ton at either plant with no limitation on supply.

The cost and production data for a typical period are as follows:

	Indiana Plant	Pennsylvania Plant
Materials: (2,800 tons used)	$ 84,000	
(3,600 tons used)		$108,000
Fixed cost per period	70,000	180,000
Variable cost (estimated to be constant per ton of output)	140,000	172,800
Total cost	$294,000	$460,800
Production	2,800 tons	3,600 tons
Cost per ton	$ 105	$ 128

The production manager would like to shift production to the Indiana plant to take advantage of the lower cost per ton. This plant is the older of the two, and the fixed costs of operation are lower.

Required:

Prepare an analysis to show the production manager how the production should be scheduled. Assume that the present output of 6,400 tons will be continued (disregard any marketing costs and assume that the total fixed cost will not change). As part of your analysis, show the cost savings that will result from your recommendation.

11-23. **Make or Buy with Complications.** Mazza MedTech Services, Inc. has been operating at below normal capacity, and opportunities for increased volume from existing services do not appear likely. The production manager suggests that a sophisticated blood test, presently being sent out to Riley Microlabs, can be done by the firm's current staff with little new training and by leasing specific additional equipment. This test costs $75.00 per test when purchased from Riley. Normally, 3,000 of these tests are done each year. The annual costs to perform these tests are estimated as follows:

Direct labor and other variable overhead	$ 90,000
Additional fixed overhead if tests are done in-house	90,000
Allocated fixed overhead (100 % of variable costs)	90,000
Total cost	$270,000

The sales manager objects to this plan, stating that Riley is also a customer and that Mazza does 500 comprehensive medical tests each year for Riley which include this particular blood test. The Riley business adds $40,000 to contribution margin each year. She says, "This market will be lost if we pull the blood tests away from Riley." Consequently, only 2,500 of these tests will be done if the Riley testing work is lost.

Required:

Based upon the information given, should Mazza MedTech Services, Inc. do its own blood tests or continue to purchase the testing from Riley Microlabs?

CASE 11A—TEDDY BEAR HOUSE

Teddy Bear House is a day-care center/preschool owned and operated as a partnership by Linda Rivera and JoAnn Clarke. The center is located in a city which has a large base of working parents who have a continuous need for quality day care. Furthermore, it is located in an area of the city that, though not affluent, is populated by college-educated professionals who have expressed a need for such care for their children.

The two women started the center at the beginning of this year. Clarke contributed $40,000 to get the business started—to purchase equipment and to operate through the first month. Rivera, who previously managed a center for Preschool, Inc., is the director of the center and draws $2,000 per month for her services. Partnership profits and losses, after Rivera's monthly salary, are split 75 percent for Clarke while Rivera gets 25 percent.

Teddy Bear House, which operates from 7 a.m. to 6 p.m., Monday through Friday, is in a single building which has a capacity limit of 120 children and meets city and state regulations. At the present time, the center has six classes, all at maximum sizes, structured as follows:

Age	Number of Classes	Children Per Class	Total Children	Monthly Tuition Per Child
2-3	2	10	20	$320
3-4	1	15	15	280
4-5	1	15	15	280
5-6	2	15	30	260

Class sizes are determined by state law which sets a limit on the number of children per instructor. The center uses one instructor per classroom.

Tuition is charged by the month. Payments are due on the first school day of the month. A 10 percent discount is also offered on the monthly charge for each additional child from the same family.

In October, the most recent month with data available, revenues were $21,500 ($22,600 less $1,100 adjustments). Monthly revenues should be rather stable since classes are full most of the time. Expenses for the center during October were as follows:

Salaries for instructors	$ 9,600
Salary of director	2,000
Salary of part-time cook	900
Building rental	1,700
Food	2,200
Staff benefits costs	2,450
Insurance	750
Utilities	500
Supplies	600
Other administrative expenses	300
Total	$21,000

Most of the expenses are fixed: salary of the part-time cook, building rent, utilities, insurance, and other administrative expenses. The salary of the director is fixed; but, in the strict sense of a partnership, this is a distribution of profit. However, it is included in the expenses for comparative purposes.

The variable expenses are food ($1.25 per student per day), and staff benefits are 10 percent of salaries plus $200 per person for benefit programs for instructors and the part-time cook. Step costs are salaries for instructors (an average of $1,600 per instructor). Supplies are $1 per student per month.

Rivera wants to increase the quality of service by decreasing class sizes and expanding the number of students enrolled. These alternatives are, however, interrelated. Rivera feels the class sizes are too large and that children are not getting the individual attention they require. Several parents who currently have children in the center would be willing to pay a higher tuition if class sizes were reduced. Rivera surveyed the parents of all 80 students to measure their support for a tuition increase tied to reduced class size. For children ages 2 to 5, 80 percent would support a 25 percent increase, and nearly 50 percent would support a 50 percent increase. Of the parents of children in the 5 to 6 age group, 70 percent really did not want any increase. The remaining 30 percent said they would support a 25 percent increase but no more.

The proper class size is a very subjective question. However, Rivera feels that the target she wants is a child/instructor ratio of 5 to 1 for the 2-3 age group; 8 to 1 for the 3-4 and 4-5 age groups; and 10 to 1 for the 5-6 age group.

The center has easily maintained the 80 student level, with each class full. A waiting list keeps children available when someone leaves the center. Rivera keeps in touch with waiting-list parents to make certain each person on the list is still interested. The current waiting list is as follows.

Age	Number of Children
2-3	5
3-4	7
4-5	4
5-6	11

Rivera does not start a new class and hire an additional instructor unless more students are on the waiting list than required per class. Thus, she can keep all of her classes full in case someone leaves. Obviously, there are enough students on the waiting list to start a new class for the 5-6 age group. Lately, however, she has wondered if the center could make a profit by starting classes with fewer than the requisite number, taking the chance that new students would appear and could be added immediately.

Information from her various surveys and telephone calls tells Rivera a potential market for quality infant care (0-24 months) exists. Since the state has a limit of a 6 to 1 infant/instructor ratio, Rivera doesn't think this expansion would be profitable. However, she has never done an analysis of the situation and has not thought about an appropriate tuition. She feels that the infant/instructor ratio in her center should be fewer than 5 infants to one instructor. It is customary for parents to furnish their own food for infants, so the center would have no food costs for the infants.

Clarke's attitude is that she will only agree to Rivera's suggested changes if the center will continue to operate at or above the current profit level.

Required:

1. Look at each decision separately, as incremental to the current situation, and evaluate the marginal profit:

   (a) If class size is decreased (keeping the same 80 students), what increase in tuition is necessary to keep the current monthly profit level?

   (b) Without regard to (a) above, is it profitable to create the new class from the waiting list?

   (c) Assuming the new fee structure as found in Part 1 (a), is it profitable to move to the smaller class sizes, if new full classes are created and existing classes are filled to their new maximums using the waiting list?

   (d) Is a class for infant care profitable if tuition is approximately the same as the small class tuition for the 2-3 age group?

2. Looking at all of the possible changes, what combination would yield the highest monthly profit for the center?

CASE 11B–NICHOLS PRODUCTS, INC.

The vice-president of production at Nichols Products, Inc., Greg Young, complains that the quality of a part used in manufacturing one of the product lines is poor. He states that this part costs $23 per unit but that 10 percent of the parts break in the assembly process. This part is now purchased from a supplier that uses a lighter gage of steel. As a result of bending operations in assembly, it often snaps at a stress point. The supplier has been willing to split the cost of replacement parts with Nichols. A search for other suppliers has not been helpful. The best alternative using the higher gage steel was a quoted price of $28. Any price increase to cover the higher costs would cause serious competitive problems for Nichols' salespersons.

Breakage of this part in assembly has caused rework and scrap costing Nichols about $150,000 in addition to the cost of the broken parts. Also, the engineering and customer service staffs estimate that about 25 percent of the firm's warranty claims of $660,000 last year were related to this part failing while in service.

Julie Kramer, the controller, states that idle plant capacity exists and suggests that we make our own parts at a higher quality level. Kramer believes that the suppliers are unwilling to reduce their profits and are cheapening their products instead of absorbing higher materials costs.

The company needs 50,000 of these parts each year. A study reveals that Nichols Products would incur the following additional costs if 50,000 units of this part were made:

Direct materials (including higher gage steel)	$1,050,000
Direct labor (15,000 labor hours).	225,000
Variable overhead (30,000 machine hours)	180,000

Engineering believes that failure rates will become negligible.

Greg Young is not convinced that the components can be made at a lower cost than the purchase cost. He thinks that the cost of quality materials is too high. Furthermore, the plant has substantial fixed overhead that must be absorbed at a rate of $10 per machine hour. In Young's opinion, use of any idle capacity should cover at least this fixed overhead.

Required:

1. Based upon the quantitative data given, what should be the source of the part? Show computations.
2. Evaluate Greg Young's argument. Does he make a valid point?
3. Discuss the possible long-term ramifications of this decision on the factory, on sales, on customers, and on profits.

Chapter Twelve

Capital Investment Decisions

 Chapter Objectives

After studying Chapter 12, you will be able to:
1. Explain the nature and importance of capital investment decisions.
2. Identify the relevant cash inflows and outflows in an investment proposal.
3. Know how to format the relevant cost and revenue data to analyze the attractiveness of an investment proposal.
4. Understand the application of both discounted cash flow methods in capital investment decisions.
5. Understand the use of the payback period and accounting rate of return methods in capital investment analysis.
6. Compare the strengths and weaknesses of the capital investment evaluation methods.
7. Know how the cost of capital is used in capital investment analysis.
8. Know how depreciation and income taxes impact the cash flows of capital investment proposals.

Capital Investment Alternatives

John Victory, President of Prestige Electronics, recently reviewed investment proposals from his key managers. He made a list on a note pad of the projects he wants to examine in detail. The variety surprised him and included:

1. An engineering R & D project to apply a recently announced semi-conductor advance to a Prestige product which now uses servo-mechanical technology. The new application would push Prestige into new markets with great sales potential but also with stiff competition.

2. A building project that would bring all administrative departments together. They are now operating in three different locations around town.

3. His production planning manager has proposed a project that would rearrange several work centers and improve production efficiency for a major family of current products.

4. Another production project would add capacity to a specialized assembly operation that would allow sales to increase.

5. A proposal from the administrative manager would lease or purchase a new copy center machine that will replace old equipment and have capabilities to do work now sent outside.

6. The plant manager indicates that an air purification system must be installed by year end to meet a new state regulation for air quality in the work place.

7. A data processing proposal would automate several manual inventory control steps, save on personnel costs, and reduce inventory investment by an estimated 10 percent.

8. His finance manager has been negotiating with a firm that has expertise in several technical areas that Prestige needs for its new product development. A controlling interest can be purchased with a sizable cash investment.

9. Marketing has proposed a major jump in advertising spending for a product line that has not met sales budget targets.

John made a quick calculation which shows that the investment funds available this year will fund less than a third of the capital investments requested in these proposals. Some proposals are very risky while others have predictable outcomes; some proposals are straightforward while others include many extraneous issues and data; and data for some proposals are overstated while the data are understated for others. Profit potential varies widely. Some generate returns tomorrow; others promise returns years from now. Cash flows, accrual net income, and returns on investment indicate conflicting priorities.

John clearly wants to spend Prestige's scarce investment dollars where the benefits are the greatest for the long run. John wants to be sure that the proposals:

1. Include only relevant investment, revenue, and cost data.
2. Are analyzed consistently and evaluated fairly.
3. Are compared using criteria that will maximize benefits to Prestige.

This chapter will continue the emphasis on differential analysis begun in Chapter 11. But the long-term nature of many decisions introduces the time value of money. Long-term decisions are called capital investments. Chapters 12 and 13 discuss:

1. Identifying relevant cash flows of capital investments.
2. Techniques for analyzing project data.
3. Other issues impacting capital investment decisions.

Chapters 12 and 13 depend on an understanding of the time value of money. Appendix B explains this concept and presents applications. It also contains present value tables necessary for **discounting** future cash flows to present values.

Making **capital investment decisions** is an extension of relevant costing analysis discussed in Chapter 11. Most relevant costing analysis had a strong short-term bias, but on many occasions the importance of long-term considerations was cited. One common long-term aspect is the need to acquire assets that will be used over a period of years. These acquisition decisions define relevant costs and revenues exactly the same as decisions with shorter time horizons. Relevant revenues are assumed to be cash inflows, and relevant costs are assumed to be cash outflows regardless of the time frame. But because the flows of money in long-term decisions extend over a period of years, the opportunity cost of the cash becomes a major factor in investing decisions.

Assume that a special sales order will earn an incremental contribution margin of $10,000 on sales of $70,000. If all decision guidelines are met, we would accept the special order. However, if the costs of the special sale ($60,000) are incurred today but the collection of the $70,000 is delayed for 2 years, the wisdom of accepting the order is seriously in doubt. If our company could earn 10 percent per year on the funds we expected to collect, we forego $7,000 of interest the first year and $7,700 the second year (assuming compound interest). Now we are losing $14,700 of interest income to earn $10,000 in additional contribution margin.

If the time frame is short, the opportunity cost is small and might be ignored. When days become years, the use of money over time becomes an important relevant cost in our investment analysis. This is called the **time value of money**. Appendix B explains the concept in detail for those unfamiliar with the time value of money.

Because capital investment analysis is a planning task, it is often linked to an organization's budgeting process. **Capital budgeting** is the process of setting the amount to be spent on long-term investment and of selecting projects to be funded. Capital investment analysis is needed to support and justify the capital spending.

The discussion of capital investment decisions first examines the typical decision characteristics, the relevant data, and the data analysis format. Then two discounted cash flow evaluation methods are explained, after which two traditional methods are presented. Depreciation, taxes, and cost of capital are briefly examined.

In Chapter 13, additional topics are presented that discuss a number of complicating factors in capital investment analysis.

THE IMPORTANCE OF CAPITAL INVESTMENT DECISIONS

Capital investment is the acquisition of earning assets with an expected life of over a year. These decisions often attract managers' time and interest and for good reasons:

1. **Long-term commitments made.** Capital decisions often lock the firm into the assets acquired for many years. Also, the future is always uncertain. So, the farther into the future a commitment extends, the greater the level of uncertainty.

2. **Large amounts of dollars required.** Many capital projects have large price tags. From Ford Motor Company with an annual capital investment budget of $7 billion to a small moving firm buying a $20,000 truck, the size of the investment requires careful analysis and evaluation of alternatives.

3. **Key areas of the firm involved.** Many investments affect vital areas of the firm. New products, new production technology, research projects, and computer systems are all examples of critical investments made to move the firm ahead competitively or to remove past limits on the firm.

4. **Source of future earnings identified.** These investments, made now, represent the base for future sales and, therefore, profits. Investing carefully and with foresight is the key to the firm's future financial performance.

5. **Difficult management problems confronted.** Many capital investment projects are one-of-a-kind and involve new technology, untested processes, or activities that managers do not perform regularly. Construction, engineering, and financial project management may not be managements' strengths. Therefore, frequent delays, cost overruns, and other difficulties appear.

6. **Scarce capital dollars allocated.** In most firms, more uses exist for capital funds than the firm can generate. Some rationing process must be used. Advocates of various projects compete for the same scarce dollars. Hopefully, the best set of opportunities can be selected and funded.

All of these issues cause capital investment decisions to get management's attention. Poor decisions can waste investment dollars, lose opportunities, and impact firm profits for many years. Excellent analysis and decisions solve problems and give the firm capacity, technology, administrative efficiency, and the financing to be a successful competitor.

These decisions require classic cost/benefit analysis. We should spend more time and money on these decisions because a better decision can pay sizable dividends in the future. In many companies, an entire department exists to review proposals, analyze estimates of the future, and monitor in-progress and completed projects. Most companies specify the amount of money each level of manager can spend without getting higher level approval. Major projects may even require board of directors' approval.

THE CAPITAL INVESTMENT DECISION

The capital investment decision generally involves a cash outflow which is the investment and cash inflows which are the returns on the investment. The decision maker expects cash inflows to exceed the cash outflows—a net cash inflow. The typical investment project will have cash outflows at the beginning of the project and cash inflows over the life of the project.

In Chapter 11, decision-making steps were outlined. The same steps apply here. The emphasis will be on collecting relevant data about the alternatives, formatting and analyzing the data, and the methods used to make decisions. Also in Chapter 11, we were making decisions based on incremental revenues and costs. We focused on the incremental contribution margin. In capital investment, the initial cost is considered to be an investment. The evaluation focus is on the rate of return on the investment. Annual incremental contribution margins from a series of years are compared to the **initial investment**. This chapter will look at methods used to compare the incremental contribution margin to the investment.

Cash Flows

Cash is used as the key financial measurement in capital investments. Cash has no inherent earning power, but it does have purchasing power. Cash, when held, has an opportunity cost, since it could have been used to buy a productive asset or a financial asset that could earn revenue for the owner. Cash also is a common denominator asset. Prices, costs, and values can all be equated to a cash amount. Attempts can even be made to quantify intangible benefits. Essentially, a non-quantitative value can be converted into an estimated cash flow.

Even more so than in Chapter 11, the assumption is that all financial flows are in cash. Because of the longer time frame, the timing of cash flows becomes a relevant factor. The opportunity cost of cash must be considered.

Cash outflows commonly include:

1. The cash cost of initial investment plus any costs incurred to acquire, implement, set up, and test the asset.
2. Any incremental cash operating costs incurred over the life of the project.
3. Any incremental investments in working capital such as inventories and accounts receivable.
4. Any additional outlays needed to overhaul, expand, or update the asset during the life of the project.

5. Any additional taxes that may need to be paid on incremental taxable income from the project.

Cash inflows include:

1. Any cash received from the sale of old assets being replaced by the new project net of any tax impacts.
2. The release of funds from any working capital accounts.
3. Any incremental cash revenues received over the life of the project.
4. Any salvage value realized from the disposition of project assets at the end of the project.

These cash flows will all occur after the "go" decision is made to proceed with the project. Therefore, we are estimating future cash flows. Perhaps near-term flows can be forecast more accurately. Certain cash flows can be estimated based on current prices and known technology; whereas others are estimates based on vague facts and unproven technology. It is said that production estimates are more accurate than marketing estimates. Production may use historical data and existing production capabilities; while marketing managers must deal with greater vagaries in the marketplace. Specific cases all have unique forecasting problems. In many situations, cost savings are not clear, benefits may not be easily quantified, and impacts on indirect costs are subjective at best. Much time and expense must be expended to develop forecast data.

Once cash flow estimates are prepared for the project, they do not change regardless of the method used to evaluate projects. Each method may analyze the cash data differently, but the cash forecasts are the same for all.

Types of Projects

Capital investment projects are similar to the relevant costing decision types in Chapter 11. The key difference is that the investment provides a base for calculating a rate of return. In Chapter 11 we were looking for the highest incremental profit (defined as incremental contribution margin). Decisions are either:

1. Accept or reject.
2. Select A or B or C or etc.

In the first type, we decide whether the rate of return on investment is acceptable or unacceptable. This is a screening decision. Is it "good enough" to accept? The second type is a preference or ranking decision—select the best alternative from a set of mutually exclusive projects. By picking A, we reject B, C, and any other alternative. To do nothing is a possible choice—the status quo.

Generally, projects are ranked according to some scale from high to low returns. The highest ranking projects will be selected, until the capital investment budget is spent. Often, not enough funds are available and many acceptable projects will go unfunded. The firm's goal will be to select the highest yielding projects available.

Time Perspective

In the real world, every conceivable combination of cash flows and timing can exist. But in our analysis, we assume a simplified timeline for most illustrations. The present point in time is Year 0. It is the point where investments are made, new assets acquired, old assets sold, and any tax consequences of these changes felt. In real life, major projects may require several years of cash outflows while the investment is built and prepared for use.

Generally in capital investment decisions, annual time periods are used. A five-year project will have a cash outflow in Year 0 and five annual net cash inflows. Shorter time periods, such as 6-month periods for a semiannual interest paying bond investment and 1-month periods for leases requiring monthly payments, also occur.

The annual flows of cash are assumed to occur at year end. In Appendix B, Tables I and II show present value factors for single amounts and for repetitive flows respectively. These are "end of period" factors. Other tables exist that can reflect the smooth flows of cash within a time period. But this fine tuning is probably necessary only in specialized situations.

Salvage values are the residual asset values at the end of the project's life and are cash inflows. These, by necessity, are probably very rough estimates of asset values well into the future. Generally, salvage values are not substantial amounts and are further reduced by the time value of money.

An Example—Equipment Replacement and Capacity Expansion

Equipment replacement and capacity expansion decisions were introduced in Chapter 11 as incremental decision types. In most cases, the decisions require new long-term assets. Replacement decisions focus on incremental, or changed, cash flows. We eliminate the old; and we put the new in its place. Net new investment and changed operating costs are the primary relevant costs. Expansion decisions generally mean adding more equipment, space, or personnel to increase sales, enter new markets, or introduce new products. The capital investment needed to support the growth is evaluated relative to the growth in contribution margin. In both types of decisions, measuring relevant cash flows focuses on "how much" and "when."

To provide an illustration for identifying and formatting relevant cash flows, assume the following situation. Quartz Timepieces is considering:

1. A $100,000 investment in a new machine to replace a technologically obsolete quality monitoring device.
    (a) The new device has an expected life of 5 years and could probably be sold at the end of year 5 for $10,000.
    (b) Also, the vendor recommends an updating overhaul in Year 3 at a cost of $20,000.
    (c) Capacity will increase by 1,000 units per year.
2. Each unit sells for $55 and has $30 of variable costs.
3. Additional inventory of $3,000 is needed, and is assumed to be released at the end of this project.

4. Operating costs will be reduced by $15,000 per year.
5. The old machine can be sold for $8,000 now, which is also its book value. If the old machine is not replaced, it could be used for the 5 years but have no salvage value or book value.
6. All other sales and operating costs will remain unchanged.

Until tax issues are discussed more carefully, taxation implications will be ignored.

Relevant Investment, Revenue, and Cost Data

The relevant investment cash flows are any incremental cash outflows that occur in Year 0 of the project. This is the cash cost of any assets purchased. A common but less obvious investment is any added working capital requirements of the investment. Additional inventory and accounts receivable are often needed to support business expansion. These funds can be recovered at some point in the future, but must be financed today just the same as the new equipment.

If, because of the new investment, old assets are disposed of or traded in, their net cash values will reduce the investment. In the example, the $103,000 equipment and inventory costs are reduced by the sale of the equipment for $8,000. The net investment is $95,000.

Relevant revenues are additional revenues received from the investment. Often investment projects are intended to expand capacity or to enter new markets. New revenues are incremental cash flows. Cost savings from greater efficiency or automation can also be treated as a revenue or as a negative cost. This is the cost savings of $15,000 in the example.

Relevant costs are the annual incremental cash costs associated with the project. Depreciation and other accounting accrual adjustments are excluded except for their impact on cash taxes. Taxes on taxable incremental income or operating savings are relevant cash outflows.

If a number of alternatives are considered, the Chapter 11 rules apply. Any cash revenue or cost that does not change is irrelevant and can be ignored. Any cash flow that differs among the alternatives is relevant.

On an annual basis, the goal is to find the incremental contribution margin earned from the investment's assets. As in Chapter 11, either the incremental analysis or total analysis approach can be used. Depending on the data available and the type of decision, one approach may be easier to apply or provide a clearer analysis of the data. Where possible, the cleaner approach is preferable. Often, this is the incremental approach which uses only incremental investment, revenues, and costs cash flows.

Formatting the Relevant Data

Adopting a uniform format for analysis of capital investments will help in organizing data and presenting it in a logical pattern. Using the data from the previous example, the time frame layout shown in Figure 12.1 will be used throughout our capital investment discussions.

Cash Flows:	Investment Year 0	Life of the Project				
		Year 1	Year 2	Year 3	Year 4	Year 5
New equipment	$(100,000)					
Salvage value						$ 10,000
Sale of old equipment	8,000					
Additional inventory	(3,000)					3,000
Incremental sales		$ 55,000	$ 55,000	$ 55,000	$ 55,000	55,000
Incremental product cost		(30,000)	(30,000)	(30,000)	(30,000)	(30,000)
Operating cost savings		15,000	15,000	15,000	15,000	15,000
Updating overhaul				(20,000)		
Net cash flow	$ (95,000)	$ 40,000	$ 40,000	$ 20,000	$ 40,000	$ 53,000

Figure 12.1   Format for Relevant Capital Investment Data—An Example

Cash outflows are indicated as negative numbers and inflows as positive numbers. All relevant cash flows for this project are captured in this format. Project years beginning with year 0, which is today, are shown as columns. Specific cash flow items are listed as rows with a brief description of each at the left side of Figure 12.1

Remember that volumes of analytical data may have been developed to support each number in Figure 12.1. The $100,000 device cost would have resulted from evaluation of other pieces of equipment and negotiations with vendors. The additional revenues and variable costs came from capacity use and marketing studies. Operating cost savings came from production planning, industrial engineering, and cost accounting analyses. Each forecast item is the best assessment that Quartz personnel can provide.

With these data presented, we are ready to analyze the cash flows using four methods of evaluation.

THE EVALUATION METHODS

The evaluation methods to be discussed here are:

1. Present value methods, including:
    (a) The net present value method.
    (b) The internal rate of return method.
2. The payback period method.
3. The accounting rate of return method.

Nearly all managerial accountants agree that methods using **present values** (the time value of money) give the best assessment of long-term investments. The two non-time value of money methods are in many respects "straw persons" that have serious flaws. But they are so commonly used for evaluation of investments or of actual results that their strengths and weaknesses must be examined.

Net Present Value Method

To evaluate a long-term investment opportunity, the time value of money should be part of the analysis. The **net present value (NPV) method** includes this cost of money by using an interest rate that sets the desired rate of return, or at least sets a minimum acceptable rate of return. The decision rule is:

Given a minimum acceptable rate of return, if the present value of incremental cash inflows is greater than the net incremental cash investment outflow, approve the project.

Using Tables I and II at the end of the book, the net cash flows for each year are brought back to Year 0 and summed for all years. An interest rate must be specified. This is often viewed as the cost of funds needed to finance the project and as the minimum acceptable rate of return. Note that the present value of cash flow in Year 0 is the amount itself—no discounting is needed. The net cash investment is subtracted from the sum of the present values of the cash inflows. When the residual is positive, the project's rate of return is greater that the interest rate used for discounting. If:

Incremental Investment Cash Outflows ≤ Present Value of Incremental Cash Inflows

then:

Minimum Acceptable Rate of Return ≤ Project's Rate of Return

The net present value is positive, and the project should be approved. When the sum is negative, the project's rate of return is less than the discount rate. If:

Incremental Investment Cash Outflows > Present Value of Incremental Cash Inflows

then:

Minimum Acceptable Rate of Return > Project's Rate of Return

The net present value is negative, and the project should be rejected.

Time Value of Money   To evaluate a project using the NPV method, we must use the time value of money. The basic present value concept and illustrations are in Appendix B. We have mentioned the opportunity cost of cash previously. By investing cash today, we expect returns in the future. Quartz Timepieces invested $95,000 today and expects to get $40,000 back in Year 1 and again in Year 2, $20,000 in Year 3, $40,000 in Year 4, and finally $53,000 in Year 5. But the first $40,000 is a year away. What is it worth today? It is $40,000 minus the interest we could earn over the next year. If Quartz had the cash today, they could retire debt, pay dividends, or invest in another project.

If Quartz management has set an expected rate of return of 12 percent, we can quantify the opportunity cost. The Year 1 $40,000 equals some present value plus 12 percent earned during the year. We can find the present value either by division or multiplication:

Division:	$40,000 ÷ (1.00 + .12)	= $35,714 or
Multiplication:	$40,000 × [1 ÷ (1.00 + .12)]	= $35,714 or
	$40,000 × .893 (from Table I)	= $35,720

Tables I and II in Appendix B were developed using the multiplication alternative. All numbers in the tables have been rounded to three decimal places which will cause minor rounding differences. The $6 difference between the multiplication amounts is from rounding. Using 12 percent, Quartz managers value the $40,000 due in one year to be $35,714 today.

The Year 2 $40,000 includes two years of opportunity cost. The calculation is:

$$\$40,000 \times [1 \div (1.12 \times 1.12)] = \$31,888$$

The present value multiplication factor from Table I is .797. This is done for each year for the life of the project. Year 5 is:

$$\$53,000 \times [1 \div (1.12 \times 1.12 \times 1.12 \times 1.12 \times 1.12)] = \$30,074 \text{ or}$$
$$\$53,000 \times .567 \text{ (from Table I)} = \$30,051$$

The difference of $23 is from rounding $\frac{1}{(1.12)^5}$ to the present value factor of .567. This means that a dollar to be received in Year 5 is worth 56.7 cents today using 12 percent interest.

The Interest Rate   An obvious question is from where does the interest rate for discounting come? This rate has many names that help explain its source and use. Among them are:

1. **Cost of capital.** Based on the calculation of the weighted-average cost of long-term investment funds, management will not accept any project that cannot earn at least what the firm must pay for its capital. Later, we illustrate a calculation of cost of capital.
2. **Minimum acceptable rate of return.** Management either logically or arbitrarily has set a particular rate as the lowest rate of return it considers satisfactory. The rate could include the cost of capital, inflation, and a riskiness factor. Generally, the rate is the cost of funds plus some safety margin.
3. **Desired rate of return, target rate of return,** or **required rate of return.** Although similar to the minimum acceptable rate of return, these imply that the rate is a target of management in reviewing project profitability.
4. **Hurdle rate.** A project's rate of return must "jump over" or be above the target rate, again often based on cost of capital plus other risk factors.
5. **Cutoff rate.** Projects are listed by rate of return from high to low. All projects with returns down to the cutoff rate are acceptable. A cutoff rate

is generally predetermined, but it could be the rate at which the capital investment budget is exhausted.

A firm will often use one or more of these terms as its way of expressing the **discount rate** Unless a special need exists, these terms will be used interchangeably. Generally, if a project's rate of return falls below this percentage, it is rejected. If it is above this rate, the project is approved. Still, whether it is funded depends on the availability of capital funds.

The cost of capital is the weighted-average cost of all long-term funds. It is important to understand that a specific project is not funded by specific debt or equity dollars. Even where a bond payable is issued for plant expansion purposes, the project should be viewed as being funded by the entire set of long-term liabilities and equity. The analysis should be blind to the source of funding. The investing decision should be separate from the financing decision. If not, it would be possible to accept a less profitable project because it was funded by debt, while a more profitable project is rejected because the cost of equity funds is greater. The answer should always depend on which projects benefit the whole company most. Chapter 13 will address alternative financing sources such as the lease-versus-purchase decision.

The Example   In the Quartz Timepieces example, let us assume that management has decided that 12 percent is the minimum acceptable rate of return. The following calculations are needed to obtain a net present value:

	Investment Year 0	Life of the Project				
		Year 1	Year 2	Year 3	Year 4	Year 5
Net cash flow	$ (95,000)	$40,000	$40,000	$20,000	$40,000	$53,000
Present value factors at 12 %	× 1.000	× .893	× .797	× .712	× .636	× .567
Present values at 12 %	$ (95,000)	$35,720	$31,880	$14,240	$25,440	$30,051
Present values—Years 1 to 5	$137,331					
Net present value	$ 42,331					

Figure 12.2   Net Present Value of Capital Investment Cash Flows

The net present value is a positive $42,331, meaning that the project earns over a 12 percent rate of return. From the net present value method, we cannot find the project's exact rate of return.

Another way to find the present values uses both Tables I and II. The $40,000 of additional contribution margin occurs each year, an **annuity**. The overhaul, salvage value, and the recovered inventory are specific amounts in particular years. The calculations could have been done as follows:

Annual incremental contribution margin (Table II)	$40,000 ×	3.605 =	$144,200
Overhaul cost (Table I)	(20,000) ×	.712 =	(14,240)
Salvage value and inventory recovery (Table I)	13,000 ×	.567 =	7,371
Total present value of future cash flows			$137,331

Use of both Tables I and II or Table I alone will produce the same present values. Minor rounding differences can be ignored.

We can check the net present values of other interest rates. At other interest rate levels, we find:

Percentage	Present Value of Cash Inflows	$-$	Investment	$=$	Net Present Value
16%	$124,328		$95,000		$29,328
20	113,246		95,000		18,246
24	103,713		95,000		8,713
28	95,523		95,000		523
30	91,797		95,000		(3,203)

Notice that, as the interest rate increases, the present value of the future cash flows decreases. The opportunity cost of money increases with the interest rate and causes the values of future dollars to decrease. At 30 percent the project is unacceptable. The project's true or internal rate of return is between 28 and 30 percent. The internal rate of return is the interest rate where the net present value equals zero.

Ranking Projects   Even though a project has a positive net present value, too many attractive projects may exist, given the amount of investment money available. A ranking system is needed. We could rank projects by the amount of net present value each generates. But this will ignore the relative size of the initial investment. An extension of the net present value method is the profitability index. The **profitability index** is found by dividing the present value of cash inflows by the original investment. The resulting ratio compares cash in and out. The higher the ratio, the more attractive the investment.

The following set of projects is ranked by both the net present value and the profitability index. Notice that an acceptable project should have a profitability index of at least 1, meaning that it has a positive net present value.

Project	Present Value of Cash Inflows	Initial Investment	Net Present Value	Net Present Value Ranking	Profitability Index	Index Ranking
A	$235,000	$200,000	$35,000	1	1.18	5
B	170,000	140,000	30,000	2	1.21	4
C	80,000	60,000	20,000	3	1.33	1
D	98,000	80,000	18,000	4	1.23	3
E	52,000	40,000	12,000	5	1.30	2

The two rankings differ considerably. We would typically accept projects with the highest profitability index until we exhaust our capital budget or our list of acceptable projects.

Now assume that this company plans to spend about $250,000, plus or minus $10,000. After reviewing all combinations, we see that Projects B, C, and E give the highest total net present value of $62,000 ($30,000 + $20,000 + $12,000). No other combination of projects can earn more than $62,000 for the initial investment. Excluded from the best combination is the project with the largest net present value. Given the budget limitation, a number of approved projects will not be funded. The goal is to maximize the profits from the available capital investment budget.

The net present value method gives managers an ability to assess all relevant data about a project and to consider the time value of money. It requires the selection of a discount rate that focuses on the firm's cost of long-term funds. Yet this method does not give a specific rate of return for a project. Many managers want to know a project's expected rate of return. This leads to the internal rate of return method.

Internal Rate of Return Method

The **internal rate of return (IRR)** method finds the project's rate of return. This is the point where the:

Incremental initial investment cash outflow = Present value of the incremental cash inflows

In other words, the net present value is zero. Without calculator or computer assistance, the specific rate of return is found by trial and error.

In the Quartz Timepieces example above, the internal rate of return was said to be between 28 and 30 percent. We know that the net present value at 28 percent is positive and at 30 percent is negative. By interpolation, we can approximate a finer-tuned rate. For example:

Rate of Return	Net Present Value	Calculations
28%	$ 523	($523 ÷ $3,725) × 2% = .28%
30%	(3,202)	28.00 % + .28 % = 28.28%
2% difference	$3,725 absolute difference	

The internal rate of return is about 28.28 percent (28 % plus .28 %). At 28.28 percent, the present value of the investment is equal to the present value of the future cash flows. In most cases, however, knowing that the rate is between 28 and 30 percent is adequate.

Estimating the Internal Rate of Return   Using Table II and knowing a set of project variables, we can estimate other unknown variables including a project's internal rate of return. This estimate requires that the annual net cash inflows are "smooth"—equal year to year. The variables and a sample set of data are:

	Variable	Example
A =	Initial Investment	$37,910
B =	Life of project	5 years
C =	Annual net cash inflow	$10,000 per year
D =	Cost of capital (or internal rate of return)	10 percent
E =	Present value factor at 10 percent (from Table II)	3.791

If we know any three of A, B, C, or D, we can find E and the missing variable. A variety of questions can be answered:

1.   What is the internal rate of return of the project?
     If we know A, B, and C, we can calculate E and find D from Table II. The formula gives the present value factor:

$$E = A \div C \quad \$37{,}910 \div \$10{,}000 = 3.791$$

     On Table II we go to the 5-period (year) row, move across until we find 3.791 in the 10 percent column. At 10 percent, the present value of the cash outflow ($37,910) equals the present value of the cash inflows (3.791 × $10,000). The internal rate of return is 10 percent.

2.   What is the annual cash inflow needed if we want a 10 percent return on the project?
     If we know A, B, and D, we can find E and calculate C. We can use the investment of $37,910 and 3.791 to find the annual cash inflow needed:

$$C = A \div E \quad \$37{,}910 \div 3.791 = \$10{,}000 \text{ per year}$$

     We need $10,000 in incremental contribution margin per year to earn a 10 percent return.

3.   What can we afford to pay for an investment that earns $10,000 each year for 5 years if we want a 10 percent return?
     If we know B, C, and D, we can find E and calculate A. The formula uses the annual cash inflow and 3.791:

$$A = C \times E \quad \$10{,}000 \times 3.791 = \$37{,}910$$

     We can pay no more than $37,910 and still earn at least a 10 percent return.

4.   How long must the project last to earn at least a 10 percent return?
     If we know A, C, and D, we calculate E and find B as follows:

$$E = A \div C \quad \$37{,}910 \div \$10{,}000 = 3.791$$

     At 10 percent, we find 3.791 on the 5-period row.

   Most business-analyst calculators and spreadsheet software have built-in functions to find the internal rate of return. This simplifies the calculation burden that has limited its use in the past.

   Ranking Projects   Since each project has a specific rate of return and the same life, the task of ranking projects under the IRR method is relatively simple. All projects are merely listed according to their rates of return from high to low. The cost of capital or a cutoff rate can be used to establish the minimum acceptable rate of return. Then, given the capital budget, projects are selected by coming down the list until the budget is exhausted. Combination problems similar to those discussed under the net present value method also occur here. Again, the goal is to pick the set of projects that maximizes profits for the entire capital budget.

Other Concerns   One other constraint is still present. The present value methods assume that cash flows are reinvested and the reinvested cash will earn the discount rate of return. While this assumption may be realistic for cost of capital rates, it may be wishful thinking for projects with high internal rates of return. Discussions of such issues are best left to finance texts and courses.

A general business concern is also leveled at high discount rates. Any project with significant long-term payoffs will not appear strong because the long-term payoffs will be discounted so severely. Even huge cash inflows due 10 years or more into the future appear to be less valuable than minor cost savings earned in the first year of another project. Concern has been expressed that high discount rates encourage managers to think only short term and to ignore research, market innovation, and product development projects. These are strategic impacts of using accounting tools in potentially wise or unwise ways.

The Payback Period Method

The **payback period method** is a "quick and dirty" evaluation of capital investment projects. It is likely that no major company makes investment decisions based solely on the payback period, but many ask for the measure as part of the analysis. Rules of thumb are set, and rough initial assessments are made using payback information.

The payback period method asks: How fast do we get our initial cash investment back?

No rate of return is given, only a return of the investment. If annual cash flows are equal, to find the **payback period** we merely divide the initial investment by the annual cash inflow. If the investment was $120,000 and the annual net cash inflow is $48,000, we have a payback period of 2.5 years. We need not know how long the project will last (beyond the 2.5 years) nor anything about the cash flows after the 2.5 years. It might last 20 years or 20 days beyond the payback point.

The payback method is viewed as a "bail-out" risk measure. If the future of the project is uncertain, how long do we need to stick with it to get our money back? It is also used frequently in short-term projects where the impact of present values is not great. Such projects as efficiency improvements, cost reductions, and personnel savings are examples. How long should these savings be counted? The "savings" could go on forever. Several major companies set an arbitrary 6-month payback period rule for certain types of cost saving projects. This is a severe test, but it eliminates the long-term counting problem.

The IRR can be estimated using the payback period and the expected project life. The payback period may be used to estimate a project's rate of return if:

1.   The project has a fairly high rate of return (over 20 percent), and
2.   The payback period is less than half of the project's life.

For example, if a $40,000 investment earns $10,000 per year and could last at least 12 years, the payback period is 4 years. The reciprocal of the payback period is 1/4 or 25 percent. From Table II for 12 years, the present value factor (payback period) of 4 indicates a rate of return of between 22 and 24 percent. If the project's life were very long, say 50 years, the **payback reciprocal** is almost a perfect estimator (see the present value factor for 25 percent and 50 periods on Table II).

If the cash flows are uneven from year to year, the payback period can be found by measuring the recovery of the investment year to year. Using the Quartz Timepieces example:

Year	Cash Flows	Unrecovered Investment
0	$(95,000)	$95,000
1	40,000	55,000
2	40,000	15,000
3	20,000	0
4	40,000	0
5	53,000	0

In year 3 the cost is totally recovered. In fact, only $15,000 of year 3's $20,000 is needed (75 percent). The payback period is 2.75 years.

When the payback period is used to rank projects, the shortest payback period is the most attractive. Thus, all projects considered can be listed from low to high. A firm's policy can say that no project with a payback period of over 5 years will be considered. This would act like the cutoff rate in the present value methods. Then, projects would be selected until capital funds were exhausted. Rarely, however, would a company trust its project selection to this rough technique.

The major complaints about the payback period method are that it:

1.   Ignores the time value of money, and
2.   Ignores the cash flows after the payback point.

These are serious deficiencies, but the method is easily applied and is a rough gauge of potential success. It is a long-standing investment evaluation technique that continues to be used despite its limitations.

Accounting Rate of Return Method

This method:

1.   Ignores the time value of money.
2.   Generally assumes smooth flows of income over the project's life regardless of the actual facts.
3.   Includes depreciation expense and other accounting accruals in the calculation of project income, losing the purity of cash flow data.

With these negatives, why is it discussed? Because most internal corporate performance reporting systems use financial accounting data. In fact, many companies use sophisticated cash flow-based capital investment analyses but report the actual results from the investment using historical costs and accrual income measures.

First, let us illustrate the method and then examine some possible implications. The **accounting rate of return (ARR) method** attempts to measure net income from the project. From the cash flows used in all other methods, the ARR subtracts depreciation expense on the initial investment from the annual cash inflows. Other accrual adjustments may also cause the project's annual net income to differ from its annual net cash inflows. The general formula is:

$$\frac{\text{Annual operating cash inflow} \; - \; \text{Annual depreciation expense on initial investment}}{\text{Average investment}} = \text{Accounting rate of return}$$

The denominator, average investment, is the average of the beginning investment base and the ending investment base (0 if no salvage value). In many cases this is the average book value of the investment over its life. Some analysts prefer to use the original cost of the investment or replacement cost as the denominator. The numerator is the incremental net income from the project. To illustrate the method, assume the following:

Initial investment	$110,000
Annual cash inflow	35,000
Depreciation expense	20,000
Salvage value	10,000
Project life	5 years

The calculations will be:

$$\frac{\$35,000 - \$20,000}{(\$110,000 + \$10,000) \div 2} = \frac{\$15,000}{\$60,000} = 25 \text{ percent}$$

The significance of 25 percent must be taken in context relative to other project's rates of return and cannot be compared to present value rates of return.

One difficulty in using the accounting rate of return for investment analysis is the appearance of increasing returns as an asset grows older. Let us look at the above project on an annual basis as a manager would see the data on annual responsibility reports.

	Average Investment (Book Value)	Project Net Income	Annual Accounting Rate of Return
Year 1	$100,000	$15,000	15.0%
Year 2	80,000	15,000	18.8
Year 3	60,000	15,000	25.0
Year 4	40,000	15,000	37.5
Year 5	20,000	15,000	75.0

By using the historical cost, straight-line depreciation, and net income, the average annual book value declines; and net income is assumed to remain constant. The older the asset, the higher the apparent rate of return. As managers see this information in their accounting reports, it is tempting to reject any proposal that will make their performance reports look less favorable. This is particularly true when managers' bonuses are tied to accrual accounting performance numbers. Managers will be biased toward sticking with older assets with higher accounting rates of return. They forego new investments that offer new technology, lower operating costs, and greater productivity.

It is impossible to compare these rates with NPV or IRR rates for new projects. If this method is used to select projects, the projects' rates of return will be ranked from high to low. Some arbitrary percentage may be set as a minimum rate, maybe even some form of the cost of capital. Project selection would attempt to maximize the rate of return on the entire capital budget.

TAXES AND DEPRECIATION

The illustrations presented thus far have ignored the issue of income taxes. And depreciation, being a noncash expense, has only been used in the accounting rate of return method. Together these two factors have major impacts on capital budgeting.

Income Taxes and Capital Investments

The real world is a tax-paying world, and capital investment analysis must consider taxes. Taxation rules are complex and impact many cash flows. The taxable inflows include:

1. Incremental sales less incremental expenses.
2. Incremental operating expense savings.
3. Gains on sales of old assets in Year 0 and of investment assets at the end of the project.

Incremental costs or losses reduce taxes and include:

1. Incremental operating expenses.
2. Repairs and overhauls of investment assets.
3. Losses on sales of assets.

The tax rate used should be the expected **marginal tax rate** for the future year being analyzed. The marginal tax rate is the tax rate paid on any incremental taxable income. Because of special deductions or rules, the average tax rate may be different—often lower than the marginal rate. But since an incremental decision is being considered, the marginal rate is the relevant rate. While the corporate federal income tax maximum rate is currently 34 percent, many companies also pay state and local income taxes. For this reason and for simplicity, we will assume that the marginal income tax rate is 40 percent for all tax-related issues.

Clearly, income taxes will reduce the rate of return on most capital projects. Taxes reduce net cash inflows. Over the years, the federal government has used incentives to encourage capital investment, has changed depreciation and other deduction approaches, and has raised and lowered rates. Specific tax laws and policies are beyond the scope of this book, but we must examine the typical tax impacts.

As an example of changing tax policy, the tax law since the early 1960s has on and off provided an **investment tax credit** for new investments. A percentage (often 7 percent) of the cost of new capital assets was allowed to be deducted immediately as a credit on a corporation's tax return. This was done to encourage economic expansion during recessionary periods. The credit effectively reduced the initial cost of an investment. At present, this provision is not available but may be reintroduced again in the future.

Depreciation Expense and Taxes

The only role that depreciation expense plays in cash flow-based capital investment analysis is as a deduction for calculating income taxes. If income taxes are ignored or are not applicable, as in non-profit organizations, depreciation expense can also be ignored.

Depreciation calculation for accounting purposes and for tax purposes took a dramatically different path in 1981. Previously, financial accounting and allowable tax depreciation methods were generally parallel, with tax rules being very complex. In 1981, a new system called the **Accelerated Cost Recovery System (ACRS)** was signed into law. Asset groupings were narrowed greatly; and deductions were generally accelerated, meaning assets could be written off faster than previously allowed for tax purposes. Traditional accelerated depreciation methods were replaced. The tax reform act of 1986 further revised ACRS's cost recovery periods and rates with the **Modified Accelerated Cost Recovery System (MACRS)**. A more extensive discussion of ACRS, MACRS, and their impacts is presented in Chapter 13. To discuss the basic depreciation expense impacts in this chapter, we will assume the continued use of straight-line depreciation. Salvage value will be ignored in depreciation expense calculations and assumed to be net of any tax consequences.

To see the impact of taxes and depreciation expense, let us look again at the Quartz Timepieces example and first apply a tax rate of 40 percent to the incremental operating cash flows. The net cash flows from Figure 12.1 and net present value analysis are recast in Figure 12.3, shown at the top of page 632.

The unexciting news is that suddenly a very profitable project (just under 30 percent on a pre-tax basis as shown earlier) now has a negative net present value using a 12 percent discount rate. Notice that we assume the machine overhaul in Year 3 is a maintenance expense and that the salvage value and inventory recovery are nonoperating items with no tax effects.

Cash flows:	Investment Year 0	Life of the Project				
		Year 1	Year 2	Year 3	Year 4	Year 5
Initial investment and cost recovery	$(95,000)					$13,000
Incremental operating cash inflows (taxable income).....................................		$40,000	$40,000	$20,000	$40,000	$40,000
Taxes on incremental taxable income (40%)		16,000	16,000	8,000	16,000	16,000
Net after tax operating cash inflows		$24,000	$24,000	$12,000	$24,000	$24,000
Net annual cash flows	$(95,000)	$24,000	$24,000	$12,000	$24,000	$37,000
Present value factors at 12%	× 1.000	× .893	× .797	× .712	× .636	× .567
Present values at 12%	$(95,000)	$21,432	$19,128	$ 8,544	$15,264	$20,979
Present values—Years 1 to 5	85,347					
Net present value	$ (9,653)					

Figure 12.3 Net Present Value Analysis With Taxes

The Tax Shield   Depreciation expense is a **tax shield**. It is a non-cash expense but is a legitimate tax deduction for tax purposes. By reducing taxable income, the cash paid out for taxes is reduced. Depreciation is, in a sense, a cash generator. The greater the depreciation expense, the lower the taxable income and, therefore, taxes. Remember, though, that cash was paid out when the asset was originally purchased.

The depreciation impact can be seen by using the Quartz example. The net increase in depreciable assets is $92,000 ($100,000 minus $8,000, the old asset's book value). At present, salvage value is ignored in most IRS depreciation expense calculations. If we assume straight-line depreciation, the annual additional depreciation expense is $18,400:

$$\text{Added depreciation expense per year} = \frac{(\$100,000 - \$8,000)}{5} = \$18,400$$

The calculation of cash flows follows:

	Year 1
Incremental revenues	$55,000*
− Incremental costs	(30,000)*
+ Operating cost savings	15,000*
Incremental cash inflow	$40,000
− Depreciation expense	18,400
Taxable income	$21,600
− Incremental taxes (40 percent)...................................	8,640*
After tax project net income	$12,960
+ Added depreciation expense	18,400
After tax cash inflow	$31,360

*Cash flows

The project's Year 1 profit, $12,960, and the incremental depreciation expense, $18,400, are added to find the Year 1 cash flow. This is similar to the indirect method of reporting cash flow from operations on the statement of cash flows discussed in Chapter 18.

Another approach is to focus on cash flow items and ignore the after tax project net income (using only the asterisked items above).

Incremental cash inflow (from above).............................	$40,000
− Incremental taxes	8,640
After tax cash inflow	$31,360

Calculation of the annual tax payment is the same for all years.

	Life of the Project				
	Year 1	Year 2	Year 3	Year 4	Year 5
Cash flows:					
Taxable cash inflows	$40,000	$40,000	$20,000	$40,000	$40,000
Less added depreciation expense	(18,400)	(18,400)	(18,400)	(18,400)	(18,400)
Taxable income......................................	$21,600	$21,600	$ 1,600	$21,600	$21,600
Incremental taxes (40%)	$ 8,640	$ 8,640	$ 640	$ 8,640	$ 8,640

Inserting the tax cash outflows for the entire project into the analysis is shown in Figure 12.4.

	Investment Year 0	Life of the Project				
		Year 1	Year 2	Year 3	Year 4	Year 5
Cash flows:						
Initial investment and cost recovery	$ (95,000)					$13,000
Incremental operating cash inflows (taxable income).....................................		$40,000	$40,000	$20,000	$40,000	$40,000
Taxes on incremental taxable income after depreciation expense deduction		8,640	8,640	640	8,640	8,640
Net after tax operating cash inflows		$31,360	$31,360	$19,360	$31,360	$31,360
Net cash flows............................	$ (95,000)	$31,360	$31,360	$19,360	$31,360	$44,360
Present value factors at 12%	× 1.000	× .893	× .797	× .712	× .636	× .567
Present values at 12%	$ (95,000)	$28,004	$24,994	$13,784	$19,945	$25,152
Present values—Years 1 to 5..............	$111,879 ◄					
Net present value	$ 16,879					

Figure 12.4 Net Present Value Analysis With Depreciation and Taxes

The increased tax deduction for depreciation moves the net present value of the project from a negative $9,653 to a positive $16,879, a $26,532 change. This can be proven by calculating the present value of the depreciation expense.

Depreciation Expense	×	Tax Rate	×	Present Value Factor (for 5 years at 12 percent)	=	Tax Shield
$18,400	×	.40	×	3.605	=	$26,533*

* Difference due to rounding.

This is the difference between the "after tax but without depreciation expense" NPV of ($9,653) and the "after tax with depreciation expense" NPV of $16,879. The benefit from the tax shield is great, but remember that the project's present value was reduced from a "no tax" net present value of $42,331 to an "after tax" net present value of $16,879.

Accelerated Depreciation Benefits   The cash saving power of depreciation can be increased by using an accelerated depreciation method. If more depreciation is deducted earlier in a project's life, the deferral of taxes has a time value of money. In a simple example, assume a $15,000 investment, no salvage value, a $5,000 cash inflow per year for 5 years, and a 12 percent desired rate of return.

	Investment Year 0	Life of the Project				
		Year 1	Year 2	Year 3	Year 4	Year 5
Cash flows	$ (15,000)	$5,000	$5,000	$5,000	$5,000	$5,000
Straight-line depreciation		(3,000)	(3,000)	(3,000)	(3,000)	(3,000)
Taxable income		$2,000	$2,000	$2,000	$2,000	$2,000
Taxes (40%)		$ (800)	$ (800)	$ (800)	$ (800)	$ (800)
After tax cash flows	$ (15,000)	$4,200	$4,200	$4,200	$4,200	$4,200
Present value—Years 1 to 5	15,141*					
Net present value	$ 141					

* Present value (12 % for 5 years): $4,200 × 3.605

Now assume that we use a sum-of-years digits method of depreciation:

	Investment Year 0	Life of the Project				
		Year 1	Year 2	Year 3	Year 4	Year 5
Cash flows	$ (15,000)	$ 5,000	$ 5,000	$ 5,000	$ 5,000	$ 5,000
Sum-of-years-digits depreciation		(5,000)	(4,000)	(3,000)	(2,000)	(1,000)
Taxable income		$ 0	$ 1,000	$ 2,000	$ 3,000	$ 4,000
Taxes (40%)		$ (0)	$ (400)	$ (800)	$(1,200)	$(1,600)
After tax cash flows	$ (15,000)	$ 5,000	$ 4,600	$ 4,200	$ 3,800	$ 3,400
Present value factors at 12%	× 1.000	× .893	× .797	× .712	× .636	× .567
Present values at 12%	$ (15,000)	$ 4,465	$ 3,666	$ 2,990	$ 2,417	$ 1,928
Present value—Years 1 to 5						
Net present value	$ 466					

Merely by changing depreciation methods, the net present value increases by $325. This is strictly from speeding up the depreciation deduction and the time value of money. Chapter 13 will further discuss the advantages of accelerated depreciation and shorter tax lives for assets. The ACRS and MACRS methods in use now provide both of these benefits.

COST OF CAPITAL

Throughout the present value methods discussion, the term **cost of capital** appeared again and again. Capital projects are long-term investments—at least longer than current assets. These capital investments are financed by long-term sources of funds, such as mortgages, bonds payable, permanent paid-in-capital, and even retained earnings.

The basic idea is that all new investments in assets should at least earn enough to cover all costs, including the cost of funds. But what do capital funds or long-term funds cost? Many financial theories have been put forth to measure cost of capital. Their relative merits are beyond this text. A basic approach is presented merely to explain the sources of such a key variable in capital investment analysis.

A **weighted-average cost of capital** attempts to pool all long-term funds that a firm uses. A weighted-average is used because the relative amount of each source of funds affects the average cost of funds. Over the years, a firm might issue or retire bonds, issue stock and change dividend policies—paying out a higher or lower percentage of earnings. Relative amounts of debt and equity may change over the years. Debt instruments might have been issued in low or high interest rate periods, and stock might have been issued when prices were higher or lower. Also, interest rates and price/earnings ratios might now be higher or lower. All of these factors can impact the average cost of long-term funds.

Debt has significant cost advantages over equity since debt is less risky and interest is deductible for tax purposes. In effect, the government shares the cost with the firm. If a firm has a before-tax cost of debt of 10 percent and a 40 percent tax rate, the after-tax cost is 6 percent. For each additional $1 of interest cost, taxes go down by 40 cents and after-tax profits go down by 60 cents.

Dividends, on the other hand, are not deductible for tax purposes. These payouts are a distribution of profits to owners and not an expense of doing business.

Let us assume that a firm has the following long-term funds structure and cost of funds:

	Book Value	Mix Percentage	Before Tax Cost	After Tax Cost	Weighted Average
Bonds payable......	$10,000,000	25%	10%	6%	1.5%
Preferred stock	4,000,000	10	12	12	1.2
Common stock	14,000,000	35	18	18	6.3
Retained earnings...	12,000,000	30	18	18	5.4
Total	$40,000,000	100%			14.4%

Based on these calculations, the weighted-average cost of capital is 14.4 percent. Specific sources and calculations of the "before-tax cost" percentages are beyond this text's scope. As new capital is added, others retired, and markets change, this figure might change. Often financially strong companies in growing but proven industries have lower cost of funds. Higher risk, financially unstable, or new firms have higher costs.

Many firms prefer to add a risk factor to their cost of capital. This may be a margin of safety or a compensating factor for perceived different levels of risk. Different risks may be faced by different divisions of the same firm.

An inflation factor could also be included, but because certain cash flows may be impacted more by inflation than others, forecasts of revenues, costs, and other flows should probably incorporate estimated inflation impacts. The impact of inflation is also discussed in Chapter 13.

SUMMARY

The capital investment decisions are critical to the firm's long-term success. The relevant data for making investment decisions are incremental cash flows. The relevant revenues and costs were defined by criteria established in Chapter 11 for incremental decisions. The major additional factor added in this chapter is the time value of money. The opportunity cost of cash to be received in the future can be a significant variable in measuring returns. This opportunity cost is a function of the discount rate used and how far into the future we must wait to receive the cash.

The data analysis format will set the timing of relevant cash flows. To analyze the data, four methods were discussed. Two use the time value of money and calculate present values for all cash flows. These are:

1. The net present value, where a rate of return is set and used to calculate present values of all future cash flows, and
2. The internal rate of return, where the rate of return is found by setting the present value of the investment (an outflow) equal to the present value of future cash inflows.

Two other methods were discussed that did not use the time value of money. The payback period method is a fast, simple way of measuring when the initial investment will be returned. The accounting rate of return method uses accrual accounting data, losing the significance of cash flows. But corporate reporting systems often report actual results in an accrual accounting format.

Several assumptions were made in this chapter to simplify the basic analysis. These include:

1. The initial investment is made in Year 0 (today) so that a project's specific starting point can be established.
2. All cash flows occur at the end of time periods so that only Tables I and II need to be used.
3. A common marginal income tax rate of 40 percent is used to include a variety of federal, state, and local tax rates.
4. Straight-line depreciation is used for tax purposes instead of the ACRS or MACRS rates to simplify calculations. Salvage value is ignored in tax depreciation calculations and is considered to be net of any taxes when realized at the end of the asset's life.

The real world may not allow these assumptions to be used. Rarely is sufficient cash available to fund all attractive projects. Generally, projects are selected based on a ranking of rates of return. The cost of capital is often used in some form as the minimum acceptable rate of return. A project must earn enough profit to at least pay for the cost of its investment funds.

Many more complicating issues surround the capital investment decision. Chapter 13 continues the discussions and examines a number of these issues.

PROBLEMS FOR REVIEW

Problem A

Baxter Plastics is considering a change in producing a specialized part used in several Baxter products. Baxter sees a need for 200,000 parts per year over the foreseeable future.

The part is currently made on a molding machine that is now 3 years old and could be used for another 5 years. It cost $160,000 new, was to last 8 years, and would have a salvage value net of taxes of $15,000. It is now worth $75,000 on the used equipment market.

A new machine will improve the operation by reducing scrap, its increased tolerances (requiring less maintenance), and automatically packing the finished units. It will cost $275,000, have a useful life of 5 years, and have a $25,000 salvage value net of taxes after 5 years. The comparative cash operating expenses are:

	Old Machine	New Machine	
Variable cost	$6.00 per unit	$5.70 per unit	.30/u
Fixed cost	$100,000	$80,000	20,000

Assume that straight-line depreciation is used and that a tax rate of 40 percent is applicable to all incremental gains, losses, and taxable income. Cost of capital is estimated to be 14 percent.

Required:

1. Find the relevant cash flows for the molding machine replacement decision.
2. Using the net present value method, should the new molding machine be acquired?
3. Find the internal rate of return, the payback period, and the accounting rate of return.

Solution:

1. We could measure the relevant cash flows of the old machine and then the new machine, and then compare the two sets. A more direct analysis is to use the differential cash flows—the differences between the relevant cash flows of the old and the new machines. The differential cash flows are:

	Investment	Life of the Project				
	Year 0	Year 1	Year 2	Year 3	Year 4	Year 5
Cash flow:						
New machine........................	$(275,000)					
Sale of old machine	75,000					
Tax savings from loss on sale...........	10,000[1]					
Incremental salvage value						$10,000[2]
Variable cost savings		$60,000[3]	$60,000	$60,000	$60,000	60,000
Fixed cost savings		20,000[4]	20,000	20,000	20,000	20,000
Incremental income taxes		(18,000)[5]	(18,000)	(18,000)	(18,000)	(18,000)
Net cash flows........................	$(190,000)	$62,000	$62,000	$62,000	$62,000	$72,000

[1]The original cost of the old asset was $160,000, with annual depreciation of $20,000. After three years, the book value is $100,000 ($160,000 − $60,000). The old machine was sold for only $75,000, creating a $25,000 loss. This is deductible against other income reducing the cash tax expense in Year 0 by 40 percent of the loss:

$$\$100,000 - \$75,000 = \$25,000$$
$$\$25,000 \times .4 = \$10,000 \text{ tax savings}$$

[2]Salvage value of the new machine minus the salvage value of the old machine.
[3]The variable cost savings is: $.30 per unit × 200,000 units = $60,000 savings per year.
[4]The fixed cost saving is $100,000 - $80,000 = $20,000 savings per year.
[5]Incremental tax payment is based on:

Variable cost savings	$60,000	Incremental depreciation expense:	
Fixed cost savings	20,000	Old machine: ($160,000 ÷ 8) ...	$20,000
Incremental depreciation expense ..	(35,000)	New machine: ($275,000 ÷ 5) ..	55,000
Incremental taxable income	$45,000	Incremental depreciation	$35,000
Incremental tax payment (40%)	$18,000		

2.   Using the Part 1 cash flows, the net present value method shows:

	Investment	Life of the Project				
	Year 0	Year 1	Year 2	Year 3	Year 4	Year 5
Cash flows:						
Net cash flows................	$(190,000)	$62,000	$62,000	$62,000	$62,000	$72,000
Present value factors at 14% ...	× 1.000	× .877	× .769	× .675	× .592	× .519
Present value of cash flows.....	$(190,000)	$54,374	$47,678	$41,850	$36,704	$37,368
Present values—Years 1 to 5 ...	217,974					
Net present value	$ 27,974					

Based on this analysis, the investment will earn a positive net present value. If we want a 14 percent rate of return or better, we should approve the investment.

3.   To find the **internal rate of return**, we will use the trial and error method. Because the cash flows are not smooth over the project's entire life, the payback period gives a close but slightly lower estimate. Using various rates of return, we find a negative net present value at 20 percent:

	14%	16%	18%	20%
Net present value	$27,974	$17,748	$ 8,244	$ (600)

The rate of return is near but under 20 percent. To find a more exact rate, tables with greater detail must be used. Interpolation can be used:

18% NPV	$8,244	($8,244 ÷ $8,844) × 2.00% = 1.86%
20% NPV	(600)	1.86% + 18.00% = 19.86%
Absolute difference	$8,844	

The internal rate of return is 19.86 percent.
The **payback period** is found by:

$$\text{Net initial investment} \div \text{Annual cash inflow} = \text{Payback period}$$
$$\$190,000 \div \$62,000 = 3.06 \text{ years}$$

The **accounting rate of return** is found by:

(Variable & fixed cost savings − Incremental depreciation − Incremental taxes) ÷ Average investment
= Accounting rate of return

$$\frac{(\$60,000 + \$20,000 - \$35,000 - \$18,000)}{(\$190,000 + \$10,000) \div 2} = 27.0\%$$

Problem B

George's Antiques is evaluating alternative alarm systems for its factory. Two suppliers have made bids on the contract. The bids contrast sharply in terms of cash flows. Both bids are for a 4-year contract. Ignore taxes.

	Cash Outflows for Bid A	Cash Outflows for Bid B
Initial payment	$ 8,000	$16,000
Year 1	8,000	5,000
Year 2	8,000	5,000
Year 3	8,000	5,000
Year 4	8,000	9,000

Required:

1. Using the net present value method with a 12 percent discount rate, recommend the lowest cost alternative to George.
2. Comment on the non-quantified variables the antique company may want to consider.

Solution:
1. Note that all cash flows are outflows. Thus, the smaller net present value is the lower cost and, therefore, the more attractive.

	Investment	Life of the Project			
	Year 0	Year 1	Year 2	Year 3	Year 4
Bid A:					
Cash outflows	$ (8,000)	$(8,000)	$(8,000)	$(8,000)	$(8,000)
Present value factors	× 1.000	× .893	× .797	× .712	× .636
Present values.............	$ (8,000)	$(7,144)	$(6,376)	$(5,696)	$(5,088)
Net present value	$(32,304)				
Bid B:					
Cash outflows	$(16,000)	$(5,000)	$(5,000)	$(5,000)	$(9,000)
Present value factors	× 1.000	× .893	× .797	× .712	× .636
Present values.............	$(16,000)	$(4,465)	$(3,985)	$(3,560)	$(5,724)
Net present value	$(33,734)				

Bid A has the lower net present value, which is the lower cost alternative. Its total cost is $1,430 less than Bid B.

2.   Other factors that George will want to consider include:

   1.   What is the risk of loss?
   2.   Are any cost estimates subject to change?
   3.   Which vendor has the better reputation for service?
   4.   What is the response time in an emergency?
   5.   What is the quality of installation and training?
   6.   How easy is each system to use?
   7.   Can the system be upgraded at low cost?
   8.   How is each system monitored?

   These are issues that may well be more important than the net present value differential.

TERMINOLOGY REVIEW

Accelerated Cost Recovery System (ACRS) (631)
Accounting rate of return (ARR) method (629)
Annuity (623)
Capital budgeting (614)
Capital investment (615)
Capital investment decisions (614)
Cost of capital (622)
Cutoff rate (622)
Desired rate of return (622)
Discount rate (623)
Discounting (614)
Hurdle rate (622)
Initial investment (616)
Internal rate of return (IRR) (625)
Investment tax credit (631)

Marginal tax rate (630)
Minimum acceptable rate of return (622)
Modified Accelerated Cost Recovery System (MACRS) (631)
Net present value (NPV) method (621)
Payback period (627)
Payback period method (627)
Payback reciprocal (628)
Present value (620)
Profitability index (624)
Required rate of return (622)
Tax shield (632)
Target rate of return (622)
Time value of money (614)
Weighted-average cost of capital (635)

QUESTIONS FOR REVIEW AND DISCUSSION

1. Why is timing important in a capital investment decision? What is meant by the time value of money?

2. Why do capital investment decisions receive so much of management's time and attention?

3. What is meant by "net investment" in a capital investment decision?

4. Can a capital investment be made when no outflow of resources is made?

5. Are the returns from an investment the same as the accounting profit? Explain.

6. What are the advantages and disadvantages of the payback method?

7. What are the advantages and disadvantages of the accounting rate of return method?

8. John Steiner, a sales representative for a machine tool company, used the following phrase over and over with his customers: "Buy this thing, depreciate it, and watch the cash come rolling in from Uncle Sam!" What does he really mean?

9. Explain the difference between the internal rate of return method and the net present value method.

10. The net present value of a certain investment is zero. Does this mean the investment earns no profit? Explain the significance of a zero net present value.

11. How can the rankings from using the internal rate of return and the profitability index differ?

12. Why can the terms cutoff rate, hurdle rate, minimum acceptable rate of return, target rate of return, and desired rate of return be used interchangeably?

13. Explain the tax shield. Tie this explanation to the comment: "Depreciation is a source of cash."

14. How would you estimate the internal rate of return if you know the life of the project? How would you estimate the internal rate of return if you do not know the life of the project?

15. Are definitions of relevant costs and revenues different for capital investment analysis than the definitions used in Chapter 11?

16. Sue Ellen Meyers is buying a car for $12,000. After a down payment of $3,000, she finances the remainder at 12 percent annual interest with monthly payments. If she signs a 50-month financing contract, what will be her monthly payment?

17. What is the advantage of accelerated depreciation over straight-line depreciation in a capital investment decision?

18. Cash, accounts receivable, and inventory are classified as current assets. How can they be considered part of a long-term capital investment?

19. Knowing the cost of capital is a necessary part of present value analysis. What does it represent? Explain one way to measure it.

20. The formula used to derive the numbers in Table I is as follows:

$$P = \frac{1}{(1 + i)^n}$$ Where: P = Present Value Factor
                                       i = Interest Rate
                                       n = Number of Periods

Present Value of $1

Explain the math in words.

EXERCISES

1. **Determining the Length of an Investment.** Edward's Electronics is considering expanding its business by adding one more store. The building will cost $1 million and generate about $150,000 in cash inflows each year. The manager feels the investment should not be made unless the store realizes a 10 percent rate of return on the cash invested.

    Required:
    How many years must the store generate $150,000 to meet the 10 percent requirement?

2. **Review of Time Value.** John McCormick has won second prize in THE BIG Lottery. Friends who he never knew he had have offered him several "opportunities of a lifetime." He would like a 14 percent annual return. The lottery prize was a check for $300,000. Friends have offered deals promising the following returns:

    1. $50,000 per year for 10 years.
    2. $400,000 on the same date in next presidential election year.
    3. $20,000 per year for the rest of his life (about 50 years).
    4. A penniless friend has indicated that a check he wrote for $1,000,000 made out to McCormick is "in the mail."
    5. $500,000 to be paid on this same date 5 years from now.

    Required:
    Considering reasonable estimates of uncertainty, which should he select?

3. **Payback Method.** Hanley Company purchased a machine for $125,000 and will depreciate it on a straight-line basis over a 5-year period with an after-tax salvage value of $15,000. The related cost savings cash flow from operations, before income taxes, is expected to be $50,000 a year.

    Required:
    1. Find the payback period ignoring taxes.
    2. Assume that Hanley's effective income tax rate is 40 percent and that salvage value is ignored when calculating depreciation. What is the payback period?

4. **Using Different Capital Investment Methods.** Miko Center Company plans to acquire equipment costing $600,000. Depreciation on the new equipment would be $120,000 each year for 5 years. The annual cash inflow before income tax from this equipment has been estimated at $220,000. The tax rate is 40 percent.

    Required:
    1. Find the payback period.
    2. Find the accounting rate of return.
    3. Find the net present value if the minimum acceptable rate of return on investment is 16 percent.
    4. Estimate the internal rate of return from Table II (e.g., between 16 and 18 percent).

5. **Determining the Required Investment.** The Wheeler Company would like to initiate an advertising campaign to increase its annual sales volume. Data show that the proposed

advertising will add $80,000 to the annual cash flow for each of the next two years, plus $30,000 in the third year.

Required:
    What is the maximum amount that Wheeler would invest in this campaign if the company sets a minimum rate-of-return objective of 18 percent?

6. **Investments With Uneven Cash Flows.** Icon Consolidated has the data on two $100,000 investment opportunities. With only $100,000 in cash available, the owners must decide which is the better opportunity. The controller has gathered the following data:

> *Alternative 1:* $30,000 of cash inflow for each of the first three years and $90,000 for each of the last three years.
> *Alternative 2:* $80,000 of cash inflow in the first year, $60,000 in the next four years, and $40,000 in the sixth year.

Required:
    If the company has a 14 percent minimum rate of return, which investment opportunity would the company prefer?

7. **Comparing Alternatives.** The Stein Company is considering a new popper for their caramel popcorn factory. The analysis is narrowed to the "Bang" or the "Pow." Information on the two devices follows:

	Bang	Pow
Purchase price	$90,000	$60,000
Annual cash inflows	$34,000	$24,000
Useful life	5 years	5 years
Salvage value in 5 years	$ 8,000	$ 5,000

    Either device will do the job equally as well as the other. Stein uses a 16 percent cost of capital. Ignore taxes.

Required:
1.   Which machine has the higher net present value?
2.   Using the profitability index, which machine is more attractive?

8. **Equipment Replacement.** By replacing an old refrigeration unit, Ann Bacon of Bacon's Produce thinks that capacity will be greater and that cash operating costs will decline by $60,000 per year. The new refrigerator will cost $350,000. With the new refrigerator, sales are expected to increase by $100,000 per year. Her variable contribution margin is 40 percent. The old equipment is fully depreciated but will be sold for $8,000. The new refrigerator will use straight-line depreciation, has a 5-year life, and is expected to have a salvage value of $40,000. Ignore taxes.

Required:
    Format the cash flows for the refrigeration unit proposal.

9. **Selecting Between Two Investments.** Meridian Township has $60,000 of surplus cash in a fund that will not be used for one year. The township treasurer has two investment possibilities available:

(a)   Invest in 12 percent treasury bills for 6 months and then reinvest the proceeds in a 16 percent corporate bond for the remaining 6 months; or

(b)   Invest now in a 16 percent corporate bond maturing in 3 months, reinvest the proceeds in 12 percent treasury bills for 6 months, and hold the proceeds in the township's 6 percent interest-bearing checking account for the remaining 3 months.

Required:
Which alternative gives the township the higher amount at the end of one year?

10.   **Net Returns and Discounted Rate of Return.** The Echols Company is considering a new production method that can reduce materials cost by an estimated $60,000 a year. The new method is also expected to result in annual savings in labor and overhead cost of $70,000. The new equipment required for this method will cost $400,000 and will be depreciated on a straight-line basis for tax purposes. The asset will have no residual value at the end of 10 years, the estimated life of the equipment. Income tax is estimated at 40 percent.

Required:
1.   Determine the annual net cash inflow from the proposed investment.
2.   Will the investment earn an 18 percent after-tax rate of return?

11.   **Sales Offer as Investment.** The owner of a mini storage business has just received an offer of $600,000 for the storage buildings. The owner is interested in another investment opportunity that can probably yield an annual discounted return of 15 percent after income tax. The storage unit is expected to continue to yield an annual cash flow, before income taxes, of $170,000 for a period of 8 years. The book value of the storage buildings is $560,000, and straight-line depreciation is used for tax purposes. Zero salvage value is predicted. A 40 percent tax rate applies.

Required:
Should the offer for the sale of the storage business be accepted or refused?

12.   **Different Investment Goals.** Three projects are being evaluated. All have the same initial investment and expected life. The following data came from the analysis of the three projects:

	Net Present Value (Using 16%)	Payback	Accounting Rate of Return
Project A	$22,000	2.8 years	18%
Project B	$23,000	2.7 years	16%
Project C	$21,000	2.6 years	17%

Required:
1.   If the time value of money and profitability are important, which project is preferred?
2.   If we want the project that will make us look best in the accrual accounting reports, which project is preferred?
3.   If avoiding risk and getting our cash investment back quickly are the key factors, which project is preferred?

13. **Relevant Costs.** Kempa Company designs and makes office equipment. The sales manager is trying to decide whether to introduce a new swivel chair. The chair will sell for $200 and have variable costs of $80. Volume is expected to be 1,000 units per year for 5 years. Additional fixed cash operating costs will be $40,000 per year. Additional machinery costing $200,000 is needed. The new machinery will have a 5-year life and have no salvage value. Kempa uses straight-line depreciation. Kempa's tax rate is 40 percent, and the company uses a "hurdle rate" of 15 percent.

Required:
1. What will be the annual after-tax cash inflow?
2. What is the net present value of the machinery investment?

14. **Uneven Cash Flows.** The following projects all require a $80,000 investment today.

	Project				
	93-A54	93-G13	93-K01	93-P56	93-S43
Cash inflows:					
Year 1	$20,000	$10,000	$40,000		$60,000
Year 2	20,000	10,000			30,000
Year 3	20,000	15,000	40,000		10,000
Year 4	20,000	15,000		$160,000	(60,000)
Year 5	20,000	25,000	40,000		
Year 6	20,000	25,000			40,000
Year 7	20,000	30,000	40,000		
Year 8	20,000	30,000			80,000

Required:
   For each of the five projects, find the payback period, the accounting rate of return, and the net present value (using a 15 percent discount rate).

15. **New Business.** Zacha Co. purchased a new machine for $50,000 to expand capacity. Sales are expected to increase by 20 percent. The only additional fixed expense is the depreciation on the new machine (straight-line over 5 years with no salvage value). The income statement for the past year is:

Sales	$ 300,000
Variable expenses	(180,000)
Fixed expenses	(100,000)
Net income before taxes	$ 20,000
Taxes (40%)	(8,000)
Net income after taxes	$ 12,000

Required:
1. What is the expected annual net cash inflow, after taxes, from the use of the new machine?
2. Find the net present value using a hurdle rate of 15% and the payback period.

16. **Equipment Replacement.** By replacing present equipment with more efficient equipment, Willie Company estimates that cash operating costs can be reduced by $65,000 a year. In addition, sales volume can be increased resulting in a larger contribution margin of $25,000 a year without considering the cost savings from improved efficiency.

Depreciation of $50,000 per year is to be taken on the new equipment. Depreciation on the present equipment is $10,000 per year. The income tax rate is 40 percent.

Required:

What will be the estimated incremental annual cash inflow net of income taxes for each year on this investment situation?

17. **Investment in Another Company.** The management of Keeling Enterprises, Inc. is considering the investment of $10,000,000 to acquire the assets of Ener-Tec Company, a small company that has developed a more economical means of using electrical energy. Last year, Ener-Tec reported net sales of $20,000,000 and operating expenses of $18,000,000. Included in the operating expenses is depreciation of assets in the amount of $800,000. This level of earnings is expected to continue for 5 years, after which the technology will be outdated and the assets will have no value.

Required:

Ignoring income taxes and using the time value of money, what is the approximate rate of return earned by the investment?

18. **Find the Missing Values.** For each of the following projects fill in the missing value, if:

A = Initial investment
B = Life of project
C = Annual net cash inflow
D = Internal rate of return
E = Present value factor from Table II for "B" periods
    at "D" internal rate of return

	A	B	C	D	E
Project 1	$118,932	6 years	$34,000	?%	?
Project 2	$?	5 years	$12,000	?%	3.605
Project 3	$ 68,000	15 years	$?	16%	?
Project 4	$ 84,750	? years	$15,000	12%	?
Project 5	$?	? years	$20,000	20%	2.991
Project 6	$111,925	20 years	$?	8%	?

19. **Ranking Projects.** The following projects have been evaluated using the capital budgeting techniques we studied. Lives, size of investments, and cash flows vary among the projects.

	Project			
	A	B	C	D
Net present value (using 16%)	$3,440	$8,550	$300	$(2,000)
Internal rate of return	18%	16%	20%	12%
Payback period	4 years	2 years	3 years	5 years
Accounting rate of return	25%	18%	22%	20%

Required:

1. Rank the projects for each of the capital investment methods shown.
2. Discuss what might cause the differences in the rankings.

20.   **Tax Shield.** Your boss is considering a new parking lot for employees that will cost $200,000. The company is in the 40 percent tax bracket, and your boss says, "It will only cost us $120,000 after taxes to put in the lot." The firm has a 14 percent cost of capital and would depreciate the lot over 8 years using the straight-line method.

Required:

Tell your boss what the net cost, in present value terms, will be to put in the parking lot.

PROBLEMS

12-1.   **Payback and Discounted Returns.** Ignore tax impacts. The manager of Timber Ridge Inc. uses a simple payback method in selecting investment alternatives. She states that if she can recover the investment in 3 years, she is virtually in the same position as another investor who requires a discounted rate of return of 18 percent on a 5-year investment. In her business, investments produce uniform returns over a 5-year period and have no residual salvage value. Three investment alternatives are outlined as follows:

	Alternatives		
	1	**2**	**3**
Investment	$90,000	$24,000	$44,000
Annual return for each of 5 years	$30,000	$ 9,000	$12,500

Required:
1.   Which, if any, of the investment alternatives meets the 3-year payback criterion?
2.   Evaluate the three alternatives by using the net present value method with a minimum rate of return of 18 percent and compare the results with those found in Part 1.

12-2.   **Relevant Costs.** The Auto Wash Company has just installed a special machine for washing cars. The machine cost $20,000. Its operating costs, based on a yearly volume of 100,000 cars, total $15,000, exclusive of depreciation. The machine will have a 4-year useful life and no residual value. After the machine has been used one day, a machine salesman offers a different machine that promises to do the same job at a yearly operating cost of $9,000, exclusive of depreciation. The new machine will cost $24,000 cash, installed. The "old" machine is unique and can be sold outright for only $8,000, less $2,000 removal cost. The new machine, like the old one, will have a 4-year useful life and no residual value.

Sales, all in cash, will be $150,000 per year and other cash expenses will be $110,000 annually, regardless of this decision.

Required:
1.   Ignore taxes. Calculate net income for each of the 4 years assuming that the new machine is not purchased and then assuming that it is purchased. Sum the net incomes for the 4 years for each alternative. What should be done?
2.   Ignore taxes, and consider the time value of money. If a 15 percent return on investment is desired, what should be done?

12-3.   **Incremental Costs and Revenues.** The Dwyer Company has the opportunity to market a new product. The sales manager believes that the firm could sell 5,000 units per year at $14 per unit for 5 years. The production manager has determined that machinery costing $60,000 and having a 5-year life and no salvage value would be required. The machinery would have fixed operating costs requiring cash disbursements of $4,000 annually. Variable costs per unit would be $8. Straight-line depreciation would be used for both book and tax purposes. The tax rate is 40 percent and the firm's cost of capital is 14 percent.

Required:
1.   Determine the increase in annual net income and in annual after-tax cash flows expected from the investment.
2.   Determine the net present value of the investment.
3.   Suppose that the firm uses sum-of-years digits depreciation, how would your answer to Part 2 change?

12-4.   **Improving Investment Returns.** For many years Emilio Perez has been successful in the retail garment industry. Recently he has learned of an opportunity to purchase a two-story brick building for $750,000. He believes that he can operate successfully by using only one of the two floors. At the present time, he is operating in an older building where he uses two floors. This presents a sales limitation, he admits, but he believes his customers have become accustomed to the situation. Yet, he estimates that the annual returns from his business after income tax would probably increase by $150,000 for each of the next 10 years if he moved.

With uncertainties about inflation and interest rates, he would hesitate to invest unless he could obtain a discounted rate of return of at least 18 percent. This investment opportunity does not appear that good to him, and he is inclined to continue the current arrangements.

His daughter, who has recently graduated from medical school, disagrees with his position: "You forget that this area is growing. We have no professional building; and I know of several doctors, dentists, and attorneys who would be happy to have offices on the second floor if you did some remodeling. I already have estimates and find that you can have the second floor remodeled for $100,000. The offices should yield annual after-tax rental income of $40,000."

Required:
1.   From the information given, what is the approximate internal rate of return on the building itself?
2.   What is the approximate internal rate of return on the building and the remodeling investment together?

12-5.   **Finding Unknowns.** Fill in the blanks for each of the following independent cases. In all cases, the investment has a useful life of 10 years and no salvage value. Ignore taxes.

	Annual Cash Inflow	Investment	Cost of Capital	Internal Rate of Return	Net Present Value
1.	$ 45,000	$188,640	14%	?	$?
2.	$ 80,000	$?	12%	18%	$?
3.	$?	$300,000	?	16%	$ 81,440
4.	$?	$450,000	12%	?	$115,000
5.	$100,000	$?	?	14%	$ (38,300)

12-6. Investment Returns and Sales Volume. Plastic Products Inc. is considering an investment of $2,000,000 in a new product line. Depreciation of $200,000 is to be deducted in each of the next 10 years. Salvage value is estimated at zero. A selling price of $50 per unit is decided upon; unit variable cost is $30. The sales division believes that a sales estimate of 50,000 units per year is realistic. The controller states that a solid market exists for only 20,000 units a year. Projects must meet a minimum rate-of-return requirement of 15 percent. Income tax is estimated at 40 percent of income before tax.

Required:

1. Evaluate the project using each of the sales volume alternatives given. Use the net present value method.
2. At what volume will the project earn exactly a 15 percent return? Use the internal rate of return method.

12-7. Change in the Value of Money. Lauren Gatewood, manager of the Town Company, states that she used to accept investment opportunities that yielded discounted returns (after income tax) at a rate of 18 percent. With a decreasing cost of capital, she now expects to earn a 12 percent discounted rate of return.

Two competing investment proposals are now waiting for her evaluation, and the data are presented as follows:

	Alternatives	
	1	2
Estimated life	6 years	6 years
Net investment	$180,000	$192,000
Estimated annual cash inflows before depreciation and income taxes:		
Year 1	$ 50,000	$ 80,000
Year 2	50,000	70,000
Year 3	50,000	60,000
Year 4	90,000	50,000
Year 5	60,000	50,000
Year 6	60,000	50,000

Depreciation is to be deducted by the straight-line method, and the estimated salvage values will equal disposal costs at the end of the project's proposed life. Taxes are estimated to be 40 percent of income before tax.

Required:

1. Do either or both of the alternatives provide an 18 percent return? Use the net present value method.
2. Do either or both of the alternatives provide a 12 percent return? Use the net present value method.

12-8. Cost Reduction Project. Ashwell Company operates several factories, one of which was built some 70 years ago and is not in good condition. The factory has a fire insurance policy covering machinery, inventory, and the building itself. Premiums on the policy are $40,000 per year.

Recently, a fire inspector from the insurance company has recommended that the premium be increased to $60,000 per year because the older factory's fire protection has been diminished. The existing sprinkler system has stopped functioning and cannot be repaired at a reasonable cost. The plant manager was told by the inspector that a new system, costing $120,000 and with a 12-year life and no salvage value, would be needed to continue the policy at the current premium level.

The system would be depreciated on a straight-line basis. The tax rate is 40 percent, and Ashwell's cost of capital is 12 percent.

Required:
1. In a quantitative sense, should the sprinkler system be installed?
2. Discuss other benefits that are either intangible or difficult to measure that might impact the decision.

12-9. **Alternative Uses.** The Savoie Company owns an office building in the business center of Metro City. The building has a large unused lobby area. The facilities manager for the firm, Karen McGriff, is planning to get a greater financial return from the unused space and believes that a convenience shop should be placed in the lobby. She has talked to managers of several other office buildings and has projected the following annual operating results if the company establishes the shop:

Sales	$85,000
Cost of sales	40,000
Salaries and benefits of clerks.....................	24,000
Licenses and permits	1,000
Share of utilities on the building	2,000
Share of building depreciation	1,000
Advertising for the shop	1,000
Allocation of Savoie's administrative expense.......	1,500

The investment required would be $50,000, all for equipment that would be worthless in ten years. Before presenting the plan to the executive manager, Karen learned that the space could be leased to an outside firm that would operate a convenience shop. The other firm would pay a commission of $5,000 per year for ten years. Because the lobby is heated and lighted anyway, Savoie would supply utilities at a minimal added cost. Savoie's cost of capital is 12 percent. Ignore taxes.

Required:
1. Determine the best course of action for Savoie.
2. Determine how much annual rent Savoie would have to receive to equalize the attractiveness of the alternatives.

12-10. **Basic Replacement Decision.** You are given the following data:

Existing machine:		Replacement machine:	
Cost	$70,000	Cost	$180,000
Book value	30,000	Salvage value..............	20,000
Salvage value (end of life)	0	Annual cash operating	
Annual depreciation	5,000	costs	8,000
Annual cash operating costs	50,000	Depreciation method	Straight line
Present fair market value	50,000	Useful life	6 years
Remaining life	6 years		

The income tax rate for all taxation issues is 40 percent. The target rate of return is 14 percent. Assume that salvage value is ignored in calculating depreciation expense.

Required:

1. Determine the net present value of the replacement decision.
2. What is the profitability index of the replacement decision?

12-11. **Value of a Business.** The Jawbreak Company makes and sells candy in large lots for other firms that package and sell the candy under various brand names. The firm could acquire a small candy exporting firm that has sold about 800,000 pounds of candy annually to Korea and Hong Kong. To operate the firm, Jawbreak would have to hire a specialized salesperson for $150,000 annually including travel and entertainment expenses. It would also need to acquire additional packaging machinery costing $200,000. The machinery would last for 5 years, have no salvage value, and would be depreciated on a straight-line basis for tax purposes.

Other data are as follows:

(a) Variable costs are $0.10 per pound.
(b) Selling price on the export business is $0.50 per pound.
(c) Annual cash costs of operating the new machinery are $40,000.
(d) The tax rate is 40 percent.
(e) Cost of capital is 16 percent.

Required:

On the basis of the information provided and using a 5-year time horizon, what is the most Jawbreak should pay for this investment opportunity?

12-12. **Expanding a Product Line.** Ghafari Brothers Company makes office equipment, such as tables, desks, computer equipment consoles, and work tables. The sales manager is trying to decide whether to expand the relatively new computer equipment console product line. The average desk will sell for $300 and has a variable cost of $140 per unit. Volume is expected to be 4,000 units per year for five years. To make the desks, the firm will have to buy additional machinery that will cost $900,000, have a 5-year life, and a $100,000 salvage value. Straight-line depreciation will be used, and salvage value is ignored in depreciation calculations. Additional fixed cash operating costs will be $200,000 per year.

The Ghafari firm is in the 40 percent tax bracket, and its cost of capital is 16 percent.

Required:

1. Determine, using the net present value method, whether the computer console line should be expanded.
2. Compute the payback period.
3. Determine the approximate internal rate of return that the firm expects to earn on the investment. Ignore salvage value.

12-13. **Changes in the Economic Environment.** Four years ago, Bolin Properties Inc. invested $10,000,000 in a venture in another country. The investment was estimated to have a 10-year life and was expected to produce a cash inflow of $2,500,000 each year before income tax. It did exactly this for 4 years. Conditions are less favorable now, and the revised estimate indicates that the annual cash flow will be only $1,300,000 but will last for 8 more years. (Because this is a foreign investment, it has a special tax status and is not subject to income tax.)

The investment can now be sold for $5,400,000. At the present time, an investment can be justified only if the discounted rate of return is expected to be no less than 18 percent.

Required:

Should the investment be sold for $5,400,000 or continued in operation? Show computations by the net present value method.

12-14. Effect of Accelerated Depreciation. The molding department of Hornsby Inc. has been investigating the possibility of acquiring a new unit of equipment at a cost of $60,000. Cash savings before income tax from the use of this equipment have been estimated at $20,000 per year for a period of 5 years. At the end of 5 years, the equipment will have no salvage value. The rate to be used in evaluating investments is 10 percent after income tax of 40 percent.

Required:

Calculate the net present value if straight-line depreciation is used for tax purposes and if sum-of-years-digits depreciation is used for tax purposes.

12-15. Break-Even Volume and Investment. For several years, Pullella Company has used a combination of its own equipment and rental equipment to handle standard materials. The company has enough of its own equipment to handle routine work but must rent equipment to handle a particular bulk material. The cost to rent equipment has been estimated to average $4,000 a year.

An evaluation of the operation indicates that the company can save $.15 per cubic yard of bulk material by using its own equipment instead of the rented equipment. An equipment manufacturer offers the necessary additional equipment at a cost of $80,000. The equipment will probably have a useful life of 6 years with no salvage value.

Uncertainty exists with respect to how much work will be required from the new equipment if it is purchased. Estimates of the number of cubic yards that might possibly be handled in each of the 6 years are 80,000 cubic yards, 100,000 cubic yards, or 120,000 cubic yards. On this type of investment, a 15 percent discounted return is considered to be appropriate.

Required:
1.   Can the investment meet the minimum rate-of-return requirement if 80,000 cubic yards are handled? If 100,000 cubic yards are handled? If 120,000 cubic yards are handled?
2.   Determine the break-even volume, that is, the number of cubic yards at which the investment can just meet the 15 percent return requirement. Round all amounts to the nearest dollar.

12-16. Ranking Investment Alternatives. Mosearo Industries has designated $1.2 million for capital investment expenditures during the upcoming year. Its cost of capital is 14 percent after tax. A number of investment opportunities have been identified. The following list shows the potential investments together with their net present values:

Project	Net Investment	Net Present Value
A	$200,000	$22,000
B	275,000	21,000
C	150,000	6,000
D	190,000	(19,000)
E	500,000	40,000
F	250,000	30,000
G	100,000	7,000
H	200,000	18,000
I	210,000	4,000
J	250,000	35,000

Required:

1. Calculate the profitability index for each of the investments.
2. Which of the projects should be accepted, considering the limit on funds available?
3. If the available investment funds are reduced to only $1,000,000:
   (a) Does the list of accepted projects change from part 2?
   (b) What is the opportunity cost of the eliminated $200,000?

12-17. Proposal Preparation. Yoder Instruments Company manufactures a variety of products. The sales manager of Yoder has stated repeatedly that he could sell more units of one of the firm's products if they were available. To prove his claim, the sales manager conducted a market research study last year at a cost of $60,000 to determine potential demand for this product. The study indicated that Yoder could sell 25,000 units annually for the next 5 years. A unit sells for $20 per unit.

The machinery currently used has capacity to product 15,000 units annually. This machinery has a book value of $80,000 and a remaining useful life of 5 years. The salvage value of the machinery is negligible now and will be zero in 5 years. The variable production costs using this equipment are $12 per unit.

New machinery could produce 30,000 units annually. The new machinery costs $250,000 and has an estimated useful life of 5 years with no salvage value at the end of the 5 years. Yoder's production manager has estimated that the new equipment would provide increased production efficiencies, reducing the variable production costs to $10 per unit. The production manager also explains that the machine's higher capacity would cause factory administrative overheads to be reallocated. He thought a charge of $4 per unit for the additional 10,000 units produced would be the amount calculated by the cost accounting department.

The sales manager felt so strongly about the need for additional capacity that he prepared an economic justification for the equipment. His analysis, as shown in the accompanying tables, excited him because it did cover all expenses including the bank's prime interest rate and "still returned a small sum to the bottom line." He was last seen on his way to the President's office to schedule a meeting with the executive finance committee. A quick peek at his analysis shows:

Initial investment:
Purchase price of new machinery............................		$250,000
Disposal of present equipment:		
Loss on disposal	$80,000	
Less benefit of tax loss (40 percent)	32,000	48,000
Market research study costs		60,000
Total new investment needed		$358,000

Additional annual profit:
  Contribution margin from product:
    New machinery output:
      30,000 units × [$20 - ($10 + 4)] $180,000
    Existing machinery output:
      15,000 × [$20 - ($12 + 4)]   60,000
    Added contribution margin $120,000
    Less depreciation on new machinery   50,000
    Increase in taxable income .... $ 70,000
    Income tax at 40 percent   28,000
    Increase in income .... $ 42,000
    Less 9 percent borrowing cost on the additional investment required
    (.09 X $358,000)   32,220
    Net annual return on the proposed new machinery .... $ 9,780

Required:

The sales manager's executive secretary, who has kept him out of "hot water" in the past, is worried about the sales manager's numbers. She asks you to review them and see if he has his "gear together." You recall that the cost of capital of the firm has been 16 percent and a 40 percent tax rate has been used, along with straight-line depreciation. Revise the sales manager's report to show:

(a)   The required net investment in the new machinery.
(b)   The additional annual cash inflow.
(c)   The net present value of the proposed investment in new machinery.

12-18. **The New Technology Arrives.** The Wildhaber Machine Shop purchased a new grinding machine one year ago at a cost of $68,000. The machine has been working very satisfactorily, but the shop manager, Fred, has just received information on an electronically controlled grinder that is vastly superior to the machine which he now uses. While both machines can meet all required existing quality standards and tolerances, the new machine's quality potential can far exceed the old machine's capabilities. Comparative data on the two machines follow:

	Present Machine	Proposed New Machine
Purchase cost new (including installation costs)	$70,000	$90,000
Salvage value today	35,000	
Salvage value at end of life	5,000	10,000
Annual costs to operate	95,000	75,000
Estimated useful life when new	7 years	6 years

Fred makes a few quick computations and exclaims, "Wow! We need that machine and its capabilities. But, no way can I sell that upstairs. When the boss sees the loss on the old machine, he'll have kittens." He's looking at this:

Remaining book value of the old machine $60,000
Salvage value now of the old machine   35,000
Net loss from disposal $25,000

Wildhaber uses straight-line depreciation and ignores salvage value in its depreciation calculations. Sales from the grinding operation are expected to remain unchanged at $300,000 per year indefinitely. Other cash costs of the grinding operation total $80,000 annually. The corporate tax rate is 40 percent.

Required:
Prepare summary income statements covering the next 6 years for the grinding operation, assuming:
(a) That the new machine is not purchased.
(b) That the new machine is purchased.
What do you recommend? Show any additional analysis needed.

12-19. Debt Restructuring. M. M. Raamon Company is a large manufacturer working as a subcontractor in the defense industry. Over the years, the cost pinch has caused the company to borrow heavily to have working capital readily available. As of January 1, 1994, the company is forecast to have the following long-term debentures outstanding, all of them with semiannual interest payments at June 30 and December 31:

$2,000,000	8% debentures due June 30, 1998
$3,000,000	10% debentures due December 31, 2002
$5,000,000	12% debentures due June 30, 2006
$4,000,000	12% debentures due December 31, 2008

It is now early fall 1993. Rex Cauley, chief financial officer, believes that the market interest rate on January 1, 1994 will be 10 percent and would like to take advantage of lower interest rates to reduce cash payments for interest and to extend the payment periods. Rex proposes issuing $8,000,000 of 10 percent debentures due December 31, 2008 and up to $6,000,000 of 12 percent debentures due December 31, 2013 in exchange for the outstanding debentures at January 1, 1994. All exchanges would take effect on that date after all interest payments on existing debt are made.

Required:
1.   Compute the present value of the existing debt as of January 1, 1994.
2.   Compute the present value of the proposed debt instruments as of January 1, 1994.
3.   Is it possible for the company to exchange the two debentures for the existing four debentures? Explain.
4.   Explain why someone holding a 12 percent bond would consider exchanging it for a bond of a lesser interest rate, such as 10 percent, all other things being equal.

CASE 12A—Westerli Avionics

Westerli Avionics specializes in electronic guidance systems for both commercial and military aircraft. For a relatively small company, Westerli has been very profitable and is currently generating excess cash from operations that it plans to use for both diversification and vertical integration. Allied Telecommunications has just offered to buy 51 percent of Westerli's 5 million outstanding shares for $35 per share. The offer calls for an exchange of Allied stock plus $15 per share cash, a total deal worth $89,250,000. The most recent market price for Westerli stock is $29 per share.

Jim Leering, CEO of Westerli Avionics, believes the market price of its stock undervalues the company. Some stockholders disagree with Leering and want the high earnings multiple represented by the offer; reported earnings for the recent fiscal year are $3.00 per share. Leering says that cash flow, not reported earnings, is the number that really matters. It is cash flow that services debt, pays dividends, and maintains and expands plant and equipment. Cash flow from operations last year was $18 million and is expected to grow at 14 percent per year for the next 10 years. The current interest rate for discounting is 12 percent. Leering thinks a 10-year time frame is reasonable for future earnings analysis.

A small group of Westerli stockholders is opposed to the Allied deal and continuing operations and instead proposes that the company liquidate and distribute the cash to the stockholders. Assets have a book value of $130 million and a replacement cost of $200 million. However, the market value of used assets, if sold currently, would be about $175 million.

Jim Leering must make a recommendation to the board of directors tomorrow morning.

Required:
1.   Calculate the present value for the future stream of cash flows from operations.
2.   Compare the three alternatives mentioned and select the one that appears best for the company and stockholders.
3.   Should Westerli make a counteroffer? If so, how much should it be?

CASE 12B—Mavis Machine Shop[1]

The management of Mavis Machine Shop is considering a project to modernize its plant facilities. The company operates out of a large converted warehouse in Salem, West Virginia, and produces assorted machined metal parts for the oil and gas drilling and production industry in the surrounding area. One of Mavis's major customers is Buckeye Drilling, Inc. which purchases specialized drill bits and replacement parts for its operations. Mavis has negotiated an annual contract with Buckeye to supply its drill bit requirements and related spare parts in each of the past 8 years. In the past, the requirements had been about 8,400 bits per year.

The present arrangement of the machine shop includes 4 large manual lathes currently devoted to the Buckeye business. Each lathe is operated by a skilled worker, and each bit requires machining at all 4 lathes. The management is considering replacing these manual lathes with an automatic machine, capable of performing all 4 machining operations necessary for a drill bit. This machine would produce drill bits at the same rate as the 4 existing lathes, and would require only one skilled operator.

The 4 existing manual lathes are 3 years old, can each produce 2,100 drill bits on a 2-shift, 5-day per week basis, and had cost a total of $570,000. The remaining useful life of these lathes, calculated on a two-shift, 5-day per week basis, is estimated to be 9 years. The salvage value at the end of their useful life is estimated to be $5,000 each and was ignored in depreciation calculations. Depreciation of $142,500 has been accumulated on the 4 lathes. Cash for the purchase of these lathes had been partially supplied by a 10-year, unsecured bank loan, of which $180,000 is still outstanding. The best estimate of the current selling price of the 4 lathes in their present condition is $240,000, after dismantling and removing costs. The loss from the sale would be deductible for tax purposes, resulting in a tax savings of 40 percent of the loss.

[1]This case was written by Thomas Graham under the supervision of Professor John Shank.

The automatic machine being considered needs only one highly skilled operator to feed in raw castings, observe its functioning, and make necessary adjustments. It would have an output from 2 shifts of 8,400 drill bits annually. Because it would be specially built by a machine tool manufacturer, no catalog price exists. The cost is estimated to be $810,000, delivered and installed. The useful life would be 10 years. No reliable estimate of its salvage value can be made. An educated guess is that the value would equal the book value of the asset at any time in its life assuming no salvage value was considered in the depreciation calculations.

As a result of a study prepared by the cost accountant for use in deciding what action to take, the following information has been compiled. The direct labor rate for lathe operations is $15 per hour. The new machine would use less floor space, which would save $1,600 annually on the allocated charges for square footage of space used, although the layout of the plant is such that the freed space would be difficult to utilize and no other use is planned. Miscellaneous cash expenses for supplies and power would be $20,000 less per year if the automatic machine is used.

If purchased, the new lathe would be financed with a secured bank loan at 14 percent. Some additional financial data for the company are given in the following table. This information is considered to be typical of the company's financial condition, with no major changes expected in the foreseeable future.

MAVIS MACHINE SHOP
SELECTED FINANCIAL INFORMATION
CONDENSED INCOME STATEMENT, 1994

Net sales	$5,364,213
Expenses	4,138,647
Profit before taxes	$1,225,566
Income taxes	502,851
Net income	$ 722,715

MAVIS MACHINE SHOP
CONDENSED BALANCE SHEET
DECEMBER 31, 1994

Current Assets	$3,051,349	Current Liabilities . .	$ 930,327
Property Assets . . .	4,239,210	10 % Bonds	
		Outstanding	500,000
Other Assets	151,491	Common Stock	1,000,000
		Retained Earnings . .	5,011,723
	$7,442,050		$7,442,050

Required:
1. Summarize the net investment and net cash flows for the proposed project. Assume that the new lathe will be depreciated using straight-line depreciation.
2. For the project, calculate the approximate internal rate of return, the payback period, the net present value (at 20 percent after taxes), and the profitability index.
3. What qualitative factors should be considered in evaluating this project?
4. What decision would you recommend?

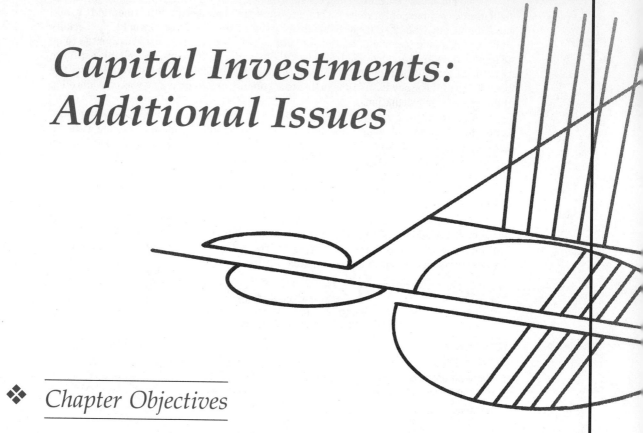

Chapter Thirteen

Capital Investments: Additional Issues

❖ *Chapter Objectives*

After studying Chapter 13, you will be able to:
1. Analyze several issues which complicate calculations used in capital investment decisions.
2. Evaluate the financing decision independent of the acquisition decision.
3. Understand the significance of accelerated depreciation and the basics of ACRS and MACRS.
4. Understand how the risks associated with various decision variables in the capital investment decision impact the evaluation of a project.
5. See the importance of a post audit of capital investment decisions both to improve control and to improve future capital investment evaluations.
6. Integrate the evaluation of social costs of capital investments into the more quantitative analysis.

■ *More Complexities in Capital Investments* ■

As mentioned at the beginning of Chapter 12, John Victory, President of Prestige Electronics, is reviewing investment proposals. He is surprised by the variety of the opportunities presented. But he also has been amazed by the complexity of the decisions. Few projects are straightforward cash out and cash in propositions. Every proposal has tax issues, gains and losses, and inflationary concerns. Alternatives may have different lives and initial required investments. Also, why purchase equipment when it could be leased? Comparisons often appear to be between apples and oranges.

Some of the projects have a fairly high degree of certainty attached to the future cash flows; but others depend on what, at best, are guesses. He knows that the success of certain projects depends heavily on one or two key variables. If estimates of a key variable are off by a small amount, the feasibility of the entire project may be in doubt.

Recent changes in the tax laws concerning depreciation appear to make capital investments more attractive. But should he make investment choices based on tax advantages or tax law changes?

Based on discussions presented in Chapter 12 about capital investment decisions, Chapter 13 moves on to more complex issues and extensions of basic analyses. The chapter begins with additional computational issues and ends with a discussion of evaluating social costs in investment decisions.

The basic methods of evaluating capital investment projects were discussed in Chapter 12. Because capital investment projects vary widely and depend heavily on estimates of the future, many additional issues and levels of complexity may need to be considered. Among these are calculation issues, consideration of financing alternatives, more concern about taxes and depreciation, and risk analysis. Finally, the planning and control cycle is closed with a post audit of the investments' results.

CALCULATION ISSUES

Enough calculation issues arise in capital investment analyses that a textbook could be written just to tackle these complications. A few of these have already been addressed in Chapter 12. Several others are now discussed.

Uneven Project Lives

When comparing alternative projects, lives of each project may not match. How can a 4-year solution to a problem be compared to a 6-year or a 10-year solution? The decision can be viewed from two sides—the time frame of the job to be done and life of the proposed solutions. Do we want a solution for 3 years, 5 years, or longer? How long can the physical asset last? Often, because of technology changes, the intended life of an asset may be shorter than its physical life. A 3-year solution is sought, while the asset's physical life might well be twice that long.

If the time period is based on the needs of the problem, the task is to find salvage or market values for assets at the end of the defined time period.

If the time period is based on the physical lives of the proposed assets, the different useful lives of the proposed solutions must be matched somehow. One approach is to use a shorter-lived project as the comparison time period. This requires finding salvage or market values for assets with longer lives of other alternatives. Another approach, using a longer-lived project, requires an assumption that the shorter-lived projects will be extended by another similar investment at the end of the first investment's life. For example, two 4-year projects might be strung together to match an alternative with an 8-year life.

While no specific rule can be set, the time frame of a problem as defined by management would seem to be a better choice. Management's intent and common sense should govern the time period choice.

Working Capital

When expansion occurs, inventories and receivables often expand. Financing working capital growth is an integral part of a project's total investment. Unlike depreciable equipment and fixed assets, **working capital** is used, is replenished, and can probably be recovered at the end of the project. Often, working capital requirements grow slowly over time. Needed increases in these accounts can easily be overlooked and omitted from a project's analysis.

Assume that Athletic Champs operates a chain of sporting goods stores in shopping malls. Opening a new store requires layout, equipment, and fixtures costing about $450,000. In addition, about $300,000 of inventory is needed to stock a new store. Experience shows that inventory and other working capital needs will grow at about $20,000 per year for the first five years. If Athletic Champs uses an 8-year time frame for evaluating a store location, an assumption will be needed about the equipment salvage value and the recovery of the working capital investment. The fixed assets' salvage values are estimated to be $50,000, and the entire working capital investment (now $400,000) is thought to be recoverable. The cash flows would look like:

	Investment	Life of the Project				
	Year 0	Year 1	Year 2	...	Year 5	... Year 8
Cash flows:						
Initial construction	$(450,000)					$ 50,000
Working capital needs	(300,000)	$(20,000)	$(20,000)	...	$(20,000)	... 400,000

Working capital recovery is not automatic. Inventory may be obsolete and receivables might not be collectible. A going-concern assumption can generally be made if the business is expected to continue past the time frame cutoff.

Inflation and Future Cash Flows

Inflation is a common economic problem. Over the past 20 years in the United States, annual inflation rates have ranged from a high of over 13 percent to a low of under 2 percent. While these levels are moderate compared to rates in numerous other countries, capital investments decisions must include inflationary impacts on future cash flows.

Two approaches have been suggested to incorporate inflation into the analysis:

1. Add the expected inflation rate to the cost of capital rate. This is simple but assumes that inflation is the same for all future time periods and that all cash flows are impacted by the same inflation rate.
2. Build the impacts of inflation into the expected future cash flows. This allows different inflation rates to be used for investments, revenues, and each cost component such as personnel and materials.

The second approach is more reflective of reality.

To illustrate inflation impacts on estimates of future cash flows, assume that Beall Motors plans to enter the motor diagnostic business in Seaview. Numerous automotive shops will be competing with Beall for business. The equipment will cost about $120,000 and should last about three years, when automotive technology advances will require more powerful computer capabilities. Beall expects revenues to be about $150,000 per year, personnel costs to be $60,000, and other support costs to run about $30,000.

Economic forecasts indicate that inflation should run about 6 percent per year for the next few years. But Beall feels that, at best, he could raise prices no more than 4 percent per year because of competition. Personnel costs will probably increase at a 10 percent rate. Other costs will increase at the average 6 percent rate. The equipment, which has no salvage value, will be depreciated on a straight-line basis. Assume a 40 percent tax rate. Also assume that estimates for Years 0 and 1 are at the current price level.

	Investment	Life of the Project		
	Year 0	Year 1	Year 2	Year 3
Cash flows:				
Initial investment	$(120,000)			
Revenues		$150,000	$156,000	$162,240
Personnel costs		(60,000)	(66,000)	(72,600)
Other costs		(30,000)	(31,800)	(33,708)
Incremental taxes*		(8,000)	(7,280)	(6,373)
Net cash flows	$(120,000)	$ 52,000	$ 50,920	$ 49,559

* Taxes in Year 1: ($150,000 − 60,000 − 30,000 − 40,000) × .40 = $8,000,
  Taxes in Year 2: ($156,000 − 66,000 − 31,800 − 40,000) × .40 = $7,280, and
  Taxes in Year 3: ($162,240 − 72,600 − 33,708 − 40,000) × .40 = $6,373.
  Taxes decline because expenses are increasing faster than revenue.

Of note is the fact that depreciation, being based on the historical cost of the investment, is $40,000 per year each year. While all other revenues and costs have inflation built into them, the tax law requires that the depreciation expense is always expressed in historical-cost dollars from the year of acquisition. Using historical cost-based depreciation in tax calculations often leads to increased levels of tax payments since profits grow from inflated revenues and other expenses.

Evaluation of Projects With Different Initial Investments

Up to this point, most of the illustrations have assumed that a single investment alternative existed. The firm had to decide whether or not to invest in that single project. Actually though, a firm may have several alternatives but still have to select only one. In such a case, care must be exercised in using the internal rate of return method, because the project with the highest internal rate of return may not be the most desirable. This can happen in those cases where the dollar investment is not the same. The dollar amount of the return from a larger investment, in many cases, will exceed the dollar return from a smaller investment having a better internal rate of return.

Assume that Vista Transit Company must choose between two projects. Each project has an estimated life of 5 years with annual returns as follows:

	Project I	Project II
Net investment	$75,000	$100,000
Annual return for each of 5 years	26,000	33,000

Investments are expected to earn a desired rate of return of at least 12 percent. Project II requires an investment of an additional $25,000 versus Project I. The approximate internal rate of return is computed for each alternative and the incremental investment as follows:

	Project I	Project II	Incremental (II − I)
Net investment	$(75,000)	$(100,000)	$(25,000)
Annual return	26,000	33,000	7,000
Payback period	2.885	3.030	3.571
Present value factor from Table II for period 5 row closest to payback period	2.864	2.991	3.605
Approximate internal rate of return from Table II	22%	20%	12%

It appears that Project I should be selected because the internal rate of return is higher. The additional $25,000 investment needed by Project II yields a much lower rate of return—12 percent. But, if the rate of return on the incremental investment is greater than the hurdle rate of return, the larger investment should still be made. In this example, an additional $7,000 per year is returned on an additional investment of $25,000. The rate of return on the incremental investment barely meets the 12 percent desired rate of return. However, other investment alternatives earning more than 12 percent and less than 22 percent may exhaust the available capital investment dollars.

Sometimes the investment problem can be understood better when the returns are depicted on a graph, as in Figure 13.1. The returns from each alternative are discounted at various discount rates. The investment is subtracted from the discounted cash inflows, and the net present values (either positive or negative) are plotted on a graph. At about 12.38 percent the two projects have the same net present values. Project I has a higher net present value at higher discount rates. Project II has a higher net present value at lower discount rates.

Conceptually, Figure 13.1 is similar to the break-even graph used in Chapter 4. Positive discounted returns are given on a vertical scale above a zero line, and negative discounted returns are shown below the line. Computations at the 10 percent rate are as follows:

	Project I	Project II
Present value of cash inflows	$96,419	$122,815
Less net initial investment	−75,000	−100,000
Net present value (positive)	$21,419	$ 22,815

The internal rate of return for each alternative is at the point where the present value line crosses the zero axis on the chart—21.66 percent for Project I and 19.40 percent for Project II. The cost of the investment is balanced by the discounted returns at the rate indicated at the point of crossover.

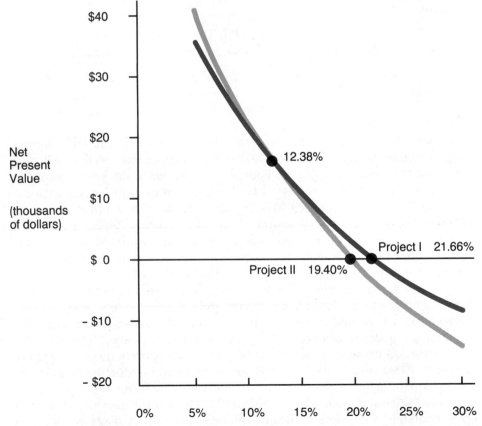

Figure 13.1   Comparison of Two Projects at Various Discount Rates

If one alternative produces larger cash inflows in the early years while the other alternative produces higher cash inflows in later years, the problem of selecting discount rates arises. Should the company forego the more immediate returns for even larger returns in the future? The answer will depend upon the rate at which future cash inflows can be reinvested as compared to the sacrifice of immediate returns. A probable solution to the problem is to discount the future cash flows at the minimum acceptable rate of return.

Gains and Losses on Asset Disposals

If assets are sold at more or less than their book values, a gain or loss on asset disposal will occur. The book value of an asset is the original cost minus the accumulated depreciation taken on the asset. In the real world, accounting book values and tax cost bases often differ. Unless, specifically mentioned, these two are assumed to be the same for illustration purposes. If the sale is for more than the book value, a gain occurs; and if the sale is for less than the book value, a loss occurs.

Aside from taxation issues, the gain or loss can be ignored since the cash from the sale of the asset is the relevant cash flow in the decision-making process. Asset disposals arise from two aspects of the capital investment decision:

1.   Old assets may be sold as part of the decision to acquire a new asset.
2.   The new asset may be sold at the end of its expected useful life.

Since the capital investment decision is a future decision, it might be considered unusual that an assumed salvage value for the new asset and its estimated market value would differ. Tax issues could well cause a difference. A planned gain or loss might arise.

In discussing disposals, sales and trade-ins are handled differently for tax purposes. In trade-ins, the market value of the old asset reduces the cash paid to acquire the new asset. The old book value is added to the cash cost of the new asset to create the new asset's book value. For example, assume that a new asset is purchased for $20,000 cash plus the trade-in of an old asset having a book value of $5,000. Also assume the asset will have a 5-year life and no salvage value. Straight-line depreciation over 5 years will be $5,000 per year ($20,000 plus $5,000 divided by 5 years). No gain or loss is recognized, and depreciation expense over the new asset's life is adjusted.

When old assets are sold and new assets are purchased in separate transactions, a gain or a loss on the old asset is recognized, and the new asset's cost is depreciated. Tax related issues surrounding gains and losses on sales depend on current legislation applicable to capital gains and losses. Many complex issues exist. At present, capital gains tax rates and ordinary income rates are the same. Most issues related to taxation of gains and deductibility of losses are beyond the scope of this text. The concern here is to recognize cash inflows from asset sales and to identify the basic tax impacts of the gains and losses. It is assumed here that gains are taxed at 40 percent and that losses are deductible against other income and reduce the firm's tax liability at a 40 percent rate.

For example, if an asset has a book value of $10,000 and is sold for $6,000, two cash flows are created (and for our purposes are assumed to occur at the time of sale): a cash inflow of $6,000 from the sale and a reduction in tax payments of $1,600. The $1,600 is 40 percent of the loss of $4,000 [.4 × ($10,000 − $6,000)].

If an asset having a $10,000 book value is sold for $16,000, the cash flows would be a cash inflow of $16,000 and a cash outflow of $2,400 for the taxes owed on the gain of $6,000.

FINANCING VERSUS INVESTMENT DECISIONS

Many capital investments are directly tied to how the investment outlay will be financed. Often debt is issued, stock is sold, bank borrowing is arranged, or leases are signed. The particular financing arrangements depend on many variables—money market conditions, debt/equity ratios, prior borrowings, and the overall financial condition of the firm. Financing major projects should be an integral part of the firm's strategic planning and long-range cash forecasting.

Even for specific projects, one alternative may include leasing while another requires a purchase with the cash coming from bank borrowings or the firm's own cash balances. Financing may require principal and interest payments, lease payments, or no cash flow if we use so-called "free" money from our own cash account.

The General Rules

The general capital investment decision rules about financing are:

1. Make capital investment decisions without regard to the method of financing. Assume that the capital investment is a cash purchase and that the funds are coming from the pool of long-term funds available to the firm.
2. Evaluate the financing alternatives after the decision to invest has been made.

Remember, we assume that the pool of long-term funds is basically all long-term debt and equity and is available to finance long-term assets. The weighted-average cost of capital results from this philosophy.

The general rule says that the "go" or "no go" decision should be dependent on the project's basic cash flows. Financing alternatives may increase or decrease the firm's costs of financing but will not change the inherent quality of the project. As discussed earlier, a project may meet all approval criteria, but because cash is scarce, we may still not fund the project. Thus, while the basic investment decision should be independent of financing alternatives, the financing side may well determine if a project is actually adopted.

Lease Versus Purchase

A common situation is the choice of using our own cash reserves, borrowing from a bank, or leasing an asset. The timing of cash flows and the interest cost of these alternatives can differ dramatically.

Taxes can also impact financing cash flows. Lease payments, containing both principal and interest components, are entirely deductible for income tax purposes. When funds are borrowed, the interest component is deductible, but the principal repayment is not. Depreciation expense can be deducted on an owned asset but not a leased asset. The traditional tax shield is available to owners but not lessees.

Leases have an interest rate embedded into the lease payment. Aside from the tax issues, the choice of financing could well depend on whether the embedded lease interest rate is higher or lower than either the firm's short-term borrowing rate or cost of capital rate. The choice of using the short-term borrowing rate or cost of capital rate may be a function of the length of the lease. A 24-month auto lease might be compared to the firm's bank borrowing rate, while a building lease for 10 years would use the cost of capital rate.

Two Examples

Assume a lease on a copying machine is $10,000 per year for five years with payments due at the beginning of each year. The alternative financing arrangement is to buy the machine for $39,140 cash. The cash flows are shown in Figure 13.2.

The **embedded interest rate** is found as follows:

Cash price − Initial cash payment = Present value of future cash flows
Present value of future cash flows ÷ Annual cash payment = Present value factor

$39,140 − $10,000 = $29,140 present value
$29,140 ÷ $10,000 = 2.914 present value factor

We use Table II and the 4 Period row because the first of five payments is made immediately. We find 2.914 in the 14 percent column. We are paying the copying equipment firm 14 percent interest for the financing arrangements.

	Investment Year 0	Life of the Lease				
		Year 1	Year 2	Year 3	Year 4	Year 5
Cash flows:						
Lease cash outflows	$(10,000)	$(10,000)	$(10,000)	$(10,000)	$(10,000)	$ 0
Present value factors (14%) ...	× 1.000	× .877	× .769	× .675	× .592	
Sum of lease present values ..	$(39,130)					
Purchase cash outflow	$(39,140)*					

* Difference due to rounding.

Figure 13.2   Financing Cash Flows for a Lease and a Purchase

If we can borrow funds for less than 14 percent, we can save money by financing the purchase. It can be argued that the cost of capital should be used since any borrowing uses the firm's financing capacities—either equity or debt. And by using bank borrowing, we consume some of the firm's debt capacity. Again, the short-term (working capital) and long-term (debt and equity) issues appear.

To compare the lease and purchase cash flows, Figure 13.3 on page 668 shows the relevant facts from the following situation. An office machine costs $1,000 or can be leased for $187.44 per year for 8 years with the first payment due at the end of the first year. Assume that the firm's cost of capital and embedded lease interest cost are both 10 percent. The user is responsible for all maintenance and repairs under either alternative. Taxes are 40 percent, no salvage value is expected, and straight-line depreciation is used. The $187.44 lease payment was set by dividing the annuity present value factor for 8 periods at 10 percent (5.335) into the principal amount of $1,000.

The net purchase advantage of $12.40 (excluding the rounding differences) is due exclusively to the time value of money and the higher interest expense in early years. Note that the use of MACRS for depreciation expense would increase the purchase advantage significantly. If the cost of funds rate and the embedded lease interest rate were different, the advantage could change direction and/or magnitude.

Thus, if the borrowing rate and the cost of funds rate are the same, the advantage is generally to purchase. If the lease's embedded rate is lower than the cost of funds rate, the advantage is often to lease. This commonly occurs in two situations.

First, some businesses use an artificially low interest rate for leases either to give them a competitive advantage or to encourage customers to lease instead of buying. It is through a promotional effort such as this that the "tail (the financing decision) might wag the dog (the acquisition decision)." In these cases, the cash purchase cost would be the present value (using the cost of capital) of the annual lease payments. The vendor's lease present value would be below its cash purchase price.

Second, the financial condition of some firms is so poor that they may have exhausted both debt and equity sources of additional funds. Leasing may be their only way to acquire needed new assets, regardless of the embedded interest rate.

Leasing and other financing alternatives often are integral parts of evaluating capital investments. Care must be taken to separate the acquisition issues and the financing issues. The key is to identify the relevant cash flows of the investment itself and the relevant cash flows of the financing arrangements.

ACCELERATED DEPRECIATION, MACRS, AND THE TAX SHIELD

Accelerated depreciation has been part of the tax law since the 1950s. Cumbersome and complex rules developed around methods, asset lives, and capitali-

| Year | Lease or Loan Cash Payment | Purchase Costs | | | | | | Leasing Costs After-Tax Lease Cost[2] | Advantage of Buying[3] | Present Value Factor | Present Value of Buying Advantage |
		Beginning Balance	Interest Expense	Principal	Depreciation	Depreciation & Interest Deduction	Tax Savings (40%)	Net Cash Cost[1]				
1	$187.44	$1000.00	$100.00	$ 87.44	$ 125.00	$ 225.00	$ 90.00	$ 97.44	$112.47	$ 15.03	0.909	$ 13.66
2	187.44	912.56	91.26	96.18	125.00	216.26	86.50	100.94	112.47	11.53	0.826	9.52
3	187.44	816.38	81.64	105.80	125.00	206.64	82.66	104.78	112.47	7.69	0.751	5.78
4	187.44	710.58	71.06	116.38	125.00	196.06	78.42	109.02	112.47	3.45	0.683	2.36
5	187.44	594.20	59.42	128.02	125.00	184.42	73.77	113.67	112.47	(1.20)	0.621	(0.75)
6	187.44	466.18	46.62	140.82	125.00	171.62	68.65	118.79	112.47	(6.32)	0.564	(3.56)
7	187.44	325.36	32.54	154.90	125.00	157.54	63.02	124.42	112.47	(11.95)	0.513	(6.13)
8	187.44	170.46	17.05	170.39	125.00	142.05	56.82	130.62	112.47	(18.15)	0.467	(8.48)
Totals			$499.59	$999.93*	$1000.00	$1499.59	$599.84	$899.68*	$899.76*	$ .08*		$ 12.40

[1] Cash payment − Tax savings

[2] The net of tax cost of the lease payment, or $(1 - .4) \times 187.44$

[3] Difference between Purchase Net Cash Cost and After-Tax Lease Cost

* Difference due to rounding

Figure 13.3   Lease Versus Purchase Financing Analysis

zation. In the early 1980s, as part of a series of so-called "tax reform" laws, a new depreciation system was introduced—the **Accelerated Cost Recovery System (ACRS)**. The system included the following changes:

1. Assets were grouped into a small number of categories (now eight).
2. Asset lives of the categories were generally shorter than previously allowed.
3. Forms of declining balance depreciation were used to determine annual percentages of deduction, and
4. A series of accounting conventions such as the half-year deduction were imposed. The half-year convention says that only one half of the first fiscal year's depreciation can be taken in the first tax year. The remaining half of the first year's depreciation is taken in the second tax year, along with half of the second year's depreciation.

The current version, **Modified Accelerated Cost Recovery System** or **MACRS**, is applicable to assets acquired in 1987 and later.

MACRS Classes and Deduction Percentages

Eight classes of assets exist with the following characteristics:

MACRS CLASSES

Class	Type (Examples and ADR Mid-Lives)*	Basic Depreciation Method
3 Year	Certain tools and assets of specialized industries and assets with an ADR mid-life of 4 years or less.	200% declining balance
5 Year	Autos and trucks, research equipment, and computers and assets with an ADR mid-life of 4 to 10 years.	200% declining balance
7 Year	Office equipment and most production equipment and assets with an ADR mid-life of 10 to 16 years.	200% declining balance
10 Year	Machinery and equipment in selected industries and assets with an ADR mid-life of 16 to 20 years.	200% declining balance
15 Year	Certain utility facilities and land improvements and assets with an ADR mid-life of 20 to 25 years.	150% declining balance
20 Year	Certain agricultural buildings and utility equipment and assets with an ADR mid-life of over 25 years.	150% declining balance
27.5 Year	Residential rental property.	Straight-line
31.5 Year	Non-residential real property.	Straight-line

* ADR mid-life is an IRS technical term for the average useful life of an asset group that has a specific asset depreciation range of life.

For each class, a specific percentage of cost can be deducted annually. The percentages for the 3-, 5-, 7-, 10-, 15-, and 20-year classes are shown in Figure 13.4.

Recovery Year	Property Class					
	3-Year	5-Year	7-Year	10-Year	15-Year	20-Year
1	33.33	20.00	14.29	10.00	5.00	3.750
2	44.45	32.00	24.49	18.00	9.50	7.219
3	14.81*	19.20	17.49	14.40	8.55	6.677
4	7.41	11.52*	12.49	11.52	7.70	6.177
5		11.52	8.93*	9.22	6.93	5.713
6		5.76	8.92	7.37	6.23	5.285
7			8.93	6.55*	5.90*	4.888
8			4.46	6.55	5.90	4.522*
9				6.56	5.91	4.462
10				6.55	5.90	4.461
11				3.28	5.91	4.462
12					5.90	4.461
13					5.91	4.462
14					5.90	4.461
15					5.91	4.462
16					2.95	4.461
17						4.462
18						4.461
19						4.462
20						4.461
21						2.231

* Year of switch to straight-line to maximize depreciation.

Figure 13.4   MACRS Accelerated Depreciation Percentages

Using the 5-year class, double-declining depreciation (2 × the straight line rate of 20%), and the half-year convention, the annual deduction percentages can be found as follows:

Tax Year and Calculations			5 Year Percentages from Figure 13.4
1st Tax Year:			
.5 × Year 1 depreciation .5 × 100% × 40%	=	20.00%	20.00%
2nd Tax Year:			
.5 × Year 1 depreciation .5 × 100% × 40%	=	20.00%	
.5 × Year 2 depreciation .5 × (100% − 40%) × 40%	=	12.00	32.00%
3rd Tax Year:			
.5 × Year 2 depreciation .5 × (100% − 40%) × 40%	=	12.00%	
.5 × Year 3 depreciation .5 × (100% − 64%) × 40%	=	7.20	19.26%
4th Tax Year (convert to straight-line depreciation):			
.5 × Year 3 depreciation .5 × [(100% − 71.2%) ÷ 2.5]	=	5.76%	
.5 × Year 4 depreciation .5 × [(100% − 71.2%) ÷ 2.5]	=	5.76	11.52%
5th Tax Year:			
.5 × Year 4 depreciation .5 × [(100% − 71.2%) ÷ 2.5]	=	5.76%	
.5 × Year 5 depreciation .5 × [(100% − 71.2%) ÷ 2.5]	=	5.76	11.52%
6th Tax Year:			
.5 × Year 5 depreciation .5 × [(100% − 71.2%) ÷ 2.5]	=	5.76%	5.76%
Total depreciation expense as a percentage of original investment cost			100.00%

The 200 percent declining-balance depreciation deduction percentage declines each year and eventually falls below the annual straight-line percentage deduction for the asset's remaining life. In that year, the MACRS method assumes a switch to straight-line depreciation for the rest of the asset's life. Also, the tax law permits continued use of straight-line depreciation for the entire life, if the half-year rule is used.

The advantage of MACRS, the current form of tax-law accelerated depreciation, is the time value of money from deducting more depreciation earlier. In absolute dollars, no more depreciation is taken; and no fewer tax dollars are paid. The key is when the tax dollars are paid.

Immediate Expensing of Assets for Small Businesses

Another feature of the tax law is to allow an immediate deduction for tax purposes of a limited amount of new assets. The maximum amount allowed is $10,000, with a limitation that an asset costing more than $200,000 must reduce the $10,000 amount by $1 for each $1 of cost in excess of $200,000. For example, a firm purchasing $250,000 of property during the year could not use the immediate deduction option. Companies immediately expensing any amount must deduct that amount from the basis of the asset to arrive at the asset's depreciable base. This deduction is intended to assist small and medium-sized firms.

An Example of MACRS

Assume that a company is considering the purchase of computer equipment costing $100,000, with an estimated useful life of six years. The income tax rate is 40 percent, and the firm's minimum acceptable rate of return on investments is 16 percent. The tax reductions and present values of those reductions are shown in Figure 13.5, using (1) 200 percent declining-balance and (2) straight-line depreciation methods. The equipment falls into the 5-year class, using the half-year convention and no salvage value. Notice that the half-year convention is also used in the straight-line portion of Figure 13.5, shown at the top of page 672. This shows the comparative advantage of the MACRS method.

The advantage of using MACRS depreciation over straight-line depreciation is $2,625. Under both alternatives $100,000 and any incremental revenues and cost savings would be included in the complete analysis.

POST AUDIT OF CAPITAL INVESTMENTS

Most capital investments are one-time activities. In many firms, project management seems to be more difficult than managing repetitive tasks. Having the right managerial tools and controls is absolutely necessary to avoid cost overruns, missed timetables, lost benefits, and disruption of normal business activities.

Cash Flow	Life of the Lease					
	Year 1	Year 2	Year 3	Year 4	Year 5	Year 6
MACRS depreciation:						
Tax depreciation expense	$20,000	$32,000	$19,200	$11,500	$11,500	$ 5,800
Tax savings (40%)	$ 8,000	$12,800	$ 7,680	$ 4,600	$ 4,600	$ 2,320
Present value factors (at 16%)	× .862	× .743	× .641	× .552	× .476	× .410
	$ 6,896	$ 9,510	$ 4,923	$ 2,539	$ 2,190	$ 951
Present value of tax savings $27,009						
Straight-line depreciation:						
Tax depreciation expense	$10,000	$20,000	$20,000	$20,000	$20,000	$10,000
Tax savings (40%)	4,000	8,000	8,000	8,000	8,000	4,000
Present value factors (at 16%)	× .862	× .743	× .641	× .552	× .476	× .410
	$ 3,448	$ 5,944	$ 5,128	$ 4,416	$ 3,808	$ 1,640
Present value of tax savings $24,384						
Differential:						
MACRS over S-L depreciation exp.	$10,000	$12,000	$ (800)	$ (8,500)	$ (8,500)	$ (4,200)
MACRS over S-L tax savings	4,000	4,800	(320)	(3,400)	(3,400)	(1,680)
Present value factors (at 16%)	× .862	× .743	× .641	× .552	× .476	× .410
	$ 3,448	$ 3,566	$ (205)	$ (1,877)	$ (1,618)	$ (689)
Advantage of MACRS over straight-line depreciation .... $ 2,625						

Figure 13.5 Comparing Tax Impacts of MACRS and Straight-Line Depreciation Methods

Once an investment proposal is approved, controls over expenditures and a reporting system to keep managers apprised of the project's status are needed. An essential key is a project-oriented accounting system. All expenditures should be traced to the project, and controls should be applied to ensure that expenditures are consistent with the approved investment proposal. The systematic data accumulation and status reporting of each project allow those managing projects, including those who approved the investment, to keep track of how well the project is doing as compared to the original plan.

After a piece of equipment has been acquired, or after a project has been completed, performance should be monitored closely. Results, both from technical and economic points of view, need to be audited or evaluated at the end of a "shakedown period." During this period, it may be found that certain corrections or changes have to be made if the project is to realize its promised potential. A postcompletion audit or evaluation shows whether or not the benefits forecast are being achieved and may indicate ways in which operation can be improved.

The audit referred to is not an audit in the strict financial accounting sense. In reality, it is a management review and, like the original evaluation, may have estimation problems. Quantification of intangible benefits after-the-fact may be just as difficult as when the original investment proposal was evaluated. The review may also be limited by the accounting information that is available. On a special project where a new segment is added, the operating results may be shown separately in the accounting records. But on an individual piece of equipment, which is only one among many, no separate accounting data may exist. In fact, it would be difficult to identify the operating results with any one piece of equipment. How much additional effort should be exerted to separate relevant revenues and costs depends on the importance of the investment and the costs of collecting additional information.

The **post audit** is a mechanism:

1.   That compares actual operating results with the forecast cash flows to improve the estimation process in future capital investment proposals.
2.   That makes employees aware of a control that will evaluate their role in preparing the capital investment proposal and their responsibility to produce the promised rate of return.
3.   That can review project management and evaluate cost and technical performance.
4.   That can detect and correct early operating problems.

The post audit closes the planning and control cycle. Both better control and improved planning should be its expected products.

PROBLEMS OF UNCERTAINTY

The future is never certain. Capital investment analysis depends heavily on estimates of future cash flows. All these estimates are risky. How can the risk be measured and incorporated into the analysis? Several steps should be taken in all cases:

1.   Test the forecast data for source credibility and reasonableness.
2.   Test the assumptions underlying the forecasts and the project itself.
3.   Create managerial responsibility for the estimates.

Responsibility for developing the proposal and for executing the project is linked to performance. An audit trail is developed. The goal of this step is to create the best analytical base possible for the decision.

Incorporating risk into the analysis is another issue. Basically, risk can be added to capital investment analysis in three ways:

1.   Adding a risk percentage factor to the cost of capital to compensate for risk and differences in risk.
2.   Performing a sensitivity analysis of key project variables.
3.   Incorporating expected values into cash flow forecasting.

Risk Percentage Factor

Adding a **risk percentage factor** to the cost of funds is an approach used by firms to recognize the risk of error in estimates. By adding a percentage to the cost of capital, a safety shield is created. The minimum acceptable rate of return is now higher than the cost of capital by the risk factor. This represents a cushion against finding that a project did not quite meet all expectations but, hopefully, still earned enough to cover the cost of funds invested.

A number of firms extend this idea still further to recognize differences among divisions or types of projects within a firm. Divisions that have histories of strong earnings and proven records of successful capital investments might be assigned a desired rate of return with a small or no risk factor. New divisions or ones in high-risk areas, such as in research and development, might be assigned a desired rate of return with a high risk factor. Following is an example:

	Cost of Capital	Risk Factor	Desired Rate of Return
High risk division	12%	8%	20%
Normal risk	12	4	16
Low risk division	12	2	14

Difficulties with this approach are:

1. Not all projects in a specific division contain the same risk.
2. Some decision rules must be established to assign risk factors to divisions.
3. Past capital project results may not be good indicators of future risks and results.

However, adding a risk factor does attempt to recognize **uncertainty** in future cash flow forecasts.

Sensitivity Analysis

All examples presented thus far assume that estimates of future revenues and costs are valid. However, there is always the possibility that every forecast variable could change. **Sensitivity analysis** measures how much key variables can change and still not affect the capital investment decision. Among the variables commonly tested are:

1. Volume of units.
2. Sales price.
3. Life of the project.
4. Materials and labor costs.

Most firms have simulation capabilities available to test "what if" scenarios. If sales volume were to drop by 5 percent, 10 percent, or 20 percent from the forecast level, should the project be rejected? If because of technological changes a particular machine's life is cut from 6 years to 4 years, will the loss of Years 5 and 6 cash flows hurt the proposal?

For example, assume that the net present value of Project 52 is $80,000. Project 52 will add 10,000 units of productive capacity to our factory. We earn a $10 contribution margin per unit. The expanded capacity should last 5 years. Our desired rate of return is 15 percent. Thus, ignoring taxes, the value of 1 unit of sales over the 5-year period is $33.52 (from Table II, 3.352 × $10). We can answer several questions:

1. *What if* sales only reach 80 percent of new capacity?

    2,000 units × $33.52 = $67,040 = Present value of the lost contribution margin

    $80,000 − $67,040 = $12,960 = Net present value of project if sales equal 8,000 units

    The project still earns better than a 15 percent return.

2. *What* sales are needed to earn at least 15 percent?

    $80,000 ÷ $33.52 = 2,386 = Units of lost sales

    10,000 units − 2,386 units = 7,614 Units of sales required to have a zero net present
    value using a 15 percent return

    This means that a 23.86 percent drop in expected new sales will cause the
    project to have a zero net present value—a return of 15 percent. A drop
    of 3,000 units would cause the project to have a negative net present
    value and to be rejected.

3. *What if* the project lasted only 4 years, not 5 years?

    10,000 × $10 × .497 = $49,700 = Present value of Year 5 sales

    $80,000 − $49,700 = $30,300 = Net present value of Project 52 if Year 5 is elimi-
    nated

    The project is still acceptable.

Cutting years off the end of a project's life is a common method of reducing
uncertainty. The further into the future an estimate goes, the less confidence
we have in it. Many companies have internal rules for certain categories of
capital projects that limit the useful lives arbitrarily. For example, cost savings
projects may be allowed to count only 3 years of savings.

Using Expected Values

Incorporating various estimates for key variables into the analysis has long
been attempted. One approach uses optimistic, most likely, and pessimistic
estimates of sales, costs, and lives. Weighted averages are then used to generate the cash flow estimates called **expected values**. Another similar approach
assigns probabilities to various values of key variables. Using the Project 52
example from the last section, a sales forecast with probabilities could be
created:

Sales Level		Probability of Occurrence			
10,000 units	×	.4	=	4,000	units
9,000 units	×	.3	=	2,700	units
8,000 units	×	.2	=	1,600	units
7,000 units	×	.1	=	700	units
Expected value of sales volume				9,000	units

Obviously, "what ifs" of many variable changes can be analyzed. Spread
sheet capabilities now make these simulations routine and an normal part of
project evaluation.

CAPITAL INVESTMENTS IN NOT-FOR-PROFIT ORGANIZATIONS

In most cases capital investment decisions in not-for-profit organizations are no different than in profit-making concerns. The goal is to obtain the highest benefit from the money spent. Often, the legislative and appropriation processes in governmental units hide the basic intent of public spending. Solving social problems, providing public services, and operating quasi-business activities must include cost and benefit analyses to help select efficient and effective solutions.

The primary difference is that in many situations profits and cash flows may not be the primary goal of the expenditure. In the case of a city government, an investment may be made for the general welfare of the citizens. A city will attempt to obtain the highest level of benefits for its citizens at the lowest possible cost. For example, neighborhood playgrounds may be formed in various sections of the city. The benefits for the children and young people of the city are evident, but how can they be measured? Intangible benefits are sometimes difficult or impossible to quantify or even to estimate. But estimation of benefits and costs can often help in selecting from among alternatives.

SOCIAL COSTS OF CAPITAL INVESTMENT DECISIONS

Social costs are growing in importance in the capital investment decisions of public and private sector firms. **Social costs** and **social benefits** are costs and benefits that the community shares. The community can be defined locally, nationally, or globally. Social cost concerns arise from a wide variety of sources and include the costs of:

1. Protecting the health of employees, consumers, and persons in the community.
2. Providing employment and training for workers in the community.
3. Handling environmentally endangering substances.
4. Evaluating environmental impacts prior to capital development.
5. Choosing among various benefits for employees, taxpayers, and other groups given limited resources.
6. Considering public policy, political pressures, and public opinion in allocating capital resources.

Many of these considerations have intangible costs and benefits, legal requirements, and no direct positive cash flow possibilities for the firm. Pollution controls are often legally required. Good citizenship would expect a firm to want to prevent air and water pollution. But few "win/win" situations exist. New regulations may impose costs on a firm that has been experiencing marginal profitability. Capital spending on pollution equipment may mean equipment to improve the firm's technology and competitiveness must be delayed or eliminated, threatening the survival of the firm.

An additional difficulty is that diverse points of view value social costs and benefits very differently. Nuclear power plants are classic examples of strong opinions on all sides, which have largely brought a halt to development. Increased and changing regulations, public protest, strong "not-in-my-backyard" reactions, and major project management problems have caused most public utilities to shelve new nuclear power plant construction plans.

The analysis task is to incorporate the relevant impacts of social costs on the firm into the capital proposal. This means recognizing tangible costs of compliance, of solving environmental problems, and even of public relations. Converting intangibles to dollar estimates can be done in some cases but not in others. Costing equipment to achieve air particulate content compliance can be estimated. Valuing clean air, a human life, and wet lands is nearly impossible (but it has been attempted), even though we know great value exists. Thus, the quantitative analysis should contain as complete an assessment of the impacts of social costs on the firm as possible.

The real difficulty arises in the analysis of the qualitative issues. Reducing social costs and maintaining the firm's short-term profitability are often in natural conflict. Enlightened managers have seen that a firm's single goal of profit maximization has evolved into a multi-pronged set of goals that includes employees', consumers', and the community's concerns.

SUMMARY

Capital investment decisions are complex. The basic analysis presented in Chapter 12 understated the difficult task of estimating future cash flows. Numerous simplifying assumptions were made. This chapter has examined several additional issues. Even after this chapter's discussion, a student of capital investment decisions can see the difficult task managers have in forecasting the future, considering all relevant costs and revenues, and assessing many qualitative competitive and social issues.

This chapter examined computational issues such as uneven lives, working capital needs, incremental investment analysis, and inflationary impacts on forecasts.

The more expanded discussion of tax and accelerated depreciation actually only scratched the surface of tax impacts on capital decisions.

A distinction was drawn between the acquisition and financing decisions. A project proposal must stand on its own merits. Selecting a financing alternative is another decision where relevant cash flows must be evaluated to find the lowest cost alternative.

Several approaches were presented to help reduce uncertainty. Risk analysis, sensitivity analysis, and expected values are tools used to incorporate risk into the cash flow analysis.

Having a post audit of capital investment projects closes the planning and control cycle. This post completion management review is a control tool to evaluate actual performance, the original proposal data, and the implementation. It is a planning tool to help improve the forecasting process for future capital proposals.

Social costs and benefits are both difficult to measure and often highly controversial. Many types of social costs bring legal, political, and community pressures to managers who make capital investment decisions. The same reasons that make capital investing critical to a firm make these decisions important to employees and to local and global communities.

Capital investment analysis is of major importance to a firm. The area is exciting because it often deals with big dollars, critical areas, new ideas, and future profits. Analysis of these decisions is, therefore, worthy of much time and effort.

PROBLEM FOR REVIEW

Amarillo Metal Works is considering the replacement of a precision cutting machine. The new machine would cost $40,000 and generate annual cost savings of about $20,000. Inflation will increase the savings by 5 percent per year. The $20,000 is the most likely estimate (a 50 percent likelihood) but could go down by 20 percent (20 percent likelihood) or go up by 20 percent (30 percent likelihood). The machine has a useful life of six years, and it qualifies as a 5-year class asset for tax purposes under MACRS. The current cutting machine has a book value of $18,000 and could be made to last 6 more years. Depreciation on this machine is straight-line. If the machine were sold now, proceeds would be $10,000. Amarillo has a cost of capital of 12 percent and has added a 4 percent risk factor. The company's current tax rate is 40 percent.

Required:

1. Calculate the net investment assuming the old machine is sold.
2. Calculate the after-tax annual cash flows assuming the new machine will be used for 6 years with tax depreciation for five years. Consider the cost savings, expected probabilities, and the estimated inflation rate. Note: Salvage value is ignored under MACRS.
3. Evaluate this investment using the net present value method.

Solution:
1. Net investment:

Investment in new machine	$(40,000)
Less proceeds from the sale of old machine	10,000
Less reduction of income tax [.40 × ($18,000 − $10,000)]	3,200
Net investment	$(26,800)

2.   Annual net cash flows for six years:

	Year 1	Year 2	Year 3	Year 4	Year 5	Year 6
Inflation adjustment:						
Cash cost savings.....................	$20,000	$20,000	$20,000	$20,000	$20,000	$20,000
Times the inflation factor	×1.0000	×1.0500	×1.1025	×1.1576	×1.2155	×1.2763
Inflated cash savings	$20,000	$21,000	$22,050	$23,152	$24,310	$25,526

Expected cost savings:

	Proba-bility %	Year 1	Year 2	Year 3	Year 4	Year 5	Year 6
Optimistic (+20%)	30% ×	$24,000	$25,200	$26,460	$27,782	$29,172	$30,631
Most likely	50 ×	20,000	21,000	22,050	23,152	24,310	25,526
Pessimistic (−20%)	20 ×	16,000	16,800	17,640	18,522	19,448	20,421
Expected value	100%	$20,400	$21,420	$22,491	$23,615	$24,796	$26,037

Incremental depreciation:

	Year 1	Year 2	Year 3	Year 4	Year 5	Year 6
New depreciation (MACRS)						
Year 1—20.0%	$ 8,000					
Year 2—32.0%		$12,800				
Year 3—19.2%			$ 7,680			
Year 4—11.5%				$ 4,600		
Year 5—11.5%					$ 4,600	
Year 6— 5.8%.......................						$ 2,320
Old depreciation (S-L)	(3,000)	(3,000)	(3,000)	(3,000)	(3,000)	(3,000)
Incremental depreciation	$ 5,000	$ 9,800	$ 4,680	$ 1,600	$ 1,600	$ (680)

Calculation of annual cash inflows:

	Year 1	Year 2	Year 3	Year 4	Year 5	Year 6
Cash cost savings.......................	$20,400	$21,420	$22,491	$23,616	$24,795	$ 26,037
Incremental depreciation	(5,000)	(9,800)	(4,680)	(1,600)	(1,600)	680
Taxable income	$15,400	$11,620	$17,811	$22,016	$23,195	$ 26,717
Incremental tax (× .4)	$ (6,160)	$ (4,648)	$ (7,124)	$ (8,806)	$ (9,278)	$(10,686)
After-tax cash flow (Cash savings − Tax) ...	$14,240	$16,772	$15,367	$14,810	$15,517	$ 15,351

3.   Net present value method:

	Year 0	Year 1	Year 2	Year 3	Year 4	Year 5	Year 6
Calculations:							
Net investment..................	$(26,800)						
Net cash inflow		$14,240	$16,772	$15,367	$14,810	$15,517	$15,351
Present value factors (16%)	×1.000	× .862	× .743	× .641	× .552	× .476	× .410
Present values...................	$(26,800)	$12,275	$12,462	$ 9,850	$ 8,175	$ 7,386	$ 6,294
Total PV of inflows	56,442						
Net present value	$ 29,642						

TERMINOLOGY REVIEW

Accelerated Cost Recovery System
(ACRS) (669)
Embedded interest rate (666)
Expected value (675)
Inflation (661)
Lease (665)
Modified Accelerated Cost Recovery
System (MACRS) (669)

Post audit (673)
Risk percentage factor (673)
Sensitivity analysis (674)
Social benefits (676)
Social costs (676)
Uncertainty (674)
Working capital (660)

QUESTIONS FOR REVIEW AND DISCUSSION

1. What capital investment analysis technique is best for ranking projects with different initial investments? Why?

2. Why is an initial investment in additional inventory different than an investment in machinery?

3. Identify two ways that inflation can be incorporated into capital investment analysis.

4. What problem arises if alternative investments have different useful lives? Identify at least one solution.

5. By incorporating the inflation factor into the discount rate, what assumption is being made?

6. A project can be divided into Phase I and Phase II. Phase II is a continuation of Phase I, cannot be developed by itself, and may or may not be developed. Phase I looks like a sure "winner," but Phase II is questionable. Capital investment analysis is done on Phase I, then on Phase II itself, and then on Phase I and II together. What might be learned from each of the analyses?

7. What is meant by financing decisions and investing decisions? Why should they be analyzed separately?

8. Why would the annual cost of leasing differ from the annual cost of buying? Identify factors on both sides.

9. What depreciation methods are built into most of the annual MACRS depreciation percentages?

10. If capital investment analysis depends so heavily on estimates of future cash flows, what controls exist to prevent over-optimistic estimates from inflating a given project's rate of return?

11. (a) ABC Company uses a 14 percent hurdle rate. XYZ Company uses a 20 percent hurdle rate. What could cause this difference in rates?
    (b) In DEF Corporation, Division G uses a 12 percent hurdle rate, Division H uses a 16 percent hurdle rate, and Division I uses a 20 percent hurdle rate. What could cause these differences in rates?

12. What information does sensitivity analysis give us that the basic estimates about future cash flows do not?

13. What does the term "expected value" mean? Is it real? How can it replace a specific estimate of a key variable?

14. How can intangible benefits and costs be incorporated into capital investment analysis?

15. A business analyst recently said "Social costs of many decisions often far outweigh the business dollars and cents amounts." What did he mean?

16. A local not-for-profit organization's director was heard to say, "Capital investment analysis works for profit making organizations but not for us. We're trying to maximize benefits to the people our organization serves and not maximize profits." Comment on the pros and cons of the quote.

EXERCISES

1. **Gains and Losses on Disposal.** A company is considering the purchase of a new machine for $200,000 which would have a 5-year life. The company would sell for $50,000 its old machine which cost $180,000 and has a book value of $20,000. Gains, losses, and profits use a tax rate of 40 percent. The new machine will require about $30,000 less raw materials inventory to operate.

   Required:
   What is the net cash outflow for the investment?

2. **Net Investment.** The management of Westport Metal Fabricators plans to replace a forming machine that was acquired several years ago at a cost of $45,000. The machine has been depreciated to its salvage value of $5,000. A new machine can be purchased for $80,000. The dealer will grant a trade-in allowance of $6,000 on the old machine. If a new machine is not purchased, the company will spend $20,000 to repair the old machine. Gains and losses on trade-in transactions are not subject to income tax. The cost to repair the old machine can be deducted in the first year for computing income tax. Income tax is estimated at 40 percent of the income subject to tax.

   Required:
   Compute the net investment in the new machine for decision-making purposes.

3. **Trade-In and Cash Flows.** McConnell Company plans to buy a piece of equipment that will have a cost basis of $75,000 after deducting the trade-in of the old machine and have a useful life of ten years with no salvage value. This machine replaces an old machine which has a remaining 10-year life and a book value of $40,000. The expected additional annual cash inflow from using the machine is $20,000 and the expected additional annual cash outflow is $5,000. Straight-line depreciation is used and a tax rate of 40 percent is in effect.

   Required:
   What is the net annual cash benefit?

4. **Working Capital.** Kim Andrews sells a very successful line of products. She can spend $100,000 now on additional inventory. The added inventory will increase earnings after taxes by $50,000 per year. She is looking at a 6-year time horizon. She expects to get the $100,000 in inventory investment back at the end of the 6 years. She must earn a 16 percent rate of return.

   Required:
   What is the net present value of this decision?

5.   **Incremental Investment and Discounted Rate of Return.** A manufacturer of equipment quotes a price of $130,000 for a unit of equipment that is being considered by Tan Products Inc. This equipment should be able to produce net returns of $40,000 each year for 5 years. Another equipment manufacturer offers a similar unit at a price of $180,000. This unit of equipment is expected to yield $55,000 in net returns each year for 5 years. These are mutually exclusive investment alternatives. An investment of this type is expected to yield a discounted rate of return of no less than 16 percent. Ignore income tax.

Required:
1.   Which investment alternative is more attractive if a minimum acceptable rate of return of 16 percent is expected? Show computations.
2.   What is the approximate internal rate of return for each project?
3.   What is the approximate internal rate of return for the incremental investment?

6.   **MACRS Depreciation.** The Buccalo Company will buy tooling equipment for research purposes for $800,000. No salvage value is expected at the end of the 5-year life. The equipment qualifies as a 3-year class asset for MACRS depreciation. Annual net cash inflow before taxes is $300,000. The tax rate is 40 percent. Buccalo wants at least a 16 percent return on investment.

Required:
Find the net present value, accounting rate of return, the payback period, and the approximate internal rate of return.

7.   **Basic MACRS Application.** Sizemore Company is considering an investment opportunity involving a cash outlay of $120,000 for new office building machinery that would last about ten years and have no estimated residual value. The machinery would reduce annual cash operating costs by $25,000. The firm's tax is 40 percent, and its cost of capital is 14 percent. The company considers this asset to be a 7-year asset for MACRS purposes.

Required:
For this project compute the payback period, the approximate internal rate of return, and the net present value.

8.   **Net Investment and Discounted Rate of Return.** A unit of equipment used in stamping out plastic parts can be acquired from an equipment manufacturer at a cost of $200,000. If this equipment is acquired, an old unit of equipment that is fully depreciated will be sold for $20,000.

Annual returns from the new equipment, before deducting depreciation or income tax, have been estimated at $80,000 for a period of 5 years. Depreciation of $40,000 is to be deducted each year, and the new equipment is expected to have no salvage value at the end of the 5 years. Income tax rate is 40 percent for all taxation items.

Required:
1.   Determine the net investment in the new equipment.
2.   Will this investment be acceptable if the minimum rate of return has been established at 16 percent?

9.   **MACRS and the Replacement Decision.** You are given the following data:

Existing machine:

Cost.........................	$70,000
Book value	30,000
Salvage value	0
Annual depreciation	5,000
Annual cash operating costs	50,000
Present sales value	50,000
Remaining life	6 years

Replacement machine:

Cost...........................	$180,000
Estimated salvage value	10,000
Annual cash operating costs	8,000
Depreciation method MACRS	5 years
Useful life	6 years

Income tax rate for all taxation issues .... 40 percent

Required:
Determine the net present value of the replacement decision assuming a desired rate of return of 16 percent.

10. **Lease Versus Purchase.** Zalka and Daughters are considering the purchase of a photo-copy machine. The dealer has offered a sale or a lease contract. Maintenance and sup-plies costs are the same under either arrangement. The cash purchase price is $45,000. The lease arrangement calls for monthly payments of $2,000 for 24 months. Zalka's annual cost of funds is approximately 12 percent (or 1 percent per month). Assume that the machine will have a technological life of two years. Ignore taxes.

Required:
Which is the more attractive financial arrangement—the lease or the purchase?

11. **Inflation and Investment Analysis.** Sittin'-in-the-Sun Health Spas is evaluating an expansion of its existing spa this fall. The proposal calls for a 6-year building rental contract at $10,000 a year. Equipment purchases and facility improvements are ex-pected to cost $60,000. Straight-line depreciation ignoring the half-year convention is used. Other cash operating expenses are estimated at $25,000 annually. Based on past experience, the company thinks new revenues should be $50,000 annually. Sittin'-in-the-Sun will not expand unless the expected return is at least 15 percent. The company has an effective tax rate of 40 percent.

Inflation is a concern. The controller thinks that revenues will be inflated by 5 percent per year, and cash operating expenses will increase by 8 percent per year.

Required:
Evaluate the project using the net present value method, and determine whether it should be adopted.

12. **Lease Versus Purchase Alternatives.** Al Williams is evaluating two vendors of similar machines. Both machines will do the same tasks and generate the same revenues. Cash operating costs, however, differ and are as follows:

	Alternative A	Alternative B
Year 1	$125,000	$ 80,000
Year 2	100,000	80,000
Year 3	80,000	120,000
Year 4	80,000	100,000
Year 5	60,000	100,000
Year 6	40,000	100,000

Both alternatives can be leased under a 6-year contract for $50,000 per year or purchased with cash for $200,000. Al can get funds at a cost of 14 percent.

Required:
1.   Which alternative is the better operating decision?
2.   Which financing alternative is better?
3.   What should be done?

13.   **Lease Financing.** Vehicle A can be leased under a 4-year contract for $16,000 per year or purchased with cash for $54,400. Vehicle B can be leased on a 6-year contract for $15,000 per year or purchased with cash for $74,900. Assume we can find cash funds at a cost of 10 percent. The first payment is due today on both vehicles. Ignore taxes.

Required:
1.   What is the embedded interest rate in each vehicle's contract?
2.   If we want the use of both vehicles, should we purchase or lease each of them?

14.   **Unequal Lives.** Having given the matter some thought, you decide that you would be equally happy buying and driving any of the following cars:

(a)   A Supreme Deluxe and trading every sixth year.
(b)   A Premium Fairmont and trading every third year.
(c)   An Economy Delight and trading every second year.

You have decided to base your decision on the present value of the expected future costs. You have predicted your costs as follows:

	Supreme Deluxe	Premium Fairmont	Economy Delight
Original cost	$30,000	$20,000	$15,000
Market value at trade-in time	8,000	8,000	8,000
Annual operating costs, excluding depreciation	2,400	2,000	1,500
Overhaul, fourth year	2,000	0	0
Overhaul, second year	0	1,000	0

You believe that you will stick with this approach for at least 6 years. Your minimum desired rate of return is 10 percent. Ignore taxes.

Required:
Select the alternative that promises you the greatest financial advantage.

15.   **Net Present Value and Expected Values.** Two competing investment alternatives are being considered by the Mills Company. One alternative costs $130,000. The other alternative costs $160,000. An investment of this type is expected to earn a discounted rate of return of at least 14 percent.

The two projects are each expected to last 5 years. Probabilities of annual revenues from each project differ as follows:

Annual Revenue Probabilities

$130,000 Investment		$160,000 Investment	
10%	$10,000	10%	$ 20,000
10%	20,000	20%	40,000
15%	30,000	40%	60,000
20%	40,000	20%	80,000
25%	50,000	10%	100,000
10%	60,000		
10%	90,000		

Required:
Determine the more desirable alternative by the net present value method. Ignore taxes.

16. **Sensitivity Analysis of Future Estimates.** Yen Industries included the following estimates on a bid for a 10-year government contract:

Investment in machinery.....................................	$800,000
Additional inventory (funds to be released when contract ends) .	100,000
Cost of equipment overhaul at the end of year 6	120,000
Machinery salvage value at the end of contract (in 10 years) ...	80,000
Annual revenue from the contract	200,000 per year
Cost of capital	14 percent

Required:
Ignoring taxes, what impact (amount and percentage change) will the following mistakes in estimation have on the net present value of this contract?
(a)   An understatement of $20,000 in the investment in machinery.
(b)   An understatement of $20,000 in the inventory needed.
(c)   An understatement of $30,000 in the cost of the overhaul.
(d)   An overstatement of $50,000 in the salvage value at the end of the contract.
(e)   An overstatement of $4,000 in the annual revenue from the contract.

17. **Value of MACRS.** Fletch Company plans to buy a piece of equipment that will cost $120,000 and have a useful life of ten years with no salvage value. The expected incremental annual cash inflows from using the new machine are $32,000 and the expected incremental annual cash outflows are $6,000. A tax rate of 40 percent is in effect. The company uses a 12 percent cut-off rate.

Required:
1.   Using straight-line depreciation and ignoring the half-year rule, what is the net annual after-tax cash benefit? Find the net present value.
2.   Using the 5-year MACRS asset class, what is the net annual after-tax benefit? Find the net present value and compare it to your answer to part 1.

PROBLEMS

13-1.   **Equipment Replacement.** The Plymouth Company owns a machine with the following characteristics:

Book value	$55,000
Current market value	40,000
Expected salvage value at end of 5-year remaining useful life	0
Annual depreciation expense, straight-line method	11,000
Annual cash operating costs	18,000

The firm's cost of capital is 14 percent, and the tax rate of 40 percent is applicable to all taxation items.

The firm is considering replacing the machine with one that has the following characteristics:

Purchase price	$80,000
Expected salvage value	5,000
Annual cash operating costs	3,000
Useful life	5 years

Straight-line depreciation at $15,000 per year would be taken on the new machine. Additionally, because the new machine is more efficient, the firm could reduce its investment in inventoried parts by $15,000.

Required:

Determine whether the new machine should be bought. Use whatever capital investment methods you believe will best present the facts to Plymouth's management.

13-2. **Mutually Exclusive Alternatives.** The Jason Company has $50,000 to invest in either of two alternatives. Investment I yields $12,000 a year in after-tax annual cash flows for 10 years. Investment II yields a one-time, after-tax return of $180,000 at the end of 10 years.

Required:

1. Using Tables I and II, find the present value for all interest columns from 4 percent through 25 percent, using the 10-year row.
2. If the minimum rate of return is in the range of 4 percent to approximately 8 percent, which investment is preferred?
3. Over which range of minimum interest rates is Investment I preferable to Investment II?
4. At approximately which rates of return are neither Investment I nor Investment II attractive?

13-3. **Net Investment and Returns.** The management of the Columbus Company has rejected an opportunity to buy new machinery costing $135,000. Although it would probably yield cash savings after income tax, including the effect of depreciation on income tax, of $40,000 each year for 5 years, it would not meet the rate-of-return objective of at least 18 percent.

The assistant manager believes that the investment could have met the standard if other factors had been considered. For example, if this equipment had been purchased, old equipment with a net book value of zero could have been sold for $30,000. The income tax rate for the year on the sale of equipment is 40 percent.

Required:

Use the net present value method to determine whether or not the assistant manager is correct in the analysis.

13-4. **Depreciation and Rate of Return.** The president of Kasner Company has been considering an investment of $600,000 in research and development equipment that should have a useful life of six years with a salvage value of zero. This type of investment is expected to yield a discounted rate of return of 12 percent.

An estimate indicates that the cash flow before income tax from this investment will probably amount to $175,000 a year. Straight-line depreciation is normally used and income tax is 40 percent.

The president has been informed that depreciation may be deducted for tax purposes by the MACRS method using a 5-year life and that this method would make the investment more favorable than if straight-line depreciation is used. He does not understand how a "bookkeeping method," as he calls it, can help to improve the investment.

Required:
1. Compute the net present value of the investment with straight-line depreciation. Ignore the half-year rule.
2. Compute the net present value of the investment with MACRS 200% declining balance depreciation.
3. Explain to the president how a "bookkeeping method" can help to improve the investment.

13-5. **Incremental Investment, Internal Rate of Return, and Incremental Internal Rate of Return.** Welton Company is introducing a product that will sell for $10 per unit. Annual volume for the next four years should be about 200,000 units. The company can use either of two machines to make the product. Data are as follows:

	Machine X	Machine Y
Per unit variable cost	$ 4	$ 2
Annual cash fixed costs	725,000	850,000
Cost of machine	800,000	1,400,000

Both machines have four-year lives and no anticipated salvage value. The firm uses straight-line depreciation, has a 40 percent income tax rate, and a 14 percent cost of capital.

Required:
1. Determine which machine has the higher approximate internal rate of return.
2. What is the approximate internal rate of return on the incremental investment needed for machine Y over machine X?

13-6. **Comparing Unequals.** Below are data relating to three possible investments:

	X	Y	Z
Cost	$34,000	$25,000	$75,000
Annual cash savings	8,111	7,458	14,011
Useful life—years	10	5	20

Required:
1. Ignoring taxes, rank the investments according to their desirability using the following:
   (a) Payback period.
   (b) Internal rate of return.
   (c) Net present value using a discount rate of 12 percent.
   (d) Profitability index.
2. Comment on the impact that the unequal lives have on the rankings.
3. Comment on the impact that the unequal investments have on the rankings.

13-7.   Sell or Use Equipment. An offer of $130,000 has been made for a unit of equipment that Herrera Products has been using to make parts for one of its divisions. The equipment is fully depreciated but can be used for 5 more years. At the end of 5 years, it is expected to have little, if any, value.

The variable cost of producing the parts is $10 per unit. A total of 10,000 units are to be manufactured each year. If the parts are not manufactured, the company must buy them from an outside supplier at a cost of $15 per unit. Also, if the parts are not produced, the space occupied by the equipment can be rented for $12,000 per year. Income tax is estimated at 40 percent of the income before tax. The company uses a 12 percent hurdle rate on this type of investment.

Required:
Should the offer for the sale of the equipment be accepted, or should the parts be manufactured? (Use the net present value method.)

13-8.   Sensitivity of Key Variables. The Richmond Company owns a machine that cost $50,000 five years ago, has a book value of $25,000, and has a current market value of $14,000. The machine costs $20,000 per year to operate and will have no market value at the end of five more years.

The firm has an opportunity to buy a new machine that costs $60,000, will last five years, have no salvage value, and costs $5,000 per year to operate. It will perform the same functions as the machine currently owned.

The firm has a cost of capital of 12 percent. Ignore income taxes.

Required:
1.   Determine the approximate rate of return that the firm would earn on the investment.
2.   Suppose that the production manager knows that the new machine is more efficient than the old, but does not know how much more. What annual cash savings would be necessary for the firm to earn 12 percent?
3.   Suppose that the estimate of annual cash flows is considered reliable but that the useful life of the new machine is in question. About how long must the new machine last in order for the firm to earn 12 percent?

13-9.   Required Investment in Current Assets. An interesting project is being considered by Deer Creek, Inc. The project will require an investment of $300,000 in equipment that is expected to have a useful life of 8 years with no salvage value. Initially, additional cash, accounts receivable, and inventory will be required in the amount of $100,000. This working capital will be released at the end of 8 years. Annual cash flow returns from this project before income tax have been estimated at $100,000.

Depreciation is to be deducted by the MACRS method assuming a 7-year MACRS class. Income tax is estimated at 40 percent of income before income tax.

The minimum desired rate of return is 14 percent.

Required:
Does the investment alternative meet the rate-of-return objective? (Use the net present value method.)

13-10.   Equipment Replacement. Guarantee Insurance Company has been operating a cafeteria for its employees at its headquarters, but it is considering a conversion from this form of food service to a completely automated set of coin vending machines, in which case the old equipment would be sold now for whatever cash it might bring. The vending machines would be purchased immediately for cash. A reputable catering firm would take complete responsibility for servicing and replenishing the vending machines and would simply pay Guarantee a contracted percentage of the gross vending receipts.

The following data are available:

Current cafeteria cash revenues per year	$240,000
Current cafeteria cash expenses per year	265,000
Present cafeteria equipment (6-year remaining life):	
Net book value	$ 60,000
Annual depreciation expense.................................	10,000
Disposal value now	10,000
Disposal value in 6 years	0
New vending machines:	
Purchase price	$120,000
Forecast disposal value	20,000
Expected annual gross receipts	180,000
Estimated useful life	6 years
Guarantee's percentage receipts	10 percent

Guarantee uses straight-line depreciation without the half-year rule, and has a tax rate of 40 percent.

Required:

1.   Evaluate the financial aspects of the change in Guarantee's approach to the cafeteria problem by measuring:

    (a)   Expected change in net annual operating cash flow.

    (b)   Payback period.

    (c)   Approximate internal rate of return.

2.   Identify the non-quantitative variables that impact this decision. Could a quantitative value for these variables be estimated by collecting more information?

13-11. **Timing the Investment.** The capital investment committee of the board of directors at Hendy Inc. is considering the acquisition of equipment costing $80,000. Shipping and installation costs are estimated at an additional $9,000. The equipment is expected to have a useful life of 7 years with no salvage value. Before considering the effect of depreciation, the annual cash flow returns after income tax from the use of this equipment are estimated at $20,000.

One member of the committee believes that the equipment now in service for this production can be used for another year, yielding cash flow after tax and depreciation of $10,000. A new and improved model is expected in another year that can be acquired at a cost of $91,000 with no salvage value at the end of the expected 6-year life. Shipping and installation costs are also estimated at $4,000. Annual cash flow returns after income tax, but before considering the effect of depreciation, are estimated at $23,000.

The company has set a minimum rate-of-return objective of 18 percent. Depreciation on either piece of new equipment is to be based on the MACRS method over five years. The income tax rate is 40 percent.

Required:

Does it appear that the equipment should be purchased now, or should the company wait a year for the new model? Use the net present value method and show computations.

13-12. **Acquisition of Equipment Using Expected Values.** A new product line is being considered by the Ingram Company. Special equipment will be required for the manufacturing process. To handle the expected volume, Ingram may need to purchase multiple machines if the project is to be accepted. Data with respect to the production of this product are:

Number of Equipment Units	Product Unit Capacity
1	60,000 units
2	120,000 units
3	160,000 units
4	200,000 units
5	240,000 units

The new product line will increase out-of-pocket annual fixed cost (excluding depreciation) by $140,000. It is estimated that this increase can be expected regardless of the number of machines purchased. The variable cost of producing a unit has been estimated at $6, and the selling price estimated at $10. The company has the physical space to install up to 5 units of equipment. Each machine sells for $300,000 per unit, and the useful life is estimated at 6 years with no salvage value.

A survey has been made to estimate the potential demand for this product. Probabilities of the estimated demand are as follows:

Sales Probability	Units of Sales
10%	40,000 units
20%	80,000 units
30%	120,000 units
20%	160,000 units
10%	200,000 units
10%	240,000 units

Required:
Using straight-line depreciation, a 40 percent tax rate, a 16 percent discount rate, and the net present value method, determine how many machines, if any, should be purchased.

13-13. **Purchase vs. Lease Decision.** Cittin Farms is considering replacing a technologically obsolete and fully depreciated tractor currently used in farming operations. The tractor in use is in good working order and will last, physically, for at least 6 years. However, the proposed tractor is so much more efficient that Cittin Farms predicts cost savings of $25,000 a year if the new tractor is acquired. The tractor's delivered cost is $80,000. Its technological useful life is six years, although the physical useful life is 15 years. The salvage value of the tractor is $10,000 in six years and zero in 15 years. The 5-year class MACRS depreciation will be used on the new tractor. If the new tractor is acquired, Cittin Farms can sell the old tractor at a capital gain of $5,000.

Cittin Farms requires a minimum of a 14 percent after-tax return on all investments. The income tax rate is 40 percent. If Cittin Farms decides to acquire the new tractor, it has the option of purchasing or leasing the tractor. The distributor will sell the tractor outright for $80,000 delivered cost or will lease the tractor at $24,000 per year for six years. Under the lease, the first payment of $24,000 is due now, and at the end of six years the tractor reverts back to the distributor.

Required:
1.   Should Cittin Farms acquire the new tractor?
2.   If Cittin Farms should acquire the new tractor, would the company prefer an outright purchase or a lease?

13-14. **MACRS and an Incremental Investment.** Klarita Walsh has an rate of return objective of 16 percent for acceptable capital investment projects and a rate of return of 18 percent on incremental investments.

At present time, she is interested in the acquisition of equipment for producing a product line which can be sold for $30 per unit with a unit variable cost of $19. Her sales manager believes that a market exists for 30,000 units each year. The equipment has an installed cost of $800,000 and should have a useful life of 8 years with no salvage value. The equipment will qualify as a 5-year group MACRS asset.

A representative of the equipment manufacturer has gone over the cost estimates that Walsh has prepared and stated that the variable cost per unit of product can be cut to $15 with an equipment addition costing an incremental $250,000. This modification will not extend the useful life of the equipment nor change the salvage value.

Required:
1. Evaluate each of the alternatives by the net present value method with MACRS, using the 16 percent rate of return objective. Which alternative is better? Assume a 40 percent income tax rate.
2. Evaluate the incremental investment to see if the higher investment meets the rate of return objective of 18 percent.

13-15. **Selection of Depreciation Methods.** Dick Austin, controller of Bellinger Manufacturing, is trying to assess the cash flow implications of two depreciation policies for a new machining facility. The facility will cost $800,000 and will be technologically obsolete at the end of 6 years, at which time it will have a salvage value of $100,000. The depreciation cash flow implications are measured by the savings in income tax, because of the depreciation's tax deductibility. Tax savings are measured by the annual depreciation expense times the company's income tax rate of 40 percent.

Austin is considering the straight-line method and a MACRS method acceptable for tax purposes. For tax purposes, depreciation will cover 6 years, including one-half year in the first and last years. Taxes also ignore salvage value. The annual percentages appropriate for each depreciation method are:

Year	Straight-line Percentage	MACRS Percentage
1	10.0%	20.0%
2	20.0	32.0
3	20.0	19.2
4	20.0	11.5
5	20.0	11.5
6	10.0	5.8

Required:
1. Calculate the savings in income tax resulting from each of the two depreciation methods.
2. Which depreciation method yields the higher present value of tax savings, assuming the company uses a 16 percent interest rate?

13-16. **Inflation Impacts.** Goslin Company designs and makes lighting fixtures. The sales manager is trying to decide whether to introduce a new line of lights. The lights will sell for $100 and have variable costs of $40. Volume is expected to be 2,000 units per year for 5 years. Additional fixed cash operating costs will be $50,000 per year. Additional machinery costing $200,000 is needed. The new machinery will have a 5-year life and have no salvage value. Goslin uses straight-line depreciation. Goslin's tax rate is 40 percent, and the company uses a hurdle rate of 15 percent.

Goslin sees a serious threat to the project's profitability—inflation. He knows competition will allow only small increases in prices, perhaps 4 percent per year. But he knows labor and materials cost pressures could cause variable costs to increase by double that rate, probably 8 percent per year. Fixed costs are likely to increase by $2,000 per year.

Required:

1. By adjusting the hurdle rate for inflation by 5 percent to 20 percent, evaluate the project.
2. By adjusting each cost and revenue element by its estimated inflation factor, evaluate the project.
3. Compare the two methods of considering inflation.

13-17. **New Product Decision.** Wieberg Corporation has spent $25,000 developing a new product with an estimated life of six years. Management is now trying to decide whether the product should be manufactured. Estimated product demand and price are as follows:

Year	Demand	Price
1	6,000	$10
2	8,000	11
3	10,000	12
4	7,000	11
5	5,000	10
6	6,000	10

The variable costs associated with this product are as follows:

Direct material	$2.00
Direct labor	1.50
Variable factory overhead	1.50
Selling and administrative	.50
Total variable costs	$5.50

Manufacturing the product requires new equipment costing $52,000 that has a useful life of five years with no scrap value. Depreciation will be under the MACRS method using 6 years. In addition, the company will expense the first $10,000 of the equipment cost for tax purposes. The equipment will be installed in an area currently used by Sales and Distribution as a finished goods warehouse. Additional warehousing space will be leased for $3,000 per year, payable at the beginning of each year. Sales and Distribution had previously been charged $1,000 per year for this area which will now be given to Production.

Fixed costs will also increase. Production will add $4,000 per year to fixed factory overhead. Advertising and other marketing costs will increase the fixed selling costs by $2,000 per year.

The tax rate is 40 percent. An after-tax discount rate of 12 percent is expected on all new investments.

Required:

1. Determine the yearly after-tax returns for this investment, and calculate the net investment.
2. Calculate a payback period.

3.   What is the net present value for this investment?
4.   Is there additional information you would like before making a final decision on whether to start production of this product? Explain.

13-18.   **Sensitivity Analysis.** Hillkirk-Lurie Corporation wants to expand a production facility because of increasing demand for its specialty line of cycling shorts. The following information is available for management's consideration in this decision:

```
Investment:
    Increase in fixed assets  . . . . . . . . . . . . . . . . . . . . . . . . . . . . . . . . .    $125,000
    Increase in working capital . . . . . . . . . . . . . . . . . . . . . . . . . . . . .       45,000

Recovery at the end of five years:
    Fixed assets . . . . . . . . . . . . . . . . . . . . . . . . . . . . . . . . . . . . . . . . .    $ 25,000
    Working capital  . . . . . . . . . . . . . . . . . . . . . . . . . . . . . . . . . . . . .       45,000
    Project life . . . . . . . . . . . . . . . . . . . . . . . . . . . . . . . . . . . . . . . . . .       5 years

Annual operations:
    Volume in units  . . . . . . . . . . . . . . . . . . . . . . . . . . . . . . . . . . . . .       10,000
    Selling price per unit . . . . . . . . . . . . . . . . . . . . . . . . . . . . . . . . . .       $28 per unit
    Variable cost per unit  . . . . . . . . . . . . . . . . . . . . . . . . . . . . . . . .       15 per unit
    Fixed cost, exclusive of depreciation  . . . . . . . . . . . . . . . . . . . . .    $ 24,000
```

Straight-line depreciation is used for tax purposes. Ignore salvage value and the half-year convention. The company's tax rate is 40 percent. On investments of this nature, the company uses a 15 percent after-tax rate of return cutoff.

Required:
1.   Determine the net present value for this investment proposal.
2.   If variable costs are underestimated, by how much can the estimates be off and the investment still return 15 percent?
3.   Holding costs and prices constant, by how much can unit volume fall and still earn 15 percent?
4.   With the original data on selling price, demand, and variable cost, how much can fixed costs increase (exclusive of depreciation on the new investment) and have the project still return 15 percent?

CASE 13A—Plastic Productions, Inc.

On Monday morning, Joe Sindelar, owner and president of Plastic Productions, Inc. (PPI), sits in his office pondering the acquisition of a new machine for the company. PPI is in need of an additional plastic injection molding press, specifically a 175 ton Cincinnati Machining injection molding press. A former coworker, who now works at a large plastics firm on the East Coast, mentioned at a recent trade show that his firm was leasing new injection molding presses. Because Joe prefers to own his production equipment, he has never considered a leasing alternative. In fact, Sindelar maintains a favorable relationship with High Plains Bank so that PPI can borrow needed cash for capital investments. Realizing he is relatively ignorant on the subject of leasing, Sindelar somewhat reluctantly calls in Claudia Ringwald, his controller.

"Claudia," says Sindelar, "I wonder if it's possible for us to lease that press instead of buying it. Trouble is, I don't know the first thing about leasing. And to tell you the truth, I've always liked owning my equipment. But, I want you to show me whether my negative gut feeling on leasing is right or wrong."

"No problem," replies Ringwald. "Consider it done."

PPI is a small, closely-held firm that employs 50 people. As a job-shop type plastics molding manufacturer, PPI offers a full service approach to its customers. The process starts when PPI receives an order from a buyer, typically a large original equipment manufacturer. An order is the design specifications for a mold. Once PPI's tooling engineers finish the mold, a product prototype is made and shipped to the buyer for inspection. When the prototype is approved, it is returned to PPI and the production process begins.

A production process typically follows these steps. Colored plastic pellets are issued from the raw materials storeroom. The pellets are automatically fed into a melting chamber that liquefies the plastic. The liquid plastic is automatically or manually forced through a pressurized valve into the mold and the hydraulic press compresses the plastic, causing it to form to the mold with great precision. Water is pumped around the mold, cooling the plastic. The press is then released and the hardened product is removed from the mold.

Driving the decision to acquire the additional injection molding press is a major strategic decision based on several factors. Two significant factors stand out.

First, the technical experience at PPI has grown greatly over the past several years to the point where the engineering staff and the production personnel feel that PPI is ready to tackle specialty low-volume, high-margin jobs that require considerably more technical and production expertise. The second factor is the increasing control high-volume buyers exercise over PPI. These buyers are typically large original equipment manufacturers (OEMs) that are facing increasingly stiff foreign competition. In an effort to stay competitive, these buyers employ just-in-time techniques. Basically, PPI has been forced to incur higher costs since it produces the entire contract amount in one run but only ships when the customer calls. Realizing that these JIT techniques will only become more prevalent with the high-volume buyers, PPI wishes to reduce its dependence on these customers.

The sales rep at Cincinnati Machining quotes Ringwald a price of $25,000 for the press. The company is willing to lease the press to PPI at $6,000 annually for six years, with the first payment due upon arrival of the equipment at PPI. If the press is leased, Cincinnati will provide free maintenance. If purchased, PPI could enter into a series of one-year maintenance contracts with Cincinnati. The initial maintenance contract offered costs $900 annually. The first annual maintenance payment would be due when the machine is delivered to PPI.

The bank officer at High Plains tells Ringwald that the bank would make a loan to PPI for $25,000. The terms would be six years at a 14 percent annual rate. Annual payments of $6,428 would be due at the end of each year.

Ringwald determines that the press will have a useful life of six years, with no salvage value, and will have to be replaced due to wear on the injection valve and the hydraulics system. She notes that the equipment is eligible for the Modified Accelerated Cost Recovery System (MACRS) using a 5-year class life. PPI's current marginal tax rate is 40 percent.

Required:

1.   Some financial managers suggest the buy alternative should not consider the cost of borrowing. In other words, financing of investments comes from some pool of dollars, the accumulation of which is independent of investment alternatives. If financing of the buy alternative is not included, should PPI buy or lease?

2.   Assume the cost of borrowing is included in the buy alternative. Compare the buy and lease alternatives.

Chapter Fourteen

Planning and Control in Decentralized Operations

❖ *Chapter Objectives*

After studying Chapter 14, you will be able to:

1. Define the components of division net income, division direct profit, division controllable profit, and division contribution margin.
2. Describe the problems of selecting an investment base for evaluating performance.
3. Evaluate a division manager's performance using a profit index and residual income.
4. Identify the criteria for developing and evaluating transfer pricing policies: goal congruency, autonomy, performance evaluation, and administrative cost.
5. Define transfer prices and identify the major guidelines and the advantages and disadvantages for applying each transfer price.
6. Explain how the importance of intracompany dealings, the existence of external markets, the relative power positions of the divisions, managerial intent, and other factors affect transfer pricing and divisional evaluations.

Dividing the Profit Pie: Whose Is Whose?

Southern States Petroleum Company is a large integrated oil company headquartered in New Orleans. The company consists of a corporate headquarters and five operating divisions: Exploration & Production, Trading & Supply, Gas Processing, Refining, and Marketing & Distribution. Each division is responsible for generating a profit and for managing its investment in assets. Debates have raged among division managers about who earned what profits, since in many cases, "Your revenues are my costs."

Exploration & Production Division has the task of finding, developing, and producing oil and gas reserves. Oil produced is sold to the Trading & Supply Division or to outside customers, depending on who offers the best prices. Gas produced is sold to the Gas Processing Division, petrochemical companies, or pipeline companies.

Trading & Supply Division has a primary responsibility for meeting the crude oil needs of the Refining Division. It purchases crude oil from the Exploration & Production Division and the open market. Crude oil not sold to refining is marketed to outside customers. Consequently, the division engages in speculative buying and selling as a major means of generating profits.

Although the Gas Processing Division may purchase gas from other companies, 90 percent of its gas needs are met by the Exploration & Production Division. Processing results in liquid petroleum gas products such as ethane, propane, and butane. These products are sold to the Marketing & Distribution Division and to petrochemical companies.

Refining Division has refineries in south Texas, on the Mississippi, and in California. The refineries have the capability to produce a full range of petroleum products and are currently operating at about 50 percent of capacity. They also have a large storage capacity. Finished products are sold either to the Marketing & Distribution Division or to a wholesale market.

Marketing & Distribution sells to utilities and resellers, plus industrial, governmental, commercial, and residential customers. It buys its products from the Refining and Gas Processing Divisions. If shortages occur, it may purchase from the wholesale market. The division is responsible for selling a wide range of products and must be prepared to store and transport the products it sells. The division has storage capacity and owns a barge fleet, tanker trucks, and some pipeline facilities. Other product shipments are contracted with railroad and pipeline companies.

Since the divisions each generate profits and have tremendous investments in assets, Southern States wants to develop an appropriate measure for evaluating the financial performance of the divisions and their managers. Among the problems each division encounters are:

1. Should the divisions be cost, profit, or investment centers?

2. What income measure should be used to calculate a rate of return on investment?
3. What transfer price policy should be used to value intracompany deals fairly?

One of the most striking characteristics of business operations and organizations over the past thirty years has been top management's desire to grow and yet retain the advantages of smallness. Companies have decentralized operations to retain this element of smallness, to build "entrepreneurial spirit," and to motivate division managers to act as the heads of their "own" companies.

In general, a **decentralized company** is one in which operating subunits are created with definite organizational boundaries and in which subunit managers have decision-making authority. Thus, responsibility for portions of the company's profits can be traced to specific subunit managers. Even though the amount of authority granted to these managers varies among companies, the spirit of decentralization is clear—to divide a company into relatively self-contained subunits or segments (usually called divisions) and allow them to operate in an autonomous fashion.

This chapter discusses two of the problem areas common to evaluating performance of subunits and their managers. Evaluation measures and how these measures can be used are covered first. Then the criteria, approaches, and problems associated with transfer prices for goods and services moving among divisions are discussed. Transfer pricing creates interesting implications for promoting the goals of the entire firm, evaluating performance, and encouraging independence, while keeping the administrative cost of the transfer pricing system reasonable.

REVIEW OF RESPONSIBILITY CENTERS

Before discussing decentralization and performance measures, it is essential to review the types of responsibility centers first introduced in Chapter 3. A **responsibility center** is any organizational unit where control exists over the occurrence of cost or the generating of revenue. Managers of **cost centers** have control only over the incurrence of cost but not over revenue. Cost centers are usually found at lower levels of an organization but may include entire plants or even entire parts of an organization, such as manufacturing or the controller's office. In contrast, managers of **profit centers** have control over both costs and revenues. These subunits are responsible for generating revenues and for the costs incurred in generating those revenues.

Investment centers are responsibility centers whose managers control costs, revenues, and the investment in assets used or managed. The investment represents plant and equipment, receivables, inventories, and, in some cases, payables traceable to the investment center's operations. Companies or subsidiaries could be investment centers or profit centers, depending on whether corporate headquarters gives investment responsibility to these levels. Asset responsibility or control is defined as authority to buy, sell, and use subunit assets.

Top management's intent often determines whether a responsibility center will be a cost, profit, or investment center. In a large company, a data processing center could be a cost center, either absorbing its own costs or allocating its costs to users of the firm's computer operations. As a profit center, it would be allowed to charge an external market rate for data processing services it provides to internal users and be expected to earn a profit on its operations. To create an investment center, the center manager would be given responsibility to acquire equipment and update services from funds generated by its charges for services provided. This is similar to a revolving fund that is common in quasi-business units of government operations. Often, organizational structures create natural cost, profit, or investment centers. But managerial intent is perhaps the most important factor in determining how a unit will be viewed and managed.

The type of responsibility center determines an organization's approach to the selection and implementation of performance measures. For example, a cost center, where no responsibility for revenues exists, is responsible for producing its product or rendering its service at the lowest cost, while balancing quality, delivery, and other qualitative factors. Financial evaluations are based on cost; thus, the emphasis is on cost control. Any responsibility center having authority over its sales as well as cost places the emphasis mainly on profit control. The amount of profits must be related to the amount of assets if a division manager has authority over asset acquisition decisions, financing, and asset utilization to generate revenues and profits.

ADVANTAGES OF DECENTRALIZATION

Decentralization is the delegation of decision-making authority to lower management levels in an organization. The degree of decentralization depends on how far top management delegates decision-making authority to successively lower managerial levels. A number of advantages are cited for decentralizing and include:

1. **Motivate managers**. Managers who actively participate in decision making are more committed to working for the success of their divisions and are more willing to accept the consequences of their actions, whether positive or negative.
2. **Speed decision making**. In a decentralized organization, managers who are close to the decision point and familiar with the problems and situations are allowed to make the decisions. Consequently, decisions can be made faster without moving data up the organization and having a decision made by a manager far removed from the action. Also, experience in

decision making at low management levels results in trained managers who can assume higher levels of responsibility when needed.

3. **Enhance specialization**. Delegating authority permits the various levels of management to do those things each does best. For example, top management can concentrate on strategic planning and policy development; middle management on tactical decisions and management control; and lower management on operating decisions.

4. **Define span of control**. As an organization increases in size, top management has more difficulty controlling the organization. Decentralizing the authority defines more narrowly the span of control of each manager and thus makes the control system more responsive to the market.

5. **Develop policy**. To give guidance to a wide-spread organization and numerous decision makers, development of policies and procedures is needed. Decision rules, degrees of latitude, training of managers, and planning and control systems contribute to creating discipline and providing direction.

To realize the full benefits of these advantages, top management must resolve three primary problems associated with decentralization which are:

1. **Competent people**. Without competent people, the best policies break down; and a lack of control reduces the efficiency and effectiveness of operations.

2. **Measurement system**. The same measurement system must be implemented and maintained for all subunits. Top management must develop policies that provide consistency in reporting periods, methods of reporting, and methods of data collection.

3. **Suboptimization**. Left to themselves, division managers will work for their own interests without consideration of benefits to the entire organization. Top management needs to focus all managers' efforts on corporate goals through planning and incentive systems.

Formulating the best method of controlling and evaluating divisions and their managers is usually more complex than any other single control activity within a company. Motivation, control, and managerial behavior are broad topics and far beyond the scope of this book.

MEASUREMENT OF FINANCIAL PERFORMANCE

In previous chapters, planning and control tools and processes were discussed. These are applied to cost, profit, and investment center evaluations. A hierarchy of control can be developed. Cost controls used in cost centers are also applied to profit and investment centers. Revenue and profit measurements used in profit centers are also applied to investment centers. Thus, the following planning and control structure can be built:

	Cost Center	Profit Center	Investment Center
Expense budgeting	X	X	X
Flexible budgets...............................	X	X	X
Plan versus actual expense comparisons	X	X	X
Standard cost variances	X	X	X
Revenue and profit budgeting		X	X
Plan versus actual controllable contribution margin ..		X	X
Plan versus actual direct contribution margin		X	X
Asset utilization and rate of return target setting....			X
Plan versus actual asset utilization comparisons ...			X
Plan versus actual rates of return comparisons			X

It is rare that financial measures alone can evaluate the performance of a responsibility center. Product or service quality, delivery reliability, minimization of wasted resources, market share, and responsiveness to customers are all nonfinancial measures critical to the overall success of a firm. Both financial and nonfinancial goals and targets are often part of a manager's business plan. Yet, for profit and investment centers, the dominant financial performance criterion for evaluating managers is profitability.

In a decentralized operation, financial performance measures are often the key information passed up to the firm's headquarters. Selecting proper measures is not an easy task. The financial measures used in reports:

1. Send messages to all managers about what is important to the firm's executive managers.
2. Are often the basis for calculating incentive compensation, personnel evaluations, and promotion decisions.
3. Influence the allocation of new capital and personnel resources.

Rate of return on investment, usually called **return on investment (ROI)**, is widely accepted as the primary measure of performance for investment centers.

Return on Investment

Return on investment is defined in terms of a ratio:

$$\text{Return on investment} = \frac{\text{Profit}}{\text{Investment}}$$

This ratio is really composed of two elements whose characteristics allow better control and evaluation. A revised form shows:

$$\text{Return on investment} = \frac{\text{Profit}}{\text{Sales}} \times \frac{\text{Sales}}{\text{Investment}}$$

The first term is the **return on sales (ROS)** (sometimes called the profit margin). It is a measure of the relationships among sales, expenses, volume, and profit. The second term is the **asset turnover**. It measures the ability to generate sales with the assets a subunit employs. These are two of the earning power ratios discussed in Chapter 17.

Implementing the ROI concept raises a number of issues. Problems exist in defining the profit numerator, investment denominator, and the ratio itself. Even then, subunits of a decentralized company may be dissimilar, creating "apples and oranges" comparisons.

The Numerator—Division Profit   The choice of the profit figure is not simple. The first problem is how the profit number will be used. Will it be used to evaluate the division as an economic unit or to evaluate the division manager's performance? A different profit measure is appropriate for each. Once the purpose is decided, the next problem is how to construct the best measure from several profit concepts commonly available. Assume that a division reports the following profit and loss data (with all numbers in thousands):

Revenue from division sales	$1,000
Direct division costs:	
Variable cost of goods sold and other operating costs.	700
Fixed division overhead—controllable at the division level	100
Fixed division overhead—noncontrollable at the division level.	50
Indirect division costs:	
Allocated (fixed) general office overhead	60

Four alternative income statements organize the data for different purposes. (The profit titles are also consistent with those used in Chapter 4.)

	Division Variable Contribution Margin	Division Controllable Contribution Margin	Division Direct Contribution Margin	Division Net Profit
Revenue	$1,000	$1,000	$1,000	$1,000
Direct cost:				
Variable cost	700	700	700	700
	$ 300			
Fixed controllable costs		100	100	100
		$ 200		
Fixed non-controllable costs			50	50
			$ 150	
Indirect cost:				
Allocated home office overhead				60
				$ 90

Division Net Profit   The best profit measure for division performance may appear to be **division net profit**. However, the net profit calculation includes allocated home office overhead. An example of this cost would be the cost of operating the president's office. Although each division benefits from these costs, they are not controllable at the division level nor traceable to specific divisions. Generally, net profit is a poor indicator of a division's performance.

The main argument for using net profit, which implies allocation of home office costs, is that the division manager is made aware of the full cost of operating the entire firm. Even though part of this full cost is not identifiable with the division, the division manager may work harder to control the costs which are controllable.

Every effort should be made to find ways to trace home office expenses to specific divisions. However, the method chosen to allocate common costs is likely to be arbitrary and open to question by the division managers. Often, a division manager may spend much time attempting to reduce his or her costs by getting top management to change the allocation procedure.

Division Direct Contribution Margin   **Division direct contribution margin** is defined as the total division revenue less the direct costs of the division. This concept avoids the main difficulty of division net profit since all common costs of the firm as a whole are excluded. The direct contribution margin is the most useful profit measure for comparing divisional performances, for resource allocation decisions, and for corporate planning purposes. All revenues and costs traceable to this unit are included. The direct contribution margin is the "bottom line" result for that division.

Often, corporate-level decision makers use the direct contribution margin to indicate where additional investments should be made to generate the greatest incremental returns. Certainly, specific projects must justify themselves as Chapters 12 and 13 demonstrate. But more attention will be paid to high performing divisions.

Division Controllable Contribution Margin   **Division controllable contribution margin** is defined as the total division revenue less all costs that are directly traceable to the division and that are controllable by the division manager. It appears that this calculation is best for managerial performance measurement, because it reflects the division manager's ability to execute assigned responsibilities. Changes in the profit figure from year to year should be a reflection of how a manager carries out division-level responsibilities. Any variances between actual and plan can be explained in terms of factors over which the division manager has control.

However, certain direct costs are included in the calculation that are traceable to a division level but cannot be controlled at that level. Costs, such as the division manager's salary, are controllable only at a higher management level. Also, some division costs, such as long-term leases and depreciation, are from past investment decisions that may have been made by higher level managers or previous division managers. These direct but noncontrollable costs should be excluded from the profit calculation for managerial evaluations. If this is not done, the division profit used for performance evaluation may be increased or decreased by actions outside the division.

Some factors in the division controllable contribution margin may be difficult for the division manager to influence; for example, the materials prices may increase. Even though the price cannot be changed, perhaps alternate materials can be used; or alternate sources of supply can be found. Problems of this nature may be difficult to solve, but they are part of the division management's responsibility. Failure to solve such problems is different from being unable to take action because of a lack of authority.

Division Variable Contribution Margin   The **division variable contribution margin** is defined as the total revenue less the variable costs. Although variable contribution margin is useful in decision making, for performance evaluation its defect is obvious; namely, direct and controllable fixed costs are excluded from the calculation. Variable costs do have an important role in intracompany pricing policies and decisions, which is discussed later in this chapter.

Some Problems   Several accounting problems must be solved for division direct and division controllable contribution margins to be good evaluation performance measures.

The division manager can increase the short-run profit of the division to the detriment of the company as a whole. For example, it may be possible to delay maintenance costs. Such an action will increase short-run profits but adversely affect long-run profitability of the division and the company. Expenditures that engender employee loyalty such as employee physical fitness programs may be eliminated. By reducing training costs, the division manager may not develop long-run top management personnel.

Controllability also has a time dimension. If the time horizon is very long, some costs may be controllable which would not be in the short run. For example, the occupancy costs of a division may be controllable by a department manager if the time horizon is at least as long as the life of the lease for the space. Conversely, if the time horizon for the profit calculation is one year, the cleaning and repair costs are controllable but the rent expenses are not. In distinguishing controllable from noncontrollable costs, the time period, as well as the level of management for which the profit report is prepared, must be considered.

The Denominator—Investment   If divisions are to be evaluated by a ROI, it is necessary to measure the investment base. Many problems are associated with this determination.

The definition of the investment base has significance. The **investment base** may be total direct assets, net direct assets, or net direct assets managed. Net direct assets would be traceable assets minus any traceable liabilities. Again, the distinction between direct and controllability is important. Certain assets may be traced to a division but not be in service or usable by division managers.

Asset Identification   The first task is to decide which assets to assign to each division. Many assets can be traced directly to a division. For example, much of a firm's physical property can be traced to a particular division. A division may handle its own receivables and inventory and may even have jurisdiction over its own cash balance. But sometimes traceable assets, such as receivables, inventories, and cash, are centrally administered and controlled. By proper account coding it may be possible to identify receivables and inventories to specific divisions. Cash, often a corporate asset, is rarely traceable to specific divisions.

For investments that are common to several divisions, no amount of coding, sorting, or classifying will provide a basis for tracing them to a single division. An example of a common investment would be the investment in administrative offices used by two product divisions. Any basis of allocation used would be arbitrary. As with common costs, avoiding these arbitrary allocations generally improves the analysis.

Asset Valuation   Once identifying assets with divisions has been determined, it is necessary to decide on the value of the assets. One might argue that replacement cost or perhaps original cost adjusted for price-level changes should be used. In inflationary periods, ROI using replacement cost may be lower than an historical-cost-based ROI. It may seem that the investment should be stated at some current value rather than on an historical-cost basis. The obvious difficulty is measurement. How can replacement costs be determined? If a common-dollar base is desirable, which price-level index should be used? It is easier to raise questions than to give answers.

Preferred Relationships   Matching an income measure and an investment base is the next step. Managerial intent and motivational potential are keys to selecting the proper ROI tool. If the purpose is to evaluate the division itself, direct contribution margin would be the natural match with net division direct assets. This would give a return on net direct assets. Traceability is important to both the numerator and denominator. Direct division assets are assets traceable to specific divisions less traceable liabilities.

To evaluate the division managers, controllable contribution margin should be matched with net direct managed assets. This gives a **return on managed assets**. Controllability is the foremost criterion. Managed assets include the assets controlled by the division manager having the authority to acquire, use, and dispose of these assets.

Additional Problems With ROI   Using the ROI concept as a means of evaluating performance raises some concerns about how effective ROI can be and about potential undesirable impacts that may arise.

Comparability Among Divisions   One of the major concerns is that ROI comparisons should use the same definitions for the same purposes. Divisions being compared should have the same or similar accounting methods.

The same depreciation method should apply to similar classes or categories of assets. Likewise, incorrect comparisons result when one division inventories under FIFO and another division uses LIFO. Also, each division being compared should have the same or similar policies for capitalizing or expensing costs. Capitalization policies have profit impacts on both current and future periods. In one division, tools are expensed whenever they are purchased. Another division capitalizes the original tools plus any increments but expenses replacement tools.

Motivational Impact on Managers   From top management's point of view, division managers should be working to achieve the overall objectives of the organization. This requires strategies, policies, techniques, and incentives to act as motivators for division managers. **Goal congruence** is the term often used to link each division manager's goals with top management's goals. Individual managers may have personal and organizational goals that differ from top management's goals. When designing managerial performance criteria, senior management must carefully select the components of ROI to promote firm-wide goal congruency. Thus, managers should be motivated to work for their own benefit while, at the same time, benefiting the whole organization.

Up to this point, ROI has been discussed in ratio form; that is, the division profit divided by the division investment. ROI may create problems simply because of the nature of the ratio. For example, suppose that one division of a company is currently earning 25 percent. The division manager may be reluctant to make additional investments at, perhaps, 20 percent because the average return of the division would drop. However, if new investments in other divisions of the company yield only 15 percent, company management may prefer that the additional investment with a yield of 20 percent be accepted. The high-earning manager may still be reluctant to lower the average ROI from 25 percent even though the company management has set 15 percent as the base rate for comparison. Thus, the use of ROI as a ratio might restrict additional investment at the expense of company-wide profitability.

Improving ROI   Since division managers are expected to improve ROI, they look to components they can control. It is obvious that ROI can be improved in three direct ways: by increasing sales, by decreasing expenses, and by reducing the level of investment. To see how individual changes affect the ROI calculation, consider the following data for the Boise Division of the Idaho Company:

Sales	$2,500,000
Variable costs	1,500,000
Contribution margin	$1,000,000
Fixed costs	600,000
Net income	$ 400,000
Investment base	$2,000,000
Return on sales	16.00 percent
Asset turnover	1.25 times
ROI	20.00 percent

Increase Sales   Looking at ROI as a product of return on sales, asset turnover might give the impression that the sales figure is neutral, since it is the denominator in the return on sales and the numerator in asset turnover. Suppose the Boise Division can increase sales with only variable expenses moving with sales; the return on sales improves. This happens anytime total expenses increase or decrease by a different amount than sales increase or decrease. This change in sales also improves the asset turnover, if the change in asset investment is not proportionate. The objectives are to wring the high-

est level of net income from a given amount of sales and the highest level of
sales from a given investment base.

Continuing the numerical example for the Boise Division, assume that sales
volume and variable costs increase by 5 percent because of the volume increase and that fixed costs and the investment base remain constant.

Sales (105 percent)	$2,625,000
Variable costs (105 percent)	1,575,000
Contribution margin	$1,050,000
Fixed costs	600,000
Net income	$ 450 000
Investment base	$2,000,000
Return on sales	17.14 percent
Asset turnover	1.31 times
ROI	22.50 percent

Reduce Expenses   Often, the easiest path to improved profitability—
thus, to increased ROI—is to implement a cost reduction program (focusing
on certain expense areas or across-the-board cuts) and introduce cost controls
(stronger budget limits or approvals for spending discretionary funds). Reducing costs is usually the first approach managers take when facing a declining
return on sales. A rather typical pattern has emerged. First, review the discretionary fixed costs, either individual cost items or programs representing a
package of discretionary fixed costs, and look for those that can be curtailed or
eliminated quickly. Second, look for ways to make employees more efficient,
hence eliminating duplication, wasted time, and downtime and increasing
individual workloads. Third, review costs of resource inputs for operations
and seek less costly choices.

Reduce Investment Base   Managers have traditionally sought to control sales and expenses. Their sensitivity to asset management, however, has
not always been at the same high level. Managers, whose performances are
evaluated using ROI, will find that trimming any excess investment can have a
significant impact on the asset turnover and, therefore, on ROI. For example,
maintaining excess inventories increases operating costs as well as financing
costs. Inventory reduction improves ROI and releases funds for use elsewhere
or reduces the firm's need for financing.

Reducing unnecessary investment depends on selling or writing off unused
or unproductive assets. Referring to the original Boise data, assume that its
managers are able to reduce the investment by 4 percent but still maintain the
same level of sales and expenses.

Sales	$2,500,000
Variable costs	1,500,000
Contribution margin	$1,000,000
Fixed costs	600,000
Net income	$ 400,000
Investment base (96 percent of original)	$1,920,000

Return on sales .... 16.00 percent
Asset turnover .... 1.30 times
ROI .... 20.83 percent

If the eliminated investment is a depreciable asset, depreciation expense will also be reduced. This causes a compound reaction: profitability increases, return on sales increases, and ROI increases by improvement in both the return on sales and the asset turnover.

Residual Income

The use of residual income has been proposed as an alternative to the ratio form of ROI. Residual income focuses attention on a dollar amount instead of a rate. The maximization of the dollar amount will tend to be in the best interest of both the division manager and the company as a whole.

In general, **residual income** is defined as the operating profit of a division less an imputed charge for the operating capital used by the division. The same measurement and valuation problems still apply to residual income. But motivational problems are hopefully eased. Assume that the current controllable contribution margin (before any imputed capital charge) is $250,000 and the relevant investment is $1,000,000. The ROI, then, is 25 percent. Suppose top management wants the division management to accept incremental investments so long as the return is greater than 15 percent—a hurdle rate.

This hurdle rate percentage is then used to calculate an imputed charge for division investment funds. The residual income would be calculated as follows:

Division controllable profit (before imputed capital charge) $250,000
Less imputed capital charge (15% x $1,000,000) 150,000

Division residual income $100,000

The advantage of this evaluation measure is that the division manager is concerned with increasing a dollar amount (in this case, the $100,000) and is more likely to accept incremental investments which have a yield of over 15 percent. Even if a budgeted level for residual income is used, the division manager will focus on comparing the budget and actual. A tendency exists to select additional investments with a yield in excess of 15 percent. Division management behavior, then, should be more congruent with company-wide objectives.

A disadvantage with residual income is the difficulty posed when comparing the performance of several divisions of different sizes. For example, a division with $50 million in assets should be expected to have a higher residual income than one with $2 million in assets.

The imputed capital charge is also called the **minimum desired rate of return**. As long as a division earns in excess of that amount, the division should continue to invest. The stage of growth and other risk factors influence the potential ROI that a division can generate. Consequently, top management might select different minimum desired rates of return for each division to recognize the unique role each plays in the organization. For example, a start-up division may be more expensive to finance than a division in the mature stage—justifying a lower initial rate of return.

PERFORMANCE EVALUATION SYSTEMS IN SERVICE ORGANIZATIONS

Service organizations also need evaluation systems to satisfy the same needs as a manufacturer or merchandiser. Evaluation criteria and measures can depend on whether the service organization is a commercial operation or a not-for-profit organization.

Profit-oriented operations have an incentive and motivation to be profitable. They may use ROI or residual income, if an appropriate profit index and investment base are available. Obviously, organizations such as CPA firms, law firms, insurance agencies, and facility management firms for hotels, computer centers, and institutional food services do not have large investment bases. They often lease equipment, space, cars, and other operating assets. Personnel is their prime asset. Using ROI or residual income in these situations will not give a realistic measure of performance for the divisions or functions within the organization. A return on revenue is a better measure and a greater management motivator than is ROI or residual income.

Not-for-profit organizations are different. Profits are not the prime interest of managers. Eliminating a profit motive removes one of the most powerful incentives for managers to perform. Other measures of efficiency and effectiveness have comparability and consensus problems. For example, the concept of Diagnosis Related Groups (DRG) was developed by the U. S. government to help control hospital health care costs. A DRG is a specific procedure performed in a hospital on a patient. The hospital is reimbursed a specific amount for that specific procedure. One goal is that hospitals should manage costs so that they can perform the procedure at an actual cost equal to or below the reimbursed "price." Cost allocation systems, marketing and pricing, budgeting processes, hospital operations organization, and billing classification systems have all been modified to maximize revenues. Hopefully, better cost control has also resulted from the changes to at least partly achieve the original goal of the DRG system.

Additionally, identifying an investment base for ROI and residual income is difficult, particularly in governmental units. Another factor is the problem of identifying relationships between inputs (resources consumed) and outputs (services rendered). Therefore, finding criteria for evaluating performance is not an easy task. Governmental units attempt to overcome this dilemma by assessing accountability through budgeting. However, governmental budgeting (rightly or wrongly) is more of a process for authorizing expenditures and obtaining funding than for planning and controlling operations. Politics, public posturing, and taxation issues tend to subvert mechanisms that many people think would make good performance evaluation indicators.

INTRACOMPANY TRANSACTIONS AND
THE TRANSFER PRICING PROBLEMS

In calculating division profit, problems arise when the divisions are not completely independent. If one division furnishes goods or services to another division, a **transfer price** must be set to determine the buying division's cost and the selling division's revenue.

Accounting has long depended on the arm's-length transaction to establish objective transaction prices and values. But reporting transactions between divisions, departments, and other subunits often requires an economic value where no independent transaction occurred. The range of intracompany dealings includes:

1. A centralized personnel department serves all subunits of a company, and its costs are allocated to subunits on the basis of number of employees in each subunit.
2. One department provides repairs and maintenance for the production departments' equipment in a factory and bills for those services at an average actual cost per hour of service.
3. A Data Processing Services Division provides computer-based information systems services to all other divisions in the company and allocates costs on the basis of predetermined prices for volumes of transactions and data handled.
4. Plant A produces components which are shipped to Plant B for assembly into an end product which is then transferred to the Sales Division for sales to outside customers. Components and products are billed at a "full cost plus a profit" basis between Plants A and B and Plant B and the Sales Division.
5. Plant J sells a strategic raw material to a variety of customers, including Plant K in the same company. Managers negotiate a special price each year for the raw material, depending on the supply and demand factors for each plant.
6. In a similar situation, Division R sells an industrial product to a broad array of customers. Division S happens to need the product and buys from the sister division because of its high quality, delivery reliability, or price advantage. Division S may or may not be aware of the common ownership of the two divisions.

This continuum of intracompany dealings is shown in Figure 14.1 on page 710. While not representing any numerical measuring scale, this line does illustrate the many varieties of intracompany business transactions. At one end is a pure cost allocation problem. At the other end is a pure market-driven pricing situation.

Roughly, the left one-third of the continuum is the cost allocation problem. Overhead costs are being redistributed to other units using cost drivers, benefits received, or even arbitrary rules. Commonly, service departments are transferring costs to producing departments.

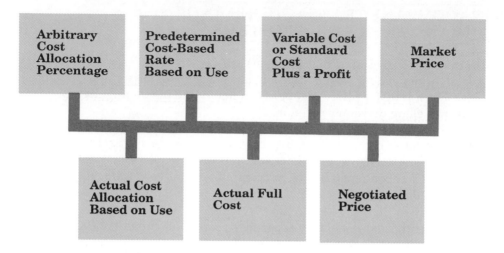

Figure 14.1   Intracompany Transactions Continuum

The middle one-third is internal sales of goods and services where external markets do not exist or where company policies force firm subunits to deal with each other internally. External prices for equivalent items either do not exist or can only be used as a surrogate for internal transfers.

The right one-third of the continuum represents situations where external markets do exist and market prices are used, in part or in total, as the exchange price. Buyers seek suppliers. Sellers seek customers. If an intracompany sale takes place, it is the best source for the buyer and a profitable sale for the seller—both subunits in the same company. In other situations, special prices to benefit both the internal buyer and seller in order to encourage them to deal with each other may be part of the company policies.

Often, top management will create a responsibility center in an organization that does not have the natural characteristics of a profit or investment center. Joel Dean, a management expert who has studied internal company dealing for decades, has suggested four criteria for marking off profit centers properly:

1.   Operational independence.
2.   Access to sources and markets.
3.   Separable costs and revenues.
4.   Managerial intent.[1]

The left third on Figure 14.1 rarely meets any of the criteria. Frequently, subunits in the middle section have trouble meeting more than the managerial intent criterion. Often, the right third meets most of the criteria.

---

[1]Joel Dean, "Profit Performance Measurement of Division Managers," *The Controller*, September 1957.

Desired Qualities of Transfer Prices and Policies

In decentralized firms, transfer prices are needed for multiple purposes. To find the best pricing policy, the desired qualities must be prioritized for a given set of intracompany dealings. The bad news is that no one price or pricing policy will meet all criteria. A manager who has spent years supervising internal sales and purchases for a major company has said: Perhaps the optimal policy is one that will produce the least amount of dysfunctional behavior or, at best, an amount that we can tolerate. Hopefully, policies encourage positive behavior. But dysfunctional behavior, actions which hurt the firm's results, can be frequent by-products.

Let us first outline the criteria for creating a transfer pricing system; second, discuss alternative transfer prices; and third, identify the ability of each price to meet the criteria. Criteria for a transfer price can be reduced to four elements:

1. **Goal congruence.** Will the transfer price encourage each manager to make decisions that will maximize profits for the firm as a whole? In decentralized organizations, perhaps one of the most difficult tasks is to get everyone to pull toward the common goal—the financial success of the whole firm. It is a misconception that success of each subunit will guarantee the optimal success for the whole firm.

2. **Performance evaluation.** Will the transfer price allow corporate-level managers to measure the financial performance of subunit managers? Ideally, market prices would allow all subunit transactions to be arm's length. With internal transfers, prices must fairly split costs and revenues for an objective evaluation.

3. **Autonomy.** Will the transfer price policy allow subunit managers to operate as if they were operating an independent business? If a division manager must ask for approval from some higher level, the firm's policies have diluted the autonomy of its managers. Arbitration of interdivisional disputes can often become time consuming, expensive, and destructive of subunit independence.

4. **Administrative cost.** Is the transfer pricing system easy and inexpensive to operate? As with all accounting costs, an incremental cost should generate a positive contribution margin. Where internal transaction volume is large and complex, a more extensive internal pricing system is justified. Administrative cost also includes waiting for decisions, hours spent haggling, and internal divisiveness.

Neutralizing power positions that certain subunits have over other subunits is another issue and forces fairness into the transfer pricing system. If one division sells its entire output to another division, the buyer can demand concessions from the seller that can cause the seller to appear unprofitable. If management intent is to keep the two divisions independent, the pricing policy must allow the seller to get a reasonable price for its output.

The four main criteria plus other concerns should be prioritized and allowed to influence the creation of the pricing policy. Different situations will demand different transfer pricing policies.

Transfer Prices

The most common transfer prices are:

1. Market price.
2. Cost-based prices including:
   (a) Actual full cost.
   (b) Target or predetermined full cost.
   (c) Cost plus a profit.
   (d) Variable cost.
3. Negotiated price.
4. Dual prices.

Each is examined and compared to the transfer price criteria.

Market Price   Market price is a price set between independent buyers and sellers. Market price meets more of the transfer pricing criteria than any other. But finding a market price may be difficult since one may not exist. Two contrasting conditions are typical:

1. A market price exists, and both buyer and seller have access to other sellers and buyers for the same products.
2. A market price is not readily available, but a pseudo-price is created either by using similar products or by getting outside bids for the same item.

Finding an appropriate market price may not be easy. Frequently, catalog prices may only vaguely relate to actual sales prices. Market prices may change often. Also, internal selling costs may be less than would be incurred if the products were sold to outsiders.

A more difficult problem arises where no real market exists at the transfer point. Examples include intermediate components, industrial supplies, and "make or buy" jobs. The buyer's purchasing department may request bids from outside suppliers. If the outside bidders are rarely considered seriously since company policy requires inside purchases, the outside bidder will not play this game for long. Bidding is an expensive process. Some companies have a policy of considering outside vendors seriously and committing a certain percentage of business to these bidders to help keep the system viable.

Despite the problems of finding a market price, managers generally agree that market prices are best for most transfer pricing situations. A market transfer price parallels the actual market conditions under which these divisions would operate if they were independent companies.

Goal Congruence   Only in achieving the maximum profit for the firm as a whole does the market price cause a possible problem. If subunits are acting like independent business firms, they are unlikely to share cost and profit information with their contracting partner. It is possible that Division A, having excess capacity and a mixture of fixed and variable product costs, could benefit greatly from additional production volume. Division A's prices are based on its current volume. Division B is looking for a supplier for a part that Division A can easily provide. Division B may ask for bids from a variety of suppliers. Company C, an unrelated firm, may be selected because of its low price. This price is still well above Division A's variable cost but below its market price bid. Managers in A and B are making the best decisions for their respective divisions as they see it, but total company profit is hurt. The firm as a whole would be better off if Division B purchased from Division A. But Division B would need to pay Division A a higher price, or Division A would have to accept a lower profit margin than its regular business generates.

Many company managements will argue that this is a small cost to incur if the individual division managers act in an aggressive, competitive style. What is lost from suboptimization is gained in greater profits from highly motivated quasi-entrepreneurs. Depending on results in specific firms, this trade off may or may not be justified.

Performance Evaluation and Autonomy   Market prices form an excellent performance indicator because they cannot be manipulated by the individuals who have an interest in profit calculation. A market price eliminates the negotiations and squabbling over costs and definitions of fairness. If market power positions exist, they also exist in the general market place.

Where market prices are less clear and are either created or massaged, the pure advantage of market prices declines. In fact, as we move away from a true market price, the price becomes a negotiated price, which is discussed below.

Administrative Cost   As part of normal buying and selling, the price is determined. It is a simple and near-costless task of recording the price for transfer pricing purposes. And as we move away from a clear market price, costs increase. Negotiations are expensive in terms of consuming executive time, getting outside bids, and creating support data for negotiating positions.

Cost-Based Prices   Unless market price is readily available, most transfer prices are based on production costs. By its nature, **cost-based transfer prices** are best suited to cost centers. Three issues stand out in cost-based transfer prices discussion:

1.   Actual cost versus a target cost, such as standard or budgeted cost.
2.   Cost versus cost plus a profit.
3.   Full cost versus variable cost.

These three issues are distinct but can also overlap. The implication of different combinations affects every transfer pricing criteria.

Actual Versus a Target or Standard Cost   A primary problem with cost-based prices is in measuring cost. Actual cost gives the selling subunit no incentive to control cost. All product costs are transferred to the buying subunit. Clearly, using actual costs merely pushes costs to the next unit. This can create a serious competitive problem for the vertically integrated firm that passes parts through numerous divisions before selling a product in a competitive market. Historically, this has been a problem for General Motors Corporation.

Moving to a target cost is not a perfect solution. First, if a budget or standard cost is used for cost control and also for transfer pricing, profit pressures may well subvert the cost system and damage its usefulness as a cost control device. Who sets the standard? Is it a tight or lax standard? Is cost reduction built into the transfer price contract? Clearly, actual cost is still less attractive than a standard or budgeted costs.

Cost Versus Cost Plus a Profit

If cost only is used as a transfer price, the selling unit cannot earn a manufacturing profit, much less cover its operating expenses. Full cost plus a profit percentage is a popular solution.

Adding a percentage to cost for a profit creates the question: "What percentage?" Somehow 10 percent seems attractive and common. This is, however, only arbitrary logic. Perhaps a markup percentage can be calculated that will cover operating expenses and provide a target return on sales or assets. Even here, full-cost prices fail to produce the kind of competitive environment that decentralization promotes.

Full Cost or Variable Cost

Another version of cost-based transfer pricing is variable cost. Only variable production costs are transferred. These costs are generally materials, direct labor, and variable overhead. Variable cost has the major advantage of encouraging maximum profits for the entire firm. By passing only variable costs along to the next division, production and pricing decisions are made based on cost-volume-profit relationships for the firm as a whole. The obvious problem is that the selling division is left holding all its fixed costs and operating expenses. That division is now a loss division, no where near a profit center.

Full cost creates problems for profit optimization. A **full-cost transfer price** makes an assumption about volume and fixed costs per unit. Just as contribution margin analysis gives much stronger decision-making power than full product cost analysis, **variable-cost transfer prices** also beat full cost.

With these issues in mind, how well do cost-based transfer prices match with the evaluation criteria?

Goal Congruence

Conceptually, full-cost transfer prices will always produce suboptimal profits for the firm as a whole. Variable-cost transfer prices will generate an optimal firm-wide profit. Often, the definition of the most goal-congruent transfer price is out-of-pocket costs plus any opportunity costs. The opportunity costs are contribution margin earned from alternative uses of the seller's capacity.

The following example contrasts decisions using variable costs and full costs. Assume that Division A sells to Division B. The output of Division A is Product A, which can be sold to an outside market or to Division B to be processed further and sold as Product B. One unit of B uses one unit of A. In both divisions, to sell more units, the price must be reduced. In Division A, variable costs are $1.20 per unit; fixed costs total $3; and normal volume is set at 10 units. In Division B, variable costs are $1 per unit; fixed costs total $3; and normal volume is set at 5 units. Note that fixed costs and volumes could be in thousands or millions. Data about different sales levels in each division are shown in Figure 14.2:

Division A

Outside Sales (Units)	Product A Selling Price to Outside Market	Division A Marginal Revenue	Product A Variable Cost Per Unit	Division A Incremental Contribution Margin	Division A Total Contribution Margin	Full Cost — Product A[1] Allocated Fixed Cost Per Unit	Full Cost — Division A Full-Cost Profit Margin
1	$3.00	$3.00[2]	$1.20	$1.80	$1.80	$.30	$1.50
2	2.80	2.60	1.20	1.40	3.20	.30	2.60
3	2.60	2.20	1.20	1.00	4.20	.30	3.30
4	2.40	1.80	1.20	.60	4.80	.30	3.60[3]
5	2.20	1.40	1.20	.20[4]	5.00	.30	3.50
6	2.00	1.00	1.20	(.20)	4.80	.30	3.00
7	1.80	.60	1.20	(.60)	4.20	.30	2.10
8	1.60	.20	1.20	(1.00)	3.20	.30	.80
9	1.40	(.20)	1.20	(1.40)	1.80	.30	(.90)

Division B

Outside Sales (Units)	Product B Selling Price to Outside Market	Division B Marginal Revenue	Product B Variable Cost Per Unit	Division B Incremental Contribution Margin	Division B Total Contribution Margin	Full Cost — Product B[5] Allocated Fixed Cost Per Unit	Full Cost — Division B Full-Cost Profit Margin
1	$6.00	$6.00	$1.20 + $1.00	$3.80	$ 3.80	$.30 + $.60	$2.90
2	5.75	5.50	1.20 + 1.00	3.30	7.10	.30 + .60	5.30
3	5.50	5.00	1.20 + 1.00	2.80	9.90	.30 + .60	7.20
4	5.25	4.50	1.20 + 1.00	2.30	12.20	.30 + .60	8.60
5	5.00	4.00	1.20 + 1.00	1.80	14.00	.30 + .60	9.50
6	4.75	3.50	1.20 + 1.00	1.30	15.30	.30 + .60	9.90[6]
7	4.50	3.00	1.20 + 1.00	.80	16.10	.30 + .60	9.80
8	4.25	2.50	1.20 + 1.00	.30[7]	16.40	.30 + .60	9.20
9	4.00	2.00	1.20 + 1.00	(.20)	16.20	.30 + .60	8.10

[1] Assumes that normal volume is 10 units and that fixed costs are $3.
[2] Marginal revenue in Figure 14.2 is found by subtracting the total revenue from selling N units at N prices from the total revenue from selling N + 1 units at N + 1 prices. For example in Division A when selling two units, revenue of $5.60 ($2.80 x 2 units) minus $3.00 for one unit is $2.60.
[3] Point where Division A's full-cost profit margin is maximized, if fixed cost per unit are applied.
[4] Last unit with a positive contribution margin per unit and point where Division A's variable contribution margin is maximized.
[5] Assumes that normal volume is 5 units and that fixed costs are $3.
[6] Point where Division B's full-cost profit margin is maximized, if fixed cost per unit is applied.
[7] Last unit with a positive contribution margin per unit and point where Division B's variable contribution margin is maximized.

Figure 14.2   Variable-Cost and Full-Cost Transfer Pricing Example

This example is simplified by using a given amount of fixed costs and setting a normal volume for each division. As volume increases, sales prices and marginal revenue per unit decline. Division total contribution margin increases to a maximum and then declines. To create a full cost, a fixed cost per unit is applied to each unit.

If variable costing is used, the optimal outside sales for Division A would be 5 units. The 6th unit would have a negative incremental contribution margin. Division B would sell 8 units and need to purchase 8 units of Product A. Thus, total production of Product A would be 13 units—5 for outside customers and 8 for Division B. The firm's optimal total contribution margin and profits are as follows:

	Division A	Division B	Total
Units sold outside	5	8	
Units transferred to Division B	8		
Outside sales:			
(5 units × $2.20 per unit)	$11.00		
(8 units × $4.25 per unit)		$34.00	
Variable costs:			
(5 × $1.20 per unit)	6.00		
(8 × $2.20 per unit)		17.60	
Variable contribution margin	$ 5.00	$16.40	$21.40
Fixed manufacturing costs	3.00	3.00	6.00
Manufacturing profit	$ 2.00	$13.40	$15.40

If full costing is used, the cost of a unit of Product A would be $1.50 (variable cost of $1.20 plus fixed cost of $.30). At that price, Division B would produce and sell only 6 units. The 6th unit has a positive full-cost profit margin ($1.30 variable contribution margin minus $.90 of fixed costs from Division A and B together), but the 7th unit has a negative manufacturing margin ($.80 minus $.90). And in Division A, full costing would tell us to stop outside sales of Product A at 4 units, the last unit that has a positive full-cost profit margin. Manufacturing profits would appear as follows:

	Division A	Division B	Total
Units sold outside	4	6	
Units transferred to Division B	6		
Outside sales:			
(4 units x $2.40 per unit)	$ 9.60		
(6 units x $4.75 per unit)		$28.50	
Full costs:			
(4 x $1.50 per unit)	6.00		
(6 x $3.10 per unit)		18.60	
Applied manufacturing margin	$ 3.60	$ 9.90	$13.50
Over- or (under-) applied fixed costs	.00	.60	.60
Manufacturing profits	$ 3.60	$10.50	$14.10

The firm as a whole maximizes profits by using a variable-cost transfer price. Both divisions use contribution margin analysis to decide what business to accept from outside customers. When a full-cost transfer price is used, Division A appears to perform better because it now at least breaks even on the units sold to Division B. Division B appears much worse off because it must pay full price to Division A and its sales volume is reduced. The firm as a whole is worse off by $1.30.

In summary, full cost does a poor job of goal congruency, and variable cost optimizes firm-wide profits.

Performance Evaluation and Autonomy   Clearly, a variable-cost transfer price provides little help in performance evaluation if the subunit is considered to be a profit center. Autonomy is also violated since close working relationships and much exchange of data are expected. When using full-cost transfer prices, an added profit percentage is necessary to get the seller to a profit position. It is difficult to support any cost-based approach as a strong performance evaluation method.

Administrative Cost   Internally, cost-based transfer prices are the cheapest and easiest prices to obtain. They are outputs of the cost accounting system. Perhaps this is why cost-based transfer pricing is the most widely used transfer pricing method. To repeat, in spite of its weaknesses full-cost transfer prices continue to be popular.

Negotiated Price   The use of **negotiated transfer prices** is often suggested as a compromise between market-based and cost-based transfer prices. Real advantages may exist in allowing two division managers to arrive at the transfer price through arm's-length bargaining. The selfish interests of the division managers in the division profit and related bonuses serve the company objectives. Negotiated prices are helpful when:

1.   Cost savings occur from selling and buying internally.
2.   Additional internal sales fill previously unused capacity allowing the buyer and seller to share any incremental profit.

Often, minimums (out-of-pocket costs plus any opportunity costs) and maximums (market prices) are clear, but they may give a wide price range. As long as the negotiators have relatively equal power positions, negotiations can create a quasi-free market. Friction and bad feelings that may arise from centrally controlled transfer prices may be eliminated.

Goal Congruence   Often, the company as a whole benefits from the buyer and seller units negotiating a price that is agreeable to both parties. Fairness is an issue that must be weighed. The firm as a whole will win if the subunits elect to enter negotiations freely.

Performance Evaluation and Autonomy   A negotiated price may be a suitable surrogate for a market price. A market atmosphere is created if buyers and sellers are free to go outside and if neither subunit has an unfair power position—such as a monopoly position for purchases or sales.

Negotiations can be between buyer and seller alone or involve the corporate office. If negotiations lead to arbitration by the corporate office or if corporate policies interfere with free negotiations, autonomy suffers. The corporate office has the delicate problem of keeping hands off and yet monitoring subunit dealings to prevent significant non-congruent behavior.

Administrative Cost   Negotiations are often expensive, consume time of key executives, and may create an internal unit to handle these relationships. If intracompany sales are important to a subunit, its managers must put a high priority on these negotiations. Its sales and profit levels are at stake. In highly integrated companies, negotiation costs can be a major operating expense.

Dual Transfer Prices   A dual system allows the selling division to "sell" at a real or synthetic market price (such as full cost plus a profit percentage). The transfer price to the buying division is the variable cost. Use of dual transfer prices has been suggested as a way of creating a profit, and thus a positive motivation, in the selling division, while transferring the goods or service to the buying division at variable cost plus identifiable opportunity costs. Variable cost is probably the best figure to guide the decisions in the buying division.

The selling division manager is motivated to sell because profit will be increased, and the buying division manager will buy internally unless the outside price is less than variable cost plus opportunity costs. Hence, the main purpose of the dual system is to motivate both the buying and selling division managers to make decisions that are consistent with the interests of the company as a whole—goal congruency.

Such a system, however, does expand the corporate office accounting task. Both the buying and selling divisions will recognize the same profits. Intracompany sales and duplicate profits have to be eliminated before the total company profit can be determined.

Goal Congruence and Performance Evaluation   The advantages of the dual transfer price system rest on being able to evaluate performance of both units as profit centers and to encourage behavior that will benefit the firm as a whole. Thus, the dual system provides the buying division with incremental cost information while at the same time allowing the selling division to show a profit. Such a system encourages the congruence of divisional goals with company-wide goals.

If the selling division has substantial fixed costs to cover, a danger does exist that the buying division will sell at cut rate prices and fail to cover all fixed costs. Here active corporate-level monitoring may be needed.

Autonomy and Administrative Cost   Cost and corporate interference are the practical considerations and the major obstacles to the use of dual transfer pricing systems. From an accounting point of view, each division records its own transactions; and the central office must monitor, record, and track intracompany dealings, a clear violation of autonomy. In financial statements for the combined company, accounts representing intracompany transactions are eliminated. For example, a selling division will record a sale and establish a receivable; a buying division will record a purchase and set up a payable. In eliminating the intracompany accounts, any intracompany profits in the buying division's inventory will be adjusted out. The home office must have a special accounting system to track all transactions of a dual pricing system. These extra costs must be outweighed by the benefits of greater congruency and decision-making performances.

Commonly, the dual transfer pricing system is an academic approach to solving transfer pricing conflicts. But occasionally, a real world firm will put a dual pricing system in place. Given the right circumstances and the intent of management, a dual system can generate the desired combination of benefits.

Grading Transfer Pricing Methods According To the Criteria

Having discussed the transfer pricing criteria and the methods commonly used, let us now assess the relative strengths and weaknesses. An evaluation is presented as follows:

	Goal Congruence	Performance Evaluation	Autonomy	Administrative Cost
Market prices	Good	Very Strong	Very Strong	Low, if available
Cost-based prices:				
Actual full cost	Poor	Poor	Poor	Very Low
Full cost plus a profit percentage . . .	Poor	Average	Average	Low
Variable cost	Strong	Very Poor	Poor	Often Low
Negotiated prices	Strong	Strong	Strong to Poor	High
Dual prices	Strong	Strong	Poor	High
	(Variable Cost)	(Market Price)		

Remember that specific cases can produce very different answers in each area. Clearly, no one transfer price serves all purposes. Managers must rank their priorities and select transfer pricing policies that fit the situation. Perhaps the goal really is to select a transfer pricing policy that creates the least disruption or adverse managerial behavior.

SUMMARY

Many companies have sought to increase their financial performance by organizing themselves into an array of profit or investment centers. Decentralizing a company involves defining boundaries for organizational units, called responsibility centers, and delegating decision-making authority to the managers of these centers. Such a structure motivates managers to work for the benefit of the company, provides for front-line decision making by those nearest the action, enhances specialization by letting managers do what they do best, and reduces the span of control for management.

A control system is necessary if management wants to motivate its division managers and to evaluate the performance of divisions and their managers. Measures of expected performance level and actual performance are the two essential ingredients for a control system. Since decentralized companies frequently place investment authority in lower levels of the organization, performance measures should be related to responsibility assignments. Return on investment and residual income are approaches to divisional financial performance evaluation and were discussed. Definition problems exist for both the numerator and denominator. Numerators include direct and controllable contribution margins. Denominators include net direct assets and managed assets.

Divisions within a company do not operate in isolation from one another; rather, they frequently do business as buyer and seller. Any time intracompany transactions occur, a transfer price must be attached to the transaction. Criteria of goal congruence, performance evaluation, autonomy, and administrative cost are developed to measure the strengths and weaknesses of each type of transfer price. Transfer prices can be market based, cost based, negotiated, or dual. Each of these possible prices has been presented, together with how each method performs versus the transfer pricing system criteria. No one method meets all criteria. Each has strengths and weaknesses depending on the importance of intracompany dealings and the priorities of management.

PROBLEMS FOR REVIEW

Review Problem A

Layton-Wells has two department stores, which are organized as divisions. One store is downtown where business activity is declining. The other store is in the South Plains Mall, located in an area of the city that is expanding rapidly. Results of operations for each store for fiscal 1993 are shown as follows:

	South Plains Mall Store	Downtown Store
Sales	$3,900,000	$1,750,000
Total costs	2,762,500	1,570,000
Average current assets	587,500	165,000
Average long-term assets (net)	4,062,500	962,000
Minimum desired rate of return	15%	10%

Required:

1. ROI for each division.
    (a) Compute the return on sales.
    (b) Compute the asset turnover.
    (c) Compute the ROI.
2. Residual income for each division.
    (a) Compute residual income.
    (b) Compute the residual income percentage.

Solution:

1.   ROI:

	South Plains Mall Store	Downtown Store
Net profit:		
Sales	$3,900,000	$1,750,000
Total costs	2,762,500	1,570,000
	$1,137,500	$ 180,000
Investment base (averages):		
Current assets	$ 587,500	$ 165,000
Long-term assets (net)	4,062,500	962,000
	$4,650,000	$1,127,000
(a) Return on sales:		
(Net profit ÷ Sales)	29.17%	10.29%
(b) Asset turnover:		
(Sales ÷ Investment base)	.8387	1.5528
(c) ROI: (Return on sales × Asset turnover) or (Net profit ÷		
Investment base)	24.46%	15.97%

2.   Residual income:

(a) Computation of residual income:		
Net profit	$1,137,500	$ 180,000
Minimum desired return (Investment base × Minimum desired rate of return)	697,500	112,700
Residual income . . . . *Net Profit − Min desired Ret*	$ 440,000	$ 67,300
(b) Residual income percentage: (Residual income ÷ Investment base)	9.46%	5.97%

Review Problem B

The Circuit Board Division of Bastion Computers manufactures an electronic circuit board used in personal computers. Sales of the board go to outsiders as well as to the new Laptop Computer Division. The circuit boards are sold for $125 to outsiders. The laptop computer sells for $900 to distributors. Results of operations for the two divisions for 1993 are as follows:

	Circuit Board Division	Laptop Computer Division
Intracompany sales (units)	10,000 ⎰ 22,000	0
Sales to outside market (units)	12,000	10,000
Variable production costs	$880,000	$3,600,000
Fixed factory overhead	880,000	1,000,000
Variable marketing expenses.	60,000	60,000
Fixed marketing & administrative expenses ..	80,000	150,000
Home office—allocated expenses	20,000	150,000

The home office expenses are allocated to the divisions and are not regarded as traceable to the divisions.

Required:

Prepare an income statement for each division under each of the following conditions:

1. Intracompany sales are made at market price.
2. Intracompany sales are made at full cost.
3. Intracompany sales are made at variable cost.
4. "What if" Laptop Computer Division can purchase a similar circuit board from a Korean electronics firm for $110, and the Circuit Board Division has alternative business that generates a contribution margin equivalent to $30 per unit. What prices should the Circuit Board Division demand as a minimum price and the Laptop Division demand as a maximum price?

Solution:

Before answering the specific requirements, let's first calculate the full cost and variable cost per unit.

| | Circuit Board Division | |
	Full	Variable
Variable production costs	$ 880,000	$880,000
Fixed factory overhead	880,000	
Total product costs	$1,760,000	$880,000
Product cost per unit	$ 80.00	$ 40.00

1. Intracompany sales at market price:

	Circuit Board Division	Laptop Computer Division
Outside selling price	$ 125.00	$ 900.00
Transfer price	$ 125.00	
Interdivisional sales (units)	10,000	0
Sales to outside market (units)	12,000	10,000
Sales to outside market	$1,500,000	$9,000,000
Sales to Laptop Computer Division	1,250,000	0
Total sales	$2,750,000	$9,000,000
Cost of goods sold:		
Cost from Circuit Board Division		$1,250,000
Variable production costs	$ 880,000	3,600,000
Fixed factory overhead	880,000	1,000,000
Total cost of goods sold	$1,760,000	$5,850,000
Gross margin	$ 990,000	$3,150,000
Operating expenses:		
Variable marketing expenses	$ 60,000	$ 60,000
Fixed marketing & administrative expense	80,000	150,000
Home office—allocated expenses	20,000	150,000
Total operating expenses	$ 160,000	$ 360,000
Net income	$ 830,000	$2,790,000

2. Intracompany sales at actual cost:

	Circuit Board Division	Laptop Computer Division
Outside selling price	$ 125.00	$ 900.00
Transfer price	80.00	
Intracompany sales (units)	10,000	0
Sales to outside market (units)	12,000	10,000
Sales to outside market	$1,500,000	$9,000,000
Sales to Laptop Computer Division	800,000	0
Total sales	$2,300,000	$9,000,000
Cost of goods sold:		
Cost from Circuit Board Division		$ 800,000
Variable production costs	$ 880,000	3,600,000
Fixed factory overhead	880,000	1,000,000
Total cost of goods sold	$1,760,000	$5,400,000
Gross margin	$ 540,000	$3,600,000
Operating expenses:		
Variable marketing expense	$ 60,000	$ 60,000
Fixed marketing & administrative expense	80,000	150,000
Home office—allocated expenses	20,000	150,000
Total operating expenses	$ 160,000	$ 360,000
Net income	$ 380,000	$3,240,000

3.   Intracompany sales at variable cost:

	Circuit Board Division	Laptop Computer Division
Outside selling price	$ 125.00	$ 900.00
Transfer price	40.00	
Intracompany sales (units)	10,000	0
Sales to outside market (units)	12,000	10,000
Sales to outside market	$1,500,000	$9,000,000
Sales to Laptop Computer Division	400,000	0
Total sales	$1,900,000	$9,000,000
Cost of goods sold:		
Cost from Circuit Board Division		$ 400,000
Variable production costs	$ 880,000	3,600,000
Fixed factory overhead	880,000	1,000,000
Total cost of goods sold	$1,760,000	$5,000,000
Gross margin	$ 140,000	$4,000,000
Operating expenses:		
Variable marketing expense	$ 60,000	$ 60,000
Fixed marketing & administrative expense	80,000	150,000
Home office—allocated expenses	20,000	150,000
Total operating expenses	$ 160,000	$ 360,000
Net income	$ (20,000)	$3,640,000

4.   Circuit Board Division's minimum price:

    The minimum price for the Circuit Board Division is the variable cost plus the opportunity cost that Circuit Board Division would incur if it sold circuits to the Laptop Computer Division: $40 plus $30 or $70 per unit.

Laptop Computer Division's maximum price is the outside price available to Laptop less any internal costs that would not be incurred if the internal sale took place: $110 minus the variable marketing cost of $5 per unit ($60,000 divided by 12,000 units sold externally) or $105 per unit.

The two divisions would negotiate a price between the maximum and minimum.

TERMINOLOGY REVIEW

Asset turnover (701)
Cost centers (697)
Cost-based transfer prices (713)
Decentralization (698)
Decentralized company (697)
Division variable contribution margin (703)
Division controllable contribution margin (702)
Division direct contribution margin (702)
Division net profit (701)
Dual transfer pricing systems (718)
Full-cost transfer price (714)

Goal congruence (705)
Investment base (703)
Investment centers (697)
Market price (712)
Minimum desired rate of return (707)
Negotiated transfer prices (717)
Profit centers (697)
Residual income (707)
Responsibility center (697)
Return on investment (ROI) (700)
Return on managed assets (704)
Return on sales (ROS) (700)
Transfer price (709)
Variable-cost transfer prices (714)

QUESTIONS FOR REVIEW AND DISCUSSION

1. What are the advantages of decentralization? What are the primary problems of decentralization?

2. Distinguish between a cost center, a profit center, and an investment center.

3. How is performance generally measured in a cost center? In a profit center? In an investment center?

4. Why is a cost budget not a good control measure in evaluating a division manager who has decision power on prices and marketing products?

5. What are some of the problems in using division profit as an evaluation measure?

6. Explain the difference between division controllable profit and division direct profit.

7. The president of Major Company has returned from an executive management seminar. He sees you in the office coffee lounge and says: "As I read and hear more and more on valuing assets, I am increasingly bewildered by the 'language of accounting.' Yes, I understand historical cost and its problems. But you accountants also mix and match terms like market value, replacement value, economic value, present value, opportunity value, disposal value, entry value, and more values! You seem to have extra time since I see you here in the lounge a lot. Maybe you could help clear up this confusion for me by writing a memo that lays out how these terms can help to make decisions about divisional performance and about keeping or selling these assets and to inform our stockholders about our performance."
    Write the president his memo.

8. Identify and explain allocation problems involved in determining a profit measure and the investment base for the purpose of calculating a ROI.

9. When comparing various divisions, why is it important that the divisions have the same or similar accounting methods? Cite three examples of accounting methods that could cause divisions' profits to differ.

10. List the components of the ROI equation, tell how they are related, and identify an action a manager can take regarding each component to improve ROI.

11. How is residual income defined? What is the major advantage of using residual income in performance evaluation versus ROI?

12. Identify the major factors necessary in conceptually defining profit centers for promoting decentralization in an organization.

13. What is a transfer price? Under what conditions are transfer prices necessary?

14. Identify four criteria that are useful in evaluating transfer prices for intracompany transactions.

15. Using the criteria for evaluating transfer prices, evaluate each of the following transfer prices.
    (a) Market price.
    (b) Actual cost.
    (c) Target full cost.
    (d) Cost plus a profit percentage.
    (e) Variable cost.
    (f) Negotiated price.

16. Explain and comment on the following paragraph from a recent publication on transfer pricing:
    A pseudo-profit center is one that is artificially carved out of an organization by management, such as making the maintenance department in a factory a profit center. The primary advantage of a pseudo-profit center is that it captures the motivational advantages of real profit centers. But an analysis of pseudo-profit centers shows that the transfer pricing techniques used to create them can cause motivational disadvantages that completely overshadow any perceived advantages. Frequently, pseudo-profit centers will motivate managers to act in a dysfunctional manner.

17. If a market transfer price can be determined, why is such a price usually considered the best one to use?

18. Briefly describe a dual transfer price. What are the advantages and disadvantages of implementing such a pricing system?

19. If the intermediate market is perfectly competitive, will a market-based transfer price ever lead to suboptimal profits in the producing division?

20. What is the disadvantage of negotiated transfer prices when no intermediate market exists for the producing division?

21. If a full-cost transfer price does not produce an optimal profit level for the firm, why is it so popular as a transfer price?

22. Two quotes were recently heard:
    "In recent years, a tendency exists to move toward corporate decentralization and is accompanied by setting individual rate-of-return targets for corporate segments."
    "The ROI tool is so hampered by limitations that we might as well forget it."
    Does the second quote eliminate the usefulness of the first? Explain.

EXERCISES

1. **Profit Measures.** The following data are from a division of Rosier Company:

Revenue from sales	$50,000
Division variable cost	32,500
Allocated home office overhead	4,600
Fixed overhead traceable to division ($4,500 is controllable, and $8,000 is not controllable)	12,500

    Required:
    Calculate division variable contribution margin, division controllable contribution margin, division direct contribution margin, and division net profit.

2. **Comparison of ROI and Residual Income.** A division of the Castillo Company reported operating income of $2,400,000 per year based on an investment of $12,000,000. The company is considering the use of ROI or residual income as an evaluation measure. At the present time, the division manager is faced with a decision on an incremental investment of $4,000,000 which will increase annual operating income by $700,000 per year.

    Required:
    Provide calculations showing the difference between the two performance measures and explain the possible advantage of using residual income assuming that a 16 percent ROI is considered minimally acceptable.

3. **ROI and Residual Income.** Provide the missing data in the following cases:

	Divisions			
	A	**B**	**C**	**D**
Net income	?	$500,000	?	$ 300,000
Investment base	$1,500,000	?	$2,000,000	$3,000,000
ROI	?	20%	12.5%	?
Imputed rate	6%	18%	?	?
Residual income	$ 15,000	?	$ (50,000)	$ 0

4. **Transfer Price Based on Full Cost.** The Stromberg Company has a division which produces a single product that sells for $26 per unit in the external market. The full cost of the product is $18, calculated as follows:

Variable materials and labor cost per unit	$14
Fixed cost per unit	4*
Total cost per unit	$18

    * Total fixed cost of $400,000 divided by current production and sales of 100,000 units.

    Another division has offered to buy 20,000 units at the full cost of $18. The producing division has excess capacity, and the 20,000 units can be produced without interfering with the current external sales volume of 100,000 units. The total fixed cost of the producing division will not change as a result of the order. However, the division manager of the producing division is inclined to reject the order, feeling that the division's profit position will not improve.

    Required:
    Explain to the producing division manager (by means of a calculation) the impact of transferring 20,000 units at the full cost of $18 per unit.

5. **Selecting a Transfer Price.** Division 1 produces 100,000 units of a product with a variable cost of $5 per unit and a fixed cost of $3 (based on $300,000 fixed cost allocated to 100,000 units of production). These units can be sold in an intermediate market for $1,000,000 ($10 per unit) or transferred to Division 2 for additional processing and sold in a finished market. The selling price processed is $14 per unit, and the additional processing cost in Division 2 is $1.50 per unit. The fixed cost in the Division 2 processing unit is $100,000. At this time, excess capacity exists in the Division 2 processing department if the units are not transferred.

Required:
Should the 100,000 units be sold by Division 1 or by Division 2? Would a transfer price based on either market price or variable cost be likely to lead to the right decision? Explain.

6. **ROI and Transfer Pricing.** You are given the following data regarding budgeted operations of a company division:

Average direct assets:

Receivables	$100,000
Inventories	300,000
Plant and equipment, net	200,000
Total	$600,000

Fixed overhead	$200,000
Variable costs	$1 per unit
Desired ROI on average direct assets	20%
Expected volume	100,000 units

Required:
1. What average unit sales price is needed to obtain the desired rate of return on average direct assets?
2. Assume that 30,000 units of the 100,000 units are to be sold to another division of the same company. The other division manager has balked at a tentative selling price of $4. He has offered $2.25, claiming that he can manufacture the units himself for that price. The manager of the selling division has examined her data. She has decided that she could eliminate $40,000 of inventories, $60,000 of plant and equipment, and $20,000 of fixed overhead if she did not sell to the other division. Should she sell for $2.25? Show computations to support your answer and briefly explain your reasoning.

7. **Transfer Pricing Problem.** The Tooele Company has a production division which is currently producing 120,000 units but has a capacity of 180,000 units. The variable cost of the product is $22 per unit, and the total fixed cost is $720,000 or $6 per unit based on current production.

    A sales division of the Tooele Company offers to buy 40,000 units from the production division at $21 per unit. The production division manager refuses the order because the price is below variable cost. The sales division manager argues that the order should be accepted since by taking the order the production division manager can lower the fixed cost per unit from $6 to $4.50 (output will increase to 160,000 units). This decrease of $1.50 in fixed cost per unit will more than offset the $1 difference between the variable cost and the transfer price.

Required:

1. If you were the production division manager, would you accept the sales division manager's argument? Why or why not? (Assume that the 120,000 units currently being produced sell for $30 per unit in the external market.)

2. From the viewpoint of the overall company, should the order be accepted if the manager of the sales division intends to sell each unit in the outside market for $27 after incurring an additional processing cost of $2.25 per unit? Explain.

8. **Profit Centers and Transfer Prices.** A large automobile dealership is installing a responsibility accounting system with three profit centers: Parts and Service, New Vehicles, and Used Vehicles. The department managers were told to run their shops as if they were in business for themselves. However, interdepartmental dealings frequently occur. For example:

   (a) The Parts and Service Department prepares new cars for final delivery and repairs used cars prior to resale.

   (b) The Used Vehicle Department's major source of inventory is cars traded in as partial payment for new cars.

Required:

The owner of the dealership has asked you to outline criteria for a company policy statement on transfer pricing, together with specific rules to be applied to the common examples cited. He has told you that clarity is of paramount importance because your criteria will be relied on for settling transfer-pricing disputes.

9. **Policy Implications.** Assume you are concerned about the coexistence of managing corporate profitability and divisional decentralization and autonomy. Comment on each of these:

   (a) From the viewpoint of the corporation, does any general transfer-pricing rule lead to the maximization of corporate profits?

   (b) Why might a division manager reject a cost reduction proposal with a positive net present value, preferring instead to retain an inefficient old asset?

   (c) Many firms use cost-plus or negotiated transfer prices even though they do not lead to optimal results for individual products. Why?

   (d) Competitive market prices are often thought to be ideal transfer prices. Is this true? Explain your answer.

   (e) Why might it be said that the goal of a divisional manager performance evaluation system should be to "create the least amount of dysfunctional behavior" by the individual manager?

10. **Evaluating Transfer Prices.** Newmill Enterprises runs a chain of drive-in hamburger stands in northern Michigan during the summer season. Each stand's manager is told to act as if the stand will be judged on its own profit performance. Newmill has set up a separate business to rent a soft ice cream machine for the summer and to supply its burger stands with ice cream for their frappes. Rent for the machine is $1,000. Newmill is not allowed to sell ice cream to other dealers because it cannot obtain appropriate licenses. The manager of the ice cream business charges the stands $3 per gallon. Operating figures for the machine for the summer are as follows:

Sales to the stands (10,000 gallons at $3)		$30,000
Variable costs, at 1.60 per gallon	$16,000	
Fixed costs:		
Rental of machine	1,000	
Other fixed costs	4,000	21,000
Operating margin.......................................		$ 9,000

The manager of the Clam Bar, one of the Newmill drive-ins, is seeking permission to sign a contract to buy ice cream from an outside supplier at $2.40 a gallon. The Clam Bar uses 2,000 gallons of soft ice cream during the summer. Frank Redmond, controller of Newmill Enterprises, refers this request to you. You determine that other fixed costs of operating the machine will decrease by $500 if the Clam Bar purchases from an outside suppliers. Redmond wants an analysis of the request in terms of overall company objectives and an explanation of your conclusion.

Required:
Evaluate these transfer prices: $3.00, $2.40, $2.10, and $1.60. Recommend a price. Explain.

11. **Intracompany Charges.** Listed below are three charges found on the monthly report of a division that manufactures and sells products primarily to outside companies. Division performance is evaluated using ROI. Are any of the following charges consistent with responsibility accounting and managerial performance evaluation?
   (a) A charge for general corporation administration at 10 percent of division sales.
   (b) A charge for the use of the corporate computer facility. The charge is determined by taking actual annual computer department costs and allocating an amount to each user based on the ratio of departmental hours used to total corporate hours used.
   (c) A charge for goods purchased from another division. The charge is based on a competitive market price for similar goods.

12. **Dual Transfer Price System.** The Crawford Company has two divisions, A and B. Division B produces a product at a variable cost of $10 per unit and sells 50,000 units to the external market at $15 per unit and 40,000 units to Division A at variable cost plus 50 percent. However, under the dual transfer price system in use, Division A pays only the variable cost per unit. The fixed cost of Division B is $160,000 per year.
   Division A sells 40,000 units of its finished product in the external market at $30 per unit and has a variable cost of $8 per unit in addition to the cost of the subassembly purchased from Division B at variable cost. The annual fixed cost of Division A is $180,000.

Required:
Show the income statements for the two divisions and the income statement for the company as a whole (assuming the company consists of only the two divisions). Explain why, under the dual transfer price system, the income for the company is less than the sum of the profit figures shown for the two divisions.

13. **Market Value Transfer Price.** The Epsilon Company has two divisions, M and S. Division M manufactures a product and Division S sells it. The intermediate market is competitive. But the product can be processed further and sold or stored for later processing and sale. Once the product is manufactured, some of it is sold by Division M;

and some is transferred to Division S which decides whether to hold or to process and sell the product. The following information pertains to the current year:

Division M manufacturing cost for 1,200,000 units	$7,200,000
Of the 1,200,000 units produced:	
Sold by M in intermediate market—600,000 units	6,000,000
Held by S for later sale—200,000 units (no additional processing work done on these units in Division S)	2,000,000
Processed by S and sold—400,000 units	7,200,000
Intermediate market value of 600,000 units at the time they were transferred to S.	6,000,000
Total additional processing cost of S	1,200,000

Assume no beginning inventories.

Required:
1. Prepare an income statement for the whole firm.
2. Prepare a separate income statement for each division using a cost-based transfer price.
3. Prepare a separate income statement for each division using a market-value transfer price.

14. **Choosing an Appropriate Transfer Price.** The Walker Oil Company has just decentralized its Refining and Marketing divisions. Refining is allowed to sell to outside wholesalers, while Marketing is permitted to buy from other refiners. Walker Oil produces only unleaded gasoline at a variable refinery cost of $.30 per gallon and a fixed refining cost of $160,000 per month for a capacity of 400,000 gallons. The market price in the intermediate market is $1.00 per gallon. Marketing sells the fuel to independent service stations at $1.20 per gallon and incurs transportation costs of $.10 per gallon.

Required:
Assuming all refined gallons are sold to Marketing, show the impact on profits for Refining, Marketing, and Walker Oil Company as a whole when using each of the following transfer prices: (a) variable cost, (b) market price, and (c) full cost. What conclusion can you draw?

15. **Decision Making in a Decentralized Operation.** The Richardson Company is planning to build its own office building. The company has a construction division which builds all buildings and equipment for the entire company. The construction division has requested bids on the elevators for the building from two companies. The O Company gives a bid of $4,500,000, and the U Company bids $4,000,000. However, the O Company would buy materials for the elevators from a fabricating division of the Richardson Company. This order would result in the fabricating division earning $600,000 after covering all costs. Since the Richardson Company is decentralized, the construction division is not aware of this possibility.

Required:
Which bid would you expect the construction division to take? Which bid would the Richardson Company prefer to have the construction division accept? Show calculations.

16. **Transfer Pricing Problem.** The tailor shop in a men's clothing store is set up as an autonomous unit. The transfer price for tailoring services is based on the variable cost which is estimated at $12 per hour. The store manager feels that the Suit and Sport Coat

Department is currently using too much tailor time and that this department could cut down on hours used by taking more care in fitting the garments. The manager has decided to double the hourly tailor rate even though this new rate will be no reflection of the real variable cost. The idea is simply to provide an incentive to the Suit and Sport Coat Department to conserve on tailor time.

Required:
1. What possible disadvantages do you see in the store manager's action? Do you agree or disagree with this means of stressing the need to conserve tailor time?
2. Would it make any difference if the various selling departments were not required to use the tailor shop and were allowed to take their work to some outside tailor shop? Explain.

17. **Opportunity Costs.** The Cook Division of Colaianne Corporation expects the following results for 1995 on sales to outsiders:

Sales (100,000 units)		$600,000
Variable cost of sales	$300,000	
Fixed cost of sales	200,000	500,000
Profit		$100,000

Yesterday, the manager of the Cole Division requested a bid from Cook for 30,000 units for 1996 delivery. Cole would "work over" each unit at a cost of $4 per unit and sell the end product for $9 per unit. Cook can make only 120,000 units per year and would have to forego some regular sales if the Cole business is taken on. Cole has an outside bid of $4.50 per unit.

Required:
1. What is the minimum bid Cook should make to Cole, and what transfer price goal is being optimized?
2. What is the maximum bid Cook should make to Cole, and what transfer price goal is being optimized?
3. If Cole buys from the outside supplier, does Colaianne gain or lose and by how much?

18. **Inside or Outside Sales.** Chiang and Childers are divisions of Copeland Global Corporation. Chiang sells a "thing" to outside customers and to Childers. Chiang's recent results are:

	Sales to Childers	Sales to Outsiders
Sales:		
100,000 units at $10		$1,000,000
50,000 units at $8	$400,000	
Variable costs ($4 per unit)	200,000	400,000
Contribution margin	$200,000	$ 600,000
Fixed costs ($480,000 at $3.20 per unit)	160,000	320,000
Profit	$ 40,000	$ 280,000

Chiang has capacity for 150,000 units. Fixed costs are common costs.

Required:

1. Chiang thinks its outside sales could grow to 110,000 if the Childers' agreement could be changed. Childers obtains a $7 per unit bid from another company. Assume Childers wants to maintain only one supplier. Should Chiang match the outside price? Show your analysis.
2. From Copeland Global Corporation's perspective what transfer price would maximize corporate profits in total? Why?
3. From the division managers' perspectives what transfer price would be the best basis for evaluating their performances? Why?

19. **Allocation of Central Corporate Office Cost.** The Horton Company has several operating divisions which are largely autonomous as far as decision making is concerned. The central corporate office consists mainly of the president and immediate staff. The annual cost is $1,000,000, and this cost is fixed. In calculating division profit, this cost is allocated to divisions on the basis of sales. The current allocation rate is $.04 per sales dollar based on the company-wide normal sales volume of $25,000,000 per year. The company controller does not consider this to be a transfer price because he feels that the divisions are not really buying anything. In the controller's view, the charge is a method of allocating cost which should be absorbed by the divisions when they calculate their annual net income.

Required:

Do you agree with the controller? In what sense is the charge a transfer price? Could the charge affect the decision of a division manager considering a new product with a variable cost of $5.50 and a selling price of $8? Explain.

20. **Intracompany Sales.** Nally Enterprises has three divisions: Fisk, Nied, and Zale. One of the products sold by Zale requires parts made by Fisk and Nied. Data on the product from Zale are as follows:

Selling price		$70
Variable costs:		
Fisk costs	$18	
Nied costs	12	
Zale costs	8	38
Contribution margin		$32
Factory fixed costs (based on volume of 10,000 units)		18
Profit		$14

Fisk charges Zale $26 per unit. Nied charges Zale $20 per unit. These prices are full manufactured cost plus $2 per unit markup. Fixed costs applied to the finished product are incurred equally by the three divisions.

Zale routinely gets outside bids on all parts used. Recent valid quotes were $21 per unit on the part made by Fisk and also $21 per unit on the Nied part.

Required:

1. Based on the above data, what profits are reported by each division?
2. What should be considered the maximum and minimum transfer prices for the Fisk and Nied parts?
   (a) What objective(s) would be met by the maximum price? Why?
   (b) What objective(s) would be met by the minimum price? Why?

21. **Finding a Transfer Price.** Badia Factory Division of Higgins Corporation produces electric motors, 20 percent of which is sold to Priss Sales Division of Higgins and the remainder to outside customers. Higgins treats its divisions as profit centers. Corporate policy requires that all interdivisional sales and purchases be recorded at variable cost as a transfer price. Badia Division's estimated sales and standard cost data for the year ending December 31, 1995, based on the full capacity of 100,000 units, are:

	To Priss	**Outsiders**
Sales	$ 900,000	$ 8,000,000
Variable costs	(900,000)	(3,600,000)
Fixed costs	(300,000)	(1,200,000)
Manufacturing margin	$(300,000)	$ 3,200,000
Unit sales	20,000	80,000

Badia has an opportunity to sell the above 20,000 "Priss" units to an outside customer at a price of $75 per unit on a continuing basis. Priss can purchase its requirements from an outside supplier at a price of $85 per unit.

Required:
1. Assume that Badia desires to maximize its manufacturing margin and sells to the new outside customer. What is the impact on Badia's, Priss', and Higgins' profits?
2. Given Higgins' desire to maximize profits, what policy should be established to accomplish that corporate goal? In the above case, what should be the transfer price?
3. Concerning goal congruency, autonomy, performance evaluation, and administrative cost, which basic criteria of transfer pricing are met and which are violated by:
    (a) A variable cost transfer price of $45.
    (b) A transfer price using a market price of $85.
    (c) A transfer price using a full cost of $60.

PROBLEMS

14-1. **Transfer Price Based on Full Cost.** The Casper Division of the Freddie Company produces a large metal frame which is sold to the Cody Division. Cody Division uses these frames in constructing metal lathes which are sold to machine tool manufacturers. In Casper Division, the frames are produced in a stamping process and are then run through a finishing process in which they are trimmed and polished before being shipped to the Cody Division.

The current estimate of the variable cost of materials and labor to produce a frame in the stamping process is $120 per frame. Fixed overhead associated with this process in the Casper division is $700,000 per year. Current production is 50,000 frames, which is full capacity for both the stamping and the trimming and polishing processes.

The variable cost of labor in the trimming and polishing process (no additional materials are required) is $12 per frame since labor in this process is paid on a piece-rate basis. The fixed overhead in this process is $300,000 per year and is largely due to equipment depreciation and related costs. The machines have almost no salvage value because of their special-purpose design.

The transfer price to the Cody Division is a full-cost transfer price and is calculated by prorating the current fixed cost in each process over the 50,000 frames being produced. The price is quoted for each process and is presented to the manager as follows:

Stamping process:
Materials and labor cost per unit $120
Fixed overhead cost per unit ($700,000 for 50,000 units) 14
$134

Trimming and polishing process:
Labor cost per unit . . . . $ 12
Fixed overhead cost per unit ($300,000 for 50,000 units) 6
$ 18

Total cost per unit $152

An outside company has offered to rent to Cody Division machinery which would perform the trimming and polishing process. The rental cost of the machinery is $200,000 per year. With the new machinery, the labor cost per frame would remain at $12. The Cody Division manager sees the possibility of obtaining the frames from the Casper Division for $134 by eliminating the $18 cost of trimming and polishing and performing these processes in the Cody Division. An analysis is as follows:

New process:
Machine rental cost per year $200,000
Labor cost ($12 x 50,000 units) 600,000
    Total Cody Division trimming and polishing costs $800,000

Current process:
50,000 units at $18 per unit, portion of the Casper Division transfer price
attributable to trimming and polishing process $900,000

The manager of the Cody Division has approached the vice-president of operations for approval to acquire the new machinery.

Required:
1.   As the vice-president, how would you advise the manager of the Cody Division?
2.   Could the transfer pricing system be improved and, if so, how?

14-2.   **Interdivisional Sales.** Patrick Corporation, manufacturer of specialized trailers for over-the-road and container shipping, is decentralized, with each product line operating as a divisional profit center. Each division head is delegated full authority on all decisions involving sales of divisional output both to outsiders and to other divisions of Patrick. The International Shipping (IS) Division has always purchased its requirements for a particular trailer platform subassembly from the Highway Division. However, when informed that the Highway Division was increasing its price to $300, IS Division management decided to purchase the subassembly from an outside supplier.

IS can purchase a similar subassembly for $260 per unit plus an annual die maintenance charge of $20,000 from a reliable supplier. Highway Division insists that owing to the recent installation of some highly specialized equipment which has resulted in high depreciation charges, Highway would not be able to make an adequate profit on its investment unless it charged $300. In fact, the IS business was part of the justification for buying the new equipment. Highway's management appealed to top management of Patrick for support in its dispute with IS and supplied the following operating data:

IS's annual purchases of subassembly	2,000 units
Highway's variable costs per unit of subassembly	$ 220
Highway's fixed costs per unit of subassembly	$ 65

Required:

1. Assume that no alternative use for Highway's internal facilities exists. Determine whether the company as a whole will benefit if IS Division purchases the subassembly from the outside supplier.
2. Assume that Highway's internal facilities would not otherwise be idle. By not producing the 2,000 units for IS, Highway's equipment and other facilities would be assigned to other production operations and would result in annual cash operating savings of $40,000. Should IS Division purchase from the outsider? Explain.
3. If the outside supplier drops the price by another $20 per unit, would your answer to either Part 1 or 2 change? If so, why?

14-3. **Allocation of Central Office Overhead.** The Wilbur Company has several departments which operate quite autonomously as far as decision making is concerned. The company allocates central office overhead to all these operating departments based on the total labor dollars incurred by each division. The central office overhead budget and the allocation rate are as follows:

Executive offices	$ 200,000
Legal	70,000
Advertising	60,000
Personnel	100,000
Accounting	70,000
Total	$ 500,000
Total estimated payroll in operating departments	$1,000,000

Allocation rate: $500,000 ÷ $1,000,000 = $.50 per labor dollar

The central office overhead of $500,000 is considered to be a fixed cost. Also, once the rate is established, it is not changed for one year.

The engineering research department conducts research on certain engineering problems related to the company's products and issues reports to clients who request this service. The manager of this department is faced with a need to hire two more technical assistants because of an increased workload. If the manager works through the company's personnel department, these positions can be filled at a cost of $1,500 per month for each employee. However, the usual $.50 per dollar of payroll will also be charged against the research department's budget for central office overhead. The manager discovers that it is possible to contract for technical services of an outside engineering firm which will furnish two technical assistants for as long as they are required, and the cost will be considered a consulting cost and not part of the division's payroll. The cost will be $2,000 per month for each assistant.

Required:

1. Is the central office overhead charge a transfer price? Explain.
2. What is the manager of the engineering research department likely to do? Show your calculations.
3. If the Wilbur Company wants to continue to allocate central office overhead, advise the president how this might be done so as not to affect the hiring decisions of the various department managers.

14-4.   Decision Making in a Decentralized Operation. The Broadway Company has several divisions. Division S produces (among other products) a metal container which is sold to customers who use it for shipping liquid chemicals. The main material used in manufacturing these containers is a metal which can be purchased from Division M, one of the other divisions of the company, or from several outside sources. Division S has received a customer order for 100 containers at $500 each. It will require two tons of materials to produce the 100 containers. The manager of Division S requests bids for the materials required to produce the containers from Division M and from two outside companies. Division M, bidding a transfer price based on full cost, bids a price of $8,000 per ton on the materials order. Division M's variable cost is only $4,500 per ton, and it has excess capacity. However, Division M regularly bases price bids on full cost, whether or not the order is from another division or from an outside customer.

The two outside companies bid $6,000 and $6,500 per ton. However, the Gairer Company, which bid $6,500, would buy the manufacturing supplies necessary to produce the materials from Division P, another division of the Broadway Company. The supplies would amount to $1,500 per ton of materials required. Division P's variable cost is about $800 per ton with a $200 freight charge for the total shipment.

Required:
1.   What would you expect Division S to do? Explain.
2.   Will Division S accept the right outside bid? Explain.
3.   Should Division M's transfer pricing policy be changed? If so, how?

14-5.   Pricing for Returns. A truck division of an auto company follows a pricing policy whereby normal activity is used as a base for pricing. That is, prices are set on the basis of long-run annual volume predictions. They are then rarely changed, except for notable changes in wage rates or material prices. You are given the following data:

Materials, wages, and other variable costs	$ 5,000	per unit
Fixed overhead	$30,000,000	per year
Desired rate of return on invested capital	20	percent
Normal volume	40,000	units
Invested capital	$90,000,000	

Required:
1.   What net income percentage based on dollar sales is needed to attain the desired rate of return?
2.   What rate of return on invested capital will be earned at sales volumes of 35,000 and 45,000 units, respectively?
3.   If sales were to drop to 35,000 units or rise to 45,000 units, by what percentage must each of the following variables change from the normal level of 40,000 units to achieve the 20 percent rate of return: sales price, fixed overhead, return on sales percentage, and invested capital?

14-6.   Changing a Cost Center to a Profit Center. The president of Morris Company has just attended a seminar on the use of responsibility centers. He is very anxious about putting "competitive zeal" into every part of the organization. He is especially interested in making some of the service centers within the company into profit centers. It is decided that the maintenance department will be the first to be made into a profit center, and it is hoped that the experience gained will be helpful if other service centers are to be converted to profit centers.

A meeting has been called to discuss setting prices to be charged by the maintenance department to the units that it serves. The manager of the maintenance department suggests a cost-plus basis for pricing, with labor and materials costs plus a 10 percent markup being charged to the unit requesting maintenance services. He argues that a markup over cost is needed to allow the department to become a profit center; otherwise there is no point in changing from the current status—that of a cost center.

Some managers of operating departments argue that a fee schedule for each kind of maintenance job should be established. Some think a reasonable approach would be to survey local industrial maintenance firms and use their prices less a percentage for cost savings. Others think that the whole idea only creates an "artificial profit center" and that the maintenance budget should just be divided among the production departments. Most do not seem to like the cost-plus idea.

Required:
1. Evaluate each position. Are there other choices? If so, what?
2. What recommendation can you make?

14-7. **Transfer Pricing Problem.** The Derrick Company has a central computer facility which is used by several operating departments for data processing and problem-solving purposes. The center's budget for the current year is given as follows:

Rentals	$1,200,000
Payroll, operators	260,000
Payroll, programmers	180,000
Payroll, supervision and secretarial	90,000
Miscellaneous supplies	120,000
Utilities	250,000
Total	$2,100,000

It is estimated that 20,000 computer time units will be available. All of the costs shown in the budget are considered to be fixed, except for utilities and miscellaneous supplies, which are variable.

During the past 5 years, the computer facility has not been operated at full capacity. The percentage of capacity has increased from 40 percent in the first year of operation to an estimated 70 percent for the current year.

A transfer price policy has been established which calls for the use of a full cost per unit of time. Thus, an operating department that needs one half of a time unit would be charged at the rate of $52.50 [1/2 x ($2,100,000 ÷ 20,000 time units)]. All operating departments do most of their own programming. The central staff has four programmers who are used to solve special problems as they arise in the center.

The associate director of the center has approached the director to revise the transfer price policy to include only the variable costs. His argument is that the operating departments would thereby be encouraged to make greater use of the facility. The director's response is that she sees no reason why this should be so. "After all," she points out, "the operating departments need only so much time anyway; and besides, the various managers cannot buy computer time outside the company. So how could the transfer price affect their behavior?"

The associate director's response is that he knows of several instances where the operating departments have secured additional outside-the-company programming services so that the program submitted would require less running time. "In fact," he says, "I know of one case where the operating manager spent $300 on additional programming to save an estimated 2 time units of running time."

The director's response is, "He should have—after all, it cost us $105 every time we run the program!"

Required:
1. Do you agree with the associate director or the director? Explain.
2. Was the behavior of the operating manager (as described by the associate director) optimal as far as the whole company is concerned?
3. Assuming that the additional programming effort could not have been done inside the company, what is the maximum price that the operating manager should have paid?

14-8. **Preparation of Divisional Income Statements.** Butler Packing Company has two divisions. Division 1 is responsible for slaughtering and cutting the unprocessed meat. Division 2 processes meat such as hams, bacon, etc. Division 2 can buy meat from Division 1 or from outside suppliers. Division 1 can sell at the market price all the unprocessed meat that it can produce. The current year's income statement for the company is as follows:

Sales			$2,600,000
Cost of goods sold:			
Beginning inventory		0	
Processing costs:			
Livestock costs, Division 1		$ 600,000	
Labor, Division 1		400,000	
Overhead, Division 1		500,000	
Processing Supplies, Division 2		200,000	
Labor, Division 2		300,000	
Overhead, Division 2		100,000	
Cost of goods available for sale		$2,100,000	
Less ending inventory cost:			
Division 1	$ 0		
Division 2	200,000	200,000	1,900,000
Gross margin			$ 700,000
Operating expenses:			
Sales & administrative, Division 1		$ 120,000	
Sales & administrative, Division 2		100,000	
Central office overhead		100,000	$ 320,000
Income before income tax			$ 380,000

The ending inventory of $200,000 is valued at the product cost incurred in Division 1. This inventory is as yet unprocessed. The market value unprocessed is $300,000. The sales for the year can be broken down as follows:

Division 1 (to outsiders)	$ 600,000
Division 2	2,000,000
	$2,600,000

The market value of the unprocessed meat actually transferred from Division 1 to Division 2 (exclusive of the ending inventory) was $1,800,000.

Required:
1. Prepare division income statements that might be used to evaluate the performance of the two division managers.

2. Explain the transfer pricing policy you have used in preparing the statements.
3. Can you see any conflict in the policy you have used if this same transfer price is to be used for decision making? Explain.

14-9. Preparation of Divisional Income Statements. A large farming company has 2 divisions; one produces grain, and the other sells the grain. As soon as the grain is produced, it is transferred to the selling division where it is stored in anticipation of future sales at a higher price.

During the year, 3 grain crops of 1,900,000 bushels each were produced. All 3 have now been sold, although some were held in inventory for various periods of time. The market price at production time was $4 per bushel for the first crop, $5 per bushel for the second, and $3 per bushel for the third. Assume no beginning inventories.

The annual income statement for the entire company is as follows:

Revenue:		
Sales (5,700,000 bushels)		$28,300,000
Cost:		
Producing division labor and materials	$13,250,000	
Selling division labor	1,500,000	
Producing division overhead	8,250,000	
Selling division overhead	900,000	
Total cost		$23,900,000
Net income		$ 4,400,000

Required:

The company president is very pleased with the total profit but wants to determine whether the price speculation activities of the selling division are earning a profit. You are requested to prepare divisional income statements for the producing division and the selling division. Decide what type of transfer price, market or cost, to use. Explain which transfer price is better. Are the division income statements useful? Explain.

14-10. Evaluation of a Division Using ROI. A company has a division which manufactures and sells furniture. The income statement of this division is as follows:

Sales		$17,000,000
Division costs:		
Variable cost	$12,000,000	
Fixed cost	4,000,000	16,000,000
Division contribution margin		$ 1,000,000
Allocated central office overhead		500,000
Net income		$ 500,000
Investment allocated to division.................		$ 5,000,000
ROI		10 percent

The management is disturbed at the low ROI. The corporate treasurer indicates that the company can earn at least 20 percent on investment funds from any number of other projects. Furthermore, the treasurer points out that the investment is actually understated because the plant and facility carried at cost of $5,000,000 could be disposed of for about $8,000,000.

An investigation reveals that 50 percent of the division's fixed cost of $4,000,000 cannot be eliminated even if the division is sold. The allocated central office overhead is a pro rata share of operating the corporate offices, and sale of the division would not affect this cost either.

Required:

1. Assuming that an expenditure of $1,000,000 annually would maintain the facility in good operating condition for at least 10 years, should the division be sold? Explain.
2. If not, does a better way of reporting the ROI exist that would alert management to consider selling if volume begins to decline?

14-11. Internal or External Sales. Wittkamp Company has the capacity to manufacture 700 units of a part used in machine tool production. This part is manufactured in batch lots of 100 units each. Division A makes this part at a uniform variable cost of $5 per unit. The manufactured batches can be sold either to outside customers or to Division B where the parts are used in machine tool assembly.

Data with respect to prices per batch from outside sales are given below along with prices charged to outsiders after further processing in Division B:

Batch No.	Division A Price to Outside Customers	Division B Price to Outside Customers After Additional Processing	Division B Additional Processing Costs Per Batch
1	$16	$35	$13
2	15	32	13
3	14	30	13
4	13	26	12
5	12	22	12
6	11	20	12
7	10	20	11

Required:

Decide which batches should be sold after production in Division A and which batches should be transferred to Division B for further processing. Show computations.

14-12. Transfer Pricing Problem. The Leisure Company has a producing division (Division 1) which supplies several parts to another producing division (Division 2) which produces the main product. These component parts are listed as follows with relevant cost information, including outside supplier prices:

Component No.	Variable Cost Per Unit	Quantity Produced	Outside Price
1	$11	25,000	$14.50
2	15	35,000	19.20
3	7	15,000	9.40
4	5	15,000	9.60

The out-of-pocket fixed cost of Division 1 amounts to $270,000. This cost consists of the salaries and other overhead. In addition, the fixed cost which is not out-of-pocket (consisting mainly of depreciation on machinery) amounts to $90,000 per period. In calculating unit cost, the total fixed cost of $360,000 is allocated based on units produced to arrive at a full cost.

A full cost transfer price is used. In Division 2, which uses the 4 components, the manager has authority to buy inside the company or to buy from an outside supplier. The outside prices vary somewhat throughout the year.

After calculating the full cost, the manager of Division 2 notices that outside purchase prices of Components 1 and 3 are lower than the transfer prices and places orders with outside suppliers. Division 1 stops producing these two components, reallocates the fixed cost to the remaining units, and adjusts the full cost transfer prices.

Required:

1.   Reallocate the fixed cost and determine the adjusted transfer prices based on full cost of the remaining products. If no communication between the two divisions occurs, what action will the manager of Division 2 likely take?
2.   Comment on the deficiencies of the full cost transfer price system.
3.   What if the items transferred to Division 2 from Division 1 are 100 percent of Division 1's business. Devise a method of assigning the fixed cost of Division 1 to Division 2 that will not cause Division 2 to buy outside when the components could be produced by Division 1.
4.   What if the items transferred to Division 2 from Division 1 are 4 percent of Division 1's total business. How would your answer to Part 3 change?

14-13. **Evaluation of Alternative Transfer Prices.** The Stratton Company has a division that manufactures shafts, some of which are sold to other divisions and to outside customers. This division is organized in two sections as follows:

Section 1—Machining and Grinding: This highly mechanized section has much heavy equipment that is used to give shape to the shafts and to perform grinding operations on shafts with special requirements.

Section 2—Cleaning and Packing: This section consists primarily of workers who clean and pack all shafts.

The costing system used by the company charges materials, direct labor, and overhead to each order. Labor, materials, and one-third of overhead in both sections are considered to be variable. The overhead is allocated on the basis of labor cost for normal activity levels. Furthermore, the rate is a division-wide rate, not by section. This rate is developed as follows:

	Direct Labor Payroll	Overhead
Section 1 (70% of capacity)	$200,000	$ 900,000
Section 2 (60% of capacity)	600,000	300,000
Total division	$800,000	$1,200,000

$$\text{Overhead rate:} \frac{\$1,200,000}{\$800,000} = 150 \text{ percent of labor cost}$$

The average wage for Section 1 is $15 per hour; for Section 2, $10 per hour. A full cost transfer price is used for selling shafts to other producing divisions. If an order is placed by another producing division that calls for $100 of materials and 2 hours of labor time in each section, the price that is quoted would be arrived at as follows:

	Hours	Total
Labor:		
Section 1	2	$ 30
Section 2	2	20
		$ 50
Overhead (150% × $50)		75
Materials		100
Transfer price		$225

The assistant to the controller has been considering a change in the costing system whereby an overhead rate would be developed for each section. It is believed that such a system would give a more equitable price for the work done for other divisions and would be a better basis for pricing outside sales. Since the shaft sold to outside customers is competitive, the price is determined by bid and negotiations; and the primary factor in deciding whether to accept or reject business is the order's profit. At times, the division is operating near enough to capacity that outside work must be stopped if inside work is to be done.

At the moment two orders are being considered and are from another division that can buy either inside or outside the company. The details on the two orders are:

	Order 1	Order 2
Materials	$500	$200
Labor:		
Section 1	3 hours	6 hours
Section 2	3 hours	1 hour

Required:

1. Calculate the transfer prices for the two orders under the present system. Then, calculate the transfer prices under the proposed system.
2. If the market price were $700 for Order 1 and $600 for Order 2, how might management decisions in both buying and selling divisions be affected by the overhead system?
3. Recalculate the transfer prices for the two orders based on variable cost only. Assume a sectional variable overhead rate is used in the manufacturing division.
4. Which system do you prefer? Why?

14-14. **Transfer Price Decision.** The Elkton Subsidiary of Nordic Instruments Inc. manufactures small printed circuit boards and has the capacity to make 100,000 units of a given model each year. At the present time, only 75,000 units are being made each year and are sold to an outside customer for $7.50 a unit.

Fixed manufacturing costs are applied on the basis of an annual production of 100,000 units each year. Total fixed cost for the year is $175,000. The total unit cost of each circuit board is $6.50. The Reeves Subsidiary has been purchasing this type of circuit board from an outside supplier at a price of $7.50 per unit. The president of the company requests that the Elkton Subsidiary deliver 25,000 circuit boards to the Reeves Subsidiary at a price equal to the variable cost.

The superintendent of Elkton states that the division gains no advantage by selling at variable cost. No contribution is made to the recovery of the fixed cost. Furthermore, the superintendent states that the company gains nothing. The fixed cost of Elkton must be recovered, and Reeves should pay the full price of $7.50 as it would by buying outside.

Required:

1. Is the argument of the superintendent valid? Explain.
2. What is the variable cost of manufacturing each circuit board?
3. Describe a pricing system that should benefit the company and be acceptable to each division.

14-15. Internal Pricing Decision. Alan William is the manager of the Sterling Division of Triple-A Machine Company. This division manufactures spring assemblies that are sold to various outside customers at a price of $32 per unit.

Recently the division has been operating below normal capacity at 550,000 machine hours. Normal capacity has been defined as 700,000 machine hours and is approximately equal to the practical capacity. Each assembly requires 15 minutes of machine time. The direct materials and direct labor cost per assembly is $16.20, and overhead varies at the rate of $8.40 per machine hour. The total fixed overhead for the year is $3,521,000.

William's division has just been awarded a contract for the sale of 400,000 units in another country at a unit price of $26. This contract will not interfere with the regular sales at a price of $32, and it is anticipated that this contract can be renewed in future years.

The Jessop Division of the company has started production of a product line that will require 400,000 units of the spring assembly made by the Sterling Division. The president of the company states that the assemblies should be transferred between the divisions at the variable cost to the Sterling Division. If Sterling Division does not furnish the units, the Jessop Division will be forced to purchase the assemblies on the outside market at $32 apiece. With higher costs, Jessop will have lower profits on the sale of the end products.

Required:

1. Determine the variable cost to produce each spring assembly.
2. Under the circumstances, should the Sterling Division supply the Jessop Division?
3. What price should be used for the internal transfer, assuming a transfer should be made?

14-16. ROI and Residual Income. Kimber-Zack Corporation is a highly diversified company organized into autonomous divisions along product lines. The autonomy permits division managers a significant amount of authority in operating their divisions. Each manager is responsible for sales, cost of operations, acquisition of division assets, management of accounts receivable and inventories, and use of existing facilities. Cash management is centralized at the corporate home office. Divisions are permitted cash for their normal operating needs, but all excess cash is transferred to the corporate home office.

Division managers are responsible for presenting requests for capital expenditures (to acquire assets, expand existing facilities, or make any other long-term investment) to corporate management for approval. Once the proposals are analyzed and evaluated, corporate management decides whether to commit funds to the requests.

Kimber-Zack adopted a ROI measure several years ago. The measure uses division direct profit and an investment base composed of fixed assets employed plus accounts receivable and inventories. ROI is used to evaluate the performance of each division, and it is the primary factor in assessing salary increases each year. Also, changes in the ROI from year to year affect the amount of the annual bonus.

ROI has grown over the years for each division. However, the company's overall ROI has declined in recent years. Cash balances are increasing at the corporate level, and investments in marketable securities are growing. Idle cash and marketable securities do not earn as good a rate of return as division capital investments.

The following data (with 000s omitted) show the operating results for the Apparel Division and the Sports Gear Division for the last three years:

	Apparel Division			Sports Gear Division		
	1992	1993	1994	1992	1993	1994
Estimated industry sales	$10,000	$11,000	$12,100	$5,000	$6,250	$7,500
Division sales..................................	$ 1,200	$ 1,380	$ 1,587	$ 500	$ 650	$ 780
Division direct costs:						
Variable costs	$ 360	$ 396	$ 467	$ 160	$ 182	$ 203
Discretionary fixed costs	480	490	500	180	210	240
Committed fixed costs	250	300	375	150	215	260
Total division direct costs......................	$ 1,090	$ 1,186	$ 1,342	$ 490	$ 607	$ 703
Division net profit	$ 110	$ 194	$ 245	$ 10	$ 43	$ 77
Investment base	$ 1,100	$ 1,200	$ 1,300	$ 125	$ 195	$ 280
ROI	10.00%	16.17%	18.85%	8.00%	22.05%	27.50%

The managers of both divisions were promoted to their positions in 1992. John Harris had been assistant division manager of the Apparel Division for six years prior to his appointment as manager of that division. The Sports Gear Division was created in 1990. Rose Knolting had served as assistant manager of the Toy Division for four years prior to becoming manager of the Sports Gear Division, when the latter position suddenly became available in late 1991.

Required:
1.   In general, is ROI an appropriate measure of performance? Explain.
2.   Explain how an overemphasis on ROI can result in a declining corporate ROI and increasing cash and marketable securities.
3.   Describe specific actions that might have caused this increase in 1994 ROI while the corporate ROI declined.
4.   Assuming the minimum desired rate of return is 12 percent for Apparel and 15 percent for Sports Gear, compute the residual income and the residual income percentage of both divisions for each year.
5.   Which division manager (Harris or Knolting) do you judge as the better manager? What are the reasons for your recommendation?

CASE 14A—Birch Paper Company[2]

"If I were to price these boxes any lower than $480 a thousand," said James Brunner, manager of Birch Paper Company's Thompson Division, "I'd be countermanding my order of last month for our salespeople to stop shaving their bids and to bid full-cost quotations. I've been trying for weeks to improve the quality of our business. And if I turn around now and accept this job at $430 or $450 or something less than $480, I'll be

[2]Copyright(C) 1957, 1985 by the President and Fellows of Harvard College. This case was prepared by William Rotch Linder under the supervision of Neil E. Harlan as the basis for class discussion rather than to illustrate either effective or ineffective handling of an administrative situation. Reprinted by permission of the Harvard Business School.

tearing down this program I've been working so hard to build up. The division can't very well show a profit by putting in bids which don't even cover a fair share of overhead costs, let alone give us a profit."

Birch Paper Company was a medium-sized, partly integrated paper company, producing white and kraft papers and paperboard. A portion of its paperboard output was converted into corrugated boxes by the Thompson division, which also printed and colored the outside surface of the boxes. Including Thompson, the company had four producing divisions and a timberland division, which supplied part of the company's pulp requirements.

For several years each division had been judged independently on the basis of its profit and ROI. Top management had been working to gain effective results from a policy of decentralizing responsibility and authority for all decisions but those relating to overall company policy. The company's top officials believed that in the past few years the concept of decentralization had been successfully applied and that company's profits and competitive position had definitely improved.

Early in 1993, the Northern Division designed a special display box for one of its papers in conjunction with the Thompson Division, which was equipped to make the box. Thompson's staff for package design and development spent several months perfecting the design, production methods, and materials that were to be used. Because of the unusual color and shape, these were far from standard. According to an agreement between the two divisions, the Thompson Division was reimbursed by the Northern Division for the cost of its design and development work.

When the specifications were all prepared, the Northern Division asked for bids on the box from the Thompson Division and from two outside companies. Each division manager was normally free to buy from whatever supplier he wished; and even on sales within the company, divisions were expected to meet the going market price if they wanted the business.

In 1993 the profit margins of converters such as the Thompson Division were being squeezed. Thompson, as did many other similar converters, bought its paperboard. Its function was to print, cut, and shape boxes. Though it bought most of its materials from other Birch divisions, most of Thompson's sales were made to outside customers. If Thompson got the order from Northern, it probably would buy its linerboard and corrugating medium from the Southern Division of Birch. The walls of a corrugated box consist of outside and inside sheets of linerboard sandwiching the fluted corrugating medium. About 70 percent of Thompson's out-of-pocket cost of $400 for the order represented the cost of linerboard and corrugating medium. Though Southern had been running below capacity and had excess inventory, it quoted the market price, which had not noticeably weakened as a result of the oversupply. Its out-of-pocket costs on both liner and corrugating medium were about 60 percent of its selling price.

Northern received bids on the boxes of $480 a thousand from Thompson, $430 a thousand from West Paper Company, and $432 a thousand from Eire Papers. Eire Papers offered to buy from Birch the outside linerboard with the special printing already on it but would supply its own inside liner and corrugating medium. The outside liner would be supplied by Southern at a price equivalent of $90 a thousand boxes and would be printed for $30 a thousand by Thompson. Of the $30, about $25 would be out-of-pocket costs.

Since this situation appeared to be a little unusual, William Kenton, manager of Northern, discussed the wide discrepancy of bids with Birch's commercial vice-president. He told the vice-president, "We sell in a very competitive market, where higher costs cannot be passed on. How can we be expected to show a decent profit and return on investment if we have to buy our supplies at more than 10 percent over the going market?"

Knowing that Mr. Brunner had on occasion in the past few months been unable to operate the Thompson Division at capacity, it seemed odd to the vice-president that Mr. Brunner would add the full 20 percent overhead and profit charge to his out-of-pocket costs. When asked about this, Mr. Brunner's answer was the statement that appears at the beginning of the case. He went on to say that having done the developmental work on the box and having received no profit on that, he felt entitled to a good markup on the production of the box itself.

The vice-president explored further the cost structure of the various divisions. He remembered a comment that the controller had made at a meeting the week before to the effect that costs which were variable for one division could be largely fixed for the company as a whole. He knew that, in the absence of specific orders from top management, Mr. Kenton would accept the lowest bid, which was that of the West Paper Company for $430. However, it would be possible for top management to order the acceptance of another bid if the situation warranted such action. And though the volume represented by the transactions in question was less than 5 percent of the volume of any of the divisions involved, other transactions could conceivably raise similar problems later.

Required:
1.   What is the economic impact to Birch Paper Company of the three alternatives for sourcing the product?
2.   Does goal congruence exist in this situation?
3.   What is an appropriate transfer price for the Thompson Division?
4.   What changes would you recommend for the transfer pricing system of the company?

CASE 14B—Erculean Electronics

Erculean Electronics is a division of a major communications equipment supplier. It designs, manufactures, assembles, and tests a wide variety of electronic linking assemblies. The largest percentage of its business is internal, meaning that about 45 percent of its assemblies becomes part of the division's own end products. But in the past few years, sales have gone to a growing array of customers including:

1.   Other sister divisions producing complementary products.
2.   Other communications companies, often direct competitors, that use similar assemblies with minor engineering changes.
3.   Automotive firms and automotive suppliers who are incorporating more electronic communications components into their products.
4.   Appliance manufacturers who use specialized linkages in their electronic products.
5.   Numerous international manufacturers in each of the above industries.

In short, Erculean is enjoying success in a very specialized market. The keys to its success are high quality products, an ability to adapt to a customer's needs quickly (sometimes in days), and highly dependable delivery to most customers on narrow just-in-time schedules. Another key has been Erculean's manufacturing prowess. It has always been cost conscious and on the edge of manufacturing technology and processes.

Manufacturing has expanded rapidly to meet the growth in demand. Also, since its original plants were in the high labor cost Midwest, it has sought relief in numerous ways. A brief description of its current manufacturing locations and capabilities introduces the problems facing Erculean managers:

1. The Jackson, Michigan plant is older but highly automated, and its production employees work under an Automotive Workers Union contract that guarantees its members 2,000 hours per year of employment. It is within 200 miles of 40 percent of Erculean customers. The number of workers at this plant has dropped from over 800 in 1974 to about 225 today. Most of these workers are very experienced and have adapted very well to the increased automation and robotics introduced in the early 1990s. Worker classifications have been reduced in the latest contract by 75 percent. But the average cash wage is over $15 per hour, and the fully-loaded rate is nearly $30 per hour.

2. A Tulsa, Oklahoma plant was built in the mid-1980s and is also highly automated; and, since 1990, its employees are represented by the International Electric Workers Union. The average cash wage is about two-thirds of the Michigan plant, and the fully-loaded rate is about half the Jackson plant. Few worker classifications exist, and the definition of "direct labor" differs considerably from the Jackson definition.

3. Outside subcontractors are used for certain products and when company plants are operating at capacity. Generally, Erculean controls materials quality by buying the materials, selling them to the subcontractors, and buying back the finished products. The subcontractors are suppliers of electronic subassemblies in other industries. These suppliers have different cost functions and may do different amounts of work depending on the contract requirements.

4. Six small border Mexican plants also produce the same linkages. These plants have extremely low labor rates, are labor intensive with little automation, produce lower volumes, but have very high quality. The wage cost is around $2.00 per hour, depending on the location and the peso exchange rate.

5. Other international production has not yet been needed, but Erculean is already negotiating for a Malaysian facility. Potential European customers are pushing for close proximity plants for sourcing.

In the U.S. plants under recent labor contracts, new employees enter at lower wage rates or under a temporary status with no benefits. This adds to the already confusing labor costing situation.

Very fundamental questions need answers:

1. Should the cost accounting system define costs the same way for all plants?
2. How should labor cost be defined?
3. What are variable production costs?
4. How should "where to produce" decisions be made?
5. On which costs should bids for new business be based?
6. What transfer pricing policies are appropriate for intracompany business?

Required:

First, suggest an approach in the form of a policy on how costs might be incorporated in the bidding and pricing procedures for external business.

Second, suggest an approach in the form of a policy to price intracompany transfers between Erculean and other divisions of the communications equipment firm.

Third, suggest an approach to match cost functions, types of production, volumes, sources of business, and sales revenues that might help Erculean optimize its profits.

Part Five

Special Topics

Chapter Fifteen

Cost Estimation

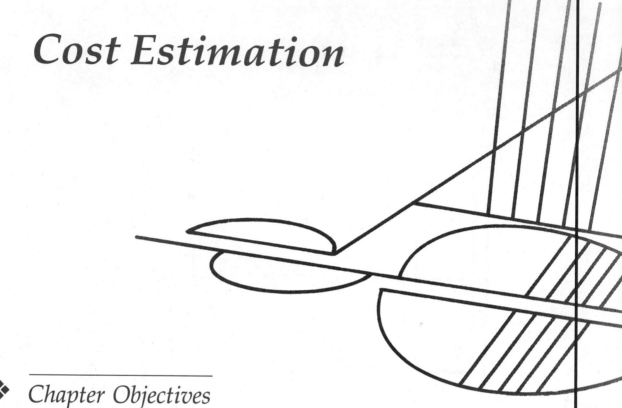

❖ *Chapter Objectives*

After studying Chapter 15, you will be able to:

1. Identify and explain the differences in the behavior of variable costs, fixed costs, semivariable costs, and step costs.
2. Identify five techniques for separating semivariable costs into fixed and variable components.
3. Separate semivariable costs into fixed and variable components by visual inspection, by the high-low method, and by regression.
4. Explain the importance of "goodness of fit" when statistically determining a formula for cost behavior.
5. Describe how the standard deviation principle can be applied in cost control.
6. Explain how multiple and nonlinear regression can be used in identifying cost behavior.
7. Describe the use of trend analyses in time series data.

■ *Cost Behavior in the Emergency Room* ■

The administrator of Methodist General Hospital believes the emergency room is costing the hospital too much to operate in light of the revenues generated by emergency patients. He is particularly concerned about an agreement with the county government to treat transient patients without demanding payment for services. The county agreed to share costs for the emergency operations related to such patients on 60/40 basis; 60 percent by the county and 40 percent by the hospital. However, the county disagrees with the costs submitted by the hospital, and the controller believes the county is not covering its fair share of the costs.

The administrator has asked the controller to prepare an analysis that shows the costs of performing the various tasks in the emergency room and where patients go from the emergency room. The controller knows that most of the emergency room costs are fixed, semivariable, or semifixed. Identifying costs with the various tasks and relating tasks to patients present a challenging analysis the hospital has not done before. She realizes that cost behavior will play a significant role in any decisions about whether to maintain or eliminate the emergency room. She knows the importance of task identification and cost driver selection to cost behavior determination. What techniques can she use to accomplish her analysis?

In Chapter 3 we learned that the existence of activities causes the incurrence of costs. Cost drivers are the means of identifying costs with activities and groupings of activities and tracing costs to cost objectives, such as products and services. Cost behavior describes the relationship between costs and an activity as the level of activity increases or decreases. Decision processes should be based on how changing activity levels affect total costs. With a knowledge of cost behavior, managers can estimate how costs are affected as future activity levels change, leading to better decisions. Determining cost behavior is also important to management's understanding of overhead costs, marketing costs, and general and administrative expenses and to the proper implementation of budgets and budgetary controls. Managers can control costs with more confidence when they take cost behavior patterns into consideration.

This chapter reviews the common cost behavior characteristics and presents approaches to estimating the cost behavior pattern for various activities. It also shows how some statistical concepts can aid the cost control process. Since forecasting activities and costs in the future is critical to many of the decisions management faces, techniques for analyzing trends will also be explored.

TYPES OF COST BEHAVIOR

Chapter 2 discussed the common cost behavior patterns and showed graphs of such patterns within the relevant range. Below is a brief review of ideas that are essential for the contents of the sections that follow. For more detail, return to Chapter 2.

Variable Cost

A **variable cost** is a cost that varies in total amount in direct proportion to changes in activity or output. A decrease in activity brings a proportional decrease in total cost; an increase in activity results in a proportional increase in total cost. For example, if the activity is typing and the cost per page is $1.50, the cost driver is the number of pages typed. The total cost of typing will increase at the constant rate of $1.50 per page. Similarly, a hospital will find that laundry costs tend to vary with the number of hospital beds occupied. An insurance company may find that some claims processing costs vary according to the number of claims processed. The point is that a variable cost is constant per unit of the cost driver representing the activity.

Fixed Cost

A **fixed cost** is constant in total amount when changes occur in activity levels within some range of activity. Fixed costs tend to be lumps of dollars rather than a rate, like variable costs. Examples of fixed costs are supervision, rent, depreciation, insurance, and property taxes.

By definition, the total fixed costs are constant, which means they do not change as the level of activity changes. Expressed using a per unit of activity basis, fixed costs vary as activity changes—unit costs decrease as activity increases; unit costs increase as activity decreases. The idea that fixed costs are constant does not mean that a fixed cost cannot be changed. As we saw in Chapter 2, outside influences or decisions by management may cause the level of fixed cost to change.

Semivariable and Semifixed Costs

Some costs are neither strictly variable nor fixed. Some of these we call **semivariable costs**. Semivariable means the cost may change in total but not in proportion to the change in activity. These costs are characterized by possessing attributes of both variable and fixed costs. The fixed cost portion is the minimum cost required if some activity takes place, but as activity increases, total costs increase above this minimum at the proportionate rate. Typical examples are utilities, telephone, and repairs and maintenance.

Semifixed costs are typified by step increases in costs with changes in activity. Increases are lumps of costs. For example, a company may operate with one design engineer up to a point where the plant is operating at 10,000 machine hours per year. After that point, one person cannot handle the design engineering workload. Therefore, at 10,000 hours, another design engineer must be hired; and the salary level is doubled. The fixed cost has reached a new plateau. When volume reaches 20,000 machine hours, a third engineer must be hired; and the salary level increases to a still higher level.

Other Cost Behavior

Some costs do not fit the behavior patterns presented above because these costs are disjointed or otherwise nonlinear in nature. For example, consider the behavior of the following two costs:

1. A lease agreement for a piece of machining equipment calls for a monthly payment schedule based on the following table:
    (a) Minimum $600 per month for 0 to 500 machine hours.
    (b) $3 per hour for 501 to 700 machine hours.
    (c) $2 per hour for 701 to 900 machine hours.
    (d) $1 per hour for 901 and above machine hours.
    A graph depicting this cost behavior appears as Graph (A) in Figure 15.1.
2. The most widely discussed nonlinear cost pattern used in accounting is based on the learning-curve phenomenon. A typical learning-curve cost pattern is presented as Graph (B) in Figure 15.1. As discussed in Appendix A to Chapter 9, the learning-curve phenomenon exists when unit or average unit manufacturing costs decline in a systematic manner as cumulative production increases. Graph (B) is based on an 80 percent learning rate.

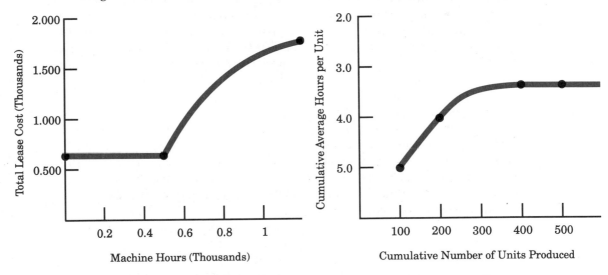

Figure 15.1   Examples of Other Cost Behavior

SIGNIFICANCE OF COST BEHAVIOR TO DECISION MAKING AND CONTROL

An alert manager will identify the cost behavior associated with a cost driver and its related activity. Such a manager is in a better position to plan, make decisions, control costs, and manage costs. To understand more fully the significance of a manager's determination and understanding of cost behavior, we look at three areas: trends in fixed costs, decision making, and planning and control.

Trends in Fixed Costs

With the many changes taking place in the manufacturing environment, organizations are finding an increasing portion of their total costs are fixed costs. A number of reasons exist for this situation. The following are a few of the more critical changes taking place.

Implementation of more automated equipment is replacing variable labor costs and a major share of the variable overhead costs. Thus, fixed costs are becoming a more significant part of total costs. Costs such as depreciation, taxes, insurance, and fixed maintenance charges are substantially higher. Some industries, for example the steel and automobile industries, are becoming essentially fixed cost industries, with variable costs playing a less important role than was once the case.

Another factor that has helped to increase fixed costs significantly is the movement in some industries toward a guaranteed annual wage for production workers. Employees who were once hourly wage earners are now becoming salaried. With the use of more automated equipment, the workers a company has may not represent "touch labor," that is work directly on the product. Instead, the production worker may monitor production by means of a television screen, or may watch to see that the equipment is operating as it should and is properly supplied with materials. The production line employee is handling more of the functions normally associated with indirect labor, and the cost is a fixed cost.

Although a significant shift to automation has occurred in many larger industries and even in some medium-sized industries, many companies and service organizations still operate in a more conventional way, without automated equipment and with direct labor on an hourly basis. Society seldom changes completely. For example, you can travel from one place to another by jet plane, but the automobile is also still used. Likewise, different cost behavior patterns will likely coexist.

Decision Making

Cost behavior affects the decisions management makes. Variable costs are the incremental or differential costs in most decisions. Fixed costs change only if the specific decision includes a change in the capacity-providing activities that result in increasing or decreasing the level of fixed costs.

Cost-based pricing requires a good understanding of cost behavior because fixed costs pose conceptual problems when converted to per unit amounts. Fixed costs per unit assume a given capacity level. If the volume of production and sales is other than the capacity contemplated in determining the cost-based price, the fixed cost component of the total cost yields a misleading price. Managers must know which costs are fixed as well as anticipated capacity levels in order to make good pricing decisions.

Planning and Control

A company plans for and controls variable costs differently than it plans for and controls fixed costs. Variable costs are planned in terms of input/output relationships, for example, for each unit produced, a price per unit of materials times the number of units of materials or the labor rate times the number of labor hours. Once operations are underway, levels of activities may change. The input/output relationships identify changes in resources necessary to respond to the change in activity. If activity levels increase, this signals that more resources (materials, labor, or variable overhead) are needed. If activity levels decrease, the resources are not needed; and procedures can be triggered to stop purchases and reassign or lay-off workers. In cases where more materials or labor time are used than are called for in the input/output relationship, inefficiencies and waste are in excess of the levels anticipated; and managers must investigate causes and eliminate or reduce the financial impact of the unfavorable variations.

Fixed costs, on the other hand, are planned for on at least an annual basis, if not longer. Control of fixed costs is exercised at two points in time. The first point is when the decision is made to incur a fixed cost. Management evaluates the need for incurrence of the cost and makes the decision to move forward or reject the proposal. Once fixed costs are incurred, another point of control enters, that being the daily decisions on how to best use the capacity provided by the cost. For example, a university makes a decision to build a new classroom and faculty office building. That decision is the first point of control. After construction, control is implemented in using the building to its maximum capacity. That will occur if classes are scheduled throughout the day and evening.

Another difference in the planning and control of variable and fixed costs is the level at which costs are controllable. Variable costs can be controlled at the lowest supervisory level. Fixed costs are often controllable only at higher managerial levels.

COST ESTIMATION

Cost estimation is the process of estimating a cost relationship with activity for an individual cost item or grouping of costs. We typically express this relationship as an equation that reflects the cost behavior within the relevant range. Although a number of techniques exist for estimating a cost-to-activity relationship, we will discuss five techniques: (1) account analysis, (2) engineering approach, (3) scattergraph and visual fit, (4) high-low method, and (5) regression analysis.

Since this book emphasizes the use of managerial accounting data, it is not the purpose of our discussion to make you an expert in the above techniques. However, we try to show you how these techniques can be used in the various management functions.

Account Analysis

In **account analysis,** accountants estimate the variable and fixed cost behavior of a particular cost by evaluating information from two sources. First, the accountant reviews and interprets managerial policies with respect to the cost. Second, the accountant inspects the historical activity of the cost. All cost accounts are classified as fixed or variable. If a cost shows semivariable or semifixed cost behavior, the analyst either (1) makes a subjective estimate of the variable and fixed portions of the cost or (2) classifies the account according to the preponderant cost behavior. Unit variable costs are estimated by dividing total variable costs by quantity of the cost driver.

Account analysis is fairly accurate for determining cost behavior in many cases. Vendor invoices, for instance, show that direct materials have a variable cost behavior, and leasing costs are fixed. A telephone bill is a semivariable cost; one portion is fixed for the minimum monthly charge, and the remainder may be variable with usage.

Account analysis has limited data requirements and is simple to implement. The judgment necessary to make the method work comes from experienced managers and accountants who are familiar with the operations and management policies. Because operating results are required for only one period, this method is good for new products or situations involving rapid changes in products or technologies.

The two primary disadvantages of this method are its lack of a range of observations and its subjectivity. Using judgment generates two potential issues: (1) different analysts may develop different cost estimates from the same data, and (2) the results of analysis may have significant financial consequences for the analyst, which means the analyst will likely show self-serving estimates. Another potential weakness in the method is that data used in the analysis may reflect unusual circumstances or inefficient operations, as is likely with new products. These factors become incorporated in the subsequent cost estimates. This method is also at the mercy of the quality of the detailed chart of accounts and transaction coding.

Engineering Approach

The **engineering approach** uses analysis and direct observation of processes to identify the relationship between inputs and outputs and then quantifies an expected cost behavior. The basic issue in manufacturing a product is determining the amount of direct materials, direct labor, and overhead required to run a given process. For a service, the question relates primarily to the labor and overhead costs.

One method of applying this approach to a product, such as a home electric generator, is to make a list of all materials, subassemblies, labor tasks, and overhead costs necessary for the manufacturing process. This is similar to "bills of material" for the materials and subassemblies and "routings" for labor and overhead. Engineering specifications and vendor information can be used to quantify the units of the various materials and subassemblies. Time and motion studies can help estimate the amount of time required for the tasks to be performed. Other analyses will be used to assess the overhead relationships to the process. Once quantities and time are determined, those amounts are priced out at appropriate materials prices, labor rates, and overhead rates.

The methodology just described does not consider the efficiency with which inputs are converted into outputs. The engineering approach goes one step further to provide a specific measure for efficiency—converting inputs to outputs. That is what makes the engineering approach valuable to most organizations.

A major advantage of the engineering approach is that it details each step required to perform a task. This permits transfer of information to similar tasks in different situations. It also allows an organization to review productivity and identify strengths and weaknesses in the process. Another advantage is that it does not require historical accounting data. It is, therefore, a useful approach in estimating costs of new products and services. The major disadvantage is the expensive nature of the approach. For example, time and motion studies require in-depth examinations of task and close observations of individuals performing each task. An additional disadvantage is that estimates made by the engineering approach are often based on near-optimal working conditions. Since actual working conditions are generally less than optimal, uncontrollable variations in cost performance are likely to occur.

Scattergraph and Visual Fit

An approach that yields rough approximations to fixed and variable costs is called **scattergraph and visual fit**. With the advent of personal computers and laptop computers, the mechanical nature of this approach loses its appeal. When the analyst has data, the computer can graph the observations and estimate cost behavior quickly. However, we present the details below because, in many cases, it can be used in a preliminary analysis and can easily be applied.

The first step in applying the approach is to graph each observation, with cost on the vertical axis and activity or cost driver on the horizontal axis. The second step is to fit visually and judgmentally a line to the data. Care should be taken so that the distances of the observations above the line are approximately equal to the distances of the observations below the line. The line represents the data as a series of conditional expected values, a line of average. The statistical term for a line of average is a line of regression. For example, Figure 15.2 shows a graph of maintenance cost and hours of operation. The data for this graph are as follows:

Hours (X)	Maintenance Cost (Y)
50	$120
30	110
10	60
50	150
40	100
30	80
20	70
60	150
40	110
20	50

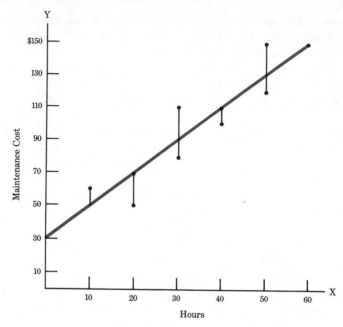

Figure 15.2 A Line of Regression (Visually Fitted)

The third step is to estimate the cost behavior from the plotted line. The variable cost per hour is indicated by the slope of the line, and the fixed cost is measured where the line begins at zero hours of activity. In the maintenance cost example, the fixed cost is at the Y-intercept and is $30. The variable costs can be calculated by subtracting fixed costs from total costs at some point along the line. Let's select 40 hours of operation. The cost indicated by the line at 40 hours is approximately $110. Compute variable costs as follows:

Total costs at 40 hours of operation	$110
Less fixed costs	30
Variable costs	$ 80

$$\frac{\$80 \text{ variable costs}}{40 \text{ hours}} = \$2 \text{ per hour of operation}$$

This analysis yields a cost estimating equation of:

$$\text{Total cost} = \$30 + \$2 \text{ per hour}$$

When used by itself, the scattergraph and visual fit approach is limited by the judgment of the person drawing the line through the data. Reasonable people will disagree on the slope and intercept for a given graph. However, most of the lines that judgment says could reasonably represent the data will converge near the center of the data. This means a visual fit may be a useful way to obtain rough approximations near the center of the data. Care should be taken with estimates away from the center, because the further from the central area, the larger the errors that may occur in estimates of fixed and variable costs.

High-Low Method

Another method for obtaining rough approximations to fixed and variable costs is the **high-low method**. Choose observations associated with the highest and the lowest activity levels, not the highest and lowest costs. The first step is to list the observed costs for various hours of activity in order from the highest number of hours in the range to the lowest. The second step is to divide the difference in hours between the highest and the lowest levels into the difference in cost for the corresponding hours to arrive at a rate of variable cost per hour. For example, the costs of supplies for several months at various hours of operation are as follows:

	Hours of Activity	Supplies Cost
High	95,000	$397,000
	90,000	377,000
	87,000	365,000
	82,000	345,000
	78,000	329,000
	75,000	317,000
	66,000	281,000
	58,000	239,000
Low	50,000	217,000

The difference in hours is 45,000 (95,000 − 50,000), and the difference in cost is $180,000 ($397,000 − $217,000). The variable supplies cost per hour is computed below:

$$\frac{\text{Cost at highest activity} - \text{Cost at lowest activity}}{\text{Highest activity} - \text{Lowest activity}} =$$

$$\frac{\text{Difference in cost}}{\text{Difference in hours}} = \frac{\$180,000}{45,000} = \$4 \text{ variable cost per hour}$$

The fixed cost is estimated by using the total cost at either the highest or lowest level and subtracting the estimated total variable cost for that level:

Total fixed cost = Total cost at highest activity − (Variable cost per unit × Highest activity)

or

Total fixed cost = Total cost at lowest activity − (Variable cost per unit × Lowest activity)

If the variable cost is calculated correctly, the fixed cost will be the same at both the high and low points. For the above illustration, the calculation of total fixed cost is as follows:

Total fixed cost = $397,000 − ($4 variable cost per hour × 95,000 hours)
                 = $397,000 − $380,000
                 = $17,000

or

Total fixed cost = $217,000 − ($4 variable cost per hour × 50,000 hours)
                 = $217,000 − $200,000
                 = $17,000

The cost estimation equation that results from the high-low method is:

Total cost = $17,000 + $4 per hour

Occasionally, either the highest or lowest activity or the cost associated with one of those points is obviously an outlier to the remaining data. When this happens, use the next high or low observation that appears to align better with the data.

The high-low method is simple and can be used in a multiplicity of situations. Its primary disadvantage is that two points from all of the observations will only produce reliable estimates of fixed and variable cost behavior if the extreme points are representative of the points in between. Otherwise, distorted results may occur. In a number of cases, only two points exist and the cost estimate must use these as high and low points.

REGRESSION AND CORRELATION ANALYSES

To this point in the chapter, we have discussed techniques that use only some of the data available and produce subjective estimates. If enough quality data are available, statistical techniques are available that use all of the data and provide objective results.

Regression and correlation analyses are statistical techniques that provide information for making business decisions. We will concentrate on using the results, not on details of the techniques.

Regression analysis fits a line to the cost and activity data using the least squares method. **Correlation analysis** deals with the "goodness of fit" in the relationship between costs and activity as identified by the **regression line**. Both analyses are important to finding relationships and establishing the significance of that relationship. Otherwise the cost estimating equation could yield distortions.

Linear regression is a statistical tool for describing the movement of one variable based on the movement of another variable. In determining cost behavior, we want to know if the movement in costs is related to the movement in activity. The dependent variable (y) is what we want to predict (costs, in our case). The independent variable (x) (the activity base for cost behavior) is used to predict the dependent variable. The cost behavior is expressed as a line of regression.

Least Squares Method

A line of regression can be fitted precisely to a large quantity of data by the least squares method. The high-low method is an average computed from data taken only at the high and low points of the range, but the least squares method includes all data within the range. The line of regression is determined so that the algebraic sum of the squared deviations from that line is at a minimum. The line of regression is derived by solving two simultaneous equations which are based on the condition that the sum of deviations above the line equals the sum of deviations below the line.

The equation for the determination of a straight line is given as follows:

$$y = a + bx$$

This equation states that the value of "y" is equal to a point "a" plus a factor of variability applied to "x." In the example on visual fit, "a" was the $30 of fixed cost. The factor "b" was the change in "y" in relation to the change in "x." In the example, "y" increased by $2 for each increase in hours. Hence, the estimating equation was:

$$y = \$30 + \$2x$$

As another illustration, assume that supplies cost for various hours of operation has been recorded and that computations have been made as shown:

Hours x	Supplies Cost y	x²	xy
30	$ 500	900	$ 15,000
50	650	2,500	32,500
20	300	400	6,000
10	300	100	3,000
60	900	3,600	54,000
50	750	2,500	37,500
40	650	1,600	26,000
60	700	3,600	42,000
30	450	900	13,500
10	350	100	3,500
40	600	1,600	24,000
20	450	400	9,000
Σ x = 420	Σ y = $6,600	Σ x² = 18,200	Σ xy = $266,000

Two equations are used in obtaining a line of regression. These equations represent all of the data. (The letter n is used for the number of items of data.)

Equation (1): $y = na + b\Sigma x$
Equation (2): $xy = xa + b\Sigma x^2$

Refer to the preceding data, substitute values and solve the two equations for a and b simultaneously:

Equation (1): $6,600 = 12a + 420b
Equation (2): $266,000 = 420a + 18,200b

To solve for *b*, multiply Equation (1) by 35 (420/12):

Equation (3): $231,000 = 420a + 14,700b

Subtract Equation (3) from Equation (2); the a values will cancel to yield the following:

$35,000 = 3,500b
b = $10, the rate of variable supplies cost per hour

Substitute the value of *b* in Equation (1) and solve for *a* as follows:

$6,600 = 12a + 4,200
12a = $2,400
a = $200, estimated fixed supplies cost

A line of regression for the data given is shown in Figure 15.3.

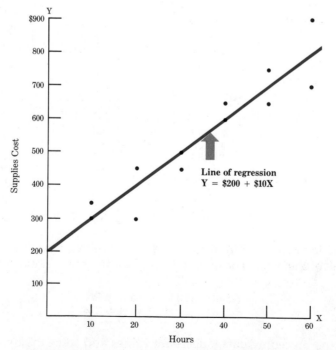

Figure 15.3   A Line of Regression (Least Squares Method)

In measuring the relationship between the cost and activity, we are interested in more than just an equation for estimating cost. We also want to know the "goodness of fit" for the correlation of the regression line to the cost and activity data and the "reliability" of the estimates of cost. This section discusses some of the measures available for assessing goodness of fit and reliability.

Goodness of Fit   The relationship between cost and activity is called correlation. At times costs may be randomly distributed and are not at all related to the cost driver used in defining the relationship. This is illustrated in Figure 15.4.

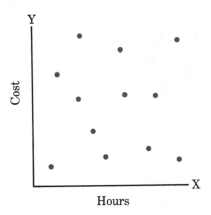

Figure 15.4   No Correlation

At the other extreme, the relationship may be so close that the data can almost be plotted on a line, as shown in Figure 15.5.

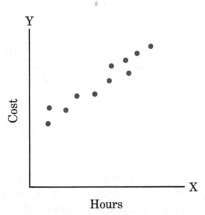

Figure 15.5   Positive Correlation

Between these extremes the degree of correlation may not be so evident. A high degree of correlation exists when the regression line explains most of the variation in the data. Assume, for example, a situation with all data lying relatively close to a line of regression for costs related to hours of operation. Cost data are plotted on the graph in Figure 15.6.

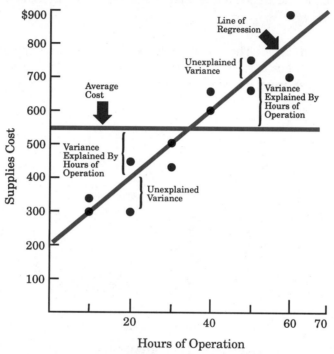

Figure 15.6   Explanation of Correlation

The average is computed in the conventional way by adding the costs and dividing by the number of items. In this case, the average is $550. Any variance between the line of regression and the average can be explained by hours of operation. The unexplained variances are the variances between the actual costs and the line of regression. In this illustration, a large part of the variance from the average can be explained by hours of operation; only a small amount is unexplained. Hence, a good correlation exists between cost and hours.

The degree of correlation is measured by the **coefficient of determination,** most frequently designated as r^2. The equation for r^2 is given as follows:

$$r^2 = 1 - \frac{\text{Unexplained variance}}{\text{Total variance}}$$

The r^2 figure can vary from 0 to 1. An r^2 close to 0 would indicate that the regression line does not describe the data. That is, the regression line is nearly horizontal, and little of the variation in y is explained by the variation in x. If the regression line is very descriptive of the data, the r^2 will be close to 1.

The unexplained variance is the sum squared of all differences between the actual cost observation (y) and the cost predicted by the regression line y' = a + bx. We put that in the arithmetic form of:

$$\text{Unexplained variance} = \Sigma\,(y - y')^2$$

The total variance is the sum squared of all differences between the actual observation (y) and the average of all cost observations, or the mean $\bar{y}$ (called y bar). We express this number in the form:

$$\text{Total variance} = \Sigma\,(y - \bar{y})^2$$

We can calculate a value for r^2 using data from the supplies cost example. The values we need for the unexplained variance and the total variance come from the following:

Hours	Actual Cost of Supplies	Predicted Cost y'	Deviations (y − y')	Deviations Squared (y − y')²
30	$500	$500	$ 0	$ 0
50	650	700	− 50	2,500
20	300	400	−100	10,000
10	300	300	0	0
60	900	800	100	10,000
50	750	700	50	2,500
40	650	600	50	2,500
60	700	800	−100	10,000
30	450	500	− 50	2,500
10	350	300	50	2,500
40	600	600	0	0
20	450	400	50	2,500
			$\Sigma\,(y - y')^2 =$	$45,000

Actual Cost of Supplies	Average $\bar{y}$	Variations (y − $\bar{y}$)	Variations Squared (y − $\bar{y}$)²
$ 500	$550	$− 50	$ 2,500
650	550	100	10,000
300	550	−250	62,500
300	550	−250	62,500
900	550	350	122,500
750	550	200	40,000
650	550	100	10,000
700	550	150	22,500
450	550	−100	10,000
350	550	−200	40,000
600	550	50	2,500
450	550	−100	10,000
$6,600	$\bar{y} = \$6,600 \div 12 = \$550$		$\Sigma\,(y - \bar{y})^2 =$ $395,000

From this information, r^2 is computed in the formula below:

$$r^2 = 1 - \frac{\$45,000}{\$395,000}$$
$$r^2 = 1 - .1139$$
$$r^2 = .8861 \text{ or } 88.61\%$$

This shows a relatively high correlation between supplies cost and hours of operation.

Measure of Variability   Because a regression equation will not result in a perfect fit on the data observations, we need a measure of variability in the data with respect to the regression equation. The **standard error of the estimate** (S_e) is a measure of the deviation between the actual observations of y and the values predicted by the regression equation. In other words, S_e gives an estimate of the amount by which the actual observation might differ from the estimate. The standard error of the estimate is calculated by the following formula:

$$S_e = \sqrt{\frac{\Sigma (y - y')^2}{n - 2}}$$

The numerator is a difference we calculated above in finding r^2. The denominator is referred to as the degrees of freedom, which is the number of observations (n) reduced by the number of parameters that must be estimated in the regression equation (two parameters—a and b).

For our example of supplies cost and hours of operation, the following calculation gives the standard error of the estimate:

$$S_e = \sqrt{\frac{\$45,000}{12 - 2}}$$

$$S_e = \sqrt{\frac{\$45,000}{10}}$$

$$S_e = \sqrt{\$4,500}$$

$$S_e = \$67.08$$

A table of probabilities for a normal distribution shows that approximately two thirds of the data (more precisely, 68.27%) lie within plus and minus one standard deviation of the mean. In this example, then, approximately two-thirds of the cost observations should lie within plus and minus one standard error of the estimate of the line of regression, or lie between $67.08 above the line of regression and $67.08 below it. To understand how this works with our data, consider the plot in Figure 15.7 of differences between the actual cost and predicted cost we call $(y - y')$:

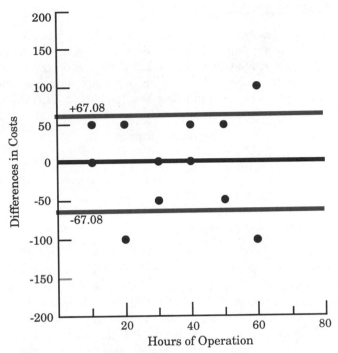

Figure 15.7   Graph of Differences

An interrelationship exists between r^2 and S_e. For example, as the deviations between actual cost and the predicted cost decrease, our measure for goodness of fit (r^2) increases in amount and S_e decreases in amount. That is, the higher the r^2, the lesser the deviation, the higher the correlation, and the closer the actual observations snug the line of regression. The significance of this interrelationship is that the higher the r^2 and the lower the standard error of the estimate, the more accurate is our estimate of b (the variable cost per hour).

Sources of Errors   The cost estimating equation derived from a set of data has a certain degree of error due to imperfections in the data, data collection, and other processing issues. These imperfections will appear in the difference between an actual cost and a cost predicted by the regression equation. Understanding the sources of errors is a step toward eliminating the impact of those errors on the results. The most common sources of errors fall in one of the following three categories: (1) major errors in the original data; (2) errors in keying data; and (3) inappropriate measure of activity.

Major errors in the original data are minimized through (1) reviewing the cutoff procedures that separate costs into periods, especially for outliers; and (2) examining the data for procedural errors, such as classification of transactions into the wrong account. For errors in keying data and calculation, look for cost outliers, observations with large differences between the actual cost and the cost predicted by the regression line. If multiple cost drivers are available in the data, try other cost drivers to locate one with a higher r^2 value.

Output from Computer Analysis

The advent of the personal computer and spreadsheets has greatly simplified application of the foregoing techniques for analyzing cost behavior. We just enter the data on a spreadsheet, enter a few function commands, and the results appear on the screen. The data for our example of supplies cost and hours of operation yield the following results with a LOTUS spreadsheet analysis:

Regression Output:

Constant	200	*Intercept a*
Std Err of Y Est	67.08203	*— Se*
R²	0.886075	
No. of Observations	12	*a + bY*
Degrees of Freedom	10	
X Coefficient(s)	10	*slope b*
Std Err of Coef.	1.133893	

The information we use can be read from the output. The constant is the fixed cost of $200. "Std Err of Y Est" is the standard error of the estimate and equals $67.08, if rounded to two decimal places. R² is r² and equals .8861 rounded to four decimal places. The number of observations is given as a check. The degrees of freedom are 10 and come from 12 − 2, where 2 is the number of parameters we are estimating (a and b). We have one cost driver (measure of activity) which has a coefficient of 10. That is our variable cost per hour, b. The "Std Err of Coef." is information on the standard deviation of the b values and is used in hypothesis testing, a subject beyond the scope of our discussion.

If data entry is correct, the output of a regression and correlation analyses can be performed quickly. The user of this information has only to apply the results to decision-making and planning and control issues.

CHECKING SOME INFERENCES

Before making use of a sample of cost data for cost estimation and control, we must have assurance that inferences with respect to cost behavior are correct. Otherwise, the cost data may be misleading.

In this chapter, the illustrations show that the cost data are represented by a straight line (linear) and not by a curve. In some situations, the linear relationship may not be appropriate. Costs, for example, may not increase at a constant rate, but instead may change at an increasing or a decreasing rate as the measure of activity increases. Hence, the cost data would be represented by a curve rather than a straight line. The shape of the line or curve can be revealed by plotting a sufficient amount of data for various hours of operation.

Also, the data may not be uniformly dispersed along the line of regression. At the extremes, for example, the data may be more widely dispersed than at the middle portion of the range. As a result, lines drawn for plus and minus one standard error of the estimated may not be parallel. This is illustrated on the graph in Figure 15.8.

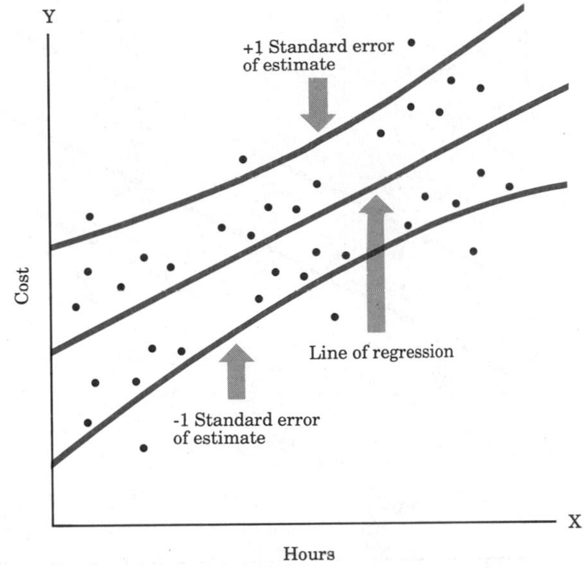

Figure 15.8 Wide Dispersion at Extremes

In each situation, the data should be plotted and inspected as a part of the total evaluation. As more data are collected, the cost estimation process can be refined. In general, more risk exists in making predictions at the extremes of the range, that is, when the costs are further from the average (total cost divided by the total hours).

In Figure 15.9 on page 770, the graph assumes that the lines for the standard error of the estimate are parallel to the line of regression over the relevant range depicted. A value for the standard error of the estimate may then be helpful in the identification of costs that should be investigated over this range of activity. (See the section on Control Limits below.) In situations where the degree of dispersion varies over the range, it will be necessary to determine the standard error of the estimate for each position in the range.

CONTROL LIMITS

From the data given in our example, the fixed supplies cost is estimated at $200, and the variable supplies cost is estimated to vary at the rate of $10 per hour. For 30 hours of operation, the total cost is estimated at $500. This is a predicted cost, however, and it is unlikely that the actual cost will be precisely $500. Because some variation in cost can be expected, management should establish an acceptable range of tolerance. Costs that lie within the limits of variation can be accepted. Costs beyond the limits, however, are identified and may be investigated.

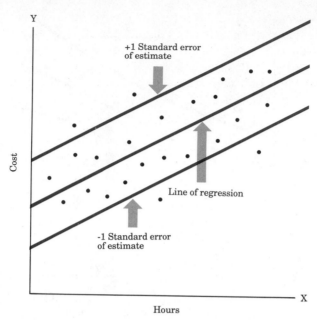

Figure 15.9   Uniform Dispersion

In dealing with cost variances, or variances in any type of data, it is necessary to consider the way the data are distributed. Statistical data may form a pattern of distribution designated as a normal distribution. In a **normal distribution,** data can be plotted on a smooth, continuous, symmetrically bell-shaped curve with a single peak in the center of distribution. Management may find that cost data are normally distributed for a given level of operation and, in deciding upon an acceptable range of cost variability, may employ the concept of standard deviation that is commonly used in statistics. The standard deviation measures the extent of variation that may be expected in a distribution of data. (In this chapter it will be assumed that cost data are normally distributed for each relevant level of operation.) Published tables show what proportion of the data may be expected to lie within plus and minus a given number of standard deviations from the mean (average).

For the supplies cost illustration, a standard error of the estimate (a standard deviation for y) is computed. We have already computed the standard error of estimate, and it amounts to $67.08. We apply it as follows. At 40 hours of operation, for example, the cost is expected to lie between $532.92 and $667.08 about two thirds of the time.

	Upper Limit Plus One	Lower Limit Minus One
Line of regression cost	$600.00	$600.00
Standard error of the estimate	+67.08	−67.08
	$667.08	$532.92

If more tolerance is permitted for control purposes, the limits may be extended. For instance, a 95 percent probability occurs for a range of costs of plus and minus 1.96 standard deviations. From the data given, the 95 percent probability is for a cost range between $468.52 and $731.48 at 40 hours of operation [$600 plus and minus $131.48 (1.96 × $67.08)]. Management must make a decision by balancing two alternatives:

1. A relatively narrow range of cost variation with a relatively low probability of a cost being within the zone.
2. A relatively wide range of cost variation with a relatively high probability of a cost being within the zone.

In other words, the wider the range, the fewer the costs that will be considered for investigation and the higher the likelihood that waste and inefficient operations will go uncorrected.

MULTIPLE AND NONLINEAR REGRESSION

Multiple Regression Model

In many situations, more than one factor will be related to cost behavior. Hours of operation, for example, may not be the only factor to be considered. A certain cost may vary not only with changes in the hours of operation but also with the weight of product produced, temperature changes, or other factors. Or, telephone service costs may be a function of the basic monthly charge, in-state long distance calls, out-of-state long distance calls, and features such as call waiting or call forwarding. Insofar as possible, all factors that are related to cost behavior should be brought into the analysis. This will provide a more effective approach to predicting and controlling costs. In simple regression only one factor is considered, but in **multiple regression** several factors are considered in combination. The basic form of the multiple regression model is:

$$y = a + b_1x_1 + b_2x_2 + \ldots + b_mx_m$$

The x's represent different independent variables, and the a's and b's are the coefficients. Any b is the average change in y resulting from a one unit change in the x_i.

The computations in regression and correlation analyses become more complex as other factors (cost drivers or measures of activity) are introduced, but the principle is the same as we presented in simple regression. Because we will use the computer for the computational side, we will not discuss the details of multiple regression calculations.

Quality of the Regression

Like simple regression, we have a coefficient of determination and a standard error of the estimate. For multiple regression, we call the coefficient of determination R^2. It still is the ratio of the explained variance over the total variance, although an adjustment is necessary for the number of coefficients that are estimated in the regression analysis. The standard error of the estimate is the same as in simple linear regression, with one exception. The degrees of freedom number, measured as n less the number of parameters estimated, will be different. Each variable will have a coefficient, and the more variables there are, the more coefficients must be estimated.

Concerns in Using Multiple Regression

Sometimes a factor affecting the amount of cost is not or only partially quantitative in nature. For example, bank charges for various services may be different for senior citizens than they are for people under 65 years of age. A multiple regression model will have one independent variable that will have a value of 1 for a senior citizen and 0 for other customers. These variables are called "dummy variables."

Another concern in using a multiple regression model is the potential existence of a very high correlation between two or more independent variables. The variables move so closely together that the technique cannot tell them apart. We call this situation multicollinearity. For example, direct labor hours and direct labor costs would be highly correlated. Multicollinearity is not an issue if we are interested only in predicting the total costs. However, when we need accurate coefficients, a definite problem exists. The coefficients on the b's in the model are variable costs for that independent variable, and accurate coefficients can be used in pricing decisions and cost-volume-profit analyses.

Multicollinearity, when severe, will be indicated by one or more of the following symptoms:

1. A coefficient is negative when a positive one is expected.
2. A coefficient is insignificant which, in theory, should be highly significant.
3. An unreasonably high coefficient exists that does not make economic sense.

If one or more of the symptoms appear, think through your theory supporting the equation. Pull out one of the independent variables that is less critical to the setting. Adding two problem variables together may be a solution in some cases.

Nonlinear Regression

Multiple regression also permits fitting certain nonlinear functions to cost data. For example, costs that follow a cubic function would appear as:

$$y = a + b_1x + b_2x^2 + b_3x^3$$

For powers higher than 4, a statistician should be consulted. Another nonlinear function found in cost data and in some financial situations is the exponential function modeled as:

$$y = ax^b$$

Examples of this type of model are learning curves and compound interest.

To use linear regression to find values for the coefficients a and b of the best-fitting equation, it is necessary to transform the equation by taking logs. A linear form results from logs, as follows:

$$\log y = \log a + b \log x$$

First, transform the data by taking the log of x and log of y. By including the log of y (instead of y itself) and the log of x (instead of x itself) in linear regression, the results are a constant (log a) and a slope (b). Taking the antilog of the constant results in a value for a. Now we have values for both a and b that can be used in decision making and in planning and control.

Output From Computer Analysis

Similar to the linear regression, computer spreadsheets have the capability to perform the multiple regression analysis. The results from a LOTUS spreadsheet appear as follows:

Regression Output:

Constant			1,200
Std Err of the Y Est			293
R^2			0.87722
Number of observations			12
Degrees of freedom			9
X Coefficient(s)	.512	.308	.165
Std Err of Coef.	.055	.05	.056

In interpreting the results, we receive the same information and just have more independent values. Here, we have three independent variables when we only had one in simple linear regression.

TIME SERIES APPROACHES

Regression and correlation analyses are concerned with the linear relationship between two or more variables. Knowledge of the independent variable(s) x is used to predict the dependent variable y. In **time series analysis**, the independent variable is time. The dependent variable y takes on different values over time. Thus, any variable classified chronologically is a time series. The time periods may be years, quarters, months, weeks, days, hours, or any other interval. Time series analysis is commonly used in budgeting and financial planning. Time series are analyzed to discover past patterns of growth and change that can be used to predict future patterns and needs for operations of an organization.

A number of time series analysis techniques exist. These techniques use historical information about the cost, its trends and movements over time, to predict future values for that cost. The advantage of time series techniques is that they are economical to use, although computers are required. The only data needed are the variable's historical information (total cost for some cost category or some performance statistic). Most of these methods require application of complex statistical computations that are beyond the scope of managerial accounting. The following sections describe an approach to analyzing trends.

Trend Analysis

The trend is the component that underlies the growth or decline in a time series. These movements can be described by a straight line or a curve. In a production operation, forces affecting the trend might be price changes, technological change, or productivity changes. In a service operation, a population change might also be a factor.

Before the analyst develops a measurement for the trend, the data are plotted on a graph. Remember that the independent variable is time. The plot gives the analyst the general shape of the data. If a plot of the series indicates a straight-line movement, a straight trend line will be fitted to the data. If a nonlinear trend is apparent, the appropriate trend curve can be developed.

The method most widely used to describe straight-line trends is the least squares method in simple linear regression; for nonlinear trends the least squares method in multiple regression is used.

As a short example of the trend line concept, consider the monthly overhead cost data for the painting cost center in a kitchen appliance manufacturer:

Month	Overhead Cost	Month x, Coded from x = 0
January	$7,170	0
February	5,955	1
March	5,982	2
April	4,655	3
May	6,041	4
June	6,577	5
July	5,855	6
August	6,939	7
September	7,571	8
October	8,065	9
November	9,314	10
December	9,009	11

The regression results for this situation are below:

Constant	5,358.65
Standard error of the estimate	960.16
r^2	0.558005
Number of observations	12
Degrees of freedom	10
X Coefficient	285.29

Figure 15.10 shows the foregoing data points plotted on a graph with the regression trend line superimposed over the data points.

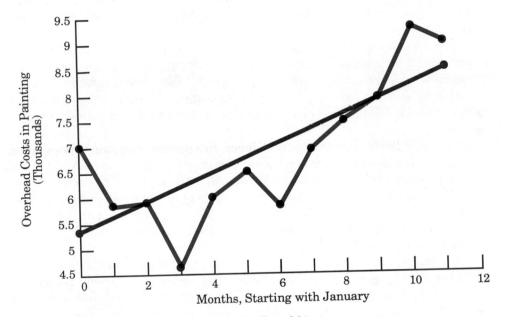

Figure 15.10   Graph of Data and Regression Trend Line

The regression trend line explains only 55.8 percent of the variability in the data. That is not as good a fit as a manager would like to have for predicting costs in the future and in setting control limits. Since the data are time series data, other factors may be included in the data, such as seasonal variations. The next section looks at decomposition as an analysis technique.

Decomposition

Because many fluctuations and variations occur that obscure the trend in data, it is necessary to identify the component factors that influence each of the periodic values in a series. This identification procedure is called **decomposition**. Four components are found in time series analysis: (1) trend, (2) cyclical variations, (3) seasonal variations, and (4) irregular fluctuations.

The cyclical component is a series of irregular wavelike fluctuations or cycles of more than one year's duration due to changing economic conditions. It is the difference between the expected values of a trend and the actual values—the residual variation fluctuating around the trend. In our previous example of 12-months, a cyclical variation would not occur because the time period was not long enough.

Seasonal fluctuations are typically found in data classified quarterly, monthly, or weekly. Seasonal variation refers to a pattern of change that recurs regularly over time. The movement is completed within the duration of a year and repeats itself year after year. In our example of the painting operations, we see costs lower than expected in February through August and higher than expected the rest of the year. This situation could be the result of seasonal fluctuations.

The irregular fluctuations component can be composed of fluctuations that are caused by unpredictable or nonperiodic events. Economic behavior, for example, is influenced by weather changes, strikes, wars, rumors of wars, elections, and the passage of certain federal or state legislation. An index for the irregular fluctuations of the past can be estimated and included in the analysis.

To study these components of a time series, we usually treat the original data of a time series as a product of the components. That is, a monthly series is a product of trend, seasonal variations, and irregular fluctuations, expressed as $T \times S \times I$. T is measured in units of actual data, and S and I are index values. The index values may be related to a price index or some other index. If the time series data were in terms of years, a C for cyclical fluctuations would replace the S for the seasonal fluctuations.

For our example, let's include a seasonal index adjustment. A number of means exist for arriving at such an index, but we will assume one is given us for incorporation in the analysis. The seasonally adjusted index for our monthly data is:

Month	Index	Adjusted Data*
January	111.45	6,433
February	90.62	6,572
March	89.15	6,710
April	67.97	6,849
May	86.46	6,987
June	92.30	7,125
July	80.61	7,264
August	93.74	7,402
September	100.40	7,541
October	105.03	7,679
November	119.15	7,817
December	113.25	7,956

* Original data × (100 ÷ index) = Adjusted data

The regression run on this adjusted data is as follows:

Constant	6,433.33
Standard error of the estimate	0.259093
r^2	0.999999
Number of observations	12
Degrees of freedom	10
X Coefficient	138.40

The r^2 value is so near perfect that we do not need to graph the adjusted data and the regression trend line to know that the points and the line are almost identical. The seasonal adjustment accounted for the original difference. We now have a trend line for predicting where costs are going in the future if something else does not change.

SUMMARY

A variable cost changes at a constant rate over a relevant range, but the rate of variability may change outside this range. A fixed cost is a constant amount over a relevant range, but the amount may increase or decrease outside the range. Many costs are neither entirely variable nor entirely fixed. Two varieties of these costs are semivariable costs and semifixed costs. For decision-making and control purposes, such costs must be segregated into variable and fixed components.

Five methods for identifying variable and fixed cost behavior are account analysis, the engineering approach, scattergraph and visual fit, the high-low method, and regression analysis (the least squares method, for most of the work we do). In account analysis, the analyst determines the cost behavior of a specific cost by reviewing and interpreting managerial policies with respect to the cost and by inspecting the historical activity of the cost. The engineering approach uses analysis and direct observation of processes to identify the relationship between inputs and outputs and then quantifies an expected cost behavior. In the scattergraph and visual fit method, the analyst graphs each observation, with cost on the vertical axis and activity or cost driver on the horizontal axis. Then, the analyst visually and judgmentally fits a line to the data. The y-intercept of the line is the estimate of fixed cost, and the slope of the line is the estimate of variable cost per unit. The high-low method is a simple method in which the rate of cost variability is determined from data taken only at the high and low points of a range of data. The least squares method, as a simple regression analysis, is more complex but takes into account all data in the range.

Before relying on a fixed cost or a variable rate, the relationship must be determined between the cost and one or more cost drivers to which we attribute cost incurrence. If correlation is very poor, the cost driver selected may not be closely related to that cost. The degree of correlation is measured by the coefficient of determination, usually designated as r^2. The coefficient of determination provides a numerical analysis of cost variance. By using the regression line, the variance is segregated into a portion that is explained by the one or more cost drivers chosen and a portion that is unexplained.

Control limits can be established in deciding when to investigate cost variances. In a normal distribution of cost data, for example, costs extending beyond plus or minus one standard deviation may be investigated. Approximately two times out of three a cost can be expected to fall within plus or minus one standard deviation of the line of regression. If desired, the range of acceptable cost variation can be made greater or smaller. The limits established depend on how tightly management wishes to control cost and how willing management is to accept the possibility that investigations may be fruitless.

In time series analysis, the independent variable is time. The dependent variable y takes on different values over time. Thus, any variable classified chronologically is a time series. The time periods may be years, quarters, months, weeks, days, hours, or any other interval. Time series are analyzed to discover past patterns of growth and change that can be used to predict future patterns and needs for operations of an organization.

PROBLEM FOR REVIEW

Blanco Casting Company estimates costs by the least squares method. Data with respect to the cost of equipment maintenance for the last year are given as follows:

Months	Hours	Actual Costs
January	800	$9,800
February	700	9,340
March	750	9,560
April	700	9,720
May	720	9,570
June	640	9,100
July	680	9,630
August	620	9,740
September	630	8,920
October	760	9,800
November	800	9,750
December	820	9,860

The company determined in an earlier period the line of regression and statistics that will be used to determine which of the last year's amounts should be investigated. In determining the line of regression, the accountant calculated the following numbers:

$$\Sigma (y - y')^2 = 2{,}700{,}000$$
$$\Sigma (y - \bar{y})^2 = 7{,}500{,}000$$
$$\text{Degrees of freedom} = (n - 2) = 30$$
$$\text{Variable cost per hour} = \$6$$
$$\text{Fixed cost per month} = \$5{,}000$$

A cost is investigated if it is more than one standard deviation from the line of regression value.

Required:

1. Compute one standard error of the estimate from the line of regression.
2. Using the rule established by the company, identify the months when the costs should be investigated.
3. If the limit had been set at 1.96 standard deviations (that is, allowing a 95% probability that the costs would lie within the range), in which months would the costs be investigated?
4. Calculate the coefficient of determination (r^2). Explain how the coefficient of determination and standard error of the estimate are related.

Solution:

1. The line of regression costs, already computed in this problem, is the most representative of average costs for the various hours of operation. By the least squares method, based upon the equation $y = a + bx$, simultaneous equations were formed to solve for a variable cost of $6 per hour plus a fixed cost of $5,000 per month. The number of cost observations was 32. The standard deviation (standard error of the estimate) from the line of regression is computed as follows:

    (a) The difference between each actual cost and the cost as computed using the line of regression (in this case, hours multiplied by $6 + $5,000) is squared. The squared values are added to become the sum of the squared deviations from the line of regression. This is given in the problem as 2,700,000. Then the number of observations reduced by 2 is divided into the sum of the squared deviations. The square root of the result is the standard deviation.

    (b) The computation follows:

$$S_e = \sqrt{\frac{\Sigma (y - y')^2}{n - 2}} = \sqrt{\frac{2{,}700{,}000}{30}} = \sqrt{900{,}000}$$
$$S_e = 300$$

2. The line of regression cost is equal to the number of hours multiplied by $6 plus $5,000. The differences between the line of regression costs and the actual costs are obtained, and each difference is compared with the standard deviation (standard error of the estimated) of $300. According to the rule established, a cost is to be investigated if it is more than plus or minus $300 from the line of regression.

Months	Hours (X)	Line of Regression Cost (5,000 + 6X)	Actual Cost	Cost Difference
January	800	$9,800	$9,800	$ 0
February	700	9,200	9,340	140
March	750	9,500	9,560	60
April	700	9,200	9,720	520*
May	720	9,320	9,570	250
June	640	8,840	9,100	260
July	680	9,080	9,630	550*
August	620	8,720	9,740	1,020*
September	630	8,780	8,920	140
October	760	9,560	9,800	240
November	800	9,800	9,750	−50
December	820	9,920	9,860	−60

* April, July, and August would be investigated.

3.   If the rule is set that costs exceeding 1.96 standard deviations from the line of regression are to be investigated, the value for this problem will be $588 (1.96 × $300). Determine the months in which costs are more than $588 from the line of regression value. In this case, costs for the month of August would be investigated.

4.   The coefficient of determination shows the degree of correlation between the hours of operation and the cost. The equation is given as follows:

$$r^2 = 1 - \frac{\Sigma (y - y')^2}{\Sigma (y - \bar{y})^2}$$

$$r^2 = 1 - \frac{2,700,000}{7,500,000} = 1 - .36$$

$$r^2 = .64 \text{ or } 64\%$$

The correlation fit between hours and costs is marginally good at 64%.

If the data are closely clustered around the line of regression, the standard error of the estimate (standard deviation) will be small. This means the amount of unexplained variance is small; hence, r^2, or the degree of correlation, will be high.

TERMINOLOGY REVIEW

Account analysis (756)
Coefficient of determination (764)
Correlation analysis (760)
Cost estimation (755)
Decomposition (775)
Engineering approach (756)
Fixed cost (752)
High-low method (759)
Least squares method (761)
Linear regression (760)

Multiple regression (771)
Normal distribution (770)
Regression analysis (760)
Regression line (760)
Scattergraph and visual fit (757)
Semifixed costs (752)
Semivariable costs (752)
Standard error of the estimate (766)
Time series analysis (773)
Variable cost (752)

QUESTIONS FOR REVIEW AND DISCUSSION

1. Why is cost estimation so important?

2. Identify the four basic cost behavior patterns.

3. Describe the two major steps involved in the account analysis method of cost estimation.

4. Explain the engineering approach in cost estimation.

5. Describe the steps for preparing an estimate of fixed and variable costs using the scattergraph and visual fit method.

6. When using the high-low method, what criteria should be used in selecting the two points?

7. Describe the high-low point method of cost segregation.

8. Distinguish between the dependent variable and independent variable in a cost-estimating equation.

9. How is regression analysis different from the other methods of cost estimation?

10. What is the coefficient of determination and what range of values can it take?

11. Does a high correlation between x and y prove that a change in x causes a change in y? Explain.

12. What does a standard error of the estimate measure and how is it related to the coefficient of determination?

13. In a normal distribution of data, what proportion of the data should lie within plus and minus one standard deviation from the mean? How can this information be used in cost control?

14. Why is it important that costs be recorded in the proper accounting period? At which points during the accounting period is it most critical to track transactions and ensure that they are in the proper period?

15. It is common practice for monthly data to be unadjusted for accruals (wages, interest, and the like). These adjustments may occur quarterly or only annually. Discuss the potential impact of this on cost behavior analysis.

16. Is it possible to predict costs beyond the range of x values used in determining a line of regression? Explain.

17. If fixed costs do not change with respect to volume, why are the fixed costs of a large retailer much higher than those of a small store?

18. When using historical data to predict the cost behavior pattern, it is possible to have a coefficient (fixed cost) that is negative. What can it mean when the estimate of fixed cost is negative?

19. What is multiple regression? When would it be used in cost estimation?

20. What is multicollinearity and how does it pose problems in multiple regression analysis?

21. Explain how a linear regression analysis can be used for an equation of the form $y = ax^b$.

22. What is a time series?

EXERCISES

1.   **Cost Segregation by High-Low Method.** The costs of equipment lubrication in the machining operation of Tellit Products Company have been recorded as follows:

Hours	Costs
18,500	$61,700
16,000	54,200
17,200	57,800
18,000	60,200
21,000	69,200
16,400	55,400
16,700	56,300
15,000	51,200
17,600	59,000
18,100	60,500

Required:
Determine the average rate of cost variability per hour and the fixed cost by the high-low point method.

2.   **High-Low method.** Joyce Mason sells various ceramics and crafts at flea markets in the area. She uses a motor home for transportation and lodging. She recognizes that travel costs with the home are relatively high and would like to estimate costs so that she can decide how far she can travel and still operate at a profit.

  Records from one round trip of 150 miles show that the total cost was $320. On another round trip of 340 miles, the total cost was $472. A local round trip of 50 miles cost $240. She is convinced that the time and cost for trips of more than 300 miles are too high unless the sales potential is very high.

Required:
Calculate the variable cost per mile and the fixed cost per trip. Use the high-low method.

3.   **Other Cost Behavior.** Luke Reeves has power saws that he uses to produce wooden components used by other companies in interior building construction and in furniture making. He would like to estimate the costs of operation as a guide in billing customers. Reeves has not been in business long enough to develop much cost information, but he senses that the variable cost per hour is somewhat higher on jobs that require less time.

  On a job that took 20 hours, the cost was $230. Another job that took 50 hours cost $275. The cost of a project that required 200 hours was only $400, and another project at 300 hours cost $500.

Required:
1.   Using the information given, what is the estimated variable cost per hour in the range extending from 20 to 50 hours? What is the fixed cost for this range?
2.   What is the estimated variable cost per hour in the range extending from 200 to 300 hours? What is the fixed cost for this range?
3.   What factors might exist that would cause the variable cost to change?

4.   **Account Analysis.** The following is a partial list of account titles found in the chart of accounts for Indiana Agricultural Products:
1.   Indirect Materials
2.   Depreciation on Office Equipment (double-declining-balance method)
3.   Depreciation on Factory Equipment (units-of-production method)
4.   Direct Labor
5.   FICA Taxes on Direct Labor Payroll
6.   Rent on Finished Goods Inventory Warehouse
7.   Repairs and Maintenance of Factory Equipment
8.   Fringe Benefits for Office Workers (as a percent of salaries)
9.   Factory Utilities
10. Insurance Expense—Comprehensive on all Facilities

Required:
1.   Classify each of the accounts according to cost behavior: variable, fixed, semivariable, semifixed, or other.
2.   For each variable and semivariable cost, give an example of the cost driver or measure of activity with which the cost would vary.

5.   **Account Analysis.** Your spouse volunteered you as the social chairman of the local United Way campaign. One of the major activities under your direction is the Christmas dinner and dance for about 220 people. Renting the hall at the local Festive Inn will cost $250. The hall will seat up to 300 people. Decorations for the head table, which will seat 16 people, will cost $50. Decorations for each table will cost $10, and each table will seat up to 8 people. For $25, you can hire the choir director from one of the local high schools to play the piano and sing softly during dinner. The dance band (a prominent college student group) will cost $250. Typesetting and printing 300 copies of the program cost $75. The caterer has offered a full-course meal for $10 per person, but you must guarantee one week in advance. To help serve the meals, you have arranged for the voluntary services of a local Campfire Girls group. These people will be given a meal for their trouble. You expect 25 people to help serve.

At the time the guarantee was required, you had 205 confirmed people attending the dinner, including all speakers and dignitaries, but not including servers. You guarantee 224 people plus the servers. Assume that the servers will eat in an adjoining room, which is furnished free of charge.

Required:
1.   Estimate the total cost of the Christmas dinner and dance for the number of people guaranteed.
2.   Estimate the total costs if you had to guarantee 272 people plus servers.
3.   Which costs vary with the number of people? Which costs vary with the number of tables (or which costs are fixed per table)? Which costs are fixed for the dinner and dance?

6.   **Least Squares Line of Regression.** The cost of maintenance for animated exhibits at Joyland Amusement Park is partly variable and partly fixed. Supplies and other materials used tend to vary with hours of operation while the salaries of the maintenance workers are fixed. Data for various hours of operation are given as follows:

Hours	Total Cost
500	$ 9,000
700	11,200
450	8,600
800	12,000
600	9,800
900	13,000

Required:

1. Compute a line of regression using the least squares method. What are the variable cost per hour and the fixed cost?
2. Compute the variable cost per hour and the fixed cost using the high-low method.
3. Explain why the variable cost per hour and fixed cost are different under the two methods of computation.

7. **Visual Fit and the Extremes.** The cost of utilities at Harrison Supply varies according to hours of operation, but a portion of the cost is fixed. Hour and cost data for several months are given as follows:

Hours	Total Cost
100	$ 800
200	700
300	800
400	900
500	1,000
600	1,100
700	1,200
800	1,300
900	1,600

Required:

1. Fit a line of regression to the data by visual fit. (Place the line so that it is representative of most of the data.)
2. Using your line, compute the variable cost per hour and the fixed cost per month.
3. Determine the variable cost per hour and the fixed cost by the high-low method.
4. Explain which of the foregoing two variable costs per hour and two fixed cost numbers you have more confidence in using for business decisions.

8. **Cost Segregation by Least Squares.** The supervisor of operations at Hugh Makel Freight Lines, Inc. is in the process of estimating the variable cost per hour and the fixed cost per month of operating an automatic conveyor system. Data for the past 10 months have been collected and organized as follows.

Number of observations	10
Sum of the hours (Σx).	5,000
Sum of the costs (Σy)	160,000
Sum of the hours multiplied by the costs (Σxy)	42,000,000
Sum of the hours squared (Σx^2)	900,000

Required:

1. From the data given, compute the variable cost per hour to operate the conveyor. (Round to the nearest cent.)
2. Compute the fixed cost per month. (Round to the nearest cent.)

9.   **Correlation.** The controller of Vance Equipment Works has estimated the variable cost to operate equipment in one area of the plant at $8 per hour, with a fixed cost per month of $1,500. Next month it is estimated that the equipment will operate 300 hours at a total cost of $3,900. Ordinarily the equipment operates each month in a range extending from 200 to 1,000 hours.

    The plant superintendent questions the degree of correlation between hours of operation and cost. Information shows that the sum of the squared deviations from the line of regression is 7,845 and that the sum of the squared deviations from the general average is 156,900.

Required:

1. Calculate the coefficient of determination r^2.
2. How would the superintendent use this information to argue his point about correlation?

10. **Correlation.** The manager of the heat treatment operation at Navaho Metals Company has obtained reasonably good results in estimating the cost of indirect materials from estimates of temperatures required in processing. The sum of the squared deviations from the line of regression has been computed at 48,819, and the sum of the squared deviations from the general average has been computed at 325,460. However, the estimates of the cost of maintenance of equipment based on temperature estimates have not been reliable. The sum of the squared deviations from the line of regression has been computed at 391,414, and the sum of the deviations from the general average has been computed at 425,450.

Required:

1. Calculate the coefficient of determination r^2 for the cost of indirect materials and temperature.
2. Calculate the coefficient of determination r^2 for the cost of equipment maintenance and temperature.
3. Why might the estimates of equipment maintenance cost be unreliable?

11. **Describing Regression Results.** As controller of Well-Kept Lawn and Garden Service, you are concerned about the cost behavior of overhead costs. You gathered the appropriate data and asked a statistician friend of yours to perform a regression analysis. She has given you the following results:

$$y = 1,750 + 7.25\,x$$
$$r^2 = .91$$
$$S_e = 24.50$$

where: y = overhead cost
x = labor hours

Required:

1. Explain the meaning of the equation: $Y = 1,750 + 7.25 x$.
2. What is the percentage of the variance of overhead cost that is associated with changes in labor hours?
3. The president wants to know what S_e means and how it might be used in evaluating actions. Give a brief answer.

12. **Explaining Regression Results.** J.D. Carter & Associates is a tax preparation service. Each month, J.D. watches the Cost of Services Rendered account which contains the direct costs and certain support costs for the various tax services performed. He believes a relationship exists between the cost of services rendered and revenues. He has asked you to analyze the cost behavior of the account. You pull together two years of data and do a spreadsheet analysis which yields the following output:

Regression Output:

Constant	870.6
Std. Err. of Y Est.	137.54
R²	.8473
No. of Observations	24
Degrees of Freedom	22
X Coefficient(s)	0.639
Std. Err. of Coef.	0.081

Required:

Explain what information this regression output gives about cost behavior and how management might use it.

13. **Control Limit.** Oakland Tree Service, Inc. uses chipper equipment to dispose of large tree branches. The cost to operate this equipment has been estimated at $6 per hour. The fixed cost per month has been estimated at $1,200. A cost is to be investigated if it is more or less than one standard error of the estimate from the line of regression. Data collected for each of the last 12 months reveal that the sum of the squared deviations from the line of regression is 324,000. Last month the total cost to operate the chipper was $3,300 for 300 hours of operation.

Required:

1. Compute the standard error of estimate from the line of regression.
2. Using the criterion established, should the cost of $3,300 for last month be investigated?

14. **Control Limit.** King of Software is a regional computer chain with stores in Kansas, Missouri, and Nebraska. The company wants to expand into other states and is interested in the costs of operating stores compared to the revenues from rentals. In particular, the CEO wants to know if the current costs reflect operations that are in control. Data have been collected on total costs per month and the number of rentals by store. The following simple linear regression results have been obtained from worksheet calculations:

Observations	11
Constant	$2,600
X coefficient	$4.99
Average y	$57,474
Average x	8,949
$\Sigma (y - y')^2$	36,754
$\Sigma (y - \bar{y})^2$	515,515
$\Sigma (x - \bar{x})^2$	295,559

Required:
1. Calculate the standard error of the estimate.
2. Calculate an estimate of total cost and a 95 percent control limit interval for the following rentals per month:
   (a) 2,500
   (b) 11,555

15. **Explaining Multiple Regression Results.** The Computer Services Department of Worldwide Market Research, Inc. provides services to all other departments. Demand by other departments has grown to a point where the manager of computer services wants to bill for services rendered. She decided to analyze computer services operating costs compared to input device time, CPU time, and output device time. Operating cost data and the various times were given to a statistician for analysis. The statistician returned the following summary:

Regression Output:

Constant	2,250
Std. Err. of Y Est.	221
R^2	0.95142
Number of Observations	12
Degrees of Freedom	8

	Input	CPU	Output
X Coefficient(s)	0.335	0.458	0.189

Required:
Explain what information this regression output gives about cost behavior and how management might use it.

16. **Trend Identification.** Using the data from Exercise 1 and assuming the data are listed in the order of the months for which the hours are reported, perform a simple regression analysis on the data to establish a regression trend line. Evaluate and interpret the results.

PROBLEMS

15-1. **Account Analysis.** The following is a partial list of account titles appearing in the chart of accounts for Edlestein Industrial Supply Company:

1. Direct Materials	11. Sales Commission
2. Supervisory Salaries—Factory	12. Travel Expenses—Sales
3. Heat, Light, and Power—Factory	13. Telephone Expenses—General and Administrative
4. Depreciation on the Building	
5. Depreciation on Equipment and Machinery (units-of-production method)	14. Magazine Advertising
	15. Bad Debt Expense
	16. Photocopying Expense
6. Janitorial Labor	17. Audit Fees
7. Repair and Maintenance Supplies	18. Dues and Subscriptions
8. Pension Costs (as a percentage of employee wages and salaries)	19. Depreciation on Furniture and Fixtures (double-declining-balance method)
9. FICA Tax Expense (employer's share)	20. Group Medical and Dental Insurance Expense
10. Insurance on Property	

Required:

1. Discuss each account title in terms of whether the account represents a variable, fixed, semivariable, or semifixed cost.
2. For accounts designated as variable or semivariable, indicate the most likely cost driver with which the cost varies.
3. Explain the problems associated with using the account analysis approach to establish cost behavior patterns.

15-2. **Rough Approaches.** Evelyn Dement, an insurance claims adjuster for Chapparal Casualty Company, notes that the cost to process a claim has both fixed and variable components. She believes that she can estimate costs more accurately if she can separate the costs into their variable and fixed components. A record of the number of claims and the costs for the past year is given as follows by months:

Month	Number of Claims	Cost
January	120	$20,600
February	134	20,670
March	142	20,710
April	156	20,780
May	160	20,800
June	220	21,100
July	250	21,250
August	330	21,650
September	114	20,570
October	280	21,400
November	274	21,370
December	230	21,150

Required:

1. Estimate the variable cost per claim and the fixed cost per month by the high-low method.
2. Estimate the variable cost per claim and the fixed cost per month by the scattergraph and visual fit method.
3. Explain the differences in variable cost per claim and the fixed cost per month.

15-3. High-Low and Least Squares. The manager of the shipping department at Gorman Fixtures Company recognizes that the cost of supplies used is partly variable and partly fixed. By using the high-low method, the manager has estimated that supplies cost about $5 per shipment and that the fixed cost is $2,500 per month. However, the cost estimates for the month are never accurate even when the number of shipments has been predicted accurately. For example, in April the manager estimated a cost of $2,800 for 60 shipments. The actual cost was $2,180. A record of the number of shipments and costs is given as follows by months:

Month	Number of Shipments	Total Cost
January	50	$2,150
February	45	2,135
March	20	2,600
April	60	2,180
May	85	2,255
June	90	2,950
July	75	2,225
August	40	2,120
September	35	2,105
October	80	2,240

Required:

1. Recalculate the variable cost per shipment and the fixed cost per month by the high-low method.
2. Calculate the variable cost per shipment and the fixed cost per month by the least squares method.
3. Exclude the high and low points of the range and compute the variable cost per shipment and the fixed cost per month by the least squares method.
4. Explain why the three calculations above yield different results in this situation.

15-4. Least Squares Method. For years, Case Metals Company paid equipment maintenance personnel on an hourly rate basis. The fixed costs of maintenance labor were relatively low. With the installation of automated equipment, the nature of their work has changed. Now, maintenance personnel monitor the operations and are paid salaries. Therefore, fixed costs have increased, but variable costs per hour have been reduced. Past records show the following monthly information with respect to hours and cost for maintenance labor:

Hours	Cost	Hours	Cost
1,500	$15,000	700	$8,000
800	9,400	500	7,600
1,200	12,600	1,100	11,800
1,600	15,800	1,000	11,000
1,400	14,200	600	7,800

More recent costs for monthly maintenance labor, since the installation of automated equipment, are given as follows:

Hours	Cost	Hours	Cost
1,200	$17,600	1,500	$17,800
1,000	16,800	900	17,000
1,700	18,400	1,200	17,500
800	16,500	1,000	17,000
2,000	19,000	1,400	17,700

Required:

1. Using the least squares method, compute the variable cost per hour and the fixed cost per month under the conditions that existed in the past. (Round to the nearest cent.)

2. Using the least squares method, compute the variable cost per hour and the fixed cost per month under present conditions with automated equipment. (Round to the nearest cent.)

3. How will management now plan for and control maintenance labor differently with the automated equipment as opposed to past practices?

15-5. **Least Squares Method.** Water is supplied to Lake Arthur Township by pumping water to a storage tank at the highest elevation in town, from which it then flows to the customers by gravity. The town council notes that the costs to pump water vary to some extent by the number of gallons pumped, but fixed costs are also included in the pumping cost. A record of gallons consumed per month and total pumping cost per month is given as follows:

Gallons Consumed (000)	Pumping Cost	Gallons Consumed (000)	Pumping Cost
1,750	$29,100	1,800	$29,700
1,900	30,800	2,300	35,900
2,150	34,000	2,000	31,800
2,050	32,600	1,500	25,500
2,000	32,100	1,600	27,400
1,950	23,700	2,100	33,200
1,800	29,200	1,900	30,700
2,200	34,400	2,000	32,000
2,500	38,500	2,400	36,600
1,700	28,200	2,100	33,200

Costs are to be segregated by the least squares method. The following computations have already been made:

Sum of the gallons consumed (in thousands)	39,700
Sum of the costs	$628,600
Sum of the gallons multiplied by the costs......................	1,263,550,000
Sum of the gallons squared	80,050,000

Required:

1. Determine the variable cost of pumping per 1,000 gallons and the fixed cost per month.

2. Using the equation y = a + bx, predict the cost for each of the gallons consumed above.

3. Plot on a graph the differences between actual costs and predicted costs (y − y'). Comment on the spread of the differences about 0.

15-6. **Choice of Cost Driver.** The company is revising its cost accounting system and wants cost drivers for each department that best relate to the incurrence of departmental costs. Your analysis shows that direct labor hours and machine hours are the likely predictors of overhead costs. You have searched through the accounting data and have 15 observations representing weekly periods, as follows:

Week	Machine Hours	Direct Labor Hours	Overhead Cost
1	120	200	$4,460
2	150	210	5,225
3	190	205	5,900
4	160	210	5,350
5	200	230	6,125
6	210	235	6,300
7	230	240	6,660
8	220	235	6,450
9	180	205	5,730
10	170	210	5,560
11	140	200	5,050
12	130	195	4,800
13	160	190	5,410
14	180	205	5,760
15	195	210	6,000

Required:
1. Calculate the coefficient of determination for each cost driver.
2. Calculate the standard error of the estimate for each cost driver.
3. Which cost driver is the better predictor of overhead costs? Explain.

15-7. **Control Limits.** The supervisor of the Heat Treatment Department at Rockville Technics, Inc. has estimated that power cost varies at the rate of $0.80 per hour and that the fixed cost for the month is $500. The standard error of the estimate from the line of regression is $60. The supervisor investigates a cost in any month that the actual cost is more or less than one standard deviation from the line of regression. Actual monthly hours and costs for the last year are given below:

Month	Hours	Cost
January	600	$ 980
February	550	970
March	600	960
April	650	1,050
May	550	940
June	500	980
July	700	1,180
August	800	1,150
September	750	1,050
October	900	1,330
November	850	1,180
December	450	900

Required:

1. Using the formula $y = a + bx$, what should the cost be for each month?
2. Calculate the difference between the actual cost and the predicted cost $(y - y')$ for each month.
3. Plot the differences in (2) on a graph and draw in lines that represent the plus or minus one standard error of the estimate.
4. According to the rule established for cost investigation, for which month or months should the cost be investigated?

15-8. **Selection of a Control Limit.** For the last five years, the management of Althauser Fasteners, Inc. has followed the practice of investigating variations from the line of regression costs if a cost differs by more than one standard error of estimate from the line of regression. One standard error of estimate is $200.

A new supervisor, hired to manage the machining operation, asks, "Did you ever consider that you may be overdoing it by investigating every cost that is over one standard deviation from the line of regression? After all, you still have a probability of about 1 in 3 that the variation will be random. Then you have gone to a lot of bother for nothing. For example, last March in this operation you investigated the cost of lubrication and found nothing wrong."

The supervisor of the fabrication operation replies, "I'll grant that we may whip a few dead horses, but your idea of investigating anything over 1.96 standard deviations would have missed a very important variance for one month that was brought under control."

The cost of lubrication is estimated to vary at $6 per hour in the machining operation with a fixed cost of $3,500 each month. The actual costs for last year that the supervisors were discussing are given as follows:

Month	Hours	Cost	Month	Hours	Cost
Jan.	1,200	$10,850	July	500	$ 6,350
Feb.	1,400	12,000	Aug.	700	7,700
Mar.	1,000	9,800	Sept.	900	9,100
Apr.	1,100	10,000	Oct.	1,000	9,850
May	1,000	9,650	Nov.	1,200	10,600
June	600	7,600	Dec.	1,300	11,450

Required:

1. Calculate the difference between the actual cost and the predicted cost $(y - y')$ for each month.
2. Identify the months which were investigated with the control limit set at one standard error of estimate from the line of regression.
3. Identify the months which would have been investigated if the control limit had been set at 1.96 standard error of estimate from the line of regression.
4. The supervisor of fabrication operation has stated that one very important month would have been missed using the rule suggested by the supervisor of the machining operation. Which month would have been missed? What was the variance for that month?

15-9. **Disagreement on Control Limits.** The plant management group at VeriAmerican, Inc. is trying to decide on a reasonable control limit. A few members of the group believe that a limit should be set at one standard deviation from the line of regression. Several others, however, believe that this rule is too rigid and that a 1.96 standard deviation should be set as a limit so that 95 percent of the data can be expected to lie within the limits. The chairman of the group states that there is nothing sacred about either 1.0 or 1.96 standard error of estimate. Perhaps a compromise can be reached at 1.5 standard deviations where there is about an 87 percent probability that the data will lie within the limits, that is, about seven times out of eight.

Line of regression costs and actual costs are given for each month of the past year for the cost of power. One standard deviation has been computed at $500.

Month	Hours	Line of Regresson Cost	Actual Cost
January	3,000	$5,000	$5,600
February	3,200	5,200	5,400
March	3,600	5,600	5,700
April	4,000	6,000	7,200
May	4,300	6,300	6,400
June	3,700	5,700	6,500
July	3,900	5,900	6,000
August	4,200	6,200	7,100
September	3,600	5,600	6,200
October	3,500	5,500	5,500
November	4,000	6,000	5,700
December	4,100	6,100	6,100

Required:

1. Calculate the difference between actual cost and the line of regression cost ($y - y'$) for each month.
2. Identify the months in which costs will be investigated if the control limit is set at one standard error. Compute the total variance for the months to be investigated under this rule.
3. Identify the months in which costs will be investigated if the control limit is set at 1.96 standard deviations. Compute the total variance for the months to be investigated under this rule.
4. Identify the months in which costs will be investigated if the control limit is set at 1.5 standard deviations. Compute the total variance for the months to be investigated under this rule.
5. If you were in favor of the 1.96 standard deviation rule, would a 1.5 standard deviation rule make a big difference?

15-10. Cost to Investigate Variances and Control. "You are spending too much to investigate cost variances," Kelli Tunnell exclaims. "Last year we sent someone to the plant four times and only once did we find a cost difference that should be controlled."

Tunnell's partner, Jeffrey Crowfoot, replies, "It costs nothing to send someone to the plant, and you admit that once we found a cost worth looking at."

"But it does cost something to send someone to the plant," Tunnell persists. "It may not be additional cost, but we lose work that the employee could have done in that time and that has a value or a cost."

The company has been following the practice of investigating the cost of steam treatment whenever the cost is more than one standard deviation from the line of regression. One standard deviation is equal to $600. Kelli Tunnell wants to investigate costs only when they are more than 1.96 standard deviations from the line of regression.

A record of line of regression costs and actual costs for last year is given below:

Month	Hours	Line of Regresson Cost	Actual Cost
January	600	$19,000	$19,350
February	850	22,750	22,980
March	580	18,700	19,350
April	740	21,100	21,600
May	800	22,000	21,700
June	850	22,750	23,550
July	900	23,500	24,700
August	930	23,950	23,700
September	920	23,800	24,200
October	870	23,050	23,750
November	760	21,400	21,500
December	720	20,800	20,600

Required:

1.   What were the four months in which the costs were investigated with the upper control limit set at a plus one standard deviation?

2.   Assume that the cost that did require control, the cost Jeffrey Crowfoot mentioned, was incurred in June. Would this variance have been investigated if the upper limit had been set at plus 1.96 standard deviations?

3.   If the upper control limit had been set at plus 1.96 standard deviations, which costs would have been investigated?

4.   Is Kelli Tunnell correct in stating that a cost of lost work occurs even if incurred cost is added? Explain.

15-11. **Correlation and Control Limits.** You have collected data for total delivery costs and number of deliveries for 30 vehicles in your company's Colorado sales district. To this data you have applied simple linear regression and have the following results:

Observations	30
Constant	$3,499
X coefficient	$6.58
Average y	$47,157
Average x	6,635
$\Sigma (y - y')^2$	43,652
$\Sigma (y - \bar{y})^2$	498,002
$\Sigma (x - \bar{x})^2$	312,312

Required:

1.   Calculate the coefficient of determination.

2.   Calculate the standard error of the estimate.

3.   Based on the above results, explain how well the regression equation fits the actual cost data.

4.   Calculate an estimate and an upper and lower 95 percent control limit interval for the following deliveries per year:

    (a)   2,890
    (b)   6,635
    (c)   10,335

15-12. Overall Analysis based on Least Squares Cost Segregation. Franco Francetti has observed that the laundry cost at University Medical Center Hospital has both fixed and variable cost portions. As a cost control manager, he has noted that the cost tends to vary with patient days. Actual costs of laundry for past months are given as follows:

Patient Days	Cost	Patient Days	Cost
800	$7,700	850	$8,000
650	6,400	760	7,280
550	5,700	750	7,000
600	6,200	900	8,400
720	6,860	840	7,950
800	7,600	820	7,740
500	5,000	750	7,200
740	7,220	600	6,100
650	6,300	500	5,200
700	7,900	800	7,500

Required:

1. Using least squares, compute the variable cost of laundry per patient day and the fixed cost per month.
2. Calculate both the coefficient of determination and the standard error of the estimate.
3. Find the difference $(y - y')$ between actual cost and the line of regression cost for each of the patient days listed above. Plot these differences on a graph.
4. Using the information in (2) and (3) above, explain how well the regression line fits the actual cost data.
5. Explain how the graph in (3) above can be used to determine control limits for plus and minus one standard deviation and plus and minus 1.96 standard deviations.

15-13. Correlation for Single and Multiple Regression. The production manager of LiteCare Container Company has observed that heat treatment costs in one operation tend to vary with the cost of indirect materials used. While hours of operation are also a factor, the cost seems to be more sensitive to indirect materials cost. The following data have been collected on the hours of operation, indirect materials costs, and the heat treatment costs:

Hours	Indirect Materials Cost	Heat Treatment Cost	Hours	Indirect Materials Cost	Heat Treatment Cost
1,100	$ 930	$ 9,000	2,300	$1,400	$13,000
1,200	900	8,750	2,400	1,450	14,800
1,400	980	9,900	2,500	1,670	16,000
1,500	1,300	12,000	2,600	1,580	15,700
1,600	1,800	13,000	2,700	1,590	16,300
1,700	1,300	11,200	2,800	1,610	16,800
1,800	1,180	11,600	2,900	1,730	18,000
1,900	1,230	13,400	3,000	1,700	17,600
2,000	1,280	12,800	3,100	1,900	18,500
2,100	1,330	13,400	3,200	1,910	19,800
2,200	1,380	14,000	3,300	1,920	19,200

Required:

1. For the relationship between heat treatment cost and indirect materials cost:
    (a) Determine the regression equation.
    (b) Compute the coefficient of determination. Remember that indirect materials cost is the independent variable and heat treatment cost is the dependent variable.
2. For the relationship between heat treatment cost and hours of operation:
    (a) Determine the regression equation.
    (b) Compute the coefficient of determination.
3. Does indirect materials or hours of operation better explain the movement in heat treatment costs? Explain.
4. Perform a multiple regression analysis for heat treatment costs (as the dependent variable) and hours of operation and indirect materials cost (as the independent variables).
    (a) What is the meaning of the multiple regression equation?
    (b) Is the multiple regression equation a better predictor of heat treatment costs? Explain.

15-14. **Multiple Regression.** Lynch Foundry, in an attempt to better forecast overhead costs, is trying to apply regression analysis. After much study the managers have concluded that both direct labor hours and machine hours are the cost drivers. The data for the past year are as follows:

Month	Overhead Costs	Direct Labor Hours	Machine Hours
January	$13,425	1,485	1,342
February	15,237	1,798	1,527
March	14,626	1,762	1,426
April	14,393	1,611	1,443
May	14,996	1,703	1,411
June	16,085	1,882	1,595
July	17,324	2,076	1,694
August	18,023	2,171	1,823
September	16,627	1,905	1,627
October	17,942	2,111	1,794
November	19,151	2,294	1,899
December	17,409	1,975	1,791

Required:

1. For the relationship between overhead cost and direct labor hours:
    (a) Determine the regression equation.
    (b) Compute the coefficient of determination.
2. For the relationship between overhead cost and machine hours:
    (a) Determine the regression equation.
    (b) Compute the coefficient of determination.
3. Which cost driver is the better predictor of overhead costs? Explain.
4. Perform a multiple regression analysis for overhead costs (the dependent variable) and direct labor hours and machine hours (the independent variables). Evaluate and interpret the results.
5. Explain what improvement the multiple regression equation gives over the better simple regression equation given in (1) or (2) above.

15-15. Trend Line. Carrie Willowbee, the controller of Madison Industries, is meeting with the production managers to review the budget performance for the first seven months of 1995. She anticipates revisions will be made in the budget expectations for the remaining months of the year. In preparation for her meeting, she is analyzing the overhead data to identify any trends. The data she has accumulated are as follows:

Month/Year	Overhead Costs	Price Index
January, 1994	$116,874	297
February	119,312	300
March	122,116	302
April	124,556	305
May	127,977	308
June	125,731	309
July	124,032	311
August	121,381	313
September	134,917	315
October	98,784	318
November	110,961	319
December	107,740	320
January, 1995	110,944	322
February	112,050	324
March	107,386	327
April	113,802	329
May	112,786	332
June	122,022	334
July	109,618	336

Required:
1. Assuming January 1994 is month zero, plot the overhead costs on a graph.
2. Perform a simple regression analysis for a time series on the overhead costs. Evaluate and interpret the results.
3. Make an adjustment for the price index and rerun the regression analysis. (The adjustment is to multiply the monthly overhead costs by the fraction: price index for month zero ÷ price index for current month.) Evaluate and interpret the results.
4. Assume a change in production methods took place effective October 1994. Repeat requirements (1) through (3) above. Treat October 1994 as month zero. That is, all data prior to October 1994 are now irrelevant.
5. Return to the original data. Perform a multiple regression analysis, assuming January 1994 is month zero, using overhead costs as the dependent variable and months and price index (without converting to an adjustment) as independent variables. Evaluate and interpret your results.
6. Return to the original data. Perform a multiple regression, assuming October 1994 is month zero, using overhead costs as the dependent variable and months and price index (without converting to an adjustment) as independent variables. Evaluate and interpret your results.

CASE 15A–WADE TOOL COMPANY

Wade Tool Company manufactures small parts for the aerospace industry. These parts must meet strict, precise requirements. Recently, the company acquired improved automated equipment that reduces the losses from parts that cannot meet the very exacting standards.

Jeff Kunsman, a recent graduate of the company's training course, has been assigned the task of estimating the cost behavior pattern for the maintenance cost of the automated equipment. Preliminary estimates show that maintenance cost should vary at the rate of $7 per machine hour with a fixed cost of $4,000 each month. Kunsman has collected cost data from the previous 18 months. Based on these data, he has estimated that the cost varies at $6 per machine hour with a fixed cost of $5,000 each month. Data for the last 18 months are given as follows:

Hours	Cost	Hours	Cost
3,200	$23,950	2,750	$21,500
2,800	21,500	2,500	20,000
2,600	20,600	2,850	21,900
2,700	21,300	3,500	26,000
2,700	21,000	3,200	24,100
3,300	24,800	3,400	24,600
3,150	23,600	3,500	25,700
2,950	22,450	2,900	22,500
2,900	22,400	2,600	20,500

Kunsman's supervisor, Dan Cronin, agreed that the cost estimates as computed by Kunsman, using the high and low points of the range, were probably about right.

"However, if we use the least squares method," Cronin stated, "it should be possible to obtain even better estimates, since more data will be considered. Also, Jeff, check to see if a good correlation exists between the cost and machine hours. We may be barking up the wrong tree, and we'll want to know before we go too far. Perhaps some other factor, or some combination of factors, may be more appropriate. But if you find a good correlation, as I suspect you will, then determine a range of cost between plus and minus 1.96 standard deviations from the line of regression cost. This will establish a range with a 95 percent probability that the cost will lie within these control limits. If a cost is outside this range, we will want to check further to find out what happened."

Required:

1. Show how Kunsman computed a variable cost of $6 per machine hour and a fixed cost per month of $5,000.
2. Determine the variable and fixed cost by the least squares method.
3. Determine line of regression costs for each of the various hours given.
4. Calculate the coefficient of determination.
5. Compute the differences between actual costs and line of regression costs $(y - y')$ for each of the various hours given. Plot these differences on a graph.
6. Calculate the upper and lower control limits as established by Dan Cronin and draw the lines on the graph that represent the control limits.
7. Which differences fall outside the line and require investigation?

CASE 15B—SAINT MARY'S HOSPITAL

Cassie Hatcher was examining the use of surgical supplies at Saint Mary's Hospital. The hospital has six general surgery rooms and four specialized rooms. From the records she has gathered the following data:

Month/Year	Surgery Hours	Surgical Supplies
March, 1994	334	$10,210
April	270	8,033
May	178	5,962
June.......................................	428	10,475
July	386	13,986
August....................................	320	7,034
September	486	18,854
October	239	7,437
November	152	15,176
December	166	5,358
January, 1995	207	5,784
February	354	11,184
March	346	10,521
April	288	9,101
May	370	11,962
June.......................................	247	5,791
July	247	14,439
August....................................	430	7,585
September	328	15,515
October	211	5,625
November	368	10,366
Average hours	303	
Average costs		$10,019

Required:

1. Prepare a simple linear regression of surgical supplies based on the hours of monthly surgical activity. Evaluate and interpret the results.

2. Using the regression in (1) above, find and list the months which need to be investigated for errors. (Look at each month that exceeds one standard deviation.)

3. Ms. Hatcher checked the data entry and found the following keying errors:
   (a) November 1994 hours should be 512 rather than 152.
   (b) July 1995 hours should be 427, not 247.
   Correct these errors and rerun the regression. Evaluate and interpret the results.

4. Using the regression in (3) above, find and list the months which need to be investigated for errors. (Look at each month that exceeds one standard deviation.)

5. Ms. Hatcher, upon further investigation, found some problems with the data for the vacation months during each of the years. She found that for the surgical supplies:

June 1994 usage recorded in July	$2,520
July 1994 usage recorded in August	280
August 1994 usage recorded in September	3,602
December 1994 usage record in January 1995	408
June 1995 usage recorded in July	2,608
July 1995 usage recorded in August	229
August 1995 usage recorded in September	6,002

   Correct the errors and rerun the regression. Evaluate and interpret the results.

6. What is the effect of keying and cut-off errors on the regression results? Specifically, what is the effect on explained variation, fixed costs, and variable costs?

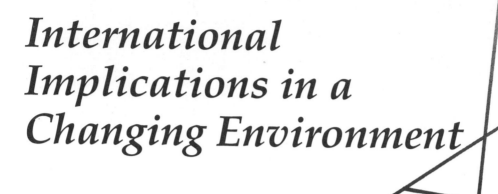

Chapter Sixteen

International Implications in a Changing Environment

 ## *Chapter Objectives*

After studying Chapter 16, you will be able to:
1. Describe the essential environmental differences influencing companies doing business in foreign countries.
2. Identify and describe the major means companies use to establish a business base in a foreign country.
3. Describe the differences in accounting rules for major cost areas in international accounting.
4. Explain the five primary purposes for international transfer prices.
5. Calculate foreign exchange gains and losses on purchase and sales transactions and hedging operations.
6. Record purchase and sales transactions that are affected by changes in foreign exchange rates, recognizing the transaction date, selected interim dates, and the settlement date.
7. Identify and describe the major issues relating to performance evaluation in and control of international operations.

▬ *All Roads Lead to South Korea* ▬

Douglas Carr, chief financial officer of International Machining Equipment, which has 16 foreign subsidiaries and affiliates operating in various countries around the world, has noticed that The Republic of South Korea is rapidly developing, and the company has no manufacturing or distribution operations directly or indirectly tied to South Korea. The CEO has ordered Carr to identify alternatives for expanding the company into South Korea.

Carr spent weeks researching his assignment and came up with three likely alternatives:

1. A large family-owned and operated business could be available for sale at the right price.
2. A major South Korean manufacturer will consider joint venturing for machining equipment aimed at a specific market niche.
3. An excellent site is available where the company can build its own manufacturing facilities.

Even after an alternative is selected, Carr knows he has to deal with a number of other issues. For example: How will the South Korean unit fit into the overall planning and control program? Will raw materials or parts be purchased outside of South Korea, and will they come from other units of the company? Will products manufactured in South Korea be sold outside the country? Will transactions be denominated in South Korean currency or one of the company's other currencies? How do the accounting rules in South Korea differ from accounting rules in the U.S.? These questions are only the tip of the iceberg of issues with which Carr will ultimately deal to create a successful South Korean unit.

Considering the influence of a global economy, it is important that a chief financial officer of a multinational company be aware of many international business issues and be able to interpret international accounting issues for top management. A few of the major concerns the executive must deal with are:

1. How to establish control systems for strategic planning, budgeting, and investment analysis at the multinational level.
2. How differences in accounting and reporting practices affect financing and investing decisions.
3. How investors, creditors, international bankers, market regulators, and rating agencies cope with change and diversity within the many countries where the company operates.
4. How internal transfer prices are used differently in multinational segments of an operation as compared to its domestic counterpart.
5. Trends that are taking place in the areas of international corporate finance, financial markets, and financial services.
6. Steps that are being taken in the international community to harmonize accounting standards.

The subjects related to international managerial accounting are diverse and would require more than one chapter to explain in detail. Therefore, this chapter presents an overview of the international environment, how companies expand into other countries, the differences in accounting issues, and selected managerial accounting concerns of a multinational company.

INTERNATIONAL ENVIRONMENT

Technology, innovation, and communication developments during the 1980s and early 1990s accelerated what many people have called a "shrinking world." Political boundaries are changing or disappearing; economic alliances among countries are expanding; and multinational businesses are almost a rule rather than an exception. Large companies know all too well that a market confined to a home country limits their ability to increase market share, to continue to grow, and to be profitable. Companies are now looking to any legal and ethical vehicle to extend markets into other countries and expand the market once it is established. Even if companies are trying to dominate the United States market, they are interested in foreign production operations as a means to lower input costs. For example, labor is cheaper in Mexico than in the United States. Many companies have manufacturing or processing facilities in Mexico to lower costs in a competitive market.

Complexities of the international environment combine to present major obstacles to managing a multinational operation. The major factors affecting the complexity of the international environment relate to communication, cultural, and environmental differences (economic, political, and business).

Communications Differences

One does not have to travel far to realize that different languages create communication challenges. Local companies manage with a great deal of face-to-face interaction and written communications. Such companies are typically blessed with a common language throughout the company. In international operations, communications become complicated and time consuming. No longer does a common language exist, although many companies are now beginning to adopt a company language. However, recruiting personnel with language skills has become common and essential to many multinational firms. Company documents must go through translation into all the languages in which the company does business. The distances between entities within the larger company make face-to-face meetings more difficult and certainly more expensive when they occur. In addition, the quality of information processing technology differs among countries. In one country computers may be commonplace while in another country labor is cheap enough that documents are processed manually. Tying the two systems together is not without challenge.

Cultural Differences

Managers in most international companies agree that qualified local managers are preferred to expatriates. Nevertheless, managers from different cultural backgrounds have culture-related attributes which impede effective and efficient operations beyond the local level. For example, in some countries, companies are like families. Employees are hired for life and know they will not be terminated. They develop a high loyalty to the company and will have considerable input into decisions. Managers in this environment have little tolerance for the independent-minded managers in another country who make decisions with little or no input from subordinates and who, when retraining is out of the question, terminate employees who do not perform well.

Other differences exist that make managing a far-flung operation difficult. Company meetings in one country are viewed as trivial and not important. In another country, meetings have social rather than management significance. Time, and thus a deadline, is of no consequence to a manager in one country, while missing deadlines will kill an operation in another country. Some managers will have a greater resistance to change, while survival of the multinational company is tied to its ability to bend and adapt to changes around the globe. As an illustration of adjusting to cultural differences, consider Japan's YKK zipper manufacturing center in Georgia:

Japan's largest zipper manufacturer, YKK, came to Macon, Georgia (pop. 106,612), in 1974, building a $15 million plant for 90 workers. The American employees proved highly capable. Today YKK runs 11 plants in Macon with 825 employees, 50 of them Japanese on long-term assignment and the rest Georgians. . . .

YKK had to unsnag several misconceptions about doing business in the U.S. to make this happen. For example, the company at first encouraged such Japanese management practices as mandatory uniforms for everyone and long, convivial evenings as a way to build team spirit among managers. The Japanese drive to make the world's best zippers, coupled with poor English, bewildered the U.S. workers. In 1979 they voted in the United Cement, Lime & Gypsum Workers Union to represent them. In response, family-owned YKK set up a personnel department largely comprising Americans already working there and began to make changes. Among them: the blue uniforms are optional (some Japanese still wear them). YKK also gave control of the daily management of the plants to Americans, believing that the workers would accept them as bosses more readily. Japanese technicians are in charge of maintaining the YKK-designed machinery, which is made in Japan. In 1984 the workers threw out the union.

After work, Japanese employees now relax and enjoy life with their families, American style. Many drive U.S. cars. Some of the men even attend PTA meetings. The children are Americanizing too, dressing in the latest fads and cheering on U.S. sports teams. Macon, meanwhile, is just a little bit Japanese. For nine years YKK has supported an annual cherry blossom festival. At this year's celebration, Tad Yoshida, executive VP of the parent company and son of the founder, presided over the parade as its grand marshal. Says he: "My father tells people assigned to Macon, 'Forget you are a Japanese and think like an American.' "[1]

Environmental Differences

Change and diversity exist to varying degrees with the environment of different countries. In one case, the environment may be relatively constant; and change will occur slowly. In another case, change is rapid; and operations must be flexible to react quickly. For the multinational company, the combination of operations in several countries and of the need to conduct business among countries amplifies greatly the environmental diversity. Management must recognize and cope with the dynamic nature of the environment. For example, individual country environments are different at a point in time and change relative to one another through time. Also, they change at different rates of speed. This means managers must treat the individual country environments as variables in decision making, planning, control, and cost management. If they do not, what is appropriate today is outdated tomorrow. Again, the emphasis is on flexibility.

Inflation   One of the most difficult aspects of environmental change and diversity in which a multinational manager must deal is inflation. Germany, Brazil, and the United States are examples of countries with diverse inflationary patterns. A high rate of local inflation means that local managers are preoccupied with the continuous necessity to find new sources of working capital, with protecting the values of local monetary assets, with frequent reassessments of product prices, and with the necessity to daily or weekly reevaluate product-line composition. Managers in this situation give nominal lip service to most other managerial chores, such as maintaining efficient operations.

Even with local inflationary differences, some help exists in multinational companies that does not exist in local companies. Tight coordination by headquarters of the operations in an inflationary environment with those in other countries can provide sources of inexpensive working capital and can reduce the amount of working capital required. Such coordination can also help protect inflation-endangered local resources and provide less expensive sources for raw materials as local prices rise.

The existence of differing rates of inflation creates another problem. The real costs of production in one country can change dynamically relative to another country. Managers at headquarters must be continuously balancing the system by shifting production and other resources among countries as costs change.

Political and Business Differences   The diversity of the political and business differences within a country's environment creates management

---

[1]Louis Kraar, "Japanese Pick Up U.S. Ideas," *Fortune*, Special Issue, Vol. 123, No. 12, Spring/Summer 1991, page 67.

challenges for the multinational managers. Differences exist in legal and tax systems, business customs and practices, types of government, types of government regulations, and national traditions. Kickbacks and bribes are normal practice in one country and illegal in another country. For example, for a company to build a plant in certain South American countries, the companies must make monetary gifts to local and provincial government employees to get construction permits, inspections, and other approvals expeditiously. Such practices in the United States are contrary to federal law.

SETTING UP BUSINESS IN OTHER COUNTRIES

Because companies in individual countries cannot always produce all of the goods and services needed within that country, they are looking for ways to procure or produce raw materials, parts, or subassemblies from cheaper foreign markets. In addition, companies want to expand their markets outside their own territory and look for ways to export the excess demand. For example, companies in the United States during the early 1990s are selling billions of dollars worth of goods and services in Canada, Japan, Mexico, Britain, Germany, South Korea, France, the Netherlands, Taiwan, Belgium-Luxembourg, and many other countries. The United States is also buying billions of dollars of goods and services from those same countries.

Companies expand into other countries in a variety of ways. The various approaches companies have used are presented below as direct investment, equity investment in other companies, joint ventures, franchising and networking, barter exchanges, and counter trade.

Direct Investment

A direct investment means the company goes into a foreign country and invests in its own operations. A direct investment may be one of the most expensive alternatives a company has, and it may be one of the most difficult alternatives. Many countries do not favor foreigners coming into their country to establish business, although that feeling is changing slowly. The governments want the foreign investment dollars while promoting local ownership and local managerial talent.

One common approach is to establish a foreign sales office which is responsible for marketing the company's products in that country. The sales office may buy, build, or lease whatever facilities it needs. Its organization may consist of a sales manager and sales representatives or merely a sales manager who coordinates activities with various wholesalers and jobbers. A sales office has no responsibility for production; orders are placed with the company's operating unit that will supply the needs of the foreign sales office.

Another approach is to buy an existing company. Many proprietorships, partnerships, and family or closely-held companies are willing to negotiate with companies who want to acquire all or some of their assets. Such companies usually have a well-established customer base and a good reputation.

A multinational company may also choose to go into a country and build manufacturing and marketing operations from scratch or build manufacturing facilities to accommodate an existing sales office. These are known as "greenfield" facilities.

Equity Investment in Other Companies

An equity investment usually means the company buys an interest in an established foreign entity. The two most common investment levels are a controlling interest of greater than 50 percent and an interest greater than 20 percent but less than the controlling interest. The first type of investment is treated as a subsidiary and is subject to consolidation rules for financial reporting. The second type of investment is an affiliate that is accounted for using the equity method for financial reporting. (The equity method is an accounting method that adjusts the investment for share of profits earned and dividends received.) Any one investor with at least a 20 percent ownership is assumed to have a significant influence on managerial decisions.

An organization that has subsidiaries and confines its activities primarily to their management is a **holding company** (sometimes called a controlling company). The multinational holding company does not perform the world-wide manufacturing and marketing functions itself. Rather, it leaves such functions to the subsidiaries. The management functions may be centralized or decentralized, depending on top management's philosophy. The subsidiaries may have been acquired by direct investment or by an equity investment. The holding company coordinates and evaluates its investments, coordinates resource acquisition, provides general and administrative services, and performs activities that are more efficiently done on a centralized basis. Holding companies gave rise to the need for consolidated financial statements widely recognized in the world today.

Joint Ventures

Another option for a company that cannot (or chooses not to) enter a country through one of the above approaches is the joint venture. A **joint venture** is an entity that is owned and operated by a small group of investors who are termed venturers or partners. Each venturer usually plays an active role in the management of the joint venture, such that no one venturer can be said to be in control. That is, control is usually joint in the sense of joint property, joint liability for losses and expenses, joint participation in profits, and joint voting power in decisions relating to major operating and financing issues.

What legal form will a joint venture take? Joint ventures may be incorporated and function as a corporation, or they may be unincorporated. A corporate joint venture operates as any corporation. Rights and rewards of ownership are determined on the basis of shares held. Several possibilities exist for unincorporated forms of organization:

1. A general partnership in which the entity is organized as a partnership with each partner (venturer) assuming unlimited liability. Rights and rewards of ownership are determined by the partnership agreement.

2.   A limited partnership in which the entity is organized as a partnership. However, one or more general partners (venturers) have unlimited liability, and one or more of the limited partners (venturers) have limited liability. Rights and rewards of ownership are determined by the partnership agreement. General partners usually manage the jointly owned net assets, subject to restrictions placed upon them by the limited partners.

3.   An undivided interest in which ownership of net assets takes neither the form of a corporation nor a partnership. Rights and rewards of ownership are determined by the contract among the venturers.

Joint ventures have been used with increasing frequency in recent years as a means of entering foreign markets. Although companies will enter into a joint venture with a foreign corporation, it is not unusual for a company to have a foreign government as a venture partner.

Franchising and Networking

Franchising and networking are two vehicles for expanding to new markets. Although both have been around for years, franchising was especially popular during the late 1970s and throughout the 1980s. Network marketing gained popularity in the mid-1980's and is growing through the 1990s.

Franchising is basically an approach where a company goes into an area and sells the right to use its name, its products, and its system of conducting business operations. The franchisee makes a significant investment in buying these privileges, and the franchiser provides the training and expertise. The franchise usually has a limited product line, as determined by the franchiser, and a limited territory. Perhaps the most famous franchise in the world is McDonalds and its golden arches. McDonalds is now in the U.S.S.R. and is moving into other formerly Eastern Bloc countries.

Networks, simply stated, are people talking to each other and sharing ideas, information, and resources. The important part is not the network but the process of communication that creates linkages among people and clusters of people. For the purpose of expanding the sale of goods or services into new foreign markets, network marketing becomes a convenient vehicle. Generally, network marketing has three characteristics:

1.   Individuals join a network where they buy products and services wholesale.

2.   Members of the network have the opportunity to invite other people to join the network and to earn an override on the products or services purchased by the members recruited.

3.   Members may specialize in marketing to people outside the network a product line or lines and earn the retail profit.

In most network marketing organizations, a corporate sponsor develops the beginnings of the network, assures payments to those earning performance bonuses, overrides, etc., and works with other companies to provide the products or services that will flow through the network.

Perhaps the most widely known network marketing organization around the world is the Amway Corporation, headquartered in Ada, Michigan. A company that would like to sell products in another country, such as Japan, can arrange with the Amway Corporation to provide the designated products to Amway's Japanese network. The use of networks to get a foot in the door is becoming a popular expansion approach.

Barter Exchanges

Bartering is simply an exchange of products or services involving something other than cash. For instance, ESPN, when a young network and short of cash, exchanged commercial time for costly broadcasting equipment. In this way, ESPN was able to use its most available resource—air time—instead of committing its cash reserves. Bartering provides a way for companies to capitalize on their abundant resources while conserving their scarce resources. In addition, it is becoming a vehicle to introduce new and existing products into new markets.

The most formal type of barter is the barter exchange. An exchange company is the focal point. It maintains a large database of individuals and companies that are members of the exchange, the goods or services members are offering for exchange, as well as the goods or services members are seeking to receive. Most barter exchanges charge a commission at some rate for each transaction consummated. Some exchanges also charge membership fees. The barter exchange is popular because it allows members the opportunity to barter for a wide range of goods or services and it provides a common arena for members to make many business contacts.

Countertrade

Countertrade can be an important part of a multinational company's worldwide marketing effort, enabling the company to enter new markets and gain an increased share in established markets. **Countertrade** is a reciprocal trade arrangement required as a condition of the principal sale and sometimes used by proactive companies as a marketing device. The term has acquired a double meaning over time. The generic term, countertrade, describes any reciprocal trading arrangement. The other more specialized meaning is a financing technique used by companies dealing with countries which lack a foreign exchange or have nonconvertible currency. In the past, such countries included certain third world and Eastern Bloc countries. Both meanings are contemplated in the following discussion. The typical countertrade techniques include in-country sourcing, export development, technology transfers, and direct investment.

As a rule, the host country company has the greatest bargaining power in any transaction involving countertrade because it is able to obtain concessions that the multinational company might not otherwise receive. If the multinational company truly has the upper hand, it can sell its products on a cash-only basis with no reciprocal obligation whatsoever.

Several degrees of national bargaining power exist in countertrade situations. Countries that require some form of offset, industrial cooperation, or industrial benefits to control market access have the greatest power. This tactic is used most frequently by socialist countries and countries with state trading monopolies, such as the U.S.S.R., Eastern European countries, China, and Algeria. It is also used by capitalist countries to control market access in the area of government defense. These countries include Canada, Australia, New Zealand, South Korea, some Latin American countries, and most of Western Europe. National bargaining power is strengthened when the country has laws requiring countertrade.

Market access is a strong national bargaining point in countries that are especially attractive markets. The People's Republic of China is the outstanding example of a country with countertrade bargaining leverage due to market attractiveness. Although most Chinese do not yet have significant disposable income, the sheer size of the market (one billion people), the country's steps towards raising the standard of living, and the lure of entering a previously closed market encourage multinational companies to agree to reciprocal trade concessions.

Establishing a joint venture may or may not increase the multinational company's bargaining power. If the country allows the joint venture only on the condition of a countertrade component (i.e., the foreign partner must agree to take back a percentage of production as partial payment for the sale of technology, equipment, and know-how), the multinational company's power is diminished. If the joint venture is not tied to countertrade, the multinational company's power is increased. It may buy back the products, sell them in the local market, or export them to third countries, depending on its business plans.

National bargaining power is at its weakest when the country requires countertrade primarily because of a shortage of foreign exchange. This normally occurs in heavily indebted developing countries, although it happens in the smaller socialist countries as well. In this situation, the more advanced developing countries, such as Brazil and Mexico, are in a better position than the lesser developed countries, such as Ethiopia, Haiti, Somalia, and the Sudan. They have a variety of marketable commodities and manufactured products to offer the multinational company as payment for imports; thus, they still have some degree of negotiating strength.

DIFFERENCES IN ACCOUNTING RULES AND FINANCIAL STRUCTURE

Accounting rules, on which information is based, and the business philosophy underlying financial structures, which influences the accounting rules, vary by country. Rules that seem reasonable in the United States might be totally inappropriate elsewhere because of differences in the business system and other elements of the environment. Although investors have major complaints about financial reporting issues, format, and timing, we are concerned about the internal reporting impact of differences. Therefore, we will not discuss the financial reporting concerns.

Accounting Rules

Studies of accounting practices around the world show many areas of differences in the treatment of costs and revenues. The following areas are examples where differences exist which have an impact on the multinational company:

1. Accounting for intangibles, especially goodwill.
2. Accounting for deferred income taxes.
3. The use of discretionary reserves.
4. Accounting for changing prices due to differences in inflation rates in many companies.
5. Accounting for pension costs by employers because of the influence of tax laws.
6. The valuation of investments in other countries.
7. Accounting for long-term leases.
8. The treatment of gains and losses from foreign currency transactions and from financial statement translation.

Let's look at the first three items on the list to understand what differences may exist.

Goodwill   Accounting for goodwill involves the timing of recognition of expenses. In the United States, it is common to write off goodwill over a period of 40 years. This is considered a conservative practice that has an insignificant impact on any annual net income. However, most other countries are more aggressive in their approach. Some countries permit expensing goodwill in the year of acquisition. Other countries use a 5-year amortization rule. Comparing the same transaction for subsidiaries in different countries yields very different results for assets and expenses.

Deferred Taxes   Deferred taxes are used extensively in Canada, the United States, and the United Kingdom but sparingly, if at all, in most other countries. Industrial countries seem to have a greater acceptance of deferred taxes than the nonindustrialized countries. However, differences still exist among the industrial countries over which expenses should be considered for deferred treatment.

Discretionary Reserves   The United States largely abandoned the use of reserves many years ago. However, reserves are used extensively internationally. Reserves mostly fall into three categories: hidden, legal, and free.

Hidden reserves arise from understating assets and overstating liabilities. The purpose is to bring more expenses into the income statement, thereby reducing taxable and distributable earnings and leading to a more liquid financial structure. Hidden reserves arise by depreciating assets very quickly, undervaluing inventories, and recognizing contingencies as actual expenses and liabilities. In some countries, such as Switzerland, management has wide discretion in determining the size of hidden reserves. In other countries, such as France and Germany, hidden reserves are a product of tax accounting that tends to show a faster write-off of plant and equipment.

Legal reserves arise from a company's articles of incorporation. Many countries require that a certain percentage of the company's earnings be appropriated in a legal reserve before dividends are declared, thus reducing the company's dividend base. This results in higher liquidity and a stronger capital base. It is also common for the company to include even higher reserve requirements in its articles of incorporation to ensure even better liquidity.

Free reserves are a variation of the legal reserves and result from a number of factors. Stockholders may vote to establish a reserve at some level; or management may choose to establish a reserve or increase the level of an existing reserve. These reserves result in a more conservative balance sheet with relatively high liquidity and high capital positions and in an income statement that is often smoothed to show whatever management wants to report.

Financial Structure

The differences in accounting rules relate to the financial structure of a company that evolves out of the environment of an individual country. Let's look at a few of examples of how the financial structure is influenced.

A commonly used ratio (see Chapter 17 for ratio analysis) is the debt to asset ratio (total liabilities divided by total assets). Since liabilities must be paid using company assets, the lower the ratio, the greater the company's ability to pay its debts, and the lower the risk for investors in the company. From the perspective of the U.S. accounting rules, creditors should be more willing to lend money to, and investors should be more willing to invest in, companies with lower debt to asset ratios. However, Japan is a different situation. Japanese companies tend to have high debt to asset ratios. In Japan, the debt to asset ratio is an indication of how much confidence the banks have in a company. Companies have low debt to asset ratios because the banks are reluctant to extend credit. Rather than indicating a risky company, a high debt to asset ratio in Japan suggests a safer investment.

In most European countries and Japan, the equity capital markets do not play a significant role in financing operations. Instead, a heavier reliance is placed on internal, as well as debt, financing. Creditors are protected by high liquidity, and banks tend to have unusual access to financial information through representation on boards of directors and a long history of interaction with the companies to which they lend. Therefore, the accounting rules are not dramatically influenced by the need for information by the outside investor. In the United States, generally accepted accounting principles focus more on the investor's needs.

In Germany, the law requires that at least 50 percent of the net income of a company must be available to shareholders to vote on at the annual meeting. This creates a strong incentive to keep reported earnings as low as possible and results in strengthening the liquidity and capital position of the company. Also in Germany, the tax laws require that the method used to value assets for book purposes also be used for tax purposes. Therefore, German companies will follow accounting practices that will keep the tax payments as low as possible.

International Accounting Standards

The existence of different accounting rules affects the decisions of management and resource providers to the extent that they fail either to understand or to trust the messages communicated by financial information. A number of international, regional, and domestic organizations recognize this problem and are working toward harmonizing accounting rules to the greatest extent possible. Perhaps the most well known of the organizations is the International Accounting Standards Committee (IASC).

The IASC was formed in 1973, by agreement of the leading professional bodies in the major western developed countries, to develop world-wide accounting standards. In essence, the IASC is trying to harmonize the world's accounting standards and eliminate those differences that cannot be explained by environmental variables.

The IASC currently represents more than 100 accountancy bodies from some 75 countries. Governments do not belong to the IASC; it is a private-sector organization with representatives from professional accounting organizations.

To date, the IASC has issued almost 30 *International Accounting Standards*. Compliance with these standards is voluntary because the IASC has no power to enforce them. Nevertheless, support for these standards is growing around the world. In fact, most of the professional organizations holding membership in the IASC have agreed to require, at some point in the future, the *International Accounting Standards* as part of their country's generally accepted accounting principles. If all multinational companies would observe the standards, significant harmonization would occur.

INTERNATIONAL TRANSFER PRICING

As discussed in previous chapters, the need for determining a transfer price arises when goods or services are exchanged between organizational units of the same company. A transfer price (a monetary value) is used when one subsidiary or affiliate of a corporation sells to another. This price is recorded by the seller unit as revenue and by the buyer unit as cost of goods sold.

Because transfer prices do not occur at arm's length, room exists for manipulation. Governments are concerned because the transfer price could affect taxes, such as excise taxes (border or value-added taxes, for example) and income taxes. Companies are concerned because transfer prices affect direct cash flows for payments of goods, taxes, cost structures influencing its competitive position, and evaluation of management's performance.

Transfer prices for a multinational company are more complex because differing conditions in each country where the company does business can lead to different transfer pricing decisions. In addition, international transfer prices serve different purposes than those used only in domestic operations. Naturally, we still want managers to make desirable decisions that enhance goal congruence, and meet the objectives of strategic planning, management control, and operational control. However, international transfer pricing goes beyond the domestic needs to include:

1. Minimization of world-wide income taxes.
2. Minimization of world-wide import duties.
3. Avoidance of financial restrictions, including the movement of cash.
4. Management of currency exchange fluctuations.
5. Approvals from the host country.

Minimization of World-wide Income Taxes

The manipulative nature of the transfer price setting process gives rise to shifting taxable profits from a country with high income taxes to a country with low income taxes. The purpose of the shift is for the multinational company to retain more of its world-wide profits. For example, assume that the tax rate in Brazil is 50 percent, while the tax rate in the U.S. is 35 percent. A U.S. subsidiary of a multinational company sells a product to one of its sister subsidiaries in Brazil. If we assume that a normal transfer price is $16 per unit but that the transfer price for units going into Brazil is set at $20 per unit, the U.S. subsidiary will have a higher profit of $4 per unit ($20 − $16) that is taxed at 35 percent. The subsidiary in Brazil now has a higher cost of goods that will be sold in the future, and its profits are less by $4 per unit. If the Brazilian subsidiary received a transfer price of $16, its profits would be higher and those amounts would be taxed at 50 percent.

Minimization of World-wide Import Duties

Import duties, called tariffs, interact with local country income taxes. Low import duties are often associated with high income taxes. The opposite is also true: high import duties with low income taxes. Most countries apply import duties whether or not a domestic company is part of a multinational company. Therefore, transfer prices can be used to reduce high import duties. For example, a company moving products into a country with high import duties can develop low transfer prices that mean lower tariff charges. Remember that the high tariffs general mean low income taxes, so the low transfer price brings a double benefit. The opposite is also true. A company may use high transfer prices when transferring goods into a country with low import duties.

Avoidance of Financial Restrictions

Foreign governments often place financial restrictions on subsidiaries or affiliates operating within their boundaries. Common restrictions apply to the amount of cash that may leave the country in the form of dividend payments and to the allowability of certain expenses charged by the parent company in computing taxes for that country. Examples of parent expenses in this category are research and development, general and administrative costs, and royalty or licensing fees. Certain governments have restrictions on moving cash out of their countries. Thus to allow moving profits and, therefore, "stuck" cash, high transfer prices will reduce those restricted profits and increase firm-wide liquidity and mobility.

Management of Currency Exchange Fluctuations

A section later in the chapter covers currency exchange gains and losses and a few things management can do to minimize losses. However, one topic not covered there is the balance-of-payment problem. When countries decide to revalue their currency downward (known as devaluation), a company can suffer major losses in international transactions that involve that country. Losses on devaluations may be avoided by using inflated transfer prices to transfer funds from that country to countries with stronger currencies. That is, transfer prices again become a cash removal method. Few financial assets are held in the volatile currency.

Gaining Host Country Approval

Most governments are becoming sophisticated and aware of the results of using high or low transfer prices. Price controls may be based on the transferred-in cost. For example, price increases may be limited to cost increases. Using unfavorable prices to a country's detriment may cause a loss of goodwill. In the long run, companies find that transfer pricing policies which satisfy foreign authorities may be in the best interest of the company than the minor profits that might be sacrificed. A foreign government's requirements about domestic ownership, locally produced content, and approval for sales to the government can be significant factors in determining how to enter an international market and how a company will operate there.

INTERNATIONAL TAXATION

International taxation occurs when a domestic government imposes taxes on income or wealth generated within its boundaries by a company of a foreign country. International taxation also includes taxes levied on income earned by a domestic company from commercial activities in foreign countries. In other words, a company may be taxed by a country where wealth or profit is produced and again by the multinational's home-base country. For example, a U.S. corporation engaged in international operations must comply with U.S. tax laws and the tax laws of each foreign country in which it does business.

International taxation has a dramatic impact on the decisions made by the management of multinational companies. It affects where a company invests, what form of business organization it selects, what products it produces, how it markets its products, the currency it selects for denominating transactions, the transfer prices it sets, and financing arrangements it establishes. Unfortunately, tax systems are as varied as the countries developing them. As a result, international taxation is constantly changing and extremely complex. Management must continually review and restructure its own tax accounting system as changes occur in tax treaties, agreements, laws, and regulations.

Most countries believe that they have the right to tax income earned by a domestic company outside the country's boundaries. For a multinational company, this means that income is taxed where it is earned and then again where the parent company is based. The result is double taxation. The ways available to multinational companies to mitigate the effects of double taxation include:

1. *Tax exemption:* A tax exemption allows certain corporations to pay no tax on certain income.
2. *Tax credits:* A tax credit allows a company to reduce the taxes paid to the domestic government by the amount of taxes paid to the foreign government. A credit is a direct reduction of the tax liability.
3. *Deferred principal:* The deferral occurs where parent companies are not taxed on foreign income until they actually receive the income, such as in a dividend.
4. *Tax havens:* A tax haven is a country with an exceptionally low or no income tax. It generally offers a company the right to earn income or to transfer income within its borders and pay little or no tax. Tax havens become especially useful for shifting income from high tax countries.
5. *Tax treaties:* A tax treaty between two or more countries establishes what items of income will or will not be taxed by the country in which the income is earned.

Most multinational companies have extensive and complex tax planning systems to minimize the world-wide tax burden. The people who are part of this system must be familiar with the tax laws and regulations of the individual countries in which their companies operate.

ACCOUNTING FOR TRANSACTIONS IN FOREIGN CURRENCY

Among the first activities of an expanding company in the international market are the buying and selling of goods and services. For example, a manufacturer of computer-aided design equipment may try to expand by selling its product to foreign customers. Or it might try to lower its product cost by buying some of its memory chips from a less expensive source in another country. Although most of the illustrations in this text are recorded in U. S. dollars, French francs, German marks, British pounds, Japanese yen, Malaysian dollars, or some other currency will be used in international markets. The value of these currencies rises and falls daily in relation to the dollar.

A **foreign currency transaction** is one in which settlement is in a foreign currency. A transaction with a foreign company that is settled in a domestic currency is not a foreign currency transaction. The more common foreign currency transactions are:

1. Importing or exporting goods or services on credit with the receivable or payable denominated in a foreign currency.

2. Borrowing from or lending to a foreign company with the amount payable or receivable denominated in a foreign currency.
3. Hedging operations.

Each of these transactions are presented in the following sections.

Importing or Exporting Goods or Services

The most common form of foreign currency transaction is the importing or exporting of goods or services. Let's now look at the financial impact of these transactions.

Foreign Purchases   When a domestic company purchases goods or services abroad, it may pay either in its own currency or in the foreign currency. If billings and payments are both in the domestic currency, no accounting problem arises. For example, assume that our U.S. company mentioned earlier buys memory chips from a company in Japan at a cost of $200,000. The accounting records of the U.S. company would reflect the following amounts on the date of purchase:

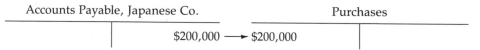

On the date of payment, the transaction would appear in the accounts as:

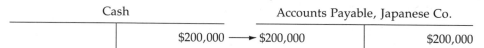

However, the Japanese company may bill the U.S. company in yen and request payment in yen. If so, the U.S. company will incur an exchange gain or loss if the exchange rate changes between the dates of purchase and payment. For example, assume that the transaction above is in yen and the exchange rates of the dates of purchase and payment are $.0050 and $.0055 per yen, respectively. This means the purchase price of $200,000 is really ¥40,000,000 (¥40,000,000 × $.0050 = $200,000). The accounts of the U.S. company would show the same amounts at the date of purchased as shown above. The date of payment results in different amounts affecting the accounts, as follows:

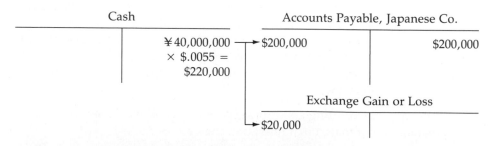

In this case, the U.S. company received an exchange loss of $20,000 because it had agreed to pay a fixed ¥40,000,000 and, between dates of purchase and payment, the exchange value of the yen in relation to the dollar increased.

Foreign Sales   Sales are the opposite of purchases. So the same rationale applies to sales except that the relationship of exchange gains or losses to the exchange rate is reversed. For example, assume that our company sells completed computer products to a company in Germany for $500,000. If the billing and subsequent payment are made in U.S. dollars, no accounting problems arise. The accounts on the date of purchase would be:

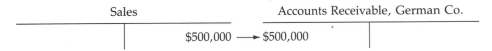

Sales		Accounts Receivable, German Co.	
	$500,000 ⟶ $500,000		

On the date of payment, the transaction would appear in the accounts as:

Accounts Receivable, German Co.		Cash	
$500,000	$500,000 ⟶ $500,000		

If the U.S. company bills in German marks (DM) and permits payment in German marks, the U.S. company will incur an exchange gain or loss if the exchange rates change between the dates of billing and payment. For example, assume that the above transaction is in German marks and that the exchange rates on dates of billing and payment are $.50 and $.45 per German mark, respectively. The sale would still be record as $500,000 and represents DM 1,000,000 (DM 1,000,000 × $.50 = $500,000). On the date of payment, in which the transaction is settled in German marks, the accounts show the following results:

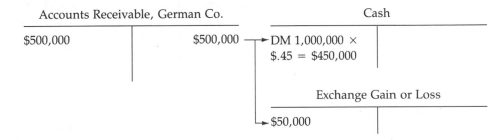

Accounts Receivable, German Co.		Cash	
$500,000	$500,000 ⟶ DM 1,000,000 × $.45 = $450,000		

		Exchange Gain or Loss	
	⟶ $50,000		

The U.S. company suffered an exchange loss of $50,000 because it agreed to receive a fixed DM 1,000,000 and the exchange rates changed between dates of billing and payment. In this case, the exchange rates decreased.

Dates of Concern to Accountants   In each foreign currency transaction, three dates are of concern to accountants: the date of the purchase or sale, a balance sheet date falling between the date of the transaction and the date of the settlement, and the date of the settlement. These dates and the appropriate exchange rates used in translating accounts denominated in foreign currencies are as follows:

1. *Date of transaction:* Each asset, liability, revenue, expense, gain, or loss arising from the transaction is measured and recorded in the domestic currency by multiplying the units of foreign currency by the current exchange rate (spot exchange rate on date of transaction).

2. *Balance sheet date:* Recorded balances that are denominated in a foreign currency are adjusted to reflect the exchange rate in effect at an interim balance sheet date.

3. *Settlement date:* In the case of a foreign currency payable, a domestic company must convert the domestic currency into foreign currency units to settle the accounts payable. For an accounts receivable in which foreign currency units are received, the foreign currency must be converted to domestic currency. Although translation is not required, a transaction gain or loss is recognized if the amount of the domestic currency paid or received upon conversion does not equal the carrying value of the related payable or receivable.

To illustrate the impact of these dates, consider that our U.S. company sold completed computer products to a French company for $100,000 at a time when the franc exchange rate was $.20. The billing to the French company was for 500,000 francs. The **spot rate**, the rate of exchange between two currencies that are being bought and sold for immediate delivery, for francs at the three dates is as follows:

Transaction date—12/1/94	$.20
Balance sheet date—12/31/94	.23
Settlement date—3/1/95	.22

1. On December 1, 1994, the U.S. company would record a sale and accounts receivable at the domestic equivalent of $100,000 (500,000 francs × $.20).

2. On the balance sheet, December 31, 1994, the receivable denominated in foreign currency is adjusted using the exchange rate in effect at the balance sheet date. In this case, the receivable is $115,000 (500,000 francs × $.23).

Commitment at 12/31	$115,000
Recorded receivable	100,000
Exchange gain	$ 15,000

Accountants will increase the receivable balance and record an exchange gain for the $15,000.

3. On the settlement date, March 1, 1995, the U.S. company receives 500,000 francs and must convert them to U.S. currency. With a conversion rate of $.22, the U.S. company receives $110,000 (500,000 francs × $.22).

Settlement at 3/1	$110,000
Recorded receivable	115,000
Exchange loss	$ (5,000)

The receivable is liquidated at $115,000, and an exchange loss is recognized for the $5,000. For the total transaction, the company realizes a net exchange gain of $10,000 ($110,000 − $100,000).

Realized and Unrealized Gains or Losses   Anytime a company enters into a foreign currency transaction and exchange rates change between date of transaction and date of settlement, an **exchange gain or loss** can occur. A company does not know whether it will really have an exchange gain or loss until the settlement date. When settlement occurs, the company may have a realized gain or loss. For instance, in the French company illustration, the realized gain is $10,000 as determined on the settlement date.

When a balance sheet date comes between the transaction and settlement dates, U.S. accounting rules require companies to identify an exchange gain or loss as of the balance sheet date. That gain or loss will appear in the income statement, and any appropriate asset or liability accounts must be adjusted. Since the transaction has not been settled, any exchange gain or loss on the balance sheet date is unrealized. In our example, the unrealized gain was $15,000, and we identify it with 1994. Because exchange rates changed after the balance sheet date, an exchange loss occurred and is identified with 1995.

The distinction between realized and unrealized exchange gains and losses is important only to identify to which accounting period we attribute the gain or loss. That is, financial reporting requirements cause us to recognize unrealized gains or losses at balance sheet dates. Incidentally, the balance sheet can be monthly, quarterly, or annually. We only assumed annual balance sheets for illustration purposes.

Borrowing or Lending

Accounting for foreign borrowing or lending transactions, other than for trade payables or trade receivables, follows the two-step approach outlined in foreign purchases and sales above. The cost of an asset acquired or revenue recognized is accounted for independently from the method of settlement. For example, if a piece of machining equipment is purchased from a foreign company on credit, the cost of the asset is the number of foreign currency units that would be paid in a cash transaction multiplied by the exchange rate at the transaction date. The cost of the asset is not adjusted for subsequent changes in the exchange rate, but the liability is adjusted at each balance sheet date on the basis of the exchange rate in effect on that date. Any adjustment to the liability will appear as an exchange gain or loss in the income statement. The amount recorded as interest expense is the equivalent number of domestic currency units needed to make the interest payment. If a receivable is involved instead of a liability, a period adjustment is made to the receivable account.

This accounting treatment suggests that companies should develop policies covering borrowings and lendings (investments) in the international environment.

Debt Policy   If currency in one country is becoming generally weaker as compared to the currency in another country, it may be advantageous to borrow in that weak currency. We can say a currency is weak relative to another currency when exchange rates are unstable, fluctuating in uncertain patterns, or tend to have a downward trend in current economic conditions. For example, assume the Canadian dollar is weak compared to the U.S. dollar and we expect the Canadian dollar to fall in value. We borrow $1,000,000 (Canadian) when the exchange rate is $.90. In terms of U.S. currency, the amount borrowed is $900,000. Then, if the exchange rate is $.80 at the time the loan is repaid, the loan can be settled for $800,000 (Canadian $1,000,000 × $.80). That is a savings due to exchange of $100,000.

Even though this strategy has certain advantages, it probably will not produce dramatic results. In general, the interest rates on loans are very high when a currency is weak and very low when a currency is strong. In addition, creditors will extend credit, if at all, over very short periods of time. The borrower will probably have little advantage when the inflation rate in a weak economy is rapid. However, a slight advantage may exist when borrowing in currencies where inflation is more gradual.

Lending (Investment) Policy   Bank balances and investments in bonds, whenever possible, should be held in strong currencies. Over the years, for instance, the Swiss franc has been considered a strong currency. As a result, Switzerland has served as a banking center. Interest rates on investments are relatively low, but the investment itself is viewed as relatively safe from the erosive effects of inflation.

Assume that $180,000 is deposited in a Swiss bank account when the exchange rate is $.30. The transaction is recorded by the Swiss bank as SF 600,000 ($180,000 ÷ $.30). At a later date, the Swiss franc trades at $.50. Assuming no interest on the deposit (a simplification for our example), the original SF 600,000 are now worth $300,000 (SF 600,000 × $.50). That is an exchange gain of $120,000.

Judgments about how currencies will move relative to each other are speculative at best. Over time, a strong currency may weaken; or a weak currency may strengthen. Much depends upon the direction of international economics and politics, and the economic health of any particular country relative to the others. Some of the speculation can be avoided by using future exchange contracts, a subject to be discussed later.

Hedging

As we have seen, a domestic company doing business with companies in other countries and engaging in foreign currency transactions faces an exchange risk. To minimize this exchange risk, companies establish hedging operations. A **hedge**, in its broadest sense, is any purchase or sale transaction having as its specific purpose the offset of gains or losses arising from changes in foreign currency exchange rates that relate to one or more purchase or sale transactions already made or under contract. The hedging transaction usually matches the same transaction and settlement dates as the transaction it is intended to offset.

Hedges can occur in a number of ways. Perhaps the most common hedge is a **forward exchange contract (forward contract)**. It is an agreement to exchange currencies of two different countries at a specified rate (the forward rate) on a stipulated future date. That is, you can buy or sell a foreign currency with delivery due in the future. A **forward rate** is the rate of exchange between two currencies being bought and sold for delivery at a future date. The exchange rate most people hear about is the spot rate, the rate of exchange between two currencies that are being bought and sold for immediate delivery.

Another hedge that companies are beginning to use more frequently is to buy or sell options in a futures market. In most developed countries, a futures market exists for commodities, metals, and currency. Buying or selling of options, like the forward contract, is betting on certain behavior in the exchange rates at some future date.

Although hedging may be used for many types of transactions, the following scenarios show an application of hedging to the purchase and sale of goods and services. In addition, our illustrations assume the use of a forward exchange contract as the hedge.

Hedge for a Foreign Currency Exposed Liability   In a purchase transaction where settlement takes place at some future date, a liability is created on the transaction date. When the transaction is denominated in a foreign currency, the exchange gains or losses relate to the liability. Therefore, we refer to the account payable as an exposed liability.

To illustrate the accounting for a forward exchange contract that hedges an exposed liability position, we will use the same set of data from the foreign purchases section above. The assumptions are as follows:

1.   Purchased memory chips for ¥40,000,000 payable in yen.
2.   Exchange rates:

Transaction date	$.0050
Forward rate (90 days)	$.0051
Settlement date	$.0055

3.   The transaction is denominated in yen.

The U.S. company has made a purchase on credit. The liability will be settled in 90 days in a foreign currency. Therefore, it must go into the foreign currency market in 90 days and exchange U.S. dollars for Japanese yen. The exchange rate for this transaction will be the spot rate on the date the U.S. company makes the exchange for yen. The hedge for this transaction is to contract today to buy the needed yen in 90 days at an agreed to exchange rate (the forward rate). A completed hedging transaction will consist of two parts: (1) a premium or discount which is measured by the difference between the spot rate on the date of transaction and the forward rate; and (2) an exchange gain or loss which is the difference between the domestic currency that would settle the debt on the transaction date and the domestic currency to settle the debt on the settlement date.

For our illustration, assume the U.S. company entered into a forward exchange contract to buy ¥40,000,000 on the settlement date for $.0051. The hedging transaction is treated separately from the transaction to purchase memory chips. (We recorded the purchase of memory chips earlier and will not repeat it here.) Recording all of the elements of a hedging transaction is straightforward but includes several accounts with which managers are not usually familiar. Therefore, we will deal only with the calculations of the appropriate amounts related to the forward exchange contract. Managers will find this approach more useful. The relevant amounts on the hedging transaction date are as follows:

Domestic currency that would be required on the transaction date to acquire the needed foreign currency. (This is an asset account called Foreign Currency Receivable from Exchange Dealer.) (¥40,000,000 × $.005)	$200,000
Domestic currency that will be paid on the date the foreign currency is delivered. (This is a liability account called Domestic Currency Payable to Exchange Dealer.) (¥40,000,000 × $.0051)	204,000
Premium paid on the contract (This is an asset account called Premium on Forward Contract.) [¥40,000,000 × ($.005 − $.0051)]	$ 4,000

On the transaction date, the U.S. company records the forward exchange contract by recognizing a liability of $204,000 for the number of dollars to be paid to the exchange dealer when the forward exchange contract matures. At the same time, the amounts to be received from the forward exchange contract are recorded as an asset. The ¥40,000,000 to be received is translated into $200,000 using the spot rate of $.0050 in effect at date of transaction. Note that the liability is for a fixed amount of dollars ($204,000) and that it is based on the contracted forward rate, while the right to receive ¥40,000,000 reflects the units to be received at the current spot rate. In future periods, the liability is not adjusted; however, the receivable is based in a foreign currency and is subject to the fluctuations in the exchange rate. We will not go through the accounting requirements, other than to say that any premium or discount amounts are amortized to the income statement over the life of the forward exchange contract on a straight-line basis and exchange gains and losses are identified with accounting periods between the transaction date and the settlement date. For managerial purposes, we are more concerned about the total impact of exchange fluctuations and hedging transactions. A summary of what has occurred follows:

Exchange loss on purchase transaction (computed earlier in chapter)		$ 20,000
Premium amortized to expense		4,000
Amount received from Exchange Dealer (settlement date) (¥40,000,000 × $.0055)	$220,000	
Receivable from Exchange Dealer (date of transaction)	200,000	
Exchange gain on forward contract		(20,000)
Net loss on exchange		$ 4,000

Notice that the net loss in this situation is the premium paid on the forward contract. The exchange gain on the hedge offsets the exchange loss on the original transaction.

Hedge for a Foreign Currency Exposed Asset   In a sale transaction where settlement takes place at some future date, a receivable is created on the transaction date. When the transaction is denominated in a foreign currency, the exchange gains or losses relate to the receivable. Therefore, we refer to the account receivable as an exposed asset.

In our example, the U.S. company entered into a forward exchange contract to hedge an exposed liability position. Handling a hedge for an exposed asset (receivable) position is based on a similar analysis. However, because the U.S. company will be receiving foreign currency in settlement of the exposed receivable balance, the company would enter into a forward exchange contract to sell foreign currency for U.S. currency with a future delivery date. In this case, the receivable from the dealer is denominated in a fixed number of dollars, the amount of which is determined by the contracted forward rate. The obligation to the dealer, on the other hand, is denominated in a foreign currency, which is translated into dollars using the current spot rate. The difference between the receivable and liability is accounted for as a discount or premium on a forward exchange contract.

To illustrate the accounting for a forward exchange contract that hedges an exposed asset position, we will use the set of data from the sale of computer products to a German company in our earlier example. The assumptions are as follows:

1. Sold DM 1,000,000 worth of computer products payable in marks.
2. Exchange rates:

Transaction date	$.50
Forward rate	$.48
Settlement date	$.45

3. The transaction is denominated in German marks.

The U.S. company has sold its products on credit. The receivable will be settled on a future date in a foreign currency. Therefore, it must go into the foreign currency market on that future date and exchange the German marks received for U.S. dollars. The exchange rate for this transaction will be the spot rate on the date the U.S. company makes the exchange for dollars. The hedge for this transaction is to contract today to sell the German marks to be received at an agreed to exchange rate (the forward rate).

For our illustration, assume the U.S. company entered into a forward exchange contract to sell 1,000,000 marks on the settlement date for $.48. The hedging transaction is treated separately from the transaction to sell the computer products. (We recorded the sale earlier and will not repeat it here.) The relevant amounts on the hedging transaction date are as follows:

Domestic currency that would be acquired from the exchange of the foreign currency received. (This is an asset account called Domestic Currency Receivable from Exchange Dealer.) (DM1,000,000 × $.48)	$480,000
Domestic currency that would be received on the transaction date from the exchange of foreign currency. (This is a liability account called Foreign Currency Payable to Exchange Dealer.) (DM1,000,000 × $.50)	500,000
Premium paid on the contract (This is an asset account called Premium on Forward Contract.) [DM1,000,000 × ($.50 − $.48)]	$ 20,000

On the transaction date, the U.S. company records the forward exchange contract by recognizing a liability of $500,000 for the number of marks to be paid to the exchange dealer when the forward exchange contract matures. At the same time, the amounts to be received from the forward exchange contract are recorded as an asset. The 1,000,000 marks to be received is translated into $480,000 using the forward rate of $.48. Note that the receivable is for a fixed amount of dollars ($480,000) and that it is based on the contracted forward rate. In future periods, the receivable is not adjusted; however, the liability is based in a foreign currency and is subject to the fluctuations in the exchange rate. Any premium or discount amounts are amortized to the income statement over the life of the forward exchange contract on a straight-line basis and exchange gains and losses are identified with accounting periods between the transaction date and the settlement date. A summary of the results of all transactions is as follows:

Exchange loss on sale transaction (computed earlier in chapter)		$ 50,000
Premium amortized to expense		20,000
Amount payable to Exchange Dealer (settlement date) DM(1,000,000 × $.45)	$450,000	
Payable to Exchange Dealer (date of transaction)	500,000	
Exchange gain on forward contract		(50,000)
Net loss on exchange		$ 20,000

TRANSLATION OF FINANCIAL STATEMENTS OF FOREIGN AFFILIATES

A major topic in accounting for international operations is restating a foreign entity's financial statements into the domestic currency. This conversion process is the first step in preparing consolidated financial statements for a domestic parent company and its foreign subsidiary and in accounting for a domestic parent company's investment in a foreign affiliate where the investment is at least 20 percent but the financial statements of the affiliate are not consolidated.

The method of translation depends on the foreign affiliate's functional currency. The **functional currency** or local currency is the currency of the place where the subsidiary conducts its business. Generally, it is the major currency in which a company earns and disburses cash. The company must decide what the functional currency is for each of its affiliates. This will have an impact on the exchange gains and losses on foreign currency transactions.

Translation or restatement of financial statements involves the use of various exchange rates to convert each item in the financial statements from one currency unit to another. This process results in translation gains or losses that will appear on the income statement. This whole process is primarily a financial reporting issue, and it only becomes a managerial issue if the translated statements become the basis for taxation or creditor and investor relationships. Translation has many rules and the subject requires much more detail than we can afford here. Therefore, the rules for translation and an example of translation are not given here.

PERFORMANCE EVALUATION IN THE MULTINATIONAL COMPANY

How can a manager compare cross-border performance statistics when the reported numbers are generated by unfamiliar measurement rules? How does a financial executive communicate on a topic with an investor in Germany, with a potential joint venture partner in Eastern Europe, and with a government regulator in Japan? All these constituents are thinking in terms of their own "local" definitions. Properly measuring the performance of an individual, a division, a subsidiary, or the entire multinational company is never simple. A number of issues are unique to the international environment that confound the use of measures commonly employed in the domestic setting. In addition, many events affecting performance are not controllable by the individual or the unit being evaluated.

The remainder of this section discusses several of the important topics relating to performance evaluation.

Financial Measures

Multinational companies use various measures to evaluate the results of operations at home and abroad. The traditional measures are profit, return on investment (ROI), and budget comparisons. Although we have discussed all of these measures in earlier chapters, a new dimension appears in the international setting: local currencies versus foreign currencies. For example, return on investment has an investment value in the ratio. Is ROI computed using the local currency or the currency where the multinational company is based? Translating local currency to a foreign currency can alter the investment measurement. The most common approach in evaluating the various measures is to separate what is controllable at the local level from what local managers cannot or do not control well—exchange rate fluctuations. That means managers in the various countries are responsible for profits, investments, etc., in local currency, leaving someone at the multinational's corporate office responsible for exchange gains and losses.

Over the last few years, additional financial measures are gaining in popularity. Managers around the world are becoming cash flow conscious. As a result, managers at all levels of the multinational organization place a heavy emphasis on cash flow and evaluate cash flow measures in periodic reports.

Profits are important as an overall measurement. However, the various types of contribution margins discussed in Chapters 4 and 14 are becoming more useful in evaluating foreign managerial talent and in assessing the corporate investment in a foreign subsidiary or affiliate. Contribution margins are more reliable measures for planning and decision making, performance evaluation and control, and cost management.

Nonfinancial Measures

Multinational companies use several nonfinancial measures in their performance evaluation. The most common ones for companies whose parent is domiciled in the United States are:

1. Increasing market share.
2. Relationship with host country government.
3. Quality control.
4. Productivity improvement.
5. Cooperation with parent company.
6. Environment compliance.
7. Employee development.
8. Employee safety.
9. Labor turnover.
10. Community service.

Notice that for some of these measures a company will have difficulty attaching a numerical value. Despite the difficulty, the measures are very important in comparing performances.

Budgets

As we have discussed in several earlier chapters, budgets are a tool for controlling operations. The budget provides a baseline for comparing the actual results of operations. This comparison produces variances that can be analyzed to evaluate performance and improve the efficiency of future operations. Often companies depend on budgets and control reports to survive currently or to set a basis for becoming more competitive. We can extend these concepts into the international setting as long as we recognize a couple of basic points about currency and tracking results, subjects presented in the following sections.

Use of Local Currency   Should the multinational company use the local currency or translate results into the domestic currency for budgeting and budgetary control purposes? In most cases, the local currency gives a more meaningful picture of the activities. The local currency recognizes the differences within countries and also differences in the relationship of the subsidiary or affiliate to the parent. The one potentially difficult problem with using local currencies is that top management of the multinational company might not interpret results properly in the light of local country differences and, therefore, may not understand and interpret the potential effects of currency exchange gains and losses.

Another potential problem occurs when comparisons are made of worldwide operations and all local currencies are translated into the currency where the multinational company is based. If the subsidiary or affiliate operates in a country with a stable currency, translation into the domestic currency should not affect comparisons. However, possible distortions can occur in comparisons when translations of results from countries with an unstable currency are present. In that case, management either excludes those results or finds another basis for comparison.

Tracking Results   When budgets and performance results are translated into a home country-based currency, questions arise as to which exchange rate to use in tracking results. Generally speaking, we have nine combinations of exchange rates when comparing budget and performance data. Three rates might be used for budgeted data and three rates might be used for tracking results. This results in nine different combinations of rates ($3 \times 3 = 9$). The rates are as follows:

Developing the Budget	
D1	Rate at budget preparation date.
D2	Projected rate at budget preparation date.
D3	Actual rate at end of budget period (through updating).

Tracking Results	
T1	Rate at budget preparation date.
T2	Projected rate at budget preparation date.
T3	Actual rate at end of budget period (through updating).

The combinations that make the most sense to consider are those that use the same rate to develop the budget and to track results. They are: D1-T1, D2-T2, and D3-T3. All three of these combinations hold the manager accountable for local activities and environmental changes while eliminating the effects of exchange gains and losses. D2-T2 has a slight twist in that someone needs to project the rates at the end of the budget period. The differences in rates are not in the variances, but someone can be held accountable for poor projections. From a conceptual point of view, the use of projected rates is the most preferred combination because it gives the best information as the period is progressing.

Some people have suggested using combinations D1-T3 and D2-T3. Both of these introduce the effects of rate differences because the rate used to develop the budget is different than the rate used to track the results. In D1-T3, the manager is responsible for the entire rate change between date of budget and end of period. Few companies give a country manager complete control of (and responsibility for) currency exchange. The D2-T3 combination holds the manager responsible only for the difference between the projected and the actual end of period rates.

If top managers want information on the exchange gains and losses, one possibility is to use D1-T1 to determine the operating variance and D1-T3 to determine the exchange gain or loss. Then a report could be prepared to explain the reason for the exchange-rate change and to discuss the impact of the change on the business for the year. Now, someone has to explain what changed and why.

As an example, consider a multinational company based in the United States that has a German subsidiary with the following situation:

Expected volume...	1,200 units
Expected price in local currency	DM3
Beginning exchange rate	$.50
Projected end of period exchange rate	$.40
Actual volume	1,000 units
Actual price in local currency..................................	DM3
Actual end of period exchange rate	$.40

The variances will be computed using combinations D2-T2 and D1-T3. The variance for projected rate as budgeted over the projected rate as tracked is:

Expected volume × Expected price × Projected rate
1,200 units   ×   DM3   × $.40   = $1,440
Actual volume   ×   Actual price   ×   Projected rate
1,000 units   ×   DM3   × $.40   =   1,200

Total variance .... $ 240

The total variance is the operating variance only; no exchange gain or loss is included. This variance is due totally to volume changes.

The variance for beginning rate over the projected rate is:

Expected volume × Expected price × Beginning rate
1,200 units   ×   DM3   × $.50   = $1,800
Actual volume   ×   Actual price   ×   Projected rate
1,000 units   ×   DM3   × $.40   =   1,200

Total variance .... $ 600

The total variance for this situation is composed of the operating variance and a variance due to exchange gains or losses. The two variances are:

Operating variance:
$(1,200 - 1,000) \times 3 \times \$.50$ $300
Exchange loss:
$1,000 \times 3 \times (\$.50 - \$.40)$ 300

Total variance $600

SUMMARY

More and more companies are moving into the international business arena. As would be expected, top managements are faced with new challenges, uncertainties, and unknowns. Before actually doing business in another country, management must assess the complexities resulting from communication, cultural, inflation, and political and business differences. Once the differences are understood, the decision of how to establish a business base in a particular country is made. The common considerations are direct investment, equity investment in other companies, joint ventures, franchising and network marketing, barter exchanges, and countertrade.

Accounting rules are different in most countries. Items like accounting for goodwill, deferred taxes, and discretionary reserves vary around the globe. These differences relate to political, cultural, and business philosophies within each country. As a result, the financial structure of any subsidiary or affiliate is dependent on the country in which it operates. Clearly, a need exists to harmonize the difference in accounting rules. An organization called the International Accounting Standards Committee is working on that task.

Transfer pricing for movement of goods and services among units of the same company but in different countries takes on a meaning different from that of domestic transfer pricing. International transfer pricing is much more concerned with minimizing world-wide income taxes and import duties, avoiding financial restrictions, managing currency exchange fluctuations, and gaining host country approval.

As companies engage in purchase and sell transactions between countries, currency exchange rates become important. Companies face the possibility of exchange gains and losses. In an effort to minimize the uncertainty in exchange rate fluctuations, some companies will engage in hedging operations, including forward exchange contracts and options trading. Consequently, foreign currency transactions require close management by multinational companies.

At some point, the individual, operation, subsidiary, or company must be evaluated. Performance measurement in the international community is more complex than in the domestic setting. Although the financial measures of profit, return on investment, and budget comparisons are important, many nonfinancial measures are also becoming significant. In addition, the traditional budget takes on a new meaning in the multinational community because the need to translate a foreign currency into a domestic currency raises issues about the appropriate exchange rate for developing the budget and tracking the results. The preferred approach is to use projected rates at the end of the period for both.

PROBLEM FOR REVIEW

International Machining Equipment had the following three transactions during December 1995:

Dec. 11 Sold two machines to a company located in Columbia for 7,738,000 pesos. The spot rate on this date was 365 pesos per U.S. dollar. Payment was made in Colombian pesos on January 10 (a 30-day arrangement).

11 Entered into a forward exchange contract from a foreign currency broker at a forward rate of $.003 as a hedge on the Colombian transaction.

12 Purchased subassemblies from a company in Taiwan. The account was denominated in 500,000 Taiwan dollars. The exchange rate on this date was $.0389. The settlement date was January 10.

Required:

1. Using T-accounts, show the U.S. dollar amounts that will appear in the records on the dates for the sale and purchase transactions. (Ignore the hedging transaction.)

2. Using T-accounts, show adjustments that must be made to receivables and payables at the December 31 balance sheet date. Assume the exchange rate on December 31 for Colombian pesos was $.00268 and for Taiwan dollars was $.0344. Ignore the hedging transaction adjustments.

3. Using T-accounts, record the sales and purchase transactions. On the settlement date, the exchange rate for Colombian pesos was $.0031 and for Taiwan dollars was $.0397.

4. Calculate the exchange gain or loss from the hedging transaction.

5. Summarize the total exchange gains and losses for all transactions covering the period of December 11 through January 10.

Solution:

1.   Transaction date:

Colombian transaction: 7,738,000 pesos ÷ 365 = $21,000

Sales		Accounts Receivable	
12/11 $21,200	12/11 $21,200	

Taiwan transaction: NT$500,000 × $.0389 = $19,450

Accounts Payable		Purchases	
12/11 $19,450	12/11 $19,450	

2.   Balance sheet date:

Colombian transaction:
Accounts Receivable balance 12/11 .... $21,200
Value of transaction at 12/31:
7,738,000 × $.00268 (rounded)   20,738
Exchange loss .... $ 462

Accounts Receivable				Exchange Gain or Loss		
12/11	$21,200	12/31	$462	12/31	$462	

Taiwan transaction:
Accounts Payable balance 12/11 .... $19,450
Value of transaction at 12/31:
500,000 × $.0344 17,200
Exchange gain .... $ 2,250

Accounts Payable				Exchange Gain or Loss		
12/31	$2,250	12/11	$19,450		12/31	$2,250

Note: The sales, purchase, and exchange gain or loss accounts are all closed out at year end. Therefore, the exchange gain or loss account will have a zero balance on January 1.

3. Settlement date:

Colombian transaction:
Accounts Receivable balance 12/31 .... $20,738
Value of transaction at 1/10:
7,738,000 × $.0031 (rounded) 23,988
Exchange gain .... $ 3,250

Accounts Receivable				Exchange Gain or Loss		
12/11	$21,200	2/31	$ 462		1/10	$3,250
		1/10	20,738			

Cash	
1/10	$23,988

Taiwan transaction:
Accounts Payable balance 12/31 .... $17,200
Value of transaction at 1/10:
500,000 × $.0397 19,850
Exchange loss .... $ 2,650

Accounts Payable				Exchange Gain or Loss		
12/31	$ 2,250	12/11	$19,450	1/10	$2,650	
1/10	17,200					

	Cash	
	1/10	$19,850

4.   Exchange gain or loss on hedging operation:

Domestic currency that would be acquired from the exchange of the
foreign currency received. (This is an asset account called Domestic
Currency Receivable from Exchange Dealer.)
(7,738,000 ÷ 365) $21,200

Domestic currency that would be received on the transaction date from
the exchange of foreign currency. (This is a liability account called Foreign
Currency Payable to Exchange Dealer.)
(7,738,000 × $.003) 23,214

Premium paid on the contract (This is an asset account called Premium
on Forward Contract.) .... $ 2,014

Amount received from Exchange Broker on settlement date
(7,738,000 × $.0031) $23,988

FC Payable to Exchange Broker on transaction date 23,214

Exchange gain on hedging... $ 774

Net loss on hedging ($2,014 − $774) .... $ 1,240

5.   Summary of exchange gains or losses on foreign currency transactions:

Colombian transaction:
   Exchange gain on transaction ($3,250 − $462) .... $ 2,788
   Exchange gain on hedging.............................. $ 774
   Less premium on hedging 2,014   (1,240)
   Net gain on Colombian transaction .... $ 1,548
Taiwan transaction:
   Exchange loss on transaction ($2,650 − $2,250) .... $ 400
   Net gain on all transactions .... $ 1,148

TERMINOLOGY REVIEW

Bartering (808)
Countertrade (808)
Exchange gain or loss (819)
Foreign currency transaction (815)
Forward exchange contract (forward
contract) (821)
Forward rate (821)
Franchising (807)
Free reserves (811)

Functional currency (824)
Hedge (820)
Hidden reserves (810)
Holding company (806)
International taxation (814)
Joint venture (806)
Legal reserves (811)
Spot rate (818)

QUESTIONS FOR REVIEW AND DISCUSSION

1.   Describe two cultural differences that can affect the manner of managing a company in a foreign country.

2. Why are inflation rates in the various countries where multinational companies operate important to corporate management?

3. How might a multinational company make a direct investment in a foreign country?

4. What is meant by an "equity investment?"

5. Describe the forms of joint ventures into which a multinational company might enter.

6. What are the main characteristics of network marketing? Why would a company use such a network?

7. What is a barter exchange? How might a multinational company use such an exchange?

8. Who has the bargaining power in a countertrade situation, i.e., a company in the host country or the multinational company? Explain.

9. Explain why accounting rules may differ from one country to another.

10. The United States accounting profession largely abandoned discretionary reserves years ago. Why would a company want to use discretionary reserves?

11. What is the difference between hidden reserves and legal reserves?

12. Describe how the business environment of an individual country will influence a company's financial structure.

13. Why are international standards especially relevant for multinational corporations?

14. Why is an international transfer price often not the result of an arm's-length transaction?

15. Why would an international transfer price be used to minimize world-wide income taxes and import duties?

16. What avenues are available to a multinational company to mitigate the effects of double taxation?

17. Explain why a company is exposed to an added risk when it enters into a transaction that is to be settled in a foreign currency.

18. If an American company does business with a German company and all their transactions take place in German marks, which firm may incur an exchange gain or loss?

19. What does it mean if the exchange rate of a French franc in terms of the U.S. dollar is $.15? If a bottle of French perfume costs 200 francs, how much will it cost in U.S. dollars?

20. Distinguish between spot and forward rates of exchange.

21. Name the three dates that are important to an accountant in handling foreign currency transactions. Explain the accounting at each date.

22. When do exchange gains and losses occur on foreign purchases and foreign sales transactions?

23. Briefly explain how hedging is achieved through forward exchange contracts.

24. What is the difference between realized and unrealized exchange gains and losses?

25.   Under what conditions should the local currency be used in developing budgets within a multinational company?

26.   Why would a manager of an Italian subsidiary not want the budget developed using actual exchange rates at the time of budget preparation and the actual operational results stated at actual exchange rates at the end of the period?

EXERCISES

1.   **Transfer Pricing Problem.** Volkswerke is a Swiss subsidiary of a German company. It makes a product that it can sell in Switzerland or transfer to another subsidiary in Germany. In a normal month, Volkswerke produces 100,000 units of product with a variable cost of 12 francs per unit and fixed costs of 8 francs per unit (based on 800,000 francs fixed cost allocated to production). These units can be sold in Switzerland for 26 francs per unit or transferred to the German subsidiary for additional processing and sold in a processed form. The selling price processed is 34 marks. The cost to complete the additional processing is 6 marks per unit. The fixed cost of processing is 300,000 marks. The current exchange rate between the francs and marks is one franc = .90 marks. If the product is not transferred, the German subsidiary would have excess capacity.

Required:

1.   Should the Swiss production be transferred to the German subsidiary or sold locally? Explain your answer.

2.   Explain how a transfer price could be used to move cash from Switzerland to Germany, assuming Switzerland does not like to see money leave the country.

2.   **Evaluating Fixed Overhead Relationships.** Juarez Medical Center, a Mexican subsidiary of a U.S. corporate hospital chain, has a radiology department that operated at 2,000 standard hours last year. The standard is 5 patients per hour, and the department actually handled 9,000 patients. Fixed overhead data are given as follows:

Fixed overhead charged to patients	630,000 pesos
Unfavorable capacity variance...............................	350,000 pesos

When this information was transmitted to the U.S. home office, it was translated into U.S. dollars. Budgeted amounts were translated at the exchange rate for preparing the budget (peso = $.0045) and the amounts charged to products were translated at the exchange rate at the end of the year (peso = $.0040).

Required:

1.   What was the fixed overhead budget last year in pesos?
2.   What was the fixed overhead rate per patient in pesos?
3.   Translate the appropriate information into U.S. dollars.
4.   How does the translation affect the unfavorable capacity variance?
5.   Where in the translated numbers can be found any exchange gain or loss?

3.   **Budget Variance for Individual Costs.** Suzi Stephens, manager of the Machining Department at Autowerke, a German subsidiary of a U.S. company, Mayfield Industries, Inc., has estimated overhead costs for August at an expected operating level of 6,000 machine hours. Past experience indicates a rate of cost variability per hour as follows:

Lubrication	DM1.50
Supplies	.60
Power	.50
Repairs	1.00
Maintenance...	1.60

Costs that are fixed for the month are budgeted as follows:

Supervision..	DM 4,500
Indirect labor	11,500
Heat and light..	3,200
Taxes and insurance.......................................	1,600
Depreciation	1,800

During the month of August, the department produced the quantity of product that should have been produced in 5,000 hours in a total of 5,500 hours and incurred the following overhead costs:

Lubrication	DM 3,900
Supplies	1,700
Power	1,500
Repairs	2,800
Maintenance...	4,300
Supervision..	4,000
Indirect labor	12,000
Heat and light..	3,200
Taxes and insurance.......................................	1,400
Depreciation	1,600
Total	DM36,400

Required:

1. Prepare a budget of overhead costs for 5,000 machine hours.
2. Compare the actual overhead costs with the budget for 5,000 machine hours. Show budget variances for each item.
3. The budget comparison in (2) above is translated into U.S. dollars for review by a corporate manager. Assume that the budget and the results will be translated at the projected exchange rate of $.50.
    (a) Show the budget and actual comparison after currency translation.
    (b) Would your evaluation of Suzi Stephens change after the translation?
    (c) What is the amount of foreign exchange gain or loss in the variances?

4. **Variances for Individual Operating Expenses.** Anemia Manufacturing Company, a U.S. subsidiary of a British corporation, uses a budget formula for estimating its marketing and administrative expenses. The fixed and variable components of this formula for individual costs are:

Cost Category	Fixed Cost Per Month	Variable Cost Per Unit Sold
Salary and wages	$1,750	$0.90
Rent of space.................................	1,000	0.60
Freight out	0	0.15
Miscellaneous	250	0.05
	$3,000	$1.70

The company budgeted 10,000 units of sales for the month. It actually sold 9,200 units and incurred the following marketing and administrative expenses:

Salary and wages	$10,230
Rent of space..	6,710
Freight out	1,280
Miscellaneous	680
	$18,900

At the end of each month, the comparisons of numbers for variance calculations are sent to the home office in London, where they are translated into British pounds. The budgeted information is translated at the projected exchange rate of one U.S. dollar = .84 pounds. The actual amounts are translated at the exchange rate at the end of the month (one U.S. dollar = .75 pounds).

Required:
1. For each of the individual cost categories, compute the spending and volume variances, and indicate whether they are favorable or unfavorable.
2. Make the translations of the data according to home office policy.
3. What impact does the translation have on how you evaluate the spending and volume variances?
4. What is your suggestion for translating the numbers so the results of the translation will be evaluated the same as the U.S. dollar results?

5. **Recording a Foreign Purchase and Sale.** Macon Manufacturing, a U.S. Corporation, had the following two transactions with foreign companies during this year:
    (a) Purchased a special-purpose machine from a German company on credit for DM30,000 (Deutche marks). At the date of purchase, the exchange rate was $.39 per mark. On the date of payment, which was made in marks, the exchange rate was $.41.
    (b) Sold a product on account to a British company for 200,000 pounds. Payment was made in pounds. The British pound was $1.20 on the transaction date and $1.28 on the settlement date.

Required:
1. Using T-accounts, record the purchase and payment on Macon Manufacturing's books related to the purchase of the machine.
2. Using T-accounts, record the sale and payment on Macon Manufacturing's books related to the sale of the product.

6. **T-Accounts and Foreign Purchases and Sales.** MARKAR Tools, Inc., a U.S. corporation, is a well-known importer/exporter of industrial tools, equipment, and supplies. The following transactions were entered into during June:

June 3 Purchased power tools on account from a Japanese wholesaler at an invoice price of 1,400,000 yen. The exchange rate for yen was $.0072.
     5 Sold supplies on credit to Machwerke, a German company, for an invoice price of $2,800. The exchange rate for German marks was $.5634.
     9 Sold hand tools on credit to Dodds Retailers in New Zealand at an invoice price of $14,200 U.S. dollars. The exchange rate for New Zealand dollars was $.576.

June 11 Purchased electric drills on account from a manufacturer in Belgium. The billing was for 746,270 francs. The exchange rate for Belgium francs was $.0268.

16 Paid 900,000 yen on account to the Japanese wholesaler for the purchase on June 3. The exchange rate for yen was $.0067.

18 Settled the accounts payable with the Belgium manufacturer. The exchange rate for Belgian francs was $.0284.

22 Received full payment from the Dodds Retailer invoice of June 9. The exchange for New Zealand dollars rate was $.0284.

30 Completed payment of the June 3 purchase. The exchange rate for yen was $.0078.

Required:

Using T-accounts, record the above transactions for June. Show calculations of any exchange gains and losses relating to these transactions. (Hint: Purchases are denominated in foreign currency; sales in U.S. currency.)

7. **Year-end Adjustments for Foreign Currency Transactions.** Clancy Wool Products Exchange, a U.S. based import/export company, had the following transactions during March:

March 6 Purchased products from a Swiss company for 500,000 Swiss francs. The exchange rate for francs was $.486.

15 Sold products to a German company located in Dresden for $100,000. The exchange rate for the German mark was $.407.

18 Sold products to a British company for 100,000 pounds. The exchange rate for British pounds was $1.505.

20 Purchased products from WOOL-Made, a British company, for $120,000. The exchange rate for British pounds was $1.498.

The company's fiscal year ends on March 31. All of the foregoing transactions were open on March 31. The exchange rates on this date were: franc = $.460; mark = $.398; and pound = $1.472.

Required:

1. Determine the amount Clancy Wool Products Exchange would report for each unsettled receivable and payable on March 31.

2. Determine the exchange gain or loss on each unsettled receivable and payable as of March 31.

8. **Calculation of Exchange Gains and Losses.** Georgia Timberline, Inc. is a North Carolina company that has a substantial import/export business as part of its operations. The following transactions occurred in November:

Nov. 1 Purchased products on account from a manufacturer in Edinburgh, Scotland, at an invoice price of 1,000 pounds. The exchange rate for pounds was $1.20.

5 Purchased products on account from British Hi-Tech. The invoice was stated at $2,000. The exchange rate for pounds is $1.21.

7 Sold products to a Canadian wholesaler in Ontario. The invoice was stated at 4,000 Canadian dollars. The exchange rate for Canadian dollars was $.80.

Nov. 15 Paid 500 pounds on account to the Edinburgh manufacturer. The exchange rate for pounds was $1.15.

20 Paid the amount due to the British Hi-Tech company. The exchange rate for pounds was $1.18.

25 Returned merchandise to the Edinburgh manufacturer and received credit of 100 pounds. The exchange rate for pounds was $1.15.

28 Received full payment on account from the Canadian wholesaler. The exchange rate for Canadian dollars was $.76.

30 Remitted final payment to the Edinburgh manufacturer. The exchange rate for pounds was $1.16.

Required:
Calculate the foreign exchange gains or losses on the transactions for each supplier and customer.

9.   **Hedging Foreign Exchange Fluctuations.** Overseas Products Company billed a customer in a foreign country at 600,000 units of that country's currency. The exchange rate at that time was 50 units of local currency to one dollar. Overseas Products Company hoped to collect the equivalent of $12,000 from the customer in three months. Economic conditions changed in three months, and the currency was quoted at 120 units to the dollar when the company received payment.

Required:
1.   Compute the loss in foreign exchange to Overseas Products Company.
2.   Explain what measures could have been taken to guard against the loss in foreign exchange.

10.   **Foreign Exchange Gains and Losses with Hedging.** Pagley Quality Exports is a wholesaler engaged in foreign trade. As a wholesaler, the company both buys and sells in international markets. The following transactions with companies in Hong Kong are typical of the company's business:

March 1 Purchased merchandise from Chang, Ltd., a Hong Kong manufacturer. The invoice was for 190,000 Hong Kong dollars, payable on June 1. The exchange rate on this date for the Hong Kong dollar was $.1285.

1 Acquired a forward exchange contract, as a hedge, to buy 190,000 Hong Kong dollars on June 1 for $.1294.

31 Sold merchandise to TSAI Retailers for 150,000 Hong Kong dollars. No hedging was involved. The exchange rate for Hong Kong dollars was $.1256.

April 30 Received 150,000 Hong Kong dollars from TSAI Retailers. The exchange rate for Hong Kong dollars was $.1372.

June 1 Submitted full payment of 190,000 Hong Kong dollars to Chang, Ltd., after obtaining 190,000 Hong Kong dollars on its forward exchange contract. The exchange rate for Hong Kong dollars was $.1430.

Required:
Calculate the exchange gains or losses associated with each of the transactions.

11.   **Foreign Exchange Gains and Losses with Hedging.** Huseman Enterprises buys and sells products in the international marketplace. As a U.S. corporation, Huseman uses the U.S. dollar as its functional currency. However, all billings are denominated in a

foreign currency. The following transactions are typical of the company's business activities:

(a) Sold merchandise to an Italian company for 2,000,000 lira when the exchange rate for lira was $.00052. Huseman also sells 1,000,000 lira for future delivery at .00052.

(b) Received payment from the Italian company in (a) when the exchange rate for the lira was $.0006. The lira sold in (a) are delivered to the exchange broker.

(c) Purchased merchandise from a British company for 5,000 pounds when the exchange rate for pounds was $1.20. Concurrently, the company purchased 5,000 pounds for future delivery at $1.20.

(d) Received the pounds in (c) from the exchange broker. The company then paid the British company for the merchandise purchased in (c) using these pounds. The exchange rate for pounds was $1.25.

(e) Sold merchandise to a Mexican company for 100,000 pesos when the exchange rate for pesos was $.0045.

(f) Purchased merchandise from another Mexican company for 200,000 pesos when the exchange rate for the peso was $.0045.

Required:
Calculate the exchange gains or losses associated with each of the transactions. The last two transactions are still open. Assume that on the date you are making your calculations, the exchange rate for the peso was $.005.

12. **Performance Evaluation after Translation.** Herb Gonzalez is the manager of a South American subsidiary of MDE International. In a recent meeting of subsidiary managers in the western hemisphere, Herb learned he was one of only a few managers in world operations to meet or exceed budget projections. The actual sales exceeded the budgeted sales, and cost of goods sold and operating expenses were lower than projected. Herb acknowledged how easy it was to meet budgeted numbers when his budget was denominated in local currency. He knew what he had to do.

The next day, the president of MDE International made a presentation of operating results of all subsidiaries world-wide. To bring comparability to the presentation, the results of all subsidiaries were translated into U.S. dollars. The subsidiaries were all ranked according to operating net income after translation. Herb found, to his astonishment, that his subsidiary was listed in the bottom ten performing subsidiaries. How could he be one of the top managers one day and the next day be one of the ten worst managers?

Required:

1. Give an explanation for why Herb's performance looks good in local currency but looks poor after translating the results into U.S. currency.

2. What are the problems with making comparisons of subsidiaries operating in different countries?

PROBLEMS

16-1. **Transfer Pricing Problem.** A large farming company has two units: the Mexican Division produces grain, and the U.S. Division sells the grain. As soon as the grain is produced, it is placed in storage areas until sold by the U.S. Division. A transfer price is used to charge the U.S. Division and to recognize the Mexican Division as a profit center.

During the year, three grain crops of 1,900,000 bushels each were produced. All three have now been sold, although some were held in inventory for various periods of time. The market prices at production time were 1,000 pesos per bushel for the first crop (peso = $.004), 1,110 pesos per bushel for the second (peso = $.0045), and 600 pesos per bushel for the third (peso = .005). No beginning inventories were on hand. The Mexican producer uses a transfer price equal to the market price in pesos.

The results for the period are:

Total company revenues (5,700,000 bushels)	$28,300,000
Costs:	
Producing division (peso = $.005):	
Labor and materials	$13,250,000
Division overhead	8,250,000
Selling division:	
Labor	$ 1,500,000
Division overhead	900,000

The company president is pleased with the total profit (stated in U.S. dollars) generated by the two divisions. He wants to determine whether the price speculation activities of the selling division are earning a profit.

Required:

1. Prepare divisional income statements for each division, using the currency of the country where each operates. Which division is more profitable?
2. Would you use the market price or cost for the transfer price? Explain.

16-2. **Overhead Variances for a Department.** The following flexible budget information has been prepared for the Fabrication Department of Abbott Industries, a Canadian subsidiary of a U.S. corporation:

Machine hours at normal capacity	5,000
Variable overhead (Canadian dollars):	
Indirect labor	$ 3,500
Supplies	2,500
Repairs and maintenance	1,000
Electricity, other than lighting	5,000
Total variable overhead	$12,000
Fixed overhead (Canadian dollars):	
Supervision	$ 3,000
Supplies	1,700
Repairs and maintenance	3,000
Depreciation on machinery	6,500
Insurance	1,800
Property taxes	1,000
Heating	600
Lighting	400
Total fixed overhead	$18,000
Total factory overhead	$30,000

Factory overhead is allocated on the basis of machine hours. The standard calls for ten units of product per machine hour. At the end of May, 4,650 machine hours were actually worked; and 48,530 units of product were produced. The following actual overhead costs were incurred:

Variable overhead (Canadian dollars):

Indirect labor	$ 3,400
Supplies	2,200
Repairs and maintenance.....................................	960
Electricity, other than lighting	4,740
Total variable overhead	$11,300

Fixed overhead (Canadian dollars):

Supervision...	$ 3,100
Supplies	1,650
Repairs and maintenance.....................................	3,200
Depreciation on machinery....................................	6,500
Insurance	1,900
Property taxes	1,100
Heating	845
Lighting	405
Total fixed overhead	$18,700
Total factory overhead	$30,000

When the financial reports are sent to the U.S. headquarters, the budget and actual amounts are translated into U.S. dollars. The budgeted amounts are translated at the projected exchange rate for the end of the period (Canadian dollar = $.80). Actual results are translated at the actual exchange rate at the end of the period (Canadian dollar = $.90).

Required:

1. Prepare a report that shows each category of overhead cost with individual budget variances.
2. Calculate an overall capacity variance for the department.
3. Translate the amounts according to the above rules and repeat (1) and (2) above.
4. Explain what differences occur in the relationship of the numbers and how you would evaluate performance.
5. Would you recommend a different approach to translation? Why? Explain your approach.

16-3. **Sales and Marketing Expense Variances.** Trujillo Distributors, a wholly-owned Mexican subsidiary of a U.S. corporation, is in the process of evaluating its selling and marketing expenses. Management has estimated that its relevant range of operations is 40,000 to 60,000 sales units. At each of these levels, management has established the following budgeted amounts:

	Sales Units	
	40,000	**60,000**
Sales and marketing expenses (pesos in thousands):		
Transportation	110,000	150,000
Credit and collections	57,000	65,000
Direct selling..	19,800	26,200
Advertising and promotion	11,000	14,000

The company planned to operate at 48,000 units during 1995. It actually achieved 50,000 units during the year. Although the president is not confident that his managers are good cost estimators and are controlling costs, the accounting systems are able to differentiate between variable and fixed costs. Actual costs incurred for sales and marketing activities are as follows:

	Variable	Fixed
Transportation	109,000	31,000
Credit and collections	23,505	42,185
Direct selling	18,730	7,485
Advertising and promotion	7,248	4,690

The budgeted and actual financial results are submitted to the U.S. headquarters at the end of each year. All amounts are translated into U.S. dollars using the projected exchange rate for the end of the year (peso = $.005).

Required:

1. Identify the budget formula for each individual sales and marketing expense.
2. Prepare an analysis for each expense that shows the spending and volume variances.
3. Restate the analysis in terms of U.S. dollars according to company policy. Does this translation change the evaluation you would make of the subsidiary's performance? Explain.

16-4. **Comprehensive Operating Expense Variance Analysis.** The Pomeroy Manufacturing Company is a U.S. subsidiary of a Japanese company. It budgeted 180,000 sales units for November. The product has a budgeted selling price of $21 and a manufacturing cost of $11.50 per unit. The company's flexible expense budget shows the following budget formulas for the operating expenses:

Administrative salaries and wages	$50,000 + $.04 per unit sold
Sales salaries and wages	$20,000 + $.06 per unit sold
Utilities	$11,500 + $.15 per unit sold
Supplies	$0.10 per unit sold
Travel and entertainment	$.95 per unit sold
Depreciation	$61,000
Property taxes	$2,000

At the end of November, the accounting records showed that the company had sold 195,000 units for a total of $4,000,000 and that cost of goods sold was $2,240,000. Actual costs for the operating expenses were:

Administrative salaries and wages	$ 56,800
Sales salaries and wages	33,600
Utilities	38,500
Supplies	19,560
Travel and entertainment	183,250
Depreciation	61,000
Property taxes	1,850
Total	$394,560

At the end of each month, the accountant translates the budgeted and actual information into yen and sends the reports to the headquarters office in Tokyo. The company uses the exchange rate at the beginning of the month (U.S. dollar = 250 yen) for the budgeted information and the exchange rate at the end of the month (U.S. dollar = 200 yen) for the actual information.

Required:
1. Prepare an income statement showing columns for both actual and budgeted results.
2. Calculate a spending variance for each of the individual operating expenses.
3. Calculate a volume variance for each of the individual operating expenses.
4. Using the translation rules given, recompute the budgeted and actual results and the spending and volume variances.
5. Is your evaluation of the variances different in the translated amounts? If yes, explain why.

16-5. **T-Account Recording of International Transactions.** Harley Import/Export, Inc. has considerable foreign business dealings. The company's fiscal year end is September 30. Over the three months of August, September, and October the company engaged in the following transactions:

Aug. 15 Purchased goods from a Japanese company for $110,000; terms denominated in U.S dollars (yen = $.0040).

17 Sold goods to a German company for $140,000; terms denominated in marks (mark = $.35).

21 Purchased goods from a Mexican company for $120,000; terms denominated in pesos (peso = $.004).

25 Paid for the goods purchased on Aug. 15 (yen = $.0045).

31 Sold goods to an Italian company for $200,000; terms denominated in lira (lira = $.0005).

Sept. 5 Sold goods to a British firm for $56,000; terms denominated in U.S. dollars (pound = $1.30).

7 Purchased goods from a Japanese company for $162,000; terms denominated in yen (yen = $.0045).

15 Received payment for the sale made on Sept. 5 (pound = $1.40).

16 Received payment for the sale made on Aug. 17 (mark = $.40).

17 Purchased goods from a French company for $66,000; terms denominated in U.S. dollars (franc = $.11).

20 Paid for the goods purchased on Aug. 21 (peso = $.003).

22 Sold goods to a British company for $84,000; terms denominated in British pounds (pound = $1.40).

30 Made year-end adjustment for incomplete foreign exchange transactions: franc = $.12; peso = $.003; mark = $.40; lira = $.0003; pound = $1.30; yen = $.0050.

Oct. 7 Paid for the goods purchased on Sept. 7 (yen = $.0045).

19 Paid for the goods purchased on Sept. 17 (franc = $.10).

22 Received payment for the goods sold on Sept. 22 (pound = $1.20).

30 Received payment for the goods sold on Aug. 31 (lira = $.0004).

Required:
Using T-accounts, record the above transactions for Harley Import/Export, Inc. Use separate receivable and payable accounts for each country involved.

16-6.   Foreign Exchange Gains and Losses. Marlow Implements of Kansas City conducts a considerable amount of its business through foreign suppliers and customers. It is a calendar year company. The following are several typical transactions for 1994 and 1995:

Oct. 14 Sold products to a Mexican company for $20,000; terms denominated in U.S. dollars (peso = $.004).

26 Purchased goods from a Japanese firm for $40,000; terms denominated in yen (yen = $.004).

Nov. 4 Sold products to a British company for $39,000; terms denominated in pounds (pound = $1.30).

14 Received payment in full for October 14 sale (peso = $.003).

15 Paid for the goods purchased on October 26 (yen = $.0044).

23 Purchased goods from an Italian company for $28,000; terms denominated in U.S. dollars (lira = $.0005).

30 Purchased products from a Japanese company for $35,200; terms denominated in yen (yen = $.0044).

Dec. 2 Paid for the goods purchased on November 23 (lira = $.0004).

3 Received payment in full for goods sold on November 4 (pound = $1.20).

8 Sold products to a French company for $66,000; terms denominated in francs (franc = $.11).

17 Purchased products from a Mexican company for $37,000; terms denominated in U.S. dollars (peso = $.004).

18 Sold products to a German company for $90,000; terms denominated in marks (mark = $.30).

31 Year-end exchange rates: franc = $.09; peso = $.003; pound = $1.10; mark = $.35; lira = $.0004; yen = $.005.

Jan. 7 Received payment for goods sold on December 8 (franc = $.10).

16 Paid for goods purchased on December 17 (peso = $.002).

17 Received payment for goods sold on December 18 (mark = $.40).

28 Paid for goods purchased on November 30 (yen = $.0045).

Required:
1.   For each transaction, show the total exchange gain or loss incurred between transaction date and settlement date.
2.   What is the total net exchange gain or loss for all transactions?
3.   Show, by individual transaction, the amount of exchange gain or loss that belongs to the year ended December 31 and how much belongs to the following year.
4.   What are the accounts receivable and the accounts payable balances for unsettled transactions at December 31?

16-7.   Foreign Exchange Gains and Losses and Hedge. On June 1, 1995, University Research Labs, a domestic research and development operation, placed an order for special laboratory equipment from a company in Holland. The purchase price was stated at 400,000 gilders and was payable in 60 days (July 30, 1995). The exchange rate for gilders on June 1 was $.21.

On this same date, University Research Labs decided to hedge its foreign currency commitment by purchasing 300,000 gilders for delivery in 60 days at a price of $.23 in the futures market.

These transactions were both settled on July 30, 1995. The exchange rate for gilders on that date was $.17.

Required:
1.   Calculate the exchange gains and losses associated with these transactions. Include in your computations, the effects of any premium or discount on the hedging transaction.
2.   Assume University Research Labs has a fiscal year end of June 30, 1995. Calculate the exchange gains and losses and the straight-line amortization of premium or discount to the fiscal year ended June 30, 1995. The exchange rate on this date was $.24.

16-8.   **Hedging Transactions.** Intermountain Grain Importers/Exporters, located in Salt Lake City, Utah, buys and sells grains in the international market. The company's fiscal year ends September 30. The following transactions where handled during 1995:

Sept. **1** Sold 1,000,000 bushels of wheat to a French cooperative for 18,000,000 francs (exchange rate = $.1464). Payment is due October 30.

    1 Management felt the franc might decline in value, so it negotiated a forward contract with an exchange broker to sell 18,000,000 francs on October 30 for $.1442.

    5 Sold 2,000,000 bushels of wheat to a company in Spain for $5,300,000 (exchange rate for Spanish peseta = $.0074). The account is to be settled in U.S. dollars on November 5.

  15 Purchased rice from an exporting company that operates in Japan. The contract provided for payment of 16,000,000 yen on October 15. Exchange rate for yen on September 15 was $.00643.

  15 Entered into a forward contract to buy 16,000,000 yen on October 15 for $.00645 per yen.

  18 Sold 500 tons of soybean meal to Quebec Meal and Flour, Ltd. for 52,000 Canadian dollars (exchange rate for Canadian dollars = $.8245). The account is to be settled December 17.

  30 Exchange rates for any unsettled transactions are:

French franc	$.1455
Spanish peseta	$.00736
Japanese yen	$.006433
Canadian dollar	$.8243

Oct. **15** Received 16,000,000 yen under terms of the forward contract and then submitted payment to pay for the rice purchased on September 15 (exchange rate = $.006435).

  30 Received 18,000,000 francs from the French company and settled the forward contract (exchange rate = $.1457).

Nov. **5** Received payment in full for the wheat sold on September 5 to the Spanish company (exchange rate = $.0073).

Dec. **17** Received payment from Meal and Flour, Ltd. for the September 18 sale (exchange rate = $.8246).

Required:
1.   Compute the exchange gain or loss at time of settlement for each purchase or sale transaction and the related hedging transaction.
2.   For transactions unsettled on September 30, show how much of the exchange gain or loss applies to the period prior to September 30 and how much to the period subsequent to September 30.

16-9.   Transaction Gains and Losses on Hedging a Purchase. Darby Refineries of Houston, Texas, purchased 2,000,000 barrels of oil from a company in Venezuela on November 15, 1995. Darby agreed to pay 160,000,000 bolivars on January 14, 1996 (60 days later). To ensure that the dollar outlay for the purchase would not fluctuate, Darby negotiated a forward contract to buy 160,000,000 bolivars on January 14 at the forward rate of $.0265. Darby Refineries is a calendar year company.

Important dates and exchange rates for bolivars are: November 15—$.0233; December 31—$.0230; January 14—$.0289.

Required:
1.   Compute the dollars to paid on November 15, 1995 to acquire the 160,000,000 bolivars from the exchange dealer.
2.   Compute the premium or discount on the forward contract.
3.   Compute the total exchange gain or loss on the forward contract.
4.   Compute the total exchange gain or loss on the exposed liability related to the oil purchase.
5.   Considering that December 31, 1995 is the year end, answer the following:
    (a)   How much of the premium or discount on the forward contract would be charged to 1995? How much to 1996?
    (b)   How much of the exchange gain or loss on the forward contract would be charged to 1995? How much to 1996?
    (c)   How much of the exchange gain or loss on the exposed liability would be charged to 1995? How much to 1996?
6.   Did the hedging transaction minimize the effects of currency fluctuations? Explain.

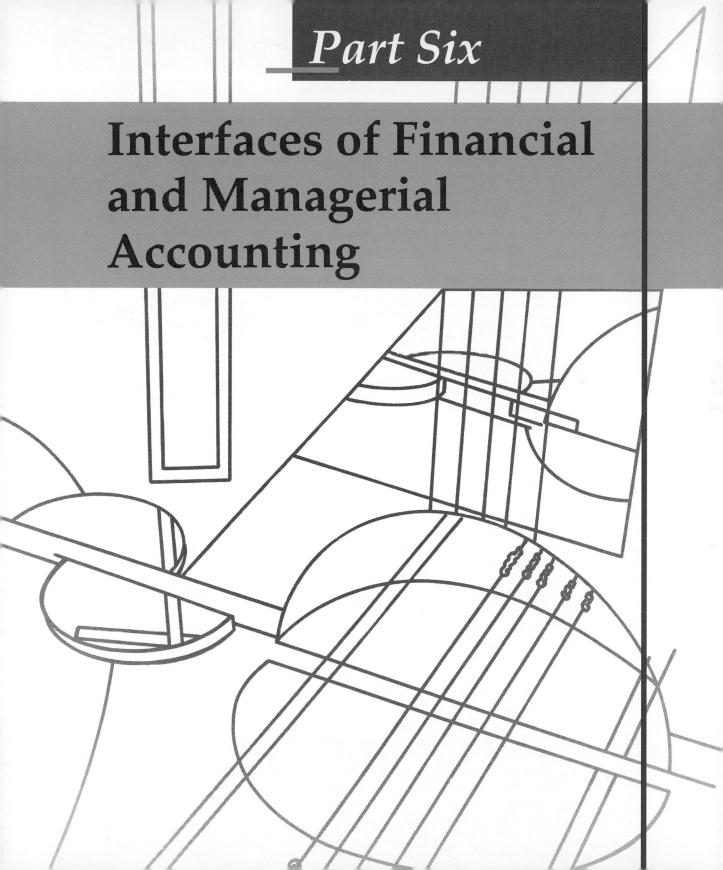

Part Six

Interfaces of Financial and Managerial Accounting

Chapter Seventeen

Financial Performance Analysis

❖ *Chapter Objectives*

After studying Chapter 17, you will be able to:
1. Understand how financial statement analysis about a firm's financial condition can give insight to both external financial analysts and its managers.
2. Prepare comparative, percentage of composition, and base-year financial statement analyses.
3. Identify the key questions in each risks area of liquidity, capital adequacy, and asset quality and in each returns area of earnings, growth, and market performance.
4. Identify and calculate specific ratios in each risks and returns area.
5. Understand that ratio interrelationships can show:
   (a) That financial strengths in one area can offset a weakness in another area.
   (b) How financial leverage can improve returns to common equity owners.
   (c) How sensitive earning-power ratios are to changes in income statement and balance sheet account balances.
6. Explain why ratio analysis has certain limitations and caveats that must be understood if the ratios are to be relevant.

Why Do They All Want to Know My Business?

Maynard Hogberg operates CAD Creations, a computer-aided-design engineering firm doing subcontracting work for the major automotive companies and other engineering firms. His firm is now 6 years old. He used his own money plus funds raised by a venture capital firm to start the firm. He has just received his quarterly financial statements.

"It's like they have radar! As soon as these statements show up, everybody wants to see them. We're doing okay; I can pay the bills; and we're making a buck." Maynard wasn't trying to hide his financial results; but he wasn't anxious to send a mass mailing of his financial statements to the world. Who are the "they," and what do they want to know? Here's who:

1. *Venture capital firm and its backers:* These people own 40 percent of the common stock in CAD Creations. Their primary motive is to reap large gains from an initially risky investment. Eventually, they will want to sell their stock for a price many times the purchase price. They want to see the revenues and the earnings growth rates from last quarter and last year.
2. *Major automotive company procurement office:* This firm is negotiating a long-term development contract with CAD Creations. The last thing this "major automotive" wants is to be in the middle of a critical project and have its supplier be in financial trouble and see development stop. Liquidity and adequacy of the capital base are its primary financial concerns.
3. *Supplier of computer equipment:* The main financial worry a seller has is whether, after the sale, the receivable will ever be collected. Normally, a seller will do a credit check on a prospective customer. If the customer has a poor credit rating, no references, or no bank credit, the seller may extend little or no credit. Even C.O.D. sales may be required. In this case, the computer equipment supplier is concerned about the large amount of equipment it has sold to CAD Creations on credit.
4. *Friendly banker:* Maynard has developed a close working relationship with a commercial lending officer at the Detroit National Bank. They meet monthly. The bank's credit administration department maintains detailed files on the financial results and forecasts for each of its clients. The bank wants to assist Maynard to meet his cash needs and yet wants to be sure that the debt CAD Creations is assuming will be paid out of operating profits.
5. *Mike, Maynard's 21-year-old son:* Mike was given a few shares of CAD Creations stock by his dad. Mike is planning to attend an expensive graduate school after his days at Major University. Without sounding too presumptuous, he asks his dad if he can expect any cash dividends soon.

These and others have a legitimate need for CAD Creations' financial data. As a publicly held company, the general public can have access to this information. Publishing financial reports is required.

Analysis of the financial statements for whatever purposes is an important part of the financial management of a firm. Published financial statements, blessed by its CPA auditor, are management's representations. Management must approve the statements, understand their contents, and communicate the results to the very broad set of financial market places that the firm faces.

Financial performance analysis is like painting a picture. Blending colors, using different strokes, drawing certain abstractions, integrating foreground and background, and linking focal points, settings, and shapes are a few of the artist's skills which are combined in just the right proportions to bring a piece of art to life. A firm's financial condition cannot be captured with one set of financial statements or financial ratios. The task of financial analysts is to use all the elements of their craft properly in order to pull the greatest understanding possible from the data available. From better analysis will come better decisions. The skills needed to create a financial picture of the firm come with knowledge of financial analysis and with practice in applications.

The primary vehicles of financial performance analysis are financial ratios. Selecting appropriate measures to assess each area of financial concern is a first step. Finding the magnitude and direction of change of different ratios gives the analyst insight into: (a) changes in financial ratios; (b) what causes specific ratios to change; (c) how these changes are related; and (d) what impact these changes have on the financial condition of the firm.

Tied to the firm's performance is how it is doing relative to its financial plan, to other firms in its industry, and in the financial market place in general.

USES AND USERS OF FINANCIAL PERFORMANCE ANALYSIS

The audience for financial performance analysis is the same group for whom we prepare the financial statements themselves. Financial performance analysis interprets the financial statement data and presents information in summary or cryptic form to simplify users' analysis. The primary users are existing or potential investors in our stock and debt issues, creditors who may extend trade credit to us or lend us cash, and customers trying to determine whether we are financially stable. In certain industries, government regulators are interested in certain financial ratios that indicate the level of financial safety or profitability a firm enjoys.

For all firms, financial performance analysis can be useful in several ways, including:

1. **To set goals and targets.** Budgets and financial plans often use financial ratios as goals for managerial performance—setting rates of return goals, sales growth percentages, and efficiency targets. Comparisons of actual to plan are summarized in reports using financial ratios. Often, performance bonuses and other compensation rewards are based on financial measurements.

2. **To compare our performance to others.** Comparisons to industry averages, to firms operating in similar environments, to competitors, and to successful firms in general give benchmarks for managers and stockholders to assess our firm's performance.

3. **To measure financial strength for credit purposes.** Firms lending money and extending credit want assurance of being paid on time. While no ratio can guarantee debt payment, the amount of liquid assets and other liabilities gives an indication of the availability of funds. It is said that bankers gladly lend money to people who don't need it and won't lend to those who do. Certainly, showing an ability to generate cash or having plenty of available cash is important in lending decisions. Also, the higher the risk, the greater the interest rate premium the lender will demand to extend credit.

4. **To measure profitability for return on investment purposes.** Owners are choosing among alternatives. Capital is attracted to profitable choices and drawn away from unprofitable ones. Investors monitor earnings relative to the investment base to decide to expand or contract their financial commitment. This is equally true of internal managerial decisions and of external equity investors.

5. **To spot trends, weaknesses, and potential problem areas.** Looking at financial data over time provides an opportunity to see change. Changes are found through comparisons. Using a series of balance sheets and income statements to produce ratios gives analysts insight over several time periods. Monthly, quarterly, and annual data can be analyzed to spot trends in profits, liquidity, and many other elements.

6. **To evaluate alternative courses of action.** Often, managers will look at the financial statement impacts of a key investment decision. Changes in financial ratios may cause the firm to appear to be more risky or more safe. Efficient use of assets and profitability are other impacts that decision makers will evaluate before a choice is made.

7. **To help understand the linkages and interactions that transactions and accounts balance changes have on the financial well being of the firm.** This implies that ratio analysis is an educational technique—the role of this chapter, in fact. Expert financial analysts have an amazing "feel" for financial statement data relationships, changes, and the underlying strengths and problems that the numbers represent. The novice will see change in one dimension, then two, and so on. The more experience analysts have, the more they can read "between the lines" and spot subtle changes.

These are the major uses of financial performance analysis. The analytical tools are versatile and easily adapted to new needs.

AN EXAMPLE COMPANY—AMBERG LIGHTING EQUIPMENT

To illustrate financial performance analysis, a comprehensive example will be used throughout the chapter. Amberg Lighting Equipment is a major distributor of electrical fixtures for commercial and retail uses. It serves retail outlets, contractors, and other wholesalers. It has had strong growth over the past five years. A portion of its common stock is closely held, but the stock is publicly traded.

It is December 31, 1995. The executive management has just approved a profit plan for 1996. Figure 17.1 presents historical balance sheets for the past three years and a forecast for December 31, 1996. Also, the past two annual income statements and the forecast 1996 statement are presented in Figure 17.2.

AMBERG LIGHTING EQUIPMENT
BALANCE SHEET
DECEMBER 31, 1995
(IN MILLIONS)

	Forecast 1996	Actual 1995	Actual 1994	Actual 1993
Cash	$ 105	$ 118	$ 100	$ 84
Marketable securities	125	118	80	37
Accounts receivable (net)	363	345	300	284
Inventories	465	310	280	234
Prepaid expenses	59	46	40	53
Total current assets	$1,117	$ 937	$ 800	$ 692
Plant and equipment	$ 559	$ 515	$ 455	$ 438
Accumulated depreciation	−120	−119	−86	−68
Net plant and equipment	$ 439	$ 396	$ 369	$ 370
Land	95	60	60	60
Other assets	44	67	59	38
Total noncurrent assets	$ 578	$ 523	$ 488	$ 468
Total assets	$1,695	$1,460	$1,288	$1,160
Accounts payable	$ 260	$ 190	$ 144	$ 139
Accrued liabilities	126	65	55	58
Short-term borrowings	120	83	34	64
Bonds payable—current portion	30	30	30	30
Total current liabilities	$ 536	$ 368	$ 263	$ 291
Bonds payable—10 percent	270	300	330	360
Total liabilities	$ 806	$ 668	$ 593	$ 651
Preferred stock—9 percent	$ 100	$ 100	$ 100	$ 0
Paid-in-capital—common	300	300	300	300
Retained earnings	489	392	295	209
Total equity	$ 889	$ 792	$ 695	$ 509
Total liabilities and equity	$1,695	$1,460	$1,288	$1,160

Other financial data:

	Forecast 1996	Actual 1995	Actual 1994	Actual 1993
Common shares outstanding (millions)	60 mil.	60 mil.	60 mil.	60 mil.
Preferred shares outstanding (millions)	1 mil.	1 mil.	1 mil.	0
Common dividends paid	$42	$36	$30	$30
Preferred dividends paid	9	9	6	0
Average price per common share	$26.25	$26.75	$23.00	$20.75

Figure 17.1 Forecast and Actual Balance Sheets and Other Financial Data

AMBERG LIGHTING EQUIPMENT
INCOME STATEMENT
FOR THE YEAR ENDED DECEMBER 31, 1995
(IN MILLIONS)

	Forecast 1996	Actual 1995	Actual 1994
Sales	$2,848	$2,454	$2,084
Cost of goods sold	1,721	1,461	1,210
Gross margin	$1,127	$ 993	$ 874
Operating expenses:			
Marketing expenses	$ 215	$ 188	$ 175
Distribution expenses	329	275	248
Depreciation expense	65	45	38
Administrative expenses	229	209	164
Total operating expenses	$ 838	$ 717	$ 625
Operating net income	$ 289	$ 276	$ 249
Interest expense	42	40	46
Net income before taxes	$ 247	$ 236	$ 203
Income taxes expense (40 percent)	99	94	81
Net income after taxes	$ 148	$ 142	$ 122

Figure 17.2 Forecast and Actual Income Statements

Amberg executives will be meeting soon with financial analysts to discuss the company's prospects for 1996. Also, the vice president of finance will be renegotiating the terms of Amberg's line of credit with its lead bank, Interstate Commerce. Final touches are being put on the comments the officers will put in the 1995 Annual Report to stockholders. Stockholders will receive this report in late March.

Along with the data in Figures 17.1 and 17.2, much more information will be included in the annual report, such as footnotes to the financial statements, an historical 10-year summary of financial data, and the auditors' report. These are not included here for simplifying purposes. Use of such detail is beyond the scope of our discussions.

TYPES OF FINANCIAL STATEMENT ANALYSIS

Financial analysts look at financial statement data in every manner possible to gain insight. Traditional formats include:

1. Comparative statements.
2. Percentage of composition statements.
3. Base-year comparisons.
4. Ratio analysis.

In reality, all four types are ratio analyses. A ratio is a numerator divided by a denominator. Any percentage is the result of dividing one number by another—a ratio expressed as a percentage. The four approaches are frequently combined to help explain changes.

Comparative Statements

Data from two time periods are compared to measure change between two time periods. Comparisons include:

1. Actual to plan or budget.
2. Between two versions of a budget.
3. Last month, quarter, or year to this month, quarter, or year.

The differences between values and percentage changes are often presented. Figure 17.3 illustrates a comparative statement for the forecast 1996 income statement compared to the actual 1995 results.

AMBERG LIGHTING EQUIPMENT
COMPARATIVE INCOME STATEMENTS
FOR THE YEAR ENDED DECEMBER 31, 1995

	Forecast 1996	Actual 1995	Difference	Percentage Change
Sales.............................	$2,848	$2,454	$394	16.06%
Cost of goods sold	1,721	1,461	260	17.80
Gross margin......................	$1,127	$ 993	$134	13.49
Operating expenses:				
Marketing expenses	$ 215	$ 188	$ 27	14.36
Distribution expenses	329	275	54	19.64
Depreciation expense.............	65	45	20	44.44
Administrative expenses	229	209	20	9.57
Total operating expenses........	$ 838	$ 717	$121	16.88
Operating net income	$ 289	$ 276	$ 13	4.71
Interest expense	42	40	2	5.00
Net income before taxes	$ 247	$ 236	$ 11	4.66
Income taxes expense (40 percent)	99	94	5	5.32
Net income after taxes	$ 148	$ 142	$ 6	4.23

Figure 17.3 Comparative Income Statements

A 16 percent increase in sales will be nearly eaten up by higher cost of goods sold and operating expenses, leaving only a 4.23 percent increase in net income after taxes. **Comparative statements** can help spot significant changes in dollar amounts and percentages quickly.

Percentage Composition Statements

Percentage composition statements are often called **common-sized statements** since all statement values are expressed as a percentage of a base number. The base number is frequently set equal to 100 percent and is total assets on the balance sheet and sales on the income statement. Percentage composition statements are used for comparing:

1. Multiple years of data from the same firm,
2. Companies that are different in size, and
3. Company to industry averages.

In the Amberg Lighting Equipment example, the common-sized balance sheets would appear in Figure 17.4 as follows:

AMBERG LIGHTING EQUIPMENT
BALANCE SHEET
DECEMBER 31, 1995

	Forecast 1996	Actual 1995	Actual 1994	Actual 1993
Cash	6.19%	8.08%	7.76%	7.24%
Marketable securities	7.37	8.08	6.21	3.19
Accounts receivable (net)	21.42	23.63	23.29	24.48
Inventories	27.43	21.23	21.74	20.17
Prepaid expenses	3.48	3.15	3.11	4.57
Total current assets.............	65.90%	64.18%	62.11%	59.66%
Plant and equipment	32.98%	35.27%	35.33%	37.76%
Accumulated depreciation	−7.08	−8.15	−6.68	−5.86
Net plant and equipment	25.90%	27.12%	28.65%	31.90%
Land	5.60	4.11	4.66	5.17
Other assets.....................	2.60	4.59	4.58	3.28
Total noncurrent assets	34.10%	35.82%	37.89%	40.34%
Total assets	100.00%	100.00%	100.00%	100.00%
Accounts payable	15.34%	13.01%	11.18%	11.98%
Accrued liabilities.................	7.43	4.45	4.27	5.00
Short-term borrowings	7.08	5.68	2.64	5.52
Bonds payable—current portion	1.77	2.05	2.33	2.59
Total current liabilities	31.62%	25.21%	20.42%	25.09%
Bonds payable—10 percent	15.93	20.55	25.62	31.03
Total liabilities..................	47.55%	45.75%	46.04%	56.12%

Preferred stock—9 percent	5.90%	6.85%	7.76%	0.00%
Paid-in-capital—common	17.70	20.55	23.29	25.86
Retained earnings	28.85	26.85	22.90	18.02
Total equity	52.45%	54.25%	53.96%	43.88%
Total liabilities and equity	100.00%	100.00%	100.00%	100.00%

Figure 17.4   Percentage Composition Balance Sheets

The most dramatic change is the increase in inventories. Inventories grew from just over 20 percent in 1993 to over 27 percent in the plan for 1996. This is an expensive asset to carry. Expansion creates a need for more inventory, but this seems to be unusually large.

If ideal mixes of assets, liabilities, and equity can be set for an industry, percentage composition statements can quickly spot deviations. We could see how competitors and successful peer firms are operating.

Base-Year Comparisons

Base-year comparisons select a starting point, the base period, and compare all other periods to that point as a percentage. Real life examples include the Consumer Price Index that sets the price level index equal to 100 for a period of time and measures inflation as the change in the index since that time period. The CPI currently uses 1982 to 1984 as the base period. In Figure 17.5, income statement data between 1993 and 1996 are compared.

AMBERG LIGHTING EQUIPMENT
INCOME STATEMENT
FOR THE YEAR ENDED DECEMBER 31, 1995

	Forecast 1996	Actual 1995	Actual 1994
Sales	136.66%	117.75%	100.00%
Cost of goods sold	142.23	120.74	100.00
Gross margin	128.95	113.62	100.00
Operating expenses:			
Marketing expenses	122.86	107.43	100.00
Distribution expenses	132.66	110.89	100.00
Depreciation expense	171.05	118.42	100.00
Administrative expenses	139.63	127.44	100.00
Total operating expenses	134.08	114.72	100.00
Operating net income	116.06	110.84	100.00
Interest expense	91.30	86.96	100.00
Net income before taxes	121.67	116.26	100.00
Income taxes expense (40 percent)	122.22	116.05	100.00
Net income after taxes	121.31	116.39	100.00

Figure 17.5   Base-Year Comparisons of Income Statement Data

Cost of goods sold is slowly increasing faster than sales. More low margin goods are being sold, or price increases are not keeping up with cost increases. In spite of increases in several operating expense accounts, operating expenses are growing slower than sales—a very positive sign in a fast sales growth period.

In one sense, **base-year comparisons** could be called **horizontal analysis** while the percentage composition comparisons could be called vertical analysis. Both show trends and relative changes.

Ratio Analysis

Ratio analysis is defined here as selecting a variable as the numerator and another variable as the denominator. The result is the ratio of one value to the other. It can be expressed as a percentage (%), a ratio (X:Y), or merely as a number.

The majority of this chapter will discuss specific ratios grouped by area of financial analysis. Before individual areas and ratios are explained, several ratio analysis issues should be mentioned.

Too Much or Too Little   Every ratio can get too high or too low. This is the "Goldilocks paradox." Remember that papa bear's porridge was too hot; momma bear's porridge was too cold; but baby bear's porridge was just right. Generally, the "just right" level is difficult to find precisely. But if a ratio is too high, financial risk will grow; and, likewise, if the ratio is too low, financial risk will also grow.

Calculation Rules   A few simple rules help in calculating ratios from balance sheet numbers (for a point in time) and income statement numbers (for a time period):

1.   When calculating a ratio using balance sheet numbers only, the numerator and denominator should be from the same balance sheet, not different time periods. The exception is in calculating growth ratios discussed later. The same is true of ratios using only income statement numbers.

2.   When a balance sheet number and an income statement number are both used, the balance sheet number should be an average for the time period represented by the income statement number. At least the beginning and ending balance sheet numbers for the period should be averaged. By using a static number (a balance sheet number) from either the beginning or the end of the period and a flow number (an income statement number), the resulting ratio can be biased because of change that could have occurred in the balance sheet account during the period.

3.   Generally, the number of days in a month or year are not critical to the analysis. Therefore, for our purposes a year will have 360 days, 52 weeks, and 12 months.

In using financial statement data, analysts should use uniform and consistent definitions for accounts and terms. Terms will be defined as they are used in ratio definitions.

Sources of Data   Many sources are available for financial statement analysis. The most obvious is the published financial statements from the firm itself. The required filings with the Securities and Exchange Commission are public data and often available from the filing company. Regulated industries' data can be obtained from the appropriate government agency. Financial data on specific firms can be purchased from credit agencies and providers of credit data.

Trade associations often generate financial ratios for their industries. Also, specialized firms prepare and sell information on specific firms, groups of firms, and industries. Brokerage firms, investment services, and financial rating organizations publish a tremendous array of information.

FINANCIAL PERFORMANCE ANALYSIS: RISKS AND RETURNS

Measuring financial performance requires a structure. Calculating tens of ratios is a futile exercise. The questions of "What do you want to know?" and "Why do you want to know?" frame an attack. The attack identifies areas of financial concern. Key questions within each area spearhead the attack. Then, specific ratios help answer the questions.

The "why" question gives the viewpoint of the asker: creditor, potential lender, common stockholder, regulator, etc. The "what" question leads to specific concerns and ratios. These areas of financial concern can be grouped by risks and returns, the natural financial trade-offs, as follows:

Risks	Returns
Liquidity	Earnings
Capital adequacy	Growth
Asset quality	Market evaluation

Risks areas measure the financial safety of the firm. Returns areas measure the financial success of the firm. Risks and returns are interrelated. Reducing a financial risk can aid financial returns success, and poor financial returns can force the firm into a risky financial position. The following sections of the chapter describe each of the risks and returns according to its major concern and how it is generally seen by the financial community.

Liquidity

The key liquidity question is:

What liquid assets are available or accessible to meet demands for cash from expected and unexpected sources?

The underlying question is: Can we pay our bills on time? The ratio answer comes from looking at ratios that try to measure assets that can be converted into cash quickly and the short-term needs for cash. Generally, current assets and liabilities are the focus of liquidity analysis. The traditional measures are the current ratio and the quick ratio. An additional ratio is included here to estimate the ability of the firm to generate cash from current operations to pay interest and debt.

Current Ratio   The **current ratio** is defined as:

$$\frac{\text{Current Assets}}{\text{Current Liabilities}} = \text{Current Ratio}$$

It indicates how many dollars of current assets are available for each dollar of current liabilities. The assumption is that current assets are converted into cash within the operating cycle. Often a one-year time frame is used. The generated cash is assumed to be used to pay current liabilities. In the Amberg case, the year-end numbers are as follows:

	Forecast 1996	Actual 1995	Actual 1994	Actual 1993
Current assets	$1,117	$ 937	$ 800	$ 692
Current liabilities	536	368	263	291
Current ratio	2.08:1	2.55:1	3.04:1	2.38:1

At the end of 1995, $2.55 of current assets were available to pay for each dollar of current liabilities. Generally, firms want to have a safety cushion by having more liquidity than is really needed. This is to cover the unexpected portion of the basic question above. It could be said that Amberg had the safest position in 1994 and by the end of 1996 is forecast to be at its riskiest position in the four years shown.

Typically, cash, accounts receivable, and inventories are the major current asset balances. Accounts payable, short-term borrowings, and the current portion of long-term debt are the major current liabilities. The difference between current assets and current liabilities is called **working capital**. These are funds that are needed to keep the current operations working smoothly. Notice that working capital is financed from long-term debt or equity—long-term funds used in current or day-to-day activities. Firms need working capital, but the funds to finance it are expensive and needed in many other places in the firm. To get more working capital, management must issue more long-term debt, sell stock, or sell noncurrent assets. This will increase current assets or reduce current liabilities—improving the current ratio.

To reduce the cost of financing working capital, firms will try to keep current assets low. But a low current ratio may mean that cash is not available to pay bills, that enough credit is not being extended to customers, or that too little inventory is available to meet sales orders. If the ratio goes too high, financing working capital is expensive, too much inventory may be held (may become obsolete or merely be overstocked), or receivables may not be collectible.

Different industries and firms have different working capital needs and have different ideal current ratios. Traditionally, a 2:1 ratio is suggested as ideal. Perhaps no firm should be at 2:1 exactly. Steel warehouses may need a

4:1 ratio to cover receivables and inventories that "turn" very slowly. Other firms with very predictable cash flows, few receivables, and low inventories can get by with nearly a 1:1 ratio. Industry averages give an indication of where this number should be.

Quick Ratio   The **quick ratio**, also called the **acid test ratio**, is defined as:

$$\frac{\text{Cash, Marketable Securities, and Receivables}}{\text{Current Liabilities}} = \text{Quick Ratio}$$

As the name implies, the quick ratio is testing a firm's ability to pay its bills quickly from readily available cash and near-cash assets. Inventories are excluded because they must be sold. Yes, since receivables must be collected, this may still be a problem; but at least we are owed the money. The Amberg numbers are:

	Forecast 1996	Actual 1995	Actual 1994	Actual 1993
Cash	$ 105	$ 118	$ 100	$ 84
Marketable securities	125	118	80	37
Accounts receivable (net)	363	345	300	284
Total quick assets	$ 593	$ 581	$ 480	$ 405
Current liabilities	$ 536	$ 368	$ 263	$ 291
Quick ratio	1.11:1	1.58:1	1.83:1	1.39:1

The 1.11:1 forecast for the end of 1996 means that **quick assets** still exceed the total current liabilities owed at that time. The questions yet to be answered are: How soon within the year are the current liabilities due and when will most of the receivables be collected?

Operations Cash Flow to Current Debt Service   A major liquidity issue is whether we are generating enough cash from our regular business to pay maturing debt principal and the interest due on debt. Chapter 18 discusses cash flow reporting and explains cash flow from operations. Cash flows from operations excluding interest expense for the Amberg data are:

		1996	1995	1994
	Net income..	$148	$142	$122
+	Depreciation and all other amortizations	65	45	38
+	Decreases in operating current assets (accounts receivable, inventories, and prepaids)			13
−	Increases in operating current assets	− 186	− 81	− 62
−	Decreases in operating current liabilities (accounts payable and accrued expenses).................			− 3
+	Increases in operating current liabilities	131	56	5
+	Eliminate interest expense	42	40	46
−/+	Nonoperating gains and losses			
=	Cash flow from operations......................	$200	$202	$159

This is cash generated from day-to-day activities. Debt service is defined as current portion of long-term debt and maturing borrowings plus interest paid on debt during the year.

The **operations cash flow to current debt service ratio** is measured as follows:

$$\frac{\text{Operations Cash Flow}}{\substack{\text{Debt Principal Maturing During the Year} \\ \text{+ Interest Expense}}} = \substack{\text{Operations Cash} \\ \text{Flow to Current} \\ \text{Debt Service}}$$

The Amberg data show:

	Forecast 1996	Actual 1995	Actual 1994
Operations cash flow	$ 200	$ 202	$ 159
Short-term borrowings (prior 12/31)	$ 83	$ 34	$ 64
Bonds payable—current portion (prior 12/31)	30	30	30
Interest expense	42	40	46
Debt service for the year	$ 155	$ 104	$ 140
Operations cash flow to debt service	1.29:1	1.94:1	1.14:1

In 1994, Amberg did generate enough cash from operations to pay principal and interest on its debt. In 1995, the rate improved considerably; and in 1996 the forecast shows a big decline. This is a critical measure for bank lenders. If the number is under 1:1, the implication is that a company must borrow or sell assets to meet debt agreements.

Other Liquidity Considerations   The missing element in all liquidity measures is the firm's ability to borrow cash when needed. This is called **off-balance-sheet financing**, meaning that liquidity sources don't appear on the asset side. These are lines of credit at banks or other borrowing agreements to generate cash. Financially strong firms can sell commercial paper. Weaker firms can sell or borrow against accounts receivable. Often, the off-balance-sheet sources are far more important than what the balance sheet accounts can show.

We can have too much or too little liquidity. Generally, the more liquid we are, the less we earn—low risk, low return. Therefore, we want to be as "invested" as possible with as little cash and near-cash assets around as possible. One of the jobs of a corporate treasurer is to minimize idle cash. Generally, long-term investments have a higher yield than short-term investments. But, liquidity is reduced with longer-maturing assets. One trade-off is to acquire only investments that can easily be sold.

Studies have shown that many more firms become bankrupt from not being able to pay their liabilities than from lack of profitability. A new business without enough financing cannot expand, cannot buy inventory to meet sales demands, cannot hire additional employees, and often falls behind in paying regular payables in addition to having debt service problems. Hard times demand balance sheet liquidity or access to cash reserves.

Increasingly, liquidity needs are being measured by forecasting cash outflows and cash inflows. Several time periods are important: near term ("Can we meet the payroll on Friday?"), annual ("Can we borrow enough when both receivables and inventories are at their seasonal highs?"), and long-term ("How will we pay for the new factory?"). These are, of course, internal concerns. As yet, the best external indications of whether a firm is in position to pay its bills on time are the liquidity ratios we have discussed here.

Capital Adequacy

Closely tied to liquidity is capital adequacy. If a firm has a problem with liquidity, a strong capital position will allow it to borrow more easily. And vice versa, if a firm has a weak capital position, it should stay very liquid to avoid any possible liquidity troubles. A firm with both liquidity and capital problems often has major financial troubles.

Capital is equity. Equity is defined as stockholders' equity and includes any preferred stock. The term **common equity** is stockholders' equity excluding preferred stock.

Two questions define the capital adequacy issues:

1. How much capital is necessary to protect creditors and stockholders against expected and unexpected losses?
2. How little capital is necessary to allow stockholders to enjoy maximum favorable return on equity and dividends?

These are conflicting positions—more capital for protection and less capital for higher rates of return. Creditors want more, owners want less. The ideal position for a specific firm is difficult to measure. But if capital relative to total assets or debt drops too low, creditors stop lending money or demand higher interest rates to cover the greater risk. If capital ratios go too high, owners are disappointed by the lower rates of return on the large equity base.

The ratios examined are: debt to equity, common equity multiplier, and times interest earned. Also, dividend payout percentage tells what portion of profits earned is given to stockholders and what portion is reinvested.

Debt to Equity   The definition of the **debt to equity ratio** is:

$$\frac{\text{Total Liabilities}}{\text{Total Equity}} = \text{Debt to Equity Ratio}$$

The Amberg data show:

	Forecast 1996	Actual 1995	Actual 1994	Actual 1993
Total liabilities	$ 806	$ 668	$ 593	$ 651
Total equity......................	889	792	695	509
Debt to equity ratio	90.66%	84.34%	85.32%	127.90%

For the past 2 years and for the 1996 forecast, Amberg has kept total debt under a 1:1 ratio. Notice that this ratio is expressed as a percentage. It could be shown as .9066:1 for 1996.

Other ratios such as equity to total assets, debt to total assets, and equity to debt tell the same story. Debt is also often defined as long-term debt, excluding operating current liabilities.

Common Equity Multiplier

If an owner invests $1, how much other money can be raised to lever that $1? **Common equity multiplier** indicates that relationship and is defined as follows:

$$\frac{\text{Total Assets}}{\text{Common Equity}} = \text{Common Equity Multiplier}$$

The data from the Amberg case show:

	Forecast 1996	Actual 1995	Actual 1994	Actual 1993
Total assets	$1,695	$1,460	$1,288	$1,160
Common equity (total equity − preferred stock).	789	692	595	509
Common equity multiplier	2.15	2.11	2.16	2.28

The higher the number, the more noncommon stockholder money we are using to finance our assets, and the more risky our position becomes. The lower, the less financial leverage we are using, and the safer we are.

Times Interest Earned

A measure of capital adequacy is whether we are earning enough from operations to pay for the cost of debt—more debt, more interest. **Times interest earned** is defined as:

$$\frac{\text{Net Income Before Interest Expense and Taxes}}{\text{Interest Expense}} = \text{Times Interest Earned}$$

The Amberg data show:

	Forecast 1996	Actual 1995	Actual 1994
Net income before interest expenses and taxes	$ 289	$ 276	$ 249
Interest expense	42	40	46
Times interest earned	6.88	6.90	5.41

The risk is not having cash to pay the interest. A higher number means more safety, and a lower number (particularly under 1.00) means more risk.

Dividend Payout Percentage

The **dividend payout percentage** shows what portion of earnings was paid out in dividends to stockholders. The definition is:

$$\frac{\text{Preferred Stock and Common Stock Dividends}}{\text{Net Income}} \quad = \quad \text{Dividend Payout Percentage}$$

The Amberg data show:

	Forecast 1996	Actual 1995	Actual 1994
Common dividends paid	$ 42	$ 36	$ 30
Preferred dividends paid	9	9	6
Net income after taxes	148	142	122
Dividend payout percentage	34.46%	31.69%	29.51%

A percentage around 30 or 40 percent is normal for a mature firm with a stable earnings record trying to fund growth internally. Rapidly growing firms will probably pay out a smaller percentage to save cash and to build equity faster. As this ratio increases toward 100 percent or above, danger is signaled.

Other Capital Adequacy Considerations   As was mentioned, capital adequacy and liquidity are often offsets for one another. The problem is that liquidity has a very short-term horizon, while capital adequacy has a longer-term time frame. Liquidity problems can arise quickly and must be solved quickly. Capital can be built from earnings which may take years. Firms with large capital bases will find borrowing much easier than already heavily levered firms. Also, firms in risky businesses (new firms, those developing technology, and those in a volatile business) typically need large capital bases as cushions for large operating losses. Mature and well-established firms in stable industries (public utilities, financial institutions, and quasi-governmental firms) may be able to take on heavier debt burdens.

Asset Quality

Asset quality examines two questions dealing with balance sheet assets:

1.   Are assets used efficiently?
2.   What risk exists that the book values will not be recovered?

Measures of efficiency or use are plentiful, but measuring value is difficult using financial statement data. Often the second question must be answered using external data to make sure that financial accounting principles that require no overstatement of asset values are followed. It is an important issue but not addressable by ratio analysis. Efficiency measures look at accounts receivable, inventories, and total assets.

Accounts Receivable Turnover and Days Sales in Receivables
Accounts receivable turnover is:

$$\frac{\text{Sales}}{\text{Average Accounts Receivable}} \quad = \quad \text{Accounts Receivable Turnover}$$

The **days sales in receivables** computation is:

$$\frac{\text{Average Accounts Receivable}}{\text{Sales} \div 360 \text{ Days}} = \text{Days Sales in Receivables}$$

Both ratios are commonly used and express the same idea. Notice that by multiplying Accounts Receivable Turnover times Days Sales in Receivables, we get 360 days.

The Amberg data show:

	Forecast 1996	Actual 1995	Actual 1994
Sales	$2,848	$2,454	$2,084
Average accounts receivable	354	323	292
Accounts receivable turnover	8.05	7.61	7.14
Days sales in receivables	44.75	47.31	50.44

Over the past 3 years, the accounts receivable turnover has increased; and the days sales in receivables have decreased. Amberg is speeding up collections. If Amberg extends "net 30 days" credit terms, a large portion of customers are not paying within 30 days, but the situation is improving.

These numbers must be compared to the credit terms extended to customers to determine whether the ratios indicate that a problem exists. In addition to these ratios, close scrutiny of the allowance for bad debts and bad debts expense must be maintained. Trends of these percentages will give an indication of potential problems. Comparisons to industry leaders will show how our experience compares to others. It also may give insight about our credit terms and whether we are too liberal or too conservative in extending credit to customers and in following up for collections. Maybe we need to be tougher in giving credit and in collecting; maybe we need a big and mean collections person!

Inventory Turnover and Days Sales in Inventory   Inventory turnover is:

$$\frac{\text{Cost of Goods Sold}}{\text{Average Inventory}} = \text{Inventory Turnover}$$

Days sales in inventory is defined as:

$$\frac{\text{Average Inventory}}{\text{Cost of Goods Sold} \div 360 \text{ Days}} = \text{Days Sales in Inventory}$$

Notice that the inventory turnover ratios are basically the same as the receivables turnover ratios except that instead of using sales, cost of goods sold is used. Sales and accounts receivable are valued using sales prices. Cost of goods sold and inventory are valued using purchase prices. This consistency is important. If sales were used for the inventory ratios, the results would be distorted by an "apples and oranges" comparison.

The Amberg data show:

	Forecast 1996	Actual 1995	Actual 1994
Cost of goods sold	$1,721	$1,461	$1,210
Average inventories	388	295	257
Inventory turnover	4.44	4.95	4.71
Days sales in inventory........................	81.16	72.69	76.46

The 1996 forecast shows a large jump in inventories with deterioration of both the inventory turnover and days sales in inventory. Whether an inventory turnover of between 4 and 5 is good or bad depends on what other firms in the industry can do—particularly very successful firms. As the turnover moves higher, more sales are generated from the same sized inventory. But if it gets too high, frequent stock outs might occur; and additional sales may be lost. A low number means the inventory is poorly used; too much is sitting around; and perhaps the physical inventory is old, the wrong items, or stale. Ideally, a middle ground is where minimum inventory is held to maximize sales.

Total Asset Turnover   One way to increase profits given our investment in assets is to increase the ratio of sales to total assets—assuming the return on sales ratio remains constant. The **total asset turnover** is:

$$\frac{\text{Sales}}{\text{Average Total Assets}} = \text{Total Asset Turnover}$$

The Amberg data are:

	Forecast 1996	Actual 1995	Actual 1994
Sales	$2,848	$2,454	$2,084
Average total assets	1,578	1,374	1,224
Total asset turnover	1.80	1.79	1.70

Amberg's operations have been generating more sales per dollar of assets each year for the past 3 years. If the profit margin on sales remains constant, the return on assets should be increasing, which we will see below. The asset turnover ratio is part of the earning power ratios—a key to measuring potential profit improvement in a firm.

Book Value Per Share   The **book value per share** indicates at least how many net asset dollars exist for each share of common stock. This ratio by itself is relatively worthless. In fact, because of historical costs used on balance sheets and real-world inflation of asset values, the book values of assets are often of little value. The definition is:

$$\frac{\begin{array}{c}\text{Common Equity}\\ \text{(Common Paid-in-Capital + Retained Earnings)}\end{array}}{\text{Total Outstanding Common Shares}} = \text{Book Value Per Share}$$

The Amberg data show:

	Forecast 1996	Actual 1995	Actual 1994	Actual 1993
Common equity	$ 789	$ 692	$ 595	$ 509
Total outstanding common shares	60 mil.	60 mil.	60 mil.	60 mil.
Book value per share	$13.15	$11.53	$9.92	$8.48

The book value per share has grown each year as common equity has grown without any increase in common shares outstanding. If the asset values were market values, the book value would give the amount of money each share would be worth if all assets were sold and all noncommon equity claims were paid. Such is rarely the case.

Other Asset Quality Considerations   These ratios use balance sheet amounts. These values are assumed to be good financial accounting amounts—not overstated. We also assume that bad debts accounting is handled fairly, that inventories are at cost and can be converted into sales in the normal business cycle, and that noncurrent assets have at least the balance sheet values attached to them. Often, financial analysts will automatically deduct intangible assets from the asset and equity totals, ignoring them in analyses. Such treatment assumes they have no sales value and are therefore not really usable assets or assets that can be converted into cash. Also, the longer an asset must be held to convert it into cash, the lower the certainty of collection. If two investments are of equal quality but have different maturity dates, the shorter-termed asset will have a higher value. Less time exists for its value to change—less risk exists.

Earnings

The key earnings question is:

> Is net income adequate to satisfy investors' dividend and rate of return expectations and to support growth?

Profitability is often the major focus of analysts. Announcements of financial performance emphasize quarter-to-quarter or year-to-year changes in net income. Earnings per share numbers receive a disproportionate share of attention. Slight deviations of actual earnings figures from expected levels send stock traders to buy or sell the firm's stock.

Clearly, long-term trends in earnings patterns reflect success or difficulties in a firm's competitive market. Rates of return are the major indicators of earnings performance: return on sales, on assets, and on common equity. Earnings per share is often the single measure of earnings that is looked to for stock price purposes. Growing in importance is the cash flow per share, which tells us how much cash was generated per share from operations. Gross margin percentage is examined for trends in operating profitability, as would be other comparative operating ratios.

Return on Sales   The **return on sales (ROS)** is defined as:

$$\frac{\text{Net Income After Taxes}}{\text{Sales}} = \text{Return on Sales}$$

The Amberg data show:

	Forecast 1996	Actual 1995	Actual 1994
Net income after taxes	$ 148	$ 142	$ 122
Sales	2,848	2,454	2,084
Return on sales	5.20%	5.79%	5.85%

The ratio shows a declining ROS for the past year which continues into the forecast year. Whether 5 to 6 percent is an adequate percentage for this firm should be measured against high quality firms in its industry.

In internal analyses and even for certain external uses, operating net income is used instead of net income. The assumption is that operating net income comes from normal operations without any special income or loss items, financing costs, and taxes.

Return on Assets   The **return on assets (ROA)** is defined as:

$$\frac{\text{Net Income After Taxes}}{\text{Average Total Assets}} = \text{Return on Assets}$$

The Amberg data show:

	Forecast 1996	Actual 1995	Actual 1994
Net income after taxes	$ 148	$ 142	$ 122
Average total assets	1,578	1,374	1,224
Return on assets	9.38%	10.33%	9.97%

The ROA is hovering around 10 percent but will drop to its lowest point in forecast 1996. In 1996, assets will grow faster than net income.

Internal analysis would use **managed assets** for the total asset denominator to evaluate a division manager. Managed assets are those assets under the control of a manager of an investment center. The earnings figure should be a controllable or direct contribution margin—excluding allocated common costs. In multidivisional firms, the rate of return on managed assets is planned, is used to compare performances, and is often used in bonus calculations.

Return on Total Equity or Common Equity   The **return on total equity (ROE)** and **return on common equity (ROCE)** are defined as:

$$\frac{\text{Net Income After Taxes}}{\text{Average Total Equity}} \quad = \quad \text{Return on Total Equity}$$

$$\frac{\text{Net Income After Taxes} - \text{Preferred Dividend}}{\text{Average Common Equity}} \quad = \quad \text{Return on Common Equity}$$

The Amberg data show:

	Forecast 1996	Actual 1995	Actual 1994
Net income after taxes	$ 148	$ 142	$ 122
Preferred dividends paid........................	9	9	6
Average total equity	841	744	602
Average common equity........................	741	644	552
Return on total equity	17.60%	19.09%	20.27%
Return on common equity	18.76	20.65	21.01

Because stockholders' equity finances only a portion of total assets, the ROE percentage will be larger than the ROA percentage. Again, the slow growth in net income as compared to other changes is causing the Amberg percentages to drop. This reaffirms a disturbing trend.

A similar ratio called return on division equity could be used internally. Division equity would be managed assets minus any liabilities attributable directly to that division, including accounts payable and possibly subsidiary debt issued in the subsidiary's name and in its control.

Earnings Per Share   **Earnings per share** is defined as:

$$\frac{\text{Net Income After Taxes} - \text{Preferred Dividends}}{\text{Average Number of Common Shares Outstanding}} \quad = \quad \text{Earnings Per Share}$$

The Amberg data show:

	Forecast 1996	Actual 1995	Actual 1994
Net income after taxes	$ 148	$ 142	$ 122
Dividends on preferred stock	9	9	6
Average common shares outstanding	60 mil.	60 mil.	60 mil.
Earnings per share	$2.32	$2.22	$1.93

The earnings per share is increasing but only slowly. Investors like to see this number grow at a steady rate. Investors would say that the 1996 forecast is disappointing.

Often, debt and preferred stock are issued with provisions to convert the securities into common stock at some point in the future. Excluding the prospect of having additional common shares outstanding might overstate the reported earnings per share. Including these shares that may never be issued might understate the earnings per share. Thus, two earnings per share figures are reported—as we have done above—as **fully diluted earnings per share** which assumes that the additional shares are issued and outstanding.

In the Amberg case, let us assume that at some time in the future two common shares would be issued for each $100 share of preferred stock. One million preferred shares are currently outstanding, meaning that 2 million new common shares would be issued to convert the preferred shares. The preferred stock was issued in mid-1994. Note that preferred dividends then would not be paid.

The Amberg data show:

	Forecast 1996	Actual 1995	Actual 1994
Net income after taxes	$ 148	$ 142	$ 122
Average fully diluted common shares outstanding . .	62 mil.	62 mil.	61 mil.
Fully diluted earnings per share	$2.39	$2.29	$2.00

The interesting point here is that at current earnings levels the common shareholder is better off if the preferred stock is converted.

Cash Flow Per Share   With increasing emphasis on cash flow, **cash flow per share** is becoming another leading indicator of the cash generating capabilities of operations. The definition is:

$$\frac{\text{Cash Flow From Operations} - \text{Preferred Stock Dividends}}{\text{Average Number of Common Shares Outstanding}} = \text{Cash Flow Per Share}$$

The Amberg data show:

	Forecast 1996	Actual 1995	Actual 1994
Cash flow from operations	$ 158	$ 162	$ 113
Dividends on preferred stock	9	9	6
Average common shares outstanding	60 mil.	60 mil.	60 mil.
Cash flow per share	$2.48	$2.55	$1.78

The great 1996 forecast growth in inventory will use operations cash and cause the forecast cash flow per share to decline.

Gross Margin Percentage   The **gross margin percentage** provides information about the relative prices received (sales) and the costs of products made or purchased (cost of goods sold). This ratio is examined for trends. Have cost increases been passed along in price increases? Is gross margin as a percentage improving or deteriorating?

The definition is:

$$\frac{\text{Sales} - \text{Cost of Goods Sold}}{\text{Sales}} = \text{Gross Margin Percentage}$$

The Amberg data show:

	Forecast 1996	Actual 1995	Actual 1994
Sales	$2,848	$2,454	$2,084
Cost of goods sold	1,721	1,461	1,210
Gross margin	$1,127	$ 993	$ 874
Gross margin percentage	39.57%	40.46%	41.94%

The percentage is declining over the past 2 years and into forecast 1996. This is a drop of 2.37 percent in 2 years. Often, very slight changes in the gross margin percentage are significant. In this case, we probably have found the major reason that net income has not grown as fast as assets and sales and the cause of the drop in the ROS and ROA ratios. Amberg management should examine this change carefully and study possible actions to correct the trend.

Other Earnings Considerations   Strong earnings overcome many other financial problems. But changes in earnings patterns create uncertainty. Volatile earnings bother analysts who like to see stable earnings percentages and growing earnings dollar amounts. Declining earnings trends are particularly upsetting.

Often earnings impacts are the result of changes in other financial performance areas. Studying earnings results from other financial and operating changes is an important part of financial performance analysis, particularly in financial forecasting. Modeling and "what if" analysis discussed in Chapter 8 make important contributions to financial analysis.

Growth

The key growth questions are:

1.   Is growth adequate given conditions in the firm's markets?
2.   Are the firm's growth patterns balanced or at least within planned growth patterns?

The first question needs external data about economic and market growth rates and cannot be answered from financial statements alone. The second question compares growth rates across a variety of balance sheet and income statement accounts. Balance implies the same relative growth rates for accounts like assets, equity, sales, and profits. The argument can be made that nearly all financial problems arise from unbalanced growth in these and other accounts.

The basic definition for all growth ratios is:

$$\frac{\text{Year 2 Account Balance} - \text{Year 1 Account Balance}}{\text{Year 1 Account Balance}} = \text{Growth Rate Percentage}$$

The Amberg data show:

	Forecast 1996	Actual 1995	Actual 1994
Growth in assets	16.10%	13.35%	11.03%
Growth in total equity	12.25%	13.96%	36.54%
Growth in debt	20.66%	12.65%	−8.91%
Growth in sales	16.06%	17.75%	
Growth in operating expenses	16.88%	14.72%	
Growth in net income	4.23%	16.39%	

The 1996 forecast growth rates show extremes in undesirable areas—the high is debt and the low is net income. The percentages for 1995 are very balanced with the difference between high and low being 5.1 percent.

If assets grow faster than equity, capital adequacy is soon in trouble. If net income growth lags behind, equity cannot be built quickly enough to support more rapid sales and asset growth. Balanced growth assumes that the firm is already in a "balanced" position. If we are in an imbalanced position already, management must control growth in the high areas and encourage more growth in the low areas.

Market Performance

The key market performance question is:

How do the financial markets evaluate the financial condition of the firm?

Stock prices and debt instrument prices give an assessment by investors and analysts of the financial risks and returns in the firm. The ratios commonly used are the price-earnings ratio and dividend yield. Another ratio, the income yield, is the inverse of the price-earnings ratio. Yields on debt instruments and preferred stock can also be calculated and compared to market averages by security type and quality.

Price-Earnings Ratio   The definition of the **price-earnings ratio** is:

$$\frac{\text{Average Market Price Per Share}}{\text{Earnings Per Share}} = \text{Price-Earnings Ratio}$$

The Amberg data show:

	Forecast 1996	Actual 1995	Actual 1994
Common stock—average market price per share	$26.25	$26.75	$23.00
Earnings per share	2.32	2.22	1.93
Price-earnings ratio	11.31:1	12.05:1	11.92:1

The price-earnings ratio (or multiple) is monitored carefully by investors, stockholders, and the firm's management itself. Generally, the higher the ratio, the greater the investor's expectation of future growth in earnings and dividends. The lower the ratio, the less faith investors have in future earnings and dividend growth.

Dividend Yield   The cash dividends paid relative to the market price is the **dividend yield**. For common stock the definition is:

$$\frac{\text{Common Stock Cash Dividends Per Share}}{\text{Average Market Price Per Share}} = \text{Common Equity Dividend Yield}$$

The same ratio could be found for preferred stock. The Amberg data show:

	Forecast 1996	Actual 1995	Actual 1994
Common stock—average market price	$26.25	$26.75	$23.00
Common dividends paid	$42	$36	$30
Average common shares outstanding	60 mil.	60 mil.	60 mil.
Common equity dividend yield	2.66%	2.24%	2.17%

Basically, the dividend yield is the cash payout on the share price. Firms with high dividend yields are attractive to investors who need immediate income from their investments. Successful firms with strong earnings and low dividend yields are attractive to investors who want to see their investment grow through capital appreciation.

INTERRELATIONSHIPS OF RISKS AND RETURNS

As a firm takes on more risk in one area, it can compensate by becoming safer in another area—protecting itself. Financial problems arise when this balance is tilted too far. Aggressive risk taking should be offset by strong fall back positions and backup alternatives. Certain strategies illustrate the tradeoffs. Included here are financial leverage, earning power ratios, and a strategic profit model.

Financial Leverage

Financial leverage is defined as the use of borrowed funds to enhance the rate of return to common equity owners. Borrowed funds can be extended to include preferred stock in these analyses. If only common equity capital is used for long-term financing, common equity owners get all the profits after taxes as their return. However, the owners must also provide all long-term funds.

If common equity owners could reduce their investment by borrowing funds and paying interest on those funds, the profits earned over and above the cost of the funds would go to the common equity owners. The rate of return on common equity should increase—perhaps dramatically. Two benefits are possible. First, the same operating profits can be earned using less equity. Second, a "profit margin" can be earned by earning more on the debt-funded assets than the debt costs.

An illustration will show these relationships. Three companies, Common Company, Preferred Company, and Debt Company, have nearly identical operations. Their condensed balance sheets are as follows:

	Common	Preferred	Debt
Total assets	$1,000,000	$1,000,000	$1,000,000
Liabilities and equities:			
Current liabilities	$ 200,000	$ 200,000	$ 200,000
Bonds payable—8%	0	0	400,000
Preferred stock—9%	0	300,000	0
Common equity	800,000	500,000	400,000
Total liabilities and equities	$1,000,000	$1,000,000	$1,000,000

The results of operations for the current year are:

	Common	Preferred	Debt
Income before interest and taxes	$ 125,000	$ 125,000	$ 125,000
Interest on bonds payable	0	0	32,000
Income before taxes	$ 125,000	$ 125,000	$ 93,000
Income taxes (40 percent)	50,000	50,000	37,200
Net income after taxes	$ 75,000	$ 75,000	$ 55,800
Preferred stock dividends	0	27,000	0
Earnings on common equity	$ 75,000	$ 48,000	$ 55,800
Total assets	$1,000,000	$1,000,000	$1,000,000
Common equity	$ 800,000	$ 500,000	$ 400,000
Return on total assets	7.50 %	4.80 %	5.58 %
Return on common equity	9.38 %	9.60 %	13.95 %

The return on common equity increases in both alternatives that use less common equity. The cost of preferred funds (9 percent) and debt funds (8 percent minus tax benefits) is lower than the return on common equity of 9.38 percent. Several generalizations can be made:

1. If the cost of debt is less than the return on the additional net investment, financial leverage will benefit the common equity owners.
2. Even if only equity financing is used, the presence of current liabilities causes the return on common equity to exceed the return on assets.
3. If the debt interest rate and the preferred dividend rate are similar, debt is less expensive because debt interest is deductible for tax purposes and dividends on preferred stock are not.
4. As the amount of debt increases, the debt interest rate will increase because the risk of default is greater. The cushion of capital as a protection to creditors becomes less relative to the amount of debt taken on.
5. By adding more debt or preferred stock, the return on assets will decline and may cause the firm as a whole to look less profitable. But the return on common equity will grow up to a point.

As with all financial performance issues, too much of a good thing turns into a bad thing. Financial leverage gains to common equity end when the cost of borrowed funds exceeds the return on the investments made. Assume in the above example that Debt Company increases the portion of debt to $600,000 and that common equity drops to $200,000. Also, assume that the cost of debt increases to 18 percent because of the higher risk. Interest expense is now $108,000; taxes are $6,800; and net income after taxes is $10,200. With common equity now $200,000, the return on common equity declines to 5.1 percent. This is a drop from the 9.38 percent total common equity example and the 13.95 percent return with $400,000 of debt at 8 percent interest. The reason for this is the after tax cost of debt is 10.8 percent [18 % × (1 − .40)] while the return on net assets (total assets after deducting current liabilities) is only 9.38 percent. Thus, the debt funds cost is more than is earned from the assets purchased with the funds.

Earning Power Ratios

Another extension of the ratio interrelationships and the leverage concept is the **earning power ratios**, which combine return on sales, asset turnover, and capital multiplier ratios to form the return on equity ratio. The basic format is:

$$\frac{\text{Net Income}}{\text{Sales}} = \text{Return on Sales}$$

$$\frac{\text{Net Income}}{\text{Sales}} \times \frac{\text{Sales}}{\text{Average Total Assets}} = \text{Return on Assets}$$

$$\frac{\text{Net Income}}{\text{Sales}} \times \frac{\text{Sales}}{\text{Average Total Assets}} \times \frac{\text{Average Total Assets}}{\text{Average Common Equity}} = \text{Return on Common Equity}$$

The expression can be broken down into:

Return on Sales x Asset Turnover x Capital Multiplier = Return on Common Equity

Again, using the Amberg data from the 1996 forecast:

$$\frac{\$148,000}{\$2,848,000} \times \frac{\$2,848,000}{\$1,578,000} \times \frac{\$1,578,000}{\$740,000} = 5.20\% \times 180.48\% \times 213.24\% = 20.00\%$$

These basic relationships have particular importance to Amberg management since earnings growth has slowed and all the rates of return have declined. To improve the ROCE, the following changes could be made:

1. Increase the return on sales by reducing operating expenses, increasing margins, minimizing taxes, and reducing interest expenses.
2. Increase sales relative to total assets while holding the ROS constant.
3. Reduce total assets while holding sales, ROS, and the capital multiplier constant.
4. Reduce common equity through greater equity leverage while holding asset turnover and ROS constant.

Thus, improving any of the three ratios while holding the others constant will improve the return on common equity. In every case, increasing the numerator and decreasing the denominator improve the return ratio.

The earning power ratios can be compared to other successful firms and industry averages to spot problem areas and to indicate a firm's relative strengths and weaknesses. Leveraging net income, sales, total assets, and equity financing into a high return to common stockholders is a major financial management responsibility. Obviously, too much leverage begins to change expense patterns, to decrease the firm's ability to generate sales from limited assets, and to create more expensive debt. Again, the too much/too little extremes create financial problems.

Strategic Profit Model

Another approach to evaluating and testing financial ratio relationships is a very traditional model, often called the Du Pont formula. A modified version is called the strategic profit model and is illustrated in Figures 17.6 and 17.7. The left hand side of Figure 17.6 is the return on assets. All the components of the ROA are arrayed and can be modeled. The model can:

1. Show the sensitivity of the earning power ratios from changes in specific account balances.
2. Identify the differences among firms and industries in terms of financial structure and financial performance.
3. Test the impacts of proposed changes in operations, debt structure, and working capital.
4. Help set long-range and near-term goals and criteria that need to be met to achieve the goals.

Increasing the understanding of financial interrelationships has made this simple analytical framework popular in financial performance analysis for over 50 years.

CAVEATS IN USING FINANCIAL PERFORMANCE ANALYSIS

As with any tool, the strengths and usefulness of performance analyses are tempered by limits and dangers of inappropriate application. Assumptions must always be tested, underlying data must have credibility, and care must be taken in generalizing from basic ratio findings. Among the caveats are:

1. **No consistently valid rules of thumb exist.** Specific industries often have very different acceptable ranges for certain key ratios. Often industry traditions call for certain financial ratios and specific numbers. An individual firm's strengths and weaknesses cause ratios to be case specific. Traditional guidelines are useful and often valid for general comparisons. Time and events cause these guidelines to change.

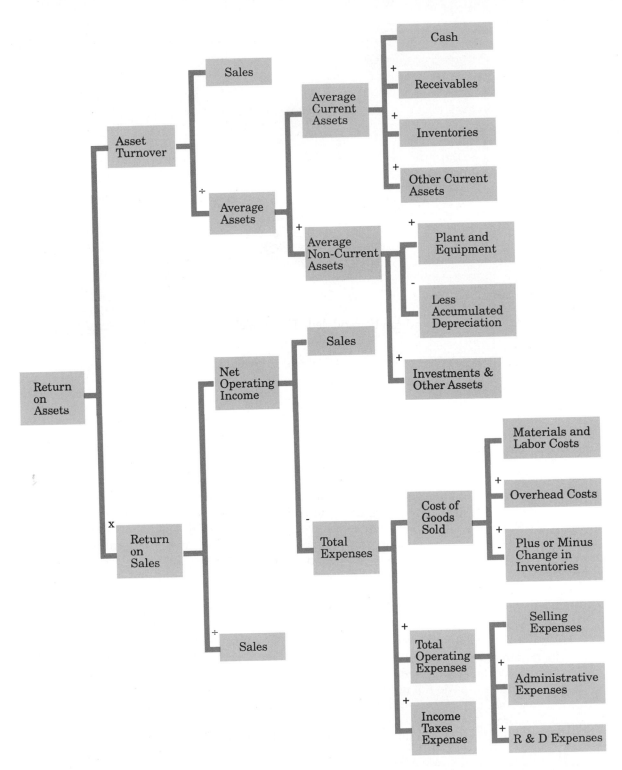

Figure 17.6   Strategic Profit Model—Return on Assets

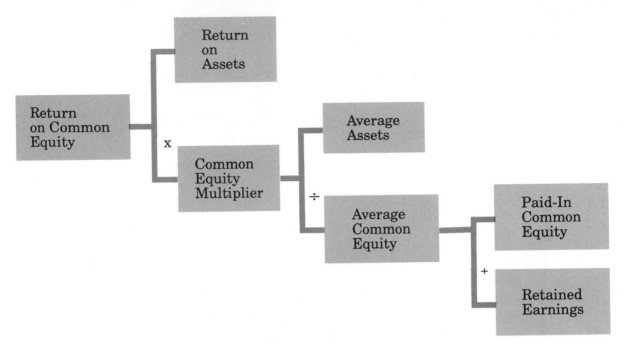

Figure 17.7   Strategic Profit Model—Return on Common Equity

2. **No one ratio can tell a story.** Sets of ratios for a given time period and over a series of time periods are needed to paint the financial picture of a firm. Knowing one number tells little about the interrelationships that exist.

3. **Industry averages are just that—averages.** Strong firms and weak firms are averaged. Firms with weak liquidity and strong capital positions are averaged with firms with strong liquidity and weak capital positions. Big and little firms often have different characteristics. Specific industry ratios give insight to the industry and are useful in beginning an analysis. But for financial planning, competitive analysis, and measuring strength, a carefully selected group of strong peer firms (similar size, competitive environment, geography, etc.) provides a more powerful comparative base.

4. **Be careful to define ratios uniformly and consistently.** Using cross firm and industry ratio data is dangerous unless common definitions are used. What is capital? How are turnovers calculated? How is cash flow defined? What is return on investment? Often, common terms have different operating definitions in different firms.

5. **More ratios do not necessarily make a better analysis.** A carefully selected set of ratios should be reported routinely with internal financial reports. Managers, officers, board members, and even stockholders should become familiar with a common set of ratios. This is often called a

key ratio report. Some firms prepare a key operating statistics report each month that includes tracking a set of key financial ratios. Hundreds of ratios could be calculated. But a small, well-understood set of ratios can tell an informed reader as much as pages of data can.

6. **Be aware of off-balance sheet events and factors that impact the interpretation of financial ratios.** Nonfinancial links, contracts, or business events may impact a firm's financial condition with no direct impacts on financial statement numbers. Law suits, lines of credit, and long-term supplier or sales contracts are a few examples. The analyst must weigh the nonfinancial issues and the nonfinancial statement situations that affect the firm's operations.

7. **Allow for accounting method differences.** Asset valuations, liability recognition, accounting policies, and different generally accepted accounting practices can cause similar firms to appear very different. Price-level impact differences may be another variable. Also, year-end balances may be poor indicators of the average balance during the year.

8. **Remember that the goal of financial performance analysis is to diagnose the firm's financial health.** Ratio analysis should not be an exercise unto itself but should measure performance.

These and other caveats bring the positive attributes back to reality. Care must be taken to avoid the pitfalls and to pull the maximum information available from the financial statements.

SUMMARY

Financial statement analysis can be used by both outside analysts and by internal management. Management is well aware of the key relationships that are used by current and prospective investors, creditors, and customers. Financial performance should be a proactive tool—part of the financial planning and control processes. Management can also use ratios to detect areas where improvements can be made.

Financial performance analysis focuses on the financial risks and returns areas of liquidity, capital adequacy, asset quality, earnings, growth, and market performance. Key ratios in each area were defined, illustrated, and discussed.

The interrelationships among various ratios and areas of risks and returns exist. Strengths in one area can offset a weakness in another area. Financial leverage as a concept that uses debt instead of equity to finance assets was illustrated. Earning power ratios are composed of return on sales, asset turnover, and capital multiplier ratios. A strategic profit model was discussed as means of testing the sensitivity of relationships and the impacts of changes in account balances on rates of return.

The advantages of ratio analysis kicked off the chapter. Caveats on the use of ratios ended the analysis. Financial performance analysis is a powerful tool but must be used carefully and with sensitivity.

PROBLEM FOR REVIEW

Lyman Products Company is a closely held company, with over 60 percent of the capital stock held by one family. The company manufactures insulating and packing materials and has recently developed decorative and maintenance-free wall and floor coverings.

For several years, the company has been successful, with results for 1994 being typical. The president of the company stated that the company could do even better but had been holding unnecessary amounts in both materials and finished goods inventories. With the release of funds held in inventory and with operating economies, the company would have resources for investment in a new plant. This plant would make it possible for the company to be an aggressive competitor in the wall and floor covering market. Also, plant investments can be made without the issuance of additional shares of stock (and the possible risk of the family losing control of the company) if investments can be made from internally-generated funds.

In 1995, management found ways to reduce inventories and operating costs while increasing sales volume by a modest amount. Income statements for 1994 and 1995 are given, along with average balance sheets for 1994 and 1995.

LYMAN PRODUCTS COMPANY **INCOME STATEMENTS** **FOR THE YEARS ENDED DECEMBER 31, 1994 AND 1995** **(IN THOUSANDS)**		
	1995	**1994**
Net sales	$7,100	$6,850
Cost of goods sold	4,682	4,794
Gross margin	$2,418	$2,056
Operating expenses	1,047	1,020
Operating income	$1,371	$1,036
Interest expense	96	84
Income before income taxes	$1,275	$ 952
Income taxes expense (40 percent)	510	381
Net income	$ 765	$ 571
Depreciation included in cost of goods sold and operating expenses	$ 224	$ 216
Cost of materials used	3,790	3,870
Dividends declared and paid	300	200
Number of common shares outstanding	200	200

LYMAN PRODUCTS COMPANY
AVERAGE BALANCE SHEETS
FOR 1994 AND 1995
(IN THOUSANDS OF DOLLARS)

	1995	1994
Assets:		
Current assets:		
Cash	$1,233	$ 686
Accounts receivable, net of uncollectibles	635	584
Inventories:		
Finished goods......................................	852	975
Materials	540	730
Total current assets....................................	$3,260	$2,975
Plant and equipment, net of accumulated depreciation	2,085	1,895
Total assets	$5,345	$4,870
Liabilities and Stockholders' Equity:		
Current liabilities:		
Accounts payable	$ 316	$ 421
Notes payable	650	650
Other current liabilities	171	191
Total current liabilities	$1,137	$1,262
Long-term notes payable	450	315
Total liabilities.....................................	$1,587	$1,577
Stockholders' equity:		
Capital stock, $1 par value............................	$ 200	$ 200
Paid-in capital in excess of par	1,300	1,300
Retained earnings	2,258	1,793
Total stockholders' equity............................	$3,758	$3,293
Total liabilities and stockholders' equity	$5,345	$4,870

New equipment costing $900,000 is to be acquired early in 1996. The family can invest $240,000, if additional capital stock is to be issued. Additional debt will be accepted if total debt will be no more than 40 percent of total liabilities and stockholders' equity.

Required:
1.   Compute the following ratios for 1994 and 1995. Show computations.
    (a)   Return on sales
    (b)   Return on assets
    (c)   Return on total equity
    (d)   Gross margin percentage
    (e)   Debt to equity ratio
    (f)   Times interest earned
    (g)   Dividend payout percentage
    (h)   Accounts receivable turnover
    (i)   Finished goods inventory turnover
    (j)   Materials inventory turnover
    (k)   Total asset turnover

      (l)   Current ratio

      (m)   Quick ratio

2.   Comment on the Lyman Products Company's financial performance in the areas of earnings, asset quality, and liquidity.

3.   Does it appear that the plant equipment can be purchased by following the conditions stated?

Solution:

1.   **Ratios:**

		1995	1994
(a)	Return on sales	10.8%	8.3%
	(Net income ÷ Net sales)	($765 ÷ $7,100)	($571 ÷ $6,850)
(b)	Return on asset	14.3%	11.7%
	(Net income ÷ Total assets)	($765 ÷ $5,345)	($571 ÷ $4,870)
(c)	Return on total equity	20.4%	17.3%
	(Net income ÷ Total equity)	($765 ÷ $3,758)	($571 ÷ $3,293)
(d)	Gross margin percentage................	34.1%	30.0%
	(Gross margin ÷ Sales)	($2,418 ÷ $7,100)	($2,056 ÷ $6,850)
(e)	Debt to equity ratio	42.2%	47.9 %
	(Total liabilities ÷ Total equity)	($1,587 ÷ $3,758)	($1,577 ÷ $3,293)
(f)	Times interest earned	14.3 times	12.3 times
	(Operating income ÷ Interest expense)	($1,371 ÷ $96)	($1,036 ÷ $84)
(g)	Dividend payout percentage	39.2%	35.0%
	(Dividends per share ÷ Earnings per share)	(1.50 ÷ 3.83)	(1.00 ÷ 2.86)
	Dividends per share:		
	$300 ÷ 200 = $1.50 per share, 1995		
	$200 ÷ 200 = $1.00 per share, 1994		
	Earnings per share:		
	$765 ÷ 200 = $3.83 per share, 1995		
	$571 ÷ 200 = $2.86 per share, 1994		
(h)	Accounts receivable turnover.............	11.2 times	11.7 times
	(Net sales ÷ Accounts receivable)	($7,100 ÷ $635)	($6,850 ÷ $584)
(i)	Finished goods inventory turnover	5.5 times	4.9 times
	(Cost of goods sold ÷ Finished goods inventory)	($4,682 ÷ $852)	($4,794 ÷ $975)
(j)	Materials inventory turnover..............	7.0 times	5.3 times
	(Cost of materials used ÷ Materials inventory)	($3,790 ÷ $540)	($3,870 ÷ $730)
(k)	Total asset turnover	1.3 times	1.4 times
	(Net sales ÷ Total assets)	($7,100 ÷ $5,345)	($6,850 ÷ $4,870)
(l)	Current ratio	2.9:1	2.4:1
	(Current assets ÷ Current liabilities)	($3,260 ÷ $1,137)	($2,975 ÷ $1,262)
(m)	Quick ratio	1.6:1	1.0:1
	[(Cash + Accounts receivable) ÷ Current liabilities]	($1,868 ÷ $1,137)	($1,270 ÷ $1,262)

2.   **Financial Performance Areas:**

    In all cases, Lyman Products Company ratios should be compared to successful peer company data and industry data to help analyze specific ratios. The trends between 1994 and 1995 show:

1. Earnings: The company was more profitable in 1995 than in 1994. The ROS, ROA, and ROE ratios all improved. A dramatic increase in the gross margin percentage and a slight savings in operating costs (in relation to net sales) are translated into better rates of return. Earnings per share improved from $2.86 to $3.83, a 33.9 percent improvement.

2. Asset Quality: Inventories have been used much more efficiently in 1995. A question may be raised as to whether or not inventories could be reduced further. Over 60 days of finished goods inventory and over 50 days of materials inventory are still on hand. Overall, the firm's ability to generate sales from total assets declined. This should be a concern, since additional plant investments are planned. Receivables turnover seems to be slowing slightly.

3. Liquidity: Liquidity was good in 1994 and even better in 1995 as demonstrated by the current ratio and the quick ratio. The interest cost is also well covered by earnings.

3. **New Plant Financing:**

The company should be able to acquire $900,000 in plant equipment with $500,000 in internally-generated funds (primarily from cash) while still holding a cash balance of over $700,000. If desired, the remaining $400,000 could be financed by debt without going over 40 percent. The debt to total assets ratio in 1994 and 1995 was 32.4% and 29.7% respectively. The additional common stock and debt will still keep the ratio well below 40 percent.

TERMINOLOGY REVIEW

Accounts receivable turnover (864)
Acid test ratio (860)
Base-year comparisons (857)
Book value per share (866)
Cash flow per share (870)
Common equity (862)
Common equity multiplier (863)
Common-size statements (855)
Comparative statements (855)
Current ratio (859)
Days sales in accounts receivable (864)
Days sales in inventory (865)
Debt to equity ratio (862)
Dividend payout percentage (863)
Dividend yield (873)
Earning power ratios (875)
Earnings per share (869)
Financial leverage (873)
Fully diluted earnings per share (870)

Gross margin percentage (870)
Horizontal analysis (857)
Inventory turnover (865)
Managed assets (868)
Off-balance-sheet financing (861)
Operations cash flow to current debt service ratio (861)
Percentage composition statements (855)
Price-earnings ratio (872)
Quick assets (860)
Quick ratio (860)
Return on assets (ROA) (868)
Return on common equity (ROCE) (868)
Return on sales (ROS) (868)
Return on total equity (ROE) (868)
Times interest earned (863)
Total asset turnover (866)
Working capital (859)

QUESTIONS FOR REVIEW AND DISCUSSION

1. Is the usefulness of financial ratios restricted to analysis of historical financial statements? Explain.

2. Identify what is meant by vertical and horizontal financial statement analysis.

3. What is asset turnover? What influence does a higher asset turnover tend to have on the rate of return on assets? What does a very low ratio imply? What is the danger of a very high ratio?

4. Explain the earning power ratios. How can each be used?

5. What can management do to increase return on equity? What are the problems with a very high and a very low return on equity?

6. If return on assets is to be used to evaluate a manager at the operating level, what adjustments should be made to net income and to assets? What adjustments should be made to net income and to assets to evaluate a segment?

7. What is the disadvantage of having more liquid assets than are needed? What is the disadvantage of having too few liquid assets?

8. What are the two conflicting questions that try to assess capital adequacy? How are answers to these two questions brought together?

9. What are the risks and returns areas in financial performance analysis? Why is each one in the "risks" or the "returns" group that it is? Could a risk become a return or a return become a risk?

10. What is the key question in assessing liquidity? What ratios are used to help answer the question? What additional off-balance sheet data might be useful?

11. What are the primary concerns in assessing asset quality? What ratios are used to answer the concerns? What do too high and too low ratios mean?

12. What is the key question regarding earnings and profitability? Are there really two needs for earnings buried in the one question? If so, what are they; and why are they important?

13. What are the concerns about growth? Are these easily answered from financial statement data? Explain.

14. Why should we be concerned with how the external financial markets assess our financial position?

15. What is financial leverage? Explain how it works.

16. Explain the difference between the market value and the book value of a share of stock.

17. List five caveats to be considered in the analysis of financial statements.

18. In general, what is being measured by the current ratio and by the acid-test ratio? What is the difference between the two ratios?

19. The strategic profit model brings together much balance sheet and income statement data to generate rates of return. Describe the model's structure. How can it be used to help set and to help achieve financial goals?

20. How is times interest earned calculated? When is it used?

21. What may be indicated by:

    (a) A sharp increase in the current ratio?
    (b) A return on stockholders' equity that is nearly equal to return on assets?

(c) A large increase in the dividend payout ratio?

(d) A drop in inventory turnover and an increase in days sales in inventory?

(e) A decline over several years of the gross margin percentage?

(f) An increase in the book value per share?

(g) An increase in the earnings per share?

(h) A decline in the price-earnings ratio?

22. If assets are growing at an annual rate of 10 percent, sales by 15 percent, net profit by 8 percent, and equity by 6 percent, what financial problems will eventually appear for this company?

EXERCISES

1. **Rate of Return.** Three Rivers Stores earned $1,500,000 on net sales of $50,000,000 in 1993. Beginning total assets were $10,000,000; and ending total assets were $12,000,000.

Required:

1. Compute the return on net sales.
2. Compute the return on the average assets.
3. Compute the asset turnover.
4. Explain why such a difference exists between return on net sales and return on the average assets.

2. **Current Asset Use.** Analyze the following data:

(a) If net credit sales for the year are $15,000,000 and the average accounts receivable are $3,000,000, how many days sales are in accounts receivable on the average? What is the receivables turnover?

(b) If the cost of goods sold is $7,200,000 and the average inventory of merchandise is $600,000, how many days sales are in inventory on the average? What is the inventory turnover?

(c) If it has been determined that accounts receivable should be collected in 40 days and that inventory turns over every 30 days, how long is the operating cycle?

3. **Turnovers.** The following selected data are taken from the Woolly Company's accounts:

Sales in 1994	$357,000
Cost of goods sold in 1994	216,000
Accounts receivable, 1/1/94	220,000
Accounts receivable, 12/31/94	242,000
Inventory, 1/1/94	130,000
Inventory, 12/31/94	70,000

Required:

1. Find the inventory turnover and the days sales in inventory.
2. Find the accounts receivable turnover and the days sales in receivables.

4. **Capital-Based Ratios.** The following data are available from the McCarthy Shipping Company. No shares were issued in 1994.

Net sales for 1994	$6,360,000
Net income for 1994	398,000
Cash dividends—on preferred.....................................	2,400
Cash dividends—on common	70,000
Average market price per common share	150
Average balance amounts:	
Common stock—par value, $100	1,500,000
Paid-in capital in excess of par—common........................	90,000
Preferred stock—par value, $100, 4 percent....................	60,000
Retained earnings	500,000

Required:
Calculate the:
(a) Earnings per share of common stock.
(b) Book value per share of common stock.
(c) Dividend yield per share of common stock.
(d) Price-earnings ratio for common stock.
(e) Return on total equity.
(f) Return on common equity.

5. **Statements from Incomplete Data.** George Bernthal of Bernthal Company found the following pieces of his balance sheet and key ratio report data in his gerbil cage:

Cash	$?			
Accounts receivable	$?	Equity to debt ratio	3
Inventory	$ 80	Current ratio	2.25
Fixed assets (net)	$?	Inventory turnover	14.4
		Days sales in receivables	
Current liabilities	$ 80	(He uses 360 days.)........	15
Common stock..............	$100	Gross margin percentage	25%
Retained earnings	$?		

Required:
Add as much data to his average balance sheet as you can.

6. **Changing the Rate of Return Relationships.** Vera Amick, chief executive officer of Seaside Resorts Corporation, notes that the corporation earned a net income of only $3,000,000 last year on sales of $75,000,000 and an average asset investment of $50,000,000. With no other changes, she states that net income can be increased to $5,000,000 by reducing waste and cutting costs.

Required:
1. What was the return on sales and assets last year?
2. If costs can be reduced as stated by Amick, what will be the return on sales and assets?

7. **The Good News and Bad News.** A change in any financial ratio can contain good news and bad news. Changes in a numerator or denominator can cause a ratio to strengthen or weaken. Financial results of 1993 and 1994 have caused the following three ratios values to move:

Ratio	1994	1993
Current ratio	3:1	4:1
Inventory turnover	6	5
Dividend payout...	30%	40%

Required:

For each ratio, indicate what the good news might be and what the bad news might be. Can you create a scenario for the three changes taken together?

8.   **Common-Size Statements.** Jess Schulman, the president of Health Care Products Company, states that large dollar amounts on financial statements confuse him. However, he finds that percentage relationships are helpful. For example, he expects cost of goods sold to be 60 percent of net sales, operating expenses to be 20 percent, income taxes to be 7 percent, and a net income to be about 10 percent.

Operating results for 1994 and 1995 are given below in summary form:

	1994	1995
Net sales	$15,140,000	$18,534,000
Cost of goods sold	9,175,000	11,523,000
Gross profit	$ 5,965,000	$ 7,011,000
Operating expenses	3,421,000	3,906,000
Operating income	$ 2,544,000	$ 3,105,000
Income taxes	1,036,000	1,233,000
Net income	$ 1,508,000	$ 1,872,000

Required:

1.   Prepare percentage composition statements for both years.
2.   Prepare a base-year comparison using 1994 as the base year.
3.   What trends exist? Were the president's expectations realized? Should he worry about certain trends?

9.   **Liquidity and Capital Adequacy Ratios.** X Business and Y Business have the following ratios:

	X Business	Y Business
Current ratio	4.5 : 1	1.5 : 1
Debt to equity ratio	.2 : 1	1.0 : 1
Quick ratio	2.5 : 1	.8 : 1
Times interest earned	10 times	3 times

Required:

What can be said about the financial strength of X Business and Y Business?

10.   **Changing the Rate of Return Relationships.** Garrett Corporation generally earns about 3 percent on net sales each year. The asset investment is usually turned over 4 times each year. More profitable product lines have been added that should increase the rate of return on the sales dollar to 6 percent. Next year, net sales have been estimated at $12,000,000 with an average investment in assets of $3,000,000.

Required:

1.   Compute the return on assets with a 3 percent return on net sales.
2.   Compute the return on assets for the next year assuming a 6 percent return on net sales.

11.   **Liquidity Impacts.** A company's current ratio and quick ratio have moved as follows:

	1993	1994	1995	1996
Current ratio	2:1	2.5:1	3:1	4:1
Quick ratio	1.5:1	1:1	.8:1	.6:1

Required:

Comment on the validity of the following statements:

(a) The stronger current ratio in 1996 reflects improved profitability.

(b) A large obsolete inventory may be a serious problem.

(c) The quick ratio change reflects a desire to pay our bills on time.

(d) The current ratio in 1996 is clearly too high.

(e) The company is more liquid in 1996 than in 1993.

12. **Equity and Market Ratios.** At December 31, 1995, Richmond Company had 100,000 shares of $10 par value common stock issued and outstanding. The number of shares outstanding during 1995 did not change. Total stockholders' equity at December 31, 1995 was $2,800,000. The net income for the year ended December 31, 1995 was $400,000. During 1995 Richmond paid $3 per share in dividends on its common stock. The quoted market value of Richmond's common stock on a national stock exchange averaged $32 during 1995.

Required:

1. What was the common stock price-earnings ratio at the end of 1995?

2. What was the dividend yield on common stock at the end of 1995?

13. **Creation of Financial Statements from Ratios.** Assume net income was $5,000. No other information is known.

Return on equity	10%
Return on sales	4%
Gross margin percentage	60%
Income tax rate	50%
Current ratio	3:1
Return on assets	5%
Inventory turnover	4
Days sales in receivables	90
Long-term debt to equity	2:3

Required:

Using the above ratios, construct a balance sheet and income statement in as detailed a form as possible. Add accounts only where needed for balancing or subtotaling.

14. **Impacts on Risks and Returns Areas.** Business events impact each financial performance area in one or more ways. Consider the following areas:

1. Liquidity

2. Capital adequacy

3. Asset quality

4. Growth

5. Earnings

Required:

Indicate the major impacts the following business events would have on the firm's financial performance categories, and whether these changes would strengthen (S), weaken (W), or have no change (NC) on each area. List each event as a row and each performance category as a column. Make a brief note in each cell (column and row intersection) to explain your answer:

(a) Lengthening credit terms to customers from 30 to 60 days.
(b) Dividend declared and paid.
(c) Long-term debt issued for cash.
(d) Issued common stock in trade for production equipment.

15. **Comparability of Data.** Walter Zarnoch boasted that he has been earning 30 percent on his investment in Boswell Industries. The net income has averaged $630,000, and the assets invested cost $2,100,000. You have examined the data and find that the depreciation charges should have been on a current dollar basis and that net income in comparable dollars of purchasing power was only $450,000. The assets when revised to current values should be shown at $5,000,000.

Required:
1. Show how Zarnoch computed the 30 percent return on assets.
2. Compute a corrected return on assets.

16. **Turnover and Rate of Return Relationships.** In each of the following situations, compute the return on net sales, the asset turnover, or the net sales as requested:
1. What is the return on sales if the asset turnover is 2.6 and 13 percent is earned on assets?
2. Sales for the year were $28,000,000, and the average asset investment was $8,000,000. Determine the asset turnover.
3. Assets are turned over 0.8 times in earning 15 percent on the sales dollar. What is the return on assets?
4. With an asset turnover of 2.5, what must be the return on sales if the return on assets is 15 percent?
5. If stockholders' equity is equal to 60 percent of total liabilities and stockholders' equity, what is the rate of return on stockholders' equity if 9 percent is earned on total assets invested?
6. The return on assets was 16 percent, and 8 percent was earned on net sales. What was the asset turnover?
7. The return on assets has been computed at 14 percent. The net income was $840,000, and the asset turnover was 2. Although you do not have the sales figure, determine the amount of sales and the return on sales.
8. If the total cost of operations, excluding income tax, amounts to $2,600,000, compute sales if net income is 5 percent of sales. The income tax has been computed at $250,000.
9. The return on sales has remained at 6 percent for the past two years. The asset turnover in the first year was 2.4 and declined to 1.8 in the second year. Compute the return on assets for each of the two years.
10. Net sales for the year were $9,600,000. Assets turned over 1.2 times during the year. Cost of goods sold and operating expenses, including income tax, amounted to $8,880,000. Compute the return on net sales and on total assets.

17. **Effect of Financial Leverage.** Deep River Brands earned a net income of $1,200,000 on sales of $30,000,000 and an average asset investment of $20,000,000. Total debt averaged $5,000,000.

Valley Brands, a competitor, also reported a net income of $1,200,000 on sales of $30,000,000 and an average asset investment of $20,000,000. However, total debt averaged $10,000,000.

Required:
1. Compute the rate of return for the stockholders for Deep River Brands.
2. Compute the rate of return for the stockholders for Valley Brands.
3. Explain why the rate of return for stockholders is better for Valley Brands.

18. **Dividends and Price-Earnings Ratio.** Last year Rapid Data Company reported a net income of $4,500,000 and paid a dividend of $.90 on each of 2,000,000 shares of common stock outstanding. The market value of each share of stock averaged $45.

Required:
1. Compute the earnings per share.
2. What was the price-earnings ratio?
3. What was the dividend payout percentage?
4. What was the dividend yield ratio?

19. **Dilution of Earnings.** The Bridger Company reported net earnings of $3,000,000 on 2,000,000 shares of common stock outstanding. The company has long-term notes outstanding bearing interest of 8 percent per year with a total face value of $10,000,000. Each note has a face value of $1,000. At the option of the holder of the note, each $1,000 of face value can be exchanged for 100 shares of common stock. Assume a 40 percent income tax rate.

Required:
1. Calculate the earnings per share of common stock before dilution.
2. Calculate the fully diluted earnings per share of common stock.

20. **Effect of Improved Inventory Turnover.** Masterson Company earned a net income of $270,000 on an average asset investment of $3,375,000. Management noted, however, that the finished goods inventory turnover of 6 represented 60 days of sales and was excessive. Average finished goods inventory was $300,000. By eliminating obsolete inventory and planning target inventory levels, the inventory was reduced to $200,000. Before the inventory reduction, current assets averaged $500,000; and current liabilities averaged $325,000. After the inventory reduction, net income is still estimated at $270,000.

Required:
1. Compute the return on assets before the inventory reduction.
2. What was the current ratio before the inventory reduction?
3. Compute the finished goods inventory turnover after reducing inventory.
4. Compute the current ratio after the inventory reduction. (Assume that both current assets and current liabilities will be decreased by the inventory reduction.)
5. What is the expected return on assets after cutting back the investment in finished goods inventory?

21. **Inventory Turnovers.** The new management at Ripley Supplies noted that the materials inventory turned over only once in 18 days. The cost of materials used during the year was $18,000,000. The work in process inventory turnover was 24. Cost of production for the year was $48,000,000.

Steps were taken to obtain prompt delivery from suppliers so that operations could be conducted efficiently with only a 12-day supply of inventory. In addition, bottlenecks in production were eliminated, with the result being that the cost of production was 30 times the work in process inventory.

Required:
1. What was the average investment in materials inventory with a turnover every 18 days? Every 12 days?
2. What was the average investment in work in process inventory with a turnover of 24? Of 30?
3. Explain why reducing inventory levels can improve the return on assets.

22. **Current Asset Turnovers.** Tech Products Company has been growing rapidly. Net income increased from $130,000 in 1994 to $288,000 in 1995. Cost of goods sold and operating expenses amounted to $1,300,000 in 1994 and $4,800,000 in 1995. The average investment in current assets was $650,000 in 1994 and $1,600,000 in 1995. The company had some difficulties in meeting delivery schedules in 1995 and in making payments to creditors.

Required:
1. Compute the return on current assets each year.
2. Compute the current asset turnover each year (use sales as the numerator).
3. Determine the rate of return per turnover each year.
4. Explain why the company may be having trouble in meeting delivery schedules and in making payments to creditors.

23. **Accounts Receivable Turnovers.** Dundon Blending Company has been having difficulty paying current obligations on time and has had to obtain additional short-term credit from the bank. Collections on accounts receivable have been slower than usual. Ordinarily, accounts receivable are turned over in 30 days. With the longer collection periods, the company is chronically short of cash to pay current creditors promptly.
Data with respect to sales and receivables are given as follows:

	1995	1994	1993
Cash sales	$385,000	$426,000	$510,000
Credit sales	576,000	752,000	960,000
Average accounts receivable	120,000	94,000	80,000

Required:
1. Compute the accounts receivable turnover for each of the three years.
2. Compute the number of days sales in receivables.
3. From the information given, explain any possible reason for the slowdown in collections.

24. **Segment Rate of Return.** Amity Products produces and sells three major product lines: electrical wiring, flexible conduits, and fiberglass control boxes. Each of these lines is manufactured in a separate division. Data pertaining to operations for last year are as follows:

Divisions	Net Income	Average Assets
Electrical wiring	$120,000	$2,400,000
Flexible conduits	870,000	5,800,000
Fiberglass control boxes	102,000	850,000

The average assets given are the assets directly identifiable with the divisions. In addition, corporate assets averaged $1,070,000 and are not directly identifiable with any division. Expenses (after income taxes) that are common to the total operation amounted to $80,000 and have not been deducted in computing division net income. In the determination of final net income for the company, however, these expenses are allocated 40:40:20.

Required:
1.   Compute the ROI for each division and for the company in total.
2.   Rank the divisions according to rate of return.

PROBLEMS

17-1.   Rate of Return Relationships. Red Ball Delivery Service reported a net income of $140,000 on net sales of $2,800,000 in 1994. The average investment in assets was $1,400,000.

   The president of the company plans to reduce the asset investment next year, observing that the company is holding some unproductive assets. Budget plans for 1995 reveal that a net income of $150,000 is to be earned on net sales of $3,000,000. The average investment in assets is to be $1,200,000.

Required:
1.   Compute the return on net sales, the asset turnover, and the return on assets for 1994.
2.   Compute the return on net sales, the asset turnover, and the return on assets from the budgeted amounts for 1995.

17-2.   Relationships. Steinhour Company's income statement and partial balance sheets for 1994 and 1995 are given below:

Sales		$98,000
Cost of goods sold		56,000
Gross profit		$42,000
Operating expenses:		
Salaries	$14,000	
Depreciation	3,500	
Interest	2,900	
Other operating expenses	8,500	28,900
Net income		$13,100

	12/31/1995	12/31/1994
Current assets:		
Cash	$ 1,200	$ 800
Accounts receivable	15,000	13,000
Inventory	23,500	18,000
Other current assets	1,400	1,600
Total current assets	$41,100	$33,400
Current liabilities:		
Accounts payable	$ 8,000	$ 7,500
Current installments of long-term debt	1,600	1,500
Interest payable	400	600
Total current liabilities	$10,000	$ 9,600

Required:

1.   Look at Steinhour's liquidity position for 1995: current ratio, quick ratio, and operations cash flow to current debt service. Comment.
2.   Look at Steinhour's asset quality for 1995: inventory and accounts receivable turnover. Comment.
3.   If the industry average for return on sales is 15 percent, gross margin percentage is 60 percent, and times interest earned is 10, comment on Steinhour's positions.

17-3.   **Financial Ratios.** The following financial statements are from Rainey Company:

	12/31/1994	12/31/1993
Cash	$ 14,000	$ 16,000
Accounts receivable (net)	22,000	28,000
Inventories	65,000	55,000
Fixed assets (net)	85,000	79,000
Total assets	$186,000	$178,000
Accounts payable	$ 30,000	$ 15,000
Bonds payable	60,000	75,000
Common stock (par value $10)	60,000	60,000
Retained earnings	36,000	28,000
Total liabilities and equity	$186,000	$178,000

	1994
Sales	$360,000
Cost of goods sold	240,000
Gross margin	$120,000
Operating expenses (including $20,000 of depreciation expense)	100,000
Income before taxes	$ 20,000
Income taxes	8,000
Income after taxes	$ 12,000

Required:

Find the following ratios (rounded to two decimal places):

(a)   Inventory turnover for 1994.
(b)   The average market price of Rainey stock, if the price-earnings ratio is 8.
(c)   The earning power ratios for 1994.
(d)   The current ratio by the end of 1994.
(e)   Cash flow per share from operations in 1994.
(f)   Gross margin percentage for 1994.

17-4.   **Rate of Return on Stockholders' Investment.** Secure Products Company reported a net income of $4,200,000 on net sales of $70,000,000 in 1995. Selected balance sheet data for 1995 follow:

Average assets	$50,000,000
Average liabilities.....................................	8,000,000
Average stockholders' equity	42,000,000

Chance Enterprises reported a net income of $6,000,000 on net sales of $100,000,000 in 1995. Selected balance sheet data follow for 1995:

Average assets	$50,000,000
Average liabilities.....................................	26,000,000
Average stockholders' equity	24,000,000

Required:

1. Compare the two companies by computing the following percentages and ratios:
   (a) Return on sales.
   (b) Return on assets.
   (c) Asset turnover.
   (d) Return on stockholders' equity.
2. Identify the company that earns a better return for stockholders. Explain the factors that enhance stockholders' rate of return.
3. Which company has more risk? Why?

17-5. **Percentage Composition Statements.** The Park Medical Services had a good year in 1995, but its earnings fell slightly from 1994. Clare Worthington, a member of Park's board of directors, states that the income statement certainly shows large amounts, but she wants to know the basic relationships. Income statements for 1994 and 1995 are as follows:

	1995	1994
Revenue	$91,000,000	$85,000,000
Materials and supplies	$ 5,920,000	$ 5,500,000
Wages and salaries	40,200,000	36,500,000
Rent	725,000	725,000
Taxes and insurance	4,200,000	3,400,000
Heat and light	980,000	850,000
Advertising	1,480,000	1,275,000
Other operating costs	13,880,000	12,700,000
Interest expense	7,250,000	7,350,000
Income taxes	6,250,000	6,300,000
Total expenses	$80,885,000	$74,600,000
Net income	$10,115,000	$10,400,000

Required:

1. Prepare percentage composition (common-sized) income statements for 1994 and 1995.
2. Comment on the expense problem areas. What items might the board want to investigate further? What data might they ask to see? Why have certain expenses decreased in amount and percentage? What was the change in the return on revenue?
3. Would a base-year comparison show similar relationships? Why or why not?

17-6. **Industry Averages.** Jimmie Gilbert has recently compared his company's financial ratios to a set of average ratios for his industry that he obtained from the National Association of Financial Ratio Analysts (NAFRA). He has lined up his data, two local competitors' data, and the NAFRA data as follows:

	Gilbert	Competitor 1	Competitor 2	NAFRA
Receivables turnover	6.3	4.9	5.6	5.8
Inventory turnover	4.2	2.6	3.1	3.1
Asset turnover	2.2	1.3	1.5	1.6
Gross margin percentage	37.0	40.6	40.3	39.6
Return on sales	.3	7.2	4.9	9.2
Return on equity	12.2	11.0	10.6	17.1
Cash flow to debt service	3.9	9.1	7.3	5.8
Current ratio	1.6	2.9	2.1	1.9

Required:
Comment on the relative strengths and weaknesses of the three local businesses as compared to the national NAFRA ratios. Using only this data, what might explain Gilbert's low return on sales? Why would the three businesses in this local area have such a low return on sales when compared to the NAFRA data?

17-7. **Segment Rate of Return.** A return on assets has been computed for each division of Alvarez Products and for the company as a whole. The company has a Metals Division and a Plastics Division.

	Metals Division	Plastics Division	Total
Sales	$1,600,000	$2,150,000	$3,750,000
Cost of goods sold	1,278,000	1,648,000	2,926,000
Direct division expenses	122,000	322,000	444,000
Allocated or indirect expenses of the division	88,000	45,000	133,000
Total	$1,488,000	$2,015,000	$3,503,000
Income from operations	$ 112,000	$ 135,000	$ 247,000
Division direct average assets	$ 800,000	$ 900,000	$1,700,000
Corporate average assets allocated to divisions	600,000	450,000	1,050,000
Total assets	$1,400,000	$1,350,000	$2,750,000
Return on assets	8 percent	10 percent	9 percent

Required:
Compute a revised rate of return for each division.

17-8. **Benefits of Financial Leverage.** A majority stockholder, who is also a member of the board of directors of Oelke Products, has had the company hold debt to a minimum. Net income each year has been approximately $7,200,000. A summary balance sheet for a typical year is as follows:

Current assets	$ 80,000,000
Plant and equipment net of accumulated depreciation	40,000,000
Total assets	$120,000,000
Current liabilities	$ 30,000,000
Stockholders' equity	90,000,000
Total liabilities and stockholders' equity	$120,000,000

A younger member of the board is irritated with such a cautious policy. "We would be better off to liquidate and invest in government securities," he exclaims. The younger board member states that with new product lines and an aggressive sales stance, the net income could easily be $15,000,000 a year. He admits that $30,000,000 in additional assets would be needed. "The additional assets should be financed by long-term notes," he adds. All other balance sheet relationships would remain unchanged.

Required:
1. Compute the typical rate of return each year on assets and stockholders' equity.
2. Compute the revised rate of return on assets and stockholders' equity by following the younger member's proposal.
3. Comment on the two strategies. Which do you favor? Why?

17-9. **Rates of Return by Segments.** The president of Metro Products Company has been reviewing financial data for 1995 and is concerned that one of the operating divisions is not doing as well as the others. The company manufactures three different product lines in three separate operating divisions. Financial data from 1995 are as follows:

	Product Divisions		
	1	2	3
Net sales.....................	$1,700,000	$2,000,000	$1,800,000
Cost of goods sold	$ 780,000	$ 940,000	$ 720,000
Operating expenses	590,000	860,000	810,000
Total expenses..................	$1,370,000	$1,800,000	$1,530,000
Net income	$ 330,000	$ 200,000	$ 270,000
Direct asset investment	$1,600,000	$2,000,000	$1,080,000
Return on assets	21 percent	10 percent	25 percent

Closer examination reveals that some of the operating expenses are common to the total operation and have been allocated to the divisions. Also, included in the assets are amounts pertaining to the total operation but not identifiable with any particular division. The amounts allocated to divisions are as follows:

Divisions	Allocated Expenses	Allocated Assets
1	$160,000	$200,000
2	350,000	800,000
3	140,000	100,000

Required:
1. From the information given, recompute the rate of return for each division and for the total operation.
2. Why was the rate of return for Division 2, as originally computed, so much lower relative to the other divisions?

17-10. **Cost Savings and Rate of Return.** Food preparation management of the State Capital Cafeterias operations is taking steps to not only reduce materials waste but to find more efficient ways to process materials in production. Last year, food materials costing $780,000 were used; and a net income of $85,000 was earned on an average asset investment of $978,000.

By improved preparation methods, the materials used for the same volume of operations will cost $636,000. This savings can increase net income to $145,000 according to estimates made.

Wayne Harder, a supervisor in the central preparation department, suggests that the company can also save by reducing the level of materials inventory. At present, for certain basic ingredients (about 50 percent of the food materials used last year) inventory for 30 days is maintained with an inventory turnover of 12. Harder points out that suppliers are able to deliver promptly and that an inventory turnover of 20 is very possible if the Purchasing Department cooperates and expedites orders. Other food materials are highly perishable and require daily or weekly deliveries and turnovers. These would not change.

Required:

1. Compute the rate of return last year on the average asset investment.
2. Compute the estimated rate of return on the average asset investment after the saving on food materials used and the reduction of the investment in materials inventory.

17-11. Rates of Return and Liquidity. Maria Cardoza, vice-president of finance of Pacific Trade Company, is concerned that the company is growing too rapidly and will be unable to support further growth by debt financing.

"We are enjoying an embarrassment of riches," she states. "Each month we must incur more costs to serve our ever-increasing sales. At the same time, we are increasing debt and must face the fact that we should finance by the sale of more capital stock."

Summarized financial data (stated in thousands) for several years are as follows:

	1996	1995	1994	1993
Current assets	$1,030	$ 870	$ 720	$ 580
Plant assets (net of depreciation)	3,150	1,770	860	770
Total assets	$4,180	$2,640	$1,580	$1,350
Current liabilities	$ 889	$ 550	$ 230	$ 210
Long-term notes payable	1,000	450	50	0
Stockholders' equity	2,291	1,640	1,300	1,140
Total liabilities and equities	$4,180	$2,640	$1,580	$1,350
Net sales	$9,870	$4,750	$3,240	
Cost of goods sold	$7,930	$3,640	$2,380	
Operating expenses	930	490	335	
Interest expense	100	45	5	
Total expenses	$8,960	$4,175	$2,720	
Income before income taxes	$ 910	$ 575	$ 520	
Income taxes	364	230	208	
Net income	$ 546	$ 345	$ 312	
Additional data:				
Average outstanding shares	500	500	500	500
Depreciation included in various expenses	$ 220	$ 140	$ 60	
Current portion of long-term debt	400	300	50	$ 0

Required:

1. Calculate the asset turnover and the return on assets and stockholders' equity for each year. Also, find the earnings per share.
2. For each year, calculate the current ratio and the operations cash flow to current debt service. (Assume current accounts are operations accounts.)
3. Comment on your findings. Identify the improvements and the declines in the ratios calculated above. Do you agree with the vice-president of finance?

17-12. Inventory and Accounts Receivable Turnovers. The president of Oberlin Stores notes that the collection of accounts receivable should be improved. He proposes that inducements should be given to customers to pay promptly. This, he argues, will increase costs somewhat; but, in the final analysis, the rate of return should increase. Also, he believes that the company is holding a larger inventory than necessary and can improve the rate of return by reducing the inventory.

Financial data for last year are summarized as follows along with the profit plan for next year as prepared by the controller:

	Last Year	Estimated Next Year
Net sales	$4,200,000	$6,000,000
Cost of goods sold	$3,000,000	$4,500,000
Operating expenses	500,000	600,000
Total	$3,500,000	$5,100,000
Income before income taxes	$ 700,000	$ 900,000
Income taxes	300,000	400,000
Net income	$ 400,000	$ 500,000

	Average Balances	
Current assets:		
Cash	$ 500,000	$ 650,000
Accounts receivable	700,000	600,000
Inventory	600,000	450,000
Total current assets	$1,800,000	$1,700,000
Plant assets (net of depreciation)	1,400,000	1,300,000
Total assets	$3,200,000	$3,000,000

Required:

1. Using the data given, compute the following relationships and ratios for both last year and the budget for next year:
   (a) Return on net sales and return on assets.
   (b) Accounts receivable turnover and inventory turnover.
2. Explain how the return on assets has been increased by improving the accounts receivable and inventory turnover rates.
3. Would the percentage composition statement comparisons be helpful? How? What would they tell us?

17-13. **Comprehensive Analysis.** Lorna Lafko, president of Troy Instrument Company, has been concerned about conditions in the general economy and the impact of these conditions on the company. She states that the company sold more during the past year, but doesn't seem to be making much progress in earning larger profits. Income statements and balance sheets for 1995 and 1994 are presented in summary form below:

	1995	1994
Net sales	$5,840	$3,750
Cost of sales	$3,796	$2,250
Operating expenses and interest	993	525
Income tax	420	390
Total expenses	$5,209	$3,165
Net income	$ 631	$ 585

	Average Balances	
	1995	1994
Current assets:		
Cash	$ 846	$ 645
Accounts receivable (net of allowance)	652	380
Inventories	860	454
Total current assets	$2,358	$1,479
Plant and equipment (net of depreciation)	2,900	2,700
Total assets	$5,258	$4,179

	Average Balances	
	1995	**1994**
Current liabilities:		
Accounts payable and accrued payables...............	$1,567	$ 819
Long-term notes payable	500	500
Stockholders' equity:		
Capital stock.......................................	300	300
Retained earnings	2,891	2,560
Total liabilities and equities	$5,258	$4,179

Required:

1. Compute the following relationships for each year considering profitability and safety. Round answers to two decimal places.
   (a) Percentage of each income statement item to net sales.
   (b) Percentage of total current assets and plant and equipment to total assets.
   (c) Return on assets and stockholders' equity.
   (d) Accounts receivable turnover and inventory turnover.
   (e) Current ratio.
   (f) Percentage of stockholders' equity to total liabilities and equity.
2. Comment on the relationships computed.

17-14. Measures of Liquidity. Vern Tanner, a member of the board of directors of Tech-Products, states that the company is becoming overextended in attempting to support a larger operation with insufficient working capital. Dave Helsel, president of the company, states that results speak for themselves. Sales volume has increased, profits have increased, and the return on stockholders' equity has increased, he points out. Financial data for the past three years are summarized as follows:

	1995	**1994**	**1993**
Net sales...........................	$4,000,000	$2,000,000	$1,200,000
Cost of goods sold	$3,400,000	$1,600,000	$ 900,000
Operating expenses, excluding			
depreciation	180,000	150,000	140,000
Depreciation expense	50,000	40,000	30,000
Interest expense	80,000	30,000	0
Income taxes	120,000	70,000	60,000
Net income	$ 170,000	$ 110,000	$ 70,000

	Average Balances		
	1995	**1994**	**1993**
Current assets	$1,930,000	$1,780,000	$1,680,000
Current liabilities	1,250,000	970,000	760,000
Long-term debt	800,000	300,000	0
Common stock ($10 par)	600,000	500,000	500,000
Retained earnings	430,000	290,000	210,000

Required:

1. Do you share Vern Tanner's concern? Or is Dave Helsel's statement of assurance on target?
2. Determine these ratios for each year to support your conclusions:
   (a) Return on net sales, return on assets, and return on stockholders' equity.

   (b)   Current ratio, cash flow from operations per share, earnings per share, and book value per share.

   (c)   Percentage of debt to equity and the common equity multiplier.

   3.   Comment on the trend revealed by your analysis.

17-15. Comparative Statements. The president of Reis Tool Supply in reviewing the financial statements for 1994 has expressed surprise and concern about a number of financial factors including:

   1.   A decrease in net working capital for the year.

   2.   Lower ROI than in prior years.

   3.   Greater dependence on debt.

   4.   A feeling that operating efficiency has dropped.

   5.   Lower return on stockholders' money.

   He expected the dividends of $20 that were paid during the year to be covered by depreciation charges. Also, he had planned to finance new plant acquisitions by the long-term debt increase and profits, leaving working capital at about the 1993 level. The comparative income statements and balance sheets are shown below:

	1995	1994	1993
Sales	$ 395	$ 340	$ 285
Cost of goods sold	279	235	201
Gross margin	$ 116	$ 105	$ 84
Operating expenses	67	60	47
Interest expense	10	9	8
Net income before income taxes	$ 39	$ 36	$ 29
Income taxes	21	19	14
Net income after income taxes	$ 18	$ 17	$ 15

	1995	1994	1993	1992
Current assets:				
Cash	$ 59	$ 64	$ 50	$ 43
Accounts receivable	77	76	62	64
Inventories	108	120	108	93
Other current assets	8	8	12	11
Total current assets	$ 252	$ 268	$ 232	$ 211
Plant assets:				
Plant	$ 210	$ 142	$ 122	$ 105
Less: Accumulated depreciation	48	34	23	21
Net plant	$ 162	$ 108	$ 99	$ 84
Total assets	$ 414	$ 376	$ 331	$ 295
Current liabilities:				
Bank loans	$ 42	$ 35	$ 20	$ 12
Accounts payable	53	58	67	65
Long-term debt—current portion	19	11	5	0
Estimated income taxes payable	12	18	13	15
Total current liabilities	$ 126	$ 122	$ 105	$ 92
Long-term debt	87	61	40	20
Owners' equity:				
Capital stock, $10 par value	$ 80	$ 80	$ 80	$ 80
Premium on stock	55	55	55	55
Retained earnings	66	58	51	48
Total liabilities and equities	$ 414	$ 376	$ 331	$ 295

Required:

Prepare a ratio analysis that will evaluate the liquidity, capital adequacy, and asset quality risks and also the earnings and growth returns. Comment on the trends that have developed over the three-year period.

17-16. **Rate of Return on Assets.** A budget has been prepared for Mendel Machine Parts Company for the year ended December 31, 1995. Two basic product lines are manufactured and sold: stamped parts and castings. Sales and production estimates in units are as follows:

	Estimated Units Sold	**Estimated Units Produced**
Stamped parts	3,000,000	3,200,000
Castings	2,000,000	1,900,000

Each unit of the stamped parts is sold for $15, with a unit variable cost of production of $10. Each unit of the castings is sold for $12, with a unit variable cost of production of $6. Total fixed manufacturing costs for the year have been estimated at $3,000,000.

The selling costs for each unit of either product line have been budgeted at $2 per unit, and the fixed selling and administrative costs are estimated at $800,000 for the year. Total average assets invested during the year have been estimated at $72,000,000.

Mr. Pizer, Mendel's president, has prepared an alternate estimate in which 3,500,000 units of stamped parts and 2,500,000 units of castings are to be sold. By substituting automated equipment for labor, the company can save $1 in variable cost per unit of castings but must accept an additional fixed manufacturing cost of $300,000. To obtain the revised product mix of an equal additional number of units sold (500,000) for each product line, the selling expense per unit for both products must be increased to $2.50.

Further examination reveals that deliveries can be made to the customers in less time, so that the production of each product line can be reduced by 200,000 units without delaying the deliveries. Inventories are recorded at variable cost of production. Beginning inventories were:

Stamped parts	600,000 units at $10 per unit
Castings	900,000 units at $6 per unit

The average assets required for operation can be reduced by the amount of the cut in required production.

Income taxes are estimated at 40 percent of income before income taxes.

Required:

1. Prepare a budgeted income statement for 1995, using the original sales and production estimates.
2. Compute the rate of return on the original estimate of average assets.
3. Prepare a budgeted income statement for 1995 incorporating all of the changes stated.
4. Compute the rate of return on the revised estimate of average assets.

17-17. Industry Data. Kathy Weber has been doing a little research on financial ratios in the electronic components manufacturing business. She has found the following financial data along with a set of financial ratios:

	Percentage of Total Assets				
	1992	1993	1994	1995	1996
Cash and equivalents	6.6	6.9	7.7	7.9	8.9
Trade receivables	30.0	29.6	28.2	29.0	27.4
Inventory	31.7	32.9	32.6	27.8	26.4
All other current assets	2.5	1.9	1.2	2.3	2.2
Total current assets	70.8	71.3	69.7	67.0	64.9
Fixed assets (net)	23.0	23.1	24.1	25.5	27.9
Intangibles (net)	1.1	.6	.9	.8	.9
All other noncurrent assets	5.1	5.0	5.3	6.7	6.3
Total assets	100.0	100.0	100.0	100.0	100.0
Notes payable—short-term	9.4	9.8	8.7	9.4	9.0
Current portion—long-term debt	2.5	2.9	2.9	2.9	3.4
Trade payables	15.3	14.2	13.3	14.0	13.6
Accrued expenses	8.8	8.8	8.4	8.5	8.4
All other current liabilities	4.2	4.6	4.0	3.8	3.5
Total current liabilities	40.2	40.3	37.3	38.6	37.9
Long-term debt	14.2	14.1	14.6	14.6	14.7
All other noncurrent liabilities	3.5	3.3	3.0	2.4	3.3
Net worth	42.0	42.4	45.2	44.4	44.1
Total liabilities and net worth	100.0	100.0	100.0	100.0	100.0

	Percentage of Net Sales				
	1992	1993	1994	1995	1996
Net sales	100.0	100.0	100.0	100.0	100.0
Cost of goods sold	66.9	65.1	65.5	65.9	66.6
Operating expenses	25.8	26.7	26.0	26.7	27.4
Interest expense	1.3	1.7	1.7	2.2	2.0
All other net expenses (income)	.0	−1.3	− .3	− .8	.3
Profit before taxes	6.0	7.8	7.1	6.0	4.3
Taxes	1.8	2.5	2.3	1.9	1.4
Profit after taxes	4.2	5.3	4.8	4.1	2.9

	Ratio or Percentage Values				
	1992	1993	1994	1995	1996
Current ratio	1.8	1.8	1.9	1.9	1.8
Quick ratio	1.0	.9	1.0	1.0	1.0
Receivables turnover	6.3	6.1	6.6	6.4	6.8
Inventory turnover	4.0	3.9	3.6	4.0	4.6
Times interest earned	5.6	5.2	5.2	3.7	3.1
Operating cash flow to debt service	5.0	4.2	4.6	4.4	3.3
Debt to equity ratio	1.4	1.3	1.2	1.2	1.3
Return on equity	20.1	22.1	20.9	16.5	14.3
Return on assets	8.5	8.9	8.4	6.9	6.1
Asset turnover	1.8	1.8	1.8	1.8	1.8
Growth in sales	5.3	6.2	7.3	5.1	6.9
Growth in assets	3.2	4.2	5.7	7.7	7.3
Growth in equity	7.3	10.3	6.6	4.6	3.4
Growth in profits	5.7	8.3	6.2	5.1	3.2

Note that because nearly 300 firms' data are summarized in the above numbers, the ratios may not correspond exactly to the statement numbers.

Required:

1. What characteristics appear to cause 1993 to be a high returns year and 1996 to be a low returns year?
2. What do the growth ratios tell Ms. Weber about the industry?
3. What changes on a balance sheet would cause the balance sheets to appear riskier than the industry ratios show?

CASE 17A–BOYER AND FREY

Dan Frey, vice-president of sales, has recommended that a new product line be added. A careful study of the market and an analysis of costs show that the new product line should yield the following results each year:

Net sales..	$2,800,000
Cost of goods sold	$1,600,000
Operating expenses	200,000
	$1,800,000
Income before income taxes	$1,000,000
Income taxes (40 percent)	400,000
Net income	$ 600,000

Depreciation of $150,000 has been included in cost of goods sold and operating expenses. The cost of goods sold and operating expenses include only the direct costs associated with the new product line.

Financial data for the last year, considered to be a typical year, are as follows:

Net sales..	$12,000,000
Cost of goods sold*	$ 7,500,000
Operating expenses*..............................	1,800,000
	$ 9,300,000
Operating income	$ 2,700,000
Interest expense	100,000
Income before income taxes	$ 2,600,000
Income taxes	1,040,000
Net income	$ 1,560,000
Total assets	$12,000,000
Current liabilities	$ 3,000,000
Long-term debt	1,000,000
Stockholders' equity	8,000,000
Total liabilities and equities	$12,000,000

* Includes depreciation of $400,000.

The investment in additional equipment for the production and sale of the new product line has been estimated at $3,000,000. "The new product line will yield a 20 percent return on assets," Frey states.

Joe Boyer, the vice-president of production, interrupts. "Are you talking about a cash flow return, Dan?" he asks.

"No," Frey answers. "When depreciation is added back, the cash flow return will be even greater."

The vice-president of finance, Linda Strohmeyer, asks, "How do you think we should finance the investment?"

"We should be able to issue long-term notes," Frey responds. "Our debt at the present time is modest. And, with debt financing, we gain the advantage of leverage."

"In your estimate, Dan, you forgot to include any interest cost. It will cost us $150,000 after income taxes to finance $3,000,000," Strohmeyer replies.

Required:
1. Does it appear that the new product line will produce a return on assets that is at least equivalent to the present rate of return? What is the cash flow as a percentage of the investment from the new product line?
2. How will the return on stockholders' equity compare with the present rate of return? (Assume that all balance sheet amounts are the same except for the new investment and the additional long-term notes.)
3. What is the percentage of debt to total equity now? What will it be if the new product line is accepted?
4. In your opinion, is the investment situation attractive? Explain your answer.

CASE 17B—SANDPIPER PROPERTIES

Sandpiper Properties owns and operates beach front hotels and condominiums. The company has 1,500,000 shares of common stock outstanding. Jay and Jane Harper, original incorporators, own 1,000,000 shares of stock.

The company issued $10,000,000 in notes payable a few years ago. Interest of 10 percent is paid on the notes annually. To hold the interest cost down and to attract investors, the holder of each $1,000 note has the option to exchange the note for 50 shares of common stock.

A summary of results of operations last year follows:

Income before interest and income taxes	$4,000,000
Interest on notes payable	1,000,000
Income before income taxes	$3,000,000
Income taxes (40 percent)	1,200,000
Net income	$1,800,000

The common stock has been increasing in price and is now selling for $18 a share. Jay and Jane Harper are concerned that they will lose control if the note holders exercise the conversion option. Prospects for the stock increasing in price are excellent. Investment letters have already mentioned the stock favorably. The Harpers hold only $1,500,000 of the notes payable and are in no position to invest more in stock or notes.

Required:
1. Compute the earnings per share before dilution and after full dilution. Should this be a major concern?
2. Compute the Harpers' percentage share of ownership after conversion of all notes to common stock.

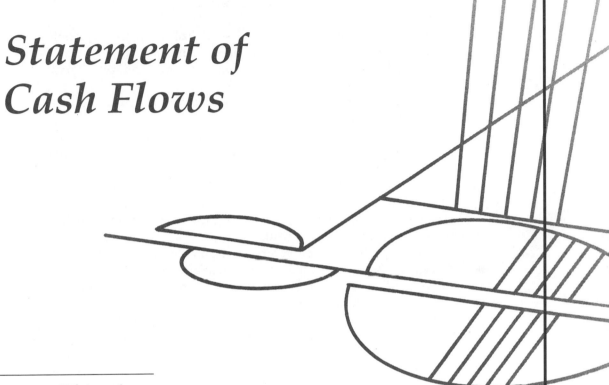

Chapter Eighteen

Statement of Cash Flows

❖ *Chapter Objectives*

After studying Chapter 18 you will be able to:
1. Prepare a statement of cash flows for a firm from its balance sheet, income statement, and additional key data.
2. Identify and group cash flows by operations, investing, and financing activities.
3. Explain why cash flow from operations is different than net income.
4. Understand the relationship between historical cash flow reporting and cash flow forecasting.
5. Interpret the ability of a firm to generate cash flows and interpret how a firm's cash flows were used.
6. Understand how cash flow reporting aids in the analysis of financial performance.
7. Develop the ability to measure cash flows for use in many managerial decisions.

◼ *The Case for Cash Flow Reporting* ◼

Lori Crandall, a partner in a CPA firm who specializes in financial planning and cash management for small and medium-sized business clients, was preparing a speech for a local Chamber of Commerce meeting. She is recalling a number of recent cash-related incidents:

Case A: Lori reviewed an article in a recent accounting journal about bankruptcies. Lack of liquidity and insufficient cash flow were listed as the causes of well over half of all small business failures. Lack of profits, low sales, poor business decisions, lack of planning, and other causes accounted for much smaller percentages.

Case B: During a regular annual planning and review retreat with key managers of a small metal parts manufacturer, Ms. Crandall found good news and bad news. The good news was a newly signed long-term relationship with a major auto industry component maker. The bad news was a sudden need for cash. As part of the new contract's requirements, the component maker, using a JIT system, wanted no more than an 8-hour supply of parts on its premises. Ms. Crandall's client had not implemented JIT completely and had built safety stocks of parts to ensure compliance with delivery requests of nearly 50 different parts. Also, the component maker requested a monthly billing for parts shipped and promised payment within 60 days of being billed. Payments thus far have been late by at least 30 days. Most vendors have net 30-day terms. Profits have gone up by nearly 50 percent in the past 6 months, but the company's bank line of credit is exhausted, and it is having trouble just meeting the payroll each week. Vendors are complaining about slow payments to them. Receivables and inventories have more than doubled since last year's meeting.

Case C: A newsletter from a client firm announced a major restructuring of its long-term financial structure. Its largest customer paid $5,000,000 for new common stock giving it a 15 percent ownership interest. A 2 for 1 stock dividend was also issued. The newsletter implied that these moves were made to repay borrowings which would reduce interest expense by $600,000 per year.

Case D: A recent article in the city's newspaper reported that a major employer in town had recently purchased over $10,000,000 of new equipment to modernize its factory. The article quotes the company's chief financial officer as saying, "We are paying for the new investment from current operations and limited short-term borrowings."

Case E: In July, the president of a local successful public relations firm called her to help get their accounting records corrected for the first half of the year. Internal staff changes had caused serious problems. No accurate statements had been prepared for the current year, and its banker had refused to renew a major loan due August 15 without historical and forecast cash flow data, as well as other financial statement information.

Case F: A friend who owns a fast growing swimming pool and spa equipment company called and started the conversation with: "Why am I always out of cash? I'm making money; sales are great; but I'm always overdrawn!"

Lori has heard these and other "cash" stories from many clients. She remembers one of her professors' "three rules of finance:"

1. Get the cash!
2. Get the cash!
3. Get the cash!

While a facetious list, it stuck in her memory and has a certain amount of ironic truth in it. Yes, she thought, all these cases had one common element: Where's the cash? Where did it come from? Where did it go?

Reporting cash flows has important impacts. Looking at historical cash inflows and outflows helps explain events within a firm to both managers and external users of financial information. Forecasting cash flows is often even more important since managerial decisions will determine the sources of financing, the uses of investment dollars, and the cash flows from day-to-day operating activities.

Chapter 18 discusses reporting cash flows. The format presented is intended primarily for historical and external reporting. But when linked to the financial planning discussions in Chapters 7 and 8, reporting cash flows is really a continuing need, whether past, present, or future.

In managerial accounting, cash flows are relevant to nearly every business decision. The size, direction, and source of cash flows can help measure the success of a business proposal. The timing of cash flows often influences the relative attractiveness of alternative investments. Sources of cash for investments and flows of cash from those investments are prime factors in measuring the financial health of a project, a segment of a business, and the firm as a whole.

Managing cash is a major activity of the firm's financial officers. Cash is an important asset with some unusual characteristics. Cash has little or no earning power and, therefore, is undesirable as an investment. However, having cash on hand is necessary to conduct business on a daily basis. Cash provides immediate liquidity—an ability to pay bills. A firm commonly needs some cash on hand, receives and pays out large amounts of cash, but will want to keep its cash balance as low as possible. Cash planning will mean that a firm wants enough cash available to pay its known obligations on time and to cover unexpected immediate demands for cash. But the firm also wants to earn as much as possible on its assets by minimizing its nonearning assets like cash. Cash balances are needed to cover the mismatching of receipts and payments.

If the cash flows match were perfect, we would need no cash on hand. The next customer's payment would exactly match the next bill to be paid. In reality, a firm will probably set a minimum and a maximum balance for its cash account. Short-term investments and bank borrowings would be used to keep the actual cash balance within that range. Cash is defined for cash flow reporting as currency, bank demand deposit and savings balances, and any highly liquid securities (often U. S. Government securities or high-grade certificates of deposit with maturities under 90 days). Cash and near-cash assets, called cash equivalents, should be available for use and free of restrictions.

For more than twenty years, publicly held companies have been required to provide three financial statements. These statements are now the balance sheet, income statement, and statement of cash flows. In 1971 the Accounting Principles Board of the American Institute of Certified Public Accountants issued **Opinion No. 19** which required a **statement of changes in financial position** for the first time. This new statement could be prepared using either a cash flow or working capital emphasis. The cash flow version used a format that listed sources of cash flows and then uses of cash flows in separate sections. The difference between the sources and uses was the change in the cash balance between the two balance sheet dates.

In 1987, the Financial Accounting Standards Board issued **Statement of Financial Accounting Standard No. 95 "Statement of Cash Flows."** This standard requires the use of the cash flow version and suggests using three groups of cash flows—operating, financing, and investing. Standard No. 95 emphasizes the growing importance of cash flow information to financial statement users.

A balance sheet gives a snap-shot picture of the firm at a specific point in time. An income statement reports revenues and expenses from operating activities plus other gains and losses for a specific time period.

Changes in balance sheet account balances between statement dates are partially explained by these revenue and expense flows. But many balance sheet changes result from investing and financing decisions, unrelated to operating activities. Also, because of the significance of cash flows to the overall health of a firm, many important transactions and flows are not reported directly or completely on either the balance sheet or income statement.

A statement of cash flows reports the inflows and outflows of cash a firm experiences between balance sheet dates. In addition, certain major noncash transactions are reported in memo fashion at the bottom of the statement after the cash flows are shown. Thus, the statement of cash flows should report all significant financial transactions and flows for the time between balance sheet dates. The timeline in Figure 18.1 shows the breadth of coverage of the income statement, the balance sheet, and the statement of cash flows.

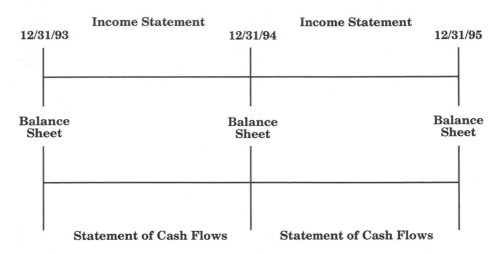

Figure 18.1   Time Periods Covered by the Three Major Accounting Statements

TYPES OF CASH FLOWS

The **statement of cash flows** reports cash flows in three groups as shown in the following table.

THE THREE GROUPS IN A STATEMENT OF CASH FLOWS

Operations

Activities:	Cash generated from the normal activities of the firm. Cash received from sales to customers and paid for purchases of merchandise and operating expenses.
Accounts Affected:	Operating current assets, such as accounts receivable, inventories, and prepaid expenses; and operating current liabilities, such as accounts payable and accrued expenses (for example wages payable and taxes payable).

Investing

Activities:	Cash paid for purchases of noncurrent assets and received from sales of noncurrent assets plus purchases and sales of short-term investments.
Accounts Affected:	All noncurrent assets and investment-type current assets.

Financing

Activities:	Cash received from issuing long-term debt and capital stock, cash paid to retire debt and equity securities, cash paid to stockholders for cash dividends, plus borrowings and repayments of short-term debt.
Accounts Affected:	All long-term debt and equity accounts and short-term borrowing and dividend payable accounts.

Figure 18.2 illustrates that the grouping of cash flows can be linked directly to the balance sheet format itself. A balance sheet account will first be identified as being related to one of three groupings. Second, a change between balance sheet dates will be explained by using additional information from within the firm or, if none is available, by making the obvious assumption about the change. For example, if the land account increased by $100,000 and no other information is known, we would assume that land costing $100,000 was purchased for cash.

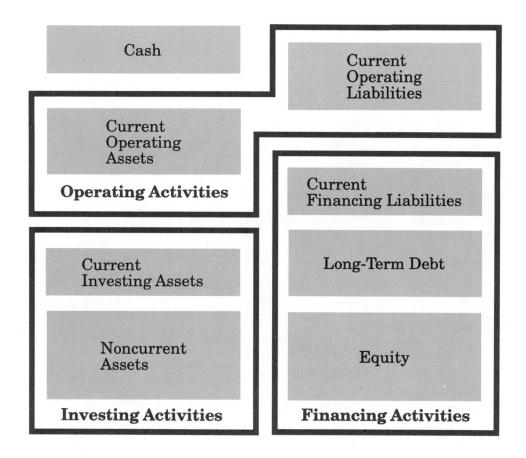

Figure 18.2   Balance Sheet Account Groups For Cash Flow Reporting

FORMAT OF THE STATEMENT

The format of the statement of cash flows emphasizes the three groups of cash flows. The "bottom line" or the "answer" is the change in the cash balance between balance sheet dates. The cash from operating, investing, and financing activities must sum to the change in the cash balance. Figure 18.3 gives a framework for the statement. Cash outflows are shown in parentheses.

This format implies that operations will have a positive net cash flow, that investing will be negative, and that financing will be positive. For a profitable and growing firm, these assumptions are commonly true. Operations should be a generator of cash to reinvest in earning (noncurrent) assets like equipment and machinery. Investing reflects these purchases as negative cash flows. These assets are generally consumed in normal business operations. For example, a dump truck is consumed through use. In the financial statements, use is estimated through depreciation expense—a noncash using expense. Generally, new assets are purchased and old assets are sold. Therefore, investing cash outflows commonly exceed cash inflows.

Cash flow from operating activities:
(assumes the indirect method discussed below)

Net income (loss)	$	
Plus and minus adjustments for converting	$	
accrual net income to cash flow	($)	
Net cash flow from operating activities		$

Cash flow from investing activities:

Purchases of noncurrent assets	($)	
Purchases of marketable securities	($)	
Sales of noncurrent assets	$	
Sales and maturities of marketable securities	$	
Net cash flow from investing activities		($)

Cash flow from financing activities:

Issues of long-term debt	$	
Issues of capital stock	$	
Increases in short-term borrowings	$	
Retirements of long-term debt and short-term borrowings	($)	
Payments of cash dividends	($)	
Net cash flow from financing activities		$
Net change in cash and cash equivalents		$

Schedule of noncash investing and financial activities:

Trades of stock or debt for assets	$	
Trades of assets for assets	$	
Trades of stock for debt	$	

Figure 18.3   Framework of the Statement of Cash Flows

The direction of net cash flows from financing activities is less certain. If the firm is growing and needs more cash than can be generated from operations, more debt or stock must be sold, producing cash inflows. The net cash flows will be positive. Yet, successful firms generating large cash inflows from operations might be able to finance all investment needs internally and still be able to pay dividends to stockholders. Retiring debt might also be possible. Here the net financing cash flows would be negative.

OPERATIONS CASH FLOWS

Normally, a business will buy merchandise on account, sell it on account, pay for the purchase, and then collect the receivable. This is the operating cycle. Operating current assets and liabilities facilitate the cycle. Their balances may increase or decrease. Accrual accounting measures the amount of revenue earned and expenses incurred so that net income can be measured. If all sales were for cash and all expenses were paid in cash when incurred, operating net income on the income statement would also be cash flow from operations. But the accounts receivable balance increases and decreases over time, as do inventories, accounts payable, accruals, and many other operating accounts. Also, certain expenses such as depreciation expenses are noncash expenses which result from accrual adjustments on the books of the firm and have no impact on the cash account.

To find cash from operations the accrual accounting-based income statement must be converted to a cash basis. Two methods can be used:

1.   **Indirect Method:** The starting point is net income, and adjustments are made to convert the accrual-based net income to cash flow from operations.
2.   **Direct Method:** Each income statement amount is adjusted to a cash basis and all cash-basis items are summed for cash flow from operations.

Both approaches produce the same cash flow from operations number. The direct method does give more specific data about cash received from customers, paid to suppliers, and paid to employees. Yet the goal of the operations section is to show the amount of cash generated by or spent on the day-to-day activities of the firm. Either method will show this. We will discuss the indirect method logic first, then apply the same logic to the direct method.

Indirect Method

Figure 18.4 presents a format of the cash flow from operations section using the indirect method. In the indirect method, the starting point is net income from the income statement. The indirect method will be used in the integrated illustration developed later in the chapter.

The task is to convert an accrual-basis number to a cash-basis number. This means reversing the adjustments made to convert the original cash flow transactions to accrual data. Accounts Receivable represents sales not collected. For example, assume that between balance sheet dates accounts receivable increased from $60,000 to $75,000 and sales were $800,000. All $800,000 in sales shown on the income statement were not collected. The increase in receivables would mean cash collections were less than sales. If all other amounts on the income statement were cash flows, the cash flow from operations was less than net income by the $15,000 that receivables increased. The $15,000 is subtracted from net income to reflect the fact that cash flows were lower than the revenue earned.

Each operating current asset and liability can be explained using the same logic. Therefore, the general rules shown in Figure 18.4 for these accounts are always valid.

Net income (loss)		$
+	Decreases in current operating assets	$
+	Increases in current operating liabilities	$
−	Increases in current operating assets	($)
−	Decreases in current operating liabilities	($)
+	Noncash using expenses	$
−	Noncash providing revenues	($)
+	Losses on financing and investing transactions	$
−	Gains on financing and investing transactions	($)
Net cash flow from operating activities		$

Figure 18.4   Indirect Method for Finding Cash Flow From Operations

Any noncash using expense on the income statement will be "added back" to net income to eliminate this expense from the cash flow analysis. Depreciation, depletion, amortization, and bad debt expense are examples of noncash expenses appearing on many income statements. Again, if all other items on the income statement except for $40,000 of depreciation expense are on a cash basis, the cash flow from operations will be greater than net income by $40,000. Thus, noncash expenses are added to net income. Any noncash revenue, such as revenue earned during this period and collected in a prior period or a following period, would be subtracted to remove it from net income for cash flow purposes.

Gains or losses appearing on the income statement that arose because of investing or financing transactions must also be eliminated from net income. Gains will be subtracted, since the gain caused net income to be larger when it was included on the income statement originally. Likewise, losses will be added, since a loss would cause net income to decline.

These gains and losses arise from sales of investment assets and from financing transactions such as debt retirements. Any cash flows from these transactions will appear in the investing and financing sections of the cash flow statement, not in operations. If a gain of $20,000 was realized from the sale of land that cost $50,000 originally, the cash received must have been $70,000. The $70,000 would be shown as a cash inflow in the investing section. And the $20,000 gain would be subtracted from net income in the operations section. If the gain was allowed to stay in net income, the $20,000 would be counted twice (both in operations and in investing). The sale of land presumably is not the normal business activity of this firm and thus not an operating activity.

Under the indirect method, adjustments to income for all changes in current operating accounts, all noncash expenses and revenues, and all gains and losses will produce the cash flow from operations.

Direct Method

The logic of finding cash flow from operations is the same as that used in the indirect method. But instead of adjusting net income, each income statement account is adjusted from accrual basis to cash basis. Certain balance sheet current operating accounts are tied directly to certain income statement accounts. The adding or subtracting logic is more difficult since sales is a positive but cost of sales and other expenses are negatives. An increase in accounts receivable will be subtracted from sales, but an increase in inventories will be added to cost of sales. Handling these positives, negatives, increases, and decreases algebraically will solve these apparent conflicts. Figure 18.5 illustrates the links between accounts and the needed pluses and minuses.

In Figure 18.5, assume that sales is a positive amount and cost of sales and all other expenses are negative. Using the rules developed in Figure 18.4 for adding to or subtracting from net income, the adjustments to each income statement account can be consistently inserted. For example, *sales* will be adjusted by the change in Accounts Receivable. If receivables increased by $15,000, the rule requires the increase to be subtracted. The positive $800,000 in sales has a negative $15,000 added to it. The result is:

Sales		Increase in Accounts Receivable		Cash Flow
$800,000	+	($15,000)	=	$785,000

Income Statement	Statement Amount		Adjustment Amount	Adjustment		Cash Flow Amount
Sales	$	+	$	Decrease in accounts receivable		
				or		
			($)	Increase in accounts receivable	=	$
Cost of sales	($)	+	$	Decrease in inventory		
			$	Increase in accounts payable		
				or		
			($)	Increase in inventory		
			($)	Decrease in accounts payable	=	($)
Operating expenses	($)	+	$	Decrease in prepaid expenses		
			$	Increase in accrued expenses		
				or		
			($)	Increase in prepaid expenses		
			($)	Decrease in accrued expenses	=	($)
Depreciation expense	($)	+	$	Depreciation expense	=	0
Gains on sales	$	+	($)	Gains on sales	=	0
Losses on sales	($)	+	$	Losses on sales	=	0
Net income	$					
Cash flow from operations						$

Figure 18.5   Calculating Cash Flow From Operations—Direct Method

Cost of sales will be adjusted by changes in inventories and accounts payable. An increase in inventories means purchases are greater than cost of sales. A decrease in inventory means we sold all we purchased plus a portion of the inventory we purchased in a prior year. Likewise, if accounts payable decrease, all the purchases plus some of the payables carried over from last year were paid in cash. An increase in payables means we did not pay for all we purchased this year. A look at the cost of sales calculation and the payables account will show the cash flow calculations.

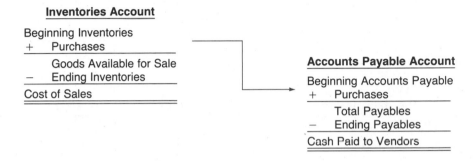

As an illustration, assume that cost of sales was $500,000, that inventories increased from $50,000 to $62,000, and that accounts payable increased from $45,000 to $65,000. Using the rules from Figure 18.4 and the format from Figure 18.5, the cash outflow from payments to vendors was:

Cost of Sales		**Increase in Inventories**		
($500,000)	+	($12,000)		

		Increase in Accounts Payable		**Cash Flow**
	+	$20,000	=	($492,000)

The same logic can be applied to *operating expenses*. Generally, operating expenses will have many separate expense accounts and be affected by various prepaid expense and accrued expense accounts. Increases in prepaids represent additional cash outlays over and above the expense shown. Decreases in prepaids mean that the prepaids (cash paid out in a prior year) were used this year. Increases in accrued expenses mean bills incurred were not paid, while decreases mean all of this year's expenses plus some from last year were paid. In Figure 18.5, these all combine to show the cash actually paid for operating expenses this year.

Depreciation expense is a negative on the income statement but is a noncash expense. By adding the negative to the positive adjustment (an "add back" to net income), a zero cash impact is the result. All *losses* and *gains* on investing and financing transactions would be treated the same way as depreciation. They have no impact on cash from operations. The adjustments delete the gains and losses from the income statement.

The result is cash flow from operations. The direct method shows more clearly the individual categories of cash flow within the operations area. The difference between the direct and indirect method is primarily a matter of preference and style. From a managerial perspective, planning and forecasting cash flows parallel the direct method but are done in much greater detail than shown on the external cash flow statement. But the intent of the statement is to show primary sources and uses of cash. These patterns can be seen by using either the direct or indirect method.

PREPARING A STATEMENT OF CASH FLOWS

A key to preparing a statement of cash flows is organization. Two balance sheets, an income statement, additional data, and many cash flows going in opposite directions can cause confusion and errors. A structured approach, as with any type of analysis, is essential. A set of steps should be followed to organize the data, the statement, and the procedures to complete the task. These are:

1.   Format the statement.
2.   Find the changes in balance sheet accounts between statement dates.
3.   Find the "answer" to the statement.
4.   Analyze any additional data available.
5.   Use T-accounts to analyze changes in more complicated accounts.
6.   When a change in an account is explained, check it off and move to the next data item or account until all accounts are checked off.
7.   Add up the operations, investing, and financing sections and balance to the change in cash, the "answer."

Following these steps carefully will not guarantee a complete and accurate statement, but the task will be organized and will help eliminate errors. And a methodology is established. These steps approach the problem in a very pragmatic way. It works best for textbook problems included here, but the same procedures will work using real-world financial reports.

AN EXAMPLE

By using the following information in Figure 18.6 from the Hakasan Corporation, the statement of cash flows will be developed using the set of procedures listed above. Initially, the example will use the indirect method for reporting cash flows from operations. The direct method will be illustrated later in the chapter. The following data have been taken from various financial statement footnotes and management comments in the annual report.

1.   Declared cash dividends of $21,600.
2.   Issued a stock dividend of $10,000.
3.   Converted bonds payable of $20,000 into common stock.
4.   Sold additional common stock with proceeds of $15,000.

HAKASAN CORPORATION
COMPARATIVE BALANCE SHEETS
DECEMBER 31, 1994 AND 1993

	1994	1993	Increase or (Decrease)	Check Off
Cash and cash equivalents	$ 22,100	$ 18,300	$ 3,800	_____
Marketable securities	14,000	15,000	(1,000)	_____
Accounts receivable	38,200	39,900	(1,700)	_____
Inventories	71,600	64,000	7,600	_____
Prepaid expenses	4,600	3,100	1,500	_____
Investment in Mace Inc.	26,000	0	26,000	_____
Plant and equipment	96,000	76,000	20,000	_____
Accumulated depreciation	(14,000)	(12,000)	(2,000)	_____
Land	5,000	5,000	0	_____
Total assets	$263,500	$209,300	$54,200	
Accounts payable	$ 50,200	$ 51,400	$ (1,200)	_____
Wages payable	8,500	8,100	400	_____
Taxes payable	11,200	7,500	3,700	_____
Dividends payable	6,000	5,000	1,000	_____
Bank notes payable	30,000	20,000	10,000	_____
Bonds payable	0	35,000	(35,000)	_____
Common stock	60,000	15,000	45,000	_____
Retained earnings	97,600	67,300	30,300	_____
Total liabilities and equity	$263,500	$209,300	$54,200	

HAKASAN CORPORATION
INCOME STATEMENT
FOR THE YEAR ENDED DECEMBER 31, 1994

Sales		$326,400
Cost of sales	$149,800	
Operating expenses	88,400	
Depreciation expense	7,000	
Interest expense	4,000	
Total costs and expenses		249,200
Net income before gain and taxes		$ 77,200
Gain on sale of equipment		3,200
Net income before taxes		$ 80,400
Income tax expense		18,500
Net income		$ 61,900

Figure 18.6   Example Financial Statements

5.   Purchased an investment in Mace Inc. for $26,000.
6.   Sold equipment costing $12,000 with accumulated depreciation of $5,000 for $10,200.

All other account balance changes arose from normal transactions and flows of cash during 1994.

Step 1: Formatting the Statement

The first step is to lay out the statement so that items can be entered as encountered. Using a blank workpaper, the framework can be written in as shown:

Cash flow from operating activities:

  Net income

Cash flow from investing activities:

Cash flow from financing activities:

Net change in cash and cash equivalents:

Schedule of noncash investing and financing activities:

At the top enter cash flow from operating activities. After giving operating activities about one-third of the page, enter cash flow from investing. Then enter cash flow from financing activities. Near the bottom enter net change in cash and **cash equivalents**. Below the net change in cash enter schedule of noncash investing and financial activities.

Step 2: Find the Change in Balance Sheet Accounts

On Figure 18.6, Step 2 has already been done. The Increase or (Decrease) column shows the balance changes that must be explained.

Step 3: Enter the "Answer" to the Statement of Cash Flows

From Figure 18.6 the change in cash is obvious—$ 3,800. This same amount is the sum of the cash flows from operations, investing, and financing, the "bottom line" of the cash flow statement. Now we know the target, the answer that the cash flows from all our efforts must equal:

Net change in cash and cash equivalents $ 3,800

Steps 4, 5, and 6: Analyze Additional Data. Use T-Accounts to Analyze Certain Accounts. When an Account's Change is Explained, Check It Off and Move to the Next Data Item or Account Until All Accounts Are Checked.

Steps 4, 5, and 6 flow continuously. They are repeated until all changes on balance sheet accounts are explained. Step 7 determines that the statement of cash flows is complete.

Often in textbook problems, additional data needed but not apparent from the financial statements are listed. In real world situations, certain facts are known that could not be detected from balance sheet changes. Also, data from supporting schedules and footnotes may be helpful. Within the firm, inquiries within the finance and accounting areas may generate data about relevant events. In the Hakasan Corporation, six pieces of additional data were found.

First Item   The first additional item says that cash dividends of $21,600 were declared. The wording is important. Terms like "paid" and "received" mean that cash flowed. Declared here would mean cash flowed if no dividends payable account appeared on the balance sheet. However, one does exist. To find the cash flow impact, we need to look at the accounts that are affected. In Retained Earnings we should typically find two types of transactions—dividends reducing the balance and net income increasing (or net loss decreasing) the balance. Step 5, **T-account** the relevant accounts, is now added to the process.

By entering the beginning and ending balances for Retained Earnings and Dividends Payable, dividend declaration and eventual payment can be tracked. The $21,600 is taken from retained earnings and added to the payable. Dividend Payable had a $5,000 balance at December 31, 1993.

Retained Earnings

	12/31/93	67,300
Cash dividend declared 21,600	Net income	61,900
?		?
	12/31/94	97,600

Dividend Payable

	12/31/93	5,000
Cash dividend paid ?	Cash dividend declared 21,600
	12/31/94	6,000

This was probably paid in early 1994. More dividends were declared and paid during 1994. Late in 1994, more were declared and are to be paid in early 1995. In the Dividend Payable T-account, we know the beginning balance, the added dividends declared, and the ending balance. With no other information about cash dividends, we can find the cash paid to stockholders. We assume the obvious:

$5,000 + $21,600 − $6,000 = $20,600 cash paid.

Another way to analyze the same facts is to begin with dividends declared of $21,600 and subtract the increase in the payable. Since more is owed at the end than the beginning, we must have paid less than the $21,600 declared. Likewise, any decrease in the payable would be added to dividends declared, meaning that we paid more than the amount declared.

Since this is a financing account (see Figure 18.3), the cash paid for dividends will appear as a cash outflow in the financing section. The dividend payable account can now be checked off on Figure 18.6. We have explained this account's change.

While working with retained earnings, we know that net income of $61,900 from the Income Statement was added in 1994. The net income can be entered in the operations section to begin the cash flow from operations calculations using the indirect method. We can also write in the item pertaining to the payment of the cash dividends like so:

Cash flow from operating activities:	
Net income	$ 61,900
•	
•	
Cash flow from financing activities:	
Paid cash dividends on common stock	$(20,600)

We have now explained the change in the dividends payable account. However, in retained earnings, the beginning balance plus the net income, minus the declared cash dividends does not equal the ending balance. Some other transaction is needed to explain the entire change.

Second Item   The second additional data item tells us that a stock dividend of $10,000 was issued. Remember that a stock dividend is merely a transfer of funds between retained earnings and common stock in Figure 18.6. The stockholder receives more shares (more pieces of paper), but no real value and no change in ownership percentage. No cash flow occurs, and it is not even considered to be a noncash event since the balance sheet is not affected financially. However, as the T-accounts show, this transaction completes the explanation of the change in Retained Earnings. It can be checked off on Figure 18.6. The common stock account is also affected, but more information is needed.

Retained Earnings

		12/31/93	67,300
Cash dividend declared	21,600	Net Income	61,900
Stock dividend issued	10,000		
		12/31/94	97,600

Common Stock

	12/31/93	15,000
	Stock dividend issued	10,000
	Issued for bonds payable	20,000
	Sold stock	15,000
	12/31/94	60,000

Bonds Payable

		12/31/93	35,000
Converted to stock	20,000		
Retired bonds	15,000		
		12/31/94	0

Third Item   The third additional item says that $20,000 of bonds payable was converted in common stock. Here is a significant noncash financial transaction. No cash changed hands; but the firm's debt decreased, and its equity increased. The $20,000 of long-term debt has been eliminated, and more shares have been issued to the former debt holders. This is a noncash financial event.

Looking at the bonds payable account, we see that the entire $35,000 has been eliminated. Seeing no other information about bonds payable, we must assume that we retired the remaining $15,000 of bonds during 1994. These bonds may have matured, or we may have repurchased them from the holders, apparently at book value. This is a financing cash outflow and completes explaining the change in Bonds Payable. Check it off.

Fourth Item   The fourth additional data item says that common stock was sold and that the proceeds were $15,000. A financing cash flow of $15,000 from sale of common stock is entered on our statement. Since no other information is available about common stock, we did not need to know that the sale netted $15,000. The T-account shows that, beyond the debt swap and the stock dividend, the common stock account increased by another $15,000. Without more information, the obvious cause was a stock sale. This transaction now completes the explanation of the change in Common Stock. Check it off.

By comparing the T-accounts and the items on the statement of cash flows, the flows of cash through the dividend, stock, and bonds payable accounts should be clear and should tie to the changes in the account balances.

Fill in the statement of cash flows to look like this:

Cash flow from financing activities:

Paid cash dividends on common stock	$(20,600)
Retired bonds payable	(15,000)
Sold common stock	15,000

Noncash investing and financing activities:

Converted bonds payable into common stock	$ 20,000

Fifth Item   The fifth item is the purchase of an investment in Mace Inc. for $26,000. Since the account changed from zero to $26,000, we can assume that the only event here was the purchase. It is an investing transaction and is a cash outflow. The Investment in Mace Inc. account can be checked off, and the item may be entered onto the statement of cash flows:

Cash flow from investing activities:

Purchased investment in Mace Inc.	$(26,000)

Sixth Item   The sixth additional data item is the sale of equipment. Typically, the noncurrent assets and accumulated depreciation accounts have numerous transactions that must be sorted out—purchases and sales. T-accounts are often essential even for the experienced accountant.

By reconstructing this sale of equipment, we can see that a gain was apparently earned on the sale. A similar gain appears on the income statement. The asset sold had an original cost of $12,000 and had accumulated depreciation of $5,000. It had a book value of $7,000 when sold. Since $10,200 was received in cash, a $3,200 gain was earned. This confirms the amount of the gain on the income statement:

Original cost	$12,000
− Accumulated depreciation	5,000
Book value	$ 7,000
Gain on sale	3,200
Sale price (cash proceeds)	$10,200

An investing cash outflow is entered on the statement of cash flows, and the gain on sale of equipment is subtracted from net income in the operations section to eliminate this investing activity gain from operations.

In the T-accounts, the sold asset must be removed from the plant and equipment account; and the accumulated depreciation must be removed from the accumulated depreciation account. The two T-accounts show that our work is not complete. But no other information is available about these assets. In the plant and equipment account, we assume additional plant and equipment was purchased for cash. The beginning balance minus the sale is subtracted from the ending balance. The difference is the amount purchased, $32,000 in this case. The $32,000 is an investing cash outflow. The change of $20,000 is explained. Check it off. The following T-accounts illustrate the changes in the affected accounts:

Plant and Equipment

12/31/93	76,000	Sold equipment	12,000
Purchase equipment	32,000		
12/31/94	96,000		

Accumulated Depreciation - Plant & Equipment

Sold equipment	5,000	12/31/93	12,000
		Depreciation expense	7,000
		12/31/94	14,000

Gain on Sale of Equipment

	Sold equipment	3,200

In the accumulated depreciation account, we need to remember that the 1994 depreciation expense would have been added to the beginning balance. The Income Statement shows Depreciation Expense as $7,000. The $7,000 was added to the beginning balance in Accumulated Depreciation. The beginning balance of $12,000, plus the $7,000, minus the $5,000 equals the ending balance of $14,000. The Depreciation Expense is added to Net Income in the operations section of the statement of cash flows since it is a noncash expense. The change in Accumulated Depreciation is explained. Check it off. The statement of cash flows looks like this:

Cash flow from operating activities:
Net income   61,900
  + Depreciation expense   7,000
  − Gain on sale of equipment   (3,200)
    •
    •

Cash flow from investing activities:
    •
Sold equipment $ 10,200
Purchased plant and equipment   (32,000)

Please note that by adding depreciation expense to net income, we are not saying that depreciation expense generates cash. In financial analysis, depreciation expense is often added to net income to provide a quick but crude estimate of cash from operations, while ignoring many other adjustments. Using a summarized version of the Hakasan Corporation income statement and *assuming all other items were on a cash basis*, the impact on net income and cash flow if depreciation expense were increased from $7,000 to $17,000 for 1994 can be seen. The net income would decrease by the $10,000 of additional depreciation. Now if depreciation expense were added back, both alternatives give the same operations cash flow. Therefore, depreciation is merely a non-cash expense and is not a source of cash itself.[1] This concept is illustrated in the following table:

	1994	With Deprecia-tion Expense at $17,000
Revenue minus expenses (assumed to be cash flow)	$ 68,900	$ 68,900
− Depreciation expense	− 7,000	−17,000
Net income	$ 61,900	$ 51,900
+ Depreciation expense	+ 7,000	+17,000
Revenue minus expenses (assumed to be cash flow)	$ 68,900	$ 68,900

Remaining Accounts   Now that all additional items have been discussed and their cash impacts recorded, the remaining balance sheet account changes can be considered. Starting at the top, we have already entered the change in cash as the "answer" to the statement. Check it off.

Marketable securities is a current asset but is an investing account (see Figure 18.3) because it is often a temporary investment of seasonally idle cash. A T-account analysis is probably not necessary but is presented below to illustrate the realism of the assumed sale of $1,000 marketable securities. With no gain or loss indicated on the income statement, the securities must have matured or were sold for face value. This is an investment cash inflow. It is assumed here that marketable securities are not a cash equivalent. Enter the inflow, and check it off:

Cash flow from investing activities:

Sold marketable securities $1,000

Marketable Securities

12/31/93	15,000		
		Sold securities	1,000
12/31/94	14,000		

Cash

Sold securities	1,000	

---

[1]It is critical to distinguish between depreciation expense and the tax benefits of the depreciation deduction. Depreciation expense is an allowable deduction for tax purposes. The greater the tax deduction the lower the tax expense will be. Therefore, a larger tax shield from a larger depreciation deduction will reduce taxes and cash payments to governments. But depreciation expense itself has no cash generating ability. See Chapters 12 and 13.

A decrease in accounts receivable means we collected more from our customers than we sold to them this year. By following this logic or the rule that says a decrease in a current operating asset is added to net income, the result is an addition of the decrease of $1,700 to net income. Check off receivables.

Inventories and Prepaid Expenses are handled the same way. Both account balances increased during 1994. In inventories, we apparently purchased $7,600 more than we sold. In prepaid expenses, the increase of $1,500 means more supplies and other prepaid items were purchased than expensed in 1994. Both amounts must be subtracted from net income in the operations section. Check them off. The table below shows how the cash flow from operating activities section of the statement of cash flows is affected:

Cash flow from operating activities:

+ Decrease in accounts receivable	$ 1,700
− Increase in inventories	(7,600)
− Increase in prepaid expenses	(1,500)

Land is the last asset account to be analyzed. The balance did not change, and no additional data on land are available. We assume that no land transactions occurred in 1994, no cash flows, no entries. Check it off.

Accounts payable is an operating current liability which decreased by $1,200. By tying Cost of Sales and the inventories and accounts payable accounts together in T-accounts, the flows of costs and cash can be seen. The decrease in Accounts Payable means an amount equal to all of this year's purchases plus some of last year's was paid out. The decrease will be subtracted from net income.

Inventories

12/31/93	64,000		
Purchases	157,400	Cost of sales	$149,800
12/31/94	71,600		

Accounts Payable

		12/31/93	51,400
Cash payments	158,600	Purchases	157,400
		12/31/94	50,200

Cost of Sales

| Cost of sales | $149,800 | |

Cash

| | Cash payments | $158,600 |

Notice from the T-accounts that since inventories increased, purchases were greater than cost of sales. And that since Accounts Payable decreased, cash payments were greater than purchases. Cash paid out for merchandise exceeded the cost of sales by $8,800, sum of the two adjustments for the change in Inventories and Accounts Payable.

Wages Payable does not have a matching wages expense on the income statement. Many expense accounts are rolled into operating expenses. The increase in Wages Payable of $400 means that the wages expense in operating expenses is $400 greater than the cash paid out for wages. Thus, the increase should be added to net income—a current operating liability increased. By Figure 18.3 rules it should be added. Check off Wages Payable. The appropriate section of the cash flow statement will look like this:

Cash flow from operating activities:

− Decrease in accounts payable	$(1,200)
+ Increase in wages payable	400
+ Increase in taxes payable	3,700

Taxes Payable is tied to the tax expense account. The increase in Taxes Payable means that the cash paid out for taxes was less than the tax expense. This increase in a current operating liability will be added to net income as was the change in Wages Payable. Check off Taxes Payable.

The last account not checked is Bank Notes Payable. These notes payable are long-term bank borrowings, probably to finance various purchases of equipment. The balance increased by $10,000 in 1994. Given no other information, we assume that new notes were signed for $10,000 and that no old notes were paid off. These are important assumptions. If, for example, $5,000 of the notes owed at December 31, 1993 had been retired and $15,000 of new notes added, both the retirement and the new borrowings would appear in the financing section. A cash outflow and a cash inflow would have occurred. In the absence of this type of information, new borrowings are assumed to total $10,000 and are shown as a financing cash inflow. Check off Bank Notes Payable. This item would be added to the cash flow from financing activities section of the statement of cash flows as shown:

Cash flow from financing activities:

New long-term borrowings	$10,000

All balance sheet accounts have now been checked off. A quick glance at the income statement indicates that all relevant cash flow items also have been analyzed and reported. Steps 4, 5, and 6 are now complete.

Step 7: Add Up the Operations, Investing, and Financing Sections and Balance to the Change in Cash, the "Answer."

Figure 18.7 presents the statement of cash flows with all the items discussed above entered. The three sections have been added, and they sum to the change in cash:

$$\$61,200 + \$(46,800) + \$(10,600) = \$3,800$$

When this equation is in agreement, the statement preparation task is presumably done, and the financial analysis of the cash flows can begin.

HAKASAN CORPORATION
STATEMENT OF CASH FLOWS
FOR THE YEAR ENDED DECEMBER 31, 1994

Cash flow from operating activities:		
Net income		$ 61,900
Adjustments for noncash transactions:		
+ Depreciation expense		7,000
− Gain on sale of equipment		(3,200)
+ Decrease in accounts receivable		1,700
− Increase in inventories		(7,600)
− Increase in prepaid expenses		(1,500)
− Decrease in accounts payable		(1,200)
+ Increase in wages payable		400
+ Increase in taxes payable		3,700
Net cash flow from operating activities		$ 61,200
Cash flow from investing activities:		
Purchased stock in Mace Inc.	$(26,000)	
Sold equipment	10,200	
Purchased plant and equipment	(32,000)	
Sold marketable securities	1,000	
Net cash flow from investing activities		$(46,800)
Cash flow from financing activities:		
Paid cash dividends to stockholders	$(20,600)	
Retired bonds payable	(15,000)	
Sold common stock	15,000	
Additional bank notes borrowing	10,000	
Net cash flow from financing activities		$(10,600)
Net change in cash and cash equivalents		$ 3,800
Noncash investing and financial activities:		
Bonds payable were converted into common stock		$ 20,000

Figure 18.7   Statement of Cash Flows

IF THE STATEMENT DOES NOT BALANCE

Step 7 came to a happy end in the analysis just completed. What if the operations, investing, and financing cash flows do not balance to the change in cash? With no promises or guarantees, a few suggestions can be offered:

1. Check for an item that was entered as a negative that should be a positive or vice versa. Divide the difference by 2 and check any item equalling that amount.
2. Check to see if an account was omitted from the analysis.
3. In complex accounts, check to see that all aspects of a transaction have been accounted for.
4. Recheck addition. Numerous pluses and minuses can be confusing.
5. Recheck the operations section rules of increase and decrease.
6. Look for items entered twice, for gains and losses, and for significant noncash financial events.

Often the error is simple but difficult to find. It is here that the discipline of following the steps outlined above becomes invaluable. Repeating the steps and checking for completeness and accuracy, you will hopefully find the discrepancy.

OPERATIONS SECTION USING THE DIRECT METHOD

The operations section in Figure 18.7 uses the indirect method. The explanations developed earlier for operating activities change very little when the direct method is used. However, it is worthwhile to illustrate the adjustments needed to prepare a direct method cash flow from operations. Figure 18.8 uses the pattern developed in Figure 18.5. The direct method calculations result in cash from operations of $61,200, the same as in the indirect method. Figure 18.9 shows the operations section as it would appear using the direct method.

Income Statement	Income Statement Amount	Adjustment Amount	Adjustment	Cash Flow Amount
Sales	$326,400	+ $ 1,700	Decrease in accounts receivable	= $328,100
Cost of goods sold	(149,800)	+ (7,600)	Increase in inventory	
		(1,200)	Decrease in accounts payable	= (158,600)
Operating expenses	(88,400)	+ (1,500)	Increase in prepaid expenses	
		400	Increase in wages payable	= (89,500)
Depreciation expense	(7,000)	+ 7,000	Depreciation expense	= 0
Interest expense	(4,000)	+ 0		= (4,000)
Gain on equipment sale	3,200	+ (3,200)	Gain on equipment sale	= 0
Taxes expense	(18,500)	+ 3,700	Increase in taxes payable	= (14,800)
Net income	$ 61,900			
Cash flow from operations				$ 61,200

Figure 18.8 Calculation of Cash Flow from Operations Using the Direct Method

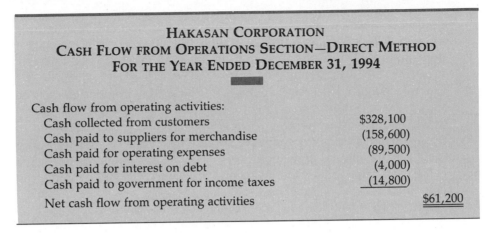

Figure 18.9   Cash Flow from Operations Section—Direct Method

THE STORY THE STATEMENT TELLS

The story the statement of cash flows tells is sometimes obvious and other times subtle. In this case, operations clearly generated cash that allowed Hakasan Corporation to purchase more equipment and to invest in Mace Inc. Changes in current asset and liability accounts did not have much impact on the cash from operations. The cash "savings" from depreciation expense was offset by inventory growth. Net income and cash from operations are nearly the same. Numerous debt and equity transactions allowed the firm to increase its equity position and reduce its long-term debt position. The net cash from stock and notes payable issuances was used primarily to retire debt. Stockholders received strong cash dividends, requiring about a third of the cash from operations.

To get a clearer picture of Hakasan Corporation's cash generating abilities and trends, several years of cash flows should be compared. Special events in a specific year may obscure the firm's long-term patterns of cash flows. In 1994, the number of flows into and out of the financing accounts may be unusual. Typically, the statement will highlight major flows of cash and can point to strengths and weaknesses. Among questions that can be examined are:

1. Is cash needed for expansion being used to pay dividends to stockholders?
2. What happened to all the profits the firm generated?
3. Is cash generated from issuing stock or long-term debt being used to support cash-losing operating activities?
4. Are operations absorbing too much cash to finance accounts receivable and inventories growth?
5. Is cash from operations growing as fast as sales are growing?

6. Is growth in noncurrent assets (investing activities) causing debt to grow too rapidly?

7. Can operations be depended upon to generate enough cash to repay maturing debt obligations?

8. Can needed growth in noncurrent assets and current operating assets be supported by internal cash flow (operations) or must external cash inflows (financing) be found?

9. Are we selling assets to cover needs for cash in operations or in financing (debt repayment and dividends)?

10. Is the cash balance itself too low or has it declined too far to handle the volume of business in the firm?

11. Are the firm's cash flows from operations, to asset purchases, and to or from investors and creditors growing in a balanced manner from year to year?

12. Are new investments being made to replace old assets and to expand capacity as sales grow?

It is clear that to answer some of these questions, data from several years and perhaps more information than the three financial statements provide are needed. Also, an experienced analyst will be able to gain more information from the data than the newcomer. But the financial analysis is definitely improved with the cash flow information.

To imply links between cash inflows in one area and outflows in others is dangerous unless more facts are known. Timing and intent may be made known by management in its annual report or through other announcements. But the usefulness of the statement is its ability to show major sources and uses of cash.

CASH FLOW FORECASTING

The major emphasis in this chapter is on analyzing historical financial statements. But as mentioned at the beginning of the chapter, managers are often more concerned with forecasting the firm's cash flow position. Several versions of cash planning exist:

1. Long-term planning: The time frame is three to five years or more into the future. Major needs and sources of cash are identified. Major plant expansion, new products and market growth, and debt maturities are examples of large cash needs that need advance planning. Sales of stock, new debt issues, and building cash surpluses to meet these needs may take years to execute.

2. Annual planning: The annual financial plan will develop a cash budget on a monthly basis for the coming year. Cash sources and uses are much like the statement of cash flows we have prepared on a historical basis. In many companies, day-to-day operations is the primary provider and

user of cash. Much effort will be spent planning sales, inventories, credit, and collections. Arrangements with banks are important to manage the seasonal highs and lows that many firms experience in their cash accounts.

3. Daily and weekly planning: Is Friday's payroll covered? This question is typical of the daily cash management process. Knowing exactly when bills should be paid, getting customer receipts into the bank quickly, arranging for lines of credit for short-term borrowing, and keeping the cash balance as low as possible without great risk of overdrafts or payless paydays are examples of short-term cash activities.

Chapters 7 and 8 developed the budgeting and cash planning concepts and methods. The same basic techniques of cash flow reporting run across the time line from future to past.

OTHER MANAGERIAL IMPLICATIONS

Cash is the basic ingredient in nearly all business transactions. Often knowing where the cash is, who gets it, and when it is received are the critical parts of many decisions. In other chapters throughout this book, incremental revenues and costs have been discussed. A term like "out-of-pocket" refers directly to cash flows. Generally, these revenues and costs are assumed to be cash. In capital investment decisions, the timing of cash flows is an absolutely critical factor in selecting projects from among many alternatives available.

The financial health of the firm as a whole is partly measured by its ability to generate and sustain cash flows. The term "cash cow" refers to a business segment that can generate large cash flows, even if the relative profitability of that segment is not high. Ability to generate cash is perhaps the primary factor that banks evaluate prior to extending credit to a business. Debt coverage, which is the ability to pay interest and principal when due, is as vital a worry for companies in international money markets as it is for a student with a car loan. These situations merely scratch the surface of managers' concerns about their cash and their cash flows.

SUMMARY

This chapter presented the statement of cash flows. The format, the procedures for preparing the statement, the logic of understanding cash flows, and interpretations of the statement were discussed. Cash flow reporting can have a future or a historical orientation. Underlying the formal statement is a multitude of uses and users. History has shown that the usefulness and, therefore, the importance of cash flows have grown tremendously in the past few decades. This trend will likely continue.

PROBLEM FOR REVIEW

Financial statements for Wade Construction Company are given for 1994 and 1995 in summary form. Harry Wade, the president of the company, is considering expansion and would like to know how much cash was provided by operations in 1995.

WADE CONSTRUCTION COMPANY
INCOME STATEMENT
FOR THE YEAR 1995
(IN THOUSANDS OF DOLLARS)

Net revenue	$8,400
Cost of goods sold	$4,320
Operating expenses, excluding depreciation	2,285
Depreciation expense	232
Interest earned	(170)
Interest expense	290
Loss on sale of temporary investments	32
Gain on sale of equipment	(146)
Expenses (net of gains and losses)	$6,843
Net income	$1,557

WADE CONSTRUCTION COMPANY
BALANCE SHEETS
DECEMBER 31, 1994 AND 1995
(IN THOUSANDS OF DOLLARS)

	1994	1995	Increase/ (Decrease)	Check Off
Assets:				
Current assets:				
Cash and cash equivalents	$ 386	$ 607	$ 221	_____
Temporary investments	920	1,320	400	_____
Accounts receivable	1,472	1,890	418	_____
Inventory	661	974	313	_____
Prepaid expenses	85	72	(13)	_____
Total current assets	$3,524	$4,863		
Plant and equipment, net of accumulated depreciation	3,762	3,816	54	_____
Total assets	$7,286	$8,679	$1,393	
Equities:				
Current liabilities:				
Accounts payable	$ 856	$ 831	$ (25)	_____
Bank loans payable	630	725	95	_____
Accrued operating expenses	252	318	66	_____
Total current liabilities	$1,738	$1,874		
Long-term notes payable	1,400	800	(600)	_____
Total liabilities	$3,138	$2,674		
Stockholders' equity:				
Capital stock, $10 par	$1,000	$1,400	400	_____
Paid-in capital in excess of par value	1,500	2,300	800	_____
Retained earnings	1,648	2,305	657	_____
Total stockholders' equity	$4,148	$6,005		
Total equities	$7,286	$8,679	$1,393	

Additional data:
1. Temporary investments with a book value of $400,000 were sold during the year.
2. Plant assets costing $746,000 were acquired during the year.
3. Long-term notes payable of $600,000 were traded for 20,000 shares of common stock. The par value of the stock issued was $200,000.
4. The company issued 20,000 shares of capital stock.
5. Retained earnings includes only the addition for net income and the deduction for dividends.

Required:
Prepare a statement of cash flows for 1995 with supporting logic for each balance sheet account change. Use the indirect method for operations and show the direct method as a supporting schedule.

Solution:
Step 1: Format the statement.
The Wade Construction Company statement that appears in this solution is outlined with the cash flow from operations, investing, and financing sections. The change in cash and the notation for the schedule for noncash activities are entered.
Step 2: Find the change in balance sheet accounts
This is most easily done right on the balance sheets presented in the problem itself. See the Increase/(Decrease) column above.
Step 3: Enter the "answer" to the statement of cash flows
On the solution statement the $221,000 increase in cash and cash equivalents is entered.
Step 4: Analyze the additional data items
Step 5: Use T-accounts to analyze certain accounts
Step 6: Check-off accounts as they are explained
(Use the space provided on the balance sheet)
Item # 1: Sold temporary investments with a book value of $400,000. The income statement shows a loss on the sale of $32,000. Wade realized $368,000 in cash, an investing source of cash. To balance the temporary investments account, Wade must have purchased $800,000 of temporary investments, an investing use of cash. The loss will be added to net income in the operations section, since this is not an operating item. The T-accounts show:

Temporary Investments				Cash			
12/31/94	920			Sale	368		
		Sale	400			Purchases	800
Purchases	800						
12/31/95	1,320						

Loss on Sale of Temporary Investments		
Sale	32	

Item # 2: Plant assets costing $746,000 were acquired, an investing use of cash. The T-accounts plus the income statement show that other events occurred in these accounts. Depreciation expense of $232,000 was added to the accumulated depreciation account, reducing the net plant and equipment account balance. Wade sold equipment having a book value of $460,000 (the residual number needed to balance the account). The gain on sale of equipment from the income statement of $146,000 means that the cash received was $606,000 ($460,000 + $146,000), an investing source.

Plant and Equipment, Net of Accumulated Depreciation

12/31/94	3,762		
Purchases of equipment	746		
		Depreciation expense	232
		Sold equipment	460
12/31/95	3,816		

Depreciation Expense		Gain on Sale of Equipment	
Expense 232			Sold equipment 146

Cash

Equipment sale	606	Equipment purchases	746

Item # 3: Long-term debt was traded for common stock. This is a noncash transaction and will be reported as a memo item at the bottom of the statement. The $600,000 in the Long-Term Notes Payable will be matched with $200,000 in the capital stock account and then $400,000 from the Paid-in-Capital in Excess of Par. Item # 3 is tied to Item # 4 to explain the changes in the paid-in-equity accounts.

Item # 4: Wade issued another 20,000 shares of common stock. Item # 3 explained where the other 10,000 shares went. Therefore, the remaining increases in the Capital Stock and the Paid-in-Capital in Excess of Par must both be the results of the sale of stock. These accounts increase by a total of $600,000 ($200,000 + $400,000). This is a financing source.

Capital Stock

12/31/94	1,000
Issued stock for notes payable	200
Issued stock for cash	200
12/31/95	1,400

Paid-in-Capital in Excess of Par

	12/31/94	1,500
	Issued stock for notes payable	400
	Issued stock for cash	400
	12/31/95	2,300

Long-Term Notes Payable

		12/31/94	1,400
Converted to capital stock	600		
		12/31/95	800

Cash

Sold stock	600

Item # 5: Retained Earnings contains only the normal transactions—net profit and dividends. By adding the net income to the beginning balance and subtracting the ending balance, the $900,000 of dividends paid appears. Note that no dividends payable account is present, thus we assume that the dividends were declared and paid. This is a financing use of cash.

Retained Earnings

		12/31/94	1,648
		Net income for 1995	1,557
Cash dividend	900		
		12/31/95	2,305

Remaining accounts:

Accounts Receivable: The increase of $418,000 is a subtraction from net income in the operations section. It means that $418,000 of 1995 sales was not collected during 1995.

Inventory: The increase of $313,000 is a subtraction from net income in the operations section. It means that inventory costing $313,000 was added during 1995.

Prepaid Expenses: The decrease of $13,000 means that Wade used and expensed prepaids purchased for cash in a prior period, not in 1995. It is an addition to net income in the operations section.

Accounts Payable: The decrease of $25,000 means that Wade paid an amount equal to all his 1995 purchases plus $25,000 he owed from prior periods. This is a subtraction from net income in the operations section.

Bank Loans Payable: Without additional information, we assume that Wade increased his borrowings at his bank by $95,000 during 1995, a financing activity. He may have paid off part of the $630,000 beginning balance and borrowed more during 1995. If he had, both the retirements and the new borrowings would be entered in the financing section.

Accrued Operating Expenses: An increase of $66,000 means that Wade used goods or services during 1995 and did not pay for all he used. This is an addition to net income in the operations section.

Step 7: Add up the operations, investing, and financing sections and balance to the change in cash.

The sum for each section is $998,000 for operations, a negative $572,000 for investing, and a negative $205,000 for financing. These sum to the $221,000 change in the cash and cash equivalents account.

The complete statement of cash flows follows:

WADE CONSTRUCTION COMPANY
STATEMENT OF CASH FLOWS
FOR THE YEAR 1995
(IN THOUSANDS OF DOLLARS)

Cash flow from operating activities:		
Net income	$1,557	
+ Depreciation expense	232	
+ Loss on sale of temporary investments	32	
− Gain on sale of equipment	(146)	
− Increase in accounts receivable	(418)	
− Increase in inventories	(313)	
+ Decrease in prepaid expenses	13	
− Decrease in accounts payable	(25)	
+ Increase in accrued expenses	66	
Net cash flow from operating activities		$ 998
Cash flow from investing activities:		
Sold temporary investments	$ 368	
Purchased temporary investments	(800)	
Sold equipment	606	
Purchased equipment	(746)	
Net cash flow from investing activities		$ (572)
Cash flow from financing activities:		
Proceeds from sale of common stock	$ 600	
Dividends declared and paid	(900)	
Proceeds from additional bank loan	95	
Net cash flow from financing activities		$ (205)
Net change in cash and cash equivalents		$ 221
Schedule of noncash investing and financing activities:		
Long-term notes payable exchanged for capital stock		$ 600

Schedule of Cash Flows from Operations Using the Direct Method:

WADE CONSTRUCTION COMPANY
CASH FLOW INCOME STATEMENT
FOR THE YEAR 1995
(IN THOUSANDS OF DOLLARS)

	Accrual Basis		Adjustment		Cash Flow Amount
Net revenue	$8,400	+	$(418)	=	$7,982
Cost of goods sold	(4,320)	+	(313)		
		+	(25)	=	(4,658)
Operating expenses	(2,285)	+	13		
		+	66	=	(2,206)
Depreciation expense	(232)	+	232	=	0
Interest income	170			=	170
Interest expense	(290)			=	(290)
Loss on temporary investments sale	(32)	+	32	=	0
Gain on sale of equipment	146	+	(146)	=	0
Net income	$1,557				
Cash flow from operations					$ 998

Explanation of Direct Method Adjustments:

(Note the similar logic for the indirect method items above.)

Net revenue: Accounts receivable increased by $418,000 ($1,890,000 − $1,472,000). This means that the company collected less than the amount billed to the customers.

Net revenue	$8,400,000
Less increase in accounts receivable	418,000
Cash collected from customers	$7,982,000

Cost of sales: Inventory increased by $313,000 ($974,000 − $661,000). The company then added to inventory by purchasing more than it sold. Add the increase to cost of sales.

Cost of sales	$(4,320,000)
Add inventory increase	(313,000)
Purchases	$(4,633,000)

Accounts payable decreased by $25,000 ($856,000 − $831,000). The decrease indicates that the company paid for more than it purchased.

Purchases	($4,633,000)
Add decrease in accounts payable	(25,000)
Cash payments to vendors and suppliers	($4,658,000)

Operating expenses: Prepaid expenses decreased by $13,000 ($72,000 − $85,000). The increase in "inventory" of prepaid expenses means that the company paid more than the amount expensed.

Accrued operating expenses increased by $66,000 ($318,000 − $252,000). The liability increased. Hence, payments were less than the amount expensed.

Operating expenses, excluding depreciation	($2,285,000)
Add decrease in prepaid expenses	13,000
Add increase in accrued operating expenses payable	66,000
Cash payments	($2,206,000)

Depreciation expense: Depreciation is a noncash expense.

Interest earned and interest expense: No prepaid assets or accrued liabilities are identified with either interest earned or interest expense. Apparently, the company collected the interest earned and paid the interest expense as stated.

Losses and gains: Each gain and loss will be reported with the total cash flow of the item to which the loss or gain pertains.

TERMINOLOGY REVIEW

Cash equivalents (918)
Cash flow from financing activities (911)
Cash flow from investing activities (911)
Cash flow from operating activities (911)
Direct method (912)
Financing activities (909)
Indirect method (912)
Investing activities (909)

Noncash financing and investing activities (911)
Operations activities (909)
Opinion No. 19 of the Accounting Principles Board (908)
SFAS No. 95 "Statement of Cash Flows" (908)
Statement of changes in financial position (908)
Statement of cash flows (909)
T-account (919)

QUESTIONS FOR REVIEW AND DISCUSSION

1. How should the balance sheet accounts be grouped for reporting cash flows?

2. Why is the change in the cash balance so important to financial reporting and managerial analysis?

3. Explain why historical reporting of cash flows is similar to cash. flow forecasting.

4. One reason that the statement of cash flows is required for financial reporting is to help explain changes in balance sheet account balances between balance sheet dates. Does the statement of cash flows explain all the changes in balance sheet account balances? Explain.

5. What is "cash and cash equivalents?"

6. Explain in general how the cash balance is increased or decreased by income statement transactions.

7. Can the cash balance be increased or decreased by transactions that affect only the noncurrent balance sheet accounts? Explain.

8. Name the common sources of cash in each activity area: operations, investing, and financing.

9. Name the common uses of cash in each activity area: operations, investing, and financing.

10. In using the indirect method, explain why losses are added to net income and gains are subtracted from net income.

11. If the cash balance increases by $10,000, does this mean that liabilities plus equity minus noncash assets decreases by $10,000?

12. Peter Leong operates a very successful and expanding party store in a growing suburban area. He has just received his yearly financial statements and tax return. He is startled to see that profits are up again, but he doesn't have enough cash in the bank to pay his taxes. What might be the problem?

13. Ralph heard someone say, "Depreciation is a source of cash." He needs more cash! He thinks he'll buy more equipment and get more depreciation expense. Comment.

14. This chapter suggests a step approach to preparing a statement of cash flows. What are the steps?

15. In a normal growing firm, should we expect to see net cash inflows or outflows from operating activities? Investing activities? Financing activities?

16. "Accumulated depreciation creates a cash reserve for replacement of assets." Do you agree or disagree with the statement? Why?

17. Explain why a decrease in a liability account indicates that the cash disbursement was larger than the amount of the related expense on the income statement.

18. If prepaid rent has increased during the year, does this indicate that more or less cash was disbursed than the amount shown as rent expense?

19. The Hopp Company paid high dividends, had zero profits, and had an unchanging cash balance for the past few years. The company probably did which of the following:

    (a) Sold assets to get cash to pay off long-term debt early.
    (b) Financed the dividends by allowing accounts receivable to rise.
    (c) Had very low operating expenses.
    (d) Had lots of depreciation expense.

    Can you suggest another possibility?

20. The manager of Best Fixtures Company states that cash dividends in the amount of $85,000 were declared but not paid this year. The manager sees that retained earnings decreased and insists that the event must appear in the financing activities section. Comment on the manager's thinking.

21. A mowing unit was sold by Valley Country Club last year at a gain of $250. The mowing unit had an original cost of $5,000 and had $4,500 of accumulated depreciation at the date of sale. Explain what impacts this sale had on the statement of cash flows.

22. Treasury bills costing $6,000 were acquired as a short-term investment. Without more detailed information, indicate two ways this might be handled on the statement of cash flows.

EXERCISES

1. **Cash Flow from Operations.** Stratos Company reported a net income of $132,000 for the year. Included as deductions on the income statement were depreciation of $46,000 and loss on the sale of equipment in the amount of $7,000. Accounts receivable increased by $6,000 and inventories decreased by $5,000.

    Required:
    Compute the cash flow from operations for the year.

2. **Cash Flow with Loss from Operations.** Valley Mining Company reported a net loss of $247,000 for the year after deducting depreciation and depletion of $437,000. Credit sales exceeded cash collections by $55,000. Accrued operating expenses increased by $40,000 during the year.

    Required:
    Compute the cash flow from operations for the year.

3. **Reporting Cash Flows** The Seg Osse Company's income statement for the year just ended included:

Net loss for the year	($4,200)
Depreciation expense during the year	8,500
Gain of sale of equipment	800

    The equipment had a net book value of $2,700. In addition, a balance sheet comparison revealed these changes between years:

Increase in inventory	$14,000
Decrease in accounts receivable	4,000
Increase in accounts payable	18,000

    Required:
    What will the statement of cash flows show as cash flow from operations?

4. **Cash Flow Reporting.** You are given below a list of several key transactions, along with other relevant information for Newman Company in 1996:
    (a) Net income for 1996 was $100,000.
    (b) Depreciation expense for the year was $25,000.
    (c) Dividends of $18,000 were paid in December.
    (d) 10,000 shares of preferred stock were issued for total cash consideration of $350,000.
    (e) A piece of land was acquired for $20,000.
    (f) A used piece of equipment was sold for $8,500. It had an original cost of $20,000 and accumulated depreciation of $11,500.
    (g) The following changes in operating accounts occurred:

Accounts receivable	$27,000 Increase
Inventory	16,000 Decrease
Accounts payable	11,000 Decrease

Required:
Prepare the statement of cash flows for 1996.

5. **Summing Cash Flows.** The following information for 1997 is provided for the Simcoe Corporation:

Proceeds from sales of building (book value $300,000)	$ 500,000
Proceeds from long-term borrowing	2,000,000
Purchases of fixed assets	1,600,000
Payment of dividends	400,000
Proceeds from sale of Simcoe common stock	1,000,000

Required:
What is the increase in cash for 1997 based on the above events only?

6. **Statement of Cash Flows from Basic Data.** Warren Bowman gives you his year-end balance sheets for June 30 for the past two years.

	June 30, 1996	June 30, 1995
Income tax payable	$ 8,130	$ 8,240
Plant and equipment	54,600	51,400
Accumulated depreciation	18,000	13,500
Accounts payable	12,140	13,610
Inventory	14,280	12,430
Cash	16,400	17,250
Capital stock................................	12,000	8,000
Accounts receivable	18,920	16,480
Wages payable	7,320	7,890
Notes payable, due June 30, 1996	24,000	30,000
Unexpired insurance	2,630	2,280
Retained earnings	19,240	13,600
Short-term bank loans	6,000	5,000

Required:
Prepare a statement of cash flows for the fiscal year ended June 30, 1996 using only the balances and the information Warren has given you.

7. **Cash Flow from Operations.** Precision Instruments, Inc. reported net income of $216,000 for the fiscal year ended September 30, 1995. Included on the income statement were deductions for depreciation expense of $41,500 and amortization of patents of $5,600. Accounts receivable and accounts payable both decreased by $12,000. Inventories increased by $18,500, while prepaids dropped by $2,500. Dividends payable increased by $2,000.

Required:
How much cash was generated during the fiscal year from operating activities?

8. **Cash Flow Transactions.** Siva Flavorings had the following transactions during the past year.

(a)   Collected an account receivable.
(b)   Purchased merchandise inventory on account.
(c)   Sold a delivery truck for book value.
(d)   Declared a dividend.
(e)   Traded capital stock to an officer in exchange for eliminating a mortgage on the firm's factory.
(f)   Paid rent on computer equipment.
(g)   Purchased new delivery truck for cash.
(h)   Sold common stock.
(i)   Borrowed money from a bank for 6 months to finance inventories.
(j)   Sold merchandise on account.
(k)   Issued stock dividend.
(l)   Purchased common stock in a company that is a long-time vendor.

Required:
For each of the following transactions, indicate whether the transaction itself is a cash inflow (I), a cash outflow (O), or has no effect (NE). Also, given the transaction's nature, indicate whether it is an operating activity (Op), investing activity (In), financing activity (Fi), or none of these (N). The question is not asking how each item is to be reported, merely what happened and what kind of activity it was.

9.   **Transactions and Cash Flows.** Transactions of Goslin Parts Company have been selected from the past year's records as follows:
(a)   Acquired equipment at a cost of $850,000.
(b)   Received cash of $62,000 from the sale of land.
(c)   Issued capital stock of $1,300,000 in exchange for an investment in the capital stock of Wait Machine Company.
(d)   Accounts receivable decreased by $120,000.
(e)   Accounts payable decreased by $54,000.
(f)   Paid dividends in the amount of $240,000.
(g)   A gain was recorded on the sale of a dump truck of $13,000.
(h)   The company repurchased shares of its stock for $50,500.
(i)   Depreciation expense of $138,000 was deducted on the income statement.
(j)   The Patent account increased by $85,000.
(k)   Received $115,000 from the sale of equipment.
(l)   Sold Goslin common stock for $400,000 and used proceeds to retire $350,000 of long-term notes payable.
(m)   Paid $200,000 to advertising agency and recorded advertising expense of $160,000 this year.

Required:
For each transaction, indicate the correct letter from the list below which best describes how that transaction will be reported on a statement of cash flow.
(a)   Added to net income to adjust net income to a cash basis.
(b)   Subtracted from net income to adjust net income to a cash basis.
(c)   As an investing source of cash.
(d)   As a financing source of cash.
(e)   As an investing use of cash.
(f)   As a financing use of cash.
(g)   Reported as a supplemental memo item.
(h)   Not reported on this statement.

10. **Determining the Missing Amounts.** In the direct method of finding cash flows from operations, additions and subtractions are performed on income statement accounts. The following cases come from the Tecante Export/Import Services Company:

Case 1: Sales for the year	$?
Accounts receivable, beginning	135,000
Accounts receivable, ending	92,000
Cash collections for the year............................	534,000
Case 2: Cost of goods sold for the year............................	$267,000
Inventory, beginning	62,000
Inventory, ending	?
Accounts payable, beginning	38,000
Accounts payable, ending	29,000
Cash payments to vendors for the year....................	295,000
Case 3: Operating expenses for the year	$145,000
Prepaid operating expenses, beginning	8,000
Prepaid operating expenses, ending	12,000
Depreciation expense on operating equipment	?
Accrued operating expenses, beginning	21,000
Accrued operating expenses, ending......................	18,000
Cash paid for operating expenses for the year..............	135,000
Case 4: Income taxes expense for the year	$35,000
Income taxes payable, beginning	14,000
Income taxes payable, ending	7,000
Income taxes paid for the year	?

Required:
Fill in each missing figure.

11. **Financing Cash Flows.** Except for the additional data items, assume that all other cash flows for the Chiddick Company are normal events.

	12/31/95	12/31/96
Long-term debt	$40,000	$33,000
Common stock..	40,000	80,000
Retained earnings	40,000	35,000

Events for this year include:
1.   Net income for 1996 was $40,000.
2.   Swapped $23,000 of common stock with creditors to retire debt.

Required:
What financing cash flows will be reported on the statement of cash flows?

12. **Measuring Cash Flows.** The following financial statements are from the Abramson Stores.

	12/31/1995	12/31/1994	Inc/(Dec)
Cash	$ 12,000	$ 12,000	$ 0
Accounts receivable (net)................	40,000	45,000	(5,000)
Inventories	65,000	45,000	20,000
Fixed assets	180,000	160,000	20,000
Less accumulated depreciation	(45,000)	(50,000)	5,000
Total assets	$252,000	$212,000	$40,000
Accounts payable	$ 15,000	$ 20,000	$ (5,000)
Bonds payable	80,000	60,000	20,000
Common stock.......................	120,000	100,000	20,000
Retained earnings	37,000	32,000	5,000
Total liabilities & equity	$252,000	$212,000	$40,000

	1995	
Sales	$800,000	
Cost of goods sold	(440,000)	
Operating expenses	(300,000)	(including $30,000 of depreciation expense)
Gain on fixed assets sold	5,000	
Net income	$ 65,000	

In addition to the information contained in the statement, you learn that Abramson sold fixed assets originally costing $50,000 and having a book value of $15,000 for cash.

Required:
1.   As defined in the chapter, what is "the answer" to the cash flow statement?
2.   Based on the above information only, what was the 1995 cash flow from financing activities?
3.   What cash was paid for purchases of fixed assets in 1995?

13.   **Incomplete Data and Cash Flows.** Incomplete data from the McGowan Company are available to you for 1995. Noncurrent account balances are given as follows:

	December 31	
	1995	1994
Plant and equipment, net of accumulated depreciation	$286,000	$290,000
Long-term debt	160,000	0
Capital stock.......................................	300,000	200,000
Retained earnings	705,000	517,000

Dividends of $148,000 were declared and paid during the year. Depreciation of $32,000 was deducted on the income statement. Equipment having a net book value of $58,000 was sold at no gain or loss.

Required:
Prepare a statement of cash flows for 1995.

14.   **Cash Flow from Operations.** Household Helpers, Inc. operates a home cleaning service. A summarized income statement for 1995 follows:

Revenue	$494,000
Salaries and wages	$215,000
Supplies used	96,000
Other operating expenses, excluding depreciation	82,000
Depreciation	14,000
Total expenses	$407,000
Income before income taxes	$ 87,000
Income taxes	40,000
Net income	$ 47,000

Current assets and current liabilities at December 31, 1994 and 1995 follow:

	December 31	
Current assets:	1995	1994
Cash	$117,000	$ 91,000
Accounts receivable	77,000	56,000
Inventory of supplies	54,000	42,000
Total current assets	$248,000	$189,000
Current liabilities:		
Accounts payable (purchase of supplies)	$ 11,000	$ 8,000
Salaries and wages payable	44,000	46,000
Income taxes payable	18,000	21,000
Total current liabilities	$ 73,000	$ 75,000

Required:
1. Prepare an operations section of a statement of cash flows using the direct method.
2. Reconcile the cash flow from operations in Part 1 with the cash flow from operations using the indirect method.

15. **Cash Flows Using Incomplete Data.** The marketing manager of Rose Industries has given you an envelope with the following financial items listed on the back. He is temporarily handling the financial reporting duties since the chief accountant took another job. He wants to know a few things about "cash." You look at the envelope and see:

Depreciation expense	$ 3,200
Decrease in accounts payable	4,000
Increase in tax liability	500
Cash from bank borrowings	19,000
Loss on sale of land	1,000
Net income	28,000
Cash from sale of land	10,000
Cash paid for acquisition of land	22,400
Cash dividends paid	15,000
Cash paid to retire preferred stock	18,500

Required:
1. What was the cash flow from operations this year?
2. Which of the following responses correctly describes the transactions involving land?

    (a)   A net loss of $2,200 would be recorded.
    (b)   Land transactions caused a net cash inflow of $9,000.
    (c)   Land transactions caused a net cash outflow of $12,400.
    (d)   The change in the land account balance was $12,400.

16.   **Changes in Noncurrent Asset Accounts.** The Crumbaugh Company showed the following entries in its trucks account and the related accumulated depreciation—trucks account:

Trucks				Accumulated Depreciation—Trucks		
1/1/96	100,000				1/1/96	40,000
3/4/96	25,000	6/6/96	?	6/6/96 ?	12/31/96	30,000
12/31/96	?				12/31/96	60,000

Required:
If a truck was sold on 6/6/96 for $13,000, creating an $8,000 gain on the sale, what is the 12/31/96 balance in the trucks account?

17.   **Direct and Indirect Methods.** The Williams Company financial statements are presented below:

	12/31/1995	12/31/1994	Inc/(Dec)
Cash	$ 10,000	$ 20,000	$(10,000)
Accounts receivable (net)	30,000	45,000	(15,000)
Inventories	75,000	55,000	20,000
Prepaid operating expenses	4,000	6,000	(2,000)
Fixed assets	201,000	154,000	47,000
Less accumulated depreciation	(45,000)	(25,000)	(20,000)
Total assets	$275,000	$255,000	$ 20,000
Accounts payable	$ 55,000	$ 20,000	$ 35,000
Bonds payable	40,000	90,000	(50,000)
Common stock	120,000	90,000	30,000
Retained earnings	60,000	55,000	5,000
Total liabilities and equity	$275,000	$255,000	$ 20,000

	For the year ended 12/31/95
Sales	$460,000
Cost of goods sold	(300,000)
Operating expenses (including $32,000 of depreciation expense)	(140,000)
Gain on fixed asset sold	5,000
Net income	$ 25,000

Additional data: The fixed assets sold by the Williams Company for cost originally cost $37,000 and had a book value of $25,000.

Required:

1. Prepare an operating activities section of the statement of cash flows using the direct method.
2. Prepare an operating activities section of the statement of cash flows using the indirect method.

18. **Statement of Cash Receipts and Disbursements.** Summarized financial statements are given as follows for Franklin County Caring Society.

Membership dues	$263,100
Banquet revenue	308,400
Total revenue	$571,500
Wages expense	$ 68,200
Supplies used	51,400
Banquet expenses	87,200
Rent	15,000
Depreciation of fixtures	1,200
Benefits paid	274,200
Total expenses	$497,200
Net income	$ 74,300

	1995	1994
Current assets:		
Cash	$100,900	$132,000
Temporary investments	320,000	215,000
Dues receivable	54,100	58,100
Supplies inventory	9,200	7,900
Prepaid rent	3,500	2,000
Total current assets	$487,700	$415,000
Fixtures, net of accumulated depreciation	142,400	137,600
Total assets	$630,100	$552,600
Current liabilities:		
Accounts payable	$ 12,900	$ 9,100
Wages payable	5,800	6,400
Total current liabilities	$ 18,700	$ 15,500
Franklin County Caring Society capital	611,400	537,100
Total equities	$630,100	$552,600

Additional data:

1. Banquet revenues and expenses are on a cash basis.
2. Fixtures costing $6,000 were acquired in 1995.

Required:
Prepare a statement of cash flows for the year.

19. **Estimated Cash Flow.** Yoder Mills, Inc. is expected to make a payment of $500,000 on equipment notes payable by December 31, 1996. Sales volume is down, and it is difficult to collect accounts receivable. The cash balance on January 1, 1996 was $130,000 and is at an absolute minimum to meet operating obligations.

The controller has estimated that the net income for 1996 will only be $18,000. Depreciation of $270,000 has been deducted in computing net income. Other estimates are given as follows:

1. Accounts receivable are to be reduced by $20,000.
2. Inventories are to be reduced by $30,000.
3. Accounts payable will increase by $10,000.
4. Equipment with a net book value of $12,000 will be sold for that amount.

Required:
From the information given, does it appear that the debt payment can be made while holding a cash balance of no less than $130,000? Prepare an estimated statement of cash flows to support your position.

20. **Reconciling Net Income and Cash from Operations.** The following items are from the accounts of a local firm.

Gain on sale of long-term investment	$133,500
Increase in accounts receivable	14,300
Increase in land	48,000
Increase in accrued expenses payable	6,800
Decrease in inventory	21,700
Decrease in accounts payable	12,000
Decrease in prepaid insurance	1,500
Increase in common stock	85,000
Net income	124,800
Depreciation of building for year	48,000
Decrease in cash	14,000
Cash received from sale of long-term investment	228,800
Cash provided by operations	43,000

Required:
Select from the list above those items that would be relevant to a reconciliation of net income and cash from operations, and prepare such a reconciliation.

21. **Operating Cash Flows.** Data from the financial statements of Donaldson Machine Company are given for 1995 and 1996.

	Balances, December 31	
	1996	**1995**
Cash	$ 27,000	$ 23,000
Accounts receivable	54,000	48,000
Inventory	46,000	71,000
Current assets	$127,000	$142,000
Accounts payable	$ 23,000	$ 29,000
Operating expenses payable	18,000	7,000
Current liabilities	$ 41,000	$ 36,000

The income statement for the year shows net sales of $620,000, cost of goods sold of $385,000, and operating expenses of $112,000. Included in operating expenses is depreciation of $14,000. Also, a gain of $8,000 is reported from the sale of equipment.

Equipment costing $248,000 was acquired, and the equipment sold had a net book value of $23,000 at date of sale. The company issued capital stock and received $60,000.

Required:

1. Prepare a statement of cash flows using the direct method.
2. Prepare an operating activities section of a statement of cash flows using the indirect method.

PROBLEMS

18-1. Cash Flows from Operating Activities. The Brown Company provided the following data from its 1995 activities:

COMPARATIVE BALANCE SHEET
DECEMBER 31, 1995 AND 1994

	12/31/95	12/31/94	Increase/(Decrease)
Cash	$ 34,000	$ 50,000	$(16,000)
Accounts receivable	68,000	60,000	8,000
Inventory	90,000	99,000	(9,000)
Plant and equipment	240,000	180,000	60,000
Accumulated depreciation	(80,000)	(65,000)	(15,000)
Total	$352,000	$324,000	$ 28,000
Accounts payable	$ 55,000	$ 66,000	$(11,000)
Bonds payable	90,000	50,000	40,000
Common stock	70,000	60,000	10,000
Retained earnings	137,000	148,000	(11,000)
Total	$352,000	$324,000	$ 28,000

INCOME STATEMENT
FOR THE YEAR ENDED 12/31/95

Sales	$300,000
Cost of goods sold	(200,000)
Operating expenses	(72,000)
Loss on sale of equipment	(8,000)
Net income	$ 20,000

Additional data:

1. Depreciation expense is $27,000.
2. Equipment costing $30,000 with accumulated depreciation of $12,000 was sold for $10,000.
3. Investors swapped $10,000 of bonds payable for $10,000 of common stock.

Required:

1. How much cash did Brown collect from customers in 1995?
2. How much cash did Brown spend on new plant and equipment in 1995?
3. What was cash flow from operations in 1995?
4. What items would Brown report in its financing activities section of its statement of cash flows in 1995?

18-2. Operating Cash Flows. The following data are from the Chappelle Company:

	12/31/1995	12/31/1994
Current assets:		
Cash	$115,000	$120,000
Accounts receivable	60,000	70,000
Inventory	18,000	15,000
Prepaid expenses	5,000	3,000
Total	$198,000	$208,000
Current liabilities:		
Accounts payable	$ 45,000	$ 35,000
Accrued operating expenses	10,000	21,000
Total	$ 55,000	$ 56,000

A summary income statement for 1995 is as follows:

Net sales	$380,000
Cost of goods sold	$250,000
Operating expenses, including depreciation expense of $25,000	80,000
Total expenses	$330,000
Net income	$ 50,000

Required:
1. What cash was paid out for operating expenses items during 1995?
2. What cash was paid for purchases of merchandise in 1995?
3. Show the cash flow from operating activities using the indirect method.

18-3. **Cash Flows By Type of Activity.** The president of Vanderpool Corp. has never worried about cash flow until recently. A small problem has caused her to worry about where her cash is coming from and going to. The following data are selected from her financial statements. Equipment costing $20,000 was sold in 1998. The equipment sold had a book value of $15,000. No other additional data are needed to explain the data presented.

Sales	$ 450,000
Cost of goods sold	−310,000
Gross profit	$ 140,000
Operating expenses	−100,000
Loss on sale of equipment	− 6,000
Net income before taxes	$ 34,000
Taxes	− 10,000
Net income	$ 24,000

Selected balance sheet accounts showed:	12/31/1998	12/31/1997
Accounts receivable	$ 50,000	$ 80,000
Inventory	60,000	85,000
Equipment	100,000	110,000
Accumulated depreciation—equipment	(28,000)	(20,000)
Accounts payable	48,000	32,000
Income taxes payable	8,000	3,000
Dividends payable	6,000	10,000
Bonds payable	100,000	80,000
Retained earnings	48,000	54,000

Required:

1. What cash flow was generated from operating activities?
2. What cash flow was provided by financing activities?
3. What cash flow was provided by investing activities?

18-4.   Revising a Cash Flow Statement. Mr. Dunny thinks cash flow is critical. He has tried to express his own company's cash flow in the following statement:

Funds provided:

Net income		$26,000
Depreciation expense		2,000
Amortization expense		1,000
Accounts receivable decrease		200
Accounts payable increase		500
Sale of land		3,000
Sale of investments		1,300
Sale of stock		4,000
Total..		$38,000

Funds applied:

Dividends paid		$15,000
Inventory increase		400
Long-term notes payable		1,000
Gain on sale of land	$500	
Less loss on sale of investments.......................	200	300
New buildings.......................................		16,000
New equipment		4,300
Change in cash		1,000
Total..		$38,000

Required:

Help Mr. Dunny get squared away with a better cash flow statement in good form.

18-5.   Statement Preparation—Cash Basis. Below is a list of items that occurred during 1995 in the Harrol Company.

Net income for the year	$356,000
Dividends paid during the year	75,000
Proceeds from sale of a ten-year bond issue	200,000
Amortization of patents	15,000
Depreciation expense	125,000
Cash received on sale of land	130,000
Decrease in inventory	44,000
Increase in accounts receivable	96,000
Loss on the sale of land	20,000
Increase in accrued expenses	18,000
Cash purchase of new equipment...............................	500,000
Cash purchase of a long-term investment	158,000
Decrease in income taxes payable	24,000
Increase in accounts payable	47,000
Purchased buildings by issuing a 20-year note payable	300,000

Required:

Prepare a statement of actual cash flows for 1995 using the items given. The treasurer of the Harrol Company has indicated that cash increased by $102,000.

18-6.   **Cash Flows From Financial Statement Data.** The following statement of income and selected balance sheet data are given for the Lichtman Company:

INCOME STATEMENT
FOR THE YEAR ENDED DECEMBER 31, 1996

Sales		$450,000
Cost of goods sold		300,000
Gross profit		$150,000
Operating expenses:		
Depreciation expense	$10,000	
Other cash expenses	90,000	100,000
Net income before taxes		$ 50,000
Tax expense		20,000
Net income		$ 30,000

SELECTED ACCOUNT BALANCES

	December 31	
	1996	**1995**
Cash	$10,000	$ 6,000
Accounts receivable	90,000	80,000
Inventory	60,000	55,000
Accounts payable	30,000	22,000
Retained earnings	60,000	55,000

Required:
1.   How much cash did Lichtman pay to suppliers for purchases in 1996?
2.   Prepare an operations section of a statement of cash flows using the indirect method.
3.   Based on the information given, Lichtman paid out how much in dividends?

18-7.   **Decrease in Cash Balance.** Jon Walgren, the president of Dunbar Instruments, Inc., cannot understand why the firm's cash balance decreased by $37,000 during the last fiscal quarter, when the cash flow from operations for the quarter was $71,000. He had expected the cash balance would increase by that amount. Depreciation expense of $25,000 was deducted on the income statement and was the only cause of difference between net income and cash from operations. Noncurrent balance sheet items from the statements at the beginning and at the end of the quarter follow:

	Beginning of Quarter	End of Quarter
Plant and equipment (net of accumulated depreciation)	$386,000	$404,000
Long-term debt	200,000	160,000
Retained earnings	317,000	338,000

Required:
Prepare a statement of cash flows that will show why Dunbar's expectations were not realized.

18-8.   **Cash Flow and Acquisitions.** The president of Van Horn Appliances can't understand how a competing company, Murphy Appliances, can invest $12,000,000 in new plant and equipment in 1996 and yet not increase debt or capital stock. Furthermore, dividend payments to stockholders were not reduced. The president asks you to determine how the competitor was able to finance these additions without borrowing or issuing capital stock.

During 1996, equipment having a net book value of $3,150,000 was sold at a gain of $420,000, net of income tax. No other plant assets were sold. Financial data from the statements for Murphy Appliances for the past three years are as follows:

| | Year Ended December 31 (in thousands of dollars) | | |
	1996	1995	1994
Net income*	$3,153	$2,732	$2,068
Depreciation deducted for the year............	1,835	887	936
Dividends declared and paid	500	500	500

*Excludes effect of gain on sale of equipment.

Required:
1. Explain to the president how cash might have been acquired for the plant additions made by Murphy Appliances.
2. For your answer to Part 1 to be true, what assumptions are you making about the current operations of Murphy Appliances?

18-9. **Sources and Uses of Cash.** Wendy Pierce owns and operates a stationery and office supply store. Next year she hopes to increase the cash balance of the business by $25,000. Net income for the year has been estimated at $76,000, and Pierce plans to withdraw $30,000 for personal use. She states that depreciation will help to provide cash for the acquisition of new store fixtures. During the coming year, fixtures costing $100,000 are to be acquired.

An estimated income statement follows:

Net sales...	$874,000
Cost of goods sold	$623,000
Operating expenses (including depreciation of $14,000)...............	175,000
Total expenses	$798,000
Net income	$ 76,000

Actual current assets and liabilities and estimated balances a year from now are as follows:

	Estimated Balances At End of Year	Actual Balances
Current assets:		
Cash	$ 73,000	$ 75,000
Accounts receivable	83,000	94,000
Inventories	146,000	147,000
Prepaid expenses	14,000	19,000
Total current assets..............	$316,000	$335,000
Current liabilities:		
Accounts payable	$ 79,000	$ 75,000
Bank loans	123,000	110,000
Accrued operating expenses	19,000	15,000
Total current liabilities	$221,000	$200,000

Required:

1.   Is Pierce correct in stating that depreciation can provide cash that will help to pay for store fixtures? Explain.
2.   Prepare an estimated statement of cash flows using just the data given.
3.   Explain why the cash balance did not increase by $25,000 as expected.

18-10.   **Cash Flow from Operations.** "Net income is fine—over 10 percent of sales!" exclaims the president of Armitage Parts Company. "But I want to know why we have to reduce our cash balance just to pay our bills on time." An income statement for 1996 for Armitage Parts Company follows:

ARMITAGE PARTS COMPANY
INCOME STATEMENT
FOR THE YEAR ENDED DECEMBER 31, 1996

Net sales..	$5,230,000
Cost of goods sold	$2,890,000
Operating expenses	940,000
Income taxes	630,000
Total expenses	$4,460,000
Net income	$ 770,000

Depreciation of $147,000 is included in operating expenses. Current assets and current liabilities are given as of December 31, 1995 and 1996:

	12/31/1996	12/31/1995
Current assets:		
Cash	$ 203,000	$ 474,000
Accounts receivable	941,000	846,000
Inventory	982,000	928,000
Prepaid expenses	16,000	12,000
Total current assets........................	$2,142,000	$2,260,000
Current liabilities:		
Accounts payable	$ 801,000	$ 719,000
Accrued operating expenses payable..............	267,000	293,000
Income taxes payable	137,000	188,000
Dividends payable	180,000	260,000
Total current liabilities	$1,385,000	$1,460,000

Dividends of $400,000 were declared in 1996. A new building was constructed at a cost of $850,000. A mortgage on the building of $290,000 was obtained to make the final payment to the building contractor. No other transactions affected noncurrent assets or equities.

Required:

1.   Prepare a statement of cash flows. Show the cash flow effect of each item on the income statement.
2.   Is the president justified in being concerned about the cash position? Explain.

18-11. **Operating Cash Flows.** White Company has completed preparation of the income statement and the balance sheet at year end, December 31, 1997. A statement of cash flows must be developed. The following data are available:

		12/31/1997	12/31/1996
(a)	From the balance sheet:		
	Current assets:		
	Cash	$17,000	$ 8,000
	Accounts receivable	17,000	12,000
	Inventory...............................	15,000	18,000
	Current liabilities:		
	Accounts payable	$10,000	$12,000
	Notes payable, short term	18,000	13,000
(b)	From the income statement for 1997:		
	Net income	$20,000	
	Depreciation expense	6,000	
(c)	From other records:		
	Purchase of long-term investment	$15,000	
	Payment of long-term note...................	5,000	
	Sale of capital stock	10,000	
	Payment of cash dividend	8,000	
	Purchased land for future plant site, issued capital stock as payment	25,000	

Required:

Prepare a statement of cash flows using the indirect method for operating activities.

18-12. **Statement of Cash Flows—Indirect Method.** The management of Clover Flavors, Inc. is planning a capital investment program and wants to evaluate its sources and uses of cash over the past year. The income statement for the past year follows:

CLOVER FLAVORS, INC.
INCOME STATEMENT
FOR THE YEAR (IN THOUSANDS OF DOLLARS)

Net sales...	$4,732
Cost of goods sold	2,964
Gross profit...	$1,768
Operating expenses	1,032
Operating income	$ 736
Interest expense	$ 43
Loss on sale of equipment....................................	19
Gain on sale of temporary investments	(34)
Net deductions	$ 28
Income before income taxes	$ 708
Income taxes	262
Net income	$ 446

Beginning and ending balance sheets are as follows:

CLOVER FLAVORS, INC.
BEGINNING AND ENDING BALANCE SHEETS
(IN THOUSANDS OF DOLLARS)

	Ending	Beginning
Assets:		
Cash and cash equivalents	$ 652	$ 567
Temporary investments	300	500
Accounts receivable	817	780
Inventory	761	746
Prepaid expenses	39	43
Investment in Gilbert Foods, Inc.....................	280	0
Land	46	38
Buildings, net of accumulated depreciation	1,739	1,781
Equipment, net of accumulated depreciation............	1,059	976
Total assets	$5,693	$5,431
Equities:		
Accounts payable	$ 650	$ 876
Short-term bank loans payable	600	400
Accrued expenses payable	94	62
Dividends payable	84	90
Income taxes payable..............................	137	121
Long-term notes payable	0	400
Capital stock.....................................	600	200
Retained earnings	3,528	3,282
Total equities	$5,693	$5,431

Additional data:
1. Buildings were not acquired or retired during the fiscal year.
2. Operating expenses include depreciation expense of $137,000.
3. The long-term notes payable were converted to capital stock.
4. Equipment costing $346,000 was acquired during the fiscal year.

Required:
Prepare a statement of cash flows using the indirect method for the management of Clover Flavors, Inc.

18-13. **Statement of Cash Flows—Direct Method.** Refer to Problem 18-12.

Required:
Prepare a statement of cash flows using the direct method for the management of Clover Flavors, Inc.

18-14. **Cash Flows—Incomplete Data.** Gibbons Transport Company plans to acquire new trucks in 1997 at an estimated cost of $4,000,000. The president of the company hopes that operations for the last year can produce at least half of the cash needed for the acquisition.

The controller of the company is out of town, but you have been able to obtain the following information from her assistant. His numbers are solid for current assets, but he could only estimate the noncurrent accounts events and balances. All figures are expressed in thousands of dollars.

	June 30, 1996	June 30, 1995
Assets:		
Cash and cash equivalents	$ 2,667	$ 1,168
Temporary investments	4,000	2,000
Accounts receivable	2,460	2,274
Prepaid taxes and insurance	78	64
Supplies on hand.........................	290	316
Total current assets.....................	$ 9,495	$ 5,822
Terminal buildings (net of accumulated depreci-ation)	1,700	1,400
Trucks and equipment (net of accumulated de-preciation)	6,000	7,500
Total assets	$17,195	$14,722
Liabilities and equities:		
Accounts payable	$ 3,633	$ 2,027
Wages and salaries payable	734	812
Interest payable	52	68
Income taxes payable	218	357
Total current liabilities	$ 4,637	$ 3,264
Mortgage payable	1,800	1,900
Long-term notes payable	1,500	1,500
Capital stock.............................	4,500	4,000
Retained earnings	4,758	4,058
Total liabilities and equities	$17,195	$14,722

You have obtained the following information:

1. An addition was made to the terminal buildings at a cost of $500,000 in March 1996.
2. The company sold trucks having a book value of $1,100,000 in April 1996. A loss of $230,000 after income taxes was taken on the sale. No trucks were purchased.
3. Net income for the year ended June 30, 1996, excluding the loss on sale of the trucks, was $1,600,000.
4. A stock dividend of $500,000 was issued in January 1996.

Required:

1. From the information given, prepare a statement of cash flows using the indirect method for the year ended June 30, 1996.
2. If a minimum cash balance of $1,500,000 is considered necessary, does it appear that at least half of the cost of the new trucks will be provided by operations and other sources during the year ended June 30, 1996?

18-15. **Cash Flow From Divisions.** Wear-Well Fabrics Company, Inc. operates with three divisions: an apparel division that sells casual wear, a sports division that sells ski jackets and other athletic clothing, and a novelty division that sells costumes and shirts with special designs or inscriptions.

Each division has complete autonomy with a minimum of control exercised by the corporate headquarters. At the end of each year, the divisions are expected to remit to corporate headquarters half of the amount of the cash flow generated by operations in that division. This requirement may be suspended if it can be shown that the funds are needed by the division for future operations.

Balances of accounts that are traceable to each division are given in thousands of dollars on July 1, 1996:

	Apparel	Sports	Novelty
Accounts receivable	$ 326	$ 68	$ 89
Inventories	636	240	277
Equipment, net of accumulated depreciation.......	784	472	217
Total traceable assets......................	$1,746	$ 780	$583
Accounts payable	$ 502	$ 145	$103
Accrued expenses...........................	32	15	15
Total traceable liabilities	$ 534	$ 160	$118

Estimated income statement and other data for the divisions are given in thousands of dollars for the year ended June 30, 1997:

	Apparel	Sports	Novelty
Net sales.......................................	$3,670	$1,720	$840
Cost of goods sold	$2,936	$1,204	$504
Operating expenses, excluding depreciation.......	342	286	138
Depreciation....................................	65	73	34
Interest expense	30	15	6
Loss on sale of fixtures........................	37	0	0
Income taxes	130	71	79
Total expenses..............................	$3,540	$1,649	$761
Net income	$ 130	$ 71	$ 79
Equipment purchases	$ 96	$ 29	$ 19

Estimated balances of the traceable accounts for each division on June 30, 1997 are as follows in thousands of dollars:

	Apparel	Sports	Novelty
Accounts receivable	$ 390	$ 105	$115
Inventories	630	368	301
Equipment, net of accumulated depreciation.......	759	423	202
Total traceable assets......................	$1,779	$ 896	$618
Accounts payable	$ 432	$ 155	$ 70
Accrued expenses...........................	55	20	4
Total traceable liabilities	$ 487	$ 175	$ 74

Required:
1. Prepare a statement that will show the cash flows from operations and investing for each division and for the company in total for the year ended June 30, 1997.
2. Determine the amount to be remitted to corporate headquarters using the established rule.
3. Assume that sales will be 10 percent lower for each division. Cost of goods sold will be the same percentage of sales as before. All other items will remain the same. Prepare a revised forecast statement of cash flows for each division under this assumption.
4. How much will be remitted to corporate headquarters under the assumption that sales revenue will be 10 percent lower?

18-16. **Long-Term Cash Flow Analysis.** The Denning Company has seen its balance sheet (in millions) grow over the past five years as follows:

	12/31/1997	12/31/1992
Cash and equivalents	$ 2	$ 37
Receivables, net	60	3
Inventories	100	50
Plant assets, net of accumulated depreciation	300	100
Total assets	$462	$190
Current operating liabilities	$105	$ 30
Long-term debt	150	0
Stockholders' equity	207	160
Total equities	$462	$190

The total net income for the 5 years was $104 million. Cash dividends paid were $57 million. Depreciation was $80 million. Fixed assets were purchased for $280 million, $150 million of which was financed with long-term debt.

Jeff Denning, the president and majority stockholder, is an effective operating executive. But he has little patience with financial matters. After examining the most recent balance sheet and income statement he muttered, "We've enjoyed 5 years of steady growth and strong profits every year. We're in the worst cash position in our history and deep in debt. This is ridiculous! The harder you work, the deeper in debt you get. And we can't afford the next phase of our expansion plan. Who stole our cash?"

Required:

1. Prepare a statement of cash flows for the 5-year period.
2. Using the cash flow statement and any other information available, outline two major causes for such a squeeze on cash.

18-17. **Finding Cash Flows From Incomplete Data.** Seaway Instrument Company, Inc. manufactures measuring instruments used in medical research and in the production of automated equipment. Henry DeBellis, the chairman of the board, states that the company has acquired land in 1996 valued at $72,000 in exchange for capital stock. A building is to be constructed on this site, and operations are to be expanded. Equipment has been acquired in 1996 at a cost of $320,000, and new patents were purchased at a cost of $30,000. No equipment or patents were sold. On January 1, 1996, the company had no land but did have equipment, net of accumulated depreciation, of $385,000 and patents of $95,000.

The controller of the company has provided you with the following data:

SEAWAY INSTRUMENT COMPANY
INCOME STATEMENT
FOR THE YEAR 1996

Net sales	$1,686,800
Cost of goods sold	$1,164,700
Operating expenses, excluding depreciation	181,200
Depreciation expense	34,000
Amortization of patents	7,000
Interest expense	31,700
Gain on sale of temporary investments	(8,500)
Net deductions from sales	$1,410,100
Income before income taxes	$ 276,700
Income taxes	113,700
Net income	$ 163,000

Current assets and current liabilities at December 31, 1995 and 1996 are given as follows.

	12/31/1996	12/31/1995
Current assets:		
Cash and cash equivalents	$52,600	$48,900
Temporary investments	25,000	65,000
Accounts receivable	63,300	76,500
Inventories	76,300	34,100
Unexpired insurance	5,400	9,700
Current liabilities:		
Accounts payable	$64,800	$35,300
Accrued operating expenses payable	38,400	14,100
Interest payable	2,700	4,900
Income taxes payable	45,300	12,500
Dividends payable	18,000	6,000

In addition, the controller furnishes the following information with respect to long-term debt and the stockholders' equity:

	12/31/1996	12/31/1995
Long-term debt	$250,000	$190,000
Capital stock	100,000	50,000
Paid-in capital in excess of par	130,000	80,000
Retained earnings	434,400	321,400

Required:
1. Prepare a statement of cash flows using the indirect method.
2. Prepare a cash flow from operations section of a statement of cash flows using the direct method.

18-18. **Explain a Cash Balance Increase.** The president of Micromite, Inc., Wade Rodland, was pleased with the increased cash balance shown on the balance sheet at year end 1996. While the net income for the year was somewhat more than expected, the greatly increased cash balance was not.

"We have been trying to build up our cash reserves for extensive equipment replacement; but with dividends of roughly $500,000 and the replacement of equipment at a cost of $126,000, I had expected a cash increase of only $400,000," Rodland stated. An income statement for 1996 is given, along with beginning and ending balance sheets.

MICROMITE, INC.
INCOME STATEMENT
FOR THE YEAR ENDED DECEMBER 31, 1996
(IN THOUSANDS OF DOLLARS)

Net sales	$12,427
Cost of goods sold (Depreciation of $120,000 included)	$ 9,273
Operating expenses (Depreciation of $28,000 included)	1,138
Interest expense	74
Loss on sale of equipment	70
Total expenses and loss	$10,555
Income before income taxes	$ 1,872
Income taxes	694
Net income	$ 1,178

MICROMITE, INC.
BEGINNING AND ENDING BALANCE SHEETS
DECEMBER 31, 1996
(IN THOUSANDS OF DOLLARS)

	Beginning	Ending
Assets:		
Cash and cash equivalents	$ 490	$1,873
Accounts receivable	482	449
Inventories	886	868
Prepaid expenses	93	50
Plant and equipment, net of accumulated depreciation	3,235	2,838
Total assets	$5,186	$6,078
Liabilities and stockholders' equity:		
Accounts payable	$ 389	$ 472
Accrued operating expenses payable	87	91
Dividends payable	115	136
Interest payable	35	40
Income taxes payable	214	345
Notes payable, due August 31, 1995	800	800
Capital stock	1,200	1,200
Retained earnings	2,346	2,994
Total liabilities and stockholders' equity	$5,186	$6,078

Required:

1. Prepare a statement of cash flows for 1996 using the indirect method.
2. Point out factors that increased the cash balance by more than the amount anticipated by Rodland.

18-19. **Estimated Cash Flow.** Dawn Porter, the president of Sunglo Products, Inc., is concerned about an installment of $2,000,000 that must be paid on long-term debt by mid-December, 1997. Declining sales volume in the past two years has reduced cash flow below earlier expectations. The following is a budgeted income statement for 1997:

SUNGLO PRODUCTS, INC.
BUDGETED INCOME STATEMENT
FOR THE YEAR ENDED DECEMBER 31, 1997

Net sales	$8,280,000
Cost of goods sold, including depreciation of $415,000	$4,915,000
Operating expenses, including depreciation of $136,000	784,000
Loss on equipment disposal	252,000
Interest expense	632,000
Interest income	(56,000)
Net deductions from sales	$6,527,000
Income before income taxes	$1,753,000
Income taxes	800,000
Net income	$ 953,000

Current assets and current liabilities at December 31, 1996 are listed, along with the forecast balances at December 31, 1997:

	12/31/1996	12/31/1997
Current assets:		
Cash and cash equivalents	$ 937,000	$1,043,000
Temporary investments	350,000	0
Accounts receivable	428,000	371,000
Inventories	384,000	415,000
Prepaid expenses	32,000	14,000
Total current assets	$2,131,000	$1,843,000
Current liabilities:		
Accounts payable	$ 494,000	$ 521,000
Accrued expenses payable	62,000	78,000
Interest payable	43,000	52,000
Income taxes payable	186,000	138,000
Total current liabilities	$ 785,000	$ 789,000

The forecast cash balance at December 31, 1997 has already been reduced by the $2,000,000 payment on long-term debt. At the very minimum, the cash balance should not fall below $800,000.

The president believes that the budgets indicate that the debt payment can be made with no reduction in the cash balance. She points out, however, that a payment of dividends of $300,000 must be made in order to satisfy shareholders. Also, property having a book value of $252,000 is to be scrapped, with no salvage value anticipated.

The treasurer admits that it will be tight, but he believes that suppliers may accept delayed payments that will result in accounts payable increasing to $557,000 and that accrued expenses payable may be allowed to increase to $94,000. Also, with a good credit record, banks may extend short-term credit of at least $100,000.

Required:

1. Prepare a forecast cash basis income statement for 1997 using the treasurer's estimates.
2. Complete a forecast statement of cash flows using the treasurer's estimates.
3. Will Sunglo be able to pay its dividend and long-term debt and still maintain at least $800,000 in cash? Explain

18-20. **Statement of Cash Flows.** Saylor Parts, Inc. expanded operations in 1995 in anticipation of increased sales volume in future years. The president of the company is concerned about liquidity and asks you to prepare a statement of cash flows for 1995.

SAYLOR PARTS, INC.
BALANCE SHEETS FOR DECEMBER 31, 1994 AND 1995
(IN THOUSANDS OF DOLLARS)

Assets	1995	1994
Current assets:		
Cash and cash equivalents	$ 6,314	$ 7,051
Temporary investments	500	1,500
Accounts receivable	5,258	3,932
Inventories	6,146	4,628
Supplies on hand	1,233	581
Total current assets	$19,451	$17,692
Property and equipment, net of accumulated depreciation	21,365	14,500
Intangibles:		
Goodwill	1,000	1,200
Patents	826	752
Total assets	$42,642	$34,144

Equities	1995	1994
Current liabilities:		
Accounts payable	$ 4,978	$ 4,338
Wages payable	236	154
Other accrued operating expenses payable	517	228
Bank loans payable	1,100	450
Dividends payable	200	500
Income taxes payable	500	750
Total current liabilities	$ 7,531	$ 6,420
Long-term debt payable	3,000	2,000
Total liabilities........................	$10,531	$ 8,420
Capital stock.............................	$ 4,000	$ 3,500
Paid-in capital in excess of par	6,200	2,500
Retained earnings	21,911	19,724
Total stockholders' equity	$32,111	$25,724
Total equities	$42,642	$34,144

SAYLOR PARTS, INC.
INCOME STATEMENT
FOR THE YEAR ENDED DECEMBER 31, 1995
(IN THOUSANDS OF DOLLARS)

Net sales......................................		$36,240
Cost of goods sold		21,585
Gross margin		$14,655
Operating expenses:		
Supplies used...............................	$2,374	
Wages and salaries...........................	3,178	
Insurance	136	
Property taxes	151	
Advertising	312	
Depreciation................................	870	
Amortization of patents	36	
Amortization of goodwill	200	
Other operating expenses	576	7,833
Operating income		$ 6,822
Interest expense	$ 176	
Loss on sale of temporary investments	85	
Loss on sale of equipment......................	127	388
Income before income taxes		$ 6,434
Income taxes		2,247
Net income		$ 4,187

Additional data:
1. Dividends were cut by 50 percent between 1994 and 1995.
2. Plant equipment at a net book value of $835,000 was sold during the year.
3. Capital stock appraised at $3,000,000 was issued in exchange for a building appraised at $3,000,000.

Required:
1. Prepare a statement of cash flows for Saylor Parts, Inc. for 1995.
2. Comment on the possible implications that the expansion may have had on the firm's financial position and its operations.

CASE 18A—ALAN WILLIAM COMPANY

Alan William Company plans to construct a building and to make some major changes in its operations in 1996. In anticipation of construction, the company has conserved cash and has not paid dividends during the past year.

Estimates show that the building will probably cost $21,000,000 and that furnishings and equipment may cost another $5,000,000. A member of the board of directors states that by the time the building is constructed, the cost may be $30,000,000 with the furnishings and equipment costing $6,000,000.

Other actions planned for 1996 are as follows:

1. Capital stock is to be issued for $4,000,000.
2. Old plant assets having a net book value of $1,680,000 are to be retired. It is estimated that $3,460,000 will be received from their sale. Costs of $100,000 will be incurred for advertising and for the sale of the assets. Income tax rate on the gain will be 40 percent.
3. An investment in Vero Chemicals, Inc. is to be sold for $4,660,000 with a 40 percent tax on the gain.
4. The company plans to have no less than $3,000,000 as its operating cash balance by the end of 1996.
5. The building can be partially financed by a long-term loan of $15,000,000, with interest at the rate of 12 percent being deducted to leave net proceeds of $13,200,000. In later years, interest of $1,800,000 is to be paid each year until the loan becomes due.
6. The following are forecast income statement data for 1996:
   (a) Net sales are forecast at $52,000,000.
   (b) Cost of goods sold and operating expenses combined, excluding depreciation, are estimated at 70 percent of net sales.
   (c) Depreciation expense has been estimated at $2,100,000.
   (d) Interest expense on the loan for building construction has been estimated at $1,800,000.
   (e) Income taxes have been estimated at 40 percent.
   Balance sheet data as of December 31, 1995 are as follows:

Assets

Cash and cash equivalents	$ 1,972,000
Temporary investments	6,000,000
Accounts receivable	4,763,000
Inventories	6,211,000
Investment in Vero Chemicals, Inc.	3,000,000
Plant and equipment, net of accumulated depreciation	10,300,000
Total assets	$32,246,000

Equities

Accounts payable	$ 5,420,000
Short-term bank loans	500,000
Accrued operating expenses payable	860,000
Interest payable	230,000
Capital stock	4,500,000
Premium on stock	8,100,000
Retained earnings	12,636,000
Total equities	$32,246,000

The president of Alan William states that sales revenue for 1996 may be only $45,000,000. In the president's opinion, sales may have been optimistically estimated at $52,000,000. Cost of goods sold and operating expenses are still budgeted at 70 percent of sales revenue.

Required:
1.   Prepare forecast statements of cash flows under four assumptions:
    (a)   Lower building and equipment cost with the optimistic sales estimate.
    (b)   Lower building and equipment cost with the lower sales estimate.
    (c)   Higher building and equipent cost with the optimistic sales estimate.
    (d)   Higher building and equipment cost with the lower sales estimate.
2.   Will the company need all or part of the long-term loan under each of the assumptions stated? Comment.

CASE 18B–ANCHOR METALS, INC.

The board of directors of Anchor Metals, Inc. is planning a complete restructuring of the company. Long-term debt at a relatively high interest rate is to be refinanced by new notes with a lower interest rate. Notes in the amount of $20 million, with a scheduled maturity in 1998, are to be replaced in part by new notes of $15 million that are to mature in 2017. The early maturity penalty is $800,000, net of income taxes.

"We will be trying to do a lot of things at once," Ralph Bonner, the board chairperson, stated. "Our loss situation in a declining market for metal products is intolerable. But, we have an opportunity to buy a lumber and building supply company for $16 million, that is, if we can raise the capital. The business has been profitable and can give us diversification. At the same time, we will reduce our dependence on metal products by selling off some of the assets in that area."

The president, Gail Preston, announces, "Some of our equipment can be sold for $12.8 million, about the same amount as shown on our books."

One of the directors states, "Our stock isn't doing well, and that's an understatement. Even so, we should be able to float 100,000 shares in the capital market and realize $15 a share. Our debt is far too large as a percentage of total equity, and a stock issue will improve the relationship."

"It will be tight going," Bonner replies. "The budget for next year shows that we will have an operating loss after tax of $340,000 even with the projected changes. Total depreciation is estimated at $9,280,000. Even so, it looks a lot better than last year's loss of $979,000. At least, we are moving in the right direction."

Financial statements for 1996 in summary form are given as follows:

ANCHOR METALS, INC.
INCOME STATEMENT
FOR THE YEAR ENDED DECEMBER 31, 1996
(IN THOUSANDS OF DOLLARS)

Sales	$62,840
Cost of goods sold, including depreciation of $7,320	$47,460
Operating expenses, including depreciation of $2,240	12,332
Interest expense	4,374
Income tax credits	(347)
Net deductions from sales	$63,819
Net loss	$ (979)

ANCHOR METALS, INC.
BALANCE SHEETS FOR DECEMBER 31, 1995 AND 1996
(IN THOUSANDS OF DOLLARS)

	1995	1996
Assets		
Current assets:		
Cash and cash equivalents	$ 2,278	$ 1,818
Accounts receivable	2,138	2,868
Inventory	5,861	5,615
Prepaid expenses	1,340	1,847
Total current assets	$11,617	$12,148
Plant and equipment, net of accumulated depreciation	36,450	34,190
Total assets	$48,067	$46,338
Liabilities and Stockholders' Equity		
Current liabilities:		
Accounts payable	$ 4,325	$ 3,036
Trade notes payable	2,500	3,100
Accrued operating expenses payable...................	339	278
Total current liabilities	$ 7,164	$ 6,414
Notes payable, maturities 2/1/98 and 6/30/01	31,280	31,280
Total liabilities	$38,444	$37,694
Stockholders' equity:		
Capital stock, $10 par value..........................	$ 1,635	$ 1,635
Premium on stock	4,220	4,220
Retained earnings	3,768	2,789
Total stockholders' equity	$ 9,623	$ 8,644
Total liabilities and stockholders' equity	$48,067	$46,338

Required:
1. Prepare a statement of cash flows for 1996. Show the cash flow from operations by making appropriate additions or deductions from the net loss.
2. Based on the information given, prepare an estimated statement of cash flows for 1997.
3. Can the company accomplish its objectives with the new capital expected?
4. Compute the percentage of total debt to total assets at the end of 1996.
5. Compute the percentage of total debt to total assets expected at the end of 1997. (Assume no change in current liabilities.)
6. Comment on the board's strategy for 1997.

❖ *APPENDIX A*

AN OVERVIEW OF THE ACCOUNTING PROCESS

The American Institute of Certified Public Accountants defined accounting as follows:

"Accounting is the art of recording, classifying, and summarizing in a significant manner and in terms of money, transactions and events which are, in part at least, of a financial character, and interpreting the results thereof."[1]

In this appendix, the recording, classifying, and summarizing aspects of accounting—that is, the accounting cycle—will be described and illustrated. This discussion includes the adjusting and closing process that occurs at the end of every accounting period.

THE ACCOUNTING CYCLE

The accounting cycle begins with an event that is reflected in a transaction and in the recording of this transaction. For accounting purposes, every transaction has two sides, and this duality is important to the recording process.

Duality

The properties of an entity and the rights in those properties are accounted for as they enter or leave the business, as they circulate within the business, or as they stand at any point in time. The properties are called **assets**, and the rights in the properties are called **equities**. The rights or equities of outsiders are called **liabilities**, and the rights of the owners are called the **owners' equity**. Examples of typical assets are listed below:

1. Cash: Cash on hand or on deposit in banks.
2. Accounts receivable: Amounts owed by customers of the business.
3. Inventory: Materials to be used in manufacturing products, or the finished or partially finished products themselves.
4. Land: Real estate owned and used by the business.
5. Building: Building owned and used in conducting business activities.
6. Equipment: Equipment owned and used in conducting business activities.

---

[1]*Accounting Research and Terminology Bulletins—Final Edition*, "Accounting Terminology Bulletins, No. 1, Review and Resume" (New York: American Institute of Certified Public Accountants, 1961), par. 9.

Examples of typical equities are as follows:

1.   Accounts payable: Amounts owed to trade creditors of the business.
2.   Notes payable: Promissory notes owed to the bank or to other outsiders.
3.   Mortgage payable: Debt owed and secured by a mortgage on business property.
4.   John Adams, capital: Designation of the interest in a business of an owner named John Adams.

Both the assets and the equities are accounted for simultaneously. A business transaction does not affect just one item alone. At least two items must be considered in each transaction. It would not be possible, for example, for a business to have a transaction that resulted only in the increase of the asset cash. An explanation as to why cash increased must also be present. Cash may be received in exchange for some other asset that left the business, or the cash may come from a loan made by some outsider, or as a result of investment by the owner.

The duality aspect of each transaction is the foundation for **double-entry accounting** . Double-entry accounting recognizes that no asset can exist without someone having a claim or a right to it. Therefore, both the specific assets and the equities are accounted for at the time transactions are recorded. Some transactions result in increases to assets and some result in decreases. The assets can be increased by:

1.   Donations.
2.   Investments by the owners.
3.   Services performed by the business.
4.   Loans or credit furnished by outsiders.

Assets obtained through loans or credit result in an increase in liabilities. The other situations increase the owners' equity. Both the increase in the assets and the increase in the rights to the assets are recorded. Assets of a business can be decreased by:

1.   Losses, such as fire or theft.
2.   Withdrawal of assets by owners, such as dividend payments.
3.   Use of assets, such as inventory, to conduct operations.
4.   Donations to others.
5.   Settlement of the claims (liabilities) of outsiders.

The use of assets to settle the claims of outsiders results in a reduction in liabilities. In all the other situations listed, the owners' equity is decreased. The decrease in the asset and the decrease in the equity are both recorded.

One asset may be exchanged for another, or one type of equity may be converted to another form. For example, an account receivable from a customer in the amount of $2,000 may be collected. Total assets remain unchanged in amount. Only a change in the composition of the assets occurred: cash increased by $2,000, and the account receivable from the customer decreased by $2,000. The holder of a note against the company may be issued stock in exchange for rights as a creditor; that is, the liability for the note payable is eliminated and is replaced with an addition to the owners' equity. The total equity in the firm is the same, but the form of the equity has changed.

Accounting Equation and Transactions

The relationship between the properties called **assets** and the rights in the properties called **equities** is expressed in the form of an equation, as follows:

$$Assets = Equities$$

The rights of outsiders called **liabilities** and the rights of the owners called **owners' equity** or **capital** are recognized and expressed as a relationship, which is known as the **accounting equation**

$$Assets = Liabilities + Capital$$

A **business transaction** is an event or condition that requires an entry in the accounting records. For accounting purposes business transactions are expressed in terms of their effect on the accounting equation. The effect of changes on the three basic elements is illustrated by examining the accounting equation and some typical transactions. The amounts are numbered so that they can be identified with the transactions.

(1) Karen Weaver begins business on October 1 by investing $75,000 in cash. After this transaction, the business has cash as an asset in the amount of $75,000; and the owners' equity, that is Weaver's claim on the assets, is $75,000.

(2) Weaver pays $900 for the rental of a store for three months. The asset cash is traded for the asset prepaid rent, representing the right to occupy the store for three months.

(3) New equipment costing $30,000 is purchased for the store on account. An asset is increased in exchange for an increase in a liability.

(4) Payments of $28,000 were made to the creditors from whom equipment was purchased. The asset cash is reduced by $28,000, and the liability, accounts payable, is reduced by $28,000.

	Cash	+	Prepaid Rent	+	Equipment	=	Accounts Payable	+	Karen Weaver, Capital
(1)	+75,000								+75,000
(2)	−900		+900						
(3)					+30,000		+30,000		
(4)	−28,000						−28,000		

Accounting Equation and Revenue and Expense

In the previous illustration, no transactions were included which required the recognition of revenue or expense. Assets are increased by revenue received for services performed by a business. **Revenue** is the consideration received by the business for rendering goods and services to its customers. Terms used for particular types of revenue, such as **sales**, indicate how the revenue was earned. Revenue is treated as an increase in capital.

Expense is a measure of the decrease in assets incurred in the process of producing revenue. Terms used for particular types of expenses, such as **rent**, indicate how the asset was used. Expense is treated as a reduction in capital.

The relationship between assets, liabilities, capital, revenue, and expense can be expressed with the accounting equation as follows:

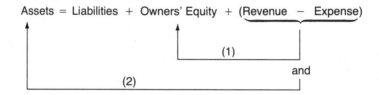

(1) (Revenue - Expense)—measurement of *net* increase or decrease in owners' equity from rendering goods or services to customers during an accounting period.

(2) (Revenue - Expense)—measurement of *net* inflow or outflow of assets as a result of rendering goods or services to customers during an accounting period.

The equation as presented above is somewhat oversimplified, but it is essentially true. Revenue and expense accounts measure aggregate increases or decreases in assets, but no specific assets are identified. More precisely, it may be stated that **net assets** (assets - liabilities) are increased or decreased when revenue and expenses are recognized. Sometimes assets are received with a corresponding liability being recorded until goods or services are delivered. When the goods or services are delivered, the liability is reduced and revenue is recorded. For example, a cash deposit may be received from a customer with a liability being recorded for the obligation to deliver goods or services in the future. Eventually, when the goods or services arrive, the liability is removed and revenue is recognized.

Often the relationship between the assets and the revenue and expenses is direct. For example, assets such as cash or accounts receivable are usually increased when sales revenue is recorded. At the same time, cost of goods sold is recorded as an expense and the inventory (an asset) is reduced.

Source Documents

A business transaction is ordinarily supported by some form, or **source document**, which serves as evidence or proof of the transaction and gives information about what has happened. Such a document is either received from an outsider or is originated within the business. A bill or an invoice received from a supplier of materials supports an entry to record an increase in the materials inventory asset and the accounts payable liability. Sometimes materials are transferred within the company. A document is usually prepared to support the transfer and to give the essential facts of the transaction. The materials inventory of one division is increased, while the materials inventory of the other division is decreased. Forms originating within the enterprise are also sent to outsiders. Bills or invoices are mailed to customers when sales are made, and checks are sent to creditors in payment of amounts owed.

Accounts

The method of accumulating data should be designed so that information can be collected easily.

Data are collected by classification in accounts. In essence, accounts are pages or cards divided into two halves by a vertical line and may appear somewhat as follows:

An account is created for each asset, liability, owners' equity, revenue, and expense. The left side of the account is called the debit side of the account, and the right side of the account is called the credit side. Debit and credit are the terms used for left and right in accounting. A book of accounts or a file of account cards is referred to as a **ledger.**

Increases in accounts are recorded on one side of the account, and decreases are recorded on the other side. The balance of the account is the difference between the sum of the items on each side of the account. A **debit balance** exists if the amounts on the left side are greater; a **credit balance** occurs if the amounts on the right side are greater.

Increases and Decreases in Accounts   Special rules for recording increases and decreases are employed for each basic type of account: asset, liability, owners' equity, revenue, and expense. The accounting equation is given once more to show the rules of increase and decrease:

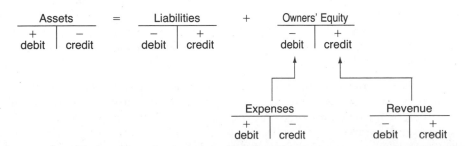

The increases and decreases are arranged so that each transaction is recorded and classified properly while maintaining an equality of debits and credits. If the recording process is carried out properly in a mechanical sense, the sum of the accounts with debit balances will equal the sum of the accounts with credit balances.

Note that the equation itself can be stated as follows:

$$\text{Assets} = \text{Liabilities} + \text{Owners' Equity} + (\text{Revenue} - \text{Expenses})$$

This merely says that assets are equal to the claims that individuals or other entities have on those assets. Revenue and expenses measure how assets enter or leave the business in performing services for customers, and the net result is eventually added to the owners' equity.

The rules followed for debiting and crediting accounts are arbitrarily defined but are logically consistent. For example, a debit means an increase in any asset, but a debit will also decrease any liability or owners' equity account. The rules of debit and credit exist so that the accounting equation will hold true, and so that debits will always be equaled by credits. Therefore, assets will always equal equities; and the sum of the amounts shown as debits will always agree with the sum of the amounts shown as credits. Note that a revenue account is credited to increase it. This is logical inasmuch as an increase in revenue is an increase in the owners' equity; and, therefore, an increase in revenue is handled in the same way as a direct increase in owners' equity. Similarly, increases in expenses reduce owners' equity and, like direct reductions in owners' equity, are recorded by debits.

Use of Accounts   The transactions previously given for Weaver are now expanded and are listed and numbered as follows:

(1)   Karen Weaver invested $75,000 in cash to begin business operations.
(2)   A $900 prepayment was made for rent of a store for three months.
(3)   Equipment was purchased on account at a cost of $30,000.
(4)   Cash of $28,000 was paid to the creditors from whom equipment was purchased.
(5)   Merchandise costing $50,000 was purchased on credit terms.
(6)   Merchandise was sold to customers on account for $48,000.
(7)   Wages of $800 were paid.
(8)   A promissory note was received for $8,000 from a customer on account.
(9)   Cash of $200 was paid for heat and light for one month.

The ledger accounts—with the transactions analyzed and entered according to the rules of increase and decrease shown by the accounting equation—are given as follows. The entries are numbered so that they can be identified with the transactions.

Assets		=	Liabilities		+	Owners' Equity	
Dr.	Cr.		Dr.	Cr.		Dr.	Cr.
+	−		−	+		−	+

Cash			Accounts Payable			Karen Weaver, Capital	
(1) 75,000	(2) 900		(4) 28,000	(3) 30,000			(1) 75,000
	(4) 28,000			(5) 50,000			
	(7) 800						
	(9) 200						

Accounts Receivable						Plus Revenue	
(6) 48,000	(8) 8,000					Dr.	Cr.
						−	+

Notes Receivable						Sales	
(8) 8,000							(6) 48,000

Prepaid Rent						Minus Expenses	
(2) 900						Dr.	Cr.
						+	−

Equipment						Purchases	
(3) 30,000						(5) 50,000	

						Wages Expense	
						(7) 800	

						Heat and Light Expense	
						(9) 200	

The Journal

The direct recording of transactions in the ledger accounts is inconvenient and errors are difficult to find. It takes time to leaf through the ledger pages or cards; and if many transactions occur, time will be insufficient to enter each transaction in the ledger cards as it takes place. Furthermore, there should be some chronological record of the transactions with the entire transaction being shown in one place. Errors can then be located with less difficulty by tracing transactions from the chronological record to the ledger accounts.

A preliminary analysis of transactions is made in a book of original entry called a **journal**. In its simplest form, the journal consists of a book with a column for dates at the left, a wide Description column for account titles and explanations, and two columns for entering monetary amounts. The first of the two monetary columns is called the Debit column, and the second is called the Credit column. A simple journal of this type is usually called a **general journal**. The preliminary record entered in the journal is called a **journal entry**.

Each transaction is analyzed to identify the accounts that are to be debited and credited. The transaction is then recorded as follows:

1. The date is entered in the Date column.
2. The name of the account to be debited is entered in the Description column, and the dollar amount is entered in the Debit money column.
3. The name of the account to be credited is entered in the Description column on the next line in an indented position, and the dollar amount is entered in the Credit money column.
4. A brief explanation of the transaction is written beneath the account titles.

The general journal entries for Weaver's transactions would appear as shown in Figure A.1 below:

GENERAL JOURNAL　　　　　　　　　　　　　　　　　　　　　　Page 1

Date		Description	Post. Ref.	Debit	Credit
1995 Oct.	1	Cash .... Karen Weaver, Capital .... Investment of $75,000 by Karen Weaver.		75,000	75,000
	1	Prepaid Rent .... Cash................................. Rent paid in advance for 3 months.		900	900
	2	Equipment .... Accounts Payable .... Equipment bought on account.		30,000	30,000
	6	Accounts Payable .... Cash................................. Creditors paid on account.		28,000	28,000
	9	Purchases........................... Accounts Payable .... Merchandise purchased on account.		50,000	50,000
	12	Accounts Receivable.................. Sales .... Merchandise sold on account.		48,000	48,000
	15	Wages Expense....................... Cash................................. Wages paid for two weeks.		800	800
	15	Notes Receivable .... Accounts Receivable .... Note received from customer on account.		8,000	8,000
	30	Heat and Light Expense .... Cash................................. Utilities paid for October.		200	200

Figure A.1　The General Journal

Posting

The number and the kind of accounts kept in the ledger depend on the information desired or required. It is advisable to keep separate accounts for each type of asset, liability, revenue, and expense. An owners' equity or capital account should be kept for information relative to the owners' equity in the business. Generally, a list of accounts, called a **chart of accounts,** is prepared and each account is assigned a number. After the transactions have been recorded in the journal, the information is transferred to the ledger accounts through a process called **posting.** When information is posted from the journal to the ledger, the date, amount of each transaction, and page number of the journal are entered in the account. The narrow column headed "Post. Ref." in the journal is a cross-reference column called the **posting reference column.** The number of the ledger account is entered in the "Post. Ref." column so that a transaction can be easily traced to the ledger accounts if that should become necessary at a later date. Space is also provided in the ledger accounts for page numbers of the journal where the transactions were first entered. Thus a transaction can easily be traced from the journal to the ledger or from the ledger back to the journal.

Posting is a process of organizing data according to account classifications from the chronological record contained in the journal. After the data are classified in the accounts and summarized, they are used in the preparation of financial statements and reports.

While the two-column journal does provide a chronological record of transactions with both parts of the transaction in one place, it is not very helpful as a labor-saving device. In fact, more accounting work is necessary because the transaction must be entered first in the journal and then it must be posted to the ledger accounts. For example, Weaver would have to make a journal entry for each transaction, then post the information from the journal to the ledger accounts before the ledger would contain the debits and the credits shown in the earlier set of T-accounts.

Special Journals

Often business transactions of a certain type are repeated time and again. There are likely to be many purchases of merchandise, sales to customers, cash receipts, and cash disbursements. To record each transaction separately in a two-column journal as an increase or as a decrease to a given account is unduly burdensome. Transactions of a similar type should be classified together, summarized for a period such as a month, and posted as one aggregate transaction for the month.

Several types of journals are available, each type being designed to serve a special purpose. For example, all sales transactions could be entered in a sales journal. Similarly, purchases, cash receipts, and cash disbursements are entered respectively in a purchases journal, a cash receipts journal, and a cash disbursements journal. Other specialized journals can be created if transactions occur frequently enough to warrant their use. A manufacturing company, for example, may use a special journal to record materials withdrawn and transferred to production. Miscellaneous transactions that do not occur often enough to merit the use of a special journal are entered in the two-column general journal.

The special journals have columns so that similar transactions can be conveniently added together and posted as one transaction. For example, sales for the month may be shown in a sales journal designed as shown in Figure A.2.

	SALES JOURNAL				Page 4
Date	Account Debited	Post. Ref.	Cash Dr.	Accounts Receivable Dr.	Sales Cr.
1995 Oct. 4	Customer A		500		500
11	Customer B			2,300	2,300
18	Customer A		800		800
25	Customer E			1,500	1,500
			1,300	3,800	5,100

Figure A.2   The Sales Journal

This design indicates that sales are often made on both cash and credit terms, since the sales journal has a column for cash debits, a column for accounts receivable debits, and a column for sales credits. At the end of the month, the sum of the two debit columns should be equal to the sum of the credit column.

All sales journals are not designed with three columns. Special journals are designed to fit the needs of the user, and special columns are provided for frequently used accounts.

Trial Balance

After posting from the journal to the ledger accounts, the balances of the accounts are calculated and are listed on a trial balance. This listing shows whether or not the debit balances are equal to the credit balances. Mechanical accuracy is verified if the total of the debit balance and the credit balance is equal. However, this does not prove that all amounts have been recorded in the proper accounts.

For example, in the Weaver illustration a balance for the cash account is computed by subtracting the sum of the credit entries of $29,900 from the sum of the debit entries of $75,000 to obtain a debit balance of $45,100. Other account balances are similarly computed, and all balances are listed to form the following trial balance.

KAREN WEAVER
TRIAL BALANCE
OCTOBER 31, 1995

	Debit	Credit
Cash	45,100	
Accounts Receivable	40,000	
Notes Receivable	8,000	
Prepaid Rent	900	
Equipment	30,000	
Accounts Payable		52,000
Karen Weaver, Capital		75,000
Sales		48,000
Purchases	50,000	
Wage Expense	800	
Heat and Light Expense	200	
	175,000	175,000

ADJUSTING PROCESS

Business transactions are accumulated over an interval of time designated as an **accounting period** or a **fiscal period.** The period of time may be a month, a quarter, a year, or any other significant time interval. Ordinarily, financial measurements are made over a period of a year, with the year being divided into months or quarters. During a fiscal period, a company records purchases, sales, cash receipts, cash disbursements, returns of merchandise from customers, payrolls, transfers of materials and labor into production, and other events that arise in the normal course of its operations. Other important information may not be recorded at all, or the information may be recorded but with the passage of time may require adjustment. The adjustments are made after the transactions for the fiscal period are recorded and after a trial balance is prepared. To illustrate the adjusting procedure, adjustment data are given along with ledger accounts.

Adjustment data:

1. Wages in the amount of $700 were earned by the employees at October 31 but have not been paid or recorded.
2. The note receivable has been outstanding for half of the month and annually earns interest at 12%. The total interest earned is $40 [($8,000 × 12%) ÷ (12 × 2)].
3. Rent of $900 was prepaid for three months beginning October 1.
4. The equipment was acquired at a cost of $30,000. Depreciation of the equipment has been estimated at $250.

5. The inventory of merchandise on hand was counted and assigned a cost of $10,000.
6. Sales in the amount of $1,500 are estimated as not collectible.

Usually, the adjustments for a company are classified under the following three general headings:

1. The accrual adjustments
2. The prepayment adjustments
3. The valuation adjustments

Accrual Adjustments

Often wages, rent, interest, and the various costs of business operations are recorded only at the time they are paid. However, some costs grow or accrue with the passage of time. For example, wages are earned by the employees each working day even though they are paid only at designated times.

Since the last payroll, wages of $700 have been earned. The additional expense and the liability are computed and the effect of the adjusting entry is illustrated in the following T-accounts.

Wages Expense		Wages Payable	
800			700
700			

Looking at accruals in another way, assets and revenue also grow or accrue. Weaver has earned a total of $40 on the note receivable. The ledger accounts after posting the adjusting entry would appear as follows:

Interest Receivable		Interest Earned	
40			40

The need for accrual adjustments arises when all of the data pertaining to the fiscal period have not been recorded. Expenses that increase with the passage of time must be recorded, whether paid or not; and the liability for unpaid expenses must also be recognized. Similarly, revenue that increases with the passage of time must be recorded, whether collected or not; and the asset representing the amount due must be recognized.

In the following accounting period, when the $40 interest receivable is collected in cash, the collection is viewed as a conversion of assets; that is, the asset cash is increased and the asset interest receivable is decreased. The revenue was recognized in the prior accounting period even though the cash was not received until the subsequent period. Revenue is viewed as being the result of the earning process. The cash collection may or may not take place at the same time that the revenue is actually recognized (recorded).

Prepayment Adjustments

Business events should be properly analyzed and recorded as they occur. For example, an asset may be recorded at the time it is acquired for cash, or a liability may be recorded when an advance collection is received from a customer. By the end of the fiscal period, however, the situation may have changed. An adjustment may be required to show the part of the asset that was used in profit-making activity. The expense will be recorded, and the asset previously entered will be reduced. Likewise, deliveries of products may have been made against advance collections received from customers. The liability initially entered in the records will be reduced, and the portion earned will be recorded as revenue. Adjustments made to separate expenses from assets and revenue from liabilities are referred to as **prepayment adjustments.** The most common prepayment adjustments that businesses will encounter separate expenses from assets and deal with prepaid expenses, depreciation, and inventory.

Prepaid Expense Adjustment   Karen Weaver has prepaid rent of $900 at the beginning of October. At the end of the month, one-third of the prepaid rent has expired. The adjusting entry to record the rent expense and the reduction of the asset will bring the accounts up to date as follows:

Prepaid Rent		Rent Expense	
900	300	300	

Depreciation Adjustment   To conduct business operations, a company normally requires buildings, fixtures, machinery, and equipment. Assets of this type have a relatively long useful life and are classified under the general heading of **plant assets** or **fixed assets.** The expense resulting from the use of these assets is designated as **depreciation expense.** Depreciation represents an estimate of the physical wear and tear as well as any obsolescence relative to the use of the asset.

Plant assets are somewhat like prepaid expenses. The cost of a plant asset, like the cost of an insurance policy, for example, is allocated over its useful life. Ordinarily the plant asset has a longer life than the prepaid expense, but the adjustment procedure is somewhat similar. Unlike the prepayment, however, the plant asset may not be paid for at the time it is acquired. Debt may have been incurred to finance the cost of the asset. But the way in which it is financed has no influence upon the allocation of its cost to operations. The cost is allocated or assigned to time periods according to the flow of benefits received from the use of the asset over its estimated useful life.

An asset such as a building or a piece of equipment has a limited useful life; it does not yield benefits indefinitely. It eventually wears out, becomes outmoded with the passage of time and changes in technology, or becomes inadequate as the company grows and requires the use of larger assets or assets with greater productive capacity. Over the total period of time the asset is in use, its cost is allocated to the various fiscal periods as depreciation expense.

Generally, the cost of a plant asset is substantial, and the asset may be in service for a number of years. Often detailed underlying records are maintained to show the original cost of the asset, the name of the company from which the asset was purchased, the history of maintenance and repair service, the depreciation that has been recorded each year, and other pertinent details with respect to the asset and its operation. Ordinarily the plant asset account itself is not credited directly when depreciation adjustments are made. Instead, a special asset reduction account called Accumulated Depreciation or Allowance for Depreciation is credited. The original cost is then preserved in the plant asset account, and the reductions, because of depreciation, are shown in a separate offsetting account. The remaining cost to be charged against future operations, or the **net book value** of the asset as it is called, is equal to the balance shown in the plant asset account minus the balance shown in the accumulated depreciation account. The accumulated depreciation account has a credit balance and is frequently referred to as a **contra-asset account**.

Assume that Weaver has estimated the useful life of the equipment at 10 years with no provision for salvage value. Each month depreciation of $250 [($30,000 ÷ 10) ÷ 12] is deducted. When an equal amount of cost is assigned to each accounting period, the company is said to be recording depreciation according to the **straight-line method**. After the adjusting entry is posted, the ledger accounts appear as follows:

	Equipment	
	30,000	

Accumulated Depreciation— Equipment		Depreciation Expense— Equipment
	250	250

A connection does not necessarily exist between the net book value of a plant asset and its market value. At the end of the first accounting period Weaver might be able to sell the equipment for more or less than the net book value of $29,750. Depreciation policy is not intended as a device for the valuation of plant assets. It is merely a means of allocating the costs to the fiscal periods during which the assets are in service. The allocation of costs is made to facilitate the determination of net income for the period.

The depreciation procedure in accounting is an estimating process and is filled with uncertainty. An estimate of the useful life and the salvage value is required, and a judgment of how to assign the cost must be made. As a result, accounting data are not as precise as they may appear. Estimates and human judgments enter into the processing operation, depreciation policy being a good example. The user of accounting information must be aware of these underlying judgments and estimates. The student of accounting should be constantly on the alert for other areas in the accounting process where estimates and judgments are filled with uncertainty.

Inventory Adjustment   Some companies maintain **perpetual inventory** records, recording purchases as additions to inventory, and withdrawals or sales as deductions from inventory and as increases in cost of goods sold. The inventory records should then show the proper balances on hand at all times. At the end of the fiscal year, a physical count may reveal errors in the book record that should be corrected. However, if the accounting system is operating properly and if proper control over the physical inventories exists, the corrections should not be substantial in amount.

Many companies do not keep a perpetual record of inventories. The purchases are recorded, but no record of the cost of items withdrawn or sold is kept. As a general rule, it is impractical to record the cost of items sold if merchandise is sold to customers over the counter in relatively small lots. At the end of the fiscal year, the physical quantity remaining in inventory can be determined by count. Cost is then identified with the inventory according to the particular costing method that is employed. The cost of goods sold during the year is computed indirectly as the sum of the beginning inventory and purchases minus the inventory at the end of the year. This method of arriving at inventory cost and the cost of goods sold is called the **periodic inventory** method.

A variety of practices may be employed in making the periodic inventory adjustment. The essential points are that the cost of goods sold should be determined as accurately as possible and that the inventory at the end of the year should be valued properly.

The inventory adjustment may be made by setting up a new account entitled Cost of Goods Sold. The balance of inventory at the beginning of the year and the purchases for the year are closed out by credits, with the debit being entered in the cost of goods sold account. At this point, the cost of goods sold account has a balance representing the cost of goods available for sale. It is converted to cost of goods sold by removing the cost attached to the inventory remaining at the end of the year. This is accomplished by a debit to the merchandise inventory account in an amount equal to the cost of the inventory at the end of the year and by a credit to the cost of goods sold account.

To illustrate using data from Karen Weaver's company: **(a)** The inventory at the beginning of the month (no inventory existed at the beginning of the month) and the purchases of $50,000 are transferred (closed) to Cost of Goods Sold; **(b)** At the end of the month, a count of the inventory reveals that the merchandise on hand cost $10,000. After the adjustments are recorded, the affected ledger accounts are shown as follows:

Merchandise Inventory		Purchases		
(b) 10,000			50,000	**(a)** 50,000

Cost of Goods Sold		
(a) 50,000	(b)	10,000

Valuation Adjustments

Another type of adjustment is a valuation adjustment. Certain assets, such as marketable securities, accounts receivable from customers, and inventories are to be realized in cash in the normal course of events. But the assets may not be realized at the amounts shown in the ledger accounts.

Accounts receivable, for example, show the amounts due from the customers; but not all of the customers will pay their accounts. Some accounts will be uncollectible. At the end of the year, the company has no way of knowing which customers will default. Yet, sales should be charged with the estimated uncollectible accounts arising out of sales operations for the year. An adjusting entry is made to record the estimated uncollectible accounts chargeable to the year, and the credit is made not to accounts receivable but to an account that may be entitled Allowance for Doubtful Accounts.

Of the total accounts receivable of $40,000, Weaver estimates that $1,500 will not be collected. When the estimate is made, no specific accounts receivable are identified as uncollectible. Therefore, the credit is made to an allowance account. The affected ledger accounts after posting the adjusting entry are given below:

Accounts Receivable

| 40,000 | |

Allowance for Doubtful Accounts		Uncollectible Accounts Expense	
	1,500	1,500	

In the next accounting period, as specific accounts are identified as uncollectible, they are written off against the allowance for doubtful accounts. Assume that one of the customers defaults during the next accounting period in the amount of $400. After recording the default, the affected ledger accounts would appear as follows:

Accounts Receivable		Allowance for Doubtful Accounts	
40,000	400	400	1,500

The estimating procedure previously illustrated is subject to errors in judgment but nevertheless tends to produce more useful data than would be the case if the estimate were not made. No logical reason exists why losses on customers' accounts should be matched against revenue of the fiscal period in which the losses are detected. The losses should be matched against the revenue recorded when the initial transaction takes place. Unfortunately, no exact determination of the losses can be made at that point. It should be possible, however, to make reasonable estimates based on past experience. Hence, this device is a method for recognizing the uncollectible accounts expense in the period in which the sale was made and not in a subsequent period when the account receivable is actually judged to be uncollectible.

Marketable securities and inventories are also subject to valuation adjustments. It is customary to value marketable securities and inventories at the lower of cost or market. If market values are lower than cost, an adjustment may be made to charge a loss to the year in which the market decline occurred. The offsetting credit may be made directly to the asset account or to an allowance (contra) account similar in concept to the allowance account used with accounts receivable.

Adjusted Trial Balance

After the adjusting entries are posted, an adjusted trial balance is prepared as follows:

KAREN WEAVER
ADJUSTED TRIAL BALANCE
OCTOBER 31, 1995

	Debit	Credit
Cash	45,100	
Accounts Receivable	40,000	
Allowance for Doubtful Accounts		1,500
Notes Receivable	8,000	
Interest Receivable	40	
Merchandise Inventory, October 31	10,000	
Prepaid Rent	600	
Equipment	30,000	
Accumulated Depreciation—Equipment		250
Accounts Payable		52,000
Wages Payable		700
Karen Weaver, Capital		75,000
Sales		48,000
Cost of Goods Sold	40,000	
Wages Expense	1,500	
Uncollectible Accounts Expense	1,500	
Rent Expense	300	
Depreciation Expense—Equipment	250	
Heat and Light Expense	200	
Interest Earned		40
	177,490	177,490

Financial Statements

Financial statements are prepared from an adjusted trial balance. A statement of revenue and expenses is called an **income statement.** Expenses are deducted from revenue. If revenue exceeds expenses, the difference is called **net income.** If expenses exceed revenue, the difference is called **net loss.** The income statement shows the net changes in owners' equity that result from operating at a profit or at a loss. The income statement is used to measure revenue and expenses for a given accounting (or fiscal) period. An income statement for Karen Weaver is given as follows:

KAREN WEAVER
INCOME STATEMENT
FOR THE MONTH ENDED OCTOBER 31, 1995

Sales		$48,000
Cost of goods sold		40,000
Gross margin		$ 8,000
Operating expenses:		
Wages	$1,500	
Uncollectible accounts	1,500	
Rent	300	
Depreciation	250	
Heat and light	200	3,750
Operating income		$ 4,250
Interest earned		40
Net income		$ 4,290

A **balance sheet** is essentially a formal classified listing of assets and equities at one point in time. As time passes and as other transactions take place, the balance sheet becomes out of date; but as of the balance sheet date, it is a statement of the financial position of the enterprise. The balance sheet for Karen Weaver on October 31 is shown below:

KAREN WEAVER
BALANCE SHEET
OCTOBER 31, 1995

Assets

Cash		$ 45,100
Accounts receivable	$40,000	
Less allowance for doubtful accounts	1,500	38,500
Notes receivable		8,000
Interest receivable		40
Merchandise inventory		10,000
Prepaid rent		600
Equipment	$30,000	
Less accumulated depreciation	250	29,750
Total assets		$131,990

Equities	
Liabilities:	
Accounts payable.....................	$ 52,000
Wages payable	700
Total liabilities	$ 52,700
Owners' equity:	
Karen Weaver, capital	79,290
Total equities	$131,990

Note that the owners' equity is $4,290 more than the owners' equity shown on the adjusted trial balance. The net income of $4,290 has been added to the $75,000 on the adjusted trial balance to yield an owners' equity of $79,290 at the end of the period.

THE CLOSING PROCEDURE

At the end of the accounting period, the revenue, expense, and cost of goods sold accounts have served their purpose. Measurements of the extent of the net increase or decrease in net assets resulting from profit-making activities during the accounting period have been taken. Now the income statement accounts can be closed; that is, the balances can be reduced to zero so that new measurements can be made in the following time period. Revenue and expense classifications are like meters that measure the flow of liquids or gases for an interval of time. When the time interval has lapsed, the dials on the meters are set back to zero so that new measurements can be made for the next period of time. The closing entry in the general journal for Karen Weaver on October 31 would be made as follows:

Sales	48,000	
Interest Earned	40	
Cost of Goods Sold		40,000
Wages Expense		1,500
Uncollectible Accounts Expense		1,500
Rent Expense		300
Depreciation Expense—Equipment		250
Heat and Light Expense		200
Karen Weaver, Capital		4,290
Entry to close revenue and expense accounts for the year and to close net income to Karen Weaver's capital account.		

After the revenue and expense accounts are closed, only the asset, liability, and owner's equity accounts have balances to be carried forward to the next accounting period and to serve as a cumulative record. The balances after closing are listed on a **post-closing trial balance**. The purpose of this final trial balance is to prove that the general ledger is in balance before transactions are entered for the new period. The ledger is now ready to receive entries for the next time period, and the cycle of processing accounting data is repeated again.

The post-closing trial balance for Karen Weaver on October 31, is given as follows:

KAREN WEAVER
POST-CLOSING TRIAL BALANCE
OCTOBER 31, 1995

	Debit	Credit
Cash	45,100	
Accounts Receivable	40,000	
Allowance for Doubtful Accounts		1,500
Notes Receivable	8,000	
Interest Receivable	40	
Merchandise Inventory, October 3	10,000	
Prepaid Rent	600	
Equipment	30,000	
Accumulated Depreciation—Equipment		250
Accounts Payable		52,000
Wages Payable		700
Karen Weaver, Capital		79,290
	133,740	133,740

FORMS OF BUSINESS OWNERSHIP

Up to this point in the discussion of the accounting cycle, a proprietorship was assumed; that is, one person owned the business. With a proprietorship, the owners' equity is simply shown in one account and designated by the name of the owner, for example, Karen Weaver, Capital or Karen Weaver, Proprietorship. Actually, various legal forms of business ownership exist. Most businesses can be classified as one of the following:

1. Proprietorship.
2. Partnership.
3. Corporation.

A business that is owned jointly by two or more individuals or entities is designated as a **partnership**. Each partner's interest is identified by name and is designated as each partner's capital.

A business may also be **incorporated;** that is, the business is given an existence apart from its owners through a charter issued by a state. The **corporation** is like a person at law, being able to transact business in its own right and having the legal rights and responsibilities of an individual in the commercial field. The owners' equity in a corporation is not identified according to the persons who have ownership rights; that is, the stockholders. Instead, the owners' equity is shown under two general classifications:

1.   The investment of the owners, which under ordinary circumstances will remain as a permanent investment. This is called paid-in capital.
2.   The accumulated retained earnings of the business. In general, the accumulated retained earnings will be the total of all profits reduced by losses and by cash dividend payments.

In the formation of a corporation, the organizers agree that a certain stated amount shall be invested for each share issued. This original investment constitutes a permanent investment, assuming, of course, that no reorganization or other drastic change in the corporate structure is under consideration. The amount of this stipulated investment is designated as **capital stock** if only one class of stock is issued. If more than one class of stock is issued, the stated amount for each class is shown separately and is appropriately designated as **preferred stock** or as **common stock**, as the case may be.

Often a corporation will receive more than the legal minimum investment per share. For example, it may be agreed that for each share issued there will be $1 invested and credited to capital stock. The shares are issued, however, for $5 each. The amount of the investment in excess of the stated value, in this case $4 per share, is credited to Paid-In Capital in Excess of Stated Value. Ordinarily, the amount credited to this account cannot be withdrawn and is looked upon as a part of the permanent investment.

The accumulated retained earnings of the corporation are reduced by net losses, distributions to the owners, or transfers to paid-in capital. Barring restrictions that may be imposed by law or by contractual agreement, the retained earnings balance establishes the amount that may be withdrawn by the owners as dividends.

SOME BASIC CONCEPTS

The mechanical features of processing accounting data have been discussed, but much more is involved in the preparation of data for the financial statements. Certain fundamental concepts are observed, some of which are discussed in this section.

Going Concern Concept

A basic assumption in accounting is that a business will continue to operate in the future and that it will not cease doing business, sell its assets, and make final payments to creditors and owners. Therefore, it is said that accounting is carried out on a **going concern** basis. The plant assets, for example, are not normally adjusted to liquidation values. Presumably the plant assets will not be sold but will be used in future business operations. On the balance sheet given for Kirby Products, Inc., later in this Appendix, the building and equipment, for example, are shown at a net amount of $254,500. This does not mean that they can be sold for that amount. The valuation of $254,500 is the undepreciated cost to be carried forward to future years. As the building and equipment are used in conducting operations, a cost of using them will be recognized in the determination of net income or net loss.

Cost Concept

Cost is conventionally used as the basis for accountability. Assets when acquired under normal circumstances are recorded at the price arrived at by negotiation between two independent parties dealing at arm's length. Simply stated, the **cost** of an asset to the purchaser is the price that must be paid now or later to obtain it. The fair value of the asset is not relevant in recording the transaction. A purchaser may acquire an asset at a cost that is greater or less than the fair value determined in the marketplace. If so, the asset is accounted for at the purchaser's cost, value notwithstanding.

Accounting for cost is an extremely complex process. In conducting business operations, some assets lose their original identity, that is, they are converted into some other form. For example, materials used in a chemical process often cannot be identified as such in the end product. Costs are traced through operations, wherever possible, as the assets are transferred or converted in the course of operations.

Realization Concept

The profit or loss of a business is measured as the difference between the consideration received from customers and the cost attached to the products or services given in exchange. In conventional accounting, profit is not recognized unless it is realized. For the most part, realization depends on an agreement with a customer to pay a stipulated amount for the product.

The point at which the revenue is realized will vary depending on circumstances. The amount of the consideration received from the customer is frequently looked upon as being realized when title to the items sold is vested in the customer. At that point there is an enforceable claim against the customer. It is not necessary that the consideration be in the form of cash; the promise of the customer to make eventual payment is sufficient. In some cases, profit realization and cash realization go together. For example, a barber will realize the amount to be received from the customer when the service is given the customer, and the consideration will be realized in cash immediately after the service has been given. For all practical purposes, it can be said that the barber would be entitled to measure profit as cash is realized. On the other hand, when merchandise is delivered to customers on installment sales, considerable doubt may exist as to whether or not the promise of the customer to make eventual payment will be fulfilled. Profit on installment sales may be looked upon as realized when cash is collected. The collections may not be made according to plan, and the merchandise may have to be repossessed. However, under most circumstances, a justification can exist for the recognition of revenue as collections are made. At that time no question about the realization of the revenue should exist.

In some cases, profit is realized before delivery is made to the customer and before cash is collected. For example, a shipbuilder may build a vessel on government contract. As the work progresses, profit may be realized by matching cost for the percentage of work completed against a corresponding percentage of the amount of the consideration to be received. This method of accounting for profit, known as the **percentage-of-completion** method, is sometimes used by contractors who build highways, buildings, bridges, and other structures and properties that are completed over a relatively long period of time.

Periodicity Concept

Ordinarily, revenue and expense are measured over a period of one year. This year does not necessarily correspond with the calendar year but instead may correspond with the natural cycle of business activity. Logically, a fiscal year should end with the close of a cycle of business activity, that is, when inventories and accounts receivable are at a minimum, before new inventory is acquired for another cycle of sales and subsequent collections. For example, a department store may choose a year extending from March 1 of one year to February 28 (or 29) of the next calendar year. The Christmas sales and the January sales for the same season will then fall within the same year, and the inventories and the accounts receivable will generally be low just before merchandise is purchased for spring and summer sales. The year chosen for financial measurements is called the fiscal year or fiscal period.

Consistency Concept

The results of an accounting system are dependent in many cases upon estimates. They are also influenced by the choice of an accounting method and the consistency with which it is applied. For example, inventories may be accounted for on a first-in, first-out basis, a last-in, first-out basis, or by some other means.

An accounting method or procedure once chosen should be followed consistently from year to year. Consistency in accounting is not advocated just for the sake of consistency, but rather to avoid the confusion that would result if profit or loss were calculated differently each year. Desirable changes should be made, of course; but when changes are made, the effect of such changes upon the financial statements should be fully disclosed.

Matching Concept

A reasonably accurate measurement of the net income or the net loss for a fiscal period depends on the matching of expenses against related revenue. The matching of revenue and expense is difficult. With a going concern there is always the possibility that a revenue or an expense should have been recognized in a previous fiscal period or that it should have been deferred until some future period. If expenses have not been properly offset against revenue, the resulting net income or net loss for the fiscal period will be reported incorrectly.

The revenue and the expense pertaining to a fiscal period may have to be estimated. A company might sell a product under an agreement to guarantee against defects and furnish future maintenance and repair services. Not only must the estimated liability to the customer be recognized, but the expense of giving this service should be estimated and offset against the revenue resulting from the initial sales transaction. The cost of giving this service to the customer is related to the sales transaction; therefore, the estimated expense and liability should be recorded during the period in which the sale was made.

When a company purchases a piece of equipment, the cost of the equipment should be matched against the revenue of the future fiscal periods that will benefit from its use. The portion of the cost which should be deferred and matched against the revenue of any given year depends upon the estimation of the useful life and salvage value of the equipment. Many similar situations arise in which matching must be done on an estimated basis, using the information available.

The Accrual Principle

Revenue and expenses are accounted for on the accrual basis. Revenue is defined as the consideration (measured in monetary terms) received for rendering goods and services. Revenue is usually recognized when the following conditions are satisfied:

1. The amount of revenue must be capable of objective measurement.
2. The earning process must be reasonably complete so that the cost of completion can be determined.
3. The revenue must be realized.

Revenue is not necessarily recognized at the time cash is collected. For example, goods and services are often sold on credit terms. At some later date, collections will be made from the customers, but collections of cash are not a realization of revenue. Instead, the collections are a realization in cash of the accounts receivable asset, which was increased at the time revenue was recorded, that is, at the date when goods or services were delivered and billed.

Occasionally, customers will pay in advance for goods and services that will be delivered later. The advance payments have not been earned and cannot be recorded as revenue. The company, in accepting these advance payments, is obligated to the customers until it makes delivery. As deliveries are made, the liability is reduced and revenue is earned. If the accounting records have not been kept up to date during the fiscal period, adjusting entries will be made at the end of the period so that the portion of the advance earned is shown as revenue while the portion still owed to the customers is shown as a liability.

Reductions in revenue should be offset against the corresponding revenue recorded. Cash discounts and allowances granted to customers should be estimated and deducted from the related revenue. The loss is related to the revenue and not to the period of time in which the discount or the allowance is finally granted.

Similarly, expenses are carefully matched against related revenue and are not necessarily recognized when cash payments are made for goods and services. An expense occurs when the asset leaves the business as a result of revenue-producing activity and not when cash payments are made to creditors. The cost of the asset becomes expense in the fiscal period that benefits from the use of the asset. For example, supplies may be purchased on credit terms. At the time of purchase the supplies are recorded as an asset, and a liability to the creditor is recorded. When payment is made for the supplies, the liability to the creditor is reduced. But the payment is not related to the use of the supplies. As the supplies are used in earning revenue, the cost of the portion used should be recorded as expense with the supplies asset account being reduced by a corresponding amount.

Often expenses will have to be estimated. Goods and services may be delivered with an agreement that defects will be corrected or that future services will be given without charge. The costs to correct the defects and to furnish the additional services should be estimated and deducted as expenses in the same period in which the related revenue is recorded.

The problem of matching expenses against revenue in the income determination process is challenging. The identification of revenue with a given interval of time is not an exact process, nor is it a simple matter to identify expenses with the resulting revenue. Judgments and estimates will have to be made in many cases, using the best information that is available to management.

Conservatism Concept

Usually the accountant takes a conservative position. Revenue is generally not recognized by recording value increases that may take place on unsold products or merchandise, even if the items in question can be sold, with certainty, at the current market prices in excess of their cost. The principles of valuing assets at cost and recognizing revenue only when the sale is made go hand in hand. If market increments were recorded, assets would be reflected at market value and not at cost.

On the other hand, losses are usually recorded when the market price declines below cost. This inconsistency in the application of accounting principles has been justified on the basis of conservatism. As a rule, the accountant is skeptical of claims that assets are worth more than cost but will be more inclined to accept evidence that assets may be realized at even less than cost. Conservatism can be carried too far, however. It has merit in that the readers of the balance sheets are not led to expect that marketable securities, for example, can be realized at cost when in reality the current market prices are below cost. But excessive undervaluation can make the business appear to be in poor financial condition when such is not the case. Investment may be discouraged if a business appears to be less valuable than it is. The accountant must recognize that persons can be injured by understatements as well as by overstatement. Excessive write downs of assets in one time period understate net income in that period and overstate net income when the assets are sold.

Valuation

The reader of the balance sheet should be acquainted with the principles of valuation that are commonly applied in arriving at the dollar amounts shown for the various assets and equities. Sometimes the basis of valuation is indicated in the body of the statement or in accompanying footnotes. In many cases, however, the basis of valuation is not given, it is assumed that the reader is familiar with conventional practices. Recently the conventional practices of valuation have been criticized. Questions have arisen as to whether or not assets should be valued at cost on the balance sheet when evidence exists that the assets are worth considerably more or less than cost. Or is the profit for a fiscal period properly measured when historical cost is matched against revenue as expense in the period of sale? The valuation problem cannot be separated from the problem of income determination. With rapid inflation in the past few years, the problem of financial measurement has been receiving increasing attention not only from accountants, but from various business groups and the average consumer.

Various asset valuation approaches are used:

1.   Historical cost.
2.   Price-level adjusted historical cost.
3.   Fair market value, realizable value, or exit value.
4.   Replacement cost or entry value.
5.   Present value of future cash flows.

BALANCE SHEET CLASSIFICATIONS

A classified balance sheet for Kirby Products, Inc. as of April 30, 1996 is illustrated on page 993.

Both the assets and the equities are usually listed separately and are not reduced by offsetting one against the other. This holds true even though specific assets may be pledged to secure the payment of a debt such as notes payable or bonds payable. Ordinarily the debt holder will receive payment in cash and will lay claim to the assets pledged only if the debtor defaults. The equity holders are said to have an **undivided interest** in the total assets. Thus, the equities are looked upon as a measurement of the extent of the rights of any individual or entity to the total assets, but not to any particular asset. In the statement given for Kirby Products, Inc. the holders of the long-term notes payable do not have a $75,000 interest in cash, accounts receivable, inventories, or any other specific asset. They do, however, have a $75,000 claim against the assets in total.

KIRBY PRODUCTS, INC.
BALANCE SHEET
APRIL 30, 1996

Assets

Current assets:

Cash....................................	$ 41,370	
Marketable securities at cost (market value, $38,250)	36,430	
Notes receivable	3,000	
Accounts receivable .... $ 68,490		
Less allowance for discounts, returns,		
allowances, and doubtful accounts..... 2,640	65,850	
Inventories	86,420	
Prepaid insurance	1,770	$234,840
Investment in stock of Rabold Mills, Inc.		165,000

Plant Assets:

Land	$ 14,600	
Building and equipment.............. $292,700		
Less accumulated depreciation........ 38,200	254,500	269,100

Intangible assets:

Organization expense.........................	$ 4,900	
Goodwill	28,000	32,900

Other assets:

Advances to company officers		8,500
Total assets		$710,340

Equities

Current liabilities:

Bank loans	$ 18,000	
Accounts payable	41,350	
Accrued payroll and other expenses	19,540	
Estimated income tax payable	28,400	$107,290
Long-term notes, due August 31, 2007		75,000
Deferred rental revenue		2,700

Stockholders' equity:

Capital stock, $10 par value, 5,000 shares issued and		
outstanding	$ 50,000	
Premium on stock	82,500	
Retained earnings	392,850	525,350
Total equities...................................		$710,340

On the balance sheet, the assets and the equities are listed under classifications according to their general characteristics and their relative liquidity. Similar assets or similar equities are listed together, so that it is a relatively simple matter to make a comparison of one classification with another or to make comparisons within a classification. Some of the most commonly used classifications are:

Assets	Equities
Current assets	Current liabilities
Investments	Long-term liabilities
Plant assets	Deferred revenue
Intangible assets	Other liabilities
Other assets	Owners' equity

Current Assets

The **current assets** include cash and other assets that in the normal course of events are converted into cash within the operating cycle. A manufacturing enterprise, for example, will use cash to acquire inventories of materials that are converted into finished products and sold to customers. Cash is collected from the customers, and the circle from cash back to cash is called an **operating cycle**. In a merchandising business, one part of the cycle is eliminated. Materials are not purchased for conversion into finished products. Instead, the finished products are purchased and are sold directly to the customers.

Several operating cycles may be completed in a year, or it may take more than a year to complete one operating cycle. The time required to complete an operating cycle depends on the nature of the business.

It is conceivable that virtually all of the assets of a business could be converted into cash within the time required to complete an operating cycle. But a current asset is an asset that is converted into cash within an operating cycle *in the normal course of events*. Assets such as buildings, machinery, and equipment that are used in conducting the business are not converted into cash in the normal course of operations. They are held because they provide useful services for the business over a number of time periods; they are excluded from the current asset classification.

On the other hand, a manufacturer or a dealer who holds assets such as buildings, machinery, and equipment for resale to customers in the regular course of the business includes these items in the inventory under the classification of current assets. The manufacturer or dealer does not hold these assets for use in the business, but holds them as an inventory of product to be converted into cash in the normal course of operations. An automobile dealer, for example, has company cars that are not to be sold but are to be used in operating the business. These cars are not included in the inventory. But the cars that are held for resale to customers are an inventory of product that should be listed under the current assets.

In many cases, the operating cycle does not extend beyond a year. However, exceptions exist. An inventory of liquor in the distilling industry must be aged, for example, and may be shown as a current asset even though it will not be converted into cash within the next year. It qualifies as a current asset inasmuch as it is converted into cash in the normal course of events within the operating cycle of the business.

Investments

Investments are funds in cash or security form held for a designated purpose or for an indefinite period of time. This classification includes investment in the stocks or bonds of another company, real estate or mortgages held for income-producing purposes, and investments held for a pension or other special fund.

Plant Assets

The assets such as land, buildings, machinery, and equipment that are to be used in business operations over a relatively long period of time are often classified as **fixed assets**, or more specifically as **plant assets** or as property, plant and equipment. It is not expected that these assets will be sold and converted into cash as are inventories. Plant assets produce income indirectly through their use in operations.

On the balance sheet for Kirby Products, Inc., land is shown separately at $14,600; building and equipment are shown at both the gross amount and at the net amount after deducting accumulated depreciation. Land does not have a limited useful life and is not reduced by depreciation. However, the cost of buildings, equipment, and other plant assets having a limited useful life are matched against revenue during the fiscal periods in which they are used.

Adjustments are usually not made in conventional accounting practice to restate plant assets at current replacement cost or at net realizable value. Plant assets, unlike the inventories, are not to be sold in the normal course of operations. Instead, they are used in performing the work of the business enterprise. The investment in plant assets is recovered gradually as the assets are used in producing profits, but it is not expected that the investment will be recovered by direct sale as is the case with inventory.

In accounting for profit, the replacement cost of a plant asset and its net realizable value are not generally considered; yet in special decision-making situations these valuations can be applied. When equipment is to be replaced, for example, management considers the current replacement cost and the amount that should be realized upon the sale or trade-in of the present equipment. During the course of operations, recognition may also be given to the possibility that new equipment may cost more in the future. Profit that would otherwise be distributed to the stockholders as dividends may be retained to the extent of the anticipated increase in replacement cost. By following this policy, the company hopes to be able to retain the purchasing power of its initial investment.

Intangible Assets

Other fixed assets that lack physical substance are often referred to as **intangible assets**. The intangible assets consist of valuable rights, privileges, or advantages. Although the intangibles lack physical substance, they have value. Sometimes the rights, privileges, and advantages of a business are worth more than all of the other assets combined.

Typical items included as intangible assets are patents, franchises, organization expense, and goodwill. **Patents** give the business an exclusive privilege of using a certain process in manufacturing. **Franchises** permit a company to handle a given product or to operate within a given territory or along a certain route. To become incorporated, a company must incur certain costs, such as the initial incorporation fee to the state and the cost of legal services in connection with the formation of the corporation. These costs are the costs of the privilege of having a corporation and are designated as **organization expense.** A company is said to possess **goodwill** if it can earn a higher-than-normal rate of return upon invested resources. The higher rate of return may be caused by various factors such as managerial skill, popular acceptance of the products, or some other favorable circumstance. In setting a selling price for a prosperous business, it is recognized that the business as such may be worth more than the fair market value of the properties listed on the balance sheet as reduced by the liabilities. In other words, a value is placed on the anticipated earnings above an established normal level.

Goodwill is recorded only when it is purchased or sold. Frequently goodwill is recorded when a profitable business is acquired or when there is a change in the form of ownership. In the balance sheet given for Kirby Products, Inc., goodwill is shown at $28,000. Perhaps the business was at one time a sole proprietorship and developed goodwill. When the business was incorporated, stockholders purchased ownership interests and in doing so recognized and paid for goodwill. Or Kirby Products, Inc. may have purchased another business, paying in excess of the values of the listed properties transferred less the liabilities assumed. This additional payment was made for anticipated future earnings above a normal level or, in short, was a payment for goodwill.

The cost of an intangible asset should be written off on the income statements over the fiscal periods during which it is estimated that the asset will yield benefits. For example, a franchise may enable a company to operate over a given route for only a stipulated period of time. The cost of the franchise should then be written off during the estimated fiscal periods that will benefit.

Other Assets

Other assets exist that cannot be classified as current assets, investments, plant assets, or intangible assets. These assets are listed as other assets. Frequently the other assets consist of advances made to company officers, cost of buildings in the process of construction, and miscellaneous funds held for special purposes.

Current Liabilities

On the equity side of the balance sheet, as on the asset side, a distinction is made between current and long-term items. The **current liabilities** are obligations that are to be discharged within the normal operating cycle of the business and, in most circumstances, are liabilities that are to be paid within the next year by using the assets now classified as current. The amounts owed under current liabilities often arise as a result of acquiring current assets, such as inventory, or acquiring services that will be used in current operations. The amounts owed to trade creditors, arising from materials or merchandise purchases, are shown as accounts payable. If the company is obligated under short-term promissory notes that support bank loans or other amounts owed, the liability is shown as notes payable. Other current liabilities may include the estimated amount payable for income tax, portions of long-term liabilities due within a year, and the various amounts owed for wages and salaries of employees, utility bills, payroll taxes, local property tax, and other services.

Long-Term Liabilities

Debts not falling due within a year of the balance sheet date are generally classified as **long-term liabilities** Notes, bonds, and mortgages are often listed under this heading. Kirby Products, Inc. has a long-term debt of $75,000 evidenced by notes that will not become due until August 31, 2007. No portion of this debt is to be paid during the next fiscal year; therefore, the entire amount is shown separately as a long-term liability.

Other Liabilities

Liabilities, like assets, cannot always be classified as either current or long-term. In some cases, the creditors will not expect to receive payment either in the near or the distant future.

Deferred Revenue

Customers may make advance payments for merchandise or services. The obligation to the customers will, as a general rule, be settled by delivery of the products or services and not by cash payment. Advance collections received from customers are usually classified as **deferred revenue** pending delivery of the products or services. On the balance sheet given for Kirby Products, Inc., rent has been collected in advance from the tenants who have leased space in the building. When Kirby Products, Inc. gives rental service to the tenants, the obligation will be removed from the balance sheet. The rentals will then be realized and shown on the income statement.

Owners' Equity

The **owners' equity** in a corporation, often called **stockholders' equity**, is subdivided.

1. One portion represents the amount invested by the owners directly, plus any portion of retained earnings converted into permanent capital.
2. The other portion represents the retention of net earnings in the business.

This rigid distinction is necessary because of the nature of a corporation. Ordinarily the owners of a corporation, that is, the stockholders, are not personally liable for the debts contracted by the company. A stockholder may lose the amount invested, but creditors usually cannot look to the stockholder's personal assets for satisfaction of their claims. Under normal circumstances, the owners may withdraw as cash dividends an amount measured by the corporate earnings. This rule gives the creditors some assurance that a certain portion of the assets equivalent to the stockholders' investment cannot be arbitrarily withdrawn. Of course, this portion could be depleted because of operating losses.

The investment by the stockholders or the paid-in capital may also be divided into two portions. One portion of the investment is the legal minimum that must be invested according to the corporate charter as approved by the state. Each share of stock may be assigned a par value such as $1, $5, or $10 per share. For each share issued, the stipulated value is to be received by the corporation. This minimum investment is generally labeled as capital stock. Any amount invested in the corporation that is in excess of par value is shown separately and is labeled as **premium on stock** or as **paid-in capital in excess of par value**.

Sometimes shares are not assigned a par value. The state may require that the entire amount received from the sale of no-par stock be held as the legal minimum investment, in which case the total amount received would be credited to capital stock. In some states, however, no-par shares are virtually equivalent to par-value shares for accounting purposes in that they are assigned a stated value per share. Any amount received in excess of the stated value can be classified as **paid-in capital in excess of stated value**.

Ordinarily, the premium on stock or the paid-in capital in excess of stated value is not reduced as a result of dividend distributions. Many states, however, allow dividends to be charged against this portion of the stockholders' investment, but some states require that the source of such dividends be revealed to the stockholders.

If stock is issued at less than its par value or its stated value, it is issued at a discount. Some states do not permit the issuance of stock at a discount, while other states hold the stockholders liable to creditors to the extent of the stock discount if the corporation cannot meet the claims of its creditors.

The accumulated net earnings of a corporation are shown under a separate heading such as **retained earnings** or **reinvested earnings**. As a general rule, this portion of the stockholders' equity may be voluntarily reduced by the distribution of dividends to the stockholders and, of course, involuntarily by losses. Net losses in excess of retained earnings are shown as a deduction in the stockholders' equity section and are labeled as a **deficit**.

The owners' equity in an unincorporated business is shown more simply. The interest of each owner is given in total, usually with no distinction made between the portion invested and the accumulated net earnings. The creditors are not concerned about the amount invested because, if necessary, they can attach the personal assets of the owners. The owners' equity in a partnership may appear as follows:

Owners' equity:
Craig Bergman, Capital	$161,000
Lucy Sutton, Capital	53,000
Total owners' equity	$214,000

INCOME STATEMENT CLASSIFICATIONS

The income statement, like the balance sheet, is a classified statement. An income statement for Kirby Products, Inc. for the fiscal year ended April 30, 1996, is illustrated as follows:

KIRBY PRODUCTS, INC.
INCOME STATEMENT
FOR THE YEAR ENDED APRIL 30, 1996

Net sales		$1,283,480
Cost of goods sold		756,560
Gross margin		$ 526,920
Selling expenses:		
Sales salaries	$79,940	
Advertising	31,870	
Travel and entertainment	6,460	
Freight and delivery	4,850	
Depreciation	6,140	$ 129,260
General and administrative expenses:		
Officers' salaries	$53,180	
Office salaries	38,870	
Taxes	7,610	
Insurance	1,740	
Utilities	6,480	
Uncollectible accounts expense	6,760	
Amortization of organization expense	2,450	
Amortization of goodwill	4,000	
Depreciation	1,050	122,140
Total operating expenses		$ 251,400
Operating income		$ 275,520
Other revenue and expense:		
Interest and dividends earned	$ 5,320	
Rent revenue	8,600	
	$13,920	
Less interest expense	9,340	4,580
Income before income tax		$ 280,100
Estimated income tax		139,600
Income before extraordinary loss		$ 140,500
Loss on fire at Woodward plant (net of tax saving of $19,000)		21,000
Net income		$ 119,500
Earnings per share of stock		$ 23.90

Operating Revenue

The revenue resulting from the predominant activities of the business is listed first and is called the **operating revenue**. The gross operating revenue is often reduced by customer returns and allowances and cash discounts in arriving at net operating revenue. Kirby Products, Inc. earns gross operating revenue by making sales to customers; and this revenue has been reduced by returns and allowances and cash discounts in arriving at the net sales of $1,283,480.

Cost of Goods Sold

If a company is engaged in selling goods, the cost of goods sold is computed and is deducted from the net sales to obtain the gross margin. The cost of goods sold can be computed quite easily as shown below:

1. Finished goods available at the beginning of the fiscal period + Cost of goods manufactured or purchased during the fiscal period = Cost of goods available for sale during the fiscal period

2. Cost of goods available for sale during the fiscal period − Finished goods available at the end of the fiscal period = Cost of goods sold

Gross Margin

The gross margin of $526,920 is equal to the net sales of $1,283,480 reduced by the cost of goods sold of $756,560. **Gross margin** measures the difference between the net revenue realized from the sale of goods and their cost. No final profit has been earned at this point, of course, because operating expenses and other revenue and expenses must be considered. However, the gross margin is significant. The relationship between the gross margin and net sales may be expressed as a percentage, and a comparison of gross margin percentages between years may reveal that selling prices are increasing or decreasing relative to the cost of goods sold. Or it may reveal a change in a mix of products sold. Under certain conditions, gross margin percentages can also be used to estimate the amount of inventory that should be available.

If an inventory has been destroyed or stolen, an insurance claim can be established by using the typical gross margin percentage to estimate the amount of the inventory loss. The cost of goods sold up to the time of the loss is estimated to be equal to the complement of the gross margin percentage multiplied by net sales. The estimated cost of goods sold is then subtracted from the cost of the goods that were available for sale to arrive at an estimated cost of the inventory at the time of the loss. The cost of the goods available for sale is equal to the cost of the inventory at the beginning of the fiscal period plus the cost of purchases or goods manufactured to the point of the loss.

Operating Expenses

The expenses of operating the business are classified according to function and are deducted from the gross margin to arrive at the operating income.

Expenses of promoting, selling, and distributing products are classified as **selling expenses** and include such items as advertising, sales commissions, delivery expense, sales supplies used, travel and entertainment, and sales office rent. The general expenses of business administration are classified as **general and administrative expenses** and include such items as officers' salaries, office salaries, office supplies used, taxes, insurance, and uncollectible accounts expense.

Other Revenue and Expense

Various incidental or miscellaneous revenue and expenses not related to the main operating purpose of the business are combined with the operating income in the computation of income before income tax. In this example, interest, dividends, and rents were earned, and interest expense was incurred.

Income Tax

Corporate federal income tax is as much an expense for an incorporated business as any other operating expense. Yet it is usually shown separately near the bottom of the statement because **(1)** it is based upon the taxable income or loss for the period, and **(2)** it is usually a significant amount.

Extraordinary Gains and Losses

Unusual gains and losses that are not expected to recur are shown as **extraordinary gains and losses.** Extraordinary items are strictly defined. In order to qualify as an extraordinary item, a transaction or event must be both unusual in nature and infrequent in occurrence; and the amount must be substantial. The definition of "unusual" depends on the nature of the business and the environment in which it operates. For example, the gain or loss from the retirement of plant assets would not be considered unusual in most circumstances and, hence, should not be reported as an extraordinary gain or loss. On the other hand, a fire loss or a loss from some natural disaster, if substantial in amount and both unusual in nature and infrequent in occurrence, would be classified as extraordinary on the income statement. Extraordinary items are shown on the income statement net of the related income tax. Note, for example, that the fire loss in the income statement would have been $40,000 before tax.

Net Income

The final result on the income statement is labeled net income if the revenue and gains exceed the expenses and losses. Otherwise, the net result is labeled a net loss.

Earnings Per Share

Those who read financial reports look for the earnings per share of stock. If only one class of stock outstanding exists with no complexities in the equity structure, the computation can be made quite easily by dividing the number of shares of outstanding stock into the net income. For Kirby Products, Inc., the earnings per share were computed at $23.90 ($119,500 net income ÷ 5,000 outstanding shares). With two or more classes of stock outstanding or with senior securities (bonds or preferred stock) that may be converted to common stock, the computation becomes more complicated. The rights to earnings by security holders other than the common stockholders must be considered before computing the earnings per share of common stock.

BALANCE SHEET, END OF FISCAL YEAR

A balance sheet for Kirby Products, Inc. at the end of the fiscal year April 30, 1996 is shown on page 1003.

A STATEMENT OF CHANGES IN RETAINED EARNINGS

The **statement of changes in retained earnings** connects the stockholders' equity in retained earnings as shown on the balance sheet with the results as shown on the income statement. Other additions or deductions are also shown in the computation of retained earnings at the end of the fiscal period. A statement of changes in retained earnings for Kirby Products, Inc. is given below. The dividends are a distribution of earnings to the stockholders and are not an expense of doing business. Hence, they are deducted on the statement of changes in retained earnings.

KIRBY PRODUCTS, INC.
STATEMENT OF CHANGES IN RETAINED EARNINGS
FOR THE YEAR ENDED APRIL 30, 1996

Balance of retained earnings, April 30, 1995	$392,850
Add net income for the year	119,500
	$512,350
Less dividends	84,000
Balance of retained earnings, April 30, 1996	$428,350

A CASH FLOW STATEMENT

In addition to a balance sheet, income statement, and a statement of changes in retained earnings, a statement of cash flows is required. Chapter 18 discusses the objectives, the format, and the report's contents.

KIRBY PRODUCTS, INC.
BALANCE SHEET
APRIL 30, 1996

Assets

Current assets:

Cash	$ 40,680	
Marketable securities at cost (market value, $74,200)	71,740	
Notes receivable	14,000	
Accounts receivable $ 94,380		
Less allowances for discounts, returns, allowances, and doubtful accounts 2,870	91,510	
Inventories	96,400	
Prepaid insurance	2,080	$316,410
Investment in bonds of Konrad Inc.		50,000

Plant assets:

Land	$ 14,600	
Building and equipment $381,150		
Less accumulated depreciation 45,390	335,760	350,360

Intangible assets:

Organization expense	$ 2,450	
Goodwill	24,000	26,450

Other assets:

Advances to company officers		8,500
Total assets		$751,720

Equities

Current liabilities:

Bank loans	$ 10,000	
Accounts payable	31,250	
Accrued payroll and other expenses	25,420	
Estimated income tax payable	46,500	$113,170
Long-term notes, due August 31, 2007		75,000
Deferred rental revenue		2,700

Stockholders' equity:

Capital stock, $10 par value, 5,000 shares issued and outstanding	$ 50,000	
Premium on stock	82,500	
Retained earnings	428,350	560,850
Total equities		$751,720

PROBLEMS

A-1. Journal Entries, Ledger, and Trial Balance. Eleanor Keefer owns and operates Western Record Store. A post-closing trial balance at June 30, 1995, is as follows:

WESTERN RECORD STORE
POST-CLOSING TRIAL BALANCE
JUNE 30, 1995

	Debit	Credit
Cash	3,450	
Accounts Receivable	1,730	
Merchandise Inventory	2,340	
Accounts Payable		2,170
Eleanor Keefer, Capital		5,350
	7,520	7,520

Transactions for the month of July are summarized as follows:

(a) Merchandise costing $6,180 was purchased on credit terms.

(b) Rent for the store and equipment in the amount of $250 was paid for the month of July.

(c) Merchandise was sold to customers on credit terms in the amount of $8,740.

(d) Payment of wages for the month was made in the amount of $980.

(e) A payment of $90 was made for electric service in July.

(f) Cash of $9,300 was collected on accounts receivable.

(g) Keefer withdrew $1,500 during the month for personal use.

Required:

1. Prepare journal entries to record the transactions.
2. Record the balances at June 30 in ledger accounts. Post the journal entries to the ledger accounts.
3. Prepare a trial balance at July 31. (Add ledger accounts as needed.)

A-2. **Adjusting Entries and Adjusted Trial Balance.** Transactions for the month of August, 1995, have been recorded by journal entry and posted to the ledger accounts of Magill Furnishings. A trial balance at August 31, 1995, appears below:

MAGILL FURNISHINGS
TRIAL BALANCE
AUGUST 31, 1995

	Debit	Credit
Cash	4,370	
Accounts Receivable	8,260	
Allowance for Doubtful Accounts		320
Merchandise Inventory, July 31	4,190	
Prepaid Insurance	330	
Equipment	11,400	
Accumulated Depreciation—Equipment		1,500
Accounts Payable		3,270
Advances from Customers		800
Thomas Magill, Capital		12,920
Sales		43,700
Purchases	31,200	
Wages Expense	1,750	
Advertising Expense	680	
Utilities Expense	330	
	62,510	62,510

Data to be used for making adjustments are given as follows:
- **(a)** Advertising incurred for the month amounted to $760, but only $680 of this amount was paid and recorded.
- **(b)** Some of the equipment was rented to another store during the month at an agreed rental of $200 for the month. Magill did not collect any of the rent during the month.
- **(c)** Customers paid $800 in advance for merchandise to be delivered at a later date. The collection was recorded as a credit to Advances from Customers. During August, deliveries of $650 were made against the advances.
- **(d)** The prepaid insurance of $330 provides insurance coverage for 11 months.
- **(e)** Depreciation for the month of August has been estimated at $50.
- **(f)** The estimated sales during August that will not be collectible are $600.
- **(g)** Inventory at the end of August has been counted and assigned a cost of $3,840.

Required:

Prepare a form with seven columns and label the column headings as follows:

Accounts	Trial Balance		Adjustments		Adjusted Trial Balance	
	Dr.	Cr.	Dr.	Cr.	Dr.	Cr.

Copy the trial balance in the first pair of columns. Enter adjustment information as debits and credits in the second pair of columns opposite the appropriate accounts. Add account titles as necessary. Combine the data in the trial balance and adjustment columns and extend final amounts to the adjusted trial balance columns.

A-3. **Adjusting Entries and Statements.** A trial balance is given for Selden Company at March 31, 1995. Financial statements and closing entries were last made on December 31, 1994.

SELDEN COMPANY
TRIAL BALANCE
MARCH 31, 1995

	Debit	Credit
Cash	14,300	
Accounts Receivable	17,600	
Merchandise Inventory	19,400	
Prepaid Rent	4,800	
Equipment	47,000	
Accumulated Depreciation—Equipment		8,000
Accounts Payable		15,300
Capital Stock		20,000
Retained Earnings		34,100
Sales		135,000
Purchases	84,600	
Wages Expense	16,700	
Taxes and Insurance	4,300	
Heat and Light	3,700	
	212,400	212,400

Adjustment data are as follows:
(a)   Rent has been prepaid for the entire year, beginning January 1.
(b)   Total wages earned by employees amounted to $18,600 in the first quarter. A large portion of this amount has been paid and recorded.
(c)   Depreciation of equipment for the quarter has been estimated at $500.
(d)   The inventory at the end of March has been counted and assigned a cost of $20,800.

Required:
1.   Set up ledger accounts from the trial balance and enter balances at March 31.
2.   Enter adjustment data directly in the ledger accounts. Open up new ledger accounts as needed.
3.   Prepare an adjusted trial balance, an income statement for the first quarter of the year, and a balance sheet at March 31, 1995.
4.   Enter closing entries directly in the ledger accounts. **5.** Prepare a post-closing trial balance at March 31, 1995.

A-4.   Financial Statements. An adjusted trial balance is given for Van Kirk Company with the accounts in random sequence.

VAN KIRK COMPANY
ADJUSTED TRIAL BALANCE
SEPTEMBER 30, 1995

	Debit	Credit
Cost of Goods Sold	146,300	
Wages Expense	18,400	
Wages Payable		1,200
Accounts Payable		32,500
Notes Payable—Long-Term		50,000
Land	6,000	
Accounts Receivable	19,200	
Cash	31,800	
Building and Equipment	145,000	
Sales		220,000
Advertising Expense	1,600	
Prepaid Rent	3,000	
Capital Stock, $1 par value		40,000
Rent Expense	1,200	
Depreciation Expense—Building and Equipment	3,000	
Merchandise Inventory, September 30	24,300	
Estimated Income Tax Payable		7,000
Accumulated Depreciation—Building and Equipment		18,000
Heat and Light Expense	2,600	
Taxes and Insurance Expense	3,400	
Income Tax Expense	17,000	
Dividends	10,000	
Retained Earnings		65,100
Interest Expense	1,000	
	433,800	433,800

Required:
    Prepare an income statement for the fiscal quarter ended September 30, and prepare a classified balance sheet for September 30.

A-5.   **The Accounting Cycle.** A post-closing trial balance for Angela Burns, Inc. at June 30, 1995 is as follows:

ANGELA BURNS, INC.
POST-CLOSING TRIAL BALANCE
JUNE 30, 1995

	Debit	Credit
Cash	14,100	
Accounts Receivable	36,500	
Allowance for Doubtful Accounts		600
Merchandise Inventory, June 30, 1995	14,800	
Prepaid Rent	2,400	
Equipment	56,000	
Accumulated Depreciation—Equipment		12,000
Accounts Payable		6,500
Notes Payable		30,000
Capital Stock		25,000
Retained Earnings		49,700
	123,800	123,800

Transactions for the following quarter ended September 30 are summarized as follows:

(1)   Sales to customers on credit terms amounted to $104,000.
(2)   An account receivable in the amount of $200 was written off as uncollectible.
(3)   Merchandise costing $58,000 was purchased on account.
(4)   Employees' wages of $8,100 were paid during the quarter.
(5)   Cash of $93,700 was collected on the accounts receivable.
(6)   Cash of $12,000 was paid to acquire new equipment.
(7)   Advertising was used and paid in the amount of $3,800.
(8)   Heat and light expense for the quarter was paid in the amount of $4,700.
(9)   Income tax for the quarter has been estimated at $10,000.
(10)   Payments on accounts payable during the quarter amounted to $61,000.
(11)   Dividends of $4,000 were paid during the quarter. Record in an account entitled Dividends.

Adjustment data:
(a)   It has been estimated that sales in the amount of $1,000 will be uncollectible.
(b)   The inventory at September 30 has been counted and assigned a cost of $15,600.
(c)   Prepaid rent at June 30 consisted of rent for the last six months of the year.
(d)   Depreciation on the equipment has been estimated at $1,400 for the quarter.
(e)   Interest on the notes payable is at the annual rate of 8%.

Required:
1.   Prepare journal entries to record the transactions for the quarter ended September 30.
2.   Post the journal entries to ledger accounts. Set up ledger accounts as needed with beginning balances when appropriate.
3.   Prepare journal entries to record the adjustments for the quarter ended September 30.
4.   Post the journal entries to ledger accounts.
5.   Prepare an adjusted trial balance.
6.   Prepare an income statement for the quarter and a balance sheet at September 30, 1995.
7.   Prepare closing journal entries and post the entries to the ledger accounts.
8.   Prepare a post-closing trial balance at September 30, 1995.

❖ APPENDIX B

THE TIME VALUE OF MONEY

An amount of money to be received in the future is not equivalent to the same amount of money to be received now. When confronted with a choice, anyone would rather have $100 today, for example, than $100 two years from now. The $100 that is available today can be invested to return more than $100 two years from now. The time value of money can be compared with the visual perspective of distance as shown in the following illustration.

$100 Two Years Later

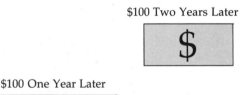

$100 One Year Later

$100 Today

Figure B.1   Future Value of Money

With physical objects at a distance, the objects appear to be smaller but are in reality as large as similar objects that are close at hand. In the case of money, however, it is no illusion. The future value of money is the compound amount of any principal for a specified time period.

A future sum of money is of less value than the same amount of money today. This is because money today will grow to a larger sum through investment. For example, $100 invested at 10 percent compound interest per year will grow to $121 at the end of two years.

$100 initial investment × 1.10 = $110, amount at the end of Year 1
$110 amount at the end of Year 1 × 1.10 = $121, amount at the end of Year 2

The $100 received today has a future value of $121 by the end of two years and thus is larger than $100 to be received at the end of two years.

The investment principal plus **compound interest** is called the **compound amount**. The compound amount of $100 in two years, with interest compounded at the rate of 10 percent annually, is $121. The formula for the compound amount of $1 follows:

$$\text{Compound amount} = (1 + i)^n$$
$$i = \text{interest rate}$$
$$n = \text{number of years}$$

In the example given, the compound amount could be computed as follows.

Compound amount of $1 $\quad = \quad (1.10)^2$

Compound amount of $1 $\quad = \quad \$1.21$

Compound amount of $100 $\quad = \quad 100 \times \$1.21$, or $121

A person who can earn 10 percent compound interest looks upon the receipt of $121 in two years as being equivalent to $100 today, assuming certainty. Such a person is indifferent as to whether he or she has $100 today or $121 in two years.

By way of comparison, assume the interest rate is zero. In this case, a person would be indifferent between $100 now and $100 two years from now, assuming no uncertainty. That is, when the interest rate is zero, $(1 + i)^2 = (1)^2 = 1$. However, when the interest rate is positive, the right to receive $1 today will be worth more than the right to receive $1 a few years from now. The strength of that preference is a measure of the magnitude of the interest rate, and it becomes a means of establishing the point of indifference between an amount of money to be received now as compared with an amount to be received in the future.

Obviously, many business decisions involve the **investment** of dollars with the expectation that more dollars will be received at some future time. In making the investment decision, the future cash inflows (returns) are compared with the investment outlay. The returns and the investment, however, are not on the same time basis. Before a comparison can be made, the present and future dollars must be stated on an equivalent time basis.[1] Present dollars can be placed on a future dollar basis; that is, the compound amount of a present investment can be computed. If a person has $100 available for investment and believes that a 10 percent return with interest compounded annually can be earned, he or she will expect to receive $121 at the end of two years from a present investment of $100. Hence, an investment opportunity that is expected to yield $115 in two years from a present investment of $100 is unacceptable if $121 can normally be expected from a $100 investment. In short, the potential investor does not believe that $115 in two years is equivalent to $100 today if he or she can expect to receive $121 from other investment opportunities.

---

[1]The adjustments to place monetary amounts of an equivalent time basis should not be confused with price-level adjustments. The two adjustments are made for different purposes. Differences in timing must be recognized even if the price level remains the same.

Let us consider some additional observations on the example just given. In a situation in which $100 can be invested to return $121 in two years, the return on investment is 10 percent compounded annually. So the compound rate of interest, 10 percent, is a measure of return on investment (ROI), or the rate of return, as it is sometimes called. Also, note that if a decision maker has a choice of investments for the $100, he or she will prefer the investment with the highest ROI (other things equal—such as the degree of uncertainty). The reason, of course, is that the investment opportunity with the highest ROI will yield the largest future amount. It is assumed that investors wish to maximize future wealth, and the highest return on investment opportunity will lead to this outcome. Consider, for example, an alternative investment which will earn 15 percent interest. Assuming certainty, the compound amount of the $100 at 15 percent for two years is:

$$\$100 \times (1.15)^2 = \$100 \times 1.3225 = \$132.25$$

Since $132.25 is larger than $121 (the compound amount of $100 in two years at 10 percent investment), the project earning 15 percent is preferred to the project earning 10 percent.

PRESENT VALUE OF MONEY

It is also possible to calculate the present value of an amount of money to be received at some point in the future. Although capital investment decisions can be analyzed using future value analysis as discussed, it is conventional and typically easier to use present value analysis.

How much money must be invested today in order to receive a certain amount of money in the future? A debtor may look at the situation from a different point of view. How much money must be paid now to settle a debt that will become due in the future? In business, a choice must often be made between having a given amount of money now or the prospect of receiving a monetary return in the future. Does the expected future return justify the investment? This can be determined by computing the present value of the future return and comparing it with the amount invested.

The **present value** of a future amount of money (compound amount) can be computed by multiplying the future amount by the present value of $1. The formula for the present value of $1 follows:

$$
\begin{aligned}
\text{Present value of \$1} &= 1 \div (1 + i)^n \\
i &= \text{interest rate} \\
n &= \text{number of years}
\end{aligned}
$$

Assume, for example, that $121 is to be received two years from now and the compound annual rate of interest is 10 percent. How much money must be invested today to get $121 at the end of two years?

Solve for the present value of $1 in two years with interest compounded annually at 10 percent.

Present value of \$1 for 2 years at 10% interest $= 1 \div (1.10)^2$

Present value of \$1 for 2 years at 10% interest $= .826446$

Present value of \$121 for 2 years at 10% interest $= \$121 \times .826446$ or \$100

The computation could also be made as follows:

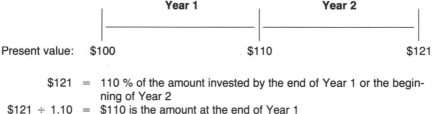

	Year 1		Year 2

Present value: \$100   \$110   \$121

$\$121 = $ 110 % of the amount invested by the end of Year 1 or the beginning of Year 2

$\$121 \div 1.10 = \$110$ is the amount at the end of Year 1

$\$110 = $ 110 % of the amount invested at the beginning of Year 1 (present value)

$\$110 \div 1.10 = \$100$ is the amount invested at the beginning of Year 1, or at time point 0

This is summarized as follows:

$$(\$121 \div 1.10) \div 1.10 = \$121 \div (1.10)^2$$

or

$$[1 \div (1.10)^2] \times \$121 = \$100 \text{ present value}$$

In comparing the future compound amount with the present value, it can be seen that the difference is the interest earned on the investment. The dollar amount of interest, of course, depends on the interest rate. At 10 percent, the total dollar interest for two years is \$21 and the following is true:

Present value (\$100) = Compound amount (\$121) − the dollar interest at 10 % (\$21)

The process of reducing a (future) compound amount to a present value is called **discounting**. The present value is sometimes called the **discounted value**. The dollar interest is called the **dollar discount**, and the rate of interest is called the **discount rate**.

It is seldom necessary to calculate either compound amounts or present values as shown here. Published tables giving both present values and future values are available. Calculators and spreadsheet software easily perform the same functions. Since it is conventional to analyze capital investment problems using present value analysis, the tables at the end of the book give present value factors for various discount (interest) rates for various time periods expressed in years. Table I gives the present value of \$1 to be received at the end of the various time periods at interest or discount rates shown across the top row of the table. Thus, it is a tabulation in decimal form of the factor $1 \div (1 + i)^n$, where n is the number of years and i is the interest or discount rate. The factor for two years at 10 percent is .826, and the present value (PV) of \$121 to be received in two years can be calculated as follows.

$$PV = \$121 \times .826$$
or
$$PV = \$100 \text{ (rounded)}$$

The factors appearing in Tables I and II are rounded to the third digit, which is sufficient precision for most capital investment problems. As is apparent, the availability of tables makes the calculation of present values much simpler than the methods used in the preceding discussion.

THE PRESENT VALUE OF A SERIES OF FUTURE CASH FLOWS

As an example, a machine investment costing $10,000 in cash produces a stream of cash inflows of $3,000 each year. A series of annual cash inflows are characteristic of the typical investment project rather than the one-time cash inflow as illustrated in the preceding section. These future cash flows represent an annuity into the future. An **annuity**, in essence, is a series of cash flows over a period of time. In capital investment decisions, it has the special meaning of a series of equal cash flows received or paid over equal time intervals. The time interval for most decisions is annual, but any time interval (a day, week, month, quarter, etc.) is appropriate, depending on the interest rate compounding and the nature of the investment alternative.

How can the present value of a series of annual cash flows be calculated? The method of calculation depends on whether the cash flows are equal (an annuity) or unequal. In either case, however, the underlying concepts are the same.

The present value of a series of annual returns is the sum of the present values of the individual returns. Assume that $1,000 is to be received at the end of each year for five years. What is the present value of these five annual receipts of $1,000 at a discount (interest) rate of 10 percent? The present value can be computed as follows:

End of Year	Returns	Computation		Explanation
1	$1,000	$1,000 \times \dfrac{1}{1.10}$	= $909	present value of $1,000 received at end of Year 1
2	1,000	$1,000 \times \dfrac{1}{(1.10)^2}$	= 826	present value of $1,000 received at end of Year 2
3	1,000	$1,000 \times \dfrac{1}{(1.10)^3}$	= 751	present value of $1,000 received at end of Year 3
4	1,000	$1,000 \times \dfrac{1}{(1.10)^4}$	= 683	present value of $1,000 received at end of Year 4
5	1,000	$1,000 \times \dfrac{1}{(1.10)^5}$	= 621	present value of $1,000 received at end of Year 5

Present value of $1,000 received at the end of each year for 5 years: = $3,790

The present value can also be computed as follows.

$$\$1{,}000 \left[\frac{1}{1.10} + \frac{1}{(1.10)^2} + \frac{1}{(1.10)^3} + \frac{1}{(1.10)^4} + \frac{1}{(1.10)^5} \right] = \$3{,}790$$

The decimal equivalents of the fractions in the equation can be found in the table of present values of $1 (Table I):

$$(.909 + .826 + .751 + .683 + .621) = 3.790$$

The sum of the present values is 3.790, and the present value of $1,000 received each year for five years at 10 percent interest compounded annually is $3,790:

$$\$1{,}000 \times 3.790 = \$3{,}790$$

Note that the factor, 3.791, can be read from Table II at the end of the book, using the 10 percent rate column and the 5 period row. The difference between the amount just calculated and the amount appearing in the table is due to rounding. The factors in Table II (Present Value of $1 Received Periodically for N Periods) are the sum of the present value factors given in Table I. The following calculations using interest rates of 6 percent, 8 percent, and 10 percent for 5 years illustrate this point.

PRESENT VALUE OF $1 RECEIVED ANNUALLY FOR 5 YEARS AT:

	6 %		8 %		10 %	
Years	Table I	Table II	Table I	Table II	Table I	Table II
1	.943		.926		.909	
2	.890		.857		.826	
3	.840		.794		.751	
4	.792		.735		.683	
5	.747		.681		.621	
Total	4.212	4.212	3.993	3.993	3.790*	3.791*

* Difference due to rounding.

When calculating the present value of a stream of equal annual cash flows, it is easier to add the yearly factors and make one multiplication than it is to make several multiplications and then add. Therefore, it is convenient to have Table II for evaluating series of equal annual cash flows.

If the annual cash flows are not of equal amounts, then it is necessary to use Table 1. For example, to calculate the present value of a series of unequal annual amounts to be received at the end of each year, the following calculation using Table I is necessary (assume a 10 percent discount rate is to be used).

Year	Amount To Be Received at the End of Each Year	Table I Present Value Factor at 10%	Present Values
1	$1,000	.909	$ 909.00
2	800	.826	660.80
3	700	.751	525.70
4	600	.683	409.80
5	200	.621	124.20
	Present value of the series of cash flows at 10 %:		$2,629.50

COMPARISON OF PRESENT VALUE AND FUTURE VALUE OF A SERIES OF CASH FLOWS

An earlier discussion illustrated the relationship between the present value and future value (compound amount) of a single amount to be received two years hence. Using a 10 percent interest (discount) rate, the present value of $121 received at the end of two years was $100. Under certainty, a person would be indifferent between $100 now and $121 two years from now at a 10 percent interest rate, because $100 would grow to $121 in two years at 10 percent compound interest.

A similar relationship exists between the present values of a stream of payments. For example, the present value of $100 received at the end of each year for five years at 10 percent is $379.10, as calculated earlier. Under certainty, the decision maker would be indifferent between $379.10 now or $100 to be received at the end of each year for five years. The $379.10 and the $100 at the end of each year for five years will both grow to the same future (compound) amount at the end of 5 years. This is shown by the following calculations:

Year	Amount of Investment at the Beginning of Each Year		Interest at 10%		Amount of Investment at End of Each Year
1	$379.10	+	$37.91	=	$417.01
2	417.01	+	41.70	=	458.71
3	458.71	+	45.87	=	504.58
4	504.58	+	50.46	=	555.04
5	555.04	+	55.50	=	610.54*

Year	Amount Invested at the Beginning of Each Year		Interest at 10%		Additional Investment at End of Each Year		Total Amount of Investment at End of Year
1	$ .00	+	$ .00	+	$100.00	=	$100.00
2	100.00	+	10.00	+	100.00	=	210.00
3	210.00	+	21.00	+	100.00	=	331.00
4	331.00	+	33.10	+	100.00	=	464.10
5	464.10	+	46.41	+	100.00	=	610.51*

* Difference of 3 cents due to rounding.

As can be seen, then, either present value or future value analysis could be used to analyze the time value of money, even when a series of annual cash flows is involved. As stated previously, it is usually easier to use present value analysis. Keep in mind that the assumed objective is to maximize future wealth. But the decision is being made now; and, generally, we want to compare cash values as of today. The present value method accomplishes that result.

PRESENT VALUE WITH CASH FLOW AT THE BEGINNING OF THE PERIOD

Up to this point, the assumption has been that cash flows occur at the end of each time interval. In many cases, the cash inflow or outflow is in advance—at the beginning of each interval. How does this change the present value analysis?

As an illustration, Dean's Office Services is in need of new word processing software. Terms of purchase are $300 at the beginning of each quarter for four quarters, with the first payment (a down payment) due now. The situation is identical to a future stream of cash flows at the end of each quarter for three quarters plus the initial investment. Assuming an interest rate of 16 percent compounded quarterly, the following calculation yields the present value of the software (the price that could be paid today in cash).

Quarter	4 % Quarterly Rate (Table 1)	Payment	Present Value
1	0.962	$300	$ 288.60
2	0.925	300	277.50
3	0.889	300	266.70
Total	2.776*		$ 832.80
Plus down payment			300.00
Present value of the software:			$1,132.80

* Table II gives a factor of 2.775. The difference is due to rounding.

As a general rule, given n payments due at the beginning of each time interval, treat the first payment to occur at time point zero and the remaining $n - 1$ payments as occurring at the end of $n - 1$ time intervals.

PRESENT VALUE ANALYSIS APPLIED

In the concluding section of this chapter, several basic applications of present value analysis will be discussed. Present values are important to a variety of analyses in business activities. Among these are:

1. Pricing and valuing fixed-return investments in securities.
2. Determining lease payments.
3. Determining monthly payments for mortgages and other borrowings.
4. Funding pension funds.
5. Making long-term relevant costing decisions (**capital budgeting** decisions).

All include cash outflows and cash inflows over a series of time payments. The primary focus will be on examples that illustrate the time value of money.

FINANCIAL DECISION EXAMPLES

Let us consider the time value of money aspects of some financial decisions. In these cases, the time value of money and financial markets interact to create security prices and accounting values which will need to be recorded.

Issuing a Bond Payable

When a bond is issued, two promises are made by the issuer to the purchaser:

1. To repay the principal amount (often called the *face value*) at maturity
2. To pay interest periodically at the rate stated in the bond agreement (often called the **coupon rate**)

The value of the bond in the market place depends on many factors such as the credit worthiness of the issuer, the length of time to maturity, the promised interest rate, and the **market rate of interest** for similar securities. The two promises are for future cash payments of specific known amounts. Thus, the sum of the present values of the two promises is the market price of the bond. The discount rate to be used is the market rate of interest. The higher the market rate of interest, the lower the value of the bond. The lower the market rate of interest, the higher the value of the bond.

Because of a likely difference between the market rate of interest and the rate stated in the bond agreement, a **discount** or **premium** occurs frequently when bonds are issued. How does the discount or premium arise? To illustrate, assume that a company issues a 10-year bond of $100,000 par value with a coupon or stated rate of interest of 10 percent. Assume that interest is paid at the end of each year rather than semiannually, which is normally the case. A bond contract of this type would call for the following schedule of cash payments.

Year	Interest at 10% of Face Value	Repayment of Principal	Total Cash Outflow
1	$10,000		$ 10,000
2	10,000		10,000
3	10,000		10,000
•	•		•
•	•		•
9	10,000		10,000
10	10,000	$100,000	110,000

If the bond is sold (issued) at par value, the interest cost to the issuer is 10 percent. The rate of interest return to the buyer of the bond is also 10 percent. The present value of the future cash payments specified by the bond contract is $100,000 at a 10 percent discount rate. This is illustrated as follows.

Promise 1:

$100,000 × present value of $1 received at the end of 10 years at 10 percent.

Promise 2:

$10,000 × present value of $1 received each year for 10 years at 10 percent.

Calculations:

From Table I:	$100,000 × .386 =	$ 38,600
From Table II:	$10,000 × 6.145 =	61,450
		$100,050*

* Difference from $100,000 due to rounding in present value factors.

As can be seen, to the buyer of the bond, the present value of the $10,000 interest payments at the end of each year for 10 years is $61,450. The present value of the principal repayment at the end of 10 years is $38,600. The total present value is $100,000, the face value of the bond (allowing for rounding error).

However, suppose that the current market rate of interest for bonds of this particular type (i.e., given the 10-year life of the bond and this particular risk) is 12 percent. In this case, an investor would not be willing to buy the bond at face value, because he or she could earn 12 percent by investing in other similar bonds selling in the current market. In order to sell the bond, the company would presumably have to increase the bond rate of interest or sell the bond at a price less than face value. Selling at below face would allow the buyer to increase the rate of return from the investment. If the $100,000, 10-year, 10 percent bond is sold at a discount, the amount of the discount would be the difference between the face value of $100,000 and the present value of the cash flow discounted at 12 percent (the market rate of interest).

Promise 1:	$100,000 × .322 (10 periods at 12% from Table I)	= $32,200
Promise 2:	$10,000 × 5.650 (10 payments at 12% from Table II)	= 56,500
	Proceeds from sale of bond	= $88,700
	Bond discount:	$100,000 − $88,700 = $11,300

The investor that purchases the bond at $88,700 (a discount of $11,300) will earn 12 percent interest on the $88,700 invested. The 12 percent earned is usually called the **yield** or the effective rate of interest. An **effective interest rate** is the actual interest earned in a year regardless of the compounding period of the stated interest rate. The accounting for the investment and interest income over the ten years by the buyer is as follows:

Year	Beginning Balance of Investment	Interest Income 12% of Investment	Cash Interest Received	Amortization of Discount	Ending Balance of Investment
1	$88,700	$10,644	$10,000	$ 644	$89,344
2	89,344	10,721	10,000	721	90,065
3	90,065	10,808	10,000	808	90,873
4	90,873	10,905	10,000	905	91,778
5	91,778	11,013	10,000	1,013	92,791
6	92,791	11,135	10,000	1,135	93,926
7	93,926	11,271	10,000	1,271	95,197
8	95,197	11,424	10,000	1,424	96,621
9	96,621	11,595	10,000	1,595	98,216
10	98,216	11,786	10,000	1,786	100,002*

* Difference from $100,000 due to rounding of present value factors.

Notice that the interest income grows annually as the investment amount grows. This in turn increases the rate of amortization of the discount until the investment reaches the face value of $100,000.

Likewise, if the current market rate of interest, or market yield, is 8 percent, an investor would be willing to pay a premium for a bond with a 10 percent coupon interest rate. The total amount to be paid would be the present value of the future cash flows at 8 percent. The premium would be the difference between the present value at 8 percent and the face value (which is the present value of the cash flow at 10 percent, as shown earlier).

Promise 1:	$100,000 × .463 (10 periods at 8% from Table I)	=	$ 46,300
Promise 2:	$10,000 × 6.710 (10 payments at 8% from Table II)	=	67,100
	Proceeds from sale of bond	=	$113,400
	Bond premium:	$113,400 − $100,000	=	$ 13,400

As noted earlier, most bonds pay semiannual interest. A 10 percent semiannual interest-paying bond would pay 5 percent twice a year. Because half of the interest each year is received after each 6-month interval instead of annually, the time value of money will cause small differences in the present values of the two promises. To find the present value for a semiannual interest paying bond, the interest rate is halved and the number of periods is doubled. In the prior example, a 10-year, 10 percent bond becomes a 20-period, 5 percent instrument for cash flow purposes. The market rate of interest of 8 percent is also halved to 4 percent (for a market return for 6 months). Investment market convention says that both the principal and interest cash flows will use the semiannual periods and rates. Repeating the prior example but assuming semiannual interest payments shows:

Promise 1:	$100,000 × .456 (20 periods at 4% from Table I)	=	$ 45,600
Promise 2:	$5,000 × 13.59 (20 payments at 4% from Table II)	=	67,950
	Proceeds from sale of bond	=	$113,550
	Bond premium:	$113,550 − $100,000	=	$ 13,550

Notice that the increase in market value is $150 ($113,550 − $113,400). This is due solely to speeding up half the interest payment each year by 6 months and the increased time value of money from that change.

Borrowing and Repaying Loans

As another example, consider a situation in which a bank is willing to loan you money for five years at 10 percent, but instead of paying annual interest, you repay the loan and the interest in one payment at the end of five years. If you need $100,000 now, how much would you have to repay in five years? The amount to be repaid in five years would have to be an amount whose present value now at 10 percent and for 5 years is $100,000 (the amount borrowed today).

$100,000	=	Amount owed in 5 years × Present value of $1 at the end of 5 years at 10 %
$100,000	=	Amount owed in 5 years × .621 (from Table I)
Amount owed in 5 years	=	$100,000 ÷ .621 = $161,031 (rounded)

As is probably apparent, future value analysis could have been used to calculate the repayment at the end of five years, but since present value tables are available, present value analysis can also be used.

It may seem a little surprising that a 10 percent loan now would require a $61,031 interest payment at the end of five years (i.e., $161,031 repaid − $100,000 borrowed). Compound interest gives some apparently deceptive results. Compound interest of 10 percent will more than double an amount in eight years. This can be seen by the 10% Column in Table I; the present value factor drops to .5 between Period 7 and Period 8 (.513 at the end of Period 7 and .467 in Period 8). If you had borrowed $100,000 for eight years, you would have to repay $214,133 ($100,000 ÷ .467 and rounded). As can be seen from Table I, even 6 percent compound interest will more than double an amount in twelve years.

As yet another example of present value analysis, consider a loan which is paid off in equal annual payments at the end of each year. For example, suppose that you need to borrow $100,000 to buy a home and the lending institutions require 15 percent interest and equal annual payments at the end of each year for the next twenty years. What will be the amount of the annual payments? The present value of the series of twenty payments would have to be $100,000 when discounted at 15 percent.

$100,000	=	Annual payment × Present value of $1 received annually for 20 years at 15 %
$100,000	=	Annual payment × 6.259 (from Table II)
Annual payment	=	$100,000 ÷ 6.259 = $15,977 (rounded)

This may seem rather high, because over the twenty years, you would pay interest and principal of $319,540 (20 years × $15,977) for the $100,000 loan. The total payments would be more than three times the amount of the loan. Keep in mind that we observed earlier that a 10 percent compound rate more than doubles an amount in eight years. In this example we are dealing with a loan of twenty years and an interest rate of 15 percent.

Funding a Pension Contract

Most pension plans are very complex, but to illustrate the basic ideas a simple example is presented. Assume that Suman Kirsh is employed by the Marine Products Corporation. Marine has developed a vested pension plan that gives an employee a retirement pension payment beginning after age 65 and continuing until death. The plan's benefits provide $1,000 per retirement year for each year an employee works for the corporation. For example, Mr. Kirsh has worked for Marine for 10 years and is 45 years old. As of now, the plan promises Mr. Kirsh, that upon his retirement at age 65, he would begin to receive $10,000 per year for his already earned 10 years of service.

Marine is now figuring the pension expense for the current year for Mr. Kirsh. What is its pension expense, and what should it pay into a retirement fund to guarantee the availability of the funds when Mr. Kirsh retires? Marine will make the payment to a pension fund trustee. The trustee currently assumes it can earn a 6 percent return on the investments it makes for Marine. Mr. Kirsh is part of a group that is rated as to life expectancy. At this time, the best estimate is that he will live until he is 85. Longevity tables indicate that he should live 20 years after age 65, requiring 20 payments. The payments begin at the end of his 65th year, on his 66th birthday.

Below is a time line illustrating the key pension events in Mr. Kirsh's career and retirement.

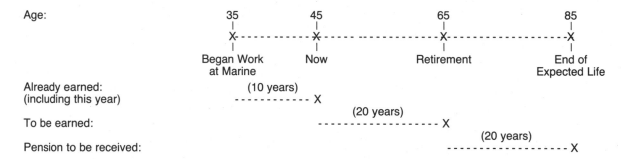

In this simplified example, if Mr. Kirsh were to work for Marine until he is 65, he would receive $30,000 per year until he dies.

This year of work, therefore, earns Mr. Kirsh an additional $1,000 per year for 20 years starting at the end of his 65th year. To calculate Marine's cost for this year (while ignoring a multitude of complicating factors), a two-step present value calculation is needed. First, we find the present value of 20 annual payments of $1,000, using 6 percent interest and Table II.

Present value at 6% of $1,000 per year for
20 periods (from age 65 to 85)   = $1,000 × 11.470 = $11,470

The $11,470 is the present value of one year's benefit as of his 65th birthday, the day he will retire. The second step will find the present value today of his retirement benefit earned this year.

Present value at 6% of a sum of $11,470 owed in 20
   periods (time between today and retirement)   = $11,470 × .312 = $3,579

This year, Marine's cost of pension benefits for Mr. Kirsh is $3,579. Marine would pay that amount to the pension trustee and record that amount as pension expense.

After some thought, it is easy to see one contributor to possible age discrimination—the rising cost of pension expense as employees grow older. Other types of pension programs mitigate this problem, but pension costs of an aging work force is a major cost problem for certain firms. The "Big 3" auto makers have this problem since seniority rules require keeping employees with more years of experience. Yet most foreign transplant auto makers have hired young work forces. The cost differences can be thousands of dollars per employee per year. Even between Chrysler and General Motors, the hourly cost differential could be as much as $5.00 higher cost for Chrysler by the end of the 1990 three-year United Auto Workers agreement with the two companies.

APPROXIMATION OF THE INTEREST RATE

In all of the examples given, the interest rate (or discount rate) was specified. Suppose that a potential investment is proposed and we wish to find the approximate interest rate of return on the investment. Such a rate is called the **internal rate of return** on investment of the project. It is the discount rate which will cause the present value of the future cash inflows to equal the amount of the initial capital investment outlay.

Assume that a friend is interested in borrowing $100 and wants to repay the loan in equal annual installments of $30 at the end of each year for five years. If you make the loan (investment), what interest rate or rate of return will you earn? To approximate the rate, we can find the internal rate of return, which is the rate that will equate the present value of $30 received at the end of each year for 5 years with the $100 investment or loan outlay at the beginning of Year 1.

$100 = $30 × (present value of $1 received annually for 5 years at i% interest)

The amount shown in parentheses is a Table II factor corresponding to the Period 5 row and an interest or discount rate which will be the internal rate of return. Using algebra, then, the Table II factor is:

(5-period factor from Table II) = $100 ÷ $30 = 3.33

To approximate the interest rate of return, we need to find the factor 3.33 in the Period 5 row in Table II. The 15 percent and Period 5 factor is 3.352 and the 16 percent and Period 5 factor is 3.274. Hence, the internal rate of return is between 15 percent and 16 percent. If a return on investment of slightly in excess of 15 percent is acceptable to you, the loan should be made. For most capital investment problems, an approximation of the rate of return is sufficient. Chapter 12 discusses applications of this concept.

PROBLEM FOR REVIEW

Asher Manufacturing Company has several outstanding notes on which it makes periodic payments and three investments in bonds from which it receives periodic income. The notes are as follows:

Note 1: A $10,000, 5-year note with annual payments of $2,638 and a 10 percent interest rate. The final payment is due in one year.

Note 2: A $15,000 note due in three years. Quarterly payments are $984 and the interest rate is 4 percent per quarter (a 16 percent annual rate adjusted to a quarterly payment frequency).

Note 3: A $50,000, 10-year note with annual payments of $8,850 and an interest rate of 12 percent. Seven years remain on the note.

The market rate of interest for bonds of similar financial quality is an effective rate of 12 percent. The bonds owned include:

Investment 1: A $10,000, 10-year, 14 percent bond with semiannual interest payments. Four years remain before maturity.

Investment 2: A $20,000, 10-year, 12 percent bond with semiannual interest payments. Six years remain before maturity.

Investment 3: A $30,000, 20-year, 10 percent bond with semiannual interest payments. Two years remain before maturity.

Required:
Calculate the present value for:

1.   Each note payable
2.   Each bond investment (using the effective interest rate)

Solution:
Part 1: *Notes payable*

The present value of any note payable with periodic payments is the present value of the remaining payments at the interest rate adjusted to the period represented by payment frequency.

Note 1: $2,638 × .909 (Table II, at 10% for 1 period)   = $ 2,397.94
Note 2: $984 × 9.385 (Table II, at 4% for 12 periods)   = $ 9,234.84
Note 3: $8,850 × 4.564 (Table II, at 12% for 7 periods)   = $40,391.40

Part 2: *Bond investments*

The present value of a bond is the present value of remaining interest payments plus the present value of the maturity value using the effective interest rate. The further from maturity date, the greater the impact of the present value of interest payments on the total present value. The closer to maturity date, the greater the impact of present value of the maturity value on the total present value.

Investment 1:	Semiannual interest income: $10,000 × 7 %	= $ 700
	Semiannual periods remaining: 4 years x 2	= 8
	Semiannual effective interest rate: 12 % ÷ 2 periods per year	= 6%
	Promise 1: Present value of principal amount	
	$10,000 × .627 (Table I, at 6% for 8 periods)	= $ 6,270
	Promise 2: Present value of interest income	
	$700 × 6.210 (Table II, at 6% for 8 periods)	= 4,347
	Present value of bond investment:	$10,617

The stated interest rate of 14 percent is higher than the effective interest rate of 12 percent. Therefore, an investor is willing to pay a premium (in this case, $617) for the bond.

Investment 2:	Semiannual interest income: $20,000 × 6 %	= $ 1,200.00
	Semiannual periods remaining: 6 years × 2	= 12
	Semiannual effective interest rate: 12 % ÷ 2 periods per year	= 6%
	Promise 1: Present value of maturity value	
	$20,000 × .497 (Table I, 6 %, 12 periods)	= $ 9,940.00
	Promise 2: Present value of interest income	
	$1,200 × 8.384 (Table II, at 6 %, 12 periods)	= 10,060.80
	Present value of bond investment:	$20,000.80

The stated interest rate of 12 percent is the same as the effective interest rate of 12 percent. Therefore, an investor is willing to pay only the maturity value for the bond. The $0.80 difference between present value and maturity value is due to rounding.

Investment 3:	Semiannual interest income: $30,000 × 5 %	= $ 1,500.00
	Semiannual periods remaining: 2 years × 2	= 4
	Semiannual effective interest rate: 12 % ÷ 2 periods per year	= 6%
	Promise 1: Present value of maturity value	
	$30,000 × .792 (Table I, at 6 % for 4 periods)	= $23,760.00
	Promise 2: Present value of interest income	
	$1,500 × 3.465 (Table II, at 6 % for 4 periods)	= 5,197.50
	Present value of bond investment:	$28,957.50

The stated interest rate of 10 percent is lower than the effective interest rate of 12 percent. Therefore, an investor requires a discount (in this case, $1,042.50) for the bond.

TERMINOLOGY REVIEW

Annuity (1012)
Capital budgeting (1016)
Compound amount (1009)
Compound interest (1009)
Coupon rate (1016)
Discount (1016)
Discount rate (1011)
Discounting (1011)
Dollar discount (1011)
Effective interest rate (1017)

Future value (1008)
Internal rate of return (1021)
Investment (1009)
Market rate of interest (1016)
Premium (1016)
Present value or discounted value (1010)
Time value of money (1008)
Yield (See effective interest rate) (1017)

QUESTIONS FOR REVIEW AND DISCUSSION

1. What is meant by the time value of money?

2. Why are the terms "present value" and "discounting" used to describe the time value of money concept?

3. Explain the basic difference between present value and future value.

4. Using an interest rate of 12 percent as an example, explain the relationship between Table I and Table II.

5. In calculating the present value of future cash inflows or outflows, what three things must either be known or estimated to make the calculation?

6. What is the internal rate of return? How would you approximate such a rate?

7. How can Table I be used to find both the present value of a future amount and the future value of a current amount?

8. What is meant by the term "discount" in time value of money discussions?

9. Why is the market rate of interest needed to find the present value of both promises in a fixed-payment financial contract, such as a corporate bond?

10. If Bond A promises 10 percent interest and pays interest semiannually, and Bond B promises 10 percent interest and pays interest annually, what is the difference between the present values of the interest payments? Assume that both have 10 years to maturity.

11. Distinguish between the coupon rate and effective rate. How is this difference accounted for on a firm's books?

12. What annual payment is needed to pay off a $15,000 loan if the interest rate is 12 percent and if:
    a. Five payments are made with the first payment beginning one year from today?
    b. Five payments are made with the first payment beginning today?

13. If a liability can be deferred forever, what is its present value?

14. Our company owes two amounts. One is $1,000,000 due in 10 years with a present value of $386,000. The other is $1,000,000 due in 9 years with a present value of $424,000. Explain the $38,000 difference.

15. Karen Smith wants to have $2,000 of savings one year from today and she must decide how much to deposit now. She has the choice of a 5 percent passbook savings account or a 6 percent interest-bearing checking account. Which of the two interest rates gives the lower present value? Explain.

EXERCISES

1. **Investment Choices.** If I have the opportunity to earn 16% on invested funds, which of the following choices should I select?

     a. $40,000 per year for 10 years
     b. $300,000 lump sum at the end of year 5
     c. $130,000 now
     d. A promise from a politician to send me $1,000,000
     e. $10 a day forever

2. **College Costs as an Annuity.** Marc Kahn will be starting college in one year. His father wishes to set up an investment for Marc to use for the $7,000 he will need each year for 4 years. Marc will make withdrawals at the beginning of the school years. If Mr. Kahn can invest at 8 percent, how much must he invest today to provide for Marc's college expenses?

3. **Time Value of Money.** Determine the following and show calculations:
     a. A person received a single payment of $12,500 as a result of an investment made 5 years ago at an annual interest rate of 10 percent. How much did the person invest?
     b. An investment opportunity requires a $5,000 payment. It will return a single payment at the end of 5 years. The annual interest rate is 14 percent. How much will be received at the end of 5 years?
     c. An investment of $4,000 returned a single payment of $10,760. The annual interest rate earned was 18 percent. How many years elapsed between the investment and the return?
     d. A person received 7 annual payments of $1,000 from an investment made 7 years ago. The annual interest rate was 10 percent. What was the amount of the investment?
     e. An investment of $5,000 returned $1,006 annually for some years. The annual rate of interest earned was 12 percent. How many payments were received?
     f. A $12,000 investment made today will provide a 12 percent annual return. The returns will be paid in equal amounts over 12 years. What is the amount of the annual payment?

4. **Career Choices.** Huge Muscle is a senior in high school who weighs 250 pounds and runs the 100-yard dash in 8.7 seconds. He has been offered $220,000 per year to play professional football but would like to go to college. He believes that if he does go to college he will be able to earn $400,000 per year playing football after he graduates. If he turns professional immediately, his playing career will be 10 years. If he goes to college, he would expect to play pro ball for 8 years.

Required:

1. Assume that going to college will cost him nothing and that his football salary would be paid at the end of each year. What should he do if the interest rate is 10 percent? Show calculations.
2. What if he is "red-shirted" for a year in college (graduates in 5 years instead of 4)? How would this impact his present value?

5. **Investment in Securities.** Wakichi Tokuda has $10,000 available for investment in one of 3 stocks to cover a period of 5 years. The stocks and their cash flows are as follows:
   a. Company K stock yields dividends annually of $4,000, but is not expected to appreciate in price over 5 years.
   b. Company L stock yields dividends of $1,000, and its price should double so that Tokuda can sell it for $20,000 at the end of 5 years.
   c. Company M stock will not yield any dividends, but its price will triple in 5 years, allowing Tokuda to sell the stock for $30,000.

Required:

In which stock should Tokuda invest, assuming his minimum rate is 15 percent? Ignore taxes. Show calculations.

6. **Winning the Lottery.** The All-National Lottery has several options for the winner of the "Big One" drawing on January 1, 1995. The options for the 1995 winner are:
   a. $1,000,000 (defined as $50,000 per year for 20 years).
   b. Year 2000 Million Dollar Pot of Gold, defined as $1,000,000 payable to the winner on January 1, 2000.
   c. A Perpetual Vacation in Paradise (defined as four homes located in Sunset City, Florida; Skitime, Colorado; Mackinaw Island, Michigan; and Betheny Beach, Delaware). Each home has a fair market value of $100,000. Assume a ready market for these properties exists.

   You have been selected as a finalist (one of three) for the "Big One" drawing tomorrow night.

Required:

1. Assuming that you are the winner and a rational decision maker, what logical steps should you take in deciding which option to select?
2. Which option would you select? Explain the numerical rationale for your decision. What is your emotional choice? Do the answers differ? Why?

7. **Effective Interest Rate.** Janice Delaney enjoys weekly strolls through shopping malls. Picking out special items here and there, she purchases most of her items with a credit card that charges 18 percent compounded monthly.

Required:

What is the effective interest rate that Delaney pays on her credit card? (Hint: Look at the computation from the point of view of the interest earned by the bank issuing the credit card.)

8. **Market Value of Bonds.** The Bryant Company plans to sell bonds with a face value of $1,000,000. The bonds will mature in 10 years. The bonds will bear an interest rate of 10 percent interest paid semiannually.

Required:
   If the market rate of interest for similar bonds is 8 percent, what will be the proceeds from selling the bonds? If the market rate of interest is 10 percent? If the market rate of interest is 12 percent?

9.   **Market Value of Bonds.** The Brazelton Company is considering 3 different corporate bond investments. All 3 have 5 years to maturity, pay semiannual interest, and have a $500,000 face value. All 3 have similar financial strengths and risks. The differential facts are:

   Investment 1: Coupon rate of 8 percent
   Investment 2: Coupon rate of 10 percent
   Investment 3: Coupon rate of 12 percent

Required:
   Assuming a 10 percent market rate of interest, what is the market value of each?

10.   **Unpaid Principal.** Brad Bauer purchased a new microcomputer system complete with appropriate software for $12,500. This upgrade in technology was intended to improve his competitive situation. If the new system results in significant cost savings, he expects to expand his small publishing company. Bauer's note calls for quarterly payments of $1,331.90 at the end of each quarter for 3 years. Interest is 16 percent compounded quarterly.

Required:
   What is the unpaid principal on the note immediately after the 7th payment? (Hint: The unpaid principal is the present value of the remaining payments.)

11.   **Mortgage Payment Schedule.** Ralph and Sue Egger have just signed a 20-year, 12 percent, $180,000 mortgage for their new "dream house." If Table II were extended to 240 months, the factors would be as follows for certain interest rates:

	Time Period	1%	6%	12%
Table II - Present Value of an Annuity of $1	240th	90.819	16.667	8.333

Required:
1.   What is the monthly payment that Ralph and Sue must make?
2.   Prepare a schedule of payments (principal and interest) for the first year. (Round to the nearest cent.)

12.   **Pay Cash or Borrow.** Juanita Christy needs a new car that she could purchase now for $12,000. Although she has the cash available, Christy would rather keep as much cash as possible for investments where there is the potential for a 20 percent rate of return. She can pay for the car on installments with a $2,000 down payment and $860 each quarter for 4 years.

Required:
   How should Christy pay for the car on time? (Hint: Compare the interest rate paid on installments with the potential returns from investment.)

13.   **Market Interest Rate on Bonds.** On July 1, the Chauez Corporation has a 8 percent, 10-year bond trading at 96.125 in the bond market. Interest on the bond is paid semiannually on June 30 and December 31. Five years remain to maturity. Betty Parker is willing to purchase $10,000 of the bonds at the current market price.

Required:
       If Parker purchases the bonds, what is her market rate of interest?

PROBLEMS

B-1.   **The Amount of an Investment in Bonds.** The Fowler Corporation is issuing $10,000,000 of 10 percent, 10-year bonds dated April 1, with interest payment dates of September 30 and March 31. Mandy Cliff is interested in purchasing $50,000 worth of the bonds on April 1. Currently, Cliff can earn 16 percent, compounded semiannually, on investments.

Required:
1.   Determine the semiannual cash flow Cliff will receive from her investment if she holds the bonds to maturity.
2.   How much is Cliff willing to invest in $50,000 face value of Fowler Corporation bonds?
3.   What is the discount or premium Cliff is demanding before she will invest her money in the bonds?

B-2.   **Equivalence of Present Value and Future Value.** Chen Ruan has 10 years before retirement. On the date of retirement, Ruan would like to have $100,000 in his personal retirement fund. The local bank has a special retirement account that guarantees 12 percent interest per year. Ruan has the option of making one deposit now into the fund or making annual deposits at the end of each year for 10 years, with deposits starting one year from now.

Required:
1.   What amount deposited now will accumulate to $100,000 in 10 years?
2.   What is the annual contribution if Ruan decides to make annual payments?
3.   Show that the annual contributions will accumulate to $100,000 by the end of 10 years.

B-3.   **Sinking Fund Contributions.** The Syner Company is authorized to issue $5,000,000 of 8-year unsecured bonds. These bonds have a stated interest of 10 percent. The bond indenture requires Syner Company to make semiannual contributions to a sinking fund each time the company makes an interest payment on the bonds. The sinking fund will grow to $5,000,000 at maturity. The sinking fund trustee can invest the semiannual contributions to earn 12 percent compounded semiannually.

Required:
       Determine the semiannual contribution that Syner Company should make to the sinking fund. (Hint: Find the present value of the $5,000,000 at 12 percent compounded semiannually, and then use Table II to determine the semiannual contribution.)

B-4. **Issuance of Bonds.** The Wendover Corporation is authorized to issue $20,000,000 of 10-year debenture bonds. The stated interest rate is 14 percent payable semiannually on June 30 and December 31. The bonds are scheduled for sale on July 1. Prior to the sale date, the market interest rate for long-term bonds increased to 16 percent compounded semiannually. (This is the rate of interest demanded by investors.)

Required:
1. What is the amount investors are willing to pay for the $20,000,000 bond issue?
2. What is the discount or premium the company must recognize for accounting purposes?

B-5. **Deficiency in a Pension Fund.** Five years ago, Mojo Valley Manufacturing Company adopted a pension plan for its salaried employees, the first of whom retires in 18 years from now. The pension fund has consistently earned 8 percent over the last 5 years but is expected to average 10 percent in the future. Contributions for the past 5 years are listed as follows:

Five years ago	$30,000
Four years ago	35,000
Three years ago	35,000
Two years ago	40,000
One year ago	40,000

The pension plan agreement currently calls for $2,000,000 as the balance in the pension fund on the date the first employee retires. Although the pension plan calls for a specified annual contribution, the amounts actually contributed depend on the available cash at the end of each year, subject to a minimum payment of $25,000. Therefore, the pension fund probably does not have a sufficient balance now.

Required:
1. Determine the current pension fund balance if contributions have earned 8 percent.
2. Calculate the current deficiency in the pension fund.

B-6. **Amortization Schedule for a Loan.** Howard Payne has $30,000 that he is willing to loan to a friend for a second mortgage on a new home. The friend will repay the loan at $9,593 at the end of each year for 5 years. Payne set up the annual payments to yield an 18 percent return on his $30,000 investment. For purposes of determining the annual interest income from this loan, Payne needs a loan amortization schedule showing how much of each annual payment is interest and how much reduces the principal.

Required:
Prepare an amortization schedule that shows the outstanding balance of the loan at the beginning of each year, the annual payment, the interest in the payment, and the reduction in principal.

B-7. **Early Retirement Decision.** Jack Pelley just finished 20 years of service with Biogen Corporation. Pelley, who has just celebrated his 55th birthday, is considering retiring now instead of waiting 7 more years. Pelley currently earns $100,000 a year and anticipates pay increases of 6 percent a year until retirement. Forecast salary and retirement benefits are as follows:

Age	Salary Plus 6 % Increase	Annual Benefit	
		Start Drawing at 62	Collect Right Away
55	$100,000	$42,300	$30,400
56	106,000	•	•
57	112,360	•	•
58	119,102	•	•
59	126,248	•	•
60	133,823	•	•
61	141,852	80,000	76,700

If Pelley retires now, he can start withdrawing $30,400 from the Biogen pension fund. The $30,400 will continue for 25 years. All annual benefits terminate at age 80. Even if Pelley doesn't live to 80, the estate will receive the benefits until the termination date.

ARO, Inc. needs a person with Pelley's skills and experience but can only afford to offer $80,000 for the first year with no pension benefits. However, at the end of each year, Pelley can expect 10 percent pay increases.

Required:

Assume that all salary and pension payments are made at the end of the year. Assuming Pelley views money to be worth 12 percent, should he:

1. Retire now, work for ARO, Inc., and begin collecting his pension from Biogen now?
2. Retire now, work for ARO, Inc., and begin collecting his pension from Biogen at age 62?
3. Continue working with Biogen until age 62?

B-8. **Redemption of Bonds.** Three years ago, the Mellor Company issued $3,000,000 of 8-year bonds with 16 percent interest payable semiannually. The company has the right to call the bonds at any time, but the call price is specified at 115. The call feature was added in the event market interest rates dropped and the company wanted to redeem the bonds early.

A drop in long-term interest rates occurred this year, bringing high-quality industrial bonds from 16 percent down to 12 percent compounded semiannually. Mellor's treasurer believes the interest rate will drop to 10 percent in another year, and that the company should redeem the bonds next year. The controller does not believe the interest rate will move lower but, instead, will turn around and rise. He recommends redeeming the bonds now.

The treasurer reminds him that the call price of 115 will require $3,450,000 now to redeem the bonds. This price assumes an interest rate just over 11 percent. She points out further that the present value of the outstanding bonds at the 12 percent interest rate is currently lower than the $3,450,000. If the interest rate drops to 10 percent, the present value of the bonds will rise above the call value.

Required:

Should the company redeem the bonds now, in one year, or wait until sometime later?

Present Value Tables

Table I
Present Value of $1

Where: P = Present Value Factor
i = Interest Rate
n = Number of Periods

$$P = \frac{1}{(1 + i)^n}$$

Periods (n)	1%	1.5%	2%	4%	5%	6%	8%	10%	12%	14%	15%	16%	18%	20%	22%	24%	25%	30%	40%
0	1.000	1.000	1.000	1.000	1.000	1.000	1.000	1.000	1.000	1.000	1.000	1.000	1.000	1.000	1.000	1.000	1.000	1.000	1.000
1	0.990	0.985	0.980	0.962	0.952	0.943	0.926	0.909	0.893	0.877	0.870	0.862	0.847	0.833	0.820	0.806	0.800	0.769	0.714
2	0.980	0.971	0.961	0.925	0.907	0.890	0.857	0.826	0.797	0.769	0.756	0.743	0.718	0.694	0.672	0.650	0.640	0.592	0.510
3	0.971	0.956	0.942	0.889	0.864	0.840	0.794	0.751	0.712	0.675	0.658	0.641	0.609	0.579	0.551	0.524	0.512	0.455	0.364
4	0.961	0.942	0.924	0.855	0.823	0.792	0.735	0.683	0.636	0.592	0.572	0.552	0.516	0.482	0.451	0.423	0.410	0.350	0.260
5	0.951	0.928	0.906	0.822	0.784	0.747	0.681	0.621	0.567	0.519	0.497	0.476	0.437	0.402	0.370	0.341	0.328	0.269	0.186
6	0.942	0.915	0.888	0.790	0.746	0.705	0.630	0.564	0.507	0.456	0.432	0.410	0.370	0.335	0.303	0.275	0.262	0.207	0.133
7	0.933	0.901	0.871	0.760	0.711	0.665	0.583	0.513	0.452	0.400	0.376	0.354	0.314	0.279	0.249	0.222	0.210	0.159	0.095
8	0.923	0.888	0.853	0.731	0.677	0.627	0.540	0.467	0.404	0.351	0.327	0.305	0.266	0.233	0.204	0.179	0.168	0.123	0.068
9	0.914	0.875	0.837	0.703	0.645	0.592	0.500	0.424	0.361	0.308	0.284	0.263	0.225	0.194	0.167	0.144	0.134	0.094	0.048
10	0.905	0.862	0.820	0.676	0.614	0.558	0.463	0.386	0.322	0.270	0.247	0.227	0.191	0.162	0.137	0.116	0.107	0.073	0.035
11	0.896	0.849	0.804	0.650	0.585	0.527	0.429	0.350	0.287	0.237	0.215	0.195	0.162	0.135	0.112	0.094	0.086	0.056	0.025
12	0.887	0.836	0.788	0.625	0.557	0.497	0.397	0.319	0.257	0.208	0.187	0.168	0.137	0.112	0.092	0.076	0.069	0.043	0.018
13	0.879	0.824	0.773	0.601	0.530	0.469	0.368	0.290	0.229	0.182	0.163	0.145	0.116	0.093	0.075	0.061	0.055	0.033	0.013
14	0.870	0.812	0.758	0.577	0.505	0.442	0.340	0.263	0.205	0.160	0.141	0.125	0.099	0.078	0.062	0.049	0.044	0.025	0.009
15	0.861	0.800	0.743	0.555	0.481	0.417	0.315	0.239	0.183	0.140	0.123	0.108	0.084	0.065	0.051	0.040	0.035	0.020	0.006
16	0.853	0.788	0.728	0.534	0.458	0.394	0.292	0.218	0.163	0.123	0.107	0.093	0.071	0.054	0.042	0.032	0.028	0.015	0.005
17	0.844	0.776	0.714	0.513	0.436	0.371	0.270	0.198	0.146	0.108	0.093	0.080	0.060	0.045	0.034	0.026	0.023	0.012	0.003
18	0.836	0.765	0.700	0.494	0.416	0.350	0.250	0.180	0.130	0.095	0.081	0.069	0.051	0.038	0.028	0.021	0.018	0.009	0.002
19	0.828	0.754	0.686	0.475	0.396	0.331	0.232	0.164	0.116	0.083	0.070	0.060	0.043	0.031	0.023	0.017	0.014	0.007	0.002
20	0.820	0.742	0.673	0.456	0.377	0.312	0.215	0.149	0.104	0.073	0.061	0.051	0.037	0.026	0.019	0.014	0.012	0.005	0.001
21	0.811	0.731	0.660	0.439	0.359	0.294	0.199	0.135	0.093	0.064	0.053	0.044	0.031	0.022	0.015	0.011	0.009	0.004	0.001
22	0.803	0.721	0.647	0.422	0.342	0.278	0.184	0.123	0.083	0.056	0.046	0.038	0.026	0.018	0.013	0.009	0.007	0.003	0.001
23	0.795	0.710	0.634	0.406	0.326	0.262	0.170	0.112	0.074	0.049	0.040	0.033	0.022	0.015	0.010	0.007	0.006	0.002	0.000
24	0.788	0.700	0.622	0.390	0.310	0.247	0.158	0.102	0.066	0.043	0.035	0.028	0.019	0.013	0.008	0.006	0.005	0.002	0.000
25	0.780	0.689	0.610	0.375	0.295	0.233	0.146	0.092	0.059	0.038	0.030	0.024	0.016	0.010	0.007	0.005	0.004	0.001	0.000
30	0.742	0.640	0.552	0.308	0.231	0.174	0.099	0.057	0.033	0.020	0.015	0.012	0.007	0.004	0.003	0.002	0.001	0.000	0.000
35	0.706	0.594	0.500	0.253	0.181	0.130	0.068	0.036	0.019	0.010	0.008	0.006	0.003	0.002	0.001	0.001	0.000	0.000	0.000
40	0.672	0.551	0.453	0.208	0.142	0.097	0.046	0.022	0.011	0.005	0.004	0.003	0.001	0.001	0.000	0.000	0.000	0.000	0.000
45	0.639	0.512	0.410	0.171	0.111	0.073	0.031	0.014	0.006	0.003	0.002	0.001	0.001	0.000	0.000	0.000	0.000	0.000	0.000
50	0.608	0.475	0.372	0.141	0.087	0.054	0.021	0.009	0.003	0.001	0.001	0.001	0.000	0.000	0.000	0.000	0.000	0.000	0.000
	0.000	0.000	0.000	0.000	0.000	0.000	0.000	0.000	0.000	0.000	0.000	0.000	0.000	0.000	0.000	0.000	0.000	0.000	0.000

Present Value Tables

Table II

Present Value of $1 Received Periodically for N Periods

$$P = \frac{1 - \dfrac{1}{(1 + i)^n}}{i}$$

Where: P = Present Value Factor
i = Interest Rate
n = Number of Periods

Periods (n)	1%	1.5%	2%	4%	5%	6%	8%	10%	12%	14%	15%	16%	18%	20%	22%	24%	25%	30%	40%
0	1.000	1.000	1.000	1.000	1.000	1.000	1.000	1.000	1.000	1.000	1.000	1.000	1.000	1.000	1.000	1.000	1.000	1.000	1.000
1	0.990	0.985	0.980	0.962	0.952	0.943	0.926	0.909	0.893	0.877	0.870	0.862	0.847	0.833	0.820	0.806	0.800	0.769	0.714
2	1.970	1.956	1.942	1.886	1.859	1.833	1.783	1.736	1.690	1.647	1.626	1.605	1.566	1.528	1.492	1.457	1.440	1.361	1.224
3	2.941	2.912	2.884	2.775	2.723	2.673	2.577	2.487	2.402	2.322	2.283	2.246	2.174	2.106	2.042	1.981	1.952	1.816	1.589
4	3.902	3.854	3.808	3.630	3.546	3.465	3.312	3.170	3.037	2.914	2.855	2.798	2.690	2.589	2.494	2.404	2.362	2.166	1.849
5	4.853	4.783	4.713	4.452	4.329	4.212	3.993	3.791	3.605	3.433	3.352	3.274	3.127	2.991	2.864	2.745	2.689	2.436	2.035
6	5.795	5.697	5.601	5.242	5.076	4.917	4.623	4.355	4.111	3.889	3.784	3.685	3.498	3.326	3.167	3.020	2.951	2.643	2.168
7	6.728	6.598	6.472	6.002	5.786	5.582	5.206	4.868	4.564	4.288	4.160	4.039	3.812	3.605	3.416	3.242	3.161	2.802	2.263
8	7.652	7.486	7.325	6.733	6.463	6.210	5.747	5.335	4.968	4.639	4.487	4.344	4.078	3.837	3.619	3.421	3.329	2.925	2.331
9	8.566	8.361	8.162	7.435	7.108	6.802	6.247	5.759	5.328	4.946	4.772	4.607	4.303	4.031	3.786	3.566	3.463	3.019	2.379
10	9.471	9.222	8.983	8.111	7.722	7.360	6.710	6.145	5.650	5.216	5.019	4.833	4.494	4.192	3.923	3.682	3.571	3.092	2.414
11	10.368	10.071	9.787	8.760	8.306	7.887	7.139	6.495	5.938	5.453	5.234	5.029	4.656	4.327	4.035	3.776	3.656	3.147	2.438
12	11.255	10.908	10.575	9.385	8.863	8.384	7.536	6.814	6.194	5.660	5.421	5.197	4.793	4.439	4.127	3.851	3.725	3.190	2.456
13	12.134	11.732	11.348	9.986	9.394	8.853	7.904	7.103	6.424	5.842	5.583	5.342	4.910	4.533	4.203	3.912	3.780	3.223	2.469
14	13.004	12.543	12.106	10.563	9.899	9.295	8.244	7.367	6.628	6.002	5.724	5.468	5.008	4.611	4.265	3.962	3.824	3.249	2.478
15	13.865	13.343	12.849	11.118	10.380	9.712	8.559	7.606	6.811	6.142	5.847	5.575	5.092	4.675	4.315	4.001	3.859	3.268	2.484
16	14.718	14.131	13.578	11.652	10.838	10.106	8.851	7.824	6.974	6.265	5.954	5.668	5.162	4.730	4.357	4.033	3.887	3.283	2.489
17	15.562	14.908	14.292	12.166	11.274	10.477	9.122	8.022	7.120	6.373	6.047	5.749	5.222	4.775	4.391	4.059	3.910	3.295	2.492
18	16.398	15.673	14.992	12.659	11.690	10.828	9.372	8.201	7.250	6.467	6.128	5.818	5.273	4.812	4.419	4.080	3.928	3.304	2.494
19	17.226	16.426	15.678	13.134	12.085	11.158	9.604	8.365	7.366	6.550	6.198	5.877	5.316	4.843	4.442	4.097	3.942	3.311	2.496
20	18.046	17.169	16.351	13.590	12.462	11.470	9.818	8.514	7.469	6.623	6.259	5.929	5.353	4.870	4.460	4.110	3.954	3.316	2.497
21	18.857	17.900	17.011	14.029	12.821	11.764	10.017	8.649	7.562	6.687	6.312	5.973	5.384	4.891	4.476	4.121	3.963	3.320	2.498
22	19.660	18.621	17.658	14.451	13.163	12.042	10.201	8.772	7.645	6.743	6.359	6.011	5.410	4.909	4.488	4.130	3.970	3.323	2.498
23	20.456	19.331	18.292	14.857	13.489	12.303	10.371	8.883	7.718	6.792	6.399	6.044	5.432	4.925	4.499	4.137	3.976	3.325	2.499
24	21.243	20.030	18.914	15.247	13.799	12.550	10.529	8.985	7.784	6.835	6.434	6.073	5.451	4.937	4.507	4.143	3.981	3.327	2.499
25	22.023	20.720	19.523	15.622	14.094	12.783	10.675	9.077	7.843	6.873	6.464	6.097	5.467	4.948	4.514	4.147	3.985	3.329	2.499
30	25.808	24.016	22.396	17.292	15.372	13.765	11.258	9.427	8.055	7.003	6.566	6.177	5.517	4.979	4.534	4.160	3.995	3.332	2.500
35	29.409	27.076	24.999	18.665	16.374	14.498	11.655	9.644	8.176	7.070	6.617	6.215	5.539	4.992	4.541	4.164	3.998	3.333	2.500
40	32.835	29.916	27.355	19.793	17.159	15.046	11.925	9.779	8.244	7.105	6.642	6.233	5.548	4.997	4.544	4.166	3.999	3.333	2.500
45	36.095	32.552	29.490	20.720	17.774	15.456	12.108	9.863	8.283	7.123	6.654	6.242	5.552	4.999	4.545	4.166	4.000	3.333	2.500
50	39.196	35.000	31.424	21.482	18.256	15.762	12.233	9.915	8.304	7.133	6.661	6.246	5.554	4.999	4.545	4.167	4.000	3.333	2.500
	100.000	66.667	50.000	25.000	20.000	16.667	12.500	10.000	8.333	7.143	6.667	6.250	5.556	5.000	4.545	4.167	4.000	3.333	2.500

8

Index

A

ABC, compared to traditional costing, 93
ABC activity groups, levels of, illustrated, 82
ABC cost linkage, illustrated, 79
ABC process, overall view of, illustrated, 80
Absorption costing
    defined, 506
    compared with variable costing, 507
    reconciliation with variable costing, 509
Accelerated Cost Recovery System (ACRS), 631, 669
Accelerated depreciation benefits, 634
Accommodation cash, defined, 316
Account analysis, defined, 756
Accountability in subsequent departments, 261, 279
Accounting
    defined, 967
    differences between managerial and financial, 13
    double entry, 968
    financial, 10
    managerial, 13
    responsibility, 101
Accounting cycle, 967
Accounting equation, defined and illustrated, 969
Accounting information, managers' need for, 3
Accounting period, defined, 977
Accounting process, overview of, 967
Accounting rate of return (ARR) method, 629
Accounting system, as a provider of information, 10
Accounts
    defined and illustrated, 971
    increases and decreases in, illustrated, 971
    use of, illustrated, 973
Accounts receivable turnover, defined, 864
Accounts structure, sample chart of, illustrated, 105

Accrual accounting versus cash, 26
Accrual adjustments, 978
Accrual principle, 990
Acid test ratio, defined, 860
Activity-based cost, comprehensive example of, 87
Activity-based costing (ABC), 76, 204, 268;
    defined, 79
    flow of costs under, 81
Activity center, defined, 79
Activity center's cash flows and product costs, diagram of, illustrated, 92
Activity cost centers, cost drivers, cost functions, and product costs, relationships of, illustrated, 84
Actual costs versus planned costs, 47
Add or delete a segment
    key decision
    rule of, 573
    qualitative factors of, 576
Adjusted trial balance, illustrated, 983
Adjusting process, 977
Administrative expense budget, 369
Alternatives in decision making, 549
Annuity, 623
    defined, 1012
Assembled products, 191
Asset, defined, 967, 969
Asset quality, 864
Asset turnover, defined, 701
Attainable standards, defined, 424
Automation of the work place, 76
Average cost, defined, 43
Average cost versus incremental costs, 42
Avoidable cost, 42

B

Balance sheet
    account groups for cash flow reporting, illustrated, 910
    classifications, 992
    defined and illustrated, 984

end of fiscal year, illustrated, 1003
Bartering, defined, 808
Base-year comparisons, 856
Base-year comparisons of income statement data, illustrated, 856
Batch-level activities, 81
Batch-size diversity, 86
Behavior of
    fixed costs, illustrated, 37
    variable costs, illustrated, 36
Bill of materials, 355
    defined, 31, 193
Bill of materials explosion, 360
Bond payable, issuing a, 1016
Book value per share, defined, 866
Break-even analysis, 136
Break-even chart, 138
    illustrated, 139
    with two breakeeven points, illustrated, 140
Break-even point, 136
Budget, 47
    administrative expense, 369
    comprehensive, 312
    defined, 4, 304
    direct labor, 361
    manufacturing overhead, 362
    master, 312
    master operating, example of, 354
    materials purchases, 360
    materials requirements, 359
    operating, 315
    preparation of, 311
    production plan and, 358
    project, 317, 324
    sales forecast and, 357
    selling or marketing expense, 368
    stress, 331
    supporting schedules, 365
Budget control system, illustrated, 6
Budget schedules, formatting, 321
Budget variance, 440
Budgetary control, defined, 5
Budgetary slack, defined, 330
Budgeting
    and planning, 304
    behavioral side of, 329
    capital, 614

institutionalizing, 331
other approaches to, 324
participatory, 307
probabilistic, 327
program, 327
purposes of, 307
zero-based, 326
Business, set-up in other countries, 805
Business ownership, forms of, 986
Business transaction, 969

C

Calculation of product cost using activity-based costing for cost assignment, illustrated, 90-91
Capacity, defined, 205
Capacity expansion decision, 577
Capacity variance, 201
    analysis of, illustrated, 442
    defined, 441
Capital
    adequacy, 862
    budgeting, defined, 614, 1016
    cost of, 635
    defined, 969
    stock, defined, 987
Capital investment
    defined, 615
    and cash flows, 616
    and income taxes, 630
    calculation issues of, 659
    decisions, 614
    depreciation expense and, 631
    evaluation methods of, 620
    example of, 618
    format for relevant data, illustrated, 620
    not-for-profit organization, 676
    post audit of, 671
    social costs of, 676
    time perspective, 618
    types of projects, 617
    uncertainty problems, 673
Cash
    accommodation, 316

equivalents, 918
excess, 316
management, defined,
   316
transaction, 316
versus accrual accounting,
   26
Cash flow
   balance sheet account
      groups for, illustrated,
      910
   direct method,
      defined, 912; 914
   forecasting, 930
   from financing activities,
      911
   from investing activities,
      911
   from operations,
      calculation using the
      direct method,
      illustrated, 928
   from operations section,
      direct method,
      illustrated, 929
   from operating activities,
      911
   indirect method, 912
   operations, 912
   statement, 1002
   types of, 909
Cash flow forecast, 316, 370
Cash flow per share, defined,
   870
Certified Management
   Accountant (CMA), 18
Changing business
   environment, 7
Chart of accounts, defined,
   975
Chart of accounts
   classifications, 104
Closing procedure, 985
Coefficient of determination
   (rFD)
   defined, 764
   equation for, 764
Commingled products, 191
Committed fixed cost,
   defined, 37
Common cost, defined, 41
Common equity, defined, 862
Common equity multiplier,
   defined, 863
Common-sized statements,
   defined, 855
Common stock, 987
Comparative departmental
   profit measurements,
   illustrated, 574
Comparative income
   statements, illustrated,
   854
Comparative statements, 854

Comparing P/V when
   variable costs differ,
   illustrated, 143
Competitive situation, 7
Compound amount, defined,
   1009
Compound interest, 1009
Comprehensive budget,
   defined, 312
Computer-aided design
   (CAD), defined, 9
Computer-aided
   manufacturing, (CAM)
   defined, 9
Conservation concept, 991
Consistency concept, 989
Constants, defined, 379
Continuous budget, 307
Contra-asset account, 980
Contribution margin
   concepts, illustration of,
      160
   controllable, 159
   defined, 136, 499
   direct or segment, 160
   division controllable, 702
   division direct, 702
   division variable, 703
   measurements, 158
   per unit of scarce
      resource, defined, 566
   per unit of the limiting or
      scarce factor, 159
Contribution margin analysis
   by store, illustrated, 161
   defined, 550
Control
   and planning, 304
   defined, 5
   limits, 769
Controllable contribution
   margin, 159
Controllable cost, defined, 45
Controllable costs versus
   noncontrollable costs, 45
Controllable variance, 440
Controller, 15
   responsibilities of, 16
Controlling, cost concepts
   for, 41
Conversion costs, 249
   defined, 33
Corporation, defined, 986
Correlation analysis, defined,
   760
Cost
   and pricing decision, 577
   average, 43
   avoidable, 42
   common, 41
   concept, 988
   controllable, 45
   conversion, 33, 249

decremental, 42
defined, 25
differential, 45
direct, 41
direct labor, 31
direct product, 32
fixed, 36, 752
full, defined, 578
incremental, 42
indirect, 41
indirect product, 32
irrelevant, 43
joint, 41
manufacturing, 35
manufacturing flows of,
   33
manufacturing overhead,
   31
marginal, 42
materials, 31
mixed, 40
nature of, 25
noncontrollable, 45
non-value-added, 95
opportunity, 45, 551
out-of-pocket, 43, 551
period, 28
prime, 32
product, 29
product life-cycle, 101
relevant, 43
semi-fixed, 40, 752
semi-variable, 39, 752
step fixed, 40
sunk, 44
traceable, 41
transferred-in, 262
unavoidable, 44
variable, 36, 752
Cost-based transfer price, 713
Cost behavior, 35
   checking inferences, 768
   examples of other,
      illustrated, 753
   significant to decision
      making and control,
      753
   types of, 751
Cost center, defined, 102, 697
Cost center control report,
   example of, illustrated,
   106
Cost concepts, 23
   for planning and
      controlling, 41
Cost control, 422
   use of cost data in, 25
Cost control system, 47
Cost determination, defined,
   6
Cost drivers defined, 25, 79
   preliminary stage, 83
   primary stage, 83

used for service centers,
   illustrated, 215
used in actual ABC
   systems, illustrated,
   85
Cost elements in a process
   cost environment, 249
Cost estimation
   account analysis, 756
   defined, 755
   engineering approach,
      756
   high-low method, 759
   regression analysis, 760
   scattergraph and visual
      fit, 757
Cost flow, from work in
   process through cost of
   goods sold, illustrated,
   251
Cost function, 38
Cost management, 422
   defined, 5
   issues, 94
   systems design, 78
Cost objective, defined 25
Cost of capital, 635
Cost of goods manufactured,
   35
Cost of goods sold, 31, 35,
   1000
Cost of production report
   for fabrication
      department,
      illustrated, 261
   for welding department,
      illustrated, 266
   illustrated, 250
   management's use of, 266
Cost of products
   manufactured and sold
   schedule, 367
Cost overrun, 196
Cost system
   hybrid, 267
   modified, 267
Cost variance, defined, 490
Cost-volume-profit analysis,
   defined, 136
Costing
   absorption, 506
   factory overhead, 196
   variable, 506
Costs, expenses, and income
   measurement, 26
Countertrade, defined, 808
Coupon rate, 1016
Credit balance, defined, 971
Current asset, defined, 994
Current liabilities, defined,
   996
Current ratio, defined, 859
Cutoff rate, 622

D

Days sales in inventory, defined, 865
Days sales in receivables, defined, 864
Debit balance, defined, 971
Debt to equity ratio, defined, 862
Decentralization
　advantages of, 698
　defined, 698
Decentralized company, defined, 697
Decision making
　process of, 548
　use of cost data in, 24
Decision objective, 549
Decision rule, 549
　basic, 550
Decomposition, defined, 775
Decremental cost, 42
Deferred revenue, defined, 997
Deficit, defined, 998
Deleting department C, total analysis of, illustrated, 575
Demand, derived, 321
Departmental overhead rates versus plant-wide rates, 203
Dependent variables, 324
Depreciation, defined, 979
Depreciation adjustment, 979
Depreciation expense, defined, 979
Derived demand, defined, 321
Desired profit
　after tax, 137
　as a percentage of sales, 138
　as an amount per unit, 138
　before tax, 137
Desired rate of return, 622
Differential analysis
　decisions, 555
　defined, 550
　examples of, 552
　incremental approach to, illustrated, 554
　total approach to, illustrated, 553
Differential cost, defined, 45
Direct cost, 41
Direct costs versus indirect costs, 41
Direct labor, 98, 194
Direct labor budget, 361
Direct labor costs, defined, 31
Direct materials, 193
Direct method, 216

Direct method for finding cash flow from operations, illustrated, 914
Direct or segment contribution margin, 160
Direct product costs, 32
Discount, 1016
Discount rate
　comparison of two projects at various rates, illustrated, 663
　defined, 623, 1011
Discounted value, 1011
Discounting, 614
　defined, 1011
Discretionary fixed costs, defined, 37
Dividend payout percentage, defined, 863
Dividend yield, defined, 873
Division controllable contribution margin defined, 702
Division direct contribution margin, defined, 702
Division net profit, 701
Division variable contribution margin, defined, 703
Dollar discount, defined, 1011
Double entry accounting, 968
Dual transfer prices, 718
Duality, 967

E

Earning power ratios, defined, 875
Earnings, 867
Earnings per share, defined, 869, 1001
Economic order quantity, 452
Effective interest rate, defined, 1017
Efficiency variance, 458
Embedded interest rate, 666
Engineering approach, defined, 756
Equities, defined, 967, 969
Equivalent unit, defined, 252
Ethical conduct, standards of, illustrated, 20
Excess cash, defined, 316
Exchange gain or loss, 819
Expected capacity, 205
Expected value, 327, 675
Expense, defined, 970
Extraordinary gains and losses, 1001

F

Fabricated products, 191
Facility-level activities, 81
Factory overhead, 31
　costing, 196
Favorable variance, 426
Financial accounting, defined 10
Financial Accounting Standards Board (FASB), 11
Financial and managerial accounting, scope of, illustrated, 11
Financial leverage, defined, 873
Financial modeling, 307
Financial performance, measurement of, 699
Financial performance analysis
　caveats in using, 876
　example company, 852
　risks and returns, 858
　uses and users of, 850
Financial planning model
　defined, 376
　elements of, 378
　illustrated, 379
　structuring the interrelationships, 380
Financial statement analysis, types of, 854
Financial statements, 983
Financing activities, 909
Financing cash flows for a lease and a purchase, illustrated, 666
Financing decisions versus investment decisions, 665
Finished goods inventory, 31
First-in, first-out (FIFO) cost method, 255
Fiscal period, defined, 977
Fixed assets, defined, 979, 995
Fixed costs, 147, 752
　behavior of, 37
　committed, 37
　defined, 36
　current emphasis on, 148
　discretionary, 37
　increase in, illustrated, 147
Fixed overhead, costing, 200
Fixed product costs, 33
Flexible manufacturing, defined, 8
Flexible overhead budget, 197, 439
Flow of costs from work in process through cost of

goods sold, illustrated, 251
Flow of units and costs for subassembly components, illustrated, 248
Flow of units and costs in a process manufacturing system, illustrated, 247
Flows of products and costs through the factory, illustrated, 34
Focused production, 8
Forecast, sales, defined 320
Forecast and actual balance sheets, illustrated, 853
Forecast and actual income statements, illustrated, 853
Forecast balance sheet, 373
Forecast financial statement, 317, 357
Forecast income statement, 372
Forecast statement of cash flows, 374
Foreign affiliates, translation of financial statements of, 824
Foreign currency transaction, 815
Forward contract, defined, 821
Forward exchange contract, defined, 821
Forward rate, 821
Franchises, defined, 995
Franchising, defined, 807
Free reserves, defined, 811
Full cost, defined, 43, 578
Full-cost transfer price, 714
Fully diluted earnings per share, 870
Functional currency, defined, 824
Future value of money, defined, 1008

G

Gain on asset disposal, 664
General and administrative expenses, defined, 1001
General journal, defined, 973
Generally accepted accounting principles, 11
Global competitiveness, 76
Globalization, defined, 8
Goal congruence, 705
Goals, defined, 304
Going concern, 987
Goods and services provided by American industry, illustrated, 4

Goods available for sale, 35
Goodwill, defined, 996
Gross margin, defined, 488, 1000
Gross margin percentage, defined, 870
Gross profit, defined, 488
Gross profit analysis, 488
   general framework for, illustrated, 489
   uses and limitations of, 496
Growth ratios, basic definition for, 871

H

Hedge
   defined, 820
   for a foreign currency exposed asset, 823
   for a foreign currency exposed liability, 821
   forward exchange contract, 821
Hidden reserves, defined, 810
High-low method, defined, 759
Holding company, defined, 806
Horizontal analysis, 857
Hurdle rate, 622
Hybrid cost system, defined, 267

I

Ideal capacity, 205
Idle capacity, 443
Income measurement, use of cost data in, 25
Income statement
   classifications, 999
   defined, 983, illustrated, 984
Income tax, 1001
Incorporated, defined, 986
Increase in fixed cost, illustrated, 147
Incremental analysis approach, defined, 551
Incremental analysis approach to differential analysis, illustrated, 554
Incremental cost
   defined, 42
   analysis, 43
   versus average cost, 42
Incremental profit, defined, 550
Independent variables, 324
Indifference point, 45, 157

Indirect cost
   defined, 41
   versus direct cost, 41
Indirect labor, 98, 194
Indirect method for finding cash flow from operations, illustrated, 913
Indirect manufacturing costs, 31
Indirect materials, 193
Indirect product costs, 32
Inflation, 661
In-house sourcing, defined, 557
Initial investment, 616
Inspection time, defined, 95
Institute of Management Accountants, 18
Intangible assets, defined, 995
Intracompany transactions continuum, illustrated, 710
Interdepartmental support, 215
Interest rate, approximation of, 1021
Internal rate of return (IRR), 625
   defined, 1021
International Accounting Standards Committee (IASC), 812
International environment, 802
   communications differences, 802
   cultural differences, 803
   differences in accounting rules and financial structure, 809
   environmental differences, 804
   transfer pricing, 812
International taxation, defined, 814
International transfer pricing, 812
   avoid financial restrictions, 813
   gain host country approval, 814
   manage currency exchange fluctuations, 814
   minimize import duties, 813
   minimize income taxes, 813
Inventories, in manufacturing, 31

Inventory adjustment, 980
Inventory turnover, defined, 865
Investing activities, 909
Investment, 1009
Investment base, defined, 703
Investment center, defined, 102, 697
Investment decisions versus financing decisions, 665
Investment tax credit, 631
Investments, defined, 994
Irrelevant cost, defined, 43

J

Job cost illustration, 207
   production environment for, 190
   system, 192
Job order, 192
Joint cost, defined, 41
Joint products, 570
Joint venture, defined, 806
Journal
   defined, 973
   general, defined, 973
   illustrated, 974
   special, 975
Journal entry, defined, 973
Just-in-time (JIT), 8
Just-in-time (JIT) philosophy, 268

L

Labor, quantitative methods for, 450
Labor content percentage, 98
Labor efficiency variance, defined, 432
Labor rate variance, defined, 432
Lead time, defined, 453
Learning curve
   defined, 456
   illustrated, 457
Learning phase, defined, 456
Lease, 665
   illustrated, 668
   versus purchase, 666
Least squares method, defined, 761
Ledger, defined, 971
Legal reserves, defined, 811
Levels of ABC activity groups, illustrated, 82
Liabilities, defined, 967, 969
Line of regression
   least squares method, illustrated, 762

visually fitted, illustrated, 758
Linear regression
   computer output, 768
   defined, 760
   equation for, 761
   explanation of correlation, illustrated, 764
   least squares method, 761
   no correlation, illustrated, 763
   positive correlation, illustrated, 763
   quality of, 763
   uniform dispersion, illustrated, 770
   wide dispersion at extremes, illustrated, 769
Liquidity, 858
Loans, borrowing and repaying, 1019
Long-range goals, defined, 306
Long-term liabilities, defined, 997
Loose standards, defined, 424
Loss on asset disposal, 664

M

MACRS
   accelerated depreciation percentages, illustrated, 670
   classes of assets, 669
   example of, 671
   tax impacts compared with tax impacts of straight-line depreciation methods, illustrated, 672
Make or buy, 556
   key decision rule of, 557
   qualitative factors of, 561
Managed assets, defined, 868
Management
   levels of, 7
   objective of, 9
   top, support, 329
Management accountant
   defined, 17
   responsibilities of, 17
   role of, 17
   standards of ethical conduct for, 20
Management by exception, 422
Management by objectives system (MBO), 306
Management complexity, 9

Management control report
    comparing actual to plan,
    illustrated, 48
Management overrides, 378
Managerial accounting,
    defined, 13
Managerial process and the
    budgeting system
    process, interaction of the
    illustrated, 305
Manufacturing, world class, 8
Manufacturing company,
    organization chart of a,
    illustrated, 15
Manufacturing costs, defined,
    35
Manufacturing cycle
    efficiency, (MCE),
    defined, 98
Manufacturing environment,
    impact of changing, 268
Manufacturing organization
    defined, 29
    compared to service and
        merchandising
        organizations, 26
Manufacturing overhead
    budget, 362
    costs, 31
    flexible budget for, 362
Manufacturing resource
    planning, (MRPII), 9
Margin of safety
    defined, 152
    relationship with
        operating leverage,
        154
Marginal cost, defined, 42
Marginal tax rate, defined,
    630
Market performance, 872
Market price, 712
Market rate of interest, 1016
Markup, 578
Markup pricing methods, 578
Master budget
    components of,
        illustrated, 314
    defined, 312
    for a manufacturer, 312
    for a nonmanufacturing
        company, 317
    structure of, illustrated,
        313
    summary of, 375
Matching concept, 989
Materials, quantitative
    methods for, 450
Materials acquisition, control
    of, 432
Materials costs, 31
Materials inventory, 31
Materials price variance,
    defined, 426

Materials purchases budget,
    360
Materials quantity variance,
    defined, 429
Materials requirements
    budget, 359
Materials requirements
    planning (MRP), 9
Materials used, 31
Measure of activity, 438
Measuring income in service,
    merchandising and
    manufacturing firms,
    illustrated, 27
Merchandising organization,
    318
    compared to service and
        manufacturing
        organizations, 26
    cost flows, illustrated, 29
    defined, 28
Minimum acceptable rate of
    return, 622
Minimum desired rate of
    return, 707
Mission, defined, 306
Mix variance, defined, 504
Mixed costs, 40
Model queries, 378
Modeling, defined, 376
Modified Accelerated Cost
    Recovery System
    (MACRS), 631, 669
Modified cost system,
    defined, 267
Move time, defined, 96
Multinational company,
    performance evaluation
    in, 825
Multiple overhead rates, 202
Multiple regression, defined,
    771

N

Negotiated transfer price, 717
Net assets, defined, 970
Net book value, defined, 980
Net income, defined, 983,
    1001
Net loss, defined, 983
Net present value analysis
    with depreciation and
        taxes, illustrated, 633
    with taxes, illustrated, 632
Net present value (NPV)
    method, defined, 621
Net present value of capital
    investment cash flows,
    illustrated, 623
Networks, 807
Noncash financing and
    investing activities, 911

Noncontrollable cost,
    defined, 45
Nonlinear regression,
    defined, 772
Non-value-added costs, 95
Normal capacity, 205
Normal distribution, defined,
    770

O

Objectives, defined, 304
Off-balance-sheet financing,
    defined, 861
Operating budget, 315
Operating cycle
    defined, 994
    illustrated, 315
Operating expense variance
    analysis, framework for,
    illustrated, 498
Operating expenses, 1000
    analysis of, 497
    defined, 497
Operating levels and break-
    even points, relationship
    between, 148
Operating leverage
    defined, 149
    in a declining market, 152
    relationship with margin of
        safety, 154
    with high fixed cost, 150
Operating leverage factor, 149
Operating revenue, defined,
    1000
Operations activities, 909
Operations cash flow to
    current debt service ratio,
    defined, 861
Operations cash flows, 912
Opinion No. 19 of the
    Accounting Principles
    Board, 908
Opportunity cost, 551
    defined, 45
Organization chart of a
    manufacturing company,
    illustrated, 15
Organization expense,
    defined, 996
Organization of the firm, 14
Other assets, defined, 996
Out-of-pocket costs, 551
    defined, 43
Out-sourcing, defined, 557
Overall view of ABC cost
    linkage, illustrated, 79
Overall view of ABC process,
    illustrated, 80
Overapplied or overabsorbed
    overhead, 201

Overhead, three-variance
    method for, 456
Overhead rate, 197
Overhead rates,
    departmental versus
        plant-wide, 203
    multiple, 202
Overhead variance,
    disposition of, 201
Owner's equity, defined, 967,
    969; 997

P

Paid-in capital in excess of
    par value, defined, 998
Paid-in capital in excess of
    stated value, 998
Parameters, 378
Partnership, defined, 986
Patents, defined, 995
Payback period, 627
Payback period method, 627
Payback reciprocal, 628
Pension contract, funding,
    1020
Percentage composition
    balance sheets,
    illustrated, 856
Percentage composition
    statements, defined, 855
Percentage-of-completion
    method of accounting for
    a profit, defined, 989
Performance evaluation,
    defined, 5
Performance measurement,
    97
Period costs, defined, 28
Periodic inventory, 981
Periodicity concept, 989
Perpetual inventory, 980
Physical flow of units,
    illustrated, 254
Planned costs versus actual
    costs, 47
Planning
    and budgeting, 304
    and control, 304
    assumptions, 307
    cost concepts for, 41
    defined, 4
    use of cost data in, 24
Planning, programming, and
    budgeting system (PPBS),
    defined, 327
Plant assets, defined, 979, 995
Plant capacity and control,
    443
Plant-wide overhead rates
    versus departmental
    rates, 203
Post audit, 673

Post-closing trial balance, 985
  illustrated, 986
Posting, defined, 975
Posting reference column,
  defined, 975
Practical capacity, 205
Preferred stock, 987
Preliminary stage cost driver,
  83
Premier Products Company's
  factory, illustrated, 30
Premium, 1016
Premium on stock, defined,
  998
Prepayment adjustments,
  defined, 979
Present value, 620
  analysis applied, 1015
  comparison with future
    value of a series of
    cash flows, 1014
  defined, 1010
  of a series of future cash
    flows, 1012
  with cash flow at the
    beginning of the
    period, 1015
Price market, 712
  transfer, 709
Price and quantity variances,
  inter-relationships of, 431
Price earnings ratio, defined,
  872
Price policy, 144
Price reduction, effect on
  profit, 146
Price standard, defined, 421
Pricing
  full cost, 578
  variable cost, 579
Pricing decision and costs,
  577
Primary stage cost driver, 83
Prime costs, defined, 32
Pro forma financial
  statement, 357
Probabilistic budgeting, 327
Process cost, production
  environment for, 191
Process cost system defined,
  246
  standard costs in, 446
Process costing of output, 246
Process manufacturing
  system, flow of units and
  costs in, illustrated, 247
Process time, defined, 95
Producing departments, 214
Product
  cost, defined, 29
  cost systems, 189
  costing, 6
  costs and product cost
    groups, illustrated, 33

diversity, 86
flow time, defined, 97
life-cycle costs, 101
mix complexity, 86
Product-level activities, 81
Production environment
  for job cost, 190
  for process cost, 191
Production order, completed,
  illustrated, 192
Profit
  analysis, 419
  center, defined, 102, 697
  division controllable, 702
  direct, 702
  net, 701
  variable, 703
  incremental, defined, 550
  plan, defined, 312
Profitability index, 624
Profit-volume (P/V) graph,
  140
  illustrated, 141
Program budgeting, defined,
  327
Project budget, 324
  defined, 317
Providing services, cost of 207
Purchase versus lease, 666
Pyramid reporting, 107

Q

Quantity standard, defined,
  421
Quick assets, 860
Quick ratio, defined, 860

R

Ratio and analysis, defined,
  857
Realization concept, 988
Regression analysis, defined,
  760
Regression line, 760
Reinvested earnings, 998
Relationships of activity cost
  centers, cost drivers, cost
  functions, and product
  costs, illustrated, 84
Relevant cost, defined, 43,
  550
Relevant costing decisions,
  policy issues affecting,
  554
Relevant range, 39, 140
Relevant revenues, 550
Replace equipment decision,
  576
Required rate of return, 622
Residual income, defined, 707

Responsibility center,
  defined, 697
Responsibilities of controller,
  illustrated, 16
Responsibilities of
  management accountant,
  illustrated, 17
Responsibility accounting,
  101
Responsibility center,
  defined, 102
Responsibility centers:
  investment centers, profit
  centers, and cost centers
  including activity centers,
  illustrated, 103
Retained earnings, 998
Return on assets (ROA),
  defined, 868
Return on common equity
  (ROCE), defined, 868
Return on investment (ROI)
  defined, 700
  improving, 705
  problems with, 704
  ratio for, 700
Return on managed assets,
  704
Return on sales (ROS),
  defined, 700, 868
Return on total equity (ROE),
  defined, 868
Revenue, defined, 970
Risks and returns,
  interrelationships of, 873
Risk percentage factor, 673
Rolling update, 307

S

Sales, 970
  forecast, defined, 320
  forecasting, 319
  journal, illustrated, 976
  mix, defined, 154
  mix variance, defined, 494
  price variance, defined,
    490
  quantity variance,
    defined, 495
  volume, 141
  volume variance, defined,
    491
Scarce resources
  key decision rule of, 567
  qualitative factors of, 569
  use of, 566
Scattergraph and visual fit,
  defined, 757
Scope of financial and
  managerial accounting,
  illustrated, 11

Security and Exchange
  Commission, 11
Sell or process further
  key decision rule of, 570
  qualitative factors of, 572
Selling expenses, defined,
  1001
Selling or marketing expense
  budget, 368
Semifixed costs, 40, 752
Semivariable and semifixed
  cost patterns, examples
  of, 40
Semivariable costs, defined,
  39, 752
Sensitivity analysis, defined,
  674
Service center costs, other
  influences, 218
Service centers and support
  functions, 214
Service organization, 318
  compared to
    merchandising and
    manufacturing
    organizations, 26
  cost flows, illustrated, 28
  defined, 27
  performance evaluation
    systems in, 708
SFAS No. 95
  "Statement of Cash Flows",
  908
Simulation, defined, 376
Slack, budgetary, 330
Social benefits, 676
Social costs, 676
Source document, defined,
  970
Special journals, 975
Special sales pricing, 562
  key decision rule of, 563
  qualitative factors of, 565
Spending variance, 458
  defined, 498
Split-off point, 570
Spot rate, defined, 818
Stage of completion, defined,
  253
Standard cost
  defined, 421
  modifications for, 496
  sheet, 425
  variances, summary of,
    illustrated, 445
Standard error of the estimate
  (Se), defined, 766
Standards advantages of, 422
  attainable, 424
  for labor, 432
  for materials, 426
  for overhead, 437
  loose, 424
  quality of, 423

revising, 424
strict, 424
use of, 421
Standards of ethical conduct, 18
illustrated, 20
Statement of cash flows, 909
format of, 910
framework of, illustrated, 911
illustrated, 927
preparing, 916
Statement of changes in financial position, 908
Statement of changes in retained earnings, 1002
Static phase, defined, 456
Step fixed cost, 40
Step (sequential) method, 217
Stockholder's equity, 997
Storage time, defined, 97
Straight-line depreciation, tax impacts compared to MACRS tax impacts, illustrated, 672
Straight-line method of depreciation, defined, 980
Strategic plan, defined, 306
Strategic profit model, 876
return on assets, illustrated, 877
return on common equity, illustrated, 878
Strict standards, defined, 424
Subassembly components, flow of units and costs for, illustrated, 248
Sunk cost, defined, 44
Synchronous manufacturing, 8

T

T-account, used in preparing statement of cash flows, 919
Target rate of return, 622
Tax shield, defined, 632
Technical evolution, 8
Time periods covered by the three major accounting

statements, illustrated, 909
Time series analysis, 773
Time value of money, 1008
defined, 614
Times interest earned, defined, 863
Timing placement of orders, illustrated, 454
Total analysis approach, defined, 551
Total analysis approach to differential analysis, illustrated, 553
Total asset turnover, defined, 866
Total costs patterns with a relevant range, illustrated, 39
Traceable cost, 41
Traditional factory versus just-in-time factory layouts, illustrated, 96
Treasurer, responsibilities of, 15
Trend analysis, 774
graph of data and regression trend line, illustrated, 775
Transaction cash, defined, 316
Transfer price cost-based, 713
defined, 709
desired qualities of, 711
dual, 718
full-cost, 714
international, 812
intracompany transactions continuum, illustrated, 710
market price, 712
negotiated, 717
variable-cost, 714
Transfer pricing, variable-cost and full-cost example, illustrated, 715
Transfer pricing methods, grading, 719
Transferred-in costs, 262

Trial balance, 976
illustrated, 977

U

Unavoidable costs, defined, 44
Uncertainty, 674
Underapplied or underabsorbed overhead, 201
Undivided interest, 992
Unfavorable variance, 426
Unit-level activities, 81
Use of scarce resources, 566

V

Valuation, 992
Valuation adjustments, 981
Value-added direct labor, 98
Value-added labor ratio, 98
Variable and fixed costs, nature of, 38
Variable contribution margin, 158
Variable costing
characteristics of, 506
compared with absorption costing, 507
defined, 506
reconciliation with absorption costing, 509
Variable cost pricing, 579
Variable costs, 142, 752
behavior of, 36
defined, 36
Variable-cost transfer price, 714
Variable product costs, 33
Variable overhead, costing, 199
Variance
budget, 440
capacity, 441
controllable, 440

cost, 490
disposition of, 446
efficiency, 458
favorable, 426
labor efficiency, 432
labor rate, 432
materials price, 426
materials quantity, 429
mix, 504
sales mix, 494
sales price, 490
sales quantity, 495
sales volume, 491
spending, 458, 498
unfavorable, 426
volume, 498
yield, 505
Variances, detailed levels of, illustrated, 420
Volume variance, 201
defined, 498

W

Wait time, defined, 97
Weighted-average cost of capital, defined, 635
Weighted-average cost method, 275
"What If" analysis, 380
Work in process inventory, 31
Work order, 192
Working capital, 660
defined, 859
World class manufacturing, 8

Y

Yield, defined, 1017
Yield variance, defined, 505

Z

Zero-based budgeting, defined, 326
Zero-stock system, 8

Management control report
comparing actual to plan,
illustrated, 48
Management overrides, 378
Managerial accounting,
defined, 13
Managerial process and the
budgeting system
process, interaction of the
illustrated, 305
Manufacturing, world class, 8
Manufacturing company,
organization chart of a,
illustrated, 15
Manufacturing costs, defined,
35
Manufacturing cycle
efficiency, (MCE),
defined, 98
Manufacturing environment,
impact of changing, 268
Manufacturing organization
defined, 29
compared to service and
merchandising
organizations, 26
Manufacturing overhead
budget, 362
costs, 31
flexible budget for, 362
Manufacturing resource
planning, (MRPII), 9
Margin of safety
defined, 152
relationship with
operating leverage,
154
Marginal cost, defined, 42
Marginal tax rate, defined,
630
Market performance, 872
Market price, 712
Market rate of interest, 1016
Markup, 578
Markup pricing methods, 578
Master budget
components of,
illustrated, 314
defined, 312
for a manufacturer, 312
for a nonmanufacturing
company, 317
structure of, illustrated,
313
summary of, 375
Matching concept, 989
Materials, quantitative
methods for, 450
Materials acquisition, control
of, 432
Materials costs, 31
Materials inventory, 31
Materials price variance,
defined, 426

Materials purchases budget,
360
Materials quantity variance,
defined, 429
Materials requirements
budget, 359
Materials requirements
planning (MRP), 9
Materials used, 31
Measure of activity, 438
Measuring income in service,
merchandising and
manufacturing firms,
illustrated, 27
Merchandising organization,
318
compared to service and
manufacturing
organizations, 26
cost flows, illustrated, 29
defined, 28
Minimum acceptable rate of
return, 622
Minimum desired rate of
return, 707
Mission, defined, 306
Mix variance, defined, 504
Mixed costs, 40
Model queries, 378
Modeling, defined, 376
Modified Accelerated Cost
Recovery System
(MACRS), 631, 669
Modified cost system,
defined, 267
Move time, defined, 96
Multinational company,
performance evaluation
in, 825
Multiple overhead rates, 202
Multiple regression, defined,
771

N

Negotiated transfer price, 717
Net assets, defined, 970
Net book value, defined, 980
Net income, defined, 983,
1001
Net loss, defined, 983
Net present value analysis
with depreciation and
taxes, illustrated, 633
with taxes, illustrated, 632
Net present value (NPV)
method, defined, 621
Net present value of capital
investment cash flows,
illustrated, 623
Networks, 807
Noncash financing and
investing activities, 911

Noncontrollable cost,
defined, 45
Nonlinear regression,
defined, 772
Non-value-added costs, 95
Normal capacity, 205
Normal distribution, defined,
770

O

Objectives, defined, 304
Off-balance-sheet financing,
defined, 861
Operating budget, 315
Operating cycle
defined, 994
illustrated, 315
Operating expense variance
analysis, framework for,
illustrated, 498
Operating expenses, 1000
analysis of, 497
defined, 497
Operating levels and break-
even points, relationship
between, 148
Operating leverage
defined, 149
in a declining market, 152
relationship with margin of
safety, 154
with high fixed cost, 150
Operating leverage factor, 149
Operating revenue, defined,
1000
Operations activities, 909
Operations cash flow to
current debt service ratio,
defined, 861
Operations cash flows, 912
Opinion No. 19 of the
Accounting Principles
Board, 908
Opportunity cost, 551
defined, 45
Organization chart of a
manufacturing company,
illustrated, 15
Organization expense,
defined, 996
Organization of the firm, 14
Other assets, defined, 996
Out-of-pocket costs, 551
defined, 43
Out-sourcing, defined, 557
Overall view of ABC cost
linkage, illustrated, 79
Overall view of ABC process,
illustrated, 80
Overapplied or overabsorbed
overhead, 201

Overhead, three-variance
method for, 456
Overhead rate, 197
Overhead rates,
departmental versus
plant-wide, 203
multiple, 202
Overhead variance,
disposition of, 201
Owner's equity, defined, 967,
969; 997

P

Paid-in capital in excess of
par value, defined, 998
Paid-in capital in excess of
stated value, 998
Parameters, 378
Partnership, defined, 986
Patents, defined, 995
Payback period, 627
Payback period method, 627
Payback reciprocal, 628
Pension contract, funding,
1020
Percentage composition
balance sheets,
illustrated, 856
Percentage composition
statements, defined, 855
Percentage-of-completion
method of accounting for
a profit, defined, 989
Performance evaluation,
defined, 5
Performance measurement,
97
Period costs, defined, 28
Periodic inventory, 981
Periodicity concept, 989
Perpetual inventory, 980
Physical flow of units,
illustrated, 254
Planned costs versus actual
costs, 47
Planning
and budgeting, 304
and control, 304
assumptions, 307
cost concepts for, 41
defined, 4
use of cost data in, 24
Planning, programming, and
budgeting system (PPBS),
defined, 327
Plant assets, defined, 979, 995
Plant capacity and control,
443
Plant-wide overhead rates
versus departmental
rates, 203
Post audit, 673

Post-closing trial balance, 985
    illustrated, 986
Posting, defined, 975
Posting reference column,
    defined, 975
Practical capacity, 205
Preferred stock, 987
Preliminary stage cost driver,
    83
Premier Products Company's
    factory, illustrated, 30
Premium, 1016
Premium on stock, defined,
    998
Prepayment adjustments,
    defined, 979
Present value, 620
    analysis applied, 1015
    comparison with future
        value of a series of
        cash flows, 1014
    defined, 1010
    of a series of future cash
        flows, 1012
    with cash flow at the
        beginning of the
        period, 1015
Price market, 712
    transfer, 709
Price and quantity variances,
    inter-relationships of, 431
Price earnings ratio, defined,
    872
Price policy, 144
Price reduction, effect on
    profit, 146
Price standard, defined, 421
Pricing
    full cost, 578
    variable cost, 579
Pricing decision and costs,
    577
Primary stage cost driver, 83
Prime costs, defined, 32
Pro forma financial
    statement, 357
Probabilistic budgeting, 327
Process cost, production
    environment for, 191
Process cost system defined,
    246
    standard costs in, 446
Process costing of output, 246
Process manufacturing
    system, flow of units and
    costs in, illustrated, 247
Process time, defined, 95
Producing departments, 214
Product
    cost, defined, 29
    cost systems, 189
    costing, 6
    costs and product cost
        groups, illustrated, 33

diversity, 86
    flow time, defined, 97
    life-cycle costs, 101
    mix complexity, 86
Product-level activities, 81
Production environment
    for job cost, 190
    for process cost, 191
Production order, completed,
    illustrated, 192
Profit
    analysis, 419
    center, defined, 102, 697
    division controllable, 702
    direct, 702
    net, 701
    variable, 703
    incremental, defined, 550
    plan, defined, 312
Profitability index, 624
Profit-volume (P/V) graph,
    140
    illustrated, 141
Program budgeting, defined,
    327
Project budget, 324
    defined, 317
Providing services, cost of 207
Purchase versus lease, 666
Pyramid reporting, 107

Q

Quantity standard, defined,
    421
Quick assets, 860
Quick ratio, defined, 860

R

Ratio and analysis, defined,
    857
Realization concept, 988
Regression analysis, defined,
    760
Regression line, 760
Reinvested earnings, 998
Relationships of activity cost
    centers, cost drivers, cost
    functions, and product
    costs, illustrated, 84
Relevant cost, defined, 43,
    550
Relevant costing decisions,
    policy issues affecting,
    554
Relevant range, 39, 140
Relevant revenues, 550
Replace equipment decision,
    576
Required rate of return, 622
Residual income, defined, 707

Responsibility center,
    defined, 697
Responsibilities of controller,
    illustrated, 16
Responsibilities of
    management accountant,
    illustrated, 17
Responsibility accounting,
    101
Responsibility center,
    defined, 102
Responsibility centers:
    investment centers, profit
    centers, and cost centers
    including activity centers,
    illustrated, 103
Retained earnings, 998
Return on assets (ROA),
    defined, 868
Return on common equity
    (ROCE), defined, 868
Return on investment (ROI)
    defined, 700
    improving, 705
    problems with, 704
    ratio for, 700
Return on managed assets,
    704
Return on sales (ROS),
    defined, 700, 868
Return on total equity (ROE),
    defined, 868
Revenue, defined, 970
Risks and returns,
    interrelationships of, 873
Risk percentage factor, 673
Rolling update, 307

S

Sales, 970
    forecast, defined, 320
    forecasting, 319
    journal, illustrated, 976
    mix, defined, 154
    mix variance, defined, 494
    price variance, defined,
        490
    quantity variance,
        defined, 495
    volume, 141
    volume variance, defined,
        491
Scarce resources
    key decision rule of, 567
    qualitative factors of, 569
    use of, 566
Scattergraph and visual fit,
    defined, 757
Scope of financial and
    managerial accounting,
    illustrated, 11

Security and Exchange
    Commission, 11
Sell or process further
    key decision rule of, 570
    qualitative factors of, 572
Selling expenses, defined,
    1001
Selling or marketing expense
    budget, 368
Semifixed costs, 40, 752
Semivariable and semifixed
    cost patterns, examples
    of, 40
Semivariable costs, defined,
    39, 752
Sensitivity analysis, defined,
    674
Service center costs, other
    influences, 218
Service centers and support
    functions, 214
Service organization, 318
    compared to
        merchandising and
        manufacturing
        organizations, 26
    cost flows, illustrated, 28
    defined, 27
    performance evaluation
        systems in, 708
SFAS No. 95
    "Statement of Cash Flows",
        908
Simulation, defined, 376
Slack, budgetary, 330
Social benefits, 676
Social costs, 676
Source document, defined,
    970
Special journals, 975
Special sales pricing, 562
    key decision rule of, 563
    qualitative factors of, 565
Spending variance, 458
    defined, 498
Split-off point, 570
Spot rate, defined, 818
Stage of completion, defined,
    253
Standard cost
    defined, 421
    modifications for, 496
    sheet, 425
    variances, summary of,
        illustrated, 445
Standard error of the estimate
    (Se), defined, 766
Standards advantages of, 422
    attainable, 424
    for labor, 432
    for materials, 426
    for overhead, 437
    loose, 424
    quality of, 423

revising, 424
strict, 424
use of, 421
Standards of ethical conduct, 18
illustrated, 20
Statement of cash flows, 909
format of, 910
framework of, illustrated, 911
illustrated, 927
preparing, 916
Statement of changes in financial position, 908
Statement of changes in retained earnings, 1002
Static phase, defined, 456
Step fixed cost, 40
Step (sequential) method, 217
Stockholder's equity, 997
Storage time, defined, 97
Straight-line depreciation, tax impacts compared to MACRS tax impacts, illustrated, 672
Straight-line method of depreciation, defined, 980
Strategic plan, defined, 306
Strategic profit model, 876
return on assets, illustrated, 877
return on common equity, illustrated, 878
Strict standards, defined, 424
Subassembly components, flow of units and costs for, illustrated, 248
Sunk cost, defined, 44
Synchronous manufacturing, 8

T

T-account, used in preparing statement of cash flows, 919
Target rate of return, 622
Tax shield, defined, 632
Technical evolution, 8
Time periods covered by the three major accounting

statements, illustrated, 909
Time series analysis, 773
Time value of money, 1008
defined, 614
Times interest earned, defined, 863
Timing placement of orders, illustrated, 454
Total analysis approach, defined, 551
Total analysis approach to differential analysis, illustrated, 553
Total asset turnover, defined, 866
Total costs patterns with a relevant range, illustrated, 39
Traceable cost, 41
Traditional factory versus just-in-time factory layouts, illustrated, 96
Treasurer, responsibilities of, 15
Trend analysis, 774
graph of data and regression trend line, illustrated, 775
Transaction cash, defined, 316
Transfer price cost-based, 713
defined, 709
desired qualities of, 711
dual, 718
full-cost, 714
international, 812
intracompany transactions continuum, illustrated, 710
market price, 712
negotiated, 717
variable-cost, 714
Transfer pricing, variable-cost and full-cost example, illustrated, 715
Transfer pricing methods, grading, 719
Transferred-in costs, 262

Trial balance, 976
illustrated, 977

U

Unavoidable costs, defined, 44
Uncertainty, 674
Underapplied or underabsorbed overhead, 201
Undivided interest, 992
Unfavorable variance, 426
Unit-level activities, 81
Use of scarce resources, 566

V

Valuation, 992
Valuation adjustments, 981
Value-added direct labor, 98
Value-added labor ratio, 98
Variable and fixed costs, nature of, 38
Variable contribution margin, 158
Variable costing
characteristics of, 506
compared with absorption costing, 507
defined, 506
reconciliation with absorption costing, 509
Variable cost pricing, 579
Variable costs, 142, 752
behavior of, 36
defined, 36
Variable-cost transfer price, 714
Variable product costs, 33
Variable overhead, costing, 199
Variance
budget, 440
capacity, 441
controllable, 440

cost, 490
disposition of, 446
efficiency, 458
favorable, 426
labor efficiency, 432
labor rate, 432
materials price, 426
materials quantity, 429
mix, 504
sales mix, 494
sales price, 490
sales quantity, 495
sales volume, 491
spending, 458, 498
unfavorable, 426
volume, 498
yield, 505
Variances, detailed levels of, illustrated, 420
Volume variance, 201
defined, 498

W

Wait time, defined, 97
Weighted-average cost of capital, defined, 635
Weighted-average cost method, 275
"What If" analysis, 380
Work in process inventory, 31
Work order, 192
Working capital, 660
defined, 859
World class manufacturing, 8

Y

Yield, defined, 1017
Yield variance, defined, 505

Z

Zero-based budgeting, defined, 326
Zero-stock system, 8

Management control report
    comparing actual to plan,
    illustrated, 48
Management overrides, 378
Managerial accounting,
    defined, 13
Managerial process and the
    budgeting system
    process, interaction of the
    illustrated, 305
Manufacturing, world class, 8
Manufacturing company,
    organization chart of a,
    illustrated, 15
Manufacturing costs, defined,
    35
Manufacturing cycle
    efficiency, (MCE),
    defined, 98
Manufacturing environment,
    impact of changing, 268
Manufacturing organization
    defined, 29
    compared to service and
        merchandising
        organizations, 26
Manufacturing overhead
    budget, 362
    costs, 31
    flexible budget for, 362
Manufacturing resource
    planning, (MRPII), 9
Margin of safety
    defined, 152
    relationship with
        operating leverage,
        154
Marginal cost, defined, 42
Marginal tax rate, defined,
    630
Market performance, 872
Market price, 712
Market rate of interest, 1016
Markup, 578
Markup pricing methods, 578
Master budget
    components of,
        illustrated, 314
    defined, 312
    for a manufacturer, 312
    for a nonmanufacturing
        company, 317
    structure of, illustrated,
        313
    summary of, 375
Matching concept, 989
Materials, quantitative
    methods for, 450
Materials acquisition, control
    of, 432
Materials costs, 31
Materials inventory, 31
Materials price variance,
    defined, 426

Materials purchases budget,
    360
Materials quantity variance,
    defined, 429
Materials requirements
    budget, 359
Materials requirements
    planning (MRP), 9
Materials used, 31
Measure of activity, 438
Measuring income in service,
    merchandising and
    manufacturing firms,
    illustrated, 27
Merchandising organization,
    318
    compared to service and
        manufacturing
        organizations, 26
    cost flows, illustrated, 29
    defined, 28
Minimum acceptable rate of
    return, 622
Minimum desired rate of
    return, 707
Mission, defined, 306
Mix variance, defined, 504
Mixed costs, 40
Model queries, 378
Modeling, defined, 376
Modified Accelerated Cost
    Recovery System
    (MACRS), 631, 669
Modified cost system,
    defined, 267
Move time, defined, 96
Multinational company,
    performance evaluation
    in, 825
Multiple overhead rates, 202
Multiple regression, defined,
    771

N

Negotiated transfer price, 717
Net assets, defined, 970
Net book value, defined, 980
Net income, defined, 983,
    1001
Net loss, defined, 983
Net present value analysis
    with depreciation and
        taxes, illustrated, 633
    with taxes, illustrated, 632
Net present value (NPV)
    method, defined, 621
Net present value of capital
    investment cash flows,
    illustrated, 623
Networks, 807
Noncash financing and
    investing activities, 911

Noncontrollable cost,
    defined, 45
Nonlinear regression,
    defined, 772
Non-value-added costs, 95
Normal capacity, 205
Normal distribution, defined,
    770

O

Objectives, defined, 304
Off-balance-sheet financing,
    defined, 861
Operating budget, 315
Operating cycle
    defined, 994
    illustrated, 315
Operating expense variance
    analysis, framework for,
    illustrated, 498
Operating expenses, 1000
    analysis of, 497
    defined, 497
Operating levels and break-
    even points, relationship
    between, 148
Operating leverage
defined, 149
in a declining market, 152
relationship with margin of
    safety, 154
with high fixed cost, 150
Operating leverage factor, 149
Operating revenue, defined,
    1000
Operations activities, 909
Operations cash flow to
    current debt service ratio,
    defined, 861
Operations cash flows, 912
Opinion No. 19 of the
    Accounting Principles
    Board, 908
Opportunity cost, 551
defined, 45
Organization chart of a
    manufacturing company,
    illustrated, 15
Organization expense,
    defined, 996
Organization of the firm, 14
Other assets, defined, 996
Out-of-pocket costs, 551
    defined, 43
Out-sourcing, defined, 557
Overall view of ABC cost
    linkage, illustrated, 79
Overall view of ABC process,
    illustrated, 80
Overapplied or overabsorbed
    overhead, 201

Overhead, three-variance
    method for, 456
Overhead rate, 197
Overhead rates,
    departmental versus
        plant-wide, 203
    multiple, 202
Overhead variance,
    disposition of, 201
Owner's equity, defined, 967,
    969; 997

P

Paid-in capital in excess of
    par value, defined, 998
Paid-in capital in excess of
    stated value, 998
Parameters, 378
Partnership, defined, 986
Patents, defined, 995
Payback period, 627
Payback period method, 627
Payback reciprocal, 628
Pension contract, funding,
    1020
Percentage composition
    balance sheets,
    illustrated, 856
Percentage composition
    statements, defined, 855
Percentage-of-completion
    method of accounting for
    a profit, defined, 989
Performance evaluation,
    defined, 5
Performance measurement,
    97
Period costs, defined, 28
Periodic inventory, 981
Periodicity concept, 989
Perpetual inventory, 980
Physical flow of units,
    illustrated, 254
Planned costs versus actual
    costs, 47
Planning
    and budgeting, 304
    and control, 304
    assumptions, 307
    cost concepts for, 41
    defined, 4
    use of cost data in, 24
Planning, programming, and
    budgeting system (PPBS),
    defined, 327
Plant assets, defined, 979, 995
Plant capacity and control,
    443
Plant-wide overhead rates
    versus departmental
    rates, 203
Post audit, 673

Post-closing trial balance, 985
illustrated, 986
Posting, defined, 975
Posting reference column,
defined, 975
Practical capacity, 205
Preferred stock, 987
Preliminary stage cost driver,
83
Premier Products Company's
factory, illustrated, 30
Premium, 1016
Premium on stock, defined,
998
Prepayment adjustments,
defined, 979
Present value, 620
analysis applied, 1015
comparison with future
value of a series of
cash flows, 1014
defined, 1010
of a series of future cash
flows, 1012
with cash flow at the
beginning of the
period, 1015
Price market, 712
transfer, 709
Price and quantity variances,
inter-relationships of, 431
Price earnings ratio, defined,
872
Price policy, 144
Price reduction, effect on
profit, 146
Price standard, defined, 421
Pricing
full cost, 578
variable cost, 579
Pricing decision and costs,
577
Primary stage cost driver, 83
Prime costs, defined, 32
Pro forma financial
statement, 357
Probabilistic budgeting, 327
Process cost, production
environment for, 191
Process cost system defined,
246
standard costs in, 446
Process costing of output, 246
Process manufacturing
system, flow of units and
costs in, illustrated, 247
Process time, defined, 95
Producing departments, 214
Product
cost, defined, 29
cost systems, 189
costing, 6
costs and product cost
groups, illustrated, 33

diversity, 86
flow time, defined, 97
life-cycle costs, 101
mix complexity, 86
Product-level activities, 81
Production environment
for job cost, 190
for process cost, 191
Production order, completed,
illustrated, 192
Profit
analysis, 419
center, defined, 102, 697
division controllable, 702
direct, 702
net, 701
variable, 703
incremental, defined, 550
plan, defined, 312
Profitability index, 624
Profit-volume (P/V) graph,
140
illustrated, 141
Program budgeting, defined,
327
Project budget, 324
defined, 317
Providing services, cost of 207
Purchase versus lease, 666
Pyramid reporting, 107

Q

Quantity standard, defined,
421
Quick assets, 860
Quick ratio, defined, 860

R

Ratio and analysis, defined,
857
Realization concept, 988
Regression analysis, defined,
760
Regression line, 760
Reinvested earnings, 998
Relationships of activity cost
centers, cost drivers, cost
functions, and product
costs, illustrated, 84
Relevant cost, defined, 43,
550
Relevant costing decisions,
policy issues affecting,
554
Relevant range, 39, 140
Relevant revenues, 550
Replace equipment decision,
576
Required rate of return, 622
Residual income, defined, 707

Responsibility center,
defined, 697
Responsibilities of controller,
illustrated, 16
Responsibilities of
management accountant,
illustrated, 17
Responsibility accounting,
101
Responsibility center,
defined, 102
Responsibility centers:
investment centers, profit
centers, and cost centers
including activity centers,
illustrated, 103
Retained earnings, 998
Return on assets (ROA),
defined, 868
Return on common equity
(ROCE), defined, 868
Return on investment (ROI)
defined, 700
improving, 705
problems with, 704
ratio for, 700
Return on managed assets,
704
Return on sales (ROS),
defined, 700, 868
Return on total equity (ROE),
defined, 868
Revenue, defined, 970
Risks and returns,
interrelationships of, 873
Risk percentage factor, 673
Rolling update, 307

S

Sales, 970
forecast, defined, 320
forecasting, 319
journal, illustrated, 976
mix, defined, 154
mix variance, defined, 494
price variance, defined,
490
quantity variance,
defined, 495
volume, 141
volume variance, defined,
491
Scarce resources
key decision rule of, 567
qualitative factors of, 569
use of, 566
Scattergraph and visual fit,
defined, 757
Scope of financial and
managerial accounting,
illustrated, 11

Security and Exchange
Commission, 11
Sell or process further
key decision rule of, 570
qualitative factors of, 572
Selling expenses, defined,
1001
Selling or marketing expense
budget, 368
Semifixed costs, 40, 752
Semivariable and semifixed
cost patterns, examples
of, 40
Semivariable costs, defined,
39, 752
Sensitivity analysis, defined,
674
Service center costs, other
influences, 218
Service centers and support
functions, 214
Service organization, 318
compared to
merchandising and
manufacturing
organizations, 26
cost flows, illustrated, 28
defined, 27
performance evaluation
systems in, 708
SFAS No. 95
"Statement of Cash Flows",
908
Simulation, defined, 376
Slack, budgetary, 330
Social benefits, 676
Social costs, 676
Source document, defined,
970
Special journals, 975
Special sales pricing, 562
key decision rule of, 563
qualitative factors of, 565
Spending variance, 458
defined, 498
Split-off point, 570
Spot rate, defined, 818
Stage of completion, defined,
253
Standard cost
defined, 421
modifications for, 496
sheet, 425
variances, summary of,
illustrated, 445
Standard error of the estimate
(Se), defined, 766
Standards advantages of, 422
attainable, 424
for labor, 432
for materials, 426
for overhead, 437
loose, 424
quality of, 423

revising, 424
strict, 424
use of, 421
Standards of ethical conduct, 18
illustrated, 20
Statement of cash flows, 909
format of, 910
framework of, illustrated, 911
illustrated, 927
preparing, 916
Statement of changes in financial position, 908
Statement of changes in retained earnings, 1002
Static phase, defined, 456
Step fixed cost, 40
Step (sequential) method, 217
Stockholder's equity, 997
Storage time, defined, 97
Straight-line depreciation, tax impacts compared to MACRS tax impacts, illustrated, 672
Straight-line method of depreciation, defined, 980
Strategic plan, defined, 306
Strategic profit model, 876
return on assets, illustrated, 877
return on common equity, illustrated, 878
Strict standards, defined, 424
Subassembly components, flow of units and costs for, illustrated, 248
Sunk cost, defined, 44
Synchronous manufacturing, 8

T

T-account, used in preparing statement of cash flows, 919
Target rate of return, 622
Tax shield, defined, 632
Technical evolution, 8
Time periods covered by the three major accounting

statements, illustrated, 909
Time series analysis, 773
Time value of money, 1008
defined, 614
Times interest earned, defined, 863
Timing placement of orders, illustrated, 454
Total analysis approach, defined, 551
Total analysis approach to differential analysis, illustrated, 553
Total asset turnover, defined, 866
Total costs patterns with a relevant range, illustrated, 39
Traceable cost, 41
Traditional factory versus just-in-time factory layouts, illustrated, 96
Treasurer, responsibilities of, 15
Trend analysis, 774
graph of data and regression trend line, illustrated, 775
Transaction cash, defined, 316
Transfer price cost-based, 713
defined, 709
desired qualities of, 711
dual, 718
full-cost, 714
international, 812
intracompany transactions continuum, illustrated, 710
market price, 712
negotiated, 717
variable-cost, 714
Transfer pricing, variable-cost and full-cost example, illustrated, 715
Transfer pricing methods, grading, 719
Transferred-in costs, 262

Trial balance, 976
illustrated, 977

U

Unavoidable costs, defined, 44
Uncertainty, 674
Underapplied or underabsorbed overhead, 201
Undivided interest, 992
Unfavorable variance, 426
Unit-level activities, 81
Use of scarce resources, 566

V

Valuation, 992
Valuation adjustments, 981
Value-added direct labor, 98
Value-added labor ratio, 98
Variable and fixed costs, nature of, 38
Variable contribution margin, 158
Variable costing
characteristics of, 506
compared with absorption costing, 507
defined, 506
reconciliation with absorption costing, 509
Variable cost pricing, 579
Variable costs, 142, 752
behavior of, 36
defined, 36
Variable-cost transfer price, 714
Variable product costs, 33
Variable overhead, costing, 199
Variance
budget, 440
capacity, 441
controllable, 440

cost, 490
disposition of, 446
efficiency, 458
favorable, 426
labor efficiency, 432
labor rate, 432
materials price, 426
materials quantity, 429
mix, 504
sales mix, 494
sales price, 490
sales quantity, 495
sales volume, 491
spending, 458, 498
unfavorable, 426
volume, 498
yield, 505
Variances, detailed levels of, illustrated, 420
Volume variance, 201
defined, 498

W

Wait time, defined, 97
Weighted-average cost of capital, defined, 635
Weighted-average cost method, 275
"What If" analysis, 380
Work in process inventory, 31
Work order, 192
Working capital, 660
defined, 859
World class manufacturing, 8

Y

Yield, defined, 1017
Yield variance, defined, 505

Z

Zero-based budgeting, defined, 326
Zero-stock system, 8

Management control report
comparing actual to plan,
illustrated, 48
Management overrides, 378
Managerial accounting,
defined, 13
Managerial process and the
budgeting system
process, interaction of the
illustrated, 305
Manufacturing, world class, 8
Manufacturing company,
organization chart of a,
illustrated, 15
Manufacturing costs, defined,
35
Manufacturing cycle
efficiency, (MCE),
defined, 98
Manufacturing environment,
impact of changing, 268
Manufacturing organization
defined, 29
compared to service and
merchandising
organizations, 26
Manufacturing overhead
budget, 362
costs, 31
flexible budget for, 362
Manufacturing resource
planning, (MRPII), 9
Margin of safety
defined, 152
relationship with
operating leverage,
154
Marginal cost, defined, 42
Marginal tax rate, defined,
630
Market performance, 872
Market price, 712
Market rate of interest, 1016
Markup, 578
Markup pricing methods, 578
Master budget
components of,
illustrated, 314
defined, 312
for a manufacturer, 312
for a nonmanufacturing
company, 317
structure of, illustrated,
313
summary of, 375
Matching concept, 989
Materials, quantitative
methods for, 450
Materials acquisition, control
of, 432
Materials costs, 31
Materials inventory, 31
Materials price variance,
defined, 426

Materials purchases budget,
360
Materials quantity variance,
defined, 429
Materials requirements
budget, 359
Materials requirements
planning (MRP), 9
Materials used, 31
Measure of activity, 438
Measuring income in service,
merchandising and
manufacturing firms,
illustrated, 27
Merchandising organization,
318
compared to service and
manufacturing
organizations, 26
cost flows, illustrated, 29
defined, 28
Minimum acceptable rate of
return, 622
Minimum desired rate of
return, 707
Mission, defined, 306
Mix variance, defined, 504
Mixed costs, 40
Model queries, 378
Modeling, defined, 376
Modified Accelerated Cost
Recovery System
(MACRS), 631, 669
Modified cost system,
defined, 267
Move time, defined, 96
Multinational company,
performance evaluation
in, 825
Multiple overhead rates, 202
Multiple regression, defined,
771

N

Negotiated transfer price, 717
Net assets, defined, 970
Net book value, defined, 980
Net income, defined, 983,
1001
Net loss, defined, 983
Net present value analysis
with depreciation and
taxes, illustrated, 633
with taxes, illustrated, 632
Net present value (NPV)
method, defined, 621
Net present value of capital
investment cash flows,
illustrated, 623
Networks, 807
Noncash financing and
investing activities, 911

Noncontrollable cost,
defined, 45
Nonlinear regression,
defined, 772
Non-value-added costs, 95
Normal capacity, 205
Normal distribution, defined,
770

O

Objectives, defined, 304
Off-balance-sheet financing,
defined, 861
Operating budget, 315
Operating cycle
defined, 994
illustrated, 315
Operating expense variance
analysis, framework for,
illustrated, 498
Operating expenses, 1000
analysis of, 497
defined, 497
Operating levels and break-
even points, relationship
between, 148
Operating leverage
defined, 149
in a declining market, 152
relationship with margin of
safety, 154
with high fixed cost, 150
Operating leverage factor, 149
Operating revenue, defined,
1000
Operations activities, 909
Operations cash flow to
current debt service ratio,
defined, 861
Operations cash flows, 912
Opinion No. 19 of the
Accounting Principles
Board, 908
Opportunity cost, 551
defined, 45
Organization chart of a
manufacturing company,
illustrated, 15
Organization expense,
defined, 996
Organization of the firm, 14
Other assets, defined, 996
Out-of-pocket costs, 551
defined, 43
Out-sourcing, defined, 557
Overall view of ABC cost
linkage, illustrated, 79
Overall view of ABC process,
illustrated, 80
Overapplied or overabsorbed
overhead, 201

Overhead, three-variance
method for, 456
Overhead rate, 197
Overhead rates,
departmental versus
plant-wide, 203
multiple, 202
Overhead variance,
disposition of, 201
Owner's equity, defined, 967,
969; 997

P

Paid-in capital in excess of
par value, defined, 998
Paid-in capital in excess of
stated value, 998
Parameters, 378
Partnership, defined, 986
Patents, defined, 995
Payback period, 627
Payback period method, 627
Payback reciprocal, 628
Pension contract, funding,
1020
Percentage composition
balance sheets,
illustrated, 856
Percentage composition
statements, defined, 855
Percentage-of-completion
method of accounting for
a profit, defined, 989
Performance evaluation,
defined, 5
Performance measurement,
97
Period costs, defined, 28
Periodic inventory, 981
Periodicity concept, 989
Perpetual inventory, 980
Physical flow of units,
illustrated, 254
Planned costs versus actual
costs, 47
Planning
and budgeting, 304
and control, 304
assumptions, 307
cost concepts for, 41
defined, 4
use of cost data in, 24
Planning, programming, and
budgeting system (PPBS),
defined, 327
Plant assets, defined, 979, 995
Plant capacity and control,
443
Plant-wide overhead rates
versus departmental
rates, 203
Post audit, 673

Post-closing trial balance, 985
  illustrated, 986
Posting, defined, 975
Posting reference column,
  defined, 975
Practical capacity, 205
Preferred stock, 987
Preliminary stage cost driver,
  83
Premier Products Company's
  factory, illustrated, 30
Premium, 1016
Premium on stock, defined,
  998
Prepayment adjustments,
  defined, 979
Present value, 620
  analysis applied, 1015
  comparison with future
    value of a series of
    cash flows, 1014
  defined, 1010
  of a series of future cash
    flows, 1012
  with cash flow at the
    beginning of the
    period, 1015
Price market, 712
  transfer, 709
Price and quantity variances,
  inter-relationships of, 431
Price earnings ratio, defined,
  872
Price policy, 144
Price reduction, effect on
  profit, 146
Price standard, defined, 421
Pricing
  full cost, 578
  variable cost, 579
Pricing decision and costs,
  577
Primary stage cost driver, 83
Prime costs, defined, 32
Pro forma financial
  statement, 357
Probabilistic budgeting, 327
Process cost, production
  environment for, 191
Process cost system defined,
  246
standard costs in, 446
Process costing of output, 246
Process manufacturing
  system, flow of units and
  costs in, illustrated, 247
Process time, defined, 95
Producing departments, 214
Product
  cost, defined, 29
  cost systems, 189
  costing, 6
  costs and product cost
    groups, illustrated, 33

diversity, 86
flow time, defined, 97
life-cycle costs, 101
mix complexity, 86
Product-level activities, 81
Production environment
  for job cost, 190
  for process cost, 191
Production order, completed,
  illustrated, 192
Profit
  analysis, 419
  center, defined, 102, 697
  division controllable, 702
  direct, 702
  net, 701
  variable, 703
  incremental, defined, 550
  plan, defined, 312
Profitability index, 624
Profit-volume (P/V) graph,
  140
  illustrated, 141
Program budgeting, defined,
  327
Project budget, 324
  defined, 317
Providing services, cost of 207
Purchase versus lease, 666
Pyramid reporting, 107

Q

Quantity standard, defined,
  421
Quick assets, 860
Quick ratio, defined, 860

R

Ratio and analysis, defined,
  857
Realization concept, 988
Regression analysis, defined,
  760
Regression line, 760
Reinvested earnings, 998
Relationships of activity cost
  centers, cost drivers, cost
  functions, and product
  costs, illustrated, 84
Relevant cost, defined, 43,
  550
Relevant costing decisions,
  policy issues affecting,
  554
Relevant range, 39, 140
Relevant revenues, 550
Replace equipment decision,
  576
Required rate of return, 622
Residual income, defined, 707

Responsibility center,
  defined, 697
Responsibilities of controller,
  illustrated, 16
Responsibilities of
  management accountant,
  illustrated, 17
Responsibility accounting,
  101
Responsibility center,
  defined, 102
Responsibility centers:
  investment centers, profit
    centers, and cost centers
    including activity centers,
    illustrated, 103
Retained earnings, 998
Return on assets (ROA),
  defined, 868
Return on common equity
  (ROCE), defined, 868
Return on investment (ROI)
  defined, 700
  improving, 705
  problems with, 704
  ratio for, 700
Return on managed assets,
  704
Return on sales (ROS),
  defined, 700, 868
Return on total equity (ROE),
  defined, 868
Revenue, defined, 970
Risks and returns,
  interrelationships of, 873
Risk percentage factor, 673
Rolling update, 307

S

Sales, 970
  forecast, defined, 320
  forecasting, 319
  journal, illustrated, 976
  mix, defined, 154
  mix variance, defined, 494
  price variance, defined,
    490
  quantity variance,
    defined, 495
  volume, 141
  volume variance, defined,
    491
Scarce resources
  key decision rule of, 567
  qualitative factors of, 569
  use of, 566
Scattergraph and visual fit,
  defined, 757
Scope of financial and
  managerial accounting,
  illustrated, 11

Security and Exchange
  Commission, 11
Sell or process further
  key decision rule of, 570
  qualitative factors of, 572
Selling expenses, defined,
  1001
Selling or marketing expense
  budget, 368
Semifixed costs, 40, 752
Semivariable and semifixed
  cost patterns, examples
  of, 40
Semivariable costs, defined,
  39, 752
Sensitivity analysis, defined,
  674
Service center costs, other
  influences, 218
Service centers and support
  functions, 214
Service organization, 318
  compared to
    merchandising and
    manufacturing
    organizations, 26
  cost flows, illustrated, 28
  defined, 27
  performance evaluation
    systems in, 708
SFAS No. 95
  "Statement of Cash Flows",
    908
Simulation, defined, 376
Slack, budgetary, 330
Social benefits, 676
Social costs, 676
Source document, defined,
  970
Special journals, 975
Special sales pricing, 562
  key decision rule of, 563
  qualitative factors of, 565
Spending variance, 458
  defined, 498
Split-off point, 570
Spot rate, defined, 818
Stage of completion, defined,
  253
Standard cost
  defined, 421
  modifications for, 496
  sheet, 425
  variances, summary of,
    illustrated, 445
Standard error of the estimate
  (Se), defined, 766
Standards advantages of, 422
  attainable, 424
  for labor, 432
  for materials, 426
  for overhead, 437
  loose, 424
  quality of, 423

revising, 424
strict, 424
use of, 421
Standards of ethical conduct, 18
illustrated, 20
Statement of cash flows, 909
format of, 910
framework of, illustrated, 911
illustrated, 927
preparing, 916
Statement of changes in financial position, 908
Statement of changes in retained earnings, 1002
Static phase, defined, 456
Step fixed cost, 40
Step (sequential) method, 217
Stockholder's equity, 997
Storage time, defined, 97
Straight-line depreciation, tax impacts compared to MACRS tax impacts, illustrated, 672
Straight-line method of depreciation, defined, 980
Strategic plan, defined, 306
Strategic profit model, 876
return on assets, illustrated, 877
return on common equity, illustrated, 878
Strict standards, defined, 424
Subassembly components, flow of units and costs for, illustrated, 248
Sunk cost, defined, 44
Synchronous manufacturing, 8

T

T-account, used in preparing statement of cash flows, 919
Target rate of return, 622
Tax shield, defined, 632
Technical evolution, 8
Time periods covered by the three major accounting

statements, illustrated, 909
Time series analysis, 773
Time value of money, 1008
defined, 614
Times interest earned, defined, 863
Timing placement of orders, illustrated, 454
Total analysis approach, defined, 551
Total analysis approach to differential analysis, illustrated, 553
Total asset turnover, defined, 866
Total costs patterns with a relevant range, illustrated, 39
Traceable cost, 41
Traditional factory versus just-in-time factory layouts, illustrated, 96
Treasurer, responsibilities of, 15
Trend analysis, 774
graph of data and regression trend line, illustrated, 775
Transaction cash, defined, 316
Transfer price cost-based, 713
defined, 709
desired qualities of, 711
dual, 718
full-cost, 714
international, 812
intracompany transactions continuum, illustrated, 710
market price, 712
negotiated, 717
variable-cost, 714
Transfer pricing, variable-cost and full-cost example, illustrated, 715
Transfer pricing methods, grading, 719
Transferred-in costs, 262

Trial balance, 976
illustrated, 977

U

Unavoidable costs, defined, 44
Uncertainty, 674
Underapplied or underabsorbed overhead, 201
Undivided interest, 992
Unfavorable variance, 426
Unit-level activities, 81
Use of scarce resources, 566

V

Valuation, 992
Valuation adjustments, 981
Value-added direct labor, 98
Value-added labor ratio, 98
Variable and fixed costs, nature of, 38
Variable contribution margin, 158
Variable costing
characteristics of, 506
compared with absorption costing, 507
defined, 506
reconciliation with absorption costing, 509
Variable cost pricing, 579
Variable costs, 142, 752
behavior of, 36
defined, 36
Variable-cost transfer price, 714
Variable product costs, 33
Variable overhead, costing, 199
Variance
budget, 440
capacity, 441
controllable, 440

cost, 490
disposition of, 446
efficiency, 458
favorable, 426
labor efficiency, 432
labor rate, 432
materials price, 426
materials quantity, 429
mix, 504
sales mix, 494
sales price, 490
sales quantity, 495
sales volume, 491
spending, 458, 498
unfavorable, 426
volume, 498
yield, 505
Variances, detailed levels of, illustrated, 420
Volume variance, 201
defined, 498

W

Wait time, defined, 97
Weighted-average cost of capital, defined, 635
Weighted-average cost method, 275
"What If" analysis, 380
Work in process inventory, 31
Work order, 192
Working capital, 660
defined, 859
World class manufacturing, 8

Y

Yield, defined, 1017
Yield variance, defined, 505

Z

Zero-based budgeting, defined, 326
Zero-stock system, 8